DATABASE MANAGEMENT SYSTEMS

About the Author

G K Gupta recently retired after a thirty-five year distinguished career in computer science education, research and academic management. He is currently Adjunct Professor of Computer Science at the Faculty of Information Technology at Monash University, Clayton.

Professor Gupta was born and raised in India and completed undergraduate studies at the University of Roorkee (now IIT, Roorkee). He did Master's in Computer Science at the University of Waterloo in Canada and then migrated to Australia in 1972 where he joined the Department of Computer Science at Monash University. While working full-time, he obtained a doctorate from the same university.

In 1986, Professor Gupta moved to James Cook University as Foundation Professor and Head to establish a new department of computer science. He also served as Dean of the School of Information Technology at Bond University from1998 to 2002. He came back to Monash University in October 2002 as Deputy Dean. Here he also served as Acting Dean before returning to the position of Professor of Computer Science. Professor Gupta was seconded by the Australian Government to the Asian Institute of Technology in Bangkok for two years 1979–1981, to help set up a new department there. He has also spent a year at the University of Illinois at Urbana-Champaign, another year at Bell Laboratories in New Jersey, eight months at International University in Germany and made two three-month visits to VIT University at Vellore in India.

Professor Gupta is a Fellow of the Association of Computing Machinery (ACM), a Fellow of the Australian Computer Society (ACS) and a Senior Member of the IEEE. He was awarded the inaugural Distinguished Service Award by the Computer Science Research and Education (CORE) society in 2004. Professor Gupta has previously authored the book *Introduction to Data Mining with Case Studies*; published in 2006.

DATABASE MANAGEMENT SYSTEMS

G K Gupta

Adjunct Professor of Computer Science
Monash University, Clayton
Australia

Tata McGraw Hill Education Private Limited
NEW DELHI

McGraw-Hill Offices

New Delhi New York St Louis San Francisco Auckland Bogotá Caracas
Kuala Lumpur Lisbon London Madrid Mexico City Milan Montreal
San Juan Santiago Singapore Sydney Tokyo Toronto

Tata McGraw-Hill

Published by the Tata McGraw Hill Education Private Limited,
7 West Patel Nagar, New Delhi 110 008.

Database Management Systems

ISBN (13): 978-0-07-133007-7
ISBN (10): 0-07-133007-0

Vice President and Managing Director —McGraw-Hill Education, Asia Pacific Region: *Ajay Shukla*

Head—Higher Education Publishing and Marketing: *Vibha Mahajan*
Manager: Sponsoring—SEM & Tech Ed.: *Shalini Jha*
Assoc. Sponsoring Editor: *Suman Sen*
Development Editor: *Surbhi Suman*
Sr Copy Editor: *Nimisha Kapoor*
Sr Production Manager: *Satinder S Baveja*
Sr Production Manager: *P L Pandita*
Dy Marketing Manager—SEM & Tech Ed.: *Biju Ganesan*
Sr Product Specialist—SEM & Tech Ed.: *John Mathews*

General Manager—Production: *Rajender P Ghansela*
Asst General Manager—Production: *B L Dogra*

Typeset at Tej Composers, WZ-391, Madipur, New Delhi 110063, and printed at Sheel Printers Pvt. Ltd., D-132, Hoisery Complex, Phase-II, Noida.

Cover Printer: Sheel Printers

RAZYCRZCDXCLA

The McGraw-Hill Companies

To

the memory of

Ammaji

who passed away on 15 May 2005
at the age estimated to be 99 years
(Her date of birth was not known)

Contents

Preface

Database technology occupies a very important position in our increasingly computerized society. Almost all computer systems whether they are supermarket checkout systems, air traffic control systems, railways seat reservation systems, planning systems in governments or automatic teller machines (ATMs) with which most of us interact in our daily lives in urban India, have a database system at their core. Therefore, all computer science, information technology, business administration and information science students need to learn about the basic theory and practice of database systems since it is fundamental to much of computer technology.

This book is intended to be a comprehensive text for undergraduate and graduate level database management courses offered in computer science, information systems and business management disciplines. It can be used as a primary read through one-semester by students pursuing BCA, MCA, BSc, MSc and related computer science courses. It can be used as a reference reading by BTech, BE and MTech students and industry professionals.

This book is based on many years of experience of teaching database courses at a number of universities including James Cook University, Monash University and Bond University in Australia, Asian Institute of Technology (AIT) in Thailand, International University in Germany, and VIT University in India. Writing this book has been a wonderful experience for me.

What makes this book unique?

The book differs from other books on database management since it is written especially for students in India and that is why the examples used in the book are primarily those that I hope will interest Indian students. One major example used to illustrate most database concepts that is carried throughout the book is based on cricket One Day International (ODI) matches. Some other real-life examples have also been included. These examples have been used to illustrate several concepts in database design, query processing, distributed databases, object-oriented databases and a number of other topics.

Instead of focusing on how to build the database management system software, this textbook focuses on how to build database applications since most students once they graduate will be developing database applications rather than building database software. Therefore in this book, we concentrate on the concepts underlying the relational data model rather than on any particular commercial DBMS, as these concepts are the foundation of database processing. In a similar way, in the portion of the book which studies transaction processing, we concentrate on the concepts underlying the properties of transactions and the technical issues involved in their implementation, rather than how they are implemented in any particular commercial DBMS.

This text has a logical flow of topics and is supplemented with numerous chapter-end pedagogical features, including multiple-choice questions with answers (409), review questions with section references for answers (342), exercises (246), and short-answer questions (348). Projects (43) and lab exercises (56) have been provided to enhance practical learning along with several examples and real-life case studies for holistic understanding of the subject. Important definitions and key terms have been emphasized in every chapter for a good grasp of concepts.

Book Overview

The contents of the book are described ahead briefly.

Chapter 1 introduces the subject with a simple example of a cricket database and its features followed by a definition of the term 'database'. A number of popular websites are listed to illustrate the amount of information that many websites now have and is required to be stored in databases. **Chapter 2** discusses the Entity-Relationship model in detail. Representing an Entity-Relationship model by an Entity-Relationship diagram is explained along with generalization, specialization and aggregation concepts. **Chapter 3** describes the relational model and its three major components, viz., data structure, data manipulation and data integrity. Mapping of the E-R model to the relational model is explained. This is supported by a brief description of older database models: hierarchical and network models. **Chapter 4** elucidates data manipulation in relational model including relational algebra and relational calculus. A number of examples of their use are also presented. **Chapter 5** on SQL discusses data retrieval features of SQL using simple examples that involve only one table, followed by examples that involve more than one table using joins and subqueries, as well as built-in functions and GROUPING and HAVING clauses. Use of SQL in enforcing data integrity is also mentioned. **Chapter 6** explains theoretical basis of normalization using the concept of functional dependency followed by a study of single-valued normalization and multivalued normalization.

The structure of information storage on a magnetic disk is described along with the most commonly used data structures, B-tree and hashing in **Chapter 7**. The query optimization process is covered in detail in **Chapter 8**. The steps involved in the process, and rules of thumb that are often used in query optimization, estimating the size of intermediate results in processing a query are presented herein. Algorithms for relational algebra operations are then discussed. In **Chapter 9**, the concept and properties of a transaction are described along with concepts of a schedule and serializability. Locking and two-phase locking (2PL) are introduced followed by definition of deadlocks, their detection, prevention and resolution. Database recovery from a failure, the concept of log, and recovery techniques are described in **Chapter 10**. Types of recovery techniques, immediate update technique, deferred update technique, system checkpoints, shadow page technique, and evaluation of recovery techniques are also presented in this chapter. **Chapter 11** elucidates security violations and sources of violations in a database system highlighting various components of database security, discretionary access control and non-discretionary control or mandatory control techniques along with security of statistical databases. **Chapter 12** gives the definition of database integrity, lists two types of integrity: syntactic integrity and semantic integrity, and explains how integrity constraints are implemented in SQL3.

Features of a distributed database are described in **Chapter 13**. Objectives in designing distributed databases and fragmentation are discussed using a number of examples. Issues in distributed query processing and transaction processing are briefly mentioned here. **Chapter 14** defines an object-oriented database as based primarily on the data structure called the *object*; the concept originated from the concept of class which was proposed in the 1960s. How object-oriented data model is an attempt to build a richer database model is explained in this chapter. **Chapter 15** gives details of type of database for management. It explains data warehouse, including design of a data warehouse and guidelines for implementation. Online analytical processing (or OLAP) is introduced and characteristics of OLAP systems are listed. The data mining process and several data mining techniques are described in **Chapter 16**. Markup languages and semistructured data followed by a description of XML including an example and introduction to XML elements, attributes, namespace, document type definition (DTD), document object model (DOM), XML Schema and XQuery are discussed in **Chapter 17**. XML databases are also discussed in this chapter. **Chapter 18** introduces emerging database technologies and discusses in detail three of these, viz., cloud computing, mobile databases and MapReduce.

To the Instructor

This book deals with the most important topics of database management. The book includes many examples which I believe are essential in getting students motivated and in helping them understand the course content. To further this aim, I have also presented varied revision exercises. At the end of each chapter, I have included a list of references in the book that encompasses some of the most highly cited papers in database management.

To the Student

Database management is an important and interesting area and I hope you will enjoy learning about it. The book is written primarily for you. I have provided many examples to help you learn the concepts and the techniques. A large number of references have been provided, highlighting a small number, specially selected for you since they are easy to read. I understand that most students do not have the time to read references other than the prescribed textbooks and lecture notes but these references should be useful if you decide to learn more about database techniques during your studies or afterwards.

Review, short-answer and multiple-choice questions, and exercises have been provided at the end of every chapter. Please try to solve all of these to better understand the material in the book.

Online Learning Centre

This book is supported by an online learning centre which can be accessed at *http://www.mhhe.com/gupta/dbms*. The centre comprises the following additional study resources for both instructors and students.

For Instructors

- Chapter-wise Power Point Slides
- Solution Manual
- Tutorial Questions with Answers

For Students

- 5 sets of Self-tests with Answers
- Solution for 5 Projects given in the book
- Links for further reading

Acknowledgements

I would like to thank a number of people who have helped in reading, correcting and giving ideas during the writing of this book. In particular Joe Incigneri read an earlier manuscript in 2009 and helped in improving the readability of the book. Jeanette Niehus has helped in drawing all the diagrams using Microsoft Visio.

I also gratefully acknowledge the suggestions given by the reviewers during the initial process. Their comments have added value to parts of this book.

S K Gupta	*Indian Institute of Technology Delhi, New Delhi*
R C Joshi	*Indian Institute of Technology Roorkee, Uttarakhand*
S K Jain	*National Institute of Technology, Kurukshetra, Haryana*
B Biswas	*Institute of Technology, Banaras Hindu University, Varanasi, Uttar Pradesh*
Amit Kanskar	*NRI Institute of Science and Technology, Bhopal, Madhya Pradesh*
Naresh K Nagwani	*National Institute of Technology, Raipur, Chattisgarh*
Ritika Wason	*Institute of Information Technology and Management, New Delhi*
Manish Mahajan	*ABES Institute of Technology, Ghaziabad, Uttar Pradesh*
Parteek Bhatia	*Thapar University, Patiala, Punjab*
Harmeet Malhotra	*Institute of Information Technology and Management, New Delhi*
Itu Snigdha	*Birla Institute of Technology, Mesra, Jharkhand*
Ranjan Mohanty	*Kalinga Institute of Industry and Technology, Bhubaneswar, Orissa*
P Paul	*Birla Institute of Technology, Mesra, Jharkhand*
Sarda Nandlal	*Indian Institute of Technology Bombay, Maharashtra*
V B Gadekar	*Vishwakarma Institute of Technology, Pune, Maharashtra*
K Sudha Sadhasivam	*PSG College of Technology, Coimbatore, Tamil Nadu*
N Jaisankar	*Vellore Institute of Technology, Vellore, Tamil Nadu*
S Chandaradekaran	*Madurai Kamaraj University, Madurai, Tamil Nadu*
Abdul Nazeer K A	*National Institute of Technology, Calicut, Kerala*
Valli Kumari	*University College of Engineering, Andhra University, Visakhapatnam, Andhra Pradesh*
Ravi Thorat	*Wesley PG College, Secunderabad, Andhra Pradesh*
M Palanivel	*Sreenivasa Institute of Technology, Andhra Pradesh*
Harish Yagneshwar	*Accenture India Ltd, Hyderabad, Andhra Pradesh*

It is always a pleasure to receive feedback from students and I am thankful to Shikha Kansal, Hemant Sharma, Abhinav Kansal, Toby L Thomas, Vivek Mittal, Varun Sharma, Abhimanyu, Divya Gupta, Richa Goyal, Deepti Goyal, Ritika Mittal, Amit Singh, Kaushal Kumar, Tarun Kumar Singh, Bijendra Tyagi, Rahul Rathore, Prerna Sharma, Nidhi Sehgal, and Anubhav Jain from Institute of Information Technology and Management, New Delhi and ABES Institute of Technology, Ghaziabad for their valuable feedback on the script.

Finally I would like to thank the editorial staff at Tata McGraw-Hill. I am grateful to Ms Surabhi Shukla for her assistance and support to develop this book during her time of service at Tata McGraw-Hill. I know it has not been easy for her to deal over a year with an author who is thousands of miles away.

I should be grateful if I could be informed of any errors discovered and any suggestions you might have about how the book could be improved for the next edition. You can write to me at *gkgupta@acm.org*.

G K Gupta

Publisher's Note

Have something to tell us? Please feel free to write to us with your comments at *tmh.csefeedback@gmail.com*. Please mention the title and author's name as the subject. We look forward to hearing from you.

visual guide

An example based on Cricket ODI matches to illustrate database concepts, is used throughout the book, to especially connect with Indian students

Example 1.1

Consider the table presented in Table 1.1 that presents a list of the top ten batsmen in one day international (ODI) cricket in terms of the total number of runs scored. The data was current on August 2010.

Table 1.1 Example of a simple database[1]

Player	*Span*	*Matches*	*Innings*	*Runs*	*Avg.*	*Strike Rate*	*100s*
SR Tendulkar	1989–2010	442	431	17598	45.12	86.26	46
ST Jayasuriya	1989–2010	444	432	13428	32.43	91.22	28
RT Ponting	1995–2010	351	342	13072	42.85	80.84	29
Inzamam-ul-Haq	1991–2007	378	350	11739	39.52	74.24	10
SC Ganguly	1992–2007	311	300	11363	41.02	73.70	22
JH Kallis	1996–2010	303	289	10838	45.72	72.72	17
R Dravid	1996–2009	339	313	10765	39.43	71.17	12
BC Lara	1990–2007	299	289	10405	40.48	79.51	19
Mohammed Yousuf	1998–2010	282	267	9624	42.39	75.15	15
AC Gilchrist	1996–2008	287	279	9619	35.89	96.94	16

It should be noted that in the above database the batting average for a player is not obtained by dividing the total number of runs scored by the total number of innings played. It is obtained by dividing the total runs scored by the total number of innings in which the player got out. The number of times the player was not out is not counted and the number of times a batsman was not out is not included in the table above because of space considerations. For example, Sachin Tendulkar was not out 38 times while Adam Gilchrist was not out only 11 times.

The information in Table 1.1 is quite interesting. There are three players in the top ten ODI batsmen order from India and none from England. Also the number of runs scored and the number of centuries made by Sachin Tendulkar are so high as compared to other players that it is unlikely he would be overtaken by another batsman, for example, Sanath Jayasuriya or Ricky Ponting, in the near future. Also, let us not forget that Tendulkar is an active cricketer who continues to score runs.

The chapter is organized as follows. We start by describing cloud computing in Section 18.2. This section includes discussion of characteristics of cloud computing, benefits of cloud computing, cloud computing architecture, some cloud computing applications, cloud computing economics, and security concerns in cloud computing. Section 18.3 is devoted to mobile databases. This section deals with characteristics of mobile devices, challenges of mobile databases and locality based services. Section 18.4 deals with MapReduce that is designed to handle huge amount of data that is usually distributed over 100s or 1000s of commodity computers.

18.2 CLOUD COMPUTING AND DATA MANAGEMENT

Cloud computing was identified as one of the emerging technologies in the Claremont Meeting.

What is cloud computing and why is there so much talk about it? In a recent interview, the new Infosys CEO Mr Gopalkrishnan identified cloud computing as one of the technologies on which Infosys is focusing.

Cloud computing is a concept we all are already familiar with since we all use emails from Hotmail, Gmail, Rediffmail, Yahoo! and so on. By using these email systems we access, store and send emails using someone else's computer and memory installed somewhere else. Gmail and Hotmail now claim to provide several gigabytes of memory to each email user for free. Therefore, we are using cloud computing! Somewhere out there someone is providing us computing and storage to use email. The comparing is in "The clouds" or we may say it is providing cloud computing for free.

Although email was first used in the 1970s as computer network became more widely used. Few people knew about email then but then networks became ubiquitous and the Web was invented. This led to the invention of Hotmail by Sabir Bhatia in California and that meant that we did not have to worry about our own computers managing the email traffic. Someone else's machine could do it all. We only had to connect to the Hotmail website and create a Hotmail account and use it from anywhere in the world. Currently we have Hotmail, Yahoo, Gmail and Rediffmail which altogether have almost one billion email accounts. From 2010, Monash University is moving all student emails to the clouds using Gmail and the university will stop worrying about some 50,000 student email accounts. The staff will also move to Gmail. It makes a lot of economic sense to do that.

In addition to email, the most popular cloud services include social networking sites (about 500 million people that use Facebook are being social in the cloud), microblogging and blogging services such as Twitter and WordPress, video-sharing sites like YouTube, photo-sharing sites such as Flickr, document and applications sharing sites like Google Docs, social-bookmarking sites like Delicious, business sites like eBay, and ranking, rating and commenting sites such as Yelp and TripAdvisor.

There are many definitions of cloud computing. We present an informal definition.

Definition—Cloud Computing
Cloud computing is computing services offered on the Internet that may provide computing resources such as processing, storage and software that are normally not physically present at the user's location and the user pays only for the computing resources and services used.

2.5 THE ENTITY-RELATIONSHIP MODEL

The Entity-Relationship model (E-R model) is a widely used database modeling technique because it is simple and relatively easy to understand. The method facilitates communication between the database designer and the end user. It enables an abstract global view (that is, the *enterprise conceptual schema*) of the enterprise application to be developed without any consideration of efficiency of the ultimate database. The Entity-Relationship model was originally proposed in 1976 by Peter Chen although many variants of the technique have subsequently been devised.

E-R modeling is based on the concept that organizations consist of people, facilities and objects. These components of an enterprise interact with each other to achieve certain goals of the enterprise. As an example, when dealing with an enterprise that deals with cricket, the batsmen interact with bowlers, fielders and umpires to achieve the aim of playing a match. Another example is to look at a book publishing business which involves books, authors, printers, distributors, editors, sales data and so on.

All such things that are of interest to the enterprise are called *entities* and their interactions are called *relationships*. To develop a database model based on the E-R model involves identifying the entities and relationships of interest. These are often displayed in an E-R diagram. Before discussing these, we need to describe an entity and a relationship.

2.5.1 Entities and Entity Sets

An entity is a real or abstract object. It may be a person, a place, a building, or an event like a contract or a concert or an order that can be distinctly identified and is of interest. An entity exists independent of what does or does not exist in an enterprise. A specific cricket player, for example, Sachin Tendulkar with player ID 89001 or a venue Eden Gardens with a venue ID 65478 or a country India are examples of entities assuming that the database application requires information about them. Although entities are often concrete like a company, an entity may be abstract like an idea, concept or an event, for example, an ODI match 2688 between India and Australia or a Delhi to Mumbai flight number IA123. Whether an entity is real or abstract, the model makes no distinction between them but they must be something about which information is important.

A discussion of new technologies like Cloud Computing and Mobile Databases

In-depth coverage of E-R Model, Relational Model, Transaction Management and Concurrency, Query Processing, Backup and Recovery

9. Discuss the responsibilities of a DBA. Explain what would happen if a DBA was not responsible for an enterprise database system? Why does the DBA need to understand query optimization? Explain the role of a DBA in a simple database like the ODI database if it is being used by many people.
10. Could a modern university be supported if a file processing system was used to manage enterprise information? List three major difficulties that are likely to arise if no database system was available to the university. Discuss the difficulties.
11. Study the role of data governance by looking at some recent literature on data governance. What benefits can be obtained by an enterprise using data governance which they cannot get with current database systems? Discuss.
12. Select an enterprise that you are familiar with (for example, a school, college, company, small business, club or association). List all the information that this enterprise uses.
13. Give examples to illustrate three major advantages and three areas of concern when using an enterprise database system. Discuss their importance.
14. List five queries you might wish to pose to the ODI database given in Tables 1.1, 1.2 and 1.3.
15. Why is data independence important? Discuss its importance by giving an example.
16. Present a conceptual view of a student database. Present some external views given by different types of end users and show the mappings of these views to the conceptual view.

PROJECTS

1. If you have access to the Indian Railways Timetable, describe how you would computerize it and how much memory space the computerized timetable would take? What other information would be useful in the timetable?
2. Select a local company large enough to have a lot of information about its operations. Arrange to meet someone in that company who can tell you about the information they have and the ways they manage and use it. Write a brief report on the same.

LAB EXERCISES

1. Northern India University (NIU) is a large institution with several campuses scattered across north India. Academically, the university is divided into a number of faculties, such as Faculty of Arts and Faculty of Science. Some faculties operate on a number of campuses. Faculties, in turn, are divided into schools. For example, the School of Physics, the School of Information Technology, etc. The schools are not divided further into departments.

   Each student in the University is enrolled in a single course of study which involves a fixed core of subjects specific to that course as well as a number of electives taken from other courses. Each course is offered by one particular school. Each school has a number of lecturing staff. Students are awarded a grade for each subject they chose.

   List all the information that you need to store in a database for NIU.

Focuses on building database applications to aid professional learning

```
SELECT [DISTINCT| ALL] <List of Columns, Functions, Constants, etc>
        FROM <List of Tables or Views>
        [WHERE <Condition(s)>]
        [GROUP BY < Grouping Columns>]
        [HAVING <Condition>]
        [ORDER BY <Ordering Column(s)> [ASC|DESC];

UPDATE <Table Name>
SET <Column Name> = <Value>
WHERE <Condition>;
INSERT INTO <Table Name> [(Column List)]
VALUES (<Value List>);
DELETE FROM <Table Name> WHERE <Condition>;
CREATE VIEW <View Name> AS <Query>;
CREATE TABLE <Table Name>
        (<Column Name> <Data Type> [(<Size>)] <Column Constraint>, ... Other Columns);
```

Tables may have a variety of constraints as listed below. These are discussed in detail in Chapter 11 on Integrity.

NULL or NOT NULL
UNIQUE
PRIMARY KEY
CHECK
DEFAULT
FOREIGN KEY
UNIQUE
TRIGGER
ASSERTION

Pedagogy featuring Projects and Lab Exercises besides Multiple Choice Questions for holistic study

Peter P. S. Chen

Peter Chen is the creator of the Entity-Relationship model (E-R model), which serves as the foundation of many systems analysis, design methodologies, and computer-aided software engineering (CASE) tools. His first paper on the E-R model was published in 1976 and was included in the '38 most influential papers in Computer Science' by a survey of over 1,000 computer scientists.

Currently, Professor Chen is a distinguished Chair Professor at NTHU, Taiwan. He held the position of M. J. Foster distinguished Chair Professor of Computer Science at Louisiana State University in the United States from 1983–2008.

Dr. Chen holds a PhD in Computer Science/Applied Mathematics from Harvard University.

Profiles of eminent scholars and professionals in the field of database management

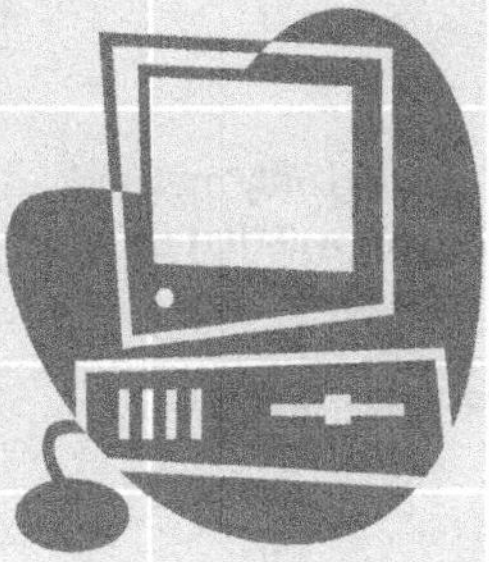

Introduction to Database Management

1

OBJECTIVES

- Introduce the importance of information for every enterprise.
- Discuss and define the concept of a database.
- Describe data governance and why databases are becoming so important.
- Briefly describe the evolution of database software.
- Describe differences between file systems and database systems.
- Explain database management systems (DBMS). The advantages and disadvantages of using an enterprise database.
- Discuss the three-level database architecture and data abstraction.
- Describe the different types of database users.
- Explain the concept of data independence.
- Present a DBMS system architecture.

KEYWORDS

Database, database management, database management systems, DBMS, data independence, data abstraction, metadata, file systems, advantages and disadvantages of using a database system, three-tier architecture, DBMS architecture and system architecture, end users, catalog, concurrency, transaction management, recovery, applications programmer, web databases, database history, database administrator, database design, requirements, testing, maintaining, importance of databases, characteristics of databases, selecting DBMS software, application programs, systems analysts, application programmers, cricket database, consistency.

The more this power of concentration, the more knowledge is acquired, because this is the one and only method of acquiring knowledge... in doing anything, the stronger the power of concentration, the better will that thing be done. This is the one call, the one knock, which opens the gate of nature, and lets out the flood of light.

Swami Vivekananda (1863–1902)

1.1 INTRODUCTION

Most modern enterprises except some small ones have data that they need to store in ways which will be easy to retrieve later. One of the most common types of database is a list of names and addresses of people who regularly deal with the enterprise. Originally when a business is small such lists may have been written on paper, then in a word processor or spreadsheet, but as the business and lists grow it becomes difficult to deal with the information stored in a word processor or a spreadsheet. Database technology may then be required.

Database management is about managing information resources of an enterprise. The enterprise may be a big company, a small business, a government department or a club; each of them generate a variety of data. The data can be, for example, about customers, credit cards, telephone calls, lottery tickets, orders, library books, students, employees, airline flights, etc. All such data (or information, we won't discuss the difference between the two) for every type of enterprise is a valuable resource and therefore, just like any other valuable resource, it needs to be managed effectively. With the advent of the World Wide Web and its widespread use in business, the amount of data that is being generated is growing exponentially, making data management even more important. Imagine the data being generated and stored by companies like amazon.com, eBay, Google, YouTube and Wikipedia that needs to be managed. On the other hand, consider the amount of data being generated by mobile phones in India. A lot of data must be stored for accounting purposes (information about every call and each sms must be stored for accounting) while other data, like the content of various sms messages, must also be stored for retrieval incase of security checks or more serious criminal proceedings. Thus, the amount of data being generated in the modern world using new technologies is mind boggling.

This chapter is organized as follows. A simple example of a cricket database is presented in the next section and a number of features of this database are discussed. In Section 1.3, the term database is defined and examples related to cricket are presented. An example of a university database is also presented. A number of popular websites are listed to show the amount of information that many websites now carry and which must be stored in databases. Section 1.4 describes a number of characteristics of databases and Section 1.5 discusses data governance and importance of databases for enterprises. Section 1.6 presents a brief history of database software.

Section 1.7 discusses the differences between file systems and database systems. A definition of database management system (DBMS) is presented along with some features of a DBMS in Section 1.8. Variety of users of database systems is described in Section 1.9. The next two sections present a number of advantages and concerns of using a centralized enterprise database system in a large enterprise as compared to the branches maintaining local database systems using conventional file systems. Sections 1.12 and 1.13 are devoted to explaining the three-level DBMS architecture, data abstraction and data independence. A typical DBMS architecture diagram is presented in Section 1.14 along with a description of its different components.

The role of the database administrator is discussed in Section 1.15. Section 1.16 explains the steps involved in designing an enterprise database system. The chapter concludes with a brief introduction to web databases followed by a number of guidelines for selecting a DBMS before making a purchase.

1.2 AN EXAMPLE OF A DATABASE

A simple example of a database is presented below.

Example 1.1

Consider the table presented in Table 1.1 that presents a list of the top ten batsmen in one day international (ODI) cricket in terms of the total number of runs scored. The data was current on 21 August 2010.

Table 1.1 Example of a simple database[1]

Player	*Span*	*Matches*	*Innings*	*Runs*	*Avg.*	*Strike Rate*	*100s*
SR Tendulkar	1989–2010	442	431	17598	45.12	86.26	46
ST Jayasuriya	1989–2010	444	432	13428	32.43	91.22	28
RT Ponting	1995–2010	351	342	13072	42.85	80.84	29
Inzamam-ul-Haq	1991–2007	378	350	11739	39.52	74.24	10
SC Ganguly	1992–2007	311	300	11363	41.02	73.70	22
JH Kallis	1996–2010	303	289	10838	45.72	72.72	17
R Dravid	1996–2009	339	313	10765	39.43	71.17	12
BC Lara	1990–2007	299	289	10405	40.48	79.51	19
Mohammed Yousuf	1998–2010	282	267	9624	42.39	75.15	15
AC Gilchrist	1996–2008	287	279	9619	35.89	96.94	16

It should be noted that in the above database the batting average for a player is not obtained by dividing the total number of runs scored by the total number of innings played. It is obtained by dividing the total runs scored by the total number of innings in which the player got out. The number of times the player was not out is not counted and the number of times a batsman was not out is not included in the table above because of space considerations. For example, Sachin Tendulkar was not out 38 times while Adam Gilchrist was not out only 11 times.

The information in Table 1.1 is quite interesting. There are three players in the top ten ODI batsmen order from India and none from England. Also the number of runs scored and the number of centuries made by Sachin Tendulkar are so high as compared to other players that it is unlikely he would be overtaken by another batsman, for example, Sanath Jayasuriya or Ricky Ponting, in the near future. Also, let us not forget that Tendulkar is an active cricketer who continues to score runs.

1. Full names of all Pakistani players have been used, since they are widely known by their full names.

There are some other things we should note about the database:

1. Each table in the database requires a name so that it can be easily identified by that name. We have named our table the *bestODIbatsmen*[2].
2. The names given to columns in the top row are of special importance in a database. They are the titles of the columns and each column is referred to by that name. If we wish to state the number of ODI matches played by a player, it will be referred to by the name *Matches*. The name *matches* with a lower case *m* will not be acceptable and other names like *Games* will also not work.
3. If some data has been typed incorrectly (and errors in databases are not uncommon), for example, if the name Tendulkar in the table above is mistyped as Tendulker, then there is no simple way to retrieve information about Tendulkar. Although any person interested in cricket would know that Tendulker is really Tendulkar, the computerized database has no intelligence.
4. The second column with the name *Span* gives entries like 1975–85 as the year the player started playing ODI cricket and the last year he played. This data is treated as one value and usually there is no simple way to separate the two dates and query the database on them separately.
5. The database above is ordered according to the total runs scored. Although such ordering is helpful when humans view the database, the ordering of data when stored in a computer is often not known and may change over time. For example, over time Ricky Ponting and Jacques Kallis are likely to make more runs and would be expected to climb up the ladder of best batsmen. Although unlikely, given the lead Sachin Tendulkar has, but Ricky Ponting in theory could take over as the highest scorer of ODI runs. In a computerized database, it is inefficient to be swapping rows of the database to maintain the desired order, when the computer can be used to sort the table, whenever the user needs it sorted on any column. For example, some users may want the table sorted on the batting average while others on the strike rate. As a corollary, there is no concept of the first row or the last row in a computerized database.
6. In the example database, a number of columns are related. For example, batting average is based on the total runs scored and the number of innings played (and the number of innings in which the player was not out), which is itself related to the number of matches played. Such relationships in a database are not desirable, since a user may by mistake increase the number of matches when a player starts a new match, and then forget to increase the number of innings, or the total number of runs scored, or the batting average. The data therefore from time to time could be inaccurate. This does not matter so much for our simple cricket database but it would not be acceptable, say, in a bank accounting database. There are ways of overcoming such problems which are discussed later.
7. A related problem with Table 1.1 is that all the information in it is an aggregation derived from information about each ODI. The example database in Table 1.1 has been used because the information is interesting for people who love cricket but it is not a very good idea to maintain tables of aggregates, since it is difficult to check the accuracy of the information, and it is easy to make a mistake in updating such summary information. If we store information about each ODI in the database then the aggregation can be carried out by the system ensuring there are no mistakes.

---

2. Once a table has a name, it may be written in a compact form by its schema. For example, Table 1.1 may be written as *bestODIbatsmen(Player, Span, Matches, Innings, Runs, Avg, Strike Rate, 100s)*. This notation has also been used later.

8. Furthermore, there are some, perhaps not so obvious, problems with our example database. Firstly, there is no convenient way to show that a player is still playing. For example, we have put 1989–2010 in *Span* for Sachin Tendulkar. This does not tell us that he is still playing. Although Adam Gilchrist played during 1996–2008, he has retired and therefore is not playing any more. Furthermore, the database assumes that a player always plays for only one country. We leave it to the reader to discover if there have been any players for which this is not true.

These issues and a variety of other issues related to computerized databases are discussed further in the following chapters.

1.3 WHAT IS A DATABASE?

Whether it is a cricket database or an airline booking database, databases have become essential in all aspects of modern life. It is often said that we live in an information society and that information is a very valuable resource (or, in other words, information is power). In this information society, the term *database* has become a rather common term although its meaning appears to have become somewhat vague, as the importance of database systems has grown. Some people use the term database of an organization to mean all the data in the organization (whether computerized or not). Other people use the term to mean the software that manages the data. We will use it to mean a collection of computerized information such that it is available to many people for various uses. A definition of a database may be given as.

A database is a well organized collection of data that are related in a meaningful way which can be accessed in different logical orders but are stored only once. The data in the database is therefore integrated, structured and shared.

According to this definition, the simple database given in the cricket example in Table 1.1 is not really a database. We may consider it a *toy database* and will continue to keep calling it a database and use it when appropriate. Similarly a *database* that someone might have for personal use on his/her home PC would not be considered a database. Also, a collection of tables that are not related to each other, for example, a table of cricket players and a table of swimmers, unless they can be related through the country they come from or in some other way, cannot be considered a database.

The main features of data in a database are as follows:

- It is well organized.
- It is related.
- It is accessible in different orders without great difficulty.
- It is stored only once.

It is assumed that operations (for example, update, insert and retrieve) on the database can be carried out in a simple and flexible way. Also, since a database tends to be a long term resource of an organization, it is expected that planned as well as unplanned applications can (in general) be carried out without great difficulty.

Example 1.2

We have noted above that a single table like Table 1.1 is not really a database. Now let us add another table. This table is also a summary of performance of a number of players in ODI matches. Consider Table 1.2 given below which gives information about the best bowlers in ODI matches based on the total number of wickets taken before 21 August 2010. Information in this table is also quite interesting. There is still no player from the UK and only one player appears in both Tables 1.1 and 1.2. Only two bowlers from India and three from Sri Lanka appear in Table 1.2.

Table 1.2 The best ODI bowlers (Table Name: *bestbowlers*)

Player	*Span*	*Matches*	*Balls*	*Runs*	*Wickets*	*Ave*	*Econ*	*ST*
M Muralitharan	1993–2010	337	18169	11885	515	23.07	3.92	35.2
Wasim Akram	1984–2003	356	18186	11812	502	23.52	3.89	36.2
Waqar Younis	1989–2003	262	12698	9919	416	23.84	4.68	30.5
WPUJC Vaas	1994–2008	322	15775	11014	400	27.53	39.4	39.2
SM Pollock	1996–2008	303	15712	9631	393	24.50	3.67	39.9
GD McGrath	1993–2007	250	12970	8391	381	22.02	3.88	34.0
A Kumble	1990–2007	271	14496	10412	337	30.89	4.30	43.0
J Srinath	1991–2003	229	11935	8847	315	28.08	4.44	37.8
B Lee	2000–2009	185	9442	7428	323	22.99	4.72	29.2
ST Jayasuriya	1989–2009	444	14838	11825	322	36.72	4.78	46.0

Now let us ask the question: Do the two tables, Table 1.1 and Table 1.2, together form a database? Although the information is well organized, the information in the two tables is difficult to relate. We do have some common data, for example, the names of those players that appear in both the tables (ST Jayasuriya is the only one) but the relationship is not strong. So it may be concluded that these two tables also do not form a database.

Example 1.3

Let us now consider a third table. Table 1.3, called *Players*, includes information about all the players given in Table 1.1 and 1.2. As we have noted earlier, there is no concept of sorting of rows in a real database. Although the information in Table 1.3 has been sorted on the column Country but it could easily be sorted according to any other column. Also, there are no duplicates in the table.

Now let us again ask the same question as we did earlier. Do the three tables, Tables 1.1, 1.2 and 1.3 together form a database? By including this table, the relationship between the three tables becomes stronger. We can now find out which players are best ODI batsmen and come from India, which could not be done before. It is also now possible, for example, to prepare a list of all Indian players who are either best ODI batsmen or best ODI bowlers. We can therefore conclude that the three tables together could be called a database since they have the properties of a database and assuming the tables are being shared.

Table 1.3 List of some players that have played in ODIs (Table Name: *Players*)

Name	*Country*	*Place of birth*	*Year of birth*
RT Ponting	Australia	Launceston	1974
AC Gilchrist	Australia	Bellingen	1971
GD McGrath	Australia	Dubbo	1970
B Lee	Australia	Wollongong	1976
SR Tendulkar	India	Mumbai	1973
SC Ganguly	India	Calcutta	1972
R Dravid	India	Indore	1973
A Kumble	India	Bangalore	1970
J Srinath	India	Mysore	1969
Inzamam-ul-Haq	Pakistan	Multan	1970
Wasim Akram	Pakistan	Lahore	1966
Waqar Younis	Pakistan	Vehari	1969
Mohammed Yousuf	Pakistan	Lahore	1974
JH Kallis	South Africa	Cape Town	1975
SM Pollock	South Africa	Port Elizabeth	1973
ST Jayasuriya	Sri Lanka	Matara	1969
WPUJC Vaas	Sri Lanka	Muttumagala	1974
M Muralitharan	Sri Lanka	Kandy	1972
BC Lara	West Indies	Santa Cruz	1969

We have included limited information in the example tables because of space considerations. For example, we could include the number of times a batsman was not out, each batsman's highest score, each bowler's best bowling performance, each player's date of first ODI played and so on.

Just like in cricket, in every modern enterprise, a large amount of data is generated about its operations. This data is sometimes called *operational data*. The operational data includes the data an organization must necessarily maintain about its operation but does not include temporary results or any transient information.

Since data is a valuable resource for every enterprise, often a great deal of money is spent collecting, storing, maintaining and using it. The running of a modern enterprise depends on proper maintenance of its operational data.

A Case Study

The case study deals with the operational data of an enterprise; the enterprise being a university. A university's operational data includes information about courses, students, academic staff, other staff, and enrolments. There is much more information of course, for example, departments, library data, financial data as well as data about research and about university facilities.

The information may include the following:

1. Student personal data (studentID, student's name, gender, current address, home address, date of birth, nationality)
2. Student academic data (studentID, student's school results, courses completed and grades, current enrolment)
3. Academic staff data (staff ID, staff member's name, gender, current address, date of birth, nationality, academic qualifications, appointment history, current appointment, salary history, current salary, sabbatical leave information, recreational leave, sick leave)
4. Research data (projectID, researcherID, funding, publications, research students)
5. Non-academic staff data (staffID, staff member's name, gender, current address, date of birth, nationality, qualifications, experience, appointment history, current appointment, salary history, current salary, recreational leave, sick leave)
6. Courses (or units) offered data (courseID, course name, department, syllabus, lecturer, quota if any)
7. Financial data (budget information, receipts, expenditure)

The above data is only a very small sample of data that a university generates (for example, data generated by the library is not included and data about facilities, for example, buildings and equipment is not included) and we leave it to the reader to think of other information that should be included for each of the items listed above. In fact, in the early 1990s, the Australian universities initiated a project to develop a unified database model for all student information that could be used by all Australian universities. After months of effort by a team of experts and spending millions of dollars, the project was cancelled in spite of the team having developed the specifications of the information which was more than 1000-pages long. The difficulty was that not all the universities agreed with the collection of information that was developed.

The above data would have a number of classes of users, for example:

1. Instructors who need information about enrolments in the courses that they teach and heads of departments about finances of their departments. These are users that use the information in the database but do not develop their own software. They are often called *end users*.
2. Programmers in the IT services unit who develop programs (called *application programs*) to produce reports that are needed regularly by the government, university administration and the departments. These programmers are called *applications programmers*. They are also responsible for developing programs that assist end users in retrieving the information that they need in their work.
3. The Registrar or some other person is in-charge of the database and makes decisions about the kind information that is to be stored in the database, and also decides who can modify and access which parts of the database.

For a large modern enterprise, it is difficult to overestimate the value of its databases. From time to time, we read stories in the press describing enterprises that were not able to handle their data effectively. In fact, in 2002, there was a case of an Australian university using the wrong database software to process its data which resulted in a loss of millions of dollars. Some interesting stories of database and software development failures are given in Glass (1997, 2001).

To conclude, we note that data

- is a valuable resource and an investment and
- should be carefully managed like other resources (for example, manpower).

Example 1.4
Very Large Databases

The example given below illustrates the amount of information currently being circulated on the Web and its fast paced growth.

Computing has changed enormously since the early days of very large and very expensive computers. This is partly because of technological developments in computer hardware and software and partly because of the development of the World Wide Web. Some of these trends can be illustrated by the popularity of the following websites:

1. Google, Yahoo and MSN—Every day, millions of people use these three websites that enable people to search the Web, use chatrooms, free email and a number of other services.
2. Ebay—A site that enables people to sell and buy new and used items by way of a person-to-person auction.
3. YouTube—Every day, millions of people watch this website that enables them to put and share videos on the Web.
4. MySpace—Every day a large number of people visit this website that facilitates social networking.
5. Facebook— It is another social networking website that connects people through social networks and encourages online interaction through groups and communities.
6. Wikipedia—A free online collaborative encyclopaedia that includes a huge amount of information on almost every topic.
7. Skype—This is a nearly free person-to-person telecommunications application that uses the Internet for making phone calls.
8. Flickr—A large number of people use this website to share photos.
9. Blogger—Free personal journal publishing tool that allows people to publish their own blogs and share them with others.
10. Fotolog—A website that enables people to share photos and blogs.

The reader is encouraged to consider the size of these sites and find out how much information each of these sites carry. Most of these sites are growing rapidly and have millions of users. For example, Facebook is reported to have more than 500 million users in September 2010[3] (less than six years after it was started) and there are 30 billion pieces of content shared each month. MySpace, also of a similar size, had 100 billion rows of data, 14 billion comments on the site, 20 billion mails, 50 million mails per day (more than Yahoo, Hotmail or Google), 10 billion friend relationships, 1.5 billion images, and 8 million images being uploaded per day as per data published in 2008.

---

3. Refer to the statistics posted at
http://www.facebook.com/press/info.php?statistic
Also look at http://blog.compete.com/2009/02/09/facebook-myspace-twitter-social-network

How would one manage such a huge amount of information?

In addition to these trends, there are a number of other new trends in computing. For example, the popularity of devices like iPod and iPhone, the digitization of millions of old books, the development of Internet TV and the availability of wireless broadband. All these developments deal with processing, storing and communicating information. Although the computer was developed to solve numerical problems, it has increasingly become an information-handling device. However, the conceptual basis of the computer architecture has not changed so significantly.

1.4 CHARACTERISTICS OF DATABASES

Various characteristics distinguish the database approach from conventional file processing systems. Some of these differences are discussed in Section 1.7. In this section a list of a various characteristics of database systems is given.

1.4.1 Persistent Data

A database only stores persistent data and once data has been stored in a database system it always stays there unless deleted by an explicit request.

1.4.2 Metadata and Self-describing Nature

A database system contains not only the database itself but also the descriptions of the data structures and its constraints. This is called *metadata* which may be defined as *data about data.* In the context of a database, metadata includes information about how the data is stored in the computer storage. Metadata, discussed in more detail later, is an integral part of the database and stored in the database itself. It is used not only by database managers but also by database end-users. This separation makes database system very different from traditional file-based systems in which data definition was a part of the application programs.

1.4.3 Data Independence

Perhaps the most important characteristic of a database system is data independence which may be defined as the ability to separate the database definition from the physical storage organization of the database. Therefore, information about the physical structure of the database is stored in the system catalog (the database metadata) and not in the application programs. Therefore any changes in the physical structure of the database do not impact the application programs. Data independence is discussed in more detail in Section 1.13.

1.4.4 Access Flexibility and Security

In modern database systems no restrictions are placed on the content the users can access unless the user is not authorized to access some data. Security is enhanced by using the concept of database views which are subsets of the database. Different views may be defined for different classes of users thereby controlling access to the database system. Each view might contain only the data relevant for a user or a group of users.

Most modern database systems, other than those used for personal use, are multiuser systems that allow multiple users to access the system at the same time. Providing this facility to the users requires concurrency control to ensure that several users accessing the same data item at the same time do so without violating the database consistency.

1.5 DATA GOVERNANCE AND IMPORTANCE OF DATABASES

An enterprise has many assets (for example, people, property, intellectual property) but an important asset whose value is often not recognized is the enterprise data. This is however changing in today's competitive world. Every enterprise needs a 'single version of the truth' but it is not always possible to find that version. Many years ago, the company, Coca Cola, could not even be sure of the number of bottles of soft drinks they were producing each day, in all their plants. Therefore, many enterprises are now recognizing the importance of *data governance*. Data governance essentially refers to decision-making regarding effective management of an enterprise's data including data quality, metadata, and data access.

Since the 1960s there has been a continual and rapid growth in the use of database technology which can deal with some aspects of data governance. Databases have become an important part of every company with data that needs to be managed. Not only has there been a dramatic growth in the number of such systems but also enormous growth in the amount of information stored in them. The complexity of applications of database systems has also being growing simultaneously. A report produced by Lyman and Varian at the University of California at Berkeley is a fascinating study on the amount of information in the world and its pace of growth.

Databases contain an enterprise's data or what we call information. As noted earlier, we do not wish to discuss the meanings of data, information and knowledge since there is no need to establish either a hierarchy or a temporal sequence in discussing data and information. It appears information is a term that is more in vogue these days than data. No one talks about the discipline of data processing any more. Instead we are more likely to use the term 'information technology'.

It is said that information is power and we live in an information society. In some sense, every society, whether developing or developed, is an information society although the more complex a society, the more central information is to its activities. Therefore as a country develops, it uses more information. We can easily understand that information has great value. Let us give some examples to illustrate that value:

- The website Google has nothing but information, and its market capitalization is well over US$100 billion.
- All the websites listed above in Example 1.4 are totally driven by information and they have significant impact on human societies all over the world.
- Warren Buffett, an American investor, has become one of the richest men in the world by just trading information.

There are many other signs of importance and growth of information. The sale of hard disks has been growing exponentially and the price per MByte has been coming down exponentially so much so that a TByte disk in India was selling for below 4,500 INR in January 2011.

Information has therefore become important and an element of commerce. Earlier, success was based on criteria as finance, manufacturing, land, food and so on, but today successful businesses are those that can manage their information. Managing information involves effective collection, organisation, storage, processing and presentation of information. For this reason effective database management and data governance in an enterprise are of great important.

1.6 HISTORY OF DATABASE SOFTWARE

In the early days of computing, computers were mainly used for solving mathematical problems. Even in solving mathematical problems, it was observed that some tasks were common to many problems that were being solved. It therefore was considered desirable to build special software modules that performed frequently occurring computing tasks such as computing Sin(x). This led to the development of mathematical software libraries that are now an integral part of any computer system and most users do not even know that such libraries exist.

By the late 1950s, storage, maintenance and retrieval of non-numeric data had become important. Again, it was observed that some data processing tasks (for example, sorting) occurred quite frequently. This led to the development of *generalized* software modules for some of the most common and frequently carried out tasks.

A general module by its nature tends to be somewhat less efficient than a module designed for a specific problem. In the late fifties and early sixties, when hardware costs were high, use of general modules was not popular since it became a matter of trade-off between hardware and software costs. In the last 30–40 years, hardware costs have been going down dramatically while the costs of building software have not. It is therefore no more a trade-off between hardware and software costs since hardware is relatively cheap and building reliable software is expensive. It therefore makes sense to build generalized software that many enterprises can use.

The earliest known use of the term *database* was in 1963 and the first database management systems were developed in the 1960s. Database management systems evolved from generalized modules for file processing (some of them were called SORT/MERGE packages) as the users demanded more extensive and more flexible facilities for managing increasing amounts of data. This development of database management systems allowed effective storage and retrieval from large databases which was not possible before. Data storage media (disks) were still quite expensive as the amount of data which businesses and governments wanted to process continued to grow. During the next 10–20 years a number of DBMS software packages became available. Most of the early DBMS software were vendor specific, for example, IBM developed a system called IMS (Information Management System) in the mid 1960s which is still being used to process data in some legacy systems. Another early DBMS was called IDMS (Integrated Data Management Store). The data models used by these were the network model based on Bachman's ideas, and the hierarchical model used in the IMS database system. Both IMS and IDMS were non-relational systems. More details about the database models used in these systems is given at the end of Chapter 3. There were other database systems that were released at the end of 1960s. For example, a DBMS called ADABAS was released by a German company, Software AG in 1970. It was initially released for IBM mainframes. It used an inverted list database.

Database technology has undergone major changes since the early database systems of the 1960s and 1970s which were based on the hierarchical and network models that were developed in the 1960s. With the proposal of the relational database model around 1970, research was started for building relational DBMS at IBM and University of California, Berkeley. Most modern systems are now based on the relational database model which is discussed in Chapter 3. An interesting early history of database systems is presented by Fry and Sibley (1976).

1.7 FILE SYSTEMS VS DATABASE SYSTEMS

There are a number of major differences between a file processing system and a database system. A file processing system often uses a relatively simple data structure to store information about one particular thing. For example, a file may be about players consisting of player records including names, date of birth and nationality while another file may be about matches consisting of match records including date, ground and the teams competing. A file may be using file management software, for example, like the widely used Indexed Sequential Access Method (ISAM) but most file processing systems are implemented for a single application. The same data may be repeated in more than one file and the physical storage structure of the same data may be different for different files if the application programs were written by different programmers.

Therefore in most file management systems, every application carries out its own file processing even if two application programs are carrying out very similar tasks. The programs may involve each user defining and using one or more files that he/she needs. For example, in a university environment, the admissions department may have defined its own files and its application programs may be making use of those files while academic departments may have their own file systems with neither of the departments knowing anything about the other departments' files although the files of both the departments are dealing with students. Such independent maintenance and processing of data not only leads to wastage of computer storage, it also leads to redundancy or replication of data which can further lead to data inconsistencies. Furthermore, the files of the two departments cannot have any inter-relationship among the data stored in their files even if the data is related.

In a database system, no application program accesses the files directly since there is a single repository of data that is defined and maintained by the database system and then accessed by all users. The access to the database is handled by the database management system. When an application program needs to access some data then it must call upon the database system to provide it the data that is required. The database system not only manages all the data, but as already noted, it also contains complete definition or description of the database structure and constraints called metadata.

A database system also allows multiple users to access the same database at the same time. Such use requires concurrency control so that several users trying to update the same data at the same time are controlled. Concurrency control is discussed in Chapter 9. This is just not possible in a conventional file system. Moreover to enforce security, virtual tables called views may be created in database systems and users are restricted to only one or more views of the data that they are allowed to see. This is discussed in Chapter 5.

In a traditional file system, if some changes are made in the structure of one or more files, the changes will affect all the application programs that use them. On the other hand, in case of a database system, the structure of the database is stored separately and therefore changes to data structure do not normally lead to changes in the application programs. This property is known as *data independence* and is discussed later in this chapter in Section 1.13.

Another major difference between file systems and database systems is that a database can represent complex relationships among the information that is stored in the database and can therefore retrieve and update related data easily which is not possible in file processing systems. Finally, there are a number of additional characteristics of a database that are not possible in a file system. These include an ability to define and enforce integrity constraints for the data that is stored in the database. A database also usually provides facilities for backup and recovery. These are discussed in Chapter 11.

In a summary, file processing systems may not be very stable over time because file processing tasks may change over time and these changes may in turn require expensive changes to be made to the files. Furthermore, in file systems, there is a possibility of information being duplicated and this can lead to redundancy and wastage of computer storage which in turn may also result in data inconsistencies. A database system on the other hand usually does not suffer from such problems since the database system does not need to be modified if new data processing is needed. A database may be shared by many users and many applications leading to higher productivity. In addition, it provides facilities for concurrency control, security, integrity and recovery.

1.8 WHAT IS A DBMS?

As discussed earlier, a database is a well organized collection of data. Before the database can be used, the database needs to be stored in the computer in some way so that data from the database may be retrieved when required and modified when necessary. Simple tables like the cricket database given above may even be stored in an Excel spreadsheet file and retrieved, viewed and printed when the need arises. However, when a database is large, for example, an airline's booking database; storing the database in a spreadsheet is not practical since the database is too large and needs to allow many users from different parts of the world to access it at the same time. The users should be able to carry out operations like insertion, deletion and retrieval (and others, for example, sorting). To provide such facilities, any large database needs to be managed by a substantial package of software. This software is commonly called a *Database Management System (DBMS)*. The primary purpose of a DBMS is to allow a user to store, update and retrieve data in abstract terms and thus make it easy to maintain and retrieve information from a database. A DBMS relieves the user from having to know about exact physical representations of data and having to specify detailed algorithms for storing, updating and retrieving data. Without a DBMS, a database would be of little use. With a DBMS, a database becomes a powerful tool to support the operations of an enterprise and to understand and analyse the enterprise.

A database management system may be defined as follows:

> ***A Database Management System (DBMS) is a large software package that controls the specification, organization, storage, retrieval and update of data in a database.***

A DBMS carries out many different tasks including the provision of various facilities to enable a user to specify and build a database, and to access and modify data once the database has been built. The DBMS is an intermediate link between the physical database, the computer and the operating system, and on the other hand, the users. To provide different facilities to different types of users, a DBMS normally provides one or more specialized programming languages often called *database languages*. Different DBMS may provide different database languages, but in recent times all DBMS are based on the same abstract model of a database, the relational data model. Given that the underlying model of almost all modern database systems is the same, a language called Structured Query Language or SQL has been declared as a de facto standard. The relational model and SQL is discussed in Chapter 3 and 5 respectively.

Let us consider a simple example of SQL, given in Fig. 1.1, for retrieving data from the database of *bestODIbatsmen*.

```
SELECT Player
FROM bestODIbatsmen
WHERE matches > 400
```

Figure 1.1 Structure of a simple SQL query

This query would retrieve the names of the batsmen that are in the table *bestODIbatsmen* (Table 1.1) and have played more than 400 ODI matches (that is, SR Tendulkar and ST Jayasuriya).

SELECT, FROM and WHERE are reserve words in SQL. Some people do not like the keyword SELECT because what is really meant is either find the names or print the names or retrieve the names but it is the keyword used in SQL. The word FROM must always be followed by the name of the table where the information is to be found (there can be more than one table containing the same information, as we will see later) and WHERE is followed by one or more conditions that the information must satisfy.

One simple way of looking at the way the DBMS processes this query is to think of the software looking at every row in the table in turn and selecting only those rows for which the WHERE condition is true. The DBMS then provides only the values from the columns whose names follow the keyword SELECT for the rows that have been selected.

It should be noted that retrieving data from a structured database like that given in Tables 1.1, 1.2 and 1.3 is quite different than retrieving data from the Web using a search engine, since the Web stores data which is not as well structured as a table.

Since a DBMS is a generalized (large) piece of software, every time a new database is set up using the software, the steps given below must be followed:

1. The database must be defined using the DBMS. Although the simple cricket database in Table 1.1 has only one table, any significant database would have much more information and many tables (more than 100 tables are not uncommon). The structure of the information (for example, number of tables and their columns and each column's type) needs to be specified to the DBMS. This logical structure of the database is often called a *schema* of the database that is to be set up. Obviously some language is required to be able to communicate the structure to the DBMS. A language that allows the database to be described to the DBMS as well as provide facilities for changing the database (for example, adding a column to the table *bestbasmen*; Table 1.1 above may need a column specifying the number of times the player was not out) and for defining and changing physical data structures is called the *data definition language (or DDL)*.
2. The database must be loaded. Put the initial data that is available into the computer using the DDL. Obviously, a database is dynamic and information is added, modified and deleted from it all the time.

3. The database may now be queried. New data can be inserted, deleted and updated, once the data has been stored in the computer. To manipulate, modify and retrieve information, a language for manipulating and retrieving data stored in the DBMS is needed. Such a language is called a *data manipulation language (DML)*.

Each DBMS needs a DDL to define the database and a DML to retrieve and modify information in the database. The two languages, DDL and DML, may be parts of a unified database language as, for example, in SQL which is discussed in Chapter 5. We also note that SQL provides facilities for use in two different ways:

1. *Query Language*—SQL provides powerful facilities to interact with the database. A query language is designed to be simple so that it can be used by nonprogrammers.
2. *Extended Host Language*—Although the SQL query language provides powerful interactive facilities to database users, it is often necessary to retrieve information from a database and process it in a way that cannot be done by the query language. It then becomes necessary for a database system to provide facilities in a standard programming language like Java or C++ to enable the user to interact with the database through software that has been developed in one of these standard programming languages. The programming language that is extended is usually called a *host language*.

To summarize, a database system consists of the items listed in Fig. 1.2.

Some years ago, as noted earlier, DBMS packages marketed by computer manufacturers (for example, IBM) were designed to run only on that manufacturer's machines. The market has changed dramatically since the 1980s and now independent software houses are designing and selling DBMS software (for example, ORACLE or Microsoft SQL Server) that can run on many different types of machines.

- The database (data)
- A DBMS (software)
- A DDL and a DML (part of the DBMS)
- Application programs

Figure 1.2 Components of a database system

1.9 USERS OF A DATABASE SYSTEM

There are several ways of classifying database users. They can be classified by the way the users interact with the system or by their roles in a database system. We will present a top-down approach, starting from the database administrators.

1.9.1 Database Administrators

We do not discuss the role of database administrators here since their role is discussed later in the chapter in detail in Section 1.15.

1.9.2 Database Designers

In large database design projects there are usually two types of designers, viz., logical database designers and physical database designers. The logical designers help in identifying data and relationships between them (as we will see in the next chapter) without taking into account the software that will be used. Once the data and relationships have been identified and modeled, the physical designers look at the ways the database model can be best mapped to physical storage (for example, hard disks) to deliver the best performance. Issues of physical storage are discussed in Chapter 7 and a number of possible data structures and their characteristics are described. The database designers may need to discuss with the database users which aspects of performance are important to them.

1.9.3 System Analysts and Application Programmers

These highly technical users determine the requirements of end users. Systems analysts develop specifications for application programs that are needed to meet these requirements. Application programmers then implement these specifications as application programs that are appropriately tested, documented and maintained. Such programs need to provide the functionality that is required by end users for whom the programs are being designed. The programmers may also be involved in designing and implementing some DBMS modules, for example, for implementing catalog, interface processors, data access, and interfaces to the software packages.

1.9.4 End Users

End users are a great variety of users that use a database in their work. They use the database for querying, updating, and generating reports. Not all end users are using a database every day, for example, I don't use the library database every day but I do use it regularly. Users like me may be called *casual end users* of the library database. In some cases, a user may be using a database even less frequently than I use the library catalogue. For example, I may check my airline bookings when I have booked a flight but this might happen only 2–3 times a year. Such users may be called *occasional end users*.

The end users normally learn only a few facilities that they use repeatedly. These facilities may include ways to use a database query language to specify their query requests. For example, while accessing the university library catalogue I need to learn the method to search it at an advanced level, reserve a book, renew a loan and browse through some electronic books and journals available in the Monash library.

1.9.5 Naive and Sophisticated Users

Some end users have jobs that require constant querying and updating a database, using standard types of queries and updates (sometime called *canned* transactions) that have been carefully programmed and tested. They do not need to understand the DBMS or the underlying database. Such users may be called *naïve users* and include, for example, a bank teller, a cashier, a policeman, or a nurse. On the other hand, some users are quite sophisticated and are familiar with the DBMS that they are using, including the underlying structure of the database. These users may be called *sophisticated users* and they are likely to be using SQL interactively or in an embedded form to perform their queries. These users include engineers, computer scientists and business analysts who are thoroughly familiar with the facilities of the DBMS and the underlying database and are able to implement its applications to meet their advanced requirements.

1.9.6 Workers Behind the Scene

They are not classified as database users since they typically do not use the database as a part of their job. They include tool developers that develop tools for database design, performance monitoring, graphical interfaces, and test data generation. Another group of users behind the scenes is operators and maintenance personnel as well as system administration personnel who are responsible for the actual running and maintenance of the hardware and software environment for the database system.

1.10 ADVANTAGES OF USING AN ENTERPRISE DATABASE

A question that often arises in large organizations is why local branches can't keep local information on a local computer using their own favourite software? Some small branches may feel that they do not need to use a DBMS since they have always managed their data using their favourite file processing system software (for example, Filemaker Pro[4]). There are many reasons why using such file processing software and maintaining information locally is often not a good idea.

In a central enterprise database system, the data is managed by the enterprise DBMS and all access to the data is through the DBMS providing a key to effective data processing. This contrasts with local data being stored and processed locally perhaps using different DBMS and without any central control. The local database may be based on considerable local knowledge of data structures being used. Although distributed database technology (discussed in Chapter 13) allows an enterprise to develop a conceptual view of the database even if the database is physically distributed, such distributed databases require considerable central monitoring and control.

In a database system, whether it is distributed or not, the enterprise DBMS provides the interface between the application programs and the data. When changes are made to data representation, the metadata[5] maintained by the DBMS is changed but the DBMS continues to provide data to application programs in the same way as before. The DBMS handles the task of transformation of data whenever necessary.

This independence between the programs and the data, as noted earlier, is data independence. Data independence is important because every time some change needs to be made to the database structure, the application programs that were being used before the change should normally continue to work. To provide

4. FileMaker Pro is a cross-platform file processing software that now allows some database functionality including SQL and web publishing support as well as support for forms and reports.
5. In the context of database, metadata is data about the database, for example, names of tables, number of columns in each of them, their types, number of rows in each table, etc. The term 'meta' comes from a Greek word that means 'alongside, with, after, next'. In addition to database systems, metadata applies to many situations. For example, when an MS Word document is created, it is automatically saved into a file with additional document metadata information that is hidden from the user. This metadata information can hint at authorship, times and dates of revisions and other tidbits. Some of this metadata can be viewed by looking at the properties of the document. Third-party programs are available that will crack open even more metadata hidden in MS Word documents. Another example of metadata is the catalogue in a library. The catalogue is metadata since it is about resources available in the library. In the context of a database, the metadata is stored in the *data dictionary*, which is a term for data describing the database. The database software uses this metadata to interpret and execute SQL queries (as discussed in Chapter 7). Metadata can also be used as a window into the database and to learn about objects and data within the database.

   Web pages also have metadata about them. Web document metadata may include the title, author, and modification date of a web document, copyright and licensing information about the document, its content rating, or the availability schedule for some shared resource. Given the importance of web metadata, a Resource Description Framework (RDF) has been designed to represent it. This metadata can itself be presented in a database.

a high degree of data independence, a DBMS must include a well-designed metadata management system.

When an enterprise uses a DBMS, all enterprise data may be integrated into one system, thus reducing redundancies (redundancy occurs when exactly the same data is stored in more than one place) and making data management more efficient. In addition, the integrated DBMS provides centralized control of the operational data. Some advantages of data independence, integration and centralized control are listed in Fig. 1.3.

- Redundancies and inconsistencies can be reduced
- Better service can be provided to users
- The cost of developing and maintaining systems is low
- Standards can be enforced
- Security can be improved
- Integrity can be improved
- A data model must be developed

Figure 1.3 Advantages of using a database system

These advantages can be elaborated as given below.

- *Redundancies and inconsistencies can be reduced*—Data inconsistencies are often encountered in everyday life. For example, I have come across situations when a new address is communicated to an organization that we deal with (for example, a bank, telephone company, or an electricity company) which results in some communications from that organization being sent to the new address while others continue to be mailed to the old address. Such situations are now less common since combining all the data in a single database results in each piece of information being stored only once. This reduces redundancy. It also reduces inconsistencies, since the enterprise does not have two different addresses anymore. And it reduces the cost of collection, storage and updating of data.
- *Better service can be provided to the users*—A DBMS is often used to support enterprise operations and to provide better service to the enterprise users of the system and to its customers. Once an enterprise establishes a centralized database, the availability of information and the possibility of its revision is likely to improve and the users can obtain new and combined information as soon as it is available. Also, use of a DBMS allows users that do not know programming to interact with the data more easily. The ability to quickly obtain new and combined information is becoming increasingly important for improving services to demanding customers in a competitive environment. Furthermore, various levels of government bodies are now requiring organizations to provide more information about their activities. A centralized DBMS makes it easy to respond to such unforeseen information requests.
- *The cost of developing and maintaining systems is lower*—Since the data and application programs are independent of each other, each of them can usually be changed without affecting the other. This can be particularly important for a website that is supported by a web database. In spite of the large initial cost of setting up a database, normally the overall cost of setting up a database and developing and maintaining application programs, for example, for increasingly important web applications is lower than using earlier technologies.
- *Standards can be enforced*—Since all access to the centralized database has to go through the DBMS, enterprise standards are easier to enforce. Standards may include the naming of the data, the format of the data, and the structure of the data. Furthermore, since all the enterprise data is stored together, data backup may be carried out more regularly and more efficiently.
- *Security can be improved*—Setting up a centralized database makes it easier to enforce security restrictions. Since the data is centralized, it is easier to control who has access to what parts of the database. However, setting up a database can also make it easier for a determined person to breach security. This is discussed in the next section.

- *Integrity can be improved*—Since the data of the organization using a database is often centralized and would be used by many users at the same time, it is essential to enforce appropriate integrity controls. Integrity may be compromised in many ways. For example, someone may make a mistake in data input and the salary of a full-time employee may be entered as Rs. 4,000 rather than Rs. 40,000. A college student may be shown to have borrowed books from the college library but he/she has no enrolment in the college. Salary of a staff member working in one department may be coming out of the budget of another department.

  If a number of users are allowed to update the same data item at the same time, there is a possibility that the result of a number of updates will not be the same as intended. For example, in an airline DBMS we could have a situation where two travel agents sell the same airline seat at the same time and the total number of bookings made is larger than the capacity of the aircraft. In Chapter 9, various ways of avoiding such situations are discussed. However, since all data is stored only once, it is often easier to maintain integrity in modern database systems than in older systems.
- *A data model must be developed*—Perhaps the most important advantage of setting up an enterprise database system is the requirement that an overall enterprise data model be built. If an enterprise were to set up several database systems, it is likely that the overall enterprise view would not be considered. Building an overall view of the enterprise data, although often an expensive and onerous exercise, is usually cost-effective in the long term. It also usually provides flexibility as changes are often necessary as the enterprise changes in response to changing demands of the clients and/or customers.

1.11 CONCERNS WHEN USING AN ENTERPRISE DATABASE

As noted earlier, a centralized enterprise DBMS provides online access to the database for many users concurrently. Because of the large number of users, (assuming that the enterprise is large), who will be accessing the enterprise database, the enterprise may incur additional risks as compared to a more restrictive older style file processing system in the areas listed in Fig. 1.4.

- Enterprise vulnerability may be higher
- Confidentiality, privacy and security may be compromised
- Data quality and integrity may be lower
- Data integrity may be compromised
- The cost of building and using a DBMS can be high
- It may difficult to change the database when necessary

Figure 1.4 Disadvantages of using a DBMS

These issues can be elaborated as given below.

- *Enterprise vulnerability*—Centralizing all the data of an enterprise in one database often means that the database becomes an indispensable resource. The survival of a large enterprise may then depend on reliable information being made available from its database on a 24/7 basis. If the database system goes down for an hour or two, the enterprise may be paralysed while the system is down. At the time of writing this book, the university computer system has been going down frequently due to installation of some new network hardware. When the network has been down, most staff members have not been able to do much work and many have just gone home. In fact an enterprise is not only dependent on its databases, it can even be dependent on information in a search engine like Google. For example, when there were problems with Google in January 2009, many staff members found it difficult to keep working effectively. The enterprise can also become vulnerable to destruction of the enterprise database or to unauthorized modification of the database.

- *Confidentiality, privacy and security*—When information is centralized and is made available to users from remote locations, it is possible to apply stringent controls on who is able to see what information and who is able to modify what information. However the possibilities of abuse can also increase because some hackers may be able to penetrate the security controls. To reduce the chances of unauthorized users accessing enterprise information, it is necessary to take technical, administrative and possibly legal measures, but an intruder with sufficient resources may still be able to breach database security. A recent University of Cambridge report[6], issued in March 2009, describes how agents of the Chinese government were able to penetrate computers in the office of the Dalai Lama as well as many other computer systems in 103 countries.[7]
- *Data quality*—Since a database provides its users the convenience to access information remotely, adequate controls are needed to control users updating data and thus control data quality and maintain integrity. With an increased number of users accessing data directly, there is an increased risk that data quality and/or integrity will be compromised partly because of input errors. For example, at the time of writing this book, it has been reported that there was an input error in the university salary database which resulted in a person who retired continuing to be paid after the retirement date.
- *The cost of building and using a DBMS*—The database approach provides a flexible approach to data management where new applications can be developed relatively inexpensively. The flexibility is not without its costs, the major cost being that of modeling and building the database, and training or employing personnel. As noted earlier, building a database for a large and complex organization can be hugely expensive but such an organization cannot operate without an effective database system. For example, building a database for an international airline like Air India or a large bank like ICICI that will continue to meet the enterprise needs in the future is a very challenging task.
- *Inability to change the database when necessary*—In a competitive global environment every business has to be able to change quickly to meet new threats from competitors. An airline may merge with another or develop a partnership with a regional airline. A bank may start an insurance business or develop a stock broking business. The database should be such that it can be modified to deal with such major changes to the business. Not all database systems are easily adaptable to new business demands, in particular when a business undergoes a merger or acquisition. If the database system is inflexible, the enterprise may lose its competitive advantage after a dramatic change like a merger or acquisition.

1.12 THREE-LEVEL DBMS ARCHITECTURE AND DATA ABSTRACTION

We now discuss a conceptual framework for a database management system. Several different frameworks have been suggested since the1970s. For example, a framework may be based on the functions that the various

6. S. Nagaraja and R. Anderson, *The Snooping Dragon: Social-Malaware Surveillance of the Tibetan Movement*, Technical Report Number 746, Computer Laboratory, University of Cambridge, UK, March 2009.
7. J. Markoff, *Vast Spy System Loots Computers in 103 Countries*, New York Times, March 28, 2009.

components of a DBMS provides to its users. It may also be based on different users' views of data that are possible within a DBMS. We consider the latter approach.

A commonly used view of data is the three-level architecture suggested by ANSI/SPARC (American National Standards Institute/Standards Planning and Requirements Committee). ANSI/SPARC produced an interim report in 1972 followed by a final report in 1977. These reports proposed an architectural framework for databases. Under this approach, a database is considered as containing data about an *enterprise*. The three-level architecture presented in Fig. 1.5 provides three different views of the data. These views are discussed in some detail below.

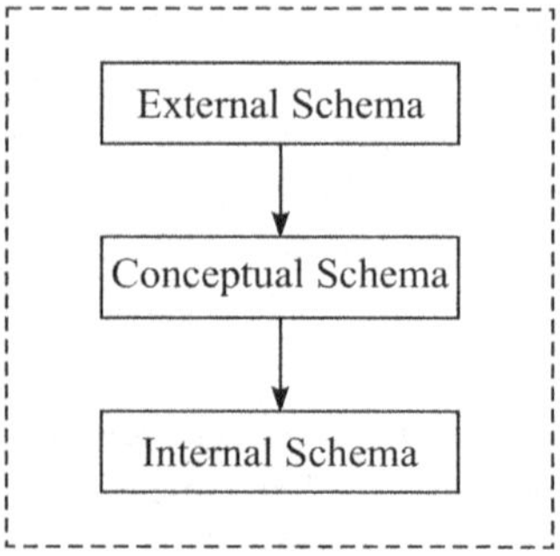

Figure 1.5 ANSI/SPARC DBMS architecture

1.12.1 External View

Each individual user has his/her own view of his/her enterprise database. This view may be a restricted view of the database and the same database is likely to provide a number of different views for different classes of users. In general, the end users and even the application programmers are only interested in a subset of the database if the database is large and complex. For example, a department head in a university may only be interested in the departmental finances and student enrolments in his/her department but not in the buildings and grounds information. The librarian would not be expected to have any interest in the information about departmental finances. The staff payroll office may have no particular interest in student enrolments in computer science unless those numbers have an impact on staff salaries.

1.12.2 Conceptual View

The conceptual view is the information model of the enterprise and contains the view of the whole enterprise without any concern for its physical implementation. This view is usually more stable than the other two views. In a database, it may be desirable to change the way some of the data is stored (internal view) to improve performance while there is no change in the conceptual view of the database. Also, from time to time, a user's view (external view) of the database will change if the user's responsibilities or needs change. The conceptual view is the overall enterprise view of the database and it includes all the information that is of interest and is to be represented in the database. The conceptual view is represented by the conceptual schema which includes details of each of the various types of data.

1.12.3 Internal View

This is the physical or storage view of the database which mostly does not need to be understood by the users. The person managing the database needs to understand this view since the efficiency of the database depends on the way it is stored. The following aspects are considered at this level:

1. What data structure will be used?
2. What access paths do users require to retrieve data, for example, specification of primary and secondary keys, indexes, and sequencing?

3. Miscellaneous, for example, data compression and encryption techniques, and optimization of the internal structures.

Efficiency considerations are the most important at the internal level and the data structures used to represent the database are chosen to provide an efficient database. The internal view does not deal with the physical devices directly. It is only necessary for the internal view to look at a physical device as a collection of physical pages and allocate storage in terms of logical pages.

The separation of the conceptual view from the internal view enables a logical description of the database without the need to specify physical structures. This is usually called *physical data independence.* When we separate the external views from the conceptual view we are able to change the conceptual view without changing the external views. This separation is sometimes called *logical data independence.* Data independence is discussed in more detail in Section 1.13.

Example 1.5

Assuming the three-level view of the database, a number of mappings are needed to enable the users working with one of the external views. For example, the staff payroll office in a university may have an external view of the database that consists of the following information only:

1. Each staff member's employee number, full name and home address.
2. Each staff member's tax information, for example, number of dependants and other relevant information.
3. Each staff member's bank information including the account number where salary is deposited.
4. Each staff member's employment status, salary level and leave information.

We have only listed a sample of information that the payroll office requires. Normally there would be other information including information that deals with payments, provident fund, retirement or pension scheme that an employee participates in.

The conceptual view of the company's database may contain detailed information about the managerial staff, full-time staff, and casual staff as well as the company's financial information and so on. A mapping will have to be created where all the staff members in the different categories are combined into one category for the payroll office. This will need to be mapped to the external view for the payroll office. Also, if there are some changes in the conceptual view, the external view will remain the same even if the mapping is changed.

1.12.4 Data Abstraction

The three-level database architecture allows a clear separation of the overall database view (conceptual view) from the external users' understanding of the database and from the physical data structure layout. A database system that is able to separate the three different views of data is likely to be flexible and adaptable. This flexibility and adaptability is called *data abstraction*. It is a powerful concept because it provides a number of advantages as mentioned below:

1. *Portability*—Portability is important since it is often desirable to be independent of a specific database vendor. The application programs need to be DBMS vendor specific, thus making it easier to replace DBMS software from one vendor to another.

2. *Flexibility and Adaptability*—Flexibility is important since enterprise requirements change according to business conditions and it is important that a database system be able to meet the requirements of new services.
3. *Application Decoupling and Data Independence*—These are important, as discussed earlier, as it is desirable to separate the underlying physical data and the applications. The applications can therefore make use of the data without specific knowledge of the database. This is called *data independence* and is discussed in more detail in the next section.

1.13 DATA INDEPENDENCE

As discussed earlier, data independence deals with independence between the way the data is structured and the programs that manipulate it. Application programs in a database system can continue to work in a certain sense independent of the storage structure of the database. Given data independence, a DBMS may change the structure of the data without having to change the application programs. This is not possible in conventional file processing systems which have a very low level of data independence since the file structure and the application programs are tightly coupled together. Also, no changes can be made to the file structure without making a corresponding change in the application programs. The programs use detailed knowledge of the file structure in manipulating data.

It is possible to have a high level of data independence in database systems only because the application programs do not deal with data in the database directly. Instead the database management software serve data to the application programs in a pre-defined and agreed manner that is independent of the way the data is stored by the system.

The three-level DBMS architecture discussed in the last section illustrates the two types of data independence possible. The first is called *logical data independence*. The second is called *physical data independence*. Logical data independence is the idea of changing the conceptual view, for example, adding a new column in a table, without affecting the external views. Thus it allows logical changes to be made to a database without worrying about the application programs. Physical data independence, on the other hand, is the idea of changing the internal view; for example, changing the data structure used for storing the database, without affecting the conceptual or the external views.

Data independence implies that the application programs should not need to know any of the following:

- The ordering of the data fields in a record
- The ordering of the records in a file
- The size of each record
- The size of each field
- The format and type of each data item
- Whether a file sorted or not
- The type of data structure being used to store some of the data

Data independence does not mean that the user does not need to know:

1. The names of files in which the relevant data is to be found
2. The names of the data fields that the user wishes to access

As noted earlier, the level of data independence of a system depends on the sophistication of metadata management in the system. A system with a sophisticated metadata management will involve changing the metadata when the physical data structure of some data is changed. Once the change is made, all the database application programs should still be able to run perfectly and find the data they use.

1.14 DBMS SYSTEM ARCHITECTURE

As noted earlier, a database management system is a complex piece of software that consists of a number of modules. The DBMS may be considered as an agent that allows communication between different types of users with the physical database and the operating system without the users being aware of every detail of how it is done.

In addition to providing facilities for defining the database and retrieving information, a DBMS provides facilities for the following:

- User communication with the system
- Authentication and authorization
- Query processing including a syntax checker and translator for the DDL and DML
- Access path selection
- Transaction management including concurrency control, logging manager, locking manager and recovery manager
- Database management including a file manager and the physical database
- Catalog manager

To provide all these facilities and some others, a DBMS has system architecture like the simple architecture shown in Fig. 1.6.

The various components of the database system architecture are discussed below.

1. **User Communication, Authentication and Authorization**
   This component deals with the user when he/she communicates with the DBMS. The communication depends on the kind of database system. It may be a two-tier system or a three-tier system. In each case, the system would include a mechanism for the user to log in and be authenticated. Once the user is allowed to access the database, the system will check the user's credentials and allow the user to access the parts of the database that he/she is authorized to.
2. **Query Processor**
   This component of a DBMS has several subcomponents including a query parser, a query rewriter, a query optimizer and a query executor. Query processor involves the DBMS interpreting the DDL and DML statements from the users and checking them for correct syntax and, if found to be correct, translate them into query execution plans. While developing query execution plans, the query optimizer attempts to efficiently find the best plan. These plans are then passed on to the database manager which then executes them. This is perhaps the most important component of a DBMS since each user is querying the database and is hoping to get results quickly. The queries are mostly submitted in a declarative language SQL and therefore its translation and optimization is very different than that of

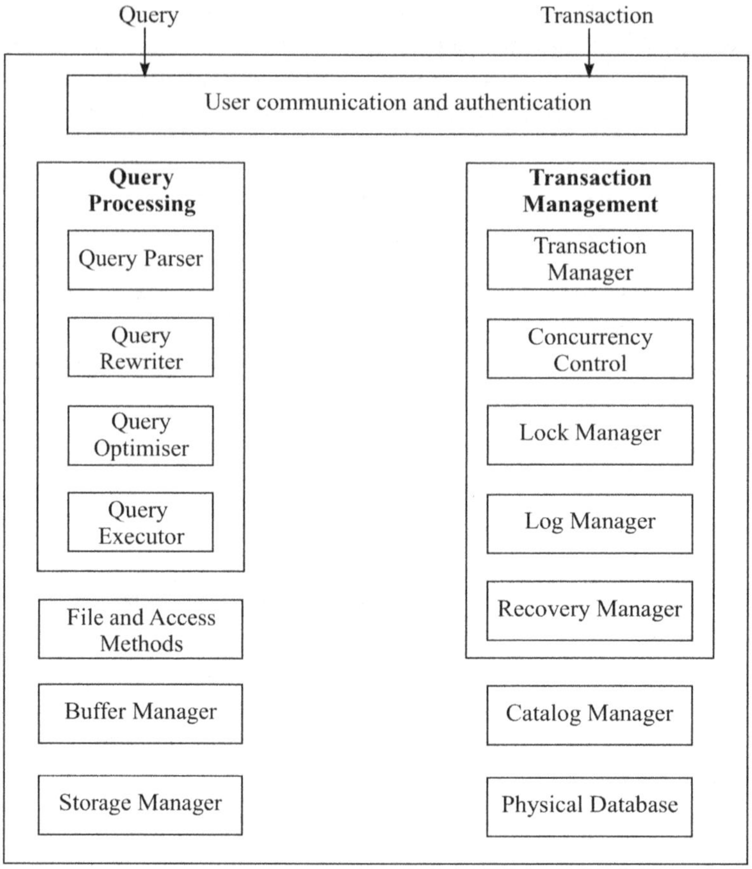

Figure 1.6 System architecture of a DBMS

procedural language programs. Query processing including details about the various components of a query processor are discussed in Chapter 7.

In a nonprocedural or a declarative language like SQL, no sequence of operations is explicitly given and therefore a query may be processed in a number of different ways, often called *plans*, where each plan might have a different sequence of operations. Optimization in declarative languages therefore is a more complex task, since it not only involves code optimization (ways to carry out operations that need to be carried out) but also selecting the best plan including selecting the best access paths. In many situations, especially if the database is large and the query is complex, a very large number of alternative plans are often possible and it is then not practical to enumerate them all and select the best. Then, it is necessary to consider a small number of possible plans and select the best option from those. Since the savings from query optimization can be substantial, it is acceptable that a DBMS spend some time in finding the best plan to process the query. Again, of course, we assume that we are dealing with queries that are expected to consume a significant amount of computing resources. There is no point in spending time optimizing queries that are so simple that almost any approach could be used to execute them in a small amount of time.

Further details of query processing are provided in Chapter 8.

3. **Transaction Management and Concurrency Control**

Modern database systems are multi-user systems. Some large systems may support thousands of users. Multiple users are able to use a single system simultaneously because the processor (or processors) in the system is shared amongst the users trying to access computer resources (including databases) simultaneously. The concurrent execution of programs is therefore interleaved, with each program being allowed access to the CPU at regular intervals. The concept of a transaction is very important since many users are using a multi-user system concurrently and the transactions must be managed so that they do not interfere with each other.

Control is therefore needed to coordinate concurrent accesses to a DBMS so that the overall correctness of the database is maintained. Efficiency is also important since the response time for interactive users ought to be short.

Our discussion of concurrency in Chapter 9 will be transaction based. A transaction is assumed to be a logical unit of work, and a unit of consistency in that preserves database consistency. Transaction processing database systems are now ubiquitous. For example, they include e-commerce, billing systems including telecommunications accounting, payroll, airline and hotel reservations, banking and electronic stock market transactions, to name a few.

Transaction management consists of a number of components including the following:

- Concurrency control
- A lock manager
- A log manager
- Recovery manager

Transaction management and concurrency control, backup and recovery, security and integrity are discussed in Chapters 9, 10, 11 and 12 respectively.

4. **File and Access Methods**

This component of the DBMS interacts with the physical storage that stores the database. The file manager is responsible for storing the database on the disk and for providing the DBA a number of data structure options for storing the database. This module also assists in maintaining the metadata of the database as well as indexes for the various files. Further details are provided in Chapter 7.

5. **Buffer Manager**

A database is normally resident on a disk although data can only be manipulated in the main memory. A part of the database therefore must be loaded in the main memory for retrieval and updates, and it must be written back to the disk once it is modified. The database therefore has a buffer manager that is responsible for handling the interfacing between the main memory and disk. The buffer manager maintains a number of pages of the same size and a large buffer size is important for the performance of a large and active database system. Further details are provided in Section 7.4.

6. **Storage Manager**

The storage manager is a DBMS subsystem that provides support for database management including management of access paths and indexes.

7. **Catalog Manager**

We have discussed earlier the role of metadata to describe the data structures (tables and their properties, users, indexes, constraints and so on) in a database. This data is maintained in the catalog and stored as relational tables. This allows the catalog to be queried in the same way as the rest of the document is queried. Further details about metadata are provided in Section 8.4.

8. **Physical Database**

   This is the physical storage of the database, normally on a disk. The database tables of the physical database are stored using a number of different file structures and indexes as discussed in Chapter 7. The performance of a large database depends critically on how efficiently the data has been structured on the disk.

The article by Hellerstein et al., provides a detailed discussion of database system architecture.

1.15 DATABASE ADMINISTRATOR

The database can meet the demands of a variety of users in the organization effectively only if it is maintained and managed properly. Usually a person (or a group of persons) centrally located, with an overall view of the database, is needed to keep the database running smoothly. Such a person is often called the *Database Administrator* (*DBA*). In a large enterprise, a DBA should be assisted by an advisory committee that includes members from relevant units of the company.

A DBA would normally understand the following:

- **What data is in the database and where did it come from?**
- **What does the data in the database mean?**
- **How reliable, accurate, and authoritative is the data?**
- **If all enterprise applications that need the data are able to use it?**
- **Who ultimately governs the definition, lifecycle, and use of data in the database?**

Given this understanding of the data, the DBA normally has a large number of tasks related to maintaining and managing the database. These tasks would generally include the tasks listed in Fig. 1.7.

These tasks can be elaborated as follows:

1. *Developing the conceptual schema*—The DBA in consultation with senior management of the enterprise (perhaps assisted by external consultants) may be responsible for defining the conceptual schema of the database. In some cases this task may be the responsibility of the Chief Information Officer (CIO) of the enterprise, if the enterprise has one. It may be necessary to make changes to the

- Developing the conceptual schema
- Deciding which DBMS to use
- Defining the database and loading the database contents
- Assisting and approving application and access
- Deciding data structures
- Backup and recovery
- Monitoring actual usage

Figure 1.7 List of tasks handled by a DBA

conceptual schema of the database periodically. The person who had responsibility for developing the initial conceptual schema should normally also be involved in making changes to it.

2. *Deciding which DBMS to use*—Once the conceptual schema has been decided, a decision regarding the DBMS to be used needs to be made. In some cases, the enterprise would have made this decision already, perhaps based on previous experience of using a DBMS within the enterprise. In some cases it may be appropriate to employ a database consultant to help in selecting a DBMS.
3. *Defining the database and loading the database contents*—Once the DBMS has been acquired and installed, the DBA would be responsible for implementing the conceptual schema by defining the conceptual schema using the DDL, and then loading the data the enterprise initially wishes to load in the database. Loading the database often is an incremental process.
4. *Assisting and approving applications and access*—The DBA would normally provide assistance to end users as well as programmers interested in writing application programs to access the database. The DBA would also approve or revoke access to the various parts of the database by different users.
5. *Deciding data structures*—Once the database contents have been decided, the DBA would normally take decisions regarding the manner in which data is to be stored and the indexes that need to be maintained. In addition, a DBA normally monitors the performance of the DBMS and makes changes to data structures if the performance justifies them. In some cases, radical changes to the data structures may be called for. Physical data structures are discussed in Chapter 6.
6. *Backup and recovery*—Since the database is such a valuable asset, the DBA must make all possible efforts to ensure that the asset is not damaged or lost. This normally requires a DBA to ensure that regular backups of a database are carried out and stored off-site and that in case of failure (or some other disaster like fire or flood) suitable recovery procedures can be used to reassemble the database with as little down time as possible. Recovery and backing techniques are discussed in Chapter 9.
7. *Monitoring actual usage*—The DBA monitors actual usage to ensure that policies laid down regarding use of the database are being followed. The usage information is also used for performance tuning.

There are many other tasks that a DBA often has to handle. These tasks may involve diagnosing, troubleshooting and resolving any database related problems. The DBA also deals with database security in addition to managing user identification, authentication and authorization.

1.16 DESIGNING AN ENTERPRISE DATABASE SYSTEM

As noted earlier, an enterprise database system is a complex and large software project. In Section 1.8 we noted ways in which a DBMS can be populated. Building a new database is just as complex as any large software project. Building a new database system usually goes through the phases shown in Fig. 1.8, just like the software development life cycle (SDLC).

These phases are discussed briefly. All design processes are usually iterative processes. For example, the second phase may discover some inconsistencies of the first phase which may need to be fixed before proceeding further.

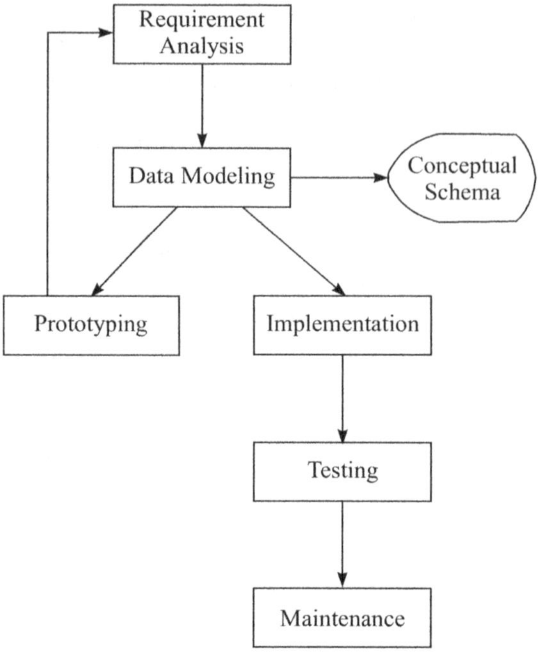

Figure 1.8 Database Design Lifecycle

1.16.1 Requirements Analysis

Each large software project involves requirement analysis to ensure that the software to be developed meets the requirements of the enterprise (or the client). For a database system, requirement analysis involves fully understanding the requirements of the proposed system and describing them precisely, including the queries that are likely to be posed. These requirements must be explored in-depth ensuring that a clear and concise description of the requirements is prepared. The description should include all the properties of the objects of interest, ways they are related to other objects and frequency of access. Nature and volume of the transactions should also be explored and documented. Furthermore, the possibility of growth of the data in future should also be considered. This can be a very challenging task.

A requirements specification document should be prepared based on all this information. This document must be accepted and signed by both parties, viz., the database designer and the client. Once signed, the document is then used in all design phases that follow.

1.16.2 Data Modeling

Once the first phase has been completed, the information content of the proposed database system is known and the requirements specification document is available, the information must be modeled using a data modeling technique. This is the most important phase of the database design because the quality of the database system and its adaptability is often significantly influenced by the quality of the data model. This is elaborated in the next chapter using a relatively simple modeling approach called the Entity-Relationship model. The primary aim of data modeling is to develop an enterprise view of the proposed database system with the ultimate aim of achieving an efficient database that is suitable for the workload and meets all the requirements. To some extent data modeling and requirements analysis go hand-in-hand because data modeling can also assist in communications between the designer and the client because of simplicity of its representation.

1.16.3 Prototyping

Prototyping can be a very helpful phase of the design life cycle because it helps enormously in improving communication between the designer and the client. A prototype should be a quick and dirty implementation of a simplified proposed database in order to confirm the specifications developed in the requirements phase.

1.16.4 Implementation

Given the data model developed in the data modeling phase which we assume is independent of the DBMS to be used, the model needs to be transformed using the DBMS that the enterprise has selected for the database. If the data modeling exercise of the last phase was successful then the implementation should also be good. We assume that the system is based on a relational database model that is discussed in Chapter 3. A suitable set of software tools should be available for users to enable them to use the system effectively.

1.16.5 Testing

Just like for any software system, a database system must also be tested to ensure that the system is reliable, efficient and correct, and meets the demands specified in the requirements document. The testing phase should discover most of the errors that may have arisen during the modeling and implementation phases. Testing may also be used to show to the client how the system is likely to appear and perform.

1.16.6 Maintenance

In spite of thorough testing, any new database system is likely to have errors and omissions and these need to be fixed during the maintenance phase. In addition, on using the system the client will almost always come up with new demands that require modifications in the design and implementation of the system. Even if no new demands are made, the client might find that some database queries or transactions are not performing well and need performance improvement. The database administrator is of course in-charge of resolving all such client requests. Maintenance of a system can become very expensive unless the system is well designed.

1.17 FUTURE OF DATABASES—WEB DATABASES

Web databases are the future of database technology. These are by far the most useful and versatile database applications currently available and most likely to be more important in the future. Most web applications involve the client requesting a web server for some information, which the web server usually finds by searching one of its databases and then serves it to the client. A variety of technologies are being used for these database interactions including CGI programs and scripts. Each copy of a CGI program connects to a web database server, which controls all requests to the databases, then returns any data retrieved to the CGI program which in turn is returned to the client.

In a typical client-server application, the user's workstation contains the software that provides the graphical user interface (for example, the browser). The server includes the database and a program to manage read and write access to it. Each module of a client-server may be developed concurrently by different teams of programmers and the database on the server can be easily moved to another server if this becomes necessary.

There are other types of databases on the Web. For example, Google has a very large database called the Bigtable, which is a distributed database system for managing structured data that is designed to scale to a very large size: petabytes of data across thousands of servers. Many projects at Google store data in a file system called Bigtable, including web indexing, Google Earth, and Google Finance. These different applications place different demands on Bigtable. Despite these different demands, Bigtable is being used successfully to provide a flexible, high-performance solution for all of the Google products.

1.18 CHOOSING A DBMS

Choosing any major piece of software is a difficult task. Certainly choosing a DBMS for a large enterprise is a challenging task since the software could even cost one crore rupees or more. Some basic information about various DBMS available in the market at the time of writing this book has been included. Oracle is the largest vendor of DBMS software. Other big vendors are Microsoft and IBM. Some DBMS packages from them as well as other vendors in the market are listed in Fig. 1.9.

- Oracle
- Microsoft Office Access
- Microsoft SQL Server 2008
- Ingres
- IBM DB2
- Sybase
- MySQL

Figure 1.9 List of popular DBMS software

Microsoft Access is part of the Microsoft Office suite of software. It is a nice implementation of relational database. For simple queries one may use QBE, Query by Example, a graphical query language which is very different from SQL. It is an easy-to-learn query language. Microsoft SQL Server 2008 is a major Microsoft database product. SQL Server 2008 has been reported to have many enhancements in comparison with its previous version. MySQL is an open source database management system software.

In selecting DBMS software, it is important to consider whether the system is to be used for business or personal use. If it is to be used for business, the size of the business, the size of the database, the number of users and response time required are the kind of issues that may need to be considered. Also, one may need to know the budget the enterprise is willing to spend and the amount of software support that will be required?

While selecting the software, in addition to the actual data management capabilities of the DBMS, it is important to consider the extent of the development environment supported by the DBMS, since the development environment supported will have a significant effect on the ability to develop new applications and to port and maintain existing applications.

Support for the standard query language SQL is now common for all DBMS although some DBMSs have added functionality not supported by the standard SQL. The added functionality can be useful but the database staff will need training in the additional features. Furthermore, using vendor-dependent features can lock the enterprise in continuing to use the same vendor which may not be desirable.

If the enterprise is large, it might be possible to undertake evaluation based on clearly identified requirements. In some cases using a database consultant might make sense. But if the organization is of small or medium size then it is crucial that the vendor selected shows a great deal of empathy and support. Another issue that also must be considered seriously is the ease of application development (or ease of finding third party applications developers). Yet another issue that may be important in some situations is how fast can the applications that are urgently needed be developed? How easy is it going to be for the employees to use? These are often difficult nontechnical issues.

For personal use, efficiency issues may not be so important since the database is likely to be small. Something like Microsoft Access might be suitable.

Some rules of thumb in selecting DBMS software for a large enterprise are as follows:

1. *Focus on effectiveness not efficiency*—Efficiency is always important, especially if the database is being used in a real-time environment where the response time is crucial. Often though one wants a system that is effective, i.e., it gets the job done satisfactorily.
2. *Focus on good end user tools*—Since a database is primarily used by the enterprise users, the software must provide tools that can provide a good user interface.
3. *Focus on good application development tools*—Most database systems require at least some application programs that need to be developed in-house. Therefore, it is important that tools be available for developing such programs.
4. *Focus on availability of third party developers.*
5. *Focus on availability of a user group support for the DBMS.*

Most DBMS products provide a 4GL (fourth-generation language) to assist in application development but the quality of the 4GL varies and may need to be evaluated.

SUMMARY

In this introductory chapter, we have covered the following topics:

- The amount of data various enterprises are collecting is growing because of increasing use of OLTP systems as well the World Wide Web.
- Database management is about management of information of an enterprise.
- A database is well organized collection of information.
- The information in a database is related, stored only once and is shared.
- Very large databases are being maintained by a number of enterprises, for example, by search engines and social networking sites.
- Database approach is different than file processing approach because file processing provides little data independence.

- A DBMS is a large software package designed to manage information.
- A DBMS has many modules including query processor, concurrency control and file manager.
- A database system has many different types of users, for example, end users, naive users and sophisticated users.
- There are a number of advantages and concerns when an enterprise database system is used, for example, reduction of redundancy and database security.
- A database system may be looked as three-level architecture; the three levels are external, conceptual and internal.
- Importance of concepts of data abstraction and data independence has been explained.
- A simple architecture of DBMS has been presented. It has many modules including query processor, concurrency control and recovery manager.
- The database administrator is responsible for managing the database system.
- The responsibilities of a DBA are described including database design, data loading and database monitoring.
- Developing a database system is similar to developing any major software since it includes requirements analysis, design and testing steps.
- Web databases are becoming increasingly important because of widespread use of the World Wide Web.
- It is important to remember a number of factors when buying a DBMS including the importance of DBMS effectiveness and database tools.

REVIEW QUESTIONS

1. Give an example of a simple database related to information that you use regularly. (Section 1.2)
2. List names of some large Indian websites that collect huge amount of information. (Section 1.3)
3. What is a database? Discuss its main features and explain the importance of each feature. (Section 1.3)
4. List the characteristics of databases. (Section 1.4)
5. What is data governance and why do enterprises require it? (Section 1.5)
6. When did database management become important in computing? When was the relational database system invented? (Section 1.6)
7. Describe the disadvantages of using a file processing system compared to a database system? (Section 1.7)
8. What is a DBMS? What tasks does a DBMS carry out? (Section 1.8)
9. What classes of users use database systems? (Section 1.9)
10. Discuss the advantages of using the DBMS approach as compared to using a conventional file system. (Section 1.10)
11. Discuss the concerns in using the DBMS approach as compared to using a conventional file system. (Section 1.11)
12. List the three views for a database system in the three-level architecture. Describe the role of these views. (Section 1.12)

13. Explain data abstraction and data independence. (Section 1.12 and 1.13)
14. List the major components of a DBMS architecture and describe their functions. (Section 1.14)
15. Describe the role of a database administrator. (Section 1.15)
16. What are the phases in developing an enterprise database system? (Section 1.16)
17. Briefly describe the role of database technology for the Web. (Section 1.17)
18. List three major considerations when buying a DBMS for an enterprise. (Section 1.18)

SHORT ANSWER QUESTIONS

The following questions are based on the assumption that a database is being shared amongst several users.

1. Name one large enterprise in your city which could not operate effectively without a database system.
2. Name one large website that you use regularly. Estimate its database in terms of number of people that use it and information about each of these users?
3. Why database systems are becoming important?
4. When were the first database management systems developed?
5. Name three popularly used DBMS.
6. List three major differences between file systems and database systems.
7. Which is the largest database company in the world?
8. How many mobile phone calls are made and SMSs are sent in India every day? Make an estimate based on some simple assumptions about the number of mobile phones in India.
9. List the major classes of nontechnical users that use a database system.
10. Who are the workers behind the scene in a database system?
11. List three benefits using an enterprise database system, compared to a file processing system.
12. List three areas of concern in using an enterprise database system.
13. What are the three levels in a three-level database architecture.
14. What is data abstraction?
15. What are the benefits of data independence?
16. List three components of query processing.
17. List three components of transaction management.
18. What does the buffer manager do?
19. What is metadata and catalog?
20. Why does a DBMS require a concurrency control module?
21. List three duties of a DBA.
22. What is the first step in designing an enterprise database system?

MULTIPLE CHOICE QUESTIONS

1. Which one of the following should be the main focus of an enterprise database?
   (a) Enterprise computers
   (b) Enterprise information
   (c) Enterprise computer network
   (d) Enterprise management
2. Which one of the following is a problem with the single table database presented at the beginning of this chapter?
   (a) It is difficult to find if a player is still playing.
   (b) A number of columns are related.
   (c) It assumes that each player plays only for one country during his lifetime.
   (d) All of the above
3. Which one of the following is the most accurate definition of a database?
   (a) A computerized record-keeping system.
   (b) A centralized collection of enterprise data.
   (c) Software designed to access and manipulate data.
   (d) None of the above
4. Due to which one of the following reason have databases become so important for all large enterprises?
   (a) Hard disks are becoming cheap.
   (b) Database technology is a mature technology.
   (c) Oracle and IBM have good database software.
   (d) The quantity of information and its importance is growing.
5. A DBMS provides a variety of facilities, some of which are listed below. Which one should not be on this list?
   (a) Data definition and manipulation
   (b) Data recovery and concurrency control
   (c) Data security and recovery
   (d) Data modeling
6. A database has a number of features. Which of the following are features of a database?
   (a) It is centralized.
   (b) It is well organized.
   (c) It is related.
   (d) It is accessible in different orders without great difficulty.
   (e) All of the above
7. Consider the following schemas of the tables:

   ODIbestbat (Player, Span, Runs, Average, Strike Rate)
   Testbestbat (Player, Span, Runs, Average, Centuries)
   ODIbestbowl (Player, Span, Runs, Wickets, Average, Economy Rate)
   Testbestbowl (Player, Span, Runs, Average, Economy rate)
   Player (Name, Country, Place of Birth, Date of Birth)
   ODImatch (Date, Host, Visitor, Result)

Testmatch (Date, Host, Visitor, Result)
Testranking (Country, Points)
ODIranking (Country, Points)

Which one of the following together satisfy the properties that a database should possess?

(a) ODIbestbat and ODIranking
(b) ODIbestbat and ODImatch
(c) ODIbestbat and Testbestbat
(d) Player, ODIranking
(e) None of the above

8. There are many advantages of using a database approach in contrast to using older data processing techniques. Which one of the following is **not** true if the database approach is used?
   (a) Data redundancy can be reduced.
   (b) Data inconsistency can be avoided to some extent.
   (c) Computing resources needed for data processing can be reduced.
   (d) Data processing standards can be enforced.
9. Which one of the following is **not** necessarily a characteristic of a database system?
   (a) Self-describing nature
   (b) Data independence
   (c) Data accuracy
   (d) Support for multiple views of the data
10. Which of the following should a good DBMS used for a large multi-user enterprise provide?
   (a) Control redundancy
   (b) Restrict unauthorized access
   (c) Enforce integrity constraints
   (d) Provide backup and recovery
   (e) All of the above
11. It is claimed that data independence is a major objective of database systems. Which one of the following statements about data independence is **not** true?
   (a) Data independence is the immunity of applications to change in physical storage structure and access strategy.
   (b) Data independence leads to difficulties in integrating data and eliminating redundancies.
   (c) Data independence makes it possible for different applications to have different views of the same data.
   (d) Data independence is necessary to enable the database to grow without affecting existing applications.
12. The ANSI/SPARC model of DBMS architecture comprise three levels, viz., internal (or physical), external and conceptual. Which of the following is **not** correct?
   (a) The internal view of a database deals with physical records and device specific considerations such as track and sector sizes.
   (b) The conceptual view of a database is the community view of the database, i.e., a view of the database *as it really is*.
   (c) The external view of a database is the individual user view, i.e., often this is a restricted view of the conceptual view.
   (d) There can be only one external view, only one conceptual view and only one internal view.

13. As a result of data independence, which one of the following is **not** true?
    (a) The user does not need to know the size of each file record.
    (b) The user does not need to know if the file is sorted.
    (c) The user does not need to know the name of the file that has the relevant information.
    (d) The user does not need to know the ordering of the fields in the records.
14. Which one of the following is a major difference between a file processing system and a database system?
    (a) File processing system files may be main memory resident while database is disk resident.
    (b) There is no data independence in file-processing systems.
    (c) File systems are able to represent relationships between various data while databases cannot.
    (d) File processing system can be used by many users.
15. Which of the following are important components of the DBMS architecture?
    (a) Query optimizer
    (b) Database manager
    (c) File manager
    (d) Physical database
    (e) All of the above are important
16. When choosing a DBMS which of the following are important?
    (a) Effectiveness
    (b) Efficiency
    (c) The name of the company
    (d) Good end user tools
    (e) All of the above are important

EXERCISES

1. Discuss the importance of information for modern enterprises. Give some examples to illustrate your answer.
2. Explain the relationship between an enterprise, its data processing needs and its database.
3. Why should you choose a database system instead of simply storing data in a spreadsheet? When would it make sense not to use a database system?
4. What is logical data independence and why is it important? Give a practical example when logical data independence is important.
5. What is meant by logical and physical structure of data? Explain the difference between logical and physical data independence.
6. Explain the difference between external view, internal view, and conceptual view in three-tier database architecture. How are these different schema layers related to concepts of logical and physical data independence?
7. Which of the following plays an important role in representing information about the real world in a database? Explain briefly.
    - **Data definition language**
    - **Data manipulation language**
8. Would a DBMS designed for use on a PC by a single user also have the same components as shown in Fig. 1.6? Explain your answer.

9. Discuss the responsibilities of a DBA. Explain what would happen if a DBA was not responsible for an enterprise database system? Why does the DBA need to understand query optimization? Explain the role of a DBA in a simple database like the ODI database if it is being used by many people.
10. Could a modern university be supported if a file processing system was used to manage enterprise information? List three major difficulties that are likely to arise if no database system was available to the university. Discuss the difficulties.
11. Study the role of data governance by looking at some recent literature on data governance. What benefits can be obtained by an enterprise using data governance which they cannot get with current database systems? Discuss.
12. Select an enterprise that you are familiar with (for example, a school, college, company, small business, club or association). List all the information that this enterprise uses.
13. Give examples to illustrate three major advantages and three areas of concern when using an enterprise database system. Discuss their importance.
14. List five queries you might wish to pose to the ODI database given in Tables 1.1, 1.2 and 1.3.
15. Why is data independence important? Discuss its importance by giving an example.
16. Present a conceptual view of a student database. Present some external views given by different types of end users and show the mappings of these views to the conceptual view.

PROJECTS

1. If you have access to the Indian Railways Timetable, describe how you would computerize it and how much memory space the computerized timetable would take? What other information would be useful in the timetable?
2. Select a local company large enough to have a lot of information about its operations. Arrange to meet someone in that company who can tell you about the information they have and the ways they manage and use it. Write a brief report on the same.

LAB EXERCISES

1. Northern India University (NIU) is a large institution with several campuses scattered across north India. Academically, the university is divided into a number of faculties, such as Faculty of Arts and Faculty of Science. Some faculties operate on a number of campuses. Faculties, in turn, are divided into schools. For example, the School of Physics, the School of Information Technology, etc. The schools are not divided further into departments.

   Each student in the University is enrolled in a single course of study which involves a fixed core of subjects specific to that course as well as a number of electives taken from other courses. Each course is offered by one particular school. Each school has a number of lecturing staff. Students are awarded a grade for each subject they chose.

   List all the information that you need to store in a database for NIU.

2. List all the information that you might require if you were in charge of a second, small airport in Mumbai that mainly handles private planes. The database is to be designed to keep track of information about airplanes, their owners, and pilots. Each plane is stored in a particular hangar which has a number and some other information about it. You will need to carefully think about the information required. A person who knows more about small private planes might be able to assist you.

BIBLIOGRAPHY

There are many good books and references on database management. The article by Fry and Sibley presents an interesting historical account of early DBMS developments. The other two articles, by Jardine and by Tsichritzis and Klug, deal with the ANSI/SPARC model. We have listed a collection of 16 database books.

For Students

The books by Churcher, Date, Stephens and Takahashi et al., are good introductory books for database management. Each of them has a different style. The book by Date has been around for a long time and is now in its eighth edition. It is simple and easy to read. The books by Pascal, Chao and Churcher are also easy to read. The book by Takahashi et al., is a translation of a popular Japanese book which includes many illustrations. The two books by Robert Glass describe some actual software disasters including some that involved database systems.

For Instructors

A comprehensive introduction to database management is provided in the book written by Elmasri and Navathe, which deals with all the topics covered in this book. The book by Ramakrishnan and Gehrke is a slightly more advanced introduction. The book by Silberchatz, Korth and Sudarshan is a comprehensive text. The books by Garcia-Molina et al., and Ullman and Widom are comprehensive introductions to database management. The article by Hellerstein, Stonebraker and Hamilton is a 120-page long article on architecture of database systems for those who want to learn more about this topic.

Chao, L., *Database Development and Management (Foundations of Database Design)*, Auerbach, 2006.

Churcher, C., *Beginning Database Design: From Novice to Professional*, APress, 2007.

Date, C. J., *An Introduction to Database Systems*, Eighth Edition, Addison-Wesley, 2003.

Elmasri, R., and S. B. Navathe, *Fundamentals of Database Systems*, Fifth Edition, Addison-Wesley, 2006.

Fry, J. P., and E. H. Sibley, "Evolution of Database Management Systems", *ACM Computing Surveys*, Vol. 8, pp 7- 42, March 1976.

Glass, R. L., Software *Runaways: Monumental Software Disasters*, Prentice Hall, 1997.

Glass, R. L., *Computingfailure.com: War Stories from the Electronic Revolution*, Prentice Hall, 2001.

Garcia-Molina, H., J. D. Ullman, and J. Widom, *Database Systems: The Complete Book*, Second Edition, Prentice Hall, 2008.

Garcia-Molina, H., J. D. Ullman, and J. Widom, *Database System Implementation*, Prentice Hall, 2000.

Hellerstein, J. H., M. Stonebraker, and J. Hamilton, "Architecture of a Database System", *Foundations and Trends in Databases*, Vol. 1, No. 2, 2007, pp 141-259. (May be downloaded from http://www.db.cs.berkeley.edu/papers/fntdb07-architecture.pdf (120 pgs))

Jardine, D. A. (Ed.), *The ANSI/SPARC DBMS Model*, North-Holland, 1977.

Kifer, M., A. Bernstein, and P. M. Lewis, *Database Systems: An Application-Oriented Approach*, Second Edition, Addison-Wesley, 2006.

Lyman, P., and H. R. Varian, "How Much Information*?*", *School of Information Management and Systems, University of California, Berkeley*, 2003. http://www2.sims.berkeley.edu/research/projects/how-much-info-2003/

Pascal, F., *Practical Issues in Database Management: A Reference for the Thinking Practitioner*, Addison-Wesley, 2000.

Ramakrishnan R., and J. Gehrke, *Database Management Systems*, Third Edition, McGraw-Hill, 2002.

Silberchatz, A., H. Korth, and S. Sudarshan, *Database Systems Concepts*, Fifth Edition. McGraw-Hill, 2005.

Stephens, R., *Beginning Database Design Solutions*, Wiley, 2008.

Takahashi, M., S. Azuma, and Trend-pro Ltd., *The Manga Guide to Databases*, No Starch Press, 2009.

Tsichritzis D., and A. Klug (Eds.), "The ANSI/X3/SPARC Framework", *Information Systems*, Vol. 3, No. 3, 1978.

Ullman, J. D., and J. Widom, *First Course in Database Systems*, Third Edition, Prentice Hall, 2007.

Michael Stonebraker—Pioneer in Database Systems

Michael Stonebraker has been a pioneer in the field of database research and technology for more than thirty years. He was the main architect of the first relational DBMS INGRES, and the object-relational DBMS, POSTGRES. These database systems were developed at the University of California at Berkeley where Stonebraker was Professor of Computer Science for twenty five years. More recently he has moved to MIT where he has been involved in working primarily on novel DBMS architectures.

Professor Stonebraker is the author of a large number of research papers and books on database technology, operating systems and the architecture of system software services. He was awarded the ACM System Software Award in 1992 for his work on INGRES. He was also awarded the first annual Innovation award by the ACM SIGMOD special interest group in 1994 and was elected to the National Academy of Engineering in 1997. He is also an ACM Fellow.

Stonebraker obtained his Bachelor's degree from Princeton University and a PhD from the University of Michigan in 1971.

Entity–Relationship Data Model

2

OBJECTIVES

- Discuss the importance of data modeling.
- Describe the different phases of database modeling.
- Explain the Entity-Relationship model for modeling a database.
- Define entity, entity sets, relationship, relationship sets, different types of relationships, and attributes.
- Describe representing entities, attributes and relationships in entity-relationship diagrams.
- Explain binary and ternary relationships.
- Discuss the concepts of generalization, specialization and aggregation.
- Describe the extended Entity-Relationship model.
- Present guidelines for building an Entity-Relationship model.
- Analyze the strengths and limitations of the Entity-Relationship model.
- Present a case study of developing an Entity-Relationship model.
- Explain evaluation criteria for different Entity-Relationship database models.

KEYWORDS

Modeling, database design, Entity-Relationship model, E-R model, entity, entity set, domain, attributes, diagrams, single-valued and composite attributes, relationship, one-to-one, one-to-many, many-to-many, binary relationship, weak entities, generalization, aggregation, specialization, E-R diagrams, extended Entity-Relationship model, EER, cardinality ratio, superkey, supertype, subtype, attribute inheritance, model evaluation.

Aag Rameshwari Aanee Bamb Someshwari.
Translation: The problem is one thing and the solution is given for something else.

Marathi proverb

2.1 INTRODUCTION

As noted in the last chapter, building a database system is a complex process that normally requires analyzing the user's requirements followed by a design process and finally concluding with an implementation. During analysis and design, the database designer normally needs to build a model of the proposed database system. Database modeling is essential to adequately manage the database development process.

Models have not been invented recently. Humans have used models for a long time for a variety of purposes and perhaps that is why modeling is interpreted differently by different people. Consider some examples of model building:

1. Architects build models of buildings to show what a building or a house would look like. Landscape architects build models of landscaping to show what a landscape or garden will look like.
2. Aeronautical engineers build models of planes to show what a plane would look like. Scaled models may also be used in testing to evaluate a plane's performance.
3. Computer architects build models of new computers or new circuit boards that are implemented in hardware.
4. Traffic engineers build models of traffic for a city or part of a city to show why there are traffic problems or how they could be solved.

The reader may think of other applications. Building models is common in science, engineering and computing. A model is an abstract (and often incomplete) representation of the design or definition of a complex product, process or situation (for example, information requirements of an enterprise). A model need not be related to one particular situation; it may model a class of situations. For example, a database model may model all kinds of libraries but often each new situation requires a customized model. A model may describe, at different levels of abstraction, an organization of the elements of a product, process or situation.

The role of data modeling in building database systems is similar to the role of an architect in building a substantial house or a building. In building a house, one does not just collect all the family members and draw some plans on a piece of paper and give it to a builder expecting it to lead to a well designed house that will meet the current and future needs of the family. Similarly, in building an enterprise database system one does not just collect all the users of the database and draw some plans on a piece of paper and give them to a database builder expecting it to lead to a well designed database system that will meet the current and future needs of the enterprise. Data modeling is therefore similar to the work of an architect whose job is to design a model that transforms the client's requirements into specifications which are then given to the database builder. Just like the architect does not disappear when the builder arrives, a database modeler also does not disappear when the database builder takes over. Both the architect and the database modeler have a role in supervising the building activity.

This chapter is organized as follows. The benefits of data modeling are discussed along with a description of various types of models in Section 2.3 and phases of database modeling in Section 2.4. In Section 2.5 the Entity-Relationship model is discussed in detail, including the definition of an entity, a relationship, different types of relationships, attributes and how to represent an Entity-Relationship model by an Entity-Relationship diagram. Generalization, specialization and aggregation are discussed in Section 2.6. The extended E-R Model is presented in Section 2.7 followed by discussion of database design in Section 2.8. Section 2.9 describes the strengths of the E-R model while Section 2.10 describes its weaknesses. A detailed case study of building an Entity-Relationship model is then presented in Section 2.11. Section 2.12 deals with evaluation of data model quality.

2.2 BENEFITS OF DATA MODELING

As noted earlier, models are built for a variety of purposes. Database modeling is essential in building any nontrivial database system for assisting communication between the client and the database designer. Modeling has the following benefits:

1. *Focusing on essentials*—Modeling often leads to developing an abstract and simple view of the product or process that is the subject of modeling. It is thus possible to ignore the details that tend to distract from the essential features. For example, when modeling a library we need to focus on the essential features, e.g., borrowers, books, serials, and at least in the beginning it may be possible to ignore that there are a variety of books (for example, some may have several editions) and serials (for example, some are published monthly while others quarterly and so on).
2. *Ease of communication and understanding*—Model building formalizes the process of reliable communication and assists in reaching an agreement. Model building therefore helps all parties involved in building a model to reach a common understanding of the subject of modeling, given that modeling formalizes communication. Communication during modeling also involves developing documentation describing what is being modeled. A model may be expressed in text or in a graphical language or it may even be more concrete like a prototype. A suitable expression medium should be chosen to assist communication. Designing a good library system would require suitable communication between the database designer, the librarians and the users (for example, academics and students, for a university library)
3. *Product or process improvement*—Since modeling involves communication between the various stakeholders, modeling can lead to improvement in the process or product that is being modeled as it provides a forum for consideration of alternative ways of doing things. For example, a process being modeled may involve enterprise customers supplying some information by completing one or more forms. Discussion during modeling may lead to these forms being improved, some forms being eliminated while others are put on the Web. In another modeling example, the design process may lead to the enterprise website being used more effectively thus improving customer service.
4. *Exploring alternatives*—In some modeling exercises, modeling can assist in answering 'what if' questions before building the database system. A user may want to explore whether it makes sense to include an aspect of the enterprise in the proposed database system. Sometimes it may be necessary to build a prototype to evaluate alternatives. For example, in a university it may be worth exploring whether the system should allow the students to enrol online if the university does not already do so.

2.3 TYPES OF MODELS

There are many different types of models. Models may be classified in the following classes according to the aim of modeling:

1. *Descriptive*—The primary purpose of such models is to describe or understand phenomena or complex machinery. For example, meteorologists build models to understand and predict weather; investment companies build models of share markets to understand the share market and to predict share prices or share index movements; and a high school teacher may build simple models to describe or explain some scientific concept to students. The aim for such models is to describe or understand what is being modeled.
2. *Prescriptive*—The primary purpose of prescriptive models is to clearly specify what a piece of machinery or software is supposed to do. In some cases prototype models may be built to specify how something is supposed to behave or look. The aim for such models is to specify what is being modeled. As an example, it has been shown that prescriptive models of human problem solving are able to explain how humans solve problems.
3. *Representative*—The primary purpose of such models is to simulate the behaviour of some phenomena or machinery. For example, computer games that simulate racing cars may be considered representative models. Representative models have been built in many other fields, for example, models of face recognition techniques. The aim for such models is to simulate what is being modeled.

A model does not have to belong to one class; it can belong to more than one class. Database models are normally prescriptive since they prescribe or specify what the database system is supposed to do although they also serve a descriptive role in helping communication between the designer and the customer by describing what the database would include. Therefore before the data available in an enterprise can be put in a DBMS, a database model or an overall abstract view of the enterprise data must be developed. The view can then be translated into a form that is acceptable by the DBMS. Although at first sight a modeling task may appear trivial, it is a very complex process for large database systems since the process often involves making compromises between what the users want and what can be realistically implemented. For example, if a user wants one single model to model all the cricket statistics that are available at the *cricinfo* website (http://stats.cricinfo.com/ci/engine/current/records/index.html), the data model would be very complex.

2.4 PHASES OF DATABASE MODELING

In the last chapter we presented the different phases of database design life cycle. One of the phases of the design life cycle was database modeling. This phase is discussed in more detail in this section.

The complexity of mapping the enterprise data to a database management system can be reduced by dividing the process into two phases. The first phase as noted above involves building an overall view (or model) of the *real world* which is the enterprise. This process is often called *conceptual modeling*. The objective of the model is to represent, as accurately as possible, the information structures of the enterprise that are of interest and independent of all physical considerations. This model is sometimes called an *enterprise conceptual schema* (a schema essentially shows the structure of the data in a database). The process of developing the model may be considered as the requirements analysis of the database development life cycle. As noted earlier, this phase assists in communication between the users and designers of the database system. This model is then mapped in the second phase, and the logical design phase, to the database schema appropriate for the database model to be used. The logical design process is an abstraction process which captures the meaning of enterprise data without getting involved in the details of individual data values or details of the DBMS to be used for implementation. Figure 2.1 shows this two-step process.

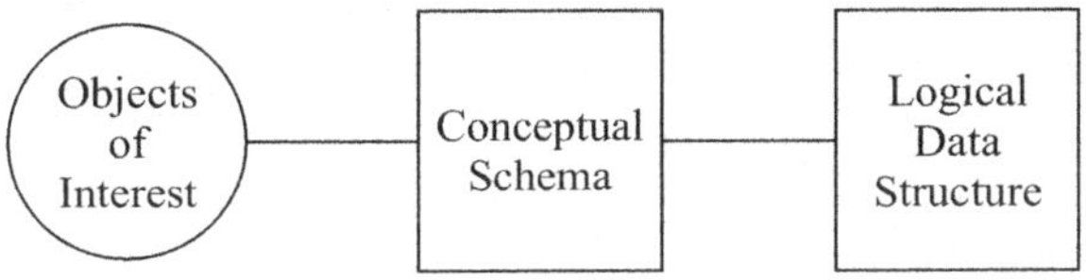

Figure 2.1 Two phases of database modeling

The process is somewhat similar to modeling in the physical sciences. In conceptual database design, a model is built to enhance understanding and to abstract details. A model should provide a reasonable interpretation of the real-life situation. A database designer therefore must explicitly consider what is to be included in the model and what is to be left out. For example, a model of employee data in an enterprise may not be able to capture the knowledge that employees Radha Rani and Krishan Kumar are married to each other. We accept such imperfections of the model since we want to keep the model as simple as possible. It is clearly impossible (and possibly undesirable or even illegal, for example, because of privacy concerns) to record every piece of information that could be available in an enterprise. We only desire that the meaning captured by a data model should be adequate for the purpose that the data is to be used for.

Data modeling often requires careful analysis of basic assumptions underlying the users' view of their world. For example, in creating a cricket database, we may need to consider the following:

- Who exactly is a batsman? Are all players in the team batsmen? Are all players in the team bowlers?
- How do we wish to interrogate the database? Would a player's full name be used or the first and the last name or just the last name or any of them? Names from different regions, for example, from north India and from south India, are quite different and a model should be able to deal with all names in a sensible way.
- Would the database allow a situation in which a player has represented more than one country during his career? If yes, how would such situations be modeled?
- Is it possible that a player could change his name during his career? For example, a player may convert from Christianity to Islam or from Hindusim to Christianity. If the database is to allow such rare incidents, how would such situations be modeled?

The person organizing the data to set up the database not only has to model the enterprise but also has to consider the efficiency and constraints of the DBMS. Implementation issues are considered in a third phase after the logical model has been completed.

As noted earlier, when the database is complex, the database design phase is likely to be challenging. A number of techniques are available for database modeling but we discuss only one such technique that is popular, and we believe, is easy to understand. The technique uses a convenient representation that enables the database designer to view the data from the point of view of the whole enterprise. This well known technique is called the Entity-Relationship model.

2.5 THE ENTITY-RELATIONSHIP MODEL

The Entity-Relationship model (E-R model) is a widely used database modeling technique because it is simple and relatively easy to understand. The method facilitates communication between the database designer and the end user. It enables an abstract global view (that is, the *enterprise conceptual schema*) of the enterprise application to be developed without any consideration of efficiency of the ultimate database. The Entity-Relationship model was originally proposed in 1976 by Peter Chen although many variants of the technique have subsequently been devised.

E-R modeling is based on the concept that organizations consist of people, facilities and objects. These components of an enterprise interact with each other to achieve certain goals of the enterprise. As an example, when dealing with an enterprise that deals with cricket, the batsmen interact with bowlers, fielders and umpires to achieve the aim of playing a match. Another example is to look at a book publishing business which involves books, authors, printers, distributors, editors, sales data and so on.

All such things that are of interest to the enterprise are called *entities* and their interactions are called *relationships*. To develop a database model based on the E-R model involves identifying the entities and relationships of interest. These are often displayed in an E-R diagram. Before discussing these, we need to describe an entity and a relationship.

2.5.1 Entities and Entity Sets

An entity is a real or abstract object. It may be a person, a place, a building, or an event like a contract or a concert or an order that can be distinctly identified and is of interest. An entity exists independent of what does or does not exist in an enterprise. A specific cricket player, for example, Sachin Tendulkar with player ID 89001 or a venue Eden Gardens with a venue ID 65478 or a country India are examples of entities assuming that the database application requires information about them. Although entities are often concrete like a company, an entity may be abstract like an idea, concept or an event, for example, an ODI match 2688 between India and Australia or a Delhi to Mumbai flight number IA123. Whether an entity is real or abstract, the model makes no distinction between them but they must be something about which information is important.

Definition—Entity
An entity is a real or abstract object that can be distinctly identified and is of interest. Whether an entity is real or abstract, it must be something about which information is important.

The kind of entities needed by a database depends on the requirements of its applications. It is usually not possible to decide which entities are of interest to an enterprise based on direct observations of things in an enterprise. That is why a model must be developed to identify all entities that are of interest to an enterprise.

An entity must of course be identifiable so it must have a name or an identifier. In addition an entity must have some information beyond its identifier for it to be an entity.

A model is only going to reflect the perspective of a certain application. Often it will not reflect the whole enterprise. The part of an enterprise that is of interest is called the *Universe of Discourse* (or U of D).

Entities are classified into different *entity sets* (or *entity types*). An entity set is a set of objects called *entity instances* or *entity occurrences*. An entity instance is an individual object of a given entity type. For example, all cricket players may constitute an entity set *Player* with a particular player (say, Ricky Ponting) being an instance of *Player* and all matches may belong to an entity set *Match* with a particular match (say, the 2003 match between Australia and India played at the MCG) being an instance of the entity *Match*. An entity may belong to one or more entity sets. For example, a cricket player would belong to *Player* and can also belong to another entity set *Captain*. Entity sets therefore are not always disjointed.

Figure 2.2 shows two instances of entity *Bestbatsmen*. Repeating what has been noted above, an entity set or entity type is a collection of (usually more than one) entity instances of the same type. A clear distinction therefore needs to be made between the terms *entity set* or *entity type* and *entity instance*.

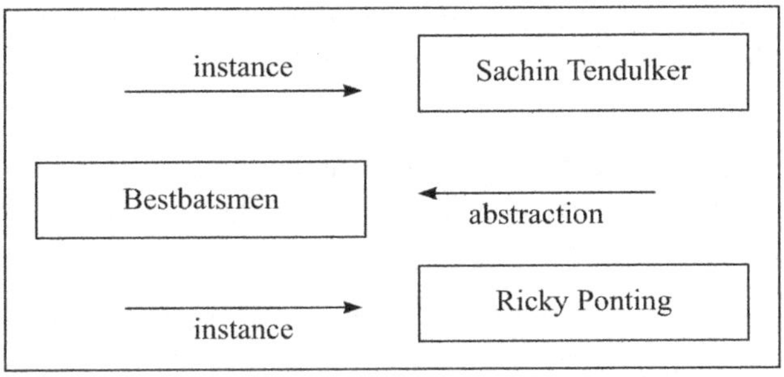

Figure 2.2 Entity instances of entity *Bestbatsmen*

As we have noted earlier, all entities have information about them that is of interest and each entity is described by the information about its properties. Instances of the same entity set are described by the same set of properties. It is, for example, not possible to have two members of an entity set *Bestbatsmen* where one player has one set of properties and the other has a different set of properties or one player is identified by his name while another by his player ID.

Real world enterprises consist of entities as well as interactions between them. Therefore a database is a collection of interrelated information about an enterprise. A database consisting of a number of entity sets also includes information about relationships between them.

2.5.2 Relationships, Roles and Relationship Sets

An enterprise database may consist of many entities, perhaps hundreds or even thousands of them in a large enterprise. All of these entities will have associations between them although some of the associations may be of no interest to the enterprise. In spite of this no entity even in a large enterprise can be on its own with no interaction with one or more other entities. As noted above, all interactions need not be represented in the database. For example, two academics in a university may have research interests in the same area but for some applications this may be of no interest to the university. Usually an association between any two or more entities will be defined for a given instant of time since associations can change with time.

This relationship can be defined as follows:

Definition—Relationship
A relationship is an association among entities.

Relationships exist between entities and may be looked upon as mappings between two or more entity sets. A relation therefore is a subset of all possible combinations of entity instances from each entity type participating in the relationship. The set of all possible combinations can be large, for example, there can be 10,000 possible relationship instances if each of the two entities has 100 entity instances. These combinations are called the cross product of the entities involved in the relationship. Let us consider an example involving an entity set *Player* and another *Match*. All possible combinations of the entity instances would be a large number of relationship instances meaning that each player had played in every match, which obviously does not make sense.

The entities associated in a relationship may be of the same type or of different types. For example, batting is a relationship between the entity sets *Player* and *Match*. Captain is a relationship between the entity set *Player* with itself.

Each entity set in a relationship has a role or a function that the entity plays in the relationship. For example, a *Player* entity in a relationship *Batting* has a role of a batsman while the role of the entity set *Match* can only be best described as match.

Often relationship names are verbs and entity names are nouns which enables one to read the entity and relationship, for example, as 'player batted in match'.

Although we allow relationships among any number of entity sets, the most common relationships are binary relationships between two entity sets. The *degree* of a relationship is the number of entity sets associated in the relationship. Unary, binary and ternary relationships therefore have degrees 1, 2 and 3 respectively.

We consider a binary relationship R between two entity types E_1 and E_2. The relationship may be viewed as two mappings $E_1 \rightarrow E_2$ and $E_2 \rightarrow E_1$. It is important to consider the constraints on these two relationships (or mappings). It may be that one object from E_1 may be associated with exactly one object in E_2 or any number of objects in E_1 may be associated with any number of objects in E_2. Often the relationships are classified as one-to-one (1-1), one-to-many (1-n) or many-to-many (m-n). For example, marriage is a one-to-one relationship (in most countries) between an entity set *Person* to itself. If an entity in E_1 can be associated with any number of entities in E_2, but an entity in E_2 can only be associated with at most one entity in E_1, the relationship is called one-to-many. In a many-to-many relationship, an entity instance from one entity set can be related to any number of entity instances in the other entity set.

We consider an example of entity sets *Employee* and *Office*[1]. Let us look at what these two entity sets might look like if all the information about them was put in two separate Tables 2.1 and 2.2.

1. Offices can be an entity only if we have some information, in addition to its identifier, about each office. The information in Table 2.2 includes the office number, building name, capacity (number of people), and area in square metres. More information like number of telephones, etc., could also be of interest.

Table 2.1 Information about *Employee*

EMPID	*Name*	*Position*	*Address*
863456	J. White	Engineer	123 Main Street
921234	M. Lal	Designer	45 Kingsway
909876	J. Blue	Architect	654 Gandhi Road
952468	S. Kale	Manager	987 GT Road
799751	G. Black	Intern	32 New Road
857623	C. Bright	Programmer	234 TN Road
897689	L. Grey	Intern	32 New Road
993579	L. Green	Director	35 Delhi Road

Table 2.2 Information about *Office*

Office Number	*Building*	*Capacity*	*Area (sqm0)*
CS101	Computing	2	25
CS103	Computing	3	35
MA201	Mathematics	2	32
MA100	Mathematics	5	50
BU212	Business	3	42
BU301	Business	1	20
BU201	Business	4	40
CS108	Computing	4	45
CS110	Computing	3	30

We have put some information in the two tables although in a real practical application there is likely to be much more information than we have displayed in the tables. Also, we have assumed that the column *Building* has no information about buildings other than their names. If there was other information of interest about the buildings, we might need another table for that information. Such issues are discussed later in this chapter.

To relate the information in the two tables we need to have a relationship between them. Let us call this relationship *occupies* (since an employee occupies an office) and consider the following possibilities:

(a) If for each employee there is at most one office and for each office there is at most one employee, the relationship is one-to-one.

(b) If an office can accommodate more than one employee but an employee has at most one office, the relationship between *Office* and *Employee* is one-to-many.

(c) If an office can accommodate more than one employee and an employee can be assigned more than one office, the relationship between them is many-to-many. For example, an engineer may have one office in the workshop and another in the design office. Also each design office may accommodate more than one staff member. The relationship is therefore many-to-many.

These three relationships are shown in Figs 2.3(a), 2.3(b) and 2.3(c).

We now define the concept of cardinality ratio of a relationship.

> ***Definition—Cardinality Ratio of a Relationship***
> *Cardinality ratio of a binary relationship is the maximum number of relationship instances that an entity can participate in.*

The cardinality ratio may be one-to-one, one-to-many, many-to-one, or many-to-many. Examples of different types of relationships are given below.

One-to-one Relationship

Figure 2.3(a) shows a one-to-one relationship between *Employee* and *Office*. The relationship shows that each instance of *Employee* in the relationship is related to at most one instance of *Office* and every instance of *Office* is related to at most one instance of *Employee.*

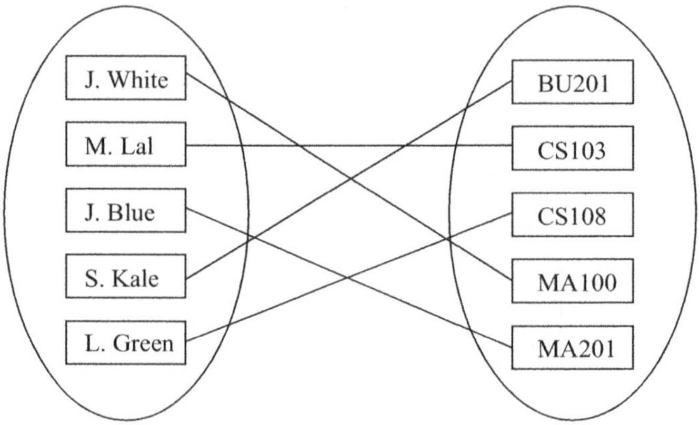

Figure 2.3(a) One-to-one relationship between *Employee* and *Office*

Note that the relationship shown in Fig. 2.3(a) does not show all the instances of entities given in Tables 2.1 and 2.2 because some *Employees* may not yet have been allocated *Offices* and some *Offices* may not yet have any *Employees* allocated to them.

One-to-many Relationship

Figure 2.3(b) shows a many-to-one relationship between *Employee* and *Office*. In this case a number of employees may occupy the same office but an employee can have only one office. Note that each instance of *Employee* is only related to one instance of *Office* but each instance of *Office* may be related to one or more instances of *Employee*. This relationship is not that unusual. For example, I am writing this while visiting VIT University in Vellore where academics share offices and a number of students (up to six, I am told) live in the same hostel room which may result in similar relationships between entities *students* and *rooms*.

Many-to-many Relationship

Figure 2.3(c) shows a many-to-many relationship between *Employee* and *Office*. In this case a number of employees may occupy the same office and an employee may have more than one office. Therefore a number

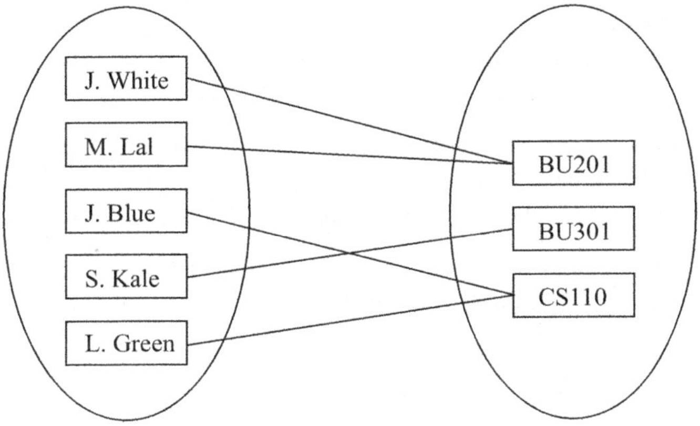

Figure 2.3(b) One-to-many relationship between *Employee* and *Office*

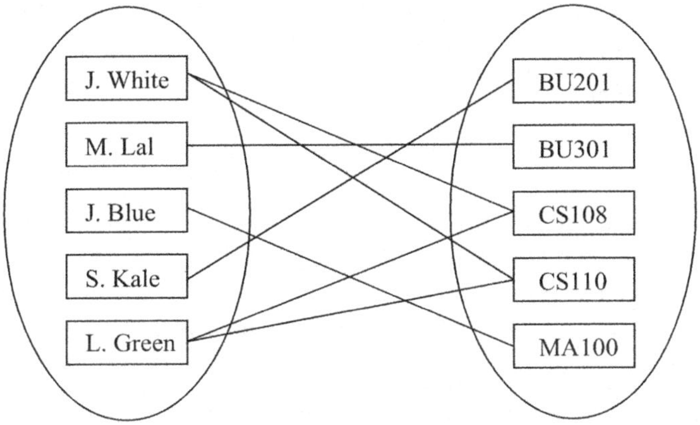

Figure 2.3(c) Many-to-many relationship between *Employee* and *Office*

of instances of *Employee* are related to one or more instances of *Office*. For example, J. White and L. Green share the office CS108 while L. Green has another office CS110 that is also shared with J. White.

The *Employee-Office* relationship is similar to many other relationships in life, for example, the relationship between lecturers and courses.

An easy way to determine the relationship type between two entities is to ask questions like the following:

- How many offices can an employee have?
- How many employees can an office hold?

As noted earlier, relationships are often binary but more than two entity types may participate in a relationship type.

Also there may be more than one type of relationship between the same two entity types. For example, there can be a number of relationship types between an entity set *employee* and another entity set *project* if one of the relationships identifies employees working on projects while the other identifies employees that are project managers for projects. Another example is two relationships, *batting* and *bowling*, between the entity types *player* and *match*.

Ternary relationships, those between three entity types, are generally more complex than binary relationships. It is however in some cases possible to replace a ternary relationship by two binary relationships between the three entity types that participated in the ternary relationship. We will discuss this further later.

Ternary relationships are more complex and may be 1:1:1 or 1:1:m or 1:m:n or p:m:n. We leave it to the reader to think of examples for each type of ternary relationship.

2.5.3 Attributes, Values and Value Set

As we have noted earlier, an E-R database model consists of entities and relationships. Since these are the objects of interest, there is always information about them that is useful to the enterprise. This information in fact describes each entity instance in an entity set and the information of interest is called entity *attributes*. For example:

- Entity's name or identifier
- Entity's location
- Entity's other properties

Entity name or identifier enables us to identify each entity instance uniquely. If an entity does not have a unique name or identifier then each entity may be identified by values of a collection of attributes. In addition, each entity instance is described by properties or a set of attributes and their values at some given time. Often we are only interested in the current values of the properties and it is then convenient to drop time from the information being collected.

In some applications, however, time is very important. For example, a personnel department of a company would wish to have access to salary history and status history of all employees of the enterprise. A number of ways are available for storing such temporal data. Further details about temporal databases are beyond the scope of this book.

Relationships may also have relevant information about them. A cricket player in an entity set *player* is likely to be described by its attributes like *player id*, *name*, *country*, etc. A relationship like *batting* between entities *player* and *match* might have attributes like the *number of runs*, *number of fours*, *number of sixes*, etc., as attributes.

Types of Attributes

Attributes can be of several different types. As discussed earlier, they can be single-valued or multivalued, simple or composite or be stored or derived. We discuss these different types briefly.

- *Simple or Composite Attributes*—Most attributes are simple (also called atomic) and can not be divided into smaller components. Such attributes include country, place of birth, player ID, and number of runs and so on. Attributes that are composite can be divided into smaller components. Typical examples of composite attributes are name (consisting of at least the first name and the last name), date of birth (day, month and year), and address (street number, street name, city and PIN).

- *Single-valued or Multivalued*—Many attributes have a single value, for example, the age of a player, his last name, the player ID and so on. Some attributes on the other hand are multivalued. For example, names of umpires in a match is multivalued since there are two umpires on the ground, there is also a TV umpire, a reserve umpire and a match referee. Other typical examples of multivalued attributes are the courses a student is enrolled in or the programming languages an employee knows.
- *Stored or Derived*—Although it is not recommended, a database may have some attribute values that are related. A simple example is the total number of ODI runs scored in a player's career or the batting average, or the number of centuries scored. These are all derived attributes based on stored attributes like the number of runs scored in each match. The age of a player may also be a derived attribute if the database has a stored attribute that gives the date of birth.
- *Required or Optional*—An attribute may be required or it may be optional. Required attributes include player ID, match ID, and player's last name and first name. Optional attribute may be the year of the first test in an ODI database since some ODI players may not have played in a test match.

For each attribute there are a number of legal or permitted values. These sets of legal values are sometimes called *value sets* or *domain* of the attribute. For example, a player id may have legal values only between 10000 to 99999 while the year value in a match date may have admissible values only between say 1930 and the current year. A number of attributes may share a common domain of values. For example, a batsman's run score and a bowler's runs conceded may have the same legal values.

An attribute may be considered as a function that maps from an entity set or a relationship set into a value set. For example, the attribute *age* may map into an integer value set with values between 15 and 45 if the attribute age belongs to an entity player. The set of (attribute, data value) pairs, one pair for each attribute, partially describe each entity instance. For example, an entity instance of entity set player may be described by

- (player id, 101122)
- (player name, Ricky Ponting)

It should be noted that a data model has no way of knowing what an attribute or property means. The data models do not have any semantic knowledge of the model. The name of the person could be *Eman* but that has no impact on the model as long as the user understands that *Eman* is the name of the person.

As an example, consider a database that includes Tables 2.1 and 2.2 as entity sets *Employee* and *Office* and two additional entity sets *Department* and *Project* which are not shown. We therefore now have the following four entity sets.

- *Employee*—the set of all employees of a company. The attributes of the entity set *Employee* are EmpID, Name, Position and Address.
- *Office*—the set of all offices in a company. The attributes of the entity set *Office* are Office Number, Building, Capacity and Area.
- *Department*—the set of all departments of the company. The attributes of the entity set *Department* are Department Number, Department Name, SupervisorID.
- *Project*—the set of all projects at the company. The attributes of the entity set *Project* are Project Number, Project Name, ManagerID.

Once again, a real-world example would include a lot more information in the database.

Note that no relationships have been included in the list above. We propose three relationships although more may be required.

- *Occupies*—this is a relationship between entity sets *Employee* and *Office*. The attributes of the relationship set *occupies* are EmpID, Office Number, Date Allocated.
- *Works_for*—this is a relationship between entity sets *Employee* and *Department*. The attributes of the relationship set *works_for* are EmpID, Department Number, Date Joined, Qualifications, and Position.
- *Works_on*—this is a relationship between entity sets *Employee* and *Project*. The attributes of the relationship set *works_on* are EmpID, Project Number, Date Joined, Status, Position.

A careful reader would have noted that all the attributes for relationships shown above need not be included in the relationships. For example, should Qualifications and Position really belong in *Works_for*? What is the meaning of Position in *Works_on*? We will not resolve such issues here but will discuss them later in this chapter and also in Chapter 5 on normalization.

It should be noted that many further attributes would be included in the entity sets and relationship sets in a real-world application. The additional entity sets and relationship sets included in the database may also be represented as tables, similar to Tables 2.1 and 2.2. We give an example of a table representation for relationship set *Occupies* in Fig. 2.3(c). It is shown in Table 2.3 although mapping of entities and relationships to tables will be discussed in detail in Chapter 3.

Table 2.3 Relationship ***occupies*** shown in Fig. 2.3(c) represented as a table

EmpID	*Office Number*	*Date Allocated*
863456	CS108	01/03/2005
863456	CS110	02/04/2008
921234	BU301	03/07/2010
909876	MA100	31/12/1999
952468	BU201	06/06/2006
993579	CS108	01/01/2000
993579	CS110	07/07/2007

Note that the office CS108 is occupied by two employees and so is CS110.

2.5.4 Representing Entities and Relationships

Since each entity set normally consists of many entity instances, it is essential to be able to uniquely identify each entity instance in every entity set. Similarly it is essential to be able to uniquely identify each relationship instance in every relationship set. Since entities are represented by the values of their attribute set, it is necessary that the set of attribute values not be identical for any two entity instances. If two entity instances from an entity set have exactly the same attribute values and the entity instances are different (although it may be difficult to imagine when such a situation might arise) then an artificial attribute may need to be included in the attribute set to assist entity identification. An artificial attribute may also be included to simplify entity identification. For example, although each instance of the entity set *Employee* in a company database perhaps can be identified by the values of its attributes *name* and *address*, it is convenient to include an artificial attribute *EmpID* to make identification of each Employee entity instance easier.

Entity Key, Candidate Key and Super Key

A group of attributes (possibly one) used for identifying each entity in an entity set is called an *entity key*. For example, for the entity set *Employee, EmpID* is an entity key and so is (*Name, Address*). Of course, if *k* is a key then so is each super set of *k*. A *superkey* is any set of attributes such that no two tuples of a relation can have the same values for *k* for every possible pair of distinct tuples.

To reduce the number of possible keys, it is usually required that a key be *minimal* in that no subset of the key should be a key. For example, *name* by itself could not be considered an entity key since two employees could have the same name. When several minimal keys exist (such keys are often called *candidate keys*), any semantically meaningful key may be chosen as the *entity primary key*.

Definition—Primary Key
The primary key of an entity is an attribute or a set of attributes that uniquely identifies a specific instance of an entity. Every entity in the Entity-Relationship model must have a primary key.

Definition—Candidate Key
When an entity has more than one attribute (or a set of attributes) that can serve as a primary key, each of such keys is called a candidate key. One and only one of the candidate keys is chosen as the primary key for the entity.

It should be noted that a superkey is unique whereas, as discussed in the next chapter, a candidate key is both unique and irreducible.

Similarly, each relationship instance in a relationship set needs to be identified. This identification is always based on the primary keys of the entity sets involved in the relationship set. The primary key of a relationship set is the combination of the attributes that form the primary keys of the entity sets involved. In addition to the entity identifiers, the relationship key also (perhaps implicitly) identifies the role that each entity plays in the relationship.

If *EmpID is* the primary key of the entity set *Employee* and *ProjNum* is the primary key of *Project*, the primary key of the relationship set *Works_on* is (*EmpID, ProjNum*). Similarly the primary key for the relationship set *Works_for* is (*EmpID, DeptNum*) since *EmpID* is the primary key of the entity set *Employee* and *DeptNum* is the primary key of *Department.* The role of the two entities is implied by the order in which the two primary keys are specified.

Weak Entity Types

In certain cases, the entities in an entity set cannot be uniquely identified by the values of their own attributes. For example, children of employees in a company may have names that are not unique. One solution to this problem is to assign unique numbers to all children of employees in the company. Another, more natural, solution is to identify each child by his/her name and the primary key of the parent who is an employee of the company. The names of the children of each employee are expected to be unique. Such an attribute(s) that discriminates between all the entities that are dependent on the same parent entity is sometimes called a *discriminator*. It cannot be called a key since it does not uniquely identify an entity without the use of the relationship with the employee. Similarly, history of employment of an employee if included in the database would not have a primary key without the support of the employee's primary key. Such entities that require a relationship to be used in identifying them are called *weak entities*. Entities that have primary keys are called *strong* or *regular entities*. Similarly, a relationship may be weak or strong (or regular). A *strong relationship* is between entities each of which is strong; otherwise the relationship is a *weak relationship*. For example, any relationship between the children of the employees and the schools they attend would be a weak relationship. A relationship between the *Employee* entity set and the *Project* entity set is a strong relationship.

A weak entity is also called a *subordinate* entity since its existence depends on another entity (called the *dominant* entity). This is called *existence dependence*. The weak entity therefore does not possess sufficient attributes to form a primary key. This is in contrast to a regular or strong entity that has key attributes and therefore does not exist because of another entity. The relationship of a weak entity to its owner entity type is called the *identifying relationship*.

It is interesting to look at the sources of weakness in a weak entity. Often it is because of the hierarchy of entity sets. For example, species name and genus name may form a key of an entity called plant.

Another example of weak entity is that a customer has several accounts with a bank. Every transaction on each account has transaction number but different transactions in different accounts could have the same number so the transaction number by itself is not sufficient to form a primary key. Therefore a transaction cannot be uniquely identified without the account number and is therefore a weak entity set. For a weak entity set to be meaningful, it must be part of a one-to-many relationship set. This relationship set should not have any descriptive attributes.

A weak entity set does not have a primary key but we need a means of distinguishing among the weak entities. The discriminator of a weak entity set is a set of attributes that allows distinction between instances of a weak entity to be made. Therefore, the primary key of a weak entity is found by taking the primary key of the strong entity on which it is existence-dependent combined with the discriminator of the weak entity set.

Although existence dependency does not imply ID dependency, a weak entity is often *ID dependent* on the dominant entity. This method of identifying entities by relationships with other entities can be applied recursively until a strong entity is reached. Although the relationship between the dominant entity and a weak entity is usually one-to-many, in some situations the relationship may be many-to-many. For example, a company may employ both parents of some children. The dependence is then may be many-to-many.

Terms that are useful:

(a) Weak entity—an entity that depends on another entity for identification.

(b) Weak entity relation—a relation that is used for identifying entities, for example, the relationship between employees and their dependants.

(c) Regular entity relation—a relation not used for identifying entities.

2.5.5 Naming Conventions

It is best to be consistent while giving names to entities, relationships and attributes. One commonly used practice is to use a singular name for all entities and use verbs for all relationships. In many respects it doesn't matter which one (singular or plural) is used as long as it is used consistently throughout the entire database schema design.

In this book we will be using the following conventions:

Entities

Entity names should have the following characteristics:

- Each entity name should come from the entity description, which has meaning to the user community.
- Each entity name should be a noun, singular and current tense. It is something about which we want to keep information.
- The first letter should be uppercase.
- Where necessary, underscores should join the words.
- Names for the entities must be meaningful and must not conflict with other entity names. Names should not be abbreviated unnecessarily making them difficult to understand.
- Example of entity names are Account, Customer, Product, Employee, Department, Player.

Relationships

- Each relationship name should be a verb that fits the sentence structure.
- Where necessary, an attribute name may use underscores to join the words.
- Example of relationship names are Occupies, Married_to, Represents, Batting.

Attributes

Each attribute name should have the following characteristics:

- Generally an attribute name should be a noun.
- Where necessary, an attribute name may use underscores to join the words.
- An attribute name must be unique with no two attributes of an entity type having the same name. Attributes of different entities can have the same name.
- For example, PID, EmpID, Course_Number (these are identifiers), Status, Reason (these are categories), Name, Description, Comment (these are textual), Date, Date_of_Birth, Year (these are date related), etc.

2.5.6 Diagrammatic Notation for E-R Model

As noted earlier, Entity-Relationship modeling facilitates communication between the database designer and the client during the requirements analysis. To assist in such communication, the designer needs good communication tools. A diagram can be such a tool since it is said that a picture is worth a thousand words.

There are a number of software tools (often called CASE tools for Computer Aided Software Engineering) available in the market which provide facilities for drawing E-R diagrams. Each tool may have its own conventions for drawing diagrams and the conventions often vary slightly from tool to tool. A diagram representing an E-R model should include the following:

- *Entities, Relationships and Attributes*—These have been discussed earlier.

- *Cardinality Constraints*—These also have been discussed earlier. For binary relationships, cardinality may be 1:1, 1:*m* or *m*:*n*.
- *Participation Constraint*—The concept of participation specifies whether an entity instance in a relationship can exist without participating in the relationship. Participation is either mandatory or optional.
- *Generalization/Specialization*—This will be discussed later, they deal with the concepts of subclass and superclass.

In addition to the above, a diagram representing an E-R model also needs to deal with the following issues.

- *Are ternary relationships allowed or only binary?*—Some notations only allow binary relationships since that makes the diagrams simpler. Some ternary relationship can be transformed into a number of binary relationships but the semantics of the relationship often change when such transformation is carried out.
- *How is cardinality to be represented?*—Cardinality can be represented in two different ways. In the first case, a lecturer teaching a number of courses and each course being taught only by one lecturer will be represented by putting 1 next to the lecturer entity and *n* near the course. In the second case, the opposite is done.
- *Are relationships allowed to have attributes?*—Some notations do not allow attributes for relationships. In such a notation, a relationship with attributes must be represented as an entity.

There are a number of different diagrammatic notations suggested in the literature. We consider only two of them. The first notation is the one that Chen recommended in his original paper and is discussed next. The second is called the Crow's Foot Notation and is discussed in Section 2.5.10.

2.5.7 Entity-Relationship Diagrams (Chen's Notation)

We call Chen's notation an E-R diagram. The original notation included notations only for entities, relationships, attributes and cardinalities. It was later extended to include generalization and participation constraints.

Building Blocks of Entity-Relationship Diagram

In an E-R diagram, as shown in Fig. 2.4, the entity sets are represented by rectangular shaped boxes and relationships are represented by diamond shaped boxes.

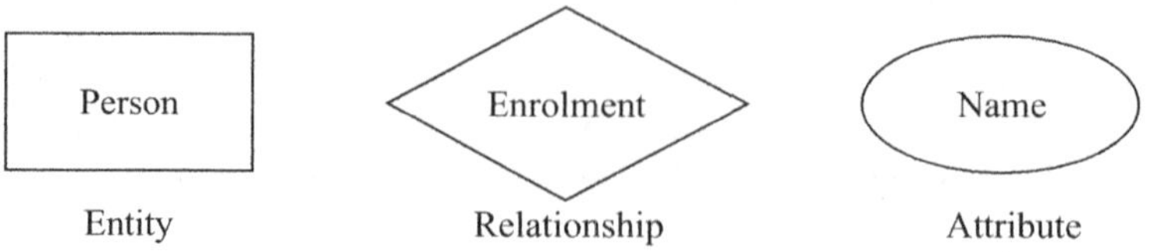

Figure 2.4 Elements of the Entity-Relationship diagram

Ellipses are used to represent attributes and lines are used to link attributes to entity sets and entity sets to relationship sets. We now present some examples of E-R diagrams.

A Simple Unary Relationship E-R Diagram

Consider a simple E-R diagram as shown in Fig. 2.5(a) that includes only one entity set which has a relationship with itself. In this relationship an employee and his/her supervisor are both instances of the entity set *Employee*. Therefore, the relationship between an employee and the supervisor is a relationship between two instances of the same entity type.

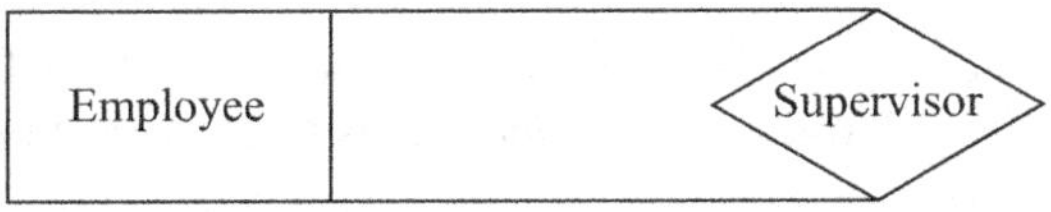

Figure 2.5(a) ERD for a unary relationship

A Simple Binary Relationship E-R Diagram

The E-R diagram as shown in Fig. 2.5(b) shows a simple relationship between two entity types *Employee* and *Department*. In this relationship an instance of the entity *Employee* works for an instance of the entity *Department*. It is not required that each instance of *Employee* be involved in this relationship. The same applies to the instances of the entity *Department* since some instances of *Employee* may not yet have been allocated to a department and some departments that are perhaps new may not have any employees.

Figure 2.5(b) ERD for a binary relationship

A Simple Ternary Relationship E-R Diagram

The E-R diagram as shown in Fig. 2.5(c) shows a simple relationship between three entity types *Employee*, *Project* and *Department*. In this relationship an instance of the entity *Employee* works for an instance of the entity *Department* as well as an instance of the entity *Project*. Such relationships between three entities are called *ternary* relationships as opposed to binary relationships between two entities. It is not required that each instance of the three entities be involved in this relationship, since as noted above, some instances of

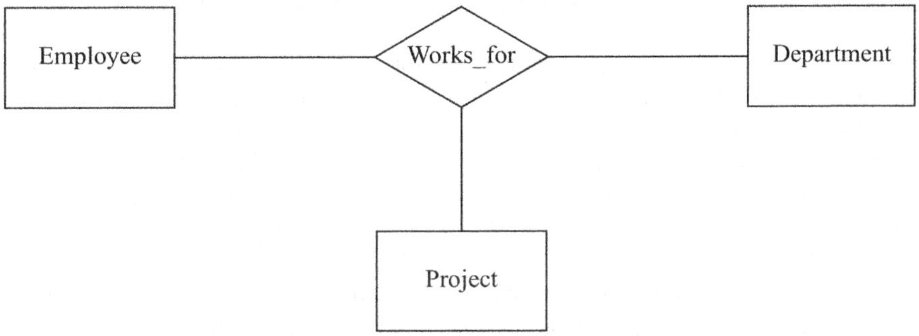

Figure 2.5(c) A ternary relationship

Employee may not yet have been allocated to a department and some departments that are perhaps new may not have any employees. Similarly, some projects may be so new that they have no employees or have not been allocated to a department.

It is important to note that ternary relationships add further complexity to a model. For example, for entity instances to participate in such relationships, each instance of the three entity types should be known. An instance of *Employee* who has been allocated to a *Department* but has no *Project* cannot participate in this relationship. Similarly, a *Project* that has been allocated to a *Department* but has no employees cannot participate in the relationship. We will discuss more about ternary relationships later in the section.

An E-R Diagram for Binary Relationship with Attributes

The E-R diagram shown in Fig. 2.5(d) presents a number of attributes for the model in Fig. 2.5(b). Another relationship *Manager* has been added between the entity *Employee* to itself. Although this E-R model is very simple, we can see that it is getting cluttered with more attributes. A more complex model obviously would require a lot of space for display.

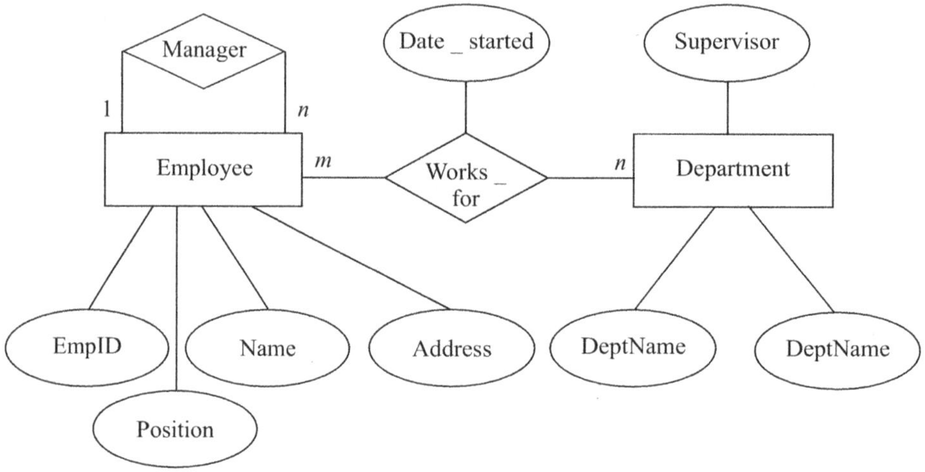

Figure 2.5(d) E-R Diagram for Fig. 2.5(b) with a number of attributes

An E-R Diagram that includes a Weak Entity and a Ternary Relationship

The E-R model shown in Fig. 2.5(e) is more complex with three additional entities including a weak entity and three additional relationships. The E-R diagram in Fig. 2.5(e) does not show the attributes because showing the attributes as well as the additional entities and relationships would make the diagram somewhat difficult to read. We should however note the following about the E-R diagram in Fig. 2.5(e):

1. The diagram shows that the relationship *Manager* is a one-to-many and the relationship *Works_on* is a many-to-many relationship and so on.
2. *Employment History* has been modeled as a weak entity since this entity depends on the entity *Employee*. If an instance of *Employee* is deleted then its dependent instances in *Employment History* would also be deleted.
3. A ternary relationship *PSP* exists between the entities *Project*, *Supplier* and *Parts*.

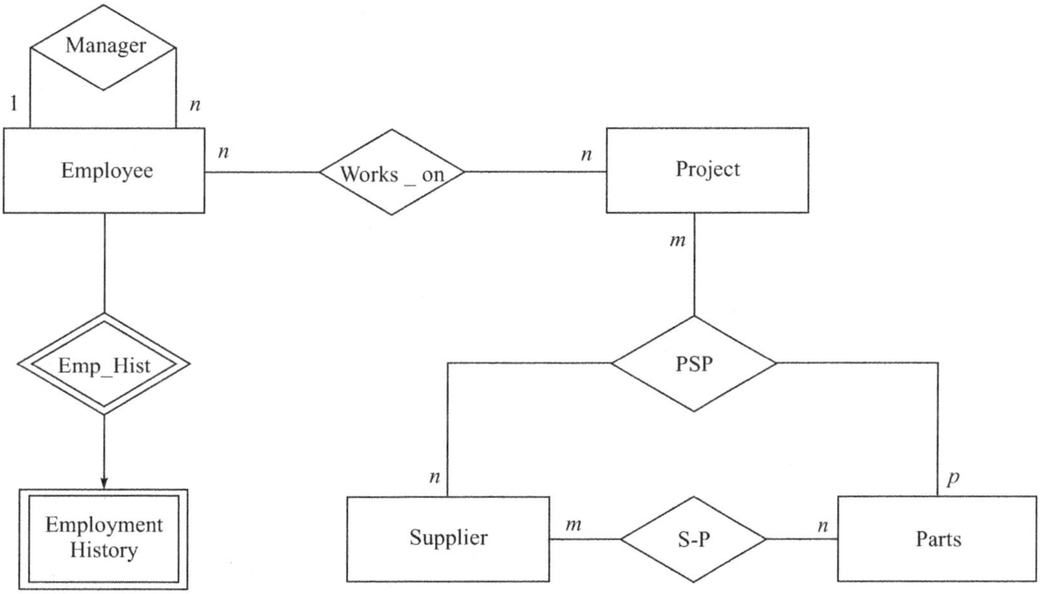

Figure 2.5(e) An E-R diagram showing a weak entity and a ternary relationship

An E-R Diagram for Two Binary Relationships between the Same Entities

We mentioned earlier that two similar entities can have more than one relationship. The simple E-R diagram in Fig. 2.5(f) presents two relationships, one being *Has_office_in* and the other *Has_proj_in* between the two entities *Staff* and *Building*.

An E-R Diagram with Two Unary Relationships for the Same Entity

A unary relationship is shown in Fig. 2.5(a) and 2.5(d). The E-R model in Fig. 2.5(g) shows that it is possible to have more than one unary relationship between a given entity and itself. The two relationships of the entity *Employee* with itself are *Coaches* and *Supervises*. Both coach and supervisor are employees. These relationships can of course have attributes. We have not shown any attributes in our diagram.

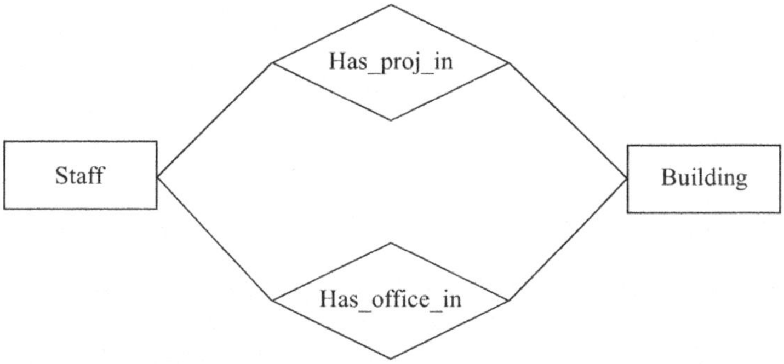

Figure 2.5(f) Two relationships between the same two entities

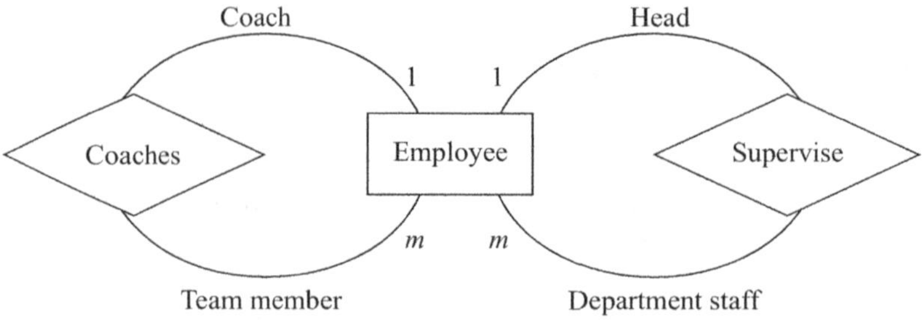

Figure 2.5(g) Two unary relationships

We briefly summarize the seven E-R diagrams presented in Figs 2.5(a) to 2.5(g). The E-R diagram in Fig. 2.5(b) only shows two entities and one relationship and not the attributes. Fig. 2.5(c) shows a ternary relationship. Figure 2.5(d) shows the same two entities but shows an additional relationship between employees and their manager. This additional relationship is between the entity set *Employee* and itself. In addition, the E-R diagram in Fig. 2.5(d) shows the attributes as well as the type of relationships (1:1, *m*:*n* or 1:*m*). The type of relationship is shown by placing a label of 1, *m* or *n* on each end of every arc. The label 1 indicates that only one of those entity instances may participate in a given relationship. A letter label (often *m* or *n*) indicates that a number of these entity instances may participate in a given relationship. The E-R diagrams may also show roles as labels on the arcs.

The E-R diagram in Fig. 2.5(e) shows a number of entities and a number of relationships. Also note that the entity *Employment History* is shown as a double box which indicates that *Employment History* is a weak entity and that its existence depends on the existence of the corresponding employee entity. The existence dependency of the entity *Employment History* on the entity *Employee* is indicated by an arrow. A ternary relationship between three entities is also shown. Note that each entity can participate in several relationships.

The E-R diagram in Fig. 2.5(f) shows two entities and two different relationships between them. Figure 2.5(g) shows two relationships also, but both these relationships are between the entity *Employee* and itself.

The above diagrams have shown entity sets and relationship sets between them. Figure 2.6 shows a number of instances of the relationship *Works_on* (*WO*) between instances of entities *Employee* (*E*) and *Project* (*P*). *E*1 to *E*6 are instances of the entity *Employee* while *P*1 to *P*4 are instances of the entity *Project*. *WO*1 to *WO*8 are instances of the relationship *Works_on*.

It should be noted that a primary key of relationship *WO*1 is (e_1, p_1) assuming e_1 and p_1 are the primary keys of the two entities *E*1 and *P*1 and so on for other instances of the relationships *WO*2 to *WO*8 shown in Fig. 2.6. It should be noted that the relationship in Fig. 2.6 is a many-to-many relationship. For example, the employee entity *E*1 is related with three project entities *P*1, *P*2 and *P*3 and the project entity *P*1 is related with two employee entities *E*1 and *E*6.

2.5.8 Ternary Relationships and Binary Relationships

As noted earlier, ternary relationships are more complex than binary relationships. One example of a ternary relationship is presented in Fig. 2.5(c). The three entities involved are *Employee*, *Department* and *Project*. We first define different types of ternary relationships. These relationships can be 1:1:1, 1:1:*m*, 1:*m*:*n* or *m*:*n*:*p*.

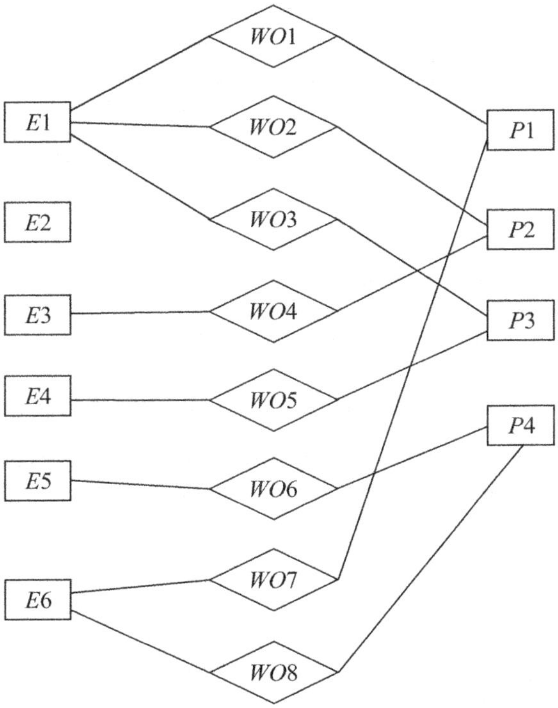

Figure 2.6 Instances of the many-to-many relationship *Works_on* (*WO*) between the entities *Employee* (*E*) and ***Project*** (*P*)

The ternary relationship in Fig. 2.5(c) is reproduced below in Fig. 2.7(a). In the simplest but unrealistic case the ternary relationship is 1:1:1, which means that for each employee there is only one department and only one project. Furthermore, a department has only one employee and only one project. And finally, each project has only one department and only one employee. This is obviously quite unrealistic but it is relatively simple to convert the 1:1:1 relationship to two binary relationships, one between *Employee* and *Project* and another between *Project* and *Department*.

If we now relax some of these constraints and allow a department to have more than one employee and more than one project while still requiring each employee to just belong to one department, each employee to work on only one project, each project to have only one employee and each project to be assigned to just one department, the relationship becomes somewhat more complex but it is still possible to transform the ternary relationship into two binary relationships. We leave this as an exercise for the reader.

The ternary relationship in Fig. 2.7(a) could have the following more realistic constraints:

1. An instance of *Employee* is related to only one instance of *Department* and only one instance of *Project*.
2. An instance of *Department* is related to many instances of *Employee* and many instances of *Project*.
3. An instance of *Project* is related to many instances of *Employee* and only one instance of *Department*.

If we now look at the three binary relationships, we find that the *Employee: Department* relationship is 1:*p*. The *Employee: Project* relationship is 1:*m*. Finally the *Department: Project* relationship is also 1:*n*. We

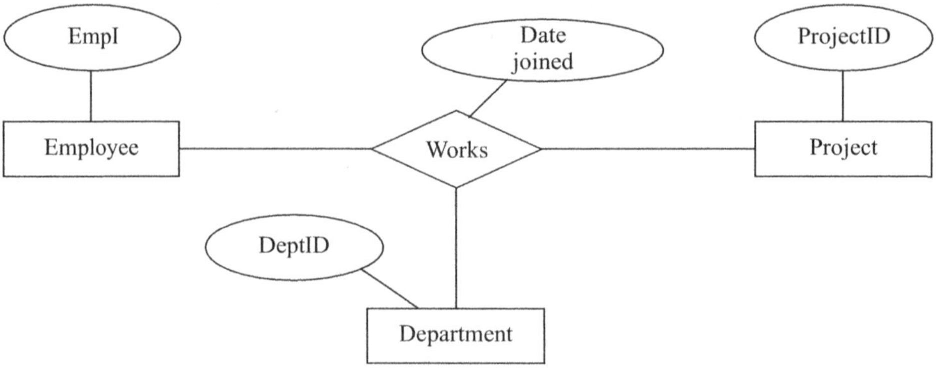

Figure 2.7(a) A ternary relation between *Employee*, ***Project*** and *Department*

therefore have three one-to-many binary relationships in the ternary relationship. Can they be represented by three binary relationships as shown in Fig. 2.7(b)?

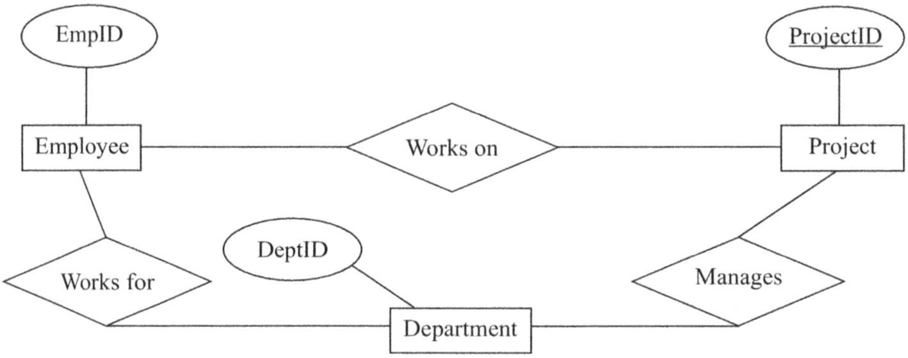

Figure 2.7(b) Three binary relations between the relations *Employee*, ***Project*** and *Department*

The three binary relationships shown in Fig. 2.7(b) are in fact not able to represent the same information as the ternary relationship in Fig. 2.7(a). What information can be represented in the E-R diagram shown in Fig. 2.7(a) that cannot be represented in the diagram shown in Fig. 2.7(b)? Is there information that the model in Fig. 2.7(b) can represent but the model in Fig. 2.7(a) cannot? We leave it to the reader to answer these questions.

Another E-R model that attempts to model the same information as the ternary relationship replaces the ternary relationship in Fig. 2.7(a) with a weak entity *Works* and three binary relationships between this entity and the other three entities.

2.5.9 E-R Diagram Conventions

A number of issues regarding conventions may arise while developing a database model. The entity-relationship model provides no guidance on how to deal with them. For example,

- Should one cross lines in the Entity-Relationship diagram when the model is complex?

- Should any derived attributes (attributes that can be computed from other attribute values) be included in the model?
- Should performance of the implemented database system be considered in modeling?
- What naming standards and abbreviations should be used? It should be clear what standards are to be used and why. Some suggestions have been made earlier in Section 2.5.5.
- Should a collection of attributes be used as a primary key or an artificial (called surrogate key) attribute be used as the primary key?

Given that no guidelines are available, we suggest such issues be resolved by the modeling team in consultation with the client and the DBA.

2.5.10 Crow's Foot Diagrammatic Notation

Although Chen's diagrammatic notation is most widely presented in literature, another widely used notation for an Entity-Relationship diagram is called the Crow's Foot notation. A similar notation is used by ORACLE in its CASE tool. In this notation, an entity is still represented by a rectangle but the attributes are written within the bottom part of the rectangle and the name of the entity is written in the top part of the rectangle while an asterisk (*) represents the attribute or the set of attributes that form the primary key. This notation is more compact than the notation used in the E-R diagrams. Some software available for E-R model use this notation.

This notation only includes binary relationships. No attributes of the relationships may be shown. Relationships are represented by lines joining entities. The cardinality of a relationship can be shown by drawing straight lines or lines with a crow's foot. Figure 2.8(a) shows the notation when used with a 1:1 relationship between *Employee* and *Office*. Note that the || symbol denotes 1 and only 1 participation.

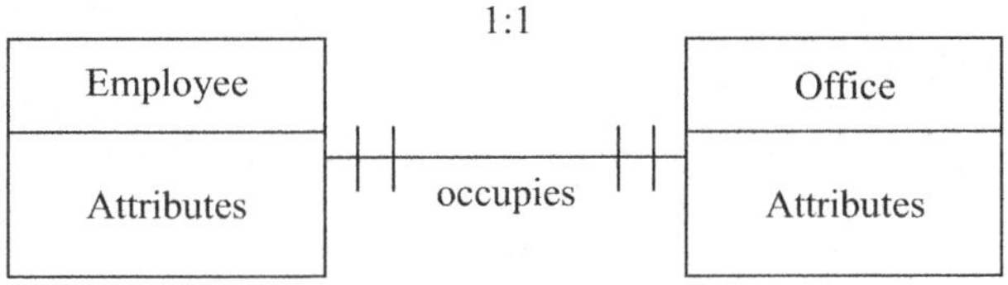

Figure 2.8(a) Crow's feet notation for two entities with 1:1 relationship

Figure 2.8(b) shows the notation when used with a *m:n* relationship between *Employee* and *Office*. Note that the | symbol denotes 1 or more participation. The crow's foot shows the many participation in a relationship.

There are many more details about the notation that we are not able to cover here. For example, the 1:1 and 1:*m* relationship attributes have to be represented by key propagation and a many-to-many relationship

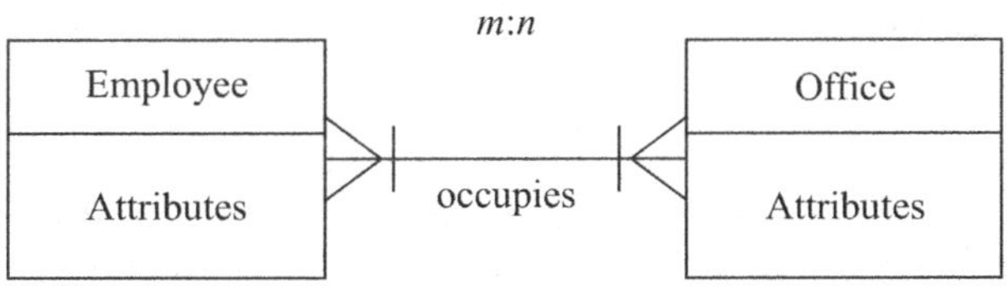

Figure 2.8(b) Crow's feet notation for two entities with 1:1 relationship

is represented by an entity called the *intersection entity* which must be put between the entities it relates. However, we will focus on using the Chen's Entity-Relationship diagrams.

2.6 GENERALIZATION, SPECIALIZATION AND AGGREGATION

The main idea in generalization/specialization is that one entity is a subset of another entity.

Although entity instances of one entity type are supposed to be objects of the same type, it often happens that objects of one entity type do have some differences. For example, as illustrated in Fig. 2.9, a company might have vehicle as an entity type but the vehicles could include cars, trucks and buses and it may then be necessary to include capacity of the bus for buses and the load capacity of the truck for trucks, information that is not relevant for cars. For cars, one may be interested in storing information regarding its type (for example, sedan or station wagon). In such situations it may be necessary to deal with the subsets separately while maintaining the view that all cars, trucks and buses are vehicles and share a lot of information. The specialization concept is a top-down concept that allows some other vehicles to be included in the entity *Vehicle* (for example, scooters) which are not an entity type in one of the specializations. Generalization is a bottom-up concept that does not allow such an option.

In Fig. 2.9 we assume that it was discovered (when the entity *Vehicle* was suggested) during initial modeling that there are likely to be a variety of vehicles and these vehicles will have some information that applies to only each group of vehicles. On the other hand, if entities: car, truck and bus, were already being considered during initial modeling and it was then realized that they were all vehicles which shared a fair bit of common information and that resulted in creation of the entity *Vehicle*, then that is generalization. Therefore, the concepts generalization and specialization are very similar; specialization being a top-down approach while generalization is the bottom-up approach.

Generalization therefore involves forming a higher-level entity type from pre-existing lower-level entity types. It is then assumed that an entity instance of the higher-level entity type must belong to one of the lower-level entity types. For example, if pre-existing entity types car and truck are combined to form a higher-level entity type vehicle then all vehicles are supposed to be either a car or a truck. Specialization on the other hand is formed by specifying subsets of a higher-level entity type. For example, if the higher level entity type was vehicle then the lower-level entity types car, truck and bus were designed then the higher-level entity type could include entity instances that do not belong to either of the lower-level entity types. So a scooter could be a vehicle although it would not be an entity instance of either of the lower-level entity types.

Primary purpose of generalization is to show similarities among a number of lower-level entity types, generalization involves the higher-level entity type inheriting attributes 'upwards' from the lower-level entity types. On the other hand, specialization involves the lower-level entity types inheriting attributes 'downwards' from the supertype entity.

In Fig. 2.9 we have shown the entity *Vehicle* which has instances v_1, v_2, ... etc., while the entity instances of bus, truck and car have been given different names to differentiate them from the instances of the entity *Vehicle* but it should be noted that v_1 and t_2 are exactly the same entity. Similarly, v_2 and t_1 are exactly the same entity and so are v_3 and c_1. It should be noted that in generalization, every instance of each subtype is related to an entity instance in the supertype while in specialization there may be some instances of supertype entity that are not related to any instance of the subtype entities, since their might be vehicles that do not belong to any of the subtypes.

Entity hierarchies are known by a number of different names. At least the following names are used in the literature, i.e., supertypes and subtypes, generalization and specialization and ISA hierarchies.

In the example above, entity type *Vehicle* will be termed a *supertype* entity and entities car or truck will each be called *subtype* entities. Subtype entities can be considered dependent entities since their existence depends on their parent, the supertype entity. Subtype entity sets are usually disjoint but can sometimes be overlapping. For example, in the somewhat unlikely situation where there was a vehicle that could be classified as a car as well as a truck then that vehicle would belong to two subtypes[2]. Another more likely example is of a supertype entity type person in a university with two subtype entity types staff and student. It is quite possible for some staff to be studying and therefore belong to both subtype entities.

There can be more than one level of supertype and subtype entities. For example, although the *Truck* entity type is a subtype, it can also be a supertype of subtype entities like forklift truck, refrigerated truck, fire truck, petrol truck, and container truck assuming these types have some information that differentiates them. The concept of entity hierarchy is important since it allows grouping of similar objects in a higher-level entity type (e.g., Vehicle) as well as allowing the user to concentrate on a lower-level entity type of interest (e.g., Bus).

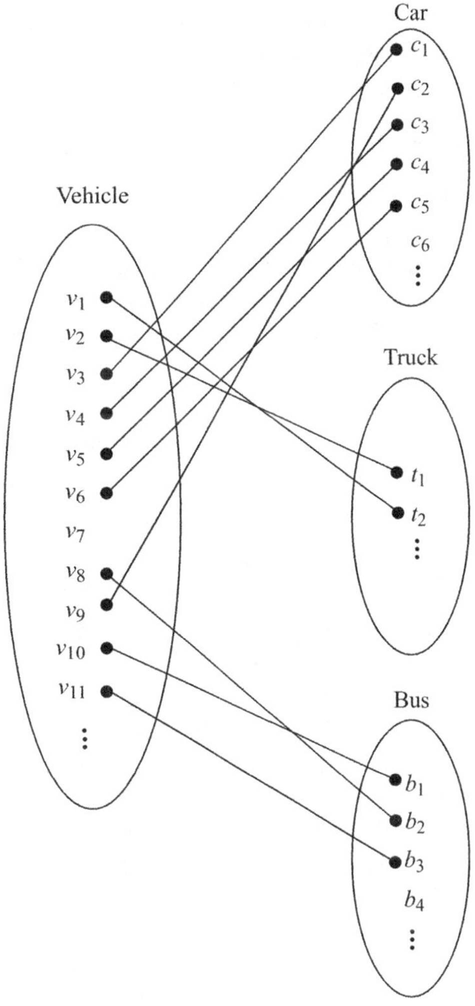

Figure 2.9 Illustrating specialization of entity vehicle

Aggregation abstraction is used in building composite entities from component entities. In aggregation, a new entity type (supertype) is defined from a set of entity types (subtypes) that represent its component parts. For example, engine, body, transmission, wheels, etc., may form an aggregation entity type vehicle. It is therefore another concept of entity hierarchy involving supertype and subtype entity types although it is different than supertype/subtype of specialization/generalization hierarchy. Supertype/subtype allows grouping of similar objects while aggregation allows grouping of several different components of the same thing to be grouped together.

2. There is in fact a vehicle called the *Ute* in Australia. It is a vehicle with the cabin of a car and the rear of a small truck. It was designed at the Ford Motor Company in Geelong, Victoria in1934. The *ute* has long been a favourite vehicle for farmers and tradesmen and is part of the Australian landscape. An Australian golfer is known to have even converted a BMW car into a ute!

Aggregation in E-R modeling may be implemented by including a relationship between the supertype entity and the component entities. It should be noted that when aggregation is used, deleting an instance of the supertype entity would normally involve deletion of all its component entity instances.

Example

Generalization

The example in Tables 2.4, 2.5 and 2.6 illustrates the concept of generalization. Table 2.4 is an entity *Person* in a university. It includes all persons at the university including students and staff since quite a lot of information about them is common. Not all such information which may include address, telephone number, date of birth, place of birth, date of joining the university, citizenship and so on is shown in the table because of space constraints.

Table 2.4 The supertype entity *Person*

ID	*First Name*	*Last Name*	*Gender*	*Status*	*Category*
67543	Arvind	Kumar	Male	FT	Student
76849	Bala	Narasimhan	Male	FT	Academic
86348	Salman	Khan	Male	PT	Both
72398	Deepaka	Dixit	Female	FT	Academic

Let us assume that the entity *Person* is a generalization of entities *Academic* and *Student*. All entity instances in *Person* also belong to one of the subtype entities, *Student* and *Academic*. The subtypes need not include information that is common to them and which is included in the supertype entity *Person*. The subtype entities only need to include information that is relevant to them because these entities will inherit the information from the supertype entity. In fact, the information in the subtype entities also need not be duplicated in the supertype entity. The supertype and subtype entities are related by their primary key.

Table 2.5 The subtype entity ***Student***

ID	*Degree Enrolled*	*Date Enrolled*
67543	BSc	1 March 2007
86348	PhD	22 July 2006

Table 2.6 The subtype entity ***Academic***

ID	*Highest Qualification*	*Discipline*	*Position*
76849	PhD	Maths	Professor
72398	PhD	Computer Science	Professor
86348	BCom(Hons)	Business	Tutor

Note that all entity instances in *Person* participate in one of the lower level entities and one entity instance participates in both *Student* and *Academic*. Therefore, this model allows overlaps in the subtype entities.

The participation constraint on a generalization and specialization is normally 1:1, since every entity instance in the subtype entities is in the supertype entity. Aggregation relationship sets have participation constraints. The constraint for each subpart class specifies how many of these parts may be related to the supertype.

2.7 EXTENDED ENTITY-RELATIONSHIP MODEL

The classical E-R model cannot fully capture the richness of real-life situations and the complexity of some newer database applications. Therefore the E-R model has been extended to provide greater semantics by including additional facilities. E-R modeling with additional modeling facilities is called the Extended Entity-Relationship model (or EER model). EER includes subset hierarchies as well as generalization hierarchies. We discuss some of these features of EER model in this section. We have discussed in the last section the concepts of generalization and specialization. These concepts are included in the EER model.

2.7.1 Supertypes, Subtypes and Inheritance

An example of generalization was presented in Fig. 2.9.

Let us consider another example. We have an entity *Student* in a large university database model. The university may decide to use just one entity type *Student* to store all the information about all students in its database. This can lead to some problems in a university like Monash which has more than 50,000 students that includes more than 15,000 postgraduate students (about 3500 research postgraduates and 12000 coursework postgraduates) and almost 20,000 international students. These different categories of students will have much information that is common to them all, for example, we assume the following information is a short list of what is common for an institute or a university in India:

- ID
- First name
- Family name
- Gender
- Citizenship
- Scheduled cast/Scheduled tribe/Backward class
- Current address
- Email address
- Telephone number
- Degree program enrolled in

There is little doubt that there will be quite a bit of information that will be different for each category of students. For example:

- For undergraduates, high school attended, current courses enrolled in
- For postgraduates, undergraduate degree, university of undergraduate degree, thesis topic, name of the supervisor, scholarship, etc.

- For international students, school/university attended, name of the country of origin, home address, home contact, etc.

There is much more information that could be listed.

We could model such a situation by describing each student by an entity type *Student* and in addition have other entity types *Undergraduate*, *Postgraduate*, *International.* Conceptually, all the common information is stored in *Student* while all the specific information is stored in entities *Undergraduate*, *Postgraduate*, and *International.* As explained in the last section, this process of modeling a group of objects and their subgroups is specialization. We could call this process as a top-down modeling process that started by identifying differences in different classes of *Student.*

In such a situation, all the attributes of *Student* will be applicable to all the subtypes but each subtype (*Undergraduate*, *Postgraduate*, and *International*) will have additional attributes that are not in the supertype entity *Student* as illustrated above. The subtype-supertype relationship specifies constraints on the entity sets since it states that the subtype must also be a member of the supertype entity and it must include all the attributes of the supertype. This is called *attribute inheritance.* The relationship between the supertype and subtype is often called *IsA* relationship.

There may be more than one level of subtype-supertype relationship. For example, *International* entity may have subtypes of *Int_undergraduate*, *Int_postgraduate* subtypes. Therefore, we have created a hierarchy in which entity *Int_undergraduate* is a subtype of *International* as well as a subtype of the entity *Student.* The hierarchy is therefore transitive which implies that an *Int_undergraduate* inherits properties from *International* as well as from *Student.*

2.7.2 Aggregation or Participation

As noted in Section 2.6, aggregation is used in modeling when an entity is the aggregate composed of other entities from the subpart classes. Aggregation therefore is used in building composite entities from component entities.

Aggregation in E-R modeling may be implemented by including a relationship between the supertype entity and the component entities. We assume that a component does not exist without the composite supertype entity which it is part of. So if the car is deleted from the database, all its parts also disappear. This type of part-relationship is called an exclusive relationship. This relationship of course is similar to the weak entity type relationship and therefore the dominant entity must also provide the identification to the weak component entities.

2.7.3 Extended Entity Relationship Diagrams

The EER Model continues to use rectangles and diamonds for entity and relationship types in the EER diagrams. EER model however also includes representation for constraints which are defined in the model and deals with situations like generalization and specialization.

All supertypes and subtypes may be represented as entity classes even if the level of the hierarchy is more than two. The common attributes are allocated to the supertype while attributes that are particular to a subtype are allocated to the subtypes. Subtypes and supertypes should participate in relationships. All subtypes and supertypes should be named as other entities are named.

The IsA relationship can also be represented in an E-R diagram. It may be represented as a diamond and is a $1{:}m$ relationship that has no attributes.

EER Diagram Conventions and Constraints

The following conventions are used in the EER diagrams:

1. The supertype/subtype relationship may be complete if an instance of supertype must also be a member of at least one subtype. This must be shown in the EER diagram by using a double line.
2. The supertype/subtype relationship may be partial if an instance of supertype need not be also be a member of at least one subtype. This must be shown in the EER diagram by using a single line.
3. The subtypes may be disjoint if an instance of supertype may be member of only one of the subtypes. This may be shown in the EER diagram by putting a *D* in the circle.
4. The subtypes may be overlapping if an instance of supertype may be member of more than one of the subtypes. This may be shown in the EER diagram by putting a *O* in the circle.

Figure 2.10 shows an example of a supertype/subtype structure in modeling specialization using an extended E-R diagram. This diagram involves a supertype entity *Student* and three subtype entities *Undergraduate*, *Postgraduate*, and *International*. The diagram shows only few of the attributes of each entity type and the attributes of entity *Student* are inherited by all the subtype entities. The relationships are one-to-one since every instance of a subtype entity must be an instance of the supertype entity.

The diagram shows that not all students need to belong to one of the subtypes since a double line has not been drawn from the entity *student*. Also the diagram shows that overlapping is possible since a student may be in subtype *International* as well as in *Postgraduate*. Furthermore, we note that all attributes of *student* are inherited by the subtypes although each subtype has some attributes that are unique for that subtype.

Figure 2.11 shows another specialization. This diagram implies somewhat different relationships between the supertype entity and the subtype entities than what is shown in Fig. 2.10 because the subtypes are disjoint and each instance of a supertype must belong to one of the subtypes. The relationship between the supertype and subtype is one-to-one.

The double line in the diagram in Fig. 2.11 shows that each computer must be either a desktop or a laptop and no overlapping is allowed. Therefore no computer can be classified as a desktop as well as a laptop. The *D* in the circle in the middle shows that the subtypes are disjoint.

2.7.4 Benefits of Supertypes and Subtypes

Supertypes and subtypes help in dealing with complexity in model building. This may be done by asking questions about the possibility of generalization and specialization during the design process. Similar entity types may be generalized into a supertype while an entity type that has many slightly different entities may be specialized into a number of subtypes.

Supertypes and subtypes may also assist in improving the presentation of an E-R model and in improving communication with the client. The higher level diagrams do not need to include the details while the lower

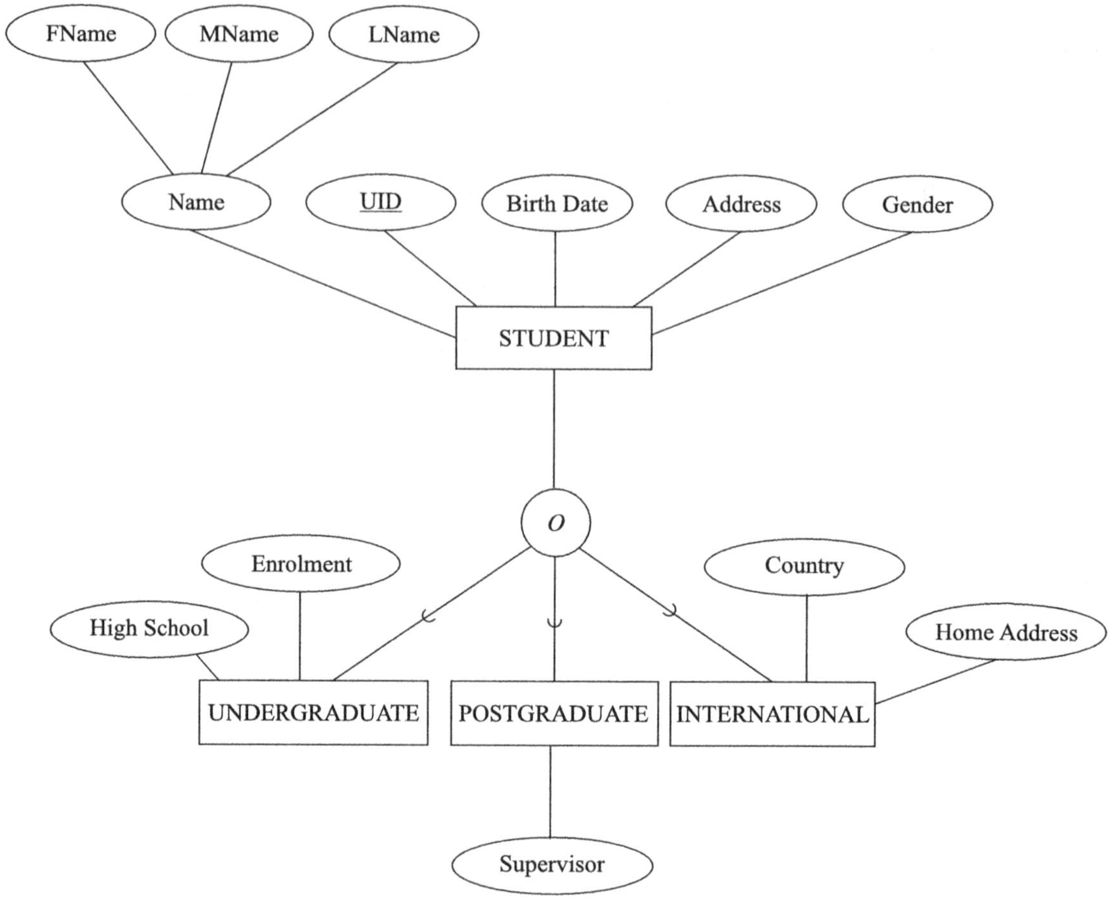

Figure 2.10 EER Diagram showing supertype and subtypes in specialization

level diagrams do. Not all such subtypes and supertypes need to be included in the database implementation; some might be just useful in helping communication.

2.8 THE DATABASE DESIGN PROCESS

As noted in Chapter 1, database design is a complex and challenging process that requires commitment of all the stakeholders including the senior management of the enterprise. In Chapter 1, we noted the following major steps which have now been modified to apply the E-R model approach.

1. *Requirements Analysis*—This step was described in Chapter 1. It involves studying the proposed database application and discussing with the client and other users what is required. A formal set of requirements specifications is prepared and documented.
2. *Identify Entity Sets*—The next step is to use the requirements specifications to identify entity sets that are of interest. This step is independent of the hardware and database software that is to be used.

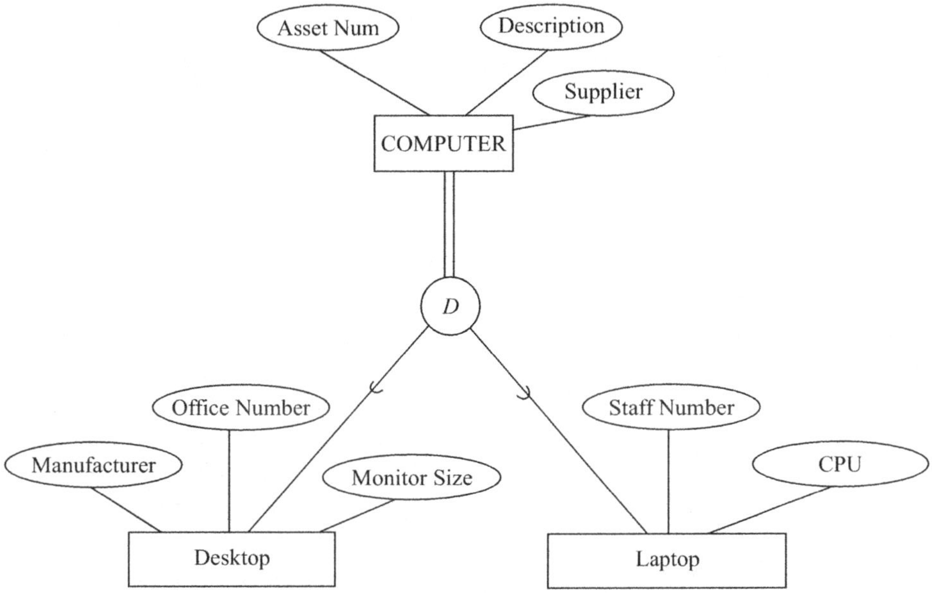

Figure 2.11 EER Diagram showing another specialization

The list of entities is then documented and discussed with the client and revised until an agreement is reached.

3. *Identify Relationship Sets*—Now identify the relationship sets that are of interest. For each relationship set, determine whether the relationship is 1:1, 1:n or m:n. These should now be discussed with the client to ensure that the database designer's understanding of the client's requirements is correct and the proposed database design meets the client's needs.
4. *E-R Diagram*—A E-R diagram is now prepared. The diagram should help the client better understand what the database design plans to implement. The model is revised if necessary until agreement between the database designer and the client is reached.
5. *Value Sets and Attributes*—Value sets and attributes for the entity sets and the relationship sets are now identified. Constraints on the values are identified. These may include domain constraints, integrity constraints and any other enterprise constraints. The model is revised if necessary until agreement is reached with the client.
6. *Primary Keys*—Primary key for each entity set is identified. These should be discussed with the client to ensure the identifiers are reasonable.
7. *Prototype*—A prototype may be developed to help communicate with the client to ensure that the design conforms to the requirements specifications.
8. *Implementation*—The E-R diagram is now mapped to the database schema for the particular DBMS and implemented.

As noted in Chapter 1, database design is an iterative process. Also, there is always the possibility that the client and/or the users will change their mind during the design process or even after thee implementation. The client may suddenly come up with new data and may suggest new applications and propose new processing.

2.9 STRENGTHS OF THE E-R MODEL

The E-R model is a very simple approach to designing a database which considers the real world as consisting of entities and relationships between them. The real world, of course, can be a lot more complex than the simple view used in E-R modeling but the E-R model approach continues to be widely used by database designers because it offers

1. *Simplicity*—As noted above, the approach is simple and easy to use with a client even if the client knows little about computing.
2. *Visual Representation*—An entity-relationship diagram provides a clear, high-level view of the proposed database.
3. *Effective Communication*—As noted above, visual representation of the model provides a clear, high-level view of the proposed database. This makes it easier to communicate with the client.
4. *Ease of Mapping to the Relational Model*—The E-R model was developed with the relational model in mind and the entity and relationship constructs map easily to the relational model as we will find in the next chapter.
5. *Focus on the Model*—The E-R model allows the database designer to focus on the complete and accurate modeling of the enterprise without having to think about efficiency of implementation. The efficiency issues should be considered in the implementation phase of database design.

2.10 WEAKNESSES OF THE E-R MODEL

As noted earlier, the E-R model is a very simple approach to designing a database. The simple approach is not always suitable for modeling database situations because of the following

1. Weaknesses of modeling in general. The database designer must understand the pitfalls of modeling since the model is not real. It is sometimes possible for people to forget that a model is only an abstraction of the reality, it is not reality itself. In fact, a model is often incomplete and could even be considered a distorted view of reality. If the database designer and the users after the system is operational start believing that the model is perfect then it can lead to a variety of problems. For example, an employee of the enterprise may insist a customer with somewhat unusual circumstances that the customer is wrong since the information in the database does not match with what the customer is saying. It could well be that the customer is right and in the unusual case the database is not correct. Just as, in physics, all laws are supposed to be hypotheses that can become invalid as soon as a better hypothesis is found. A database model is also a kind of hypothesis that could be replaced by a better model and a better hypothesis.

   Furthermore, no modeling technique is perfect. All modeling techniques have a number of weaknesses. This again means that a database model cannot fully capture a real life enterprise which can be very complex.
2. Although we have discussed the concept of an entity and presented a simple definition, a rigorous definition is not possible since there is no absolute distinction between entity types, relationship types

and even attributes. For example, an entity has been defined in many different ways. A sample of definitions from the literature are given below to illustrate the confusion.

- *An entity is a thing that can be distinctly identified*
- *Entities are things that exist independently of other entities*
- *An entity means anything about which we store information*
- *An entity is a person, place or thing about which we store information*

Even in his original 1976 paper, Chen notes that *'some people may view something (e.g. marriage) as an entity while other people may view it as a relationship. We think that this is a decision which has to be made by the enterprise administrator. He should define what are entities and what are relationships so that the distinction is suitable for his environment.'*

Therefore, it is not always easy to decide when a given thing should be considered an entity. For example, in the employee database, one may have the following information about each employee:

- Employee number
- Name
- Address
- Date of birth
- Citizenship
- Telephone number
- Salary

This is only a very small list of likely information that a company would want to store for each of its employees. Assume that there is an additional attribute called residence city. Although it is assumed that city is an attribute, it may be that city should really be an entity. The rule of thumb that should be followed in such situations is to ask the question "Is city an object of interest?" If the answer is yes, there must be some more information about each city in addition to the city name and then city should be considered an entity. If however we are only interested in the city's name, city should be considered an attribute of employee.

As noted earlier, each entity should contain information about its properties. If an object has no information other than its identifier that is of interest, the object should be an attribute but this is not always possible as we show later in this section.

3. A relationship type normally shows an association between two or more entity types but relationships are allowed to have attributes which makes them look similar to entity types. There is a distinction in that a relationship is unable to exist on its own. For example, a relationship *Works_on* cannot be expected to exist on its own without the entity sets *Employee* and *Project*. Nevertheless, a number of experts, including E. F. Codd, have noted that one person's entity can legitimately be regarded as another person's relationship. This flaw makes modeling using the E-R approach a bit of an art.
4. Although an attribute exists only as a property of an entity type, in some contexts an attribute can also be viewed as an entity. For example, some attributes like address, telephone number and some time even name can have several values. Address may be current address as well as permanent address. Telephone number may include business phone, home phone and mobile phone. Some people even carry more than one mobile phone. Consider a name like B. Ramamuralikrishna where B stands for place of birth, Bangalore. Assume that the person gets tired of using such a long name and starts using

B. R. Krishna or B. R. M. Krishna. A database may need to include all these versions of the name. How should one store them as attributes?

The guideline for multivalue attributes in entity-relationship is that such an attribute should be considered an entity. Although conceptually multivalue attributes create no difficulties, problems arise when the E-R model is translated for implementation using a relational database system discussed in Chapter 3. As an example, suppose we have an entity called project in a company database and one of the attributes is funding code. If the database model allows a number of funding codes for one project then we have a difficulty and it might be best to have another entity called funding code and then have a relation between the entity type project and the entity type funding code.

Although we have indicated above that an entity set should normally contain information about its properties, a multivalue attribute even if it has no properties other than its value has to be considered an entity.

5. Complexity. E-R models for nontrivial database applications can become rather complex since entity sets tend to have many attributes which contribute to the complexity of the model. The difficulty can be overcome by using a top-down approach so that the model is displayed at several different levels of abstraction with the top level just showing entities or even groups of entities and with the details provided by models at lower levels.

   Finally, the E-R model offers limited constraint representation, limited relationship representation, no representation of data manipulation and in some cases results in loss of information. A detailed discussion of weaknesses of the E-R model is presented in the book by Thalheim.

2.11 A CASE STUDY OF BUILDING AN E-R MODEL

We now consider a nontrivial example of building an E-R model. In this example we will attempt to model the information that is generated in a cricket ODI match. We cannot fully model the information generated in an ODI match so our model will be quite limited in scope.

The primary aim in presenting this long example is to provide the reader some understanding about the complex art and science of model building. For this reason the example will include early models with a variety of errors in them. The models will then be improved to hopefully overcome all the problems identified. We emphasise that no solution for a significantly complex problem is unique and there is never a perfect solution.

Normally, an ODI match information is presented as a scorecard as described in the Tables 2.7 to 2.13 below. The information in this example comes from an ODI match played between Australia and India in Sydney in March 2008. India won this match. We present a part of the scorecard which shows the batting and bowling performances of both innings. Surprisingly, there is no standard definition of a scorecard. For example, some may include the number of minutes a batsman was at the crease while others do not, but we assume that the scorecard given below is acceptable. *R* in the scorecard stands for number of runs scored by the batsman, *M* for the number of minutes the player was batting, *B* is the number of balls the batsman faced and 4s and 6s are the number of fours and sixes scored. *SR* is the strike rate obtained by dividing *R* by *B* (converted to a percentage).

Table 2.7 gives details of the Indian inning's scorecard.

Table 2.7 Indian inning's scorecard (Batting first, 50 overs maximum)

One Day International (ODI) Match held in Sydney, March 2008

Batsman	*How out?*	*R*	*M*	*B*	*4s*	*6s*	*SR*
RV Uthappa	c Hopes b Clark	30	99	49	1	0	61.2
SR Tendulkar	c Ponting b Clarke	91	176	121	7	0	75.2
G Gambhir	c Johnson b Clarke	15	21	16	1	0	93.8
Yuvraj Singh	c Hayden b Symonds	38	27	38	2	2	100
MS Dhoni	c Clarke b Bracken	36	52	37	2	1	97.3
RG Sharma	c Symonds b Clarke	2	6	5	0	0	40
IK Pathan	b Bracken	12	24	20	1	0	60
Harbhajan Singh	lbw b Lee	3	7	3	0	0	100
P Kumar	c Ponting b Bracken	7	7	7	1	0	100
PP Chawla	not out	6	8	2	1	0	300
S Sreesanth	not out	1	4	2	0	0	50
Extras	**(lb 5, w 12)**	**17**					
Total	**(9 wickets; 50 overs; 220 mins)**	**258**	**(5.16 runs per over)**				

Table 2.8 gives details of the fall of wickets for the Indian inning given in Table 2.7.

Table 2.8 Fall of wickets in the Indian inning

Fall of wickets: 1-94 (Uthappa, 20.5 ov), 2-121 (Gambhir, 25.2 ov), 3-175 (Yuvraj Singh, 34.6 ov), 4-205 (Tendulkar, 39.2 ov), 5-209 (Sharma, 41.1 ov), 6-237 (Pathan, 47.2 ov), 7-240 (Dhoni, 47.6 ov), 8-249 (Harbhajan Singh, 48.5 ov), 9-255 (Kumar, 49.3 ov)

Table 2.9 gives details of the Australian bowling in the Indian inning in the ODI match.

Table 2.9 Australian bowling in the Indian inning

Bowling	*O*	*M*	*R*	*W*	*Econ*
B Lee	10	0	58	1	5.8
NW Bracken	9	1	31	3	3.44
SR Clark	6	0	32	1	5.33
MG Johnson	6	0	33	0	5.5
JR Hopes	6	0	20	0	3.33
MJ Clarke	10	0	52	3	5.2
A Symonds	3	0	27	1	9

Looking at the scorecard we find that in the bowling figures, *O* stands for number of overs, *M* stands for number of overs in which no runs were scored (called maidens), *R* stands for the number of runs scored by the batsmen off the bowler's bowling. Finally, *W* is the number of players (wickets) that the bowler dismissed during the innings and *Econ* is the economy rate which is equal to *R*/*O*.

Table 2.10 gives details of the Australian inning's scorecard.

Table 2.10 Australian innings (Target: 259 runs from 50 overs)

Batsman	*How out?*	*R*	*M*	*B*	*4s*	*6s*	*SR*
AC Gilchrist	c Dhoni b Kumar	2	3	3	0	0	66.7
ML Hayden	run out (Yuvraj Singh/Harbhajan Singh)	55	122	68	7	0	80.9
RT Ponting	c Yuvraj Singh b Kumar	1	9	7	0	0	14.3
MJ Clarke	b Kumar	17	29	22	1	0	77.3
A Symonds	lbw b Harbhajan Singh	42	81	56	2	1	75
MEK Hussey	c Dhoni b Sreesanth	44	66	42	3	0	105
JR Hopes	c Chawla b Pathan	63	105	80	4	1	78.8
B Lee	b Kumar	7	20	12	0	0	58.3
MG Johnson	c Dhoni b Sreesanth	8	9	6	1	0	133
NW Bracken	c Chawla b Pathan	1	7	2	0	0	50
SR Clark	not out	0	2	0	0	0	-
Extras	**(lb 2, w 7)**	**9**					
Total	**(all out; 49.4 overs; 230 mins)**	**249**	**(5.01 runs per over)**				

Table 2.11 gives details of the fall of wickets in the Australian inning.

Table 2.11 The Fall of wickets in the Australian inning

Fall of wickets: 1-2 (Gilchrist, 0.3 ov), 2-8 (Ponting, 2.3 ov), 3-32 (Clarke, 8.6 ov), 4-121 (Hayden, 25.4 ov), 5-123 (Symonds, 25.6 ov), 6-199 (Hussey, 41.6 ov), 7-228 (Lee, 46.4 ov), 8-238 (Johnson, 48.2 ov), 9-247 (Bracken, 49.2 ov), 10-249 (Hopes, 49.4 ov)

Table 2.12 gives details of the Indian bowling in the Australian inning.

Table 2.12 Indian bowling in the Australian inning

Bowling	*O*	*M*	*R*	*W*	*Econ*
P Kumar	10	2	46	4	4.6
S Sreesanth	9	0	43	2	4.77

Contd.

Table 2.12 Contd.

Bowling	*O*	*M*	*R*	*W*	*Econ*
IK Pathan	8.4	0	54	2	6.23
Harbhajan Singh	10	0	44	1	4.4
PP Chawla	9	0	45	0	5
Yuvraj Singh	3	0	15	0	5

There is more information about a match that one may want to include in the database. Where was the match played? Was it a day match or a day-night match? On which date was the match played? Who were the umpires? Who was the match referee? Who was the TV umpire? Who won the toss? What was the result? Who won the Player of the Match award? Some may even want to know how many people attended the match. Also, one might want to include who the 12th man was and who the substitute fielder was, if substitutes were needed. There is also ball-to-ball information that could be included in an ODI database. There is thus an enormous amount of information that is generated in each ODI match. Some of this information is listed in Table 2.13.

Table 2.13 Other information about the ODI

• Toss: India won and chose to bat first
• Series: India won the best-of-3-finals 2-0
• Player of the match: P Kumar (India)
• Player of the series: NW Bracken (Australia)
• Umpires: AL Hill (New Zealand) and SJA Taufel
• TV umpire: BNJ Oxenford
• Match referee: JJ Crowe (New Zealand)
• Reserve umpire: TP Laycock

We will now try to simplify the above information for our case study. We don't want it to be so complex that the model becomes so large that it cannot be used in this book. The simplifications listed in Table 2.14 are made with a view that they do not reduce the case study to a toy example.

Table 2.14 List of assumptions made in designing the ODI database model

1. The number of extras made is not considered.
2. The date the match was played is not considered.
3. Questions like who were the umpires, who was the match referee and who was the TV umpire are ignored.
4. The toss result is not considered.
5. The Player of the Match award is not considered.
6. No information is stored about the number of people who attended the match.
7. No information about the 12th man and substitute fielders is considered in our model.

This list of assumptions is perhaps not complete. We should add any other assumptions we discover to this list.

The situation is still quite complex. First, all the information about fall of wickets (FOW) given above appears unstructured. We will now structure it so that we can understand it better. To do so we transform the given information to a tabular form as given in the two Tables 2.15 and 2.16, for the two innings. This information is now easier to comprehend and model.

Table 2.15 Fall of wickets in the Indian inning

FOW	*Player out*	*Score when out*	*Over when out*
1	Uthappa	1/94	20.5
2	Gambhir	2/121	25.2
3	Yuvraj Singh	3/175	34.6
4	Tendulkar	4/205	39.2
5	Sharma	5/209	41.1
6	Pathan	6/237	47.2
7	Dhoni	7/240	47.6
8	Harbhajan Singh	8/249	48.5
9	Kumar	9/255	49.3

The column *Score when out* is given as scores like 1/94, which means the score was 94 with one wicket down. It should be noted that the information on how many wickets were down is redundant but we will not deal with it at this time. The column *Over when out* has information like 20.5, which means that the player was out on the fifth ball of the 21st over.

Table 2.16 Fall of wickets in the Australian Innings

FOW	*Player out*	*Score when out*	*Over when out*
1	Gilchrist	1/2	20.5
2	Ponting	2/8	25.2
3	Clarke	3/32	34.6
4	Hayden	4/121	39.2
5	Symonds	5/123	41.1
6	Hussey	6/199	47.2
7	Lee	7/228	47.6
8	Johnson	8/238	48.5
9	Bracken	9/247	49.3
10	Hopes	10/249	49.4

Example Requirement

We want to look at possible ways of modeling the above ODI match information. We want all the information in a scorecard to be part of our model including fall of wickets and bowling performance. How do we model it?

Option 1

What is the simplest model that we can design for the problem? What are the entities? What are the relationships? One possibility is to try to model the match information in a similar way to what is presented in the scorecard. That is, we have an entity *Match* that provides some basic information about the match. The batting performance can be represented by an entity *Batsman* and the bowling performance by *Bowler* and the fall of wickets by an entity *FOW*. The entities and relationships are then as follows:

Entities

The entities in the current E-R model are given in Fig. 2.12

Match
Batsman
Bowler
FOW

Figure 2.12 List of entities

Relationships

Figure 2.13 gives the list of relationships between the entities listed in Fig. 2.12.

M_Batting – between Match and Batsman
M_Bowling – between Match and Bowler
M_FOW – between Match and FOW

Figure 2.13 List of relationships

The E-R model then looks like that shown in the E-R diagram in Fig. 2.14.

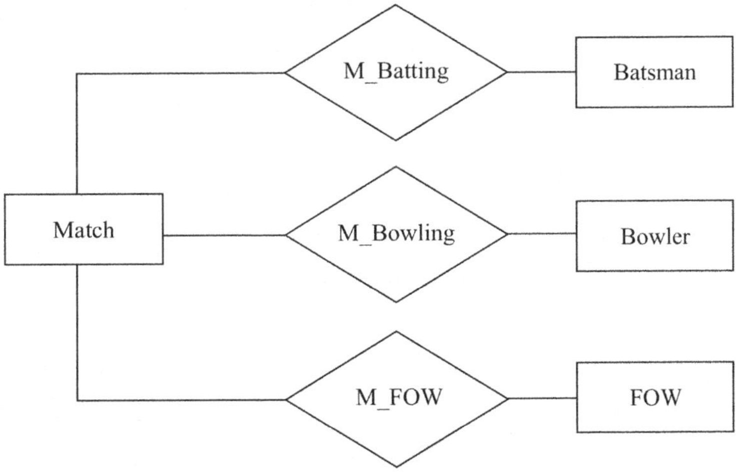

Figure 2.14 Option 1: E-R model for the ODI match database

We now list attributes for each entity.

Match

Match needs to have the attributes listed in Fig. 2.15.

Home team Visiting team Ground Date Result (Other attributes like Umpires, Referee Player of the match, etc., may be included)

Figure 2.15 List of attributes of *Match*

Batsman

Batsman needs to have the attributes listed in Fig. 2.16.

Batsman name and How out Number of runs Number of minutes Number of balls Number of fours Number of sixes

Figure 2.16 List of attributes of *Batsman*

Bowler

Bowler needs to have the attributes listed in Fig. 2.17.

Bowler name Number of overs Number of maidens Number of runs Number of wickets

Figure 2.17 List of attributes of *Bowler*

FOW

FOW needs to have the attributes that are listed in Fig. 2.18.

Wicket number Score Over Batsman out

Figure 2.18 List of attributes of *FOW*

Note that we have not included information about the strike rate for batsmen or economy rate for bowlers since these can be computed given the other information.

All the relationships are one-to-many and we assume that there are no attributes for each of the three relationships. These relationships can therefore be represented by migrating the *Match* primary key to all the other relations. This concept will be discussed in detail in the next chapter.

Let us now discuss what is wrong with this design. Readers are encouraged to list all the mistakes in this design before reading Option 2 below.

Option 2

The above design has many problems. Here is a list of some of them:

1. Although *Match* has a primary key (consisting of the attributes Home Team, Visiting Team and Date), the other entities do not.
2. **None of the entities includes the country that the player is representing.**

To fix the first problem regarding primary keys we introduce an artificial identifier in the *Match* entity. We will call it the Match ID. Artificial identifiers may be included in other entities as well but we will fix the primary key problem in the remaining entities in another way. The second problem is solved by including the country attribute where needed. We now obtain the following model:

Match ID
Home Team
Visiting Team
Ground
Date
Result
(Other attributes, like Umpires, Referee, Player of the match, etc. may be included)

Figure 2.19 List of attributes of ***Match***

Match

Match now has the attributes listed in Fig. 2.19 (Primary key is Match ID).

Batsman

Batsman now has the attributes listed in Fig. 2.20 (Primary key is Match ID, Player order. Why?).

Match ID
Player order
Batsman name and How out
Country
Number of runs
Number of minutes
Number of balls
Number of fours
Number of sixes

Figure 2.20 List of attributes of *Batsman*

Bowler

Bowler now has the attributes listed in Fig. 2.21 (Primary key is Match ID and Bowler name, assuming the name is unique).

Match ID
Bowler name
Country
Number of overs
Number of overs
Number of maidens
Number of runs
Number of wickets

Figure 2.21 List of attributes of *Bowler*

FOW

FOW (Primary key is Match ID and Wicket number)

Match ID Wicket number Score Over Batsman out

Figure 2.22 List of attributes of *FOW*

As noted earlier, the primary keys that we have identified in *Batsman, Bowler* and *FOW* are not the only way to identify each entity instance in these entities. We could have introduced artificial identifiers in each entity just as we did for the entity *Match*.

Option 3

Option 2 provides a reasonable solution but there are still problems with it because we have essentially copied the printed version of the scorecard and translated it into entities and relationships. It is possible to do better.

Match ID Player order Batsman name and How out Country Score when out Number of runs Number of minutes Number of balls Number of fours Number of sixes

Figure 2.23 List of attributes of *Batsman*

First of all do we really need an entity *FOW*? Most of this information already exists is in the entity *Batsman*. The only information missing is the score at which each batsman got out. We could include that information in the entity *Batsman* and we can then derive the information that is given in the *FOW* table. So the *Batsman* entity now has the attributes that are listed in Fig. 2.23.

There is no change in the entity *Match* or *Bowler* but the entity *FOW* is now not needed.

Perhaps a more serious problem still remains. This has to do with the attribute 'Batsman Name and How out' in the *Batsman* entity. Given that this attribute has values like 'SR Tendulkar c Ponting b Clarke' leads to the following difficulties:

- Each attribute value is considered atomic and it is then assumed that different components of the value cannot be looked at separately.
- The names Tendulkar, Ponting and Clarke are not unique because they are presented in a form suitable for people to read them and not for computer processing. For example, Ponting is written as RT Ponting in the batting performance of the Australian team. Such differences make it difficult to process this information while ensuring that Ponting and RT Ponting refer to the same player.
- Other problems may arise in uniquely identifying players if, for example, the player Sachin Tendulkar is included in the scorecard as SR Tendulkar.

These problems are not really serious if our model is simply designed to print the scorecard as is printed in the newspapers because our current model can do that. However, a question now arises and should be asked: 'Do we need, or may need in the future, to answer a query like how many runs were scored by MS Dhoni in the March 2008 ODI in Sydney?'

Option 4

To be able to uniquely identify players, we need to have a unique identifier for each player. We can introduce an attribute called Player ID for each player and if we wanted to be able to search on a player's last name then we could establish an entity called *Player*.

Let us assume the entity *Player* includes the attributes listed in Fig. 2.24.

Player ID
Player last name
Player first name
Country
When born
Place of birth
Year of first test

Figure 2.24 List of attributes of *Player*

The *Batsman* entity's attributes will change to those listed in Fig. 2.25.

Match ID
Player order
Player ID
How out
Score when out
Number of runs
Number of minutes
Number of balls
Number of fours
Number of sixes

Figure 2.25 List of attributes of *Batsman*

The *Bowler* entity will also change to as given in Fig. 2.26

Match ID
Player ID
Number of overs
Number of maidens
Number of runs
Number of wickets

Figure 2.26 List of attributes of *Bowler*

The *Match* entity will not change.

Option 5

Let us now critically review the solution. Clearly *Match* and *Player* need to be entities. Do *Batsman* and *Bowler* need to be entities? Could they be relationships between the entity *Player* and the entity *Match* since

each batting and bowling performance is related to a player and an ODI match? Making them relationships changes the E-R model to the simple model displayed in Fig. 2.27.

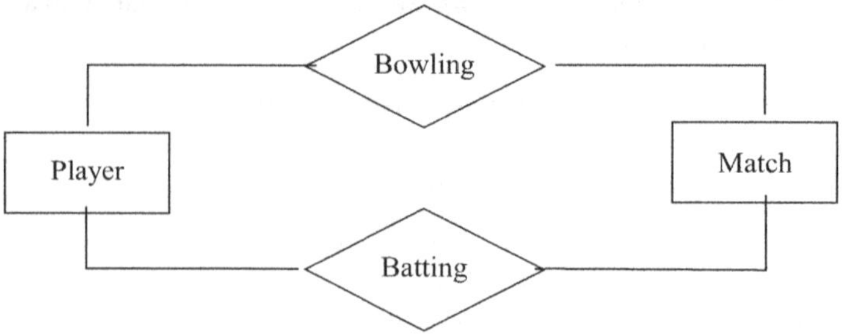

Figure 2.27 E-R diagram for Option 5

The two relationships are many-to-many since each player bats and bowls in many matches and each match has more than one batsman and bowler.

There is no change in the list of attributes for the entities *Player* and *Match*. The attributes for the relationships are given below:

The *Batting* relationship's attributes will change to those listed in Fig. 2.28.

Player ID
Match ID
Player order
How out
Score when out
Number of runs
Number of minutes
Number of balls
Number of fours
Number of sixes

Figure 2.28 List of attributes of ***Batting***

The *Bowling* relationship's attributes will also change to those listed in Fig. 2.29.

Player ID
Match ID
Number of overs
Number of maidens
Number of runs
Number of wickets

Figure 2.29 List of attributes of ***Bowling***

How do we find out *FOW*?

We leave this as the final solution. Although some problems remain and further modifications will be required.

Final Critique

As noted there are many problems with the final solution. It only shows that modeling is quite a challenging task. Let us list some of the problems that we are able to identify:

1. No information on extras, byes, leg byes, wides and no balls is included.
2. No information on the 12th man and substitutes is included.
3. No information is included about batsmen who did not bat in an innings.
4. In fact it is not possible to list the teams that played in a given match.
5. It is not possible to represent who was the captain of the team in a match and who was the wicketkeeper.
6. The total runs scored in an innings may be derived but is not included as an attribute.
7. The 'How out' attribute does not provide sufficient information to print the scorecard.
8. The Duckworth–Lewis (or D/L) system of deciding a match winner when the game is interrupted by rain and the second team is not able to bat for the same number of overs as the first team is not considered.
9. More ODI matches are now being played at neutral venues (for example, Kuala Lumpur or Dubai). There are also triangular ODI series where two visiting teams play each other. These issues are not considered in our model.

We leave it to the reader to list other weaknesses of the final model and to attempt to improve the model.

2.12 EVALUATING DATA MODEL QUALITY

As we have noted, building a conceptual model of an enterprise can be very complex. Building a data model can be more of an art than a science. Once a model has been built, one may want to evaluate the quality of the model and validate how faithfully the model represents the enterprise that is being modeled. If more than one model is available then how does one select the best model?

Evaluating model quality is a difficult issue. Researchers who have investigated the issue of model quality have often proposed that the quality be judged based on a list of desirable properties. Unfortunately these lists almost always lack any fundamental basis and are often based on a person's modeling experience. Another difficulty with such lists of desirable properties is that the properties are often quite subjective and difficult to measure. For example if we consider readability to be an important quality feature then how can we measure readability so as to conclude that one model is more readable than another?

Nevertheless, a list is useful in providing some guidance on what a modeler should keep in mind while developing a model. We present a consolidated list based on some of the references cited at the end of this chapter. The properties include many commonsense syntactic and semantic properties that one would expect of high quality models. Firstly, one expects that the model be simple and easily understandable by the users of the model. For example, it is expected that the names of the entities and relationships reflect enterprise knowledge and therefore be self-documenting. The model has to be syntactically correct, that is, the model constructs have not been used incorrectly; for example, a construct using a relationship between an existing relationship and an entity has not been used. The model must be complete in that every piece of information that is required in the database has been included in the model and no unnecessary information has been included. Minimality and nonredundancy require that information normally be included only once. If subclass and superclass structures are used in the model then each subclass must have some property that is not in the superclass for a subclass to be justified. Given that almost every computer system is modified during its lifetime as enterprise requirements change, some suggest that it is desirable that the model be flexible and extendible so that the model is adaptable to changing enterprise requirements, although it is not quite clear how one could judge if a given model is indeed flexible.

Table 2.17 List of data model quality criteria

• Completeness
• Correctness
• Consistency
• Minimality
• Readability
• Self-explanation
• Extensibility
• Performance

Table 2.17 provides a list of quality criteria.

These criteria can be described as given below:

1. *Completeness*—A good model should be complete as far as the client's requirements are concerned. Assessing completeness should be possible with the support of the client as well as assistance from a number of users who understand the proposed model well. An external expert may also be required. The temptation to incorporate requirements beyond what has been agreed to should be curbed.
2. *Correctness*—A good model should model all aspects of the proposed database system as well as business rules of the enterprise. Assessing correctness is not subjective but would require assistance of the client and may require assistance from an expert with knowledge of the database application as well as of database systems.
3. *Consistency*—A good model must not have any contradictions. Consistency, correctness and completeness are the three basic requirements of any good model. Consistency is perhaps more technical than correctness and completeness, although correctness and completeness can also be quite technical. The client may not be able to assist much in checking consistency. Assistance of a number of users who understand the proposed model well may be required. An external expert may also be required.
4. *Minimality*—A good model ought to be compact and should not include redundancy. To assess minimality it is necessary to have assistance from a number of users who understand the proposed model well. An external expert who has good knowledge of data modeling may also be required.
5. *Readability*—A good model should not only be understandable to users who have been involved in the database design but also by users who have not been involved (for example, by a user who takes over the responsibility of the database system after the data modeler is gone and the system has been implemented). Readability can be a somewhat subjective quality. The client's views about readability may also be useful.
6. *Self-explanation*—Related to readability, this criterion proposes for entity, relationship and attributes' names to be such that users can easily understand them. The client's views about self-explanation may be useful. Users may also be consulted since some of them are going to be unsophisticated users and their ability to understand the model is important.

7. *Extensibility*—A good model should be able to accommodate business changes because enterprise requirements change as the enterprise changes but it is almost impossible to judge extensibility without knowing what kind of extensions might be required.
8. *Performance*—Although a data model is developed without considering its performance, it should be possible to make some changes to a model without impacting the model's logical structure.

There are a number of other properties that some experts suggest should be added to this list. These include simplicity, validity, flexibility, understandability, implementability, expressiveness, normality (or normalization), scope, reusability, transformability and levels of detail. We do not discuss these since some of them overlap with the properties we have already described above. For example, are simplicity and understandability similar to readability and self-explanation? Is flexibility similar to extensibility?

For a good discussion of quality in database modeling, refer to Chapter 6 of the book by Batini, Ceri and Navathe.

SUMMARY

In this chapter we have discussed the following topics:

- Models have been used by people for a long time, for example, by architects, scientists and engineers.
- There are many benefits of modelling before building including focussing on the essentials, product or process improvement and exploring alternatives.
- Models can be of three different types, viz., descriptive, prescriptive or representative.
- Database modelling has at least two phases. The first phase involves building an enterprise conceptual model. In the second phase, the conceptual model is mapped to the database model to be used.
- A simple approach of database modeling is called the Entity-Relationship modeling (ERM).
- ERM involves identifying entities (like a person, a player or a book), relationships (like batting, marriage) and attributes (like age, address).
- Relationships may be unary (e.g., employee and supervisor), binary (like employee and the company) or ternary (like employee, project, and department).
- Binary relationships may be 1-1, 1-*m* or *m*-*n*.
- Attributes may be of several types including simple or composite, single-valued or multivalued, stored or derived.
- An E-R model may be represented as Chen's E-R diagram or as Crow's Foot diagram.
- Different notations are used for both types of diagrams. In the E-R diagram a rectangle represents an entity and a diamond a relationship. In the Crow's Foot notation, lines joining entities represent relationships.
- A number of examples have been used to illustrate the diagrams. One of the examples is about employee-department-project.
- All entities and relationships must have a primary key that identifies each instance of the entity set and each entity of a relationship set.
- The concepts of generalization, specialization and aggregation have been explained.

- Extended Entity Relationship modeling and diagrams have been presented.
- Strengths and weaknesses of the ERM have been described. The strengths include the simplicity of the approach while one of the weaknesses is the difficulty of precisely defining an entity.
- A case study to model ODI scorecard is described to illustrate the ERM is presented.
- Finally data quality of a model was discussed and a number of criteria, for example, completeness, correctness and consistency were discussed.

REVIEW QUESTIONS

1. Describe some fields in which modelling is used successfully. (Section 2.2)
2. What are different types of models? (Section 2.3)
3. Describe the phases of database modeling. (Section 2.4)
4. What is an Entity-Relationship model? (Section 2.5)
5. What is an entity and an entity set? (Section 2.5.1)
6. List some naming conventions for an entity and a relationship. (Section 2.5.1)
7. What is a relationship between entities? What are their roles? (Section 2.5.2)
8. Explain, 1-1 relationship, 1-*m* relationship and *m*-*n* relationship? (Section 2.5.2)
9. What is cardinality ratio? (Section 2.5.2)
10. What is an attribute and value sets? (Section 2.5.3)
11. Explain Chen's an Entity-Relationship diagram? (Section 2.5.5)
12. What are ternary relationships? Case a ternary relationship be converted into a number of binary relationships. (Section 2.5.6)
13. What is the purpose of generalization, specialization and aggregation? (Section 2.6)
14. Give two examples of additional features of the Extended Entity-Relationship model? (Section 2.7)
15. List the steps that should be taken in the database design process. (Section 2.8)
16. What are the strengths of the Entity-Relationship model? (Section 2.9)
17. What are the weaknesses in database modeling? (Section 2.10)
18. How can one evaluate an Entity-Relationship model's quality? (Section 2.12)

SHORT ANSWER QUESTIONS

1. What is an entity?
2. What is a relationship?
3. Name three entities that you know should be part of any university database.
4. Name the primary key for each of the entities.
5. Name a superkey of each of the three entities.
6. Name three attributes of each entity you have identified.
7. Identify any relationships that exist between the three entities you have identified.
8. Name the primary key of each of the relationships.

9. List the phases of database modeling.
10. Give examples of 1-1 relationships, 1-m relationships and m-n relationships?
11. What symbol represents a m:n relationship in a E-R diagram?
12. What is a superkey? How does it differ from a primary key?
13. What is cardinality ratio?
14. Give an example of an Entity-Relationship diagram?
15. What are ternary relationships?
16. Can every ternary relationship be represented as a set of binary relationships without adding any more entities?
17. Give an example of a binary relationship by showing an E-R diagram.
18. Give an example of three entities and a ternary relationship by drawing an E-R diagram.
19. Give an example of a unary relationship. Draw its diagram.
20. List some naming conventions for an entity.
21. Give an example of an extended Entity-Relationship model?
22. Explain the steps that should be taken in the database design process.
23. List two major weaknesses of the Entity-Relationship model.

MULTIPLE CHOICE QUESTIONS

1. Which of the following professionals build models in their profession?
   (a) Teachers (b) Architects (c) Engineers (d) Computer architects
   (e) All of the above
2. Which of the following are benefits of modeling?
   (a) It helps focus on the essentials.
   (b) It helps communication and understanding.
   (c) It helps explore alternatives.
   (d) It can help product or process improvement.
   (e) All of them
3. Models may be classified into a number of classes. Which one of the following is **not** one of these classes?
   (a) Descriptive (b) Prescriptive (c) Representative (d) Prototype
4. Which one of the following is **not** correct?
   (a) The E-R model was first proposed by E. F. Codd.
   (b) The E-R model is a popular high-level conceptual data model.
   (c) The E-R model is used for conceptual design of database applications.
   (d) The major strength of the E-R model is its simplicity and readability.
5. E-R modeling is part of the database design process. Which one of the following the E-R modeling process does **not** include?
   (a) Requirements analysis
   (b) Conceptual design
   (c) Logical design
   (d) Security and authorization design
6. Which one of the following is most **unlikely** to be an entity?
   (a) A person (b) A job or position (c) A travel plan (d) An address

7. Which two of the following are most **unlikely** to be relationships?
   (a) A lecture (b) An enrolment (c) A city (d) A shipment
   (e) A date
8. Which one of the following is **unlikely** to be an attribute?
   (a) Location (b) Enrolment (c) Address (d) Date of birth
9. Which one of the following is **not included in the classical E-R model?**
   (a) Entities (b) Relationships
   (c) Integrity constraints (d) Attributes
10. Which one of the following is **not correct?**
    (a) Each entity must have attributes. (b) Each relationship must have attributes.
    (c) Some attribute or attributes must be able to uniquely identify each entity instance.
    (d) Identifiers of the entities participating in the relationship are sufficient to uniquely identify each relationship instance.
11. Which of the following are correct?
    (a) Relationships represent real-world associations among one or more entities.
    (b) Relationships have a physical or conceptual existence other than that inherited from their entity associations.
    (c) Relationships are described in terms of their degree, connectivity and cardinality.
    (d) Each entity participating in a relationship plays a role.
    (e) All of the above are correct.
12. Depending on the nature of an attribute, it may belong to one of the pair of types below. Which of the following pair could **not be considered to be an attribute type?**
    (a) Simple or composite (b) Single-valued or multivalued
    (c) Stored or derived (d) Null or non-null
    (e) All of them
13. Which one of the following is a correct notation in E-R diagrams?
    (a) Entities are ovals (b) Relationships are rectangles
    (c) Attributes are diamonds (d)Weak entities are double rectangles
14. Which of the following is **not** correct?
    (a) The E-R model helps to avoid looking at the details and concentrate on the nature of the problem.
    (b) The E-R model avoids looking at database efficiency.
    (c) The E-R model helps carry out communication with the client.
    (d) The E-R model is the only technique available for database design.
15. Which two of the following are **not** correct?
    (a) A ternary relationship can sometimes be represented by two binary relationships.
    (b) Any two entities may have any number of binary relationships between them.
    (c) Generally attributes of relationships are assigned only to many-to-many relationships and not to one-to-one or one-to-many relationships.
    (d) Each entity participating in a relationship must have a relationship instance for each entity instance.

16. Which one of the following is correct?
    (a) All relationships may be converted to binary relationships.
    (b) All relationships may be converted to 1:1 relationships.
    (c) All relationship attributes may be attached to one of the participating entities.
    (d) All relationships may be represented by a table in a database.
17. For each of the following relationships, indicate the type of relationship (i.e., 1:1, 1:m, m:n).
    (a) Enrolment (a relationship between entities student and subject)
    (b) Works in (a relationship between entities department and staff)
    (c) Marriage (a relationship between entities person and person)
    (d) Manager (between employee and department)
    (e) Dependent (a relationship between entities person and person)
18. Which one of the following comments about the Entity-Relationship model is correct?
    (a) Differences between entity and attribute are always clear.
    (b) The procedure of identifying entities and attaching attributes to them is an iterative process.
    (c) Differences between an entity and a relationship are always clear.
    (d) Differences between an attribute and a relationship are always clear.
    (e) None of the above
19. Consider two E-R models about courses, lecturers and time of lecture. Each course has only one lecturer while each lecturer teaches several courses. Model A consists of two entities and one relationship joining them. The entities are lecturer and course and the relationship is lectures. Model B consists of three entities; the first and the third are the same as above but the second entity is called lecture. The first and second entity are joined by a relationship called 'gives' while the second and the third entities are joined by a relationship called 'of'.

    Which of the following are correct?
    (a) Both models allow a course to have more than one lecture from the same lecturer.
    (b) Model B is more appropriate if information about all lectures, past and present, is to be stored.
    (c) Model A does not allow lecture date and time to be stored.
    (d) Both models provide exactly the same information.
20. Which one of the following is correct?
    (a) A ternary relationship must either be 1:1:1, 1:1:m or p:m:n.
    (b) 1:1:1 ternary relationships exist commonly.
    (c) Crow's foot notation makes the E-R diagram more compact.
    (d) It is not possible to represent ternary relationships using Crow's foot notation.
21. Which one of the following is correct?
    (a) If a model includes a supertype vehicle and subtypes car, truck and bus then that must be generalization.
    (b) If a model includes a supertype vehicle and subtypes car, truck and bus then that must be specialization.
    (c) If a model includes a supertype computer and subtypes monitor, keyboard, motherboard then that must be specialization.
    (d) If a model includes a supertype vehicle and subtypes car, truck and bus then that may be generalization or specialization.

22. EER model extends the E-R model. Which one of the following is **not in the EER model?**
    (a) Supertypes and subtypes
    (b) Inheritance
    (c) Aggregation
    (d) Objects
23. Which of the following comments about the E-R model are correct?
    (a) Attributes of 1:1 relationships can be represented as attributes of either of the participating entity types.
    (b) Attributes of 1:n relationships can be represented as attributes of either of the participating entity types.
    (c) Attributes of a relationship involving more than two entity types can be represented as attributes of either of the participating entity types.
    (d) Ternary relationships normally do not have attributes.
    (e) None of the above.

EXERCISES

1. Identify which of the following are entities, relationships and attributes. List any assumptions that you have made in making your choices and list any attributes that are appropriate for each. What might be the primary key for each entity and relationship that has been identified?
    (a) Employees
    (b) Customers
    (c) Patients
    (d) Shares
    (e) Houses
    (f) Offices
    (g) Employment position
    (h) Lecture
    (i) Examination
    (j) Grade
    (k) Address
    (l) Telephone number
    (m) Dependents
2. Show how an entity, a relationship and an attribute are represented in E-R diagrams. Draw a diagram showing the entities university department, degree, course, lecture theatre, and instructor and a number of relationships between them.
3. Explain by drawing a diagram of how you would model a course that has many prerequisites and which is a prerequisite for many courses?
4. Explain by drawing a diagram of how you would model a student that is enrolled in many courses and each course has many enrolments.
5. Explain by drawing a diagram of how you would model a driving license which may be for driving a car, bus, truck, taxi, scooter or a tourist bus. Use a superclass/subclass model. List all the information that each entity should possess.
6. Develop an Entity-Relationship model for Indian movies. It should include where it was shot, details of the actors, directors, producers, the movie language and so on.
7. Can the E-R model express a relationship between two or more relationships? Would such a relationship ever be required in real life?
8. Construct an E-R diagram for student information in a Department of Computer Science in a university. This should include personal information about the student, enrolment information, and assessment information. Do not include information about library or finances.

9. Briefly describe the database design process described in this chapter. Explain why the design process is often iterative.
10. Build an E-R model for major banks of the world. Choose may be the top 500 banks or a 1000 or more. Study what are the major pieces of information about these banks available on the Web. Use the information to build a model. Are there any relationships that you can find?
11. Can a weak entity itself have a weak entity dependent on it? Give an example.
12. The two E-R diagrams (Figs 2.30 and 2.31), of the employees, departments and projects are given below. Consider the following queries:

    (a) Which employees work on project J1?
    (b) Which departments are involved in project J1?
    (c) Which parts are being supplied to project J1?
    (d) How many employees of department D1 working on project J1?
    (e) Are there parts that S1 can supply but is not supplying currently?
    (f) Are there parts that J1 uses but are not being supplied currently?

    - Which of the above queries can be made if the first model is used? ________ (Write appropriate query labels *A*, *B*, ..., etc., in the space above)
    - Which of the above queries can be made if the second model is used? ________
    - Which of the above queries cannot be answered by any of the models? ________

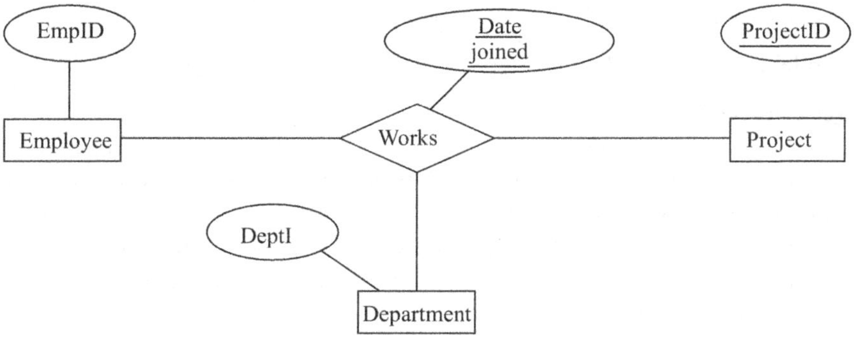

Figure 2.30 A ternary relation between Employee, Project and Department

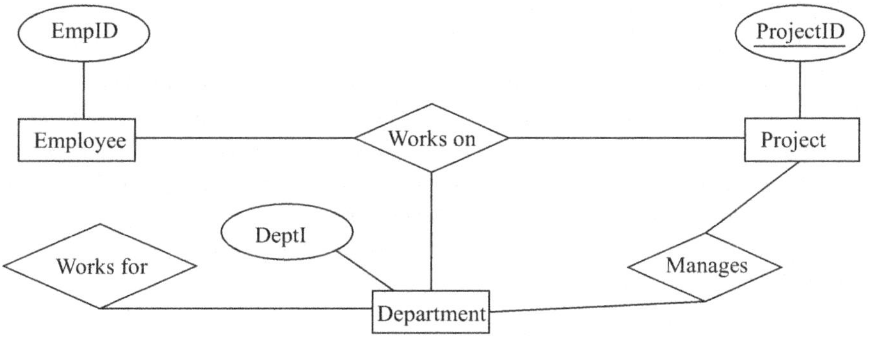

Figure 2.31 Three binary relations between Employee, Project and Department

13. Describe how the following two sets of entities may be included in a generalization hierarchy.
    (a) Book, journal, magazine, newspaper
    (b) Truck, car, bicycle, scooter, rickshaw, bus, airplane
14. Describe how the entity animal (in a zoo) can be developed into a specialization hierarchy.

PROJECTS

For each E-R modeling project, present assumptions, develop a model and discuss strengths and weaknesses of the model that you have designed.

1. Western India Medical Clinic (WIMC)

Design a database for WIMC located in Mangalore. The clinic has a number of regular patients and new patients come to the clinic regularly. Patients make appointments to see one of the doctors. Several doctors attend the clinic and they each have their own hours when they attend the clinic. Some doctors are general practitioners (GPs) while others are specialists (for example, cardiologists, dermatologists, endocrinologists). Doctors' hours are defined and fixed by each doctor but can be changed if necessary. Different doctors may charge different fees. Doctors send patients to other clinics for X-Rays and blood tests. These reports are sent from the clinics to doctors electronically. Doctors write medical certificates. Patients have families and the family relationships are important. Medical records of each patient need to be maintained. Information on prescriptions, insurance, allergies, etc., needs to be maintained.

Design an E-R model for the medical clinic.

2. Country/Rivers/Deserts/Mountains/Animals

A database of countries, their rivers, deserts, mountains and animals is to be developed. We want to store a variety of information about the countries depending on availability of information, e.g., name, population, leader's name, number of newspapers per 1000 people, amount of alcohol consumed per person, energy consumed per person, pollutants generated per person, etc. For rivers, we would want to store information like name, country or countries it passes through, source of the river, destination, how long, etc. For mountains, we would want to store information like name, height, country, part of which mountain range, etc. For animals, we need to store information like name, type (mammal, bird, etc.), found in which countries, and some of their characteristics.

Design an E-R model for this problem.

3. All India Mega Constructors (AIMC)

AIMC is an international company that specializes in large-scale construction. They build such things as bridges, dams, office blocks, hotels and factories. The company is divided into a number of departments. Each department specializes in one form of construction. For example, department 654 deals exclusively with the building of bridges, regardless of their geographical location. Head office, however, is interested in the activities of the various geographical areas in which the company operates. This is for political and financial reasons. Each individual construction activity is termed a project. Each project is given a code, which is used to uniquely identify the project in any reports.

Prior to the commencement of construction, the project is analysed into a number of tasks. This is done by the project leader and his or her assistants. Each task is given a code, unique to that project. For each task, a time estimate is made. A monthly budget is developed for the expected lifetime of the project. As each project progresses, actual expenditure is monitored.

There are several types of reports to be produced. For example, a departmental summary is often needed, a project status report may be required and a summary of projects in a particular area is often asked for.

Design an E-R model for the company.

4. The New Programming Company (NPC)
NPC started a venture capital company that decided to employ a number of unemployed computing graduates from the Northern India University (NIU). These graduates were unfortunate enough to graduate in the middle of the global financial crisis (GFC) in 2008. Having become part of the new venture, the graduates started advertising as the best programming company in India even before they had completed any programming job. Although their company name had the word 'new' in it, they claimed that had expertise in old programming languages like FORTRAN, COBOL, Algol, Pascal and Lisp.

The company has three branches called P1, P2 and P3 located in Patna, Kochi and Bhubaneswar. The company's Kochi branch has recently applied to develop software for Qatar Telecom.

The company operates in the following manner. Each time an employee starts on a task, he/she is given a job card on which the employee records the number of hours worked each day. The job card is returned to the supervisor once the assignment is completed. The job card has a variety of information on it including the job card ID, employee ID, job ID, and for each day, the date, the number of hours involved and the nature of work done.

Once the job is completed, NPC sends a bill for services to the customer company. The total charge is computed by adding the number of hours devoted to the job based on the job card multiplied by Rs. 750 which is the company's hourly rate. Once a payment is received the company issues a receipt.

At the end of each month, each employee's performance is evaluated based on the job cards. Total number of hours worked is computed and the income generated by each employee for the company is computed. Bonuses are awarded based on a complex formula for each employee who earns more than one lakh for that month.

Develop an Entity-Relationship model for the company.

LAB EXERCISES

1. Study the E-R diagram (Fig. 2.32) on the next page and do the following:
   (a) Describe the database that is modeled by the diagram.
   (b) Are the naming conventions being followed in this diagram? If not, suggest change of names wherever appropriate.
   (c) Find any mistakes that you can identify in the diagram. Explain and correct them.
   (d) List all the constraints that the model imposes on the database.

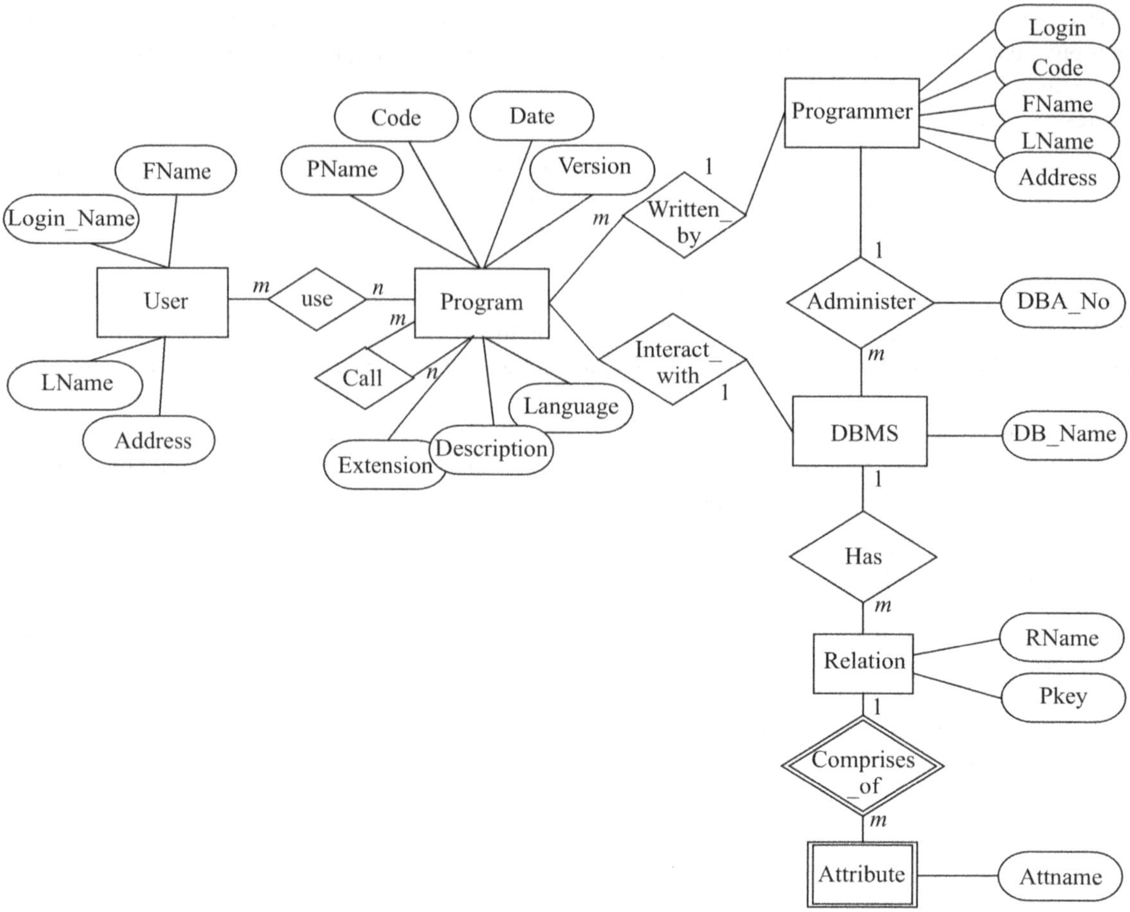

Figure 2.32

(e) Should the entity relations be a weak entity? If it is and therefore the relationship 'Maintains data in' is a weak relationship, what will be the primary keys of the weak relationships and weak entities.

(f) Modify the E-R model by using generalization

2. Consider the case study described in Section 2.11.
   (a) What were the requirements of the case study?
   (b) Were the requirements met by the model developed?
   (c) If not, modify the model to ensure that it does meet the requirements.
3. Consider the two E-R diagrams (Figs 2.33 and 2.34) below that model a simple horse-racing database.
   (a) Describe the database by studying these two diagrams.
   (b) Find any mistakes that you can identify in each of the diagrams. Explain and correct the mistakes in them.
   (c) Which one of the diagrams models the database better? Are there constraints that apply to one diagram but not the other? Are there queries that could be answered by one of the diagrams but not the other?

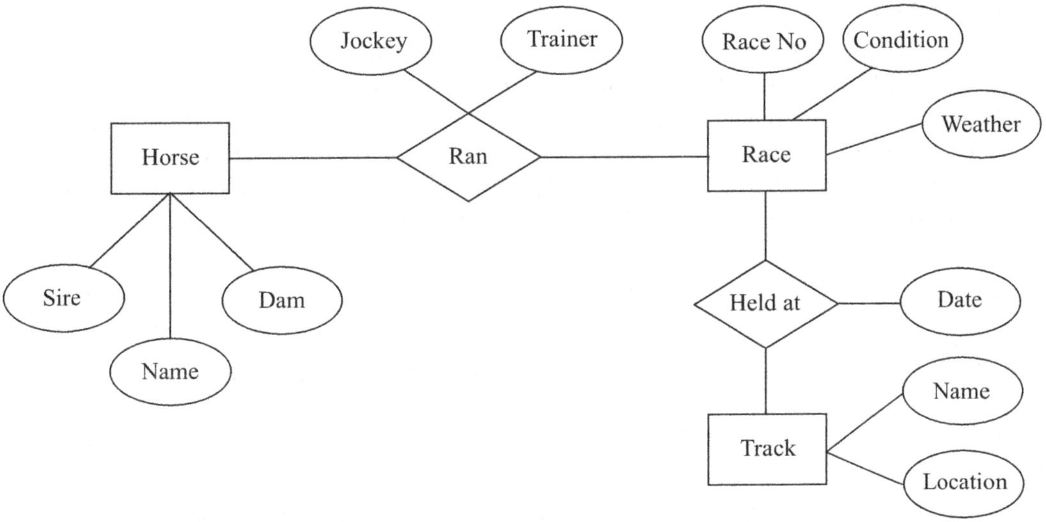

Figure 2.33

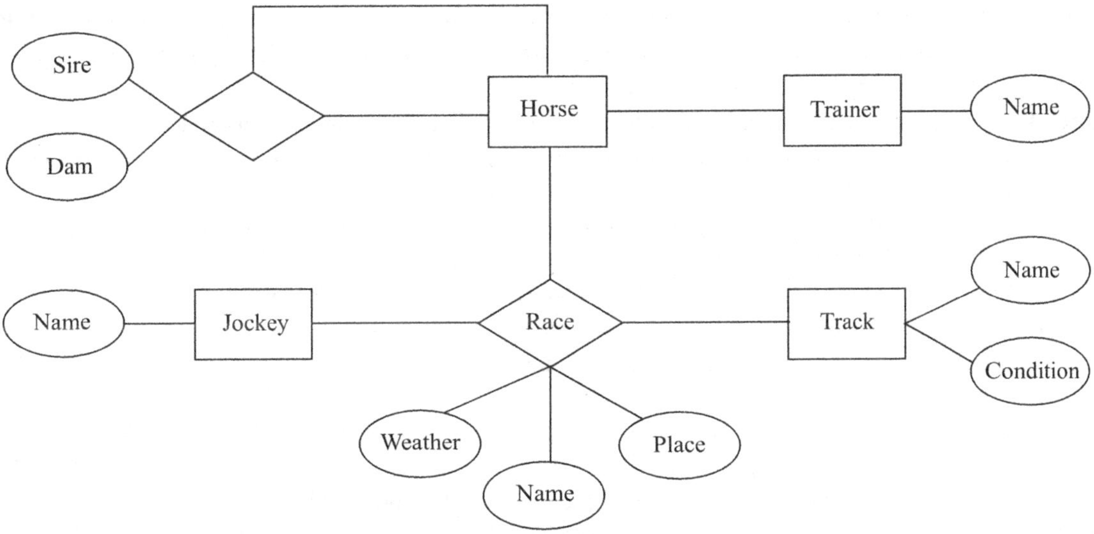

Figure 2.34

BIBLIOGRAPHY

For Students

The book by Batini, Ceri and Navathe and the book by Theorey are good introductions to E-R database modeling. The book by Baqui and Earp is also good. Most database textbooks have chapters on E-R modeling. The notes by Jung and Reddy are also worth consulting.

For Instructors

There are a number of good textbooks on database modeling. On Entity-Relationship modeling, the original 1976 paper by Chen is listed below. The books by Batini, Ceri and Navathe, by Thalheim and by Simsion are excellent. Halpin's book is different since it deals with the Object Relational Model (ORM) rather than with the E-R model and is worth reading if you want to look at another approach to database modeling. The paper by Herden looks at the quality of database models and presents an approach to measuring quality of a model. The papers by Burkett and Herden are good surveys of a number of approaches to database model quality.

Baqui, S., and R. Earp, *Database Design Using Entity-Relationship Diagrams*, Auerbach, 2003, 264 pp.

Batini, C., S. Ceri, and S.B. Navathe, *Conceptual Database Design: An Entity-Relationship Approach*, Benjamin Cunnings, 1992.

Burkett, W. C., "Database Schema Design Quality Principles". http://wwwscf.usc.edu/ wcb/dmq/dmqmain.html, 1998.

Chen, P. P., "The Entity-Relationship Model: Towards a unified view of data", *ACM Trans. Database Systems*, Vol. 1, pp 9-36, 1976.

Chen, P. P., *Entity Relationship Approach to Logical Database Design*, Monograph Series, QED Information Sciences Inc., Wellesley, Ma, 1977.

Chen, P. P. (Ed.), *Entity-Relationship to Systems Analysis and Design*, North-Holland, New York/Amsterdam, 1980.

Elmasri, R., and S. B. Navathe, *Fundamentals of Database Systems*, Fifth Edition, Addison-Wesley, 2006.

Halpin, T., *Information Modeling and Relational Databases: From Conceptual Analysis to Logical Design, using ORM with ER and UML*, Morgan Kaufmann, 2001.

Herden, O., "Measuring quality of database schemas by reviewing – concept, criteria and tool", *Proceedings of the 5th International ECOOP Workshop on Quantitative Approaches in Object-Oriented Software Engineering*, Budapest (Ungarn), pp 59-70, 2001. http://www.iro.umontreal.ca/~sahraouh/qaoose01/Herden.PDF

Hernandez, M. J., *Relational Design for Mere Mortals: A Hands-on Guide to Relational Database Design*, Second Edition, Addison-Wesley, 2003.

Jung, A., and U. Reddy, "Entity-Relationship Modeling", School of Computer Science, University of Birmingham, 2009. http://www.cs.bham.ac.uk/~udr/db2/handout2.pdf

Ng, P., "Further analysis of the entity-relationship approach to database design", *IEEE Transactions on Software Engineering*, Vol. DE-7, No. 1, pp 85-98, 1981.

Simsion, G.C., and G. C. Witt, *Data Modeling Essential*, Third Edition, Morgan Kaufmann, 2005.

Spaccapietra, S. (Ed.), *Entity-Relationship Approach: Ten Years of Experience in Information Modelling*, Proceedings of the Entity-Relationship Conference, North-Holland, 1987.

Song, I. Y., M. Evans, and E. K. Park, "A comparative analysis of entity-relationship diagrams", *Journal of Computer and Software Engineering*, Vol. 3, No. 4, 1995, pp 427-459.

Theorey, T. J., *Database Modelling and Design: Logical Design*, Fourth Edition, Morgan Kaufmann, 1999.

Theorey, T. J., D. Yang, and J. P. Fry, "Logical Design Methodology for Relational Databases", *ACM Computing Surveys*, pp 197-222, June 1986.

Thalheim, B., *Entity-Relationship Modelling*, Springer, 2000.

The University of Texas at Austin, "Introduction to Database Modelling", *Information Technology Services*. http://www.utexas.edu/its/database/datamodeling.

Peter P. S. Chen

Peter Chen is the creator of the Entity-Relationship model (E-R model), which serves as the foundation of many systems analysis, design methodologies, and computer-aided software engineering (CASE) tools. His first paper on the E-R model was published in 1976 and was included in the '38 most influential papers in Computer Science' by a survey of over 1,000 computer scientists.

Currently, Professor Chen is a distinguished Chair Professor at NTHU, Taiwan. He held the position of M. J. Foster distinguished Chair Professor of Computer Science at Louisiana State University in the United States from 1983–2008.

Dr. Chen holds a PhD in Computer Science/Applied Mathematics from Harvard University.

Relational Model 3

OBJECTIVES

- Introduce the relational model and its three components.
- Discuss the data structure used in the relational model.
- Define the properties of a relation and explain relational terminology.
- Describe how an Entity-Relationship model may be mapped to the relational model.
- Describe how information is retrieved and modified in the relational model.
- Explain how data integrity is maintained in the relational model.
- Discuss the advantages and disadvantages of using the relational model.
- Discuss the older database models, the network and hierarchical models.

KEYWORDS

Relational model, mapping E-R model, relations, tables, atomic domain, domains, tuples, cardinality, degree, attributes, rows, tables, columns, schema, constraints, candidate key, primary key, foreign key, existential integrity, referential integrity, domains, nulls, integrity, hierarchical model, network model.

Earth provides enough to satisfy every man's need, but not every man's greed.

Mahatma Gandhi

3.1 INTRODUCTION

In the last chapter we discussed the Entity-Relationship (E-R) model, a technique for building a logical model of an enterprise. Logical models are high level abstract views of an enterprise data. In building these models little thought is given to representing the database in the computer or retrieving data from it. At the next lower level, a number of data models are available that provide a mapping for a logical data model like the E-R model. These models specify a conceptual view of the data as well as a high level view of the implementation of the database on the computer. They do not concern themselves with the detailed bits and bytes view of the data.

In the 1960s, there were two widely used data models at this intermediate level. These were the *hierarchical model* and the *network model*. These are briefly discussed in Section 3.7. Readers interested in a more detailed discussion on the hierarchical and network models should refer to some of the older database books. As noted in the first chapter, a new model called the relational model was proposed by E. F. Codd in 1970. The model is based on the concept of *mathematical relation* which looks like a table of values. In the beginning the computing industry was sceptical of the relational approach; many computing professionals thought the approach could not be efficient for managing large databases. This however changed as prototypes of relational database systems were built and shown to be efficient. The first two prototypes were the Model R at IBM San Jose Research Lab in California and INGRES at the University of California at Berkeley. With the success of the prototypes, a number of commercial relational database management systems became available and the hierarchical and network models were superseded by the relational model. Some computing installations however continue to use the old DBMS to process their legacy data. During the last 30 years or so, a number of other new models have also been proposed. Some are based on an object oriented approach to viewing the data, others consider an object relational approach while the development of XML itself is leading to another way of looking at databases. These topics will be discussed in Chapters 14 and 17 respectively. The main focus of this chapter is the relational model.

All the data models provide facilities for representing entities and their attributes as well as relationships. The data about entities and their attributes is handled in a similar way in all the models. The representation is a record which is a collection of attribute values (including an identifier of the entity) although the structure of the record may be somewhat different. The relationships are however represented very differently in the models. We start by looking at the simplest model, i.e., the relational model.

One might ask the question why we should bother about the relational model when we already have the E-R model. In some ways, the two models are quite different. Using the E-R model allows us to define the structure of the enterprise data more easily than using the relational model but the simplicity of the relational model allows powerful query languages to be designed that could not be employed with the E-R model. Essentially the E-R model is used to build a conceptual view of the database that is implemented using the relational model.

This chapter is organized as follows. Section 3.2 deals with the data structure used in the relational model. Mapping of the E-R model to the relational model is described here. Data manipulation is briefly discussed since it is discussed in detail in Chapter 4. The final component of the relational model, data integrity is discussed in Section 3.4 including existential integrity, referential integrity, domains and nulls. Advantages of the relational model are presented in Section 3.5. Codd's rules for fully relational systems are then listed in Section 3.6 followed by a brief description of older database models; hierarchical and network models in Section 3.7.

3.1.1 The Relational Model

As noted earlier, the relational model was proposed by Codd in 1970. The model deals with database management from an abstract point of view. It provides specifications of an abstract database management system. The model is very easy to understand although it is based on a solid theoretical foundation that includes predicate calculus and the theory of relations. However, to use a database management system based on the relational model, users do not need to master these theoretical foundations.

Codd defined the relational model as consisting of the following three components:

1. *Data Structure*—A collection of data structure types for building a database.
2. *Data Manipulation*—A collection of operators that may be used to retrieve, derive, build a database or modify data stored in the data structures.
3. *Data Integrity*—A collection of rules that implicitly or explicitly define a consistent database state or change of state.

Each of the three components are discussed in Sections 3.2, 3.3 and 3.4 respectively.

3.2 DATA STRUCTURE

The beauty of the relational model is the simplicity of its data structure. The fundamental property of the relational structure is that all information about the entities and their attributes as well as the relationships is presented to the user as tables (called *relations*[1]) and nothing but tables. A database therefore is a collection of relations. Each row of each table consists of an entity occurrence or a relationship occurrence. Each column refers to an attribute. The model is called relational and not tabular because tables are a lower level of abstraction than the mathematical concept of relation. Tables give the impression that positions of rows and columns are important. In the relational model, it is assumed that no ordering of rows and columns is defined.

Figure 3.1 gives number of properties of a relation:

The properties listed in Fig. 3.1 are simple and based on practical considerations. The first property ensures that only one type of information is stored in each relation. The second property ensures that each column is named uniquely. This has several benefits. The names can be chosen to convey what each column is and the

1. We will use the two terms *table* and *relation* interchangeably.

- Each relation contains only one record type.
- Each relation has a fixed number of columns (attributes) that are explicitly named. Each attribute name within a relation is unique.
- No two rows (tuples) in a relation are the same.
- Each item or element in the relation is atomic, that is, in each row, every attribute has only one value that cannot be decomposed into smaller components.
- Rows have no ordering associated with them since a relation is a set of rows and sets have no ordering associated with them.
- Columns have no ordering associated with them (although most commercially available systems do) since each column has a unique name and that column' s value in each row can be easily identified by the column name.

Figure 3.1 Properties of a relation in the relational model

names enable one to distinguish between the column and its domain. Furthermore, the names are much easier to remember than the position of each column if the number of columns is large.

The third property of not having duplicate rows appears obvious but is not always accepted by all DBMS users and designers. The property is essential since no sensible context free meaning can be assigned to a number of rows that are exactly the same.

The fourth property requires that each element in each relation be atomic and that it cannot be decomposed into smaller elements. For example, if an attribute value is 1976–90 then it is not possible to look at just the first part of the value (i.e., 1976). In the relational model, the only composite or compound type (data that can be decomposed into smaller pieces) is a table. This simplicity of structure leads to relatively simple database languages.

The fifth property deals with ordering of the rows in a relation. A relation is a set of rows. As in other types of sets, there is no ordering associated with the rows in a table. Just like the second property, the ordering of the rows should not be significant since in a large database no user should be expected to have any understanding of the positions of the rows of a table. Also, in some situations, the DBMS should be permitted to reorganize the data and change row orderings if that is necessary for efficiency reasons. The columns are identified by their names. The rows on the other hand are identified by their contents, possibly the attributes that are unique for each row.

A table is a set of rows and is closely related to the concept of relation in mathematics. Each row in a relation may be viewed as an assertion. For example, a row in a relation *Player* may assert that a player by the name of *Sachin Tendulkar* has *player_id 89001* and represents *India*. Similarly, a row in a table *Match* may assert that one of the ODI matches was held on *2 March 2008* in *Sydney*. The tables in our ODI database will be presented a little later in this section.

As noted earlier, in the relational model, a relation is the only data structure. The relational terminology is defined in Fig. 3.2.

- *Relation* — It is essentially a simple table. It may be defined as set of rows (or tuples), each row therefore has the same columns (or attributes). Since a relation is a sort of tuple, there is no ordering associated with the tuples. (As noted earlier, we will continue to use both terms relation and table to mean the same).
- *Tuple* — It is a row in the relation (we will use both the teems tuple and row to mean the same).
- *Attribute* — It is a column in the relation.
- *Degree of a relation* — It is the number of columns in the relation.
- *Cardinality of a relation* — It is the number of rows in the relation.
- *N-ary relation* — It is the a relation with degree *N*.
- *Domain* — It is a set of atomic (that is, indivisible) values that each element in a column is permitted to take. Domains may be given unique names. The same domain may be used by a number of different columns.
- *Candidate key and Primary key* — It has been discussed in the last chapter and defined below.

Figure 3.2 Relational Terminology

A formal definition of candidate key is given below:

Definition—Candidate Key

An attribute (or a set of attributes) is called a candidate key of the relation if it satisfies the following properties:

(a) the attribute or the set of attributes uniquely identifies each tuple in the relation (called the uniqueness property), and
(b) if the key is a set of attributes then no subset of these attributes has the property (a) (called the minimality property).

There may be several distinct sets of attributes that may serve as candidate keys but every table must always have at least one.

Primary key may be defined as follows:

Definition—Primary Key

One (and only one) of the candidate keys is arbitrarily chosen as the primary key of the table. Primary key therefore has the properties of uniqueness and minimality.

We will often use symbols like R or S to denote a table and r and s to denote a row. When we write $r \subset R$, we are stating that row r is a row in table R.

3.3 MAPPING THE E-R MODEL TO THE RELATIONAL MODEL

In the relational model, information about entities and relationships is represented in the same way, that is, by tables. Since the structure of all information is the same, the same operators may be applied to them.

We consider the following ODI cricket database, developed in the last chapter, to illustrate the mapping of an E-R model to the relational model as well as basic concepts of the relational data model. We first reproduce the E-R diagram for the database as shown in Fig. 3.3.

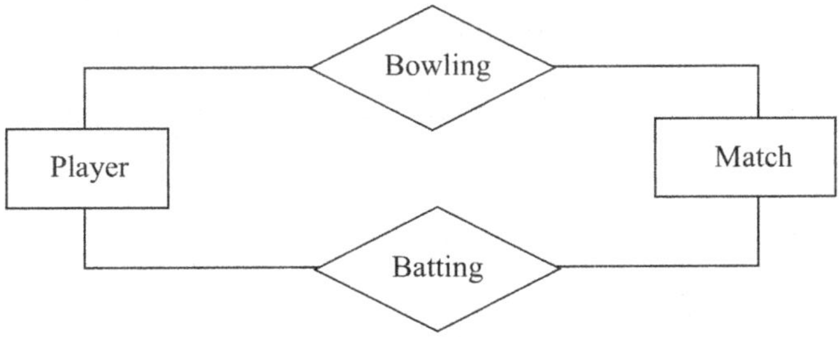

Figure 3.3 E-R diagram for ODI matches

We have not included the attributes in the E-R diagram in Fig. 3.3. The attributes are given below. Some of the attribute names have been changed so that there are no spaces in the names and the names are shorter for ease of display.

The entity *Match* has the attributes given in Fig. 3.4 (its primary key is *Match ID*). We have made some minor changes to the attribute names used in the last chapter to make the names a bit more meaningful.

MatchID Team1 Team2 Ground Date Winner

Figure 3.4 The attributes for the entity *Match*

We have changed the attribute names *Home Team* and *Visiting Team* to *Team1* and *Team2* respectively because many ODI matches are being held in third countries, for example, India and South Africa played on 1st July 2007 in Belfast. We will not discuss such matches in the examples that follow. We will also change the names of attributes to remove spaces within names that are not acceptable in SQL and will shorten several names and replace some by names used by the cricinfo (www.cricinfo.com) website, for example, http://contentaus.cricinfo.com/engvind/engine/series/258449.html to make it easier to use them in the examples that follow.

PlayerID LName FName Country YBorn BPlace FTest

Figure 3.5 The attributes for the entity *Player*

The entity *Player* has its attributes listed in Fig. 3.5 (The primary key is *Player ID*):

The relationship *Batting* has its attributes listed in Fig. 3.6 (The primary key is *Match ID* and *PID* together).

MatchID
PID
Order
HOut
FOW
NRuns
Mts
NBalls
Fours
Sixes

Figure 3.6 The attributes for the relationship *Batting*

The relationship *Bowling* entity has its attributes listed in Fig. 3.7 (The primary key is *MatchID* and *PID* together).

MatchID
PID
NOvers
Maidens
NRuns
NWickets

Figure 3.7 The attributes for the relationship *Bowling*

Now that we have all the details of the E-R model, we consider mapping it to the relational model. The mapping is quite straightforward since the relational model closely approximates the E-R Model. We will show this by transforming the E-R model in Fig. 3.3 (including the attribute lists in Figs 3.4 to 3.7) into a set of relations.

We will follow the steps given below for mapping an E-R diagram into a relational model.

3.3.1 Step 1–Mapping Strong Entities

Each strong entity in an E-R model is represented by a table in the relational model. Each attribute of the entity becomes a column of the table. For example, the entities *Player* and *Match* in Fig. 3.3 may be directly transformed into two tables of the same names given in Tables 3.1 and 3.2 respectively. We have populated these tables using real ODI data. We have only selected matches in which India has played. Note that in almost all entries one of the teams, either *Team 1* or *Team 2*, is the winner but other results are possible including abandoned, no result, draw or cancelled.

Table 3.1 below is the representation of the entity *Match* in the E-R model of Fig. 3.3.

Table 3.1 The relation *Match*

MatchID	*Team 1*	*Team 2*	*Ground*	*Date*	*Winner*
2324	Pakistan	India	Peshawar	6/2/2006	Team 1
2327	Pakistan	India	Rawalpindi	11/2/2006	Team 2
2357	India	England	Delhi	28/3/2006	Team 1
2377	West Indies	India	Kingston	18/5/2006	Team 2
2404a	Sri Lanka	India	Colombo	16/8/2006	Abandoned
2440	India	Australia	Mohali	29/10/2006	Team 2
2449	South Africa	India	Cape Town	26/11/2006	Team 1
2480	India	West Indies	Nagpur	21/1/2007	Team 1
2493	India	West Indies	Vadodara	31/1/2007	Team 1
2520	India	Sri Lanka	Rajkot	11/2/2007	Team 2
2611	England	India	Southampton	21/8/2007	Team 1
2632	India	Australia	Mumbai	17/10/2007	Team 1
2643	India	Pakistan	Guwahati	5/11/2007	Team 1
2675	Australia	India	Melbourne	10/2/2008	Team 2
2681	India	Sri Lanka	Adelaide	19/2/2008	Team 1
2688	Australia	India	Sydney	2/3/2008	Team 2
2689	Australia	India	Brisbane	4/3/2008	Team 2
2717	Pakistan	India	Karachi	26/6/2008	Team 2
2750	Sri Lanka	India	Colombo	24/8/2008	Team 2
2755	Sri Lanka	India	Colombo	27/8/2008	Team 2

Table 3.2 below is the representation of the entity *Player* in E-R model of Fig. 3.3.

Table 3.2 The relation *Player*

PlayerID	*LName*	*FName*	*Country*	*YBorn*	*BPlace*	*FTest*
89001	Tendulkar	Sachin	India	1973	Mumbai	1989
90001	Lara	Brian	West Indies	1969	Santa Cruz	1990
95001	Ponting	Ricky	Australia	1974	Launceston	1995
96001	Dravid	Rahul	India	1973	Indore	1996
96002	Gibbs	Herschelle	South Africa	1974	Cape Town	1996
92001	Warne	Shane	Australia	1969	Melbourne	1992
95002	Pollock	Shaun	South Africa	1973	Port Elizabeth	1995
99003	Vaughan	Michael	England	1974	Manchester	1999

Contd.

Table 3.2 Contd.

PlayerID	*LName*	*FName*	*Country*	*YBorn*	*BPlace*	*FTest*
92003	Ul-Huq	Inzamam	Pakistan	1970	Multan	1992
94004	Fleming	Stephen	New Zealand	1973	Christchurch	1994
93002	Streak	Heath	Zimbabwe	1974	Bulawayo	1993
90002	Kumble	Anil	India	1970	Bangalore	1990
93003	Kirsten	Gary	South Africa	1967	Cape Town	1993
95003	Kallis	Jacques	South Africa	1975	Cape Town	1995
94002	Vaas	Chaminda	Sri Lanka	1974	Mattumagala	1994
92002	Muralitharan	Muthiah	Sri Lanka	1972	Kandy	1992
97004	Vettori	Daniel	New Zealand	1979	Auckland	1997
25001	Dhoni	M S	India	1981	Ranchi	2005
23001	Singh	Yuvraj	India	1981	Chandigarh	2003
96003	Ganguly	Saurav	India	1972	Calcutta	1996
99002	Gilchrist	Adam	Australia	1971	Bellingen	1999
24001	Symonds	Andrew	Australia	1975	Birmingham	2004
99001	Lee	Brett	Australia	1976	Wollongong	1999
91001	Jayasuriya	Sanath	Sri Lanka	1969	Matara	1991
21001	Sehwag	Virender	India	1978	Delhi	2001
98001	Afridi	Shahid	Pakistan	1980	Khyber Agency	1998
98002	Singh	Harbhajan	India	1980	Jalandhar	1998
27001	Kumar	Praveen	India	1986	Meerut	NA
27002	Sharma	Ishant	India	1988	Delhi	2007

3.3.2 Step 2–Mapping Weak Entities

Although Fig. 3.3 E-R diagram does not include a weak entity, we must deal with weak entities if they are in the model. Each weak entity may be mapped to a relation that includes all simple attributes of the entity as well as the primary key of the dominant entity. The primary key of the relation representing a weak entity will be the combination of the primary key of the dominant entity and the partial key of the weak entity.

3.3.3 Step 3–Mapping Relationships

As noted in Chapter 2, there can be three types of relationships, viz., 1:1, 1:*m* and *m*:*n*. We deal with each of them.

Step 3(a)–Mapping-One-to-one Binary Relationships

Figure 3.3 does not include any 1:1 relationships but some situations are likely to give rise to such relationships.

We should note that although each relationship may be mapped to a table in the relational model, not all relationship types need to be represented by separate tables. For 1:1 key propagation may be used. In a 1:1 relationship, each instance of the first entity in a relationship is only related to one instance of the other entity. Therefore it is straightforward to represent the relationship by either putting the primary key of the first entity in the second entity or the primary key of the second entity in the first. This is called *key propagation*.

Such situations of 1:1 relationship may occur in *Department* and *Manager* entities since each department must have a manager and each manager must manage one department. We may choose one of the entities say entity *Department* which should already been mapped into a relation and include the primary key of the other entity, *Manager* (which would also have been mapped to a relation) in the *Department* relation. This is then a foreign key in the relation (that represents *Department*). If the relationship has simple attributes, those may also be included in this relation that represents *Department*.

In some situations when mapping 1:1 relationship between entities *Department* and *Manager*, both entities and the relationship may be merged into one and represented by one relation. As noted earlier, the other extreme solution of course is to represent the relationship as a table that includes primary keys of both entities as well as all the attributes of the relationship.

Step 3(b)–Mapping One-to-many Relationships

Figure 3.3 does not include any 1:*m* relationships but many situations give rise to such relationships.

In a 1:*m* relationship, one entity instance of the first entity may be related to a number of instances of the second entity but each instance of the second entity is related to only one instance of the first entity. This may be the case if we had entities *Employee* and *Manager*. Key propagation is therefore also possible in 1:*m* relationships. We cannot put the primary key of the related instances of *Employee* in the entity *Manager* because for this instance of the entity *Manager* there are likely to be a number of related instances of the *Employee*. We can however propagate the primary key of *Manager* to the related instance because each instance of *Employee* is related to only one instance of *Manager*. The primary key of *Manager* in *Employee* then becomes a foreign key in the relation *Employee*. If the relationship has simple attributes, those may also be included in the relation *Employee*.

Step 3(c)–Mapping Many-to-many Relationships

Key propagation is not possible for *m*:*n* relationships because it is not possible to propagate primary keys of instances of a related second entity to an instance of the related first entity, since there may be more than one such instance of the second entity. Similarly, it is not possible to propagate primary keys of a related first entity to the related second entity since there may be more than one such instance of the first entity. Many-to-many relationships therefore must be represented by a separate table.

Therefore each binary *m*:*n* relationship must be represented by a new relation. The primary keys of each of the entities that participates in the relationship are included in this relation. The combination of these keys will make up the primary key for the relation. Also include any attributes of the relationship in this relation.

For example, when the relationship *Batting* in Fig. 3.3 is transformed into Table 3.3 *Batting*, the primary key of the table is the combination of the primary keys of the two entities *Match* and *Player*. Similarly when *Bowling* in Fig. 3.3 is transformed into Table 3.4 *Bowling*, the primary key of the table is the combination of the primary keys of the two entities *Match* and *Player*. The primary keys of both tables *Batting* and *Bowling* therefore are the same which does not create any problems.

The relationships *Batting* and *Bowling* are both many-to-many relationships since each batsman and each bowler plays in more than one match and each match has more than one batsman and more than one bowler. We therefore transform these two relationships into Table 3.3 and Table 3.4 respectively.

We have again populated the two tables, Table 3.3 and Table 3.4, with real ODI data. The data in both these tables is very limited given the space limitations. We have included part of the batting and bowling information from only two ODI matches, one between Australia and India in Brisbane in March 2008 (Match ID 2689) and the other between Sri Lanka and India played in Colombo on 27th August 2008 (Match ID 2755). India won both these matches. More data for these tables is presented in the appendix at the end of Chapter 5. This data may be useful for some examples and exercises in Chapters 4 and 5.

The relationship *Batting* is mapped to the relational model as shown in Table 3.3.

Table 3.3 The relation *Batting*

MatchID	*PID*	*Order*	*HOut*	*FOW*	*NRuns*	*Mts*	*NBalls*	*Fours*	*Sixes*
2755	23001	3	C	51	0	12	6	0	0
2755	25001	5	C	232	71	104	80	4	0
2755	91001	1	C	74	60	85	52	8	2
2755	94002	7	LBW	157	17	23	29	1	0
2755	92002	11	NO	NO	1	11	7	0	0
2689	89001	2	C	205	91	176	121	7	0
2689	23001	4	C	175	38	27	38	2	2
2689	25001	5	C	240	36	52	37	2	1
2689	99002	1	C	2	2	3	3	0	0
2689	95001	3	C	8	1	9	7	0	0
2689	24001	5	C	123	42	81	56	2	1
2689	99001	8	B	228	7	20	12	0	0
2689	27001	9	C	255	7	7	7	1	0
2755	27001	9	B	257	2	7	6	0	0
2689	98002	8	LBW	249	3	7	3	0	0
2755	98002	8	RO	253	2	7	4	0	0

The relationship *Bowling* in the E-R model given in Fig. 3.3 is mapped to the relational model in Table 3.4.

The above database schema may also be written as in Fig. 3.8.

The E-R diagram in Fig. 3.3 has now been mapped into the relational schema in Fig. 3.8 consisting of four tables. Each table schema presents the structure of the table by specifying its name and the names of its attributes enclosed in parenthesis. The primary key of a relation may be marked by underlining although we have not done so in Fig. 3.8.

Table 3.4 The relation *Bowling*

MatchID	*PID*	*NOvers*	*Maidens*	*NRuns*	*NWickets*
2689	99001	10	0	58	1
2689	24001	3	0	27	1
2689	23001	3	0	15	0
2755	94002	9	1	40	1
2755	92002	10	0	56	1
2755	91001	4	0	29	0
2755	23001	10	0	53	2
2755	98002	10	0	40	3
2689	98002	10	0	44	1

Match(MatchID, Team1, Team2, Ground, Date, Winner)
Player(PlayerID, LName, Country, YBorn BPlace FTest)
Batting(MatchID, PID, Order, HOut, FOW, NRuns, Mts, NBalls, Fours, Sixes)
Bowling(MatchID, PID, NOvers, Maidens, NRuns, NWickets)

Figure 3.8 Database schema for the ODI cricket database

Now to summarize the mapped relational model, we note that the four tables, Table 3.1 to Table 3.4, *Match*, *Player*, *Batting* and *Bowling*, have degree 6, 7, 10 and 6 respectively and cardinality 20, 29, 14 and 7 respectively. The primary key of the table *Match* is MatchID, of table *Player* is PlayerID, of table *Batting* is (MatchID, PID) and finally the primary key of the table *Bowling* is (MatchID, PID). The table *Match* has another candidate key (Ground, Date) as well one or two others. If we can assume the names to be unique then *Player* has (LName, FName) as a candidate key. If the names are not unique but the names LName, FName and FTest together are unique, then the three attributes together form a candidate key. Note that both PlayerID and (PlayerID, Country) cannot be candidate keys, only PlayerID can.

3.3.4 Key Propagation

We further illustrate the use of key propagation by considering the simple E-R model in Fig. 3.9.

Figure 3.9 A simple database

Let the relationship *Occupies* be many-to-one, that is, one employee may occupy only one office but a room may be occupied by more than one employee. Let the attributes of the entity *Employee* be employee number (*e_num*), name (*name*) and *status*. Attributes of the entity *Office* are office number (*o_num*), *capacity* and *building*. *Occupies* has attributes *date*, *e_num* and *o_num* that include the primary keys of the two entities *Employee* and *Office*. One way to represent the above database is to have the three tables whose schema is given in Fig. 3.10.

Employee(e_num, name, status)
Occupies(e_num, o_num, date)
Office(o_num, capacity, building)

Figure 3.10 Three relations representing the E-R diagram in Fig. 3.9

There is of course another possibility. Since the relationship *Occupies* is many-to-one, that is, each employee occupies only one office, we can represent the relationship by including the primary key of the table *Office* in the entity *Employee*. This is propagation of the key of the entity *Office* to entity *Employee*. We then obtain the database schema given in Fig. 3.11.

Employee(e_num, name, status, o_num, date)
Office(o_num, capacity, building)

Figure 3.11 Two relations representing the E-R diagram in Fig. 3.9

Note that key propagation would not work if the relationship *Occupies* is many-to-many.

As noted earlier, if the relationship *Occupies* is 1:1, key propagation is possible in both directions.

3.3.5 A More Complex Example of Mapping an E-R Diagram

We now look at a larger example. An E-R diagram for a programming database project was presented in the last chapter. We reproduce the E-R diagram in Fig. 3.12. Although it looks quite complex, it is not really as complex as one would find for a relatively small real-life database. For a database of a large company, the E-R diagram might even cover the whole wall of a large room!

We now try to map the diagram in Fig. 3.12 into the relational model using the method we have already described. We first look at all the entities and then at all the relationships.

Step 1–Strong Entities

There are five strong entities according to the Entity-Relationship diagram in the figure. These five entities are directly converted into relations as below. The relations are shown with their attributes. Note that different entities may have the same attribute names since this does not create any confusion.

1. User (FName, LName, Login_Name, Address)
2. Program (PName, Code, Date, Version, Extension, Description, Language)
3. Programmer (Login, Code, FName, LName, Address)
4. DBMS (DB_name)
5. Relation (RName, PKey)

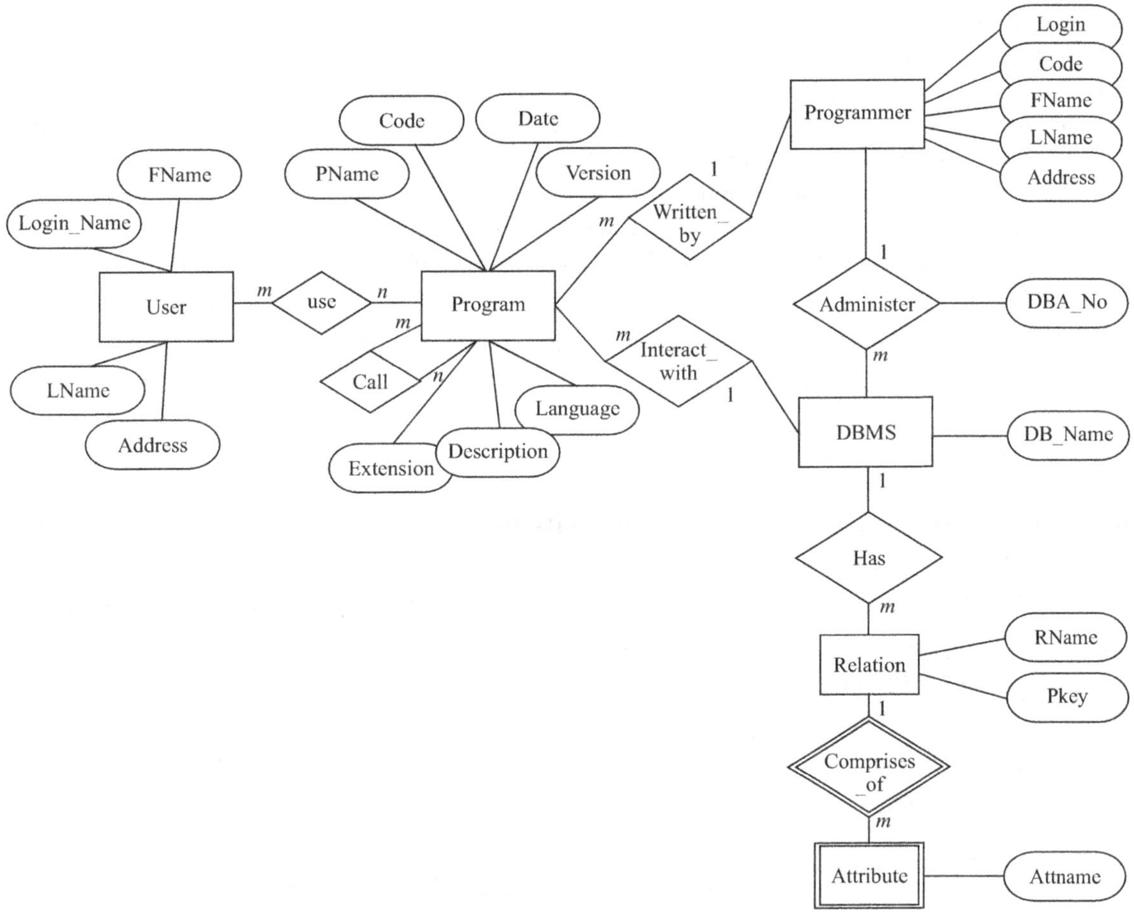

Figure 3.12 An E-R Diagram for a programming database

Step 2–Weak Entities

We do have a weak entity called attribute since it depends on there being a relation whose attributes this entity represents. Note that the primary key of the dominant entity is in this relation.

6. Attribute (RName, Attname)

Step 3(a)–One-to-one Relationships

There are no 1:1 relationships in this model

Step 3(b)–One-to-many Relationships

Two solutions are possible for each of these relationships. One possibility is key propagation. The other possibility is to map each relationship into a new relation.

(i) Either represent the relationship Written_by using key propagation which involves moving primary key of programme (*Login*) to *Program* or the relationship may be mapped to a new relation that has primary key of both entities that it joins; Written_by (PName, Login). There is a clear assumption here that a program has only one programmer.

(ii) Either represent the relationship Interact_with by key propagation which involves moving DB_name to Program or the relationship may be mapped to a new relation that has primary key of both entities that it joins Interact_with (PName, DB_name)

(iii) Either represent the relation Administer by key propagation which involves moving Login to DBMS or the relationship may be mapped to a new relation that has primary key of both entities that it joins Administer (Login, DB_name). There is a clear assumption here that each DBMS has only one administrator.

Therefore we have the following three relations if we do not use key propagation:

7. Written_by (PName, Login)
8. Interact_with (PName, DB_name)
9. Administer (Login, DB_name)

Step 3(c)–Many-to-many Relationships

Now we deal with the four *m*:*n* relationships. All such relationships must be mapped to new tables. These tables include primary keys of both joining relations as well as any attributes that the relationship might have.

10. Use (Login_name, PName)
11. Call (PName1, PName2)
12. Has (DB_name, Relation, RName, PKey)
13. Comprises_of (RName, Attname)

This E-R model therefore translates to 13 tables in the relational model.

Once the E-R diagram has been mapped into relational tables, the tables should be created using the CREATE TABLE command discussed in Chapter 5 but an important task remains before the tables may be created. For each attribute we need to determine the attribute types.

3.4 DATA MANIPULATION

The data manipulation part of the relational model makes set processing facilities available to the user. Since relational operators are able to manipulate tables, the application programs do not need to use loops. For example, to read one row and then the next and then the one after until there are no more rows left. Avoiding loops can result in a significant increase in the productivity of application programmers.

The primary purpose of a database in an enterprise is to be able to provide information to the users within the enterprise. The process of querying a relational database is in essence a way of manipulating the tables that are the database. For example, in the cricket database presented in Tables 3.1 to 3.4, one may wish to find the names of all players from India, or a list of all the matches played by Brian Lara.

We will show how such queries may be answered by using data manipulation languages that are available for relational databases. Two formal languages were presented by Codd when he proposed the relational model. These are called *relational algebra* and *relational calculus*. They are discussed in the next chapter, Chapter 4. These formal languages are followed by a detailed discussion of the commercial query language SQL in Chapter 5.

3.5 DATA INTEGRITY

We noted at the beginning of the chapter that the relational model has three main components: data structure, data manipulation and data integrity. The aim of data integrity is to specify rules that implicitly or explicitly define a consistent database state or change of state. These rules may include facilities like those provided by most programming languages for declaring data types which constrain the user from operations like comparing data of different data types and assigning a variable of one type to another of a different type. This is done to stop the user from doing things that generally do not make sense and to help in ensuring that the data in a database is consistent. In a DBMS, integrity constraints play a similar role.

The integrity constraints are necessary to avoid situations like the following:

1. Some data has been inserted in the database but it cannot be identified (that is, it is not clear which object or entity the data is about).
2. A player is shown to have played in a match but no data about him is available in the table *Player* that has information about players.
3. During processing a query, a player ID is compared with a match ID (this should never be required).
4. A player has retired from cricket but is still shown to be playing in a match.
5. In the table *Batting*, a player is shown to be batting at order greater than 11.
6. In the table *Batting* a player's FOW is lower than the number of runs he scored.
7. In the table *Bowling* a bowler has bowled more than 10 overs in an ODI.

We may define an integrity constraint as a condition specified on a database that restricts the data that can be stored in the database. A database system then enforces these constraints. Many different kinds of constraints may be defined on a database to overcome problems like those listed above. We discuss some constraints in this section and others in Chapter 11.

First we note that integrity constraints on a database may be divided into the following two types:

1. *Static Integrity Constraints*—These are constraints that define valid states of the data. These constraints include designations of primary keys.
2. *Dynamic Integrity Constraints*—These are constraints that define side-effects of various kinds of transactions (for example, insertions and deletions) carried out in the database. Full discussion of such constraints is outside the scope of this book but we will discuss the SQL *trigger* operation and others in Chapter 11.

We now discuss certain static integrity features of the relational model. We discuss the following features:

1. Primary Keys
2. Foreign Keys and Referential Integrity
3. Domains
4. Nulls

3.5.1 Entity Integrity Constraint (or Primary Key Constraint)

We have earlier defined the concepts of candidate key and primary key. From the definition of a candidate key, it should be clear that each table must have at least one candidate key even if it is the combination of all the columns in the table, since all rows in a table are distinct. Often a table may have more than one candidate key.

As discussed earlier, the primary key of a table is an arbitrarily but permanently selected candidate key. The primary key is important since it is the sole identifier for the rows in a table. Any row in a database may be identified by specifying the table name, the primary key and its value. Also for a row to exist in a table it must be *identifiable* and therefore it must have a primary key value. After all, each relation has information about real world things and therefore each row must be identifiable. Also no two rows in the table *Player* can have the same value of the primary key of the table. Furthermore, primary key values serve as references to the rows that they identify. Given the fundamental importance of the primary keys, the database design should always identify the primary key of a table.

Not having a primary key value specified is equivalent to saying that some entity has no identity. This is not acceptable.

We have earlier defined a candidate key of a relation as an attribute (or a set of attributes) if it satisfies the properties in Fig. 3.13.

- The attribute or the set of attributes uniquely identifies each tuple in the relation (called the *uniqueness* property).
- If the key is a set of attributes then no subset of these attributes has the uniqueness property (called the *minimality* property).

Figure 3.13 Essential properties of a candidate key

The first of these two properties of a candidate key (and therefore of the primary key) of a table requires that each key value uniquely identify only one row in the table. For example, more than one player may have the same name but they must have a unique player ID.

The second property requires that no collection of attributes that include the primary key may be called a key in spite of that collection being able to uniquely identify each tuple since they include the primary key which by itself can uniquely identify each row.

As a result of the candidate key properties listed in Fig. 3.13, the relational data model imposes the integrity constraints given in Fig. 3.14 on primary keys.

- No component of a primary key value can be null.
- No two rows can have the same primary key.
- Attempts to change the value of a primary key must be carefully controlled.

Figure 3.14 Integrity constraints for primary keys

The first constraint is necessary because when we want to store information about some entity, then we must be able to identify it to avoid difficulties. For example, if a table *Batting* has (MatchID, PID) as the primary key then allowing rows like those shown in Table 3.5 is going to lead to ambiguity since two rows in the table may or may not be for the same player or for the same match and the integrity of the database is therefore compromised. Having NULLS for attributes other than the primary key attributes does not create any difficulties although one might find the missing information odd in this case.

Table 3.5 Problems with NULLs in primary key

MatchID	*PID*	*NOvers*	*Maidens*	*NRuns*	*NWickets*
2689	NULL	10	NULL	58	1
NULL	24001	NULL	0	27	1
2689	23001	3	0	15	0

The problem identified above may be overcome by SQL commands. For example, we consider the following CREATE TABLE command in SQL.

```
CREATE TABLE Match
      (MatchID INTEGER,
      Team1 CHAR(15),
      Team2 CHAR(15),
      Ground CHAR(20),
      Date CHAR(10),
      Result CHAR(10)
      UNIQUE (MatchID)
      CONSTRAINT MatchPK PRIMARY KEY (MatchID))
```

Figure 3.15 Applying a primary key constraint in SQL

Such commands are discussed in more detail in Chapter 5 and Chapter 12.

The second constraint deals with changing of primary key values. Since the primary key is the identifier of an entity instance, changing it needs very careful controls. For example, consider the information in the fragment of table *Bowling* in Table 3.6. Suppose we decide to change the primary key of the first row from (2689, 24001) to (2690, 24005) for some reason (it is difficult to think of a reason in this instance). Clearly this should not be allowed without strict controls.

Table 3.6 Problems with changing the primary key

MatchID	*PID*	*NOvers*	*Maidens*	*NRuns*	*NWickets*
2689	24001	3	0	27	1
2689	23001	3	0	15	0
2755	91001	4	0	29	0

Codd has suggested the following three possible approaches:

Method 1

Only a select group of users should be authorized to change primary key values.

Method 2

Updates on primary key values are banned. If it was necessary to change a primary key, the row should first be deleted and a new row with a new primary key value but the same other values should be inserted. Of course, this does require that the old values of attributes be remembered and be reinserted in the database.

Method 3

A different command for updating primary keys is made available in the DBMS. Making a distinction between altering the primary key and another attribute of a table would remind users that care needs to be taken in updating primary keys.

3.5.2 Foreign Keys and Referential Integrity

We have discussed some problems related to modifying primary key values. Additional problems can arise in modifying primary key values because one table may include references to another. These references include the primary key value of a row which may be referred to in one or more other tables of the database. The integrity constraints generally include that every value of the primary key of one table (sometimes called the *referenced* table) that appears in another table (i.e., the *referencing* table) must occur as a value of the primary key in the referenced table. Furthermore, when a primary key is modified (for example, a row from the table might be deleted), each of these references to a primary key must either be modified accordingly or be replaced by NULL values. Only then can we maintain referential integrity.

Before we discuss referential integrity further, we define the concept of a *foreign key*. The concept is important since a relational database consists of tables only (no pointers) and relationships between the tables are implicit, based on references to primary keys of other tables. These references are called *foreign keys*.

> ***Definition—Foreign Key***
> *The foreign key in table R is a set of columns (possibly one) whose values are required to match those of the primary key of some table S. R and S are not necessarily distinct.*

It should be noted that the foreign key and primary key must be defined on the same domains. As an example, let us consider the database schema in Fig. 3.16.

```
Match(MatchID, Team1, Team2, Ground, Date, Winner)
Player(PlayerID, LName, FName, Country, YBorn, BPlace, FTest)
Batting(MatchID, PID, Order, HOut, FOW, NRuns, Mts, NBalls, Fours, Sixes)
Bowling(MatchID, PID, NOvers, Maidens, NRuns, NWickets)
```

Figure 3.16 Database schema for the ODI cricket database

We now note the following:

1. The table *Match* has the primary key MatchID but no foreign key.
2. The table *Player* has the primary key PlayerID but no foreign key.
3. The table *Batting* has the primary key (Match ID, PID) and foreign keys MatchID and PID.
4. The table *Bowling* has the primary key (Match ID, PID) and foreign keys MatchID and PID.

Several questions now arise. What do the foreign keys refer to? Could (MatchID, PID) be foreign keys as well as primary keys in tables *Batting* and *Bowling*?

Well, the answers are relatively straightforward. MatchID is referring to the primary key of the table *Match* while PID is referring to the primary key of the relation *Player*. (MatchID, PID) together are not foreign keys because *Batting* and *Bowling* do not refer to each other.

In some cases like the following, there may be a foreign key that refers to its own table, for example, if the *supervisor-no* is an *empno*.

Employee (empno, empname, supervisor-no, dept)

Therefore, foreign keys are the implicit references in a relational database. The following constraint is called the referential integrity constraint:

> ***Definition—Referential Integrity***
> *If a foreign key F in table R refers to and matches the primary key P of table S then every value of F must either be equal to a value of P or be wholly NULL.*

The justification for the referential integrity constraint is simple. If there is a foreign key in a relation (that is, the table is referring to another table) then the foreign key value must match with one of the primary key values in the table to which it refers. That is, if an object or entity is being referred to, the constraint ensures the referred object or entity exists in the database. It is not required that the foreign key values be always non-null. Sometimes a foreign key may be null, for example, a supervisor may not yet be assigned for an employee. Often a foreign key may be a component of a primary key and then the existential integrity constraint prohibits the appearance of nulls.

A foreign key in some DBMS may refer the column(s) of another table that have a combined UNIQUE constraint as well as the NOT NULL constraint.

Just as primary key updates need to be treated in a special way, one must deal with foreign key updates carefully. Foreign key updates do not need to be restricted in quite the same way as primary key updates. The system does need to ensure that the update values appear in the referenced table. Otherwise the update should be rejected.

The foreign key constraint may be specified in SQL as given in Fig. 3.17.

```
CREATE TABLE Match

(MatchID INTEGER,
Team1 CHAR(15),
Team2 CHAR(15),
Ground CHAR(20),
Date CHAR(10),
Winner CHAR(10)
UNIQUE (MatchID)
PRIMARY KEY (MatchID)
FOREIGN KEY (MatchID) REFERENCES Match
FOREIGN KEY (PID) REFERENCES Player)
```

Figure 3.17 Applying the foreign key constraint in SQL

3.5.3 Domains

We have noted that not all commercial database systems provide facilities for specifying domains. Domains could be specified as in Table 3.7.

Table 3.7 Specifying domains

CREATE DOMAIN NAME1	CHAR(10)
CREATE DOMAIN Player1	INTEGER
CREATE DOMAIN NAME2	CHAR(10)
Etc.	

Note that *NAME1* and *NAME2* are both character strings of length 10 but they belong to different (semantic) domains. It is important to denote different domains to

(a) constrain unions, intersections, differences and equi-joins of tables, and
(b) let the system check if two occurrences of the same database value denote the same real world object.

The constraint on union-compatibility and join-compatibility is important so that only those operations that make sense are permitted. For example, a join on class number and student number would make no sense even if both attributes are integers. The user should not be permitted to carry out such operations (or at least be warned when it is attempted).

3.5.4 Nulls

The issue of null values in a database is extremely important. A value in a database may be null for several reasons. The most obvious reason is that the value is not known at the present time. For example, a new employee's home telephone number will not be known until a phone is connected to his/her residence. Another reason why some values in a database may be null is that the attribute may not be applicable. For example, an employee database may have an attribute spouse which is not applicable for a single employee. For female employees the maiden name column might be inapplicable if the employee is single or if the employee did not change her name after marriage. In yet another situation, some information may not be known and will never be known. It is possible that an older migrant or a refugee may not know their date of birth. The person may not even know where he/she was born. We know of a situation when a student did not even know what his nationality was. His mother was from Bangladesh and his father from Burma and neither of the two countries was willing to provide him with a passport!

Having null values in a database creates a variety of issues beginning from simple ones like how to define the average of a collection of values if some are null to comparing null values with non-null values.

Further discussion of this interesting and complex issue is beyond the scope of this book.

3.6 ADVANTAGES OF THE RELATIONAL MODEL

Codd in 1970 indicated that there were four major objectives in designing the relational data model. These are

1. *Data Independence*—To provide a sharp and clear boundary between the logical and physical aspects of database management.

2. *Simplicity*—To provide a simpler structure than was being used at that time. A simple structure is easy to communicate to users and programmers and a wide variety of users in an enterprise can interact with a simple model.
3. *Set-Processing*—To provide facilities for manipulating a set of records at a time so that programmers are not operating on the database record by record.
4. *Sound Theoretical Background*—To provide a theoretical background for the database management field.

3.7 RULES FOR FULLY RELATIONAL SYSTEMS

If a system supports all relational algebra operators and the two integrity constraints (entity integrity and referential integrity) then the system may be called *fully relational*. Codd provided 12 rules (plus rule 0) to evaluate the properties of a relational model. A fully relational DBMS needs to satisfy these rules. The rules are

1. *Rule* 0—For any system that is advertised as, or claims to be, a relational database management system, that system must be able to manage databases entirely through its relational capabilities.

   This basic rules states that all database management should be based on the relational model. The rule is included only because when relational database systems were becoming popular, some of the nonrelational database systems started advertising their systems as relational systems.

Data Structure Rules

2. *Rule* 1—All information in a relational database is represented explicitly at the logical level and in exactly one way, by values in tables.

   There are many advantages in having this simple data structure. The data manipulation language can be simple. Additional software that interfaces with a relational DBMS can be based on the assumption that all data is represented in tables. The early nonrelational systems had much more complex data structures and the application programs were then also complex.
3. *Rule* 2—Each and every datum (atomic value) in a relational database is guaranteed to be logically accessible by resorting to a combination of table name, primary key value and column name.

   This rule requires that the only way to access data in a relational model is by specifying the name of the table, the column(s) and its primary key value(s). No other traversing of the database, for example row-by-row, should be required.
4. *Rule* 3—Null values (distinct from the empty character string or a string of blank characters are distinct from zero or any other number) are supported in fully relational DBMS for representing missing information and inapplicable information in a systematic way, independent of data type.

   Most database systems have some data that is unavailable or inapplicable. The relational model requires that this data be treated more systematically than by defining a special value, for example -9999, for each attribute.
5. *Rule* 4—The database description is represented at the logical level in the same way as ordinary data, so that authorized users can apply the same relational language to its interrogation as they apply to the regular data.

This rules deals with the database metadata which should be able to be manipulated in the same way as the regular data making it easier for database users to interrogate it.

Data Manipulation Language Rules

6. *Rule* 5—A relational system may support several languages and various modes of terminal use (for example, the fill-in-the-blanks mode). However, there must be at least one language whose statements are expressible using some well-defined syntax, as character strings and that is comprehensive in supporting all of the following items:
   - Data definition
   - View definition
   - Data manipulation (interactive and by program)
   - Integrity constraints
   - Transaction boundaries (such as begin, commit and roll-back)

   This rule requires that the user has access to at least one language that carries out all relational database operations
7. *Rule* 6—All views that are theoretically updatable are also updatable by the system.

   This is a difficult requirement since it is not easy for a database system to determine if the update request by the user to update a view is reasonable.
8. *Rule* 7—The capability of handling a base table or a derived table as a single operand applies not only to the retrieval of data but also to the insertion, update and deletion of data.

   As we will show in the next two chapters, insertion, update and deletion are able to use a table as a single operand enabling a set of tuples to be inserted, updated or deleted in one command.

Data Independence Rules

9. *Rule* 8—Application programs and terminal activities remain logically unimpaired whenever any changes are made in either storage representations or access methods.

   This rule deals with data independence, one of the most important characteristic of a relational database system. It may be defined as the ability to separate the database definition from the physical storage structure of the database. Therefore any changes in the physical structure of the database should not impact the application programs.
10. *Rule* 9—Application programs and terminal activities remain logically unimpaired when information-preserving changes of any kind that theoretically permit unimpairment are made to the base tables.

    This again relates to data independence.
11. *Rule* 10—Integrity constraints specific to a particular relational database must be definable in the relational data sub-language and storable in the catalog, not in the application programs.

    This rule requires that integrity constraints should not be included in the application programs and therefore application programs are easier to write. Also, it ensures that all application programs are subjected to exactly the same integrity constraints.
12. *Rule* 11—A relational DBMS has distribution independence.

    This rule relates to distributed database systems which are discussed in Chapter 13.

13. *Rule* 12—If a relational system has a low level (single-record-at-a-time) language, that low level cannot be used to subvert or bypass the integrity rules and constraints expressed in the higher level relational languages (multiple-records-at-a-time).

    This rule essentially requires that no low level language be used since that may bypass the rules of a relational system.

3.8 EARLIER DATABASE MODELS – HIERARCHICAL AND NETWORK MODELS

As noted earlier, the relational database model replaced the earlier models in the1980s. Two database models that were popular in the late 1960s and 1970s and now superseded by the relational DBMS is also now discussed. Some database systems even today use these old database systems. IMS, IDMS and TOTAL are examples of DBMS that were based on these models and were used widely. Some DBMS that were not based on either of these two models were also in use in the 1970s. These included ADABAS from a German company called Software AG. ADABAS was an inverted list database.

3.8.1 Network Data Model

The network model was developed by Charles Bachman and his colleagues at the General Electric Company in 1964. The model was standardized in 1971 by the CODASYL group (Conference on Data Systems Languages). The model used directed acyclic graphs (called Bachman diagrams) with nodes and edges where nodes represent the entity sets and edges (or links) represent the relationships between the entity sets. The links could be either 1:1 or 1:*m* so many-to-many relationships had to be decomposed into simpler relationships. The model allowed each child record to have multiple parents allowing 1: *n* relationships. The major problem with the network model was the complexity of designing a database system and its maintenance.

In the network model, we can represent each player as a node and their batting and bowling records also as nodes. They are then connected by edges or links. Finding batting and bowling information for a player was relatively easy since it only required searching for the relevant player node record and then finding his bowling and batting records by following the edges. Finding the names of players who scored a century involved searching the nodes for batting and finding nodes that had a score of more than 99 and then following the edges to find player nodes.

As noted above, a number of widely used database systems were based on the network model. These included IDMS (Computer Associates), IDS II (Honeywell) and DMS-1100 (Unisys).

Some typical commands used in a network database system are presented in Fig. 3.18.

Command Name	Description
FIND	Locate record
GET	Transfer record to memory
OBTAIN	Combine FIND and GET
STORE	Insert a new record
ERASE	Delete record

Figure 3.18 Examples of commands used in a network database model

A simple example of a network model database is presented in Fig. 3.19.

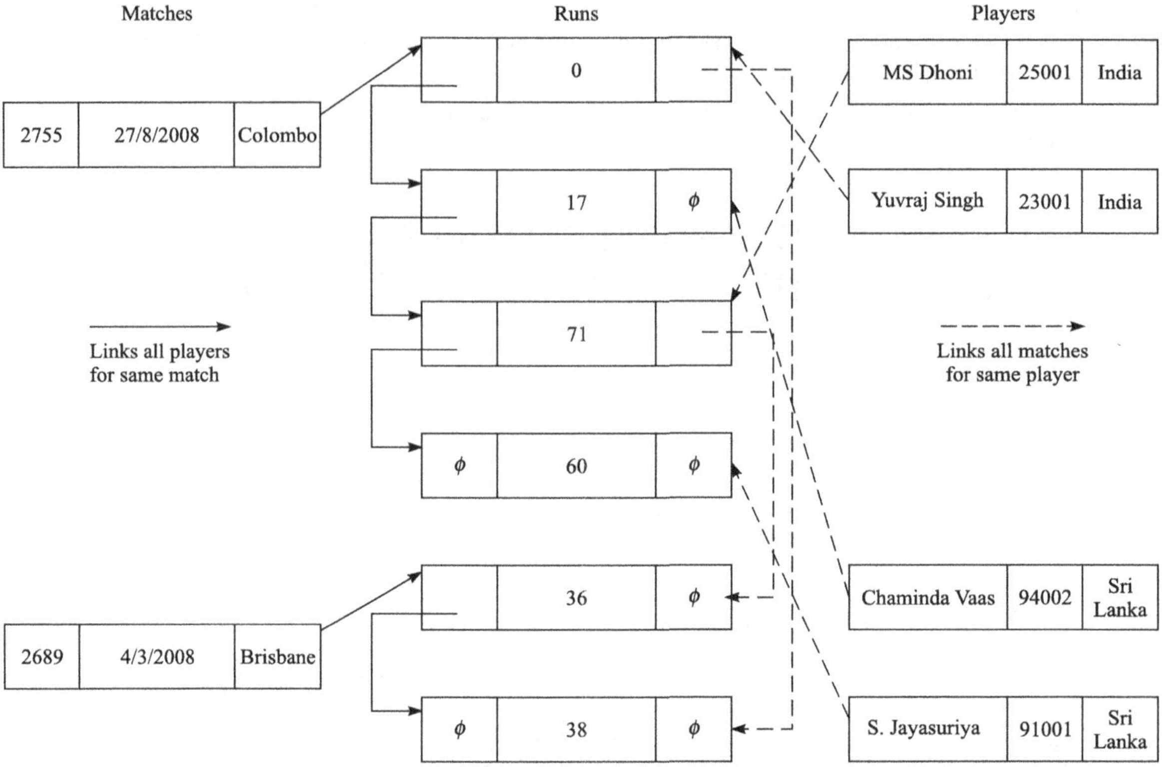

Figure 3.19 A typical network database model

Figure 3.19 shows a few records in a network model for the cricket database. There are two matches at the left-hand side and four players on the right-hand side. The players and matches are connected by the records in the middle which gives details of batting. We have only shown runs in these records but other information could be included. All the batting records of a match are linked in a chain with solid lines while all the batting records of a player are linked by the dotted lines on the right-hand side. Similar records could include all the bowling information. These chains allow one to traverse through all batting records of a match as well as all batting records of a player and these chains must be followed if one wanted to know how many runs Jayasuriya scored in match 2755. This is clearly very different than what happens in the relational model.

We leave it as an exercise for the reader to work out how insertions, deletions and updates take place in the two models and also compare these models with the relational model.

In summary, the network model was conceptually simple, efficient for some database problems and provided sufficient flexibility in that all relationships could be represented without much redundancy. Given that the network model was navigational, the performance of network DBMS was generally not high and some changes to the underlying database were difficult to implement. For example, changing relationships required physical reorganization of the data as well as changes to the application programs and therefore provided only limited data independence. Also these early DBMS were not robust. For example, a failure in the system occasionally left dangling references to data which had to be recovered.

3.8.2 Hierarchical Data Model

The hierarchical model was another model that formed the basis of the earliest database systems. It was a somewhat more restrictive model and could be considered a subset of the network model.

The hierarchical model was developed at IBM and was the basis of the IMS database system. IBM never supported the network model. IMS was based on the thinking that all views in life are hierarchical and therefore any database application could also be modelled as a hierarchy. The basic building block of the hierarchical model was called a *Physical Database Record* (PDBR) which consisted of a root segment and a hierarchy of segments (called *child segments*). Each segment was like a row in a table consisting a set of related fields. Each PDBR was defined by a database description (DBD) that was coded by a programmer.

Since IBM already had some file processing packages, the IMS hierarchical model used them for storage and retrieval of data. These included the Sequential Access Method (SAM), Indexed Sequential Access Method (ISAM), Virtual Sequential Access Method (VSAM) and Overflow Sequential Access Method (OSAM). The IMS data manipulation used Data Language I (DL/I) that had a set of commands used with a host language like COBOL. DL/I commands essentially involved traversing the hierarchical database structure.

The hierarchical model was based on a tree structure which may be defined as follows.

Definition—Tree
A tree is a hierarchical structure that is a finite set of nodes connected by edges such that there is one specially designated node called the root of the tree. The remaining nodes are partitioned into n ($n \geq 0$) disjoint sets, each of which is also a tree.

It represented data as relationships between tree nodes called parent records (also called *segments* in the hierarchical model) and child records (or segments) as a tree. These relationships between the two record types may only be one-to-many. For example, we could represent each player as a parent segment and their batting and bowling records as child segments. Finding batting and bowling information for a player is relatively easy since it only requires searching for the relevant parent record and then finding his bowling and batting child records, but many other types of queries are more difficult. For example, finding names of players who scored a century in Melbourne is more difficult because it involves going through each player's parent record then searching the child records to check if there is a record that has more than 99 runs and is about a match in Melbourne. In summary, the following should be noted about the hierarchical model:

1. The model was efficient for searching the parent records and their child records since there was less redundant data.
2. Searching through the child records was more complicated and very different than in the relational model.
3. There were difficulties in representing many-to-many relationships.

Some commands used in IMS, a well-known hierarchical database system, are presented in Fig. 3.20.

In using the hierarchical model to represent the cricket database including the tables *Player*, *Match*, *Batting* and *Bowling* difficulties arise because the hierarchical model assumes all information to be hierarchical in nature. In the cricket database it is not clear which entity may be considered the parent entity and which as the child entity.

Command Name	Acronym	Description
GET UNIQUE	GU	Retrieve record
GET NEXT	GN	Sequential retrieval
GET NEXT WITHIN PARENT	GNP	Sequential retrieval of same parent
DELETE	DLET	Delete existing segment
INSERT	ISRT	Add new segment

Figure 3.20 Examples of commands used in a hierarchical database model

We will attempt to model the information assuming that the *Match* entity is parent, *Player* is the child of the entity *Match* and *Batting* and *Bowling* are child entities of *Player*.

The cricket database in the hierarchical model is presented in Fig. 3.21.

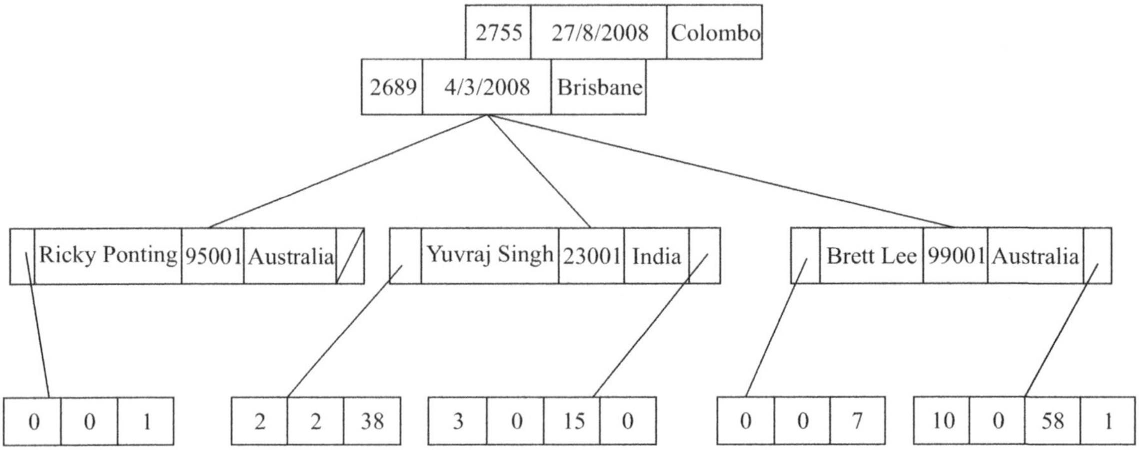

Figure 3.21 A typical hierarchical database model

Figure 3.21 shows only a few records. There are two matches at the root. One of them is shown to have three children players that the parent entity points to and each player has one or two children which are the batting or bowling records of the player. The first field is a pointer to the batting child record and the last field is a pointer to the bowling child record.

Given the above structure, the hierarchical model requires the following:

1. A parent record type may own an arbitrary number of chid record types.
2. No single occurrence of a record type may have more than one parent record type.

In summary, software based on the hierarchical model provided an efficient representation of hierarchical structures, efficient single key search (if the hierarchical structure was the application view of the data), fast update performance for some updates. It was a conceptually simple model. On the other hand, hierarchical database systems had difficulty with many-to-many relationships, it lacked flexibility (nonhierarchical relationships were difficult to represent), performance for nonhierarchical accesses was poor, lack of maintainability, for example, changing relationships often required physical reorganization of data as well as changes to the application programs.

3.8.3 Comparison of Hierarchical, Network and Relational Models

Both the network and hierarchical models were developed in the 1960s and were conceptually simple when they were proposed but suffered from a number of serious disadvantages partly because both were navigational systems. The disadvantages included low level of data independence, difficulty in representing many-to-many relationships. For a large database, the logical data model became very complex and since the data manipulation languages were procedural the application programs became complex as well and difficult to maintain. In both hierarchical and network models, physical and logical data independence was difficult to achieve, since the data manipulation languages and therefore the application programs often contained a wide variety of information about the physical organisation of the database.

Hierarchical model's single parent rule forces redundancy. It can be eliminated in the network model since the network model allows more flexibility and a record type may have an arbitrary number of parents.

The three models are compared in Fig. 3.22 below.

Item	**Hierarchical**	**Network**	**Relational**
Data structure	Hierarchy	Tree of records	Tables
Data Access	Navigational	Navigational	Non-navigational
Method of access	Procedural First access the root and then navigate to the record of interest.	Procedural Data access may start from any entity.	Nonprocedural SELECT, FROM, WHERE
User must know	Structure of the database	Structure of the database	Names of the tables
Performance	Was fast for some simple queries	Was fast for some simple queries	Good for many types of queries
Mathematical basis	None	None	Has mathematical foundation
Query language	Use DI/I through COBOL	COBOL based commands	SQL
Data integrity	None	None	Basic integrity is part of the model
Modifying the database	Difficult	Difficult	Relatively easy
Data independence	None	None	Part of the model

Figure 3.22 A comparison of the three database models

SUMMARY

This chapter has covered the following points:

- The relational data model was invented by E. F. Codd in 1970. The three major components of the model are data structure, data manipulation and data integrity.
- Data structure component of the relational model required that all information presented in a database be as relations (essentially tables).
- Each relation must meet a number of properties, for example, atomic values, no duplicate tuples, no ordering of tuples, etc.
- Relational terminology includes terms like a relation (or a table), tuple (or a row), degree (number of columns), cardinality (number of rows), attribute (column), domain, candidate key and primary key.
- The primary key of a relation has the properties of uniqueness and minimality.
- An Entity-Relationship model discussed in Chapter 2 may be mapped to relational model. Mapping includes mapping each entity and each many-to-many relationship to a table.
- Data integrity in the relational model includes constraints relating to primary keys (called existential integrity) and foreign keys (called referential integrity) as well as domains and NULLs.
- Relational data model has the advantages of data independence, simplicity, set processing and sound theoretical background.
- Codd defined 13 rules that a fully relational model must satisfy including data structure rules, data manipulation rules and data independence rules.
- The basic concepts of two older database models, the network model and the hierarchical model, have been presented. The hierarchical model is based on the concept that all data has hierarchical nature.
- Disadvantages of the hierarchical and network database models have been described and the models are compared to the relational model. These include different data structures, different database languages, lack of integrity in the older models, and low level of data independence in the older models.

REVIEW QUESTIONS

1. What are the major components of the relational model? (Section 3.1)
2. What is the meaning of the terms relation, tuple, degree, cardinality, attribute, domain, candidate key and primary key? (Section 3.2)
3. Give two example to illustrate the properties of a primary key? (Section 3.2)
4. Present an E-R model and show how it should be mapped to the relational model. How is an entity mapped? How is a relationship mapped? (Section 3.2.1)
5. Describe constraints related to the primary key, foreign key, domains and NULLs. (Section 3.4)
6. List some of the advantages of the relational model. (Section 3.5).
7. List five rules for fully relational systems. (Section 3.6)
8. Describe the main features of the hierarchical data model. (Section 3.7)
9. Describe the main features of the network data model. (Section 3.7)

10. Using an example, illustrate the features of the hierarchical and the network model. List some of the disadvantages of these models. Why do you think the products based on these models could not compete with the products based on the relational model? (Section 3.7)

SHORT ANSWER QUESTIONS

1. What are the three components of the relational model?
2. List three properties of a relation.
3. What is the data structure used in the relational model?
4. List three major properties that a relation must have?
5. What is the cardinality of a relation? What is the cardinality of the relation in Fig. 3.3?
6. What is the degree of a relation? What is the degree of the relation in Fig. 3.2?
7. Define the candidate key of a relation.
8. How is an entity in an E-R model mapped to the relational model?
9. How is a many-to-many relationship in an E-R model mapped to the relational model?
10. How is a one-to-one relationship in an E-R model mapped to the relational model?
11. How is a weak entity in an E-R model mapped to the relational model?
12. What is a primary key and existential integrity?
13. What is a foreign key and referential integrity?
14. Why DBMS products based on the network model and the hierarchical model were not able to compete with relational DBMS?
15. What is the major difference between the network model and hierarchical model?

MULTIPLE CHOICE QUESTIONS

1. The main components (more than one) of the relational model are
   (a) data structure
   (b) data manipulation
   (c) data recovery
   (d) data integrity
2. Which one of the following is correct?
   (a) A relation may have duplicate rows.
   (b) A relation may have duplicate columns.
   (c) A relation may have ordering associated with the rows.
   (d) A relation may have non-atomic attribute values.
3. Which one of the following is allowed in the relational model?
   (a) Repeating groups
   (b) Pointers
   (c) Record identifiers other than the primary key
   (d) Specification of domains

4. Which two of the following are correct? Rows in the relational data model are required to be unordered because
   (a) it makes the database more efficient.
   (b) the user should not be burdened with having to remember which row is next to which row.
   (c) numbering rows is expensive.
   (d) changes in ordering may have to be made for a variety of reasons.
5. Which one of the following is correct? In using a relational database consisting of a number of tables, a user only needs to know
   (a) the number of rows in each relation.
   (b) the number of columns in each relation.
   (c) the access paths to the data in each relation.
   (d) the names of the tables and the names of their relevant columns.
6. The concept of domain is fundamental to the relational data model. Which of the following statements regarding domains is **not** correct?
   (a) Conceptually, domains play a role similar to data types in programming languages.
   (b) Domains are user defined while the data types are built into the system.
   (c) A domain is a set of scalar or atomic values, all of the same type.
   (d) There can be no more than one attribute in each relation defined on each domain.
7. Which two of the following properties must belong to the primary key of a relation?
   (a) It identifies each row uniquely.
   (b) It is an attribute or a set of attributes on which an index is built.
   (c) It is an attribute or a set of attributes for which missing values are not allowed.
   (d) A proper subset of it cannot be a key.
8. Which one of the following is correct?
   (a) Each candidate key is a primary key.
   (b) Each primary key is a foreign key.
   (c) Each foreign key is a primary key in some relation.
   (d) Each foreign key is a candidate key.
9. Which one of the following is correct?
   (a) Referential integrity requires that a foreign key may not be NULL.
   (b) Referential integrity requires that a foreign key may not be partially NULL.
   (c) Existential integrity requires that a primary key may not be NULL although it may be partially NULL.
   (d) A high level of integrity requires that there be no NULL values in the database.
10. Consider the following relation that stores information about offices, telephones and occupants of offices:

    office(OfficeNum, TelephoneNum, Occupant)

    Each office has a unique office number.

    There is only one telephone in each office and the telephone number is unique. Each office is occupied by only one person although a person may have more than one office. Occupant is a unique identification for persons occupying rooms.

Which one of the following is correct?

(a) OfficeNum and TelephoneNum are both candidate keys.
(b) OfficeNum, TelephoneNum and (OfficeNum, TelephoneNum) are all candidate keys.
(c) (OfficeNum, occupant) and (TelephoneNum, occupant) are the candidate keys.
(d) OfficeNum must be the primary key.

11. Consider again the relation *office(OfficeNum, TelephoneNum, Occupant)*. Now assume that each office may have more than one occupant and more than one telephone and a telephone may be shared between two or more occupants. Furthermore, each occupant may have more than one office. OfficeNum, TelephoneNum and occupant names are unique.

    Which one of the following is correct?

    (a) OfficeNum and TelephoneNum are both candidate keys.
    (b) OfficeNum, TelephoneNum and OfficeNum, TelephoneNum are all candidate keys.
    (c) (OfficeNum, occupant) and (TelephoneNum, occupant) are the candidate keys.
    (d) (OfficeNum, TelephoneNum, occupant) is the candidate key.

12. Which of the following are true? The value of an attribute in a table may be NULL because
    (a) the value is not known.
    (b) the value is not applicable.
    (c) the value will never be available.
    (d) All of the above

13. Which one of the following is correct?
    (a) Every subset of a relation is a relation.
    (b) Every subset of a tuple is a tuple.
    (c) Every subset of an attribute is an attribute.
    (d) Every subset of a foreign key is a foreign key.

14. Which of the following are included in Codd's rules for fully relational systems?
    (a) NULL values are independent of data type.
    (b) All views that are theoretically updatable are also updatable by the system.
    (c) A relational database has distribution independence.
    (d) All of the above

15. Which of the following are correct?
    (a) Hierarchical model was developed before the relational model.
    (b) Object-oriented database model was developed before the relational model.
    (c) The network database model was developed before the relational model.
    (d) The Entity-Relationship model was developed before the relational model.

16. Which one of the following is **not** correct?
    (a) The network model used acyclic graphs with nodes and edges.
    (b) The hierarchical model was based on a tree structure in which there was one specially designated node called the root of the tree.
    (c) Hierarchical model had difficulty representing many-to-many relationships.
    (d) The network model is navigational while the hierarchical model is not.

17. When a row is deleted which one of the following techniques should be used to maintain integrity?
    (a) The row is deleted and nothing else is done.
    (b) The row is deleted and the references to the deleted primary key, if any, are replaced by NULL.
    (c) The delete operation is not allowed if the row's primary key is a target of a foreign key.
    (d) The row is deleted as well as the rows from other tables that have foreign keys that have the deleted primary key as their target.

EXERCISES

1. What are the properties of a relation? Discuss each property and explain why it is important.
2. Define a candidate key, a primary key and a foreign key. Can the primary key have null values? Can the foreign key have null values? Can one relation have more than one candidate key? Can one relation have more than one primary key? Can one relation have more than one foreign key? Explain and give examples to illustrate your answers.
3. Discuss the following concepts and explain their importance.
    (a) Integrity constraint
    (b) Referential integrity
    (c) Existential integrity
4. Relate each of the relational terms on the left-hand side to their informal equivalents on the right-hand side. Note that not all terms on the right-hand side have a matching term on the left-hand side.

Table 3.8 Terminology

Relation	*Pointer*
Tuple	Table
Primary key	Record or row
Candidate key	Link
Attribute	Field or column
Domain	File
Cardinality	A unique identifier
Degree	Pool of legal values Current values Number of attributes in a table Number of tuples Number of fields in the primary key

5. Consider the following student database:
   Student(ID, Name, Address, City, Tutor)
   Enrolment(ID, Code, Marks)
   Course(Code, Title, Department)

Formulate the following queries in relational algebra using the student database above. Assume that the attribute *Tutor* is the ID of the tutor.

(a) List all the student names.
(b) List all school and course names.
(c) Find student names of students that have no tutor.
(d) Find student names of students that are doing computer science courses.
(e) Find student names of students that have Suresh Chandra as tutor.

6. Consider the following relations in a student database:

Table 3.9 The relation Student

ID	*Name*	*Address*	*City*	*Tutor*
8700074	Svaty Krishna	9, Gandhi Hall	Green Park	NULL
8900020	Arun Kumar	90, Nehru Hall	Green Park	8700074
8801234	Preeti Mukerjee	80, Tata Hall	Green Park	8612345
8612345	Kamal Gupta	11, College Street	Noida	NULL
9082545	Praveen Kothari	54, M. G. Road	Chennai	8700074
9038593	B. V. Narasimhan	25 Chandni Chowk	Delhi	8612345

Table 3.10 The relation *Enrolment*

ID	*Code*	*Marks*
8700074	CS100	72
8900020	MA111	54
8900020	CS150	NULL
8700074	CH100	NULL
8801234	CS300	89
8801234	BU299	NULL

Table 3.11 The relation *Course*

Code	*Title*	*Department*
CS300	Database Management	Computer Science
CS100	Introduction to Computer Science	Computer Science
CH100	Introduction to Chemistry	Chemistry
MA111	Linear Algebra	Mathematics
BU150	Introduction to Economics	Business
BU299	Project	Business

For each relation, write the degree of the relation, its cardinality, all the candidate keys and the primary key.

7. Consider the following two relations in an example database with EmpID and DeptID as primary keys of the two tables respectively:

Table 3.12 The table Emp

EmpID	*Ename*	*ManagerID*	*DeptID*
126	Krishna Kumar	129	22
NULL	Prakash Patel	NULL	22
129	Milkha Singh	NULL	26
135	Rabindra Singh	173	99
149	Nizam Khan	129	NULL
173	David Abraham	NULL	NULL

Table 3.13 The table Dept

DeptID	*Dname*	*MgrID*
22	Sales	128
26	Production	126
75	Finance	129
81	Deliveries	149
89	NULL	173

(a) Identify all foreign keys.

(b) Do the above relations satisfy the existential and referential integrity constraints? Discuss.

(c) If the tuple with EmpID = 129 in the *Emp* table is deleted, what should be done to maintain integrity of the database?

8. Consider the cricket database in Tables 3.1 to 3.4. List some integrity constraints that should apply to these tables.

9. A simple database is to be designed to store information about rooms and telephone numbers in an enterprise. The only information to be stored is room numbers and telephone numbers in each of them. Room numbers and telephone numbers are assumed to be unique.

One way to represent the information is to have a relational schema *room(RoomNum, PhoneNum)*. Is this relation adequate to represent the information in each of the following cases? If not, present an alternative database design consisting of one or more relational schemas for each of the cases below.

Consider the following four situations:

(a) Each phone number is assigned to only one room and each room has a unique phone number.

(b) A phone number may (with extensions) be assigned to more than one room and a room may have more than one phone each with a different number.

(c) Each phone number is assigned to only one room but some rooms do not have any phones while others may have one or more phones.

(d) Each phone number is assigned to only one room and each room has at least one phone. Some rooms have more than one phone.

PROJECTS

We now present a number of projects that may be used by instructors as a basis for designing projects for their course. We have used similar projects successfully for many years in our classes. A methodology for projects which may suit some instructors is proposed below.

Project Implementation Suggestion
It is proposed that each project should consist of the following three stages:

Stage 1
In the first stage, students are required to design an Entity-Relationship model for one (possibly allocated by the lecturer) of the database applications described below as well as others that are suggested by the lecturer.

Students should make suitable assumptions where necessary when implementing their project.

The following should be included with the Entity-Relationship diagram:

1. A discussion of the needs of the enterprise. A collection of typical queries that the system is expected to answer.
2. A list of all assumptions.
3. A list of all entities and relationships and their attributes and primary keys (most of this information can be included in the Entity-Relationship diagram).
4. A discussion of the strengths and weaknesses of the proposed solution.
5. And, of course, the complete Entity-Relationship diagram.

The design and the accompanying documentation should be submitted by the given date.

Stage 2
Revise the E-R diagram based on comments received from the lecturer. Build a set of ten sensible queries, some easy, some more complex that use subqueries, GROUP BY and aggregation functions. Submit these by the due date for Stage 2.

Stage 3
Implement the database using Oracle (or another system that is available). Populate the database. Formulate the queries and run them using the database. Submit a report including the results of the queries by the given date. The report should clearly identify objectives, discuss methodology, present assumptions and present results and discuss conclusions.

Bonus marks may be given to students who build a suitable user interface for their system.

A significant component of the assignment marks should be awarded on the basis of the quality of documentation.

1. A Small Airport

Design a database for a small airport, for example, in a place like Haridwar in Uttarakhand or Puri in Orissa. The database is designed to keep track of private airplanes, their owners, airport employees and pilots. Each airplane has an identification number, is of a particular type and has a parking space in a particular hangar. Each plane has a purchase date, its type has a model number, and a capacity in terms of number of passengers. Each hangar has a number and the number of planes that may park in it. The database also needs to keep track of owners of the planes and the employees that have worked on each plane and on what date. The maintenance record of each plane that includes the number of hours spent servicing the plane and a code for the type of service done. Some planes provide charter services to large companies like Infosys or Reliance. The database stores details of each such flight.

2. College of Pharmacy

Design a database system for a College of Pharmacy, Faculty of Medicine of the North Indian University (NIU) located in Mussorie[2]. The faculty has research projects in various stages of development, i.e., current, pending and complete. Each project is funded by a single grant by the Indian Government. Usually, the major portion of this research grant is used to pay the salaries of research assistants and study's subjects. The various drugs and equipment used in the experiments are often provided by one or more drug companies, for example, Dr. Reddy's Pharmaceutical company or Ranbaxy Laboratories Ltd. A project studies the effects of the drug on many subjects, some of whom have unequal therapeutic regimens. Several employees of the College of Pharmacy work on each project, which is led by a principal investigator (PI). Each principal investigator may control several projects. When a study is completed, a research report is written describing the results of the study.

3. Bus Company Routes

Design a database system for managing information about routes supported by a bus company called The All India Bus Company with head office in Nagpur. Each route served by the company has a starting place and an ending place, but it can go through several intermediate stops. The company is distributed over several branches. Not all the cities where the buses stop have a branch. However, each branch must be at a city located along the bus routes. There can be multiple branches in the same city and also multiple stops in the same city. One bus is assigned by the company to one route; some routes can have multiple buses. Each bus has a driver and a conductor, who are assigned to the bus for the day.

4. Bus Company Office

Design the database for the administration and reservation office of a bus company called The All India Bus Company. Each passenger can book a seat on a given portion of the routes serviced by each bus; routes have a starting place, an ending place and several intermediate places. Passengers can specify whether they want to be in the smoking or non-smoking section. Some passengers can get on the bus even if they do not have a reservation, when some seats are left vacant. With each reservation, the last name, initials and telephone number of the passenger are stored. Sometimes, trips are not made because of bad weather conditions; in this case, passengers holding reservations are notified. At the end of the trip, the driver's assistant reports to the company the total number of tickets purchased on the bus by passengers and also report these figures to the administrative office of the branch at the route's destination.

---

2. All names used in these project descriptions are fictitious

LAB EXERCISES

1. List the properties of the relational model. For each property describe the consequences if a database system did not follow that property.
2. Map the E-R diagram (Fig. 3.23) given on the next page to relational model tables. List any problems you discover with the model and explain how to fix them.
3. Would some additional syntactical or semantic integrity help in maintaining database integrity? Try to think of situations when a database's integrity is violated and suggest integrity constraints that will prevent that violation.
4. Discuss why the relational databases became so popular in the 1980s and DBMS based on network and hierarchical models disappeared.

BIBLIOGRAPHY

For Students

A number of books listed below are easy to read for students. A fascinating account of the history of IBM's System R is available in the paper by Chamberlain et al.

For Instructors

Codd's papers and his out-of-print book (which may be downloaded from the Web) are the authoritative documents on the relational model. C. J. Date's books are also a good source of information. The 1982 book by Ullman is a somewhat advanced treatment of database systems.

Chamberlain, D., et al., "A History and Evaluation of System R", *Communications of the ACM*, Vol. 24, No. 10, 1981, pp 632-646.

Codd, E. F., "A relational model of data for large shared data banks", *Communications of the ACM*, Vol. 13, No. 6, 1970, pp 377-387.

Codd, E. F., "Relational Database: A practical foundation for productivity", *Communications of the ACM*, Vol. 25, No. 2, 1982, pp 109-117.

Codd, E. F., "Extending the relational model to capture more meaning", *ACM Transactions on Database Systems*, Vol. 4, No. 4, 1979, pp 397-434.

Codd, E. F., *The Relational Model for Database Management: Version 2*, Addison-Wesley Publishing Company, Inc, 1990. (This book is out of print now but may be downloaded from http://portal.acm.org/citation.cfm?id=77708.)

Date, C. J., *An Introduction to Database Systems*, Eighth Edition, Addison-Wesley, 2003.

Date, C. J., *Database in Depth: Relational Theory for Practitioners*, O'Reilly Media, 2005.

Maier, D., *The Theory of Relational Databases*, Computer Science Press, 1983. http://web.cecs.pdx.edu/~maier/TheoryBook/TRD.html

Ramakrishnan, R., and J. Gehrke, *Database Management Systems*, Third Edition, McGraw-Hill, 2002.

Silberchatz, A., H. Korth, and S. Sudarshan, *Database Systems Concepts*, Fifth Edition, McGraw-Hill, 2005.

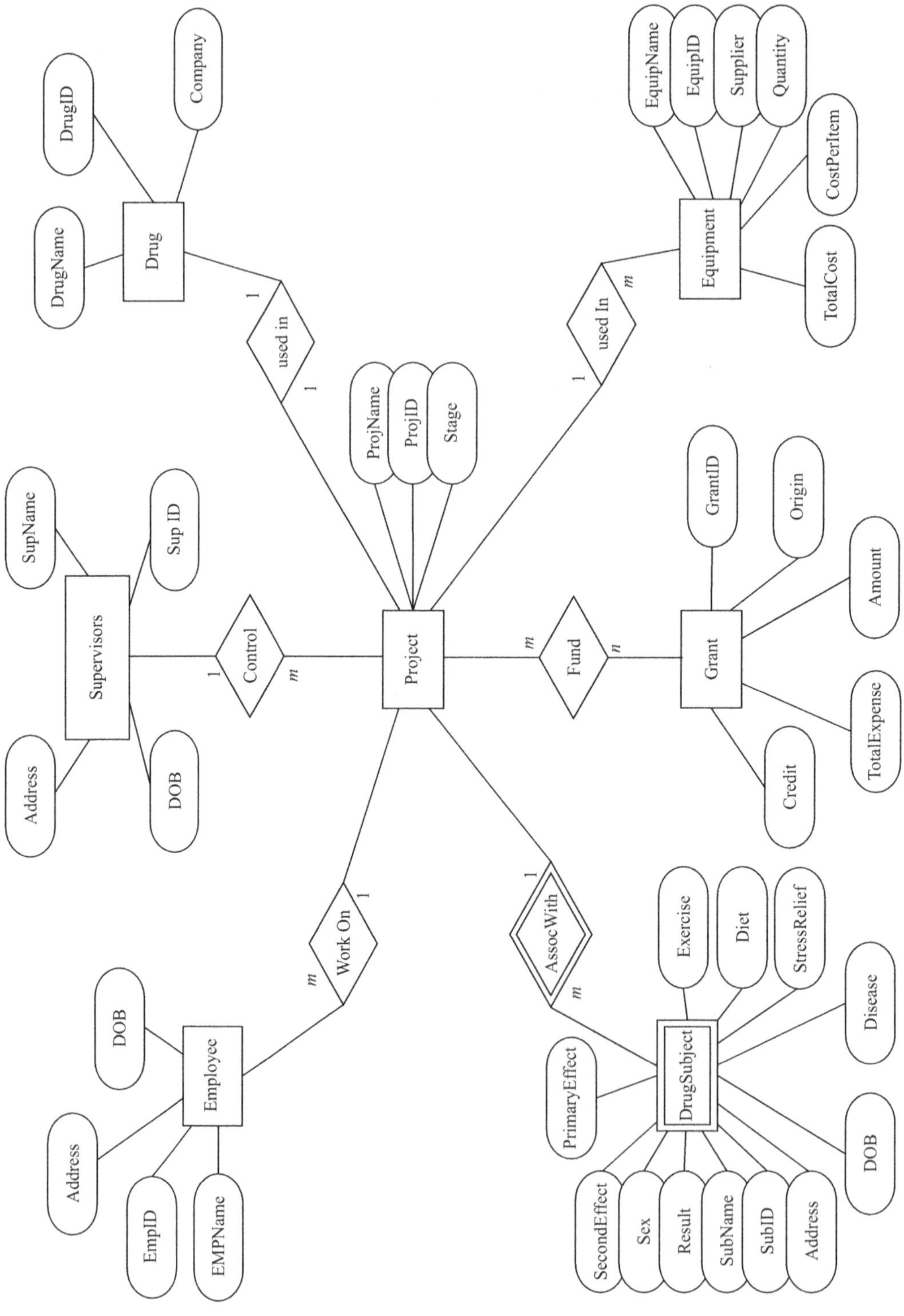
Drug
DrugName
DrugID
Company
used in
1
1
Equipment
EquipName
EquipID
Supplier
Quantity
CostPerItem
TotalCost
used In
m
1
Project
ProjName
ProjID
Stage
Supervisors
SupName
Sup ID
Address
DOB
Control
1
m
Fund
m
n
Grant
GrantID
Origin
Amount
TotalExpense
Credit
Work On
m
1
Employee
DOB
Address
EmpID
EMPName
AssocWith
1
m
DrugSubject
Exercise
Diet
StressRelief
Disease
DOB
PrimaryEffect
SecondEffect
Sex
Result
SubName
SubID
Address

Figure 3.23

Garcia-Molina, H., J. D. Ullman, and J. Widom, *Database Systems: The Complete Book*, Prentice Hall, 2002.

Kifer, M., Bernstein A., and P. M. Lewis, *Database Systems: An Application-Oriented Approach*, Second Edition, Addison-Wesley, 2006.

Ullman, J. D., *Principles of Database Systems*, Computer Science Press, 1982. (May be downloaded from http://www.filestube.com/d/database+systems+ullman)

Edgar (Ted) Codd (1923–2003)—Inventor of the Relational Model

In the 1960s and 1970s, Ted Codd worked on his theories of database management publishing his paper *A Relational Model of Data for Large Shared Data Banks* in 1970. In that paper he proposed replacing the hierarchical or navigational structure with simple tables containing rows and columns. In order for the relational model to be accepted, it had to be proved by an implementation. This was the goal of the System R project at IBM's San Jose Research Laboratory in 1973. Other pioneers who rushed to exploit Codd's relational concepts in the 1970s included Mike Stonebraker at the University of California Berkeley who developed the database system Ingres.

Ted Codd was born in England. He studied mathematics and chemistry at the Oxford University and served as a pilot in the Royal Air Force during World War II. After the war, in 1948, he moved to New York and joined IBM as a programmer. He received his doctorate in computer science from the University of Michigan. He worked for many years at the IBM's Almaden Research Center in San Jose.

Relational Algebra and Relational Calculus

4

OBJECTIVES

- Describe how information is retrieved and modified in the relational model.
- Describe relational algebra.
- Present examples of using operators used in relational algebra.
- Describe relational calculus.
- Explain tuple relational calculus (TRC) and present examples.
- Explain domain relational calculus (DRC) and present examples.
- Present foundations for SQL.
- Discuss relative advantages and disadvantages of relational algebra and relational calculus.

KEYWORDS

Relation, relational algebra, relational calculus, selection, restriction, projection, cross product, join, natural join, equi-join, division, union, intersection, difference, procedural language, declarative language, well-formed formulas, queries, tuple relational calculus, TRC, domain relational calculus, DRC, universal quantifier, existential quantifier.

I measure the progress of a community by the degree of progress which women have achieved.

B. R. Ambedkar (Author of the Indian Constitution, 1891–1956)

4.1 INTRODUCTION

Codd in 1970 presented the relational model and with it two formal languages, called relational algebra and relational calculus. Both data manipulation languages provide facility to retrieve information from a relational database. Relational algebra is a procedural language that uses certain primitive operators that take tables as inputs and produce tables as outputs. The language may be considered operational, that is, it provides a step-by-step procedure for computing the result. Each relational algebra operator is either unary or binary, that is, it performs data manipulation on one or two tables. Relational algebra is not similar to programming languages like C or C++, that is, it does not include a looping construct.

The basic relational algebra commands were introduced in the 1970 paper by Codd. These are as follows:

- SELECT
- PROJECT
- UNION
- PRODUCT
- JOIN
- DIVIDE

The relational calculus as opposed to the relational algebra is a declarative language. A statement in relational calculus essentially specifies which tuples (or their columns) are to be retrieved. Therefore relational calculus does not provide a step-by-step procedure. We consider two slightly different forms of relational calculus. These are called *Domain Relational Calculus* (DRC) and *Tuple Relational Calculus* (TRC).

This chapter is organized as follows. The next section, Section 4.2 deals with relational algebra. All relational algebra operators are explained using a number of examples. Section 4.3 deals with relational calculus. The domain relational calculus and the tuple relational calculus are explained along with a number of example queries.

4.2 RELATIONAL ALGEBRA

Database queries in relational algebra are based on specifying operations on tables. The relational algebra expressions are similar to algebraic expressions (for example, $2*a + b*c$) that we are familiar with except that we are now dealing with tables and not numbers or simple variables.

We will define a number of operations that can be applied to tables of all sizes for selecting data from a relational database. The operations include the usual set operations like union and intersection as well as operations for selecting a number of rows or one or more columns from a table.

The result of applying one or more relational operations to a set of tables (possibly one) is always a new table.

We first discuss three relational algebra operations that are sufficient for formulating a large number of useful queries. These operations are *selection, projection* and *join*. We will also discuss *Cartesian product* since it is needed in defining the join. Further relational operators are discussed later in the section.

4.2.1 Unary Relational Operator—Selection (also called Restriction)

Unary relational algebra operators operate on a single specified table and display results in table form all or some rows or column of the table.

The operation of selecting certain rows from a table is called *selection* (or *restriction*). Usually one wants to select rows that meet a specified condition, for example, players from India. Selection may then be used. It is a unary operator since it operates only on a single table.

We illustrate this simple concept by showing a table in Fig. 4.1 which has five columns labelled *A*, *B*, *C*, *D* and *E* and five rows. A selection condition (for example, attribute *C* not being equal to c_2) results in selecting three rows of the table.

A	B	C	D	E
a_1	b_1	c_2	d_1	e_1
a_2	b_2	c_1	d_1	e_1
a_3	b_1	c_2	d_2	e_2
a_4	b_1	c_1	d_3	e_3
a_5	b_1	c_3	d_1	e_4

Figure 4.1 Selection—Selecting three rows in a table

More formally, selection of a table *R* is a subset table *S* that includes all those rows in *R* that meet a condition specified by the user. The number of columns (degree) in *S* is the same as that of *R*. The number of rows (cardinality) of *S* is equal to the number of rows in *R* that meet the specified condition.

The result of applying selection to a table *R*, such that the column *A* (which may be one or more columns) has value *a* will be denoted by *R*[*A*=*a*]. Similarly, *R*[*A*>*a*] is a selection on *R* such that column *A* has values greater than *a*. A more mathematical way of writing selection is to use the notation $\sigma_{A=a}[R]$ to denote *R*[*A*=*a*][1]. More generally $\sigma_p[R]$ is used to denote a restriction on table *R* which selects rows that satisfy the condition *p*.

Let us now consider two examples of the use of the operator selection. Suppose we wish to find all the Indian players that are in the database, we do so by selecting rows in table *Player* where the value of the attribute *Country* is India. We write the selection as in Fig. 4.2.

Player [*country* = *'India'*] *or* $\sigma_{\text{country = 'India'}}[Player]$

Figure 4.2 Using SELECTION in relational algebra

1. The Greek symbol is easy to remember since the operator selection and the Greek letter sigma (σ) both start with the letter *s*. We will from time to time use Greek symbols since they are often used in advanced database textbooks but this notation may be skipped if the reader feels uncomfortable with it.

The result of applying the above selection operation to Table 3.2 *Player* is presented in Table 4.1.

Table 4.1 Result of a selection operator

PlayerID	*LName*	*FName*	*Country*	*YBorn*	*BPlace*	*FTest*
89001	Tendulkar	Sachin	India	1973	Mumbai	1989
96001	Dravid	Rahul	India	1973	Indore	1996
90002	Kumble	Anil	India	1970	Bangalore	1990
25001	Dhoni	M. S.	India	1981	Ranchi	2005
23001	Singh	Yuvraj	India	1981	Chandigarh	2003
96003	Ganguly	Saurav	India	1972	Calcutta	1996
21001	Sehwag	Virender	India	1978	Delhi	2001
98002	Singh	Harbhajan	India	1980	Jalandhar	1998
27001	Kumar	Praveen	India	1986	Meerut	NA
27002	Sharma	Ishant	India	1988	Delhi	2007

Similarly, if we wish to find out what matches have been played in Australia, we select those rows from table *Match* that have column *Team1* value equal to 'Australia' assuming that *Team1* is the home team and these matches are not being played at a neutral country. We could write it in relational algebra as in Fig. 4.3.

Match [Team1 = 'Australia'] or $\sigma_{\text{Team1} = \text{'Australia'}}$*[Match]*

Figure 4.3 Using the selection operation in relational algebra

The result of applying the selection operation in Fig. 4.3 to Table 3.1 *Match* is presented in Table 4.2 which has only two rows in it.

Table 4.2 Result of applying a selection operator to *Match*

MatchID	*Team1*	*Team2*	*Ground*	*Date*	*Winner*
2688	Australia	India	Sydney	2/3/2008	Team2
2689	Australia	India	Brisbane	4/3/2008	Team2

4.2.2 Another Unary Relational Operator—Projection

Projection is the relational algebra operation of selecting certain columns from a table *R* to form a new table *S*. For example, one may only be interested in the list of names from a table that has a number of other attributes. Projection may then be used. Like selection, projection is a unary operator that is applied to only one table.

We illustrate the concept of projection by showing the table given in Fig. 4.4 which has four columns labeled *B*, *C*, *D* and *E* and five rows. A projection of the table on attributes *C* and *E* results in selecting the two highlighted columns of the table. Note that the first and second rows in the table with two columns are duplicates.

B	C	D	E
b_1	c_1	d_1	e_1
b_2	c_1	d_1	e_1
b_1	c_2	d_2	e_2
b_1	c_1	d_3	e_3
b_1	c_3	d_1	e_4

Figure 4.4 Projection—Projecting two columns in a table

R[*A*] is a projection of *R* on *A*, *A* being a list of columns, say three columns *a*, *b* and *c* (the columns do not need to be distinct). Although the table *R* has no duplicate rows (since no table is permitted to have duplicate rows), a projection of *R* might have duplicate rows as illustrated by the projection in Fig. 4.4. The duplicate rows, if any, are removed from the result of a projection. The degree of $S = R[A]$ is equal to the number of columns in *A*. The number of rows in *S* is equal to the number of rows in *R* if no duplicates are present in *R*[*A*]. If duplicates are present then the number of rows in *S* is equal to the number of rows in *R* minus the number of duplicates removed from the result. Removal of duplicates from large tables can be computationally expensive.

A projection of *R* on columns *a, b, c* is denoted by *R*[*a,b,c*]. Some authors use $\pi_{a,b,c}[R]$ to denote the projection[2]. More generally, $\pi_s(R)$ is a projection of table *R* where *s* is a list of columns, possibly only one column.

Let us now consider a simple example. If we wish to obtain a list of names of players, we may apply the projection operator to the table *Player* on attributes *FName* and *LName*. We write this projection as in Fig. 4.5.

Player [Fname, LName] or $\pi_{\text{Fname, LName}}$ *[Player]*

Figure 4.5 Using the projection operator in relational algebra

The result of applying the projection operator as given in Fig. 4.5 to Table 3.2 *Player* would lead to the result presented in Table 4.3.

Table 4.3 The result of applying the projection in Fig. 4.5 to Table 3.2

FName	*LName*
Sachin	Tendulkar
Brian	Lara
Ricky	Ponting
Rahul	Dravid
Herschelle	Gibbs
Shane	Warne
Shaun	Pollock
Michael	Vaughan
Inzamam	Ul-Huq

Contd.

2. Once again, the Greek symbol for projection is easy to remember since the operator projection and the Greek letter pi (π) both start with the letter *p*.

Table 4.3 Contd.

FName	*LName*
Stephen	Fleming
Heath	Streak
Anil	Kumble
Gary	Kirsten
Jacques	Kallis
Chaminda	Vaas
Muthiah	Muralitharan
Daniel	Vettori
MS	Dhoni
Yuvraj	Singh
Saurav	Ganguly
Adam	Gilchrist
Andrew	Symonds
Brett	Lee
Sanath	Jayasuriya
Virender	Sehwag
Shahid	Afridi
Harbhajan	Singh
Praveen	Kumar
Ishant	Sharma

Note that in the above query we have changed the ordering of the attributes to print the names of the players as first name followed by the last name. Similarly, a list of player, last names and their player ID could be obtained by applying the projection given in Fig. 4.6 to the table *Player*, Table 3.2.

Player [PlayerID, LName] or $\pi_{\text{PlayerID, LName}}$ *[Player]*

Figure 4.6 Another example using the projection operator

The result of applying the projection operation given in Fig. 4.6 to Table 3.2 is presented in Table 4.4. To save space we only show the first 18 players, not all the 27 players.

To find the player IDs of all the players that have batted in either match in the database, we apply the projection given in Fig. 4.7 to the Table *Batting*, Table 3.3.

Batting[PID] or π_{PID} *[Batting]*

Figure 4.7 Projection applied to the *Batting* table

Table 4.4 The result of applying the projection in Fig. 4.6 to Table 3.2

PlayerID	*LName*
89001	Tendulkar
90001	Lara
95001	Ponting
96001	Dravid
96002	Gibbs
92001	Warne
95002	Pollock
99003	Vaughan
92003	Ul-Huq
94004	Fleming
93002	Streak
90002	Kumble
93003	Kirsten
91003	Kallis
94002	Vaas
92002	Muralitharan
97004	Vettori
More...	More...

The result of applying the projection given in Fig. 4.7 to Table 3.3 *Batting* is presented in Table 4.5.

We obtain Table 4.9 once the duplicate rows from the resulting table are removed. Also, it should be noted that appropriate names of the columns and tables must be used in the relational algebra expressions. The player ID is given the name *PID* in the table *Batting* to save space to fit the table on a page. Also, note that this projection cannot give us a list of player names that have batted since the table *Batting* does not include player names. We will later discuss how to obtain player names of those who batted using information from two tables, Tables 3.2 and 3.3.

It should be noted that the ordering of rows in Tables 4.7, 4.8 and 4.9 is not defined and should not be expected to be the same as displayed in Tables 3.1, 3.2 and 3.3.

Table 4.5 The result of applying the projection given in Fig. 4.7 to Table 3.3

PID
91001
94002
92002
89001
23001
25001
99002
95001
24001
99001
27001

The two unary operators, selection and projection, may be used together to first select some rows of a table and then select only some of the columns of the selected rows. We will consider such examples later in the chapter.

4.2.3 Binary Relational Operation—Cartesian Product

The *Cartesian product* (also known as the *cross product*) of any two tables R and S (of degree m and n respectively) is a table $R \times S$ of degree $m + n$. This product table has all the columns that are present in both the tables R and S and the rows in $R \times S$ are all possible combinations of each row from R combined with each row from S. The number of rows in $R \times S$ therefore is pq if p is the number of rows in S and q in R. As noted earlier, the number of columns of $R \times S$ is $m + n$ if m and n are the number of columns in R and S respectively.

Consider the Cartesian product of the tables *Player* and *Batting*. We first reproduce the schema for the two tables below:

Player(PlayerID, LName, FName, Country, YBorn, BPlace, FTest)
Batting(MatchID, PID, Order, HOut, FOW, NRuns, Mts, NBalls, Fours, Sixes).

The product will have the following attributes:

Product(PlayerID, LName, FName, Country, YBorn, BPlace, FTest, MatchID, PID, Order, HOut, FOW, NRuns, Mts, NBalls, Fours, Sixes)

We cannot show what this table looks like since the number of columns is too large to fit on a page. The number of rows is also quite large. How many rows does the product have? Therefore, we will use simpler relations that have only a few columns and only a few rows as shown in Tables 4.6, 4.7 and 4.8. These tables have been given the names *Player2*, *Batting2* and *Bowling2* to differentiate them from *Player*, *Batting* and *Bowling* in Tables 3.3, 3.4 and 3.5.

Table 4.6 The relation *Player2*

PlayerID	*LName*	*FName*
89001	Tendulkar	Sachin
24001	Symonds	Andrew
99001	Lee	Brett
25001	Dhoni	MS

Table 4.7 The relation *Batting2*

MID	*PID*	*Order*	*NRuns*
2689	89001	2	91
2689	99001	8	7
2689	24001	5	42
2755	25001	5	71

Table 4.8 The relation *Bowling2*

MatchID	*PID*	*NWickets*
2689	99001	1
2755	91001	0
2689	24001	1

Table 4.9 shows the Cartesian product of Tables 4.6 and 4.7.

Table 4.9 Cartesian product of tables *Player2* and *Batting2*

PlayerID	*LName*	*FName*	*MID*	*PID*	*Order*	*NRuns*
89001	**Tendulkar**	**Sachin**	**2689**	**89001**	**2**	**91**
24001	Symonds	Andrew	2689	89001	2	91
99001	Lee	Brett	2689	89001	2	91
25001	Dhoni	MS	2689	89001	2	91
89001	Tendulkar	Sachin	2689	99001	8	7
24001	Symonds	Andrew	2689	99001	8	7
99001	**Lee**	**Brett**	**2689**	**99001**	**8**	**7**
25001	Dhoni	MS	2689	99001	8	7
89001	Tendulkar	Sachin	2689	24001	5	42
24001	**Symonds**	**Andrew**	**2689**	**24001**	**5**	**42**
99001	Lee	Brett	2689	24001	5	42
25001	Dhoni	MS	2689	24001	5	42
89001	Tendulkar	Sachin	2755	25001	5	71
24001	Symonds	Andrew	2755	25001	5	71
99001	Lee	Brett	2755	25001	5	71
25001	**Dhoni**	**MS**	**2755**	**25001**	**5**	**71**

The number of columns of the Cartesian product in Table 4.13 is 7 (=3 + 4) and the number of rows is 16 (4 × 4). The product may not appear to be a terribly useful operator to the reader since it combines many rows that have no association with each other, except the four rows highlighted. We will now show that a Cartesian product followed by a selection operation that selects the highlighted rows is a very important operator called the *join*. This is discussed below.

4.2.4 Binary Relational Operator—Join

The join operator may be considered as the most powerful of the relational algebra operations. The join of two related tables *R* and *S* ($R \bowtie S$) is a restriction of their Cartesian product $R \times S$ such that a specified condition is met. The result is a single table. The join is normally defined on a column *a* of table *R* and a column *b* of table *S*, such that the attributes are from the same domain and are therefore related. The specified condition (called the *join condition* or *join predicate*) is a condition on columns *R.a* and *S.b*[3].

The most commonly needed join is the join in which the specified condition is equality of the two columns ($R.a = S.b$) in $R \times S$. This join is called an *equi-join*. The rows highlighted in Table 4.9 are the rows that

3. The terminology *R.x* is used to denote column *x* of table *R*.

form the equi-join. Since the equi-join by definition has two equal columns one of these may be removed by applying the projection operator. The resulting table is called the *natural join*.

Equi-Join

As noted earlier, the number of columns in the equi-join is $m+n$ if the degrees of R and S are m and n respectively. The degree of the natural join is $m + n - 1$ since one column has been removed from the equi-join. The number of rows in the result table of the join depends on the number of rows that satisfy the join condition.

To illustrate equi-join and natural join, we consider the tables *Player2* and *Batting2* (Tables 4.10 and 4.11). There is an implicit association between the two tables since the table *Player2* provides personal information about players while *Batting2* provides information about their batting. One may be wondering why the two tables are separate. The reason becomes clear if we consider what would happen when the two tables are combined. The personal information of a player is now repeated for each *Batting* (and *Bowling*) row for the player. This is not desirable not only because it wastes storage. This is discussed in more detail in Chapter 6.

The Cartesian product of *Player2* and *Batting2* has two columns that are from the domain *PlayerID*. If the column names in the two tables were the same (they are not in this case), we would need to give one of them a different name in the Cartesian product since each column name in a table must be unique.

If we look at Table 4.9, we find that the Cartesian product table has many rows that are unlikely to be of any use. The relationship between the two Tables 4.6 and 4.7 is based on the two columns *PlayerID* and *PID* and therefore all the rows in the Cartesian product table that do not have the same values of these two columns are of little use.

If we apply a selection to the Table 4.9 such that the values of the two attributes *PlayerID* and *PID* (the highlighted columns) are the same, we obtain Table 4.10.

Table 4.10 Equi-join of tables *Player2* and *Batting2*

PlayerID	*LName*	*FName*	*MID*	***PID***	*Order*	*NRuns*
89001	Tendulkar	Sachin	2689	**89001**	2	91
99001	Lee	Brett	2689	**99001**	8	7
24001	Symonds	Andrew	2689	**24001**	5	42
25001	Dhoni	MS	2755	**25001**	5	71

Note that players will not appear in the above table if they have not batted in a match in our database. Also a player appearing in the *Batting2* table and not in the *Player2* table (which should not normally happen) will also not appear in the equi-join table.

Table 4.10 is an *equi-join* since it has been obtained from the Cartesian product by applying the restriction that the values of the two columns that are from the same domain be equal. These are the columns on which the tables are said to be joined. Note that a player may appear in Table 4.6 *Player2* but may not appear in the join Table 4.10 if he did not have an entry in Table 4.7 *Batting2*.

Natural Join

If we now apply a projection to Table 4.10 so that one of the two identical columns is removed, the resulting table is the *natural join* of the Table 4.6 and Table 4.7. The natural join is shown in Table 4.11.

Table 4.11 Natural join of tables *Player2* and *Batting2*

PlayerID	*LName*	*FName*	*MID*	*Order*	*NRuns*
89001	Tendulkar	Sachin	2689	2	91
99001	Lee	Brett	2689	8	7
24001	Symonds	Andrew	2689	5	42
25001	Dhoni	MS	2755	5	71

Table 4.11 provides the names and the runs scored in each match by the players in Table 4.6 and 4.7.

One might be wondering if a natural join is possible between two tables when the tables have more than one column in common. The formal definition of natural join does in fact include that possibility. The natural join may be defined as follows.

Definition—Natural Join

The natural join of two tables R and S (written as R $\bowtie$ S) is obtained by applying a selection and a projection to the Cartesian product R × S as follows:

1. *For each column 'a' that is common to both tables R and S, we select rows that satisfy the condition R.a = S.a.*
2. *For each column 'a' that is common to both tables R and S, we project out the column S.a. Therefore if there are 'm' columns common to both tables, 'm' duplicate columns are removed from the Cartesian product.*

4.2.5 Join on More Than One Column

To illustrate the natural join of tables that have more than one common column, we consider the tables *Batting2* and *Bowling2*. These two tables have two columns in common, namely the match ID and the player ID. What would be the meaning of joining *Batting* and *Bowling* requiring that both the columns be equal?

We first present the Cartesian product of the two relations (Tables 4.7 and 4.8) in Table 4.12. Note that we have to use the column name *BPID* since duplicate column names are not allowed.

To obtain the natural join we first find the equi-join by deleting all the rows in which the match IDs and player IDs do not match. The highlighted rows are the only rows where both columns match and we obtain Table 4.13 by applying a selection to obtain the highlighted two rows. All other rows in the table are deleted as a result of the equi-join condition.

Table 4.12 Cartesian product of *Batting2* and *Bowling2*

MID	*PID*	*Order*	*NRuns*	*MatchID*	*BPID*	*NWickets*
2689	89001	2	91	2689	99001	1
2689	**99001**	**8**	**7**	**2689**	**99001**	**1**
2689	24001	5	42	2689	99001	1
2755	25001	5	71	2689	99001	1
2689	89001	2	91	2755	91001	0
2689	99001	8	7	2755	91001	0
2689	24001	5	42	2755	91001	0
2755	25001	5	71	2755	91001	0
2689	89001	2	91	2689	24001	1
2689	99001	8	7	2689	24001	1
2689	**24001**	**5**	**42**	**2689**	**24001**	**1**
2755	25001	5	71	2689	24001	1

Table 4.13 Equi-join of the tables *Bowling2* and *Batting2* on two common attributes

MID	***PID***	*Order*	*NRuns*	***MatchID***	***BPID***	*NWickets*
2689	**99001**	8	7	**2689**	**99001**	1
2689	**24001**	5	42	**2689**	**24001**	1

To obtain the natural join, the two duplicate columns that are highlighted in Table 4.13 are removed from the table and we obtain Table 4.14 as the result:

Table 4.14 Natural join of the tables *Bowling2* and *Batting2* on two common attributes

MID	*PID*	*Order*	*NRuns*	*NWickets*
2689	99001	8	7	1
2689	24001	5	42	1

So what does Table 4.14 tell us?

Essentially this table provides us with information for those players that have both batted and bowled in a particular ODI match. The table provides us with their batting performance as well as their bowling performance. If a player only bowled in a match and did not bat in that match or only batted but did not bowl then that player would not appear in this table.

Let us summarize. We obtained the natural join by taking the Cartesian product and then removing those rows that did not have matching values of the common columns resulting in an equi-join followed by removal of the duplicate attributes. The result is called the natural join.

We repeat that an equi-join or a natural join of two matching tables is possible only if both tables have one or more columns that are from the same domains. It would make no sense to have an equi-join on number of wickets in *Bowling2* with batting order in *Batting2*, even if both columns are integers.

Before concluding this discussion of the operation join, we note that when a join is needed to process a query, the procedure used is much more efficient than that which we have used to illustrate the join above in tables 4.10 to 4.14. A simple and more efficient join algorithm involves the following steps:

1. Take the first row from the first table.
2. Search the second table for a row that matches the value of the column on which the tables are being joined in the first table. When a match is found, the two rows are put together to form a row of the join table.
3. The search of the second table is continued for further matches till the second table is exhausted.
4. Now, the next row of the first table is selected and steps 2 and 3 are carried out. This process is continued until the first table is exhausted.

This algorithm is called the *nested scan* method.

In the above algorithm, we have assumed that we are forming an equi-join. A number of other join algorithms are available to process equi-joins more efficiently. These algorithms will be discussed in Chapter 7.

As noted earlier, a major criticism of the relational model for several years was that systems based on the model would always be inefficient because of the high cost of performing joins. In recent years it has been shown that joins can be computed efficiently, particularly so when indexes are available. This has resulted in a number of commercial relational DBMS products that have been shown to have very good performance.

In addition to the operators that we have discussed, there are a number of other relational operators. These are discussed now.

4.2.6 Theta Join

A join of R and S with join condition $a = b$ or $a < b$ is usually written as in Fig. 4.8.

$$R[a = b]S \text{ or } R[a < b]S$$

Figure 4.8 Specifying the join condition

Let *theta* be one of the operators <>, <, >, ≥, ≤. We may now define a more general concept of *theta-join* of table R (on attribute a) and table S (on attribute b). The theta-join is a restriction on the Cartesian product of R and S such that the condition $a\ \theta\ b$ is satisfied where θ is one of the above operations. We do not consider theta join any further.

4.2.7 Outer Join

The join operations presented so far only deal with tuples from the two tables that match the join condition. The remaining tuples from both tables are eliminated in computing the join although these tuples can often have useful information. For example, if we are joining the *Player* table with the *Batting* table using *PID* equality as the joining condition then a player that has never batted will not be included in the join. This might be useful information in some situations. For instance, if a student table is joined with an enrolment table, we may be interested in finding out the names of students who have not enrolled. In joining enrolment with courses, we may be interested in finding names of courses that have no enrolments.

There are a number of variants of the outer join. As noted above, the join of the *Player* table with the *Batting* table using *PlayerID* equality as the joining condition does not include the players that have never batted. A join including this information is called the *left outer join*. If the join also included batting information on players that batted but were not in the *Player* table (normally there should be no such rows in *Batting*) then the join is called a full outer join. If the join did not include information about players that did not bat but included information about players that batted but were not in the *Player* table then the join is called a *right outer join*.

We leave it as an exercise to find the left outer join of *Player2* and *Batting2*. Outer join is discussed again in Chapter 5 with its implementation in SQL.

4.2.8 Set Operations

Set Union

The union operator is the usual set union of two tables *R* and *S* which are union-compatible. Two tables are called union-compatible if they are of the same degree *m* and are written as

$$R(a_1, a_2,.. a_m)$$
$$S(b_2, b_2, \ldots b_m)$$

For each i ($i = 1, 2, \ldots m$), a_i and b_i must have compatible domains (e.g., either both are integers or both are strings of the same length). The number of columns in the union of *R* and *S*, $R \cup S$, is the same as that of *R* and *S* and the number of rows is $a + b$ if *a* and *b* are the number of rows in *R* and *S* respectively and there are no duplicate rows in *R* and *S*. $R \cup S$ therefore consists of all rows that are either in *R* or *S* or common in both *R* and *S*. As an example, consider two tables, Table 4.15 and Table 4.16, given below obtained by applying projection to the tables *Batting* (Table 3.3) and *Bowling* (Table 3.4). Table 4.15 *Batting3* gives the columns *MatchID* and *PID* from the table *Batting* while the projection on *Bowling* results in *Bowling3* with columns *MatchID* and *PID* in Table 4.16.

Table 4.15 *Batting3* obtained by projection of the Table 3.3 *Batting*

MatchID	*PID*
2755	23001
2755	25001
2755	91001
2755	94002
2755	92002
2689	89001
2689	23001
2689	25001
2689	99002
2689	95001
2689	24001
2689	99001
2689	27001
2755	27001

If we were interested in finding all the players who have batted or bowled or both, we can take a union of the two tables *Batting3* and *Bowling3* (Tables 4.15 and 4.16) and obtain the result in Table 4.17.

There are many duplicates in Table 4.17 and the duplicate pairs have been highlighted in the table and therefore the table does not satisfy the definition of a relation. We have not removed duplicates from the above union to illustrate that duplicates may occur after union. The rows have been sorted to make it easier

Table 4.16 *Bowling3* obtained by projection of the Table 3.4 *Bowling*

MatchID	*PID*
2689	99001
2689	24001
2689	23001
2755	94002
2755	92002
2755	91001
2755	23001

to identify duplicates which must be removed if the result is to satisfy the properties of a relation. There are 14 duplicate rows and therefore seven of them need to be removed.

A projection of the above table, Table 4.17, on attribute *PID* now provides the list of players that have either batted or bowled or both in the matches in the database. The duplicates have been removed and the list in Table 4.18 has been sorted. Table 4.18 therefore has only 11 rows after removing duplicate rows for players 23001, 24001, 99001, 91001, 92002 and 94002.

Table 4.17 Union of Tables 4.15 and 4.16

MatchID	*PID*
2689	**23001**
2689	**23001**
2689	**24001**
2689	**24001**
2689	25001
2689	27001
2689	89001
2689	95001
2689	**99001**
2689	**99001**
2689	99002
2755	**23001**
2755	**23001**
2755	25001
2755	27001
2755	**91001**
2755	**91001**
2755	**92002**
2755	**92002**
2755	**94002**
2755	**94002**

4.2.9 Set Intersection

The intersection relational operator is the usual set intersection of two tables *R* and *S* which are union-compatible. The result of the intersection is a table consisting of all the rows that are common to both tables *R* and *S*. The number of columns in the intersection $R \cap S$ is the same as that of *R* and *S* and the number of rows in the intersection is equal to the number of rows common to both *R* and *S*.

As an example, let us again consider the earlier example of Tables 4.15 and 4.16, *Batting3* and *Bowling3*. Suppose now that we wish to find those players that bowled as well as batted in the same matches. One way is to formulate the query would be to find the intersection of the two tables. The intersection is formulated in Fig. 4.9.

Table 4.18 Projection of Table 4.17 which was a union of two tables

PID
23001
24001
25001
27001
89001
91001
92002
94002
95001
99001
99002

Bowling3 $\cap$ *Batting3*

Figure 4.9 Intersection of the tables *Batting3* and *Bowling3*

The result of the intersection is a table with two columns (*MatchID, PlayerID*) for the players that are common to both tables *Bowling3* and *Batting3*, and hence have batted and bowled in the same match. The result of the intersection is given in Table 4.19.

Table 4.19 Result of the intersection operation in Fig. 4.9

MatchID	*PID*
2689	99001
2689	24001
2689	23001
2755	94002
2755	92002
2755	91001
2755	23001

Note that Table 4.19 is the same as Table 4.16 since every player that bowled in that table also batted in Table 4.15.

Furthermore, we should note that we could not take an intersection of the tables *Batting2* and *Bowling2* (Tables 4.7 and 4.8) since the number of columns in those two tables are not the same.

4.2.10 Set Difference

The difference operator when applied to two tables *R* and *S* (written as $R - S$) results in a table that consists of all the rows in the first table that are not also in the second table. If the intersection of *R* and *S* is null then $R - S = R$, otherwise $R - S = R - R \cap S$, that is, $R - S$ is obtained by removing from *R* the rows that are also in *S*. The number of columns in $R - S$ is the same as that of *R* and *S* and the number of rows in the intersection is equal to the number of rows of *R* minus the number of rows in the intersection $R \cap S$.

Batting3 – *Bowling3*

Figure 4.10 Difference of two tables

We again consider the example of the two Tables 4.15 and 4.16. If we want to find the players that batted in a match but did not bowl in it, we could formulate the query by the difference as presented in Fig. 4.10.

The result given in Table 4.20 is obtained when we take the difference of Tables 4.15 and 4.16.

Table 4.20 Difference of the Tables 4.15 and 4.16, *Batting3* and *Bowling3*

MatchID	*PID*
2689	25001
2689	27001
2689	89001
2689	95001
2689	99002
2755	25001
2755	27001

Let us now look at the meaning of the difference *Bowling3*—*Batting3*. This difference would be a table that consists of all the rows in the first table that are not also in the second table. Therefore it is the list of players that have bawled but not batted in a match. For Tables 4.15 and 4.16, the difference *Bowling3* – *Batting3* is null since there are no bowlers in Table 4.16 that have not also batted.

4.2.11 Division[4]

The concept of division is related to the concept of Cartesian product in that $R \times S$ divided by *S* yields *R*. Division therefore is essentially an inverse of Cartesian product in the same way as arithmetic division is the inverse of multiplication.

4. Part of this section may be omitted without loss of continuity.

Example

Before discussing the division operator further, we present an example.

Consider a table R and a table S as given in Tables 4.21 and 4.22.

To simplify our example, we have chosen a very simple table S that consists of only two rows as given in Table 4.22.

Table 4.21 The table *R*

MatchID	*PID*
2755	23001
2755	25001
2755	91001
2755	94002
2755	92002
2689	89001
2689	23001
2689	25001
2689	99002
2689	95001
2689	24001
2689	99001
2689	27001
2755	27001

Table 4.22 The table *S*

PID
99001
27001

The result of dividing relation R by relation S is given below in Table 4.23.

Table 4.23 gives the match IDs (in this case, only one) in which both players listed in Table 4.22 have played. That is the function of the division operator.

We first define division for a simple case when a table R has only two columns and the table S has only one column. Let the domain of the second column of R be the same as of the column of S. The division of R by S, or R/S is then a table with only one column that has the same domain as the first column of R, such that each row in R/S occurs in R concatenated with every row of S.

Table 4.23 The result of dividing table *R* by table *S*

MatchID
2689

When the tables R and S are of degree greater than 2, division can be defined similarly. For example, if R was $R(a_1, a_2, \dots a_n, b_1, b_2, \dots b_n)$ and S was $S(b_1, b_2, \dots b_n)$ then R/S would be a table $T(a_1, a_2, \dots a_n)$ such that R had at least all rows that $T \times S$ would have. We may write R as having columns $R[A, B]$ and S having column B only where A and B each could consist of more than one column.

Finding those values of attribute A that appear with each value of B in S is not directly possible in relational algebra because relational algebra does not have a direct divide operator. Therefore the division algorithm involves finding values of attribute A in R that do not appear with all values of B in S. This is complex but is possible as shown below. R divided by S is then given by a relation T given the relational algebra expression in Fig. 4.11.

$$T = R\,[A] - ((R\,[A] \times S) - R)\,[A]$$

Figure 4.11 Relational algebra expression for division

Let us now explain what the above difficult to understand expression means. Before the explanation, we repeat that $R[A,B]/S[B]$ is a table $T[A]$ such that the relation R includes each value of A in T with every value of B in the table S. How does the expression in Fig. 4.11 find those values of A? We will use a step-by-step description of the expression in Fig. 4.11.

1. We first find a table that has each value of attribute A that exist in R appearing with every value of attribute B that exists in S. This can be done by first finding all values of A in R which is $R[A]$ and then computing $R[A] \times S$, the Cartesian product of $R[A]$ and S. The product has two columns, A and B, same two columns as R does, with each value of column A in R combined with every value of column B in S.
2. We now find the values of attribute A that do not appear with each value of attribute B in S. This can be done by using the product relation found above (the product has each value of column A in R combined with every value of column B in S) and subtract the relation R from it. That means we find $R[A] \times S - R$ which is a table that has only those rows that are in the Cartesian product but not in R. In other words, these are the rows that are not in R because the A value in each of these rows does not appear with each value of B that appears in S.
3. Carry out a projection to find the values of attributes A that do not appear with every value of attributes B in S. This is simply done by taking the projection $(R[A] \times S - R)[A]$ which is a table with only one column, A. It only has those values of column A that are present in R but which do not appear with every value of column B in S.
4. Find the result of the division. To obtain the result we subtract the values of A found above from values of A in R since that gives us the values of A that do appear with every value of B in S. Therefore $R[A] - (R[A] \times S - R)[A]$ are the values of column A that are present in R and each of which appears with every value of B in S. Hence this is the result of dividing R by S.

Let us now again consider the tables R and S given in Tables 4.21 and 4.22 above.

We now illustrate how the formula $T = R[A] - ((R[A] \times S) - R)[A]$ is used in computing the division. $R[A]$ is given in Table 4.24. All the duplicates have been removed. There are only two ODI matches in R.

Table 4.24 The table $R[A]$

MatchID
2755
2689

Now the Cartesian product $R[A] \times S$ is given in Table 4.25. This table shows what R would look like if all the players in S had played in all the matches in R.

Now $(R[A] \times S - R)$ is given by Table 4.26. These are rows that are in the product $R[A] \times S$ but not in R. That is, these rows show the matches in which players in S did not play. There is only one such row in this table.

Table 4.25 The table $R[A] \times S$

MatchID	*PID*
2755	99001
2689	99001
2755	27001
2689	27001

Now we take the projection of Table 4.26 on *MatchID* and subtract it from column A of R. This gives us the result of the division.

The division R/S is given by $R[A] - (R[A] \times S - R)[A]$ which is now given by Table 4.27.

Table 4.26 The table $R[A] \times S - R$

MatchID	*PID*
2755	99001

Table 4.27 The table $R/S = T = R[A] - (R[A] \times S - R)[A]$

MatchID
2689

This is the result of the division. It is a list of all matches that the players in *S* given in Table 4.22 have played together. In this case, for simplicity, Table 4.22 had only two players.

We note that $R/S = T$ does not imply that $S \times T = R$, since *R* could well include other rows. These rows are discarded in the same way as the remainder is discarded in the integer division.

The division of *R* by *S* where the attributes *x* in *R* and *y* in *S* are union-compatible is written as in Fig. 4.12.

R [x / y] S

Figure 4.12 Division of *R* by *S* on attributes *x* and *y*

If the division also involves a projection operator as is often necessary, then it may be written as given in Fig. 4.13.

R [Ax] [x / y] S[y]

Figure 4.13 Division involving projections

This concludes our discussions of relational algebra operators.

The relational algebra described above does not include capabilities like counting and summing. Such capabilities are obviously needed in a practical system. They are included in the commercial language SQL which is discussed in the next chapter.

4.3 RELATIONAL ALGEBRA QUERIES

We now present a number of queries on the cricket database presented in Tables 3.1 to 3.4. The queries range from very simple to quite complex and have been formulated using relational algebra that we have discussed.

4.3.1 Only Projection

- (*A*1) Find the match IDs of matches that do have some bowling.
  This is a simple query that only involves a projection on table *Bowling*. It is formulated in Fig. 4.14.

Bowling[MatchID]

Figure 4.14 Relational algebra formulation for query *A*6

The result is given in Table 4.28. Note that all duplicates have been removed.

Table 4.28 Result of query *A*1 - Match IDs of matches that do have some bowling

MatchID
2689
2755

4.3.2 Selection combined with Projection

- (*A*2) Find the names of all players who played their first test after 2000.

In relational algebra notation, the query may be written as in Fig. 4.15[5]

Player[Fname, LName][FTest > 2000] or $\pi_{Fname,\, LName}(\sigma_{FTest>2000}[Player])$

Figure 4.15 Relational Algebra for query *A*2

Note that the query in Fig. 4.15 involves a projection which projects the result to display the first and last name of the selected players. Before the projection a selection is carried out which selects the players who played their first test after 2000. Clearly the projection cannot be done before the selection because the projection would then have discarded the FTest column.

The result of query in Fig. 4.15 is given in Table 4.29.

Table 4.29 Result of the projection in query *A*2

FName	*LName*
MS	Dhoni
Yuvraj	Singh
Andrew	Symonds
Virender	Sehwag
Ishant	Sharma

- (*A*3) Find the player IDs of all players who batted in the match 2755.

This query involves a selection and a projection to be applied to the table *Batting*. We carry out the selection first to find all players that have batted in match 2755 and then carry out the projection to get their IDs. The projection could not be carried out before the selection since the *MID* column will then be lost in projection and we could not apply selection.

The query may be written as given in Fig. 4.16.

Batting[MatchID = '2755'][PID]

Figure 4.16 Relational algebra formula for query *A*3

The result of relational algebra operation in Fig. 4.16 is given in Table 4.30.

Table 4.30 Result of the selection and projection in query *A*3

PID
23001
25001
91001
94002
92002
27001

4.3.3 Using the Join of Two Tables

- (*A*4) Find the names of all players who batted in match 2755.

This is a more complex query since it involves information that cannot be accessed without looking at two tables since the table *Batting* has the batting information and the table *Player* has information about players' names. To answer the query, we carry out a natural join of the tables *Player* and *Batting* on the attribute *PlayerID* and then apply selection *MatchID* = 2755. This is followed by a projection on attributes *FName* and *LName*.

In relational algebra notation, we may write the above query as in Fig. 4.17.

We are using the symbol $\bowtie$ to indicate the natural join operator. The result of the query posed in Fig. 4.17 is given in Table 4.31.

5. The Greek symbol notation for relational algebra queries are only used for some selected queries.

(Player [PlayerID = PID] Batting) [MatchID = '2755'] [Fname, LName]
or $\pi_{Fname,\ Lname}$ [$\sigma_{MatchID='2755'}$(Player ⋈ Batting)]

Figure 4.17 Relational algebra expression for query *A*4

Table 4.31 Result of query *A*4—Names of all players who batted in match 2755

FName	*LName*
Chaminda	Vaas
Muthiah	Muralitharan
MS	Dhoni
Yuvraj	Singh
Sanath	Jayasuriya
Praveen	Kumar

These are the names of players whose player IDs were in Table 4.30.

4.3.4 Using Joins of Three Tables

- (*A*5) Find the ground names and dates of all matches in which any player with last name Dhoni has batted.

  This query is even more complex since it must involve the three tables *Match*, *Player* and *Batting*. The player name information is in table *Player*, the batting information is in table *Batting* and the ground names are available in table *Match*. One approach to formulating this query is to join *Player* and *Batting* on attribute *PlayerID* and then join the resulting table with table *Match* on the attribute *MatchID*. We then apply a selection that the player name is Dhoni and then take the projection to find names of matches. We assume that the attributes *Ground* and *Date* provide the information required. In relational algebra, the query may be written as in Fig. 4.18.

(Player ⋈ Batting) ⋈ Match) [LName = 'Dhoni'] [Ground, Date]

Figure 4.18 Relational algebra formula for query *A*5

The result of query formulated in Fig. 4.18 is given in Table 4.32.

Table 4.32 Result of query *A*5—Ground names and dates of all matches in which Dhoni has batted

Ground	*Date*
Brisbane	4/3/2008
Colombo	27/8/2008

4.3.5 Using Difference

- (*A*6) Find the player IDs of all Indian players who have not batted in any match.

  Since *Batting*[*PID*] is the list of players that have batted in one or more of the matches, the difference between *Player*[*PlayerID*] of Indian players and *Batting*[*PID*] is the list of Indian players that have not batted in any match in the database because the difference consists of all the rows in the first table that are not also in the second table.

  The above query may therefore be formulated as follows in Fig. 4.19.

(Player[Country = 'India']) [PlayerID] – Batting [PID] or

$\pi_{PlayerID}[\sigma_{Country=\text{india}}\, Player] - \sigma_{\text{PID}}[Batting)]$

Figure 4.19 Relational algebra expression for query *A6*

Note that the selection is done first in the query in Fig. 4.19.

We are only considering information in Tables 3.2 and 3.3 which include only part of the information of the two ODI matches. For example, Harbhajan Singh's ID is not in the result table below although he did bat in match 2755.

The result is given in Table 4.33.

Table 4.33 Result of query *A6*—Player IDs of Indian players who have not batted in any match

PlayerID
96001
90001
96003
21001
98002
27002

- (*A*7) Find the player IDs of players who have bowled only in match 2755.

  To find players who have bowled only in match 2755 we must ensure they have not bowled in any other match in our very small database. Therefore, the query involves finding the difference between the set of players who have bowled in match 2755 and those who have bowled in matches other than 2755. Any player who has bowled in 2755 as well as other matches will appear in both sets and will therefore not appear in the difference.

Bowling[MatchID = '2755'] [PID] – Bowling[MatchID <> '2755'] [PID]

Figure 4.20 Relational algebra expression for query *A7*

The result of query posed in Fig. 4.20 is given in Table 4.34.

Table 4.34 Result of query *A7*—Player IDs of players who have bowled only in match 2755

PID
94002
92002
91001
23001

- (*A*8) Find the match IDs of matches that include all Indian players in our player table that were born after 1985.

  We first find the list of all Indian players born after 1985 by applying a restriction and a projection to the table *Player*. Then we find a list of all player IDs and match IDs for all players that have batted and divide that list by the list of Indian players born after 1985 in the database. The result of the division will be those matches that had all Indian players batting in them.

Batting [PID, MatchID] / (Player[Country = 'India'] ^ Yborn > 1985] [PlayerID])
or $\pi_{PID,\ MatchID}[Batting]/\pi_{PlayerID}\ (\sigma_{Country\ =\ \text{'India'}}[Player])$

Figure 4.21 Relational algebra expression for query A8

The result is given in Table 4.35.

Table 4.35 Result of query *A8*—Match IDs of matches that include Indian players born after 1985

MatchID
2689
2755

The above queries would have given the reader a flavour of how relational algebra can be used to answer user queries. We would like to note that the formulations presented above are not the only possible formulations for the queries that we had. A query may often be formulated in more than one way.

A question that often arises at this point is, are there better (that is, more efficient) sequences of operations than those listed above to answer the queries? For example, in query *A*3 above, could we carry out the restriction on the table *Player* before the join? This is clearly an important question but we will not deal with it here. There are usually a number of different sequences that may be used to process a query. Some of these sequences would obviously be more efficient than others. This topic is presented in detail in Chapter 7 on query optimization.

Relational algebra is like the assembler programming language. Just as there are many higher level programming languages like C++, there are other relational query languages as well. We discuss relational calculus next since this was another language proposed by E. F. Codd.

4.4 RELATIONAL CALCULUS[6]

Relational algebra provides a collection of operators and a relational algebra expression explicitly states what operations are to be done first and followed by other operations, and so on. Relational algebra, therefore provides a procedural language that can be used in specifying a sequence of operations that ought to be used in obtaining the result that the user wants. Algebra is thus like a procedural programming language where a program written in the language clearly provides a sequence of instructions that the machine follows to obtain the result. In contrast, relational calculus involves specifying conditions (predicates) that the result must satisfy. Relational calculus, therefore is a nonprocedural language for defining the table of information that the user wants to retrieve. The commercial query language SQL is also a nonprocedural language based on relational calculus.

We will briefly discuss how to define conditions using predicate calculus since it provides the basis for relational calculus. Predicate calculus is a powerful technique for logical reasoning. To introduce it, we need to discuss propositional logic first. The reader need not worry about terms like 'predicate calculus' or 'propositional logic' since they are simple concepts that are explained ahead. The background given in the next few pages can be skipped by readers not interested in the background.

6. The first part of this section may be skipped without any loss of continuity.

4.4.1 Propositions

A proposition is just a statement. It could be 'Tendulkar has batted in match 2755' or 'Shane Warne was born in Melbourne'. These are atomic propositions and may be denoted by symbols like *A* and *B* and their value is either true or false. Compound propositions contain two or more atomic propositions.

A compound proposition with two components may be of the type (*A* AND *B*) or it may be of the type (*A* OR *B*). Such propositions are called *formulas*. Their truth depends on the truth values of their components. When a sequence of propositions is joined by ANDs (e.g., *A* AND *B* AND *C*) we call it a *conjunction* of propositions and the conjunction is true only if all atomic propositions are true. When a sequence of propositions is joined by ORs (e.g., *A* OR *B* OR *C*), we call it a *disjunction* of propositions. The disjunction is true when at least one of the atomic propositions is true and false only when all the propositions are false.

Since we are dealing with propositions that have values true or false, the theorems of Boolean algebra apply. We assume the reader is familiar with, for example, De Morgan's Laws which are given in Fig. 4.22.

NOT (*A* AND *B*) = (NOT *A*) OR (NOT *B*)
NOT (*A* OR *B*) = (NOT *A*) AND (NOT *B*)

Figure 4.22 De Morgan's Laws

Consider the first expression. (*A* AND *B*) is true only if *A* and *B* both are true. It is false if either *A* or *B* is false or both *A* and *B* are false. The opposite of (*A* AND *B*), therefore is false only if (*A* AND *B*) is true which implies that *A* and *B* both are true or both (NOT *A*) as well as (NOT *B*) are false. We can similarly explain the second equation.

4.4.2 The Implies Operator

We now consider formulas that have the form 'if *A* then *B*'. The formula specifies that *B* must be true if *A* is. It does not say anything about the value of *B* if *A* is false. The truth table for 'if *A* then *B*' is

Table 4.36 Truth table for 'if *A* then *B*'

A	*B*	*If A then B*
T	T	T
T	F	F
F	T	T
F	F	T

It can be shown that *if A then B* is equivalent to *(not A) or B*. *If A then B* may be conveniently written as $A \rightarrow B$ (that is, *A* implies *B*). It may be shown that $A \rightarrow B$ is equivalent to (not *B*) $\rightarrow$ (not *A*).

The above notation can be quite useful in logical reasoning but is limited in its power of expression as we shall soon see. We first briefly note how the process of reasoning occurs. Reasoning is based primarily on two rules:

1. If *A* is true and we are given $A \rightarrow B$, then *B* must be true.
2. If $A \rightarrow B$ and $B \rightarrow C$, then $A \rightarrow C$.

The first rule is called *modus ponens* and the second rule is called the *chain rule*. Logical reasoning involves proving the truth of a proposition, given a set of propositions that are true. For example, we may be given propositions as follows:

1. If it rains (*A*), it must be cloudy (*B*).
2. If it is cloudy (*B*), I don't play golf (*C*).

3. It is raining (A)
4. Derive – I don't play golf (C)

The above propositions may be written as follows:

- $A \rightarrow B$
- $B \rightarrow C$
- A is true
- B is therefore true given $A \rightarrow B$
- C is therefore true given $B \rightarrow C$

Similarly, we may be given a set of propositions about players and their batting and bowling and we may, for example, wish to prove the truth in 'Dravid has played with Tendulkar'.

Sometimes we may face a situation, such that the proposition that we wish to prove can be shown to be true for all values of atomic propositions in it. Such a proposition is called *tautology*.

As we noted earlier, propositional calculus is useful but limited in power. In the next two sections we present facilities that improve the power of propositional logic. The more powerful logic is called *predicate calculus* or *first order logic*.

4.4.3 Parameterized Propositions

Propositions may be generalized by parameterization. For example, 'Tendulkar played in match 2755' may be written as M2755(Tendulkar) and its value is true if Tendulkar did play in match 2755. We assume M2755 is a predicate meaning 'playing in 2755'. Similarly, M2755(Dravid)) would be false if Dravid did not play in match 2755.

By introducing parameterization we have introduced a more compact notation. Rather than assigning new variables to all propositions regarding players who played in match 2755 we may now use M2755(.). Parameterization gives us a power similar to that provided by a looping facility in a programming language. If a programming language does not have any looping facility, we could still do what we wish but it would require writing similar statements over and over again, which would be very tedious. Parameterization helps us to overcome such tedious repetition.

A parameterized proposition is called a *predicate*.

Once we introduce parameters in propositions, we need a mechanism to specify what values these variables might take. This is done by the *universal* and *existential quantifiers*.

4.4.4 Universal and Existential Quantifiers

The universal quantifier (*for all* or $\forall$) and the existential quantifier (*there exists* or $\exists$) allow use of variables in the predicates enabling very compact representation of propositions. Suppose we want to express the following statement 'If a player is a captain in match 2755 then he is a player in that match', we may write it as in Fig. 4.23.

$$\forall x(\mathrm{C2755}(x) \rightarrow \mathrm{M2755}(x))$$

Figure 4.23 Using the universal quantifier

We assume C2755(x) in Fig. 4.32 is a proposition that x is a captain in match 2755 and M2755(x) states that x has played in match 2755.

Similarly, to express the statement that 'some players in match 2755 are captains', we may write as in Fig. 4.24

$$\exists x(\text{M2755}(x) \text{ and } \text{C2755}(x))$$

Figure 4.24 Using the existential quantifier

The statement in Fig. 4.33 means 'there is at least one person who is a player in match 2755 and is a captain in that match'.

It should be noted that the statement in Fig. 4.25 following is not equivalent to the above statement

$$\exists x(\text{M2755}(x) \rightarrow \text{C2755}(x))$$

Figure 4.25 Using the existential quantifier

The reason is as follows: the statement in Fig. 4.25 means '*there does exist a player for whom M2755 (x) → C2755(x) is true*'. This will always be true since one of the players will always be a captain.

This leads us to a rule of thumb in writing predicate calculus statements; a universal quantifier usually goes with an implication while the existential quantifier goes with a conjunction.

We note that expressions containing the universal quantifier may be replaced by equivalent expressions containing existential quantifiers. For example, consider the formula in Fig. 4.26.

$$\forall x(\text{P}(x)) \text{ is equivalent to Not}(\exists x(\text{Not P}(x))$$

Figure 4.26 Relation between existential and universal quantifiers

Each variable appearing in a formula is either *free* or *bound*. The bound variables are those that have been defined in one of the quantifiers. Others are called free. For example, consider the formula in Fig. 4.27.

$$\forall x(\text{P}(x) \rightarrow \text{R}(x, y))$$

Figure 4.27 Using the universal quantifier

x is a bound variable while y is free. Bound variables are like formal parameters, the variable name being legal only within the scope of the variable and the name of the variable being immaterial. That is, the above formula in Fig. 4.36 may be written as in Fig. 4.28.

$$\forall a(\text{ P}(a)\rightarrow \text{R}(a, y))$$

Figure 4.28 Using the universal quantifier

The formula in Fig. 4.28 has the same meaning as in Fig. 4.27. A formula that has no free variables is called a *sentence*.

4.4.5 Relational Calculus

Relational calculus is closely related to predicate calculus since tables in a relational database may be thought of as predicates. For example, given a table

Player(PlayerID, LName, FName, Country, YBorn, BPlace, FTest)

the expression *Player(a,b,c,d,e,f,g)* may be thought of as a predicate which is true if a row with values *a,b,c,d,e,f,g* exists in the table *Player*.

As noted in the introduction of this chapter, there are two variants of relational calculus; tuple relational calculus (TRC) and domain relational calculus (DRC). These are described now.

The difference between TRC and DRC may be described as follows. TRC, the original relational calculus presented by E.F. Codd, specifies queries in terms of variables that range over rows of the relations in the database while DRC specifies queries in terms of variables that range over columns (or domains) of the relations in the database. Commercial language SQL is closely related to TRC while DRC is related to a graphical language that is used in Microsoft Access. It is called Query by Example (QBE) and was designed at IBM Yorktown Height research centere in the 1970s. QBE is quite different than SQL since it uses a graphical interface that shows tables in which a user can specify queries by providing input which essentially provides an example of the output that user wants. It is easy to translate most SQL queries into TRC and most QBE queries into DRC although TRC and DRC do not include functions.

4.4.6 Tuple Relational Calculus

We now describe the concept of a tuple (or row) variable that is basic to the calculus defined by Codd in 1972. A tuple variable *r* is essentially a row. It is a variable that is said to range over some table *R* if the only values that *r* can take are the rows in table *R*. An indexed row has the form *r.A* where *r* is a tuple variable and *A* is an attribute. To retrieve rows that meet a given condition, the format of queries in calculus is ($r \mid P(r)$), that is, retrieve those values of tuple variable *r* that satisfy the predicate *P(r)* (or for which *P(r)* is true). *r* of course could be a list *(x,y,z)* and is called the *target list*, P is sometimes called the *qualification expression*. For example, a query in tuple relational calculus might be written as in Fig. 4.29.

{s.*Lname* | s∈ *Player*}
or {s.*PlayerID* s∈ *Player* ∧ s.*Country* = 'Australia'}

Figure 4.29 A query in tuple relational calculus

The first expression in Fig. 4.29 specifies that we are interested in column *LName* of rows *s* such that the rows are in table *Player*. We therefore get a list of last names of all players that are in the table. The second expression specifies that we are interested in column *PlayerID* of rows *s* such that *s* is in table *Player* and the value of the column *Country* is 'Australia'. Essentially these expressions are the same queries as we posed in relational algebra but the primary difference is that this formulation does not specify the order of operations as the queries in relational algebra.

As above, we will use small case letters *r, x, y,* etc., to denote row variables and *r.LName, x.PID,* etc., to identify a column of the row variable. As noted above, the format of queries in relational calculus is of the form $\{(x,y,z) \mid P(x,y,z)\}$ where *x,y,z* are tuple variables or indexed tuple variables such that the condition *P* is satisfied.

We may sometimes omit the brackets, { }, since this does not lead to any confusion. To illustrate relational calculus, we again consider the database in Fig. 4.30.

Match (MatchID, Tram1, Tram2, Ground, Date, Winner)
Player (PlayerID, LName, FName Country, Yborn,Bplace,FTest)
Batting (MatchID, PID, Order, HOut, FOW, NRuns Mts, NBalls, Fours, Sixes)
Bowling (MatchID, PID, NOvers, Maidens, NRuns, NWickets)

Figure 4.30 Schema for the ODI cricket database

We now present a number of queries and formulate them in relational calculus.

- (*C*1) **Find the names and IDs of all players.**

  The relational calculus formulation of query *C*1 is given in Fig. 4.31.

  {s.Fname, s.Lname, s.PlayerID | s∈ Player}

  Figure 4.31 Tuple relational calculus expression for query *C*1

  The above calculus expression specifies that we are interested in the values of the columns *FName, LName* and *PlayerID* of all rows *s,* such that *s* is in table *Player* (that is, all players). The result is presented in Table 4.37.

Table 4.37 Names and IDs of all players

FName	*LName*	*PlayerID*
Sachin	Tendulkar	89001
Brian	Lara	90001
Ricky	Ponting	95001
Rahul	Dravid	96001
Herschelle	Gibbs	96002
Shane	Warne	92001
Shaun	Pollock	95002
Michael	Vaughan	99003
Inzamam	Ul-Huq	92003
Stephen	Fleming	94004
Heath	Streak	93002
Anil	Kumble	90002
Gary	Kirsten	93003
Jacques	Kallis	95003
Chaminda	Vaas	94002
Muthiah	Muralitharan	92002
Daniel	Vettori	97004
MS	Dhoni	25001
Yuvraj	Singh	23001
Saurav	Ganguly	96003
Adam	Gilchrist	99002
Andrew	Symonds	24001
Brett	Lee	99001
Sanath	Jayasuriya	91001
Virender	Sehwag	21001
Shahid	Afridi	98001
Harbhajan	Singh	98002
Praveen	Kumar	27001
Ishant	Sharma	27002

- ($C2$) Find IDs of all players from India.

  The tuple relational calculus formulation of query $C2$ is given in Fig. 4.32.

$$\{e.PlayerID \mid e \in Player \wedge (e.Country = \text{'India'})\}$$

Figure 4.32 Tuple relational calculus expression for query $C2$

The above tuple relational calculus expression specifies that we wish to retrieve values of the column *PlayerID* of all rows *e*, such that *e* is a member of the table *Player* and the value of the column *Country* of *e* is India.

The result of the query in Fig. 4.32 is presented in Table 4.38.

Table 4.38 Result of query $C2$ posed in Fig. 4.32

PlayerID
89001
96001
90002
25001
23001
96003
21001
98002
27001
27002

- ($C3$) Find the names of all players from India who have batted in a match.

  The tuple relational calculus formulation of query $C3$ is given in Fig. 4.33.

$$\{s.FName, s.LName \mid s \in Player \wedge \exists y(y \in Batting \wedge s.PlayerID = y.PID \wedge s.Country = \text{'India'})\}$$

Figure 4.33 Tuple relational calculus formulation for query $C3$

The above expression specifies the columns that we wish to retrieve. The columns that we are interested in are *FName* and *LName* and we want all rows *s*, such that *s* is a member of table *Player* and there exists a row *y* that is in table *Batting* such that the value of the column named *PlayerID* in *s* which is in *Player* and *PID* in *y* which is in *Batting* is the same and the value of the column *Country* of row *s* is India. In other words, *s* is retrieved only if it names a player from India and there is an entry for this player in *Batting*.

The result is presented in Table 4.39.

Table 4.39 Result of query *C*3 posed in Fig. 4.33

FName	*LName*
Sachin	Tendulkar
Rahul	Dravid
Anil	Kumble
MS	Dhoni
Yuvraj	Singh
Saurav	Ganguly
Virender	Sehwag
Harbhajan	Singh
Praveen	Kumar
Ishant	Sharma

- (*C*4) Find player IDs of players who have batted in either match 2755 or 2689. The tuple relational calculus formulation of this query is given in Fig. 4.34.

$$\{e.PlayerID \mid e \in Player \wedge \exists j(j \in Batting \wedge e.PlayerID = j.PID \wedge j.MatchID = \text{'2755'} \vee j.MatchID = \text{'2689'})\}$$

Figure 4.34 Tuple relational calculus expression for query *C*4

We are now looking for values of the column *PlayerID* from rows *e*, such that *e* is a row in the table *Player* and there exists a row in table *Batting* for that player, such that the Match ID is either 2755 or 2689. Note that the above formulation will not retrieve any duplicates of *PlayerID* even if the player has batted in both matches 2755 and 2689 (why not?). This query could also have been formulated by specifying only the table *Batting*, such that PIDs could be retrieved from that table for rows that met the given condition.

The result of query *C*4 as formulated in tuple relational calculus in Fig. 4.34 is presented in Table 4.40. It should be noted that the result has no duplicates. We would obtain duplicates if we directly retrieve all the PIDs from the table *Batting* since some players have played in both matches 2755 and 2689.

Table 4.40 Result of query *C*4 as posed in Fig. 4.34

PID
23001
25001
91001
94002
92002
89001
99002
95001
24001
99001
27001

- (*C*5) Find player IDs of players batting in both matches 2755 and 2689.

  This query is little bit different than the queries we have seen so far and may be formulated as in Fig. 4.35.

{e. *PlayerID* | e∈*Player* ∧ ∃j, k(j∈*Batting* ∧ k∈*Batting* ∧ e.*PlayerID* = j.*PID* ∧ e.*PlayerID* = k.*PID* ∧ j.*MatchID* = '2755' ∧ k.*MatchID* = '2689')}

Figure 4.35 Tuple relational calculus expression for query *C*5

In this query formulation, we are looking for values of the column *PlayerID* from rows *e*, such that *e* is a row in the table *Player* and there exist two rows *j* and *k* in table *Batting* for that player (the formulation ensures that player ID in all three rows *e*, *j* and *k* from the two tables are identical), such that one of them corresponds to match 2755 and the other to match 2689. The result of query *C*5 is presented in Table 4.41.

Table 4.41 Result of query *C*5 as posed in Fig. 4.35

PID
23001
25001
27001

- (*C*6) Find player IDs of players bowling in 2755 but not in 2689.

This query is also different than the two earlier queries and may be formulated as in Fig. 4.36.

{e. *PlayerID* | e∈*Player* ∧ ∃j ∧ not (∃ k) (j, k ∈*Bowling* ∧ e.*PlayerID* = j *PID* ∧ e. *PlayerID* = k. *PID* ∧ j. *MatchID* = '2755' ∧ k.*MatchID* = '2689'}

Figure 4.36 Tuple relational calculus expression for query *C*6

In this query formulation, we are looking for values of the column *PlayerID* from rows *e*, such that it is a row in table *Player* and there exists a row *j* in table *Bowling* for that player, such that the Match ID is 2755 and, in addition, there does not exist a row *k* in *Bowling* for him, such that the Match ID is 2689. Note the construct *not (∃ k)* which means that a row *k* meeting the condition specified does not exist.

Table 4.42 Result of query *C*6 as formulated in Fig. 4.36

PlayerID
91001
92002
94002

The result of query *C*6 is presented in Table 4.42.

- (*C* 7) Find the names of the cricket grounds that Dhoni has batted on.

This query is somewhat more complex because player names are in the table *Player*, batting information is in the table *Batting* and ground information is in the table *Match*. The query may be formulated in tuple relational calculus as presented in Fig. 4.37.

{s.*Ground* | s∈*Match* ∧ ∃y, z (y∈*Player* ∧ z ∈*Batting* ∧ z. *PID* = y. *PlayerID* ∧ z.*MatchID* = s.*MatchID* ∧ y.LName = 'Dhoni')}

Figure 4.37 Tuple relational calculus formula for query *C*7

The above tuple relational calculus formula specifies that we wish to retrieve values of the attribute *Ground* from rows *s*, such that *s* is in table *Match* and there exist rows *y* and *z*, such that *y* is in table *Player* and *z* is in table *Batting* meeting the conditions specified. The conditions are that the row *y* is the row in table *Player* for a player whose last name is Dhoni and *z* is a row in *Batting* for the player y (that is, it is for the player with player ID of Dhoni) in match s. Note that we have not checked the first name of Dhoni assuming that there is only one player by that last name. The result of query $C7$ is presented in Table 4.43.

Table 4.43 Result of Query $C7$

Ground
Brisbane
Colombo

- ($C8$) Find the names of players who have not batted in any match in the ODI cricket database given in Tables 3.1 to 3.4.

This query can be formulated in a simple way because it only requires checking that a player has not batted.

$$\{s.\ FName, LName \mid s \in Player \wedge \text{Not } \exists e\ (e \in Batting \wedge e.\ PID = s.\ PlayerID)\}$$

Figure 4.38 Tuple relational calculus formula for query $C8$

The above tuple relational calculus expression specifies that we wish to retrieve values of the columns *FName* and *LName* from rows s, such that row s is in the table *Player* and a row e does not exist in the table *Batting*, such that this row e is for the player s.

The result of query $C8$ is given in Table 4.44.

Table 4.44 Result of query $C8$ as formulated in Fig. 4.38

FName	*LName*
Brian	Lara
Rahul	Dravid
Herschelle	Gibbs
Shane	Warne
Shaun	Pollock
Michael	Vaughan
Inzamam	Ul-Huq
Stephen	Fleming
Heath	Streak
Anil	Kumble
Gary	Kirsten
Jacques	Kallis
Daniel	Vettori
Saurav	Ganguly
Virender	Sehwag

- ($C9$) Find the match IDs of matches that have batting records.

This is a simple query using only one table. It can be formulated as given in Fig. 4.39.

The formula in Fig. 4.39 simply finds the values of the column *MatchID* of each row s such that the row s is in table *Batting*.

There is however a weakness in the above formulation. It will lead to many duplicate tuples since a match has many batting records. If we wish to eliminate the duplicates, a better formulation of the query *C*9 would be as in Fig. 4.40.

$$\{s.MatchID \mid s \in Batting\}$$

Figure 4.39 Tuple relational calculus expression for query *C*9

$$\{s.\ MatchID \mid s \in Match \wedge \exists e\ (e \in Batting \wedge e.\ MatchID = s.\ MatchID\}$$

Figure 4.40 A better tuple relational calculus expression for query *C*9

This formulation retrieves rows from table *Match* (not from *Batting* which is likely to have duplicate values of *MatchID*) and this ensures that there will be only one row for each match in the table *Match*.

The result of the tuple relational calculus formulation in Fig. 4.40 is given in Table 4.45.

Table 4.45 Result of query *C*9 as posed in Fig. 4.40

MatchID
2689
2755

- (*C*10) Find the player IDs of players who have only bowled in match 2755.

In this query, we need to check that a player has bowled in match 2755 but has not bowled in any other match in the database. The tuple relational calculus formulation for this query is given in Fig. 4.41.

$$\{e.\ PlayerID \mid e \in Player \mid \exists j \wedge not(\exists k)\ (j, k \in Batting \wedge e.\ PlayerID = j.\ PID \wedge e.PlayerID = k.PID \wedge k.MatchID = \text{'2755'} \wedge k.MatchID <> \text{'2755'})\}$$

Figure 4.41 Tuple relational calculus formulation for query *C*10

In the formulation in Fig. 4.50, we look for values of the attribute *PlayerID* of each row *e,* such that it is in the table *Player* and there exists a row *j* in table *Batting* for the same player as in *e* that is for batting in match 2755 and, in addition, there does not exist a row *k* in *Batting,* such that the batting is for the same player as in *e* in a match other than 2755.

The result is given in Table 4.46.

Table 4.46 Result of query *C*10 as posed in Fig. 4.41

PID
99001
24001
23001
94002
92002
91001
23001

- (*C*11) Find the player IDs of players who have bowled in all the matches played in Australia.

We found in the discussion on relational algebra that queries involving 'all' usually involve the relational algebra operator division which was somewhat difficult to understand. It is easier to formulate such queries in tuple relational calculus.

The query may be formulated as in Fig. 4.42.

$$\{k.PlayerID \mid k \in Player \wedge \forall e(e \in Match \wedge e.Team1 = \text{'Australia'} \wedge \exists\ s(s \in Bowling \wedge s.PID = k.PlayerID \wedge s(MatchID) = e(MatchID)\}$$

Figure 4.42 Tuple relational calculus expression for query *C*11

In this query, the tuple relational calculus expression specifies that the values of the attribute *PlayerID* are to be retrieved from each row *k*, such that *k* is in the table *Player* and for each match *e* that is played in Australia there exists a row *s* in the table *Bowling*, such that it is a bowling performance for the player *k* in the match *e*. The ∀*e* (for all *e*) expression makes solving the problems which were more difficult to solve in relational algebra since there was no operation similar to the operation for all in tuple relational calculus. Unfortunately SQL also does not have an operator similar to for all and therefore problems that involve such operations in SQL are rather painful.

The result is given in Table 4.47.

Table 4.47 Result of query *C*11 posed in Fig. 4.42

MatchID	*PID*
2689	99001
2689	24001
2689	23001

4.4.7 Domain Relational Calculus

As noted earlier, domain relational calculus (DRC) is very similar to the tuple relational calculus that we have presented in the last section except that rather than using variables. ranging over tuples in TRC, the variables range over single domains of attributes in DRC. Therefore to specify a relation with *n* attributes it is necessary to specify *n* domain variables one for each attribute.

The basis of DRC essentially is that a relational database consists of the domains that represent the sets of objects in the database. A query language based on DRC therefore consists of variables that range on a single domain of the relational database. It is claimed that DRC therefore manipulates the basic database objects since domain values interact more directly with the semantics expressed by the relations and produces simpler and more English-like languages.

The following query shows the general form of a DRC query

{<*PlayerID, LName, FName, Country, YBorn, BPlace, FTest, F*(*PlayerID, LName, FName, Country, YBorn, BPlace, FTest*) }

In this query *PlayerID, LName, FName, Country, YBorn, BPlace, FTest* represent domain variables that the user wishes to retrieve and *F*(.) is a formula that specifies the condition. The formula *F* may be very simple, for example, stating that all these domains together form the relation *Player*. The formula *F*(.) is shown below.

<*PlayerID, LName, FName, Country, YBorn, BPlace, FTest*> ∈ *Player*

We now present a number of queries and formulate them in domain relational calculus.

- (*D*1) Find the names and IDs of all players.

  The domain relational calculus formulation of query *D*1 is given in Fig. 4.43.

{<Fname, Lname, PlayerID> | ∃ *Country, YBorn, Bplace, FTest* (<*PlayerID, LName, FName, Country, YBorn, BPlace, FTest*>) ∈ Player}

Figure 4.43 Domain relational calculus expression for query *D*1

- (*D*2) Find IDs of all players from India.
  The domain relational calculus formulation of query *D*2 is given in Fig. 4.44.

> {<PlayerID> | ∃ *LName, FName, Country, YBorn, BPlace, FTest* (<*PlayerID, LName, FName, Country, YBorn, BPlace, FTest*>) ∈ *Player* ∧ Country = 'India'}

Figure 4.44 Domain relational calculus expression for query *D*2

The above domain relational calculus expression specifies that we wish to retrieve values of the domain *PlayerID* of all rows from *Player* such that they have the value of the domain *Country* India.

- (*D*3) Find the names of all players from India who have batted in a match.
  The Domain relational calculus formulation of query *D*3 is given in Fig. 4.45.

> {<FName, LName> | ∃ (*PlayerID, Country, YBorn, BPlace, FTest* (<*PlayerID, LName, FName, Country, YBorn, BPlace, FTest*>) ∈ *Player* ∧ ∃ MatchID, PID, Order, HOut, FOW, NRuns, Mts, NBalls, Fours, Sixes (<MatchID, PID, Order, HOut, FOW, NRuns, Mts, NBalls, Fours, Sixes> ∈ *Batting* ∧ Country = 'India' ∧ PlayerID = PID)}

Figure 4.45 Domain relational calculus formulation for query *D*3

The above expression looks complex because of the number of attributes in the two relations *Player* and *Batting*. Essentially the domain relational calculus specifies the columns that we wish to retrieve from those tuples from *Player* for whom the domain *Country* is India and there exists a tuple in *Batting* for the same player. In other words we retrieve only the names for a player from India if there is an entry for this player in *Batting*.

- (*D*4) Find player IDs of players who have batted in either match 2755 or 2689.
  The tuple relational calculus formulation of this query is given in Fig. 4.46.

> {<PlayerID> | ∃ *LName, FNane, Country, YBorn, BPlace, FTest* (<*PlayerID, LName, FName, Country, YBorn, BPlace, FTest*>) ∈ *Player* ∧ ∃ MatchID, PID, Order, HOut, FOW, NRuns, Mts, NBalls, Fours, Sixes (<MatchID, PID, Order, HOut, FOW, NRuns, Mts, NBalls, Fours, Sixes> ∈ *Batting* ∧ MatchID = '2755' ∨ MatchID = '2689')}

Figure 4.46 Domain relational calculus expression for query *D*4

> {<PlayerID> | ∃ *LName, FNane, Country, YBorn, BPlace, FTest* (<*PlayerID, LName, FName, Country, YBorn, BPlace, FTest*>) ∈ *Player* ∧ ∃ MatchID, PID, Order, HOut, FOW, NRuns, Mts, NBalls, Fours, Sixes (<MatchID, PID, Order, HOut, FOW, NRuns, Mts, NBalls, Fours, Sixes> ∈ *Batting* ∧ ∃ MatchID1, PID1, Order1, HOut1, FOW1, NRuns1, Mts1, NBalls1, Fours1, Sixes1 (< MatchID1, PID1, Order1, HOut1, FOW1, NRuns1, Mst1, NBalls1, Fours1, Sixes1> ∈ *Batting* ∧ MatchID = '2755' ∧ MatchID = '2689'

Figure 4.47 Domain relational calculus expression for query *D*5

We are now looking for values of the domain *PlayerID* from the relation *Player* such that there exists a row in table *Batting* for that player where the *Match ID* is either 2755 or 2689. Note that the above formulation will not retrieve any duplicates of *PlayerID* even if the player has batted in both matches 2755 and 2689 (why not?). This query could also have been formulated by specifying only the table *Batting* such that *PIDs* could be retrieved from that table for rows that met the given condition.

- (*D*5) Find player IDs of players batting in both matches 2755 and 2689.

  This query is little bit different than the queries we have seen so far and may be formulated as in Fig. 4.47.

  In this query formulation, we are looking for values of the domain *PlayerID* from rows the table *Player* for which there exist two rows in the table *Batting* for that player, such that one of them corresponds to match 2755 and the other to match 2689.

4.4.8 Well-Formed Formula (WFF)

The queries formulated in tuple relational calculus and domain relational calculus above should have given the reader some idea about the features of the two variants of relational calculus. We have however not specified what expressions in calculus are acceptable. This is elaborated ahead.

We have already discussed the concept of free and bound variables. Also we have indicated earlier, that the general form of relational calculus expressions is $\{(x,y,z) \mid P(x, y, z)\}$ where P is a formula in which the variables x, y, z are free. An acceptable formula is called a *well-formed formula* or WFF. WFFs may be defined recursively as in Fig. 4.48.

1. Any term is a WFF (a term is either an indexed tuple or a comparison of two indexed tuples).
2. If F and a WFF, so is (not F).
3. If F and G are WFFs, so are $(F \wedge G)$ and $(F \vee G)$.
4. If F is a WFF in which x appears as a free variable, then $\exists x(F)$ and $\forall x(F)$ are WFFs.
5. No other formulas are WFFs.

Figure 4.48 Definition of well-formed formulas in tuple relational calculus

4.5 RELATIONAL ALGEBRA VS RELATIONAL CALCULUS

It is useful to discuss the selective power of relational algebra and relational calculus. Any language that has the power of relational calculus is called *relationally complete*. Codd in his paper in 1970 proposed that any language that was not relationally complete should be considered inadequate. He showed that relational algebra is equivalent to relational calculus and is therefore relationally complete. It is in fact possible to design algorithms that will translate a relational algebra expression into an equivalent relational calculus expression and vice versa. These algorithms are called *reduction algorithms*. We will not discuss them here, but the reader can refer to Codd (1970) or Ullman (1982).

Given that relational algebra and relational calculus have equivalent selective power, one may now ask which one of these two languages should be preferred. Codd, in his 1971 paper, claimed that relational calculus was superior to algebra although the algebra did not require use of quantifiers for all (∀) and there exists (∃). He gave four reasons for preferring relational calculus:

1. *Ease of Augmentation*—Since the algebra and the calculus provided only basic selective power, it is necessary to augment that power by providing a facility to invoke a number of library functions (for example, average, sum, maximum). This augmentation is more easily done in relational calculus than in algebra.
2. *Scope for Search Optimization*—Since the calculus only specifies what is to be retrieved and not how it is to be retrieved, it is easier for a database system to optimize database search to answer queries that are posed in calculus. Queries posed in relational algebra can also be optimized but such optimization is likely to be only local since it would be difficult for a system to derive the properties of the data that needs to be retrieved given the operators that the user has specified.
3. *Authorization Capability*—It is likely to be easier to specify authorization by using relational calculus since authorization is likely to be based on the properties of the data that a user may be authorized to access or update.
4. *Closeness to Natural Language*—It is much more natural for users in relational calculus to specify what data they wish to retrieve than how the data is to be retrieved. Thus a language based on relational calculus is likely to be more user-friendly and easier to use for users with limited computing background.

As noted above, the relational model requires that the language available to the user should at least provide the power of relational algebra without making use of iterations or recursion statements. Relational calculus does that. So does the commercial language, SQL, which we will discuss in detail in Chapter 5.

SUMMARY

This chapter has covered the following:

- Codd defined two formal languages, viz., relational algebra and relational calculus.
- Relational algebra is a procedural language that includes the operators selection, projection, Cartesian product, equi-join, natural join, outer join, union, intersection, difference and division.
- Relational algebra notation has been presented. For example, a selection may be written as Players [Country = 'India'] and the notation has been used to formulate a variety of queries.
- Selection and projection are unary operators, operating on a single table.
- Cartesian product and join are binary operators, operating on two tables. Join is used to combine two related tables on a join condition, for example, the table *Player* and *Batting*.
- Outer join is a join operator in which matching rows from two tables as well as rows that do not match are shown. An outer join may be left outer join or a right outer join or a full outer join.
- It is possible to use set operations in relational algebra including union, intersection and difference.
- Division operator may be applied to two tables and is related to the Cartesian product operator, it may be considered the opposite of the product.

- Background of predicate calculus and relational calculus is presented including meaning of propositions, the implied operator and parameterized propositions.
- Meaning of the existential and universal quantifiers is explained and use of calculus to formulate a variety of queries is illustrated using a number of examples.
- Two notations of relational calculus, viz., the tuple relational calculus (TRC) and domain relational calculus (DRC) are presented.
- TRC uses tuple variables (rows of a table) while DRC uses variables that range over domains to formulate queries.
- Well-formed formulas (WFF) are the acceptable expressions in calculus; WFF is defined.
- Relative merits of algebra and calculus and their relative power to express queries are discussed. The calculus may be preferred for ease of augmentation and for better scope for optimization.

REVIEW QUESTIONS

1. What is the functoin of operations restriction, projection, Cartesian product, equi-join, natural join, outer join, union, intersection, difference, and division? (Section 4.2)
2. Describe the relational algebra notation for restriction, projection and natural join. (Section 4.2)
3. Give examples to explain a database query? Show how to use relational algebra to formulate a variety of queries. (Section 4.2)
4. What is the function of division operation? Can it be expressed in terms of other relational algebra operations?
5. Explain the relational calculus notation and well-formed formulas. (Section 4.3)
6. Explain the notation used in expressing queries in tuple relational calculus. (Section 4.3)
7. Give examples to explain the meaning of the existential quantifier and universal quantifier. (Section 4.4)
8. Describe how to use tuple relational calculus to formulate a variety of queries. (Section 4.4)
9. Give a number of examples of using domain relational calculus to formulate a variety of queries. (Section 4.4)
10. Select two queries and formulae them using tuple relational calculus and the domain relational calculus. (Section 4.4)
11. Explain the relative merits of algebra and calculus and their relative power to express queries. (Section 4.5)

SHORT ANSWER QUESTIONS

1. What is relational algebra?
2. What is relational calculus?
3. What is relational algebra operator selection?
4. Give an example of using selection in Table 4.5.
5. What is relational algebra operator projection?

6. Give an example of applying projection to Table 4.13.
7. What is relational algebra operator Cartesian product?
8. What is the Cartesian product of Tables 4.11 and 4.12?
9. How is the equi-join different from natural join?
10. Define the properties of two relations to be union-compatible.
11. Are Figs 4.11 and 4.12 union-compatible?
12. Find the natural join from Cartesian product of Tables 4.11 and 4.12.
13. What is the left outer join? What does the operation do?
14. What is the right outer join?
15. Find the full outer-join of Tables 4.10 and 4.11. What does the result tell us?
16. What is the relational operator division used for?
17. Give an example of two small relations and divide them to illustrate division.
18. Give examples of universal and existential quantifiers.
19. Express the query 'find all the information about players from India' using TRC and DRC.

MULTIPLE CHOICE QUESTIONS

1. Which one of the following is **not** correct?
   (a) A restriction selects one or more rows of a relation.
   (b) A projection selects one or more columns of a relation.
   (c) A join glues each row of one relation with all the rows of the other.
   (d) A difference gives all the rows in the first relation that are not in the second.
2. Which one of the following is correct?
   (a) A Cartesian product of two relations is the same as their union.
   (b) A join of two relations is a selection on their Cartesian product.
   (c) A join is always an equi-join or a natural join.
   (d) The degree of the equi-join of two relations is the same as the degree of the natural join of the same relations.
3. Consider the following query:

   (((P WHERE COLOUR = 'RED') [P#] JOIN SP) [S#] JOIN S) [SNAME]

   Which one of the following set of operations does the above query involve?
   (a) 1 selection, 2 joins, 3 projections
   (b) 1 projection, 2 joins, 3 selections
   (c) 2 selections, 2 joins, 3 projections
   (d) 1 selection, 2 joins, 3 intersections
4. Which one of the following does not always have the same list of attributes that the operands have?
   (a) Project (b) Select (c) Union (d) Difference
5. Which one of the following always results in fewer rows than the relation *R*? Assume neither of the two relations is empty.
   (a) $R \bowtie S$ (b) $R - S$ (c) R/S (d) *R* intersection *S*
   (e) None of the above

6. Which one of the following always results in at least as many rows as in the relation R? Assume neither of the two relations is empty.
   (a) $R \bowtie S$ (b) R union S (c) $R - S$ (d) R/S
   (e) R intersection S
7. Which two of the following operators require elimination of duplicates?
   (a) Projection   (b) Intersection   (c) Difference   (d) Union
   (e) Join
8. Which one of the following is a complete set of algebra operations?
   (a) selection, projection, union, difference and Cartesian product
   (b) selection, projection and join
   (c) selection, projection and Cartesian product
   (d) selection, projection, division and Cartesian product
9. Consider the following binary operators. Which one of the operator does not require the two operands to be union-compatible (that is, having exactly the same number and types of attributes)?
   (a) Intersection   (b) Difference   (c) Union   (d) Division
10. Relational division has operands and results named as given below. Which of the following is not a relation?
   (a) Dividend   (b) Divisor   (c) Quotient   (d) Remainder
   (e) None of the above
11. $R[A \text{ op } B]S$ is a join of the relations R and S. Which one of the following is **not** correct?
   (a) $R[A = B]S$ may be empty even when R and S are not
   (b) $R[A = B]S = S[B = A]R$
   (c) $R[A < B]S = S[B > A]R$
   (d) $R[A < B]S = R \times S - R[A > B]S - R[A = B]S$
   (e) $R[A < B]S = R \times S - S[B < A]R$
12. Which of the following are correct?
   (a) $R \bowtie S = S \bowtie R$ (b) $R - S = S - R$
   (c) $R/S = S/R$ (d) $S \cup T = (S - T) \cup (S \text{ intersect } R) \cup (T - S)$
13. Consider the join of two relations R and S that are of degree x and y respectively. Which one of the following is correct?
   (a) The degree of an equi-join of relations R and S is $x + y$.
   (b) Degree of a natural-join of relations R and S is always $x + y - 1$.
   (c) If the cardinality of R is a and of S is b, then the cardinality of the division R/S is a/b.
   (d) A projection of relation R has the same cardinality as R but the degree of the projected relation is equal to the number of attributes that the projection specifies.
14. Which one of the following is correct? Note that $\cup$ represents union while $\cap$ represents intersection.
   (a) $(R \cup S) \cap T = (R \cap T) \cup S$ (b) $R - S = S - R$
   (c) $(R/S) \times S = R$ (d) $S \cup T = (S - T) \cup (S \cap R) \cup (T - S)$
15. Let $T = R/S$ where R is an enrolment relation and S is a subject relation with degrees 2 and 1 and cardinalities m and n respectively. The attributes of R are student_id and subject_id and the attribute of S is subject_id. Which of the following are correct? (Note: $T \times S$ is the Cartesian product of T and S).

(a) T is of degree 1.
(b) T has cardinality no larger than m/n.
(c) $(R - T \times S)$[student_id] does not include any student who is in T.
(d) T are all the students doing all the subjects in S.
(e) All of the above

16. Let R be an enrolment relation and S be a subject relation. The relation R has two attributes student_id (call it A) and subject_id (call it B) while the relation S consists of only one attribute subject_id (call it also B).
Which one of the following is correct?
(a) $((R[A] \times S) - R)[A]$ is the list of student_id values (attribute A) in R.
(b) $R[A] - ((R[A] \times S) - R)[A]$ is a null relation.
(c) $(R - R[A] \times S)[A]$ is the list of all the student IDs for those doing all the subjects in S.
(d) The expression $R[A] - ((R[A] \times S) - R)[A]$ is the list of all the student IDs for students not doing all the subjects in S.

17. Which one of the following is **not** correct?
(a) Relational algebra provides a collection of operations that can actually be used to build some desired relation; the calculus provides a notation for formulating the definition of that desired relation.
(b) In relational algebra, one specifies what operations must be executed while in relational calculus, the specification of operations is left to the system.
(c) Relational algebra is procedural while relational calculus is nonprocedural.
(d) Using relational calculus one may specify more complex queries than using relational algebra.

EXERCISES

1. Consider the following student database:
Student(ID, Name, Address, City, Tutor)
Enrolment(ID, Code, Marks)
Course(Code, Title, Department)
Formulate the following queries in relational algebra using the student database above. Assume that the attribute *Tutor* is the ID of the tutor.
(a) List all the student names.
(b) List all school and course names.
(c) Find student names of students that have no tutor.
(d) Find student names of students that are doing computer science courses.
(e) Find student names of students that have Suresh Chandra as tutor.

2. The following questions deal with Cartesian product and join:
(a) Consider the relations in the student database exercise above. How many rows will there be in the Cartesian product of the three tables?
(b) How many attributes does the natural join of the two tables *Student* and *Enrolment* have? Explain.

3. Express
   (a) Division R/S in terms of projection, Cartesian product and difference.
   (b) Natural join in terms of projection, Cartesian product and selection.
   (c) Intersection in terms of projection, union and difference.
4. Consider the following two queries for the cricket database:
   (a) Find the youngest player in Table 3.1
   (b) Find the oldest player in Table 3.1

   Can the above two queries be formulated using relational calculus? If yes, formulate the two queries.
5. Explain the motivation for TRC and DRC and discuss the differences between the two approaches.
6. Show how a TRC query may be written as SQL and SQL query may be written as a TRC query.
7. Study the basics of QBE and use QBE in Microsoft Access to understand it and relate it to DRC. Can a DRC be translated to QBE? Show by using an example.
8. Write a query that involves a division and show how it may be expressed in TRC.

PROJECTS

1. Write algorithms and then implement them in the programming language of your choice for all the relational algebra operations. This could be a group project.
2. Using the Web, search for open source software for relational calculus (TRC or DRC). Install the software and test it by posing some queries to it.

LAB EXERCISES

1. Formulate the following queries for the ODI database using relational algebra:
   (a) Find the player's last name that was the youngest amongst the players in the database when he played in his first test match.
   (b) Find the ID of the player that hit the largest number of sixes in an ODI match in the example database.
   (c) Find the list of names of players that have scored a century in the example ODI database.
   (d) Find the average strike rate of players that have scored a century in the example ODI database.
   (e) Find the names of players that have taken four wickets or more in the example ODI database.
   (f) What is the maximum number of wickets that a bowler has taken in an ODI match in the example database? Find the ID of that bowler.
   (g) Find the name of the youngest player in the example database.
   (h) Find the IDs of players that have never scored a four or a six in all matches they have batted in.
2. Formulate the above queries in Tuple Relational Calculus.

BIBLIOGRAPHY

For Students

A number of books listed below are easy to read for students.

For Instructors

Codd's papers and his out-of-print book (which may be downloaded from the Web) are the authoritative documents on the relational model. C. J. Date's books are also a good source of information.

Codd, E. F., "A relational model of data for large shared data banks", *Communications of the ACM*, Vol. 13, No. 6, 1970, pp 377-387.

Codd, E. F., "Relational database: a practical foundation for productivity", *Communications of the ACM*, Vol. 25, No. 2, 1982, pp. 109-117.

Codd, E. F., *The Relational Model for Database Management: Version 2*, Addison-Wesley Publishing Company, Inc, 1990. (This book is out of print now but may be downloaded from http://portal.acm.org/citation.cfm?id=77708.)

Date, C. J., "The Outer Join", In *Relational Database: Selected Writings*, Addison-Wesley, 1986.

Date, C. J., *Database in Depth: Relational Theory for Practitioners*, O'Reilly Media, 2005.

Garcia-Molina, H., J. D. Ullman, and J. Widom, *Database Systems: The Complete Book*, Prentice Hall, 2002.

Garcia-Molina, H., J. D. Ullman, and J. Widom, *Database System Implementation*, Prentice Hall, 2000.

Kifer, M., Bernstein, A., and P. M. Lewis, *Database Systems: An Application-Oriented Approach*, Second Edition, Addison-Wesley, 2006.

Ullman, J. D., *Principles of Database Systems*, Computer Science Press, 1982. (May be downloaded from http://www.filestube.com/d/database+systems+ullman)

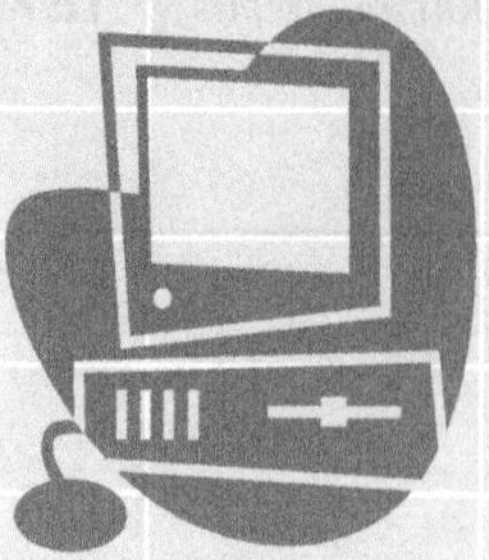

Structured Query Language (SQL) 5

OBJECTIVES

- To explain how SQL is used for data definition.
- To describe how SQL is used for retrieving information from a database.
- To explain how SQL is used for inserting, deleting and modifying information in a database.
- To explain the use of SQL in implementing correlated and complex queries including outer joins.
- To discuss embedded SQL and dynamic SQL.
- To discuss how data integrity is maintained in a relational database using SQL.

KEYWORDS

Queries, SQL, CREATE TABLE, CREATE INDEX, CREATE VIEW, CREATE DOMAIN, DDL, DROP TABLE, DROP INDEX, DROP VIEW, DROP DOMAIN, SELECT, INSERT, WHERE, GROUP BY, DELETE, UPDATE, VIEW, grouping, aggregation, functions, AVG, COUNT, MIN, MAX, SUM, nested queries, subqueries, outer join, integrity constraints, primary key, secondary key, domain, NULL, embedded SQL, dynamic SQL, complex queries, correlated queries, existential integrity, referential integrity, UNIQUE, triggers, active databases.

An eye for an eye makes the whole world blind.

Mahatma Gandhi

5.1 INTRODUCTION

We have discussed the relational model in Chapter 3, which is a model for implementing a database that has been modeled using Entity-Relationship modeling or a similar modeling methodology. The relational model is widely used because of its simplicity. It is a conceptual view of the data as well as a high level view of the implementation of the database on the computer. The model does not concern itself with the detailed bits and bytes view of the data.

In the last chapter, we studied two formal data manipulation languages in detail, viz., relational algebra and relational calculus. It is not appropriate to use either of them in a commercial database system that would be used by users with a computing background as well as by those that have little computing knowledge because calculus and algebra are not user-friendly languages and they do not provide facilities for counting or for computing averages, or maximum and minimum values. In this chapter we discuss another query language called the Structured Query Language (SQL) that is much easier for users. It is a commercial query language based on relational calculus.

The query language SQL is used in almost all commercial relational DBMS. Although other query languages exist, SQL has become a de facto standard for relational database systems.

SQL is a nonprocedural language that originated at IBM during the building of the well-known experimental relational DBMS called System R. Originally the user interface to System R was called SEQUEL designed by Donald Chamberlain and Raymond Bryce in 1974. The language was later modified in 1976–77 and its name changed to SEQUEL2. These languages have undergone significant changes over time and the current language was named the Structured Query Language (SQL) in the early 1980s.

Just as for other programming languages, the American National Standards Institute (ANSI) published a standard definition of SQL in 1986 which was subsequently adopted by the International Organization for Standardization (ISO) in 1987. Since then there have been a number of SQL standards, the most recent being SQL : 2003. We will give more details about the SQL standards at the end of this chapter. The focus of this chapter is on the basic SQL constructs. We will not discuss some of the newer features included in the more recent standards.

This chapter is organized as follows. After introducing SQL next the data definition features of SQL are described in Section 5.3. Section 5.4 covers data retrieval features of SQL. This section includes some simple examples of SQL that involve only one table followed by examples that involve more than one table using joins and subqueries, examples using built-in functions followed by explanation of correlated and complex SQL queries. GROUPING and HAVING are presented next. SQL update commands and additional data definition commands are then discussed. Views are described in Section 5.5 and Section 5.6 discusses embedded SQL and dynamic SQL. Section 5.7 explains how SQL may be used for enforcing the final component of the relational model and data integrity. Existential integrity, referential integrity, domains, and nulls have also been discussed here. Triggers are briefly described in Section 5.8. Authentication and authorization is discussed briefly in Section 5.9. Additional data definition commands are described in Section 5.10. A summary of SQL commands is presented in Section 5.11 and SQL standards are discussed in Section 5.12.

5.2 SQL

As noted above, SQL is designed to support data definition, data manipulation, and data control in relational database systems.

A user of a DBMS using SQL may use the query language interactively or through a host language like C++. An interactive web page could also be the front end of the SQL query in which the user supplies some parameters before the query is executed by the server. We will mainly discuss the interactive use of SQL although SQL commands embedded in a procedural language will also be discussed briefly.

SQL consists of the following facilities:

- *Data Definition Language (DDL)*—Before a database can be used, it must be created. Data definition language is used for defining the database to the computer system. The DDL includes facilities to create and destroy databases and database objects, for example, for creating a new table or a view, deleting a table or a view, altering or expanding the definition of a table (by entering a new column) and creating an index on a table, as well as commands for dropping an index. DDL also allows a number of integrity constraints to be defined either at the time of creating a table or later.
- *Data Manipulation Language (DML)*—These DML facilities include commands for retrieving information from one or more tables and updating information in tables including inserting and deleting rows. The commands SELECT, UPDATE, INSERT and DELETE are available for these operations. The SELECT command forms the basis for retrieving data from the database. The command UPDATE forms the basis for modifying information that is already in the database. INSERT is used for inserting new information in the database while DELETE is used for removing information from the database.
- *Data Control Language (DCL)*—The DCL facilities include database security control including privileges and revoke privileges. Therefore DCL is responsible for managing database security including management of which users have access to which tables and what data.
- *New Features*—Each new standard has introduced a variety of new features in the language. For example, SQL:2003 includes XML. Unfortunately we will not be able to cover these features in this book.

It should be noted that SQL does not require any particular appearance of SQL queries and is not case sensitive except for object names. Although it is much easier to read queries that are well structured and indented, SQL does not require it. In fact, the whole query could be typed in one long line if that is what the user wishes to do. Sometimes though different DBMS may use somewhat different conventions. We will use the convention of writing SQL commands as upper case letters like we did in the last paragraph and names of tables and their columns in lower case. In our view this makes it easier to read the queries.

We first study some of the data definition features of the language in the next section.

We will continue to use the ODI cricket database to illustrate various features of the query language in this section. As a reminder, the schemas of the four tables *Match*, *Player*, *Batting* and *Bowling* are reproduced in Fig. 5.1 and the tables are reproduced in Tables 5.1, 5.2, 5.3 and 5.4. Additional data for these tables is presented at the end of this chapter. For example, Appendix 5.1 includes information on another 50 players. Appendix 5.2 includes another 35 rows for the table *Batting* and Appendix 5.3 includes another 35 rows for the table *Bowling*. These may be used for exercises that require more data.

Match (MatchID, Team1, Team2, Ground, Date, Winner)
Player (PlayerID, LName, FName, Country, YBorn, BPlace, FTest)
Batting (MachID, PID, Order, HOut, FOW, NRuns, Mts, Nballs, Fours, Sixes)
Bowling (MatchID, PID, NOvers, Maidens, NRuns, NWickets)

Figure 5.1 Database schema for the ODI cricket database

We now reproduce the sample tables for the database that were presented in Chapter 3. The first table, Table 5.1, is *Match*.

Table 5.1 The relation *Match*

MatchId	*Team1*	*Team2*	*Ground*	*Date*	*Winner*
2324	Pakistan	India	Peshawar	6/2/2006	Team1
2327	Pakistan	India	Rawalpindi	11/2/2006	Team2
2357	India	England	Delhi	28/3/2006	Team1
2377	West Indies	India	Kingston	18/5/2006	Team2
2404a	Sri Lanka	India	Colombo	16/8/2006	Abandoned
2440	India	Australia	Mohali	29/10/2006	Team2
2449	South Africa	India	Cape Town	26/11/2006	Team1
2480	India	West Indies	Nagpur	21/1/2007	Team1
2493	India	West Indies	Vadodara	31/1/2007	Team1
2520	India	Sri Lanka	Rajkot	11/2/2007	Team2
2611	England	India	Southampton	21/8/2007	Team1
2632	India	Australia	Mumbai	17/10/2007	Team1
2643	India	Pakistan	Guwahati	5/11/2007	Team1
2675	Australia	India	Melbourne	10/2/2008	Team2
2681	India	Sri Lanka	Adelaide	19/2/2008	Team1
2688	Australia	India	Sydney	2/3/2008	Team2
2689	Australia	India	Brisbane	4/3/2008	Team2
2717	Pakistan	India	Karachi	26/6/2008	Team2
2750	Sri Lanka	India	Colombo	24/8/2008	Team2
2755	Sri Lanka	India	Colombo	27/8/2008	Team2

The second table, Table 5.2, is *Player*.

Table 5.2 The relation *Player*

PlayerID	*LName*	*FName*	*Country*	*YBorn*	*BPlace*	*FTest*
89001	Tendulkar	Sachin	India	1973	Mumbai	1989
90001	Lara	Brian	West Indies	1969	Santa Cruz	1990
95001	Ponting	Ricky	Australia	1974	Launceston	1995
96001	Dravid	Rahul	India	1973	Indore	1996
96002	Gibbs	Herschelle	South Africa	1974	Cape Town	1996
92001	Warne	Shane	Australia	1969	Melbourne	1992
95002	Pollock	Shaun	South Africa	1973	Port Elizabeth	1995
99003	Vaughan	Michael	England	1974	Manchester	1999
92003	Ul-Huq	Inzamam	Pakistan	1970	Multan	1992
94004	Fleming	Stephen	New Zealand	1973	Christchurch	1994
93002	Streak	Heath	Zimbabwe	1974	Bulawayo	1993
90002	Kumble	Anil	India	1970	Bangalore	1990
93003	Kirsten	Gary	South Africa	1967	Cape Town	1993
95003	Kallis	Jacques	SouthAfrica	1975	Cape Town	1995
94002	Vaas	Chaminda	Sri Lanka	1974	Mattumagala	1994
92002	Muralitharan	Muthiah	Sri Lanka	1972	Kandy	1992
97004	Vettori	Daniel	NewZealand	1979	Auckland	1997
25001	Dhoni	MS	India	1981	Ranchi	2005
23001	Singh	Yuvraj	India	1981	Chandigarh	2003
96003	Ganguly	Saurav	India	1972	Calcutta	1996
99002	Gilchrist	Adam	Australia	1971	Bellingen	1999
24001	Symonds	Andrew	Australia	1975	Birmingham	2004
99001	Lee	Brett	Australia	1976	Wollongong	1999
91001	Jayasuriya	Sanath	Sri Lanka	1969	Matara	1991
21001	Sehwag	Virender	India	1978	Delhi	2001
98001	Afridi	Shahid	Pakistan	1980	Khyber Agency	1998
98002	Singh	Harbhajan	India	1980	Jalandhar	1998
27001	Kumar	Praveen	India	1986	Meerut	NULL
27002	Sharma	Ishant	India	1988	Delhi	2007

The third table is Table 5.3 *Batting*.

Table 5.3 The relation *Batting*

MatchID	*PID*	*Order*	*HOut*	*FOW*	*NRuns*	*Mts*	*Nballs*	*Fours*	*Six*
2755	23001	3	C	51	0	12	6	0	0
2755	25001	5	C	232	71	104	80	4	0
2755	91001	1	C	74	60	85	52	8	2
2755	94002	7	LBW	157	17	23	29	1	0
2755	92002	11	NO	NO	1	11	7	0	0
2689	89001	2	C	205	91	176	121	7	0
2689	23001	4	C	175	38	27	38	2	2
2689	25001	5	C	240	36	52	37	2	1
2689	99002	1	C	2	2	3	3	0	0
2689	95001	3	C	8	1	9	7	0	0
2689	24001	5	C	123	42	81	56	2	1
2689	99001	8	B	228	7	20	12	0	0
2689	27001	9	C	255	7	7	7	1	0
2755	27001	9	B	257	2	7	6	0	0
2689	98002	8	LBW	249	3	7	3	0	0
2755	98002	8	RO	253	2	7	4	0	0

The fourth and the last table, Table 5.4, is *Bowling*.

Table 5.4 The relation *Bowling*

MatchID	*PID*	*NOvers*	*Maidens*	*NRuns*	*NWickets*
2689	99001	10	0	58	1
2689	24001	3	0	27	1
2689	23001	3	0	15	0
2755	94002	9	1	40	1
2755	92002	10	0	56	1
2755	91001	4	0	29	0
2755	23001	10	0	53	2
2755	98002	10	0	40	3
2689	98002	10	0	44	1

We will now discuss the various features of SQL.

5.3 DATA DEFINITION—CREATE, ALTER AND DROP COMMANDS

As noted in the last section, DDL includes commands to create and destroy databases and database objects. The basic DDL commands available in SQL are discussed below. Additional DDL commands are presented later in this chapter in Section 5.4.12.

5.3.1 CREATE Command

CREATE is the most commonly used DDL command. It may be used to create a database, a schema, a new table, a new index, a new view, a new assertion or a new trigger.

We only look at creating an empty table. To create the tables *Match, Player, Batting* and *Bowling*, we use the CREATE TABLE command. Before formulating a CREATE TABLE command, it is necessary that each column type be looked at and likely values considered so that its data type be defined. In Fig. 5.2, we have arbitrarily assumed that *Team*1 and *Team*2 are 15 characters long but that will not be sufficient if we wanted to write one of the teams as Republic of South Africa. Therefore, care must be taken in defining data types for each column. Similarly, the data type of *Ground*, CHAR(20), is not able to represent names like Melbourne Cricket Ground or M.A. Chidambaram Stadium in Chennai or Vidarbha Cricket Association Stadium in Nagpur. CHAR(60) might be a better data type if full ground names are to be used for the column *Ground*. In addition to data type for each column, it is necessary to define the primary key and any foreign keys as well as any columns that are NOT NULL or UNIQUE.

```
CREATE TABLE Match
(MatchID INTEGER,
Team1 CHAR(15),
Team2 CHAR(15),
Ground CHAR(20),
Date CHAR(10),
Result CHSR(10),
PRIMARY KEY (MatchID))
```

Figure 5.2 SQL for Data Definition including specification of primary key

The basic form of the CREATE TABLE command is given in Fig. 5.2.

The CREATE TABLE command as shown in Fig. 5.2 is used to create a new table *Match*. It includes a specification of the names of the table as well as name of all its columns, separated by comma, and their data types. For each column, a name and data type must be specified. SQL data types are discussed in Section 5.3.4. Integrity constraints may also be specified in this command. In the above data definition, we have specified that the column *MatchID* is the primary key of the table and as noted earlier it will not allow a row with a NULL primary key.

Each column name is unique starting with a letter and made up of letters, numbers or an underscore (_) but no SQL reserve words.

The CREATE command also allows default values to be assigned to the columns. If no default value is specified, the system will usually provide a NULL as the default. It is also possible to specify constraints in the CREATE TABLE command. We will discuss constraints later in this chapter.

There are several other CREATE commands, for example, CREATE DOMAIN, CREATE INDEX, CREATE VIEW. We will discuss them later in this chapter in Section 5.6.

5.3.2 ALTER Command

The ALTER command may be used to modify an existing table. ALTER may be used for adding or dropping a column, changing the column definition as well as adding or dropping a table constraint. For example, Fig. 5.3 shows how to add a column to the table *Batting* to include information on how many times a batsman was not out.

```
ALTER TABLE Batting
ADD COLUMN Not_Out INTEGER
```

Figure 5.3 Adding a Column to a Table

The new column appears as the rightmost column in the table. Once the table definition has been changed, the values of the column would need to be inserted. The default value is NULL.

```
ALTER TABLE Batting
DROP COLUMN Not_Out
```

Figure 5.4 Dropping a Column in a Table

A column in a table may be dropped if required as illustrated in Fig. 5.4.

If several columns need to be dropped then several ALTER commands are required. More examples of ALTER are given in Section 5.7.

5.3.3 Destroying a Table using the DROP Command

A table may be destroyed by using the DROP TABLE command as given in Fig. 5.5.

```
DROP TABLE Batting
```

Figure 5.5 Dropping a Table

Dropping a table may have side effects. An index or a view may have been defined on the table and one or more columns in the table may be foreign keys in other tables. We may specify CASCADE like in Fig. 5.6 if we want all references to the table to be dropped as well. It is also possible to use RESTRICT which will not allow the DROP command to be executed if there are dependencies on the table.

There are several other DROP commands, for example, DROP DOMAIN, DROP INDEX, DROP VIEW. We will discuss them later in this chapter in Section 5.7.1.

```
DROP TABLE Batting CASCADE
```

Figure 5.6 Dropping a Table using CASCADE

5.3.4 SQL Data Types

As shown in Fig. 5.2, it is required that the data type of each column be specified when a table is defined. Data types deal with numbers, text, date, time and binary objects. There are a large number of data types defined in SQL3. We list only the most commonly used data types. We have divided them in three categories.

Numerical Types

There are a variety of numerical data types available in SQL. We list some of them in Fig. 5.7.

Data Type	Description
SMALLINT	Integer, precision 5
INTEGER	Integer precision 10
REAL	Mantissa about 7
FLOAT(p)	Mantissa about 16
DOUBLE PRECISION	Same as FLOAT

Figure 5.7 SQL numerical data types

Several other numerical types are available including INTEGER(p), DECIMAL(p, s), NUMERIC(p, s) and FLOAT (p) all of which allow the user to specify precision.

Character Strings and Binary Data Types

A list of some character strings and binary data types is given in Fig. 5.8.

Data Type	Abbreviation	Description	Comments
CHARACTER(n)	CHAR(n)	Fixed length character string of length n (max n = 255 bytes). Padded on right.	CHAR(5) may be 'India' but not 'Kerala'
CHARACTER VARYING(n)	VARCHAR(n)	Variable length character string up to length n (max n =2000).	VARCHAR(10) may be 'India' or 'Kerala'
CHARACTER LARGE OBJECT(n)	CLOB(n)	Variable length character string (usually large)	May be a book. n specified in Kbytes, Mbytes or Gbytes.
BINARY VARYING (n)	VARBINARY(n)	Variable length character string up to length n	n can be between 1 and 8000.
BINARY LARGE OBJECT(n)	BLOB(n)	Variable length binary string (usually large)	May be a photo. n specified in Kbits, Mbits or Gbits.

Figure 5.8 SQL string and binary data types

As shown above, quotes must be used when dealing with character strings. Comparison of character strings in SQL queries is explained later.

BLOBs may be used for large multimedia objects, for example, photos. CLOBs may be used for objects like a book. BLOBs as well as CLOBs may not be compared with others and may not be part of a relation's primary key and may not be used in DISTINCT, GROUP BY and ORDER BY clauses.

Date and Time Data Types

We now list the date and time data types in Fig. 5.9. In addition, data types TIMESTAMP and INTERVAL are also available.

Data Type	Description	Example	Comments
Date	YEAR, MONTH and DAY in the format YYYY-MM-DD. Less than comparison may be used.	2010-05-25 or 25-May-2010	Year varies from 0001 to 9999.
Time	HOUR, MINUTE and SECOND in the format HH:MM:SS. Less than comparison may be used.	22:14:37 (fraction of a second may also be represented)	Hour varies from 00 to 23.
TIMESTAP(n)	Used to specify time of an event in the format YEAR, MONTH, DAY, HOUR, MINUTE, and SECOND	The format is YYYY-MM-DD-HH:MM-SS[.s.]	The length is 26.
INTERVAL	Used to represent time intervals like 9 days or 20 hours and 37 minutes.	Can be YEAR-MONTH or DAY-TIME.	

Figure 5.9 SQL date and time data types

Other complex data types have also been defined by SQL. These include user defined types (UDTs) and structures.

5.4 DATA MANIPULATION–SQL DATA RETRIEVAL

As noted above, the SELECT command is used for retrieving information from a database. The basic structure of the SELECT command is as given in Fig. 5.10.

```
SELECT something _of _interst
FROM table(s)
WHERE condition holds
```

Figure 5.10 The Basic SELECT Command in SQL

The SELECT clause specifies what column values are to be retrieved and is therefore equivalent to specifying a projection by listing one or more column names. There can often be confusion between the SELECT clause and the relational algebra operator called selection. The selection operator selects a number of rows from a relation given a condition that the rows satisfy while the SQL SELECT clause is similar to the relational algebra projection operator as it specifies the columns that need to be retrieved. A SELECT clause is mandatory in all SQL queries.

The FROM clause includes a list of one or more table names that are needed to answer the query. If more than one table is specified, a join operation must be specified. Having more than one table without specifying a join is rarely useful. A FROM clause is mandatory in all SQL queries.

The condition in the WHERE clause in an SQL query is optional. The clause provides qualification for the rows that are to be selected. If a WHERE clause is not specified, there is no qualification and the whole table is selected. Normally the WHERE clause is the heart of an SQL query. It specifies the condition(s) that identify the rows the user wishes to retrieve. It is therefore like the condition in the relational algebra selection operator. The condition specified in the WHERE clause is either true or false for each row in the table. The rows for which the condition is true are selected and the rows for which the condition is false are rejected. A number of other optional clauses may follow the WHERE clause. These may be used to virtually group the rows in the table and to specify group conditions and to order the table retrieved if necessary. These are discussed later in this chapter.

The result of each SQL query is a table and may therefore be used like any other table. There is however one major difference between a base table and a table that is retrieved from an SQL query. The table retrieved by an SQL query may have duplicates while the rows in a base table are unique.

SQL is case insensitive although we will continue to use upper case for the SQL reserve words like SELECT, FROM and WHERE which could well be written as select, from and where. Also, it should be noted that all table names and column names in a query are one word and do not have spaces within them. The names must be unique. Usually each query ends with a semicolon but the user should check the documentation of the DBMS that is being used to ensure correct notation.

5.4.1 SQL Aliases

A table or a column may be given another name in a SQL query by using an alias. This can be helpful if there are long or complex table or column names which may be converted to short names using aliases, in particular in complex queries using several tables. Also, for some reasons, we may want to change the columns' names in the output from the names used in the base tables. SQL aliases may then be used. A column alias in the column list of the SELECT statement may be specified by using the AS keyword.

The syntax of table name aliases is as shown in Fig. 5.11.

```
SELECT column_name(s)
FROM table_name AS alias_name
```

Figure 5.11 Alias used in the FROM clause in SQL

The syntax for column names is as shown in Fig. 5.12.

```
SELECT column_name AS alias_name
FROM table _name
```

Figure 5.12 Alias used in the SELECT command in SQL

SQL column aliases are used to make the output of an SQL query easy to read and more meaningful. An example is shown in Fig. 5.13.

```
SELECT Team1 AS HomeTeam
FROM Match
```

Figure 5.13 Alias used in the SELECT command in SQL

A query like the one above may be used to change the output of the query. It will now have the heading *HomeTeam* instead of *Team*1.

We now present a number of examples to illustrate different forms of the SELECT command.

5.4.2 Simple Queries—Selecting Columns and Rows

We will first present some simple queries that involve only one table in the database. The simplest of such queries includes only a SELECT clause and a FROM clause.

Retrieving the Whole Table using*

- (*Q*1) Print the *Player* table.

Figure 5.14 shows how this query can be formulated in SQL.

When the WHERE clause is omitted, all the rows of the table are selected.

```
SELECT *
FROM Player
```

Figure 5.14 SQL for Query Q1

The asterisk following SELECT indicates that all columns of the table specified in the FROM clause are to be retrieved. We could have written all the column names but the wild card * provides a convenient way to print them all. If all columns are not required then we can formulate a query like the next one.

The result of this query is very similar to the table *Player* given in Table 5.2 at the beginning of this chapter although the ordering of the rows cannot be predicted. As noted in the last chapter, the relational model does not define an ordering of the rows and the ordering in a result is system dependent.

Using Projection to Retrieve Some Columns of All Rows from One Table

- (*Q*2) Find the IDs and first and last names of all players.

Figure 5.15 shows how this query can be formulated in SQL.

The above query is equivalent to specifying a projection operator in relational algebra to the table *Player* such that only columns *PlayerID, FName,* and *LName* are retrieved.

```
SELECT PlayerID, FName, LName
FROM Player
```

Figure 5.15 SQL for query Q2

The result of this query is presented in Table 5.5.

Retrieving All Information about Certain Rows from One Table

Often we may not want information about all the rows. Instead we need information only about some rows based on specific criteria. The criteria may be specified by using the WHERE clause.

- (*Q*3) Find all the information from table *Player* about players from India.

Figure 5.16 shows how this query can be formulated in SQL. Since we are only interested in players from India, the WHERE clause is used to specify the condition.

Table 5.5 Result of query *Q2*

PlayerID	*FName*	*LName*
89001	Sachin	Tendulkar
90001	Brian	Lara
95001	Ricky	Ponting
96001	Rahul	Dravid
96002	Herschelle	Gibbs
92001	Shane	Warne
95002	Shaun	Pollock
99003	Michael	Vaughan
92003	Inzamam	Ul-Huq
94004	Stephen	Fleming
93002	Heath	Streak
90002	Anil	Kumble
93003	Gary	Kirsten
95003	Jacques	Kallis
94002	Chaminda	Vaas
92002	Muthiah	Muralitharan
97004	Daniel	Vettori
25001	MS	Dhoni
23001	Yuvraj	Singh
96003	Saurav	Ganguly
99002	Adam	Gilchrist
24001	Andrew	Symonds
99001	Brett	Lee
91001	Sanath	Jayasuriya
21001	Virender	Sehwag
98001	Shahid	Afridi
98002	Harbhajan	Singh
27001	Praveen	Kumar
27002	Ishant	Sharma

Only those rows that have the *Country* column value equal to India are selected. All columns of these rows are presented to the user. Note that when an attribute value is text, the value in the WHERE clause is surrounded by single quotes.

```
SELECT *
FROM Player
WHERE Country = 'India'
```

Figure 5.16 SQL for query *Q3*

The result of this query is all the details of Indian players and is the relation given in Table 5.6.

Table 5.6 Result of query Q3

PlayerID	*LName*	*FName*	*Country*	*YBorn*	*BPlace*	*FTest*
89001	Tendulkar	Sachin	India	1973	Mumbai	1989
96001	Dravid	Rahul	India	1973	Indore	1996
90002	Kumble	Anil	India	1970	Bangalore	1990
25001	Dhoni	MS	India	1981	Ranchi	2005
23001	Singh	Yuvraj	India	1981	Chandigarh	2003
96003	Ganguly	Saurav	India	1972	Calcutta	1996
21001	Sehwag	Virender	India	1978	Delhi	2001
98002	Singh	Harbhajan	India	1980	Jalandhar	1998
27001	Kumar	Praveen	India	1986	Meerut	NULL
27002	Sharma	Ishant	India	1988	Delhi	2007

In the query posed in Fig. 5.16, it is possible to use "WHERE Country <> 'India'" if all players who are not from India were to be retrieved. Many other conditions may be used in the WHERE clause as discussed later.

• (*Q*4) Find all the information from table *Player* about players from India who were born after 1980.

```
SELECT *
FROM Player
WHERE Country = 'India'
AND YBORN > 1980
```

Figure 5.17 SQL for query Q4

Figure 5.17 shows how this query may be formulated in SQL.

In this query we are not only interested in players from India but also those born after 1980. The WHERE clause is used to specify both these conditions.

Only those rows that have the *Country* column value equal to India and players born after 1980 are selected.

The result of this query is all the details of Indian players who were born after 1980 and is the relation given in Table 5.7.

Table 5.7 Result of query Q4

PlayerID	*LName*	*FName*	*Country*	*YBorn*	*BPlace*	*FTest*
25001	Dhoni	MS	India	1981	Ranchi	2005
23001	Singh	Yuvraj	India	1981	Chandigarh	2003
27001	Kumar	Praveen	India	1986	Meerut	NULL
27002	Sharma	Ishant	India	1988	Delhi	2007

Retrieving Certain Columns of Certain Rows from One Table

• (*Q*5) Find details of matches that have been played in Australia.

First we note a weakness of our example data model. There is no way to obtain sufficient detail about each ODI match as we do not include a variety of useful information, for example, which ODI matches were played as part of the "2007-8 ODI Series between Australia and India". Also in the last few years many triangular ODI series have been held and some matches have been held in neutral venues like Dubai, Belfast or Kuala Lumpur. It is thus difficult to identify where each ODI match was played but we do so for the example database by assuming that the *Team*1 name is also the name of the country where the match is being played.

```
SELECT Team1, Team2, Ground, Date
FROM Match
WHERE Team1 = 'Australia'
```

Figure 5.18 SQL for query *Q*5

Figure 5.18 shows how this query may be formulated in SQL.

Again, a WHERE clause specifies the condition that *Team*1 is Australia.

One way of looking at the processing of the above query is to think of a pointer going down the table *Match* and at each row asking the question posed in the WHERE clause. If the answer is yes, the row being pointed at is selected, otherwise rejected. Since we have not included the name of the country where a match is being played in this example database, as noted above, we have to assume that if *Team*1 is Australia then the match is being played in Australia.

The result of this query providing details of matches played in Australia is given below in Table 5.8.

Table 5.8 Result of query *Q*5

Team1	*Team 2*	*Ground*	*Date*
Australia	India	Melbourne	10/2/2008
Australia	India	Sydney	2/3/2008
Australia	India	Brisbane	4/3/2008

• (*Q*6) List matches played in which India or Australia was *Team*1.

The condition in this query is slightly more complex. Figure 5.19 shows how this condition can be formulated in SQL.

In this query also, match information is retrieved when *Team*1 column value is either Australia or India. Any number of values may be included in the list that follows IN.

```
SELECT Team1, Team2, Ground, Date
FROM Match
WHERE Team1 = IN {'Australia','India'}
```

Figure 5.19 SQL for query *Q*6

The result of query *Q*6 above is given in Table 5.9.

Constants like 'Australia' or 'India' are often called a *literal tuple*. A literal tuple of course could have a number of values. For example, it could be

WHERE {2675, Australia, India, Melbourne, 10/2/2008, Team1} IN Match

Table 5.9 Result of query *Q6*

Team1	*Team2*	*Ground*	*Date*
India	England	Delhi	28/3/2006
India	Australia	Mohali	29/10/2006
India	West Indies	Nagpur	21/1/2007
India	West Indies	Vadodara	31/1/2007
India	Sri Lanka	Rajkot	11/2/2007
India	Australia	Mumbai	17/10/2007
India	Pakistan	Guwahati	5/11/2007
Australia	India	Melbourne	10/2/2008
India	Sri Lanka	Adelaide	19/2/2008
Australia	India	Sydney	2/3/2008
Australia	India	Brisbane	4/3/2008

The set of columns in the list before IN must match the list of columns in the list that follows IN for the set membership test carried out by IN to be legal (the list in the example above being a table).

```
SELECT Team1, Team2, Ground, Date
FROM Match
WHERE Team1 = 'Australia'
      OR Team1 = 'India'
```

Figure 5.20 SQL for query *Q6*

The above query in Fig. 5.19 is equivalent to the following SQL query shown in Fig. 5.20.

SQL allows some queries to be formulated in a number of ways. We will see further instances where a query can be formulated in two or more different ways.

The above query could use aliases if the headings in Table 5.9 are to be changed. For example,

```
SELECT Team1 AS HTeam, Team2 AS Visitors, Ground, Date
FROM Match
WHERE Team1 = 'Australia'
      OR Team1 = 'India'
```

Figure 5.21 SQL for query *Q6* using aliases for column names

Removing Duplicates from the Information Retrieved

• (*Q7*) Find IDs of all players that have bowled in an ODI match in the database.

Figure 5.22 shows how this query may be formulated in SQL. A WHERE clause is not required since we want IDs of all players in the table *Bowling*.

```
SELECT DISTINCT (PID)
FROM Bowling
```

Figure 5.22 SQL for query *Q7*

The above query is a projection of the table *Bowling*. Only the *PID* column has been selected and DISTINCT is used to remove duplicate values.

The result of query *Q*7 is given in Table 5.10.

Table 5.10 Result of query *Q*7

PID
99001
24001
23001
94002
92002
91001
23001
98002

DISTINCT may also be used when the query retrieves more than one column. The next query presents an example illustrating this fact.

- (*Q*8) Find names of teams and grounds where India has played an ODI match outside India.

We need to make a number of assumptions in formulating this query. We assume that if *Team*2 is India then India is playing outside India. We also assume that India could have played the same country at the same ground more than once (for example, Australia at Melbourne) and therefore we should remove the duplicates.

The query may now be formulated as in Fig. 5.23 in SQL.

```
SELECT DISTINCT (Team1, Ground)
FROM Match
WHERE Team2 = 'India'
```

Figure 5.23 SQL for query *Q*8

Obviously the list obtained by specifying DISTINCT *(Team1, Ground))* would be smaller than that obtained by specifying *(Team1, Ground)* without the DISTINCT clause although our database is so small that it had only one duplicate, playing Sri Lanka in Colombo.

The result of query *Q*8 is the teams and grounds on which India has played ODI matches outside India as given in Table 5.11.

Table 5.11 Result of query *Q*8 formulated in Fig. 5.23

Team1	*Ground*
Pakistan	Peshawar
Pakistan	Rawalpindi
West Indies	Kingston
Sri Lanka	Colombo
South Africa	Cape Town
England	Southampton
Australia	Melbourne
Australia	Sydney
Australia	Brisbane
Pakistan	Karachi

- (*Q*9) Find IDs of all players that batted in match 2755.

To formulate this query, we require a WHERE clause that specifies the condition for rows in the table *Batting* such that the rows are for match 2755. Figure 5.24 shows how this query may be formulated in SQL.

```
SELECT PID
FROM Batting
WHERE MatchID = '2755'
```

Figure 5.24 SQL for query *Q*9

This query also involves a selection as well as a projection. Note that the *MatchID* attribute is being treated as a string.

The result of this query is given in Table 5.12. Our small sample database has only seven batting records for match 2755.

Table 5.12 Result of query Q9

PID
23001
25001
91001
94002
92002
27001
98002

Sorting the Information Retrieved

- (*Q*10) Display a sorted list of ground names where Australia has played as *Team*1.

This is a query that uses a WHERE clause to specify the condition that Australia is *Team*1 and using ORDER BY to sort the result.

Fig. 5.25 shows how this query can be formulated in SQL.

```
SELECT Ground
FROM Match
WHERE Team1 = 'Australia'
ORDER BY Ground
```

Figure 5.25 SQL for query Q10

The list returned by the query in Fig. 5.25 would include duplicate names if more than one match had the same ground name (our example database is rather small and does not contain information on many ODI series played in a country). DISTINCT could be used to remove duplicates if required.

The above query produces Table 5.13 as the result:

Table 5.13 Result of query Q10

Ground
Adelaide
Brisbane
Melbourne
Sydney

The ORDER BY clause used in the query above returns results in ascending order (that is the default). Descending order may be specified by using

ORDER BY *Team1* DESC

The order ascending may be specified explicitly. When the ORDER BY clause is not present, the order of the result depends on the DBMS implementation as discussed earlier.

The ORDER BY clause may be used to order the result by more than one column. For example, if the ORDER BY clause in a query was ORDER BY *Ground, Date*, then the result will be ordered by *Ground* and the rows with the same *Ground* will be ordered by *Date*. The ordering may be ascending or descending and may be different for each of the fields on which the result is being sorted.

String Matching

SQL provides string pattern matching facilities using the LIKE command. LIKE is a powerful string matching operator that uses two special characters (called *wildcards*). These characters are underscore (_) and percent (%). They have special meanings; underscore represents any single character while percent represents any sequence of *n* characters including a sequence of no characters. For example, LIKE 'Del%' matches any string that starts with Del followed by any number of character or no character. LIKE 'Gup_' matches a four character string starting with Gup at the beginning. Other possibilities are LIKE '%ing%' (any string with at least three characters with ing in it) or LIKE '_ing_' (a five character string with 'ing' in the middle, for example Singh) or LIKE '%mes_' (a string of at least four characters with 'mes' followed by another character at the end, matching Ramesh or any word ending in, for example 'mesh').

It should be noted that LIKE is not always the same as equality of two strings. The test of equality first pads the smaller of the two strings if they are of unequal length by blanks and then compares them. LIKE does no padding.

There are a number of string operations available in SQL. These include the operations given in Fig. 5.26.

Operation	Meaning
UPPER (string)	Converts the string into uppercase
LOWER (string)	Converts the string into lowercse
INITCAP (string)	Converts the intial letter to uppercase
LENGTH (string)	Finds the string length
SUBSTR (string, n, m)	Get the substring starting at position n

Figure 5.26 Some SQL string operations

We now consider a simple query to illustrate the use of LIKE.

• (*Q*11) Find the names of all players whose last name starts with Sing.

In this query we need to use the LIKE command. The expression that follows LIKE must be a character string. The character percent (%) represents any sequence of characters including a sequence of no characters.

```
SELECT FName, LName
FROM Player
WHERE LName LIKE 'Sing%'
```

Figure 5.27 SQL for query *Q*21

Figure 5.27 shows how this query can be formulated in SQL.

This query produces Table 5.14 as result.

Table 5.14 Result of query *Q*11

FName	*LName*
Yuvraj	Singh
Harbhajan	Singh

In Fig. 5.27, the last statement may be changed to WHERE *LName* NOT LIKE 'Sing%' to find players whose name does not start with Sing. WHERE *LName* LIKE 'Sing_' would find only those names that have one character following 'Sing'.

Also LIKE '%ing%' would find any string that has the substring 'ing' in it.

SQL also provides more complex pattern matching facilities using SIMILAR but we do not discuss that SQL command here.

5.4.3 Different Forms of the WHERE Clause

So far we have only used the equality comparison in the WHERE clause. Other relationships are available. These include greater than (>), less than (<), less than equal (≤), greater than equal (≥) and not equal (<>).

We show below a number of different forms of the WHERE clause.

Some of the common forms are as follows:

- WHERE *C*1 AND *C*2—Each selected row must satisfy both the conditions *C*1 and *C*2.

- WHERE *C*1 OR *C*2—Each selected row must satisfy either the condition *C*1 or the condition *C*2 or both conditions *C*1 and *C*2.

  AND and OR operators may be combined, for example, in a condition like *A* AND *B* OR *C*. In such compound conditions the AND operation is done first. Parentheses could be used to ensure that the intent is clear, for example, (*A* AND *B*) OR (*C*). A more complex example may help: *A* AND *B* OR *C* AND *D* OR *E* AND *F* would be processed as (*A* AND *B*) OR (*C* AND *D*) OR (*E* AND *F*) and will be true if any one or more of the conditions *A* AND *B*, *C* AND *D*, *E* AND *F* is true.
- WHERE NOT *C*1 AND *C*2—Each selected row must satisfy condition *C*2 but must not satisfy the condition *C*1.
- WHERE *A* IN—Each selected row must have the value of *A* in the list that follows IN. NOT IN may be used to select all that are not in the list that follows NOT IN.
- WHERE *A* operator ANY—Each selected row must satisfy the condition for any of the list that follows ANY. Any of the following operators may be used in such a clause: greater than (>), less than (<), less than equal (≤), greater than equal (≥) and not equal (<>).
- WHERE *A* operator ALL—Each selected row now must satisfy the condition for each of the list that follows ALL. Any of the following operators may be used in such a clause: greater than (>), less than (<), less than equal (≤), greater than equal (≥) and not equal (<>).
- WHERE *A* BETWEEN *x* AND *y*—Each selected row must have value of *A* between *x* and *y* including values *x* and *y*. NOT BETWEEN may be used to find rows that are outside the range (*x*, *y*).
- WHERE *A* LIKE *x*—Each selected row must have a value of *A* that satisfies the string matching condition specified in *x*. The expression that follows LIKE must be a character string and enclosed in apostrophes, for example 'Delhi'.
- WHERE *A* IS NULL—Each selected row must satisfy the condition that *A* is NULL, that is, a value for *A* has not been specified.
- WHERE EXISTS—Each selected row be such that the subquery following EXISTS does return something, that is, the subquery does not return a NULL result.
- WHERE NOT EXISTS—Each selected row be such that the subquery following NOT EXISTS does not return anything, that is, the subquery returns a NULL result.

5.4.4 Queries Involving More than One Table—Using Joins and Subqueries

Many relational database queries require more than one table because each table in the database is about a single entity. For example, player information including player name is in table *Player* while batting and bowling performances are provided in tables *Batting* and *Bowling*. Therefore any time we wish to retrieve information about the batting or bowling performance of a player by using the player's name (and not the *Player ID*) we have to use two tables as shown in the examples that follow.

There are two possible approaches to using more than one table. One approach is to use a join. The other approach is to use one or more subqueries as shown in the next few examples. When using a join, most queries below only consider an inner equi-join.

Subqueries

A subquery is a query that is a part of another query. Subqueries may also include subqueries and this may continue to any number of levels. The queries presented below use subqueries in the WHERE clause but subqueries may also be used in the FROM clause instead of a table name as we will show later.

When a subquery is used in the WHERE clause, it normally tests for two types of conditions. The first type of condition usually tests a condition on the result from the subquery. For example, it may use formulation like "PID IN <subquery>" or "PID NOT IN <subquery>". The second type of condition is like "EXISTS <subquery>" or "NOT EXISTS <subquery>" to test that a non-null result is returned by the subquery or a null result is returned. We illustrate these conditions now.

- (*Q*12) Find Match IDs of all matches in the database in which Tendulkar batted.

As noted above, this query needs to use two tables as the player name is given only in the table *Player* and the batting performance is given only in the table *Batting*. We will use a subquery to obtain the *PID* of Tendulkar and use that information to obtain *Match IDs* of matches that he has played in.

This query is a simple use of a subquery. The subquery only returns a single constant which is compared with another value in the WHERE clause. If the comparison's result is true then the row in the outside query is selected otherwise it is not.

In a query like this in which the subquery returns only one value, *PID* IN could be replaced by *PID* = but if we are not certain that the result of the subquery will be a constant then it is best to use the IN operator.

Figure 5.28 shows how this query may be formulated in SQL.

```
SELECT MatchID
FROM Batting
WHERE PID IN
      (SELECT PlayerID
      FROM Player
      WHERE Lname = 'Tendulker')
```

Figure 5.28 SQL for query *Q*12

The above formulation of the query has a subquery (or a *nested query*) associated with it. The subquery feature is very useful and as noted earlier, a subquery may itself have a subquery within it and queries may be nested to any level.

The result of the above query is given in Table 5.15. Due to very limited data in our database only one ODI is found.

Table 5.15 Result of query *Q*12

MatchID
2689

It may be appropriate to briefly discuss how such a query is processed. The subquery is processed first resulting in a new table (in the present case a single column table with only one row). We have of course assumed that the last name Tendulkar is unique in the database. This is unlikely to be true if the last name of the player was Singh or some other common name. This resulting table is then used in the outer query in which the WHERE clause becomes true if the *PID* value of the player in the *Batting* table is in the set of *PIDs* that is returned by the subquery. Of course, in this case there is only one member in the set returned by the subquery. The IN operation in the WHERE clause tests for set membership. The clause may also use construct NOT IN instead of IN when appropriate.

Another format for the IN condition is illustrated in the following query.

- (*Q*13) Find the match information of all matches in which Dhoni has batted.

Now we show how a subquery may itself use a subquery in its WHERE clause.

This query must involve the three tables *Match*, *Batting* and *Player* as the match information is in table *Match*, the player names are in table *Player* and batting information is available only in table *Batting*. In this query we use a subquery that itself uses a subquery within it. The innermost subquery obtains the *Player ID* of Dhoni, then the next level subquery is used to obtain the *Match ID* of matches he has batted in and then use those *Match IDs* in the outermost query to obtain information about the matches.

```
SELECT MatchID, Team1, Team2, Ground, Date
FROM Match
WHERE MatchID IN
        (SELECT MatchID
        FROM Batting
        WHERE PID IN
                (SELECT PlayerID
                FROM Player
                WHERE LName = 'Dhoni'))
```

Figure 5.29 SQL for query *Q*13

Figure 5.29 shows how this query may be formulated in SQL.

This query results in the last subquery (or innermost subquery) being processed first. This subquery involves a selection of table *Player* which results in a table with only one row that is the *Player ID* of Dhoni. This result is then used to find a list of *Match IDs* from table *Batting* in which Dhoni has batted. These *Match IDs* are then used to find match information from the table *Match*.

Note that each subquery is executed only once and its result is used as a constant or a relation in the next outer query.

The result of the query is only two matches in our example database. The results are presented in Table 5.16.

Table 5.16 Result of query *Q*13

MatchId	*Team1*	*Team2*	*Ground*	*Date*
2689	Australia	India	Brisbane	4/3/2008
2755	Sri Lanka	India	Colombo	27/8/2008

We now look at how these queries can be formulated using a join. Additional queries that use subqueries are presented following the discussion of join.

Join Queries

It is possible to combine rows from two tables (or any number of tables) listed in the FROM clause by specifying the join condition(s) in the WHERE clause. We illustrate join by reformulating the last two queries.

```
SELECT MatchID
FROM Batting, Player
WHERE PID = PlayerID
AND LName = 'Tendulkar'
```

Figure 5.30 SQL query using a join for query *Q*12

The two queries, *Q*12 and *Q*13, involving subqueries may be reformulated using the join operator as given in Figs 5.30 and 5.31 respectively.

Reformulation of query *Q*13 is given in Fig. 5.31.

It is worth discussing how the join operator is used in the above queries. When the FROM clause specifies more than one table name, the query processor (conceptually) forms a Cartesian product of those tables and applies the join condition specified in the WHERE clause. Any other conditions in the WHERE clause are then also applied. In practice, the algorithm used is not that simple (and inefficient). Fast algorithms, to be discussed in Chapter 8, are used for computing joins.

```
SELECT Team1, Team2, Ground, Date
FROM Match, Batting, Player
WHERE Match.MatchID = Batting.MatchID
AND PlayerID = PID
AND LName = 'Dhoni'
```

Figure 5.31 SQL query using a join for query *Q*13

In both joins in Figs 5.30 and 5.31, the join condition is an equality condition and therefore equi-join is used in both SQL formulations.

We should also note that, in queries like those in Figs 5.30 and 5.31, it may sometimes be necessary to qualify some of the column names if the same name is used in more than one table in the FROM clause. For example, if the column *MatchID* was called by the same name in *Match* and *Batting* then one of the equalities in the WHERE clause will have to be *Match.MatchID* = *Batting.MatchID*. Such qualifications are needed only when there is a chance of ambiguity.

As noted earlier, it is possible to give aliases to some table names (for example, *Batting* may be given an alias *b1*) when names are long or more than one instance of the same table is used in a query.

- (*Q*14) Find the player ID of players who have made a century in each of the ODI matches 2755 and 2689.

The table *Batting* has a separate row for every batsman in each innings. We can therefore either use a subquery or use a join. We use a join of table *Batting* with itself.

Figure 5.32 shows how this query may be formulated in SQL.

There are no players that have scored a century in our database and therefore the result is null.

```
SELECT PID
FROM Batting b1, Batting b2
WHERE b1. PID = b2. PID
AND b1. MatchID = 2755
AND b2. MatchID = 2689
AND b1. NRuns > 99
AND b2. NRuns > 99
```

Figure 5.32 SQL for query *Q*14

This query is presented to illustrate that sometimes we may need to join a table to itself. In this query we have joined the table *Batting* to itself such that the join column is *PID*. In addition we have ensured that the first score is from the Match 2755 and the second score is from Match 2689 and both scores are 100 or more. We then retrieve the *Player IDs*.

The resulting join table in the query above would have rows such that each row has two scores of a player from the two ODI matches and both scores are 100 or more.

The query formulation in Fig. 5.32 also shows, as discussed earlier, that a table may be given an alias if necessary. In this case one instance of table *Batting* is given the name *b1* while the other is given the name *b2*.

More Subqueries

- (*Q*15) Find IDs of players that have both bowled and batted in the ODI match 2689.

This query needs to access both the tables *Batting* and *Bowling*. We will use a subquery formulation in which the subquery finds player IDs of those players that bowled in match 2689. The outer subquery then finds player IDs of those players that batted in match 2689 if they are also in the list of players that bowled in that match. Note that the inner subquery is executed only once.

Figure 5.33 shows how this query may be formulated in SQL.

As noted above, the subquery finds the player IDs of those players that have bowled in Match 2689 while the outside subquery finds from this list of bowler player IDs those players that have also batted.

The result of this query is given in Table 5.17.

```
SELECT PID
FROM Batting
WHERE MatchID = '2689'
AND PID IN
        (SELECT PID
        FROM Bowling
        WHERE MatchID = '2689')
```

Figure 5.33 SQL for query Q15

This query could also be formulated as an intersection of the two queries, one that finds the player IDs of all the bowlers and the other that finds the player IDs of all the batsmen. The intersection then gives the player IDs of those players that are in both player ID lists.

Table 5.17 Result of query Q15

PID
99001
24001
23001
98002

• (*Q*16) Find IDs of players that have either bowled or batted (or did both) in the ODI match 2689.

This query is similar to the last query, again requiring both tables *Batting* and *Bowling*. In this case, a subquery formulation is presented in which the subquery finds player IDs of all those players that bowled in match 2689. The outer query then finds player IDs of all those players that batted in match 2689 or if they are on the list of players that bowled in that match. Note that the inner subquery is executed only once.

Figure 5.34 shows how this query may be formulated in SQL.

```
SELECT PID
FROM Batting
WHERE MatchID = '2689'
OR PID IN
        (SELECT PID
        FROM Bowling
        WHERE MatchID = '2689')
```

Figure 5.34 Incorrect SQL for query Q16

Using UNION, INTERSECT and MINUS (or EXCEPT)

The query *Q*16 may also be written using the UNION operator as given in Fig. 5.35.

```
SELECT PID
FROM Batting
WHERE MatchID = '2689'

UNION

(SELECT PID
FROM Bowling
WHERE MatchID = '2689')
```

Figure 5.35 SQL for query Q16

The result of this query is given in Table 5.18.

Table 5.18 Result of query Q16

PID
89001
98002
23001
25001
99002
95001
24001
99001
27001

Figure 5.35 SQL formulation of the query would produce duplicates in the result because some players would appear in both the lists, the list of bowlers for match 2689 and the list of batsmen for match 2689. We should note that when UNION is used the data type of the columns in the first SELECT command must match the data type of the corresponding column in the second SELECT command. In the above query there is no difficulty as we are retrieving only one column which obviously matches.

Can this query be formulated in another way; perhaps using the table match in addition to tables *Batting* and *Bowling?*

What would the query become if UNION was replaced by INTERSECT or MINUS in Fig. 5.35?

Let us first consider replacing UNION with INTERSECT as shown in Fig. 5.36.

```
SELECT PID
FROM Batting
WHERE MatchID = '2689'

INTERSECT

(SELECT PID
FROM Bowling
WHERE MatchID = '2689')
```

Figure 5.36 SQL query using INTERSECT

Set intersection of any two sets results in those members of the two sets that are common to both sets. Therefore the query in Fig. 5.36 results in giving us a list of *PIDs* for players who have batted as well as bowled in Match 2689. The result therefore is the same as Table 5.17.

Let us now use EXCEPT, which is the same as MINUS, in Fig. 5.37.

```
SELECT PID
FROM Batting
WHERE MatchID = '2689'

EXCECT

SELECT PID
FROM Bowling
WHERE MatchID = '2689'
```

Figure 5.37 SQL query using EXCEPT

Set difference of any two sets, results in those members of the first set that are not in the second set. Therefore the query in Fig. 5.37 results in giving us a list of *PIDs* for players who batted but did not bowl in Match 2689. This is reformulated in the next query and its result is the same as in Table 5.19.

- (*Q*17) Find IDs of players that have batted in match 2689 but have not bowled.

Figure 5.38 shows another way this query may be formulated in SQL. Given the difficulty in formulating the query *Q*16, we must formulate this one carefully.

This query is equivalent to the query in Fig. 5.37 using EXCEPT to select those players that are selected by the outer query (i.e., those that have batted in the match) as long as they are not in the list of players that are returned by the subquery, that is, the list of players that bowled in that match. This has been done by using the "*PID* NOT IN" in the WHERE clause. Note that the subquery is only executed once.

```
SELECT PID
FROM Batting
WHERE MatchID = '2689'
AND PID NOT IN
      (SELECT PID
      FROM Bowling
      WHERE MatchID = '2689')
```

Figure 5.38 SQL for query *Q*17

The result of this query is given in Table 5.19.

Table 5.19 Result of query *Q*17

PID
89001
25001
99002
95001
27001

5.4.5 Using Subquery in the FROM Clause

A subquery may also be used in the FROM clause. We illustrate this use by an example given in Fig. 5.39.

- (*Q*18) Find the *Match IDs* of matches in which Sachin Tendulkar has played.

This subquery in Fig. 5.39 uses a subquery in the FROM clause which returns a table as its result and is therefore treated like a virtual table. In this particular case, the table returned has only one element which is the *PlayerID* of Sachin Tendulkar. This subquery table must be given a name which is ST in this query. We can now use this name in the WHERE clause.

```
SELECT MatchID
FROM Batting, (SELECT PlayerID
              FROM Player
              WHERE LName = 'Tendulkar') ST
WHERE PID = ST.PlayerID
```

Figure 5.39 Using a subquery in the FROM Clause

This use of subquery in the FROM clause is helpful in answering a variety of queries that use multiple aggregate functions as we will show later in this chapter.

We are now ready to illustrate the use of different forms of the WHERE clause in example queries that follow.

- (*Q*19) Find Match IDs of those matches in which player 27001 bats and makes more runs than he made at every match he played at Brisbane.

To formulate this query we first find all the scores of the player 27001 when he batted in Brisbane. This requires two subqueries, the innermost subquery and the middle subquery, since batting performance is given in table *Batting* and the name of the ground is available only in the table *Match*. Once the Brisbane scores are available, the outermost query finds Match IDs of matches where he scored more.

Figure 5.40 shows how this query may be formulated in SQL.

```
SELECT MatchID
FROM Batting
WHERE PID = '27001'
AND NRuns > ALL
        (SELECT NRuns
        FROM Batting
        WHERE PID = '27001'
        AND MatchID IN
              (SELECT MatchID
              FROM Match
              WHERE Ground = 'Brisbane'))
```

Figure 5.40 SQL for query *Q*19

As noted earlier, when ALL is used in the WHERE clause as in Fig. 5.40 above, the value in the outer query must satisfy the specified condition with all the rows that are returned by the subquery. In this particular query the outermost query condition *NRuns* > ALL would be true only if the value of attribute *NRuns* is larger than the largest value of *NRuns* returned by the middle subquery.

It should also be noted that the outermost query will scan the whole table *Batting* including the matches played in Brisbane but none of the Brisbane scores would meet the condition.

The result of this query is given in Table 5.20.

Table 5.20 Result of query *Q*19

MatchID
2755

- (*Q*20) Find IDs and scores of players who scored less than 75 but more than 50 in Colombo.

Once again we need to use a subquery because the information about the grounds is given in table *Match* while the batting information is in *Batting*. We will use the clause WHERE something BETWEEN *x* AND *y* although we could also use two WHERE conditions such as WHERE something ≥ *x* AND something ≤ *y*.

Figure 5.41 shows how this query may be formulated in SQL.

```
SELECT PID, NRuns
FORM Batting
WHERE NRuns BETWEEN 51 AND 74
AND MatchID IN
        (SELECT MatchID
        FROM Match
        WHERE Ground = 'Colombo')
```

Figure 5.41 SQL for query *Q*20

Note that we are looking for scores between 51 and 74 and not between 50 and 75. This is because (*A* BETWEEN *x* AND *y*) has been defined to mean $A \geq x$ and $A \leq y$.

The result of this query is given in Table 5.21.

Table 5.21 Result of query *Q*19

PID	*NRuns*
25001	71
91001	60

• (*Q*21) Find the player IDs of those players whose date of first test match (*FTest*) is not given in the database.

As noted earlier, SQL provides a special command for checking if some information is missing as shown in Fig. 5.42 below.

```
SELECT PlayerID
FROM Player
WHERE FTest IS NULL
```

Figure 5.42 SQL for query *Q*21

It should be noted that the column value being NULL is very different than it being zero. The value is NULL only if it has been defined to be NULL.

The result of this query is given in Table 5.22.

Table 5.22 Result of query *Q*21

PlayerID
27001

5.4.6 Correlated Subqueries and Complex Queries

A number of queries above have used subqueries. The subqueries used were needed to be evaluated only once. Such subqueries are called *noncorrelated subqueries*. There is another type of subqueries that are more complex and are called *correlated subqueries*. In these subqueries the value retrieved by the subquery depends on a variable (or variables) that the subquery receives from the outer query. A correlated subquery thus cannot be evaluated once and for all since the outer query and the subquery are related. It must be evaluated repeatedly; once for each value of the variable received from the outer query.

The correlated subqueries are most often used to check for existence or absence of matching rows in the parent table and the related table in the subquery. A correlated subquery therefore always refers to one or more columns from a table in the outer query. We illustrate such queries in examples ahead.

• (*Q*22) Find the names of players who batted in match 2689.

The query *Q*8 required finding the player IDs of players who batted in a match. This query is a little bit different since in this query we wish to find the names (not player IDs) of players who have batted. We now need to use the two tables *Player* and *Batting* because player names are available only in the table *Player* while batting information is given in table *Batting*. In this query we look at each player in the table *Player* and then check, using a subquery, if there is a batting record for him in the table *Batting*.

```
SELECT FName, LName
FORM Player
WHERE EXISTS
        (SELECT *
        FROM Batting
        WHERE PlayerID = PID
         AND MatchID = '2689')
```

Figure 5.43 SQL for query *Q*22

Figure 5.43 shows how this query may be formulated in SQL.

The WHERE EXISTS clause returns true if the subquery following the EXISTS returns a non-null result. Similarly a WHERE NOT EXISTS clause returns true only if the subquery following the NOT EXISTS returns nothing, that is, a null table.

This query produces Table 5.23 as result.

Table 5.23 Result of query *Q*22

FName	*LName*
Sachin	Tendulkar
M. S.	Dhoni
Yuvraj	Singh
Adam	Gilchrist
Andrew	Symonds
Brett	Lee
Praveen	Kumar
Ricky	Ponting
Harbhajan	Singh

Again, the above query can be formulated in other ways. One of these formulations uses a join. Another uses a different subquery. Using the join, we obtain the SQL query given in Fig. 5.44.

The join table would have rows only for players that have batted in match 2689 since a selection has been applied after the join.

```
SELECT FName, LName
FORM Player, Batting
WHERE PlayerID = PID
AND MatchID = '2689'
```

Figure 5.44 SQL for query *Q*22

• (*Q*23) From the example database, find the player IDs of players who have scored more than 30 in every ODI match that they have batted.

SQL provides no direct way to check that for a given player all his batting or bowling performances satisfy some condition like all scores being above 30 but we can obtain the same information by reformulating the question. Instead of asking for players that have scored more than 30 every time they have batted, we ask for players that have batted but never scored less than 31.

Reformulating the question makes the query somewhat complex. The SQL query below formulates the query as "find the *Player IDs* of players that have no score of less than 31 in any ODI innings that they have batted"!

Figure 5.45 shows how this query may be formulated in SQL.

```
SELECT PID AS PlayerID
FORM Batting bl
WHERE NOT EXISTS
        (SELECT *
        FROM Batting b2
        WHERE b1.PID = b2.PID
        AND NRuns < 31)
```

Figure 5.45 SQL for query Q23

Note that the subquery in Fig. 5.45 cannot be executed only once since it is looking for rows in batting that satisfy the condition *NRuns* < 31 for each player in the table *Batting* whose *PID* has been supplied to the subquery by the outside query. The subquery therefore must be evaluated repeatedly; once for each value of the variable *PID* received by the subquery. The query is therefore using a correlated subquery.

Note that the condition in the WHERE clause will be true only if the subquery returns a null result and the subquery will return a null result only if the player has no score which is less than 31.

Note that we have used aliases in Fig. 5.28 to label two instances of *Batting* as *b1* and *b2*. Also the heading of the query output has been changed to *PlayerID* by using an alias in the SELECT clause.

The result of this query in presented in Table 5.24.

Table 5.24 Result of query Q23

PlayerID
25001
80001

It is worth considering why we used the table *Batting* in the outside query. Should we have used the table *Player* in it? The reason for using the table *Batting* in the outside query is that we want to first find a player that has batted and then check if the player has ever scored less than 31. We do not need to check a player that has never batted according to our example database.

Some further explanation might be helpful. The outer query looks at each row of the table *Batting* and then checks if the player qualifies. The checking is done in the subquery which checks if the players in Table *b1* have ever scored below 31.

We also wish to note that the above query formulation has a weakness that an alert reader would have already identified. The above query would retrieve *PID* of a player that qualifies for each value of *NRuns* that is greater than 30 that the player has. Therefore if a player has batted five times and has scored more than 30 every time, his ID will be retrieved five times in the result. DISTINCT may be used to remove such duplicates. Another approach would be to use the table *Player* instead of table *Batting b1* in the outside query but this leads to another problem that we discussed earlier.

• (*Q24*) Find the names of all players that have batted in all the ODI matches in Melbourne that are in the database.

This is a complex query that uses a correlated subquery because of the nature of SQL as it does not include the universal quantifier (*forall*) that is available in relational calculus. Once again we need to reformulate the question we are asking and this time it becomes quite ugly with a double negative. The reformulated question is "Find the names of players for whom there is no ODI match played in Melbourne that they have not batted "! The SQL query that solves it is shown in Fig. 5.46.

```
SELECT FName, LName
FORM Player
WHERE NOT EXISTS
        (SELECT *
        FROM Match
        WHERE Ground = 'Melbourne'
        AND NOT  EXISTS
                (SELECT *
                FROM Batting
                WHERE PID = PlayerID
                 AND (Batting.MatchID = Match.MatchID))
```

Figure 5.46 SQL for query *Q24*

This nested query consists of three components: the outermost query, the middle subquery and the innermost (or the last) subquery. Conceptually, the outermost part of the query starts by looking at each row in the table *Player* and for that player under consideration evaluates whether the NOT EXISTS clause is true. The NOT EXISTS clause will be true only if nothing is returned by the middle subquery. The middle subquery will return a null table only if for each of the matches played in Melbourne, the NOT EXISTS clause in it is false. Of course, the NOT EXISTS clause in it will be false only if the innermost subquery returns a non-null result. That is, there is no row in *Batting* for the player who has played in Melbourne that the middle subquery is considering for the player of interest to the outermost query.

Although the middle subquery does not use any variable from the outermost query, the last two lines in the innermost subquery use variables from both the outer queries. It uses *PlayerID* from the *Player* table from the outermost part of the query and *MatchID* from the *Match* table in the middle subquery. The query therefore includes a correlated subquery and the query is quite complex.

The scoping rules of the names used in a nested query needs to be understood. For example, in Fig. 5.44, the innermost query uses the table *Batting* and therefore all attribute names of that table may be used within that subquery. Attribute names from the outer subqueries may only be used if those names are unique or they are qualified by the name of the table.

SQL does not have a universal quantifier (*forall*) but does have an existential quantifier (*there exists*). As considered in the last chapter, the universal quantifier may be expressed in terms of the existential quantifier. The query formulation above implements a universal quantifier using the existential quantifier. Effectively, for each player, the query finds out if there exists a match in Melbourne in which the player has not batted. If such a match exists then the player is not selected for inclusion in the result.

Since our example database is very small, the result of this query is null. A larger database is presented in the Appendix at the end of this chapter.

More correlated and complex queries are presented after we have discussed the aggregate functions and the GROUP BY and HAVING commands.

5.4.7 Using SQL Aggregate Functions

SQL provides a number of built-in functions to carry out computations or summarizations. Some arithmetic can be carried out in the SELECT clause of an SQL query as well but it is rather limited and is not be discussed here.

The built-in functions are presented in Fig. 5.47.

As the names imply, the AVG function is for computing the average for a column that is of numeric type ignoring the NULL values, COUNT counts the occurrences of rows, MIN finds the smallest value ignoring the NULL values, MAX finds the largest value ignoring the NULL values, and SUM computes the sum. AVG, SUM and COUNT may also be used as COUNT (DISTINCT *A*) to count only unique values, AVG (DISTINCT *A*) to compute average of only unique values and finally SUM (DISTINCT *A*) to sum only unique values.

```
AVG
COUNT
MIN
MAC
SUM
```

Figure 5.47 SQL aggregate functions

Some systems allow additional functions, for example, STDDEV for computing standard deviation and VARIANCE for computing variance. These functions also ignore rows with NULL values.

We consider a number of queries that use these functions.

• (*Q*25) Find the number of players that bowled in the ODI match 2689.

```
SELECT COUNT (*) AS NBowlers
FROM Bowling
WHERE MatchID = '2689'
```

Figure 5.48 SQL for query Q25

Figure 5.48 shows how this query may be formulated in SQL.

The above query uses the function COUNT to count the number of rows that satisfy the condition in the WHERE clause. We have again used an alias for the heading of the query output.

The result of the query is presented in Table 5.25.

Table 5.25 Result of query Q25

NBowlers
4

• (*Q*26) Find the average batting score of all the players that batted in the ODI match 2689.

Figure 5.49 shows how this query may be formulated in SQL.

```
SELECT AVG(NRuns) AS AveRuns_2689
FROM Batting
WHERE MatchID = '2689'
```

Figure 5.49 SQL for query Q26

This query uses the function AVG to compute the average of the values of the column *NRuns* for all rows that satisfy the condition specified.

The result of the query is presented in Table 5.26.

Table 5.26 Result of query Q26

AveRuns_2689
25.2

• *Q*(27) Find the youngest player in the database.

We do not have the player's age as an attribute in our *Player* table. The only attribute related to age is the player's year of birth (*YBorn*) in the table *Player*. To find the youngest player we will find the player who was born last according to *YBorn*. To find the player born last, we need to find the player, whose year of birth is the largest, assuming this attribute is an integer.

```
SELECT LName AS Youngest_Player
FROM Player
WHERE YBorn =
        (SELECT MAX(YBorn)
        FROM Player)
```

Figure 5.50 SQL for query Q27

Figure 5.50 shows how this query may be formulated in SQL.

This is not a correlated query since the subquery does not use a variable from the outer query and is executed only once.

The result of the query *Q*27 is presented in Table 5.27.

Ishant Sharma is the youngest player having been born in 1988.

Table 5.27 Result of query *Q*27

Youngest_Player
Sharma

We note that we have used the equality comparison "YBorn =" just outside the subquery. Technically this is comparing an atomic attribute value of *YBorn* with the result of a subquery which only returns a table as the result, like all queries. In this query however it is clear that the result of the subquery is an aggregation MAX and therefore an atomic value. Even if more than one row has the same MAX value, only a single value will be returned which may be compared with an attribute value.

When we need to find the row with an attribute value that is the largest or smallest, the functions MAX and MIN are used but SQL does not allow us to formulate the query in a straightforward manner as that given in Fig. 5.51.

```
SELECT LName, MAX(YBorn)
FROM Player
```

Figure 5.51 An illegal formulation of query *Q*27

This SQL query is illegal although some systems will produce an output that will include all values of *LName* combined with the value of MAX(*YBorn*). The reason it is illegal is that when an aggregate operation is used in the SELECT clause then only aggregation operations may be used except when the GROUP BY clause is used. When the system finds the value of MAX(YBorn), it only looks at the *YBorn* column and values of other attributes corresponding to rows with the MAX value are then not available. We therefore must first find what the MAX(*YBorn*) value is and then find the row which has the attribute value equal to that MAX value.

Further queries using the built-in functions are presented after we have considered a mechanism for grouping a number of rows having the same value of one or more specified column(s).

5.4.8 Using the GROUP BY and HAVING Clauses

So far we have considered relatively simple queries that use aggregation functions like MAX, MIN, AVG and SUM. These functions are much more useful when used with GROUP BY and HAVING clauses which divide a table into virtual tables and apply qualifications on those virtual tables.

GROUP BY and HAVING clauses allow us to consider groups of records together that have some common characteristics (for example, players from the same country) and compare the groups in some way or extract information by aggregating data from each group. The group comparisons also are usually based on using an aggregate function.

```
SELECT something_of_interest
FROM table(s)
WHERE condition_holds
GROUP BY column_list
HAVING group_condition
```

Figure 5.52 The basic SELECT command in using GROUP BY

The general form of a GROUP BY query is as shown in Fig. 5.52.

The SELECT clause must include column names that are in the GROUP BY column list (other column names are not allowed in the SELECT clause) and aggregate functions applied to those columns. These results of aggregate functions should normally be given a column name for output. The HAVING clause must be such that the condition can be easily checked, for example, AVG(*NRuns*) > 50. Note that AVG(*NRUNS*) will always have one value for each group and therefore the comparison is straightforward. We cannot use HAVING *NRuns* > 50 because each group has many values of *NRuns*.

The presence of the WHERE clause in the above query should be noted. This clause applies to the table before GROUP BY and HAVING and therefore results in a pre-selection of rows.

As noted earlier, GROUP BY allows a table to be divided into several virtual tables followed by use of any one of the following common aggregations:

- Count rows in each virtual group.
- Obtain the sum of values from a single column in each virtual group.
- Calculate average values from a column by choosing all the rows from each virtual group.
- Find maximum and minimum values from a column for each virtual group.

The procedure in executing a GROUP BY and HAVING clause works as follows:

- *All the rows that satisfy the WHERE clause (if given) are selected.*
- *All the rows are now grouped virtually according to the GROUP BY criterion.*
- *The HAVING clause including aggregation is applied to each virtual group.*
- *Groups satisfying the HAVING clause are selected.*
- *Values for the columns in the SELECT clause and aggregations are now retrieved.*

By default all the rows in a table are treated as one group if a GROUP BY is not specified. As noted earlier, WHERE may be used to pre-exclude rows before dividing the table and using the GROUP BY and HAVING clauses. GROUP BY must have one or more column names.

- (*Q*28) Find the number of players in the database from each country.

To find the number of players from each country, we need to partition the *Player* table to create virtual subtables for players from each country. Once the table has been so partitioned, we can count them.

```
SELECT Country, COUNT(*) AS NPlayers
FROM Player
GROUP BY Country
```

Figure 5.53 SQL for query *Q*28

Figure 5.53 shows how this query may be formulated in SQL.

The GROUP BY clause groups the rows by the specified column *Country* and the function COUNT then counts the number of rows in each virtual group. Note that the SELECT statement includes the column name *Country* which is the column which is used in the GROUP BY.

The result of the query is given in Table 5.28.

Table 5.28 Result of query *Q*28

Country	*NPlayers*
South Africa	4
Australia	5
England	1
Pakistan	2
New Zealand	2
Zimbabwe	1
India	10
Sri Lanka	3
West Indies	1

It should be clear that the above table could not be obtained without the GROUP BY clause which has many uses in formulating SQL queries. If the GROUP BY command was not available, we would need to find the number of players from each country by formulating a separate query for each country.

In the output we used an alias '*NPlayers*' for Count(*) because aggregate functions in the SELECT list do not have column names.

• (*Q*29) Find the batting average of each player in the database. Present the *PID* of each player.

To find the batting average of each player, we need to partition the table to create virtual subtables for each player. Once the table has been so partitioned, we can find the average of each player.

Figure 5.54 shows how this query may be formulated in SQL.

```
SELECT PID, AVE(NRuns) AS Ave
FROM Batting
GROUP BY PID
```

Figure 5.54 SQL for query Q29

The GROUP BY clause groups the rows by the specified column *PID* and the function AVE then computes the average of *NRuns* in each virtual group. Note that the SELECT statement includes the column name *PID* which is the column which is used in the GROUP BY.

The result of the above query is given in Table 5.29.

Table 5.29 Result of query Q29

PID	*Ave*
23001	19
24001	42
25001	54
27001	5
89001	91
91001	60
92002	1
94002	17
95001	1
98002	3
99001	7
99002	2

• (*Q*30) Find the batting average of each player from India in the database. Present the first name of each player.

To find the batting average of each Indian player, we need to join the tables *Player* and *Batting* and then select the rows for Indian players. The resulting table is now partitioned to create virtual subtables for each player. Once the table has been so partitioned, we can find the average of each player.

Figure 5.55 shows how this query may be formulated in SQL.

Before the GROUP BY the query removes all the rows for which *Country* is not India. Now the GROUP BY clause groups the rows by *LName* and the function AVE then computes the average runs for each virtual group.

The result of the above query *Q*30 is given in Table 5.30.

```
SELECT FName, AVE(NRuns) AS AveRuns
FROM Player, Batting
WHERE PlayerID = PID
AND Country = 'India'
GROUP BY FName
```

Figure 5.55 SQL for query Q30

It should be noted that we could not have used *FName* in the SELECT clause if we had used GROUP BY *PlayerID* because the system has no way of knowing that for each *PlayerID* there is a unique *FName*.

It should be noted that if we used GROUP BY *LName* then the average for singh would include runs for both Yuvraj Singh and Harbhajan Singh.

Table 5.30 Result of query Q30

FName	*AveRuns*
Yuvraj	38
M.S.	36
Kumar	7
Sachin	91
Harbhajan	3

• (*Q*31) Find the average score for each player when playing in Australia.

Figure 5.56 shows how this query may be formulated in SQL.

```
SELECT PID AS PlayerID, AVG(NRuns) AS AveRuns
FROM Batting
WHERE MatchID IN
        (SELECT MatchID
        FROM Match
        WHERE Team1= 'Australia')
GROUP BY PID
```

Figure 5.56 SQL for query Q31

This query first finds all rows in *Batting* that are for matches played in Australia by using the subquery. Then the rows are grouped by *PID* and the average score for each player is computed. Unfortunately our example database has batting information from only one ODI that was played in Australia (although *Match* table has information on matches 2675 and 2688 also) and therefore the average scores are the same as the score in that match.

The result of the query is given in Table 5.31.

Table 5.31 Result of query *Q*31

PlayerID	*AveRuns*
89001	91
23001	38
25001	36
99002	2
95001	1
24001	42
99001	7
27001	7
98002	3

• (*Q*32) Find the ID of players that had a higher average score than the average score for all players when they played in Sri Lanka.

Figure 5.57 shows how this query may be formulated in SQL.

```
SELECT PID AS PlayerID, AVG(NRuns) AS AveRuns
FROM Batting
GROUP BY PID
HAVING AVG(NRuns) >
        (SELECT AVG(NRuns)
        FROM Batting
        WHERE MatchID IN
            (SELECT MatchID
            FROM Match
            WHERE Team1= 'Sri Lanka')
        GROUP BY PID)
```

Figure 5.57 SQL for query Q32

This query first finds the average score for all players that have batted in Sri Lanka and then the outermost query selects those players that have average scores that are greater than that score.

The result of query *Q*32 is given in Table 5.32.

There was only one match in Sri Lanka so the average in the middle query are equal to the number of runs scored in that match.

Table 5.32 Result of query *Q*32

PlayerID	*AveRuns*
25001	53.5
91001	60.0
89001	91.0
24001	42.0

Multiple Aggregate Functions

In some situations, more than one function may be required. Let us illustrate it by an example.

• (*Q*33) In the query *Q*28, we found the number of players in the database from each country. Now we find the average number of players from this list in Table 5.28.

```
SELECT AVG(COUNT(*)) AS NAvePlayers
FROM Player
GROUP BY Country
```

Figure 5.58 An illegal SQL query for *Q*33

Once we have counted the number of players from each country, as in query *Q*28, the result is a table to which one may be tempted to apply another function to compute the average number of players.

Figure 5.58 shows how one might formulate this query. The formulation is however incorrect.

How do we then formulate this query?

One approach is to use a subquery in the FROM clause. This subquery then produces the table given in Table 5.28. Once we have that table, we may compute the average as shown in Fig. 5.59.

```
SELECT AVG(NPlayers) AS NAvePlayers
FROM
        (SELECT Country, COUNT(*) AS NPlayers
        FROM Player
        GROUP BY Country) NP
```

Figure 5.59 Legal SQL for query Q31

In the subquery, the table *Player* is divided into groups, each group with the same *Country* value. The number of rows in each group is counted resulting in the table *NP* in the FROM clause. Now we can find the average of the *NPlayers* column of this table.

The result of the above query *Q*33 is given in Table 5.33.

Table 5.33 Result of query *Q*33

NAvePlayers
3.2

Later in the chapter we will show how this query may be formulated using a view.

5.4.9 Outer Join

The concept of outer join was discussed in the last chapter. Further details are now presented including some examples in SQL to illustrate the concept.

We will use two new tables. Figure 5.60 lists the top 10 batsmen in ODI matches and Fig. 5.61 lists the top 10 batsmen in Test matches (both based on the total number of runs scored and current on 1st January 2010). The cricket database we have been using does not illustrate the outer join as well as these tables.

The best ODI batsmen in the world on 1st January 2010 are given in Fig. 5.60.

The best test batsmen in the world on 1st January 2010 are given in Fig. 5.61.

As noted earlier the natural join command finds matching rows from the two tables that are being joined and rejects rows that do not match. For example, if we needed to find the names, the total number of runs scored and the number of centuries scored by each player in ODI matches and Test matches we would join *bestODIbatsmen* and *bestTestbatsmen* and then carry out a projection. The SQL query is given in Fig. 5.62.

Player	Span	Matches	Innings	Runs	Ave	Strike Rate	100s
SR Tendulkar	1989-2010	440	429	17394	44.71	85.90	45
ST Jayasuriya	1989-2010	444	432	13428	32.43	91.22	28
RT Ponting	1995-2010	330	321	12311	43.19	80.50	28
Inzamam-ul-Haq	1991-2007	378	350	11739	39.52	74.24	10
SC Ganguly	1992-2007	311	300	11363	41.02	73.70	22
R Dravid	1996-2010	339	313	10765	39.43	71.17	12
BC Lara	1990-2007	299	289	10405	40.48	79.51	19
JH Kallis	1996-2010	295	281	10409	45.25	72.01	16
AC Gilchrist	1996-2008	287	279	9619	35.89	96.94	16
Mohammed Yousuf	1998-2009	276	261	9495	42.96	75.30	15

Figure 5.60 The table *bestODIbatsmen*

Player	Span	Matches	Innings	TRuns	Ave	T100s
SR Tendulkar	1989-2010	162	265	12970	54.72	43
BC Lara	1990-2006	131	232	11953	52.88	34
RT Ponting	1995-2010	140	236	11550	55.26	38
AR Border	1978-1994	156	265	11174	50.56	27
SR Waugh	1985-2004	168	260	10927	51.06	32
R Dravid	1996-2010	137	237	11256	53.60	28
JH Kallis	1995-2010	133	225	10479	54.57	32
SM Gavaskar	1971-1987	125	214	10122	51.12	34
GA Gooch	1975-1995	118	215	8900	42.58	20
Javed Miandad	1976-1993	124	189	8832	52.57	23

Figure 5.61 The table *bestTestbatsmen*

```
SELECT ORuns, 100s, Player, TRuns, T100s
From bestODIbatsmen AS b1, bestTestbatsmen AS b2
WHERE b1.Player = b2.Player
```

Figure 5.62 SQL query involving a join

The result of this query is given in Table 5.34.

This result of course only gives information about players that are in both the tables given in Figs 5.60 and 5.61. No information is provided about players that are in one table but not the other. The outer join provides information about rows that match in the two tables and also about rows that do not match.

Table 5.34 Result of the inner join query

ORuns	*100s*	*Player*	*TRuns*	*T100s*
17394	45	SR Tendulkar	12970	43
12311	28	RT Ponting	11550	38
10405	19	BC Lara	11953	34
10765	12	R Dravid	11256	28
10409	16	JH Kallis	10479	32

Consider the Fig. 5.63 which explains the concept of inner and outer joins. The figure shows the distribution of join attribute values for two relations *R* and *S*. The rows for which the join attribute values match are shown in the middle and these rows form the natural join of the two tables. The remaining rows of the two relations are rows that did not find a matching row from the other relation. There are therefore three groups of rows from the two relations:

- Rows from both relations that have matching join attribute values and are therefore combined to form the (inner) natural join of *R* and *S*.
- Rows from relation *R* that did not match rows from *S*.
- Rows from relation *S* that did not match rows from *R*.

These three regions are shown in Fig. 5.63. It shows that the left outer join of tables *R* and *S* has all the rows of relation *R* including those that are in the natural join as well as those that are not. The right outer join has all the rows of relation *S* including those that are in the natural join as well as those that are not. Finally, the full outer join of the join has all the rows of *R* and *S* as well as those that form the natural join. We now illustrate these concepts using the example.

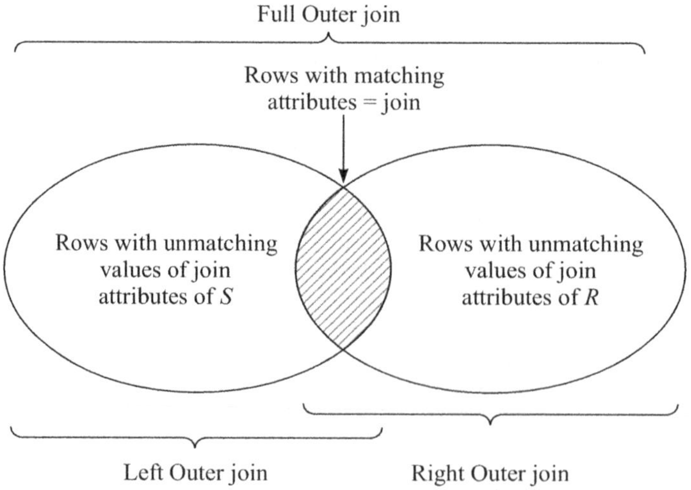

Figure 5.63 Inner join and outer joins

• (*Q*34) Find the left outer join of the tables in Figs 5.60 and 5.61 and find the total number of runs scored, total number of centuries, and the strike rate in the ODIs for each player.

Consider the left outer join between the two tables *bestODIbatsmen* and *bestTestbatsmen*. It is formulated in SQL using the FROM clause as given in Fig. 5.64. We find the total number of runs scored in both types of the game and the total number of centuries scored in the query in Fig. 5.64.

```
SELECT ORuns+TRuns AS TR, 100s+T100s AS TC, SR, Player
From bestODIbatsmen AS b1 LEFT OUTER JOIN bestTestbatsmen AS b2
ON b1.Player = b2.Player
```

Figure 5.64 SQL query involving a left outer join

The result of this query *Q*34 is given in Table 5.35 which gives the total number of runs (TR), total number of centuries (TC) and strike rate for players that have made it to the list of top ten batsmen in both ODI matches and test matches but it also shows those players that appear in the list of top 10 ODI batsmen but do not in the list of top 10 test batsmen. Since they do not appear in both tables, some of the information for them is given as NULL. These entries did not appear in the result of a natural join in Table 5.34.

Table 5.35 Result of the left outer join query in query *Q*34

TR	*TC*	*SR*	*Player*
30364	88	85.90	SR Tendulkar
23861	66	80.50	RT Ponting
22358	53	79.51	BC Lara
22021	40	71.17	R Dravid
20888	48	72.01	JH Kallis
NULL	NULL	91.22	ST Jayasuriya
NULL	NULL	74.24	Inzamam-ul-Haq
NULL	NULL	73.70	SC Ganguly
NULL	NULL	96.94	AC Gilchrist
NULL	NULL	75.30	Mohammed Yusuf

Similarly we can carry out a right outer join of the two tables which will give us a list of players who are in both tables as well as those that are in the test batsmen table but not in the ODI table. We leave it as an exercise for the reader to find the right outer join.

• (*Q*35) Find the full outer join of the tables in Figs 5.60 and 5.61 and find the number of runs scored in ODIs and tests, total number of centuries in ODIs and tests, and the strike rate in the ODIs for each player.

The full outer join is illustrated in the query in Fig. 5.65 which is formulated once again using the FROM clause.

```
SELECT ORuns, 100s, SR, Player, TRuns, T100s
From bestODIbatsmen AS b1 FULL OUTER JOIN bestTestbatsmen AS b2
ON b1.Player = b2.Player
```

Figure 5.65 SQL query involving the full outer join

The result of this query is given in Table 5.36 which gives the number of ODI runs, number of ODI centuries and strike rate as well as number of test runs and test centuries. Table 5.36 shows players who are in both lists (which is what we got in the natural join) as well as players who are in either of the lists but not in both. Some information about the top 10 test players that are not in top 10 ODI batsmen in the left three columns is NULL while batsmen who are in the ODI list but not the test list have two rightmost columns as NULL. These players would not appear in the result of a natural join which will only have players that are in both lists.

The result of a full join is quite useful since it allows us to easily identify players who appear in the list *bestODIbatsmen* and not *bestTestbatsmen* and also the other way around.

Table 5.36 Result of the full outer join query formulated in Figure 5.63

ORuns	*100s*	*SR*	*Player*	*TRuns*	*T100s*
17394	45	85.90	SR Tendulkar	12970	43
12311	28	80.50	RT Ponting	11550	38
10405	19	79.51	BC Lara	11953	34
10765	12	71.17	R Dravid	11256	28
10409	16	72.01	JH Kallis	10479	32
13428	28	91.22	ST Jayasuriya	NULL	NULL
11739	10	74.24	Inzamam-ul-Haq	NULL	NULL
11363	22	73.70	SC Ganguly	NULL	NULL
9619	16	96.94	AC Gilchrist	NULL	NULL
9495	15	75.30	Mohammed Yousuf	NULL	NULL
NULL	NULL	NULL	AR Border	11174	27
NULL	NULL	NULL	SR Waugh	10927	32
NULL	NULL	NULL	SM Gavaskar	10122	34
NULL	NULL	NULL	GA Gooch	8900	20
NULL	NULL	NULL	Javed Miandad	8832	23

Table 5.36 shows that there are a total of 15 batsmen that are either in the top ten list of ODI batsmen or in the top ten list of test batsmen or both. Only five of them are in both the lists. These players are Tendulkar, Ponting, Lara, Dravid and Kallis and they are, in my view, the batting superstars. Since three of these five

players are still playing, this table will probably look a bit different by the time you are reading it. There is very little chance of new players appearing in the two top ten lists since only a small number of players are close to the bottom of these lists at the time of writing. S. Chanderpaul of the West Indies is the only one who is still playing and has 9063 test runs and 8664 ODI runs on 21 February 2011.

5.4.10 Modifying Data in SQL—Update Commands

SQL update commands include the following:

- **Adding new data—Adding new rows to tables using the INSERT command.**
- **Modifying existing data—Modifying column data in existing rows using the UPDATE command.**
- **Deleting data—Removing rows from existing tables using the DELETE command.**

We now illustrate the INSERT, UPDATE and DELETE commands.

Adding New Data

The INSERT command is a very simple way to insert a row into a table. The next query illustrates INSERT.

• (*Q*36) Insert a new player Michael Clarke with player ID 200311 in the table *Player*.

Figure 5.66 shows how this row insertion to the table *Player* may be formulated in SQL.

```
INSERT INTO Player(PlayerID, LName, FName, Country, YBorn, BPlace, FTest)
<200311, 'Clarke', 'Michael', NULL, NULL, NULL, NULL>
```

Figure 5.66 SQL for row insertion Q36

Note that the above insertion procedure is somewhat tedious since it requires all column names to be listed and all corresponding matching values specified. The order of the column names does not need to be the same as given in the CREATE TABLE statement. Furthermore, it is possible to omit some column names from the list and their value is assigned to be NULL. The INSERT statement can be made a little less tedious if the list of column values that are to be inserted are in the same order as specified in the CREATE TABLE definition and all the column values are present. We may then write as given in Fig. 5.67.

```
INSERT INTO Player <200311, "Clarke", 'Michael', NULL, NULL, NULL, NULL>
```

Figure 5.67 SQL for row insertion Q36

It should be noted that when one wishes to insert a row, one may not have all the values of the columns. These columns, unless they are part of the primary key of the table, may be given NULL values. If there is relevant data in other tables, that data may be inserted into another table by using results of a query. For example, an INSERT like that given in Fig. 5.68 may be used.

```
INSERT INTO NEWBowling
SELECT PID, MatchID FROM bowling
WHERE NWickets > 4;
```

Figure 5.68 SQL for row insertion using information from another table

Modifying Existing Data

Every database will need modification of data from time to time; the data may have been input incorrectly or may be out-of-date. For example, an employee address or salary may have changed. The UPDATE command is used to carry out modifications.

The basic form of UPDATE command is as given in Fig. 5.69.

The table is the name of the table to be modified. SET Newvalues provides a list of new values for each table column specified while the WHERE condition selects the rows that are to be modified. An UPDATE statement may be used without a WHERE clause in which case the column values are modified for all the rows of the table. This is useful only infrequently.

```
UPDATE Table
    SET Newvalues
    [WHERE condition]
```

Figure 5.69 SQL for UPDATE of rows

• (*Q*37) Modify the number of centuries made by Tendulkar in Tables 5.61 to 51.

Figure 5.70 shows a case of modifying existing data as required in *Q*37.

```
UPDATE bestTestbatsmen
SET T100s = 51
WHERE Player = "SR Tendulkar"
```

Figure 5.70 SQL for UPDATE of row for query *Q*37

• (*Q*38) Modify the number of matches and innings played by Tendulkar to 177 and 290, respectively.

We are modifying some more data in Table 5.61. This is shown in Fig. 5.71.

```
UPDATE best Testbatsmen
SET Matches = 177,
Innings = 290
WHERE Player = 'SR Tendulkar'
```

Figure 5.71 SQL for UPDATE of more than one colum

Deleting Data

Similar to UPDATE, all or some selected rows of a table may be deleted by a command illustrated in Fig. 5.72.

• (*Q*39) Delete Match 2689 from the table *Match*.

Figure 5.72 shows how this delete operation to delete a row corresponding to match 2689 may be formulated in SQL.

```
DELETE Match
WHERE MatchID = '2689'
```

Figure 5.72 SQL for Delete Q39

The format of the DELETE command is very similar to that of the SELECT command. The DELETE command goes down the table *Match* row by row and deletes rows that meet the condition *MatchID* = '2689'. DELETE may therefore be used to either delete one row or a group of rows that satisfy the given condition.

It should be understood that DELETE commands like that in Fig. 5.72 and the one in Fig. 5.73 below are likely to have side effects if the rows deleted by these commands are being referenced by rows in the other tables.

• (*Q*40) Delete all bowling records of Brian Lara.

Once again the query is similar to some we have seen before. We use a subquery to find the player ID of Brian Lara and then delete all rows for that *Player ID* from the table *Bowling*.

Figure 5.73 shows how this delete operation may be formulated in SQL.

```
DELETE Bowling
WHERE PID =
        (SELECT PlayerID
        FROM Player
        WHERE LName = 'Lara')
```

Figure 5.73 SQL for Delete Q40

We have assumed that the last name Lara is unique.

5.5 VIEWS–USING VIRTUAL TABLES IN SQL

When a database is defined using the CREATE TABLE command in SQL, the user is instructing the DBMS to create tables and store them on disk. These tables can then be retrieved, updated or deleted as the user wishes. These are real tables or base tables that make up the database. The database also, as noted earlier, creates a lot of temporary tables when the database is queried. We have noted earlier that the result of any SQL query is itself a table. In normal query sessions, a query is executed and a table is materialized, displayed; and once the query is completed, discarded. In some situations it may be convenient to store the query definition as a definition of a table that could be used in other queries. Such a table is called a *view* of the database. A view is a virtual table that does not really exist physically as the base tables do, and it has no real existence, as it is defined as a query on the existing base tables. The user is able to treat a view like a base table that would be returned when the view definition is executed and all SELECT-FROM query commands may query views just like they query the base tables. Since a view is a virtual table, it is automatically updated when the base tables are updated. The user may in fact also be able to update the view if desired, and update the base tables used by the view, but, as we shall see later, not all views can be updated.

The facility to define views is useful in many ways. It is useful in controlling access to a database. Users may be permitted to see and manipulate only that data which is visible through some views. It also provides logical independence as the user dealing with the database through a view does not need to be aware of the tables that exist, since a view may be based on one or more base tables. If the structure of the base tables is changed (e.g., a column added or a table split in two), the view definition may need to be changed as well but the user's view will not be affected.

5.5.1 Defining Views

Views may be defined in a very simple way in SQL. As an example of view definition we define *Batsmen* as in Fig. 5.74.

```
CREATE VIEW Batsmen (PID, FName, LName, Country, MID, Score)
AS SELECT PlayerID, FName, LName, Country, MatchID, NRuns
FROM Player, Batting
WHERE PlayerID = PID
```

Figure 5.74 Creating a view in SQL

Another example is the following view definition that provides information about all the bowlers in ODI match 2689. Figure 5.75 shows how this can be created in SQL.

```
CREATE VIEW Bowling2689 (PID, FName, LName, Country, NOvers, NWickets)
AS SELECT PlayerID, FName, LName, Country, NOvers, NWickets
FROM Player, Bowling
WHERE PlayerID = PID
AND MatchID = '2689'
```

Figure 5.75 Creating a view for match 2689

Note that we can use column names for the view that are different than the column names in the base tables.

5.5.2 Querying Views

As noted earlier, views may be used in retrieving information as if they were base tables although views do not exist physically. When a query uses a view instead of a base table, the DBMS retrieves the view definition from meta-data and uses it to compose a new query that would use only the base tables. This query is then processed. Let us consider some examples.

- (*Q*41) Find the names of all players who have scored centuries.

Figure 5.76 shows how this query may be formulated in SQL using a view. In this case the view *Batsmen* defined in Fig. 5.74 is being used.

```
SELECT FName, LName
FROM Batsmen
WHERE Score ≥ 100
```

Figure 5.76 Using the view *Batsmen*

- (*Q*42) Find the names of bowlers that have taken five wickets or more in an ODI match 2689.

Figure 5.77 shows how this query may be formulated in SQL using a view. In this case the view *Bowling2689* defined in Fig. 5.75 is being used.

```
SELECT FName, LName
FROM Bowling2689
WHERE NWickets ≥ 5
```

Figure 5.77 Using the view *Bowling2689*

The above queries on views are transformed by the system by using the view definitions and then processed. The transformation is relatively easy as it only requires the view name to be replaced by the tables' names in the FROM clause of the view definition. A WHERE clause of the view definition is included in addition to the WHERE clause specified in the query on the view.

After transformation, the queries in Figs 5.76 and 5.77 would look like what is given in Figs 5.78 and 5.79.

```
SELECT FName, LName
FROM Player, Batting
WHERE PlayerID = PID;
WHERE NRuns ≥ 100
```

Figure 5.78 Query in Fig. 5.76 after transformation of the view definition

Transformation of the query in Fig. 5.77 is given in Fig. 5.79.

Now the queries may be processed as normal SQL queries.

```
SELECT FName, LName
FROM Player, Bowling
WHERE PlayerID = PID
AND MID = '2689'
AND NWickets ≥ 5
```

Figure 5.79 Query in figure 5.77 after transformation of the view definition

Earlier in Section 5.4.8 we considered how to pose queries in SQL when multiple aggregate functions are required in the query. Query *Q*33 was formulated using a subquery in the FROM clause. The subquery in the FROM clause could in fact be defined as a view and the view used in the FROM clause to obtain exactly the same result.

We formulate another query to illustrate the use of multiple aggregate functions using views.

- (*Q*43) Find the country that has the maximum number of players in the database.

This query requires counting of players in each country and then finding the country that has the maximum number of players. We will first define a view that does the counting of the players and then use that view to find the country with maximum number of players.

Figure 5.80 defines the view *NPlayers* that we require for obtaining the names of countries and the number of players from each of them.

```
CREATE VIEW NPlayers (Country, Count (*) as C)
AS SELECT Country, COUNT (*)
FROM Player
GROUP BY Country
```

Figure 5.80 Creating a view for number of players from each *Country*

NPlayers can now be used as in Fig. 5.81.

```
SELECT Country, COUNT(*)
FROM Player
GROUP BY Country
HAVING COUNT(*) =
        (SELECT MAX(C)
        FROM NPlayers)
```

Figure 5.81 Finding the *Country* that has maximum number of players

Figure 5.81 shows how the two aggregate functions MAX and COUNT may be used together in a query by using a view.

5.5.3 Updating Views

A number of interesting questions arise regarding views since they are virtual tables. For example:

- Can queries use views as well as base tables?

- Can views be updated?
- Can rows be inserted or deleted in a view in spite of views being virtual tables?

The answer to the first question is yes. There is no difficulty in using views and base tables in the same query as the query is going to be transformed into a query that uses base tables anyway.

The answer to the second and third question is maybe! Essentially if the view definition is such that a row in a view can directly identify one or more rows in the base tables then the views may be updated and rows be inserted in the view. It means the view must have a primary key of one or more base tables. The following points are worth noting about modifying data through views:

- A view to be modified must not contain any aggregate functions although a subquery used in the view may.
- The view to be modified must not use the duplicate removal DISTINCT.
- The view must not include calculated columns.
- A view may be deleted in a similar fashion as deleting a table.

Further discussion of this topic is beyond the scope of this book.

5.6 USING SQL IN PROCEDURAL PROGRAMMING LANGUAGES—EMBEDDED SQL AND DYNAMIC SQL

We have so far covered the interactive use of SQL in which the SQL queries are submitted from a terminal, executed and results returned to the terminal (sometime called *Direct SQL*). Although SQL provides powerful features to build programs, SQL is sometimes inadequate for writing application programs. Embedding SQL commands to access and manipulate the database in a conventional programming language (called the *host language*) like C or C++ allows power of SQL to be combined with the facilities of a programming language, for example, looping, to be used together to build application programs that use a database.

5.6.1 Embedded SQL

Use of embedded SQL is common in some application development environments. Embedded programming is useful when a previously written program in a procedural language needs to access a database or because SQL is not providing the facilities, for example, it has no looping facilities like IF..THEN..ELSE. On the other hand using SQL in a procedural programming language like C or C++ also creates some problems because the procedural languages are not equipped to deal with collections of multiple rows as a single operand. To overcome this difficulty, a facility is needed for stepping through a collection of rows returned by a SQL query, one row at a time. This is done by introducing the concept of a *cursor*.

It is possible to use SQL from within a program written in almost any of the conventional programming languages. Since conventional programming languages know nothing about SQL, no database table names may be used in a host language program outside the embedded SQL commands. An SQL query in a host language can appear anywhere in the host program but it must be identified by beginning it with EXEC SQL command followed by SQL statements or declarations. For example, the embedded SQL in a host language may look like the query in Fig. 5.82 with the semicolon usually terminating the command. This query does not deal with the problem of going through the results step by step. We shall discuss that soon.

```
EXEC SQL
SELECT *
FROM Player
WHERE Country = 'India';
```

Figure 5.82 A simple incomplete SQL query in embedded SQL

SQL statements in a procedural language are handled by the language preprocessor (sometime called the precompiler) for that language before the resulting program may be compiled. A preprocessor is therefore required if one wishes to use SQL in a host language. When necessary, SQL variables may be declared within a SQL declaration section by starting the declaration section by EXEC SQL BEGIN DECLARE SECTION and ending it by the command EXEC SQL END DECLARE SECTION. When a program with a SQL query is preprocessed, the SQL query becomes a procedure call of the host language and the program may then be executed. Such a use of SQL is called *embedded SQL*.

This process is explained in Fig. 5.83 that shows the preprocessor phase, followed by the compilation phase and finally the execution phase of the program.

A number of issues arise when using embedded SQL. Two of them are as follows:

1. There needs to be an error detection mechanism when using SQL in a host language.
2. The host language does not have any working storage allocated for SQL results. Some working storage is required.

We now consider how these problems are resolved in embedded SQL

5.6.2 Error Handling Using SQLCA, SQLCODE and SQLSTATE

As noted earlier a program in a host programming language knows nothing about the database it uses and thus there is considerable data independence between the program and the database. To make this interface between the host program and SQL work, the host program needs some communication working storage. Although implementation may vary from one DBMS to another, a communication area is provided to communicate between the database and the embedded program. This communication area may be accessed in the host program by including the following statement where SQLCA stands for SQL communication area.

```
EXEC SQL INCLUDE SQLCA;
```

Once SQLCA has been declared, two variables SQLCODE and SQLSTATE may now be used to detect error conditions in an embedded program.

All variables used to store database column values that are retrieved must be declared in the host language between the declaration statements as noted earlier.

```
EXEC SQL BEGIN DECLARE SECTION
int PlayerID;
char FName[20], LName[20];
EXEC SQL END DECLARE SECTION
```

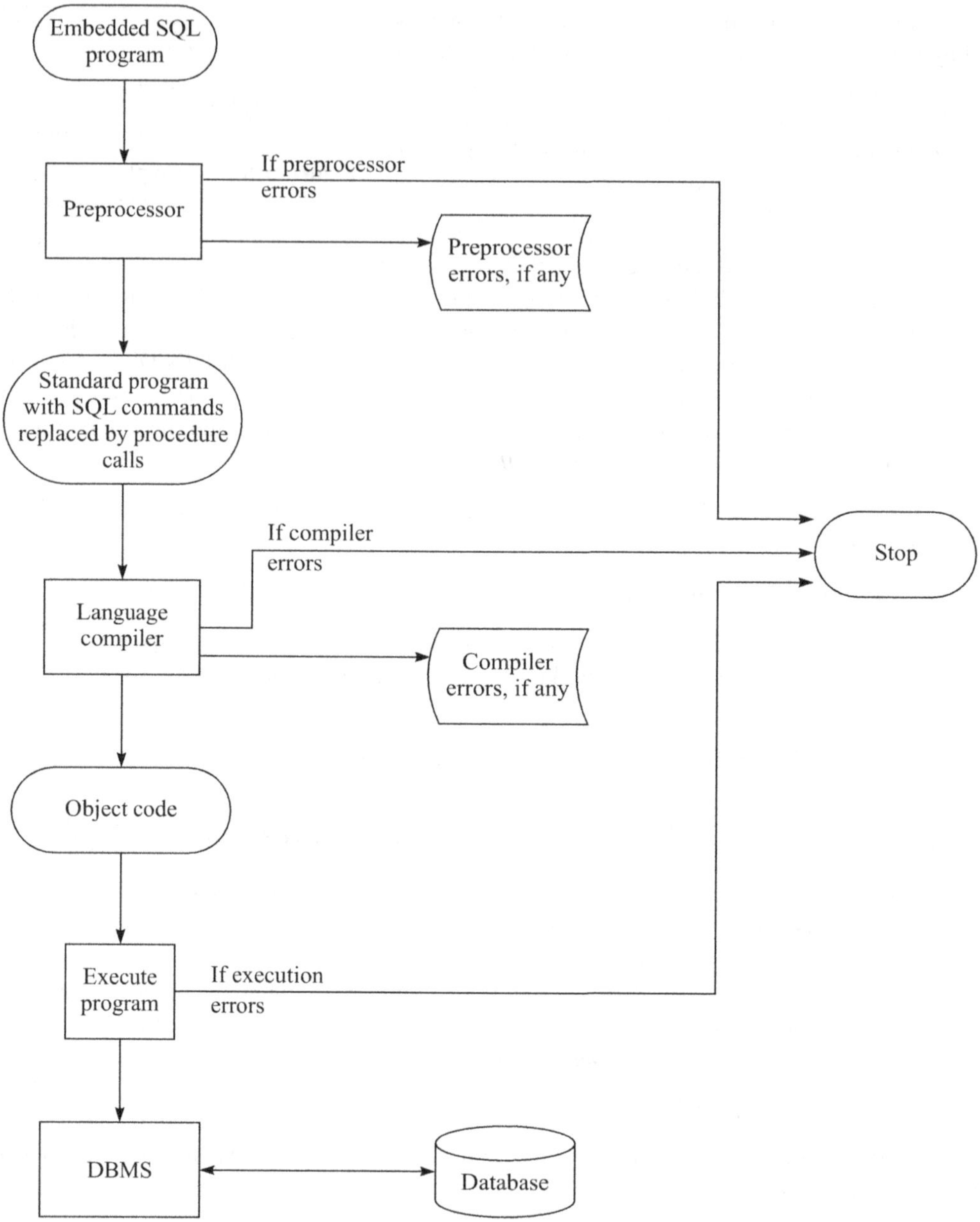

Figure 5.83 Preprocessing and compilation of an embedded SQL program

The host variables declared here are used in the SQL queries embedded in the host language program. Note that these variables are called shared variables and they are prefixed by a colon (:) when used.

5.6.3 Impedance Mismatch and Cursors

As noted above, the host language does not have any working storage for SQL results that are tables, usually with more than one row. Some SQL commands like UPDATE, DELETE and INSERT of course do not require any additional storage in the host program as shown below.

Update

```
EXEC SQL
UPDATE bestTestbatsmen
T100s = T100s + 4
WHERE Player = 'SR Tendulkar'
```

Select

When a number of rows are selected by an embedded SQL query then the concept of *cursor* as defined below must be used. As noted earlier, a cursor is needed since most conventional host programming languages are record-based, while SQL is set-based. This is called *impedance mismatch.* Therefore we need a binding mechanism that makes it possible to retrieve one record at a time as well as map the attribute values to the host language variables. A cursor (it may be thought of as a pointer) allows us to do that by essentially holding the position of the current tuple of the table that is the result of the SQL query while the host language deals with the table one row at a time. The cursor is not associated with any tables in the database, it is only associated with the table that is the result of an embedded SQL query.

Once a cursor is defined, it may be opened to point at just before the first row of the resulting table. There are two other operations available, *fetch* and *move*. Fetch gets the next row of the result while move may be used to move the cursor. Close may be used to close the cursor.

```
EXEC SQL DECLARE cursor1 CURSOR FOR
SELECT PlayerID, FName, LName
FROM Player
WHERE Country = "India";
```

Now we may issue the following commands:

```
OPEN cursor1
FETCH cursor1 INTO :var1, :var2, :var3
MOVE cursor1
CLOSE cursor1
```

Embedded SQL allows further processing of each tuple to be carried out in the host programming language.

Summary of Using Embedded SQL

1. First the declarations:

```
EXEC SQL INCLUDE SQLCA;
EXEC SQL BEGIN DECLARE SECTION;
```

```
Int PlayerID
Char LName[20], FName[20]
EXEC SQL END DECLARE SECTION;
```

2. Queries (with multiple rows result)

```
EXEC SQL DECLARE scursor CURSOR FOR
(SELECT PlayerID, FName, LName
FROM Player
WHERE Country = 'India');
EXEC SQL OPEN scursor;
do {
EXEC SQL FETCH scursor INTO <vars>;
} while (SQLCODE == 0);
EXEC SQL CLOSE scursor;
```

5.6.4 Dynamic SQL

Dynamic SQL is a programming technique that enables a program to build SQL statements dynamically at runtime. Thus more general purpose flexible applications may be created.

In some cases when using embedded SQL in a host programming language it becomes necessary to use and build the SQL query dynamically at runtime. Building SQL queries dynamically provides the user a flexible environment because the full details of a SQL query may not be known at the time of writing the program. For example, the name of the table that is to be used in the query may not be known prior to running the program. This can happen, for example, if the application program is accessing daily sales figures which are stored in tables that are named with the date, as Sales20100627 for 27 June 2010. Similar problems may arise in a reporting application, in a data warehouse application where the table name changes every time the reporting program is run. In some situations a query on the Web might allow the user to select the sort order. Instead of coding the query a number of times, with different ORDER BY clauses, a dynamic SQL query including a user specified ORDER BY clause might be the preferred solution.

Dynamic queries are useful where one of the following conditions holds:

- *An application program needs to allow users to input or choose query search or sorting criteria at runtime.*
- *An application program queries a database where the data definitions of tables are changing regularly.*
- *An application program queries a database where new tables are being created frequently and these tables are used in the queries.*

We now describe the difference between static SQL and dynamic SQL. Static SQL statements do not change from execution to execution. The full static SQL query is known when the query is processed, which provides the following benefits:

- Query processing can verify that the SQL query references valid database objects.

- Query processing can verify that the user has necessary privileges to access the database objects.
- Performance of static SQL is generally better than that of dynamic SQL.

Because of these advantages, dynamic SQL should be used only if static SQL will not achieve the query goals or if using static SQL is cumbersome compared to using dynamic SQL. However, as noted earlier, some table names may not be known when the program is written and the program is run frequently.

Dynamic SQL programs can handle changes in data definitions, without the need to recompile. This makes dynamic SQL much more flexible than static SQL. Dynamic SQL allows reusable code to be written because the SQL can be easily adapted for different environments.

5.7 DATA INTEGRITY AND CONSTRAINTS

We noted at the beginning of Chapter 3 that the relational model has three main components: data structure, data manipulation and data integrity. We have so far discussed the data structure, three data manipulation languages (relational algebra and relational calculus in the last chapter and SQL in this chapter) and data integrity. We now discuss how SQL may be used in maintaining integrity by specifying integrity constraints.

The CREATE TABLE command may include specification of integrity constraints which are usually either *column constraints* (associated with a single column) or *table constraints* (usually associated with more than one column). Any column constraint may also be defined as a table constraint.

We will look at the following types of constraints.

- Primary Key
- Foreign Key
- Domains
- Nulls

5.7.1 Primary Key Constraint

We have defined the concepts of candidate key and primary key in Chapter 3. From the definition of a primary key, it is required that each table have one primary key even if it is the combination of all the columns in the table, since all rows in a table are defined to be distinct.

One or more columns of a table may be defined as primary keys. The primary key of course is unique for each row of the table. No two rows can have the same primary key value.

One may consider the primary key definition as a constraint on the table that is being created. The primary key may be defined in the CREATE TABLE simply by using the PRIMARY KEY command as follows:

```
PRIMARY KEY (PlayerID)
```

In enforcing the existential integrity constraint the database system ensures that the primary key values are unique.

5.7.2 UNIQUE Constraint

As discussed above, a primary key has to be unique but columns that are not included in the primary key may also be defined as UNIQUE. For example, names of players may be unique and may be declared as such. A column defined as UNIQUE does not need to be NON NULL; it only needs to have all values that are not null as unique.

5.7.3 Foreign Key Constraint

As discussed in Chapter 3, the concept of a foreign key and referential integrity is important since a relational database consists of tables only (no pointers) and relationships between the tables are implicit, based on references to the primary keys of other tables. These references are called *foreign keys*.

The foreign key constraint applies on the column or columns in the referencing table, which is the table that refers to the primary key of another table. For example, it applies to the *PID* columns in tables *Batting* and *Bowling* since they refer to the *PlayerID* column in the table *Player*. It may be declared in the *Bowling* table definition as in Fig. 5.84.

```
CREATE TABLE Bowling
(MatchID INTEGER NOT NULL,
PID INTEGER NOT NULL,
NOvers INTEGER,
Maidens INTEGER,
NRuns INTEGER,
NWickets INTEGER,
PRIMARY KEY (MID, PID)
FOREIGN KEY (MatchID) REFERENCES Match
FOREIGN KEY (PID) REFERENCES Player)
```

Figure 5.84 SQL for data definition specifying foreign keys

This foreign key constraint will ensure that no row may be inserted in the table *Bowling* if the *PID* does not match with a *PlayerID* that is already in the table *Player* and *MatchID* does not match with the column *MatchID* in the table *Match*.

As mentioned earlier, a foreign key of a table may also refer to the primary key of the same table.

5.7.4 Domains

As noted earlier, the value of an attribute of a table must be drawn form a given set of values or be of specific data type. Domains can be specified as shown in Fig. 5.85. It should be used that although NAME1 and NAME2 in Fig. 5.85 are both declared as CHAR(10). They are different domains.

CREATE DOMAIN NAME1	CHAR(10)
CREATE DOMAIN Player1	INTEGER
CREATE DOMAIN NAME2	CHAR(10)

Figure 5.85 SQL for specifying domains

5.7.5 NULL Values

The issue of null values in a database is extremely important. A value in a database may be null for several reasons. The most obvious is that the value is not known at the present time. For example, a new employee's home telephone number will not be known until a phone is connected to his/her residence. Another reason some values in a database may be null are that the attribute may not be applicable. For example, an employee database may have an attribute spouse which is not applicable for a single employee.

If some attributes are not allowed to be NULL then NOT NULL should be appended to the definition of those attributes in table definition. Certainly the primary keys of tables should not be allowed NULL values.

5.8 TRIGGERS AND ACTIVE DATABASES

Triggers are an event handling mechanism for enforcing some types of data integrity.

Let us first define a trigger. A trigger is a kind of special procedure that is associated with a particular table and it executes automatically when data in the table is modified because some types of data modification may require special attention. A number of triggers may be defined on the same table. It may be that for some table one would like to be warned when a new row is inserted or deleted or updated.

A trigger, that is the procedure, may be fired before an event or after an event. A trigger may also be executed instead of an event.

Triggers provide reactive behaviour which is motivated by the occurrence of some event, typically a database operation. Triggers therefore are a practical way to check for integrity constraints and will be discussed in more detail in Chapter 12. Triggers also have other applications, for example, scheduling and real-time applications. Databases that use triggers are often called active database systems. The term can be defined as

Definition—Active Databases
A database that is designed to react to an internal or external stimulus is called an active database.

Active databases have a variety of applications. For example, an inventory control system could generate an alert when the number of a product in the inventory falls below some specified number.

The chapter on database integrity (Chapter 12) includes more information on triggers.

5.9 DATA CONTROL—DATABASE SECURITY

Databases store a large amount of personal and valuable business information. It is therefore essential that this information be protected from unauthorized access. Security of information is a complex subject and therefore we are able to only briefly introduce the subject here. There are two fundamental concepts of security, viz., authentication and authorization.

Authentication deals with uniquely identifying users, for example, as done by using a user name and password to access a computer or using a card and pin number for accessing an account through an ATM. More recently, it has been suggested that biometric techniques like fingerprints can provide a more secure method of authentication. To establish an authentication procedure there must be a facility to set up an account for each user that is to be authenticated and a password be provided to the user.

Authorization deals with the decision making regarding what parts of a database an authenticated user is allowed to access. For example, anyone can access the library catalogue but to be able to access student files in a university, a user must not only be an authenticated user but also have permission to access student files. To establish an authorization procedure, there must be procedures to allow a user permission to access some part of the database for reading only or for reading and writing. Views may be defined for a user to limit the content that a user can access.

In addition to identification, authentication and authorization, we need additional security facilities to protect a database. SQL provides two major techniques to provide security. These are the view mechanism and the GRANT/REVOKE mechanism.

We now briefly describe the GRANT and REVOKE commands available in SQL for authorization. There are no commands for authentication since it is assumed the DBMS provides facilities for authentication. View is a very useful security mechanism which allows a part of the database to be defined so that a user may be authorized to access only that part. Although the cricket database is not a good example to illustrate security mechanisms, let us assume that for some security reasons a user is only allowed to access information from the cricket database about players from his/her own country. A view may then be defined which will allow such an information to be available. GRANT command may then be used to grant authorization.

The GRANT command in SQL is used to authorize a user to carry out the specified operations (for example, SELECT, CREATE, INSERT, UPDATE and DELETE) on the listed tables or views. A user must have appropriate privileges before whatever operation the user wishes to carry out on some tables in the database.

The basic form of GRANT and REVOKE is shown in Fig. 5.86.

```
GRANT privilege ON resource TO username
REVOKE privilege ON resource TO username
```

Figure 5.86 SQL for granting and revoking privileges

The chapter on database security (Chapter 11) includes more information on these issues.

5.10 FURTHER DATA DEFINITION COMMANDS

In Section 5.3, at the beginning of this chapter, we discussed the most important data definition commands in SQL. These included CREATE TABLE, ALTER TABLE and the DROP commands. We now discuss a number of DDL commands in more detail.

5.10.1 The CREATE Command

As described in Section 5.3.1, the CREATE TABLE command is used to define a new table to the database. The CREATE command may also be used to create a view as shown in Section 5.5.1. It may also be used to create an index, an assertion, a domain, and a trigger.

Although the details of how a query is processed and how a database is stored are discussed in the following chapters, we briefly discuss the CREATE INDEX command that can assist in accessing data in the database faster. Details of how an index works are given in Chapter 7.

Suppose we have a large cricket database with a large number of players and many rows in the tables *Bowling* and *Batting*. Since most queries regarding batting and bowling access the database by using the *Player ID*, it may make sense to improve the efficiency of such queries. This can be achieved by creating an index on column *PID* in both tables.

Figure 5.87 shows how the index may be created in SQL.

```
CREATE INDEX PID1_INDX
ON Bowling (PID)
```

Figure 5.87 SQL for index creation on *Bowling*

And similarly on *Batting*.

```
CREATE INDEX PID2_INDX
ON Batting (PID)
```

Figure 5.88 SQL for index creation on *Batting*

Creation of indexes assists in efficient retrieval since a search is carried out using the index rather than each row of the table.

5.10.2 The DROP Command

Dropping a Table

We described how a table may be dropped or destroyed in Section 5.3.3. It can be done by using the DROP TABLE command. Any data that was in the dropped table is lost. As noted in Section 5.3.3, CASCADE and RESTRICT specifications may follow the DROP TABLE command to deal with the problem of disposition of other objects dependent on the table. These objects may include a view whose specification references the dropped table. Another dependency is a table that references the dropped table in a constraint, a CHECK constraint or REFERENCES constraint.

The RESTRICT clause ensures that the table is not, dropped if any dependencies exist. The CASCADE clause specifies that any dependencies be removed before the table is removed.

We also noted in Section 5.3.3 that there are several other DROP commands, for example, DROP DOMAIN, DROP INDEX, and DROP VIEW. We briefly discuss them now.

Dropping Views

A view may be dropped just as a table is dropped from a database. For example, we can drop view Bowling2689 as in Fig. 5.89.

```
DROP VIEW Bowling2689
```

Figure 5.89 Dropping the view Bowling 2689

Dropping Domain

It may at some stage become necessary to drop one of the domains which can be easily done by the command given in Fig. 5.90.

```
DROP DOMAIN NAME1
```

Figure 5.90 Dropping the Domain NAME1

Dropping Index

It may at some stage become necessary to drop one of the indexes which can be easily done by the command given in Fig. 5.91.

```
DROP INDEX PID1_INDX
```

Figure 5.91 Dropping the Index PID1_INDX

5.10.3 The ALTER Command for Modifying Table and Column Definitions

Earlier in Section 5.3.2 we discussed how the ALTER table command may be used for adding a column to a table or dropping a column. The ALTER command may also be used for changing the column definition as well as adding or dropping a table constraint. For example, Fig. 5.3 shows how to add a column to the table *Batting* to include information on how many times a batsman was not out.

The ALTER table command may also be used to add or drop an integrity constraint for a table. The ADD and DROP commands are similar to the ALTER command in Section 5.3.2 as shown in Fig. 5.92.

```
ALTER TABLE table_name <action>

<action> may include
DROP [Column] column_name
ADD [column] column_name
DROP CONSTRAINT  constraint_name
ADD CONSTRAINT constraint_definition
```

Figure 5.92 ADD or DROP commands for modifying a table

5.11 SUMMARY OF SOME SQL COMMANDS

The following list provides a summary of some of the commonly used SQL commands. SQL : 2003 is a much more complex language that includes many more commands.

SELECT [DISTINCT| ALL] <List of Columns, Functions, Constants, etc>
    FROM <List of Tables or Views>
    [WHERE <Condition(s)>]
    [GROUP BY < Grouping Columns>]
    [HAVING <Condition>]
    [ORDER BY <Ordering Column(s)> [ASC|DESC];

UPDATE <Table Name>
SET <Column Name> = <Value>
WHERE <Condition>;
INSERT INTO <Table Name> [(Column List)]
VALUES (<Value List>);
DELETE FROM <Table Name> WHERE <Condition>;
CREATE VIEW <View Name> AS <Query>;
CREATE TABLE <Table Name>
    (<Column Name> <Data Type> [(<Size>)] <Column Constraint>, … Other Columns);

There are a number of commands available for dropping a table, altering a table, creating an index, dropping an index and for creating and dropping a view.

CREATE DOMAIN—used for defining the domain for a column.
DROP DOMAIN—used for dropping a domain.
ALTER DOMAIN—used for changing an already defined domain.
DROP TABLE—to drop the whole table.
ALTER TABLE—used to drop or add columns or constraints.
DROP INDEX—to drop an already created index.
DROP TRIGGER—to drop an already created trigger.
DROP VIEW—to drop an already created view.
TRUNCATE TABLE—to remove the contents of a table.

Tables may have a variety of constraints as listed below. These are discussed in detail in Chapter 11 on Integrity.

NULL or NOT NULL
UNIQUE
PRIMARY KEY
CHECK
DEFAULT
FOREIGN KEY
UNIQUE
TRIGGER
ASSERTION

5.12 SQL STANDARDS

As noted at the beginning of this chapter, ANSI published the first standard definition of SQL in 1986 which was subsequently adopted by ISO in 1987. The 1987 standard is sometimes called SQL1. It included what most SQL implementations were providing at that time. In case of disagreement amongst the vendors, the areas were not defined by the SQL1 standard. SQL1 specified facilities for using SQL through host languages Cobol, Fortran, Pascal and PL/I, the most widely used languages at that time. SQL1 was defined to have two levels of compliance, viz., entry level (level 1) and full level (level 2). SQL1 unfortunately did not insist on meeting referential integrity requirements. In 1989, a new standard that provided only minor enhancements to SQL1 was published. This standard provided some additional features and defined support for two additional host languages, Ada and C. The two levels of the standard were retained although referential integrity was added to level 2.

The next standard for the language was published in 1992. It included a significant number of new features, was almost six times as long as the previous SQL1 standard, and was defined at three levels, viz., entry, intermediate and full. Some people have called this standard SQL : 1992 while others prefer to call it SQL2. The standards continue to evolve as some vendors implement additional language features to compete with other vendors and the international user community proposes new features to be included. A new standard was published in 1999 (called SQL3 or SQL : 1999). A number of advanced features including object-table features were included in the 1999 standard. Enhanced constraints including full referential integrity constraints were added to the entry level. The higher levels included assertions, domains, outer join, union and intersect operations.

At the time of writing this chapter, the latest SQL standard is SQL : 2003. It has been claimed that this standard does not include many new features although all parts of the SQL : 1999 standard have been revised to correct mistakes of the previous standard. In addition, a new part (Part 14) SQL/XML defines extensions related to XML documents.

The standards are strongly influenced by the vendors (and others) and once a standard is released the vendors do not necessarily implement all of it. Some vendors continue to include features that are not in the standard but are demanded by the user community.

SUMMARY

In this chapter we have discussed the query language SQL in detail. The following topics have been covered:

- SQL is the de facto standard query language for relational databases.
- SQL includes a data definition language (DDL), a data manipulation language (DML) and a data control language (DCL).
- SQL may be used in interactive mode as well as with a host programming language.
- Simple SQL queries may use only one table and use SELECT something FROM tables WHERE a condition is met. SQL is based on relational calculus.

- Data definition in SQL includes updates, data insertion, deletion, and authorization using commands that include CREATE, UPDATE and DELETE.
- SQL provides a variety of data types including INTEGER, REAL, CHARACTER, BLOB, DATE and TIME.
- WHERE clause may be of many different forms, for example, WHERE C1 and C2, WHERE EXISTS, WHERE A LIKE x.
- SQL queries that require information from more than one table are formulated using a join and/or subquery.
- Subqueries are usually used in the WHERE clause but may also be used in the FROM clause.
- SQL queries may use set processing commands UNION, INTERSECT and MINUS.
- Formulation of SQL queries that use subqueries may use EXISTS and NOT EXISTS.
- Some SQL queries require GROUP BY and HAVING clauses.
- Aggregate function like AVE, SUM, MIN, MAX and COUNT may be used in SQL queries. The functions are particularly useful when GROUP BY and HAVING clauses are used.
- Removing duplicates by using DISTICT, sorting results by using ORDER BY and string matching using LIKE is possible in SQL queries.
- Correlated subqueries and complex queries have been discussed. Correlated subqueries are subqueries that use one or more attribute values from the outer query.
- The important concept of outer join has been presented so that when a join is carried out not only the matching rows are shown but also the rows that do not match are displayed.
- The concept of view which is a virtual table has been explained. There are many benefits of views, the most important being to allow users only that part of the database that they need to use. Some views may be updated but not all.
- Advantages and disadvantages of SQL are described including its simplicity.
- The use of SQL as a host language, use of cursors, dynamic SQL is described. These facilities are required when the interactive SQL is not powerful enough for a given application.
- The role of data integrity in the relational model as implemented in SQL is described including existential integrity (primary key constraints), referential integrity (foreign key constraints), domains and NULLS.
- SQL was standardized in 1986, and 1987, followed by the SQL : 1999 standard. Further revisions include significant work on SQL with Java and XML. This resulted in SQL : 2003. Further revisions have been proposed and draft SQL : 2008 has been released.

REVIEW QUESTIONS

1. Where was SQL developed and when did it become an ISO standard? (Section 5.1)
2. Describe the structure of SQL queries and explain the different parts of the query. (Section 5.2)
3. Explain the data definition commands CREATE, ALTER and DROP. Give an example of each of them. (Section 5.3)
4. How are aliases used in SQL queries? What is the purpose of using an alias? (Section 5.4.1)

5. Give an example of formulating a simple SQL query that only selects some rows and columns from a table. (Section 5..4.2)
6. Give an example illustrating the use of DISTINCT to remove duplicates from the result of an SQL query? (Section 5.4.2)
7. Explain how string pattern matching is done in SQL to find the name starting with *Tend* and finishing with *ar*. (Section 5.4.2)
8. List five different forms used in the WHERE clause. (Section 5.4.3)
9. Write an SQL query which finds the names of players whose place of birth is not specified in the database. (Section 5.4.3)
10. How does an SQL use subquery in querying more than one table? Give an example. (Section 5.4.4)
11. Give an example of using a join in an SQL query. (Section 5.4.4)
12. Explain the use of UNION, INTERSECT and EXCEPT in SQL queries. (Section 5.4.4)
13. Show how a subquery may be used in the SQL FROM clause. (Section 5.4.5)
14. What is a correlated SQL subquery? Give an example. (Section 5.4.6)
15. What aggregate functions are available in SQL? (Section 5.4.7)
16. How can data be virtually grouped in SQL queries? Explain how GROUP BY, HAVING and WHERE can be used in the same SQL query. (Section 5.4.8)
17. Give an example of using multiple aggregate functions in an SQL query. (Section 5.4.8)
18. Explain the difference between inner join and outer join. (Section 5.4.9)
19. What is a left outer join, a right outer join and a full outer join? (Section 5.4.9)
20. What commands are used in SQL for data update, data insertion, and data deletion? (Sections 5.4.10)
21. Explain the motivations for using view? (Section 5.5)
22. Describe how the concept of views may be used for security control. (Section 5.5)
23. Is it possible to update views? (Section 5.5.3)
24. Explain how SQL may be used in a procedural programming language. (Section 5.6)
25. What is impedance mismatch? (Section 5.6)
26. Explain when is a dynamic SQL needed. Give an example. (Section 5.6.2)
27. Describe the basic data integrity requirements: existential integrity (primary keys), referential integrity (foreign keys), domains and nulls. (Section 5.7)
28. How can SQL be used in maintaining the above integrity constraints? (Section 5.7)
29. What is a trigger? What is it used for? (Section 5.8)
30. Explain the role of SQL in authentication and authorization. (Section 5.9)
31. Give a list of all CREATE, ALTER and DROP commands in SQL. (Section 5.10)

SHORT ANSWER QUESTIONS

1. Write an SQL query to retrieve all rows of the table *Player*.
2. Write an SQL query to retrieve only the last name of all players from *Player*.
3. What major data types are available in SQL?
4. Write an SQL query to retrieve only the rows of Indian players from *Player*.
5. Write an SQL query to retrieve only the last name of all Indian players from *Player*.

6. What is DISTINCT?
7. Write an SQL query to retrieve the last name of players born after 1980 from *Player*.
8. Write an SQL query to retrieve the player ID of players who scored a century in a match from *Batting*.
9. How can the result of a query be sorted?
10. Write an SQL query to retrieve the last name of players who have not played a test match from *Player*.
11. Write an SQL query to retrieve the player ID of players who have taken more than five wickets in a match from *Bowling*.
12. Write an SQL query to retrieve the number of times Tendulkar has batted in our database from table *Batting*.
13. Write an SQL query to find the highest score of Dhoni from the information in table *Batting*.
14. What is an uncorrelated subquery? Give an example.
15. What is a corelated subquery? Give an example.
16. What aggregate functions are available in SQL?
17. Use an example to explain left outer join, right outer join and full outer join.
18. Give examples of queries involving UNION and INTERSECT.
19. How does view help in database security? Give an example of its use.
20. What is primary key constraint? Give an example.
21. What is referential constraint? Give an example.
22. What does the CREATE TABLE command do? Give an example.
23. Are there other CREATE commands?
24. What does the DROP command do? Give an example.
25. What does the ALTER command do? Give an example.
26. What is a cursor used for?
27. What is impedance mismatch?
28. What is dynamic SQL useful for?
29. What is inclusion dependency?

MULTIPLE CHOICE QUESTIONS

1. Which of the following is **not** true?
   (a) SQL was called SEQUEL before the name SQL was chosen.
   (b) SQL was first designed by E. F. Codd.
   (c) SQL was developed as part of a relational DBMS prototype at IBM San Jose Research Laboratory.
   (d) SQL was first defined around 1974.
2. Which of the following are correct for SQL?
   (a) SQL may be used for data definition as well as data retrieval.
   (b) SQL may be used for defining base tables as well as view tables.
   (c) SQL may be used for defining primary keys as well as foreign keys for each table.
   (d) SQL may be used for creating as well as dropping indexes.
   (e) All of the above

3. Which two of the following statements are true about SQL?
   (a) It is a language very much like relational calculus.
   (b) It is a language very much like relational algebra.
   (c) It is a nonprocedural language.
   (d) It is a procedural language like C++.
4. Which one of the following data definition commands is **not** an SQL command?
   (a) CREATE TABLE
   (b) DROP TABLE
   (c) MODIFY TABLE
   (d) DROP DOMAIN
   (e) CREATE DOMAIN
5. Which one of the following is true about domains in SQL?
   (a) SQL domains are user-defined data types.
   (b) SQL domains must be used in data definition.
   (c) SQL domains provide strong typing.
   (d) SQL domains are only syntactic shorthand for system-defined data types.
   (e) SQL domains allow users to define allowed operations on each domain.
6. Which of the following are true about SQL?
   (a) SQL tables cannot have duplicate rows inserted in them.
   (b) SQL tables do not have any column orderings.
   (c) SQL tables do not have to have atomic column values.
   (d) SQL tables can have a default value defined for each column.
7. Which one of the following is true about SQL?
   (a) SQL automatically eliminates duplicate rows from results .
   (b) SQL automatically sorts the rows from results.
   (c) SQL does not provide commands to compute all relational algebra operators directly.
   (d) SQL does not allow any join other than an equi-join.
8. Which one of the following cannot be included in the CREATE TABLE command in SQL?
   (a) Names and data types of the table columns.
   (b) Primary key and foreign keys of the table.
   (c) Default values for the table columns.
   (d) Who is authorized to access the table.
9. Which one of the following is allowed in SQL?
   (a) Adding or deleting a column from an existing table.
   (b) Adding or deleting a constraint from an existing table.
   (c) Changing a column definition.
   (d) All of the above
10. Which one of the following is **not** true?
   (a) An SQL query must not have more than one join in one query.
   (b) All column names in an SQL query must be qualified by the table name.
   (c) All table names given in an SQL FROM clause must be distinct.
   (d) An SQL query must not have an aggregation function in the HAVING clause.
   (e) All of the above

11. SQL provides a number of special aggregate functions. Which one of the following is **not** included in SQL?
    (a) COUNT (b) SUM (c) MAX (d) MIN
    (e) MEDIAN
12. When functions are used in SQL statements, which one of the following is **not** correct?
    (a) DISTINCT must be used if the duplicates are to be eliminated before the function is applied.
    (b) All cases of COUNT *must* include DISTINCT.
    (c) Any NULLS in the argument column are ignored when functions like AVG, MAX, and MIN are used.
    (d) If the argument happens to be an empty set, COUNT returns zero while other functions return null.
13. Which of the following is **not** correct?
    (a) GROUP BY logically partitions the table; no physical rearranging is done.
    (b) Each expression in the SELECT clause must be a single value per group when GROUP BY is used.
    (c) It is not possible to use WHERE and then use GROUP BY in the same query.
    (d) HAVING is to GROUP BY as WHERE is to SELECT.
    (e) The WHERE clause selects the rows which satisfy the given condition, the HAVING clause selects a group that satisfies the condition using aggregation.
14. Which of the following is **not** true?
    (a) A query may have as many as six or more different SQL formulations.
    (b) Different versions of the same query are guaranteed to be processed equally efficiently.
    (c) Subqueries may be nested to any depth.
    (d) SQL is not a faithful implementation of the relational model.
15. Which of the following is **not** correct?
    (a) Views are virtual tables, tables that do not exist in their own right.
    (b) The user does not see any difference between a base table and a view.
    (c) Any retrieval operations on views are translated into equivalent operations on the base tables.
    (d) Views may be updated in the same way as base tables.
    (e) None of the above

The following database will be used in a number of questions that follow.

```
student(student_id, student_name, address)
enrolment(student_id, subject_id, mark)
subject(subject_id, subject_name)
```

16. Consider the following query:

```
SELECT subject_name, Count(*)
FROM subject, enrolment
WHERE subject.subject_id = enrolment.subject_id
AND mark > 40
GROUP BY subject_name
HAVING Count(*) > 5
```

Which one of the following is true about the query above?

(a) The query is illegal.

(b) The query retrieves the subject names and number of students in each subject.

(c) The query retrieves the subject names and number of students in each subject that has more than five students.

(d) The query retrieves the subject names and number of students in each subject that has more than five students, each of them with more than 40 marks.

17. Consider the following query:

```
SELECT subject_name, Count(*)
FROM subject, enrolment
WHERE subject.subject_id = enrolment.subject_id
AND mark > 40
AND subject_id IN
        (SELECT subject_id
        FROM enrolment
        GROUP BY subject_id
        HAVING Count(*) > 5 )
GROUP BY subject_name
```

Which one of the following is true?

(a) The query is illegal.

(b) This query is equivalent to the last query.

(c) The query retrieves the subject names and number of students in each subject that has more than five students.

(d) The query retrieves the subject names and number of students in each subject that has more than five students, each having more than 40 marks.

18. Consider the following query:

```
SELECT subject_id
FROM subject
WHERE subject_id IN
 (SELECT subject_id
        FROM student, enrolment
        WHERE student.student_id = enrolment.student-Id
        AND student_name = 'Ravi Kumar')
OR subject-id IN
        (SELECT subject-id
        FROM subject, enrolment
        WHERE subject.subject_id = enrolment.subject_id
        GROUP BY subject_id
        HAVING count(*) > 100)
```

Which of the following is true?

(a) The above query is illegal.

(b) The query retrieves the subject id of subjects that have a student by the name of Ravi Kumar and have an enrolment of over 100.

(c) The query retrieves the subject id of subjects that have a student by the name of Ravi Kumar or have an enrolment of over 100.

(d) The query retrieves the subject id of subjects that have a student by the name of Ravi Kumar and do not have an enrolment of over 100.

19. Consider the following query:

```
SELECT student_name, avg(mark)
FROM student, enrolment
WHERE student.student_id = enrolment.student_id
```

Which one of the following is correct for the query?

(a) The query is not legal.

(b) The query retrieves student names and their average mark.

(c) The query retrieves student names and the class average mark for each student.

(d) The query retrieves student names and the mark in each subject.

20. Consider the following query:

```
SELECT subject_name
FROM subject, enrolment
WHERE subject.subject_id = enrolment.subject_id
AND AVG(mark) >70
```

Which one of the following is correct for the query?

(a) The query is not legal.

(b) The query retrieves subject names where the average mark is greater than 70.

(c) The query retrieves subject names which have some mark greater than 70.

(d) The query retrieves subject names which have a student with an average mark greater than 70.

21. Consider the following query:

```
SELECT student_name, subject_name, AVG(mark)
FROM subject, enrolment
WHERE subject.subject_id = enrolment.subject_id
GROUP BY subject_id
HAVING AVG(mark) >70
```

Which one of the following is correct for the query?

(a) The query is not legal.

(b) The query retrieves student name, subject name and the subject average mark.

(c) The query retrieves student name, subject name and the student average mark.

(d) The query retrieves student name, subject name and the student average mark only for those subjects where the average mark is greater than 70.

22. Consider the following query:

```
SELECT subject_id
FROM subject, enrolment
WHERE subject.subject_id = enrolment.subject_id
GROUP BY subject_id
HAVING AVG(mark) >70
```

Which one of the following is correct for the query?
(a) The query is not legal.
(b) The query retrieves subject id of all subjects.
(c) The query retrieves subject id of subjects that have an average mark greater than 70.
(d) The query could not be written without a join or a subquery.

23. Consider the following query:

```
SELECT subject_name
FROM subject, enrolment
WHERE subject.subject_id = enrolment.subject_id
GROUP BY subject_name
HAVING mark > 70
```

Which one of the following is correct for the query?
(a) The query is not legal.
(b) The query retrieves subject names of all subjects.
(c) The query retrieves subject name of subjects that have an average mark greater than 70.
(d) The query retrieves subject name of subjects where some mark is greater than 70.
(e) None of the above

24. Consider the following query:

```
SELECT subject_name
FROM subject, enrolment
GROUP BY subject_id
```

Which one of the following is correct for the query?
(a) The query is not legal.
(b) The query retrieves subject names of all subjects.
(c) The query retrieves (once?) subject names of all subjects that have students enrolled in them.
(d) The query could not be formulated without a join or a subquery.
(e) None of the above

25. Consider the following query:

```
SELECT student_name
FROM student, enrolment
WHERE student.student_id = enrolment.student_id
AND mark IS NULL
```

Which one of the following is correct for the query?

(a) The query is not legal.
(b) The query retrieves student name of each of those students who have no mark given for all their subjects.
(c) The query retrieves once, the student name of each of those students who have no mark given for some of their subjects.
(d) The query retrieves student name every time an enrolment in a subject has no mark given.
(e) The above query does not retrieve any duplicate student names.

26. Consider the following query:

```
SELECT subject_name
FROM subject, enrolment
GROUP BY subject_id
HAVING MAX(AVG(mark)) > 60
```

Which one of the following is correct for the query?

(a) The query is not legal.
(b) The query retrieves subject names for subjects where the maximum mark is greater than 60.
(c) The query retrieves subject names where the maximum average mark is greater than 60.
(d) The query retrieves subject names where the average mark is maximum of all subjects and is greater than 60.

27. Consider the following query:

```
SELECT AVG(mark)
FROM enrolment
WHERE subject_id = 'IT302'
```

Which one of the following values is returned by the above query if the mark values in IT302 are 90, 60 and NULL?

(a) 75 (b) 50 (c) NULL (d) Not defined

28. Consider the following query:

```
SELECT student_id
FROM enrolment
WHERE subject_id = 'IT1500'
AND subject_id = 'IT1200'
```

Which one of the following is correct?

(a) The query is not legal.
(b) The query retrieves student IDs of students doing both IT 1500 and IT1200.
(c) The query returns a NULL result.
(d) None of the above.

29. Consider the following query:

```
SELECT student_id
FROM enrolment
```

There are 100 students and 500 enrolments although 5 students have not yet enrolled in any course. The number of rows returned by the above query is:

(a) 100 (b) 500 (c) 95 (d) Unable to determine

30. Consider again the database in the last question and consider the following query that involves a join.

```
SELECT student_id
FROM enrolment, student
WHERE enrolment.student_id = student.student_id))
```

The number of rows obtained by running the above query is?

(a) 100 (b) 500 (c) 95 (d) 50,000
(e) Unable to determine

31. Consider the following query:

```
SELECT subject_name
FROM subject
WHERE subject_id IN
        (SELECT subject_id
        FROM enrolment
        WHERE student_id IN
                (SELECT student_id
                FROM student
                WHERE student_name = 'Prem Kumar'))
```

Which one of the following is correct about the query above?

(a) The query is not legal.
(b) The query retrieves all subject names of subjects in which Prem Kumar is enrolled.
(c) The query retrieves all subject names of subjects in which Prem Kumar is not enrolled.
(d) None of the above

32. Consider the query:

```
SELECT subject_name
FROM enrolment, student, subject
WHERE student.student_id = enrolment.student_id
AND enrolment.subject_id = subject.subject_id
AND student.name = 'Prem Kumar'
```

Which one of the following is true?

(a) The query is not legal.
(b) The query retrieves all subject names of subjects in which Prem Kumar is not enrolled.
(c) The query is equivalent to the last query.
(d) None of the above

33. Consider the query:

```
SELECT student_id
FROM enrolment
WHERE subject_id = 'IT302'
AND student_id IN
        (SELECT student_id
        FROM enrolment
        WHERE subject_id = 'IT304')
```

Which one of the following is true about the query above?
(a) The query is not legal.
(b) The query retrieves student IDs of students doing both IT302 and IT304.
(c) The query retrieves student IDs of students doing IT302 or IT304.
(d) The query returns a NULL result.
(e) None of the above

34. Consider the following query:

```
SELECT student_id
FROM enrolment e1
WHERE NOT EXISTS
        (SELECT *
        FROM enrolment e2
        WHERE e1.student_id = e2.student_id
        AND mark < 50))
```

Which one of the following is true about the query above?
(a) The query is not legal.
(b) The query returns the student ID of students who have a mark of below 50 in each subject that they are doing.
(c) The query returns the student ID of students who have a mark of below 50 in some subject that they are doing.
(d) The query returns the student ID of students who have a mark of 50 or above in each subject they are enrolled.

35. Consider the following query:

```
SELECT student_name
FROM student
WHERE NOT EXISTS
        (SELECT *
        FROM subject
        WHERE department = 'Comp. Science'
        AND NOT EXISTS
                (SELECT *
                FROM enrolment
                WHERE student.student_id = enrolment.student_id
                AND subject.subject_id = enrolment.subject_id))
```

Which one of the following is true about the query above?

(a) The query is not legal.

(b) The query returns the student name of all students who have passed all computer science subjects are doing.

(c) The query returns the student name of each student who is enrolled in every subject that is offered by the department of computer science.

(d) The query returns the student name of each student who is enrolled only in subjects offered by the department of computer science.

EXERCISES

1. Write SQL statements for the following queries on the company database and determine whether it's a correlated or noncorrelated query.
   (a) Retrieve the names of players whose maximum score is higher than the average score of all players.
   (b) Find the names of all employees who have a supervisor with the same birthday as theirs.
   (c) Find the names of all employees who are directly supervised by Franklin Wong.
   (d) Find the country of the player which has the highest maximum score in the database.
2. Formulate the following queries for the ODI database used in this chapter:
   (a) Find the player's last name who was the youngest amongst the players in the database when he played in his first test match.
   (b) Find the ID of the player who has made the highest number of runs in the example database.
   (c) Find the details of the ODI match in the example database where Tendulkar scored a century but India lost the match.
   (d) Find all the IDs of matches where India won the match.
   (e) Find the ID of the player who hit the largest number of sixes in an ODI match in the example database.
   (f) Find the ID of the player who had the highest strike rate in an ODI match in the example database.
   (g) Find the list of names of players who have scored a century in the example ODI database.
   (h) Find the average strike rate of players who have scored a century in the example ODI database.
   (i) Find the names of players who have taken four wickets or more in the example ODI database.
   (j) What is the maximum number of wickets that a bowler has taken in an ODI match in the example database? Find the ID of that bowler.
   (k) Find the name of the youngest player in the example database.
   (l) Find the IDs of players who have never scored a four or a six in all matches they have batted.
   (m) Find the ID of the player who scored the largest percentage of his runs in fours and sixes.
   (n) Find the ID of the player who has the highest average score in the matches he has batted. Ensure that *Not Out* scores are not counted in computing the average.

3. Consider the following two queries. The first query is as follows:

```
SELECT PID
FROM Batting b1
WHERE NOT EXISTS
        (SELECT *
        FROM Batting b2
        WHERE b1.PID = b2.PID
        AND (SCORE < 51))
```

The second query is given below.

```
SELECT PID
FROM Player
WHERE NOT EXISTS
        (SELECT *
        FROM Batting
        WHERE Player.ID = PID
        AND (NRuns < 51))
```

Explain the difference between the two queries.

4. Formulate in SQL the query 'Find IDs of players who have either bowled or batted (or did both) in the ODI match 2689'.

Is the formulation given below correct? Explain the reasons for your answer.

```
SELECT PID
FROM Batting
WHERE MatchID = '2689'
OR PID IN
        (SELECT PID
        FROM Bowling
        WHERE MatchID = '2689')
```

Formulate this query in two other ways and show that those formulations are correct. One of these formulations should use the table *Match* in addition to tables *Batting* and *Bowling?*

5. Consider the query 'Find the player IDs of players who have scored more than 30 in every ODI match that they have batted in the example database'. We now present two different SQL formulations for this query.

The first formulation is given below:

```
SELECT PID
FROM Batting b1
WHERE NOT EXISTS
        (SELECT *
        FROM Batting b2
        WHERE b1.PID = b2.PID
        AND NRuns < 31)
```

The second formulation is given below and it shows how the query may be formulated in another way.

```
SELECT PID
FROM Player p1
WHERE NOT EXISTS
        (SELECT *
        FROM Batting b1
        WHERE p1.PlayerID = b1.PID
        AND NRuns < 31)
```

Is there another way we can formulate this query in SQL? If yes, show the formulation.

Compare and contrast the weaknesses and strengths of the two formulations. Modify each of them to remove the weaknesses of the formulation.

6. Formulate a query in SQL using the left outer join to retrieve names of players that have never batted according to the ODI database.
7. Give an example of two relations that would give a meaningful result of carrying out a full outer join. Formulate the full join using SQL.
8. Explain a situation when embedded SQL would be useful rather than using a direct SQL query. Show how the embedded SQL will be used in that case.
9. Explain a situation when dynamic SQL would be useful. Show how the dynamic SQL will be helpful rather than using a direct SQL query.
10. List as many conditions as you can think of, where a view can be safely updated.

PROJECTS

1. Find out if there are other languages for querying a relational database systems. One possibility is to explore Query-by-Example or QBE that was designed at IBM. A version of it has been implemented in Microsoft Access. Study the language you have chosen and write a number of queries presented in this chapter using that language. If you are using QBE then you may wish to refer to: pages.cs.wisc.edu/~dbbook/openAccess/thirdEdition/qbe.pdf
2. Implement all the queries listed in this chapter using a DBMS that you can access. Present a report. List any errors.

LAB EXERCISE

1. Consider the following relational database in which *CName* is a company name:

Lives(Name, Street, City)
Works(Name, CName, Salary)
Located-in(CName, City)
manages(Name, Manager-name)

Formulate the following queries in SQL.

(a) Find the names of all people who work for Bank of India.
(b) Find the name and city of all people who work for Bank of India.
(c) Find the name, street and city of all people who work for Bank of India and earn more than Rs. 55,000.
(d) Find all people who live in the same city as the company they work for.
(e) Find all people who live in the same city and on the same street as their manager.
(f) Find all people who do not work for Bank of India.
(g) Find all people who earn more than every employee of Small Bank Corporation.
(h) Assume the companies are located in several cities. Find all companies located in every city in which Small Bank Corporation is located.
(i) Find all people who earn more than the average salary of people working in their company.
(j) Find the company employing the most people.
(k) Find the company with the smallest payroll.
(l) Find the companies that pay more, on average, than the average salary at Bank of India.
(m) Modify the database so that Agarwal now lives in Shastri Nagar.
(n) Give all employees of Bank of India a 10 percent raise.
(o) Give all managers a 10 percent raise.
(p) Give all managers a 10 percent raise unless the salary becomes greater than Rs. 58,000. In such cases, give only a 3 percent raise.
(q) Delete all rows in the *Works* table for employees of Bank of Bihar.

BIBLIOGRAPHY

For Students

A number of books listed below are readable and suitable for students. The book by Beaulieu is good for learners. Chapters in database textbooks can also be a good starting point to learn SQL. A fascinating account of people, projects and politics involved in developing SQL is given in the report by Paul McJones.

For Instructors

A number of books listed below are suitable for instructors. The book by Faroult and Robson is excellent. The book by Cumming and Russell and the one by Celko is good for an experienced SQL programmer. There are many other books on SQL, some of them deal with a specific system, for example, SQL Server, ORACLE, MySQL and so on.

Beaulieu, A., *Learning SQL*, O'Reilly Media, 2005, 306 pp.

Celko, J., *SQL for Smarties,* Third Edition, Morgan Kaufman, 2005, 808 pp.

Cumming, A., and G. Russell, *SQL Hacks,* O'Reilly Media, 2006, 410 pp.

Patrick, J. J., *SQL Fundamentals*, Third Edition, Prentice Hall, 2008, 832 pp.

McGrath, M., "SQL in Easy Steps", In *Easy Steps Limited*, Second Edition, 2005, 192 pp.

Bowman, J. S., S. L. Emerson, and M. Darnovsky, *The Practical SQL Handbook: SQL Variants*, Fourth Edition, Addison-Wesley, 2001, 512 pp.

Date, C. J., and H. Darwen, *A Guide to the SQL Standard*, Third Edition, Addition Wesley, 1993, 414 pp.

Earp, R., and S. Bagui, *Learning SQL: A step-by-step guide using Oracle*, Addison-Wesley, 2002, 368 pp.

Eisenberg, A., J. Melton, K. Kulkarni, J. Michels and F. Zemke, "SQL: 2003 has been published", *SIGMOD Record*, Vol. 33, No. 1, March 2004, pp. 119-126.

Faroult, S., and P. Robson, *The Art of SQL*, O'Reilly Media, 2006, 367 pp.

Gennick, J., SQL *Pocket Guide*, O'Reilly, 2003, 154 pp.

Groff, J. R., and Weinberg, P. N., *SQL: The Complete Reference*, Second Edition, McGraw-Hill, 2002, 1080 pp.

Gulutzan, P., and Pelzer, T., *SQL-99 complete, really.*, CMP Books, 1999, 1104 pp.

Kline, K., D. Kline, and B. Hunt, *SQL in a Nutshell: A Desktop Quick Reference*, Second Edition, O'Reilly, 2004, 700 pp.

Kreines, D. C., *Oracle SQL: The Essential Reference*, O'Reilly, 2000, 418 pp.

McJones, P. (Ed.), "The 1995 SQL Reunion: People, Projects, and Politics", SRC Technical Note, 1997-08, Digital Systems Research Center, Palo Alto, 1997. http://www.mcjones.org/System_R/SQL_Reunion_95/sqlr95.html

Tow, D., *SQL Tuning*, O'Reilly, 2003, 314 pp.

Viescas, J. L., and M. J. Hernandez, *SQL Queries for Mere Mortals: A Hands-On Guide to Data Manipulation in SQL*, Second Edition, Addison-Wesley, 2007, 672 pp.

Lans, R. F. van der, *Introduction to SQL: Mastering the Relational Database Language*, Fourth Edition, Addison-Wesley, 2006, 1056 pp.

Don Chamberlin—Co-inventor of SQL

Don Chamberlin is the co-inventor of SQL (Structured Query Language), the most widely-used database language. SQL was developed in the mid 1970s by Don Chamberlin and Raymond Boyce. It was the first database language to take a unified approach to data definition, manipulation and control. Chamberlin also was one of the managers of the System R project which developed much of IBM's relational database technology including the world's first cost-based query optimizer.

A native of San Jose, California, Chamberlin earned his BS in Engineering in 1966 at Harvey Mudd College in Southern California and his MS and PhD in Electrical Engineering in 1967 and 1971 at Stanford University. He joined IBM Research at the T. J. Watson Research Center, Yorktown Heights, NY, in 1971. In 1973 he moved to San Jose and today works at IBM's Almaden Research Center there.

Among his honors, Chamberlin was named ACM Fellow in 1994, elected to National Academy of Engineering in 1997, named an IBM Fellow in 2003 and given an honorary doctorate by the University of Zurich in 2005.

Appendix 5.1 Player Table

PlayerID	*LName*	*FName*	*Country*	*YBorn*	*BPlace*	*FTest*
28001	Kohli	Virat	India	1988	Delhi	NULL
24007	Gambhir	Gautam	India	1981	Delhi	2004
28003	Raina	Suresh	India	1986	Ghaziabad	NULL
28004	Sharma	Rohit	India	1987	Nagpur	NULL
20007	Khan	Zaheer	India	1978	Shrirampur	2000
26005	Patel	Munaf	India	1983	Ikhar	2006
29020	Nayar	Abhishek	India	1983	Secunderabad	NULL
29022	Pathan	Yusuf	India	1982	Baroda	NULL
25007	Kulasekara	Nuwan	Sri Lanka	1982	Nittambuwa	2005
23007	Thusara	Thilan	Sri Lanka	1981	Balapitiya	2003
28005	Mendis	Ajantha	Sri Lanka	1985	Moratuwa	2008
27007	Warnapura	Malinda	Sri Lanka	1979	Colombo	2007
20005	Sangakkara	Kumar	Sri Lanka	1977	Matale	2000
97005	Jayawardene	Mahela	Sri Lanka	1977	Colombo	1997
26007	Kapugedera	Chamara	Sri Lanka	1987	Kandy	2006
99005	Dilshan	Tilakaratne	Sri Lanka	1976	Kalutara	1999
28007	Uthappa	Robin	India	1985	Coorg	NULL
23009	Pathan	Irfan	India	1984	Baroda	2003
26008	Chawla	Piyush	India	1988	Aligarh	2006
26009	Sreesanth	S	India	1983	Kothmangalam	2006
23005	Bracken	Nathan	Australia	1977	Penrith	2003
26006	Clark	Stuart	Australia	1975	Sutherland	2006
27008	Johnson	Mitchell	Australia	1981	Townsville	2007
28008	Hopes	James	Australia	1978	Townsville	NULL
24005	Clarke	Michael	Australia	1981	Liverpool	2004
94005	Hayden	Mathew	Australia	1971	Kingaroy	1994
25005	Hussey	Michael	Australia	1975	Morley	2005
23010	Butt	Salman	Pakistan	1984	Lahore	2003
21010	Malik	Shoaib	Pakistan	1982	Sialkot	2001
20010	Khan	Younis	Pakistan	1977	Mardan	2000
27010	Sohail	Tanvir	Pakistan	1984	Rawalpindi	2007
23011	Gul	Umar	Pakistan	1984	Peshawar	2003
26010	Anjum	Iftikhar	Pakistan	1980	Khanewal	2006
29010	Alam	Fawad	Pakistan	1985	Karachi	NULL
24010	Amla	Hashim	SouthAfrica	1983	Durban	2004
26010	Botha	Johan	South Africa	1982	Johannesburg	2006
98010	Ntini	Makhaya	South Africa	1977	Mdingi	1998
22010	Prince	Ashwell	South Africa	1977	Port Elizabeth	2002
22011	Smith	Graeme	South Africa	1981	Johannesburg	2002

Contd.

Appendix 5.1 Contd.

PlayerID	*LName*	*FName*	*Country*	*YBorn*	*BPlace*	*FTest*
98011	Flintoff	Andrew	England	1977	Preston	1998
25011	Pietersen	Kevin	England	1980	Pietermaritzburg	2005
24012	Strauss	Andrew	England	1977	Johannesburg	2004
24013	McCallum	Brendon	New Zealand	1981	Dunedin	2004
28010	Ryder	Jesse	New Zealand	1984	Masterton	2008
97010	Vettori	Daniel	New Zealand	1979	Auckland	1997
94010	Chanderpaul	Shivnarine	West Indies	1974	Unity Village	1994
20011	Gayle	Chris	West Indies	1979	Kingston	2000
20012	Sarwan	Ramnaresh	West Indies	1980	Wakenaam Island	2000
24013	Bravo	Dwayne	West Indies	1983	Santa Cruz	2004

Appendix 5.2 Batting Table

MatchID	*PID*	*Order*	*HOut*	*FOW*	*NRuns*	*Mts*	*Nballs*	*Fours*	*Six*
2755	23001	3	C	51	0	12	6	0	0
2755	25001	5	C	232	71	104	80	4	0
2755	91001	1	C	74	60	85	52	8	2
2755	94002	7	LBW	157	17	23	29	1	0
2755	92002	11	NO	NO	1	11	7	0	0
2689	89001	2	C	205	91	176	121	7	0
2689	23001	4	C	175	38	27	38	2	2
2689	25001	5	C	240	36	52	37	2	1
2689	99002	1	C	2	2	3	3	0	0
2689	95001	3	C	8	1	9	7	0	0
2689	24001	5	C	123	42	81	56	2	1
2689	99001	8	B	228	7	20	12	0	0
2689	27001	9	C	255	7	7	7	1	0
2755	27001	9	B	257	2	7	6	0	0
2717	98001	6	C	290	9	17	8	0	0
2717	21001	2	C	231	119	150	95	12	5
2717	23001	4	C	294	48	54	47	1	3
2717	25001	5	NO	NULL	26	38	30	0	1
2619	96001	1	C	150	53	105	60	7	1
2619	89001	2	C	156	94	120	81	16	1
2619	23001	4	C	209	18	28	24	1	0
2619	96001	5	C	216	4	3	5	0	0
2619	25001	6	B	294	35	50	37	3	0
2618	96001	1	C	150	59	119	79	7	2
2618	89001	2	C	116	71	87	59	13	0
2618	23001	4	C	266	72	72	57	10	2
2618	25001	5	C	311	24	60	17	3	0
2618	96001	6	RO	318	24	41	17	3	1

Appendix 5.3 Bowling Table

MatchID	*PID*	*NOvers*	*Maidens*	*NRuns*	*NWickets*
2689	99001	10	0	58	1
2689	24001	3	0	27	1
2689	23001	3	0	15	0
2755	94002	9	1	40	1
2755	92002	10	0	56	1
2755	91001	4	0	29	0
2755	23001	10	0	53	2
2689	23005	9	1	31	3
2689	26006	6	0	32	1
2689	27008	6	0	33	0
2689	28008	6	0	20	0
2689	24005	10	0	52	3
2689	27001	10	2	46	4
2689	26009	9	0	43	2
2689	23009	8.4	0	54	2
2689	98002	10	0	44	1
2689	26008	9	0	45	0
2755	25007	9	1	40	1
2755	23007	8.4	0	47	5
2755	28005	10	1	43	1
2755	27001	4	0	25	0
2755	20007	9.3	3	27	1
2755	26005	9	0	48	2
2755	98002	10	0	40	3
2755	28004	4	1	13	0

6 Normalization

OBJECTIVES

- Discuss the problems that can occur in a database system due to poor database design.
- Describe the anomalies that can arise if there is information redundancy.
- Explain the concept of functional dependencies, closure and minimal cover.
- Discuss the concept of Normal Forms, in particular the Third Normal Form (3NF) and the Boyce-Codd Normal Form (BCNF) and their purpose.
- Present techniques for normalizing relations.
- Discuss the desirable properties of decompositions.
- Describe the concepts of the Fourth Normal Form (4NF) and the Fifth Normal Form (5NF).
- Explain the concept of inclusion dependency.

KEYWORDS

Redundancy, anomalies, insertion anomaly, deletion anomaly, update anomaly, functional dependency, normal forms, first normal form, 1NF, second normal form, 2NF, third normal form, 3NF, Boyce-Codd normal form, BCNF, multivalued dependency, join dependency, fourth normal form, 4NF, fifth normal form, 5NF, decomposition, lossless, dependency preservation, inclusion dependency.

A mind all logic is like a knife all blade. It makes the hand bleed that uses it.

Rabindra Nath Tagore

6.1 INTRODUCTION

In Chapter 3, we considered the primary features of the relational database model. We noted that relations that form a database must satisfy some properties, for example, relations have no duplicate rows, rows have no ordering associated with them, and each element in the relation is atomic. We have also so far assumed that each relation has a group of attributes that belong together. Relations that satisfy these basic requirements may still have some undesirable properties, for example, data redundancy and update anomalies. We illustrate these undesirable properties and study how relations may be transformed or decomposed (or *normalized*) to eliminate them. Most of these undesirable properties do not arise if database modeling has been carried out carefully using a technique like the Entity-Relationship model. It is still important to understand the techniques in this chapter to check the model that has been obtained is good and ensure that no mistakes have been made in modeling. The basis of this checking is called *functional dependency*, a formal mathematical constraint between the attributes of a relation. We will discuss the functional dependency theory in this chapter.

Of course, mistakes can be made in database modeling especially when the database is large and complex or one may, for some reason, carry out database schema design using techniques other than a modeling technique. For example, one could collect all the information that an enterprise possesses and build one giant table (often called the *universal relation*) to hold it. This bottom-up approach is likely to lead to a table that suffers from problems we have noted above. For example, the table is highly likely to have redundant information and update, deletion and insertion anomalies. Normalization of such large tables will then be essential to avoid (or at least minimize) these problems.

To summarize, normalization plays only a limited role in the database schema design if a top-down modeling approach like the Entity-Relationship approach is carefully used. Normalization can however play a major role when the bottom-up approach is used. Normalization is then essential to build appropriate tables to hold the information of the enterprise. Whatever approach is used, normalization helps in measuring the quality of the database design based on some theoretical concepts.

The basic bottom-up design methodology, not used as commonly as the top-down design methodology, is based on relationships between the attributes (that is why this approach is sometimes called *design by synthesis*) while the top-down design is based on identifying entities and relationships between them (that is why it is sometimes called *design by analysis*). Therefore constructing a relational schema using a bottom-up design follows quite a different approach and involves grouping of related attributes into relations. It therefore becomes important to analyse the result of an initial bottom-up design to ensure that the design is good and this can be done by using normalization.

Some aspects of design quality have been discussed in Section 2.8 previously. These included aspects like correctness, completeness, readability and self-explanation. Although those aspects of quality are obviously important, assessing some aspects of quality, for example, structure and semantics of the relational schema, of a database design can be carried out using the concept we will now discuss. The concept of *functional dependency* depends on understanding the semantics of the data and can be very effective in determining if the grouping of attributes in a relational schema is appropriate. Functional dependencies deal with what information in a table is dependent on other information in that table.

This chapter is organized as follows. In the next section, an example table is presented to illustrate problems that can arise if the database is not carefully designed. A number of anomalies are discussed. A sample decomposition of the table is presented to show how normalization can overcome some of the anomalies. The theoretical basis of normalization using the concept of functional dependency is then defined in Section 6.3. We discuss how to reason with functional dependencies. This is then followed by a study of single-valued normalization in Section 6.4. It will be shown how dependencies information can be used to decompose tables when necessary without losing any information in the original tables. The section includes topics like the First Normal Form (1NF), the Second Normal Form (2NF), the Third Normal Form (3NF) and finally the Boyce–Codd Normal Form (BCNF). Section 6.5 describes some desirable properties of decomposition of relations. The following section deals with multivalued dependencies and the Fourth Normal Form (4NF) and the Fifth Normal Form (5NF). Section 6.7 briefly explains the concept of denormalization. Section 6.8 explains inclusion dependency which concludes the chapter.

6.2 POSSIBLE UNDESIRABLE PROPERTIES OF RELATIONS AND SCHEMA REFINEMENT

Let us consider the following table, which we will label *ODIplayers* that gives details of runs scored and wickets taken by ODI players during various ODI matches.

Table 6.1 The table *ODIplayers*

PID	*LName*	*Country*	*Team 1*	*Team 2*	*MID*	*Date*	*Ground*	*NRuns*	*NWickets*	*YBorn*	*Place*
89001	Tendulkar	India	Australia	India	2689	4/3/2008	MCG	91	NULL	1973	Mumbai
89001	Tendulkar	India	Australia	India	2689	4/3/2008	MCG	91	NULL	1973	Mumbai
23001	Yuvraj	India	Pakistan	India	2717	26/6/2008	Karachi	48	0	1978	Delhi
23001	Yuvraj	India	Pakistan	India	2717	26/6/2008	Karachi	48	0	1978	Delhi
21001	Sehwag	India	Pakistan	India	2717	26/6/2008	Karachi	119	NULL	1978	Delhi
99002	Gilchrist	Australia	Australia	India	2689	4/3/2008	Gabba	2	NULL	1971	Bellingen
95001	Ponting	Australia	Australia	India	2689	4/3/2008	Gabba	1	NULL	1974	Launces
99001	Lee	Australia	Australia	India	2689	4/3/2008	Gabba	7	1	1976	Wollongg
91001	Jayasuriya	Sri Lanka	Sri Lanka	India	2755	27/8/2008	Colombo	60	0	1969	Matara
27002	ISharma	India	Pakistan	India	2717	26/6/2008	Karachi	NULL	0	1988	Delhi
25001	Dhoni	India	Sri Lanka	India	2755	27/8/2008	Colombo	71	NULL	1981	Ranchi
95003	Kallis	South Africa	South Africa	Australia	2839	9/4/2009	Cape Town	70	0	1975	Cape Town
23001	Yuvraj	India	Pakistan	India	2717	26/6/2008	Karachi	48	0	1978	Delhi
24007	Gambhir	India	Australia	India	2689	4/3/2008	Gabba	15	NULL	1973	Mumbai

We briefly describe the meaning of each attribute name although we have used these attribute names before. *PID* is player ID, *LName* is player's last name (there is no space in the table for player's first name), *Country* is the name of the country that the player represents, *Team1* and *Team2* are the two teams playing the match (usually *Team1* is the host and *Team2* is the visiting team), *MID* is match ID, *Date* is the date on which the match was played, *Ground* is where the match was played, *NRuns* is the number of runs scored by the player, *NWickets* is the number of wickets taken by the player, *YBorn* is the year of birth of the player while *Place* is where he was born. The space on the book page is so limited that we have to cut short some long place names.

Note the use of NULL values in the table. A value is NULL only if the player did not take part in bowling or batting in a match. A value of 0 means that the player did bowl or bat but the result was 0.

The table *ODIplayers* in Table 6.1 satisfies the properties of a relation that we discussed in Chapter 3 and any such relation is said to be in *first normal form (or 1NF).* The main properties of relations concerned here are structural and therefore we note that all attribute values of 1NF relations must be atomic. We acknowledge that relations have other important properties like no ordering of rows, no duplicate rows and unique names of columns but in this chapter we are not particularly concerned with such properties.

As in Table 6.1, conceptually it is convenient to have all the information in one table since it is then easier to query the database. But the above table has the following undesirable features.

6.2.1 Redundant Information

One of the aims of a good database design is that redundancy of information should be eliminated. Redundancy exists when same data is stored in several places in the database. In some cases although there is no duplicate data it may be possible to derive certain information from other information in the database. Some information in Table 6.1 is being repeated, for example, information about players, like *LName*, *YBorn*, *Place*, are being repeated for Tendulkar and Yuvraj Singh. We cannot show too many rows that have repeated information but if the table was large, for example, consisting of thousands of rows of players' batting and bowling, then *LName* will be repeated many times for the same *PID*; *Team1*, *Team2* and *Ground* will be repeated for the same *MID*. Every time we wish to insert a batsman's score we must insert values of the columns *Team1*, *Team2*, as well as the name of the batsman, his year and place of birth, in addition to *PID* and *MID*. Repetition of information results in waste of storage as well as problems we discuss below.

6.2.2 Update Anomalies

Redundant information makes updates more difficult, for example, changing the name of the ground sounds strange but such things do happen. For example, the name of Bombay was changed to Mumbai. Such a change would require that all rows containing information about that ground be updated. If for some reason, all rows are not updated, we might have a database that gives two names for the same ground. This difficulty is called the *update anomaly*.

6.2.3 Insertion Anomalies: Inability to Represent Certain Information

Let the primary key of the above table be *PID, MID*. Any new row to be inserted in the table must have a value for the primary key since existential integrity requires that a key may not be totally or partially NULL.

However, if one wanted to insert the number and name of a new player in the database, for example, a new player who has been selected to tour overseas, it would not be possible until the player plays in a match and we are able to insert values of *PID* and *MID*. Similarly information about a new ODI match that is already scheduled cannot be inserted in the database until a player has played in the match. These difficulties are called *insertion anomalies*.

6.2.4 Deletion Anomalies: Loss of Useful Information

In some instances, useful information may be lost when a row is deleted. For example, if we delete the row corresponding to a player who happens to be the only player selected for a particular ODI, we will lose relevant information about the match (viz., ground name, date, etc). Similarly deletion of a match from the database may remove all information about a player who was playing in only that ODI. Such problems are called *deletion anomalies*.

The above problems arise primarily because the table *ODIplayers* has information about players, their batting and bowling performance as well as ODI matches. The semantics of the relation is not quite clear; is it about players? Is it about matches? Is it about players' performance in various matches? If we can resolve the semantics of the relations then none of the above anomalies would occur in them. One solution to deal with the problems is to decompose the table into two or more smaller tables.

Decomposition may provide further benefits. For example, in a distributed database different tables may be stored at different sites, if necessary. Of course, decomposition does increase the cost of query processing as the decomposed tables will need to be joined, sometimes frequently.

The above table may be decomposed into three tables as shown below in Tables 6.2 to 6.4 so that the semantics of each decomposed table are clearer. It has been noted earlier that Table 6.1 appears to include information about players, matches and players' performances. Therefore the decomposition is based on that understanding of the table and removes most of the undesirable properties listed above.

Player2(PID, LName, Country, YBorn, Place)
ODIMatch(MID, Team1, Team2, Date, Ground)
Performance(PID, MID, NRuns, NWickets)

Figure 6.1 The schema of decomposed Table 6.1

The decomposed tables are given below. Table 6.2 presents information about players.

Table 6.2 The decomposed table *Player2*

PID	*LName*	*Country*	*YBorn*	*Place*
89001	Tendulkar	India	1973	Mumbai
21001	Sehwag	India	1978	Delhi
99002	Gilchrist	Australia	1971	Bellingen
95001	Ponting	Australia	1974	Launces

Contd.

Table 6.2 Contd.

PID	*LName*	*Country*	*YBorn*	*Place*
99001	Lee	Australia	1976	Wollongg
91001	Jayasuria	Sri Lanka	1969	Matara
27002	ISharma	India	1988	Delhi
25001	Dhoni	India	1981	Ranchi
95003	Kallis	South Africa	1975	Cape Town
23001	Yuvraj	India	1978	Delhi
24007	Gambhir	India	1973	Mumbai

Table 6.3 presents information about matches.

Table 6.3 The decomposed table *ODIMatch*

MID	*Team 1*	*Team 2*	*Date*	*Ground*
2689	Australia	India	4/3/2008	MCG
2717	Pakistan	India	26/6/2008	Karachi
2689	Australia	India	4/3/2008	Gabba
2689	Australia	India	4/3/2008	Gabba
2689	Australia	India	4/3/2008	Gabba
2755	Srin Lanka	India	27/8/2008	Colombo
2717	Pakistan	India	26/6/2008	Karachi
2755	Sri Lanka	India	27/8/2008	Colombo
2839	South Africa	Australia	9/4/2009	Cape Town
2717	Pakistan	India	26/6/2008	Karachi
2689	Australia	India	4/3/2008	Gabba

Table 6.4 presents information about players' performance.

Table 6.4 The decomposed table *Performance*

PID	*MID*	*NRuns*	*NWickets*
89001	2689	91	NULL
21001	2717	119	NULL
99002	2689	2	NULL
95001	2689	1	NULL
99001	2689	7	1
91001	2755	60	0

Contd.

Table 6.4 Contd.

PID	*MID*	*NRuns*	*NWickets*
27002	2717	NULL	0
25001	2755	71	NULL
95003	2839	70	0
23001	2717	48	0
24007	2689	15	NULL

Such decomposition is called *normalization* and in some cases, for example in Table 6.1, decomposition is essential if we wish to overcome undesirable anomalies. The normalization process essentially assists in representing the data required for an application with as little redundancy as possible such that efficient updates of the data in the database are possible and useful data is not lost by mistake when some other data is deleted from the database.

As noted earlier, normalization can have an adverse effect on performance. Data which could have been retrieved from one table before normalization may require several tables to be joined after normalization. Normalization does however lead to more efficient updates since an update that may have required several rows to be updated before normalization could well need only one row to be updated after normalization.

Although in the above example we were able to look at the original table and intuitively propose a suitable decomposition that eliminates the anomalies that we discussed, in general this intuitive approach is not effective. A table may have one hundred or more columns and it is then almost impossible for a person to conceptualize all the information and suggest a suitable decomposition. We therefore need an algorithmic approach to find if there are problems in a proposed database design and how to eliminate them if they exist.

There are several stages of the normalization process. These are called the *first normal form (1NF)*, the *second normal form (2NF)*, the *third normal form (3NF)*, *Boyce–Codd normal form (BCNF)*, the *fourth normal form (4NF)* and the *fifth normal form (5NF)*. For all practical purposes, 3NF or the BCNF are quite adequate since they remove the anomalies discussed above for most common situations. It should be clearly understood that there is no obligation to normalize tables to the highest possible level. Performance should be taken into account and this may result in a decision not to normalize, say, beyond second normal form.

The normalization process involves applying a number of tests to each table that is being normalized. If the table does not meet the tests then it may be decomposed in two or more tables as illustrated above such that the decomposed tables meet the tests. The tests are essentially based on the concepts of functional dependency and primary keys of the tables which are discussed in Section 6.3.

It should be noted that all normal forms are additive. That is, if a table is in 3NF then it is by definition guaranteed to be in 2NF which in turn by definition guarantees 1NF.

Intuitively, the first normal form ensures that the table satisfies the structural properties required of a table in the relational model (in particular, all values are atomic). The second and third normal forms are designed to ensure that each table contains information about only one thing (either an entity or a relationship). That is, all nonkey columns in each table provide a fact about the entity or the relationship that is being identified by the key. Again, a sound E-R model of the database would ensure that all tables either provide facts about an entity or about a relationship resulting in tables that are obtained from an E-R model being in 3NF.

It should be noted that decomposition of each table always has to be based on principles that ensure that the original table may be reconstructed from the decomposed tables if and when necessary. If we are able to reduce redundancy and not lose any information, this implies that all redundant information can be derived given the other information in the database. Therefore information that has been removed must be related or dependent on other information that still exists in the database; this is why the concept of redundancy is important. Careless decomposition of a table can result in loss of information. We will discuss this in detail later in Section 6.5.

To define the normal forms more formally, we first need to define the concept of functional dependency.

6.3 FUNCTIONAL DEPENDENCY—SINGLE-VALUED DEPENDENCIES

A database is a collection of related information and it is therefore inevitable that some items of information in the database would depend on some other items of information. The information is either single-valued or multivalued. The name of a person or his/her date of birth are single-valued facts (we are not concerned that the date of birth has three components, the day, the month and the year). Also, qualifications of a person or courses that an instructor teaches are multivalued facts assuming the instructor teaches more than one course. We first deal only with single-valued facts and discuss the important concept of functional dependency.

The concept of some information being dependent on other information is quite basic. For example, at any time in a database, a student number would always determine the student name (a person may change his/her name but at any one time the person's name can be determined by the student number) and a course with a given course number would always have the same course name. We formalize this concept.

6.3.1 Functional Dependency

Functional dependency (FD) is an important concept in designing a database or assessing a given database design. It is a constraint between two sets of attributes of a relation. The idea of functional dependency is a relatively simple one. Consider a table R that has two attributes A and B. The attribute B of the table is *functionally dependent* on attribute A if and only if for each value of A no more than one value of B is associated. Functional dependency therefore may be considered a kind of an integrity constraint.

> ***Definition—Functional Dependency (FD)***
> *Let a table R have two attributes A and B. The attribute B of the table is functionally dependent on attribute A (that is, $A \rightarrow B$) if and only if for each value of A no more than one value of B is associated.*

In other words, the value of column A uniquely determines the value of B and if t_1 and t_2 are two rows in the table R and $t_1(A) = t_2(A)$ then we must have $t_1(B) = t_2(B)$.

The attributes A and B need not be single columns. They could be any subsets of the columns of the table R (possibly single columns). If B is functionally dependent on A (or A functionally determines B), we may then write

$$R.A \rightarrow R.B$$

The set of attributes $R.A$ are called the left-hand side of the functional dependency (FD) while $R.B$ is called the right-hand side of the FD. Each FD in a relation reveals something about the semantics of the relation.

Note that functional dependency does not imply a one-to-one relationship between A and B (since one value of B may be related to more than one value of A) although a one-to-one relationship may exist between A and B.

A simple example of the above functional dependency is when A is a primary key of an entity (e.g., PID) and B is some single-valued property or attribute of the entity (e.g., date of birth). $A \rightarrow B$ then must always hold.

Functional dependencies also arise in relationships. Let C be the primary key of an entity and D be the primary key of another entity. Let the two entities have a relationship with a primary key (C, D) since they are the keys of the two relations. If the relationship is one-to-one, we must have $C \rightarrow D$ and $D \rightarrow C$. If the relationship is many-to-one, we would have $C \rightarrow D$ but not $D \rightarrow C$. For many-to-many relationships, no functional dependencies hold. For example, if C is player number and D is ODI match number, there is no functional dependency between them.

If we consider the table *Batting* which includes the number of runs scored by each batsman, then we may write

$$(PID, MID) \rightarrow NRuns$$

For example, in the *ODIplayers* in Table 6.1 the following functional dependencies exist

$$PID \rightarrow Lname$$

$$PID \rightarrow Country$$

$$MID \rightarrow Ground$$

These functional dependencies imply that there can only be one last name for each *PID*, only one country for each player and only one ground name for each *MID*. It is of course possible that several players may have the same name and several players have played in the same ODI match. If we consider $MID \rightarrow Ground$, the dependency implies that no ODI match can have more than one ground. Functional dependencies therefore place constraints on what information the database may store. In the above example, one may be wondering if the following functional dependencies hold

$$Lname \rightarrow PID$$

$$Ground \rightarrow MID$$

Certainly there is nothing in the instance of the example database presented in Table 6.1 above that contradicts the first of these functional dependencies. However, whether this FD holds or not would depend on whether the database we are considering allows duplicate player last names (for example, Singh). The second FD does not hold because it implies that a cricket ground cannot have more than one ODI match which does not make a lot of sense.

Functional dependencies arise from the nature of the real world that the database models. Often A and B are facts about an entity where A might be some identifier for the entity and B some characteristic. Functional dependencies cannot be automatically determined by studying one or more instances of a database. They can be determined only by a careful study of the real world and a clear understanding of the semantics of the attributes in the table.

We have noted above that the definition of functional dependency does not require that *A* and *B* be single attributes. In fact, *A* and *B* may be collections of attributes. For example:

$(MID) \rightarrow (Team\,1,\ Team\,2)$

When dealing with a collection of columns, the concept of *full functional dependence* is important and can be defined as follows:

Definition—Full Functional Dependence
Let A and B be distinct collections of columns from a table R and let R.A → R.B. B is then fully functionally dependent on A if B is not functionally dependent on any subset of A.

The above example of batsmen and ODI matches would show full functional dependence if runs scored by a batsman are not functionally dependent on either player number (*PID*) or ODI match number (*MID*) alone. This implies that we are assuming that a player may have played in more than one ODI match and an ODI match would normally have more than one batsman. Furthermore, it has been assumed that there is at most one number of runs value of each batsman in the same ODI match inning.

The above example illustrates full functional dependence. However, the following functional dependency

$(PID,\ MID) \rightarrow Ground$

is not full functional dependence because $MID \rightarrow Ground$ holds.

As noted earlier, the concept of functional dependency is related to the concept of the candidate key of a table as the candidate key is an identifier which uniquely identifies a row and therefore determines the values of all other columns in the table. Therefore, for any subset *X* of the columns of a table *R* that satisfies the property that all remaining columns of the table are functionally dependent on it (that is, on *X*), *X* is a candidate key as long as no column can be removed from *X* and still satisfy the property of functional dependence. In the example above, the columns (*PID, MID*) form a candidate key (and the only one) of the table *ODIPlayers* since they functionally determine all the remaining columns.

As noted earlier, functional dependence is an important concept and a large body of formal theory has been developed about it. We discuss the concept of *closure* that helps us derive all functional dependencies that are implied by a given set of dependencies. Once a complete set of functional dependencies has been obtained, we will study how these may be used to build normalized tables.

6.3.2 Closure

We first define the concept of closure.

Definition—Closure
Let a table R have some functional dependencies F specified. The closure of F (usually written as F^+) is the set of all functional dependencies that may be logically derived from F.

Often F is the set of the most obvious and important functional dependencies and F^+, the closure, is the set of all the functional dependencies, including F, that can be deduced from F. The closure is important and may, for example, be needed in finding one or more candidate keys of the table.

We will use the example table in Table 6.1 given below as a relational schema.

ODI players (PID, LName, Country, Team1, Team2, MID, Date, Ground, NRuns, NWickets, YBorn, Place).

This relation has the functional dependencies listed in Fig. 6.2.

$PID \rightarrow LName$
$PID \rightarrow Country$
$MID \rightarrow Team1$
$MID \rightarrow Team2$
$PID \rightarrow YBorn$
$PID \rightarrow Place$
$MID \rightarrow Date$
$MID \rightarrow Ground$
$(PID, MID) \rightarrow NRuns$
$(PID, MID) \rightarrow NWickets$

Figure 6.2 Functional dependencies in table *ODIplayers*

Let these dependencies be denoted by F. We can derive the closure of F. We first discuss the Armstrong's axioms that assist in deriving the closure.

6.3.3 Armstrong's Axioms

To determine F^+, we need rules for deriving all functional dependencies that are implied by F. A set of rules that may be used to infer additional dependencies was proposed by Armstrong in 1974. These rules (or axioms) are a complete set of rules in that all possible functional dependencies may be derived from them. The rules are as follows:

1. *Reflexivity Rule*—If X is a set of attributes and $Y \subseteq X$, then $X \rightarrow Y$ holds.
   The reflexivity rule is the simplest (almost trivial) rule. It states that each subset of X is functionally dependent on X.
2. *Augmentation Rule*—If $X \rightarrow Y$ holds and W is a set of attributes, then $WX \rightarrow WY$ holds.
   The augmentation rule therefore is also quite simple. It states that if Y is determined by X then a set of columns W and Y together will be determined by W and X together. Note that we use the notation WX to mean the collection of all columns in W and X and write WX rather than the more conventional (W, X) for convenience.
3. *Transitivity Rule*—If $X \rightarrow Y$ and $Y \rightarrow Z$ hold, then $X \rightarrow Z$ holds.
   The transitivity rule therefore states that if X functionally determines Y and Y functionally determines Z, then X functionally determines Z. Transitivity is perhaps the most important rule.

These rules are called *Armstrong's Axioms*.

Further axioms may be derived from the above although the above three axioms are *sound and complete* as they do not generate any incorrect functional dependencies (soundness) and generate all possible functional dependencies that can be inferred from F (completeness). The most important additional axioms are

1. *Union Rule*—If $X \rightarrow Y$ and $X \rightarrow Z$ hold, then $X \rightarrow YZ$ holds.
2. *Decomposition Rule*—If $X \rightarrow YZ$ holds, then so do $X \rightarrow Y$ and $X \rightarrow Z$.
3. *Pseudotransitivity Rule*—If $X \rightarrow Y$ and $WY \rightarrow Z$ hold then so does $WX \rightarrow Z$.

Based on the above axioms and the functional dependencies specified for table *ODIplayers*, we may write additional functional dependencies. Some of these are given in Fig. 6.3.

(PID, MID) → *PID*	Reflexivity Rule
(PID, MID) → *MID*	Reflexivity Rule
PID → *(LName, Country)*	Union Rule
MID → *(Team1, Team2)*	Union Rule
PID → *(YBorn, Place)*	Union Rule
MID → *(Date, Ground)*	Union Rule

Figure 6.3 Additional functional dependencies

Often a very large list of dependencies can be derived from a given set *F* since Rule 1 itself will lead to a large number of dependencies. Since we have twelve attributes (*PID, LName, Country, Team1, Team2, MID, Date, Ground, NRuns, NWickets, YBorn, Place*) there are 4096 (that is, 2^{12}) subsets of these 12 attributes. These 4096 subsets could form 4096 values of *X* in functional dependencies of the type $X \rightarrow Y$. Of course, each value of *X* will then be associated with a number of values for *Y* (*Y* being a subset of *X*) leading to several thousand dependencies. These numerous dependencies are not particularly helpful in achieving our aim of normalizing tables.

Although we could follow the present procedure and compute the closure of *F* to find all the functional dependencies, the computation requires exponential time and the list of dependencies is often very large and therefore not very useful. There are two possible approaches that can be taken to avoid dealing with the large number of dependencies in the closure. One is to deal with one attribute or set of attributes at a time and find its closure (i.e., all functional dependencies relating to them). The aim of this exercise is to find what attributes depend on a given set of attributes and therefore ought to be together. The other approach is to find the *minimal covers*. We will discuss both approaches briefly.

As noted earlier, we do not need to deal with the large number of dependencies that might arise in a closure as often one is only interested in determining closure of a set of attributes given a set of functional dependencies. Closure of a set of attributes *X* is all the attributes that are functionally dependent on *X* given some functional dependencies *F* while the closure of *F* is all functional dependencies that are implied by *F*. Computing the closure of a set of attributes is a much simpler task if we are dealing with a small number of attributes. We will denote the closure of a set of attributes *X* given *F* by X^+.

6.3.4 Minimal Cover

We now define the concept of minimal cover.

Definition—Minimal Cover

The minimal cover for a set of functional dependencies F is given by a set of functional dependencies E such that:

1. *Every dependency in E is of the form X → Y where Y is a single attribute.*
2. *No dependency X → Y can be replaced with a dependency Z → Y where Z is a proper subset of X and still have a set of dependencies that is equivalent to E.*
3. *No dependency from E may be removed and still have a set of dependencies that is equivalent to E.*

The minimal cover of a set of functional dependencies is minimal in two ways as defined above. Firstly, according to requirement 1 above, each dependency is as small as possible such that the RHS is a single attribute and the LHS cannot have any attribute removed from it, according to Rule 2. Secondly, each FD in the minimal cover is required and thus there are no redundancies.

Algorithm to Obtain Minimal Cover

A simple algorithm may now be devised for obtaining minimal cover of FDs F based on the definition above. It is given below

1. Transform each functional dependency in F to one or more equivalent FDs with RHS having only one attribute.
2. Minimize the LHS of each FD obtained in Step 1.
3. Delete redundant FDs from the list of FDs obtained in Step 2.

For every set of FDs there always exists an irreducible set of FDs.

We now define the concept of equivalence of functional dependencies.

Equivalent Functional Dependencies

Let F_1 and F_2 be two sets of functional dependencies. The two functional dependencies are called *equivalent* if $F_1^+ = F_2^+$. Of course, it is not always easy to test that the two sets are equivalent as each of them may consist of hundreds of functional dependencies. One way to carry out the checking would be to take each dependency $X \rightarrow Y$ in turn from F_1^+ and check if it is in F_2^+.

Irreducible Set of FDs

We now define the concept of an irreducible set of functional dependencies. A set of FDs is irreducible if and only if the set satisfies the following properties:

1. The right-hand side of every FD is just one attribute.
2. The left-hand side is irreducible (that is, no attribute from the left-hand side may be omitted without changing the meaning of the set).
3. No FD from the set of functional dependencies may be discarded without changing the content of the set.

Now that we have the necessary background in functional dependencies, we may define the normal forms. Since normalization may involve decomposition of tables as shown above, the concept of functional dependencies is important in ensuring decompositions which preserve dependencies.

6.4 SINGLE-VALUED NORMALIZATION

Codd (1972) presented three normal forms (1NF, 2NF and 3NF) all based on functional dependencies among the attributes of a table. Later Boyce and Codd proposed another normal form called the Boyce–Codd normal form (BCNF). The fourth and fifth normal forms are based on multivalue and join dependencies and were proposed later.

We now discuss the normal forms and the tests which each table must meet. It should be remembered that the primary objective of normalization is to avoid some of the anomalies that we discussed at the beginning of the chapter.

6.4.1 The First Normal Form (1NF)—Atomic Attribute Values

A table satisfying the properties of a relation as discussed in Chapter 3 is said to be in first normal form. As discussed in Chapter 3, a relation cannot have multivalued or composite attributes. The 1NF requires the same condition.

Definition—1NF

A relation is in 1NF if and only if all underlying domains contain atomic values only.

The first normal form deals only with the basic structure of the table and does not resolve the problems of redundant information or the anomalies discussed earlier. All tables discussed in this chapter are in 1NF. Some tables may have multiple valued attributes but such tables must be modified to meet the requirements of the relational model. The modified tables are then in *first normal form*.

For example, Table 6.1 presented earlier is in 1NF since all attribute values in this table are atomic and indivisible. For example, a 1NF table could not have included more than one value of *NRuns*.

PID	*LName*	*Country*	*Team1*	*Team2*	*MID*	*Date*	*Ground*	*NRuns*	*NWickets*	*YBorn*	*Place*
89001	Tendulkar	India	Australia	India	2689	4/3/2008	MCG	91	NULL	1973	Mumbai
21001	Sehwag	India	Pakistan	India	2717	26/6/2008	Karachi	119	NULL	1978	Delhi
99002	Gilchrist	Australia	Australia	India	2689	4/3/2008	Gabba	2	NULL	1971	Bellingen
95001	Ponting	Australia	Australia	India	2689	4/3/2008	Gabba	1	NULL	1974	Launces
99001	Lee	Australia	Australia	India	2689	4/3/2008	Gabba	7	1	1976	Wollongg
91001	Jayasuria	Sri Lanka	Sri Lanka	India	2755	27/8/2008	Colombo	60	0	1969	Matara
27002	ISharma	India	Pakistan	India	2717	26/6/2008	Karachi	NULL	0	1988	Delhi
25001	Dhoni	India	Sri Lanka	India	2755	27/8/2008	Colombo	71	NULL	1981	Ranchi
95003	Kallis	South Africa	South Africa	Australia	2839	9/4/2009	Cape Town	70	0	1975	Cape Town
23001	Yuvraj	India	Pakistan	India	2717	26/6/2008	Karachi	48	0	1978	Delhi
24007	Gambhir	India	Australia	India	2689	4/3/2008	Gabba	15	NULL	1973	Mumbai

Table 6.1 is in 1NF as long as every attribute is considered an atomic value. For example, if one of the attributes was a player's date of birth, then it could not be considered as consisting of three components (*day, month, year*) for it to be considered atomic.

The above table of course suffers from all the anomalies that we have discussed earlier and needs to be normalized. We first discuss the *second normal form* (2NF) which will resolve most of the anomalies.

6.4.2 The Second Normal Form (2NF)–Candidate Keys

The second normal form attempts to deal with the problems that were identified in Table 6.1. The aim of the second normal form is to ensure that all information in one table is only about one thing.

> ***Definition—2NF***
> *A relation is in 2NF if it is in 1NF and every nonkey (also called nonprime) attribute is fully functionally dependent on each candidate key of the relation.*

To understand the above definition of 2NF, we need to define the concept of *key* attributes. Each attribute of a table that participates in at least one candidate key is a *key* attribute of the table. All other attributes are called *nonkey* attributes.

The concept of 2NF requires that all attributes that are not part of a candidate key be *fully* dependent on each candidate key. Being fully dependent requires that a functional dependency $A \rightarrow B$ must be such that it if an attribute from A is removed (assuming A to be a composite attribute) then the dependency does not hold. This condition essentially involves A being a candidate key (often the primary key) and B being any of the nonkey attributes.

If we consider the table

ODIplayers(PID, LName, Country, Team1, Team2, MID, Date, Ground, NRuns, Nwickets, YBorn, Place)

and the functional dependencies below, given earlier in Fig. 6.3.

$PID \rightarrow LName$
$PID \rightarrow Country$
$MID \rightarrow Team1$
$MID \rightarrow Team2$
$PID \rightarrow YBorn$
$PID \rightarrow Place$
$MID \rightarrow Date$
$MID \rightarrow Ground$
$(PID, MID) \rightarrow NRuns$
$(PID, MID) \rightarrow NWickets$

Let us assume that *(PID, MID)*[1] is the only candidate key (and therefore the primary key), the table is not in 2NF since *LName, Team1, Team2* and *Ground* are not fully dependent on the key. To resolve difficulties we could remove those attributes from the table *ODIplayers* that are not fully dependent on the candidate keys of the table and put them in a separate table. Therefore we decompose the table into a number of tables based on our understanding that the table includes information about players as well as about ODI matches. We now

1. Does the relation *ODIplayers* have only one candidate key (*PID, MID*)? Look carefully and we may discover others. For example, could (*PID, Date, Ground*) be a candidate key? What about (*LName, MID*)?

have a table about players, another about ODI matches and finally another about the relationship between the two, resulting in the following decomposition of the original table:

Player2 (*PID, Lname, YBorn, Place, Country*)
ODI (*MID, Team1, Team2, Date, Ground*)
Performance (*PID, MID, NRuns, NWickets*)

We may recover the original table by taking the natural join of the three tables.

6.4.3 The Third Normal Form (3NF)

Although transforming a table that is not in 2NF into a number of tables that are in 2NF removes many of the anomalies that appear in the table that was not in 2NF, but not all anomalies are removed and further normalization may sometimes be needed to ensure removal of all anomalies. These anomalies arise because a 2NF table may have attributes that are not directly related to the thing that is being described by the candidate keys of the table. Let us first define 3NF.

> ***Definition—3NF***
> *A relation R is in third normal form (3NF) if it is in 2NF and every nonkey attribute of R is nontransitively dependent on each candidate key of R.*

To understand the third normal form, we need to define *transitive dependence* which is based on one of Armstrong's axioms. Let A, B and C be three attributes of a table R, such that $A \rightarrow B$ and $B \rightarrow C$. From these functional dependencies, we may derive $A \rightarrow C$. As noted earlier, this dependence $A \rightarrow C$ is *transitive*.

The 3NF differs from the 2NF as all nonkey attributes in 3NF are required to be *directly* dependent on each candidate key of the table. The 3NF therefore insists that all facts in the table are about the key (or the thing that the key identifies), the whole key and nothing but the key. If some attributes are dependent on the key's transitivity then that is an indication that those attributes provide information not about the key but about a nonkey attribute. So the information is not directly about the key, although it obviously is related to the key.

The tables we get after decomposing for 2NF actually meet the test of 3NF and are therefore in 3NF.

To illustrate the concept of 3NF, consider the following tables that are slight modifications of those we got after normalization to 2NF. We have added the ground capacity to the table ODI. The other tables have not been modified.

Player2 (*PID, Lname, YBorn, Place, Country*)
ODI (*MID, Team1, Team2, Date, Ground, Capacity*)
Performance (*PID, MID, NRuns, NWickets*)

The following new functional dependency now exists:

$Ground \rightarrow Capacity$

This FD may be used to derive the following FD:

$MID \rightarrow Capacity$

Since the FD $MID \rightarrow Ground$ holds. Because we can derive $MID \rightarrow Capacity$ from the above functional dependencies, the above table is in 2NF. The table is however not in 3NF since *Capacity* is not directly dependent on the primary key of the relation which is *MID*. This transitive dependence is an indication that the table has information about more than one thing (viz., ODI and *Ground*) and should therefore be decomposed. The primary difficulty with the above table is that a ground will have many matches played in it and therefore the capacity will need to be repeated many times. This leads to all the problems that we identified at the beginning of this chapter. To overcome these difficulties we need to decompose the table ODI given above into the following two tables:

ODI1(MID, Team1, Team2, Date, Ground)
Ground1(Ground, Capacity)

ODI1 is now in 3NF and so is *Ground1*. The primary keys of the two relations are *MID* and Ground respectively.

An alternative decomposition of the table *ODI* is possible:

A (MID, Team1, Team2, Date)
B (Ground, Capacity)
C (MID, Ground)

The decomposition into three tables is not necessary as the original table is based on the assumption that each ODI is played on only one ground.

Usually the 3NF is quite adequate for most relational database designs. There are however some situations, for example, the table *Player(PID, Lname, YBORN, MID)* discussed in 2NF above, where 3NF may not eliminate all the redundancies and inconsistencies. The problem with the table *Player(PID, LName, YBORN, MID)* is because of the redundant information in the candidate keys. This is resolved by further normalization using the BCNF.

6.4.4 The Boyce-Codd Normal Form (BCNF)

Consider the following table:

Player3(PID, LName, MID, Date, Ground)

Player3 has all attributes participating in candidate keys as all the attributes are assumed to be unique. We have assumed *LName* to be unique and assumed (*Date, Ground*) to be also unique since only one match can be held on a ground on a particular day, so it is a reasonable assumption. We therefore have the following candidate keys:

(*PID, MID*)
(*LName, MID*)
(*PID, Date, Ground*)
(*LName, Date, Ground*)

Since the table has no nonkey attributes, the table is in 2NF and also in 3NF, in spite of the table suffering the problems that we discussed at the beginning of this chapter.

The difficulty in this table is being caused by dependence within the candidate keys. The second and third normal forms assume that all attributes not part of the candidate keys depend on the candidate keys but do not deal with dependencies *within* the keys. BCNF deals with such dependencies.

> ***Definition—BCNF***
> *A relation R is said to be in BCNF whenever $X \rightarrow A$ holds in R, and A is not in X, then X is a candidate key for R.*

It should be noted that most tables that are in 3NF are also in BCNF. Infrequently, a 3NF table is not in BCNF and this happens only if

(a) the candidate keys in the table are composite keys (that is, the keys are not single columns),
(b) there is more than one candidate key in the table, and
(c) the keys are not disjoint, that is, some columns in the keys are common.

Consider for example, the following relationship again:

Player3(PID, LName, MID, Date, Ground)

We now present the functional dependencies in this table.

PID $\rightarrow$ *LName*
MID $\rightarrow$ *Date*
MID $\rightarrow$ *Ground*

The table is in 3NF but not in BCNF because there are dependencies where attributes that are part of a candidate key are dependent on part of another candidate key. Such dependencies indicate that although the table is about some entity or association that is identified by the candidate keys, for example *(PID, MID)*, there are attributes that are not about the whole thing that the keys identify. For example, the above table is about an association (an ODI match) between players and matches and therefore the table needs to include only one identifier to identify players and only one identifier to identify matches. Providing three identifiers about players *(PID, LName, YBorn)* means that some information about players that is not needed is being provided. This provision of information will result in repetition of information and may lead to the anomalies that we discussed at the beginning of this chapter. If we wish to include further information about players and matches in the database, it should not be done by putting the information in the present table but by creating new tables that represent information about the entities *player* and *match*.

These difficulties may be overcome by decomposing the above table in the following three tables:

(PID, LName)
(PID, MID)
(MID, Date, Ground)

We now have a table that only has information about players, another only about matches and a third one about relationship between players and the matches they have played. All the anomalies and repetition of information have been removed.

BCNF has therefore ensured that no redundancy can be detected in the relation. Given the FDs for the relation being normalized, BCNF is the one that ensures no redundancy. 3NF in fact allows some redundancy within the composite candidate keys. It should be noted that although FDs give a clear signal that a 3NF relation has redundancies, it does not always point to a unique BCNF decomposition.

Summary of Normal Forms

Table 6.5 Summary of normal forms 1NF, 2NF, 3NF and BCNF

Normal Form	*Test*	*Remedy*
First Normal Form (1NF)	A relation is in 1NF if and only if all underlying domains contain atomic values only.	Ensure that all values are atomic
Second Normal Form (2NF)	A relation is in 2NF if it is in 1NF and every nonkey (also called nonprime) attribute is fully functionally dependent on each candidate key of the relation.	Decomposition based on nonkey attributes that are not fully dependent on the keys
Third Normal Form (3NF)	A relation R is in third normal form (3NF) if it is in 2NF and every nonkey attribute of R is nontransitively dependent on each candidate key of R.	Decomposition based on transitive FDs
Boyce–Codd Normal Form (BCNF)	A relation R is said to be in BCNF whenever $X \rightarrow A$ holds in R, and A is not in X, then X is a candidate key for R. This normally happens when a relation has more than one candidate key and the keys are composite.	Decomposition based on FDs within composite keys.

6.5 DESIRABLE PROPERTIES OF DECOMPOSITIONS

So far our approach has involved looking at individual tables and checking if they belong to 2NF, 3NF or BCNF. If a table was not in the normal form that was being checked for and we wished the table to be normalized to that normal form so that some of the anomalies could be eliminated, it was necessary to decompose the table into two or more tables. The process of decomposition of a table R into a set of tables $R_1, R_2, \ldots R_n$ was based on identifying different FDs and using that as a basis of decomposition, the decomposed tables $R_1, R_2, \ldots R_n$ are projections of R and are of course not disjoint, otherwise the glue holding the information together would be lost. Decomposing tables in this way based on a recognise and split method is not a particularly sound approach as we do not even have a basis to determine that the original table can be constructed if necessary from the decomposed tables. We now briefly discuss desirable properties of good decomposition and identify difficulties that may arise if the decomposition is done without adequate care. The next section will discuss how such decomposition may be derived given the functional dependencies.

Desirable properties of decomposition are as follows:

1. Attribute preservation
2. Lossless-join decomposition
3. Dependency preservation
4. Lack of redundancy

These properties are discussed in detail ahead.

6.5.1 Attribute Preservation

This is a simple and an obvious requirement that involves preserving all the columns that were present in the table that was decomposed.

Definition—Attribute Preservation

Therefore, decomposition of a table R into a set of tables R_1, R_2, KR_n must ensure that each attribute of R will appear in at least one relation schema R_i so that no attribute of R is lost. This is the property called attribute preservation.

6.5.2 Lossless-Join Decomposition

So far we have normalized a number of tables by decomposing them. We sometimes decomposed them intuitively but we used functional dependencies. We need a better basis for deciding decompositions since intuition may not always be correct. We illustrate how a careless decomposition may lead to problems including loss of information.

As a new example, consider the following table:

enrol(sno, cno, date-enrolled, room-no, instructor)

Consider decomposing the above table into two tables *enrol1* and *enrol2* as follows:

enrol1 (sno, cno, date-enrolled)

enrol2 (date-enrolled, room-no, instructor)

There are problems with this decomposition but we wish to focus on one aspect at the moment. Let an instance of the table *enrol* be as in Table 6.6.

Table 6.6 Table *enrol* before decomposition

S.no.	*C.no.*	*Date-enrolled*	*Room no.*	*Instructor*
830057	CP303	1FEB2004	MP006	Pranay Bose
820159	CP302	10JAN2004	MP006	Krishna Gupta
825678	CP304	1FEB2004	CE122	Prem Kumar
826789	CP305	15JAN2004	EA123	Inderjit Singh

Let the decomposed relations *enrol1* and *enrol2* be as given in Tables 6.7 and 6.8.

Table 6.7 Table *enrol1*

S.no.	*C.no.*	*Date-enrolled*
830057	CP303	1FEB2004
820159	CP302	10JAN2004
825678	CP304	1FEB2004
826789	CP305	15JAN2004

Table 6.8 Table *enrol2*

Date-enrolled	*Room no.*	*Instructor*
1FEB2004	MP006	Pranay Bose
10JAN2004	MP006	Krishna Gupta
1FEB2004	CE122	Prem Kumar
15JAN2004	EA123	Inderjit Singh

All the information that was in the table *enrol* appears to be still available in *enrol1* and *enrol2* in Tables 6.7 and 6.8 but this is not so. Suppose we wanted to retrieve the student numbers of all students taking a course from Prem Kumar, we would need to join *enrol1* and *enrol2*. The join would have six rows as follows:

Table 6.9 Join of *enrol1* and *enrol2*

S.no.	*C.no.*	*Date-enrolled*	*Room no.*	*Instructor*
830057	CP303	1FEB2004	MP006	Pranay Bose
830057	CP303	1FEB2004	CE122	Prem Kumar
820159	CP302	10JAN2004	MP006	Krishna Gupta
825678	CP304	1FEB2004	MP006	Pranay Bose
825678	CP304	1FEB2004	CE122	Prem Kumar
826789	CP305	15JAN1984	EA123	Inderjit Singh

The join contains two spurious rows that were not in the original table *enrol* in Table 6.6. Because of these additional rows, we have lost information about which students take courses from Prem Kumar. (Yes, we have more rows but less information because we are unable to say with certainty who is taking courses from Prem Kumar). Such decompositions are called *lossy* decompositions. A *nonloss* or *lossless* decomposition is that which guarantees that the join will result in exactly the same table as was decomposed. The join must not produce spurious rows. One might think that there might be other ways of recovering the original table from the decomposed tables but no other operators can recover the original table if the join does not.

We need to analyse why some decompositions are lossy. The common attribute in the above decomposition was *date-enrolled*. The common attribute is the glue that gives us the ability to find the relationships between different tables by joining the tables together. If the common attribute is not unique, the relationship information is not preserved. If each row had a unique value of *date-enrolled*, the problem of losing information would not have existed. The problem arises because several enrolments may take place on the same date.

A decomposition of a table R into tables R_1, R_2, $\ldots R_n$ is called a *lossless-join* decomposition with respect to functional dependencies F if the table R is always the natural join of the tables R_1, R_2, ..., R_n. It should be noted that natural join is the only way to recover the table from the decomposed tables. There is no other set of operators that can recover the table if the join cannot. Furthermore, it should be noted when the decomposed tables R_1, R_2, $\ldots R_n$ are obtained by projecting on the table R, for example, R_1 by projection $\Pi_1(R)$, the table R_1 may not always be precisely equal to the projection since the table R_1 might have additional rows called the *dangling* tuples.

It is not difficult to test whether a given decomposition is lossless-join given a set of functional dependencies F. We consider the simple case of a table R being decomposed into R_1 and R_2.

Definition—Lossless Decomposition

Let R be a relation with functional dependencies F. The decomposition of R into two relations with attribute sets R_1 and R_2 is lossless if and only if F^+ contains one of the following two FDs.

$R_1 \cap R_2 \rightarrow R_1$

$R_1 \cap R_2 \rightarrow R_2$

That is, the common attributes in R_1 and R_2 must include a candidate key of either R_1 or R_2.

We can now go back to the example in Tables 6.6 to 6.9. The attribute sets and the decomposed relations are given below.

enrol1 (sno, cno, date-enrolled)

enrol2 (date-enrolled, room-no, instructor)

The intersection of these two tables is (*date-enrolled*) since that is the only attribute that is common to both. Clearly it is not a key of either of the two relations *enrol1* or *enrol2*.

Loss decomposition may also be defined in terms the join of all decompositions. This definition requires that the natural join of all decomposed relations results in exactly the original relation with no spurious tuples.

6.5.3 Dependency Preservation Decomposition

It is clear that each decomposition must be lossless so that we do not lose any information from the table that is decomposed and a natural join of all decomposed relations results in the original relation.

Definition—Dependency Preservation
Dependency preservation is another important requirement since a dependency is a constraint on the database and if $X \to Y$ holds then we know that the two (sets) attributes are closely related and it is expected that both X and Y would appear in the same table so that the dependency can be checked easily.

Let us consider a table $R(A, B, C, D)$ with dependencies F that include the following:

$A \to B$

$A \to C$

If we decompose the above table into $R1(A, B)$ and $R2(B, C, D)$ the dependency $A \to C$ cannot be checked (or preserved) by looking at only one table since A and C are now in different tables. It is desirable that decompositions be such that each dependency in F may be checked by looking at only one table and that no joins need be computed for checking dependencies. In some cases, it may not be possible to preserve each and every dependency in F but as long as the dependencies that are preserved are equivalent to F, it should be sufficient.

Let F be the dependencies on a table R which is decomposed into tables $R_1, R_2, \ldots R_n$.

We can partition the dependencies given by F, such that $F_1, F_2, \text{K} F_n . F_n$ are dependencies that only involve attributes from each of the tables $R_1, R_2, \ldots R_n$ respectively. If the union of dependencies F_i imply all the dependencies in F, then we say that the decomposition has preserved dependencies, otherwise not. This checking would normally require first finding all the FDs from each table and then taking all the dependencies together and finding the closure of their union. If the closure is equivalent to the closure of FDs F, then we can say all dependencies have been preserved.

In the example of normalizing in Table 6.1, ODIplayers was decomposed into the following three relations:

Player2 (PID, LName, Country, YBorn, Place)

ODIMatch (MID, Team1, Team2, Date, Ground)

Performance (PID, MID, NRuns, NWickets)

We now use the list of FDs for the relation in Table 6.1 and check that all dependencies have been preserved.

Table 6.10 Checking dependency preservation for Table 6.1

FDs for Table 6.1	*Which Relation?*	*FD Preserved?*
PID → Name	*Player2*	*Yes*
PID → Country	*Player2*	*Yes*
MID → Team1	*ODIMatch*	*Yes*
MID → Team2	*ODIMatch*	*Yes*
PID → YBorn	*Player2*	*Yes*
PID → Place	*Player2*	*Yes*
MID → Date	*ODIMatch*	*Yes*
MID → Ground	*ODIMatch*	*Yes*
(PID, MID) → NRuns	*Performance*	*Yes*
(PID, MID) → NWickets	*Performance*	*Yes*

It was easy to check dependency preservation in this case since each dependency could be checked by looking at only one table.

6.5.4 Lack of Redundancy Decomposition

We have discussed the problem of repetition of information in a database. Such repetition should be avoided as much as possible.

Lossless-join, dependency preservation and lack of redundancy are not always possible with BCNF although 3NF can be used for lossless-join, dependency preservation and lack of redundancy.

6.6 MULTIVALUED DEPENDENCIES

Consider the following table *employee* that represents an entity employee that has one mutlivalued attribute *project*.

employee (ID, department, salary, project)

We have so far considered normalization based on functional dependencies, dependencies that apply only to single-valued facts. For example, *ID → department* implies only one *department* value for each value of *ID*. Not all information in a database is single-valued, for example, *project* in an employee database may be the list of all projects that the employee is currently working on. Although *ID* determines the list of all projects that an employee is working on, *ID → project* is not a functional dependency since *project* is not single-valued.

Recall that when we discussed database modeling using the E-R modeling technique, we noted difficulties that can arise when an entity has multivalue attributes. It was because in the relational model all attribute values must be atomic and therefore, if all the information about such an entity is to be represented in one table, it is necessary to repeat all the information other than the multivalue attribute value. This results in many rows about the same instance of the entity in the table and the table having a composite key (the entity ID and the mutlivalued attribute). The other option suggested was to represent this multivalue information in a separate table as if it was a separate entity.

The situation becomes much worse if an entity has more than one multivalued attribute and these values are represented in one table by a number of rows for each entity instance, such that every value of one the multivalued attributes appears with every value of the second multivalued attribute to maintain consistency. The multivalued dependency relates to this problem when more than one multivalued attribute exists in a table.

So far we have dealt with multivalued facts about an entity by heeping a separate table for that multivalue attribute and then inserting a row for each value of that fact. This resulted in composite keys since the multivalued fact must form a part of the key. In none of our examples so far have we dealt with an entity having more than one multivalued attribute in one table. This condition is discussed below.

The fourth and fifth normal forms deal with multivalued dependencies. Before discussing these normal forms we discuss the following example to illustrate the concept of multivalued dependency. We are now using an example which has little to do with ODI cricket. We have decided to find something different, another preoccupation in India, namely Bollywood!

We present a relation *BStars*, presented in Table 6.11, that gives information about some Bollywood stars, the cities they have lived in and names of their children. The information is not complete but the number of children and their names are correct.

Table 6.11 The relation *BStars*

Names	*Cities*	*Children*
Amitabh Bachchan	Allahabad	Abhishek
Amitabh Bachchan	Mumbai	Shweta
Madhuri Dixit	Mumbai	Arin
Madhuri Dixit	Los Angeles	Ryan
Shah Rukh Khan	Delhi	Aryan
Shah Rukh Khan	Mumbai	Suzana

The above table includes two multivalued attributes of entity *BStars*: *Cities* and *Children*. There are no functional dependencies[2].

The attributes *Cities* and *Children* are assumed to be independent of each other but Table 6.11 appears to show that there is some relation between the *Cities* and *Children* attributes. How can this be resolved? If we were to consider *Cities* and *Children* as separate entities, we would have two relationships (one between *Names* and *Cities* and the other between *Names* and *Children*). Both the above relationships are one-to-many.

2. Can we be sure about this? Could *Children* → *Name* be a functional dependency? It can only be so if we assume that the children's names are unique. We are assuming children's names are not unique in a large table.

That is, one Bollywood star is assumed to have lived in several *Cities,* though we have included only two cities for each person, and may have several children, though every film star we have used has only two children. Also many Bollywood stars may have lived or be living in the same city, for example, Mumbai. This is not an issue that concerns us.

Table 6.11 above is therefore in 3NF, it is even in BCNF, but it still has some disadvantages. We cannot decompose it based on FDs since there are no FDs in this table. So how should this information be represented? There are several possibilities. One is given in Table 6.11. Another possibility is given in Table 6.12 in which every value of *Cities* is combined with every value of *Children.* That at least overcomes the problem that the two attributes *Cities* and *Children* appeared related in Table 6.11.

Table 6.12 Another representation of the relation *BStars*

Names	*Cities*	*Children*
Amitabh Bachchan	Allahabad	Abhishek
Amitabh Bachchan	Mumbai	Shweta
Amitabh Bachchan	Allahabad	Shweta
Amitabh Bachchan	Mumbai	Abhishek
Madhuri Dixit	Mumbai	Arin
Madhuri Dixit	Los Angeles	Ryan
Madhuri Dixit	Mumbai	Ryan
Madhuri Dixit	Los Angeles	Arin
Shah Rukh Khan	Delhi	Aryan
Shah Rukh Khan	Mumbai	Suzana
Shah Rukh Khan	Delhi	Suzana
Shah Rukh Khan	Mumbai	Aryan

The two representations that have been presented in Tables 6.11 and 6.12 have some disadvantages. If the information is repeated we face the same problems of anomalies that we did when second or third normal form conditions were violated. If there is no repetition, there are still some difficulties with search, insertions and deletions. For example, if a Bollywood star had several values of *Cities*, more than the values of *Children*, then the value of *Children* in Table 6.11 for some values may have to be NULL. The role of NULL values then is confusing. Also the candidate key in the above tables is (*Names*, *Cities*, *Children*) and existential integrity requires that no NULL be allowed in the key. In a representation like in Table 6.12, every value of *Cities* (there may be five or more) will need to be repeated for every value of *Children*. This leads to a lot of redundancy. These problems may be overcome by decomposing a table like the one above in the following manner.

The basis of the decomposition is the concept of multivalued dependency (MVD). Functional dependency $A \rightarrow B$ relates one value of A to only one value of B while multivalued dependency $A \twoheadrightarrow B$ defines a relationship in which a set of values of attribute B is determined by a single value of A.

Let us now define the concept of multivalued dependency.

Definition—Multivalued Dependency (MVD)
The multivalued dependency X —>> Y is said to hold for a relation R(X, Y, Z) if for a given set of values (set of values if X is more than one attribute) for attribute(s) X, there is a set of (zero or more) associated values for the set of attributes Y and the Y values depend only on X values and have no dependence on the set of attributes Z.

We can define MVD in another, somewhat more formal, way as well.

Another Definition—Multivalued Dependency (MVD)
The multivalued dependency X —>> Y is said to hold for R(X, Y, Z) if, whenever t_1 and t_2 are two rows in R that have the same values for attributes X and therefore $t_1[x] = t_2[x]$ then R also contains rows t_3 and t_4 (not necessarily distinct), such that

$$t_1[x] = t_2[x] = t_3[x] = t_4[x]$$
$$t_3[Y] = t_1[Y] \text{ and } t_3[Z] = t_2[Z]$$
$$t_4[Y] = t_2[Y] \text{ and } t_4[Z] = t_1[Z]$$

In other words, if t_1 and t_2 are given by

$$t_1 = [X, Y_1, Z_1], \text{ and}$$
$$t_2 = [X, Y_2, Z_2]$$

then there must be rows t_3 and t_4, such that

$$t_3 = [X, Y_1, Z_2], \text{ and}$$
$$t_4 = [X, Y_2, Z_1]$$

We are therefore requiring that every value of *Y* appears with every value of *Z* to keep the table instances consistent. In other words, if *Y* and *Z* are determined by *X* alone and there is no relationship between *Y* and *Z* then *Y* and *Z* must appear in every possible pair, as shown in Table 6.12. These pairings present no information and are of no significance except that they show there is no relationship between *Y* and *Z*. If some of these pairings were not present, there would be some significance in the pairings because this is likely to mean that the two attributes are not independent.

The theory of multivalued dependencies is very similar to that for functional dependencies. Given *D* is a set of MVDs, we may find D^+, the closure of *D* using a set of axioms. We do not discuss the axioms here.

In the example above, if there was some dependence between the attributes *Cities* and *Children*, for example, perhaps the *Children* were born in the *Cities* or they studied there or live there; the table would not have MVD and cannot be decomposed into two tables as is described below.

In the above Table 6.12 whenever *X* —>> *Y* holds, so does *X* —>> *Z* as the role of the attributes *Y* and *Z* is symmetrical.

It should be noted that if *Z* was a single-valued attribute then there is no MVD and we deal with *R(X, Y, Z)* as before by entering several rows about each entity because *R* does not have MVD.

6.6.1 Multivalued Normalization—Fourth Normal Form

We have considered the example of the table *BStars*(*Name, Cities, Children*) and discussed the problems that may arise if the table is not normalized further. The table could be decomposed into *BS1*(*Names, Cities)* and *BS2*(*Names, Children*) to overcome these problems. The decomposed tables are in fourth normal form (4NF) which we now define after considering the concept of trivial MVDs.

The concept of multivalued dependencies (MVD) was developed to provide a basis for decomposition of tables like the one in Table 6.12. Therefore, if a table like *enrolment(sID, subjectID)* has a relationship between *sID* and *subjectID* in which *sID* uniquely determines the values of *subjectID*, the dependence of *subjectID* on *sID* is called a *trivial* MVD since the table *enrolment* with only two attributes cannot be decomposed any further. More formally, MVD $X \rightarrow\rightarrow Y$ is called a trivial MVD if either Y is a subset of X or X and Y together form the table R. The MVD is trivial since it results in no constraints being placed on the table.

A table having nontrivial MVDs must have at least three attributes, and two of them must be multivalued. Nontrivial MVDs result in the table requiring some constraints, otherwise all possible combinations of the multivalue attributes are required to be in the table.

4NF can be defined as follows:

Definition—Fourth Normal Form 4NF
A table R is in 4NF if, whenever a multivalued dependency X —>> Y holds in the table R, then either
(a) the dependency is trivial, or
(b) X is a candidate key for R.

As noted earlier, the dependency $X \rightarrow\rightarrow \phi$? or $X \rightarrow\rightarrow Y$ in a table $R(X, Y)$ is trivial since they must hold for all $R(X, Y)$. Similarly, $(X, Y) \rightarrow Z$ must hold for all tables $R(X, Y, Z)$ with only three attributes.

In fourth normal form, we have a table that has information about only one entity. If a table has more than one multivalue attribute, we decompose it to remove difficulties with the multivalued facts. Table 6.12 is therefore not in 4NF and needs to be decomposed in the following two tables that we have discussed before.

BS1 (*Names, Cities*)
BS2 (*Names, Children*)

The tables *BS1* and *BS2* are given below in Tables 6.13 and 6.14.

Table 6.13 A 4NF relation *BS1*

Names	*Cities*
Amitabh Bachchan	Allahabad
Amitabh Bachchan	Mumbai
Madhuri Dixit	Mumbai
Madhuri Dixit	Los Angeles
Shah Rukh Khan	Delhi
Shah Rukh Khan	Mumbai

Table 6.14 A 4NF relation *BS2*

Names	*Children*
Amitabh Bachchan	Abhishek
Amitabh Bachchan	Shweta
Madhuri Dixit	Arin
Madhuri Dixit	Ryan
Shah Rukh Khan	Aryan
Shah Rukh Khan	Suzana

These tables are clearly in 4NF since any table with only two attributes has no MVD.

Intuitively *R* is in 4NF if all dependencies are a result of keys. When multivalued dependencies exist, a table should not contain two or more independent multivalued attributes because the multivalued attributes must then be part of the key. The decomposition of a table to achieve 4NF would normally result in not only a reduction of redundancies but also avoidance of anomalies.

We leave it as an exercise for readers to find the join of relations in Table 6.13 and 6.14 and check if the join matches the original table.

6.6.2 Join Dependencies and the Fifth Normal Form

The normal forms discussed so far required that the given table *R* if not in the given normal form be decomposed into two tables to meet the requirements of the normal form. In some rare cases, a table can have problems like redundant information and update anomalies but cannot be decomposed into two tables to remove the anomalies. In such cases it may be possible to decompose the table into three or more tables using the 5NF.

The fifth normal form deals with join-dependencies which is a generalization of the MVD. The aim of fifth normal form is to have tables that cannot be decomposed further. A table in 5NF cannot be constructed from several smaller tables.

Definition—Join Dependency
*Let a relation R have subsets of its attributes A, B, C, ... Then R satisfies the Join Dependency (JD) written as *(A, B, C, ...) if and only if every possible legal value of R is equal to the join of its projections A, B, C, ...*

Before we define 5NF, we present an example in Table 6.15 below that deals with names of some movies, and names of their heroes and heroines. We have chosen a small sample of movies from Bollywood.

Table 6.15 *Movies, Heroes* and *Heroines*

Movies	*Heroes*	*Heroines*
Lagaan	Aamir Khan	Gracy Singh
Ghajini	Aamir Khan	Asin Thotumkal
God Tussi Great Ho	Salman Khan	Priyanka Chopra
God Tussi Great Ho	Amitabh Bachchan	Manisha Koirala
Hey Ram	Kamal Hasan	Rani Mukerjee
Paheli	Shah Rukh Khan	Rani Mukerjee

Note that Table 6.15 has information on a number of movies; each movie has a hero and a heroine except in one case two heroes and two heroines are given. All three fields are needed to represent the information.

Table 6.15 does not show MVDs as the attributes *Movies, Heroes* and *Heroines* as independent. They are related to each other and the pairings have significant information in them. If we try to decompose the relation into the following two:

(Movies, Heroes), and

(Movies, Heroines)

the relations given in Tables 6.16 and 6.17 are obtained by carrying out the decomposition.

Table 6.16 The decomposed relation (*Movies, Heroes*)

Movies	*Heroes*
Lagaan	Aamir Khan
Ghajini	Aamir Khan
God Tussi Great Ho	Salman Khan
God Tussi Great Ho	Amitabh Bachchan
Hey Ram	Kamal Hasan
Paheli	Shah Rukh Khan

Table 6.17 The decomposed relation (*Movies, Heroines*)

Movies	*Heroines*
Lagaan	Gracy Singh
Ghajini	Asin Thotumkal
God Tussi Great Ho	Priyanka Chopra
God Tussi Great Ho	Manisha Koirala
Hey Ram	Rani Mukerjee
Paheli	Rani Mukerjee

If the two relations are now joined (on the attribute *Movies*), we obtain the relation in Table 6.18.

Table 6.18 The join of relations 6.16 and 6.17

Movies	*Heroes*	*Heroines*
Lagaan	Aamir Khan	Gracy Singh
Ghajini	Aamir Khan	Asin Thotumkal
God Tussi Great Ho	Salman Khan	Priyanka Chopra
God Tussi Great Ho	Salman Khan	Manisha Koirala
God Tussi Great Ho	Amitabh Bachchan	Manisha Koirala
God Tussi Great Ho	Amitabh Bachchan	Priyanka Chopra
Hey Ram	Kamal Hasan	Rani Mukerjee
Paheli	Shah Rukh Khan	Rani Mukerjee

The result of the join in Table 6.18 has two additional rows that were not in the original relation, Table 6.15. Therefore the decomposition is not lossless although it has more rows than the original relation. Other decompositions are possible but they also lead to exactly the same problem.

Table 6.15 can however be decomposed into the following three relations:

(*Movies, Heroes*),

(*Movies, Heroines*),

(*Heroes, Heroines*).

The first two relations are as given in Tables 6.16 and 6.17 and the third is given in Table 6.19.

Table 6.19 The decomposed relation (*Heroes, Heroines*)

Heroes	*Heroines*
Aamir Khan	Gracy Singh
Aamir Khan	Asin Thotumkal
Salman Khan	Priyanka Chopra
Amitabh Bachchan	Manisha Koirala
Kamal Hasan	Rani Mukerjee
Shah Rukh Khan	Rani Mukerjee

Now if the three relations, given in Tables 6.16, 6.17 and 6.19 are joined, a different result is obtained. Table 6.18 gives the result of a join of (*Movies, Heroes*) and (*Movies, Heroines*) so we can join this result with the relation given in Table 6.19 (on both attributes in Table 6.19). Now we find that the two additional rows that appeared in Table 6.18 disappear and we obtain exactly the relation in Table 6.15.

Therefore relations presented in Tables 6.16, 6.17 and 6.19 show the join dependency of the relation in Table 6.15.

We are now able to define the fifth normal form.

Definition—Fifth Normal Form (5NF)
A relation R is in 5NF (also called the project-join normal form or PJNF) if for all join dependencies at least one of the following conditions holds:
- *(a) The decomposed tables (A, B, C, ...) are a trivial join-dependency, that is one of the A, B, C, ... is itself the relation R)*
- *(b) Every A, B, C, ... is a candidate key for R.*

It can be shown that the second condition of the definition above is met if the decomposition of *R* into (*A, B, C,* ...) leads to a lossless join.

It was shown earlier that the decomposition of the relation in Table 6.15 into Tables 6.16, 6.17 and 6.19 is lossless. Therefore these three relations are in 5NF. They cannot be decomposed any further.

It should be noted that there is a significant difference between the nature of functional dependencies and multivalue and join dependencies. The functional dependencies deal more with the semantics in the relational table which results in deriving decompositions. The mutlivalue and join dependencies give little semantics information about the tables. It has more to do with the way information has been structured than with the semantics.

As noted earlier, 4NF and 5NF are often not necessary and normalization can be terminated after BCNF has been achieved.

6.7 DENORMALIZATION

So far we have considered the process of normalization which involves decomposing relations so that relations were at least in 3NF. Further normalization to BCNF, 4NF and 5NF has also been also been discussed and recommended. The primary aim of normalization is to overcome anomalies that can exist in relations that are not normalized. Although normalization aims to overcome anomalies, it does not consider database performance. Normalization involving decomposing relations can have a performance penalty since many queries require additional joins and join is an expensive operation. Query performance can often be improved by joining relations together if the relations are being joined frequently and the join is expensive to compute. For example, if every query that is using the relation *Batting* is requiring a join with the relation *Player* then it may be appropriate to either join the two tables and put the player names in the *Batting* table as well as in *Player*. This technique for improving performance is called *denormalization*. This is defined as follows:

Definition—Denormalization

Denormalization is the intentional duplication of information in the database tables leading to increased data redundancy but improving query processing performance by reducing the number of joins.

As noted above, normalizing tables is generally the recommended approach in database design but some applications require information from both tables that were on the table before normalization. The premise of normalization is that the information can be retrieved by joining the two tables. The problem is that normalization may lead to too many joins for some applications. As the number and sizes of tables increase, the access costs also increase because the join of large tables takes too much time. When this happens, denormalization is worth considering.

Denormalization should only be considered after a good understanding of the data and the access requirements of all frequently used applications is known. These may involve expensive decision support applications including report generation. It may be necessary to consult the application developers before deciding to denormalize tables. Data updates should also be considered because redundancy may lead to increased cost of updates. It is best to remember that even if denormalization solves one part of dealing with performance, it may create possible problems in some other areas like updates. Total performance needs to be evaluated before denormalization. Furthermore, data integrity risks should also be considered.

Denormalization may involve inclusion of some additional columns in a table or it may involve combining two entities and the relationship between them into one table. For example, if two entities have a one-to-one relationship then they could be denormalized into one table to reduce the number of joins if the queries are frequently accessing both tables together. Also, two entities that have a many-to-one relationship may also be denormalized into one table to reduce the number of joins if many queries are accessing both tables together. Denormalizing one-to-one and one-to-many relationships between two entities does not create too much redundancy and may be useful in improving query performance. Two entities that have a many-to-many relationship should perhaps not be denormalized because of significant redundancy that is likely to be introduced.

As an example consider the three tables in Fig. 6.4 that are in 2NF.

Player2(PID, Lname, YBorn, Place, Country)
ODI(MID, Team1, Team2, Date, Ground)
Performance(PID, MID, NRuns, NWickets)

Figure 6.4 A database schema in 2NF

If most common queries to the database are about bowling and batting performance using the player's last name then it might make sense to put the name in the *Performance* table and obtain the schema given in Fig. 6.5.

Player2(PID, Lname, YBorn, Place, Country)
ODI(MID, Team1, Team2, Date, Ground)
Performance(PID, Lname, MID, NRuns, NWickets)

Figure 6.5 Denormalized database schema for schema in Fig. 6.4.

This clearly increases the level of redundancy because a player like Tendulkar or Jayasuriya has played more than 400 ODIs and so their names will appear more than 400 times but it will improve the performance of some queries.

We now summarise our discussion in Fig. 6.6.

Item	Normalize	Denormalize
Retrieval Performance	High	Higher for some queries
Update Performance	High	Slower
Storage Performance	Efficient	Not so efficient
Level of Normalization	3NF or higher	3NF or lower
Typical Applications	OLTP	OLAP
Preserving Integrity	Yes	Not always

Figure 6.6 Comparing normalization and denormalization

In most cases, denormalization does not improve query performance significantly but there are always exceptions. Generally a normalized database delivers good performance and preserves data integrity which may be compromised when the database is denormalized.

6.8 INCLUSION DEPENDENCY

The concept of inclusion dependency was first presented in 1984 by Casanova, Fagin and Papadimitriou. Inclusion dependency (IND) is somewhat different than functional dependency and join dependency as inclusion dependency may deal with attributes in one table or from more than one able. Inclusion dependency may involve comparison of column values from the same table or from different tables. Inclusion dependency deals with the semantics of a database schema. INDs are basic constraints that are necessary in a database to represent relationships. While the focus of functional dependencies was the primary key, the focus of inclusion dependency is the concept of foreign keys (and referential integrity) in a database schema.

Definition—Inclusion Dependency

An inclusion dependency on a database is a statement where X and Y are compatible sequence of attributes in relations R and S respectively, then the dependent attribute X is a subset of referenced attribute Y.

A simple example of inclusion dependency is in the tables *Player, Match, Batting and Bowling. PID* in tables *Batting* and *Bowling* are a subset of *PlayerID* in *Player* while *MatchID* in *Batting* and *Bowling* are subsets of *MatchID* in *Match.*

A unary inclusion dependency is an inclusion dependency in which exactly one column appears on each side. Therefore, *X* and *Y* are single columns. Unary INDs are common when a primary key is a single attribute like in the examples presented above. A foreign key constraint is an example of inclusion dependency.

SUMMARY

In this chapter we have discussed the problems that can occur in a database system due to poor database design. We have described the following:

- Database modeling may be top-down (design by analysis) or bottom-up (design by synthesis).
- An example has been used to illustrate problems that can occur in a database system due to poor database design.
- Problems that may arise include redundancies, update anomalies, deletion anomalies, and insertion anomalies.
- The problems may be overcome by normalization of relations that contain information about more than one thing.
- The concepts of functional dependencies, closure and minimal cover are required in carrying out normalization.
- Functional dependencies (FD) show which attributes are dependent on which other attributes and FDs form the basis of normalization.
- Normalization has a number of steps. The first four steps of normalization are based on single valued dependencies. These are called First Normal Form (1NF), Second Normal Form (2NF), Third Normal Form (3NF0 and Boyce–Codd Normal Form (BCNF). Definitions of these normal forms are presented.
- Normalizing a relation involves decomposing the relation.
- Relation decomposition must meet a number of desirable properties of relation decompositions. These desirable properties are attribute preservation, lossless-join decomposition, dependency preservation and lack of redundancy.
- The concept of multivalued dependencies was described and Fourth Normal Form (4NF) was discussed.
- The concept of join dependency and motivation for Fifth Normal Form (5NF) was described.
- Denormalization is the internal duplication of information in database relations in an attempt to improve system performance.
- Concept of inclusion dependency has been introduced.

REVIEW QUESTIONS

1. What are top-down and bottom-up approaches to database design? (Section 6.1)
2. Explain the reasons for the update, insertion and deletion anomalies? (Section 6.2)
3. Why is there a need for normalization of a relation that contains information about more than one thing? (Section 6.2)
4. Describe the problems that may arise if the relations are not normalized beyond 1NF, i.e., redundancies, update anomalies, deletion anomalies, and insertion anomalies. (Section 6.2)
5. Explain the concept of functional dependency. (Section 6.3)
6. What is closure and minimal cover? (Section 6.3)

7. What are Armstrong's axioms? (Section 6.3)
8. Explain how minimal cover may be derived. (Section 6.3)
9. Explain the role of functional dependencies in normalization. (Section 6.3)
10. Explain the basis of the first normal form, the second normal form and the third normal form. (Sections 6.4.1, 6.4.2, 6.4.3)
11. Explain what the Boyce–Codd normal form achieves and the inadequacy of BCNF in some situations. (Section 6.4.3)
12. What are the differences between 1NF, 2NF, 3NF and BCNF? (Section 6.4)
13. What is decomposition? (Section 6.5)
14. What is attribute preservation? (Section 6.5.1)
15. What is lossless-join decomposition? (Section 6.5.2)
16. What is dependency preservation? (Section 6.5.3)
17. What is lack of redundancy in decomposition? (Section 6.5.4)
18. Show how to normalize a simple familiar example. (Section 6.4)
19. Describe multivalued dependency by presenting an example. (Section 6.6)
20. Use the example to illustrate the fourth normal form. (Section 6.6.1)
21. Describe join dependency. (Section 6.6.2)
22. Explain fifth normal form and its motivation. (Section 6.6.2)
23. When should denormalization be used? What are its disadvantages? (Section 6.7)
24. What is inclusion dependency? (Section 6.8)

SHORT ANSWER QUESTIONS

1. What is update anomaly?
2. What is insertion anomaly?
3. What is deletion anomaly?
4. Give an example to illustrate the need for normalization of a relation?
5. Why do we need to normalize relations beyond 1NF?
6. Use the example above and identify three functional dependencies.
7. What is the purpose of the three Armstrong's axioms?
8. List the three properties of irreducible FDs.
9. Define the first normal form.
10. Define the second normal form.
11. Define the third normal form.
12. List two desirable properties of decompositions.
13. What is multivalued dependency?
14. Define the fourth normal form?
15. Give an example of use of the fifth normal form.
16. What is the major aim of denormalization?

17. Explain inclusion dependency using a simple example.
18. How does inclusion dependency differ from functional dependency?

MULTIPLE CHOICE QUESTIONS

1. Which two of the following are the primary aims of normalization?
   (a) Avoid data redundancies.
   (b) Avoid certain update, insertion and deletion anomalies.
   (c) Decompose large relations into smaller ones.
   (d) Determine functional and multivalue dependencies.
2. Which one of the following is correct?
   (a) All functional dependencies are many-to-many relationships.
   (b) All functional dependencies are many-to-one relationships.
   (c) All functional dependencies are one-to-one relationships.
   (d) None of the above.
3. Which one of the following is correct?
   (a) All functional dependencies must involve attributes of the same table.
   (b) All functional dependencies must involve only a single attribute on the left side.
   (c) All functional dependencies must involve only a single attribute on the right side.
   (d) All functional dependencies must involve only single attributes on both sides.
4. Which of the following is **not** correct if the table *R* is a binary table?
   (a) There can be no functional dependencies in *R*.
   (b) There must be two functional dependencies in *R*.
   (c) There can be no multivalue dependencies in *R*.
   (d) *R* cannot be in BCNF.
5. Some facts are single-valued facts while others are multivalue facts. For example, we will consider a person's name to be single-valued although it would normally consist of a first name, a last name and possibly one or more middle names. If a person had more than one different name then of course the name becomes a multivalue fact.
   Given the above, which two of the following are single-valued facts?
   (a) Place of birth of a person (b) Date of birth of a person
   (c) Courses taught by an instructor (d) Qualifications of an instructor
6. Once again we consider single-valued and multivalued facts. A person's address would normally be single-valued but may also be multivalued for some persons. For example, for a student who has a permanent address as well as an address during the academic year. Which one of the following is always a single-valued fact?
   (a) A player's telephone number (b) Number of ODI centuries scored
   (c) Countries a player has played against (d) None of the above

7. Which of the following is correct?
   (a) Functional dependencies are not associated with tables; they are based on the semantics of information that we are dealing with.
   (b) If a table has no redundant information, its attributes must not have any functional dependencies.
   (c) Functional dependencies may be determined if we are given several instances of a table.
   (d) None of the above
8. Consider a relationship Z between two entities X and Y. Let C be the primary key of X and D be the primary key of Y. Which one of the following is **not** correct
   (a) If the relationship is one-to-one, we must have $C \rightarrow D$ and $D \rightarrow C$.
   (b) If the relationship is many-to-one, we would have $C \rightarrow D$ but not $D \rightarrow C$.
   (c) For many-to-many relationships, no functional dependencies between C and D hold.
   (d) Let C be *student number* and D be *subject number*, and suppose there was an attribute *mark* in the table representing the relationship *enrolment* then no functional dependencies exist between C, D and *mark*.
   (e) None of the above
9. Which of the following is one of the three Armstrong's axioms?
   (a) Transitivity Rule: If $X \rightarrow Y$, $Y \rightarrow Z$ then $X \rightarrow Z$
   (b) Commutativity Rule: If $X \rightarrow Y$ then $Y \rightarrow X$
   (c) Union Rule: If $X \rightarrow Y$, $X \rightarrow Z$ then $X \rightarrow YZ$
   (d) Pseudotransitivity Rule: If $X \rightarrow Y$, $WY \rightarrow Z$ then $WX \rightarrow Z$
10. Let R be a relation with attributes (A,B,C,D,E,F) and let the following functional dependencies hold:

    $A \rightarrow B$
    $A \rightarrow C$
    $CD \rightarrow E$
    $CD \rightarrow F$
    $B \rightarrow E$

    Given the above functional dependencies, which of the following functional dependencies does **not** hold?
    (a) $A \rightarrow E$ (b) $CD \rightarrow EF$ (c) $AD \rightarrow F$ (d) $B \rightarrow CD$
11. Let a table R have three candidate keys A, B and (C, D). Which of the following *must* **not** be correct?
    (a) $A \rightarrow B$ (b) $B \rightarrow A$ (c) $A \rightarrow C$ (d) $C \rightarrow AB$
12. Let the functional dependencies of a table R be given by:

    sno → *sname*
    cno → *cname*
    sno → *address*
    cno → *instructor*
    instructor → *office*

    Given the above functional dependencies, how many functional dependencies are likely to be in the closure?
    (a) 5 (b) More than 5 but less than 15
    (c) More than 15 but less than 50 (d) Over 100

13. Which of the following is **not** correct?
    (a) Given a set of functional dependencies F, F^+ is the closure of F and includes all functional dependencies implied by F.
    (b) F^+ is useful since it enables us to find if some FD $X \rightarrow Y$ is implied by F.
    (c) Given a large set of functional dependencies F, it can be very time-consuming to compute F^+.
    (d) Given F and a set of attributes X, the closure of X (X^+) is the set of all attributes that are functionally dependent on X given F.
    (e) None of the above
14. Consider the following functional dependencies:

$$A \rightarrow B$$
$$B \rightarrow A$$
$$B \rightarrow C$$
$$A \rightarrow C$$
$$C \rightarrow A$$

Which of the above dependencies will be removed if we were to compute the minimal cover of the functional dependencies?
    (a) $B \rightarrow A$
    (b) $A \rightarrow C$
    (c) $B \rightarrow C$
    (d) Either $B \rightarrow A$ and $A \rightarrow C$ or $B \rightarrow C$ but not all three
15. Which of the following are true? A set of functional dependencies is irreducible if and only if
    (a) The left-hand side of every FD is just one attribute.
    (b) The right-hand side of every FD is just one attribute.
    (c) Both the left and right-hand side of every FD is just one attribute.
    (d) The left-hand side is irreducible.
16. A relation R is decomposed in two relations $R1$ and $R2$ during normalization. Which of the following must be correct if the decomposition is nonloss?
    (a) Every FD in R is a logical consequence of those in $R1$ and $R2$.
    (b) The common attributes of $R1$ and $R2$ form a candidate key for at least one of the pair.
    (c) $R1$ and $R2$ together have all the attributes that are in R.
    (d) $R1$ and $R2$ have no attributes that are common.
17. Which of the following properties the decomposition of a relation R into a number of relations must have?
    (a) It must be a nonloss decomposition.
    (b) It must be a dependency preserving decomposition.
    (c) The original relation R can always be recovered from the decomposed relations.
    (d) All of the above
18. A relation is required to be decomposed during normalization into tables that are lossless and dependency preserving. Which one of the following is true?
    (a) The highest normal form possible is 1NF.
    (b) The highest normal form possible is 2NF.
    (c) The highest normal form possible is 3NF.
    (d) The highest normal form possible is BCNF.

19. When R is decomposed into S and T, which of the following is true?
    (a) Joining S and T will always produce a table that includes all the rows that were in R but may include some others.
    (b) The decomposition is lossless if the join of S and T is precisely R.
    (c) $R(A, B, C)$ and $A \rightarrow B$ then (A, B) and (A, C) are lossless.
    (d) S and T are independent, that is, there are no inter-relation dependencies.
    (e) The decomposition is lossless even if the join of S and T does not recover R because in some cases other operators on S and T can recover R.
20. Consider the table *student*(sno, sname, cname, cno) where (sno, cno) and (sname, cname) are the candidate keys of the relation. Which one of the following is **not** true?
    (a) The above table is in 1NF.
    (b) The above table is in 2NF.
    (c) The above table is in 3NF.
    (d) The above table is in BCNF.
21. Which one of the following is **not** correct?
    (a) If a table is a relation, it is in 1NF.
    (b) If a table is in 3NF and does not have a composite key, it is in BCNF.
    (c) If an E-R model is mapped to a set of tables, the tables thus obtained are *normally* in 3NF.
    (d) If a table has no multivalued dependencies, the table is in 4NF.
22. Which of the following is **not** correct
    (a) 2NF and 3NF are based on functional dependencies.
    (b) BCNF and 4NF are based on multivalue dependencies.
    (c) 5NF is based on join dependencies.
    (d) 1NF is based on the structure of the data.
23. Which one of the following is a difference between a relation in BCNF or in 3NF?
    (a) A relation in BCNF has two or more candidate keys.
    (b) A relation in BCNF has composite candidate keys.
    (c) A relation in BCNF has overlapping candidate keys.
    (d) A relation in BCNF has all of the above.
24. Which of the following are correct?
    (a) All normal forms are additive.
    (b) 1NF satisfies the structural properties of a table.
    (c) 2NF and 3NF ensure that each table contain information about only one thing.
    (d) Decompositions must ensure that the original table may be reconstructed from the decomposed tables.
    (e) All of the above are correct.
25. Which of the following are correct?
    (a) Tables in a relational database are required to be normalized to the highest normal form.
    (b) 2NF and 3NF are designed to result in tables in which each nonkey attribute in each table provides a fact about the entity or relationship being identified by the key.
    (c) While normalizing tables, it is essential to decompose tables such that the original table can be constructed from the decomposed tables.

(d) Functional dependencies cannot be automatically derived from an instance of the table under consideration. Careful study of the real world is needed to derive the functional dependencies.

26. Consider the following table that provides details about shipments. The attributes are supplier ID, supplier name, part ID and the quantity supplied. The first three of the four attributes are unique. Also, there may be a number of shipments from the one supplier but they must involve different parts. Two shipments from the same supplier supplying the same part are not permitted.

SP(sid, sname, pid, qty)

Which of the following is true about the relation above?

(a) SP is in 2NF but not 3NF.
(b) SP is in 3NF but not BCNF.
(c) SP is in BCNF but not 4NF.
(d) SP is in 4NF.

27. If a table *R* consists only of its primary key (which may consist of a number of attributes) and has no other attributes, the table would always be in

(a) 2NF but may not be in 3NF.
(b) 3NF but may not be in BCNF.
(c) BCNF but may not be in 4NF.
(d) 4NF.

28. Which of the following is **not** correct for a table $R(X, Y, Z)$ where X, Y, and Z are not necessarily single attributes.

(a) $X \twoheadrightarrow Y$ then $X \twoheadrightarrow Z$
(b) $X \rightarrow Y$ implies $X \twoheadrightarrow Y$
(c) $X \twoheadrightarrow Y$ and $X \twoheadrightarrow Z$ imply $Y \rightarrow Z$
(d) $X \twoheadrightarrow Y$ and $Y \twoheadrightarrow Z$ imply $X \twoheadrightarrow Z - Y$

29. MVD requires that there be at least three attributes. Which one of the following is correct if the table is $T(C, H, R)$ where C is the course number and H is the time it is held and R is the room in which it is held:

(a) The only MVD is $C \twoheadrightarrow H$
(b) The only MVD is $C \twoheadrightarrow R$
(c) The only MVD is $C \twoheadrightarrow HR$
(d) There are no multivalue dependencies

30. Consider the relation *Enrolment* (sno, sname, cno, cname, date enrolled). Which one of the following is true about the table Enrolment?

(a) The table is in 3NF.
(b) The table is in 3NF only if sname and cname are unique.
(c) The table is not in 2NF if sname is not unique.
(d) The table is in BCNF if sname and cname are unique.

31. Which one of the following is **not** true?

(a) MVD arises because the relational model does not allow non-atomic attribute values.
(b) MVD attempts to solve the problem of more than one multivalue attribute in one table; problems caused by having to store all possible combinations of the multivalue attribute values.
(c) MVD arises when two independent relationships are mixed together in one table.
(d) MVD arises when the values of the multivalue attributes cannot be determined by the primary key value.

32. Which one of the following is **not** correct about decomposition of a table in two or more tables:

(a) Attribute preservation is required so we do not lose any information.
(b) Dependency preservation is required so we do not lose any information.
(c) Lossless join is required so we do not lose any information.
(d) Lack of redundancy is required so we do not lose any information.

EXERCISES

1. Is a table with only one column always in 3NF? What about a table with two columns and a table with three columns? Explain your answer and give examples to support it.
2. Is a table with only two columns that is in 3NF always in BCNF? What about a table with three columns that is in 3NF? Explain your answer and give examples to support it.
3. Explain the concept of functional dependency. Does every relation have some functional dependencies? If not, give an example of a relation that has no functional dependencies.
4. Discuss the properties of decomposition including attribute preservation, dependency preservation and lossless join. Explain why each of these properties is important? Give an example of table decomposition which is not lossless.
5. Explain clearly what is meant by multivalued dependency? What types of constraint does it specify? When does it arise? Give an example of a relation with multivalued dependency.
6. Define BCNF. How is it different from 3NF? Present an example of a relation in 3NF that is not in BCNF.
7. Give an example of a table that is in BCNF but not in 4NF. Explain briefly.
8. A table R has attributes A, B, C, D, E and satisfies the following functional dependencies:

$$A \rightarrow BC$$
$$B \rightarrow D$$
$$CD \rightarrow E$$
$$E \rightarrow A$$

   (a) What are the candidate keys?
   (b) Is this table in 2NF? 3NF? BCNF?
   (c) Show that (A, B, C) and (A, D, E) are a lossless decomposition of R.
   (d) Show that (A, B, C) and (A, D, E) are not a dependency preserving decomposition of R.
9. Normalize the relation given below to the highest normal form possible. Are there any functional dependencies in this relation? Are there any multivalued dependencies? Does the relation have join dependencies? Explain the normalization process.

Directors, Movies and *Actors*

Directors	*Movies*	*Actors*
Mani Ratnam	Aayutha Ezhuthu	Madhvan
Mani Ratnam	Aayutha Ezhuthu	Suriya
Mani Ratnam	Guru	Abhishek Bachchan
Ashutosh Gowarikar	Lagaan	Aamir Khan
Mani Ratnam	Bombay	Manisha Koirala
Ashutosh Gowarikar	Jodha Akbar	Hrithik Roshan
Ashutosh Gowarikar	Jodha Akbar	Aishwarya Rai
Shankar	Sivaji	Rajnikanth

Contd.

Contd.

Shankar	Sivaji	Shriya Saran
Shankar	Anniyan	Vikram
Shankar	Anniyan	Yana Gupta
Mani Ratnam	Guru	Aishwarya Rai

10. Could the relation in the last exercise be normalized into the following three relations? Clearly explain the basis of your answer. If decomposition into these three relations is not suitable then what decomposition is needed for normalization?

The first decomposed relation has *Directors* and *Movies* as columns:

The decomposed relation (*Directors*, *Movies*)

Directors	*Movies*
Mani Ratnam	Aayutha Ezhuthu
Mani Ratnam	Guru
Ashutosh Gowarikar	Lagaan
Mani Ratnam	Bombay
Ashutosh Gowarikar	Jodha Akbar
Shankar	Sivaji
Shankar	Anniyan

The second decomposed relation has *Directors* and *Actors*:

The decomposed relation (*Directors*, *Actors*)

Directors	*Actors*
Mani Ratnam	Madhvan
Mani Ratnam	Suriya
Mani Ratnam	Abhishek Bachchan
Ashutosh Gowarikar	Aamir Khan
Mani Ratnam	Manisha Koirala
Ashutosh Gowarikar	Hrithik Roshan
Ashutosh Gowarikar	Aishwarya Rai
Shankar	Rajnikanth
Shankar	Shriya Saran
Shankar	Vikram
Shankar	Yana Gupta
Mani Ratnam	Aishwarya Rai

The third decomposed relation has *Movies* and *Actors*:

The decomposed relation (*Movies*, *Actors*)

Movies	*Actors*
Aayutha Ezhuthu	Madhvan
Aayutha Ezhuthu	Suriya
Guru	Abhishek Bachchan
Lagaan	Aamir Khan
Bombay	Manisha Koirala
Jodha Akbar	Hrithik Roshna
Jodha Akbar	Aishwarya Rai
Sivaji	Rajnikanth
Sivaji	Shriya Saran
Anniyan	Vikram
Anniyan	Yana Gupta
Guru	Aishwarya Rai

PROJECT

1. The following schema gives information about students, instructors and courses. Some of the names are defined below.

   University (SID, Sname, gender, caddress, haddress, dob, nationality, ssresults, ccompleted, ccgrades, cenrolment, staffID, staffname, gender, saddress, sdob, nationality, qualifications, appointment, courseID, cname, department, syllabus, instructor, quota)

   - caddress = current address
   - haddress = home address
   - ssresults = student's school results
   - ccompleted = courses completed
   - ccgrades = grades in courses completed
   - cenrolment = current enrolment
   - saddress = staff address
   - sdob = staff date of birth

   Make suitable assumptions and list them. Now find all the FDs in this schema and normalize the relations to 1NF, 2NF, 3NF and BCNF.

LAB EXERCISES

1. Are there a set of FDs, MVDs and JDs that are always true for all relations? Describe them.
2. Prove or disprove the following:
   (a) If $AB \rightarrow C, A \rightarrow D, CD \rightarrow EF$ then $AB \rightarrow F$
   (b) If $XW \rightarrow Y$ and $XY \rightarrow Z$ then $X \rightarrow (Z - W)$
3. A table R has attributes P, Q, R, S, T, U, V, W and satisfies the following functional dependencies:

   $$PQR \rightarrow S$$
   $$PQ \rightarrow U$$
   $$Q \rightarrow V$$
   $$R \rightarrow W$$

   What are the candidate keys? Is this an irreducible set of functional dependencies?
4. What is inclusion dependency? Give an example to illustrate the concept.

BIBLIOGRAPHY

For Students

The books by Churcher, Teorey and Date are a good start for a student who wants to learn more about normalization. The article by Kent is a good introduction to normal forms. It is available on the Web.

For Instructors

The book by Simsion is excellent and the book by Hoberman is easy to read. A number of original papers on normalization have been included in the bibliography below. Chapters 6 and 7 of the book by Maier are a somewhat advanced discussion of normal forms. The whole book is available free online.

Beeri, C., and P. A. Bernstein, "Computational Problems Related to the Design of Normal Form Relational Schemas", *ACM Transactions of Database Systems*, Vol. 4, No. 1, September 1979, pp 30-59.

Bernstein, P. A., "Synthesizing Third Normal Form Relations from Functional Dependencies", *ACM Transactions of Database Systems*, Vol. 1, No. 4, October 1976, pp 277-298.

Churcher, C., *Beginning Database Design: From Novice to Professional*, APress, 2007, 300 pp.

Date, C. J., *Date on Database: Writings 2000-2006*, APress, 2006, 568 pp.

Fagin, R., "Multivalued Dependencies and a New Normal Form for Relational Databases", *ACM Transactions of Database Systems*, Vol. 2, No. 3, September 1977, pp 262-278.

Fagin, R., "A normal form for relational databases that is based on domains and keys", *ACM Transactions of Database Systems*, Vol. 6, No. 3, Sept. 1981, pp 387-415.

Hoberman, S., *Data Modeling Made Simple: A Practical Guide for Business & Information Technology Professionals*, Technics Publication, 2005, 144 pp.

Kent, W., "A simple guide to five normal forms in relational database theory", *Communications of the ACM*, Vol. 26, No. 2, February 1983, pp 120-125. http://www.bkent.net/Doc/simple5.htm

Maier, D., "Databases and Normal Forms", In *Theory of Relational Databases*, Chapter 6. http://www.dbis.informatik.hu-berlin.de/~freytag/Maier/C06.pdf

Maier, D., "Multivalued Dependencies, Join Dependencies and Further Normal Forms" *Theory of Relational Databases*, Chapter 7. http://www.dbis.informatik.hu-berlin.de/~freytag/Maier/C07.pdf

Simsion, G., *Data Modeling Theory and Practice*, Technics Publication, 2007, 416 pp.

Teorey, T. J., S. S. Lightstone, T. Nadeau, and H. V. Jagdish, *Database Modeling and Design: Logical Design*, Fourth Edition, Morgan Kaufmann, 2005, 296 pp.

Scamell, R. W., and N. S. Umanath, *Data Modeling and Database Design,* Course Technology, 2007, 720 pp.

Ronald Fagin—Contributed to DB Theory and Normalization

Ronald Fagin made influential and lasting contributions to the principles and the practice of database systems over a period spanning nearly three decades. Fagin is one of the founders of relational database theory. His first seminal contribution to this area was the introduction of the fourth normal form, based on the concept of multivalued dependencies, which capture crucial desirable aspects of database design. In particular, Fagin's fourth normal form formalizes the intuition that in a well-designed database schema unrelated data should not be stored in the same table. Fagin also contributed in defining inclusion dependency in 1982. Fagin's contributions to relational databases also include the co-invention of extendible hashing discussed in the next chapter.

In recent years, Fagin has made pioneering contributions to the area of accessing and retrieving fuzzy data from multimedia databases, such as 'graded' data about color and shape. Some of Fagin's algorithms have become part of the Garlic Information System developed at the IBM Almaden Research Center. Although this work was originally carried out with multimedia systems in mind, it turned out to have applications in other fields, including multicriterion decision-making in economics.

Fagin went to Dartmouth College and then to Berkeley where he completed a PhD in Mathematics in 1973.

Physical Storage and Indexing

7

OBJECTIVES

- Briefly discuss the types of computer storage, primary memory, secondary memory and tertiary storage, available for storing a database.
- Discuss the types of disks, hard disks and RAID, available for storing and accessing data in a DBMS.
- Introduce buffer management.
- Discuss unstructured and unordered files.
- Explain ordered sequential files.
- Describe the concept of indexing and different types of indexes.
- Discuss indexed-sequential files.
- Discuss the B-tree data structure and algorithms for search, insertion and deletion.
- Derive expressions for B-tree's performance.
- Explain the B^+-tree data structure for storing databases on disk.
- Discuss static hashing schemes.
- Describe dynamic hashing schemes including extendible hashing and linear hashing for storing files on disks.
- Introduce inverted file and its uses.

KEYWORDS

Storage media, primary memory, secondary memory, tertiary storage, main memory, disks, RAID, efficiency of storage structures, files, records, unstructured files, sequential files, indexing, primary index, clustering index, secondary index, indexed sequential files, B-tree, insertion, deletion, search, B^+-tree as an indexed sequential files, performance of B-tree, internal hashing, external hashing, linear hashing, extendible hashing, inverted files.

There are seven sins in the world: Wealth without work, Pleasure without conscience, Knowledge without character, Commerce without morality, Science without humanity, Worship without sacrifice and Politics without principle.

Mahatma Gandhi (1869-1948)

7.1 INTRODUCTION

We have so far discussed the Entity-Relationship and relational data models and have discussed query languages such as relational algebra, relational calculus as well as SQL. In our discussions so far, we have not considered how the information is represented physically in a database system and how it is accessed and modified. The focus of this chapter is on techniques for physical storage and retrieval of information from storage.

Much information in a database system is resident on a disk and is transferred from the disk to the main memory of the computer when required. The computer's operating system carefully orchestrates modifications of data by moving data from disk storage to the main memory, modifying it and then writing it back to the disk. Disk storage is often called *persistent* or *nonvolatile* storage because the information stored on a disk can survive system crashes like a power failure even for an indefinite amount of time. Other types of nonvolatile memory are CD-ROM and DVD. These memories are nonvolatile as well as relatively cheap and relatively slow.

However, computers also need faster memories to store large amounts of information such as the instructions of the DBMS being executed, and the bulk of the data on which the users are accessing and modifying. Computers therefore have large memory, not quite as large as a disk, made from faster but more expensive technology. This memory called the *main* memory (and *cache* memory) is *volatile* storage because the contents of such storage are always lost with a power failure and other types of computer failures. The disk-resident nonvolatile information can also be lost although it happens only rarely. To protect against loss of nonvolatile information it is desirable to have a copy of the information backed up and stored carefully.

In addition to the main memory and the disk memory, computers have registers which are part of the CPU and which are usually constructed from the fastest available technology. This makes them quite expensive, and so each computer has only a small number of registers that are used mainly to hold information which is required frequently. In this chapter we will discuss the different types of computer memories and how information is stored in them by the DBMS.

This chapter is organized as follows. After introducing the different types of computer memories in Section 7.2, storage on a magnetic disk and RAID disk systems are discussed in Section 7.3. Section 7.4 describes how data transfer from and to disk takes place using buffers. Section 7.5 deals with basics of file structures. The following sections discuss different types of file organizations starting with unstructured and unordered files in Section 7.6 and sorted sequential files in Section 7.7. Index and index types including primary index, clustering index, secondary index, multilevel index and ordering of composite index, are discussed in Section 7.8 followed by a description of indexed-sequential files in Section 7.9. The most commonly used data structure in databases, the B-tree, is introduced in Section 7.10. The algorithms for searching, deleting and inserting keys are described here. Performance of the B-tree is theoretically analysed in Section 7.10.4. A modified B-tree, B^+-tree is described in Section 7.11. Section 7.12 deals with advantages and disadvantages of B-tree and B^+-trees. Section 7.13 deals with static hashing followed by a brief discussion of external hashing in Section 7.14. Section 7.15 describes two dynamic hashing techniques, extendible hashing and linear hashing. The chapter concludes with a brief discussion of inverted files in Section 7.16.

7.2 DIFFERENT TYPES OF COMPUTER MEMORIES

We briefly discuss computer storage media which may be classified as follows:

1. Primary storage
2. Secondary storage
3. Tertiary storage

7.2.1 Primary Storage

Primary storage is directly connected to the CPU and is the fastest and most expensive. It includes the main memory, cache memory and the registers. These memories are volatile (that is, information is lost when the power is switched off) and therefore are suitable only for temporary storage of data.

The registers (usually less than 100) are usually the fastest and most expensive amongst the primary storage. The cache memory (usually around one MB) is also very fast and an expensive computer memory, often used to store frequently accessed data, thereby speeding up the execution of programs. There are a number of different types of cache memory. They are called L1, L2 and L3, depending on the nearness to the CPU with L1 being the closest. The main memory (or RAM—Random Access Memory) is the bulk of primary storage and can be as large as 4 GB or more. The data in the main memory, like that in the registers and the cache, can be directly accessed by the CPU. The access is quite fast although not as fast as the registers or the cache.

Normally, RAM is used to hold the instructions and the data for execution in a computer. As RAM can be altered very easily (as can data), it is ideal for this situation. RAM can be either *static* RAM or *dynamic* RAM (DRAM). DRAM is less expensive, uses less power and can be more compact than static RAM, although static RAM can be faster. Since CPU speeds have been growing quickly, faster RAM is needed to improve performance. One faster memory technology is RDRAM (Rambus Direct RAM) which is very fast and expensive; another is DDR RAM (Double Datarate RAM) which is also expensive like RDRAM.

7.2.2 Secondary Storage

The secondary storage devices used in the early computer systems included paper tapes, cards and magnetic tapes. Paper tapes and cards have disappeared now. Magnetic tapes perhaps are still in use at some computer installations but their use is often restricted to legacy files and archiving.

Secondary storage is not directly connected to the CPU. The CPU interacts with the secondary storage devices through controllers to read or write information. Secondary storage devices are used for more permanent and larger amounts of data. It is much cheaper than the cheapest primary memory which is the RAM. The secondary storage devices include the hard disk (which is the most widely used), flash memory, CD ROM, DVD ROM, and USB mass storage devices.

All online processing now uses disks; even personal computers are based on disks of one type or another. The reasons for storing information on disk are twofold. Although the main memory has data that can be directly accessed by the CPU, the access is quite fast but is almost always *volatile* while the secondary storage is not volatile (sometimes called *persistent*). The other reason is the size of the secondary storage which is often orders of magnitude bigger than the primary storage (the computer I am using has one terabyte disk!) because secondary storage is cheaper than the primary storage (although large main memories are becoming more common). If the amount of information being manipulated is so large that it cannot be accommodated in the main memory, secondary storage must be used. Primary memory costs continue to decline faster than the cost of the secondary storage, and eventually the cost of primary and secondary storage will become similar. Diskless computer systems can become a possibility if the problems of archiving the database can be resolved. This will have substantial impact on the nature of file systems.

To permanently store data, secondary memory uses a magnetic or optical medium. The transfer of data from secondary memory to the CPU is slower than transfer from the main memory because the information has to be mechanically read from the secondary media. Magnetic disks are metal or plastic platters usually coated with ferric oxide. The oxide can be magnetised at different points on a disk's surface. The orientation of the magnetised spots defines the organisation of the information on the disk.

In order to store information on the surface of the disk effectively a format has to be defined in which the surface can be magnetised. A hard disk is typically a number of disks stacked on top of one another. The name hard disk comes from the centre of the disk being metal or possibly hard plastic. The sector method is typically used for single plattered disks. Each track on the disk is divided into a number of sectors, each of which stores some information. To access any information, the computer needs to know the surface number, the track number and the sector number of where the information is stored. More details on this are provided in the next section.

Different rules apply to different types of disks. We will list the major considerations for handling disks as well as special considerations for handling hard disks, soft covered floppies and hard covered floppies. One of the most important things to remember when handling a disk is that the read/write heads that put information on and get information off the disk are situated very close to the surface of the disk. When the disk is spinning at hundreds or thousands of revolutions per minute, any direct contact between the head and the disk will mean that substantial damage both to the disk and more importantly to the head will occur. Such a moment of contact of head and disk is called a *head crash*.

Magnetic disks, as the name suggests, are magnetic media and therefore the data stored on the disk will be lost if a strong magnet is placed near the disk. The disk will not be damaged in any physical manner but the data stored on the disk will be erased. Sources of strong magnetic fields include any speaker whether from stereo equipment or a telephone, and electric motors.

7.2.3 Tertiary Storage

Tertiary storage is the third level of computer storage whose defining characteristic is low cost. It is often separate removal media that cannot be accessed directly by the computer system. It is usually suitable for storing large amounts of data for archival or backup purposes but is also being used in applications that generate huge amounts of data. The primary benefit of using tertiary storage is that it is often cheaper than secondary storage. It may be a stack of hard disks, optical disks like CD-ROM, DVD or even magnetic tapes. Tape is a very economical medium but access to tape is very slow. Tertiary storage devices are often sequential, not random access, as all primary and secondary storage devices.

Just as compact disks have changed the way we listen to music, optical disks are changing the way data is stored. Some benefits of optical storage over magnetic media are as follows:

- Higher capacity than magnetic storage
- Cheaper
- More compact
- More versatile

Data is stored on the surface of a metallic disk by using a series of lasers. One laser hits a metallic surface spread over a disk and burns tiny spots into the surface. Another laser can then be used to scan these spots and the differences in light reflections can be detected.

CD-ROM

They are plastic disks sealed with a protective coating. They are written from centre to the outside edge using a single spiralling track. Data is stored in 2352-byte sectors along the track. A CD ROM is a low cost storage option and is also easily available. It is widely used for archiving purposes. A CD ROM can store about 700 MB of data.

DVD

DVDs (or Digital Versatile Disks) can store much more information than CD-ROMs. A single-side DVD can store 4.78 GB of data.

Magnetic Tapes

Magnetic tapes have been around for a long time. They resemble conventional audio cassettes which have essentially disappeared now. The earlier tapes were more like tapes that were used on very old tape recorders. Tapes were one of the first storage systems used on computers. They are cost-effective storage systems that provide large cheap storage but are quite slow in reading and writing data. They are most commonly used for backup and archiving databases.

7.2.4 Summary of Computer Storage

A simple computer memory hierarchy representing different types of memories is shown in Fig. 7.1

The primary reason for having several levels of memory hierarchy is to obtain good performance economically. Database systems do not access data uniformly and most users spend majority of their time in one small part of the database. If this data can be moved to a faster (and more expensive) memory, a DBMS's performance is likely to improve significantly without using a large amount of expensive memory. For this reason the registers and the cache memory store the most frequently used instructions and data. This is somewhat similar to a browser cache on a computer which stores the frequently used pages in the browser cache thereby saving time to retrieve pages from the Web.

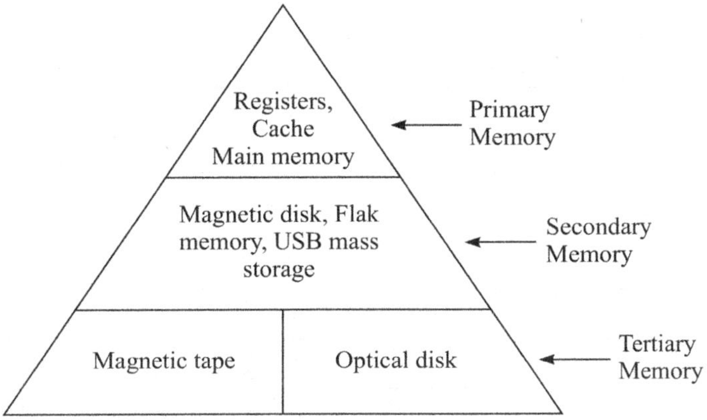

Figure 7.1 Memory hierarchy

In Table 7.1, we present another view of the memory hierarchy given in Fig. 7.1. There are of course other types of memories as well. Recently flash memory (for example, USB memory sticks) has become very popular.

Table 7.1 Different types of memories and their characteristics

Type of memory	*Size*	*Speed*	*Cost*
Registers	Very small	Very fast	Very high
Cache memory	Small	Very fast	High
Main memory	Large	Fast	Moderate
Disk storage	Very large	Medium	Cheap
Tertiary storage	Very large	Slow/Medium	Cheap

Before discussing each type of memory we note that memory costs have been going down for many years. It therefore follows that computer manufacturers can put larger and larger memories of each type in contemporary computers. The total annual disk storage sales over the last few years have been growing rapidly as shown in Fig. 7.2. Total annual disk sales in 2003 were almost 16,000 petabytes (or 16 exabytes) of storage compared to only around 4000 petabytes in 2000. Some of these disks, one assumes, are for storing increasingly large databases. Annual disk sales in 2003 were close to 3 GB per person in the world per year! In a keynote presentation at the 2005 International Conference in Data Engineering (ICDE) it was suggested that 250MB of data was being generated every year for each person in the world and the cost of disk storage was now much lower than cost of storing information on paper. Secondary storage is discussed ahead in more detail.

7.3 SECONDARY STORAGE–HARD DISKS

The first disk was invented by IBM in 1956. The current disk drives are very different from the first disks. The 1956 disk stored 5 MB of characters. Today's disks can perhaps store 100,000 times more in a very

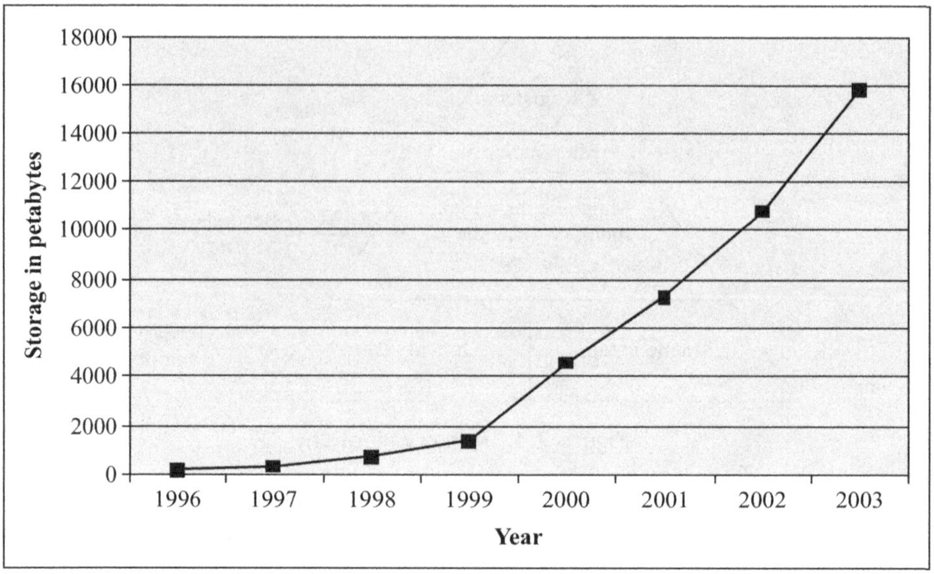

Figure 7.2 Annual disk storage sales in Petabytes

compact and much cheaper disk assembly. We first briefly discuss magnetic disk technology and then the RAID technology.

7.3.1 Magnetic Disk Technology

A hard disk normally consists of a spindle holding one or a number of hard rotating disk platters that usually spin at up to 10,000 revolutions per minute (RPM). An extremely thin polished magnetic coating is layered onto the surface of the platter. The platter usually cannot be bent or flipped and hence it is called a hard disk. Modern disks usually consist of a number of platters that use both surfaces for storing information.

A disk consists of bits that are very small magnetized areas. The bits are so small that a disk with 5" diameter can store more than a 100 GB of information. The storage density appears to be growing at the rate of 100% per year and the cost of hard disk in USA is now 0.1 per cent megabyte. Even a disk with a terabyte (1000 GB) is now available for less than Rs 5000. As noted above, disk capacities have been growing and price/MB continues to fall. A single platter 1.8 inch disk with 160 GB capacity has been announced in late 2009. A 3.5 inch single platter disk with capacity of 500 GB is also now available (at the time of writing) and it is expected that single platter disks with two terabyte capacity might be available soon.

As shown in Fig. 7.3, a disk has a number of concentric circles called *tracks* which often consist of *sectors* which are normally 512 bytes of data, the basic unit of data storage on the disk. Each sector also stores information about the sector's id, error correcting code as well as additional information required by the disk drive controller. For convenience, most disks store the same number of bytes on each track although the size of the inner tracks is smaller than the outer tracks. Each track has the same number of sectors and each sector has the same number of bytes. The tracks and sectors within them are numbered. The outermost track is numbered track 0, the next track is numbered 1 and so on. There can be more than a thousand tracks on a small disk. Sector numbers depend on the disk controller and may start with 0 or 1 or even 129.

Information is stored in tracks so that it can be read while the disk is rotating. Sectors may be combined into blocks by the operating system so that the block size on the disk is same as used by the system. This is sometimes called formatting the disk. Therefore a disk formatted by one operating system cannot usually be read by another operating system unless the disk is reformatted. The file on a disk is divided into blocks to save space as well as improve efficiency. A block is a fixed size of information (often 512 bytes to 4 KB) that may be read from the secondary storage at one time (reading one block is called a disk access). Often a block is much bigger than a record in a file. There is however no reason why in some applications a block can not be smaller than a record if the records are very large, for example, records that include images.

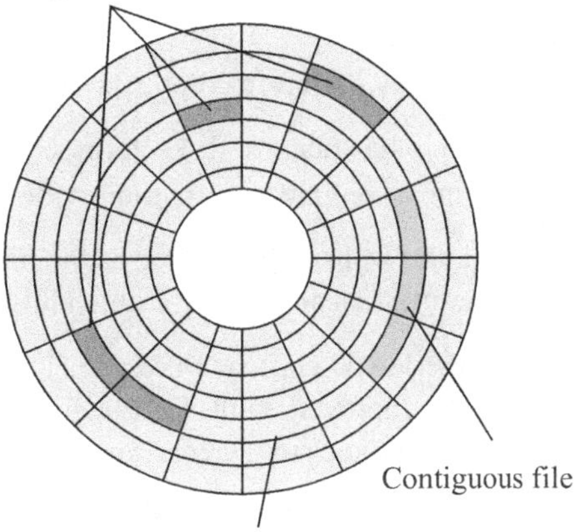

Figure 7.3 **Organization of files on a magnetic disk**

A hard disk normally contains 1 to 10 identical platters that are stacked on a spindle to form a cylinder which is all the tracks directly above and below each other. There is usually one Read Write (RW) head designated per platter face which hovers close to the face of the platter never touching the platter, and all the heads move in unison and carry out reading or writing of data. If a head ever touches a platter then, as noted earlier, it is called a head crash. When the disk is turned off, the heads retract to a side by the disk mechanism and are parked away from the platter surfaces.

Accessing a disk involves the following:

Seek Time

This is the time it takes for the disk head to position itself over the required track. Some very high performance disks eliminate this time by providing a disk head for each track. Such disks are called *fixed head disks*.

Rotational Delay

This is the waiting time it takes for the required sector to come under the disk once it is positioned over the required track.

Transfer Time

This is the time it takes the disk head to read the information and transfer it.

7.3.2 RAID (Redundant Arrays of Independent Disks)

A redundant array of independent disks or RAID is a single logical disk system that uses a stack of magnetic disks to share or replicate data amongst the disks. The initial idea, proposed in 1988 by David Patterson, Garth Gibson and Randy Katz at Berkeley, was to develop a disk system with an array of small, inexpensive disks to replace large expensive disks that were being used with large mainframe computers. Furthermore, the idea was to improve reliability and improve performance of disk systems since a disk head crash meant that all the data on the disk was lost and the file system or the database had to be rebuilt from the point of the last backup.

RAID technology therefore combines the following two ideas:

1. Multiple inexpensive disks accessed in parallel to give higher throughput.
2. Storage of redundant data to provide improved fault tolerance.

The second idea is just as important as the first since cost of disk failure is high and using a suitable redundant data scheme, RAID can provide a much higher fault tolerance.

Therefore, the RAID approach provides increased capacity, increased throughput, improved data, improved integrity and improved fault tolerance. RAID disks can provide a vast storage capacity. As the CPU performance continues to increase, increased disk throughput is required to overcome the disk I/O bottleneck. RAID technology is a part of the solution of this bottleneck.

Since the RAID systems have many disks, it makes sense to chop every file (in particular, the large ones) into pieces and store these pieces across the entire disk drives in the system. This is called *striping*. RAID disks use the concept of striping files into segments of logically sequential data so that the segments may be written across different disks to improve reliability. Striping can be done at the byte level or at block level.

There are a number of levels of RAID implementation, proposed to go from RAID level 0 to RAID level 10 although the original paper suggested only levels up to 5. We list the first five levels as well as level 10 below.

- **RAID Level 0—Striping but no redundancy**

RAID 0 is a scheme that uses a striped disk array and distributes data segments across all the different disk drives. It achieves maximum throughput with no redundancy. Because of lack of redundancy, there is no disk overhead but level 0 is not a true RAID system.

- **RAID Level 1—Mirroring and Duplexing**

RAID 1 is the simplest RAID system. It provides complete redundancy by storing mirror copies of all files on a pair of disks with writing of duplicate copies carried out in parallel. 100% redundancy means that any single disk failure does not result in loss of data and the system can continue to perform without any down time. Level 1 involves high disk overhead because of 100% redundancy. Level 1 is suitable for many database systems that need 100% mirroring.

- **RAID Level 2—Error Correction**

This RAID system stores the Hamming Code of each data word on a separate disk. Level 2 is not used in commercial database systems.

- **RAID Level 3—Parallel Transfer and Bit-interleaved Parity**

This is a high performance RAID system. It involves striped segments written on two or more disks in parallel and an additional disk to store parity information. It is similar to RAID 2 but is more economical and uses only one drive for data protection. It is not suitable for transaction-oriented databases.

- **RAID Level 4—Block Interleaved Parity using Shared Parity Disk**

This is not used widely because if implemented it would perform poorly. It uses stripes of uniform size, storing them all across the disk drives. It also uses a parity disk. One could think of it as RAID 0 plus a parity disk to provide some fault tolerance.

- **RAID Level 5—Block Interleaved Distributed Parity**

Perhaps the most widely used RAID system that is similar to RAID 3 except read and write do not take place in parallel. Parity information is spread across all disks. RAID 5 is a high performance disk system. It is suitable for most database systems.

- **RAID Level 10—Striped Mirrors with High Reliability and High Performance**

The concept of RAID 10 combines the features of RAID 0 and RAID 1. RAID 10 may be able to sustain more than one disk failure at the same time. It is suitable for high performance and fault tolerant databases.

7.4 BUFFER MANAGEMENT

We briefly discussed buffer management in Chapter 1. In this chapter we have noted that transfer of data between the main memory and a disk takes place in units of *blocks*. The disk is divided into blocks (or pages), usually of size 4 KB or 8 KB. When data is read from a disk drive, it is copied to the main memory which is itself divided into blocks to enable data to be copied into a block. This area is called a *buffer*. To read data, data from the disk is read into a main memory buffer. To write to the disk, the data in the main memory buffer is copied to a block on the disk. When several blocks need to be read from the disk, a main memory must allocate a number of buffers from the buffer pool for the transfer. This allocation of main memory for buffers is handled by an operating system module called *buffer manager* which makes decisions like how many buffers to allocate, which buffer block needs to be replaced when new data is being transferred from the disk. The buffer manager maintains a variety of information for each block in the buffer pool. This includes the number of times each buffer has been accessed as well as a flag if the buffer has been modified. Modified buffer blocks are often called *dirty*. There is a considerable range of techniques that a buffer manager uses in deciding which buffer block must be replaced when a new block is read from the disk and there is no free space in memory. We briefly discuss techniques for replacing blocks when a new request needs a block.

A number of techniques have been proposed for replacing a buffer with the aim of reducing the disk traffic and enhancing system performance. The two most commonly used techniques are LRU and FIFO described below.

LRU—Least Recently Used

The buffer manager may use the LRU approach to replace an old buffer that has not been used for the longest time. This can be done by the buffer manager maintaining a list or queue of buffers in the memory that has been inactive for the longest time. The basic idea behind LRU is locality of reference which implies the following:

- **Pages that have been requested recently will very likely be requested again soon.**
- **Pages that have not been requested recently are unlikely to be requested soon.**

The LRU scheme is not as simple as it sounds since the queue will change every time one of the buffers on the LRU queue gets used in a read or a write. This can be done by replacing the buffer at the front of the queue and moving the buffer to the back of the queue. Some schemes also include the free buffers in the LRU queue while others maintain a separate free list. Some other schemes maintain more than one LRU queue so that every request for buffer does not need to go to the same queue.

FIFO—First In First Out

This scheme is based on the idea that the age of the buffer is the most important and therefore the oldest buffer page should be replaced when another buffer is requested. FIFO may be implemented by a simple queue in which the oldest block is at the front of the queue and the most recent at the back of the queue. When the next buffer is requested, the front of the queue is replaced and the new block is put at the rear of the queue. FIFO is therefore the simplest buffer replacement scheme but it may create problems in some situations. Databases can have hot spots but FIFO will keep replacing the hot spot pages after some time, resulting in another buffer request being made for the recently replaced page which will have to be reread.

Studies have been carried out to compare LRU, FIFO and other buffer replacement schemes. In one study the LRU and FIFO schemes were compared and the LRU scheme was found to be close to optimal if access probabilities were known but was always better than FIFO if the probabilities were not known.

Much of the DBMS implementation does not need to know anything about buffer management, since it is only the lower level modules managing the files and main memory that need to directly deal with the buffer manager. A variety of information is transferred from the disk to the main memory and main memory to disk including the database files, the database metadata and the database indexes.

A database normally has a number of structures available to store the data that it contains. The structure chosen would normally depend on the application and most DBMS provide the DBA with a number of options for physical storage. These are discussed in detail later in this chapter.

We now discuss simple file structures. These include unstructured and serial files presented in Section 7.6 and sequential files in Section 7.7.

7.5 INTRODUCTION TO FILE STRUCTURES

A database consists of a variety of files and a file consists of a collection of records. It is therefore important that files be stored efficiently. We first define a record and a file.

> ***Definition—Record***
> *A record consists of a non-empty set of attributes that identify it uniquely (often called the identifier or the key) and a set of related values (often called the fields).*

> ***Definition—File***
> *A file is a collection of similar records usually stored on a secondary memory device.*

As an example of records and a file consider a table. If the table is stored as a file, each row of the table is then a record. Files may consist of fixed-length records or variable-length records. In relational database systems when a table is stored as a file, it is always a fixed-length record file.

Efficiency of Storage Structures

The most common operations on files are updates, insertions, deletions and searches. Therefore to determine efficiency of a storage structure the factors listed in Fig. 7.4 are commonly evaluated.

1. *Cost of insertion*—Usually an insertion operation involves inserting one row in a table. This includes identifying the table in which the new row will be inserted in and where. It involves fetching the block where the row will be inserted, inserting the row in it and writing the block back. It may require reading, modifying and writing blocks of data.
2. *Cost of retrieval*— Retrieval can involve a variety of data retrieval. The simplest retrieval involves fetching all rows of a table that satisfy an equality condition. For example, finding all *Player IDs* for players with scores over 99.
3. *Cost of deletion*—Deletion may involve deleting one row of a table or deleting a set of rows meeting a given condition. This involves identifying the table that has the row or rows to be deleted, then fetching the block or blocks that include rows to be deleted, modifying them and writing the blocks back.
4. *Cost of update*—Update may involve updating one row of a table or may involve updating a set of rows meeting a given condition. A number of blocks may have to be read, modified and written back.
5. *Storage utilization*—Although storage is now relatively cheap, the cost of storage is still a consideration for large databases.
6. *Cost of report generation*—Some types of reports can be very time consuming.

Figure 7.4 Factors that determine efficiency of a storage structure

We will discuss these efficiency measures for each file structure we study. The efficiency will normally be measured by the number of disk accesses since that often dominates the cost of typical database applications, for example, retrieval. We will initially assume that a retrieval involves only simple queries, for example, finding the record with key value *k*. A technique called indexing is often used for efficient retrieval. We will discuss indexing later in this chapter.

Other types of queries are frequently posed, for example:

- Find names of all players that have played in the ODI match 2755 (sometimes called *associative* search).
- Find IDs of all players who scored between 75 and 86 runs in the ODI match 2689 (called *range* query) or find all players who have scored more than 50 in a match.
- Find IDs of all players who scored below the mean score in the match 2755 (called *function* queries) or find the maximum number of runs scored by each player in all the matches in the database.
- Find all the articles from a document database that have "index" or "file" or "hashing" in their title (called *partial match* query) or find all the articles that have words starting with "comput".

Even more complex queries may sometimes be posed but we will not consider techniques for dealing with them here.

7.6 UNSTRUCTURED AND UNORDERED FILES (HEAP FILES)

These are the simplest and often the most inefficient techniques for storing information in files. These files have a number of names, for example, unstructured files, unordered files, serial files or heap files.

An unstructured file may be used for storing raw data, for example, data dumped directly from some sensors or the computer memory. It may consist of records stored one after another as the data arrives. The records are assumed to have no fixed structure or length. Each record therefore needs to include some information about its length as well as its attributes. If the records in the file do have a fixed structure, but the records are stored one after another as they arrive, the file is called a *serial file*.

A serial file is also usually a sequence of varying length records. As data is written to the file, records are added at the end of the file. The records are normally accessed sequentially. Any data may be written to a serial file. Byte count is usually used to determine the size of each record. The record size is saved at the start of each record. To retrieve information from such a file, some attribute values would have to be specified. These may then be searched in the file sequentially.

Unstructured files are useful for collecting information before the data is organized based on the requirements of an application. Unstructured files are also sometimes used when data is collected without any particular application in mind, for example, text retrieval, military intelligence, etc. Serial files also have similar applications and are often used for storing temporary or historical data.

7.7 SEQUENTIAL FILES (SORTED FILES)

Sequential files differ from the unstructured and serial files as in addition to the records having a similar structure (that is, the fields are in the same order and often of the same length), the records are arranged in position according to some key order. Two familiar examples of sequential files are a dictionary and a phone book. We give an example of a sequential file *Player* for the cricket database. Only a part of the file is given in Fig. 7.5. The file is ordered on the attribute *LName*. We assume the relation has been stored as a sequential file with each row being a record.

PlayerID	LName	FName	Country	YBorn	BPlace	FTest
96001	Dravid	Rahul	India	1973	Indore	1996
94004	Fleming	Stephen	New Zealand	1973	Christchurch	1994
96002	Gibbs	Herschelle	South Africa	1974	Cape Town	1996
95003	Kallis	Jacques	South Africa	1975	Cape Town	1995
93003	Kirsten	Gary	South Africa	1967	Cape Town	1993
90002	Kumble	Anil	India	1970	Bangalore	1990
90001	Lara	Brian	W Indies	1969	Santa Cruz	1990
92002	Muralitharan	Muthiah	Sri Lanka	1972	Kandy	1992
95002	Pollock	Shaun	South Africa	1973	Port Elizabeth	1995
95001	Ponting	Ricky	Australia	1974	Launceston	1995
93002	Streak	Heath	Zimbabwe	1974	Bulawayo	1993
89001	Tendulkar	Sachin	India	1973	Mumbai	1989
92003	Ul-Huq	Inzamam	Pakistan	1970	Multan	1992
94002	Vaas	Chaminda	Sri Lanka	1974	Mattumagala	1994
99003	Vaughan	Michael	England	1974	Manchester	1999
92001	Warne	Shane	Australia	1969	Melbourne	1992

Figure 7.5 A sequential file ordered on attribute *LName*

The main attraction of sequential organization is that it is conceptually simple and provides efficient access to successive records. Sequential files were originally developed for storing information on magnetic tapes. The structure has continued to be popular for storing files on disks because of its simplicity.

To retrieve a record from a sequential file, the entire file is normally scanned until the desired record is found. For a large file, binary search could be used. Even if binary search is used, several disk accesses will be required necessarily before the desired record is found.

Inserting a record in a sequential file requires that the record be inserted into its proper place according to the key. Therefore insertion of a record involves the insertion point to be identified, the records after the insertion point to be copied, the new record to be inserted and the copied records to be written back after the newly inserted record. Consider the case of adding a new player, say M S Dhoni or Ishant Sharma to the file shown in Fig. 7.5. A similar algorithm must be used in updating records if the file is not ordered on an attribute that is unique. Deletion of a record also leads to similar problems although a simple technique that is often used is to leave the deleted record on the disk but mark it as deleted. The record can then be removed when the next major update (sometimes called the *master update*) is carried out.

Insertion, update, deletion and retrieval of a single record at a time are therefore expensive when the sequential file structure is used. The cost of insertions may be reduced by keeping a separate small file (called the *overflow area*) of insertions. This is merged with the main file when the next major update is carried out. Another technique for overcoming the problem of expensive insertions, updates and deletions is to accumulate transactions, say for one day, and then sort them according to the same key as the file at the end of the day. All the sorted transactions (called the *transaction file*) are then processed together. Such batching techniques can make the sequential file structure very efficient. The structure however is not appropriate when an application requires quick response from the system (e.g., online applications).

The main advantages of sequential files are as follows:

- Sequential files are easy to implement.
- They provide fast access to the next record using lexicographic order.

However, sequential files have the following major disadvantages:

- Sequential files are difficult to update. Inserting a new record may require moving a large proportion of the file.
- Random access in sequential files is extremely slow.
- Sequential files are not appropriate for online applications.

Sometimes a file is considered to be sequentially organized despite the fact that it is not ordered according to any key. The date of acquisition may be considered the key value; the newest entries are added to the end of the file and this poses no difficulty to updating.

As noted above, the performance of a sequential file is usually poor if an application requires random processing of records. The primary technique used for enhancing the performance of sequential files is based on addition of an index to the file. We discuss indexing and index types in the next section.

7.8 INDEX AND INDEX TYPES

A sequential file with an associated index is like an old library card catalogue and is called an *indexed-sequential* (or ISAM) file.

> ***Definition—Index***
> *A file index is a data structure that improves the speed of common operations on the file. Indexes can be created using one or more columns of the file.*

Indexes assist in rapid retrieval of records. Index often only stores values of the key or some other attribute(s) of the file and therefore the memory space required to store an index is substantially less than that required to store the whole file. This can sometimes lead to an index being stored in the main memory for a large file stored on disk, further improving the efficiency of file processing.

Several variations of indexed-sequential files exist and we will discuss one commonly used simple version that involves an index as well as an overflow area. As noted earlier, the overflow area provides a facility to handle insertions more efficiently than an ordinary sequential file.

In addition to the indexing technique ISAM, a commonly used indexing technique is based on a tree structure called *B-tree*. We will discuss both techniques later in this chapter.

The choice of a file index can have significant impact on the performance of a database system, especially if the database tables are large. The type of index should normally be decided based on the types of queries that are made to the given database system. For example, if we look at the type of queries discussed above, a simple query involving an equality condition may require a different type of index than range queries over the same table. The situation becomes more complex if queries involve more than one condition, for example, find rows from a table *Batting* such that they have scores of more than 50 in match number 2755.

In the simplest case of indexing, the index in an indexed-sequential file consists of one entry for each data record in the sequential file. This is called *full indexing*. Since a record in a file usually would have substantially more information than its key, the index would still be much smaller than the file, as each entry in the index would consist only of a key value and an address. (The index is normally effective only when the file is large with a substantially smaller index so that the index can be a main memory resident or can be read from the disk in a few accesses at most.) If the index is large, it is common to have a higher level index so that the appropriate part of the index can be accessed directly after the higher level index has been accessed. In practice, the size of a higher level index would often depend on the size of buffers and disk blocks. Also, there may be more than two levels of indexing if the file is very large. More details of multilevel indexes are presented later in this section.

Another approach of reducing the size of an index and keeping the size as small as possible is based on maintaining one index entry for a group of records rather than for each record. Since every time the disk is accessed, a block of records rather than a single record is usually read, one index entry for each record is not really necessary. Instead one index entry for each block is sufficient. This is sometimes called *partial indexing*. An example of partial indexing is a dictionary as shown in Table 7.2. The index in this file (that is, the dictionary) is very small; one entry for each letter of the alphabet. One could consider a dictionary as having a two-level index, the high level one for each letter and then the lower level index for each page.

Table 7.2 Example of an index used in a dictionary

Index	*Dictionary*
A	All words starting with letter A
B	All words starting with letter B
C	All words starting with letter C
D	All words starting with letter D
E	All words starting with letter E
F	All words starting with letter F
G and so on	All words starting with letter G and so on

We first define some terminology for indexing. A *primary index* is specified on the ordered key attribute of a table. In this index it is clear that the values of the key attribute are unique and so indexing is relatively simple. A primary index normally is built on the primary key of the table. If the indexing attribute does not have unique values then the type of index is somewhat different. It is called a *clustering index*. It is assumed that the indexing attribute is still ordered. For some attributes ordering may not be possible, for example, the file could be ordered according to the primary index although it is required that there be another index on another attribute that is not unique. The second index is then called a *secondary index*.

These indexing techniques are now discussed.

7.8.1 Primary Index

As noted above, a primary index is specified on an ordered key attribute of a table. In this index the values of the key attribute are unique. An example of the primary index is shown in Table 7.3. The index consists of two fields, viz., the index entry and a pointer to the block on the disk.

Table 7.3 An example of a primary index

Highest Record Number on Track	*Track Number*
20	1
60	2
85	3
120	4

Therefore, to search for a row with key 90 we find the first entry in column 1 that is bigger than 90 (that is, 120) and go to the track number given (that is, 4). We can then search for 90 on that track. It should be noted that this index is much smaller than the table which probably has many attributes and therefore each row of the table is much larger than the attributes on which the index has been built.

7.8.2 Clustering Index

If the values of the indexing attribute are not unique but the attribute is still ordered and is searched frequently, a clustering index may be used to improve searching on the attribute. An example of the clustering index is shown in Table 7.4. It also consists of two fields, viz., the index entry and a pointer to the block on the disk.

The index shown in Table 7.4 usually has an entry for each record and therefore the index is relatively large but much smaller than the actual file. The entries in Table 7.4 indicate that for the attribute value 22, track number 3 should be searched which might have several records with the attribute value 22. For an attribute value 25 the index shows that there is no record with such value.

This type of index is expensive to maintain as records are updated, inserted and deleted but the index is efficient for a variety of queries, for example, searches, scans and range queries on the indexed attribute. Clustering indexes therefore should be used only where the cost of maintaining them can be justified by the savings in queries.

Table 7.4 A simple example of a clustering index

Clustering Attribute Value on Track	*Track Number*
15	1
18	2
22	3
29	4

7.8.3 Secondary Index

If the values of an attribute that justifies an index are not ordered, a secondary index may be used to improve searching on the attribute. As noted earlier, it is assumed that a primary index already exists on the search key which specifies the sequential order of the file. All other indexes on the file, of which there may be several, are called *secondary indexes*. The secondary index may be on a nonkey attribute which may also have duplicate values. A secondary index also has two values, viz., the indexing field and a pointer to the block or to the appropriate record. The secondary index then looks like that shown in Table 7.5. Since the secondary index attribute may have duplicate values, the index must take that into account by perhaps creating an entry for each duplicate value. Although the file is not ordered according to the secondary index attribute, the index is usually ordered according to the attribute so that the index can be searched quickly. It should be noted that the secondary index requires all values of the index attribute to be included in the index and therefore the index is usually relatively large and requires a longer search period than a primary index.

Table 7.5 An example of a secondary index

Secondary Attribute Value on Track	*Track Number*
15	1
18	2
25	1
49	4

It should be noted that a table may have one primary index and more than one secondary index, if appropriate.

As an example, with the file *Player* it may be desirable to build a primary index on *PlayerID* and a secondary index on *LName* while in the file *Match* it may be appropriate to have a primary index on *MID* and secondary indexes on attributes *Ground* and *Date* but this should be done only after a careful analysis of the likely queries.

Secondary indexes improve the performance of queries that use attributes other than the attribute used in the primary index, but the overhead costs of indexing are higher.

7.8.4 Multilevel Index

Since some indexes can be very large, as noted earlier, a multilevel (two levels or more) index is sometimes created to improve searching the index. If the index is stored on the disk then a multilevel index can substantially reduce the number of disk accesses needed by first retrieving the highest level index and then the lower level indexes until an entry is found in the lowest level index.

An example of a multilevel index is presented in Fig. 7.6. The index looks like a tree, with the top node being the highest level index which is searched first (it may be main memory resident) and then the appropriate block of the next level index is read from the disk followed by reading the appropriate block at the lowest level of the index, which then points to the block (the index in Fig. 7.6 is a very simplified version of an index that does not show pointers) that has the record.

Consider an example of searching using this index. Suppose we are searching for 60. First the top level of the index is searched[1]. Since 60 is larger than 50, we go to the next level on the right and search that part of the index which has only 70 and 90 keys. So the search continues to the left of 70 and the next level of the index is accessed. We find 60 and then follow the pointer (not shown in the figure) to access the block on disk which has the record.

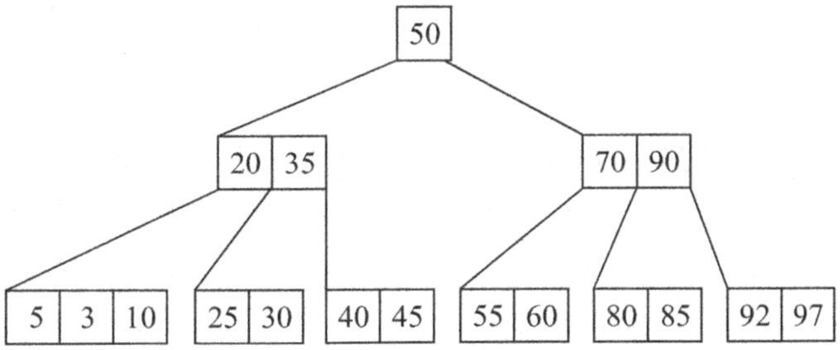

Figure 7.6 A multilevel index

Once again we emphasize that Fig. 7.6 is a simplified version of an index that would be used in practice. It does not show any pointers and each node is small with a maximum of only 3 keys.

7.8.5 Ordering Composite Index

Often a query would require search on more than one column when the WHERE clause has two conditions. To speed up such a query, a composite index that is made up of more than one column may be useful. In some cases, a composite index may include all the columns of a table. Such index is called a *covering index*. To speed up a query, the index should be on the columns that match the columns used in the WHERE clause. Composite indexes tend to be much larger than a single column index because, for example, the number of distinct values of, say (*PID*, *MID*), would be much larger than for *PID* or *MID* alone.

When a query uses a composite index, the order of the columns of the key in the index is important. The index is usually most efficient when the composite index has the columns in order from most to least distinct. Therefore, the column with the most number of distinct values should come first in the composite index.

Let us consider an example. Suppose several queries are posed on the cricket database about the number of runs scored by a batsman in a match. It has been decided to set up an index on *MID* and *PID*. Should this

1. Usually a node in the index would be bigger, for example, equal to the size of a block and include many values of the indexed attribute as well as pointers to the next level indexes. We assume that the pointers to the records are included only in the leaf nodes and therefore 50 does not point directly to a record. Furthermore, we have not stated whether this multilevel index is a full index to the file or a partial index.

index be (*PID*, *MID*) or (*MID*, *PID*)? We can make a decision if we look at the data in the database. Assume that the database includes information on all the ODIs that have been held so far. So we have 3000 different values of *MID*. Further assuming that many matches have 22 batsmen records when everyone bats while some have only, say, 10 batsmen records when only a few batsmen bat, in each of the two innings. Therefore, we may assume that there are on average 15 batting records for each match, giving us a total of 45,000 batting records in the table *Batting*. How many distinct values of *PID* are there? Let us assume there are 500, so that on average each player has 90 batting records. Some players have played more than 400 ODIs while many have played well below 100.

When a query involves *PID* and *MID*, we want to use the index to quickly get these records. If we use *PID* first then we narrow the search to 90 rows in *Batting* on average but it may be close to 400 for some values of *PID*. If on the other hand we use *MID* first, then the search is narrowed to no more than 22 records. Therefore, it is better to set up the index as (*MID*, *PID*).

7.9 THE INDEXED-SEQUENTIAL FILE

The indexed-sequential file organization has been successfully used in many business applications. IBM's well known ISAM file organization was based on using an ordered primary file and a two-level index. As described below the ISAM file structure uses an overflow area.

The organization of an indexed-sequential file is discussed below in more detail. The file usually consists of the *prime area* (the main file), the *overflow area* and the *index area*. When the file is created or reorganized, all the records reside in the prime area and the overflow area is empty. As in the sequential organization, records in an indexed-sequential file are ordered by a key value and therefore a primary index is being used as discussed above.

We illustrate the organization by a simple example. We assume that the size of the records is such that each block (we will also use the term *track* for block since normally a block is the size of a track) of the disk on which the file is resident stores only four records. Let the prime area of the file at some instance be as shown in Table 7.6.

Let the overflow area at this instance be empty. The track index then looks like Table 7.7.

Table 7.6 Records in the prime area of an indexed-sequential file

Track Number	*Records*			
1	REC10	REC14	REC18	REC20
2	REC26	REC31	REC41	REC60
3	REC72	REC74	REC75	REC76
4	REC77	REC78	REC79	REC82

Table 7.7 Index of the indexed-sequential file in Table 7.6

Track Number	*Highest Record Number on Track*
1	20
2	60
3	76
4	82

To locate record number 79, we first consult the index in Table 7.7 and find that record numbers greater than 76 and up to 82 are on track 4. Track 4 is read in the main memory and a search for record 79 is carried out. The search terminates successfully if the record is located in the block, otherwise the search terminates unsuccessfully.

Using the index does not completely eliminate the sequential search (as the block must still be searched sequentially) but it does reduce the magnitude of the search substantially. We now only need to search one track of records rather than the whole file.

The above search process was particularly simple since there were no overflow records. In a dynamic file, there will be deletions and insertions and almost always some of the tracks will overflow. The search procedure is then somewhat more complex and we discuss it now using an example.

Let us assume that record numbers 15, 30 and 90 are inserted to the file above and assume that track 5 has been designated as the overflow area. The prime area after inserting the three records then looks like the file in Table 7.8.

Table 7.8 An indexed-sequential file with overflow area

Track Number	*Records*			
1	REC10	REC14	REC15	REC18
2	REC26	REC30	REC31	REC41
3	REC72	REC74	REC75	REC76
4	REC77	REC78	REC79	REC82
The overflow track has the following records:				
5	REC20	REC60	REC90	

Note that the key sequences in each block have been preserved when records have been added although sequence preservation generally incurs additional costs. For example, the addition of record number 30 above required reading and writing track number 2 as well as track 5.

The index must now include some information about overflow records. The index may appear as shown in Table 7.9.

Table 7.9 Index for an indexed-sequential file with overflow area

Track Number	*Highest Record Number on Track*	*Highest Record Number in Overflow*	*Address of First Overflow*
1	18	20	5
2	41	60	5
3	76	Nil	Nil
4	82	90	5

Indexed-sequential files can be very efficient, however, the technique can become inefficient when the file is dynamic, since deletions and insertions are difficult and regular reorganization of the file becomes necessary to preserve efficient operations. We now consider a technique that is more suited to dynamic files.

7.10 THE B-TREE

The indexed-sequential file is not a particularly satisfactory solution for dynamic files although IBM's ISAM system using overflow areas became very popular during the 1960s and 1970s. As noted earlier, ISAM used a two-level index which may be considered as a shallow tree with the top level index being the root of the index tree and the next level being the tree leaves. We now consider another tree data structure for the index. This tree structure does not have a fixed number of index levels. It allows as many levels as are needed and allows the index to grow and shrink gracefully.

We first consider the classical B-tree structure which combines the index and the file. Later we will look at modifications of this structure that may be more suitable for use as an indexing technique.

We assume that the reader is familiar with binary search trees. The binary search tree is not suitable for storing information on disk due to the following reasons:

(a) In a binary search tree, one node of the tree is examined at a time and the node to be inspected next depends on the result of the comparison at the present node. This process would, on average, require reading ten nodes to search a file of only 1000 records.

(b) As noted earlier, information stored on a disk is read one block at a time. One block would normally include several nodes but the binary tree scheme does not readily take advantage of this feature of reading disks.

The B-tree is a multiway tree which appears like that in Fig. 7.7 below.

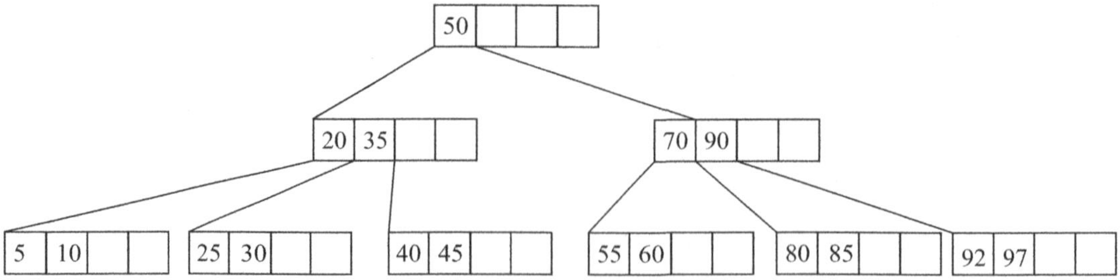

Figure 7.7 A typical B-tree

This tree shows each block having a capacity to store four keys or records. A block with k keys has $k + 1$ pointers to its children. We will consider B-trees in more detail soon.

Figure 7.7 can be looked at as an attempt to modify the binary tree structure so that the above problems are overcome. The technique includes a number of records in one node; the node size is usually equal to that of a block.

We first consider the binary tree in Fig. 7.8. In an attempt to store the tree on the disk, we may partition the binary tree as shown.

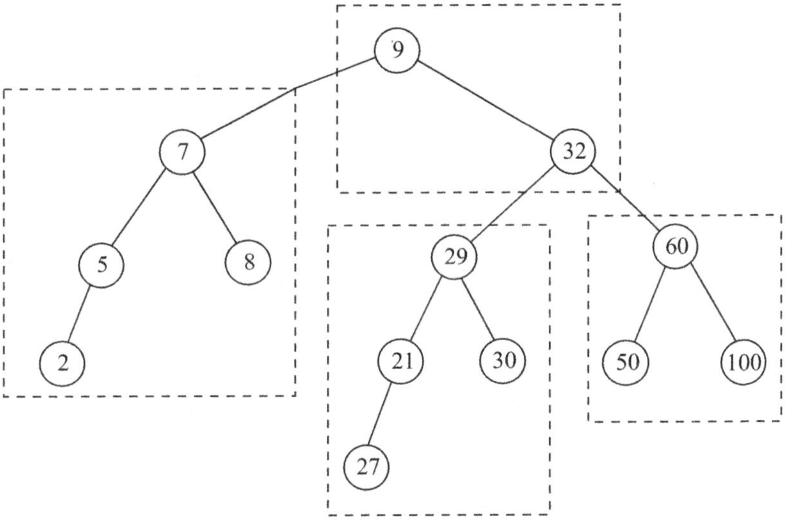

Figure 7.8 A binary search tree

The binary tree in Fig. 7.8 can be represented as a multiway tree in which each node is allowed to have more than one key. The tree is presented in Fig. 7.9.

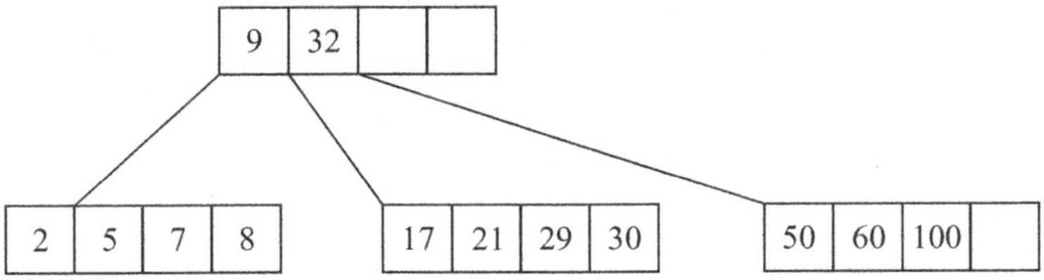

Figure 7.9 A B-tree representation for the binary tree of Fig. 7.8

The multiway tree in Fig. 7.9 is a representation of the binary search tree in Fig. 7.8. Each node in the multiway tree has a number of nodes of the binary search tree. In the binary tree scheme, it was necessary to use some technique like height-balancing to keep the tree balanced. The B-tree on the other hand uses a technique that keeps it always balanced but the cost of keeping it balanced is that the nodes are not required to be full to capacity. We will explain this in more detail soon. Let us first define a B-tree of order *m*.

Definition—B-tree

A B-tree of order m is a multiway search tree such that

(a) Every node except the root has at most (m – 1) keys and at least [m/2] – 1 keys.
(b) The root may have as few as one key.
(c) Every node with k keys has k+1 descendants except the leaves.
(d) All leaf nodes are on the same level.

Figure 7.10 presents a B-tree of order 5. Note that the root has only one key in it and every other node of the tree is only half full. A full capacity tree will have every node containing four keys and five pointers to the nodes at the next level.

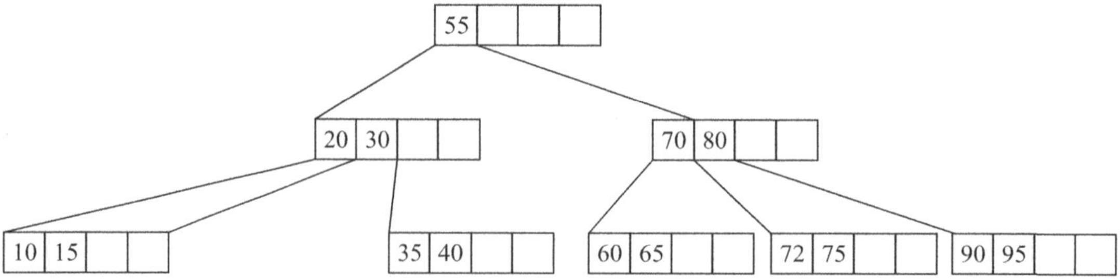

Figure 7.10 A B-tree of order 5

We now discuss how a B-tree can be searched and how insertions and deletions are made to it.

7.10.1 Searching a B-Tree

Consider searching keys from the B-tree in Fig. 7.10. Let us assume we wish to search for 95, 55, 30, 27, and 100. It does not matter in what order these searches are carried out since a search leaves the B-tree unchanged[2].

To search for 95, we start by comparing it with the key in the root. Since 95 is larger than 55, the only key in the root, the right branch is taken and the node on the right is accessed. This node has keys 70 and 80, and 95 is bigger than 80, so the rightmost branch is taken. The key 95 is located in this node and therefore the search has concluded successfully.

To search for 55, we start by comparing it with the key in the root. Since the root has the key 55, the search concludes successfully.

To search for 30, we start by comparing it with the key in the root. Since 30 is smaller than 55, the only key in the root, the left branch is taken and the node on the left is accessed. This node has keys 20 and 30 and therefore the search has concluded successfully.

To search for 27, we start by comparing it with the key in the root. Since 27 is smaller than 55, the only key in the root, the left branch is taken and the node on the left is accessed. This node has keys 20 and 30 and therefore we take the middle branch to reach the node that has 25 and 27. Therefore, the search has concluded successfully.

To search for 100, we start by comparing it with the key in the root. Since 100 is larger than 55, the only key in the root, the right branch is taken and the node on the right is accessed. This node has keys 70 and 80, and 100 is bigger than 80, so the rightmost branch is taken. This node has keys 90 and 95 and therefore the search has concluded unsuccessfully.

---

2. Not all data structures are left unchanged by a search. There are a number of data structures that every search will normally modify in an attempt to improve the structure's search performance. *Splay* trees are one such data structure.

7.10.2 Insertion to a B-tree

Let us consider an example of building a tree of order 5, that is, the maximum number of keys in each node is 4 and the minimum number is 2.

We build the tree by inserting records with keys 1, 3, 5, … 21 (all the odd numbers up to 21) followed by 2, 4, 6, … 20 (all the even numbers up to 20) in that order. Initially, starting from a null tree, one node is all that is needed as the first four keys are inserted in it to obtain the B-tree in Fig. 7.11[3].

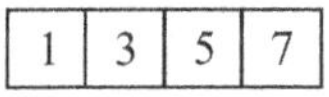

Figure 7.11 A B-tree of order 5 with only four keys and one node

The node is now full and cannot accommodate the next key. When an attempt is made to insert 9, the node *overflows* and is split into two nodes such that the middle key of the five keys migrates to a newly created root. The following algorithm is used:

1. The middle key of the *m* keys (*m* – 1 keys in the node and the key that is being inserted) is found. If *m* is even, then either of the two middle keys may be chosen.
2. This middle key partitions the keys into two groups: keys that are smaller than it and keys that are greater.
3. One of these groups is put in the present node and the other in a new node. The middle key migrates to the parent node. If there was no parent node, a new root node is created.

The above procedure is called *node splitting*. We now obtain the B-tree in Fig. 7.12 after splitting the single node shown in Fig. 7.11.

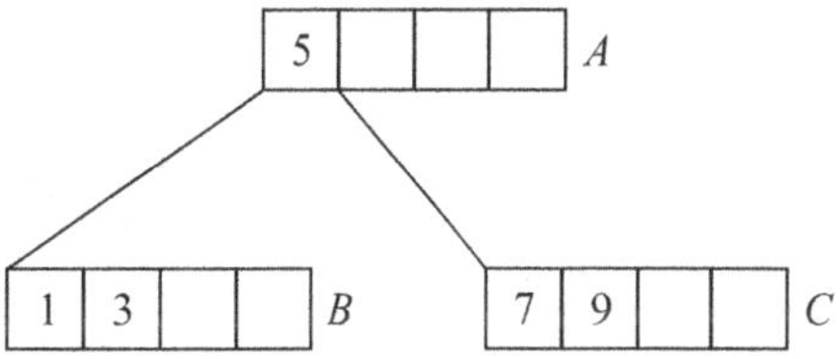

Figure 7.12 A B-tree of order 5 after a node split

Let us label the nodes *A*, *B*, *C* as in Fig. 7.12 with *A* being the root node and *B* and *C* being the two leaf nodes. To insert keys 11 and 13, we look at the root and find that keys 11 and 13 must go to node *C* (since 11 and 13 are larger than 5, the only key in the root). We insert 11 and 13 and find that node *C* is full to capacity. Inserting key 15 now causes node *C* to split since 15 must also go to node *C*. We now obtain the B-tree shown in Fig. 7.13 after splitting node *C* into nodes *C* and *D*.

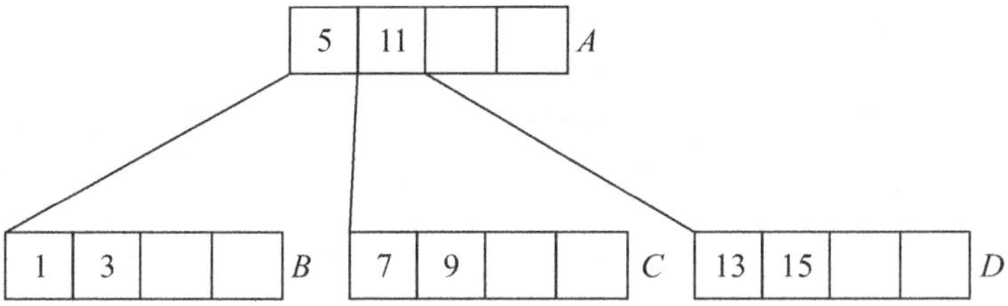

Figure 7.13 The B-tree of order 5 after node *C* is split

3. Hopefully the difference between a node and a key is clear but to ensure that it is, a node is a collection of keys while a key is often the primary key of a record although it may be another attribute or even a combination of attributes used for searching the file.

We may now insert keys 17 and 19 (in node *D*) without split, but 21 leads to splitting of node *D* sending key 17 to the root and creating a new node *E* with keys 19 and 21 in it. We now continue insertions starting with the even numbered keys and keys 2 and 4 are inserted in node *B* filling it to capacity, 6 and 8 are inserted in node *C* filling it to capacity as well, but insertion of 10 causes node *C* to overflow. A split takes place sending 8 to the root and creating a new node (node *F*). Keys 12 and 14 are now inserted in node *D* and this node is also now full. The B-tree is given in Fig. 7.14.

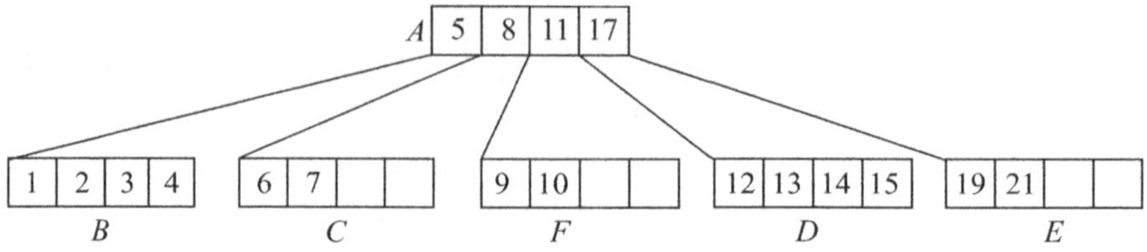

Figure 7.14 The B-tree of order 5 after more insertions

Now insertion of 16 leads to an interesting situation. It needs to be inserted in node *D* which is already full and so causes a split of node *D* sending key 14 to the root and creating a brother node *G*. Unfortunately, the root itself is full to capacity and it must also be split resulting in a new node *H* and a new root node *I* containing the middle key. The B-tree is given in Fig. 7.15.

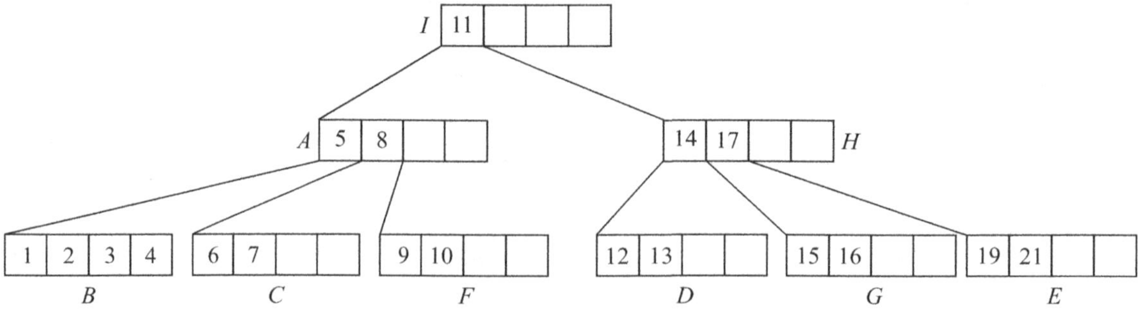

Figure 7.15 The final B-tree of order 5

We may now insert keys 18 and 20 to node *E* of the tree in Fig. 7.15 without any further node splitting and obtain a tree similar to that shown in Fig. 7.15 except that the node *E* is full with keys 18, 19, 20, 21. We note that the tree grows only when the root node is split which results in a new root node. Also we note that the final tree obtained in the above example has poor storage utilization since most nodes are only 50% full. In fact the root is only 25% full.

7.10.3 Deletion from a B-tree

We now discuss deletion of keys from the B-tree in Fig. 7.15. Node *E* is full and has keys 18, 19, 20 and 21. First the keys 4, 7, 9, 10 and 8 are deleted in that order.

To delete 4, it is searched by comparing it with the key in the root (node *I*). Since 4 is smaller than 11, the only key in the root, the left branch is taken and node *A* is accessed. Node *A* has keys 5 and 8, and since 4 is smaller than 5, the leftmost branch is taken to reach node *B*. The key 4 is located in this node and is deleted. The node is still more than 50% full and therefore no further action is needed.

To delete 7, we search for it through the root *I*, then node *A* and locate it in node *C* which is only half full and delete key 7 from it. Node *C* now violates the B-tree definition by being less than half full, it has *underflowed*, that is, it has less than the minimum number of keys allowed for a node in a tree of the order 5. To overcome this problem we look at the brother nodes of node *C* (nodes *B* and *F*) and either coalesce with one of them if that brother node is also close to underflowing or borrow some keys from one of them. To coalesce requires the keys from both the nodes that have underflowed and the brother node as well as the one key that is the separator key in the parent node to be put in one node. Therefore, the total number of these keys must be less than or equal to $m-1$, m being the order of the tree. If the total number of keys is greater than $m-1$, then coalescing is not possible and it is necessary to redistribute the total keys from the two nodes amongst them, such that both nodes have an almost equal number of keys, and the separator key from the parent node is included in the redistribution with the middle key again going to the parent node.

In this particular case, it is decided to coalesce the two nodes *C* and *F* and remove the separator key (key value 8) from node *A* and include it in the newly combined node *C*. Node *F* has been removed. This results in node *A* underflowing since it is left with only one key. The B-tree at this stage appears as given in Fig. 7.16.

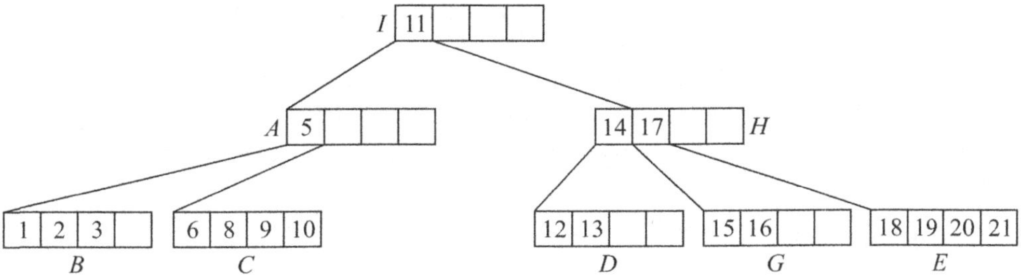

Figure 7.16 The B-tree after a number of deletions (Node *A* has underflown)

Because node *A* has now underflowed, we must consider redistributing keys between it and a brother node (that is, node *H*) or coalesce it with that node. In this case we have no option since node *H* is also only 50% full and redistribution is not possible. Therefore, we must coalesce nodes *A* and *H*. In combining *A* and *H*, we need to include the separator key from the parent node (the root) but the root node (node *I*) has only one key and therefore merging nodes *A* and *H* results in the root node as well as node *H* disappearing as shown in the B-tree in Fig. 7.17.

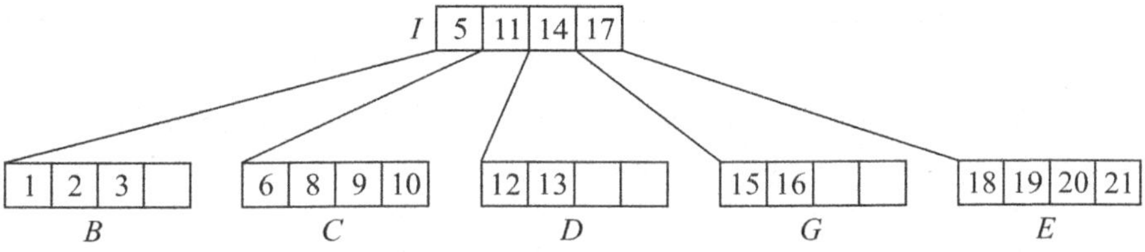

Figure 7.17 The B-tree after further deletions

Next the key 9 is deleted from node *C* and then key 10 from *C* reducing node *C* to only two keys. Deletion of 8 from node *C* causes node *C* to underflow. We look at the brother node (node *B*) and see if the two nodes can be merged together. Node *B* has three keys and cannot be coalesced with the underflowed node *C* which has only one key since the coalesced node must also include the separator key from the node above. We therefore redistribute the four keys in the two nodes and the separator key from the parent, which is key 5. Now the new middle key is sent to the parent, this is key 3, and we obtain the B-tree in Fig. 7.18.

Redistribution of keys in nodes *B* and *C* involved moving only one key (key 3) from node *B* to the parent node (root in this case) and the separator key (key 5) from the root to node *C* since we are dealing with a B-tree of order 5. In a tree of higher order, enough keys will be moved from the brother node to the node that has underflowed to make the number of keys in each node almost equal.

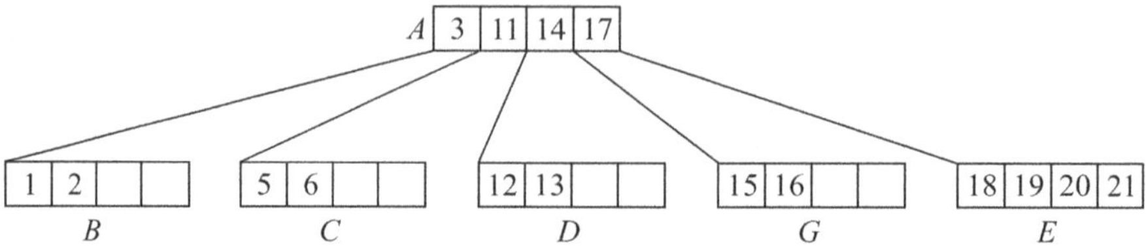

Figure 7.18 The B-tree after deleting keys 9, 10 and 8

In general, if a deletion at level k leads to a combination of two nodes, it may also lead to underflow of a parent node resulting in two nodes at level $k - 1$ coalescing or redistributing keys. This in extreme cases may lead to underflows at levels $k - 1$, $k - 2$ and so on, and eventually reduce the tree height by one.

7.10.4 Analysis of B-tree Performance[4]

We now consider the cost of insertion, deletion and retrieval in a B-tree. These costs are directly related to the height of the tree. We first consider the worst case height of a B-tree with n nodes.

The Worst Case

Let the top level of the tree (i.e., level of the root) be 0 and let the level of any other node be one higher than the level of its parent. We wish to compute the largest value of height h that a B-tree with n keys might have.

To simplify the analysis below, we will assume the order m to be odd and further assume $m = 2d + 1$.

The B-tree of height h with the worst storage utilization would have only one key in the root node and all other nodes would be only 50% full. That is, if the order of the tree is $2d + 1$, then the number of *nodes* (not keys) in the worst B-tree of height h would be given by the equation on the next page.

Note that the root is one node (with only one key) and it has two children nodes. Since we are considering the worst case, these nodes are only half full (i.e., they only have d keys) and each has exactly $(d + 1)$ children nodes [note that a node with d keys must have $(d + 1)$ children]. Since each of these nodes is also only half full, each will also have $(d + 1)$ children nodes and so on. Therefore,

4. This section may be left out without any loss of continuity.

Table 7.10 The number of nodes in a B-tree that is half full

Level	*Number of Nodes*	*Number of Keys*	*Comment*
0	1	1	Root is allowed only one key
1	2	$2d$	Each node is only half full
2	$2(d + 1)$	$2d(d + 1)$	Each node has $d + 1$ children
3	$2(d + 1)^2$	$2d(d + 1)^2$	Each node is only half full
4 etc	and so on		

Given these, we may now compute the total number of nodes in the B-tree of height h as follows. Note that a height h tree will have h levels 0, 1, 2, … $(h - 1)$.

$$N_{\min} = 1 + 2[1 + (d + 1) + (d + 1)^2 + \text{K} + (d + 1)^{h-1}]$$
$$= 1 + 2\frac{(d+1)^h - 1}{(d+1) - 1}$$

The number of keys in $N_{\min}$ nodes is $1 + (N_{\min} - 1)(d)$ since in the worst case the root has only one key. If a B-tree of height h has n keys, we may write

$$1 + (N_{\min} - 1)(d) < n$$

Substituting for $N_{\min}$ and cancelling out d from numerator and denominator, we obtain

$$1 + 2[(d + 1)^h - 1] < n$$

$$\boxed{h < \log_{(d+1)} \frac{n+1}{2}}$$

This is the worst height a B-tree of order m (or $2d + 1$) with n keys could have. We now look at the best case.

The Best Case

A B-tree with the best storage utilization would have all the nodes full. This means that the number of nodes (*not* keys) in a tree of height h would be the root (which is assumed full) that has m children that are also all full, each in turn has m children and so on. Note that in the following, we do not need to use the notation $m = 2d + 1$ since it is easier to use m as the order of the tree.

Table 7.11 The number of nodes in a B-tree that is half full

Level	*Number of Nodes*	*Number of Keys*	*Comment*
0	1	$(m - 1)$	The root is full
1	m	$m(m - 1)$	Every node is full ($m - 1$ keys)
2	m^2	$m^2(m - 1)$	Every node has m children
3	m^3	$m^3(m - 1)$	Every node has m children
4 etc.	and so on		

Given these, we may now compute the total number of nodes in the best case B-tree of height h as follows:

$$N_{\max} = 1 + m + m^2 + \text{K} + m^{h-1}$$
$$= \frac{1}{m-1}(m^h - 1)$$

Let the number of keys in the above tree of height h be n. Since each node is full and has $(m - 1)$ keys, we must then have

$$N_{\max}\,(m - 1) \geq n$$

Substituting for $N_{\max}$ and cancelling out $(m - 1)$, we obtain

$$(m^h - 1) \geq n \text{ or}$$
$$\boxed{h \geq \log_m (n+1)}$$

The above expression provides a lower bound for h for a B-tree of order m with n keys. Therefore, the height of a B-tree of order m ($m = 2d + 1$) with n keys must be such that

$$\boxed{\log_{(2d+1)}(n+1) \leq h \leq \log_{(d+1)}\frac{n+1}{2}}$$

Example

Let us consider a tree of order 101 (this order is not too large since a node is often equal to a block and a block is often 4 KB). Table 7.12 lists the minimum and the maximum number of keys that may be stored in such a tree of height h.

Table 7.12 Minimum and maximum number of keys in a B-tree of order 101

Height (h)	*Minimum Number of Keys*	*Maximum Number of Keys*
0	1	100
1	101	102,000
2	5201	1,030,300
etc.		

It is clear from the above figures that only 3 or 4 accesses of disk will be necessary for even the largest file if the order of the tree is close to 100. Clearly if the storage utilization in the B-tree is high, the height of the B-tree for the same number of keys will be smaller and the cost of insertion, deletion and retrieval will be lower. If the storage utilization is low, the height of the tree would be larger and the cost of insertion, deletion and retrieval will be higher. We are therefore interested in knowing the average storage utilization of B-trees that are built randomly. The derivation of average storage utilization is beyond the scope of this book. We only present the final result. The storage utilization of randomly built B-trees is $\log_e 2 = 69\%$ on average.

The B-tree therefore is an efficient data structure for storage of information on disk. The structure is always balanced and is efficient for insertion, deletion and retrieval but it should be noted that the B-tree is not very efficient for sequential processing. For example, if we want to traverse the keys in the B-tree in Fig. 7.15 we would need to start from the root, then visit A then B, back to A then C, back to A then to F and so on. In sequential processing, the B-tree structure that we have discussed is quite different from the indexed-sequential file structure.

The indexed-sequential structure is very convenient when the file needs to be accessed sequentially. As the above example shows, it is possible to use the B-tree structure for sequential processing but it is not as efficient as the indexed-sequential file. B-tree sequential traversing requires first finding the leftmost leaf and then processing the key that separates it from the next leaf (this separator key is in the parent node). The next leaf may now be processed followed by the next separator key in the parent node and so on. Any modification of the B-tree structure that permits more efficient sequential processing is clearly desirable. We now discuss one such modification.

7.11 THE B$^+$-TREE

This B-tree modification, called the B$^+$-tree is based on the observation that when a B-tree is searched for a key, the chances of finding the key before reaching the leaf are quite low if the order of the tree is high (say, 100). For $m = 101$, level $i + 1$ would contain at least 51 times the number of nodes at level i since each node must have at least 50 keys and 51 children. Therefore, the number of nonleaf nodes is not expected to be more than 1/50th (or 2%) of the number of leaf nodes. This suggests a simple modification of the B-tree scheme that has some useful properties in addition to the B-tree properties.

The modification involves duplicating every key that would normally appear in a nonleaf node in the appropriate leaf node. As noted earlier, this should not require much additional storage if the order is high (say, higher than 10).

In addition to putting all the keys in the leaf nodes, each leaf node is now required to have a pointer to the next leaf node in sequence. The structure given in Fig. 7.14 therefore looks like the Fig. 7.19. Note that each key in the root node in Fig. 7.14 has been duplicated in the appropriate leaf node so that all the keys are now resident in the leaves and form a sequential file.

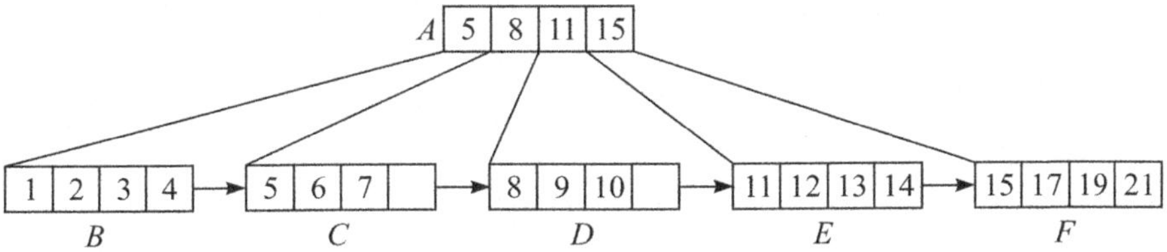

Figure 7.19 A B-tree modified for sequential processing

The modified B-tree structure is called the B$^+$-tree and it provides another very useful property. If we look at the B$^+$-tree without the leaf nodes (for a tree that has more than two levels, for example, the tree in Fig. 7.20), this is really an index for the sequential file which is the leaf nodes. The sequential file is stored in the leaf nodes (often the leaf nodes will have pointers to the records from the keys in them although the pointers are not shown in the figure) by linking the leaf nodes through pointers from one leaf node to the next. The B$^+$-tree structure may therefore be considered an indexed-sequential file.

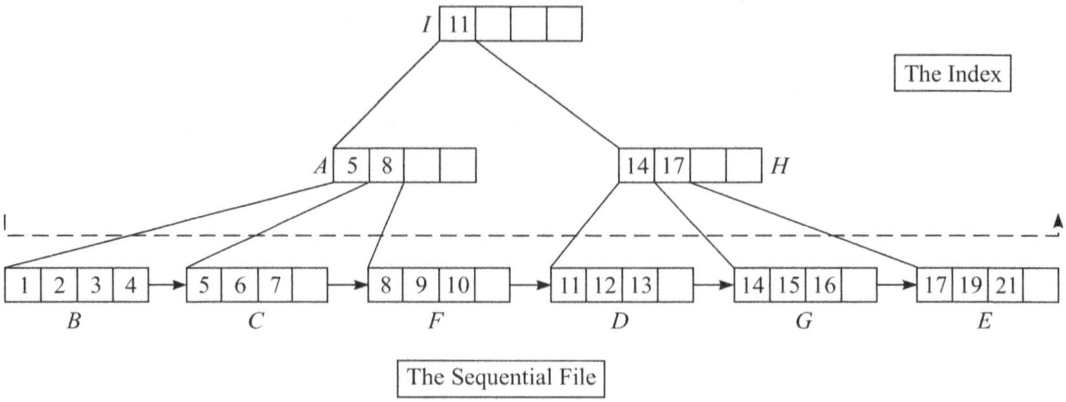

Figure 7.20 A B^+-tree of order 5 as an indexed sequential file

Since the internal nodes of a B^+-tree are the index and the leaves are the sequential file, more entries may be packed into the internal nodes by, for example, using only the first four letters of the keys in the internal nodes. As noted earlier, a higher order B^+-tree structure means that the index is more compact and faster to search, since the height of the index could well be smaller by packing the keys in the internal nodes. Also, by linking the leaf nodes, the B^+-tree structure makes it easy to traverse the sequential file.

A number of other modifications of the B-tree have been proposed to improve the efficiency of the basic tree. A commonly used modification is to change the condition that the nodes must be at least half full to the condition that they be at least two-third full. This improves the storage utilization and for large indexes reduces the index tree depth, thus making it more efficient.

The B^+-tree indexed-sequential file has a number of advantages over the conventional indexed-sequential file. These advantages and disadvantages are listed in the following section.

7.12 ADVANTAGES AND DISADVANTAGES OF B-TREES AND B^+-TREES

B-trees have substantial advantages over other file structures. The main advantages are as follows:

1. B-trees are efficient external storage structures. If the node access time far exceeds search time within nodes, the B-tree structure is usually efficient.
2. B-trees are good for searches in dynamic files since they are always balanced.
3. The only disadvantage of the B-tree and B^+-tree structure is that storage utilization tends to be close to 70% but this can be improved if the modification described above is used.
4. Developing insertion and deletion algorithms can be somewhat complicated in B-trees and B^+-trees.
5. As compared to indexed-sequential files, the performance of B^+-trees does not degrade as the file grows, since the file grows and shrinks gracefully.
6. As compared to indexed-sequential files, the B^+-tree file requires no overflow area and no periodic reorganization to maintain good performance.

We now discuss another data structure that is also commonly used in databases. It is called hashing. Static hashing followed by dynamic hashing is discussed in the sections ahead.

7.13 STATIC HASHING

We have so far studied sequential and indexed-sequential files. Indexed-sequential files are quite efficient for inserting, deleting and accessing a particular record from a file as well as for processing the whole file sequentially although for very large files the index becomes large impacting the efficiency of indexed-sequential files. Another major file organization technique that is often better for retrieval is called *hashing*.

7.13.1 Basics of Hashing

Hashed files can often lead to better performance in insertion, deletion and retrieval but the performance of sequential processing of the file is very poor. For example, a file *Player* that is stored using hashing on the last name *LName* can very quickly find the record for player with *LName* = *Sehwag*, much faster than even an indexed-sequential file would if the file is large.

File organizations based on hashing were developed as early as the mid 1950s. It has been reported that the idea of hashing originated at IBM in 1953. Significant developments have taken place since then. We will discuss classical hashing techniques briefly and then some more recent developments in dynamic hashing.

Dynamic hashing is used extensively for file organizations on external storage but hashing is equally applicable for organizing tables in the main memory. For example, static hashing is often a suitable technique for organizing a symbol table in a compiler.

The idea behind hashing techniques is to use the key of a record or another important attribute of the file and calculate the storage location from it. The transformation from the key to the storage location is done using a formula that is called a *hash function*.

Let k be the key of a record (or value of another attribute which is frequently used in search[5]) and let $h(.)$ be the hash function being used. $h(k)$ is then the address of the record whose key is k. The hash function can be as simple as dividing by a prime number N and using the remainder for numeric keys. Clearly it is necessary that the function $h(.)$ demonstrate some useful properties. Some of these are as follows:

1. The addresses generated by the function are within a given interval which specifies the acceptable addresses. For a table of size N, or file of size N, the addresses are 0, 1, 2, ... $N - 1$.
2. The hashed address often refers to a *bucket* which may be able to store a number of records. The size of the bucket may be equal to a block when the hashed file is stored on the disk.
3. The hash function should generate addresses that are approximately uniformly distributed over the range of acceptable addresses and should break-up naturally occurring clusters of key values.

5. We will keep using the term key for the attribute on which the file is hashed. This attribute does not need to be the primary key of the table that is being stored using hashing.

4. The hash function transformation should use all the characters or digits in the key to compute the address.
5. The hash function should be easy and fast to compute.

We will discuss several hash functions that satisfy the above requirements.

We first define some terms that are used in this context. We assume that the records or rows of a table are being stored in a table of size N (as noted earlier, each entry in the table could be an address of a block or bucket on secondary storage, a bucket being a collection of one or more blocks of storage connected by pointers). Therefore, only addresses from 0 to $N - 1$ are acceptable.

Figure 7.21 shows a very simple hashed file with a table of only 4 addresses that are pointing to buckets that store a number of records each. The hash table entry 2 has currently no records hashed to it.

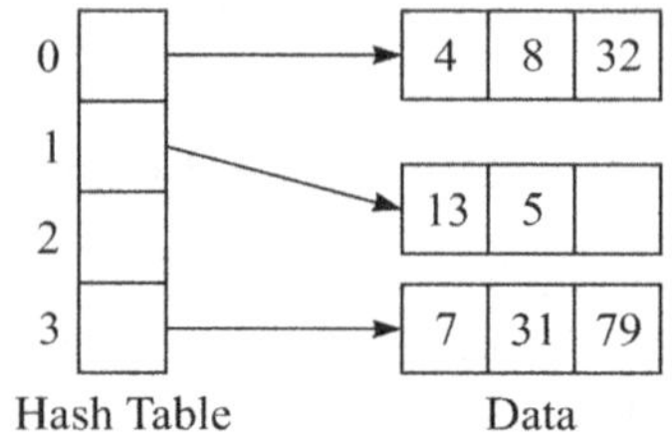

Figure 7.21 A simple static hashing file

The address generated by the hash function for a record is called the record's *home address* and the block to which the record is hashed is sometimes called the *primary block* for the record. If a record is hashed to an address where there is no space for it, we call it a *collision*. Records having the same home address are called *synonyms*.

Search

We now briefly discuss how to search the key for a record given. Let the key be K.

1. The key K is first hashed using the hash function used in building the hash table. Let the address be A.
2. The hashed address A refers to a *bucket* which stores a number of records. Search the bucket at address A for the record with key K.
3. The search concludes successfully if the key K is found otherwise unsuccessfully.

Of course, it is not as simple as the above algorithm shows because we often need to deal with collisions. If the hash table has collisions then the search algorithm becomes more complex depending on the collision technique used in building the hash table.

Collision

When a collision takes place, some technique of collision resolution is needed. We will consider the collision resolution techniques listed in Fig. 7.22.

1. Linear probing
2. Double hashing
3. Chaining

Figure 7.22 Collision resolution techniques

These collision resolution techniques will be discussed after we describe some hashing functions.

7.13.2 Hash Functions

As explained earlier, a hash function $h(.)$ transforms the attribute value k such that $h(k)$ has a value between 0 and $N - 1$ if N is the size of the hash table. Often N is a power of 2 and the function $h(k)$ produces a bit string of length b such that $N = 2^b$ and therefore the addresses generated are from 0 to $2^b - 1$.

As noted earlier, we desire that the hash function generate addresses that are uniformly distributed over the table even if the key values are not uniformly distributed. If some addresses are generated more frequently than others, we call the phenomenon *primary clustering*.

We now discuss some hash functions that have been found to perform satisfactorily for many different types of data. A reader familiar with pseudorandom number generators would have noticed the similarities between the requirements of hashing functions and pseudorandom number generators. This similarity enables us to use the techniques that have been developed for pseudorandom number generation in designing hash functions.

Most hash functions assume that a binary representation of the key (the key could well be alphanumeric or it may be another attribute of interest) is available for transformation. We therefore assume that a key k may be interpreted as an integer that is represented in binary form. Let this integer be z.

We now discuss three commonly used hash functions, viz., integer divide, mid-square and compression.

Integer Divide

The simplest hash function involves dividing z (the integer representation of the key k) by the size of the table N and using the remainder as the address. Therefore, $h(k) = z \bmod N$.

The above hash function is simple and fast to compute. The computation can be made even faster if N was 2^b for some suitable b. $h(k)$ is then given by the least significant b bits of the binary representation of z and the distribution of the computed addresses would be dependent on the distribution of these bits. It can be shown that when an integer divide is used, choosing $N = 2^b$ often does not provide a good distribution of computed addresses although the approach is very efficient. The reasons for this behaviour is not hard to find. Let the key of records be names having three components (first name, middle initial, last name). If the b least significant bits were used as the hashed address, all records with the same last name could well be mapped to the same location and the hash function may ignore the first name and the middle initial in the transformation. This is not desirable since some last names (for example, Singh) might be very common. That is why one of our requirements is that the hash function must use the entire key (not just a part of it) in computing the address.

It can be shown that by choosing N as a prime number, the problem described above usually disappears and the distribution is often uniform.

Mid-Square Function

Another quite commonly used hash function is based on squaring z (the integer representation of k) and then selecting the middle b bits as the home address of the record in a table of size 2^b.

The function satisfies the requirement that the mapping be based on all characters in the key and it has been observed that the middle b bits are usually distributed uniformly even if the keys are not.

Compression Function

This function involves partitioning the binary representation of k (that is, z) into several sections that are b bits long. These sections are then added together and the least significant b bits are taken as the address in a table of size 2^b.

Example

Consider a simple example to illustrate the use of the above hash functions. Let the key value be only two characters long. We only use uppercase letters and transform the keys to numeric values by replacing *A* by 1, *B* by 2, ... *Z* by 26. We will then apply the three hash functions to the numeric representation of the key.

Our table size is assumed to be 10 for hash functions mid-square and compression and 11 for the integer divide function, since integer divide requires table size to be a prime number for good performance.

Table 7.13 A simple example of three hash functions

Key (*k*)	*Numeric Representation* (*z*)	*Integer Divide*	z^2	*Mid-digit of* z^2	*Compression Function*
AB	0102	3	0010404	0	3
AZ	0126	5	0015876	5	0
BN	0214	5	0045796	5	7
NB	1402	5	1965604	5	7
CD	0304	7	0092416	2	7
EF	0506	0	0256036	6	1
GH	0708	4	0501264	1	5
HK	0811	8	0657271	7	0

The integer divide hash function was z mod 11. The mid-square function involved squaring z and extracting only one middle digit since the table is of size 10. We chose the 4th digit from the right (it being one of the two middle digits). The compression function also needs to transform z into one digit since the table size is 10. We achieve the transformation by adding the digits of z and then taking the least significant digit.

The above example had a hash table of size 10 for mid-square and compression functions, and size 11 for integer divide. The number of keys that were hashed to the table was 8. Although the tables were not quite full, we found that there were several collisions whatever hash function was used. We now discuss techniques for collision resolution.

7.13.3 Collision Resolution

It should be noted that collisions are an unavoidable consequence of the use of a hash function. We are after all trying to map a very large range of key values onto a much smaller hash table range. Unless we know beforehand the key values of the records to be inserted (and it is very rarely that we do), we cannot hope to devise a function which maps each key value into a unique position in the table.

Since collisions cannot be avoided, the best we can hope for is to reduce the number of collisions and spread the collisions uniformly across the table. We have already discussed hash functions that usually perform well in distributing records over the table. In most cases, no prior knowledge is available about the distribution of key values and then one of the commonly used hash functions may be used.

Before we discuss collision resolution techniques we need to consider the definition and discuss a minor problem that has to be resolved.

We define the term *load factor* as the ratio of the records in the table to its capacity. Load factor α is thus given by S/N where S is the number of records in the table which has a capacity of N records.

When hashing is used, some locations in the table have records in them while other locations are vacant. When inserting an element into the table or searching for an element, it becomes necessary to check whether a location in the table is vacant. Some simple mechanism is therefore needed to initialize a table before records can be inserted in it. If the key value is never expected to be zero then it may be used to indicate a vacant location. If this is not possible, some other value or a flag bit may have to be used. In addition, some techniques require that an empty location be differentiated from a location that has become empty due to deletion. It may be possible to represent a deleted entry by –1.

We now discuss collision resolution techniques.

Linear Probing

When a collision takes place on insertion of a new key, the linear probing method involves storing the new key k in the address $h(k) + 1$ if the home address of the key is $h(k)$. Should the address $h(k) + 1$ also be full, we continue looking at the next address till an address is found that can store the record. Of course, if we reach the end of the table, we wrap around to the top of the table. If all the addresses are full, we declare the table to be full and no insertions can be made.

Consider Table 7.14 of size 11:

Our hash function is k mod 11. If we now try to insert 238, 195 and 75 in that sequence, we find that 238 is hashed to location 7 and results in a collision. Since location 8 is also occupied, we insert 238 in location 9. The element 195 hashes to location 8 and is inserted in location 10 since that is the first vacant location. The element 75 is hashed to 9 and is inserted in location 0 producing Table 7.15.

Table 7.14 An example of a hash table using linear probing

0	
1	716
2	
3	25
4	509
5	
6	
7	40
8	30
9	
10	

Table 7.15 An example of the hash table after collisions using linear probing

0	75
1	716
2	
3	25
4	509
5	
6	
7	40
8	30
9	238
10	195

If we now want to insert 51, which hashes to location 7, it would have to be inserted in location 2 since all locations before 2 are occupied.

Searching for 51 would involve first searching if 51 already exists in the table. It therefore involves looking at location 7 and then going down the table till 51 is found or an empty location is found. The empty location could also have been created by a deletion after a previous insertion of 51 and therefore a vacant location and a deleted entry need to be differentiated. The search for an element in the table can terminate only at a vacant location or after the whole table has been searched.

Deleted elements create difficulties not only in searching but also in insertion. To illustrate the difficulty, let us assume that 238 has been deleted from the table and has been replaced by –1 to indicate a deleted entry. If we now wish to insert 51 into the table, we hash it to the table (location 7). Since location 7 is occupied, we look at location 8 which is also occupied. Location 9 however is free, having a deleted flag, and so we insert 51 in location 9. If this algorithm was followed, we could have a table with two key values 51 which probably was not what was intended! The correct insertion procedure would have involved a search for 51 and if unsuccessful, following it by insertion.

We now briefly discuss how the average cost of successful and unsuccessful search is computed. Consider the cost of searching each key in the last table. It is the average number of comparisons needed to find a key. For example, searching for 75 needs 3 comparisons; 716 needs 1 comparison; and 25 needs 1 comparison. Similarly searching for 509, 40, 30, 238 and 139 require 2, 1, 1, 3 and 4 comparisons respectively. The average cost of successful search therefore is

$$s = \frac{3+1+1+2+1+1+3+4}{8} = 2$$

Similarly, we can find the average cost of unsuccessful search in the above table. The unsuccessful search could start at any of the 11 locations with equal probability. The home address of the key being searched unsuccessfully and the cost of unsuccessful search starting at that address are presented in Fig. 7.23.

	Cost of each table address
1	search starting at address 0 would cost 3 comparisons.
2	search starting at address 1, costs 2 comparisons
3	search starting at address 2, costs 1 comparison
4	search starting at address 3, costs 3 comparisons
5	search starting at address 4, costs 2 comparisons
6	search starting at address 5, costs 1 comparison
7	search starting at address 6, costs 1 comparison
8	search starting at address 7, costs 7 comparisons
9	search starting at address 8, costs 6 comparisons
10	search starting at address 9, costs 5 comparisons
11	search starting at address 10, costs 4 comparisons

Figure 7.23 The cost of searching each hash table entry

The average cost of unsuccessful search therefore is given by

$$u = \frac{3+2+1+3+2+1+1+7+6+5+4}{11} = \frac{35}{11} \approx 3.2$$

It should now be clear that linear probing will perform well as long as the load factor is not high. Let the load factor be α, then the average number of comparisons needed for successful search and an unsuccessful search using linear probing for collision resolution are given by the expressions in Fig. 7.24.

$$s \approx \frac{1}{2}\left(1+\frac{1}{1-\alpha}\right)$$

$$u \approx \frac{1}{2}\left(1+\frac{1}{(1-\alpha)^2}\right)$$

Figure 7.24 Average number of comparisons needed for successful search and unsuccessful search using linear probing

For derivations of the above results, the reader is referred to the book by Knuth (1973).

Double Hashing

The major problem with linear probing is that collisions upset adjacent locations which in turn upset further adjacent locations when insertions occur. This results in long scans when a search is initiated and is called *secondary clustering*.

To minimize this clustering effect, double hashing handles collision by stepping along the table using variable step sizes based on the key value rather than with a unit increment as in linear probing.

For example, for a table of size 11 using an integer divide hash function, 18, 29, 40 and 51; all hash to the location 7. If a second hash function z mod 7 was used to determine the step length, we would obtain values of step length to be 4, 1, 5 and 2 for the key values 18, 29, 40 and 51 respectively. This reduces secondary clustering since it splits the path that keys hashed to the same location follow. A hash function like z mod 7 is however not satisfactory since it would map some keys to 0 and a step length of 0 obviously would create problems. Therefore, we must insist that the second hash function satisfy $1 \leq h(z) \leq N$.

Table 7.16 An example of the hash table after collisions using double hashing

0	232
1	716
2	236
3	25
4	509
5	242
6	244
7	40
8	30
9	250
10	252

Let us now consider Table 7.16 to illustrate double hashing.

We now wish to insert 57 and 238 both hashing to location 7. We therefore need to use a second hash function to find the step length. Let the step function be (1 + z mod 7). This maps 51 to 3 and 238 to 1. 51 can therefore be inserted in location 7+3 (if this location was occupied, we would have tried 7+3+3 (mod 11). 238 need to be inserted in location 7+1 but location 8 is also occupied. We try 8+1 and are successful in placing 238 in that location. If we now wish to insert 195 and 75, we compute their home addresses to be 8 and 9 respectively. Both these addresses are occupied. We therefore use the second hash function to find the step length. The hash function (1+ z mod 7) maps 195 and 75 to 7 and 6 respectively. We now try location 8+7 (mod 11) for 195. This location (4) is occupied and we therefore try 4+7 and insert the element there (location 0). For 75, we need to try location 9+6 (mod 11) but this is occupied. We now try 9+6+6 (mod 11) and find that this location (5) is available and insert 75 there. It should be noted that if N is prime, and there is a vacant space in the table, the double hashing technique will automatically find it.

The average cost of a successful search and an unsuccessful search using double hashing are given by the expressions in Fig. 7.25.

$$s \approx \frac{1}{\alpha}\ln\left(\frac{1}{1-\alpha}\right)$$

$$u \approx \frac{1}{1-\alpha}$$

Figure 7.25 Average number of comparisons needed for successful search and unsuccessful search using double hashing

Once again, for details of derivations of the above formulas, the reader should consult Knuth (1973).

The above two techniques resolve collisions by finding a free space within the hash table (this type of techniques are called *open addressing*). This leads to more and more probing as the table fills. If the elements on collision are put not in the table itself but somewhere else, then the behaviour of the hash table should improve markedly (as compared to when open addressing is used) as the table becomes full.

Chaining

The chaining scheme involves making each entry in the hash table either null or a pointer to a chain of synonyms. For example, a hash table of size 10 is shown in Fig. 7.26. This figure shows the hash table with six null entries and four entries that are pointers to chains. Three of the chains include only one entry each, while one entry has two items in the chain.

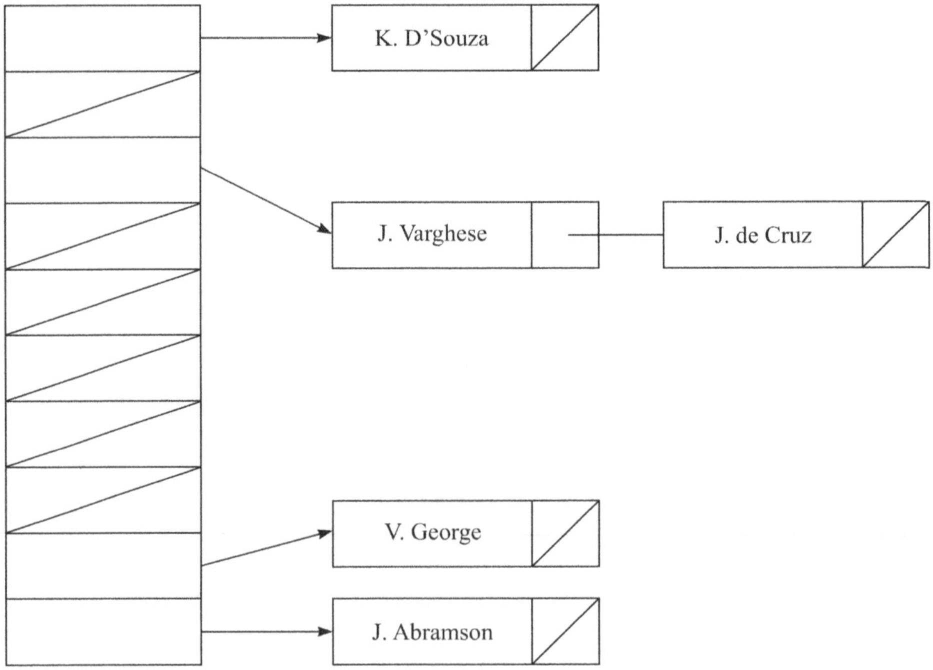

Figure 7.26 An example of open chaining to deal with collisions

Chaining also allows much easier deletion of records than open addressing since the record to be deleted must occur in the chain originating at the home address of the key value.

There are several different ways chaining may be implemented. The most common approach is to have a table, each element of which is a list header (possibly null). When elements are mapped to the table, an element is attached to the chain being pointed to by the header and the pointers are updated accordingly. We are assuming that the table and records are main memory resident.

A successful search then involves hashing the key to the table and then searching the chain that starts at that location. The cost of a successful search is the number of comparisons needed to find the element; the cost of accessing the header pointer is not included in the cost.

An unsuccessful search involves mapping the key to the table and searching the chain till the end of the chain. Of course, there may be no chain at all starting at the home address of the key being searched and then the search concludes immediately. The cost of an unsuccessful search is the number of comparisons needed to reach the end of the chain. In the case of a null chain, the cost is assumed to be zero although some authors assume the cost to be one.

The costs are then given by the expressions in Fig. 7.27.

In chaining, the load factor could become larger than 1 and the above formulas still apply. This is another advantage of chaining. The file does not overflow when the number of elements is one greater than the table capacity.

$$s \approx 1 + \frac{1}{2}\alpha$$

$$u \approx \alpha$$

Figure 7.27 Average number of comparisons needed for successful search and unsuccessful search using chaining

The primary disadvantage of chaining is that additional storage is needed for pointers. But a higher load factor could be used with chaining without much degradation in performance. Also deletion and an unsuccessful search are much faster when chaining is used.

Comparing Performance

We have presented formulas that give the approximate cost of successful and unsuccessful searches for each of the three collision resolution techniques that we have discussed. We now compare these costs for several different values of the load in Tables 7.17 and 7.18.

Table 7.17 Comparing performance of the three methods for a successful search

Load Factor	0.4	0.6	0.8	0.9
Linear Probe	1.3	1.7	3.0	5.5
Double Hashing	1.2	1.5	2.0	2.5
Chaining	1.2	1.2	1.3	1.4

Table 7.18 Comparing performance of the three methods for an unsuccessful search

Load Factor	0.4	0.6	0.8	0.9
Linear Probe	1.8	3.5	9.0	50.0
Double Hashing	1.6	2.5	4.0	10.0
Chaining	1.1	1.2	1.3	1.4

We have assumed that the table size is large, well above 50. The comparison in Tables 7.17 and 7.18 clearly shows that linear probe and double hashing are not very effective in dealing with collisions.

7.14 EXTERNAL HASHING–FILES ON DISK

As we have noted earlier in the chapter, when information is stored on a disk, a block of information is transferred to the primary memory (and from memory) at any one time. The information on disk therefore is organized in blocks; each block usually consisting of a number of records.

Hashing techniques discussed so far have assumed that the hash table is in main memory although the techniques are applicable for files residing on a disk. Rather than having a table in which each entry has a capacity of one record, we could view a file on a disk as a table in which each entry in the table is a block (sometimes called a bucket, as noted earlier) on the disk. In fact, we normally would have a table in the main memory that would at each location in the table store the disk address of the primary bucket corresponding to the home address. Let the capacity of each bucket be b so that the capacity of the file is Nb if N buckets are allocated to the file.

We now have a situation where each home address can accommodate several records and therefore the insertion and deletion algorithms are somewhat different. When inserting a record, we compute the home address and then read the bucket corresponding to that address, and insert the record in the bucket if there is a vacancy. If the bucket is full, we must insert the record elsewhere.

When discussing a hashed file on secondary storage, the term *overflow* is often used. An overflow is said to occur when a record is mapped to a bucket that is full. When an overflow occurs, techniques similar to those for collision resolution discussed earlier can be used to find a suitable location for the new record.

It can be shown that if there were two tables of the same size (that is, same Nb) one with bucket size of 1 and another with bucket capacity of b, the performance of the larger bucket file is much better at the same load factor.

We now discuss two techniques for dynamic hashing, viz., extendible hashing and linear hashing.

7.15 DYNAMIC HASHING FOR EXTERNAL FILES

The static hashing techniques discussed in Section 7.8 work satisfactorily if the table is not close to being full and the table size is not changing. A major problem with these traditional hashing schemes is that the storage must be statically allocated based on an estimate of the size of the file. The difficulty with this approach is that very often performance deteriorates if the file grows, and then the size of the file is not close to the estimate used initially to allocate storage. If the storage requirements are underestimated, the number of collisions will be large. On the other hand, if the storage requirements are overestimated, storage utilization will be low and storage will be wasted. Many files are dynamic in nature, that is, they grow and shrink dynamically by several orders of magnitude during their lifetime. For these files, reorganization of the whole file is required at regular intervals in order to maintain good performance if static hashing is used.

This major difficulty with static hashed files can be overcome by using one of the *dynamic hashing* schemes. With these schemes, the size of the hash file grows (and shrinks) dynamically as records are inserted and deleted from the file. No periodic reorganization of the file is required. The dynamic schemes maintain good performance independent of the size of the file.

It is possible to categorize dynamic hashing methods into two classes. The first class consists of those methods which use a directory structure; the second class of methods that do not use a directory. The best known methods based on directory structures are variations of a scheme called *extendible hashing*. The most well known methods that do not use a directory are based on a dynamic hashing scheme called *linear hashing*.

We note that it is possible to design a sequence of hashing functions h_i such that

$$h_i(k) = h_{i-1}(k), \text{ or}$$
$$h_i(k) = h_{i-1}(k) + 2^{i-1}$$

And both events are equi-probable.

The functions h_i, for example, could be generated if some function $H(k)$ was first used to generate a binary string and then h_i was the last $i + 1$ bits of that string.

A bucket that has records assigned to it using a hashing function h_i will be said to have been *split* if the records in it are redistributed in the file using the next hashing function $h_i + 1$. Records that are placed in more than one bucket (usually two buckets) using a hashing function h_i are said to *group* if they are collected and placed in one bucket using the hashing function h_{i-1}.

We now describe extendible hashing and then linear hashing.

7.15.1 Extendible Hashing

The data structure in extendible hashing consists of two components: a set of *buckets*[6] and a *directory*. The buckets reside on secondary storage and contain the data records. The directory is an array of pointers to the buckets. If the directory is not too large, it should reside in the main memory. An example is given in Fig. 7.28.

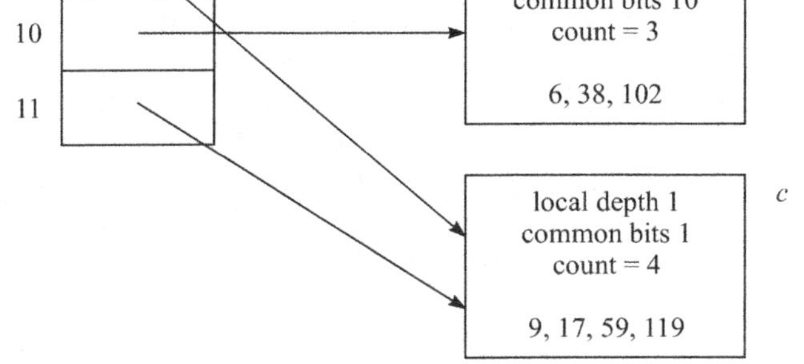

Figure 7.28 A simple example of extendible hashing

6. The term buckets is used in hashing for a block or a page on disk due to historical reasons.

Here, the directory consists of only four entries. At any time, the size of the directory will be of the form 2^d where d is called the *depth* of the directory.

In order to determine the location of a record with key k, a hash function is used to generate a very long bit pattern or *pseudokey* when it is applied to k. The rightmost d bits of this pseudokey determine the entry in the directory which must be examined. This entry contains a pointer to the appropriate data bucket. At most two disk accesses are required to locate any record in the file. If the directory can be held in the main memory, then only one access is required.

Note that more than one directory entry can point to one bucket. Associated with each bucket is a parameter called its *local depth* (*ld*). The number of directory entries pointing to a bucket is given by 2^{d-ld}. The local depth indicates that the pseudokeys contained within that bucket agree in that number of bits. We denote these bits as the *common bits* in Fig. 7.28. In an actual implementation of extendible hashing, the local depth is stored in each bucket but the common bits need not be stored. In our implementation we also store a counter *count* which shows how many keys are stored in each bucket.

As insertions occur, a bucket can become full. A new bucket is then allocated when an insertion is made to a full bucket and the contents of the original bucket and the newly inserted key are distributed over the two buckets. If the local depth of the original bucket was *ld*, then the placement of a record from this bucket will be determined by the bit $ld + 1$ of its pseudokey (numbering from the right starts at 1). The local depths of the two new buckets will be $ld + 1$ and the directory is updated so that the appropriate entry points to the newly allocated bucket. When the local depth of the original bucket is equal to the directory depth d (so that only a single directory entry pointed to it), then the directory doubles in size to enable the new bucket to be added and the depth increases by one.

Figure 7.29 shows what happens when keys 8, 13 and 16 are added to the file in Fig. 7.28. The first insertion 8 goes to bucket a making it full while 13 goes to c which is already full. A new bucket c' therefore must be added and the local depth of these two buckets becomes equal to the depth of the directory. When 16 is inserted, it goes to the bucket which is already full and therefore a new bucket a' is inserted in the file but given that bucket a had a local depth 2 which was equal to the depth of the directory, the directory must also be doubled and we obtain the result as shown in Fig. 7.29.

We recommend that the reader carefully go through the insertions 8, 13 and 16 to the file shown in Fig. 7.28 to arrive at the file in Fig. 7.29.

Similar to creation of new buckets during insertions, deletions may result in two buckets being merged. This in turn may require halving the directory and reducing its depth by one. Halving the directory is possible when the depth of the directory is greater than the local depths of each data bucket. In order to ascertain when the directory should be halved, one possibility is to store a count of the number of buckets for which the local depth equals the depth d. This count is referred to as the *depth count* (*d_count*). This is not discussed in detail here and is recommended as an exercise for the reader.

Search

In order to search for a record with key k, the hash function used in building the file is used to generate a long bit pattern or *pseudokey* when it is applied to k. Once we know the directory depth d, the rightmost d bits of this pseudokey determine the entry in the directory which must be first read from the disk (unless it is main memory resident) and then examined. This entry contains a pointer to the appropriate data bucket. The record

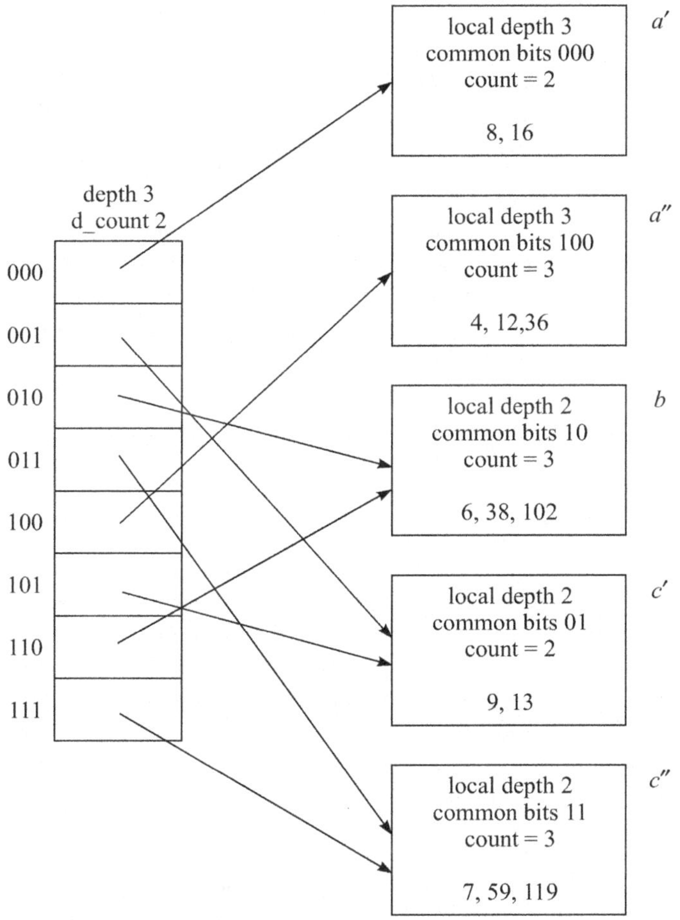

Figure 7.29 An example of bucket splitting and directory doubling in extendible hashing

with key k must be searched in that bucket. If found, we have a successful search, otherwise an unsuccessful search. Note that at most two disk accesses are required to locate any record in the file.

The performance of extendible hashing has been analysed by several researchers. We will only quote some of the important results. If N is the number of records in the system, and if the capacity of a bucket is b records, then the number of data buckets $L(N)$ required by extendible hashing is given asymptotically:

$$L(N) \sim N/(b \log_e 2)$$

If the directory can be stored in the main memory, then it follows that the storage utilization for extendible hashing is approximately $\log_e 2 \sim 0.69$. Again, assuming that the directory can be stored in the main memory, the insertion cost is two disk accesses for those insertions that do not require a bucket split, and three accesses for those that do. It can be shown that asymptotically, the average insertion cost, $I(N)$, approximates:

$$I(N) \sim 2 + 1/(b \log_e 2)$$

Deletion costs are similar to insertion costs.

Of course, if the directory is stored on disk, then these costs are higher. It can be shown that the probability that more than 2048 directory entries will be needed for a file of 40,000 records when $b = 40$ is practically 1, whereas the probability that more than 4096 entries will be needed is practically zero (it is in fact less than 0.00001). Thus, if we are satisfied with a reliability level of 10^{-5}, we can allocate 4096 entries for the directory for a file of 40,000 records with bucket capacity of 40.

Various extensions of extendible hashing have been proposed. One of these, called Bounded Exponential Hashing (BEH) is based on the argument that a desirable feature of any scheme proposed for dynamic files is that performance should be even throughout the life of the file. However, it is not quite true for extendible hashing since the pseudokeys are distributed uniformly and therefore data buckets with the same local depth are likely to contain similar numbers of records. Hence during insertion, a large number of buckets tend to split at about the same time (the time when the directory doubles). Thus the space utilization and cost of insertion in extendible hashing tends to exhibit oscillatory behaviour. BEH proposes a solution which involves distributing the pseudokeys non-uniformly to the buckets, but we will not discuss BEH further.

7.15.2 Linear Hashing

Unlike extendible hashing, linear hashing does not require a directory. Linear hashing was proposed by Witold Litwin in 1980 and is based on a hashing function which changes dynamically with the size of the file. In the extendible hashing scheme, a bucket which undergoes collision was split. This is natural but the buckets split were randomly distributed and then an index was necessary. The index is not needed if the buckets are split in a predefined order. Splitting the buckets in a predefined order is reasonable since, as noted above, when one bucket is full, all the others are also likely to be close to full, assuming a good hashing function is being used that distributes records uniformly. Therefore, the bucket where a collision takes place need not be split immediately. In linear hashing, it is split only when its turn comes in a predefined fashion after some delay.

In linear hashing, the file goes through a number of *expansions*. At the start of the dth expansion[7], the file contains $s = 2^d$ home pages (see Fig. 7.30 where there are 16 buckets, $s = 16$ and d is 4). Associated with each bucket is perhaps 1 or more overflow buckets. At this stage, the bucket address for the record with key k is given by the rightmost d bits of the address generated by hashing the key k. Let us denote the address formed by these d bits as $h_d(k)$. We are using a simple hash function mod(s) which is known to be not a good hash function but is used here only for illustrating the technique. Figure 7.30 assumes bucket capacity of 2.

Now, as further records are inserted into the file, new buckets will be added to the end of the file. The rate at which new buckets are created is determined by a system parameter called the *load control*, L. With this approach a new bucket is appended to the end of the file after every L insertions. At a typical stage during the dth expansion, the file will contain $s + p$ home blocks, assuming $16 < s + p < 32$. Figure 7.31 shows a linear hashing file undergoing an expansion.

A pointer, called the *split pointer*, which at the start of the dth expansion points to bucket 0 of the file, now points to bucket p of the file. When another bucket is due to be appended to the end of the file, the following process takes place. Bucket p is split so that the records which previously had home address p are distributed using the value $h_{d+1}(k)$ between pages p and $s + p$. Here $h_{d+1}(k)$ is the integer formed from the rightmost

7. An expansion essentially doubles the file starting from just one bucket for which $d = 0$. In the first expansion the file goes to 2 buckets ($d = 1$) then to 4 buckets ($d = 2$) and so on.

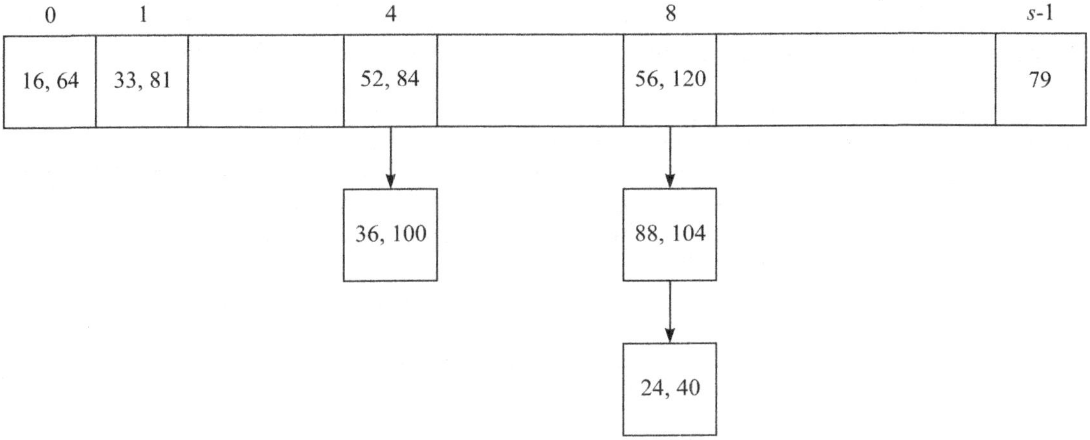

Figure 7.30 An example of a file using linear hashing

$d + 1$ bits of the address obtained by the hashing function. The split pointer is then incremented by 1. When the split pointer reaches s and the file size has doubled, the split pointer returns to the beginning of the file ($p = 0$) and the next expansion begins.

The number of expansions a file has undergone is called its *depth, d*. Initially $d = 0$. It can be seen that the current state of the file is characterized by the two variables d and p.

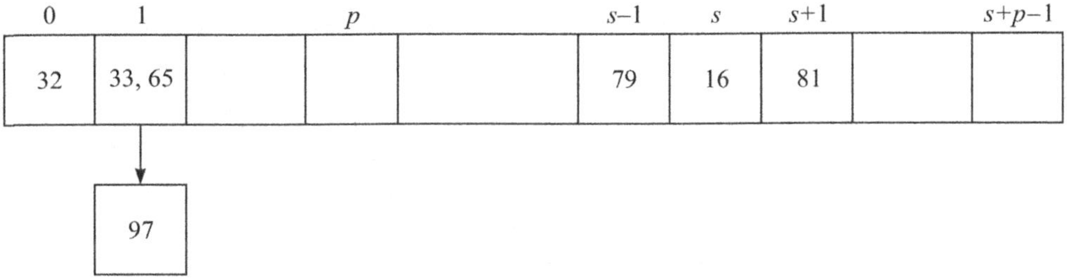

Figure 7.31 Start of the dth expansion of the file

Figures 7.32(a), (b), (c) and (d) show how a full expansion, or doubling of the file size, consists of a number of partial expansions. At the start of the dth full expansion, the file consists of 2^d bucket, and the split pointer is positioned at the first bucket of each group (see Fig. 7.32(a)).

When a new bucket is appended to the end of the file, the records in the buckets indexed by the split pointer are redistributed among these buckets and the newly created bucket. The split pointer is then advanced to the next set of buckets. The file grows this way until, at the end of the first partial expansion which as shown in the Fig. 7.32(b) expands the file by 50%. The next partial expansion begins with the split pointer positioned at the first page in each of the three groups. The pointers during the second partial expansion are shown in Fig. 7.32(c).

Suppose now that the file has g+1 groups, and when a new page is added, the records in these pages are distributed among the g+2 pages. At the end of the partial expansion, the file will have grown to g+2 groups of 2^d pages. Finally, after g partial expansions, the size of the file will have grown to 2g groups of 2^d pages.

At this stage the file is repartitioned into g groups of 2^{d+1} pages and the process starts over again. Thus a full expansion consists of g partial expansions. As in Litwin's scheme, overflow pages are used together with bucket-chaining in this method.

When expanding a set of buckets, the old buckets are scanned and only those records which are to be relocated in the new bucket are collected. Thus there is no allocation of records to the old buckets. With this approach the number of buffer pages required is minimized. However, in order to locate a record with this method, the history of the record's movements through all the previous expansions must be traced.

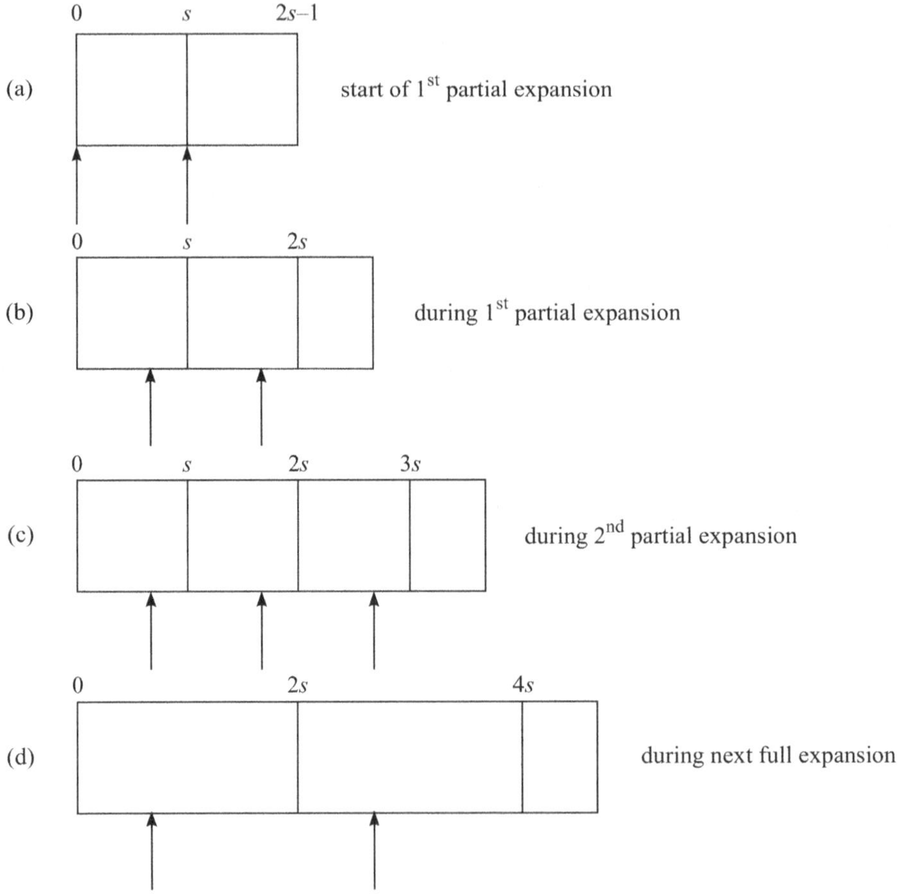

Figure 7.32 An example of file expansion using partial expansions

In Fig. 7.32, the first part shows a file that has been doubled from 16 buckets (assuming $s = 16$) to 32 buckets and is now being expanded to 64 buckets. In doubling by 100%, a partial expansion increases the size of the file by 50%. The first new bucket collects some records from bucket number 0 and bucket number 16 to put them in bucket number 32. The records collected are those that would hash to bucket 32 using the new hash function (for example, mod 64). This continues until the file is 48 buckets in size. Now the second partial expansion starts, which adds another 16 buckets to the file. The full expansion doubles the file. Once the file is 64 buckets large after the full expansion, a new partial expansion starts when the file grows further.

Linear hashing, like extendible hashing, also suffers from the problem of oscillatory behaviour. There are a number of other difficulties with linear hashing. First, there are a number of problems associated with the use of overflow buckets which necessitate the provision and management of a large, dynamically changing storage pool. The costs of maintaining such a storage pool can be high, yet these costs are often not included in performance evaluations of schemes which use overflow buckets. Also, if the size of the overflow buckets is the same as the size of the home bucket, then performance will, in general, be poor. Thus, an overflow bucket with size different from the home bucket's size should be used. Although this will improve performance, the complexity of storage management is increased. Moreover, the optimal overflow bucket size depends on a number of file parameters and is difficult to calculate.

For a complete description of linear hashing the reader is referred to the paper by Litwin, in which various strategies for splitting a page and for deciding when to expand the file are described. In all strategies, the file grows linearly till it is as large as needed. At any stage, only few overflow buckets exist, and therefore a record on the average can be found in one access to the secondary storage. We have not defined a scheme for shrinking the file, but a load control parameter may be used for this purpose. For example, when a deletion leaves a bucket less than half full, the last bucket could be removed. The operation of removing a bucket and combining the records in it with another bucket in the file is called *grouping*. The split pointer moves one address backward when a grouping operation is performed.

Hashing techniques achieve the best performance when the records are distributed uniformly over the pages in the file. With linear hashing, the number of records per page can vary by factors of two or more over the length of the file, since a recently split bucket can have only half the number of records of a bucket about to be split. As a consequence, linear hashing suffers from the same sort of oscillatory behaviour as does extendible hashing.

Another issue related to linear hashing is as follows. Logically, a linear hashed file consists of buckets with consecutive page numbers. However, no operating system will support a large dynamic file of contiguously allocated pages without considerable cost overheads. Typically, the logical linear hashed file will be mapped onto a physical file made up of several quanta of contiguously allocated pages. The mapping will be done by means of a translation table stored in the core. An efficient implementation of recursive linear hashing, the amount of physical storage claimed at any time is just fractionally greater than the minimum required. The implementation is also designed so that split pages are written onto consecutive locations on disk. Litwin's original paper also proposes an implementation of linear hashing, for his original scheme.

Physical Address Computing

Although linear hashing techniques do not require an index, some information about the addresses of the various buckets must still be maintained. Storage on secondary storage devices is usually allocated in quanta. These quanta may be all of the same size or different sizes. Several schemes are possible.

1. *Contiguous*—address calculation is very simple.
2. *Noncontiguous*—we need a table which gives the address of each quantum. The table of addresses will need to be stored on disk if the allocation is so distributed that the table is quite large.

Table 7.19 Average performance of linear hashing with uncontrolled linear hashing

Performance

	$b = 10$	$b = 50$
Successful Search	1.07	1.00
Unsuccessful Search	1.19	1.06
Insertion Cost	3.14	2.35
Split Cost	5.99	5.98
Load Factor	0.61	0.59

(Note that 2 accesses are needed to store the overflow record and 3 to split during splitting)

Table 7.20 Average performance of linear hashing with controlled linear hashing

	$b = 10$		$b = 50$	
	$g = 0.75$	$g = 0.90$	$g = 0.75$	$g = 0.90$
Successful Search	1.14	1.57	1.05	1.35
Unsuccessful Search	1.37	2.48	1.27	2.37
Insertion Cost	3.42	4.68	2.62	3.73
Split Cost	6.34	9.48	6.24	9.02

Concluding Remarks about Hashing

Hashing is an important data organization technique that has several advantages over indexing methods. Firstly, hashing usually requires no index (and therefore no storage for an index). Secondly, insertion and searching are usually very fast when hashing is used although deletion may not always be fast. Thirdly, the performance of hashing techniques is generally not dependent on the size of the table; the performance only depends on the file load factor. The primary disadvantage of hashing is that sequential processing and range queries are usually very expensive.

7.16 INVERTED FILES

A file with secondary indices is often called an *inverted* file. Rather than listing attributes for each record, we now list records for each attribute value. The roles of records and attributes have therefore been 'inverted'. This description is not quite accurate because an inverted file normally still maintains the normal file which includes full records, including all values of all attributes. This file could well be a sequential file on the primary key. A good example of an inverted file is a review journal which has a list of article titles, their reviews and a keyword index which lists keywords and lists of article numbers that contain each keyword.

Inverted files are particularly useful for searching documents, for example, through a search engine like Google. An inverted file essentially consists of lists (called inverted lists) of files (or documents) for each query term. For example, for a query term 'Mumbai' the inverted list corresponding to it will consist of one entry for each document that has the term 'Mumbai' in it.

In search engines, a search would often involve a number of keywords. The simplest approach is to build an inverted index on every conceivable keyword (there are obviously millions of keywords since they not only include all the words in the language but also names of people, places and things like medicines) and then use these inverted indexes to find the list of documents that have each of the keywords specified in the search and then find the intersection of the lists. This final list then gives us the records that have all the keyword values, which have been specified. For large collections of documents, for example, a web document collection crawled by a search engine like Google (estimated to be above 10 billion in 2008), not only the number of inverted lists very large but each inverted list can be large. Since the number of lists is in millions, an index is needed to find the inverted list corresponding to each keyword. To reduce the number of inverted lists and the size of the lists, the search engines do not make inverted lists for common words like "the", "an", "is", "are" and the words are usually stemmed to reduce the number of keywords (for example, computing, computation, computer and computerization may all be stemmed to compute).

For example, if one were to search for keywords "Gopal" "Gupta" and "database", it will be necessary to first find inverted lists for each of the three keywords and then find the intersection of the three. The first two lists might be somewhat smaller (although "Gupta" is a common name in India and even outside India) than the inverted list for "database". It would be interesting to design efficient algorithms that would retrieve a number of inverted lists of different lengths that are to be intersected.

SUMMARY

This chapter has covered the following topics:

- The efficiency of a database depends on how it is physically stored in computer storage.
- Different types of storage or memories are available for storing databases. These include primary memory, secondary memory and tertiary memory.
- Primary memory includes registers, cache memory and RAM.
- Secondary storage includes hard disks, external disks, flash memories, CD, DVD.
- Tertiary storage includes low cost storage like magnetic tapes.
- Magnetic disks are usually a spindle holding a number of rotating hard platters each of which consists of tracks that are divided into sectors.
- Data is stored on a magnetic disk as blocks and data transfer from a disk and to a disk is carried out by a buffer manager.
- RAID are Redundant Array of Independent Disks that provide increased capacity, increased throughput, improved data integrity and fault tolerance. There are a number of levels of RAID technology. Level 5 is commonly used for database systems.
- Buffer management including policies for replacing buffer pages is described. The policies include LRU and FIFO.
- The efficiency of file structures is measured by their efficiency in update, insertion, deletion and search.

- Unstructured and unordered files are simple file organization techniques.
- Sequential or sorted files have records arranged in some order which must be maintained in insertions and deletions.
- File performance may be improved by using an index which may be of different types (including primary and secondary indexes).
- An indexed sequential file is an efficient structure.
- A B-tree can form the basis of an indexed sequential file since it is efficient for search, insertion and deletion.
- The algorithms for search, insertion and deletion are presented and performance of B-tree is analyzed.
- An indexed sequential file based on a B-tree is called the B^+-tree. This structure improves the efficiency of the B-tree index.
- Another data structure for storing files is called hashing. The basic concepts of static hashing, hash functions and collision resolution are described.
- Performance of static hashing techniques is discussed and it is shown, for example, that linear probe and double hashing do not perform well when the load is high.
- Static hashing is only suitable for tables in the main memory. For dynamic files on external storage, dynamic hashing may be used. Two types of dynamic hashing are extendible and linear hashing.
- Concept of inverted files in which records are listed for each keyword are suitable for searching large collections of documents and are used by search engines.

REVIEW QUESTIONS

1. Explain computer memory hierarchy; and primary, secondary and tertiary storage. Give examples of each and explain the major differences between them. (Section 7.2)
2. Describe the types of storage media that can be used for storing a database. (Section 7.2)
3. Where is database normally stored? What are the reasons for storing it there? (Section 7.2)
4. Given that large main memories are becoming available, could the whole database be stored in one large memory? Discuss. (Section 7.2)
5. How is data stored on a magnetic disk? What is a track, sector, cylinder, and block? (Section 7.3.1)
6. What is RAID? What are the major benefits of using RAID compared to an ordinary magnetic hard disk? (Section 7.3.2)
7. Describe RAID Level 0, Level 1 and Level 5. For each level RAID list at least one suitable application and give reasons for the suitability. (Section 7.3.2)
8. What are the basic processes needed in memory buffer management? (Section 7.4)
9. How should one measure the performance of a storage structure? (Section 7.5)
10. Describe unstructured and sequential files. When are they useful? Could a relational database be stored as a collection of unstructured files? Explain. (Section 7.6 and 7.7)
11. Explain the concept of index and index types. What type of indexes may be created in SQL? (Section 7.8)
12. Describe primary index, clustered index and secondary index. (Section 7.8)

13. Give an example showing when a composite index may be useful. (Section 7.8.5)
14. Explain the basic features of an indexed-sequential file. Why is it better than the sequential file? (Section 7.9)
15. Explain the concept of a B-tree and discuss why tree-structured files are efficient for some types of searching. (Section 7.10)
16. How can one determine a suitable order for a B-tree? Would an order of 100 be suitable for all type of large tables stored on disk? (Section 7.10)
17. Describe insertion, deletion and search algorithms for a B-tree. (Section 7.10.1, 7.10.2, 7.10.3)
18. Explain node splitting and node coalescing algorithms in a B-tree. When are they required? (Section 7.10.2, 7.10.3)
19. Derive the expressions for the worst case and the best case performance of a B-tree of order *m*. (Section 7.10.4)
20. Describe the B^+-tree and why it is used more commonly than the B-tree? (Section 7.11)
21. Can the B^+-tree be modified to improve performance? Give details. (Section 7.11)
22. How does a B-tree perform in terms of searching, insertion, deletion and storage utilization? What type of queries is the B-tree efficient for in large databases? (Section 7.12)
23. Explain the concepts of static hashing, hash functions and collision resolution. (Section 7.13)
24. Explain the concept of dynamic hash files in contrast to static hash files. What is the main motivation for using dynamic hashing? (Section 7.14, 7.15)
25. Describe the extendible hashing technique. Explain how search, insert and delete operations are carried out. Do we need node splits in this scheme? (Section 7.15.1)
26. Explain the concept of linear hashing. Explain how search, insert and delete operations are carried out. Do we need node splitting in linear hashing? (Section 7.15.2)
27. When is it advisable to use a hashed file in storing a database? (Section 7.14)
28. Describe an inverted file. What is it used for? (Section 7.16)

SHORT ANSWER QUESTIONS

1. Give two examples of primary storage.
2. Give two examples of secondary storage.
3. Give two examples of tertiary storage.
4. What operations are carried out on data that is stored in a database?
5. Where is a database resident most of the time?
6. What are the two major differences between the main memory and hard disk storage?
7. How much data can be stored on a single platter hard disk?
8. What is the main purpose of creating an index on a file?
9. What is a covering index?
10. What are the advantages of using an index and what are its disadvantages?
11. Give examples of two different types of indexes?
12. Give an example to show that ordering of a composite index can impact performance.

13. Explain the basic features of an indexed-sequential file.
14. How many keys would a B-tree of order 100 accommodate if its height was 2 and it was full?
15. Briefly explain how to search a B-tree.
16. What is node splitting in a B-tree?
17. What are the advantages of using the B-tree compared to an indexed sequential file?
18. Describe B^+-tree.
19. Explain the concept of static hashing.
20. What is collision resolution?
21. What are dynamic hash files designed to achieve?
22. What is the major difference between extendible hashing and linear hashing?
23. Give an example of an application of an inverted file.

MULTIPLE CHOICE QUESTIONS

1. Which one of the following is **not** a type of computer memory?
   (a) Primary storage (b) Secondary storage (c) Tertiary storage (d) Permanent storage
2. Which of the following are correct?
   (a) Cache is primary storage.
   (b) Flash memory is secondary storage.
   (c) Magnetic disk is tertiary storage.
   (d) Magnetic tape is secondary storage.
3. Which one of the following is correct?
   (a) RAID Level 2 has stripping but no redundancy.
   (b) RAID Level 0 uses error correction using Hamming Code.
   (c) RAID Level 1 is not suitable for database systems.
   (d) RAID Level 5 is suitable for most database systems.
4. Which of the following are features of RAID 3?
   (a) It is a high performance RAID system.
   (b) It involves striped segments written on two or more disks.
   (c) It involves an additional disk to store parity information.
   (d) It is not suitable for transaction-oriented databases.
   (e) All of the above are correct.
5. Which of the following are techniques used for replacing buffer pages?
   (a) Least recently used (b) Last in first out (c) First in first out (d) Most recently used
6. Which of the following are normally used to evaluate storage structures?
   (a) Cost of insertion (b) Cost of retrieval (c) Cost of deletion (d) Storage utilization
   (e) All of the above
7. Which one of the following is correct?
   (a) Sequential files provide fast access to the next record.
   (b) Sequential files provide fast access for random access.
   (c) Sequential files provide fast updates of file.
   (d) Sequential files are difficult to implement.

8. Which one of the following is **not** an indexing technique?
   (a) Primary index (b) Secondary index (c) Multilevel index (d) Sequential index
9. Which one of the following is correct about an indexed sequential file?
   (a) The file has a prime area. (b) The file has an overflow area.
   (c) The file has an index area. (d) All of the above
10. Which one of the following is **not** true about a B-tree?
    (a) All nodes including the root must be at least half full.
    (b) All leaf nodes must be at the same level.
    (c) All nodes with k keys except the leaves must have $k + 1$ descendents.
    (d) The height of the tree grows when the root splits.
11. The maximum number of keys in a B-tree of order 11 of height 2 is (the root is at level 0):
    (a) Less than 2,000 (b) Between 2,000 and 6,000
    (c) Between 6,000 and 18,000 (d) Between 18,000 and 50,000
    (e) More than 50,000
12. A B-tree of order 5 is built by inserting the keys 10, 20, 30, 25, 15, 5, 17, 27, 37, 35, 32 and 22 in that order to a null tree.
    Which one of the following statements is correct about the resulting tree?
    (a) The tree is of height 2. (b) The root node has keys 10, 20, 25 and 30.
    (c) The root node has keys 20 and 30. (d) Altogether there are 5 nodes in the tree.
13. A B-tree is built up by inserting the keys in the last question in the reverse order (that is, by first inserting 22 to a null tree, then inserting 32, 35, 37 and so on).
    Compare the resulting tree with the tree obtained in the last question. Which one of the following statements is correct?
    (a) The two B-trees are identical.
    (b) The number of nodes in the two trees is the same.
    (c) The storage utilization in the two trees is the same.
    (d) The height of the two trees is the same.
14. Which one of the following is **not** correct?
    (a) Composite indexes are larger than single indexes.
    (b) Composite indexes should be ordered from most distinct to least distinct.
    (c) Consider a composite index on the table *Batting* on *MID* and *PID*. Let there be 3000 matches and 50,000 batting records which include only 500 distinct *PIDs*. An index on (*PID*, *MID*) would be better than an index on (*MID*, *PID*).
    (d) There is not much advantage in having a composite index on the table *Player.*
15. Which one of the following is correct?
    (a) A binary tree is not suitable for storing information on a disk since disk read/write are by a block.
    (b) A binary tree is effective for small files on the disk since binary tree looks at one node at a time .
    (c) A binary tree is a special case of a B-tree.
    (d) B-tree is not suitable for secondary indexing.
16. Which one of the following is **not** true about extendible hashing?
    (a) It consists of an index as well as a data file.
    (b) The technique can be modified to make sequential access easier.

(c) If the index is kept in the main memory, retrieval from an extendible hashing structure requires only one access to the disk.
(d) Storage utilization is approximately 69%.
(e) None of the above

17. Which of the following statements is **not** true?
    (a) Linear hashing does not need an index as extendible hashing does.
    (b) Linear hashing has better storage utilization than extendible hashing.
    (c) Linear hashing files shrink and grow as required.
    (d) Linear hashing requires overflow buckets.
    (e) None of the above
18. Linear hashing and extendible hashing have a number of common features. Which one of the following is **not** true?
    (a) They both involve splitting the block where an overflow occurs.
    (b) They both allow the file to expand or shrink dynamically as required.
    (c) They both change the hashing function dynamically with the size of the file.
    (d) They both combine the node-splitting feature of B-trees with that of conventional hashing.
    (e) None of the above
19. Some B-tree structures store all the records in the leaves only. Such trees are called B^+-trees. Which one of the following statements is **not** correct?
    (a) In a B^+-tree the records and the index are separate.
    (b) Sequential processing of the records is facilitated in B^+-trees.
    (c) If the order of the tree is large, say 100, storing all the records in the leaves does involve substantially more storage than used by conventional B-trees.
    (d) Since the index needs to store only the keys and not the records, the order of the index can be higher and therefore searching can be faster in B^+-trees.
    (e) None of the above
20. What is the maximum number of nodes in a B-tree (of order 5) of height 2?
    (a) 128 (b) 255 (c) 129 (d) 127
    (e) None of the above
21. Which of the following advantages apply to files organized using a B-tree scheme rather than using hashing?
    (a) B-tree files can be sequentially processed with much lower cost than the hashed files.
    (b) B-tree files are better because with such files it is possible to carry out range queries at much lower cost.
    (c) B-tree files are better because with such files it is easier to have multiple attribute retrieval.
    (d) B-tree files are better than hashed files because they do not involve using overflow buckets.
22. Which one of the following is **not** correct?
    (a) The optimum node size for disk resident B-trees should be selected based on rotational delay time, seek time, transfer rate and key size.
    (b) A file organization based on B-trees is guaranteed to have at least about 50% storage utilization.
    (c) A file organization based on B-trees on average has storage utilization of about 69%.
    (d) A B^*-tree guarantees storage utilization of at least about 75.0%.

23. The following tree only shows the keys present in each node. It does not show the size of the nodes or their capacity. All the nodes are of equal size.

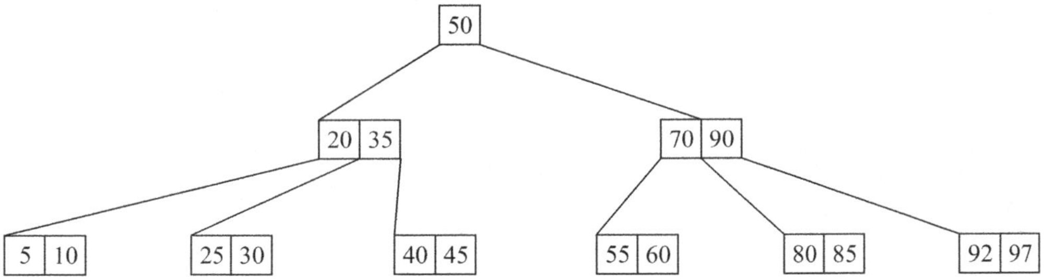

Figure 7.33

Which one of the following statements is correct?

(a) The above tree is not a B-tree since the storage utilization is less than 50%.
(b) The above B-tree must be of order 3.
(c) The above tree must be of order 3 or 4.
(d) The above tree could be of order 2, 3 or 4.
(e) The above tree could be of order 3, 4 or 5.

24. This question also refers to the B-tree displayed in the last question. Which one of the following statements is **not** correct?

(a) The above B-tree has the minimum number of nodes possible in a B-tree of order 5 and height 2.
(b) The above B-tree has the maximum number of nodes possible in a B-tree of order 3 and height 2.
(c) If the order of the above B-tree is 5, the height of the tree may not increase even if 100 keys are inserted in the tree.
(d) If the order of the above B-tree is 5, insertion of another 40 keys may increase the height of the tree.

25. Which one of the following statements is **not** correct?

(a) The height of a B-tree grows only when the root is split.
(b) In the worst case, only 4 accesses are necessary if a file of about 2 million records is stored as a B-tree of order 200.
(c) In the best case, about 16 million records could be stored in a B-tree of order 200 and height 3.
(d) In the worst case, a B-tree of height 2 may contain only half the number of records that can be stored in a B-tree, of the same height, in which storage utilization is 100%.

26. Which one of the following is **not** correct regarding $T1$ and $T2$ below?

(a) If key 30 is deleted from the tree $T2$, either 22 or 32 is moved to the root node.
(b) If key 32 is deleted from the tree $T1$, two rightmost nodes at level 1 and key 30 from the root node are combined.
(c) If key value 2 is inserted into the tree $T2$, the left node at level 1 is split and the key 10 is moved to the root.
(d) If key value 22 is deleted from the tree $T1$, 20 is moved to the leaf node which underflows and 17 is moved to the root.
(e) None of the above

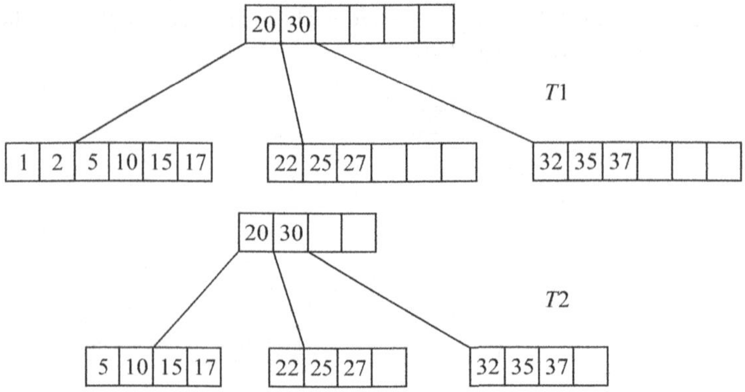

Figure 7.34

27. Given the B-tree of order 5 in Fig. 7.35, which one of the following sequence of operations is correct when the keys 25, 26 and 24 are deleted?
    (a) The key 25 is deleted from the tree, the root disappears and the nodes *B* and *C* are combined. Deletion of 26 results in borrowing of key 29 from the node *C* and moving of 32 to the node *C*. Deletion of 24 similarly involves moving of 19 down to the node *F* and of 18 up to the node *B*.
    (b) The key 25 is deleted and a key from the leaves is moved to the root. If 26 is moved to the root, the key 29 moves down to the node *G* while 32 moves up to the node *C*. Deletion of 26 then involves moving 27 to the root and concatenation of the nodes *G* and *H* and key 32. Deletion of 24 then causes 19 to be moved to the node *F* and 18 to be moved to the node *B*.
    (c) When the key 25 is deleted, 26 is moved to the root. The node *G* underflows and this results in key 29 moving down to the node *G* while 32 moves up to the node *C*. Deletion of 26 then involves moving 27 to the root and concatenation of the nodes *G* and *H* and key 32. This makes the node *C* underflow and this results in concatenation of the node *C*, node *B* and the root to form the new root. The height of the tree is therefore reduced. Deletion of 24 now involves moving 19 to the node *F* and 18 to the node *B*.
    (d) None of the above

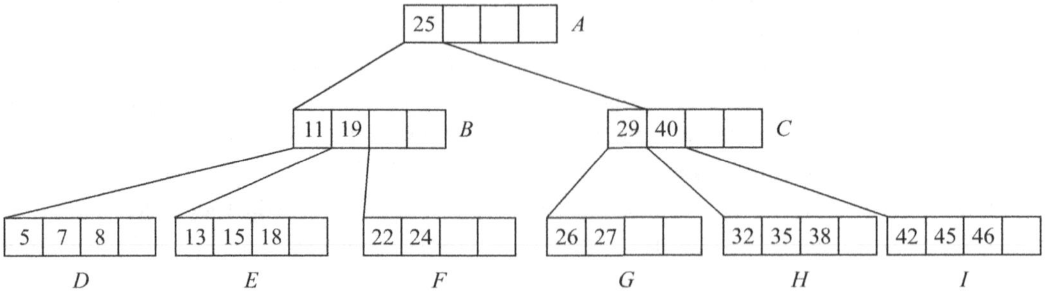

Figure 7.35

28. Which of the following are correct about conventional hashing?
    (a) It is difficult to find hashing functions that will uniformly distribute keys over the hash table.
    (b) Even when the hash table is of a reasonable size, overflow chains become long.

(c) If the file size grows beyond what was expected, the performance will decline rapidly.
(d) If the file shrinks much below what was expected, storage utilization will be low.
(e) None of the above

EXERCISES

1. What is the main storage media for databases? Why? Could a flash drive be used for storing a database? Explain.
2. Explain how reading from a disk and writing to the disk is carried out? What is a block? Why do we need a disk to be divided into blocks?
3. Explain the role of a buffer manager in a database system.
4. How are tables of a database stored in a computer system? How is data on a disk transferred to the main memory and vice versa?
5. What operations are carried out on data that is stored in a database?
6. List some different data structures that are possible for storing data on disk.
7. What is an index? Describe the different types of indexes and give examples to illustrate when each of them is useful. Given the cricket database in Chapter 3, give a set of queries and then discuss what data structure might be the best if the database is quite large.
8. Give an example of an indexed-sequential file and show how insertion, deletion and search are carried out in such a file.
9. Discuss the major differences between an indexed-sequential file and B-trees.
10. How does the B^+-tree differ from a B-tree in terms of search, insertion and deletion? Which of the two structures is preferred as an access structure in database management and why?
11. Suggest a modification to improve the performance of B^+-tree indexing. Write an algorithm to show how the modification will work.
12. How do dynamic hashing schemes differ from the classical hashing schemes? Why is the classical technique not suitable for storing information on disk?
13. Discuss extendible and linear hashing. How can they be used for constructing an index?
14. Implement one of the following schemes including modules for insertion, update, retrieval and deletion of records. The programs should be able to deal with alphanumeric keys and be able to store records that have several attribute values in addition to the key. You should also evaluate the performance of the technique that you have implemented. For example, you should be able to compute the average cost of insertion, deletion and retrieval as well as the average storage utilization.
    1. Indexed-sequential file
    2. B^+-tree
    3. Extendible Hashing
    4. Linear Hashing
15. Suggest two schemes that would improve the efficiency of a B^+-tree scheme.
16. How is the cost of different data structures for storing databases compared?
17. Show how an indexed-sequential file is maintained when rows are being inserted and deleted from a table.

18. A B-tree of order 5 is built by inserting the keys 1,2,3,4,...20 in some order.
    (a) Which order of insertion of the keys would lead to the resulting tree having as high storage utilization as possible?
    (b) Write the keys in that order.
19. Consider the B-tree shown in Fig. 7.11. Describe what will happen if the key 11 is deleted from the tree. Show the tree after the deletion.
20. Consider a file being built with bucket capacity of 4. The key values are integers and the hashing function to be used is (key value) mod 2^i (i.e., least significant i bits) for a suitable i. The following key values are added to a null file: 1, 2, 17, 20, 39, 40, 5, 6, 9, 11, 22 and 21.

    Using extendible hashing:
    (a) What is the size of the directory after these insertions?
    (b) How many buckets are in the file?
21. Consider the file built-up in the last question using extendible hashing. The following keys are now deleted from the file: 5, 9, 1 and 11. How many buckets have been removed from the file?
22. Consider a file being built with bucket capacity of 4. The key values are integers and the hashing function to be used is (key value) mod 2^i for a suitable i. The following key values are added to a null file: 1, 2, 17, 20, 39, 40, 5, 6, 9, 11, 22, 21, 19, 23, 7, 13 and 15.

    If the file is built-up using linear hashing with uncontrolled splitting (that is, a split occurs every time a record goes to an overflow bucket), answer the following:
    (a) How many buckets are in the file?
    (b) What was the maximum number of overflow buckets used at any one time?
23. Consider the file built-up in the last question using linear hashing. The following keys are now deleted from the file: 5, 7, 9, 1 and 11. How many buckets have been removed from the file?

PROJECTS

1. Given the decreasing cost of main memory, it is possible to store a whole database in the main memory. Explore the changes that would be necessary to make the database perform well. What physical storages should be used? Would B-tree and dynamic hashing schemes still be suitable? What bucket size would now be appropriate?
2. Implement the classical B-tree in C++. Carry out random searches after building it and carry out some random deletions and insertions in order to evaluate its performance.

LAB EXERCISES

1. Suppose we have a database in which two attributes are the latitude and longitude of the location of the entity. A lot of queries involve the latitude and longitude. Explore how the data should be stored. What index would be most effective?

2. Consider a database like that used in the search engines. Most queries involve one or two words but some queries include several search words. What data structure is most suitable for such a document database and the queries?

BIBLIOGRAPHY

For Students

Comer's paper is a good reference on B-trees.

For Instructors

We have presented some original papers, for example, by Fagin, Nievergelt, Pippenger and Strong. Knuth's Volume 3 book has a lot of detail about file structures. The book by Frake and Baeza-Yates is also useful and so is the book by Lightstone, Teorey and Nadeau.

Comer, D., "The Ubiquitous B-Tree", *ACM Computing Surveys*, Vol. 11, No. 2, June 1979.

Dippert, B., and M. Levy, *Designing with Flash Memory*, Annabooks, 1993.

Elmasri, R., and S. B. Navathe, *Fundamentals of Database Systems*, Addison-Wesley, Chapters 13 and 14, Fifth Edition, 2003.

Enbody, R. J., and H. C. Du, "Dynamic hashing schemes", *ACM Computing Survey*, Vol. 20, June 1988, pp 850-113.

Fagin, R., J. Nievergelt, N. Pippenger, and R. Strong, "Extendible Hashing – A fast access method for dynamic files", *ACM Transactions of Database Systems*, Vol. 4, pp 315-344, 1979.

Frake, W. B., and R. Baeza-Yates, *Information Retrieval: Data Structures and Algorithms*, Prentice Hall, 1992.

Knuth, D. E., "The Art of Computer Programming", *Sorting and Searching*, Vol. 3, Addison-Wesley.

Lightstone, S., T. Teorey, and T. Nadeau, *Physical Database Design: The Database Professional's Guide to Exploiting Indexes, Views, Storage, and More*, Morgan Kaufmann/Elsevier, 2007.

Litwin, W., "Virtual Hashing: A Dynamically Changing Hashing", *Proceedings 4th Conference on Very Large Data Bases*, Berlin, 1978, pp 517-523.

Ruemmler, C., and J. Wilkes, An Introduction to Disk Drive Modelling, *IEEE Computer*, 27:3, March 1994, pp. 17-27.

Vitter, J. S., "External Memory Algorithms and Data Structures: Dealing with Massive Data", *ACM Computing Survey*, Vol. 33, June 2001, pp 209-271.

Zobel, J. A., A. Moffat, and K. Ramamohanrao, "Inverted File Versus Signature Files for Databases", In *Proceedings International Conference on Very Large Data Bases*, Vol. 18, Vancouver, 1992.

Rudolf Bayer—Inventor of the B-tree

Rudolf Bayer (with E. McCreight) invented the B-tree in 1972.

After working at Boeing Research Labs he became an Associate Professor at Purdue University. He is a Professor of Informatics at the Technische Universität München since 1972 and Head of the Research Group Knowledge Bases at the Bavarian Research Center for Knowledge Based Systems (FORWISS). Bayer served as an Associate Editor of ACM TODS and of Informatik Forschung und Entwicklung. He was awarded the Bundesverdienstkreuz of the Federal Republik of Germany and received the ACM SIGMOD Innovations Award in 2001.

Rudolf Bayer studied Mathematics in Munich and at the University of Illinois, where he received his PhD in 1966.

Query Processing 8

OBJECTIVES

- Discuss the concept of query optimization.
- Describe the kind of information a DBMS stores in its catalog.
- Explain how different query plans can have very different costs.
- Describe query transformation including tree representation of a query.
- Discuss heuristic optimization.
- Briefly discuss algorithms for carrying out relational operations selection, projection and join.
- Compare the algorithms for computing the join of two relations.
- Present methods for estimating the size and cost of relational operations in a query as used in System R.
- Explore how correlated subqueries may be processed efficiently and discuss decorrelation.
- Introduce the concept of semantic query optimization.

KEYWORDS

Query optimization, catalog, metadata, query plans, transforming a query to a tree, heuristic optimization, size estimation, cost estimation, selection, projection, join algorithms, nested scan, sort merge, hash join, pushing selection, joins, decorrelation, correlated subqueries, nested iteration, semantic query optimization.

There is more to life than increasing its speed.

Mahatma Gandhi

8.1 INTRODUCTION

When a program written in a procedural language, for example, Java or C, is executed, the program is first translated by a compiler into a machine language. The translation involves taking the source code and generating equivalent machine code that preserves the sequence of operations that the source code specifies. As part of the translation process, the compiler carries out code optimization to generate as efficient a machine code as possible. This might include elimination of unnecessary writing of values to the memory and reading them to the registers, some clever unrolling of the loops, and so on.

In a nonprocedural or a declarative language like SQL, no sequence of operations is explicitly given and therefore, a query can be processed in a number of different ways, often called *plans*, where each plan might have a different sequence of operations. Optimization in nonprocedural languages therefore, is a more complex task since it not only involves code optimization (how to carry out the operations that need to be carried out) but also selecting the best plan as well as selecting the best access paths. In many situations, especially if the database is large and the query is complex, a very large number of alternative plans are possible and it is then not practical to enumerate them all and select the best. Often then, it is necessary to consider a small number of possible plans and select the best option from those. Since the savings from query optimization can be substantial, it is acceptable that a database spend some time in finding the best strategy to process the query. It should be noted that such a strategy may not be the optimum strategy. We assume that we are dealing with queries that are expected to consume a significant amount of computing resources; there is no point in spending time optimizing queries that are so simple that almost any approach could be used to execute them in a small amount of time.

Most query processing approaches in DBMS first check that the user is authorized to run the query submitted to it and once authorized, it translates the given SQL query in a form that is more like relational algebra but includes aggregation functions. An SQL query has a variety of commands, for example, SELECT, INSERT, WHERE, GROUP BY, HAVING, DELETE, CREATE TABLE and CREATE INDEX. The DDL commands are usually not processed by the query optimizer. Since translation of a query to relational algebra like commands is not unique, a number of alternative extended relational algebra expressions may be obtained from a single SQL query. It is then the aim of query processing to choose the best query plan from the plans available. This, however, becomes complex given that each relational algebra operation may also be executed using any one of a number of algorithms using alternative access methods for the files storing the database tables. We will now discuss how alternate plans can be obtained and describe some algorithms for relational operators like selection, projection and join.

The focus of this chapter is on read-only queries and update queries are not considered explicitly. However, the techniques of query processing discussed are also applicable to update queries since an update also requires a search before it can be processed.

The chapter is organized as follows. First, a number of SQL queries are presented to illustrate the issues in query optimization. The steps involved in query optimization process are discussed in Section 8.3. Section 8.4 describes the system catalog or metadata and its importance for query optimization. Query parsing is described in Section 8.5 including an example of a query tree. Once the query has been parsed, optimization can proceed. This is discussed in Section 8.6. This section includes comparison of the costs of different query plans for the same query. Also, logical transformations are discussed in detail. This is followed, in Section 8.6.3, by rules of thumb that are often used in query optimization. Estimating the size of intermediate results in processing a query is then discussed in Section 8.6.4. Access paths are discussed in Section 8.7 followed by query code generation Section 8.8 which is illustrated by using a query tree. Algorithms for relational algebra operations, selection and projection are discussed in Section 8.10. Section 8.11 describes a number of algorithms for computing a join. Computing aggregation functions are briefly described in Section 8.12 followed by a discussion of cost based query estimation in Section 8.13. Optimization of correlated queries is discussed in Section 8.14. Finally, Section 8.15 briefly introduces the topic of semantic query optimization.

8.2 ISSUES IN QUERY OPTIMIZATION

To illustrate the issues involved in query optimization, we consider the following cricket database that we have used in earlier chapters:

```
Match(MatchID, Team1, Team2, Ground, Date, Winner)
Player(PlayerID, LName, FName, Country, YBorn, BPlace, FTest)
Batting(MatchID, PID, Order, HOut, FOW, NRuns, Mts, NBalls, Fours, Sixes)
Bowling(MatchID, PID, NOvers, Maidens, NRuns, NWickets)
```

Figure 8.1 The example ODI database schema

Now consider the query 'find the names of grounds where Sachin Tendulkar has batted'. As we have shown earlier, this query may be formulated in a number of different ways. Three possible formulations of the query are as follows:

1. The first formulation involves two joins. First carry out a join of the relations *Match* and *Player* and then another join of the result with the relation *Batting*. The formulation is given in Fig. 8.2.

```
SELECT Ground
FROM Match, Player, Batting
WHERE PlayerID = PID
AND MID = MatchID
AND LName = 'Tendulkar'
```

Figure 8.2 An example SQL query

2. The second query involves using two subqueries. This formulation is presented in Fig. 8.3.

```
SELECT Ground
FROM Match
WHERE MatchID IN
        (SELECT MID
        FROM Batting
        WHERE PID IN
                (SELECT PlayerID
                FROM Player
                WHERE LName = 'Tendulkar'))
```

Figure 8.3 Second formulation of the SQL query

3. The third query also involves using two subqueries. This formulation is presented in Fig. 8.4.

```
SELECT Ground
FROM Match
WHERE EXISTS
        (SELECT MID
        FROM Batting
        WHERE MID = MatchID
        AND EXISTS
                (SELECT PlayerID
                FROM Player
                WHERE PID = PlayerID
                AND LName = 'Tendulkar'))
```

Figure 8.4 Third formulation of the SQL query

The three query formulations above suggest the following three different query plans:

(a) The first formulation suggests a plan in which the natural join of tables *Player* and *Batting* is carried out followed by the join of the result with the table *Match*. This is in turn followed by a selection *LName* = 'Tendulkar' of the result followed by a projection.

(b) The second formulation suggests a plan that involves first applying a selection and a projection to the table *Player* to obtain a table that has only the *PlayerID* of Tendulkar in it. This is then followed by a selection and a projection of the table *Batting* and finally a selection and a projection of the table *Match*.

(c) In the third query formulation, the table *Match* is scanned one row at a time and the row is selected only if there is a corresponding row in the table *Batting*. To find if there is a corresponding row in *Batting*, the table *Batting* is scanned one row at a time and a row is selected only if it has a corresponding row in the table *Player* with the name Tendulkar.

The differences between the costs of implementing the above query plans is quite large, without even considering the various access methods that might be available, as we will show later in this chapter.

Given that the same query may be formulated in several different ways and each query formulation may be processed in several different ways, the following questions arise:

1. How does a DBMS process a query?
2. Does the formulation of the query determine the query processing plan?
3. Is it possible to recognize different semantically equivalent queries?
4. What is the most efficient plan to process the above query?

This chapter addresses these questions as well as questions dealing with efficient methods of computing relational algebra operators like selection, projection and join.

It is not important for the user to know which query can be formulated in different ways, or which is the most efficient. Users can not be expected to have a prior knowledge about the workings of a DBMS to be able to predict efficiency of a formulation. It is therefore essential that the burden of finding an efficient execution plan be placed on the DBMS itself and not on the user. For this reason, query optimization is one of the most important tasks of a DBMS. A user may express a query in any of the different possible forms but one expects that the DBMS will execute the query efficiently.

We assume, the database that we are dealing with is too large to fit in the main memory. The database therefore primarily resides in the secondary memory and parts of it are copied to the main memory as necessary. The secondary storage (disk) is assumed to be partitioned in blocks, each block typically storing a number of rows from a table, and the data movements between the main and secondary memory take place in blocks. The typical size of a block is assumed to be 1 KB although recent machines tend to use larger block sizes.

Often the cost of secondary memory access is the main bottleneck in a database system and therefore the number of blocks read or written is usually taken as the cost of carrying out a particular operation. We assume that processing of each block takes much less time than reading or writing it to the secondary storage although this is not always the case.

8.3 STEPS IN QUERY PROCESSING

As noted earlier, DBMS queries are posed in a nonprocedural language SQL and as such queries do not involve any reference to access paths or the order of evaluation of operations. The query processing of such queries usually involves the four phases given in Fig. 8.5.

Each of these four topics is discussed in the following sections but we first discuss the DBMS system catalog which maintains a variety of information about the database. This information is required in query processing.

8.4 SYSTEM CATALOG OR METADATA

The concept of metadata was introduced in Chapter 1. We present more details here since it is important for efficient query processing.

An important part of the optimizer is the component that consults the metadata stored in the database to obtain statistics about the referenced tables and the access paths available on them. These are used to determine the most efficient order of the relational operations and the most efficient access paths. The order of operations and the access paths are selected from a number of alternative possibilities that normally exist so that the cost of query processing is minimized. More details about query optimization are presented in the next section.

A database system contains not only the database itself but also its metadata, the descriptions of the data structures and constraints. An informal definition of metadata is given below.

Definition—Metadata
Metadata is descriptive information about an object or resource whether it is physical or electronic. In case of a database, metadata may be defined as 'data about data'.

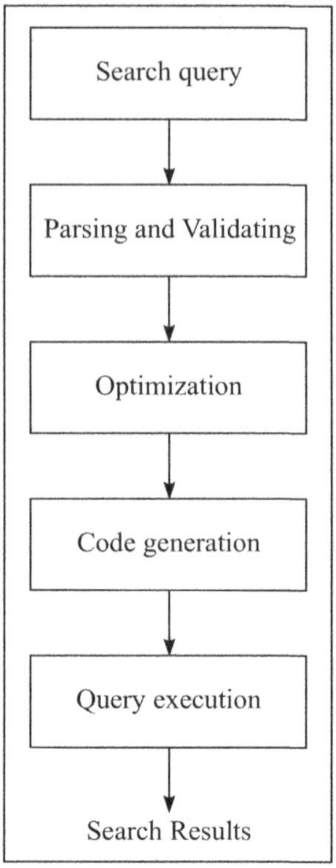

Figure 8.5 Phases in query processing

The term 'meta' is derived from a Greek word which means 'alongside, with, after, next'. In addition to database systems, metadata applies to many situations. For example, when an MS Word document is created, it is automatically saved into a file with document metadata information that is hidden from view. This metadata information can hint at authorship, times and dates of revisions and other tidbits. Some of this metadata may be viewed by looking at the properties of the document. Another example of metadata is the description of books on amazon.com. Web pages also have metadata about them. A web page metadata may include the title, author, and modification date of a web page, copyright and licensing information and its content rating.

In the context of a database, metadata includes information about how data is stored in the computer storage. The metadata is an integral part of a database and is stored in the database itself. It is used not only by the database managers but also by the database end-users. The metadata includes names of tables, number of columns in each table, their types, number of rows in each table, and so on, as listed later in this section. In the context of a database, the metadata is stored in the *data dictionary*, which is a term for data describing the database.

In formulating query plans, the query optimizer obtains relevant information from the metadata and attempts to model the estimated costs of performing many alternative query plans and then selects the best amongst them. The cost of these alternatives is estimated and the best plan is selected.

The metadata or the database catalog consists of descriptions of each database that a DBMS maintains. The following information is often available in the catalog:

1. *For Each Table*—The name of each table, the name of the file it is stored in, the data structure used for storing it, all its attributes and their domains.

2. *For Each Table*—In addition to the information listed above, the metadata also stores information about the primary key and foreign keys, if any, of each table. Furthermore, the cardinality of each table and the number of pages or blocks a table occupies on the disk is also included in the catalog.
3. *For Each View*—The name of the view and its definition.
4. *For Each Index*—The name of the index, description of its storage structure, the size of the index in terms of number of blocks on the disk.
5. *Security*—Information about ownership of the database and various tables, views, indexes and any other security issues.
6. *Histograms*—Some DBMS also store histograms of ranges of attribute values of various tables in the database. This information can help in making better estimates of the sizes of relational operations and thus the cost of query processing.

Often the statistics are updated only periodically and not at every update/insert/delete. Also, the system catalog is often stored as a relational database itself, making it easy to query it if a user is authorized to do so.

Information in the catalog is very important since query processing makes use of this information extensively. Therefore, more comprehensive and more accurate information is desirable but maintaining the same also introduces additional overheads and therefore, a balance must be found.

8.5 QUERY PARSING

The first step in query processing is query parsing. The main role of the parser is to check the query for correct syntax, resolve names and references and translate the query into a conventional parse-tree (often called a *query-tree*) or some other internal representation. To simplify query translation, queries are decomposed into query blocks. Each query block normally consists of a SELECT FROM WHERE block with some blocks also including GROUP BY and HAVING clauses. Each block of a complex query can then be translated into a query tree which in turn can be combined with other trees to form a query tree of the whole query. In the query tree we also need to deal with aggregate operations which are not present in relational algebra.

In addition, the parser may also check if the user is authorized to execute the query or not.

A query tree is an internal representation of an SQL query when translated to an extended relational algebra. Consider the query in Fig. 8.6 which finds the IDs and number of runs scored by each Indian player when they played at MCG.

```
SELECT PlayerID, NRuns
FROM Match, Player, Batting
WHERE PlayerID = PID
AND MID = MatchID
AND Country = 'India'
AND Ground = 'MCG'
```

Figure 8.6 An example SQL query

The query tree for this query is given in Fig. 8.7. This tree shows the three relations that are used in the query: *Match*, *Player* and *Batting*. There is a selection on the relation *Match* to find matches played at the MCG and there is a selection on *Player* to find all Indian players, which are then joined to *Batting* to find their batting records. Finally, these are then joined with the MCG matches to find batting records of Indian players at the MCG. Now the projection may be carried out. Therefore, the result of this query is *PlayerID* and *NRuns*.

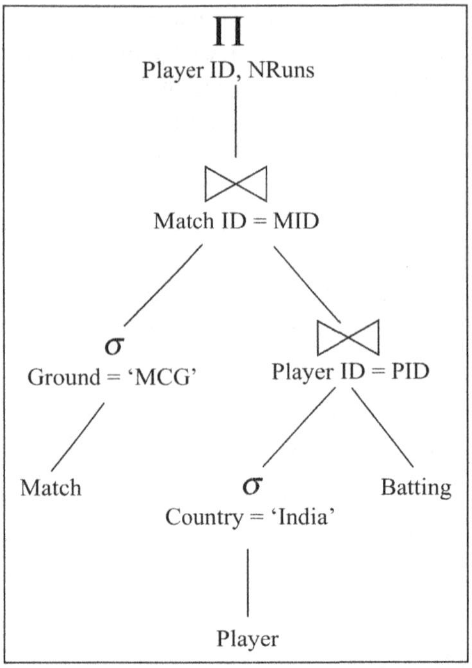

Figure 8.7 Query tree for the SQL query in Fig. 8.6

As noted earlier, the first thing the parser does is to check each of the table names in the FROM clause of the query. If the table names are found to be correct and registered in the database catalog and the attribute names used in the query are also correct, the names may be converted to full names for the database. If the parser returns with no errors, and the query uses some user-defined views, it is necessary to expand the query by making appropriate substitutions for the views. It is then necessary to check the query for semantic correctness by consulting the system catalogs to check for semantic errors and type compatibility in both expressions and comparisons in the query. Finally, the parser checks for authorization to make sure the user has appropriate permissions to carry out the query.

8.6 QUERY OPTIMIZATION

Once the query parser validates the query, the query in its internal format, possibly represented as a query-tree, is passed to the query optimizer. The query optimization module may carry out some transformation of the internal representation received from the parser.

The optimizer is then invoked with the internal representation of the query as input so that a query plan or execution plan may be devised for retrieving the information that is required. The optimizer carries out a number of operations. It relates the symbolic names in the query to database objects and checks their existence. Since current DBMS software is designed to run on many different platforms, it is necessary that the query plan be represented in a form that can easily be translated to each computer's internal instructions.

As noted earlier, the query optimizer is a very important component of a DBMS because the efficiency of the system depends a lot on the performance of the optimizer. Before we discuss query evaluation in detail, we should note that queries to the database may be posed either interactively or in a batch mode. When queries are posed interactively, the needs to optimize processing of each query separately. In case of batches, where an application program may include a number of queries, it may be desirable to attempt global optimization. In this section we only deal with individual query optimization.

Before query optimization is carried out, one needs to decide what is to be optimized. The goal of achieving efficiency itself may be different in different situations. For example, one may wish to minimize the processing time but in many situations one would wish to minimize the response time. In other situations, one may wish to minimize the I/O, network time, memory used or some combination of these, for example, total resources used. Generally, a query processing algorithm *A* will be considered more efficient than an algorithm *B* if the measure of cost being minimized for processing the same query, given the same resources using *A*, is generally less than that for *B*.

Although it is customary to use the term *query optimization* for the heuristic selection of strategies to improve the efficiency of executing a query, query optimization does not attempt to exactly optimize the cost of query processing. Exact optimization of the query processing cost is usually computationally unfeasible. Also, given that many statistics about the database available to the optimizer are likely to be estimates, an exact optimization is not necessarily a desirable goal. The goal, therefore, often is to select an execution plan that is reasonably efficient and hopefully close to optimal.

8.6.1 An Example

To illustrate the desirability of optimization, we now present an example of a simple query that can be processed in several different ways. The query in Fig. 8.8, similar to the one discussed earlier in Section 8.2, retrieves ground names of all matches that Tendulkar batted in and were played in Australia (*Team1* was therefore Australia). We have added another condition to help illustrate the query costs.

```
SELECT Ground
FROM Match, Player, Batting
WHERE PlayerID = PID
AND MID = MatchID
AND Team1 = 'Australia'
AND LName = 'Tendulkar'
```

Figure 8.8 An example SQL query

As noted earlier, to process the above query, two joins and two selections need to be performed. There are a number of different ways these may be performed including the following:

1. Join the tables *Player* and *Batting*, join the result with *Match* and then do the selections followed by a projection.
2. Join the tables *Player* and *Batting*, do the selections, join the result with *Match* followed by a projection.
3. Do the selections, join the tables *Player* and *Batting*, join the result with *Match* followed by a projection.
4. Join the tables *Match* and *Batting*, join the result with *Player* and then do the selections followed by a projection.

Before we attempt to compare the costs of the above four alternatives, it is necessary to understand that estimating the cost of a plan is often nontrivial. Since normally a database is disk-resident, often the cost of reading and writing to disk dominates the cost of processing a query. We would therefore estimate the cost of processing a query in terms of disk accesses or block accesses. Estimating the number of block accesses to process even a simple query is not necessarily straightforward since it would depend on how the data is stored and which, if any, indexes are available. In some database systems, tables are stored in packed form, that is, each block only has rows of the same table while other systems may store rows from several tables in each block making it much more expensive to scan the entire table.

Let us now compare the costs of the above four options. Since exact cost computations are difficult, we will use simple estimates of the cost. We consider a situation where the database consists of 1,000 rows in the table *Player*, 50,000 in *Batting*, and 1,000 in the table *Match*. For simplicity, let us assume, that the tables *Player* and *Match* have rows of similar size of around 200 bytes each and therefore we can accommodate 5 rows per block if the block is assumed to be 1 KB in size. For the table *Batting*, we assume a row size of 100 bytes and thus we use a figure of 10 rows/block. There are thus 200 blocks in *Player*, 5,000 in *Batting* and 200 blocks in *Match*. In addition, we assume that Sachin Tendulkar has 200 batting records and let there be 100 matches played in Australia. We can now estimate the costs of the four plans listed above.

The cost of query plan (1) above may now be computed. Let the join be computed by reading a block of the first table followed by a scan of the second table to identify matching rows. This method of computing a join is called *nested-scan* and is not particularly efficient. This is then followed by the reading of the second block of the first table followed by a scan of the second table and so on. The cost of $R \bowtie S$ may therefore be estimated as the number of blocks in *R* times the number of blocks in *S*. Since the number of blocks in *Player* is 200 and in *Batting* 5,000, the total number of blocks read in computing the join of *Player* and *Batting* is 200 × 5,000 = 1,000,000. The result of the join is 50,000 rows since each row from *Batting* matches with a row from *Player*. Assume that the joined rows will be of size approximately 300 bytes since each row in the join is a row from *Player* joined with another from *Batting*. Given the row size of 300 bytes, we can only fit 3 rows in a block and therefore, we need about 17,000 blocks to store all 50,000 joined rows. The cost of computing the join of this result with *Match* is 17,000 × 200 = 3,400,000 block accesses. Therefore, the total cost of plan (1) is approximately 4,400,000 block accesses which appears rather large.

To estimate the cost of plan (2), we know the cost of computing the join of *Player* and *Batting* has been estimated above as 1,000,000 block accesses. The result is 17,000 blocks in size. Now the result of applying the selections to the result of the join reduces this result to about 5 to 10 rows, that is about 5 blocks. The cost of this selection is about 17,000 disk accesses. Also the result of applying the selection to the table *Match* reduces that table to 20 rows (2 blocks). The cost of this selection is about 100 block accesses. The join now only requires about 4 block accesses. The total cost therefore, is approximately 2,017,200 block accesses.

To estimate the cost of plan (3), we need to estimate the size of the two results Team = 'Australia' and *LName* = 'Tendulkar' of selections and their cost. The cost of the selections consist of reading the tables *Player* and *Match* and writing the results. The reading costs are 10,200 block accesses. The writing costs are very small since the size of the results is 1 row for *Player* and 20 rows for *Match*. The cost of computing the join of *Player* and *Batting* primarily involves the cost of reading *Batting*. This is 200 block accesses. The result is quite small in size and therefore the cost of writing the result back is small. The total cost of plan (3) is therefore about 10,400 block accesses, better than the cost of plan (1) and plan (2).

Similar estimates may be obtained for processing plan (4). We will not estimate this cost, since the above estimates are sufficient to illustrate that a brute force method of query processing is unlikely to be efficient. The cost can be significantly reduced if the query plan is optimized. The issue of optimization of course is much more complex than estimating the costs in the way we have done above, since in the above estimation the various alternatives for computing the joins and using various access paths that might be available to the system to access each table were not considered.

The above cost estimates assumed that the secondary storage access costs dominate the query processing costs. This is often a reasonable assumption although the cost of communication can be important if we are dealing with a distributed system. The cost of storage can be important in large databases since some queries may require large intermediate results. The cost of CPU is of course always important and it is not uncommon for database applications to be CPU bound rather than I/O bound as is normally assumed. In the present chapter, we assume a centralized system where the cost of secondary storage access is assumed to dominate other costs although we recognize that this is not always true. For example, System R used the following cost estimate:

$$\text{Cost} = \text{Page fetches} + w \times \text{CPU utilization}$$

where w was some factor.

When a query is specified to a DBMS, the optimization part of query processing generally involves the following operations:

1. Logical transformation of the query
2. Selection of the alternatives based on heuristics
3. Estimate costs and select best

We now discuss the above steps.

8.6.2 Logical Transformations

At the beginning of this chapter, we showed that the same query may be formulated in a number of different ways that are semantically equivalent. It is clearly desirable that all such queries be transformed into the same query representation. To do this, we need to translate each query to some canonical form (that is, a form that is standard) and then simplify.

This involves transformations of the query and selection of an optimal sequence of operations. The transformations that we discuss in this section do not consider the physical representation of the database and are designed to improve the efficiency of query processing using whatever access methods might be available. An example of such transformation has already been discussed in the examples given. If a query involves one or more joins and a selection, it is always going to be more efficient to carry out the selection first since that will reduce the size of one of the tables (assuming that the selection applies to only one table) and therefore reduce the cost of the join, often quite significantly.

We now discuss heuristic optimization in which the query tree is transformed by using a sequence of operations so that the query execution time improves.

8.6.3 Heuristic Optimization

Heuristic optimization often includes making transformations to the query tree by moving operators up and down the tree so that the transformed tree is equivalent to the tree before the transformations. Before we discuss these heuristics, it is necessary to discuss the following rules governing the manipulation of relational algebraic expressions:

1. *Joins and Products are Commutative*[1]—For example,

$$R \text{ X } S = S \text{ X } R$$
$$R \bowtie S = S \bowtie R$$

where $\bowtie$ is a natural join or theta-join. The order of attributes in the two products or joins may not be quite the same but the ordering of attributes is not considered significant in the relational model since the attributes are referred to by their name not by their position in the list of attributes.
We look at a simple example of joining two relations *Player* and *Batting*.

$$Player \bowtie Batting = Batting \bowtie Player$$

2. *Selection is Commutative*—For example,

$$\sigma_P(\sigma_q(R)) = \sigma_q(\sigma_P(R))$$

For example, if a query involves the following two conditions, then it does not matter which selection is carried out first.

WHERE *Team1* = 'Australia'
AND *LName* = 'Tendulkar'

3. *Joins and Products are Associative*[2]—For example,

$$(R \text{ X } S) \text{ X } T = R \text{ X } (S \text{ X } T)$$
$$(R \bowtie S) \bowtie T = R \bowtie (S \bowtie T)$$

The associativity of the above operations guarantees that we will obtain the same results whatever be the ordering of computations of the operations product and join. In the example above, we may compute the join of *A* and *B* followed by a join with *C* or join *B* and *C* and then join the result with *A*. Union and intersection are also associative.
Once again, we consider an example involving two joins. It does not really matter whether the first join is computing followed by the second or the second join is computed followed by the first.

$$(Player \bowtie Batting) \bowtie Match = Player \bowtie (Batting \bowtie Match)$$

Also, using the commutativity of the join discussed in 1 above, this expression may be written as:

$$(Player \bowtie Batting) \bowtie Match = Match \bowtie (Player \bowtie Batting)$$

4. *Cascade of Projections*—For example,

$$\pi A(\pi B(R)) = \pi A(R)$$

---

1. Commutativity is the mathematical name for the condition that a group of quantities connected by an operator give the same result irrespective of the order of the quantities.
2. Associativity is another mathematical term for the condition that a group of quantities connected by operators gives the same result irrespective of their grouping, as long as their order remains the same.

where the attributes A are a subset of the attributes B. The above expression formalizes the obvious that there is no need to take the projection with attributes B if there is going to be another projection which is a subset of B that follows it.

5. *Cascade of Selections*—For example,

$$\sigma_P(\sigma_q(R)) = \sigma_{P\wedge q}(R)$$

The above expression also formalizes the obvious that if there are two selections, one after the other, then there is no need to carry out the selections one at a time (since each will require processing a table) and instead both selections could be combined and carried out together.

6. *Commuting Selections and Projections*—For example,

$$\sigma_P(\pi_A(R)) = \pi_A\sigma_P(R)$$

or

$$\pi_A\,\sigma_P(R) = \sigma_P(\pi_A(R))$$

There is no difficulty in commuting selection with a projection since we are then doing the selection before the projection. However, if we wish to commute the projection and then the selection, that is possible only if the selection used no attributes other than those that are in the projection.

7. *Commuting Selections with Cartesian Product*—In some cases, it is possible to apply the commutative law to selections and a product. For example,

$$\sigma_P(RXS) = \sigma_P(R)XS$$

or

$$\sigma_{P\wedge q}(RXS) = \sigma_P(R)X\sigma_q(S)$$

In the above expressions we have assumed that the condition p has only attributes from R and q has attributes only from S.

8. *Commuting Selection with a Union*—Since selection chooses some rows from one of the tables or both tables, selection can be carried out before the union of the rows that remain after selection.
9. *Commuting Selection with a Set Difference*—Since selection chooses some rows from one of the tables or both tables, selection can be carried out before the difference of the rows that remain after selection.
10. *Commuting Projection with a Cartesian Product or a Join*—We assume that the projection includes the join predicate attributes and therefore the join may be carried out before the product or the join to reduce the size of the tables being joined.
11. *Commuting Projection with a Union*—Since the projection chooses some columns from both tables, projection may be carried out before the union of the tables with columns that remain after projection.

The above heuristics may now be used to transform the query tree to reduce the query processing cost by reducing the size of intermediate results. Since the cost is assumed to be closely related to the size of the tables on which the operations are carried out, one of the primary aims of the transformations that we discuss is to reduce the size of intermediate tables.

8.6.4 Rules of Thumb

The basic transformations include the following rules of thumb:

(a) *Moving selections down the tree as far as possible*—The idea is to carry out selections as early as possible. If the query involves joins as well as selections, moving the selections down the tree is likely to lead to substantial savings since the tables that are joined after selections are likely to be smaller (in some cases much smaller) than before selection. This is clearly shown by the example that we used earlier in this chapter to show that some query plans can be much more expensive than others. The query plans that cost the least were those in which the selection was carried out first. There are of course situations where a selection does not reduce the table significantly. For example, a selection selecting only women from a large table of customers or clients may result in a table that is only 50% of the size of the original table.

(b) *Projections are executed as early as possible*—In real-life databases, a table may have one hundred or more columns and therefore the size of each row is relatively large. Some tables can even have columns that are images, making each row very large. In such situations, if a projection is executed early and it leads to elimination of many columns, then the resulting table has rows of much smaller size, and the amount of data that needs to be read in from the disk for the operations that follow could be reduced substantially leading to cost savings. It should be noted that the only columns that we need to retain from the tables are those that are either needed for the result or those that are to be used in one of the operations that is to be carried out on the table.

(c) *Optimal ordering of the joins*—We have noted earlier that the join operator is associative and therefore when a query involves more than one join, it is necessary to find an efficient ordering for carrying out the joins. An ordering is likely to be efficient if we carry out those joins first that are likely to lead to small results rather than carrying out those joins that are likely to lead to large results.

(d) *Cascading selections and projections*—Sometimes it is convenient to carry out more than one operation together. When selections and projections have the same operand, the operations may be carried out together, thereby saving the cost of scanning a table more than once.

(e) *Projections of projections are merged into one projection*—Clearly, if more than one projection is to be carried out on the same operand table, the projections should be merged. This could lead to substantial savings since no intermediate results need to be written on the disk and then read again from the disk.

(f) *Combining certain selections and Cartesian product to form a join*—A query may involve a cartesian product followed by a selection rather than specifying a join. The optimizer should recognize this and execute a join using an efficient algorithm since this is likely to be much cheaper to perform.

(g) *Sorting is deferred as much as possible*—Sorting is normally an $n\log n$ operation and by deferring sorting, we may need to sort a table that is smaller than it would have been if the sorting was carried out earlier.

(h) A set of operations is reorganized using commutativity and distribution if a reorganized form is more efficient.

Most of these rules of thumb are straightforward. The main objective of these rules is to reduce the size of intermediate results, since query cost is directly related to the size of these results.

8.7 ACCESS PATHS

In the last chapter, Chapter 7, we discussed various ways of physically organizing data in a database. Different methods were considered and a DBMS may use more than one access method to store the same file, and then a suitable method must be selected for the given query. Each of these methods is called an *access path*. Access paths to a table may include one or more B-tree indexes, sequential scan and hashing. There has been considerable research in selecting optimal access paths since it is important to access data efficiently. The user, of course, does not know what physical access path should be used, or what might be available, to access the data that he/she wishes to retrieve. Often, an efficient program for retrieving data may be written only if one knows the access paths available but one of the major advantages of using database systems is data independence which removes the need for the user to know such details. It is therefore up to the DBMS to decide the most appropriate access method for the query at hand. Such decisions are made by a DBMS module called the *query processor*. The query processor of course does more than just select a suitable access method for the data.

As noted above, when a user poses a query in a language like SQL, the user does not know how the tables[3] are physically stored and what access paths are available or the order in which relational algebra operations are to be performed. It is the responsibility of the query processor to select the access paths to be used and to determine the order of the operations that need to be carried out.

As noted in Chapter 1, when we described the DBMS architecture, a software component of the DBMS maintains the physical storage of tables and provides access paths to these tables. Often, tables in a database are stored as records in a file which may be accessed through a block of records at a time along a given access path. The access paths may involve an index on one or more attributes of the table. The indexes are often implemented as B-trees which we have discussed in Chapter 6. An index may be scanned record by record providing sequential access along the columns on which the index has been built. The records may of course be scanned using a sequential scan. As discussed in the last chapter, B-trees perform well for range queries as well as for sequential access. Hashing performs very poorly for queries that require sequential access or range access on a column.

A file may have one or more indexes available on it. In fact, a table with many columns could well have many indexes and the storage occupied by the indexes can become as large as the storage occupied by the table. Indexes allow very efficient search when the row with a given value of a column needs to be found.

A query may involve a number of operations and there would often be a number of different ways these operations could be processed. A number of steps are usually involved in selecting appropriate access paths. One possible set of steps may be as follows:

1. Generate a set of basic access paths required to process the query.
2. For each access path, collect all the relevant information including statistical information about number of rows and columns of tables involved in the query, information about the indexes, information about any fields on which a table may have been sorted and estimates of selectivities of relational operations involved in the query.

---

3. In this chapter we will use the table and file interchangeably to mean a file that stores one or more of the tables in the database.

3. Estimate the cost of each access path given the information.
4. Select the cheapest access paths for the query.

The DBMS therefore estimates the cost of the different access path alternatives and chooses the alternative with the least cost. As noted earlier, the estimates of costs are often based on statistics about the sizes of the tables and distribution of key values (or ranges). The planner then produces a plan that presents a suggested sequence of operations as well as details of how the operations should be carried out. For example, the access paths to be used and when an index is to be used.

8.8 QUERY CODE GENERATION

Query code may be generated from the query tree once optimization has been carried out and access methods have been assessed and algorithms for relational algebra operators have been chosen. Figure 8.9 shows a query tree with annotations about how the relational algebra operators in Fig. 8.7 query tree will be carried out.

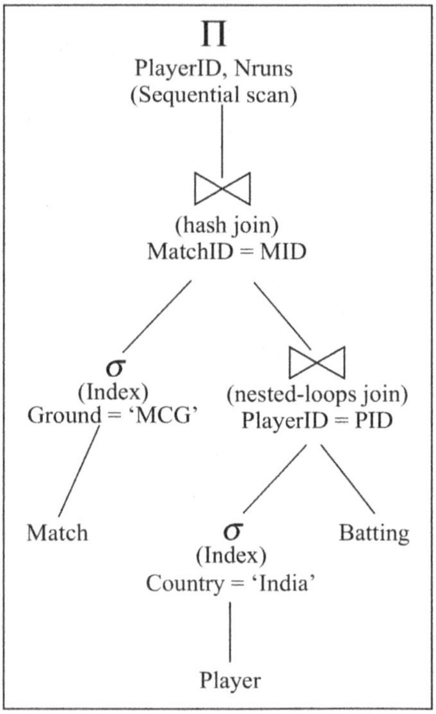

Figure 8.9 Query tree including details for a query execution

The query tree in Fig. 8.9 provides details of query processing which were not given in the query tree in Fig. 8.7. This tree is essentially the query pseudocode which may be written in a procedural form as follows:

1. Access the file *Match* and use its index on *Ground* to find all rows that meet the condition "*Ground* = '*MCG*'."
2. Save the intermediate result from Step 1 in file *M*1.
3. Access the file *Player* and use its index on *Country* to find all rows that meet the condition "*Country* = '*India*.'"
4. Save the intermediate result from Step 3 in file *P*1.
5. Access the files *Batting* and *P*1 and carry out their natural join on the attributes *PlayerID* and *PID* using the nested loops method.
6. Save the intermediate result from Step 5 in file *J*1.
7. Access the files *M*1 and *J*1 and carry out their natural join on the attributes *MatchID* and *MID* using the hash join method.
8. Save the intermediate result from Step 7 in file *J*2.
9. Carry out a sequential scan of *J*2 and extract attributes *PlayerID* and *NRuns*.
10. Display the results to the user.

We have provided a simple code. In practice many more details will be needed, for example, the name of each file and where the intermediate results will be stored but we ignore such details in our example.

8.9 QUERY EXECUTION

Now the fully specified query tree, for example, the pseudocode derived from the query tree in Fig. 8.9, can be executed. As shown above, the code includes details of tables that are to be accessed and how and what processing of that information is to be carried out. There are a variety of complexities in query execution. For example, how will the data be accessed from the disk and how memory buffers will be managed? The query may involve some writing of data after modification. This involves another set of issues which are not discussed here.

We will now discuss how the relational operations are computed and how the size and cost of carrying out an operation may be carried out in the next two sections.

8.10 ALGORITHMS FOR COMPUTING SELECTION AND PROJECTION

The efficiency of query processing in a relational database system depends on the efficiency of the relational operators. Even the simplest operations can often be executed in several different ways and the cost of different algorithms can be quite different. For all relational operators no algorithm is universally superior given a variety of access paths. Although the join is frequently used and is the most costly operator and therefore worthy of detailed study, we will also discuss other operators to show that careful thought is needed in efficiently implementing the simpler operators as well.

Implementing each relational operator involves accessing information about one or more tables involved in the operation. As discussed earlier, the efficiency of accessing information would depend on the access paths available. An access path may involve scanning the whole table or if an index is available, using the index which is likely to be more efficient in most cases. In some cases, hashing may be available which can be very efficient in retrieving given rows of a table. While discussing relational algebra operations, we will always need to consider what access paths are available. We are not able to discuss all possible algorithms but will present the most commonly used techniques.

8.10.1 Computing Selection

The selection operation is a simple operation that results in retrieving a number of rows from a table given the condition in the WHERE clause of the SQL query.

Let us consider the following simple query:

SELECT *A*
FROM *R*
WHERE *p*

The above query may involve any of a number of types of conditions in the WHERE clause as discussed in Chapter 4. We list some conditions here.

	Possible conditions in WHERE clause
1	attribute *A* = value *v*
2	attribute *A* = attribute *B*
3	attribute *A* > value *v*
4	attribute *A* between value *v*1 and value *v*2
5	attribute *A* IN (list of values)
6	Attribute A IN subquery
7	WHERE attribute *A* condition *C*1 OR condition *C*2
8	WHERE attribute *A* condition *C*1 and condition *C*2
9	WHERE *A* IS NOT NULL

Therefore, deciding which algorithm to use for a SELECT operation is not always easy. Even in the simple case of equality, a number of different approaches may be possible depending on how the table has been stored. We list some possibilities below.

1. *File Scan*—Traversing a file to find the information of interest. A *file scan* may be the most inefficient way to retrieve the information required.

   In some situations there may be no other option than to scan the whole table *R* to find the rows that satisfy the given condition. This may not be so expensive, if the table is not very large and the rows are stored in packed form but could be expensive if the table is large and the rows are stored such that each block has rows from several different tables.
2. *Using an Index*—If the condition *p* involves equality on a single attribute and there is an index on that attribute, it is most efficient to search the index and find the row or rows where the attribute value is equal to the value given. That should be very efficient since it will only require accessing the index and then perhaps accessing only one block. If the attribute of interest is the primary key, then only one row will be retrieved as a result of the equality condition.

   Of course, it is possible that there is no index on the column of interest, for example, there may be no index on *LName* in the cricket database, or the condition in the WHERE clause is not quite as simple as an equality condition on a single column. For example, the condition might be an inequality or specify a range. The index may still be useful if one exists but the usefulness would depend on the condition that is posed in the WHERE clause.
3. *Using Hashing*—Another possibility is of course that the table *R* is stored as a hash file using the attribute of interest and then again one would be able to hash on the value specified and find the record very efficiently.
4. *Secondary Index*—The file may have an index on an attribute other than the primary key and this attribute might be the attribute which may be used to retrieve a record or a number of records.

As noted above, often the condition may be a conjunction or disjunction of several different conditions: it may be like p_1 and p_2 or p_1 or p_2. For example, WHERE NRuns > 99, and Ground = 'MCG'. Sometimes such conjunctive queries can be efficiently processed if there is a composite index based on the columns that are involved in the two conditions but this is an exception rather than a rule. Often, however, it is necessary to assess which one of the two or more conditions can be processed efficiently. Perhaps one of the conditions can be processed using an index. As a first step then, those rows that satisfy the condition that involves the most efficient search (or perhaps that which retrieves the smallest number of rows) are retrieved and the remaining conditions are then tested on the rows that are retrieved. Processing disjunctive queries of course requires somewhat different techniques since in this case we are looking at a union of all rows that satisfy any one of the conditions, and therefore each condition will need to be processed separately. Hence, it is going to be of little concern which of the conditions is satisfied first since all must be satisfied independently of the other. Of course, if any one of the conditions requires a scan of the whole table then we can test all the conditions during the scan and retrieve all rows that satisfy any one or more conditions.

8.10.2 Computing Projection

Projection is also conceptually a simple operation which only requires selecting one or more columns of a table. Selecting columns require a scan of the whole table and discarding the unwanted columns.

SQL does not remove duplicates unless the user specifies DISTINCT. Removal of duplicates is then necessary. Duplicate removal is an expensive operation. If the projection includes a candidate key of the table, duplicate removal is then not necessary since each row in the projection is then guaranteed to be unique. Of course, more often the projection would not include a candidate key and may then have duplicates. Duplicates may be removed by sorting the projected table and then identifying the duplicates and eliminating them.

Duplicate removal may also use hashing which may be desirable if the tables are particularly large since hashing would hash identical rows to the same bucket and would therefore only require sorting the rows in each bucket to find the duplicates, if any. If there are few duplicates, hashing may be more efficient. If however there are many duplicates then sorting may be more efficient.

8.11 ALGORITHMS FOR COMPUTING A JOIN

Join is of course an important and expensive operation in relational query processing. It is also a common operation for a database that has many tables since join is needed whenever information from two or more tables is to be combined.

We assume that we wish to carry out an equi-join of two tables R and S that are to be joined on attributes a in R and b in S. Let the number of rows in R and S be m and n respectively. We do not count join output costs since these are identical for all methods. We assume R is the smaller table, that is, $|R| \leq |S|$. We further assume that all selections and projections of R and S have already been carried out and neither R nor S is ordered or indexed unless explicitly noted.

Because of the importance of the join operator in relational database systems and the fact that the join operator is considerably more expensive than operators like selection and projection, a number of algorithms have been suggested for processing the join. The more commonly used algorithms are as follows:

1. The nested scan method

2. Using indexes in nested scan
3. The Sort-Merge algorithm
4. Hashing algorithm
5. Variants of hashing

8.11.1 Nested Scan

We first briefly discuss the naive nested scan method that accesses every pair of rows and concatenates them if the equi-join condition (or for that matter, any other join condition) is satisfied. The algorithm essentially enumerates the cross-product of the two relations. The cost of the naive algorithm is $O(mn)$ assuming that R and S both are not ordered. The cost of the join can be large when m and n are large.

We will assume that the table R is the *outer table*, that is, R is the table whose rows are retrieved first. Table S is then the *inner table* since in the nested scan loop, rows of S will only be retrieved when a row of R has been read.

The nested scan algorithm may be written as given in Fig. 8.10.

```
for i = 1 to m do
        begin
        access ith row of R ;
        for j = 1 to n do
                begin
                access jth row of S ;
                compare ith row of R and j th row of S ;
                if equi-join condition is satisfied
                then concatenate and save;
                end
        end.
```

Figure 8.10 The nested scan join algorithm

This method basically scans the outer table (R) first and retrieves the first row. The entire inner table S is then scanned and all the rows of S that satisfy the join condition with the first row of R are combined with that row of S and output as result. The process then continues with the next row of R until R is exhausted.

This has cost $(m + mn)$ which is order(mn). If $m = 1000$ pages and $n = 500$ pages then the cost of the join operation will be 500,000 disk accesses. This is obviously too expensive to be useful.

If the memory buffers can store two or more blocks, one from R and one from S, the cost will go down by a factor rs where r and s are the number of rows per block in R and S respectively. The technique is sometimes called the *nested block* method. Some cost saving is achieved by reading the smaller table in the outer block since this reduces $(m + mn)$. The cost of the method would of course be much higher if the tables are not stored in a packed form, since then we might need to retrieve many more rows.

Efficiency of the nested scan (or nested block iteration) would improve significantly if an index was available on one of the join attributes. If the average number of blocks of table S accessed for each row of R was c then the cost of the join would be $(m + mc)$ where $c \ll n$.

8.11.2 Using Indexes in Nested Scan or Indexed Nested Loop Join

The nested scan method may be made more efficient if indexes are available on both join columns in the tables *R* and *S*.

Assume that we have available indexes on both join columns *a* and *b* in the tables *R* and *S* respectively or on only one of them. If both indexes are available, we may scan both the indexes to determine whether a pair of rows, one from each relation, has the same value of the join attribute. If the value is the same, the row from *R* is selected and then all the rows from *S* with the same join attribute value are selected. This is done by scanning the index on the join attribute in *S*. The index on the join attribute in *R* is now scanned to check if there is more than the one row with the same value of the attribute. All the rows of *R* that have the same join attribute value are then selected and combined with the rows of *S* that have already been selected. The process then continues with the next value for which rows are available in *R* and *S*.

If an index is available only on relation *S* then we may use the following algorithm.

For each tuple in the outer relation *R*, use the index to look-up tuples in *S* that satisfy the join condition with the tuple in *R*.

$$\text{Cost of the join with one index: } B_R + \mathrm{N_R}\ \alpha N_S$$

αN_S is the cost of traversing the index of *S* and fetching all matching tuples for one tuple from *R*.

If indices are available on join attributes of both *R* and *S*, use the relation with fewer tuples as the outer relation. Clearly this method requires substantial storage so that we may store all the matching rows from *R* and *S* that have the same join attribute value. The cost of the indexed nested loop join when both the indexes are used may be estimated as follows. Let the cost of reading the indexes be αN_R and βN_S, and then the total cost of the join is

$$\text{Cost of the join with two indexes: } \alpha N_R + \beta N_S + B_R + B_S$$

B_R and B_S are the number of blocks in each relation. Cost savings by using indexes can be large enough to justify building an index when a join needs to be computed.

8.11.3 The Sort-Merge Method

The nested scan technique is simple but involves matching each row of *R* with every row of *S* thus essentially enumerating the cross product of the two relations. This can be avoided if both tables were ordered on the join attribute and then rows that match were merged. The sort-merge algorithm was introduced during the development of System R at IBM. It is a classical technique that has been the preferred algorithm for joining tables that have no index on either of the join attributes.

This method involves sorting the tables *R* and *S* on the join attributes, storing them as temporary tables and then scanning them row by row or block by block and merging those rows that satisfy the join condition. The advantage of this scheme is that in contrast to nested scan, the entire inner table does not need to be read for each row of the outer table. This saving can be substantial if the outer table is large although sorting *R* and *S* at the beginning can be expensive.

We now consider the algorithm in some detail assuming that the two relations have been sorted already. The cardinality of R is m and that of S is n. Also, let R be the outer relation and S be the inner relation, then the sort-merge method may be written as in Fig. 8.11.

1. Sort R and S on the join attribute.
2. Start by setting first row of R (r) and first row of S (s) to be 1. So $r = 1$ and $s = 1$.
3. If r and s match then output them and set $s = s + 1$.
4. Otherwise if $r > s$ on the join attribute, set $s = s + 1$, otherwise $r = r + 1$.
5. Stop if the end of relation R or S, that is, $r > m$ or $s > n$.
6. Go to Step 3 if not finished.

Figure 8.11 The sort-merge algorithm for join

Let the cost of sorting R and S be C_s and C_r. The costs C_s and C_r are given by $O(m\log m)$ and $O(n\log n)$ respectively. The cost of merging them by reading the two tables in main memory is m and n accesses respectively. The total cost of the join therefore is as given below:

$$C_r + C_s + m + n$$

As an example, we again consider $m = 1000$ pages and $n = 500$ pages. The cost of sorting R is $m\log m$ which is approximately 10,000 disk reads while sorting S would cost about 4,500 pages. The total cost therefore is approximately 15,000 disk accesses, much smaller than 500,000 for the nested scan method. The cost in both cases is a very crude estimate since the cost could be lowered if the number of buffers is large which is often possible given that large main memories are becoming common.

If one or both of the tables are already sorted on the join attribute then the cost of the join reduces.

8.11.4 Simple Hash-Join Method

This is a very different join algorithm. To identify matching rows from the two tables, the method involves hashing both relations on the join attribute, using the same hash function. The implementation of the method would depend on the size of the relations and the size of the available main memory.

One approach would be to build the hash table of the smaller table R by hashing each row on its join attribute. We assume that the smaller of the two tables R is too large to fit in the main memory; the hash table would also in general not fit into the main memory. The hash table therefore must be built in stages. A number of addresses of the hash table are first selected such that the rows hashed to those addresses can be stored in the main memory. The rows of R that do not hash to these addresses are written back to the disk. Let these rows be table R'. Now the algorithm works as follows:

(a) Scan table R and hash each row on its join attribute(s). If the hashed value is equal to one of the addresses that are in the main memory, store the row in the hash table. Otherwise write the row back to the disk in a new table R'.

(b) Scan the table S and hash each row of S on its join attribute(s). One of the following three conditions must hold:

1. The hashed value is equal to one of the values in the hash table in the memory, and one or more row of R with the same join column value exists. We combine the rows of R that match with the row of S and output as the next rows in the join.
2. The hashed value is equal to one of the values in the hash table in the memory but there is no row in R with the same join attribute value. Such rows of S are rejected.
3. The hashed value is not equal to one of the selected hash table values. These rows are written back to the disk as a new table S'.

The above step continues till S is finished.

(c) Repeat steps (a) and (b) until either table R' or S' or both are exhausted.

8.11.5 Grace Hash-Join Method

This method is a modification of the simple hash-join method in that the partitioning of R is completed before S is scanned and partitioning of S is completed before the joining phase. The method consists of the following three phases:

1. *Partition R*—Since R is assumed to be too large to fit in the main memory, a hash table for it cannot be built in the main memory. The first phase of the algorithm involves partitioning the table into n buckets, each bucket corresponding to a hash table entry. The number of buckets n is chosen to be large enough so that each bucket will comfortably fit in the main memory.
2. *Partition S*—The second phase of the algorithm involves partitioning the table S into the same number (n) of buckets, each bucket corresponding to a hash table entry. The same hashing function as for R is used.
3. *Compute the Join*—A bucket of R is read in and the corresponding bucket of S is read in. Matching rows from the two buckets are combined and output as part of the join.

8.11.6 Comparing Join Algorithms

Comparing the join algorithms discussed above is governed by how large the two relations are and how big is the size of main memory available for buffers. The nested scan method is generally not efficient even if large main memory is available. The sort-merge algorithm mainly involves the cost of sorting the two relations if a large main memory is available. If the relations are very large, the sorting would require many disk accesses. If hashing is used, the algorithm is efficient only if the hash function hashes the table rows uniformly. The performance of the hashing method also depends on the size of the main memory available.

8.12 COMPUTING AGGREGATION FUNCTIONS

Aggregation is frequently used in queries given the frequency of use of the functions supported in SQL for computing the average, minimum, maximum, count, and sum (AVG, MIN, MAX, SUM and COUNT). Aggregation can itself be of different types including aggregation that only applies to one table. For example, finding the maximum number of runs scored in a match, or it may involve a table that requires finding the number of players from each country. The latter aggregation would require GROUPing the rows in the table into virtual tables before aggregation can be applied to each.

Aggregate operations return a single value from a table (in case of GROUP BY, a single value for each group) although it must go through the whole table. Therefore aggregation normally involves scanning of the whole table and collecting the information required. For example, COUNT requires counting the number of rows meeting the condition. It may also involve the GROUP BY clause which will require several counters to be maintained concurrently for each element of the group. SUM on the other hand requires the sum of a column to be computed while scanning the table. MIN and MAX require smallest and largest values found while AVG involves finding the SUM and counting the non-NULL values of that attribute.

Some aggregate operations may be able to use an index if available on the attribute. For example, a GROUP BY may be able to use an index depending on the type of index.

8.13 COST BASED QUERY OPTIMIZATION IN SYSTEM R

System R database system was built in the 1970s as a research project at IBM San Jose Research (which later changed its name to Almaden Research Center). As noted earlier, System R project was responsible for developing the SQL language. The cost-based query optimization technique was also developed there.

The cost-based query optimization approach is described in the 1979 paper by Selinger et al. Our discussion in this section is based on that paper. This optimization approach involves the following steps:

1. Generate a number of reasonable query execution plans.
2. Estimate the cost of each plan.
3. Execute the least cost plan.

As noted earlier, the cost of a query evaluation plan depends on the size of the basic tables referenced as well as the size of the intermediate results. To obtain reasonable cost estimates of alternative plans, the query optimizer needs estimates of the various intermediate results.

Since we are going to consider only a rough estimate of the cost, we will not consider the storage cost of storing intermediate results and cost of memory usage because the cost of query processing is generally dominated by the cost of disk access which is proportional to the size of intermediate results.

To estimate sizes of the intermediate results, we define the concept of *selectivity factor*.

Definition—Selectivity Factor
The selectivity factor roughly corresponds to the fraction of rows which are expected to satisfy a condition in the WHERE clause.

Selectivity factor is important in computing the cost of selection. A high selectivity means more rows of the table are selected and the cost is higher.

To compute the cost of an operation, the query optimizer first looks up the database catalog to retrieve statistical information about the relations used in the query. For example, we use information like the number of rows in a table, number of distinct values of an attribute, record size of each table and number of blocks occupied by a file on disk. Let us consider tables *R* and *S* with n_R and n_S being the cardinality or the number of rows respectively. Let b_R and b_S be the number of rows per block for the two tables respectively. Also, further, let *d*(*A*, *R*) be the number of distinct values of attribute *A* in table *R*.

Item	Description
n_R	Cardinality of relation *R*
p_R	Number of pages in *R*
b_R	The number of rows of relation *R* per block
f_R	Fraction of data pages in the segment that hold rows of *R*
d_I	Number of distinct keys in index *I*
p_I	Number of pages in index *I*
d(A, R)	Number of distinct values of attribute *A* in table *R*

Figure 8.12 Terminology used in computing the cost of relational operations

We now start by estimating the size and cost of the selection operation followed by a brief discussion on estimating cost of other operations.

8.13.1 Size and Cost of a Selection

For the selection operation, the selectivity factor is the ratio of the number of rows of the result to the cardinality of the base table. Selectivity factor of a selection is estimated by the DBMS by maintaining profiles of attribute value distribution or by making suitable assumptions of the distribution.

As noted earlier, a selection may involve a number of types of conditions in the WHERE clause. The list in Fig. 8.13 gives the most common conditions that were listed earlier.

	Possible conditions in WHERE clauses
1	attribute *A* = value *v*
2	attribute *A* = attribute *B*
3	attribute *A* > value *v*
4	attribute *A* between value *v*1 and value *v*2
5	attribute *A* IN (list of values)
6	Attribute *A* IN subquery
7	WHERE attribute *A* condition *C*1 OR condition *C*2
8	WHERE attribute *A* condition *C*1 AND condition *C*2
9	WHERE *A* IS NOT NULL

Figure 8.13 A list of possible conditions in the WHERE clause

Let us first consider the simplest condition (attribute A = value v) and consider a table R that has the attribute A on which an equality condition has been specified. If we assume that values of attribute A are distributed uniformly, we would expect the result of the first selection above to have approximately $n_R/d(A, R)$ rows where $d(A, R)$, as noted above, is the number of distinct values that attribute A takes in table R and n_R is the cardinality of R. Although the assumption of uniform distribution is almost always unrealistic, the above estimate is easily obtained and is often quite useful.

For other selection conditions, the estimation of size becomes somewhat more complex. For example, in selections like "WHERE attribute A condition $C1$ OR condition $C2$" we would need to estimate how many rows meet the condition $C1$ and how many of those meet condition $C2$.

Figure 8.14 lists selectivity factors for all the possible conditions listed in Fig. 8.13.

	Conditions in WHERE clause	**Selectivity Factors**
1	attribute A = value v	$1/p_I$ if there is an index on A or $1/d(A, R)$ if there is no index, 1/10 if no information
2	attribute A = attribute B	$1/\text{MAX}(p_{IA}, p_{IB})$ if there are indexes on both columns A and B $1/p_{IA}$ if there is only one index, on column A Otherwise 1/10
3	attribute A > value v	(High key value – v)/(High key value – Low key value) Otherwise 1/3
4	attribute A between value $v1$ and value $v2$	($v2$ – $v1$)/(High key value – Low key value) Otherwise 1/4
5	attribute A IN (list of values)	(Number of items in list) × (Selectivity factor for column = Value) Max value = 0.5
6	Attribute A IN subquery	(Expected cardinality of the subquery result)/(Product of the cardinalities of all tables in the subquery FROM clause)
7	WHERE attribute A condition $C1$ OR condition $C2$	$F(C1) + F(C2) - F(C1) \times F(C2)$
8	WHERE attribute A condition $C1$ AND condition $C2$	$F(C1) \times F(C2)$
9	WHERE A IS NOT NULL	$1 - F(\text{NULL})$

Figure 8.14 Selectivity factors for the selection operation

Notes on Fig. 8.14

- It is assumed that attribute values are uniformly distributed.
- $F(C1)$ means selectivity factor for the condition $C1$.
- In 3 above, it is assumed that linear interpolation provides a good estimate. Also the value 1/3 is not significant.
- In 6 above, a number of assumptions have been made about how many values will match values of attribute A.

We now present the cost of single relation queries in Fig. 8.15. These cost factors are derived using the selectivity factors in Fig. 8.14 but often there is more than one access path available and then the cost of each access path may need to be evaluated and the cheapest path is chosen. A number of access methods were discussed in Section 8.10. Here again, we consider a number of different situations. The costs are derived based on the following:

$$\text{Cost} = \text{Cost of page fetches} + W \times (\text{CPU cost})$$

This includes the cost of pages fetched from disk and the cost of CPU utilization which in System R calculations is based on the number of times the CPU interacts with the disk. W is a factor that deals with relative costs of page fetches and CPU utilization. Other symbols have been defined in Fig. 8.12.

Situation	**Cost (in pages)**
Using file scan, equal condition	$P_R/2 + W \times$ (CPU cost)
Using hashing, equal condition	$1 + W$
Unique index, equal condition	$1 + 1 + W$
Clustered index matching one or more Boolean factors	$F(C) \times (p_I + p_R) + W \times$ (CPU cost)
Nonclustered index matching one or two Boolean factors	$F(C) \times (p_I + p_R) + W \times$ (CPU cost)
Clustered index not matching any Boolean factors	$(p_I + p_R) + W \times$ (CPU cost)
Nonclustered index not matching any Boolean factors	$(p_I + p_R) + W \times$ (CPU cost)
Segment scan	$p_R/P + W \times$ (CPU cost)

Figure 8.15 Estimates of the cost of some selection operations

8.13.2 Size and Cost of a Projection

The projection operation removes a number of columns from a table and since the DBMS has information about the domain of each column, the system usually has enough information to estimate the size of the projected table if the result has no duplicates. When duplicates occur, as often is the case, estimation of the size of the projected table is more difficult since sorting may be required before duplicates are removed. One approach is based on the number of different values in each column which can be used to estimate the probability of any two rows; the result being the same.

8.13.3 Size and Cost of a Cartesian Product

Estimating the size of a Cartesian product of two relations R and S is relatively simple since the number of rows in the Cartesian product is $n_R \times n_S$ with number of columns being approximately equal to the sum of the number of columns in R and S. The size of the Cartesian product can thus be estimated by assuming the size of each row to be equal to the sum of the row size of R and row size of S. The size of each row can be found in the catalog.

8.13.4 Size and Cost of a Join

A different selectivity factor may be defined for the join between two relations.

Definition—Join Selectivity Factor
Join selectivity factor is defined as the ratio of the number of rows participating in the join to the total number of rows in the Cartesian product of the relations.

We therefore need to estimate the join selectivity factor for two relations R and S. To obtain this estimate, we consider if the join attribute(s) of the table R is the key of the table. Then the number of rows of the join cannot be bigger than the number of rows of the other table S.

When neither of the join columns are a key, finding the size of the resulting table is more difficult. One approach that is then often used is to make use of the statistics from metadata. For example, information like $D(A, R)$ which is an estimate of the number of different values of the attribute A in table R. If A is the join attribute between tables R and S, we may be able to assume that each value of the join attribute in R also appears in S and given that there are n_S rows in S and there are $d(A, S)$ distinct values of A in S, we can assume uniform distribution and conclude that for each value of A in R there will be $n_S/d(A, S)$ matching rows in S. Therefore, an estimate of the size of the join is $n_R n_S/d(A, S)$. Another estimate would of course be $n_R n_S/ d(A, R)$. Often the two estimates are not identical since the assumption of all rows from one table participating in the join does not apply equally well to both tables. For example, only 80 rows in R might be participating in the join while only 50 are participating from S. We list the join selectivity factors in Fig. 8.16.

Although the cardinality of the join of n tables is the same regardless of the join order, the costs of joining in a different order can be substantially different. If we are dealing with tables $R(A, B)$ and $S(B, C)$, we need to estimate the probability of a row of S matching with a row of R.

Symbol Used	**Condition**	**Join Selectivity Factor**
J_{KS}	Join attribute is key of S	Smaller than $n_R/R \times S$
J_{KR}	Join attribute is key of R	Smaller than $n_S/R \times S$
J_{NK}	Join attribute is not a key of either relation	One estimate is $1/d(A, S)$, another is $1/d(A, R)$

Figure 8.16 Join selectivity factors

In estimating the cost of a join, we need to consider the method used to compute the join. We discussed the cost of some join methods in the last section. For example, in nested scan, the cost of reading both tables many times is quite high. In the case of a sort-merge algorithm, the cost includes the cost of sorting both tables and the cost of joining them both which is approximately equal to the sum of reading each table once. Much better estimates of cost using a variety of assumptions are possible.

Methods	**Cost (in pages)**
Nested scan	$(n_R + n_R\, n_S) + J_{KS} \times (R \times S) + W$ (CPU cost)
Sort-merge	$n_R \log n_R + n_R \log n_R + n_R + n_R + J_{KS} \times (R \times S) + W$ (CPU cost)
Hash-Join	$(n_R + n_S) + J_{KS} \times (R \times S) + W$ (CPU cost)

Figure 8.17 Estimates of cost of computing a join

The following should be noted about the cost formulas in Fig. 8.17.

1. All estimates include the cost of storing the result of the join. We assume that one of the relations is being joined on its primary key. A different join selectivity factor will be required if this is not the case.
2. We have included the factor $W \times$ (CPU cost) although the CPU cost will be different for different methods.
3. We assume a simple hash-join method that involves reading both relations and hashing them. The CPU cost here includes the cost of hashing as well as creating a hash table. There are too many hash join methods to cover them all here.

Given these cost estimates, the cost of processing a query plan may be estimated and the cheapest plan can be selected.

8.14 CORRELATED SUBQUERIES

As noted in Chapter 5, the concept of subquery is important in SQL. In uncorrelated subqueries, the subquery is independent of the outside query and is usually executed only once. Optimization of uncorrelated subqueries is usually straightforward since they can be converted into equivalent queries using joins. A correlated subquery, like that in Fig. 8.18, on the other hand is different, since it contains a correlated reference to one or more columns, called *correlated columns*, of one or more tables in the outside query. These columns' references change and therefore the correlated subquery is usually executed many times.

```
SELECT FName, LName
FROM Player
WHERE EXISTS
        (SELECT *
        FROM Batting
        WHERE PlayerID = PID
        AND MatchID = '2689')
```

Figure 8.18 A simple correlated query

Some correlated queries can in fact be rewritten using a join. For example, Fig. 8.18 presents a correlated query that finds the first and last name of players that batted in ODI Match 2689.

This correlated subquery can be rewritten as in Fig. 8.19.

```
SELECT FName, LName
FROM Player, Batting
WHERE PlayerID = PID
AND MatchID = '2689'
```

Figure 8.19 Rewriting SQL query in Fig. 8.18

This type of query rewriting is called *decorrelation*.

It is important that queries with correlated subqueries be executed efficiently due to the following reason:

1. Correlated queries can be expensive to execute.
2. Many queries are required to be formulated as correlated queries.
3. Increasing applications in decision support systems and OLAP use correlated queries to deal with complex requests.

Correlated queries are therefore posed frequently.

Different types of correlated queries may need different approaches for optimization. There may be just one level of subquery but many queries have more than one level. The subquery may or may not have aggregates in it. The subquery may be linked with the outside query with any of the following operators: IN, NOT IN, EXISTS, NOT EXISTS and comparison operators, for example, > ALL, < ALL, > ANY, < ANY, ≤ ALL, ≥ ALL and so on. The result of the subquery may be null or it may not be. Some of these operators pose special problems, for example, ALL and NOT EXISTS.

The brute force approach of executing correlated queries is called *nested iteration* which involves tuple-at-a-time approach. For each tuple in the outer query, the correlated columns' values are passed on to the subquery and the subquery is executed. The process continues until all the rows of the outer table have been exhausted. For example, in the correlated query in Fig. 8.20, for each row of table *b*1 the subquery is executed and depending on the result of the subquery the row is selected or rejected. If the batting table *b*1 has, say 15,000 rows (given that there have been around 3,000 ODIs so far), the subquery will need to be executed 15,000 times. It could of course be optimized so that the outside query checks for each player only once but nested iteration is likely to be expensive for any correlated query that has many rows in the outside query table and the subquery involves table scans, joins or aggregate functions.

```
SELECT PID AS PlayerID
FROM Batting b1
WHERE NOT EXISTS
        (SELECT *
        FROM Batting b2
        WHERE b. PID = b2.PID
        AND NRuns < 31)
```

Figure 8.20 A correlated query

To overcome the problem of high cost of nested iteration when the outer query has many rows, query decorrelation involving rewriting the correlated query can be used. Decorrelation essentially removes outer query references to the subquery. Although query decorrelation does not always work, it can be an effective technique for many types of correlated subqueries.

A number of techniques for decorrelation have been proposed. In one approach, all the distinct values from the outer query are extracted and all the possible results from the subquery are materialized. These results can then be joined with the table in the outer query using the results obtained from the subquery. As we have seen earlier this approach does not always work. For example, for the query in Fig. 8.20 we find all the distinct values from the outer query, which are all the *Player IDs* and find all the players that have *NScore* < 31 but the condition outside the subquery NOT EXISTS creates difficulty in making this approach work.

There is considerable research carried out in this area but more details of this topic are outside the scope of this textbook.

8.15 SEMANTIC QUERY OPTIMIZATION

So far the query optimization techniques we have presented have not considered the semantics of the query that is being optimized. All techniques have essentially involved translation of relational operators using their properties and then comparing a variety of their implementation alternatives. Therefore, these query optimization techniques may be called *syntactic query optimization*. Although semantic query optimization is currently not being used in relational databases, it has been claimed that many queries can be processed much more efficiently if the semantics of the queries in addition to the syntax were considered.

We now define semantic query optimization.

Definition—Semantic Query Optimization
Semantic query optimization is the process of using the semantic information available in the query and its database to transform the original query into one which is more efficient and semantically equivalent.

A query is semantically equivalent to an original query if they both produce exactly the same result for the same database at a given state of the database. Semantic query optimization is often based on the use of integrity constraints and other rules about the database to optimize queries.

Semantic query optimization is not being used by the current DBMS because semantic query optimization is expected to be more time consuming than the current query optimization techniques that appear to work satisfactorily. Furthermore, it is often assumed that semantic query optimization is more suitable for deductive database systems and object oriented systems. With the continuing improvement in computer hardware, semantic query optimization could well become useful for relational database systems.

SUMMARY

Query processing is perhaps the most complex component of a DBMS. In this chapter we have discussed various aspects of query processing including:

- There are similarities between query processing and compilation in procedural languages. The similarities include both of them requiring parsing and code generation.
- Query processing has a number of steps which include parsing, optimization, code generation and execution.
- Importance of query optimization has been illustrated by showing an example of a query that may be processed in a number of ways which involve very different costs.
- Database catalog plays an important role in query optimization since it includes a variety of information about the database including information about each table.
- Query parsing deals with query correctness and validation and converts the query to an internal representations as a query tree.
- A number of logical transformations may be used for transforming a query.
- A number of heuristic optimization techniques based on rules of relational algebra have been described. These include rules like join, and products are commutative as well as associative.
- Simple rules of thumb for query optimization have been presented. These include moving selections and projects as far down the query tree as possible.
- Rules governing the manipulation of relational algebra expressions are presented. These include join, products and selection operations being commutative.
- Rules to transform a query tree to obtain a more efficient plan have been presented. These include the rules of thumb.

- Access paths also have a significant influence on the cost of executing a query.
- A number of algorithms for computing relational algebra operations have been presented. These include nested-scan, sort-merge and hash-based algorithms for computing joins.
- Estimating the cost of a query plan is nontrivial including estimating the cost of each operation using information in the database catalog. The information used includes the number of distinct values of an attribute, cardinality of a table, size of an index and so on. Selectivity factors are then computed.
- Correlated queries are those that have subqueries that include correlated reference to one or more columns from an outer query and the subquery is executed many times. Such queries are usually expensive to execute.
- Some correlated queries may be decorrelated by transforming the query into one that uses a join.
- The semantics of a query is not normally considered by the query processor. The concept of a different approach of query processing called semantic query optimization is briefly described.

REVIEW QUESTIONS

1. Explain how query processing is similar to compilation in procedural languages and how it is different. (Section 8.1)
2. What is the importance of query optimization? What is its objective? (Section 8.2)
3. Describe the different steps of query processing. Are these the same as steps of a procedural language compiler? Explain (Section 8.3)
4. What is metadata and catalog? How is it stored in a database? What is it used for? (Section 8.4)
5. Explain how query parsing is carried out in a DBMS. (Section 8.5)
6. What logical transformations may be used for transformation of a query? (Section 8.6.2)
7. What rules govern the manipulation of relational algebra expressions. (Section 8.6.3)
8. List five simple rules of thumb of query optimization. (Section 8.6.4)
9. How are different access paths used in query optimization? (Section 8.7)
10. How is the query code generated? (Section 8.8)
11. Describe algorithms for computing a selection and a projection. What if an index has been created on the relation? (Section 8.10)
12. Explain two different algorithms for computing the join of two tables. (Section 8.11)
13. Explain the nested scan method of computing a natural join. How expensive will it be if the number of rows in the two relations are m and n respectively? (Section 8.11.1)
14. Explain the sort-merge method of computing a natural join. How expensive will it be if the number of rows in the two relations are m and n respectively? (Section 8.11.3)
15. Explain the idea behind the hash-join method. How expensive will it be if the number of rows in the two relations are m and n respectively? (Section 8.11.4)
16. Compare the different algorithms for computing a join. (Section 8.11.6)
17. Describe an algorithm for computing the aggregation functions in a query. (Section 8.12)
18. Describe the basic approach used in cost-based query optimization used in System R. (Section 8.13)
19. How may one estimate the size and cost of the various relational algebra operation? (Section 8.13.1)

20. What is selectivity factor and the join selectivity factor? (Section 8.13)
21. What is the nested iteration for executing a correlated query? Why is it not considered an efficient algorithm? (Section 8.14)
22. What is the main idea behind decorrelation? Why is it useful? Does it work for all types of correlated queries? (Section 8.14)
23. Give an example to explain the benefits of semantic query optimization. (Section 8.15)
24. Why is semantic query optimization not used in most current DBMS? (Section 8.15)

SHORT ANSWER QUESTIONS

1. Why is query optimization important for databases?
2. Give an example of metadata outside the field of database?
3. Which operators are commutative?
4. What are the different steps of query processing?
5. Name two methods used for computing a join?
6. Describe how the operation selection is computed.
7. Describe how the operation projection is computed.
8. Given a query-tree, show how the query plan is optimized using various rules presented in heuristic query optimization.
9. What is nested scan method for computing the natural join of two relations?
10. Explain how the aggregate operations COUNT and AVERAGE are computed for a relation.
11. What is selectivity factor?
12. How is the size of a selection estimated?
13. How is the size of a projection estimated?
14. How is the cost of a join computed?
15. Give an example of how the cost of a selection may be estimated. What information is required in estimating the cost?
16. What is decorrelation? Can a query processor carry out decorrelation?
17. What is semantic query optimization?

MULTIPLE CHOICE QUESTIONS

1. Which of the following are issues in query processing?
   (a) How does a DBMS process a query?
   (b) Does the formulation of the query determine the query processing plan?
   (c) Is it possible to recognize different semantically equivalent queries?
   (d) What is the most efficient plan to process the above query?
   (e) All of the above

2. Which of the following is **not** a step in query processing?
   (a) Parsing and validating
   (b) Compiling
   (c) Optimization
   (d) Code generation
3. Which of the following are true?
   (a) Metadata is data about data.
   (b) Metadata includes statistics about each table.
   (c) Metadata has statistics about each view.
   (d) Metadata has information about ownership of tables, views, indexes.
   (e) All of the above
4. Which one of the following is correct?
   (a) The main role of the parser is to check the query for correct syntax.
   (b) The parser resolves names and references.
   (c) The parser translates the query into a parse-tree.
   (d) The parser may also check if the user is authorized to execute the query.
   (e) All of the above are correct.
5. Which one of the following is **not** correct?
   (a) The parser passes the parse-tree to the optimizer.
   (b) The optimizer checks the existence of all objects in the query.
   (c) The optimizer then optimizes the query processing.
   (d) The optimizer formulates a number of query processing plans.
6. Which one of the following is **not** correct regarding rules of thumb?
   (a) Use optimal ordering of joins.
   (b) Use optimal ordering of selections.
   (c) Cascade selections and projections.
   (d) Merge projections of projects into one projection.
7. Which one of the following is correct?
   (a) Selections and projects may not be commuted.
   (b) Selections and Cartesian products may not be commuted.
   (c) Selections and union may be commuted.
   (d) Projection with union may not be commuted.
8. Which one of the following is the most inefficient for computing a selection?
   (a) File scan
   (b) Using an index
   (c) Using hashing
   (d) Secondary index
9. Which one of the following is the most inefficient method for computing a join?
   (a) Sort-merge
   (b) Hashing
   (c) Using indexes
   (d) Nested scan
10. Which one of the following is correct?
   (a) The selectivity factor roughly corresponds to the fraction of rows which are expected to satisfy a condition in the WHERE clause.
   (b) Selectivity factor for WHERE attribute $A = v$ may be assumed to be one-tenth if there is no index.
   (c) Selectivity factor for WHERE attribute $A > v$ is usually 1/4.
   (d) Selectivity factor for WHERE attribute A condition $C1$ AND condition $C2$ is $F(C1) + F(C2)$ where $F(C)$ is the selectivity factor for condition C.

11. In estimating a query plan's cost a number of assumptions are made. Which one of the following assumption is correct?
    (a) Attribute values are not uniformly distributed.
    (b) Linear interpolation does not provide a good estimate.
    (c) The cost estimate of a selection is based on the cost of pages fetched from the disk and the cost of CPU utilization.
    (d) Some selectivity factors may be assumed to be 1/2.
12. Which one of the following is correct?
    (a) The cost estimate of a selection is COST = W*Cost of page fetches + CPU cost, where W is a factor that deals with relative cost of page fetch and CPU cost.
    (b) Cost of a projection using hashing is $1 + W$.
    (c) Cost of a join using an index is $1 + 1 + W$.
    (d) Cost of using a file scan for equality condition is $P_R/2 + W$ * (CPU cost).
13. Which one of the following is correct?
    (a) Join selectivity factor is defined as the ratio of the number of rows participating in the join to the total number of rows in the Cartesian product of the relations.
    (b) The cost estimate of nested scan join is $(n_R + n_R\, n_S)$.
    (c) The cost estimate of sort-merge join is $n_R \log n_R + n_R \log n_R$.
    (d) The cost estimate of hash join is $(n_R + n_S)$.
14. Which of the following are correct?
    (a) Denormalization is the intentional duplication of information in the database tables leading to increased data redundancy but improving query processing performance by reducing the number of joins.
    (b) Denormalization does not have any impact on integrity.
    (c) Semantic query optimization is the process of using the semantic information available in the query and its database to transform the original query into one which is more efficient and semantically equivalent.
    (d) All of the above are correct.
15. Which one of the following is the *most accurate* description of query optimization?
    (a) Query optimization involves finding the exact optimum plan that minimizes the query processing cost.
    (b) Query optimization involves heuristic selection of a strategy to efficiently process a given query.
    (c) Query optimization involves minimizing the disk I/O cost of the given query.
    (d) Query optimization involves minimizing the CPU cost of the given query.
16. A table R has 1,000 rows while a table S has 10,000 rows. What is the best upper bound on the number of rows in the join of R and S if the equi-join attribute in S is its primary key.
    (a) 1000 (b) 10,000 (c) 1,000,000 (d) 10,000,000
    (e) None of the above
17. A table R has 1,000 rows while a table S has 10,000 rows and let the size of a block be such that only 10 rows of R or S fit in a block. The nested-scan method of joining the two tables is used and there are

no indexes and the main memory is too small to fit even *R*. What is the approximate cost of the join in terms of number of blocks read?

(a) 1,000,000 blocks (b) 100,000 blocks
(c) 10,000 blocks (d) 1,000 blocks
(e) None of the above

18. In the above question, instead of nestedscan, the sort-merge method is used and the tables are not sorted, and there are no indexes, and the main memory is too small to fit even *R*. Assume $\log_2(1{,}000) = 10$ and $\log_2(10{,}000) = 13$. What is the approximate cost of the join in terms of number of blocks read?
    (a) 500,000 blocks (b) 50,000 blocks
    (c) 20,000 blocks (d) 5,000 blocks
19. Which one of the following rules is **not** true?
    (a) Selections and joins are commutative.
    (b) Difference and intersection are commutative.
    (c) Selections and projections may be commuted.
    (d) Projections and joins may be commuted.
    (e) Selections and joins may be commuted.
20. Which of the following rules of heuristic query optimization are correct?
    (a) Carry out selections as early as possible.
    (b) Carry out projections as early as possible.
    (c) Carry out sorting as early as possible.
    (d) Carry out unions as early as possible.
21. When estimating the size of the result of applying a relational operator, which one of the following is correct?
    (a) The size of the result of applying a selection on a table *R* is $n_R/D(A, R)$, where $D(A, R)$ is the number of distinct values that appear in the table *R* for attribute *A*
    (b) The cardinality of a projection of *R* is the same as the cardinality of *R*
    (c) The cardinality of a join of *R* and *S* is $m \times n$ where *m* and *n* are the cardinalities of the two tables
    (d) The cardinality of a join of *R* and *S* cannot be greater than the cardinality of *R* or *S*, whichever is greater
22. Which of the following information is **not** stored in the database catalog?
    (a) The number of rows of each table. (b) The number of pages in each table.
    (c) The number of distinct keys in each index. (d) The number of pages in each index.
23. Consider the following query which retrieves *Match IDs* of all ODI matches played in Colombo in which Suresh Raina batted.

```
SELECT MatchID
FROM Player, Batting, Match
WHERE Player.PlayerID = Batting.PID
AND Match.MatchID = Batting.MatchID
AND Match.Ground = 'Colombo'
AND Player.Lname = 'Raina'
```

The query processor may process the above query in one of several different ways. Which of the following is the best way to process the query?

(a) Join the tables *Player* and *Batting*, then join the result with *Match* and then do the selections followed by the projection.

(b) Join the tables *Player* and *Batting*, do the selections, join the result with *Match* and the carry out the projection.

(c) Do the selections first, then join the tables *Player* and *Batting*, then join the result with *Match* and finally do the projection.

(d) Do the selections, then some projections followed by the joins and then the final projection.

EXERCISES

1. Let tables *R* and *S* have 20,000 and 45,000 rows respectively. 25 rows of *R* and 30 rows of *S* fit on one disk block. Estimate the number of block accesses required for computing the join of *R* and *S* using the nested scan and the sort-merge methods.
2. Discuss briefly how the cost of processing a query that involves a selection, a projection and a join may be estimated.
3. Show that join, union, and intersection are commutative and difference is not.
4. Show that join, union, and intersection are associative and difference is not.
5. Show that the equation $(R - S)[p] = R[p] - S[p]$ is not valid in general.
6. Consider three tables $R1(A, B, C)$, $R2(C, D, E)$ and $R3(E, F)$ with A, C and E being the primary keys in the three tables respectively. Assume that the cardinality of the three tables is 1000, 1500 and 750 respectively. Estimate the size of the join of the three tables.
7. Consider three tables $R1(A, B, C)$, $R2(C, \text{D}, E)$ and $R3(E, F)$ with all of the attributes together in each table being the only primary key. Let the number of different values of C in $R1$ be 900, number of different values of C in $R2$ be 1100, number of different values of E in $R2$ be 50 and the number of different values of E in $R3$ be 100. Assume that the number of rows in each of the three tables is 1000, 1500 and 750 respectively. Estimate the size of the join of the three tables. What is an efficient strategy to compute the join?
8. Let there be the following tables used in a query:

$R1\ (A, B)$	$R2\ (B, C, D)$	
$R3\ (D, E)$	$R4\ (B, F, G)$	
$R5\ (F, H, I)$	$R6\ (I, K)$	$R7\ (H, J)$

The query involves taking a join of all seven tables on common attributes and then taking a projection that retrieves attributes (A, E, J, K). Construct a query-tree for the above query. Show how the query-tree may be transformed to process the query efficiently.

9. What is meant by heuristic optimization? Discuss the main heuristics that may be applied during query optimization.
10. Discuss the different algorithms for implementing the selection operation given that the selection condition may vary from equality to a specification of a range.

11. Discuss the nested scan, sort-merge, and hashing algorithms for computing the join of two tables.
12. Let R and S be two tables. Let n_R and n_S be the number of rows in R and S. Also assume that b_R and b_S are the number of rows of R and S respectively that fit on a block and the main memory has m blocks. How many block accesses are required for computing the Cartesian product of R and S.?
13. Show that the equation

$$\pi_p(R - S) = \pi_p(R) - \pi_p(S)$$

is not valid in general.
14. Consider the query:

$$\sigma_{A=d}(AB) \bowtie BC$$

Present an example of tables (AB) and (BC) where computing the join first would be desirable.
15. Let there be the following tables used in a query:

R_1 (A, B)	R_2 (B, C, D)
R_3 (D, E)	R_4 (B, F, G)

Consider the following query (the syntax of the query is not important):

```
SELECT B, E, G
FROM R1, R2, R3, R4
WHERE R1 .B = R2 .B
AND R2 .B = R4 .B
AND R2. D = R3 .D
AND A = 42
AND G = 97
```

Construct a query-tree for the above query. Show how the query-tree may be transformed to process the query efficiently.
16. Consider the queries used in Chapter 5. List all the queries that would benefit if the relations in the cricket database were denormalized. What denormalization do you recommend? List any problems that might arise due to the denormalization recommended.
17. Select two queries from Chapter 5 that involve correlated subqueries. How would you decorrelate them? Check that the correlation is correct and estimate how much faster each of the decorrelated query executes.

PROJECTS

1. Compare the algorithms for computing a join as far as efficiency is concerned. Implement nested-scan and sort-merge algorithms and compare their performance by running the programs on some simple database with each table having say 100 rows or more.
2. Choose a correlated query from Chapter 5. Carry out decorrelation if possible. Compare the performance of the original query with that of the decorrelated query for a large database.

LAB EXERCISE

1. Consider the following 13 tables that we obtained by mapping an E-R diagram to the relational model in Chapter 3. The E-R diagram is given in Chapter 3.
   - User (FName, LName, Login_Name, Address)
   - Program (PName, Code, Date, Version, Extension, Description, Language)
   - Programmer (Login, Code, FName, LName, Address)
   - DBMS (DB_name)
   - Relation (RName, PKey)
   - Attribute (RName, Attname)
   - Written_by (PName, Login)
   - Interact_with (PName, DB_name)
   - Administer (Login, DB_name)
   - Use (Login_name, PName)
   - Call (PName, PName)
   - Has (DB_name, Relation, RName, PKey)
   - Comprises_of (RName, Attname)

   (a) List 10 queries for this database.
   (b) Draw query trees for them and explain how the queries may be processed efficiently.
   (c) Estimate the cost of some of the queries that you have given above. Make suitable assumptions about the cardinality of each table in the query and how many rows may be accommodated in a disk block.
   (c) If a query you have formulated includes more than two joins, determine which sequence of joins is the best and why?

BIBLIOGRAPHY

For Students

Most database books include a chapter on query evaluation.

For Instructors

A number of references in the list below provide detailed discussion of query evaluation. The paper by Selinger et al., is one of the first significant papers dealing with query optimization. The paper by Yao, the survey by Graefe and the papers by Surajit Chaudhuri are worth consulting. Some chapters in the book by Lightstone, Teorey, and Nadeau are useful.

Blasgen, M., and K. Eswaran, "Storage Access in Relational Databases", *IBM Systems Journal,* Vol. 16, No. 4, pp 363-378.

Chaudhuri, S., "Query Optimizers: Time to Rethink the Contract?", *ACM SIGMOD International Conference on Management of Data*, 2009, pp 961-968.

Chaudhuri, S., "An Overview of Query Optimization in Relational Databases", *ACM Symposium on Principles of Database Systems (PODS)*, 1998, pp 34-43.

Gotlieb, L.R., "Computing Joins of Relations", *ACM-SIGMOD*, 1975, pp 55-63.

Graefe, G., "Query Evaluation Techniques for Large Databases", *ACM Computing Surveys*, Vol. 25, No. 2, June 1993, pp 73-170.

Graefe, G., "Implementing Sorting in Database Systems", *ACM Computing Surveys*, Vol. 38, No. 3, September 2006, Article No. 10.

Jarke, M., and J. Koch, "Query Optimization in Database Systems", *ACM Computing Surveys*, Vol. 16, No. 2, 1984, pp 111-152.

Kim, W., "On Optimization an SQL-like Nested Query", *ACM Transactions on Database Systems*, Vol. 7, No. 3, 1982, pp 443-469.

Kim, W., J. Garza, and D. Batory (Ed.), *Query Processing in Database Systems*, Springer-Verlag, 1981.

Lightstone, S., T. Teorey, and T. Nadeau, *Physical Database Design: The Database Professional's Guide to Exploiting Indexes, Views, Storage, and More,* Morgan Kaufmann/Elsevier, 2007.

Misra, P., and M. H. Eich, "Join Processing in Relational Databases", *ACM Computing Surveys*, Vol. 24, Issue 1, 1992, pp 63-113.

Sanders, G. L., and S. Shin, "Denormalization Effects on Performance of RDBMS", *Proc. 34th International Conference on System Sciences*, 2001.

Selinger, P. G., M. M. Astrahan, D. D. Chamberlin, R. A. Lorie, and T. G. Price, "Access Path Selection in a Relational Database Management System", *Proceedings of the 1979 ACM SIGMOD Conference on Management of Data, ACM-SIGMOD Record*, 1979, pp 23-34.

Yao, S. B., "Optimization of Query Evaluation Algorithms", *ACM Transactions of Database Systems*, Vol. 4, No. 2, June 1979, pp 133-155.

Patricia Selinger—Pioneer of Query Processing Methods

Patricia Selinger was a leading member of the IBM Research team that produced the System R, the world's first relational database system. System R established the basic architecture for the highly successful DB2 DBMS. Selinger's innovative work on cost-based query optimization for relational databases has now been used by nearly all relational database systems and is taught in virtually every university's database management course. Dr. Selinger ran the IBM Almaden Research Computer Science Department and then established and managed the Database Technology Institute whose mission is to accelerate technology into IBM's database products.

Pat Selinger is the Vice President of Information Management Architecture and Technology. Currently, she is responsible for establishing and coordinating research in information management, unstructured information and user interface technology areas. In 1994, she received the title of IBM Fellow for her exceptional technical work and leadership in relational databases. She was elected to the National Academy of Engineering in 1999.

Transaction Management and Concurrency 9

OBJECTIVES

- Explain the concept of a transaction.
- Describe the four properties of DBMS transactions.
- Explain why concurrency is important.
- Discuss when concurrent execution of two transactions leads to conflict.
- Give examples of concurrency anomalies.
- Explain the concept of a schedule.
- Study the concepts of serializability, final state serializability (FSR), view serializability (VSR) and conflict serializability (CSR).
- Discuss how to test for CSR.
- Describe how serializability can be enforced using locking and timestamping.
- Discuss the concept of deadlocks, their prevention and resolution.
- Explain the concept of lock granularity, multiple granularity.
- Describe use of intention locking in multiple granularity.
- Describe timestamping concurrency control.
- Describe the optimistic concurrency control.
- Briefly look at evaluation of concurrency control techniques.

KEYWORDS

Concurrency, transactions, ACID, atomicity, consistency, isolation, durability, concurrency anomalies, lost update, inconsistent retrievals, schedule, serial schedule, serializability, final state serializability FSR, view serializability VSR, conflict serializability, CSR, testing for CSR, precedence graphs, recoverability, hierarchy of serializability, 2PL, locking, timestamping, deadlocks, prevention, resolution, detection, wait-for graph, granularity, fine granularity, coarse granularity, multiple granularity locking, intention locking, intention shared (IS), intention exclusive (IX), recoverability, optimistic concurrency control, evaluation.

A moment comes, which comes but rarely in history, when we step out from the old to the new; when an age ends; and when the soul of a nation long suppressed finds utterance.

Jawaharlal Nehru (on the independence of India, 15 August 1947)

9.1 INTRODUCTION

Most modern database systems, except personal databases, are multi-user systems. Some large systems support thousands of users. Multiple users are able to use a single system simultaneously because of multiprogramming in which the processor (or processors) in the system is shared amongst a number of users trying to access computer resources (including databases) simultaneously. The concurrent execution of programs is therefore interleaved, with each program being allowed access to the CPU at regular intervals. This also enables a program to access the CPU while another program is doing input/output. In this chapter, we first discuss the concept of a transaction which may be defined as execution of a user program in a database. Since many users are using a multiuser system concurrently, the transactions must be managed so that they do not interfere with each other. In this chapter we discuss the problem of synchronization of access to shared objects in a database while supporting a high degree of concurrency.

Concurrency control in a database system permits many users, assumed to be interactive, to access a database in a multiprogrammed environment while preserving the illusion that each user has sole access to the system. Control is needed to coordinate concurrent accesses to a DBMS so that the overall correctness of the database is maintained. Efficiency is also important since the response time for interactive users ought to be short. The reader may have recognized that the concurrency problems in database management systems are related to the concurrency problems in operating systems although there are significant differences between the two.

Clearly no problem would arise if all users were accessing the database only to retrieve information and no one was modifying it as, for example, when accessing census data or a library catalogue. If one or more users are modifying the database, for example, a bank account or airline reservations, an update performed by one user may interfere with an update or retrieval by another. For example, users A and B both may wish to read and update the same record in the database around the same time. The relative timing of the two transactions may have an impact on the state of the database at the end of the transactions. The end result can be an inconsistent database.

Our discussion of concurrency will be transaction based. A transaction T is a sequence of actions $[t_1, t_2, \ldots t_n]$. A transaction is assumed to be a logical unit of work and a unit of consistency as it preserves database consistency. Transaction processing database systems are now ubiquitous. For example, they include e-commerce, billing systems like telecommunications accounting, payroll, airline and hotel reservations, banking and electronic stock market transactions, to name a few.

This chapter is organized as follows. The concept of a transaction is defined followed by a discussion of the properties of a transaction and the importance of concurrency control. Examples of concurrency anomalies, lost updates, inconsistent retrieval, and uncommitted dependency, are described in Section 9.3. Sections 9.4 and 9.5 present the major concepts of concurrency control. Section 9.6 defines serializability and deals with techniques of concurrency control by enforcing serializability. Section 9.7 deals with hierarchy of serializable schedules. Section 9.8 describes concurrency control and enforcing serializability including the concepts of locking and two-phase locking (2PL). Definition of deadlocks, their detection, prevention and resolution are discussed in Section 9.9. Section 9.10 explains lock granularity while Section 9.11 explains multiple granularity and intention locking. Sections 9.12 and 9.13 describe nonlocking techniques of concurrency control. Section 9.12 deals with timestamping control and Section 9.13 with optimistic control. The chapter concludes with a brief look at transaction support in SQL in Section 9.14 and evaluation of concurrency control techniques in Section 9.15.

9.2 THE CONCEPT OF A TRANSACTION

We first need to define the concept of a *transaction.*

Definition—Transaction
A transaction is defined as a logical unit of work which involves a sequence of steps but which normally will be considered by the user as one action and which preserves consistency of the database.

For example, transferring an employee from department *A* to department *B* may involve updating several tables in a database but would be considered a single transaction. Transactions are straight-line programs devoid of control structures. The sequence of steps in a transaction may lead to an inconsistent database temporarily but at the end of the transaction, the database is expected to be in a consistent state. It is assumed that a transaction always carries out correct manipulations of the database.

The concept of a transaction is important since the user considers it as one unit and assumes that a transaction will be executed in isolation from all other transactions running concurrently that might interfere with the transaction. We must therefore require that actions within a transaction be carried out in a prespecified serial order and in full, and if all the actions do not complete successfully for some reason then the partial effects must be undone. A transaction that successfully completes all the actions is said to *commit.* It otherwise aborts and must be *rolled back.* For example, when a transaction involves transferring an employee from department *A* to department *B*, it would be unacceptable if the result of a failed transaction was that the employee was deleted from Department *A* but not added to Department *B*.

We summarize the ACID properties of a transaction now.

9.2.1 Atomicity

As noted above, although a transaction is conceptually atomic, it usually consists of a number of steps. It is necessary to make sure that the outside world and other transactions do not see partial results of a transaction execution and therefore either all actions of a transaction are completed without any errors or the transaction is abnormally terminated and has no effect on the database. Therefore, a transaction is either completed successfully and commits or is rolled back as if it had never been invoked. This is sometimes called *all-or-nothing.* In the section on recovery we will discuss how to recover from a crash while transactions are being executed.

9.2.2 Consistency

Although a database may become inconsistent during the execution of a transaction, it is assumed that a completed transaction preserves the consistency of the database. This consistency preservation cannot be completely automatic[1] and often requires the application program running the transaction to carry out a variety of checks which ensure that database consistency is preserved. For example, when a user carries out a bank transaction, it is assumed that the consistency of the bank accounts is not violated. When a transaction is run on an ATM, strange incidents can happen. For example, the power might go off after the card is returned but before the cash is dispensed. The transaction must maintain consistency in such unusual situations. Further, we will discuss how to recover from such database crashes while one or more transactions are being executed. Any transaction that does not pass the checks of the application program is abnormally terminated. Whether a transaction completes or is terminated, the consistency of the database is thus ensured.

9.2.3 Isolation

As noted earlier, no other transactions should be able to view any partial result of the actions of a transaction since intermediate states may violate consistency. It is essential that other transactions only view results of committed transactions. Also, no transaction should interfere with the actions of another transaction. Each transaction must be executed as if it was the only transaction being carried out and the user should feel as if all transactions are being carried out one after another. This requirement ensures that the detail of concurrency are hidden from the application developers making their task of writing application programs easier.

9.2.4 Durability

A transaction that is for some reason interrupted in the middle of its execution must be aborted so that the database is left consistent. Also, once a transaction has been completed successfully and has committed, its effects must persist and a transaction must complete before its effects can be made permanent. The results of a committed transaction are durable. A committed transaction cannot be aborted and its effects cannot be undone by a subsequent software or hardware failure. Also a committed transaction may have seen the effects of other transactions but we assume those transactions had committed before the present transaction saw the effects.

The result of all transactions following the ACID properties is that the users can rely on the consistency of the data they see whether the database is a centralized system or a distributed system. Furthermore, as noted above, these properties make it easier for application developers to develop applications. These ACID properties represent the first letters of the four properties above. A summary of these properties in presented in Fig. 9.1.

When an application program specifies a transaction we assume that it is specified in the format given in Fig. 9.2.

---

1. Some tasks of checking consistency can be automatically carried out by the DBMS since the DBMS will check a variety of constraints that are declared for the database including those declared in triggers. We discussed integrity constraints in Chapter 3 and 5 and will discuss them in more detail in Chapter 13.

	Property	What is it?
A	Atomicity	All or nothing.
C	Consistency	Each transaction leaves the database consistent; otherwise rolled back.
I	Isolation	Each transaction is executed as if it was the only one running.
D	Durability	A committed transaction cannot be aborted and its effects cannot be undone.

Figure 9.1 A summary of the ACID properties of transactions

All the actions between the Begin and Commit are now considered part of a single transaction. If any of these actions fail, all the actions carried out before the failure must be undone. We assume that transactions are not nested.

Begin Transaction (details of the transaction) Commit

Figure 9.2 Format of a DBMS transaction

We will use the classical example of a bank account transfer transaction to illustrate some of the concepts used in transaction management. The transaction is given in Fig. 9.3.

Begin Transaction Transfer Rs. 100 from account *A* to account *B* Commit

Figure 9.3 An example of a transaction

It is clear that there needs to be a transfer program in the system that will execute the transaction. The steps given in Fig. 9.4 are involved in carrying out the transaction.

Step	Action
1	Read account *A* from disk
2	If balance is less then Rs. 100, return with an appropriate message
3	Subtract Rs. 100 from balance of account *A*
4	Write account *A* back to disk
5	Read account *B* from disk
6	Add Rs. 100 to balance of account *B*
7	Write account *B* back to disk

Figure 9.4 Actions of an example transaction

We have ignored several small details. For example, the steps in Fig. 9.4 do not check if accounts *A* and *B* exist. Also it has been assumed that the application program has the authority to access the accounts and transfer the money.

In the above algorithm, a system failure at step 5 or step 6 would leave the database in an inconsistent state since both would result in Rs. 100 being subtracted from account *A* and not added to account *B*. A recovery from such failure would normally involve the incomplete transaction being rolled back.

We assume that all transactions complete successfully and any problem of transaction failures are resolved by the recovery mechanisms discussed in Chapter 9. The only detail of transactions that is of interest right now is the reads and writes although other computations would often be carried out between the reads and writes. We therefore assume that all actions t_i that form a transaction are either a read or a write. The set of items read by a transaction are called its *read set* and the set of items written by it are called its *write set*. Two transactions T_i and T_j are said to *conflict* if some action t_i of T_i and some action t_j of T_j access the same object and at least one of the actions is a write. Two situations are possible as presented in Fig. 9.5.

1.	The write set of one transaction intersects with the read set of another. The result of running the two transactions concurrently will clearly depend on whether the write is done first or the read. The conflict is called a *RW Conflict*.
2.	The write set of one transaction intersects with the write set of another. Again, the result of running the two transactions concurrently will depend on the order of the two writes. The conflict is called a *WW Conflict*.

Figure 9.5 Two conflict situations

A concurrency control mechanism must detect such conflicts and control them. Various concurrency control mechanisms are available. The mechanisms differ in the way they detect the conflict and the way they resolve it. We will consider concurrency control algorithms later in this chapter. First we discuss some examples of concurrency anomalies to highlight the need for concurrency control.

We have noted already that in the discussion that follows we will ignore many details of a transaction. For example, we will not be concerned with any computation other than the reads and the writes and whether the results of a read are being stored in a local variable or not.

We now discuss concurrency anomalies.

9.3 EXAMPLES OF CONCURRENCY ANOMALIES

There are three classical concurrency anomalies. These are lost updates, inconsistent retrievals and uncommitted dependency.

9.3.1 Lost Updates

Consider an example of two transactions *A* and *B* which simultaneously access an airline database wishing to reserve a number of seats on a flight. Let us assume that transaction *A* wishes to reserve five seats while transaction *B* wishes to reserve four seats. The reservation of seats involves booking the seats and then updating the number of seats available (*N*) on the flight. The two users read-in the present number of seats, store it in their local storage, and modify their local copy and write back resulting in the situation presented in Fig. 9.6.

Every row in Fig. 9.6 represents one time instance and one action of one of the transactions. We move down in time as we go down in the figure with time = 1 being the earliest time and time = 6 being the latest. No two actions of the two transactions are carried out at the same time. Also, we assume that these two transactions execute in isolation from all other transactions that might be running at the same time.

Transaction *A*	Time	Transaction *B*
Read *N*	1	–
–	2	Read *N*
$N := N - 5$	3	–
–	4	$N := N - 4$
Write *N*	5	–
–	6	Write *N*

Figure 9.6 An example of lost update anomaly

If the execution of the two transactions were to take place as shown in Fig. 9.6, the update by transaction *A* is lost although both users read the number of seats, get the bookings confirmed and write the updated number back to the database. This is called the *lost update anomaly,* since the effects of one of the transactions were permanently lost.

9.3.2 Inconsistent Retrievals

Consider another example of two transactions *A* and *B* accessing a department database simultaneously. Transaction *A* is updating the database to give all employees in the department a 3% raise in their salary while transaction *B* is computing the total salary bill of the department as shown in Fig. 9.7. The two transactions interfere since the total salary bill changes as the transaction *A* updates the employee records. The total salary retrieved by transaction *B* may be a sum of some salaries before the raise and others after the raise. This could not be considered an acceptable value of the total salary but the value before the raise or the value after the raise is acceptable.

Transaction *A*	Time	Transaction *B*
Read employee 100	1	–
–	2	Sum = 0.0
Update salary	3	–
–	4	Read employee 100
Write employee 100	5	–
–	6	Sum = sum + salary
Read employee 101	7	–
Update salary	8	–
Write employee 101	9	–
–	10	Read employee 101
–	11	Sum = sum + salary
etc.	–	etc.

Figure 9.7 An example of inconsistent retrieval

The problem illustrated in Fig. 9.7 is called the *inconsistent retrieval anomaly*. During the execution of a transaction, therefore, changes made by another transaction that has not yet committed should not be visible since that data may not be consistent.

9.3.3 Uncommitted Dependency

Consider an example of two transactions *A* and *B* running on the system as shown in Fig. 9.8.

Transaction *A*	Time	Transaction *B*
–	1	Read *Q*
–	2	Update *Q*
–	3	Write *Q*
Read *Q*	4	–
–	5	Read *R*
Update *Q*	6	–
Write *Q*	7	–
–	8	Failure (rollback)
–	9	–

Figure 9.8 An example of uncommitted dependency

Transaction *A* has read the value of *Q* that was updated by transaction *B* but was never committed. The result of transaction *A* writing *Q* therefore will lead to an inconsistent state of the database. Also if transaction *A* does not write *Q* but only reads it, it would be using a value of *Q* which never really existed. Yet another situation would occur if the rollback happened after *Q* was written by transaction *A*. The rollback would restore the old value of *Q* and therefore lead to the loss of updated *Q* by transaction *A*. This is called the *uncommitted dependency anomaly*.

We will not discuss the problem of uncommitted dependency any further since we assume that the recovery algorithms presented in the chapter will ensure that transaction *A* is also rolled back as transaction *B*. The most serious problem facing concurrency control is that of the lost update. The commonly suggested solutions are

1. Once transaction *A* reads a record *Q* for an update, no other transaction is allowed to read it until the transaction *A* update is completed. This is usually called *locking*.
2. Both transactions *A* and *B* are allowed to read the same record *Q* but once *A* has updated the record, *B* is not allowed to update it as well since *B* would now be updating an old copy of record *Q*. *B* must therefore read the record again and then perform the update.
3. Although both transactions *A* and *B* are allowed to read the same record *Q*, *A* is not allowed to update the record because another transaction (transaction *B*) has the old value of the record.
4. Segregate the database into several parts and schedule concurrent transactions such that each transaction uses a different portion. There is thus no conflict and the database stays consistent. Often this is not feasible since most databases have some parts, called *hot spots,* which most transactions want to access.

These are in fact the major concurrency control techniques. We discuss some of them in detail later in this chapter. We first need to consider the concept of *serializability* which deals with correct execution of transactions concurrently.

9.4 SCHEDULES

The concept of a transaction has already been discussed. A transaction must have the ACID properties of atomicity, consistency, isolation and durability. We have also noted earlier that each transaction normally consists of a number of steps or actions including reads and writes; an example is shown in Fig. 9.4.

When two or more transactions are running concurrently, the steps of the transactions would normally be *interleaved* because if one transaction is carrying out some I/O there is no reason for all the other transactions to wait for it to finish. Interleaving therefore improves the response time of the database system. The interleaved execution of transactions is decided by the database system concurrency control software called the *scheduler* which receives a stream of user requests that arise from the active transactions.

We now define a schedule.

Definition—Schedule
A particular sequencing (usually interleaved) of the actions (including reading and writing) of a set of transactions is called a schedule (or history). The order of actions of every transaction in a schedule must always be the same as they appear in the transaction.

We have discussed earlier that each transaction maintains the integrity of the database. It therefore follows that a serial execution of a number of transactions will also maintain the integrity of the database.

The serial schedule is defined as follows.

Definition—Serial Schedule
A serial schedule is a schedule in which all the operations of one transaction are completed before another transaction begins (that is, there is no interleaving).

For performance reasons, serial schedules are of little interest but they are useful as a measure of correctness because a serial schedule is always correct given our basic assumption that each transaction maintains the integrity of the database. That is what we will use them for.

We will soon present some interleaved schedules, for example, in Figs 9.11, 9.12 and 9.13. A serial transaction is presented in Fig. 9.10. We will show more different schedules of two transactions later in this chapter.

It is the responsibility of the scheduler to maintain database integrity while allowing maximum concurrency. The scheduler must make sure that only correct schedules are allowed. To have a mechanism or a set of conditions that define a correct schedule is unfortunately not possible since it is always very complex to define a consistent database. The assertions defining a consistent database (called *integrity constraints* or *consistency constraints*) could well be as complex as the database itself and checking these assertions, assuming one could explicitly enumerate them after each transaction commits, would not be practical. The simplest approach to maintaining database consistency is based on the notion of each transaction being correct by itself transforming a consistent database to another consistent database and a schedule of concurrent executions being able to preserve their correctness.

9.5 SCHEDULES AND RECOVERABILITY

Normally we assume that if a transaction has been aborted or has failed for some reason then the transaction may be rolled back and all its action may be undone leaving the database in a condition as if the transaction never existed. In some situations aborting a transaction so that all its actions are undone may not be possible, perhaps because it had modified some data item which was subsequently modified by another transaction and that transaction has already committed. Such a schedule is called *unrecoverable* and hence should not be permitted.

On the other hand, *recoverable* transactions are such that another transaction is not able to modify contents that it has modified and commit. Recoverability is therefore used to enhance concurrency and maintain consistency when transactions abort.

We first define recoverability.

Definition—Recoverability
A schedule is said to be recoverable if it does not allow a transaction A to commit until every other transaction B that wrote values that were read by A has committed.

Therefore a schedule is recoverable as long as transaction *A* does not commit until every transaction that wrote values read by *A* has committed. In other words, a schedule is recoverable if it never requires a committed transaction to be rolled back.

Transaction *A*	Time	Transaction *B*
–	1	Read *Q*
–	2	Update *Q*
–	3	Write *Q*
Read *Q*	4	–
–	5	Read *R*
Update *Q*	6	–
Write *Q*	7	–
Commit (*A*)	8	
–	9	Failure (rollback)
–	10	–

Figure 9.9 An example of uncommitted dependency

Let us consider the example given in Fig. 9.8 where we discussed uncommitted dependency. A slightly modified version of Fig. 9.8 is reproduced in Fig. 9.9. Uncommitted dependency actually dealt with the problem of recoverability and as we show in Fig. 9.8 that transaction *A* commits before transaction *B* carries out a *dirty write* and *aborts*. Concurrency control therefore must ensure that all tractions are recoverable and situations like that shown in Fig. 9.9 are not permitted.

9.6 SERIALIZABILITY

As noted above, a serial schedule is always correct since serial transactions do not depend on each other. As noted earlier, we further assume that each transaction when run in isolation transforms a consistent database into a new consistent state and therefore a set of transactions executed one after another (i.e. serially) must also be correct. A database may not be consistent during the execution of a transaction, but it is assumed the database is consistent at the end of each transaction. Although using only serial schedules to ensure consistency is a possibility, it is not a realistic approach as noted earlier, since one transaction may be waiting for some input/output from secondary storage or from the user while the CPU remains idle, wasting a valuable resource. Another transaction could have been running while the first transaction was waiting and this would obviously improve the system efficiency. In some cases, a complex transaction if run serially could monopolize the CPU for a long period resulting in all other transactions waiting for it to finish. We therefore need to investigate schedules that are not serial but result in database consistency being maintained. However, since all serial schedules are correct, interleaved schedules that are equivalent to them must also be considered correct. There are in fact $n!$ different serial schedules for any set of n transactions. Note that not all serial schedules of the same set of transactions result in the same consistent state of the database. For example, an airline seat reservation system may result in different allocations of seats for different serial schedules although each schedule will ensure that no seat is sold twice and no request is denied if there is a free seat available on a desired flight. However, one serial schedule could result in 200 passengers on the plane while another could result in 202, as shown below.

Let us consider an airline reservation system. Let there be 12 seats available on flight IA32 at some stage. Three requests arrive, viz., transaction T_1 for 3 seats, transaction T_2 for 5 seats and transaction T_3 for 7 seats. Any of the six serial schedules of the three transactions presented in Fig. 9.10 are correct.

$T_1\ T_2\ T_3$
$T_1\ T_3\ T_2$
$T_2\ T_1\ T_3$
$T_2\ T_3\ T_1$
$T_3\ T_1\ T_2$
$T_3\ T_2\ T_1$

Figure 9.10 Six possible different schedules for three transactions

If the transactions are executed in the order $\{T_1, T_2, T_3\}$ then we allocate 8 seats but cannot meet the third request since there are only 4 seats left after allocating seats for the first two transactions. If the transactions are executed in the order $\{T_2, T_3, T_1\}$ then we are able to allocate all the 12 remaining seats but the request of transaction T_1 cannot be met. If the transactions are instead executed in the order $\{T_3, T_1, T_2\}$ then we allocate 10 seats but are unable to meet the request of transaction T_2 for 5 seats. In all there are 3! (that is 6) different serial schedules possible. The remaining three are $\{T_1, T_3, T_2\}$, $\{T_2, T_1, T_3\}$ and $\{T_3, T_2, T_1\}$. They lead to 10, 8 and 12 seats being sold respectively. All the above serial schedules must be considered correct although they produce different results and any one of the three possible results may be obtained as a result of running these transactions.

We have seen that some sets of transactions when executed concurrently without any controls may lead to problems, for example, the lost update anomaly. Of course, any set of transactions can be executed concurrently without leading to any difficulties if the read and write sets of these transactions do not intersect.

We want to discuss sets of transactions that do interfere with each other. To discuss correct execution of such transactions, we now define the concept of *final state serializability* which is a requirement when more than one transaction is being executed concurrently.

9.6.1 Final State Serializability

Before we define final state serializability, we define final state equivalence which is required in defining final state serializability.

> ***Definition—Final State Equivalence***
> *Two schedules S1 and S2 are called final state equivalent if both include the same set of operations and result in the same final state for any given initial state.*

Let T be a set of n transactions $T_1, T_2, \dots T_n$. If the n transactions are executed serially (call this execution S), we assume they terminate properly and leave the database in a consistent state.

> ***Definition—Final State Serializability***
> *A concurrent execution of n transactions $T_1, T_2, \dots T_n$ (call this execution S) is called final state serializable (FSR) if the execution is final state equivalent to a serial execution of the n transactions.*

The final state serializable schedule may be equivalent to any serial schedule. For example, Fig. 9.9 shows six possible different schedules of any three transactions. Therefore the concurrent execution C always produces exactly the same effect on the database as S does, where S is any serial execution of T, not necessarily the order $T_1, T_2, \dots T_n$. As shown in a serializable schedule in Fig. 9.11, if a transaction T_i writes a data item A in the interleaved schedule C before another transaction T_j reads or writes the same data item, the schedule C must be equivalent to a serial schedule in which T_i appears before T_j. Therefore, in the interleaved transaction, T_i appears logically before T_j; the order is the same as in the equivalent serial schedule. The concept of serializability defined here is sometimes called *final state serializability*; other forms of serializability also exist. Final state serializability has sometimes been criticized for being too strict while at other times it has been criticized for being not strict enough!

If a schedule of transactions is not serializable, we may be able to overcome the concurrency problems by modifying the schedule so that it is serializable. The modifications are made by the database scheduler.

We now consider a number of examples of possible schedules of two transactions running concurrently. Consider a situation where a couple has three accounts (A, B, C) with a bank. The husband and the wife maintain separate personal savings accounts while they also maintain a joint loan account on their house. A is the husband's account, B is the wife's account and C is the housing loan. Each month a payment of \$500 is made to account C. To make the payment on this occasion, the couple walks to two adjoining automatic teller machines and the husband transfers \$200 from account A to C (Transaction 1) while the wife on the other machine transfers \$300 from account B to C (Transaction 2). Several different schedules for these two transactions are possible. We present the following four schedules for consideration.

A careful look at these schedules will show that the third schedule (Fig. 9.12) is not serializable while the other three are.

Another Notation for Schedules

Although we will continue to use tabular representations for presenting schedules, a much more compact form is often used. In the tabular form, each schedule is ordered by time with time starting at the top increasing down to the bottom of the table. In the linear representation that we now describe, time goes from the left to the right.

A transaction is a sequence of steps. From the sequence, this representation first extracts the read and write steps from the schedules since they are the only steps that concern us here; ignoring all other actions. After extracting the reads and writes, these actions are represented by symbols like $r_1(A)$ for reading A by transaction number 1. Let us now look at two transactions as follows:

$$\text{Transaction 1} = r_1(A)w_1(A)r_1(C)w_1(C)c_1$$
$$\text{Transaction 2} = r_2(B)w_2(B)r_2(C)w_2(C)c_2$$

Note that we have added symbols c_1 and c_2 to indicate that transactions 1 and 2 commit respectively.

The schedule in Fig. 9.12 may then be represented as

$$\text{Schedule in Fig. 9.12} = r_1(A)w_1(A)\ r_2(B)w_2(B)\ r_1(C)w_1(C)r_2(C)w_2(C)$$

This list representation of the schedule indicates that a read and a write of item A by Transaction 1 takes place followed by a read and write of item B by Transaction 2 and so on.

We will continue to use the tabular representation for the moment since it is easier to see what is in the schedule at a glance, but we may use the compact notation later when convenient.

We first present a serial schedule in Fig. 9.11.

Transaction 1	**Time**	**Transaction 2**
Read A	1	–
$A := A - 200$	2	–
Write A	3	–
Read C	4	–
$C := C + 200$	5	–
Write C	6	–
–	7	Read B
–	8	$B := B - 300$
–	9	Write B
–	10	Read C
–	11	$C := C + 300$
–	12	Write C

Figure 9.11 A serial schedule without interleaving

Clearly all the actions of Transaction 1 are carried out first followed by actions of Transaction 2. There is no interaction between the transactions. This is not so in the next schedule in which the actions of the two transactions are interleaved.

We present an interleaved serializable schedule in Fig. 9.12.

Transaction 1	Time	Transaction 2
Read *A*	1	–
$A := A - 200$	2	–
Write *A*	3	–
–	4	Read *B*
–	5	$B := B - 300$
–	6	Write *B*
Read *C*	7	–
$C := C + 200$	8	–
Write *C*	9	–
–	10	Read *C*
–	11	$C := C + 300$
–	12	Write *C*

Figure 9.12 An interleaved serializable schedule

Figure 9.13 shows another interleaved schedule that is not serializable because it includes a lost update.

Transaction 1	Time	Transaction 2
Read *A*	1	–
$A := A - 200$	2	–
Write *A*	3	–
Read *C*	4	–
–	5	Read *B*
–	6	$B := B - 300$
–	7	Write *B*
–	8	Read *C*
–	9	$C := C + 300$
–	10	Write *C*
$C := C + 200$	11	–
Write *C*	12	–

Figure 9.13 An interleaved nonserializable schedule

Figure 9.14 shows yet another serializable schedule that has taken care of the lost update by writing C before the second transaction reads and writes it.

Transaction 1	Time	Transaction 2
–	1	Read B
–	2	$B := B - 300$
–	3	Write B
Read A	4	–
$A := A - 200$	5	–
Write A	6	–
Read C	7	–
$C := C + 200$	8	–
Write C	9	–
–	10	Read C
–	11	$C := C + 300$
–	12	Write C

Figure 9.14 Another interleaved serializable schedule

It is therefore clear that many interleaved schedules would result in a consistent state while many others will not. All correct schedules of the two transactions T_1 and T_2 are serializable only if they are equivalent to either serial schedule (T_1, T_2) or (T_2, T_1).

9.6.2 Testing for FSR

There is no simple way to test for FSR. Conceptually testing for FSR involves looking at the schedule that we want to test and comparing it with each of the permutations of the n transactions that are in it. For example, if there are three transactions in a schedule then we may compare the schedule with each of the six serial schedules of the three transactions. If the schedule matches one of them then the schedule is correct according to FSR. However, as the number of transactions grows, the number of permutations grows exponentially and then comparison becomes quite inefficient.

9.6.3 View Serializability

The final state serializability requires that a schedule be equivalent to a serial schedule as both result in the same final state for a given initial state. In FSR we do not know what happens at every step of the schedule. Does each transaction read the same values as the other? It is not unreasonable to require that they do, since it will ensure that both transactions have the same view of the database.

Definition—View Equivalence

Two schedules S1 and S2 are called view equivalent if both comprise the same set of operations and result in the same final state for any given initial state and in addition each operation has the same semantics in both schedules.

Given the definition of view equivalence, we can now define view serializability.

> ***Definition—View Serializability***
> *A concurrent execution of n transactions T_1, T_2, ... T_n (call this execution S) is called view serializable (VSR) if the execution is view equivalent to a serial execution of the n transactions.*

View serializability is a stricter condition than FSR since in addition to the requirement of FSR view serializability require that each corresponding read operation in each schedule return the same values. We now describe conflict serializability which is a stricter condition still.

9.6.4 Testing for VSR

There is no simple algorithm available for testing VSR. We could of course follow the same brute force approach as we did for FSR and compare a given schedule with each permutation of the transactions in it for view equivalence but this approach is not very practical. For this reason VSR has limited practical use.

9.6.5 Conflict Serializability

It should now be clear that there are a number of notions of serializability. We have discussed final state serializability and view serializability but FSR and VSR have limited practical value since it is difficult to test whether a given schedule is in FSR or VSR. We therefore discuss another concept of serializability called conflict serializability. Conflict serializability has a number of useful theoretical and practical properties and is therefore more widely used.

The definition of conflict serializability uses the concept of conflict equivalence. Two schedules are defined to be conflict equivalent if they have the same set of operations and the same order of conflicting operations. We first define conflict.

Conflict serializability is a stronger requirement than requirements for FSR and VSR.

> ***Definition—Conflict***
> *Two data operations belonging to two different transactions in a schedule are in conflict if they access the same data item and at least one of them is a write.*

Based on this concept of conflict, we may now define conflict equivalence and conflict serializability.

> ***Definition—Conflict Equivalence***
> *Two schedules are called conflict equivalent if they have the same set of operations and the same conflict relations.*

> ***Definition—Conflict Serializability***
> *A concurrent execution of n transactions T_1, T_2, ... T_n (call this execution S) is called conflict serializable if the execution is conflict equivalent to a serial execution of the n transactions.*

Conflict serializability is a stronger condition than view serializability and therefore all schedules that satisfy the requirements of CSR also satisfy the requirements of VSR.

9.6.6 Testing for Conflict Serializability—The Precedence Graph

In contrast to testing FSR and VSR, it is easier to test for CSR.

We now present an algorithm for testing conflict serializability. The algorithm involves constructing a *precedence graph* (also called *conflict graph* or *serialization graph*). The precedence graph is a directed graph in which there is a node for each transaction in the schedule and an edge between T_i and T_j exists if any of the conflict operations given in Fig. 9.15 appear in the schedule.

1. T_i executes WRITE(X) before T_j executes READ(X), or
2. T_i executes READ(X) before T_j executes WRITE(X), or
3. T_i executes WRITE(X) before T_j executes WRITE(X).

Figure 9.15 List of possible conflicts in two transactions

A schedule is serializable only if a cycle is not found in the precedence graph. We give an example of a precedence graph in Fig. 9.16. Each edge has a label which indicates the name of the object involved in the conflict. This graph shows that the transactions carry out one of the conditions 1–3 between T_1 and T_3, T_2 and T_3, T_1 and T_5 as well as T_3 and T_4, T_4 and T_6 and T_5 and T_6.

The precedence graph in Fig. 9.16 has no cycle and therefore the schedule shown in this figure is serializable. The reader is encouraged to write down a schedule that results in the given precedence graph.

It should be noted that all objects A, B, C, D, E and F are distinct objects because if say C was the same as A then there must have been edges between T_1 and T_4, and T_1 and T_6 as well since there would be additional conflicts because of transactions T_4 and T_6 operating on the object A.

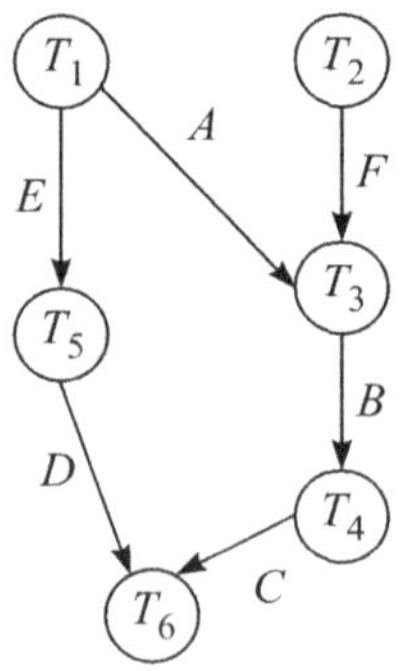

Figure 9.16 An example of a precedence graph

Assuming a simple concurrent execution of two transactions T_i and T_j, it is clear that the graph can only have a cycle if there is an edge between T_i and T_j as well as an edge between T_j and T_i. For this to happen, one of the above conditions must be met for an object X followed by the schedule meeting one of the conditions given in Fig. 9.17 for an object Y, where the objects X and Y need not be distinct.

4. T_j executes WRITE(Y) before T_i executes READ(Y), or
5. T_j executes READ(Y) before T_i executes WRITE(Y), or
6. T_j executes WRITE(Y) before T_i executes WRITE(Y).

Figure 9.17 List of possible conflicts in two transactions

These two sets of conditions provide a total of nine different combinations of conditions which could lead to a cycle. It can be shown that none of these combinations are possible if 2PL discussed later in Section 9.8.2 is used. For example, assume the two conditions given in Fig. 9.18 have been satisfied by a schedule.

7. T_i executes WRITE(X) before T_j executes READ(X),
8. T_j executes WRITE(Y) before T_i executes WRITE(Y).

Figure 9.18 List of possible conflicts in two transactions

It can be shown that none of the eight combinations of conditions are possible if 2PL is used.

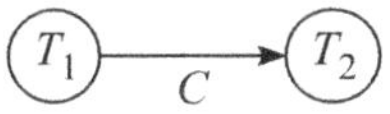

Figure 9.19 Precedence graph for the schedule in Fig. 9.11

It is interesting to draw precedence graphs for some schedules that we have presented. The schedule in Figs 9.11 and 9.12 are like that shown in Fig. 9.19.

The precedence graph for the schedule in Fig. 9.13 is presented in Fig. 9.20. Note that this graph has a cycle in it and is therefore not serializable. The precedence graph for the schedule in Fig. 9.13 is similar to that given in Fig. 9.20 and that schedule is also not serializable.

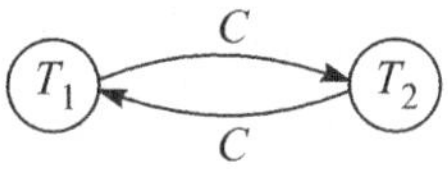

Figure 9.20 Precedence graph for the schedule in Fig. 9.13

Several versions of 2PL have been suggested. Two commonly used versions are called *static* two-phase locking and *dynamic* two-phase locking. The static technique basically involves locking all items of information needed by a transaction before the first step of the transaction is executed and unlocking them all at the end of the transaction. The dynamic scheme locks items of information needed by a transaction only immediately before using them. All locks are released at the end of the transaction.

9.7 HIERARCHY OF SERIALIZABLE SCHEDULES

We have explained the concepts of FSR, VSR and CSR and relationships between them. We illustrate them in Fig. 9.21.

Figure 9.21 shows that serial schedules are the most restrictive serializable schedules, since no interleaving of transactions is permitted in serial schedules. Amongst the serializability requirements we have discussed earlier, CSR is the next most restrictive, followed by VSR and FSR is the weakest requirement of serializability amongst the techniques discussed. There are a number of other serializability techniques presented in the literature that we have not discussed.

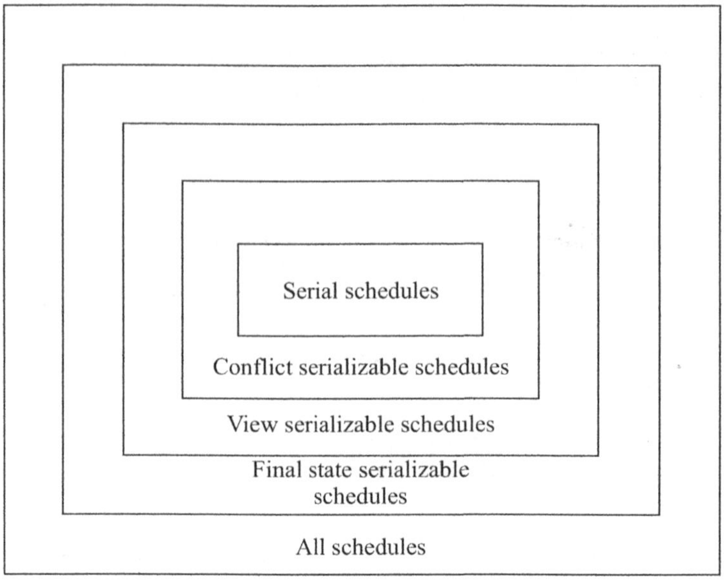

Figure 9.21 Hierarchy of serializable schedules

9.8 CONCURRENCY CONTROL AND ENFORCING SERIALIZABILITY

As noted earlier, a schedule of a set of transactions is serializable if computationally its effect is equal to the effect of some serial execution of the transactions. A DBMS must ensure that only serializable schedules are allowed and the durability property of transactions is also ensured. Therefore, any transaction that commits must not be allowed to be undone.

One way to enforce serializability is to insist that when two transactions are executed, one of the transactions is assumed to be older than the other. Now the only schedules that are accepted are those in which data items that are common to the two transactions are seen by the junior transaction only after the older transaction has written them back. The DBMS module that controls which schedules are permitted is called the *scheduler*.

The three basic techniques used in concurrency control (locking, timestamping and optimistic concurrency control) enforce this in somewhat different ways. The only schedules that these techniques allow are those that are serializable. We now discuss locking followed by these concurrency control techniques.

9.8.1 Locking

Locking is a common technique by which a database may synchronize execution of concurrent transactions. Using locking, a transaction can obtain exclusive or shareable access rights (called *locks*) to an object. If the access provided by the lock is shareable, the lock is often called a *shared lock* (sometimes called a *read* lock). On the other hand, if the access is exclusive, the lock is called an *exclusive lock* (sometimes called a *write* lock). If a number of transactions need to read an object and none of them wishes to write that object, a shared lock would be the most appropriate. Locks may be acquired or released for data items by making requests to the scheduler. The locks are granted by database system software called the *lock manager.*

Of course, if any of the transactions were to write an object, the transaction must acquire an exclusive lock on the object to avoid any concurrency anomalies that we have discussed earlier. A number of locking protocols are possible. Each protocol consists of the following:

1. A set of locking types.
2. A set of rules indicating what locks can be granted concurrently.
3. A set of rules that transactions must follow when acquiring and releasing locks.

We will use the simplest approach that uses shared and exclusive locks, where a transaction would set a read lock on the data item that it reads and an exclusive lock on the data item that it needs to update. As the names indicate, a transaction may obtain a shared lock on a data item even if another transaction is holding a shared lock on the same data item at the same time. Of course, a transaction cannot obtain a shared or exclusive lock on a data item if another transaction is holding an exclusive lock on it. The shared lock may be upgraded to an exclusive lock (assuming no other transaction is holding a shared lock on the same data item at that time) for items that the transaction wishes to write. This technique is sometimes also called *blocking* because if another transaction requests access to an exclusively locked item, the lock request is denied and the requesting transaction is blocked.

A transaction can hold a lock on one or more items of information. The transaction must unlock these data item(s) before the transaction commits. As noted earlier, the locks are granted by the database system software called the *lock manager* which maintains information on all locks that are active in a lock table and controls access to the locks. The lock table contains a variety of information. For example, the identifier for each locked object, the number of locks on each object and their type and identifiers of transactions holding locks. As noted earlier, several modes of locks may be available. For example, in shared mode, a transaction can read the locked data item but cannot update it. In an exclusive lock mode, a transaction has exclusive access to the locked data item and no other transaction is allowed access to it until the lock is released. A transaction is allowed to update the data item only as long as an exclusive lock is held on it.

If transactions running concurrently are allowed to acquire and release locks as data items are read and updated, there is a danger that incorrect results may be produced in spite of the locks. Consider the example in Fig. 9.22.

In Fig. 9.22, exclusive lock (called XL) is a request for an exclusive lock and UL is releasing the lock (sometimes called unlock). SL is a request for a shared lock. In the example shown in Fig. 9.22, the result displayed by Transaction 2 is incorrect because it was able to read *B* before the update but read *A* only after the update. The above schedule is therefore not serializable. As discussed earlier, the problem with this schedule is inconsistent retrieval.

The problem arises because the above schedule involves two RW-conflicts. The first one involves *A* in which Transaction 1 logically appears before Transaction 2 since Transaction 1 reads *A* before Transaction 2. The second conflict involves *B* in which Transaction 2 logically appears before Transaction 1 since Transaction 2 reads *B* before Transaction 1. Therefore, the schedule is not serializable.

Transaction 1	Time	Transaction 2
XL(A)	1	–
Read(A)	2	–
$A := A - 50$	3	–
–	4	SL(B)
Write(A)	5	–
–	6	Read(B)
UL(A)	7	–
–	8	UL(B)
–	9	SL(A)
XL(B)	10	–
–	11	Read(A)
Read(B)	12	–
–	13	UL(A)
$B := B + 50$	14	–
–	15	Display ($A + B$)
Write (B)	16	–
UL(B)	17	–

Figure 9.22 Unserializable schedule using locks

Such problems may be overcome by using a technique called the two-phase locking (2PL), which we now discuss.

9.8.2 Two-Phase Locking (2PL)

To overcome the problem illustrated in Fig. 9.22 a two-phase locking (2PL) scheme is used. 2PL is the most commonly used concurrency control technique in commercial databases. In 2PL, a transaction cannot request a new lock after releasing a lock. The two-phase locking protocol involves the following two phases:

1. *Growing Phase* (*Locking* phase)—During this phase, locks may be acquired but not released.
2. *Shrinking Phase* (*Unlocking* phase)—During this phase, following the growing phase, locks may be released but not acquired. All locks are released when the transaction is completed.

In a summary, the main feature of two-phase locking is that conflicts are checked at the beginning of the execution and resolved by waiting. This leads to safe interleaving of transactions.

Using the 2PL method we can modify the schedule presented in Fig. 9.22. The modified schedule is given in Fig. 9.23. This schedule acquires all locks before any lock is released.

Unfortunately, although the above schedule would not lead to incorrect results, it has another difficulty, i.e., both the transactions are blocked waiting for each other. Transaction 1 in Fig. 9.23 is waiting (at Step 7) for Transaction 2 to unlock B while Transaction 2 cannot do so until it obtains a lock on A (at Step 9). A classical *deadlock* situation has occurred! Deadlocks arise because of circular wait conditions involving two or more

Transaction 1	Time	Transaction 2
XL(A)	1	–
Read(A)	2	–
$A := A - 50$	3	–
–	4	SL(B)
Write(A)	5	–
–	6	Read(B)
XL(B)	7	–
UL(A)	8	–
–	9	SL(A)
–	10	UL(B)
–	11	Read(A)
Read(B)	12	–
–	13	UL(A)
$B := B + 50$	14	–
–	15	Display ($A + B$)
Write (B)	16	–
UL(B)	17	–

Figure 9.23 A schedule using two-phase locking

transactions as above. A system that does not allow deadlocks to occur is called *deadlock free*. In two-phase locking, we need a deadlock detection mechanism and a scheme for resolving the deadlock once a deadlock has occurred. We will look at such techniques in Section 9.9.

The attraction of the 2PL algorithm derives from a theorem which proves that 2PL always leads to serializable schedules that are equivalent to serial schedules in the order in which each transaction acquires its last lock. This is a sufficient condition for serializability although it is not necessary.

We now discuss how deadlocks can be detected, prevented and resolved.

9.9 DEADLOCKS

We first define a deadlock.

> ***Definition—Deadlock***
> *A deadlock can be defined as a situation in which each transaction in a set of two or more concurrently executing transactions is blocked circularly waiting for another transaction in the set.*

Therefore, none of the transactions will become unblocked unless there is some external intervention.

As noted earlier, the locks are granted and managed by the database system software called the lock manager and the lock manager maintains a lock table to manage the locks. This table maintains a variety of information about each lock including how many locks are held on each object, assuming these are shared locks, and which locks are held by which transaction. A queue of lock requests that are waiting is also maintained.

One experimental study has suggested that deadlocks are not very common. Of course the instance of deadlocks goes up as more and more transactions try to access the same object. For example, booking tickets on a train or a flight at the time of holidays like Deepawali. Such objects are called *hot spots*. Normally though, it has been found that less than 1% of the transactions are involved in deadlocks.

Deadlock detection requires a technique to detect a deadlock. Usually deadlocks are detected by building and analyzing a waits-for graph (WFG) as shown in Fig. 9.24. Deadlock detection may take place every time a transaction's lock request is not granted. This is called *continuous detection*. On the other hand one may prefer a *periodic detection* scheme, for example, once every second, although results of experiments seem to indicate that the continuous scheme is more efficient.

9.9.1 Wait-For Graph (WFG)

A wait-for graph is presented in Fig. 9.24. When a transaction T_i requests a data item that is currently being held by T_j, then the edge T_i to T_j is inserted in the wait-for graph. This edge is removed only when T_j is no longer holding a data item needed by T_i.

The system in Fig. 9.24 is in a deadlock state because the wait-for graph given in the figure has a cycle since T_1 is waiting for T_2, which is waiting for T_3 and T_4 while T_3 is waiting for T_5, which in turn is waiting for T_2 which is already waiting. The letters on the edges in the figure indicate the names of the objects that transactions are waiting for. For example, T_1 is waiting for T_2 for object b. Therefore, there is a cyclical wait between transactions T_2, T_3 and T_5.

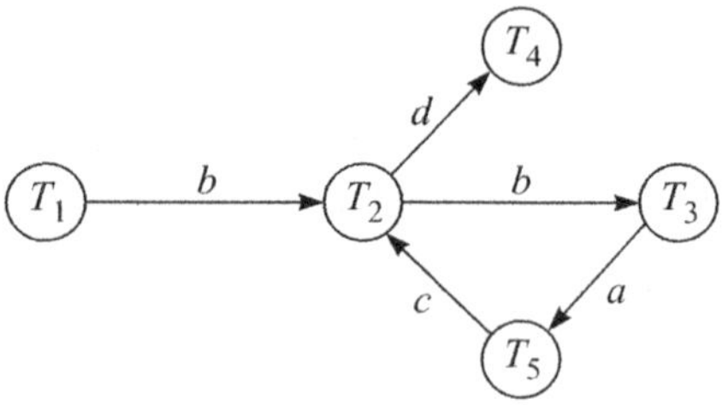

Figure 9.24 An example of a wait-for graph (WFG)

As noted earlier, a deadlock can only be detected by periodically checking the WFG for cycles. We will soon discuss how to resolve deadlocks once a deadlock has been detected.

A deadlock is clearly undesirable but deadlocks are often unavoidable in concurrency controls based on locking. Two-phase locking is not deadlock free. We therefore must deal with deadlocks when they occur. There are several aspects of dealing with deadlocks, viz., one should prevent them if possible (deadlock *prevention*), detect them when they occur (deadlock *detection*) and resolve them when a deadlock has been detected (deadlock *resolution*). Deadlocks may involve two, three or more transactions. To resolve deadlocks, one must keep track of what transactions are waiting and which transaction they are waiting for.

Once a deadlock is detected, one of the transactions in the deadlock must be selected and rolled back (such a transaction is called a *victim*) thereby releasing all the locks that the transaction held and thus breaking the deadlock. We first discuss deadlock prevention followed by discussion on deadlock detection and resolution.

9.9.2 Deadlock Prevention

Deadlocks occur when some transactions wait for other transactions to release a resource and the wait is circular (for example, as already discussed, in Fig. 9.24, T_1 is waiting for T_2, which is waiting for T_3 and T_4 while T_3 is waiting for T_5, which in turn is waiting for T_2 which is already waiting). Deadlock prevention does not involve deadlock detection. Instead deadlocks are prevented by ensuring that circular waits do not occur. This can be done either by defining an order on who may wait for whom or by eliminating all waiting. We first discuss two techniques that define an ordering on transactions.

Wait-die Algorithm

When a conflict occurs between T_1 and T_2 (T_1 being the older transaction), if T_1 possesses a lock then T_2 (the younger one) is not allowed to wait for the resource that T_1 has a lock on. T_2 must roll back and restart. If, however, T_2 possessed the lock at conflict, the senior transaction is allowed to wait. The technique therefore avoids cyclic waits and generally avoids *starvations* (a transaction's inability to secure resources that it needs). An older transaction may however find that it has to wait for every resource that it needs, and it may take a while to complete.

Wound-die Algorithm

To overcome the possibility of a senior transaction having to wait for every item of data that it needs, the wound-die scheme allows a senior transaction to immediately acquire a data item that it needs, even if it is being controlled by a younger transaction by having a lock on it. The younger transaction is then restarted. A younger transaction waiting for a lock that is held by a senior transaction however is allowed to wait.

Immediate Restart

In this scheme, no waiting is allowed. If a transaction requests a lock on a data item that is being held by another transaction (younger or older), the requesting transaction is restarted immediately. This scheme can lead to starvation if a transaction requires several popular data items since every time the transaction restarts and seeks locks on a number of popular items, it is likely to find that one or more of those data items have been locked by other transactions resulting in it being rolled back and restarted.

We now illustrate these techniques in Fig. 9.25. We assume that transactions arrive in the sequence 1, 2 and 3. Therefore, *T*1 is the oldest and *T*3 is the youngest.

The figure shows that the three techniques result in different actions. For example, when a senior transaction wishes to lock an object that has a lock by a junior transaction then wait-die allows it to wait, wound-die aborts the younger transaction while immediate restart aborts the senior transaction.

9.9.3 Deadlock Detection and Resolution

Once a deadlock has been detected using the WFG as shown in Fig. 9.24, it must be resolved. The most common resolution technique requires that one of the transactions in the waits-for graph be selected as a *victim* and be rolled back and restarted. The victim may be selected on the basis of any of the following:

1. *Randomly*—A transaction from the cycle is picked randomly.
2. *Last blocked*—The transaction that blocked most recently.

Trans. *T1*	Trans. *T2*	Trans. *T3*	Comments	Wait-die	Wound-die	Immediate Restart
XL(*A*)	1	–	*A* locked			
	XL(*C*)	–	*C* locked			
UL(*A*)	3	–	*A* unlocked			
XL(*C*)	4	–	Conflict	*T*1 waits for *C*	*T*1 locks *C*; *T*2 aborted	*T*1 aborted
–	5	XL(*B*)	*B* locked			
–	XL(*A*)		*A* locked			
–	XL(*B*)		Conflict	*T*2 waits for *B*	*T*2 locks *B*; *T*3 Aborted	*T*2 aborted
–	8	XL(*C*)	Conflict	*T*3 aborted	*T*3 waits	*T*3 aborted

Figure 9.25 Example illustrating deadlock prevention techniques

3. *Youngest*—Since this transaction is likely to have done the least amount of work.
4. *Minimum work*—The transaction that has written the least data back to the database, since all the data written must be undone in the rollback.
5. *Least impact*—The transaction that is likely to affect the least number of other transactions, that is, the transaction whose rollback will lead to least other rollbacks (in cascade rollback).
6. *Fewest locks*—The transaction that has the smallest number of locks.

It has been found that a technique that selects the victim with the fewest locks to resolve a deadlock provides the best performance. Also, it has been suggested that if deadlock prevention with immediate restart is to be used, database performance suffers. Furthermore, it has been suggested that locking smaller objects improves performance because chances of a deadlock occurring are reduced.

9.10 LOCK GRANULARITY

Lock granularity was first studied by Jim Gary and his colleagues. Our discussion is based on their 1976 paper cited at the end of this chapter.

In addition to selecting a locking mechanism, the nature and size of the individual data item that may be locked must be decided upon. A lockable data item could be as large as a table or as small as a column value of a row. The lockable item could also be of a size in between. For example, a page of a relation or a single row. The larger the size of the items that are locked, the smaller is the concurrency that is possible, because when a transaction wants to access one or more rows of a table, it is allowed to lock the whole table and another transaction wanting to access some other rows of the same table is denied access. On the other hand, coarse granularity reduces the overhead costs of locking since the lock table that maintains information on the locks is smaller since large objects are being locked and the number of transactions holding locks is smaller. Fine granularity of the locks involving individual row locking or locking of even smaller items allows greater concurrency at the cost of higher overheads. Therefore, there is a trade-off between the level of concurrency and overhead costs.

We now define lock granularity.

> ***Definition—Lock Granularity***
> *The size of the data unit that is locked is called lock granularity. The granularity is fine if the data unit is small and coarse if it is large.*

Typically the finest granularity involves locking a row at a time. A coarser granularity is locking a block or a page of the table. A coarse granularity involves locking the whole table.

9.10.1 Fine vs Coarse Granularity

The following points are worth noting:

1. Fine granularity reduces contention and therefore increases concurrency since granularity is fine, and therefore each transaction is locking only a small part of the database. This helps performance but is suitable only for simple transactions which access only a few rows of a table. Fine granularity may not be suitable for complex transactions which access a large number of rows because such a transaction would need to acquire many locks to get its work done.
2. Since fine granularity is locking only small data units, the number of locks at any one time is larger than it would be with a coarser granularity since each transaction is likely to hold many locks. Therefore, lock management overhead including space required by the lock manager to maintain information about locks is higher.
3. Coarse granularity results in fewer locks and lower overheads of maintaining the locks but usually leads to lower concurrency since each transaction is holding on to a larger chunk of the database. This is particularly true if there are some hot spots in the database and transactions are allowed to lock large data units. Coarse granularity is more suitable for complex transactions that access many rows at a time.

Because of this tension between the benefits and disadvantages of fine and coarse granularity, both types of units of locks or even more than two levels of granularity may be offered by a database system. We discuss this approach now.

9.11 MULTIPLE GRANULARITY AND INTENTION LOCKING

We earlier suggested that a database could use several different granularities not just within the database but also within an application, perhaps depending on the nature of each transaction. Multiple granularity locking solves some problems but leads to other problems because now locked items with different granularities must be compared to check conflicts. For example, if one user has been allocated a fine granularity lock, for instance, on one row, and another user requests to lock the whole table then the system needs to efficiently check that there is no conflict between the fine granularity lock and the coarse granularity lock.

9.11.1 Hierarchy of Lock Units

Lock units may be organized in a hierarchy, starting from the whole database going down to a single row or even a single cell as follows:

1. The database
2. Database areas
3. Tables
4. Blocks or Pages
5. Rows

This hierarchy may be considered as a tree with the whole database as its root and other data units as its descendents. The database then is a superset of areas which are supersets of tables. Tables contain blocks or pages and each page contains rows.

Each item in the hierarchy can be locked. It should be noted that as a transaction acquires an exclusive lock on an item then it also acquires exclusive locks on all its descendents.

9.11.2 Intention Locks

To overcome the problem of checking locks in a multiple granularity locking system, a new type of lock called the *intention lock* is used. When a fine granularity lock is taken, a weak coarse granularity lock, the intention lock, is also taken. Hence, an intention lock is used to lock all ancestors of a data unit to be locked either in a shared or exclusive mode. An intention lock is a flag to the lock manager that locking is being done at a finer level thus preventing conflicts.

We now show how an intention lock works.

1. When a transaction *A* wishes to obtain a fine granularity lock on a table *P*, it must first request an intention lock on *P*. This essentially flags to the system lock manager that *A* is going to request a fine granularity lock on table *P*.
2. The intention lock requested is an intention shared (IS) lock if the transaction wishes to request a shared lock on say a row in table *P*. If *A* needs an exclusive lock on a row in *P* then it requests an intention exclusive (IX) lock on the table *P*.
3. A special case of intention lock called shared intention lock (SIX) is available for transactions that read a lot of rows of a table but change only a small number. This resolves the problem of exclusively locking the whole table by granting a shared lock as well as an exclusive lock.

The conflict matrix for the locks is given in Fig. 9.26. It shows the following:

- *S Lock*—If transaction *A* has acquired a share lock on a table *P* then another transaction is allowed to lock descendents of data unit locked by *A* in *S* or IS mode.
- *X Lock*—If transaction *A* has been granted an exclusive lock on a table *P* then no other transaction is allowed to lock descendents.
- *IS Lock*—If transaction *A* has acquired an intention share IS lock on a table *P* then another transaction is allowed to lock descendents of the data unit locked by *A* in S, IS or IX mode.

- *IX*—If transaction *A* has been granted an intention exclusive IX lock on a table *P* then another transaction is allowed to lock descendents in IS or IX mode.
- *SIX Lock*—If transaction *A* has been granted an intention share and exclusive lock SIX on a table *P* then another transaction is allowed to lock descendents in IS mode.

Requested Lock Type						
		S	X	IS	IX	SIX
Lock Type Granted	S	Y	N	Y	N	N
	X	N	N	N	N	N
	IS	Y	N	Y	Y	Y
	IX	N	N	Y	Y	N
	SIX	N	N	Y	N	N

Figure 9.26 Conflict matrix using intention locking

Locks are requested from the highest level to the lowest level and released from the lowest to the highest. Therefore, a higher level lock cannot be released without a lower level lock being released first.

The table in Fig. 9.27 illustrates how request sequences would work.

Locking Request	**Database**	**Area**	**File**	**Block**	**Row**
Lock row *R* for read	IS	IS	IS	IS	S
Lock row *R* for write-exclusive access	IX	IX	IX	IX	X
Lock a file *P* for read and write access	IX	IX	X		
Lock a file *P* for complete scan and occasional update	IX	IX	SIX		

Figure 9.27 Request sequence using intention locking

Clearly intention locks involve additional locks that must be managed by the system but it is possible to achieve better performance since intention locks allow other transactions much more freedom to lock database objects.

9.12 NONLOCKING TECHNIQUE–TIMESTAMPING CONTROL

The two-phase locking technique relies on locking to ensure that each interleaved schedule that is executed is serializable and that makes 2PL attractive. Now we discuss a technique that does not use locks and is therefore deadlock free, and works quite well when the level of contention between transactions running concurrently is not high. It is called *timestamping*. It should be noted that this technique works well only under specific conditions. Its performance can degrade when the conditions are very different.

The timestamping technique gets rid of locks by assigning a unique timestamp, which is a number indicating the time of start of the transaction or just a counter that is incremented every time a new timestamp is requested, for each transaction at the start of the transaction. It then insists that the schedule executed is always serializable to the serial schedule in the chronological order of their timestamps. This is in contrast to two-phase locking where any schedule that is equivalent to some serial schedule is acceptable.

Since the scheduler will only accept schedules that are serializable to the serial schedule in the chronological order of the timestamps, the scheduler must insist that in case of conflicts the junior transaction processes information only after the older transaction has written it. Note that the transaction with the smaller timestamp is the older transaction. For the scheduler to be able to carry out this control, the data items also need to have read and write timestamps. The read timestamp of a data item X is the timestamp of the youngest transaction that has read it and the write timestamp is the timestamp of the youngest transaction that has written it. Let the timestamp of a transaction T be TS(T).

Consider a transaction T_1 with timestamp = 100. Suppose the smallest unit of concurrency control is a table and the transaction wishes to read or write some rows from a table named R. Let the read timestamp of R be RT(R) and the write timestamp of R be WT(R). The following situations may then arise:

1. T_1 wishes to read R. The read by T_1 will be allowed only if $\text{WT}(R) < \text{TS}(T_1)$ or $\text{WT}(R) < 100$. That is, the last write was by an older transaction which had a smaller timestamp. This condition ensures that a data item read by a transaction has not been written by a more recent transaction. If the write timestamp of R is larger than 100 (that is, a younger transaction has written it), then the older transaction is rolled back and restarted with a new timestamp.
2. T_1 wishes to read R. The read by T_1 will be allowed if it satisfies the above condition that R has been last written by an older transaction even if $\text{RT}(R) > \text{TS}(T_1)$, that is, R has been read by a younger transaction. Therefore, reading a data item that has been read by a younger transaction is quite acceptable as long as it has not been written by a younger transaction.
3. T_1 wishes to write some rows of table R. The write will be allowed only if the last read of the transaction was by an older transaction and no younger transaction has read the table R. Therefore, the write is allowed if $\text{RT}(R) < \text{TS}(T_1)$.
4. T_1 wishes to write some rows of table R. The write need not be carried out if the last write was by a younger transaction, that is, $\text{WT}(R) > \text{TS}(T_1)$. The reason this write is not needed is that in this case the younger transaction has not read R, since if it had, the older transaction T_1 would have been aborted. If R had been read by a younger transaction, the older transaction would have been rolled back and restarted with a new timestamp. It is not necessary to check the write since if a younger transaction has written the relation, the younger transaction would have read the data item, and the older transaction operated on an old data item can be ignored. It is possible to ignore the write if the second condition is violated since the transaction is attempting to write an obsolete data item.

Now we illustrate these points in Fig. 9.28. A schedule with two transactions is shown in this figure. We assume transaction T_1 to be older and therefore $\text{TS}(T_1) < \text{TS}(T_2)$.

Let us first explain the information given in the figure. The first column presents the actions carried out by transaction 1. In addition, we have presented the read and write timestamp values of the objects that the transaction reads or writes. For example, the first value in the first row "Read A (TS=95)" tells us that the transaction wishes to read object A which has a read timestamp (RT) of 95 before the object is read. The second column gives all values to be equal to the timestamp of the transaction which is 100 after the transaction has read or written the object values, since that is the last transaction to have accessed those objects.

Transaction 1 (Old timestamp)	**New Timestamps TS(T_1)=100**	**Time**	**Transaction 2 (Old timestamp)**	**Timestamps TS(T_2)=150**
Read A (TS=95)	100	1	–	
$A := A - 200$		2	–	
Write A (TS=97)	100	3	–	
–		4	Read B (TS=102)	150
–		5	$B := B - 300$	
–		6	Write B (TS=105)	150
Read C (TS=98)	100	7	–	
$C := C + 200$		8	–	
Write C (TS=99)	100	9	–	
–		10	Read C (TS=110)	150
–		11	$C := C + 300$	
–		12	Write C (TS=115)	150

Figure 9.28 Example of concurrency control using timestamping

We note that if the RT(C) value at time 7 was 102, the transaction will be allowed to read C but if WT(C) is 105 then the transaction is rolled back.

Read (A) by transaction T_1 is permitted since A has not been written by a younger transaction. Write (A) by transaction T_1 is also permitted since A has not been read or written by a younger transaction. Read (B) by transaction T_2 is permitted since B has not been written by a younger transaction. Read (B) by transaction T_1 however is not allowed since B has been read by (younger) transaction T_2 and therefore transaction T_1 is rolled back.

9.13 NONLOCKING TECHNIQUE–OPTIMISTIC CONTROL

The locking concurrency control and the timestamping concurrency control both implicitly assume that conflicts are frequent between the transactions and therefore concurrency controls are needed to control the conflicts and maintain database consistency. If on the other hand we assume that our database environment is such that conflicts are uncommon then we might be able to use a different type of concurrency control mechanism. Such an environment could well exist for a database system like that of an Internet trader amazon.com or eBay where most visitors to the site only access parts of the database to check the price or read product reviews and only a few visitors, as a percentage of visitors, buy products or modify data in other ways (for example, by writing book reviews).

The optimistic concurrency control approach is suitable for database applications where the number of conflicts between the transactions is expected to be low. The technique is not suitable for intensive applications like the airline reservation system where write operations frequently occur at 'hot spots'. For example, status of the flight for the next few days or for holiday periods. In the optimistic control technique, transactions are allowed to execute unhindered and are validated only after they have reached their commit points. If the transaction validates, it commits, otherwise it is restarted.

The optimistic control may be summarized as involving checking at the end of the execution and resolving conflicts by rolling back. One possible algorithm involves the following three phases:

1. *The Read Phase*—Each active transaction is allocated a private space which cannot be accessed by other transactions or by the outside world. Each transaction is then allowed to execute such that all writes are carried out only in the private space. At the end of this phase the transaction is ready to commit and the concurrency controller knows the read and write sets of each transaction.
2. *The Validation Phase*—The transaction is now validated by the scheduler which checks if the transaction violates any serializability conditions. If the transaction is found to be correct, it is validated otherwise aborted. The correct transaction goes to the next phase.
3. *The Write Phase*—The private space data of the validated transaction is now transferred to the database and the transaction has committed.

Optimistic concurrency control does not involve any checking before or during the execution of the transaction. Usually any updates carried out by the transaction are carried out to a local copy of the objects and not carried out directly to the database objects. At the completion of the transaction, validation is carried out. Validation requires certain information be retained by the system. This information may be transaction timestamps as well as a list of objects that are read and written by each transaction. We do not provide further details of validation.

If at the time of validation, it is discovered that the transaction wanting to commit had read a data item that has already been written by another transaction, the transaction attempting to commit would be restarted. These techniques are also called validation or certification techniques.

It is possible to combine two or more concurrency control techniques, for example, very heavily used objects could be locked, and others could follow optimistic control.

9.14 TRANSACTION SUPPORT IN SQL

SQL provides a number of facilities for transaction management. Three characteristics of a transaction may be specified in a SET TRANSACTION command by the user. These characteristics are as follows:

- Access mode
- Diagnostic area size
- Isolation level

1. *Access Mode*—A transaction may be specified not to modify the database by specifying READ ONLY. It may otherwise be specified to be READ WRITE which is also the default.
2. *Diagnostic Area Size*—The diagnostic area size specifies the number of error conditions that can be held simultaneously.
3. *Isolation Level*—This transaction characteristic specifies the extent to which the transaction is exposed to the actions of the other transactions. The default value of this characteristic is SERIALIZABLE which provides the highest level of isolation. This isolation level ensures that the transaction reads the results of only committed transactions. Locks are obtained before reading or writing objects and released at the completion of the transaction thus ensuring 2PL.

The choices available under isolation level are as follows:

- READ UNCOMMITTED
- READ COMMITTED
- REPEATABLE READ
- SERIALIZABLE

READ UNCOMMITTED allows the transaction to read changes made by another transaction that has not committed. This is called dirty read and is the lowest isolation level. READ COMMITTED is often the default isolation in DBMS. It ensures that the transaction only reads the changes made by committed transactions and no data that has been changed by another transaction but not yet committed will be read. Shared locks are used in READ COMMITTED. REPEATABLE READ also ensures that the transaction reads only the changes made by committed transactions and dirty data is not read. SERIALIZABLE is the most restrictive isolation level. It ensures that no other user is able to insert or update rows into the data set until the first transaction is completed.

Some problems (for example, dirty read) can occur if an isolation level lower than serializable is specified. Therefore, serializable is the safest isolation to use in transaction processing.

9.15 EVALUATION OF CONCURRENCY CONTROL MECHANISMS

A number of researchers have evaluated the various concurrency control mechanisms that have been discussed here. It was found that the level of resources available has significant impact on which concurrency method performs the best. It is generally accepted that a technique that minimizes the number of restarts (like the two-phase locking technique) is superior when the physical resources are limited and number of conflicts is high. Two-phase locking performed much better than timestamping and optimistic algorithms under medium to high conflict levels since timestamping and optimistic methods tend to waste the most resources through restarts. When the conflict level is low and there are sufficient resources, then restart-oriented methods are better since they can provide a higher degree of concurrency. The optimistic algorithm was found to perform the best in such an environment. Deadlock prevention techniques like those based on immediate restart tend to make the database slow down somewhat. It has been found that deadlock detection techniques help. At low loads, it does not really matter much which technique is used, although some studies show that the optimistic technique then is more efficient. It is of course possible to use more than one technique in a system. For example, two-phase locking may be combined with optimistic techniques to produce hybrid techniques that work well in many situations.

SUMMARY

In this chapter we have considered the concept of transaction and its ACID properties and have discussed the importance of concurrency control. The following topics have been covered:

- The concept of transaction and its ACID properties (atomicity, consistency, isolation and durability) are important in transaction management and concurrency control.
- Conflicts may arise during concurrent execution of two transactions including RW conflict and WW conflict.
- The conflicts can lead to concurrency anomalies (lost update, inconsistent retrievals and uncommitted dependency).
- An important concept in concurrency control is the concept of a schedule and a serial schedule.
- For concurrent execution, a schedule must be a serializable schedule.
- For a schedule to be serializable, it must meet the requirements of serializability.
- Three types of serializability are described, viz., final state serializability (FSR), view serializability (VSR) and conflict serializability (CSR).
- CSR may be tested using a precedence graph.
- A number of concurrency control methods depend on the concept of locks, shared locks and exclusive locks to enforce serializability.
- Simple (or single-phase) locking is not always satisfactory and therefore the concept of two-phase locking (2PL) has been proposed.
- 2PL can lead to the problem of deadlocks.
- A number of methods are available to prevent deadlocks or for detecting and resolving these using wait-for graphs.
- It is necessary to deal with the issue of lock granularity, should lock granularity be fine or coarse.
- Another approach is multiple granularity using intention locks.
- It is possible to use concurrency control methods that do not use locks; two such methods are timestamping and optimistic concurrency control.
- Research has been carried out in performance evaluation of timestamping and 2PL to find when timestamping performs better than 2PL and when 2PL performs better.

REVIEW QUESTIONS

1. List the properties that a transaction must have. Briefly explain them. (Section 9.2)
2. Why is the concept of a transaction important in concurrency? (Section 9.2)

3. When does concurrent execution of two transactions lead to conflict? (Section 9.1 and 9.6.5)
4. What concurrency anomalies (lost update, inconsistent retrievals, uncommitted dependency) are possible if there is no concurrency control? (Section 9.3)
5. Give an example of a schedule of three transactions. How many different serial schedules are possible? List them. (Section 9.4)
6. What is a recoverable schedule? Define it. (Section 9.5)
7. When do two transactions running concurrently conflict? Explain RW and WW conflicts. (Section 9.6.5)
8. What is final state serializability? (Section 9.6.1)
9. Explain view serializability (VSR). Is it possible to test for VSR? (Section 9.6.2)
10. What is conflict serializability and how it differs from VSR? (Section 9.6.3)
11. What is a precedence graph? What does it show? (Section 9.6.4)
12. What is a serializable schedule? Why are serializable schedules considered correct? (Sections 9.6 and 9.7)
13. What are the issues in determining locking granularity? What is multiple granularity? (Section 9.10)
14. What is intention locking? How is it used in multiple granularity? (Section 9.11)
15. What is two-phase locking and how does it guarantee serializability? Why simple (or single-phase) locking is not satisfactory? (Section 9.8.2)
16. Explain how do you determine that a given schedule will lead to deadlock. What is wait-for graph? (Section 9.9.1)
17. How can deadlocks be prevented and how can deadlocks be resolved? (Section 9.9.2 and 9.9.3)
18. What is the basis of the timestamping technique? How does the timestamping technique differ from 2PL? (Section 9.12)
19. When does timestamping perform better than 2PL and vice versa? (Section 9.12)
20. Explain the basis of optimistic concurrency control. When does it work well? (Section 9.13)
21. Explain how SQL supports transaction. (Section 9.14)
22. Explain how different concurrency control techniques are evaluated. (Section 9.15)

SHORT ANSWER QUESTIONS

1. What is concurrency?
2. What problems may arise if concurrency control is not used in a database system?
3. Is concurrency important in a library catalogue database? Why?
4. What are the ACID properties of a transaction?
5. Why is the concept of transaction important in database systems?
6. Give an example of a schedule of three example transactions.
7. Give an example of a schedule that is not recoverable.
8. What is serializability?
9. Give an example of a serial schedule.
10. Define final state serializability (FSR).

11. Why do we need other types of serializability?
12. What is VSR?
13. What is CSR?
14. Which one of the three—FSR, VSR and CSR, is the strictest?
15. What does 2PL do?
16. What are locks?
17. Give an example of a precedence graph with a cycle.
18. What is meant by granularity?
19. Give an example of coarse granularity.
20. What is intention locking?
21. What is the main feature of timestamping concurrency control?
22. What is the main feature of optimistic concurrency control?
23. Give one example of deadlock prevention.
24. How can one detect a deadlock?
25. Give an example of a wait-for graph.
26. What is the aim of multiple granularity locking?
27. What may be specified in SET TRANSACTION mode in SQL?
28. What isolation levels may be specified in SQL?
29. What was discovered by evaluating concurrency control methods?

MULTIPLE CHOICE QUESTIONS

1. Which of the following problems does concurrency controls deal with?
   (a) lost updates
   (b) inconsistent retrievals
   (c) uncommitted dependency
   (d) All of the above
2. Which of the following are correct?
   (a) If two transactions are accessing the same object and writing them at the same time without any controls then one of the updates can be lost.
   (b) If one transaction is updating a number of items and another transaction is reading them without any controls then that may result in inconsistence retrievals.
   (c) If one transaction reads something that is written by another transaction and commits before the other transaction commits then it is called uncommitted dependency.
   (d) All of the above
3. In the following list, mark all properties that a transaction must have.
   (a) Serializability
   (b) Consistency
   (c) Atomicity
   (d) Isolation
4. Which one of the following is **not** correct?
   (a) A transaction is an atomic unit of work, all its subtasks must be processed together one after another.
   (b) A transaction may not be nested.

(c) A transaction is a logical unit of work which preserves the consistency of the database.
(d) A transaction is usually a serial program devoid of loops.

5. Three transactions attempt to book seats on a flight that has 12 seats available. The transactions are transaction T_1 for 3 seats, transaction T_2 for 5 seats and transaction T_3 for 7 seats. If a schedule that is serializable is executed, the number of seats sold cannot be
(a) 7 (b) 8 (c) 10 (d) 12
(e) None of the above

6. Which of the following are correct?
(a) Although transactions appear atomic, they consist of a sequence of more elementary steps.
(b) Although operations may be happening concurrently in the middle of a transaction, it is the role of concurrency control that each transaction is isolated from other operations.
(c) To manage concurrency, the database must be partitioned into items which are the units of data to which access is controlled.
(d) All of the above

7. Which of the following is **not** correct?
(a) A schedule for a set of transactions is a specification of the order in which the elementary steps of the transactions are carried out.
(b) A schedule is serial if all the steps of each transaction occur consecutively.
(c) A schedule is serializable if its effect is equivalent to that of some serial schedule.
(d) Each schedule that is serializable is allowed by 2PL.

8. Which of the following is correct? Two transactions running concurrently and accessing the same data item do **not** conflict if
(a) both transactions are reading the data item but neither is writing it.
(b) the first transaction is reading the data item and the second writing it.
(c) the first transaction is writing the data item and the second reading it.
(d) both transactions are writing the data item.

9. Consider the following schedule:

Transaction 1	Time	Transaction 2
Read (A)	1	–
$A := A - 50$	2	–
Write (A)	3	–
–	4	Read (B)
–	5	Read (A)
Read (B)	6	–
$B := B + 50$	7	–
–	8	Write ($A + B$)
Write (B)	9	–

Which of the following is correct?

(a) The schedule is serializable.

(b) A deadlock happens if 2PL is used to execute the above schedule.

(c) If timestamping is used to execute the above schedule then assuming that Transaction 1 is the older transaction, Transaction 1 is rolled back.

(d) None of the above

10. Which of the following schedules are serializable schedules? $r_i(K)$ means a read by transaction i of data item K. w indicates a write.

(a) $r_1(A)w_1(A)\, r_2(B)w_2(B)\, r_3(D)w_3(D)\, r_1(C)w_1(C)\, r_2(C)w_2(C)$

(b) $r_3(D)w_3(D)\, r_1(A)w_1(A)\, r_1(C)w_1(C)\, r_2(B)w_2(B)\, r_2(C)w_2(C)$

(c) $r_1(A)w_1(A)\, r_2(B)w_2(B)\, r_1(C)w_1(C)\, r_2(C)w_2(C)\, r_3(D)w_3(D)$

(d) All of the above

11. Which one of the following schedules is **not** a recoverable schedule? In the schedules below Y indicates a transaction commit while X denotes a transaction abort. The subscripts show the transaction numbers.

(a) $r_1(C)w_1(C)\, r_2(B)w_2(B)\, r_2(C)w_2(C)(Y_2)\, r_3(D)w_3(D)\, r_1(A)(X_1)$

(b) $r_1(A)w_1(A)\, r_2(B)w_2(B)\, r_1(C)w_1(C)\, r_2(C)w_2(C)\, r_3(D)w_3(D)$

(c) $r_1(A)w_1(A)\, r_3(D)w_3(D)(Y_3)\, r_2(B)w_2(B)\, r_1(C)w_1(C)\, r_2(C)w_2(C)(X_1)$

(d) All of the above

12. Which one of the following is true?

(a) There are no schedules that are acceptable to a two-phase locking scheme but not to a timestamping scheme.

(b) A timestamping schedule is always equivalent to the serial schedule in the order of the timestamps of the transactions.

(c) Timestamping concurrency control works well even when the level of contention in the database is high.

(d) Timestamping allows no schedules that would not be permitted by 2PL.

13. Which one of the following is true?

(a) 2PL schedules are equivalent to serial schedules in the order of the acquisition of the last locks.

(b) 2PL schedules are equivalent to serial schedules in the order of the acquisition of the first locks.

(c) Timestamping is a more strict concurrency control mechanism (in that it allows less concurrency).

(d) A timestamping technique allows fewer sets of schedules than a dynamic two-phase locking scheme.

14. Which of the following are true?

(a) All serial schedules are serializable.

(b) All FSR schedules are serial schedules.

(c) All VSR schedules are FSR schedules.

(d) All of the above are true.

15. Which one of the following is true?

(a) All schedules are FSR schedules.

(b) CSR is the most stringent serializability requirement we have discussed.

(c) All FSR schedules are VSR schedules.

(d) All VSR schedules are CSR schedules.

16. Which one of the following is true?
    (a) If a schedule is not at least FSR then it is not serializable.
    (b) A serializable and correct schedule must be CSR.
    (c) All FSR schedules can be easily tested for FSR.
    (d) All serializable schedules are correct.
17. Which one of the following techniques is **not** guaranteed to prevent deadlocks?
    (a) The younger transaction is not allowed to wait for a lock if the data item is held by an older transaction.
    (b) The older transaction is not allowed to wait for a lock if the data item is held by a younger transaction.
    (c) Some transactions are selected randomly and not allowed to wait for a data item that is already locked.
    (d) No transaction is allowed to wait for a lock if the data item is held by another transaction.
18. In timestamping, consider the smallest unit of concurrency control to be a relation and let transaction T at time t wish to read or write some rows from the relation R. Let the read and write timestamps of R be r and w respectively.
    Which of the following is *not* correct?
    (a) If $r < t$, the read by T will be allowed only if $w < t$.
    (b) If $r > t$, the read by T will not be allowed.
    (c) If $w < t$, the write by T will be allowed only if $r < t$.
    (d) If $w > t$, the write by T need not be carried out if $r < t$.
    (e) All of the above are correct.

EXERCISES

1. Three transactions A, B and C arrive in the time sequence A, then B and then C. The transactions are run concurrently on the database. Can we predict what the result would be if 2PL is used? Explain briefly.
2. Show whether the given schedule is possible if 2PL is used or if timestamping is used.
3. Can a schedule that is not serializable be correct? Give an example.
4. Show an example of a schedule that is final state serializable but not conflict serializable.
5. Explain the use of intention locks in multiple granularity and describe lock conflicts when intention locking is used.
6. Is the following schedule serializable? Show what happens if 2PL is used to execute the schedule.

Transaction 1	Time	Transaction 2
Read (A)	1	–
$A := A - 50$	2	–
Write (A)	3	–

Contd.

Contd.

–	4	Read (*B*)
–	5	Read (*A*)
Read (*B*)	6	–
$B := B + 50$	7	–
–	8	Write ($A + B$)
Write (*B*)	9	–

7. Explain the hierarchy of serializable schedules. Why are view serializable schedules a subset of FSM schedules and CSR schedules are a subset of the VSR schedules? Can you think of any serializable schedules that are a subset of the CSR schedules?
8. What is a recoverable schedule? Discuss what happens when a schedule is not recoverable. Explain the situation when two transactions have committed before a transaction having carried out a dirty write aborts.
9. Can a schedule that is not serializable be correct? Give an example.
10. Find out what other types of serializability has been proposed. How do they compare to final state serializability and conflict serializability?
11. Give an example of a schedule that is final state serializable but not conflict serializable.
12. Illustrate what happens if timestamping is used to execute the above schedule. Assume that Transaction 1 is the older transaction.
13. Explain why deadlocks occur and the role of the lock manager.
14. Briefly explain one deadlock prevention and one deadlock detection algorithm. Compare the efficiency of the two.
15. Does timestamping use locking? What is the motivation for timestaming and in what type of database environment it works best? Explain briefly.
16. What is the single most significant difference between two-phase locking and the timestamping technique of concurrency control? Explain briefly.
17. Under what conditions do you think deadlock prevention is better than deadlock detection and resolution?
18. If deadlock is prevented, is starvation still possible? Explain clearly.
19. Give an example schedule for two transactions that is allowed under timestamping control but not under 2PL.
20. Consider the following transactions:

T_1	T_2
read(x)	read(x)
$x := x - n$	$x := x + m$
write(x)	write(x)
read(y)	
$y := y + n$	
write(y)	

How many different schedules of the two transactions are possible? How many of these are serializable?

PROJECTS

1. Consider an airline booking system and let us assume we have implemented the following schema which is a rather primitive system:

    Customer(CustomerID, Title, First name, Last name, Gender, Age, Address, TelephoneBH, TelephoneAH, Email)

    Flight(FlightNUM, DepartureDate, DepartureTime, ArrivalDate, ArrivalTime)

    Seat(FlightNUM, CustomerID, DepartureDate, SeatNUM, Class)

    Ticket(SerialNUM, FlightNUM, DepartureDate, SeatNUM, CustomerID)

There is little doubt that this schema has a number of weaknesses but we will ignore them at the moment. The table *Customer* includes the details of each customer. No customer can make a booking unless the person is in the *Customer* table. There is a separate row in the table *Flight* for each flight and departure date and time. Seats are allocated when booking is made. The ticket is assumed to be for only one flight and only one customer.

Which tables in the above schema are likely to be hot spots? How should the concurrency be controlled for the system to work efficiently? Discuss the issues of serializability, granularity, deadlocks and recoverability. Suggest how the database design could be modified to deal with concurrency more effectively.

LAB EXERCISES

1. Consider a bank, say ICICI, which, let us assume, has more than 1000 branches and more than 5000 ATMs all over India. What time of the day is the peak traffic time for the ATMs? Make an assumption on how many ATM transactions are carried out at peak time and then make an assumption of a simple schema for the bank customer database. What concurrency problems might arise? Discuss.
2. It has been estimated that close to four trillion SMS will be sent all over the world in 2011 and there will be 700 million mobile customers in India in 2011. Annual SMS traffic in India might be estimated to grow to 500 billion messages per year. Estimate how many messages per second might be sent on Diwali or 1st January all over India. Discuss the concurrency problems of such high traffic for mobile phone databases in India.
3. Are the ACID properties of transactions always required? Discuss a situation when it may be possible not to worry about one or more of them.
4. The conditions in Figs 9.15 and 9.17 provide a total of nine combinations of conditions which can lead to a cycle in the precedence graph. Show how each of these combination may be avoided if 2PL is used.

BIBLIOGRAPHY

For Students

The paper by Thomasian is good. The book by Bernstein et al., is quite good for an introduction. An older version is available free on the Web.

For Instructors

There are a number of books that deal exclusively with transaction processing and these books provide a much more detailed discussion on concurrency control and other transaction processing topics. Some of these books are listed below including the classic book by Gray and Reuter and the one by Papadimitriou. The book by Kifer et al., is also good. The book edited by Kumar has 21 papers in it with a focus on performance of concurrency control techniques. The paper by Agarwal, Carey and Livny deals with performance evaluation of concurrency control methods in detail.

Agarwal, R., and D. DeWitt, "Integrated Concurrency Control and Recovery Mechanisms: Design and Performance Evaluation", *ACM Transactions of Database Systems*, Vol. 10, pp 529-564, 1985.

Agarwal, R., M. J. Carey, and M. Livny, "Concurrency Control Performance Modeling: Alternatives and Implications", *ACM Transactions on Database Systems,* Vol. 12, December 1987.

Agarwal, R., M. J. Carey and L. McVoy, " The performance of alternative strategies for dealing with deadlocks in database management systems", *IEEE Transactions on Software Engineering*, Vol. 13, Issue 12, pp 1348-1363 , 1987.

Bernstein, P. A., V. Hadzilacos, and N. Goodman, *Concurrency Control and Recovery in Database Systems*, 1987 version. http://research.microsoft.com/~philbe/ccontrol/

Bernstein, P. A., and E. Newcomer, *Principles of Transaction Processing*, Morgan Kaufmann Series in Data Management Systems, Second Edition, 2009, pp 400.

Eswaran, K. P., J. Gray, R. A. Lorie, and I. L. Traiger, "The notions of consistency and predicate locks in a database system", *Communications of the ACM*, Vol. 19, pp 624-633.

Gray, J., "The Transaction Concept: Virtues and Limitations", *Proceedings of the 7th International Conference on Very Large Database Systems*, September 1981.

Gray, J., and A. Reuter, *Transaction Processing: Concepts and Techniques*, Morgan Kaufmann Series in Data Management Systems, 1993.

Gray, J. N., R. A. Lorie, G. R. Putzolu, and I. L. Traiger, "Granularity of locks and degrees of consistency in a shared data base", *Modeling in Data Base Management Systems*, edited by G. M. Nijssen, North Holland, 1976, pp 365-394.

Kumar, V. (Ed.), *Performance of Concurrency Control Mechanisms in Centralized Database Systems*, Prentice Hall, 1996.

Kung, H. T., and C. H. Papadimitriou, "An Optimality Theory of Concurrency Control in Databases", *Proc. ACM SIGMOD Conference*, pp 116-126, 1979.

Kifer, M., A. Bernstein and P. M. Lewis, *Databases and Transaction Processing: An Application-Oriented Approach*, Second Edition, Addison-Wesley, 2006.

Papadimitriou, C. H., "The Serializability of Concurrent Database Updates", *Journal of the ACM*, Vol. 26, 1979, pp 631-653.

Papadimitriou, C. H., *The Theory of Database Concurrency Control*, Computer Science Press, New York, 1986.

Thomasian, A.,"Concurrency Control: Methods, Performance, and Analysis", *ACM Computing Surveys*, Vol. 30, No. 1, 1998, pp. 70-119.

Weikum, G., and G. Vossen, *Transactional Information Systems: Theory, Algorithms, and the Practice of Concurrency Control and Recovery*, Morgan Kaufmann, 2002.

Jim Gray (1944–2007)—Pioneer in Database Transaction Processing

As explained in this chapter, a transaction is the fundamental abstraction underlying database system concurrency and failure recovery. Gray's work led to the definition of the desired key transaction properties as atomicity, consistency, isolation and durability. His locking and recovery work demonstrated how to build database systems that exhibit these properties. His fault tolerance work explained how to use transactions to achieve high system availability. The work he did on data cubes with a number of colleagues at Microsoft is also very important. At Microsoft his research focus was building super-servers and workgroup systems from commodity software and hardware.

Jim Gray worked at IBM and AT&T on database and transaction processing systems. He has co-authored the book *Transaction Processing Concepts and Techniques*. He has been a Member of the National Academy of Engineering, Fellow of the ACM, a member of the National Research Council's Computer Science and Telecommunications Board, President's Information Technology Advisor Committee, Trustee of the VLDB Foundation, and Editor of the Morgan Kaufmann series on Data Management.

Jim Gray was awarded the ACM Turing Award in 1998 for contributions to database systems and transaction processing research and technical leadership in system implementation.

Jim Gay mysteriously disappeared at sea in 2007 when he went to scatter his mother's ashes in his yacht.

Database Backup and Recovery 10

OBJECTIVES

- Explain the various causes of database system failures.
- Explain the concepts of backup and recovery.
- Describe the concepts of physical and logical backups.
- Explain different types of database backup.
- Discuss what needs to be considered in designing a database backup plan.
- Discuss the types of database recovery.
- Discuss the concept of a log.
- Discuss a number of recovery techniques including immediate update and deferred update recovery techniques.
- Describe what a checkpoint is and what it does.
- Describe shadow page technique.
- Introduce the ARIES recovery approach.
- Briefly discuss evaluation of various recovery techniques.
- Explain how to recover from a media failure.

KEYWORDS

Database recovery, database failures, causes of failures, backup, backup types, backup plan, Physical backup, logical backup, system recovery from failure, buffer management, transaction recovery, log, checkpoint, immediate update, deferred update, do, undo, redo, shadow paging, optimistic concurrency, evaluation, Do, REDO, UNDO, dirty pages, forcing pages, media recovery, ARIES.

An error does not become truth by reason of multiplied propagation, nor does truth become error because nobody sees it.

Mahatma Gandhi

10.1 INTRODUCTION

Given that an enterprise's database is a valuable asset, it is essential that a DBMS provide adequate mechanisms for reducing the chances of a database system failure and for recovery from a failure when it occurs, thus improving reliability and availability of the system. In many enterprises 24 × 7 availability of a database system is essential. For such mission-critical systems as well as for other database systems, suitable procedures for database recovery when the system does fail due to software or hardware problems are required. These procedures are called *recovery techniques*. The recovery techniques use saved information to restart the database system from an intermediate state.

In this chapter, as before, we assume that we are dealing with a multiple user database system and not a single user system as commonly found on personal computers. The problems of database recovery can be much simpler in a single user system than recovery in a multi-user system.

The primary aim of database recovery is to ensure that the ACID properties of a database transaction are not violated. A database crash can violate any or all of the ACID properties. For example, we noted earlier, strange incidents can happen while using an ATM. For example, power to the ATM might go off after the user's ATM card is returned but before the cash is dispensed. The transaction must maintain consistency in such unusual situations. Another possibility is that the power might go off before the card is returned to the user. The machine then retains the card and the user is not sure what will happen to the card. This is obviously unacceptable because another user using the ATM later, when the power returns, may be able to find the card. Once again such a situation is not acceptable. What the user wants is that the ACID properties are not violated. In particular, consistency and durability of a transaction must be maintained.

After a database crash, the recovery manager is given full control of the database system so that it can bring the database to a consistent state. In this chapter we discuss the operation of the recovery manager.

Before we discuss causes of database systems' failures and the techniques to recover from them, we should note that in our discussion we shall assume that the database is resident normally on a disk and a part of it is transferred from the disk to the main memory when accessed. A database system carefully orchestrates modification of data by moving data from disk storage to the main memory, modifying it and then writing it back to the disk. As noted in Chapter 7, disk storage is accessed randomly in units of blocks. Disk storage may however be destroyed by incidents like a head crash which happen only rarely. A subset of the database that is being used by the users will always be resident in the main memory. To protect against such loss, although it happens only rarely, it is desirable to have a copy of the database stored in what is sometimes called *stable storage*. Stable storage is assumed to be reliable and unlikely to lose information with any type of system failure. No media like disk or tape can be considered truly stable although disks are now the medium of choice for stable storage. Perhaps stable storage can be implemented as several independent nonvolatile storage media replicating information; some of it stored off-site.

This chapter is organized as follows. Database failures are discussed next followed by database backup in Section 10.3 including backup types and backup plan. Physical and logical backup are described in Section 10.3.1. System recovery from a failure is then discussed in Section 10.4. Since major recovery techniques use a log, the concept of log is discussed in Section 10.5. Recovery and buffer management is discussed in Section 10.6. Recovery techniques are discussed in Section 10.7. Sections following including Section 10.8 are the heart of the chapter and include a number of types of recovery techniques including immediate update technique in Section 10.9, deferred update technique in Section 10.10, system checkpoints in Section 10.11, a brief introduction to ARIES recovery system in Section 10.12, a summary of log-based methods in Section 10.13, and shadow page technique in Section 10.14. Section 10.15 deals with evaluation of recovery techniques. Section 10.16 discusses recovering from a media failure.

10.2 DATABASE SYSTEM FAILURE

A database system failure may occur due to any of the factors listed in Fig. 10.1. These include incorrect transactions in spite of our assumption that all transactions are correct and transform a consistent database into another consistent database.

- Power failure
- User and system administrator input errors
- Hardware and media failure
- System failure
- Unrecoverable failure
- Other causes, for example, operator error, fire or flood

Figure 10.1 Major causes of database system failure

We discuss these causes briefly.

1. *Power Failure*—This is perhaps the most common cause of failure. Such failures result in the loss of information in the volatile main memory. However, with battery-backed uninterruptible power supplies (UPS) power failures are often not such a serious problem.
2. *User and System Administrator Input Errors*—These failures are not always easy to detect although they can lead to an inconsistent database. User errors can occur when a user's incorrect transaction results in data in a database being changed or deleted incorrectly. User errors are estimated to be the greatest single cause of database failures. These errors can be simple localized errors, for example, deleting data for Suresh Patel when it was data for Surendra Patel which needed to be deleted. Users' errors can also be more serious when, for example, data about all the ODI matches played in 2009 is deleted by mistake. Such mistakes may require drastic action to avoid major database downtime.
3. *Hardware and Media Failure*—Media failures are failures that result in the loss of some or all of the information stored on disk storage. Such failures can occur due to a hardware failure, for example, disk head crash; or by a software failure, for example, bugs in the disk writing modules in the operating system. Such failures can only be recovered if the archived version of the database, plus a log of activities since the time of the archive, is available. Most hardware failures also result in the loss of information in the main memory.

4. *System Failure*—A system failure may be classified as *soft-fail* or *hard-fail*. A soft-fail is a more common failure usually involving only the loss of information in the main memory. A soft-fail leaves the data on the disk memory intact. A hard-fail usually occurs less frequently but is harder to recover from since it may involve loss or corruption of information stored on the disk.

   System failures can sometimes be the most serious database failures and their causes can be difficult to track down. Most of these failures are due to either hardware, or DBMS or operating system failure. Recovery from system failure often involves reconstructing the database using the recovery information saved on the disk.
5. *Unrecoverable Failures*—These are failures that result in loss of data that cannot be recovered and happen usually because of operational mistakes, for example, failure to store regular archive copies of the database offsite or disasters like an earthquake or a flood which damages the building in which the database system has been installed.
6. *Other causes like operator errors, fire, flood*—Some unusual disasters can lead to loss of all information stored in a computer system. Recovery from such major failures can be difficult, sometimes impossible, unless the enterprise follows policies that will protect against such risks. Every enterprise needs to develop a disaster recovery plan to protect against catastrophic data loss, for example, the loss of an entire database host in a flood or fire. For Example, the recent (February 2011) earthquake in New Zealand destroyed most of the buildings in the Christchurch CBD. How would companies recover their databases if the databases were stored in computers in these buildings and if they did not plan for such a disaster?

We now present a definition of a database system failure.

Definition—DBMS Failure
A failure of a DBMS occurs when the database system does not meet its specification, that is, the database is in an inconsistent state.

Database backup ands recovery may be defined as follows.

Definition—Database Backup and Recovery
Database backup and recovery techniques are designed to protect the database against data loss and to reconstruct the database after data loss.

In addition to database failures discussed above, a transaction may fail to complete for a number of reasons. For example, a user may cancel the transaction before it completes or the user may enter erroneous data or the DBMS may instruct the transaction to be abandoned and rolled back because of a deadlock or an arithmetic division by zero or an overflow. Normally a transaction failure does not involve loss of the contents of the main memory or the disk storage and the recovery procedure only involves undoing changes caused by the failed transaction.

In a study conducted in 1981, it was found that 97 per cent of all transactions execute successfully. Most of the remaining 3 per cent failed because of incorrect user input or user cancellation. System crashes were found to occur every few days and almost all of these crashes were due to hardware or operating system failures. Several times a year, the integrity of the disk was lost although disk technology has improved significantly since then.

We now discuss database backup that is needed to ensure database recovery from a disaster.

10.3 DATABASE BACKUP

A database backup is a copy of the database, or a database snapshot, made on the date and time of the backup. A backup is like an insurance policy which is nice to have when a disaster strikes. Since a database can be very large, performing regular backups of a database is a time consuming and painful job. There is always the temptation to ignore backups since a computing professional who is in-charge of a database system may believe that given modern computer systems and reliable disks the system is very unlikely to crash. But database systems do crash and often most companies are so reliant on their computer systems that some cannot even continue to operate effectively without their database system.

A backup should include all database information of interest including tables, indexes, views, database catalog, stored procedures and archived log files. Backing up a database is the act of making a physical copy of the database on some media, perhaps using one or more tape drives, disk drives, removable disks or CDs depending on the size of the database. Database backups are usually created by using appropriate third party software which is available from many vendors. A database backup is usually carried out under the supervision of senior technical staff to ensure that the enterprise data stored in a database is not lost. Data in the database is not easy to replace.

Every database administrator who carries out database backups hopes that the backup will never be needed to restore the database and in fact most backups are never used even when kept for a long time. In spite of this the robustness of backups is critical because if a backup is not done correctly there is a very good chance that when a backup needs to be used the restoration process will not work correctly. Many horrifying restoration stories have been reported in the literature.

As defined above, the role of database backup is to protect the database against data loss and to help reconstruct the database after data loss. Effective database backup involves setting up a backup schedule, monitoring the backup techniques and troubleshooting backup problems. Database backup may also be used for creating a database copy for long-term storage or data transfer, involving moving data from one database to another or one host to another.

As noted earlier, database failures do occur and that is why backup and recovery are the most important aspects of protecting a database. For example, in May 2009 when this book was being written, newspapers in Australia reported that doctors at more than 100 hospitals in the state of New South Wales (which includes Sydney) could not access patient records including vital test results for up to 36 hours after a power failure crippled the NSW Health's database system. Some records were lost because all backups could not be restored and X-ray and pathology results could not be accessed. Medical staff members were forced to use whiteboards to keep track of emergency patients after the main database server shut down. It is not clear why some backups could not be restored but the incident highlights the importance of database backups.

A disaster like that described above illustrates the importance of planning for the worst disasters for important database systems. Although we do not know the cause of the NSW medical disaster, disasters can occur because of a number of causes including user errors, hardware failure, software failure, intrusions by unauthorized people, and finally due to natural disasters. The worst scenarios include fire in the database computer room or flood in the city where the computer system is located due to unexpected heavy rain storm perhaps due to heavy monsoon. A United Nations report on natural hazards in Asia-Pacific region lists cyclones, floods, landslides, earthquakes and tsunamis amongst the major natural hazards. This report concludes that China and India are ranked first and second respectively based on the total number of deaths due to natural disasters. In the current world political environment we cannot afford to forget the threat of a manmade disaster, i.e., terrorism. An important database system needs to be protected against all such disasters.

A report by Dell Computers lists a number of actions that an organization needs to take to prepare for serious disasters. The report includes the following advice:

- Make sure it is possible to communicate with your employees whatever disaster happens.
- Make sure all email addresses and email files are recoverable.
- Make sure current contact information for all employees and important clients are quickly recoverable.
- Make sure it is possible to recover the database system in a remote location if the current database location is not usable.
- Make sure the disaster recovery plan is regularly tested.

Some of the information listed above should be kept on another computer, perhaps using a system like Gmail, so that it is never lost.

A database backup may be done through a scheduled hierarchy of daily, weekly and monthly backups depending on the importance of the database and the rate of change of the data. For example, a telephone company would want to protect its accounts data by frequent backup and reliable recovery procedures. Since backup can be large, old backups are usually expired in time to make media available for new backups although media is relatively cheap now. Backups must be frequently tested for recovery. Most failed recoveries, as in the case of NSW hospitals noted above, are a result of lack of proper testing, organizational errors and miscommunication.

10.3.1 Backup Types

No one likes doing backups and it is one of the most difficult jobs in a database organization so the temptation is always to do as little backup as you might get away with and still pretend backups are being done. Such attitude should never the permitted if a valuable database is being managed. We discuss database backup planning next but it is necessary to discuss different types of backups which we do now.

1. *Level 0 – A full backup*—It involves backing up all the database files or files that have been selected. Backup flags are set to indicate what has been backed up.
2. *Level 1 – An incremental backup*—This involves backing up all the database files that have changed since the most recent full backup. Backup (or archival) flags are set to indicate what has been backed up and when.
3. *Level 2 – A differential backup*—This level of backup is essentially the same as incremental backup but backup flags are not reset when this backup is made. Therefore, the next differential backup will backup all files that have been modified since the most recent Level 1 backup.
4. *Level 3 – Copy*—This is essentially making a copy of some important files in spite of incremental or differential backups.

These are only the basic backup types. Other backup types, including Level 3, Level 4 and other higher level backups, have been defined.

A minimum backup must include a Level 0 backup at regular intervals and a Level 1 backup every night. A maximum backup would include running a mirror hot-swappable database system on another computer system and regular backup stored at another site.

We now discuss what issues need to be considered in designing a backup plan.

10.3.2 Backup Plan

A backup plan should include what types of backups will be carried out and when as well as a number of other issues. In designing a backup plan the following questions need to be asked before a plan is developed.

1. *Why?*—The aims of a database backup should be clearly documented. What kind of risk do we want to protect the database system against? The risks should also be clearly documented. How much will it cost the enterprise if some of the contents of the database were lost?
2. *What?*—What will be backed up? As noted earlier, a backup should include all database information that is important to the enterprise. How frequently and what type of backup will be carried out? A backup schedule is needed, for example, an incremental backup is required every night and a full backup needs to be carried out weekly or monthly.
3. *How fast is it changing?*—What is the rate of change of the database? A database that is changing fast should be backed up daily if not more frequently.
4. *When?*—What is the most convenient time to schedule the database backup? Usually backups are scheduled for off-peak hours when the load on the system is low. For example, one may do backup at 3 a.m. but if the system is being accessed by international users then this may not be the best time.
5. *How fast is the recovery required?*—An important question is how quickly is the restoration of the database after a crash required? In some critical applications quick restoration in minutes may be required while in other applications, for example, a library, even a restoration taking an hour or two may be acceptable.
6. *Where?*—Where will the backups be stored? It is strongly recommended that one copy of the database backup be stored off-site to protect against a disaster and another copy be stored in a fireproof safe on-site. All backup copies should be numbered properly. Given database disaster stories, it appears that it is not uncommon to not be able to find some part of a backed-up large database when the need arises.
7. *Who?*—Who is responsible for database backup software, hardware and the backup itself? Database backup or for that matter any kind of system backup is not the most sought after job but given its importance a trustworthy competent professional should be entrusted with the responsibility.
8. *How to test it works?*—All computer installation carries out backups but not many test their procedures regularly. More than once I have found that when I needed to recover a file I was not able to. Therefore, a backup and recovery system must be regularly tested for many different types of recovery requirements, for example, restoring a single table, a single index or the whole database.

Just to present a very simple example of importance of backup consider the backup of files that are this book. I am usually keeping the files and all related materials on a 2GB memory stick since I can take it home or even overseas when travelling and keep working on it. But what happens if the memory stick is lost or destroyed? How would I recover the valuable files? One time, the stick was in my pocket and I ran to cross a busy road and the stick popped out of my pocket and fell on the road! Actually I was lucky and no harm was done but I do keep a copy of the memory stick on my desktop computer's hard disk and also try to keep a copy on the external hard disk. I don't do a full backup every day because it takes time and is a bit of a pain but ensure that I backup the chapters I am working on. Even for such simple backup 'system' things can go wrong if I do not maintain proper protocols of which media has the latest files and therefore which ones can I modify. For a large database computer system, a backup protocol must include which media has the latest Level 0 backup and which media has the Level 1 backups and so on. These media must be stored properly on-site and/or off-site and clearly labeled and identified so there is no confusion where the latest backups are when recovery is required. Details of these media should perhaps be kept on a system like Gmail so that the information is never lost.

A new backup approach is now being considered by the University here at Monash, Australia. Since the desktop computer hard disks have no backups other than those done by users themselves which are mostly non-existent, the University is looking at ways of backing up all desktop computers. That will certainly help.

Database recovery is a complex task which must be done with care and tested regularly otherwise when data is lost the recovery from backup may not be possible. In addition to the backup, which is done only periodically, other procedures are needed to recover from database failures. These recovery procedures are discussed in Section 10.4. We first discuss physical and logical backups.

10.3.3 Physical and Logical Backup

Database backups may be divided into physical backups and logical backups.

Physical Backup

A physical backup involves making physical copies of the database files on backup media. It consists of copying disk blocks that make up the database. A physical backup does not interpret what is being backed up since the physical backup copies everything that is on the disk including database metadata and any other files.

A physical database may be carried out in a simple way by shutting down the database and doing the backup (this is called a *cold backup*). This is only practical if the database is not being used 24/7. A cold database backup can take a long time if the database is very large. A database may also be backed up while it is running (this is called a *hot backup*). This is of course not as simple as a cold backup since the database is being backed up as the users are changing the database. Most commercial DBMS provide utilities to carry out a hot backup.

Logical Backup

A logical backup on the other hand involves making a copy of each file that is in the database metadata to the backup media. Logical backup is simpler than physical backup but the backup does not record locations of various files on the disk. Logical backup however has the advantage of easier recovery from human errors, for example, dropping a table by a user by mistake. Recovery from a logical backup may be customized to recover from such user errors.

Logical backup may also be useful when it is required to move some files from one database to another.

Some DBMS allow both physical and logical backups to be carried out. It has been reported that physical backup is faster than a logical backup.

10.4 RECOVERY FROM A FAILURE

We have listed the types of failures earlier in Fig. 10.1. The failures are conveniently divided into three types of failures as transaction failures that occur due to incorrect transactions; system failures that occur, for example, when the power goes off; and media failures when all or some the disk is lost. We discuss these failures briefly in this section.

As noted earlier, proper design of a recovery system would be based on clear assumptions about the types of failures expected and the probabilities of those failures occurring. Most modern database systems are able to recover from a soft-fail by a system restart which takes only a few seconds or minutes. A hard-fail requires rebuilding of the database on the disk using one or more backup copies. This may take minutes or even hours depending on the type of failure and the size of the database. We should note that no set of recovery procedures can cope with all failures and there will always be situations when complete recovery may be impossible. This may happen if the failure results in corruption of some part of the database as well as loss or corruption of redundant data that has been saved for recovery.

The recovery requirements in different database environments are likely to be different. For example, in banking or in an airline reservation system or in a telecommunications accounting system, it would be a requirement that the possibility of losing any information due to a system failure be made very small. On the other hand, loss of information in an inventory database may not be quite so critical. Mission-critical databases may require fault tolerant hardware that may, for example, involve maintaining one or more duplicate copies of the database coupled with suitable recovery procedures. We know of one large lottery system which maintained two live identical database systems to ensure that if one system crashed the other system would continue to provide service to the lottery customers.

10.4.1 Transaction Failure

As noted above, transaction failures occur when an incorrect transaction fails and must be aborted. The values changed by the aborted transaction must then be restored to their values before the transaction changed them. Techniques for doing this are discussed later in this chapter.

10.4.2 System Failure

As noted above, a system may fail because of power failure, hardware failure and other causes like operator error. Recovery from a system failure is possible only if the DBMS maintains redundant data (called *recovery data*) including data about what users have been doing.

We assume that the recovery process will restore the database to a consistent state as close to the time of failure as possible but this depends on the type of failure and the type of recovery information that the database maintains.

We should note that a database system would often interact with the outside world. For example, a bank database system behind an automated teller machine (ATM) allows a customer to withdraw (some ATMs allow deposits as well) money. An airline database system would allow a travel agent (and increasingly a customer directly, using the Internet) to purchase a ticket and print it. A recovery technique obviously cannot rollback such interactions with the outside world and the technique must ensure consistent system behaviour in spite of such interactions.

The reliability of a database system may be measured by estimating the availability of the system which may be defined as the ratio of the mean time to failure (MTF) to the sum of MTF and the mean time for recovery (MTR). For example, if a database system on average fails once a month and takes on average two hours to recover then MTF is 720 hours (assuming 30 days in a month) and availability is given by 720 divided by MTF + MTR which is 722 resulting in availability of 99.72 per cent. If the recovery time was on the average only one hour, the availability rises to 99.86 per cent. Even such high reliability involving 24 hours or 12 hours downtime in a year may not be acceptable for some mission-critical database systems.

10.4.3 Media Failure

To be able to recover from media failures, for example, a disk head crash, a backup copy of the database must be kept in a safe place. The recovery process can only restore the database to the state it was in when the database was last archived. More details are presented in Section 10.16.

The component of a DBMS that deals with recovery is often called the *recovery manager*. Most recovery techniques are based on using a log. Therefore, before discussing some recovery techniques we discuss the concept of a database log.

10.5 THE CONCEPT OF A LOG

In Section 10.7 we will discuss some techniques for rolling back a partially completed transaction and redoing a completed transaction that may not have been written to disk when a failure occurred during its execution. It should be clear that to be able to rollback a transaction we need to store information about what that transaction had done before the failure. This is usually done by keeping a *log* or a *journal* which is normally stored on stable storage[1] (the most recent log could in fact be resident in the main memory although frequently the log is forced to disk) although recovery techniques that do not use a log also exist. A log is a history of updates made to the database resident in the volatile memory. It is like a tape recorder which records every change made to the database which can be played back if the system crashes so that lost transactions may be re-applied. The log stores sufficient information needed to implement the atomicity and durability properties of transactions. The log is designed to survive a database crash or a media failure.

1. Stable storage is storage that is robust against failures. Although disk is not considered stable storage, writing data to a disk in two places in a specific way may be considered stable storage. Stable storage functionality may be better achieved by mirroring data on separate disks.

A definition of log is now presented.

Definition—Log

A log is a linear ordered history of updates made to the database that is resident in the volatile memory and stored in a stable storage.

The DBMS module that manages the database log is called the *log manager*. Logs are logically an append-only sequence of unstructured records stored on disk to which an insert is generated at each insert, delete and update. Some systems maintain fair bit of information in each log record and therefore a log record is much longer than the one line record that we employ in this chapter. A log can therefore become very large quite quickly and may become a system performance problem. Each record appended to the log is assigned a unique *log sequence number* (LSN) for identification.

Figure 10.2 shows one possible arrangement for managing log files in a database system. In this system copies of log files are regularly archived to improve recovery reliability. This is done by the recovery manager in the main memory using the log buffer to save changes to the database. The system eventually flushes the log buffer to disk once a commit operation occurs. The size of the log buffers can influence system performance since a small buffer will require frequent writes to the disk, while a large buffer involves risk of loosing recovery data when the system crashes. The log files are regularly archived since these files can grow very quickly in a large busy database. Log files and the archived log files require considerable storage but large inexpensive disk systems, for example, RAID may be used.

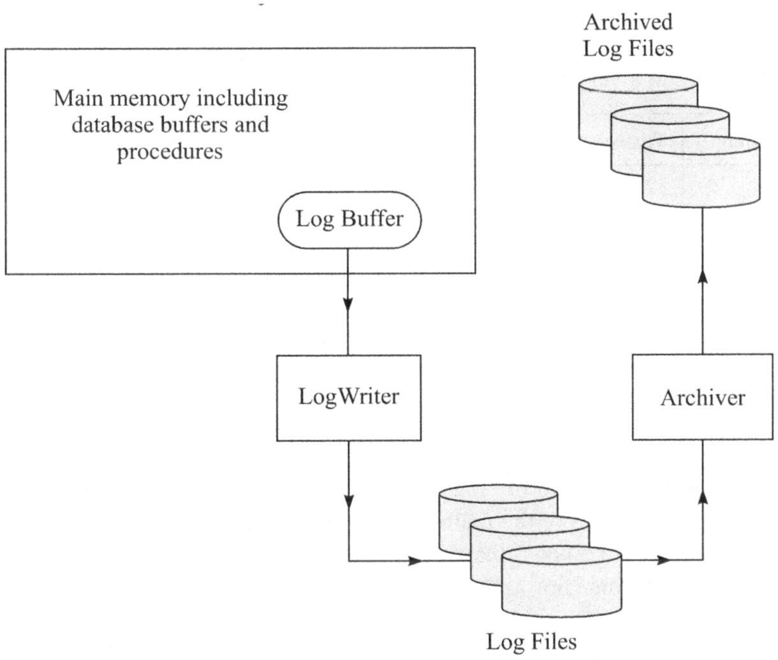

Figure 10.2 Management of log files in a database

Log-based recovery techniques essentially enable the database system to replay, after a failure has occurred, the execution of transactions just before the failure.

When a database failure occurs, each transaction could be in one of the following situations:

(a) *No action needed*—The transaction did not modify the database and therefore no rollback is required. The transaction could be resubmitted if required.
(b) *Rollback needed*—The transaction modified the database but was not completed. In this case the changes made by the transaction must be rolled back and the transaction may then be resubmitted if required.
(c) *Redo is needed*—The database was modified and the transaction was completed but it is not clear if all the modifications made by the transaction were written to the disk. In this case there is a need to ensure that all updates carried out by the completed transaction are durable.

As noted earlier, to ensure that the uncompleted transactions can be rolled back and the completed transactions are durable, most recovery mechanisms require maintenance of a log on a nonvolatile medium. Without the log, or some other similar technique, it would not be possible to discover whether a transaction updated any items in the database. The log maintains a record of all the changes that are made to the database, although different recovery methods that use a log may require the maintenance of a somewhat different log. Typically the log will maintain entries about updates, transaction commits, and transaction aborts. These entries have a variety of information. For example, for an update, the transaction ID and the old and new values may be written in the log record. On a transaction commit, the log entry will have information about the transaction and that it has committed. Similarly, on a transaction abort, the log entry will have information about the transaction and that it has aborted.

We now present an example of a very much simplified log that includes entries of the type given in Fig. 10.3.

Log Sequence Number	**Transaction ID**	**Action**	**Details**
LSN 23876	12345	Begun	
LSN 23877	12345	Update	old value 1000 and new value 2000
LSN 23878	12345	Commit	
LSN 23879	23456	Aborted	
LSN 23880	23460	Completed	

Figure 10.3 Entries in a simplified log

Once a completing transaction writes to the log that it has committed, it is assumed to commit even if all changes have not been propagated from the main memory to the disk. On commit, the log record is forced out to the disk. It should however be noted that when an entry is made to the log, the log record may not be immediately written to the disk since normally a system will only write a log block when it is full. A system crash therefore may result in some part of the log that was not yet written to disk also being lost but this does not create any problems. Most systems insist that log blocks be forced out at appropriate times.

If the log maintains information about the database before the updates and after the updates, the information in the log may be used to undo changes when a failure occurs and redo changes that a committed transaction has made to the database that may not have been written to the disk. As we will discuss in Section 10.7, another approach is possible in which the log only maintains information about the database after the updates but the changes are made to the database only if the transaction has completed successfully. We will discuss both techniques.

Recovery is often a significant cost in maintaining a database system. A major component of the recovery cost is the cost of maintaining the log which is needed only when a crash occurs.

We note that the maintenance of a log is sometimes needed for auditing purposes so a log may be used for both auditing and recovery. The log may also be used for performance analysis. If a database contains sensitive personal or enterprise data, it may be necessary to maintain a log of what information is read by whom and what is written back. This could then be used for auditing the usage of the system. This is sometimes called an *audit trail*. Database audit is discussed in more detail in the next chapter, in Section 11.6.

Since a log is the complete history of the database processing, access to the log should also be carefully controlled. Read access to a log could provide a user with indirect access to the whole database.

At the time of recovery we cannot normally look at the entire log since the last failure, as the log might be very long. Markers are therefore often put on the log to ensure that the entire log need not be looked at when a failure occurs. We will discuss this further later in this chapter, in Section 10.11.

We now briefly discuss buffer management which is required in describing the recovery techniques.

10.6 RECOVERY AND BUFFER MANAGEMENT

Although we have discussed the components of a database system in earlier chapters, it is convenient to list the major components of a database that are involved in recovery:

1. *The Nonvolatile Database*—This is the persistent database normally stored on one or more disks and is organized as a set of blocks. The nonvolatile database is usually resilient to soft failures of the system.
2. *The Volatile Memory Database Subset*—This subset of the database is copied from the nonvolatile database so that it may be read by users and modifications may be made before the changes are propagated to the nonvolatile database. Some blocks stored in the volatile memory are likely to be more recent than corresponding pages in the nonvolatile database since the volatile pages may have been modified but not written back to the disk.
3. *The Nonvolatile Log*—This is the primary log that is nonvolatile, and is usually stored in stable storage as discussed earlier. No modifications are permitted to the log.
4. *The Volatile Log*—This subset of the log that is not yet written to the disk and is usually lost when there is a system failure. It is frequently force written to the disk.

Figure 10.4 shows these components of the database. In the figure, the volatile memory and nonvolatile memory are shown as separate components of the database system. The flow of information in the system that takes place is also shown. The users are issuing queries that may include reads, insertions and updates of the database. In response to these queries the main memory brings in some database blocks from the disk. The main memory also maintains the log buffer or a set of log pages that stores information on all the changes to the database including beginning of a transaction, changes that each transaction makes to the database and finally transaction commit for a successful transaction or rollback for an unsuccessful transaction. These changes, as noted earlier, are flushed out to disk when the buffer is full or a transaction commits. The whole database and the database log are stored on the disk that does not lose the information when power goes off or when the database crashes because of some other reason.

As noted in Chapter 7, the part of the main memory that is available for storage of copies of disk blocks (also called pages) is called the *buffer*. The buffer is usually managed by software called the *buffer manager*. The primary purpose of a buffer management strategy is to minimize the number of disk accesses. An easy way to reduce disk traffic is to allocate a large fraction of the main memory to storing blocks of the nonvolatile database but there clearly is a limit to how much main storage can be assigned to buffers. A database buffer manager is a specialized memory manager as the needs of a database are somewhat more specialized than an ordinary operating system.

The buffer manager interacts with the crash recovery system to decide on what can be written back to disk. A crash recovery system may insist that some blocks be forced output before a particular buffer can be output.

To understand the various recovery mechanisms fully, it is necessary to understand the buffer management strategies used by a DBMS. An operating system uses algorithms like the LRU (least recently used) and MRU (most recently used) in managing buffers. Similar strategies may be used in database buffer management but database management has some peculiar requirements that make some techniques that are suitable for operating systems unsuitable for database management.

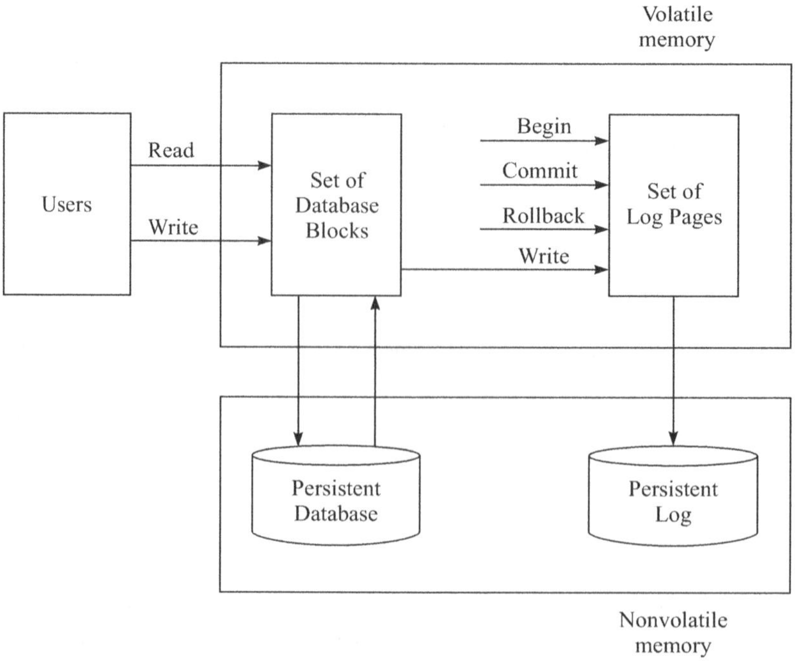

Figure 10.4 Major components in database recovery

As discussed later, all log based recovery algorithms follow the *write-ahead* log principle. This involves writing the recovery data for a transaction to the log before a transaction commits and the log must be written from main memory to the disk. To enforce the write-ahead principle, the recovery manager needs to be integrated with the buffer manager. Some recovery algorithms permit the buffer manager to *steal* dirty main memory pages by writing them to disk before the transaction that modified them commits. The write-ahead principle requires that the log records referring to the dirty pages must be written before the pages are cleaned. *No-steal* buffer management policies result in simpler recovery algorithms but limit the length of the transactions. Some recovery algorithms require the buffer manager to *force* all pages modified by a transaction to disk when the transaction commits. Recovery algorithms with *no-force* buffer management policies are more complicated, but they do less I/O than those that force buffers at commit.

Terminology

Some terminology used in buffer management is now defined.

1. *Dirty page*—A page in which data has been updated by a transaction that has not been committed.
2. *Pinned page*—A page that is not available for flushing.
3. *Unpinned page*—A pinned page that has been released.

We are now ready to discuss recovery techniques.

10.7 LOG-BASED TRANSACTION RECOVERY TECHNIQUES

Before we discuss a number of recovery techniques, we define what a log-based recovery technique is expected to achieve.

> ***Definition—Database Recovery***
> *A database recovery technique is a technique that guarantees that after a failure the volatile memory database system recovers to be equivalent to a serial order of the committed transactions that coincides with the serialization order of the transaction history as recorded in the log.*

Consider the following schedule assuming three transactions T_1, T_2 and T_3 accessing the database:

Now assume that a system failure occurs at time 12. Since transactions T_1 and T_3 have committed before the crash, the recovery procedure should ensure that the effects of these transactions are reflected in the database (that is, the transactions are durable). On the other hand T_2 did not commit and it is the responsibility of the recovery procedure to ensure that when the system restarts the effects of the partially completed T_2 are undone forever.

The following three protocols are needed by the recovery procedure to deal with various recovery situations:

The actions listed in Fig. 10.6 are sometimes called *DO-UNDO-REDO* protocols. They play a slightly different role in the two recovery techniques that we discuss in Sections 10.9 and 10.10.

Time	T_1	T_2	T_3
0	Begin	–	–
1	–	–	Begin
2	Read N	–	–
3	–	–	Read P
4	$N := N - 5$	–	–
5	–	Begin	–
6	–	–	$P := P - 4$
7	–	Read M	–
8	Write N	–	–
9	Commit	–	–
10			Write P
11	–	Write M	–
12	–	–	Commit
13	–	M := M * 1.5	–
14	–	Temp := M	–
15	–	$B := B + 1$	–

Figure 10.5 Three transactions running concurrently

1. DO(T_i, action) — This procedure carries out the action specified. The log is written before an update is carried out.
2. UNDO(T_i) — This procedure undoes the actions of the transaction T_i using the information in the log. It involves forcing the undo information for each block in the volatile memory to the disk.
3. REDO(T_i) — This procedure redoes the actions of the committed transaction T_i using the information in the log. It involves forcing the redo information of a transaction to the disk when the transaction is committed.

Figure 10.6 The DO-UNDO-REDO protocol

When a transaction aborts, the information contained in the log is used to undo the transaction's effects on the database. Logging disciplines require that a transaction be undone in reverse of the order that its operations were performed.

We now discuss two recovery techniques that use a log. Another technique that does not use a log is discussed later. Before discussing these techniques we briefly discuss steps involved in Redo and Undo operations. These operations are identified by examining the most recent part of the system log. A decision is made, we will discuss later how this is done, about how far back the log will be examined and then examination of the log continues forward to the most recent log record. This is sometimes called the analysis phase which identifies all transactions that need to be REDOne or UNDOne. Once this phase is over, the REDO operations are carried out. Finally all the UNDO operations are carried out.

REDO Operations

The REDO operation involves redoing of all transactions that had committed before the crash took place. REDO applies all the changes in the order they were carried out by the transaction that committed.

UNDO Operations

The UNDO operation involves undoing all transactions that had not committed before the crash took place. UNDO applies all the changes in the opposite order that they were carried out by the transaction that committed, reversing the most recent changes first.

10.8 TYPES OF RECOVERY TECHNIQUES

A number of recovery techniques have been proposed. The most popular techniques use a log but techniques that do not use a log have also been proposed. We provide a brief list of recovery techniques.

1. *No-undo and No-redo Techniques*—Although these techniques do maintain a log they essentially do not require a log since they ensure that the database contains only the actions of the committed transactions. On recovery therefore no undo or redo is required and recovery from a soft-fail is very quick.
2. *No-undo and Redo Techniques*—These techniques essentially do not propagate any actions of an uncommitted transaction to the disk. Only changes made by the committed transaction are propagated. On recovery therefore no undo is required although redo may be required. This is also called the *deferred update* recovery technique.
3. *No-redo and Undo Techniques*—These techniques essentially ensure that all changes made by the committed transactions are force propagated to the database. On recovery therefore some undo may be required but no redo is required. This is also called the *immediate update* recovery technique.
4. *Undo and Redo Techniques*—These techniques essentially require information for both the undo and redo to be logged. On recovery therefore both undo and redo are required.
5. *Techniques without using a log*—Techniques in this category include the shadow page techniques. The shadow page technique involves two versions of the database page addressing table, the table that translates page numbers into disk addresses. Another approach, called the versioning approach, involves maintaining a differential file which is used to update the database when a transaction commits. More details of the shadow page technique are presented later in the chapter.

Our brief discussion above has left several questions regarding the log-based techniques unanswered, for example:

(a) Is the write-ahead principle necessary?
(b) If a crash occurs, how does recovery take place?
(c) What happens if a failure occurs as the log is being written to the disk?
(d) What happens if another crash occurs during the recovery procedure?

We now answer these questions.

10.8.1 Write-Ahead Principle

If the updated data item is written back to disk before the log, a crash between updating the database and writing a log would lead to problems as the log would have no record of the update. Since there would be no record, the update could not be undone if required. If the log is written before the actual update item is written to disk, this problem is overcome. Also if a failure occurs during the writing of the log, no damage would have been done as the database update would not yet have taken place. A transaction would be regarded as having committed only if the logging of its updates has been completed, even if all data updates have not been written to the disk.

We first define the write-ahead principle.

Definition—Write-Ahead Principle
Write-ahead loggings (WAL) involves a redo and/or undo log entry written to the log before an update item is written to disk.

10.8.2 The Recovery Process

We now discuss how the recovery takes place on failure. Assuming that the failure results in the loss of the volatile memory only, we are left with a log file and database that may not be consistent since some transformations that did not commit may have modified the database. It is now the responsibility of the recovery procedure to make sure that those transactions that have log records stating that they were committed are in fact committed (some of the changes that such transactions made may not yet have been propagated to the database on the disk). Also effects of partially completed transactions, that is, transactions for which no commit log record exists, are undone. To achieve this, the recovery manager inspects the log when the system restarts and REDOes the transactions that were committed recently (we will later discuss how to identify transactions that are recent) and UNDOes the transactions that were not committed. This rolling back of partially completed transactions requires that the log of the uncommitted transactions be read backwards and each action is undone. The reason for undoing uncommitted transactions backwards becomes clear if we consider an example in which a data item is updated more than once as in Fig. 10.7 below.

Log Sequence Number	Transaction ID	Action	Details
LSN 238	1135	Begin	
LSN 239	1135	Update	Account A - old value 1000 and new value 900
LSN 240	1135	Update	Account A - old value 900 and new value 700
LSN 241	1135	Update	Account B - old value 2000 and new value 2100

Figure 10.7 An example of a log

Only backward UNDOing can ensure that the original value of 1000 is restored.

10.8.3 Crash during the Recovery Process

It is always possible that the system will crash again during the analysis phase or the REDO phase or the UNDO phase. Fortunately no problems arise if another crash happens during recovery. If the crash happens during the analysis of the log, then the analysis can be done on restart after the crash. If the crash happens during the REDO phase then the REDO can be done again. Also if the crash happens during the UNDO phase then this phase can also be done again.

Several failures may occur in a short span of time and we may REDO transactions again and again and UNDO transactions several times. It is therefore essential that UNDO and REDO operations be *idempotent,* that is, the effect of doing the same UNDO or REDO operations several times is the same as doing it once. An operation like add $35 to the account obviously is not idempotent while an operation setting the account balance to $350 obviously is.

We now discuss two log-based recovery techniques, namely the Immediate Update Recovery Technique and the Deferred Update Recovery Technique.

10.9 LOG-BASED IMMEDIATE UPDATE RECOVERY TECHNIQUE

As noted earlier, one possible recovery technique is to allow each transaction to make changes to the database as the transaction is executed and maintain a log of these changes. This is sometimes called *logging only the UNDO information*. The information written in the log would include the identifiers of items updated and their old values. For a deleted item, the log would maintain the identifier of the item and its last value. As discussed above, the log must be written to the disk before the updated data item is written to disk.

Definition—Immediate Update Recovery Technique
Immediate Update Recovery technique applies write operations to the database as a transaction is executing and writes are saved in the log before being applied to the database. A transaction is not allowed to update the database until all UNDO entries have been written to the log and the transaction is not allowed to commit until all REDO and UNDO log entries are forced-written to disk. This is sometimes called logging only the UNDO information.

We consider a simple example of a bank account transfer discussed earlier. When the transaction is ready to be executed, the transaction number is written to the log to indicate the beginning of a transaction, possibly as shown in Fig. 10.8.

Log Sequence Number	Transaction ID	Action	Details
LSN 23876	12345	Begin	
LSN 23877	12345	Update	Account A - old value 1000 and new value 900
LSN 23878	12345	Update	Account B - old value 2000 and new value 2100
LSN 23879	12345	Commit	

Figure 10.8 Entries for a bank transfer example

Let us consider another simple example of the log.

Log Sequence Number	Transaction ID	Action	Details
LSN 23876	12345	Begin	
LSN 23877	12345	Update	Account A - old value 1000 and new value 900
LSN 23878	12345	Update	Account B - old value 2000 and new value 2100
LSN 23879	12345	Commit	
LSN 23880	12400	Begin	
LSN 23881	12400	Write	Account C - old value 2500 and new value 2000
LSN 23882	12400	Write	Account D - old value 1500 and new value 2000
LSN 23883	12405	Begin	
LSN 23884	12400	Commit	

Figure 10.9 Entries for another bank transfer example

Let the log consist of the 9 records in Fig.10.9 at failure. The recovery procedure first checks which transactions have been committed (transactions 12345 and 12400) and REDOes them by the following actions:

REDO (T = 12345)
REDO (T = 12400)

Transaction 12405 was not committed. UNDO (T = 12405) is therefore issued. In the present example, transaction 12405, however, does not need to be rolled back since it did not carry out any updates.

The reason for REDOing committed transactions is that although the log states that these transactions were committed, the log is written before the actual updated data items are written to disk and it is just possible that an update carried out by a committed transaction was not written to disk. If the update was in fact written, the REDO must make sure that REDOing the transaction does not have any further effect on the database. Also, as noted earlier, several failures may occur in a short span of time and we may REDO transactions 12345 and 12400 and UNDO transaction 12405 several times. It is therefore essential that UNDO and REDO operations be *idempotent*, that is, the effect of doing the same UNDO or REDO operations several times is the same as doing them once. An operation like add $35 to the account obviously is not idempotent while an operation setting the account balance to $350 obviously is.

Let us consider another example of UNDO. Let the log have only the first seven log records in Fig. 10.9 at failure. We therefore issue:

REDO (T = 12345)
UNDO (T = 12400)

Once REDO is completed, UNDO reads the log backwards. It reads a record of the log and restores the old value of Account D, then reads record 6 of the log and restores the old value of Account C.

Note that the recovery procedure works properly even if there is a failure during recovery since a restart after such a failure would result in the same process being repeated.

10.10 LOG-BASED DEFERRED UPDATE RECOVERY TECHNIQUE

The immediate update scheme requires that before-update values of the data items be logged. Therefore the updates carried out by the transactions that have not been committed may have to be undone. In the deferred update scheme, the database on the disk is not modified until the transaction reaches its commit point although all modifications are logged as they are carried out in the main memory and therefore the before-update values do not need to be logged. Only the after-update data values of the database are recorded on the log as the transaction continues its execution but once the transaction completes successfully (called a *partial commit*) and writes to the log that it is ready to commit, the log is force written to disk and all the writes recorded in the log are then carried out. The transaction then commits. This is sometimes called *logging only the REDO information*. The technique allows database writes to be delayed but involves forcing the buffers that hold transaction modifications to be pinned in the main memory until the transaction commits.

Definition—Deferred Update Recovery Technique
Deferred update Recovery technique records the write operations of a transaction to the log. The writes are applied to the database only when the transaction commits. A transaction cannot change any items in the database until it commits. A transaction may not commit until all the write operations are forced-written in the log. This is sometimes called logging only the REDO information.

There are several advantages of the deferred update procedure. If a system failure occurs before a partial commit, no action is necessary whether the transaction logged any updates or not. A part of the log that was in the main memory may be lost but this does not create any problems. If a partial commit had taken place and the log had been written to the disk then a system failure would have virtually no impact since the deferred writes would be REDOne by the recovery procedure when the system restarts.

The deferred update method can also lead to some difficulties. If the system buffer capacity is limited, there is the possibility that the buffers that have been modified by an uncommitted transaction are forced out to disk by the buffer management part of the DBMS. To ensure that the buffer management will not force any of the uncommitted updates to the disk requires that the buffer must be large enough to hold all the blocks of the database that are required by the active transactions. We again consider the bank account transfer example used earlier. When the transaction is ready to be executed, the transaction number is written on the log to indicate the beginning of a transaction, possibly as follows:

<T = 1235, BEGIN>

This is then followed by the write commands in the log, for example, as shown in Fig. 10.10.

Note that the deferred update only requires the new values to be saved since recovery involves only REDOs and never any UNDOs. Once this log is written to the disk, the updates may be carried out. Should a failure

Log Sequence Number	Transaction ID	Action	Details
LSN 23876	12345	Begin	
LSN 23877	12345	Update	Account A - new value 900
LSN 23878	12345	Update	Account B - new value 2100
LSN 23879	12345	Commit	

Figure 10.10 Entries for a deferred update log

occur at any stage after writing the log and before updating the database on the disk, the log would be used to REDO the transaction.

Similar to the technique used in the last section, the recovery manager needs a procedure REDO which REDOes all transactions that were active recently and committed. No recovery action needs to be taken about transactions that did not partially commit (those transactions for which the log does not have a commit entry) before the failure because the system would not have updated the database on the disk for those transactions. Consider the example given in Fig. 10.11 below.

Log Sequence Number	Transaction ID	Action	Details
LSN 35876	12111	Begin	
LSN 35877	12111	Update	Account C - new value 950
LSN 35878	12111	Commit	
LSN 35879	12340	Begin	
LSN 35880	12340	Write	Account A - new value 900
LSN 35881	12340	Write	Account B - new value 2100
LSN 35882	12340	Commit	
LSN 35883	12400	Begin	
LSN 35884	12400	Write	Account C, new=2000
LSN 35885	12400	Write	Account D, new=2000
LSN 35886	12405	Begin	
LSN 35887	12400	Commit	

Figure 10.11 Another example of deferred log

Now if a failure occurs and the log has the above entries, the recovery manager identifies all transactions that were active recently and have been committed (Transactions 12111, 12340 and 12400). We assume the recovery manager does not need to worry about transactions that were committed well before the crash (for example, Transaction 1111). In the next section, we will discuss how we identify *recent* transactions.

If another failure occurs during the recovery, the same transactions may be REDOne again. As noted earlier, the effect of redoing a transaction several times is the same as doing it once.

10.11 SYSTEM CHECKPOINTS

In the discussion above, the immediate update methods involves REDOing all recently committed transactions and UNDOing transactions that were not committed while the deferred update methods only requires REDOing and no UNDOing. We have so far not defined how *recent* transactions are identified. We do so now.

One technique for identifying recent transactions might be to search the entire log and identify recent transactions on some basis, for example, time. This is of course certain to be very inefficient since the log may be very long. Also, it is likely that most transactions that are selected for REDOing have already written their updates into the database and do not really need to be REDOne. REDOing all these transactions will cause the recovery procedure to be inefficient.

To limit the number of transactions that need to be reprocessed during recovery after a failure, a technique of marking the log is used. The markers are called system *checkpoints* and putting a marker on the log (called taking a checkpoint) consists of the following steps:

(a) Write a <begin checkpoint> record to the log.
(b) Write all log records currently residing in the main memory to the disk followed by writing to the disk all modified pages in the buffer. Also identifiers (or names) of all active transactions are written to the log.
(c) Write an <end checkpoint> record to the log.

Now when the recovery procedure is invoked on a failure, the last checkpoint is found (this information is often recorded in a file called the *restart file*) and only the transactions active at the time of checkpoint and those after the checkpoint are processed.

A simple recovery algorithm requires that the recovery manager identify the last checkpoint and build two lists, one of the transactions that need to be REDOne and the other of transactions that need to be UNDOne. Initially, all transactions that are listed as active at the checkpoint are included in the UNDO list and the log is scanned forward. Any new transaction that becomes active is added to the UNDO list and any transaction that is logged to have committed is removed from the UNDO list and placed on the REDO list. At the end of the log, the log is scanned backwards and all the actions of those transactions that are on the UNDO list are UNDOne in the backward order. Once the checkpoint is reached, the log is scanned forward and all the actions of the transactions on the REDO list are REDOne.

10.12 IMPLEMENTING A LOG-BASED RECOVERY SYSTEM–ARIES

ARIES (Algorithms for Recovery and Isolation Exploiting Semantics) is a widely used implementation of log-based recovery management developed at IBM. ARIES is a flexible and efficient system and it is possible to generalize it to meet different recovery needs. The method is used by IBM DB2, SQL Server and a number of other database systems. It has the following major characteristics:

- A write-ahead log is implemented that logs all updates to all pages. Every database page has a Log Sequence Number (LSN) and this LSN is placed in the log record when a page is updated. Logs during partial or total rollbacks are also kept. The log is written to stable storage before the changes are written to disk.
- It uses a steal/no-force approach and hence requires both undo and redo.
- It maintains various data structures to identify dirty pages, pages that are changed but not written to disk, in the memory buffers and the active transactions.
- On restart after a crash, ARIES goes through three phases, viz., ANALYSIS, REDO and UNDO. ARIES scans the database log from the last checkpoint to the end of the log.
- During the analysis phase, information about transactions that were in progress at the time of the crash and information about dirty pages is collected. Based on this information, the analysis phase determines which transactions must be rolled back during UNDO.
- During the REDO phase, ARIES redoes the actions of all transactions to restore the state at the time before the failure.
- ARIES then scans the log backwards and undoes the actions of all uncommitted transactions. Changes made to the database while undoing transactions are logged to ensure such an action need not be repeated in the event of repeated restarts.

The principal designer of ARIES was C. Mohan. Our description is based on the 1992 paper published by the group. Details of ARIES are complex; it also includes issues related to concurrency control as well as description of several versions of ARIES. It is necessary to read the original papers to develop full understanding of the system.

10.13 SUMMARY OF LOG-BASED METHODS

Although log-based recovery methods vary in a number of details, there are a number of common requirements on the recovery log. First, all recovery methods adhere to the write-ahead log procedure. Information is always written to the log before it propagates to nonvolatile memory and before transactions commit. Second, all recovery methods rely on the ordering of operations expressed in the log to provide an ordering for the REDO and UNDO operations. Third, all methods use checkpoints or some similar technique to bound the amount of log processed for recovery. Some recovery methods scan the log sequentially forward during crash recovery. Others scan the log sequentially backwards. Still others use both forward and backward scans.

A log manager may manage a log as a file on the secondary storage. When this file has reached a prespecified length, the log may be switched to another file while the previous log is copied to some archive storage. The approach used by System R is to take a large chunk of disk space and lay it out for the log as a circular buffer of log pages. The log manager appends new blocks sequentially to the circular buffer as the log fills. Although an abstract log is an infinite resource, in practice the online disk space available for storing the log is limited. Some systems will spool truncated log records to archival storage for use in media recovery. Other systems will provide enough online log space for media recovery and will discard truncated log data.

ARIES is a widely known and used example of a log-based recovery technique. As noted earlier, a number of versions of ARIES have been developed and are used in a number of database systems.

10.14 SHADOW PAGE SCHEMES

Not all recovery techniques make use of a log. Shadow page schemes (or *careful replacement* schemes) are recovery techniques that do not use logging for recovery. To simplify the description we assume that only one transaction is running at any one time and when a page of storage is modified by the transaction a new page is allocated for the modified data and the old page is retained as a *shadow* copy of the data. This is easily achieved by maintaining two tables of page addresses, one table called the *current page table* and the other called the *shadow page table*.

> ***Definition—Shadow Page Recovery Scheme***
> *Shadow paging is an alternative to log-based recovery techniques that introduces a level of indirection between logical pages and physical pages by using two page tables, a current page table and a shadow page table, of the database that is being used by a transaction. The current page table points to modified database. In case of a transaction failure, the current page table is removed. In case of a transaction commit, the shadow page table is removed.*

At the beginning of a transaction the two page tables are identical but as the transaction modifies pages new pages are allocated and the current page table is modified accordingly while the shadow page table continues to point to the old pages. The current pages may be located in the main memory or on the disk but all current pages are output to the disk before the transaction commits. If a failure occurs before the transaction commits, the shadow page table is used to recover the database state before the transaction started. When a transaction commits, the pages in the current page table (which now must be on the disk) become the pages in the shadow page table. The shadow pages must be *carefully replaced* with the new pages in an atomic operation. To achieve this, the current page table is output to the disk after all current pages have been output. Now the address of the shadow page table is replaced by the address of the current page table and the current page table becomes the shadow page table committing the transaction. Should a failure occur before this change, the old shadow page table is used to recover the database state before the transaction started.

In the example shown in Fig. 10.12, as described above, two tables, one called the *current page table* and the other called the *shadow page table,* are maintained. Initially, both tables point to pages that have been brought into the main memory from the disk and their contents have not been modified. When a page of the database is modified by a transaction a new page is allocated for the modified data and the current page table points to this page. The modified new page may be written back to the disk but it does not overwrite the old page which remains as a *shadow* copy of the data.

In the example, Pages 3, 4 and 7 have been modified and therefore new pages are allocated for these modified pages. Now if a failure occurs before the transaction commits, the shadow page table is used to recover the database state before the transaction started. Nothing else needs to be done. If the transaction commits, each modified page is flushed to the disk. Once flushed, the pages in the current page table become the new page table and the old shadow table is replaced. It may be appropriate to save the old shadow table until the commit procedure finishes. The current page table is output to the disk after all current pages have been output. The address of the shadow page table is replaced by the address of the current page table as it becomes the new shadow page table for the next transaction.

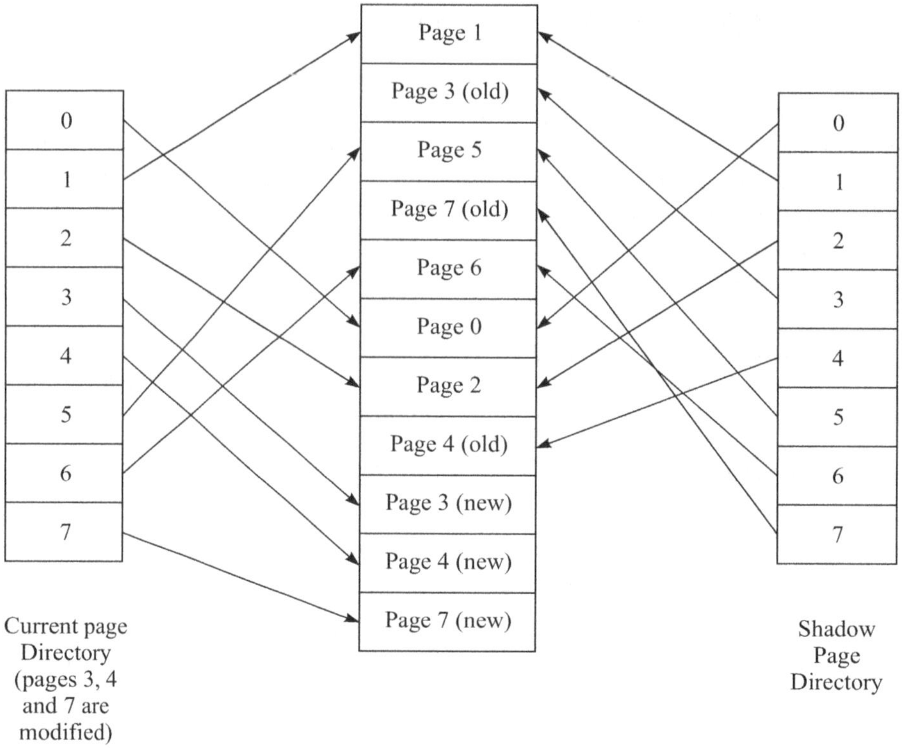

Figure 10.12 An example of shadow page technique

The shadow page recovery technique therefore eliminates the need for the log although the technique is sometimes criticized as having poor performance for normal processing. However, the recovery is often fast when a transaction aborts. Also the shadow paging technique requires a suitable garbage collection technique to remove all the old shadow pages.

In spite of the attractive feature of shadow paging that a log is not required, most database systems used recovery techniques based on write-ahead logging rather than shadow paging.

10.15 EVALUATION OF RECOVERY TECHNIQUES

Gray et al. (1981) describe their experience with developing and using a recovery system. They note that the recovery system was comparatively easy to write and added about 10 percent to the DBMS code. In addition, the cost of writing log records was typically of the order of 5 percent. The cost of checkpoints was found to be minimal and restart after a crash was found to be quite fast. Different recovery algorithms have varying costs, both during normal processing and recovery. For log algorithms, the costs of the algorithms during normal processing include the volume and frequency of the log writes and the influence of the algorithms on buffer management. Recovery algorithms which force the buffer pool have comparably poor performance. The costs of crash recovery include the number of log records read, and the number of pages of data that must be paged into main memory, restored and paged out. No-force recovery algorithms were found to read more data pages during recovery than force algorithms. Recovery algorithms with steal buffer pool management policies may read data pages for both REDO and UNDO processing, while no-steal buffer managers mainly read pages for REDO processing.

10.16 RECOVERING FROM A MEDIA FAILURE

So far, our discussion about recovery has assumed that a system failure was a soft-failure in that only the contents of the volatile memory were lost and the disk was left intact. Of course, a disk is not immune from failure and a head crash may result in all the contents of the disk being lost. Other, stranger, failures are also possible. For example, a disk pack may be damaged by a careless operator or there may be some other disaster as noted before. We therefore need to be prepared for a disaster involving loss of the contents of the nonvolatile media.

As noted earlier, the primary technique for recovery from such a loss of information is to maintain a suitable backup copy of the database possibly on a separate disk system and ensure its safe storage possibly in a fireproof and waterproof safe, preferably at a location some distance away from the database site. Such backup may need to be done every day or may be done less or more frequently depending upon the value the organization attaches to loss of some information when a disk crash occurs.

As databases tend to be large, a complete backup is usually quite time consuming. The database may be backed up incrementally, that is, only copies of altered parts of the database are backed up. A complete backup is still needed regularly but this would not need to be done frequently. After a system failure, the incremental system tapes and the last complete backup tape may be used to restore the database to a past consistent state.

SUMMARY

In this chapter we have discussed different types of database system failures and how to recover from such failures. The following topics have been covered:

- There are different types of database system failures when a database consistency is compromised, for example, power failures and hardware and media failures. Since a database is a valuable asset, it needs to be protected.
- In this chapter a number of techniques to recover from such database failures are presented.
- One approach is to carry out a database backup regularly to protect against data loss.
- There are a number of types of backups including a full backup and an incremental backup.
- It is necessary to develop a backup plan for an enterprise database system. The plan should include when the backups will be carried out, who is responsible for the backups and where the backup copy will be stored.
- A backup may be a physical backup or a logical backup. A physical backup is a backup of the whole database while a logical backup is a backup of each file in the database.

- There are a number of different techniques for database recovery. Some of them use a log.
- The log is a record of each important step of each transaction. It is used during database recovery.
- Some concepts of buffer management are relevant to recovery techniques.
- Two recovery techniques that use a log are the immediate update method and the deferred update method.
- Recovery systems using the log to repair the database and to bring it to a consistent state after a database crash using the DO, UNDO and REDO protocols in database recovery.
- The need for the DO, UNDO and REDO protocols to be idempotent is explained.
- The immediate update recovery technique applies updates to the database after writing them to log.
- The deferred update recovery technique applies updates to the database after writing them to the log only after the transaction has committed.
- Check-pointing is used to mark the log so that recovery only looks at the recent transactions and this assists log-based recovery.
- The shadow page technique does not use a log. It maintains two page tables, a current page table and a shadow page table. If the transaction commits then the current page is the table that points to the modified pages and the shadow page table is removed.
- Major features of the ARIES system are briefly described.
- Possible failure of a disk system and recovering from it is discussed.

REVIEW QUESTIONS

1. Why is it so important to ensure that an enterprise database be protected? (Section 10.1)
2. What is a database failure and what are major causes for database failures? (Section 10.2)
3. What is database backup and database recovery? (Section 10.2)
4. What is required to carry out a database backup? (Section 10.3)
5. List three backup types. Which ones are the most common? (Section 10.3.1)
6. What should be included in a backup plan? (Section 10.3.2)
7. Describe the differences between physical and logical backup. (Section 10.3.3)
8. What does a recovery technique aim to achieve? (Section 10.4)
9. Explain the concept of a log and how it helps with database recovery. (Section 10.5)
10. Explain why buffer management is relevant to recovery. (Section 10.6)
11. How does a recovery technique using the DO, UNDO and REDO protocols work? (Section 10.7)
12. Why is it important that the DO, UNDO and REDO protocols be idempotent? (Section 10.7)
13. What different states can a transaction be in when a failure occurs? (Section 10.8)
14. What is the basis of the immediate updates recovery technique? (Section 10.9)
15. What does the deferred updates recovery technique involve? (Section 10.10)
16. Given a part of the log, explain what needs to be done to carry out recovery if immediate updates or deferred updates techniques are being used. (Sections 10.9 and 10.10)
17. Explain the concept of a checkpoint and how checkpointing assists log-based recovery. (Section 10.11)
18. Briefly explain the ARIES recovery approach. (Section 10.12)

19. Describe the shadow page technique that does not use a log. (Section 10.14)
20. Given an example of shadow paging and explain what needs to be done when the transaction commits or a failure occurs. (Section 10.14)
21. Explain how to recover from a media failure. (Section 10.16)

SHORT ANSWER QUESTIONS

1. What is the aim of database backup?
2. What is the aim of database recovery?
3. List three types of database failures.
4. List three database backup types.
5. What questions must be asked when designing a backup plan for a database system?
6. What is physical backup?
7. What is logical backup? How is different from physical backup?
8. Define a database log.
9. What are the three conditions that a transaction might be in when a failure occurs?
10. What is the role of buffer management in database recovery?
11. What are REDO, UNDO and DO operations?
12. What is write-ahead principle?
13. What happens if there is a crash during the recovery process?
14. What is the main concept behind immediate update recovery method?
15. What is the main concept behind deferred update recovery method?
16. Why do log recovery methods need checkpoints?
17. Does shadow page recovery scheme need a log? If not, why not?
18. What are three major principles behind ARIES?
19. Explain a situation in which there was a media failure.

MULTIPLE CHOICE QUESTIONS

1. Which one of the following is **not** a reason for a database system failure?
   (a) Hardware and media failure
   (b) Power failure
   (c) User input errors
   (d) Database loading errors
2. Which one of the following is true about database backup?
   (a) The purpose of a database backup is to protect the database against data loss and help reconstruct the database after data loss.
   (b) A database backup is a copy of the database.
   (c) A backup system requires suitable testing.
   (d) All of the above are correct.

3. Which one of the following is **not** correct?
   (a) A full backup is called Level 9 backup.
   (b) Level 1 backup is an incremental backup.
   (c) Level 2 backup is a differential backup.
   (d) Level 3 backup only makes copies of the important files.
4. Which one of the following is correct?
   (a) The aims of database backup should be clearly documented.
   (b) The most convenient time for a database backup should be clearly documented.
   (c) Backups and the backup procedure must be tested from time to time.
   (d) All of the above are correct
5. Which one of the following is correct?
   (a) A physical backup involves making physical printed copies of the database files.
   (b) A logical backup involves making copy of each file that is in database metadata to the backup media.
   (c) A hybrid backup involves doing both the physical backup as well as logical backup.
   (d) All of the above are correct
6. Which of the following components of a database system are involved in recovery?
   (a) The nonvolatile database
   (b) The volatile memory database subset
   (c) The nonvolatile log
   (d) All of the above
7. Which one of the following is correct?
   (a) Dirty page is a page in which maintains a list of pages that have been updated by a transaction that has not been committed.
   (b) Pinned page is a page that is not available for flushing.
   (c) If a requested page is not in the buffer pool, it needs to replace either an unpinned page or a dirty page.
   (d) A page replacement policy does not have a significant impact on the disk traffic.
8. Which one of the following is correct? A database failure may involve the loss of information in the
   (a) main memory
   (b) disk
   (c) memory cache
   (d) All of the above
9. Which one of the following is correct? All log-based recovery techniques
   (a) use write-ahead log.
   (b) use checkpoint or a similar technique.
   (c) use the order of the log records to UNDO and REDO.
   (d) All of the above
10. Which one of the following is correct? The primary reason why checkpoints are needed in the log is to
   (a) reduce log processing
   (b) maintain consistency
   (c) maintain transaction durability
   (d) reduce database archiving
   (e) All of the above
11. Computer storage is often classified according to the reliability of the storage. Which of the following is **not** one of the storage classes?

(a) Permanent
(b) Volatile
(c) Nonvolatile
(d) Stable

12. Which one of the following is the most accurate definition of recovery?
    (a) Restoring the database to a prior consistent state.
    (b) Restoring the database to a state such that queries may be posed again.
    (c) Restoring the database to a state such that the log may be written again.
    (d) Restoring the database to a state such that no earlier transaction is lost.
13. Which one of the following is correct? A database failure is said to have occurred when
    (a) the system crashes.
    (b) the database system is not accessible.
    (c) the database is in an inconsistent state.
    (d) All of the above
14. Which one of the following is **not** a database failure?
    (a) Transaction failure
    (b) Application software failure
    (c) System failure
    (d) Media failure
15. Which of the following is **not** true about logs?
    (a) Each log record has a timestamp.
    (b) A log is an append-only sequence of unstructured records.
    (c) A log includes a record for each insert, delete and update.
    (d) Each log record has a unique log sequence number.
16. At recovery time, which of the following transactions does the recovery manager **not** need to identify?
    (a) Those that committed before the checkpoint.
    (b) Those that did not commit before the crash.
    (c) Those that aborted before the crash.
    (d) Those that completed before the crash but did not commit.
17. Which one of the following is true about UNDO-REDO-DO protocols?
    (a) UNDO, REDO are idempotent.
    (b) REDO is done backwards.
    (c) UNDO is done in the same sequence as done previously.
    (d) UNDO is necessary because all updates of committed transactions may not have been written to the disk.
18. Which one of the following is correct?
    (a) Deferred update may be called logging only the REDO.
    (b) Deferred update requires that modified pages in memory be pinned in the main memory until the transaction commits.
    (c) Deferred update does not need any UNDO procedure.
    (d) All of the above
19. Which one of the following is **not** true about the shadow page technique?
    (a) No log is maintained.
    (b) Two page tables, one for shadow and the other for current pages are maintained.
    (c) The current page table is used to REDO a transaction.
    (d) The shadow page table is used to rollback a transaction.

20. Which one of the following is **not** correct?
    (a) It is difficult to keep related database pages together on disk when shadow paging is used.
    (b) Shadow paging requires significant garbage collection at the end of each transaction.
    (c) Even in a multiple-user environment, shadow paging does not require logs and checkpoints.
    (d) Shadow paging may be called a No-Undo/No-Redo recovery technique.

EXERCISES

1. What is a system log? What is the purpose of the system log in system recovery? Show what a typical log entry might look like.
2. What is the difference between the two log-based recovery schemes: Immediate Update and Deferred Update? What are the similarities?
3. Compare the two log-based recovery schemes in terms of ease of implementation and overhead cost.
4. What is the purpose of the checkpointing technique?
5. How does the frequency of checkpointing affect:
    (a) System performance when no failure occurs?
    (b) The time it takes to recover from a system crash?
6. Give an example of a log and then explain which transaction in the log need to be REDOne or UNDOne if a failure occurs at the end of the log. Assume that the immediate update technique is being used.
7. What difference is expected if the deferred update procedure is being used?
8. Explain what would happen if a failure occurred during the recovery procedure in Exercise 6.
9. Give an example of each of the following:
    (a) Transaction failure
    (b) System failure
    (c) Media failure
    (d) Unrecoverable failure
10. Describe the shadow page recovery scheme. How does it compare with log-based recovery techniques in terms of ease of implementation and overhead costs?
11. What is the major difference between the Immediate Update recovery scheme and the Deferred Update recovery scheme? Explain briefly.
12. What is the *single most significant* difference between the shadow page recovery scheme and the immediate update recovery scheme? Explain briefly.
13. When the system recovers from a database failure, in what order must transactions be UNDOne and REDOne? Why is this order important?

PROJECTS

1. Consider the schema of an airline reservation database given under 'Projects' in the last chapter. What should the company do to protect the valuable information in its database and how can quick recovery take place when a failure occurs?

2. Consider the backup and recovery problems of the Indian Railways Passenger Reservation System (PRS) databases. How many different computers do the Railways use for PRS? How would you ensure that all booking information in PRS is protected when a crash or a disaster hits the computer system in Delhi? Details of Indian Railways Centre for Railways Information System (CRIS) are available at http://www.dw.indianrail.gov.in/crisbro.pdf.
3. How should a telephone company deal with the issue of backup and recovery given that all information about telephone calls made and accounting is stored in a company database?

LAB EXERCISES

1. List all failure possibilities of the Indian Railways booking system databases. Where are all the databases stored?
2. Estimate the cost of one of the Railways computer system going down for two hours.
3. Can you think of a company which might go bankrupt if a serious disaster was to hit its main office, for example, a fire or flood or an earthquake? What should this company do to protect itself?
4. Find out what kind of backup planning does your college or university has? Try testing it to recover a file if you are allowed to do it.

BIBLIOGRAPHY

For Students

The book by Hart and Freeman provides a good introduction to Oracle recovery. The book by Preston provides an interesting introduction to backup and recovery for computer systems and provides a number of case studies. It has a chapter on database backup and recovery.

For Instructors

The book by Kumar and Hsu is a good collection of papers on recovery. The 70-page 1992 paper by Mohan et al., provides an excellent detailed introduction to the ARIES recovery system. It is the basic paper on ARIES. The 1999 paper summarizes ARIES, its significance, and its subsequent applications and generalizations. The book by Preston provides a solid introduction to backup and recovery for computer systems. It also provides some interesting disaster stories. It has a chapter on database backup and recovery and includes chapters on backup and recovery for Oracle, Sybase, DB2, SQL Server, Exchange, Postgres and MySQL. The collection of papers in the book by Kumar and Hsu is useful. It includes the 1992 ARIES paper as well as the 1981 paper by Gray et al. Altogether there are 31 papers in this book.

Bernstein, P., N. Goodman, and V. Hadzilacos, *Concurrency Control and Recovery in Database Systems*, Addison-Wesley Pub. Co., 1987.

Fernandez, I., *Beginning Oracle Database 11g Administration: From Novice to Professional*, APress, 2009.

Gray, J., "The Transaction Concept: The Virtues and Limitations", *Proceedings of the Very Large Database Conference*, Cannes, France, 1981, pp 144-154.

Gray, J., McJones, P., Blasgen, M., et al., "The Recovery Manager of the System R Database Manager", *ACM Computing Surveys*, Vol. 13, June 1981, pp 223-242.

Gray, J., and A. Reuter, *Transaction Processing: Concepts and Techniques*, Morgan-Kaufmann, 1993.

Guise P. De, *Enterprise Systems Backup and Recovery: A Corporate Insurance Policy*, Auerbach Publications, 2008, 308 pp.

Haerder, T., and A. Reuter, "Principles of Transaction-Oriented Database Recovery", *ACM Computing Survey*, Vol. 15, December 1983, pp 287-318.

Hart, M., and R. Freeman, *Oracle Database 11g RMAN Backup & Recovery*, McGraw-Hill, 2010.

Kent, J., H. Garcia-Molina, and J. Chung, "An Experimental Evaluation of Crash Recovery Mechanisms", *ACM-SIGMOD*, 1985, pp 113-122.

Kumar, V., and M. Hsu, (Ed.), *Recovery Mechanisms in Database Systems*, Prentice Hall, 1997.

Mohan, C., D. Haderle, B. Lindsay, K.Pirahesh and P. Scwarz, "ARIES: A transaction recovery method supporting fine-granularity locking and partial rollbacks using write-ahead logging", *ACM Transactions on Database Systems*, Vol. 17, 1992, pp. 94-162.

Mohan, C., "Repeating History Beyond ARIES", Proc. 25th VLDB Conf., Edinburgh, 1999.

Preston, W.C., *Backup and Recovery*, O'Reilly, 2007.

Preston W. C., *Backup and Recovery: Inexpensive Backup Solutions for Open Systems*, O'Reilly, 2007, 768 pp.

Verhofstad, J. S. M., "Recovery Techniques for Database Systems", *ACM Computing Surveys*, Vol. 10, December 78, pp 167-196.

C. Mohan—Developer of ARIES Recovery System

Mohan is the primary inventor of the ARIES family of recovery and locking methods and the industry-standard Presumed Abort commit protocol.

Dr C. Mohan joined IBM Almaden Research Center in 1981. He was named an IBM Fellow in 1997 for being recognized worldwide as a leading innovator in transaction management. He received the 1996 ACM SIGMOD Innovations Award in recognition of his innovative contributions to the development and use of database systems.

Mohan received his PhD in Computer Science from the University of Texas at Austin in 1981. Mohan has also worked as the Chief Scientist for IBM India.

Database Security

11

OBJECTIVES

- Discuss why database security is a serious concern.
- Describe the main database security violations.
- Explain how a database may be protected from security threats using identification, authentication and authorization.
- Discuss a number of techniques for identification and authentication.
- Describe the discretionary access control for authorization.
- Describe SQL support for discretionary access control authorization.
- Discuss mandatory control for authorization.
- Discuss special security concerns for statistical databases.
- Describe the role of the audit policy.
- Explain the basics of security of Internet applications and encryption.
- Introduce the topic of security of outsourced databases.

KEYWORDS

Security, database security, identification, verification, cards, password, user name, authentication, biometrics, discretionary access control, privileges, GRANT, REVOKE, SQL, subjects, mandatory access control, statistical databases, tracker, inference, Internet security, encryption, decryption, symmetrical encryption, asymmetrical encryption, outsourced databases, audit policy.

My grandfather once told me that there were two kinds of people: those who do the work and those who take the credit. He told me to try to be in the first group; there was much less competition there.

Indira Gandhi

11.1 INTRODUCTION

We have noted earlier that a database is a very valuable resource of an enterprise and it is essential that its consistency be maintained at all times. Also, database systems often include valuable enterprise information along with employees' personal information that must be protected from unauthorized retrieval.

The importance of database and computer security may be highlighted by what has been discovered by a number of research teams in UK, Canada and USA during 2008–10. These researchers found that many computers, perhaps several thousands, were compromised by hackers that were based in China. The researchers in Toronto learned what kinds of material had been stolen, including classified assessments about security in several Indian states, and confidential embassy documents about India's relationships in West Africa, Russia and the Middle East. The intruders breached the systems of independent analysts, taking reports on several Indian missile systems. They also obtained a year's worth of Dalai Lama's personal e-mail messages. The reports describing these research are 'Capability of the People's Republic of China to Conduct Cyber Warfare and Computer Network Exploitation' prepared by the US–China Economic and Security Review Commission dated October 9, 2009 (URL for the full 88-page report is http://www.uscc.gov/index.php) and 'Shadows in the Cloud: Investigating Cyber Espionage 2.0' from the University of Toronto (The full report can be downloaded from http://deibert.citizenlab.org/2010/04/new-iwm-report-shadows-in-the-cloud/. A New York Times report dated 6 April 2010 is available at this site http://www.nytimes.com/2010/04/06/science/06cyber.html).

Maintaining database consistency requires many techniques. Some of these have already been discussed in Chapters 9 and 10. For example, in Chapter 9 on concurrency, we discussed techniques for maintaining consistency when a number of transactions are being carried out concurrently. In Chapter 10 on recovery, we discussed how consistency could be maintained in spite of an accidental failure or damage to the database.

We now discuss two further problem areas and solutions to deal with them. These are database security and integrity. Security is discussed in this chapter and integrity is discussed in Chapter 12. A database may become inconsistent as a result of deliberate sabotage of the database system. In addition, the database system needs to be protected against deliberate unauthorized retrieval, corruption or update of data in the database by unauthorized persons. The protection of a database in this context is called *database security*. Also, a database may become inconsistent as a result of errors and mistakes on the part of authorized users. A database system should protect the database from such errors and mistakes. The protection of a database in this context is called maintaining database *integrity*.

In this chapter we discuss database security measures that need to be taken to protect the confidentiality, integrity and availability of the database against intervention by unauthorized persons. Chapter 12 is devoted to a discussion of techniques for maintaining database integrity.

We first define database security violation and database security.

Definition—Database Security Violation
A database security violation takes place when someone carries out an unauthorized retrieval, modification or destruction of information in a database.

Database security involves allowing or disallowing user actions on the database and the objects within it. It is defined as.

Definition—Database Security
Database security is the system, processes and procedures that protect a database from unintended activity including loss of confidentiality, loss of privacy, loss of database integrity or loss of database availability to the users.

Security violations include a number of activities that are listed in the next section. Security is sometimes confused with privacy, a related concept. Privacy, called *information privacy* in the context of databases, deals with the right of individuals to control the flow of information about them. Privacy protection measures will not be discussed here but we note that privacy protection does require that adequate security measures be in place.

This chapter is organized as follows. Security violations and sources of violations in a database system are discussed next. This follows a discussion of various components of database security. Section 11.3 deals with identification and authentication while Section 11.4 deals with authorization which includes discussion on discretionary access control and nondiscretionary control or mandatory control techniques. Security of statistical databases is discussed in Section 11.5. Database audit policy is discussed briefly in Section 11.6 followed by brief discussions on security of internet applications and use of encryption. Finally, a brief discussion on outsourced databases is presented.

11.2 SECURITY VIOLATIONS

As noted earlier, an enterprise database infrastructure is subject to a range of threats. There are a number of ways for classifying database security threats. One approach classifies security violations in the following classes:

1. Loss of Integrity
2. Loss of Availability
3. Loss of Confidentiality

In our approach, security violations may be classified into the more detailed classes presented in Fig. 11.1. Each of these classes may of course be labeled as one of the three classes above (classes 3, 2, 3, 1, 2, and 3 respectively for the six classes in Fig. 11.1).

- Unauthorized disclosure of data (class 3)
- Destruction of data or database (class 2)
- Trojan horse (class 3)
- Corruption or destruction of data (class 1)
- Deliberate interruption of service (class 2)
- Inference (class 3)

Figure 11.1 Security violations in databases

For each class, we present an example.

1. *Unauthorized disclosure of data*—For example, in a university student database, a student looking at assessment records of other students compromises the database security. A lecturer looking at assessment records of students that he/she is not authorized to access also compromises security. A security violation would occur if in a police database, an officer of the department accesses police information of a person to find the address of the person. Also, it has been found that many large organizations assign lower priority to the protection of customer and employee data and a vast majority of security breaches involved confidential customer and employee information.
2. *Destruction of data or database*—A person breaks into a computer system and destroys database files on the computer system.
3. *Trojan horse*—This refers to a transaction that is hidden in another transaction. The hidden transaction becomes active and may breach security when the main transaction is executed. For example, consider a program called *who* that is commonly used by Unix users. A user could put a modified version of *who* in the home directory of the user so that whenever *who* was executed, it not only did what it was supposed to but also copied some of the files into the other user's directory.
4. *Corruption or modification of data*—In a bank database, an employee updates the information in some accounts with a view to embezzling funds. In an interesting example of unauthorized modification of data, an employee of Qantas airlines many years ago managed to regularly modify passenger lists of some flights after the flight had landed. He added his name to these flights and collected millions of frequent flyer points. He was eventually arrested.
5. *Deliberate interruption of service*—A major computer installation is destroyed by a deliberate fire or a bomb thereby destroying a valuable database. As an example, students at a Canadian university in the 1970s destroyed the central computers, interrupting the computer services of the university.
6. *Inference*—A person is able to derive confidential or sensitive information about an individual by accessing information about other individuals or groups from a census database.

These security violations usually lead to either loss of confidentiality, loss of privacy, loss of database integrity or loss of database availability to the users. They can also lead to an enterprise suffering considerable damage.

The motivations behind a deliberate security violation of a computer system are varied. For example, the violator might hope to benefit financially or to cause damage to the enterprise that owns the database perhaps because of hostility towards the enterprise or just wishing to prove that it is possible to penetrate the system security. Whatever the motivation, books and articles on computer crime provide sufficient evidence to support the view that computer security problems are real and extremely important. Computer crime studies have also exposed the vulnerability of some organizations, for whom the loss of their database may result in the collapse of the organization itself.

Sources of Security Threats

Once again, a number of different studies have investigated the sources of database security threats. These studies have shown that in commercial systems the primary threats to database security, in order of importance, are given in Fig. 11.2.

- Errors and omissions
- Dishonest employees
- Fire
- Disgruntled employees
- Water
- Strangers

Figure 11.2 Threats to database security

Trusted insiders therefore remain a significant risk. A majority of organizations have been found to be ineffective in managing the insider threat and therefore most database fraud or crime is perpetrated by employees of the organization, employees who use their access to the system to commit a crime. One possible solution to insider misuse is careful auditing of databases that have sensitive information in them. Auditing is discussed in Section 11.6. A few years ago, a police employee during the night time tried accessing information about some person in the sensitive database that had information about drug traffic suspects. This database was audited and the employee was caught when someone looked at the auditing data several days later.

Searching for problems that the FBI has with its own employees, I found the following security incidents (for more details, refer to http://www.copwatch.org/TechTV%20%20Top%2010%20List%20of%20Police%20Database%20Abuses%20html.htm):

- Cop Suspected of Using Database to Plan Murder of Ex-wife
- Australian Rookie Cop Checks on 'Potential Girlfriends': 6,900 Database searches in only two months
- FBI Files Sold to mob and international criminals by Nevada Attorney General's Office employee and former FBI agent
- Indiana Police Department banned From FBI database due to misuse
- Prosecutor's office uses database to smear prosecutor's political opponent
- Police Lieutenant charged with abusing database to influence elections

Therefore every database organization has to be very careful in monitoring the security of the database including monitoring of insiders if the information is sensitive. In addition to database auditing, intrusion detection that uses user profiling and data profiling may be used.

In practice, only a small number of problems deal with the remaining security problems like unauthorized access or willful damage to a database system. In spite of the small numbers, the security of a database must be taken seriously.

Computer security concerns can be divided into two broad classes; *internal* security and *external* security. Internal security deals with the operations of the computer system itself and with, for example, access to the system, access to the files, access to networks and inference control. External security on the other hand deals with operations outside the computer system. These, for example, include physical security of the computer server room, the computers that access the database and the rooms in which the computers are placed, security clearance of the personnel accessing the database, security of the network lines, procedures to protect passwords and audit trails. External security problems are beyond the scope of this book.

It should however be made clear at the outset that absolute security is an unrealistic goal. Just as the most well protected banks are sometimes robbed, an adversary with sufficient motivation, resources and ingenuity can compromise the most sophisticated database security safeguards. Also, a disaster of sufficient severity would result in destruction of the database irrespective of the security precautions. An optimum security policy is one in which the cost of implementing protective mechanisms has been balanced against the reduction in risk achieved. The process to achieve a tolerable level of risk at the lowest possible cost is referred to as *risk management*. Furthermore, a DBMS exists to provide flexible and efficient facilities for retrieval, aggregation and manipulation of stored data. Security and integrity controls should be such that an authorized user does not encounter unnecessary problems in accessing the system. This places demands on the system that are often inconsistent with demands to enforce security measures.

While security measures can be costly, experience shows that adequate security is inexpensive compared with the potential consequences of failure to provide adequate protection. Usually an enterprise needs to identify the possible security threats that it might be subjected to and develop a security plan based on those threats. Rare threats should not be ignored if the likely damage due to the threats is very large.

Security policies for different database systems are likely to be different, for example, a bank database, a library database and a police database are likely to have different security concerns and policies. Each security policy would however have a number of components. Some of the components are listed in Fig. 11.3.

1. Identification and authentication
2. Authorization policy
3. Statistical inference policy for statistical databases
4. Encryption
5. Database audit policy

Figure 11.3 Components of database security

Each of the components are now discussed.

11.3 IDENTIFICATION AND AUTHENTICATION

Every database must provide a mechanism that makes sure that the system only allows access to authorized users and each user is allowed to run only those transactions that he/she is authorized to carry out. Therefore a database system must have a comprehensive identification, authentication and authorization mechanism.

Definition—Identification and Authentication
Identification involves a user indicating to the computer system who he/she is while authentication involves the computer system obtaining further information from the user to verify if the user is the person that he/she claims to be.

User identification and authentication are standard means of establishing identity. They are standard operating system problems and most operating system texts provide a discussion on relevant issues.

- Knowledge
- Objects
- Actions
- Physiology

Figure 11.4 Four classes of identity verification

In general, methods for establishing the identity of an individual can be divided into four classes:

1. *Knowledge*—Identification and authentication based on knowledge is the most common form of authentication for computer systems. Common examples of such identification and authentication are username/password and card/PIN number. In username/password authentication, the username may be public but the user is assumed to be the only person who knows the password. The username/password technique does not work particularly well as has been demonstrated by the comparative ease with which hackers have managed to penetrate even so called well secured systems. In one study it was found that passwords were not that difficult to guess as users tend to use passwords that are easy to remember (e.g., same as the username, the user's

name, name of the street the user lives on, name of a relative). When a list of first names, last names, city names, street names and words from a moderate size dictionary were collected it was found that some 86 percent of all passwords on the systems that were checked were on this list. The password authentication can be improved by some simple precautions. For example, it might be possible to check the password a user is using against a dictionary of names and words and not allow common names or words to be used. Some sites are now insisting on an 8-digit password with some numeric or special characters to improve security of passwords.

Username/password authentication continues to be used widely because it is simple and easy to implement.

2. *Objects*—Identification and authentication can be based on objects in the possession of the individual, for example, a card. Each card has a unique identifier stored on it to establish the user's identity. Unfortunately this approach only confirms the identity of the object, not of the user. Objects can be lost, stolen and may be forged allowing a person with someone else's object to gain access. The scheme is considerably improved if the object is combined with some knowledge (e.g., PIN or password). This is the approach being followed by the banks in using a card and a PIN for allowing customers to access ATMs. Even then there have been problems as some people write down their PIN on the card or on a piece of paper. Most ATM cards use a four-digit PIN but many banks now allow use of longer PINs to improve security.
3. *Actions*—It is possible to base authentication on users' actions. For example, handwritten signatures have been used for hundreds of years and the approach has worked quite well. A user may be required to sign on an electronic tablet and the signature may then be compared with the one (or more) stored in the machine. It is also possible to use patterns of computer use behavior once the user is logged on to authenticate the person's identity by comparing the behaviour with the user's profile. These techniques may involve keystroke dynamics (for example, in a 1990 study reliable results were obtained by looking at keystroke latencies when users typed their username and password) and other human-computer interactions.
4. *Physiology*—The most reliable authentication techniques are based on physiology. These are also called biometric techniques and include fingerprints, retinal pattern, face recognition and voice pattern. After the 9/11 terrorist attacks, use of biometrics is becoming more common. The usual approach in biometric techniques is to obtain from the user a sample of the characteristic that is being used and measure this characteristic when the user presents himself/herself for authentication. If the match is close enough then the user is authenticated. Some of the biometric techniques, for example, face recognition, are not particularly reliable. Also, biometrics often requires expensive equipment and are not always suitable for a user wanting to access a database system using a desktop PC.

Most computer systems restrict identification and authentication to the first two categories because of the ease of implementation of the techniques they are based on. Generally, computer systems require a user to identify himself/herself by either typing a login name or by inserting a machine readable card in the client computer. This is then followed by an authentication phase that usually involves the user providing a password or a PIN which is supposed to be known only to the user.

Other authentication schemes are of course possible. For particularly sensitive information, a computer system may use special terminals that are locked or kept in a physically secure location or require the user to carry a machine readable card like a plastic credit card as well as specify login name and password. More recently, inexpensive devices attached to computers are able to read fingerprints of a person for authentication purposes. Handwritten signature verification is another area in which considerable research has been going on during the last twenty years or so. One bank in Australia is using another approach. For transfer of large amounts of money or for transferring money to a new person, the bank will seek confirmation by sending an SMS message to the account holder's registered mobile phone requesting him/her to type in the code sent via the SMS into the user's computer bank account.

A number of other precautions may also be considered. For example, if appropriate, the system should lock out a user who has failed login on say three successive attempts in a short period of time. Password may be given a lifetime of say three or six months. When a password is changed it may be appropriate to ensure that one of the old passwords is not used.

Furthermore, it should be noted that most computer systems including database systems come with a number of preset default accounts which can lead to security breaches. These default passwords should be changed to secure passwords immediately after the system has been installed.

To conclude the discussion on identification and authentication, the following simple rules should be noted.

(a) To protect an enterprise database strong identification and authentication must be used. In most systems usernames like guest, client, and visitor are often available. All such usernames should be removed from the system. Authentication must use strong passwords with a minimum of eight characters. In addition, users should be encouraged to use lower and upper case characters, as well as numbers, and punctuation marks in their password. Passwords should be regularly changed and each new password should be checked.

(b) System privileges should be allowed only to employees that need to have such privileges.

(c) An account should be locked out after three failed attempts to login to the system.

(d) Unused accounts should be locked or simply deleted after some reasonable amount of time.

11.4 AUTHORIZATION OR ACCESS CONTROL

In contrast to identification and authentication, authorization deals with controlling the type of access that a user is allowed. It may be that we only wish to allow a user by the name *X* to access some parts of the database or employees at level *Y* to some predefined level of access. In addition to access, authorization may also include specification of what a user may do with the access. In the discussion below the users are referred to as *subjects* and the database contents (e.g., tables, views, indexes) are referred to as *objects*.

> ***Definition—Authorization***
> *Database authorization involves allowing certain users to access, process or alter specified parts of the database subject to certain limitations placed on them regarding resources and objects in the database.*

Authorization may be based on either subject profiles or object profiles or both:

1. *Subject profiles*—In this scheme the DBMS maintains information on each user and what objects they may access. The information called the *subject profile* enables the DBMS to grant or refuse authorization to carry out a particular transaction.

2. *Object profiles*—In this scheme the DBMS maintains information about each data object. This information called the *object profile* is then used to decide whether a user is allowed access to the objects that he/she wishes to access. The simplest example of object profiles is the file protection mechanism that is provided by most operating systems. For example, in UNIX file management, a file may be readable, writable or executable either by the person whose directory the file is in, or by a group of users specified to the system by the user or by everyone (public). This is not particularly satisfactory as this type of file protection mechanism is very simplistic. In regard to the database, the protection provides only four options as far as the data is concerned:
    - Cannot read or write data
    - Can read but not write data
    - Can read and write data
    - Cannot read but can write data

File protections apply to a file as a whole and therefore different protections for parts of a file are not possible. In the database environment, one may wish to allow selective access to not only parts of the database but also parts of individual tables to a user or a group of users. A technique other than the file protection mechanism described above is then needed.

A database security problem can be compared with a university campus security problem. The database consists of many tables just like a campus consists of many buildings. A simplistic example of security on campus may be something like:

1. People are allowed to enter the campus or not (similar to being allowed to login to a database system).
2. People who are allowed to enter the campus, are either allowed to enter a building (in which case they can enter all rooms in that building) or not allowed to enter the building at all (similar to being able to access a table).

Such simple mechanisms are clearly inadequate in practice and we like to make finer decisions regarding a person's entry to buildings (probably based on each office). Similarly, we would like to make fine-grained decisions on access to a database among different classes of users. In the campus example, students may be allowed to enter the labs and lecture theatres in a building but can enter staff offices only with the permission of the staff member concerned. Locks on each of the offices as well as on the buildings help implement this regulation. Decisions on access to buildings involve things like:

- What day and time of the day it is
- Whether an office has a staff member in it
- Whether the office is locked, and so on

Similar possibilities exist regarding access to a database. For example, a database may allow access to different classes of users on the following basis:

1. All users that have an account may access statistical information from the database.
2. Only users with rating AAA can access and update the personal files of employees.
3. Users with rating AA can access (but not update) the personal files of employees.
4. Users with rating A can access information about employees in their own department.
5. Users that are supervisors may write an assessment of employees they supervise in their departments.

We now provide two techniques that enable fine-grained authorization. These are called *Discretionary Access Control* and *Nondiscretionary (or Mandatory) Access Control*. Most commercial products currently only implement discretionary access control since discretionary access control (DAC) provides simple and flexible security. However increasingly, perhaps due to the 9/11 terrorism attack in the USA and requirements of the US Department of Defense, database vendors are exploring the possibility of providing mandatory control facilities as well in their products.

11.4.1 Discretionary Access Control (DAC)–Access Matrix Model

A discretionary policy involves providing access to users based on their need-to-access, where the need is determined by someone authorized to determine each user's need. The need may be determined by the user's supervisor or some higher authority in the enterprise that is charged with the responsibility of determining such need and granting and revoking privileges to access and/or update the database as necessary. The database administrator often implements it. In practice in SQL, a user who owns an object (often the database administrator) has the discretion[1] to give permission to others based on their need. The concept of *authorization or access matrix* in a discretionary access control model was proposed by Conway, Maxwell and Morgan in 1972.

Definition—Discretionary Access Control
A discretionary policy involves providing access to users based on their need-to-access, where the need is determined by someone authorized to determine each user's need.

The authorization essentially is a set of triplets (s, o, a) where s is the user, o is the object and a is the action s is authorized to carry out.

The (s, o, a) triples are usually represented by a two-dimensional matrix presenting sets of users, objects and actions (S, O, A) as shown in Fig. 11.5 with columns corresponding to data objects O (not necessarily disjoint) and the rows corresponding to users S may be used to specify access rights A. Each element in the matrix specifies the access rights a user has to a data item. Access rights represent operations performed by users on data items and may include retrieve, insert, delete and update. The data item may be a table, a row or an attribute. Data items may also be defined using views. The model may of course be extended where the access rights might include predicates describing a condition under which the user may access the data item. Discretionary access control therefore is flexible. An example is presented in Fig. 11.5, and allows fine-grained security controls, although not fine-grained enough for some applications, but such controls generally require a person to manage the controls on a day-to-day basis.

	Player	**Match**	**Batting**	**Bowling**
Suresh	–	r	r	r
Anilkumar	r	–	r	–
Saraswati	rw	rw	rw	rw
Inderjit	rwx	rw	–	rw

Figure 11.5 An example of a discretionary matrix

In Fig. 11.5 the symbols r, w and x correspond to the privileges of reading, writing and executing the database object whose name is given at the top of each column. The names of subjects are given in the first column.

1. According to the Oxford Dictionary, discretion means "*the freedom to decide what should be done in a particular situation*". DAC therefore needs someone in the enterprise deciding what privileges should be granted to whom.

This is similar to the use of symbols *r*, *w* and *x* in the UNIX file protection system. This matrix with a large number of objects and a large number of users is often sparse since every user would normally deal with only a small number of objects. Therefore, storing the matrix as a two-dimensional array is not viable.

The matrix may be stored as a table with only non-empty entries or it may be stored either by columns or by rows. A system that stores by columns is commonly known as an access control list (ACL), for example, the UNIX file system is such a system in which each file is accompanied by a list containing subjects and their rights to that file. An implementation that stores by rows is commonly known as a *capability list* in which each subject maintains a list of their rights to objects. The underlying philosophy in discretionary access control is that subjects owning database objects can determine who has access to their database objects, e.g., tables.

Since the authorization matrix can be large, typically DAC supports user groups and object groups which may be hierarchically organized. Once groups are used, it may be necessary to define exceptions. Unfortunately the discretionary access control method can only deal with a coarse granularity of database objects. Also, DAC only deals with users and not processes. A process essentially is given the privileges that are available to the user who generated the process. The process may then execute some malicious programs violating the database security.

Using the SQL GRANT Mechanism

SQL provides facilities for discretionary access control. The owner of a table is automatically granted all privileges to the table. The owner may then grant privileges to other users who in turn may grant privileges to others. Once a user has been granted some privilege by the database system, normally the system would allow that user to grant the same privilege to some other user and the privileges may then be propagated. Of course, if the first user revokes the privilege to the second user, the system should revoke all the privileges that the second user has propagated. The system therefore must not only maintain a table of who has what privilege but also who has granted what privilege and check these every time some privilege is revoked.

It is worth noting that privileges should be granted only when absolutely necessary and should be revoked as soon as the need for a privilege is over.

The granting of privileges may be represented by a graph like the one in Fig. 11.6 below[2].

To simplify the graph, we will only deal with all the privileges on the four tables *A*, *B*, *C* and *D*. Brahma has all privileges on tables *A* and *B*, Vishnu on tables *B* and *C* while Shiva has all privileges on *C* and *D*.

Saraswati has been granted privileges on *A* by Brahma, on *B* by Vishnu and on *C* by Shiva. Lakshmi has been granted privileges on *C* by Vishnu and Parvati has been granted privileges of tables *B* and *C* by Vishnu. Figure 11.6 also shows that the user Hanuman has been granted privileges on table *D* by user Shiva. Rama has been granted privileges on table *A*, Krishna has been granted privileges by three other users, on tables *B* and *C* by Saraswati, on *C* by Lakshmi and on *B* by Parvati.

Now consider what happens if the privileges to Parvati were revoked. She now has no privileges according to our example and as a result Ganesh also loses privilege on *C* but Krishna is not affected since he has privileges on *B* from Saraswati as well. We have assumed that all privileges are of the same type since using privileges for write, read and execute will further complicate the example.

2. In this example, we are using names of users who have been named after some important Hindu gods.

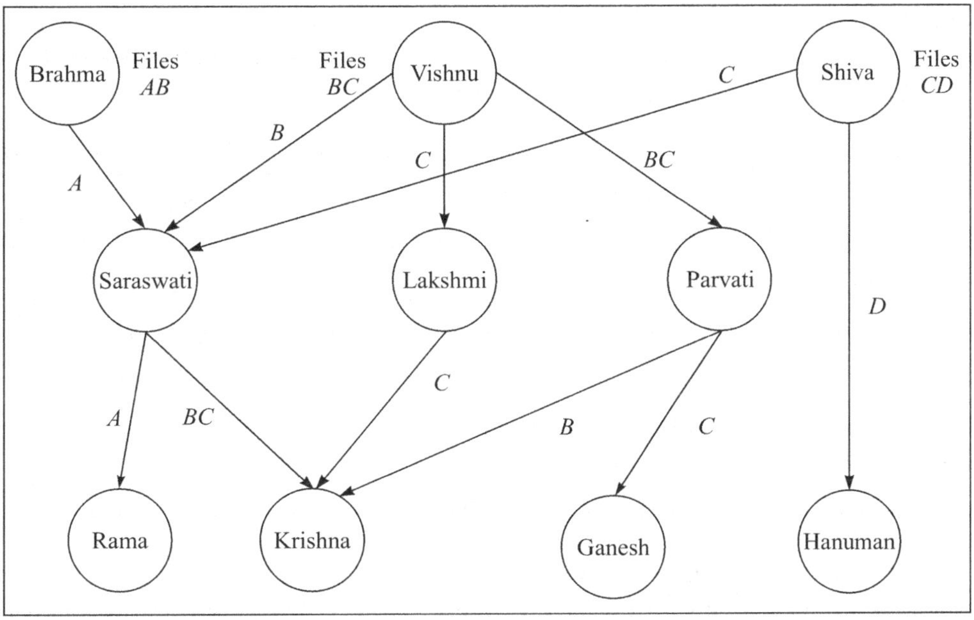

Figure 11.6 Example of an authorization graph

The granularity of many systems is quite coarse as access can be controlled only on the basis of tables. The newer systems are however able to control access as finely as each cell. One may nonetheless wish to have additional security features including value-dependent controls.

A typical SQL GRANT command looks like that shown in Fig. 11.7.

```
GRANT SELECT ON Player, Match
TO Ganesh, Vishnu
```

Figure 11.7 An example of the GRANT command

This grants a privilege to Ganesh and Vishnu to use the SELECT operation on tables named *Player* and *Match*.

A component of the DBMS called the Security Manager deals with authorizations that are issued and also compiles them. It then enforces security based on the rules given by the DBA. It is assumed that the user granting a privilege holds that privilege on the object. SQL allows privileges to be granted for SELECT as well as for other operations, for example:

1. SELECT—This provides rights to read any part of the given table to the user specified.
2. INSERT—This provides rights to the user specified to insert new rows to the given table.
3. DELETE—This provides rights to the user specified to delete rows from the given table.
4. UPDATE—This provides rights to the user specified to update rows in the given table.
5. REFERENCES—This provides the right to the user specified to refer to the table in an integrity constraint.
6. USAGE—This privilege deals with domains of attributes and allows a user to use an element in other users' declarations.
7. TRIGGER—This privilege allows the creation of a trigger on the specified table.
8. EXECUTE—This privilege allows the use of a specified function.

Some simple examples of GRANT and REVOKE are given below in Fig. 11.8.

It is also possible to GRANT ALL PRIVILEGES. SQL does not allow privileges to be granted to CREATE, ALTER and DROP a table since these privileges are retained by the owner of the table. They can only be granted by the system administrator.

```
GRANT SELECT ON Player TO Shiva
GRANT INSERT ON Match TO Krishna
GRANT DELETE ON Batting TO Parvati
GRANT UPDATE ON Bowling TO Lakshmi
REVOKE SELECT ON Match FROM Natrajan
```

Figure 11.8 Examples of GRANT and REVOKE commands

Privileges may be REVOKED as shown in Fig. 11.9.

```
REVOKE PRIVILEGES ON Player
FROM Ganesh, Vishnu
```

Figure 11.9 Another example of the REVOKE command

As noted earlier, a REVOKE command may result in withdrawal of privileges from other users who have been granted privileges by these two users Vishnu and Ganesh unless those users have been grated similar privileges by some other users as well. This is illustrated in Fig. 11.6.

A major weakness of discretionary access control is that it relies on each user to understand the security issues when they pass on privileges to other users. A clever user may persuade another user who has authorizations for a more sensitive part of the database to pass on his authorization to him/her thereby gaining access to information that he/she was not supposed to have. Nondiscretionary access overcomes this weakness by not allowing discretion to any person in the enterprise to grant privileges to others.

11.4.2 Using the SQL View Mechanism

Another useful DAC security mechanism is to provide each user with a tailor-made view (or views) of the database and restrict his/her access to the database through these views. Although the view mechanism allows data to be hidden (including data based on values), we still require control on who is allowed to write into the database through their view. This can be done by using GRANT and REVOKE commands.

Consider the following two views that may be appropriate for some users[3]. Figure 11.10 is a view about Indian Players.

Figure 11.11 presents another view. This is about batting information of Indian players.

```
DEFINE VIEW IPlayers AS
    SELECT PID, FName, LName
    FROM Player
    WHERE Country = 'India'
```

Figure 11.10 A view IPlayers for players from India

```
DEFINE VIEW IBatting AS
    SELECT PID, MID, NRuns
    FROM Batting
    WHERE PID =
        (SELECT PID
        FROM Player
        WHERE Country = 'India')
```

Figure 11.11 A view IBatting for players from India

3. We will continue to use the cricket database although in reality there is no need to control reading access to the tables. We would of course like to ensure that only authorized users can write into them.

Privileges may now be granted on these views as shown in Fig. 11.12.

GRANT all privileges on *IPlayers* to Durga
GRANT SELECT on *IBatting* to Balaji

Figure 11.12 GRANTING privileges on views

The first view is about players from India, the information being made available to users that need it. The second view allows some users access batting information for the Indian players.

A user granting privileges on any views must hold privileges on the tables used in the views.

The view approach is flexible and allows access control to be defined at a level of description close to the requirements. Views allow enforcement of data-dependent policies. It is easy to control read access through views without the granularity of a table. A view is a program and it is possible to control its invocation. However, view based security controls are complicated and slow.

We now discuss a very different approach to authorization, i.e., the nondiscretionary mandatory control model.

11.4.3 Nondiscretionary Control—Mandatory Control Model

In contrast to the need-to-access basis of the discretionary policy, in which the owner of a table or the database has discretion to grant access permissions to others, the nondiscretionary or mandatory access control (MAC) policy involves system-wide policies based on regulations of an enterprise's central authority that do not allow any discretion to any user including table owners and supervisors.

The most commonly used MAC is the multilevel MAC policy, discussed in more detail later. It is based on classifications of both users (called the *subjects*) and objects in the database system. Each subject is then authorized to access all objects that have a classification that is lower or equal to his/her classification.

As noted earlier, mandatory control involves assigning each database object to a security *class* and each user or subject a security *clearance*. The security classes may be like those used in the military as shown in Fig. 11.13 and they may range from *unclassified* (anyone can see this) to *confidential* to *secret* and finally *top secret*. Each subject is also assigned a clearance class. Based on these classifications of subjects and objects and a set of rules decided by the enterprise, the DBMS then automatically decides what a subject might or might not be able to do.

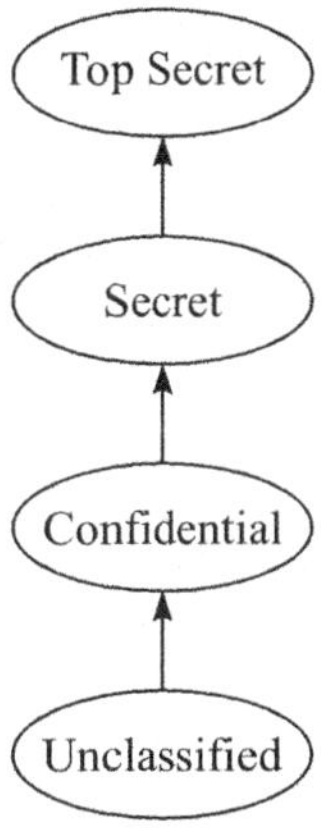

Figure 11.13 A typical classification of database objects

> ***Definition—Mandatory Control***
> *Mandatory control involves assigning each database object to a security **class** and each user or subject a security **clearance**. Each user is then authorized to access all objects that have a classification that is lower or equal to his/her classification.*

Mandatory control policy is sometimes preferred because it does not provide discretion to anyone to grant privileges to anyone else, in other words a flexibility, which may lead to problems discussed earlier. The mandatory control policy therefore may be considered more reliable. The policy is also called the

Bell–LaPadula model since David Bell and Len LaPadula created the model in 1973 in response to the US Air Force's concerns over the security of time sharing computer systems. It is possible to combine the discretionary access control technique with the mandatory control to enforce additional restrictions, but all users must still follow the basic rules of the mandatory control policies.

Multilevel Bell–LaPadula Model

The *multilevel Bell–LaPadula model* is an example of the mandatory control policy and the model is similar to what is commonly used in security organizations and some industrial organizations. As noted above, basic to such a mandatory security model is a set of *access classes* or *security levels* that represent the classifications associated with the objects in the database as shown in Fig. 11.13 and a set of *clearances* associated with the subjects of the database. Every data object in the database is assigned an access class and each user is assigned a clearance. These clearance classes could be unclassified, confidential, secret and top secret as shown in Fig. 11.13 or they could be denoted as class 1, 2, ...10, where class 1 is the lowest and 10 the highest. For example, class 10 could be top secret in military terms and clearance 10 could be the top secret security clearance.

Bell and LaPadula (BLP) gave a formal model of multilevel security. This model enforces the policy that *information cannot leak to subjects who are not cleared for the information.*

The access classes associated with the data items have a partial ordering associated with them. Let the classes be C_i, $i = 1, 2, \dots n$ where if for any two classes $C_i > C_j$, then class C_i is said to dominate C_j. To access data in the database, the subject's clearance must dominate the access class of the object. For example, if a subject had a clearance S and a data object has class O then the subject may access the data object as long as $S \geq O$.

The Bell–LaPadula model imposes the following two conditions:

- *No Read Up*—A subject S may read object O only if level(O) $\leq$ Level(S). As noted above, subjects are not allowed to *read up*.
- *No Write Down*—A subject S may write object O only if level(S) $\leq$ level(O). In other words, a subject may not *write down*.

The second condition may appear counter-intuitive but the rationale is to ensure that a subject with higher level security information does not write information in a lower level security object. For example, consider two subjects S and R with S having a lower level clearance. If R reads an object O which S is not allowed to read and then writes it as object P at a lower level which S is able to read; sensitive information may leak through P. A subject must never be able to learn information about some highly-labeled object O by reading another low-labeled object P.

A direct implementation of such a system allows the author of a top secret report to retrieve information entered by subjects operating at secret or confidential and merge it with top secret information. The subject with the secret clearance cannot read up to see the top secret result, since the data only flows in one direction between secret and top secret. Some may argue that top secret subjects should be trusted not to do such a thing. Unfortunately, this argument does not take into account the risk of a Trojan horse[4] which we shall now discuss.

4. According to the Oxford Dictionary, a Trojan horse is "*something intended to undermine or secretly overthrow an enemy or opponent*". In the computing context, it is the computer software that appears to perform a desirable function but in fact performs undisclosed malicious functions.

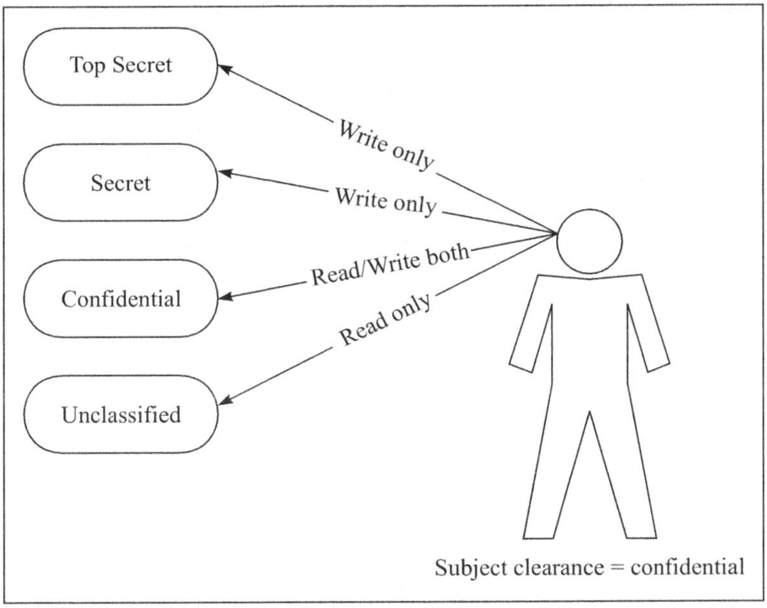

Figure 11.14 Illustrating BLP model rules

For example, consider what would happen if an attacker inserts a macro function with a Trojan horse capability into a word processing file. The attacker has stored the macro function in a confidential file and has told a top secret subject to examine the file. When the subject opens the confidential file, the macro function starts running and copies files from the top secret subject's directory into confidential files belonging to the attacker.

We now discuss weaknesses of the mandatory control model. First, researchers and system developers have found it to be extremely difficult and perhaps impossible to completely prevent information flow between different security levels in the MAC system. Furthermore, it has been reported that the end user community has found a number of cases where the BLP model did not entirely satisfy their operational and security needs. A second serious problem is the virus threat because the MAC system does not prevent a virus introduced at a lower clearance level from propagating into higher clearance levels.

Furthermore, the rules of the Bell–LaPadula model allow 'blind writes'. Subjects can 'write up' and not be able to 'read back' what they have written. Therefore, a subject unsuitable for reading an object is permitted to make changes to that object. One solution to this problem is to insist that writes be restricted to the same security level as the subject allowing a subject to write and read what he/she has written.

A mandatory control mechanism can be implemented in a database in a number of different ways. Perhaps the simplest method would be to treat each table as a data object that is given a security level while each subject is given a clearance level, and to use the rule given above or something similar to control access to the database. Often however this approach is not satisfactory since it does not allow fine-grained security controls. Therefore, it may be necessary to either treat each attribute as a data object with its own security level or treat each row as a data object. The latter would of course result in fairly high security overheads for tables with high cardinality. Nevertheless, a table may contain data of different security classes and it should be possible to specify that a subject who does not have high enough clearance to view the whole table should have access to only a part of the table. It may be possible to use a mechanism similar to that defining a different view for different classes of users.

In summary, mandatory access control mechanisms allow less flexible security controls than discretionary access control but there is less need for an administrator incharge of the database to manage the security controls on a day-to-day basis. A security system must be robust enough to resist determined attacks but sufficiently economical so it does not degrade the system performance.

If a security system is too expensive (for example in terms of computer time) it will not be used except where the need justifies the cost.

11.4.4 Controlling Database Access in Oracle

Database security in Oracle is based on discretionary access control. A system of privileges is used where a privilege is a permission to access some part of the database to a defined level.

Oracle uses a variety of authentication mechanisms for user authentication. These include authentication by the operating system, by a network service, and by the database system. Techniques are used to control the use of passwords, for example, an account is locked if the user fails to login to the system within a specified number of attempts. The database administrator is allowed to specify a lifetime for passwords, after which passwords expire. Password history is maintained so a user may not reuse a password for a specified amount of time. Passwords are checked for complexity, for example, it is required that a password include an alphabet character, one numeric character, one punctuation mark and differ from the previous password in at least three characters.

In Oracle, a privilege is a right to execute a particular type of SQL statement or to access another user's object. The privileges include the right to retrieve information from another person's table or execute another person's procedure.

A user may grant privileges to other users. Privileges may include system privileges which can only be granted by users that have been granted ADMIN OPTION. There are over 60 system privileges which include privileges such as that to delete a specified row from a specified table in the database.

Oracle also has a concept of role in which a group of privileges may be granted to another user. This is often useful in reducing the security administration work involved in granting similar privileges to many users.

11.5 SECURITY OF STATISTICAL DATABASES

The primary reason for creating statistical databases is to supply statistical or aggregate information about groups of individuals to users without revealing confidential information about any individual. For example, a census database maintained by the Bureau of Statistics is designed for use by various types of researchers. Although the census database would have been built from sensitive and confidential information about all citizens, the statistical database normally would have stripped all the personal information from the database and therefore, not be expected to allow any personally identifiable information which can be retrieved. One may think that since a statistical database has no personally identifiable information that may be directly retrieved by a user, there is little need to worry about the security of such information. We will now show that it is possible and relatively easy to derive personal information from summaries of statistical information.

To preserve the confidentiality of personal information in a statistical database, *statistical inference controls* are required. Compromise of a statistical database must be defined in relative terms. It is generally accepted that an estimate of salary of an individual that is in error by more than say 50% will probably not be considered as a database compromise. For example, an estimate of Rs.15,000 for a salary of Rs. 30,000 could not really be considered to be a compromise while an estimate of Rs. 85,000 for a salary of Rs. 100,000 might be. If the statistical database allows arbitrary queries then it is possible that if we know sufficient information about a person then we will be able to pose one or more queries that will retrieve information about that person.

> ***Definition—Positively Compromised and Negatively Compromised***
> *A database is said to be positively compromised if someone is able to derive a value of a particular data item. It is negatively compromised if someone is able to find that a data item does not have a particular value.*

Positive Compromise

For example, consider a query given in Fig. 11.15 that finds the number of people in New Delhi earning more than Rupees one crore[5] and the average tax that they pay. We assume the census data is available in a table *Census*.

```
SELECT COUNT(*), AVG(Tax)
FROM Census
WHERE Income > 1,00,00,000
AND City = 'New Delhi'
```

Figure 11.15 An example query leading to a positive compromise

Let us assume that the query results in 1 and 750,000, that is, there is only one person in New Delhi with such a high income and the person paid tax of Rs. 750,000. We have therefore derived the tax paid by the only person that qualified. The security of the database and the privacy of that person (whose name is not revealed) therefore have been *compromised*.

Negative Compromise

The query in Fig. 11.16 illustrates that a query may lead to a negative compromise if the result of the query is zero.

```
SELECT COUNT(*), AVG(Tax)
FROM Census
WHERE Income > 1,00,00,000
AND City = 'New Delhi'
AND Tax > 10,00,000
```

Figure 11.16 An example query leading to a negative compromise

Let us assume that the query returns a null result. It is now clear that anyone earning more than one crore rupees did not on average pay more than ten lakhs in tax. It does not tell us a lot if the number of people earning that amount is more than, say 10, since we have only managed to find their average tax was above ten lakhs.

Suitable Queries

A commonly suggested solution for this problem of compromising statistical databases is that any query which retrieves less than *w* rows (or *w* individuals) should not be allowed. This unfortunately does not work because proceeding as follows would also compromise the database. To illustrate that putting a limit of *w*

5. This is only a fictitious example. The numbers used have nothing to do with real incomes in India and these numbers may be changed if the reader wishes to do so.

people does not work, let us assume that we believe that only one person in New Delhi has an income of more than one crore. We will now pose two queries that retrieve information about more than w individuals and infer the tax paid by the person earning more than one crore.

We first obtain the number of people in New Delhi and average tax paid by them if they had income of more than ninety lakhs, as shown in Fig. 11.17.

```
SELECT COUNT(*), AVG(Tax)
FROM Census
WHERE Income > 90,00,000
AND City = 'New Delhi'
```

Figure 11.17 First query to illustrate that number of rows does not work

Suppose we find that the result is 51 and 500,000. That is, there are 51 people with an income more than 50 lakhs and pay on average a tax of five lakhs. We know that 50 of the 51 individuals are earning below one crore since we suspect only one person has an income of more than one crore.

Suppose we now pose a query to find the number of people and their average tax if their income is more than 90 lakhs and less than one crore. This query is presented in Fig. 11.18.

```
SELECT COUNT(*), AVG(Tax)
FROM Census
WHERE Income > 90,000,000
AND Income < 1,00,00,000
AND City = 'New Delhi'
```

Figure 11.18 Second query to illustrate that number of rows does not work

Let us assume that we now find that the result of the query in Fig. 11.18 is 50 and 500,000. That is, there are 50 people with an income greater than 90 lakhs and less than one crore. For convenience we have assumed both average tax figures to be five lakhs, which means the person earning more than one crore also paid tax of only five lakhs.

If the two values of average tax were 5,00,000 and 5,00,100 then we can deduce the tax paid by the one person with income of one crore or more. It works out to be $51 \times 5{,}00{,}000 = 2{,}55{,}00{,}000$ and subtracting from the total tax paid by the 50 people retrieved in query in Fig. 11.18, which is $50 \times 5{,}00{,}100 = 2{,}50{,}05{,}000$), and therefore obtain the figure Rs. 4,95,000.

One may of course suggest other restrictions on the queries, for example, no query should retrieve information about less than w rows or more than $n - w$ rows since it is desirable to exclude queries on a large number of individuals close to the size of the database as well. We assume n is the total number of individuals.

We now define the concept of *suitable queries.*

> ***Definition—Suitable Queries***
> *Queries whose set size falls between (w, n - w) are sometimes called suitable.*

Suitable queries also do not prevent compromise as illustrated ahead. We first define what is meant by a *characteristic formula.*

> ***Definition—A characteristic formula***
> *A characteristic formula C is a condition for describing a subgroup of the population (e.g., all people living in New Delhi).*

Another term which is used in this context is *query set*. It can be defined as.

> ***Definition—Query Set***
> *The rows that satisfy a characteristic formula are called a query set.*

The concept of *tracker* is now defined.

> ***Definition—Tracker***
> *A tracker is a set of auxiliary attributes which are added to the original query.*

The auxiliary attributes enable the user to pad the query set so that a query can be formulated to return a result that is larger than that the original query would have returned and the query may be then suitable, and therefore answerable. The effect of the auxiliary characteristics can then be subtracted and the answer to the original query may be obtained. We now define the term *individual tracker*.

> ***Definition—Individual Tracker***
> *A condition like Income > 1,00,00,000 and NOT(City = 'Mumbai') is called an individual tracker.*

Generally, if a condition p identifies a single individual in a statistical database and p can be written as $p1$ *and* $p2$ then $p1$ *and not* ($p2$) is called a *tracker* as it lets us track down information on the person we are interested in.

Another Example of Tracking

The basic idea is to find two queries such that one retrieves information about p individuals and another about $p + 1$ individuals. Let us assume that an attacker knows that there is a person who has the following attributes:

1. Gender = Male
2. Age < 40
3. Lives in Mumbai
4. Marriage status = Married
5. Income > 1,00,00,000

Let us select the third condition as $p2$ and the remaining four as $p1$. Since we cannot pose a query with the five conditions given above as it results in identifying only one individual, we pose a query ($p1$ and NOT $p2$) as follows.

We should obtain a large number of individuals. Let us assume the result is 1000 and 7,00,000. If we now pose another query which includes all individuals in India, as shown in Fig. 11.20, which does not include the City condition then we should get the above result, plus the person in Mumbai.

Suppose the result now is 1001 and 7,00,015. We can now deduce the tax paid by the one person in Mumbai.

Other approaches have been suggested to overcome such inference problems. One approach suggests adding some random noise to each result but it can be shown that even that approach can lead to a compromise.

```
SELECT COUNT(*), AVG(Tax)
FROM Census
WHERE Sex = 'M'
AND Age < 40
AND City <> 'Mumbai'
AND Status = 'Married'
AND Income > 1,00,00,000
```

Figure 11.19 An example of an individual tracker

```
SELECT COUNT(*), AVG(Tax)
FROM Census
WHERE Sex = 'M'
AND Age < 40
AND Status = 'Married'
AND Income > 1,00,00,000
```

Figure 11.20 An example of an individual tracker

We will not discuss compromise in statistical databases any further. A reader interested in further study on this topic may refer to the bibliography at the end of the chapter.

11.6 AUDIT POLICY

An effective tool in database security is the maintenance of an *audit trail*. An audit trail is a record of every transaction that has been executed in a database system. An audit trail usually includes the transaction, the access operations carried out by the transaction and the identification of the user who executed the transaction. Automated recording of at least all sensitive and/or unusual database transactions should be part of any database deployment. Weak database audit policy represents a serious organizational security risk.

In case of suspicion or detection of a database security violation, the audit trail may be analyzed to find the identity of the violator. The knowledge that an audit trail is maintained often deters violators from breaching a system's security. The data generated by an audit trail is very large and effective management of such data is necessary. The large amount of data generated by a busy database system often makes it expensive to analyze the audit trail and this suggests that some method of selective auditing or selective recoding should be considered. We do not discuss these problems any further.

Auditing is generally used for the following:

- Future accountability of current actions on the database.
- Investigations of suspicious activity (for example, some years ago a person working on police computer systems in New Zealand tried to access drug-related records of a friend. He was discovered when a routine audit of the police database activities was carried out).
- Gathering statistics about database activity which can be used for tuning the database.
- Auditing one single user, all the users or a group of users.

Audit records include a variety of information, normally including the following:

(a) *Login, logoff to the database*—The username, date and time of the day, client IP from where the connection is originating. Failed logins also need to be logged and monitored.

(b) *During database usage*—Which application is being used, what information was retrieved, what information was updated? If data was updated, old and new values may need to be saved.

(c) *Data definition usage*—What tables were created and what were dropped, if any? What other DDL commands, if any, were executed?
(d) *Errors*—What errors, if any, occurred during the time the user was logged in?
(e) *Other actions*—Were some integrity constraints changed? Were some security settings changed?
(f) *Highly confidential data*—Was some sensitive data accessed? What database objects were accessed?

Assuming that database auditing is enabled, an audit record including items like those listed above is generated during the execution phase of each statement execution. Often a database audit mechanism on a large and busy database will consume a large amount of CPU and disk resources. The performance decline experienced when an audit is enabled may force an enterprise to scale back or altogether eliminate auditing.

We have only introduced the concepts of database auditing. A reader interested in further information should refer to book by Natan and Afyouni.

11.7 INTERNET APPLICATIONS AND ENCRYPTION

New challenges must be faced when a database is being accessed via the Internet. The Internet is a public network and security risks can expose passwords, accounts, and personal information to unauthorized individuals. In the age of electronic commerce and electronic banking much confidential information, for example, credit card numbers, is communicated via the Internet. Security of such communications is obviously important. Encryption of the data is often used to ensure security. We first define encryption.

Definition—Encryption
Encryption is the process of transforming information using a key and a mathematical algorithm so as the coded information is unintelligible to an unauthorized reader

Encryption is a mathematical algorithm that helps in maintaining secure data in an insecure environment like the Internet. The encryption approach involves scrambling of a message using an encryption algorithm and a key value so that the only person (or device) that can read the message is the device having the corresponding key. Therefore, it cannot be read by an unauthorized person.

The sender transforms given data (called *clear text*) into a new unrecognizable encrypted data set using a secret encryption key which may be created randomly or transformed from a password. The original data cannot be recovered from the encrypted data without the knowledge of a corresponding secret decryption key. Therefore, unless the decryption key is revealed, an adversary who steals the encrypted data cannot succeed in retrieving the unencrypted data. Encryption is most effective in situations like Internet applications where data is communicated online and not physically secured. Indeed, in Internet applications, encryption is the only effective means to prevent data from being stolen as long as the decryption key is not revealed. The decryption key must be conveyed securely to whoever needs to decrypt the data.

Encryption can be symmetric encryption or asymmetric encryption. In symmetric encryption, the data is encrypted and decrypted with the same key which is not revealed to anyone other than the users communicating. In asymmetric encryption, different encryption and decryption keys are used. The encryption key is called the *public key* and is available to everyone while the decryption key, called the *secret or private key*, is only held by the specific user. The private key is never revealed to anyone and never transmitted over the network.

The process followed in symmetric encryption is illustrated in Fig. 11.21. The sender has some data that is in cleartext form that he/she wishes to send to a receiver. The cleartext is encrypted using a key that is known to both the sender and the receiver. Once the data is encrypted, it is transmitted to the receiver who uses his symmetric key to decrypt the data and obtains the cleartext data that the sender had sent to him/her.

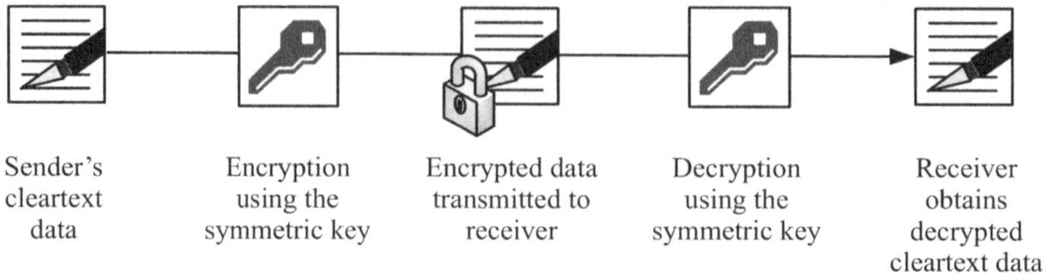

Figure 11.21 An illustration of symmetric encryption

The public/private key algorithms tend to be slow for large amounts of data while the symmetric algorithms are much faster. The public key (often 128-bit long) may be stored on the computer hard disk but the private key needs to be secured carefully, perhaps by storing it after some secure encryption. Communication of keys between the two parties requires careful protocols for both symmetric and asymmetric techniques. Since keys must be communicated via messages, the messages must be communicated in a secure environment, perhaps using encryption. Two issues need to be considered in public/private algorithms. How to communicate the public key and how to communicate the private key? In symmetric algorithms we only need to be concerned about communicating the symmetric key.

We do not discuss the issues of key distribution in this chapter but we illustrate the difficulty of communicating keys by using an example of communicating the public key for a session. Since the key is public, can we communicate it in cleartext? No, since an adversary might be able to intercept such a message and replace the intended key with another public key. The adversary is now able to intercept all messages using the fake public key and decode them!

Implementing a suitable encryption policy should consider the following issues.

(a) *What to encrypt?*—Since encryption involves additional storage costs and performance penalties, it is necessary to identify which part of each table needs to be encrypted. It is best to encrypt selectively.

(b) *Symmetric or Asymmetric?*—Symmetric encryption is faster but asymmetric encryption is more robust and has become the industry standard.

(c) *Key distribution*—A reliable system of key distribution is essential for the success of any encryption system.

(d) *Impact on database performance*—What impact would encryption have on the database performance? Encryption and decryption involve additional processing and therefore there will be some performance degradation.

(e) *Impact on recovery*—How does encryption impact recovery? Could the keys be lost if the system fails? How would key recovery take place?

11.8 SECURITY OF OUTSOURCED DATABASES

One of the major recent developments in the IT industry has been outsourcing. In particular a significant amount of IT work from USA and Europe is now done in countries like India to save cost. Data outsourcing also provides data storage and management. Therefore sensitive data is being managed on remote servers maintained by third party outsourcing vendors in an attempt to save the cost of data management although the service provider may not be fully trustworthy. It has been estimated that the total cost of data management is perhaps five times the cost of initial acquisition of the data.

Database outsourcing clearly poses significant challenges as far as correctness of information returned, confidentiality of information, privacy of personal information stored in the database and transportation via conventional transport or via networks[6] is conserned. In the last few years, this has been demonstrated by cases of data misuse when database management has been outsourced. Clients are therefore reluctant to place sensitive data under the control of a foreign outsourcing company without satisfactory database security assurances. To ensure security of database information, strict security protocols are needed. It may also be desirable to use selective encryption wherever appropriate. If data is encrypted then a user that is allowed to access some parts of the database must be provided with the encryption key. Therefore, different keys must be used for different resources and a user that has access to a number of resources must then manage a number of encryption keys.

We will not discuss these issues any further here. A reader interested in further study on this topic should refer to two chapters given in a recent book edited by Michael Gertz and Sushil Jajodia.

SUMMARY

- There are a number of different ways database security may be violated. Security violation may lead to loss of database integrity, loss of database availability and loss of database confidentiality.
- A list of primary threats to a database system includes dishonest employees, disgruntled employees, fire, etc.
- Some fundamental database security concepts and techniques include identification and authentication.
- The role of authorization or access control is discussed. There are two major access control methods for database systems.
- First discretionary access control method for authorization is discussed. In this approach some senior person in an enterprise has the discretion to give privileges to all employees who themselves may pass to others the privileges they have been given.
- The discretionary access control is possible using the SQL GRANT and REVOKE commands. Some DBMS including Oracle use this approach.
- Views may be used for fine grained database access control.

6. In a 2005 article "Personal Data for 3.9 Million Lost in Transit" the *New York Times* describes one of the largest breaches of data security. A number of other cases of breach of data security have also been reported although most of them appear to involve losing the magnetic media when data was being transported.

- The second access control is called the non-discretionary access control method. In this method, all users and database objects are classified and access is controlled based on this classification. This is similar to military classification of documents as TOP SECRET, SECRET, CONFIDENTIAL, and UNCLASSIFIED.
- Non-discretionary control (also called Mandatory Access Control, MAC) is based on the principles of information must not leak to users that are not cleared to have it. It is implemented by imposing the conditions "No read up" and "No write down".
- Security risks also exist in statistical databases and statistical inference controls are required to preserve confidentiality of personal information in statistical data.
- An audit policy that involves keeping records of who is accessing or modifying what data can help discover violation of a database system.
- Given that there is a lot of data that is stored in databases and interchanged via the Internet, it is important to protect security of such databases. Encryption is a widely used technique that scrambles the data when it is being transmitted. Two types of encryption techniques are available, viz., symmetric and asymmetric encryption techniques.
- The growing importance of cloud computing and outsourced databases requires that sensitive databases be protected when databases are stored and managed offsite.

REVIEW QUESTIONS

1. Explain how the security of a database may be compromised. (Section 11.1)
2. What types of security violations may occur in database systems? (Section 11.2)
3. Describe the role of identification and authentication in maintaining database security. (Section 11.3)
4. What is the role of authorization in database security and what techniques of authorization are available? (Section 11.4)
5. Explain authorization table, access control list (ACL) and capability list when used in discretionary access control. (Section 11.4.1)
6. How can the SQL view mechanism and GRANT and REVOKE commands be used in database security? (Sections 11.4 and 11.4.2)
7. What does nondiscretionary or mandatory control technique of authorization try to do? (Section 11.4.3)
8. Explain multilevel Bell–La Padula MAC policy and how it works. (Section 11.4.3)
9. Can statistical databases be compromised? How? Give an example. (Section 11.5)
10. Explain the concept of suitable queries and a tracker in statistical databases. (Section 11.5)
11. Give an example of how an audit policy may help in discovering a security violation in a database? (Section 11.6)
12. Estimate how much audit data will be generated for a bank like ICICI when users access its accounts database.
13. Give an example of a website that requires sensitive information like credit card information and discuss security concerns for it. (Section 11.7)
14. What is symmetric encryption and asymmetric encryption? Which is a better technique? (Section 11.7)
15. Briefly explain security concerns when a company in USA outsources its database applications to India. (Sections 11.8)

SHORT ANSWER QUESTIONS

1. Give an example of a database security violation that you have heard about.
2. List three most common security violations.
3. List three major sources of security threats.
4. What is database user identification?
5. What is database authentication?
6. Give an example illustrating the use of discretionary access control in a database system.
7. Give an example of an access control list?
8. What is an authorization graph?
9. What facilities does SQL provide for database security?
10. Give an example of nondiscretionary control.
11. What are No-Read-Up and No-Write-Down policies?
12. Why is No-Write-Down necessary?
13. Why do we need security controls in statistical databases?
14. What is a negative compromise?
15. Define tracker in statistical databases.
16. Can an audit policy help in protecting a database system against violations?
17. List six items of information that an audit process must save when a user is logged in to a database.
18. When a person buys books from amazon.com, what is the major security concern of the company and the customer?
19. What is meant by encryption and decryption?
20. What is a key in encryption?
21. List two major examples that illustrate security concerns when database applications are outsourced to India.

MULTIPLE CHOICE QUESTIONS

1. Which one of the following is **not** normally a source of database system security threats?
   (a) Dishonest employees
   (b) Dishonest customers
   (c) Disgruntled employees
   (d) Water and fire
2. Which one of the following is correct?
   (a) Identification involves a user indicating to the computer system there identity, or simply who he/she is.
   (b) Authentication and authorization are the same.
   (c) Database authentication involves allowing certain users to access, process or alter specified parts of the database subject to certain limitations.
   (d) None of the above

3. Which one of the following is correct regarding authorization?
   (a) Authorization may be based on either subject profiles or object profiles but not both.
   (b) A discretionary authorization policy involves providing access to users based on their need-to-access as specified by the users themselves.
   (c) Mandatory control involves assigning each database object to a security class and each user a security clearance. Each user is then authorized to access all objects that have a classification that is lower or equal to his/her clearance.
   (d) Authorization does not include specification of what a user may do with the access.
4. Which one of the following privileges may not be granted using SQL?
   (a) GRANT SELECT
   (b) GRANT DELETE
   (c) REVOKE SELECT
   (d) REVOKE VIEW
5. Which one of the following is **not** correct?
   (a) In integrity we are concerned with nonmalicious data errors and their control.
   (b) In security we are concerned with only malicious damage to the database.
   (c) In concurrency we are concerned with controlling access to the database by authorized users.
   (d) In recovery we are concerned with recovering to a consistent database after a failure.
6. Which of the following are normally considered a security threat?
   (a) Unauthorized disclosure of data
   (b) Corruption of data
   (c) User errors and omissions
   (d) Trojan horse
   (e) All of the above
7. Which one of the following is not normally a component of a database security policy?
   (a) User authentication
   (b) Network monitoring
   (c) Authorization
   (d) Statistical inference control
8. Which one of the following is **not** correct?
   (a) Discretionary access control involves granting or revoking of read/write privileges.
   (b) Discretionary access control involves granting or revoking of separate passwords for different parts of the database.
   (c) Nondiscretionary access control does not involve a supervisor assessing the data needs of the users.
   (d) Discretionary access control allows access rights to be propagated.
9. Given a large number of users and a large number of objects, the size of the security matrix may become prohibitively large. Which one of the following can help in reducing the size of the matrix?
   (a) Defining groups of users with identical security authorization and groups of objects that need identical protection.
   (b) Specifying a general rule and listing only the exceptions in the matrix.
   (c) Storing the security matrix using a sparse matrix data representation.
   (d) None of the above
10. Which of the following are involved in mandatory (nondiscretionary) access control?
   (a) Each user and data object is classified.
   (b) Each user can read data objects equal to or below his/her level.

(c) Each user can write data objects at his/her level.
(d) All of the above.

11. Which of the following may be involved in access matrix control model of authorization?
    (a) Each user's access rights to each object are specified.
    (b) Each group of user's access rights to each group of objects are specified.
    (c) Each user's security clearance is specified.
    (d) Each object's security level is specified.
12. Which one of the following is **not** true about SQL privileges?
    (a) GRANT and REVOKE may be granted to a view.
    (b) GRANT and REVOKE may be granted to an existing trigger.
    (c) GRANT and REVOKE may be granted to insert new rows.
    (d) GRANT and REVOKE may be granted to update a given table.
13. Which of the following principles is the basis of the mandatory control method?
    (a) No read up (b) No write down (c) No distribution down (d) No read down
14. Which of the following are correct?
    (a) Queries whose set size falls between (w, $n - w$) are sometimes called suitable.
    (b) A characteristic formula C is a condition for describing a subgroup of the population (e.g., all people living in New Delhi).
    (c) A condition like Income > 1,00,00,000 and NOT(City = 'Mumbai') is called an individual tracker.
    (d) All are correct
15. Which of the following are **not** a concern in deciding a database encryption policy?
    (a) What parts of the database need encryption?
    (b) Should symmetric or asymmetric encryption be used?
    (c) Should public domain software or vendor software be used?
    (d) What is the likelihood of someone intercepting a message?
16. Which one of the following is correct?
    (a) A statistical database may not be positively compromised.
    (b) A statistical database may not be negatively compromised if a zero result query is not permitted.
    (c) A tracker is a set of auxiliary attributes added to the original query to assist in compromising the database.
    (d) Queries who size falls between (w, $n - w$) ensure that the database is not compromised.
17. Which of the following are purposes of auditing?
    (a) Investigations of suspicious activity (b) Auditing one single user
    (c) Tuning the database system (d) All of the above
18. Which one of the following is **not** the type of information that is likely to be recorded for auditing?
    (a) Username, date and time of login and logoff.
    (b) Which application is being used by each user.
    (c) Which tables were created and which were dropped.
    (d) Which locks were granted to the user.

19. Which of the following are true?
    (a) Encryption is the process of transforming information using a key so that the coded information becomes unintelligible to an unauthorized user.
    (b) Encryption must always be symmetric.
    (c) The public/private key algorithms are normally very fast.
    (d) Encryption must involve distribution of a key.
20. Which of the following need to be considered in implementing a suitable encryption policy?
    (a) How to distribute the keys in a reliable way?
    (b) What impact would encryption have on the database performance?
    (c) What impact would encryption have on recovery?
    (d) All of the above

EXERCISES

1. Authentication mechanisms may be based on one of the following. Give an example of each of them.
   (a) Objects in the possession of the user
   (b) Knowledge that the user has
   (c) Actions of the user
   (d) Physiology of the user
2. Explain the differences between discretionary and nondiscretionary access control policies for authorization. State which is easier to implement and which is more reliable?
3. What is an access matrix? What does it specify? Give an example and discuss it.
4. Given a large number of users and a large number of objects, the size of the security matrix may become prohibitively large. What problem does this lead to? How can the size be reduced?
5. Describe some weaknesses of the discretionary access control and the mandatory access control techniques for protecting database security. How can these problems be overcome?
6. Briefly explain security problems that may arise in statistical databases. Give examples.
7. What is an individual tracker? Give an example of an individual tracker.
8. Consider the following statistical database and assume that the system will only respond to queries with a result set cardinality between 3 and 6. Suppose that we know from outside sources that Bhardwaj is the only female programmer in the database. Write a series of queries to find Bhardwaj's income.

Name	*Sex*	*Dependants*	*Occupation*	*Income*
Ahmed	M	3	Programmer	40k
Bhardwaj	F	2	Programmer	50k
Chandra	F	0	Clerk	30k
De Cruz	M	2	Lawyer	60k
Lal	F	2	Clerk	35k
Singh	M	1	Clerk	25k
Gupta	M	0	Lawyer	70k
Patel	M	2	Programmer	45k
Iyer	M	0	Programmer	35k

PROJECTS

1. Study the two reports on cyber espionage published by the University of Toronto and prepare a summary of 1000 words listing the hackers, place of origin of and the sites in India that were the potential targets. What did they discover? Are there any similar cyber attacks originating from some other countries that the researchers discovered?
2. Consider an example that we presented in Chapter 1. It relates to a database in a university. The database includes the following information.

    - Student personal data (for example, each student's name, gender, current address, home address, date of birth, nationality)
    - Student academic data (each student's school results, academic history, current enrolment)
    - Academic staff data (each academic staff member's name, gender, current address, date of birth, nationality, academic qualifications, appointment history, current appointment, salary history, current salary, sabbatical leave information, recreational leave, sick leave)
    - Non-academic staff data (each non-academic staff member's name, gender, current address, date of birth, nationality, trade qualifications and experience, appointment history, current appointment, salary history, current salary, recreational leave, sick leave)
    - Courses (or units) offered data (each course's name, course code, department, syllabus, lecturer, quota if any)
    - Financial data (budget information, receipts, expenditure)

    (a) List all the security concerns that you can identify with such a database.
    (b) Identify all the people in the university and outside the university who might be interested in violating the database security.
    (c) Explain in detail all the security controls that the database must have to properly protect it from unauthorized users.

LAB EXERCISES

1. Consider the Indian Railways Passenger Reservation System (PRS) database. List the major security concerns with this database. What actions must be taken to provide basic security for it? Details of the Indian Railways Centre for Railways Information System (CRIS) are available at http://www.dw.indianrail.gov.in/crisbro.pdf.
2. Consider a very basic airline booking system that we used in Chapter 9 and let us assume we have implemented the following schema which is a rather primitive system:

    Customer(CustomerID, Title, First name, Last name, Gender, Age, Address, TelephoneBH, TelephoneAH, Email)
    Flight(FlightNUM, DepartureDate, DepartureTime, ArrivalDate, ArrivalTime)
    Seat(FlightNUM, CustomerID, DepartureDate, SeatNUM, Class)
    Ticket (SerialNUM, FlightNUM, DepartureDate, SeatNUM, CustomerID)

(a) What are the biggest security threats to this database system?

(b) Few years ago, an employee of Qantas was able to access passenger lists of flights after the flights had landed and add himself as a passenger thus enabling him to claim frequent flyer points for flights he never took! How would you ensure such security breaches do not take place?

BIBLIOGRAPHY

For Students

The book of Castano et al., is useful. The article by Schuman is worth studying. The papers by Denning deal with statistical databases.

For Instructors

There are a variety of articles and books on database security. The article by Denning and Denning is good. The book by Fernandez et al., covers database security in detail. The book by Gertz and Jajodia is a collection of some useful papers on database security. Katz and Lindell is a detailed look at cryptography, perhaps a little too detailed for our needs. The book by Natan is also worth consulting. It is one of the few books that discuss auditing in detail as well as present examples from Oracle, SQL Server, DB2 and Sybase.

Afyouni, H. A., *Database Security and Auditing: Protecting Data Integrity and Accessibility*, Course Technology, 2005, 448pp.

Beck, L. L., "A Security Mechanism for Statistical Databases", *ACM Transactions of Database Systems*, Vol. 5, 1980, pp 316-338.

Castano, S., M. Fugini, G. Martella, and P. Samarati, *Database Security*, Addison-Wesley, 1995, 456pp.

Conway, R. W., W. L. Maxwell, and H. L. Morgan, "On the implementation of security measures in information systems", *Communications of the ACM*, Vol. 15, 1972, pp 1-12.

"Database Security 2007: Threats and Priorities within IT Database Infrastructure", *Ponemon Institute*, 2007. http://www.appsecinc.com/techdocs/whitepapers/2007-Ponemon-Database-Security-Study-Sponsored-by-Application-Security-Inc.pdf

Vimercati, S. di., P. Samarati, and S. Jajodia, "Hardware and Software Data Security", In EOLSS *The Encyclopedia of Life Support Systems*, D. Kaeli and Z. Navabi (Eds.), EOLSS Publishers, 2001.

Denning, D. E., and P. J. Denning, "Data Security", *ACM Computing Surveys*, Vol. 11, 1979, pp. 227-250.

Denning, D. E., "Secure Statistical Databases under Random Queries", *ACM Transactions of Database Systems*, Vol. 5, 1980, pp 291-315.

Denning, D. E., and J. Schlorer, "Inference Controls for Statistical Database Security", *IEEE Computer*, Vol. 16, 1983, pp 69-82.

Fagin, R., "On an authorization mechanism", *ACM Transactions of Database Systems*, Vol. 3, 1978, pp 310-319.

Fernandez, E. B., R. C. Summers, and C. Wood, *Database Security and Integrity*, Addison-Wesley, 1981.

Gertz, M., and M. Gandhi, "Security Re-engineering for Databases: Concepts and Techniques", In *Handbook of Database Security: Applications and Trends*, M. Gertz and S. Jajodia (Eds.), Springer Verlag, 2008.

Gertz, M., and S. Jajodia (Eds.) *Handbook of Database Security: Applications and Trends*, Springer Verlag, 2008.

Katz, J., and Y. Lindell, *Introduction to Modern Cryptography*, Chapman & Hall/CRC, 2008, 534pp.

Kenan, K., *Cryptography in the Database: The Last Line of Defence*, Addison-Wesley, 2005, 312pp.

Natan, R. B., *Implementing Database Security and Auditing*, Elsevier Digital Press, 2005, 413pp.

Schulman, A., "Top Ten Database Security Threats: How to Mitigate the Most Significant Database Vulnerabilities", *Imperva White Paper*. http://www.infosec.co.uk/ExhibitorLibrary/383/WP_TopTen_Database_Threats_1106LK_20.pdf.

Wood, C., E. B. Fernandez, and R. C. Summers, "Database Security: Requirements, Policies and Models", *IBM Systems Journal*, Vol. 19, 1980, pp 229-252.

12 Integrity Constraints and Active Databases

OBJECTIVES

- Explain the importance of integrity in database systems.
- Describe the concepts of syntactic and semantic integrity.
- Discuss the techniques for enforcing integrity constraints including what to enforce, where to enforce, when to enforce and how to enforce.
- Describe SQL support for syntactic integrity including primary key, foreign key, NOT NULL, Default, Domain and UNIQUE.
- Explain the different types of semantic constraints.
- Describe SQL support for semantic integrity including CHECK, ASSERTION, TRIGGER.
- Discuss active database systems.

KEYWORDS

Integrity constraints, syntactic integrity, semantic integrity, primary key, existential integrity, foreign key, referential integrity, NULL, DEFAULT, UNIQUE, CHECK, ASSERTION, domains, Triggers, column-based constraints, table-based constraints, active databases, event-condition-action (ECA), event definition, detection and reaction.

Gaadhava pudhe vaachli Geeta, Kaalcha gondhal baraa hota (Marathi proverb)
Translation: It's no use wasting wisdom on a fool who thinks and acts like he is the only correct person in the world.

12.1 INTRODUCTION

Given that an enterprise database is a very valuable resource, it is essential that its consistency be maintained at all times. Maintaining database consistency requires many techniques. Some of these have already been discussed. For example, we have discussed how consistency can be maintained in spite of an accidental failure or damage to the database. This was discussed in Chapter 10 on recovery. In Chapter 9, we discussed concurrency control techniques to maintain consistency when a number of transactions are being carried out concurrently. Finally, in Chapter 11, we have discussed security measures that need to be taken to protect the database against deliberate penetration or corruption by an unauthorized person.

In all the discussions on recovery, concurrency and security, it has always been assumed that a transaction that is run by an authorized person transforms a consistent database to another consistent state of the database. This is in fact not always true because even when an authorized user runs what he/she believes is a legal transaction the transaction may lead to transforming the database into an inconsistent state. Not all authorized users can be expected to know all the complexities of an enterprise all the time. Furthermore a mistake may be made in inputting data. I have myself made a mistake in typing the amount of money when using an electronic banking system.

Of course, a new senior appointment in a company may not recognize proper accounting procedures for the company he/she has just joined. A procedure legal in one company may not be legal in another. It is therefore necessary that the DBMS recognize illegal transactions and reject them.

The topic of integrity constraints was first discussed in Chapter 3 (Section 3.5) when we discussed the relational model and again in Chapter 5 (Section 5.7) while discussing integrity constraint features of SQL. The discussion about integrity constraint issues in this chapter is much more comprehensive.

The notion of integrity constraints is strongly related to the notion of a transaction. As discussed in Chapter 9, a transaction is a sequence of operations that performs a single logical function in a database application and obeys the ACID properties of a transaction. Some integrity constraints may be validated during the execution of a transaction and some at the time when the transaction completes its execution. A transaction should be committed only if it satisfies all the integrity constraints otherwise it should be aborted and rolled back. In summary, integrity constraints describe conditions that every instance of a relation in a database must satisfy when it is modified by a transaction.

Semantic correctness of data basically deals with the issue of how the data managed by a database system reflects the real world. The specification of what data is semantically correct is one of the most important tasks in the database design process. To specify integrity constraints they must be formulated in some language used in the database design and then these constraints on the database objects have to be satisfied in order to correctly reflect the real world. Integrity constraint specifications are usually translated into constraint enforcing mechanisms provided by the DBMS. We will discuss the support provided by SQL:1999 for integrity enforcement.

This chapter is organized as follows. First, basics of database integrity are discussed. A definition of database integrity is presented and two types of integrity, syntactic integrity and semantic integrity are discussed in some detail. Enforcement principles are described in Section 12.3 including what to enforce, where to enforce, when to enforce and how to enforce. Section 12.4 explains how integrity constraints are implemented in SQL:1999. This includes implementation of syntactic integrity constraints in Section 12.5 and semantic integrity constraints including the CHECK constraint, the Assertion constraint and the Trigger constraint in Section 12.6. Section 12.7 deals with active database systems.

12.2 WHAT IS DATABASE INTEGRITY?

Integrity is defined in different ways by different experts. We present one definition below. Essentially integrity is concerned with protecting the database from improper insertion of new information and improper deletion of existing information.

Definition—Integrity
Integrity deals with ensuring that the transactions that the users are running are correct and therefore ensures that every database insertion, deletion and update is accurate, valid and consistent according to the constraints specified.

Integrity may be syntactic integrity or semantic integrity. We discuss each of them now.

12.2.1 Syntactic Integrity

Syntactic integrity is usually specified when creating a table. It may include rules about valid values, for example, specifying the domain for each column, the primary and foreign keys, and some alternate keys. We have already discussed two integrity constraints: the existential integrity constraint and the referential integrity constraint.

Such syntactic constraints are, of course, independent of the database that is being created. The complete list of syntactic constraints is given below:

- PRIMARY KEY—As discussed earlier in Chapters 3 and 4, this specifies the primary key for the table. As noted there, the primary key is an attribute or set of attributes that uniquely identify each tuple in the relation (called the uniqueness property), and if the key is a set of attributes then no subset of these attributes has the uniqueness property (called the minimality property).
- FOREIGN KEY—Again as discussed in Chapter 3, the foreign key in a table *R* is a set of columns (possibly one) whose values are required to match those of the primary key of some table *S*. *R* and *S* are not necessarily distinct. This is the basis of referential integrity. We also need to specify actions to be taken if referential integrity is violated during a delete or an update.
- NOT NULL—As explained in Chapter 3, the issue of null values in a database is extremely important. A value in a database may be null for several reasons. The most obvious reason is that the value is not known at the present time. If an attribute is defined to be NOT NULL then it cannot accept a NULL value.
- DEFAULT—This allows specification of a default value for a column. Without a DEFAULT clause, the default value is NULL.

- UNIQUE—This constraint ensures that a column or a group of columns in a table have a distinct value. When some columns are defined to be unique, it may be considered as a specification of an alternate key although UNIQUE allows NULL values.
- DOMAIN—This allows a column domain to be defined. These domains include INTEGER, SMALLINT, DECIMAL, VARCHAR or DATE.

Later in this chapter, in Section 12.3, we will show how each of the constraints may be specified using SQL.

12.2.2 Semantic Integrity

Semantic integrity involves compliance of the database with constraints which are derived from users' understanding of the database and what is and what is not allowed in the database. The *maintenance* or *enforcement* of semantic integrity involves preventing data which represents a disallowed state from being inserted in the database. A disallowed state is determined by rules about the actions that may be performed when an event like update, delete or insertion takes place. When rules are enforced automatically, the stored data becomes more *active* because an active database waits on data in order to react to it.

The rules or constraints specify semantics of data. The constraints are usually business rules and it is difficult to discriminate between constraints and business rules. Business rules tend to be more complex than syntactic constraints. These rules may impose simple constraints, for example, involving only one attribute of a table. More complex constraints usually involve more than one attribute and often more than one table.

While discussing integrity constraints we will assume the database to be consistent before the update and specify constraints that result in a consistent database after the update. This is often called *incremental* integrity constraint checking. The semantic integrity constraints are specified in terms of conditions that must hold after an update. Arbitrary conditions can be quite difficult to deal with and most techniques only allow a simplified specification. Integrity constraints can be of several different types. For example, consider the following possible constraints that an employee database may be required to obey:

- No employee in the company earns a monthly salary of more than Rs. 2,00,000 a month.
- No employee in the company is given a cut in salary.
- No employee in the company is given a raise of more than 50% in any one instance.
- No updates are allowed on the record of retired employees.

One may classify semantic integrity constraints into the following two classes:

- *State constraints*—These are time independent constraints for a particular database. The constraints are independent of the update at hand and are usually specified by a single predicate[1] that specifies the state of the current database. Therefore these integrity constraints may be checked when a single database state is available.
- *Transitional constraints*—These constraints, again specified as predicates, apply to the update at hand. The scope of integrity constraints can vary greatly from being applicable to a single attribute in a

1. The Oxford Dictionary defines predicate as "something which is affirmed or denied concerning an argument of a proposition". In our context, we will use predicate and condition interchangeably.

single relation to involving several attributes in several relations. Checking of each such constraint requires two consecutive database states, the state just before a transaction and the state just after the transaction.

The examples listed above include examples of both types of constraints.

The scope of the constraints can be classified as follows:

- *Single variable, aggregate free*—These are single relational constraints involving single variables and are therefore the simplest to implement. An example of such a constraint could be 'each full-time employee must be paid at least Rs. 10,000 a month'.
- *Multivariable, aggregate free with only one tuple variable being updated*—These could be domain constraints or intra-relation dependencies. For example, 'every employee's salary shall be greater than any recorded salary value for that employee in the salary history'.
- *Multivariable multirelational constraints without aggregates*—These constraints involve relationships between relations (for example, referential integrity or inclusion dependencies). An example of such a constraint is 'every employee must earn less than his manager'. We are assuming managers' information is in another table.
- *Data aggregate assertions*—These are often the most expensive because of the need to process the aggregates. An example of such a constraint is that 'total salaries cannot exceed the departmental budget'.

A straightforward approach to maintenance of semantic integrity involves:

1. Specifying the semantic integrity constraints in a suitable language.
2. Vetting the data which is presented for insertion or modification of the database based on the constraints that have been specified.

The database system ideally should maintain semantic integrity constraints automatically. If we want to maintain the consistency of the database, we will need to identify as many features of database consistency as we can. These are stated in the form of integrity constraints.

12.2.3 Enforcing Integrity in Applications Programs

Almost always a database would have a number of integrity constraints that would be desirable to enforce in addition to the syntactic constraints listed above. Specification of semantic integrity constraints if done comprehensively could form a very large part of the database definition. In the absence of a mechanism for specifying these additional integrity constraints, it becomes the responsibility of the application programs to ensure integrity constraint enforcement. This is not desirable. Ideally one would like the constraints to be enforced globally by the DBMS itself. Although the embedding of integrity constraints in the application program is an efficient mechanism for enforcing the constraints, it does mean the following:

- Application programmers must clearly understand the integrity assertions.
- Since each table in a database may be used by a number of application programs, each application program would need to include similar constraints for the same table.
- Consistency is based on the assumption that each application program modifies the database correctly. Errors in application programs can lead to an inconsistent database.

- **Application programs including semantic constraints turn out to be more complex than they ought to** be since each program must include the appropriate integrity constraint checking.
- **There is little global control of database consistency.**
- **It is almost impossible to add or modify integrity constraints since to do so requires modification of** many application programs.

One of the main problems facing semantic integrity constraints enforcement is the cost of enforcement. A lot of research work in this area therefore deals with the efficiency of enforcement techniques. The constraints are often described as conditions that define consistent database states (they are only necessary conditions, they are not sufficient). The constraints are time independent facts about the database.

12.3 ENFORCEMENT PRINCIPLES

We now discuss the principles involved in enforcing constraints, when to enforce the constraints, where to enforce them and how. The usual procedure for integrity constraint checking does not involve full integrity constraint checking at each update since this is likely to be very time consuming. It is therefore assumed that all integrity constraints are satisfied by the current database and the update does not violate any integrity constraints.

We note that most integrity constraints need to be enforced dynamically since most constraints require that updated values be obtained and then a check be made on whether the new values violate the integrity constraints. However, some constraints can in fact be checked statically. For example, if an integrity constraint was that a salary could not be below 10,000, then a transaction attempting to update the salary to 7,000 could be checked without executing it. We assume that the constraints specified for enforcement by the database system are syntactically and semantically correct. Syntactic correctness may be checked using a conventional syntax checker for the language used to specify the constraints but verifying semantic correctness is a much harder problem.

It is important to verify that each constraint can be satisfied by any nontrivial database state. This is called *satisfiability*. If no database state can satisfy the constraint, the constraint is incorrect and is called *unsatisfiable* and should be rejected by the database.

Integrity enforcement has costs associated with it. The costs consist of the following:

- **Additional I/O costs if the integrity enforcement requires additional I/O.**
- **Additional computational costs to evaluate the integrity assertions. In addition, there would be** additional communication costs if the database was distributed over a number of machines.

12.3.1 What to Enforce?

The semantic integrity constraints must be specified for the database enforcer to be able to understand and enforce them. Since the constraints are predicates they can be expressed in a high level language like predicate calculus. As noted earlier, these constraints may include primary and foreign key constraints as well as semantic constraints. For example, no employee in the company earns a monthly salary of more than

Rs. 2,00,000 a month. The constraints can be more complex, for example, an AC Coach in a train must not have more passengers than its specified capacity or in a Shatabdi train each seat in the train must be allocated to a passenger before bookings are refused.

12.3.2 Where to Enforce?

An integrity constraint can be seen as an assertion verified by the data. Since the database is divided into relations, each time an insertion, delete or update is carried out on a relation one needs to check that the modified relation satisfies the constraints that have been specified for it. The individual assertions can be enforced when the updates are being processed but aggregate type assertions, for example, a constraint specifying that the number of passengers on a flight must not be more than the seating capacity of the plane being used on the flight, and can only be checked at the end of the transaction before the transaction commits. If an inconsistency is found the transaction would need to be rolled back.

12.3.3 When to Enforce?

Integrity constraints can be enforced before a transaction is executed by evaluating what a transaction is going to do or during the execution or after the transaction has completed its execution, or partially during each of the three phases.

- *Before the transaction execution*—It is possible to carry out integrity constraints enforcement before the transaction is executed. This requires obtaining new values of the data items that are going to be modified by the transaction and carry out the checking. If the checking fails, the transaction is not executed; otherwise the transaction is allowed to proceed. For example, a flight booking transaction can be rejected before execution if the flight is fully booked. No rollback of executed transactions is necessary. Since integrity checking and transaction execution are carried out sequentially to ensure that integrity is properly enforced, no other transaction can be allowed to access data items between the integrity checking and transaction execution. Essentially then the data items must be locked before integrity checking and released only after transaction execution (or transaction abort).
- *During the transaction execution*—Integrity checking can be carried out concurrently with transaction execution. As the transaction updates data items, integrity checking can be evaluated as part of the updates. A transaction is not allowed to commit until all integrity constraints have been checked. Again, no transaction rollback is necessary since integrity checking is carried out if the updates are propagated to the database only after the transaction commits.
- *After the transaction execution*—Many integrity checking techniques carry out the checking after a transaction has executed. If the checking fails, the transaction is rolled back or some other corrective action is taken at the end of the transaction. For example, the aggregate assertions can only be checked at the end of the transaction. For long transactions, it may be necessary to carry out checks of aggregate assertions during the transaction so that if an integrity violation has already occurred, it is identified early and the transaction is rolled back.

SQL's default policy is to check constraints at the end of execution of each SQL statement. So, essentially SQL requires that no constraint be violated at the end of a SQL statement. If a constraint is violated, SQL returns an error and restores the database to the state that existed before the statement was executed. It is also possible to defer SQL constraint checking, since in some cases a SQL statement may violate a constraint only to be restored by the next statement. Deferred constraints are checked at the end of each transaction.

SQL statements that violate a constraint are usually undone at the end of the statement.

12.3.4 How to Enforce?

An algorithm that enforces integrity could consist of a trigger condition being generated at each update. Any constraints that apply to the relation being modified are then checked on update and suitable action taken if a violation occurs. Some systems carry out updates only if the constraints are satisfied and on violation, reject the updates. Others allow updates but roll back transactions on violation. A suitable constraint enforcement algorithm could consist of specification of the constraints and if necessary, transform to a canonical form. This is very similar to the first step in query optimization. On each insert or update, the tuple(s) are checked against the constraints. If any constraint is relevant to the update, the updated tuple(s) is used to evaluate the constraint. **Results of studies in integrity enforcement techniques indicate that in most situations, run-time** enforcement is the best technique. Only if the integrity enforcement requires few input/output operations from the secondary memory, could before execution enforcement, perform well. After execution, techniques consistently perform poorly and much worse than other techniques if the transaction rejection rates are high. In addition to being able to specify constraints, a constraint language should also provide facilities for specification of what needs to be done at violation. The constraint could in fact be considered to have the following two components:

- A constraint condition
- A validation failure response

Semantic integrity constraints enforcement requires an integrity subsystem within the DBMS. It has been suggested that the subsystem should be part of the query processing component of the DBMS. Since integrity assertions use a language similar to the query language, it is appropriate to process the assertions when the queries are processed. Constraints on a database need to be compiled and stored with the database metadata for use with all insertion, deletes and updates on the database.

12.4 INTEGRITY CONSTRAINTS IN SQL:1999

We now discuss the support SQL:1999 provides for integrity constraints. We first discuss the support for syntactic integrity constraints, some of which were discussed earlier in Chapters 3 and 5, followed by support for semantic integrity constraints. Some of the constraints discussed below may be defined as column constraints or table constraints.

12.4.1 Constraint Names

SQL allows each individual constraint to be given a constraint name to uniquely identify each constraint from other constraints. Since the constraint names are optional, in our examples below we will not give names to the constraints that we define but in a more complex situation with large number of tables and each table having many constraints, it is helpful to give name to each constraint. Even if the user does not assign a name to a constraint, SQL assigns names to all constraints. It is therefore recommended that each constraint be given a name even if names are optional. The names are also useful when the user needs to DROP a constraint.

12.5 SQL AND SYNTACTIC INTEGRITY

We consider the syntactic integrity facilities provided by SQL:1999 for each of the following. The facilities provided are similar to those provided in SQL2. Very few extensions for syntactic integrity were provided in SQL:1999. The syntactic integrity constraints are the most important basic constraints that every database needs to satisfy.

- PRIMARY KEY
- FOREIGN KEY
- NOT NULL
- DEFAULT
- UNIQUE
- DOMAIN

As noted in the last section, integrity constraints may be checked either in the *immediate* mode or in the *deferred* mode. In the immediate mode, the checking is carried out at the beginning of each statement that might violate the constraint. In the deferred mode, the checking is carried out at the end of the transaction.

12.5.1 Column Constraints and Table Constraints

Some constraints may be specified within a column definition of a table by specifying the constraint after the column definition. They are called column constraints and may be specified for the primary key constraint, the foreign key constraint, the NOT NULL constraint and the CHECK constraint, if these constraints involve only one attribute. If more than one attribute is involved, the table constraint must be used, but a table constraint can also be used for constraints on only one attribute. When a single attribute constraint is used as a table constraint, the constraint is likely to be checked more frequently as it will be checked every time an insert, deletion or update is made to the table. A column constraint will not be checked if values in other columns are being updated.

We will illustrate the specification of various constraints below.

12.5.2 Primary Key Constraint

The primary key constraint is perhaps the most important and the most basic integrity constraint. This integrity is also called *existential integrity*. The primary key constraint may be specified either as a column constraint or a table constraint. We give examples of both. Figure 12.1 shows how it can be specified as a column constraint by specifying the constraint on the primary key attribute *MatchID* for the table *Match*. As noted earlier, this works only if the primary key is a single attribute and the primary key is declared after the declaration of the column in CREATE TABLE command for the table.

Primary key may also be specified using UNIQUE as we will see later.

As noted earlier, the approach proposed in Fig. 12.1 cannot be used if the primary key is more than one column, since it is then confusing if we say something like the following, since it is not clear if both columns together are the primary keys or each of the column is a primary key which, of course, is not permitted.

```
MatchID INTEGER PRIMARY KEY,
Team1 CHAR(15) PRIMAR KEY
```

A table constraint approach therefore must be used when a primary key consists of two or more columns. Figure 12.2 shows the table constraint approach for specifying a primary key constraint. This approach involves specifying a constraint on the whole table, not just the attribute that forms the primary key. A single column primary key may also be specified as a table constraint.

As discussed earlier, declaring a primary key constraint essentially means that no two tuples in the relation can have the same value of the primary key attributes and no column that is part of the primary key value can be NULL.

```
CREATE TABLE Match
    (MatchID INTEGER PRIMARY KEY,
    Team1 CHAR(15),
    Team2 CHAR(15),
    Ground CHAR(20),
    Date CHAR(10),
    Result CHAR(10));
```

Figure 12.1 Specifying primary key as a column constraint in SQL

```
CREATE TABLE Bowling
    (MID INTEGER,
    PID INTEGER,
    NOvers INTEGER,
    Maidens INTEGER,
    NRuns INTEGER,
    NWickets INTEGER,
    PRIMARY KEY (MID, PID));
```

Figure 12.2 Specifying primary key as a table constraint in SQL

Existential integrity is enforced by the system by checking every time a new tuple is inserted to a relation or a tuple, including its primary key, is modified. Some DBMS allow tables to be declared without a primary key being declared. It is however strongly recommended that for every table a primary key be declared.

12.5.3 Foreign Key

The foreign key constraint has been discussed in Chapters 3 and 5 and is also called *referential integrity*. We first consider a situation in which the foreign key is only one attribute. The cricket database does not have a table that has one column as its foreign key. Therefore we will use an *Employee* table which has a foreign key *Dept* referring to the *Department* table. This constraint may be specified as a column constraint in SQL by identifying the column, referencing the primary key in another table as shown in Fig. 12.3. For a column to be defined as a foreign key it should be referring to a primary key in the table which it is referring to, and both must have the same domain and the referenced table must always have the values that are in the referencing table.

```
CREATE TABLE Employee
    (EmpID NUMBER(6) PRIMARY KEY,
    Name CHAR(20),
    Dept CHAR(10), REFERENCES Department (DeptID),
    Address CHAR (50)
    Position CHAR (20));
```

Figure 12.3 Specifying foreign key as a column constraint in SQL

If the foreign key refers a table's primary key then the reference to the column may be omitted and the fourth line in Fig. 12.3 may be replaced by the following.

Dept CHAR(10), REFERENCES *Department*,

Again, as noted earlier for primary key constraint, the foreign key constraint that includes more than one column cannot be specified as a column constraint. It must be specified as a table constraint. Figure 12.4 illustrates how to specify a foreign key constraint as a table constraint when a foreign key involves more than one column. It is essential that the number of columns in the foreign key and their domains be the same as the number of columns and their respective domains in the primary key being referred to.

```
CREATE TABLE Bowling
    (MatchID INTEGER,
    PID INTEGER,
    NOvers INTEGER,
    Maidens INTEGER,
    NRuns INTEGER,
    NWickets INTEGER,
    PRIMARY KEY (MID, PID)
    FOREIGN KEY (MatchID) REFERENCES Match,
    FOREIGN KEY (PID) REFERENCES Player);
```

Figure 12.4 Specifying foreign key as a table constraint in SQL

As noted in Chapter 3, a column in a table may refer to the primary key of the same table. Figure 12.5 shows such a situation. We use an employee table in which the manager is also an employee.

```
CREATE TABLE Employee
    (EmpID NUMBER(6) PRIMARY KEY,
    Name CHAR(20),
    Dept CHAR(10),
    ManagerID(6) REFERENCES Employee(EmpID),
    Address CHAR (50)
    Position CHAR (20));
```

Figure 12.5 Specifying a foreign key referring to its own primary key

It should be noted that violation of referential integrity can occur if rows are modified either in the referencing table or in the referenced table. Once a violation takes place, referential integrity must be maintained by either setting the foreign key to NULL or by cascading the update/deletion of a referenced row.

Referential integrity implies that the referenced attribute(s) must be declared as primary key (or UNIQUE) for the referenced relation and values of the foreign key appearing in the first relation must also appear in the referenced relation unless the foreign key has been declared NULL in the first relation. A new foreign key value cannot be inserted in a table unless there is a corresponding primary key value it references. A foreign key value cannot be updated unless the updated value appears as one of the values of the primary key it references. Furthermore, a primary key value that is referenced by a foreign key may not be deleted without some further action. These actions may include the following:

- One way of enforcing referential integrity is to reject any modification of the foreign key if the modified value does not also appear in the referenced relation. This is called the *Default Policy.*
- Another way when the value being referenced by a foreign key is modified or the row deleted is to set the foreign key value to NULL. This is called the *Set-NULL policy.*
- Finally, the third way is when the value being referenced by a foreign key is modified or the row deleted is to modify the referencing foreign key as well. This is called the *Cascade Policy.*

All referential update and delete actions happen after the update or the delete have been carried out. If the constraints are violated then SQL returns an error and the database is restored to the state that existed before the update or the delete.

We now discuss the NOT NULL constraint.

12.5.4 NOT NULL

NOT NULL is a simple integrity constraint which may be specified for one or more attributes of a relation in CREATE TABLE command when appropriate. Figure 12.6 shows how to specify a NOT NULL constraint as a column constraint in a table. We have defined both attributes *Team1* and *Team2* of the table *Match* as NOT NULL.

```
CREATE TABLE Match
    (MatchID INTEGER PRIMARY KEY,
    Team1 CHAR(15) NOT NULL,
    Team2 CHAR(15) NOT NULL,
    Ground CHAR(20),
    Date CHAR(10),
    Result CHAR(10));
```

Figure 12.6 Specifying NOT NULL as a column constraint in SQL

Enforcing NOT NULL involves the system ensuring that any tuple inserted into the table does not include a NULL value for the attributes that have been declared NOT NULL. Also, modifying a value that has been declared NOT NULL to NULL will not be permitted by the system.

12.5.5 Default

A default for a column may be specified when the table is defined or in the domain definition. Default is needed when we do not have values for all values in a column. Often the system would add NULL values for column values that are not specified by the user. An example of default definition is given in Fig. 12.7. Since many of the ODIs in the database used in this book relate to matches played in India we may want to put India as the default value for *Team1*. The default value is NULL if not specified.

```
CREATE TABLE Match
    (MatchID INTEGER PRIMARY KEY
    Team1 CHAR(15) DEFAULT 'India',
    Team2 CHAR(15),
    Ground CHAR(20),
    Date CHAR(10),
    Result CHAR(10));
```

Figure 12.7 Specifying a default value as a column constraint in SQL

The default value may be specified for any column except for the primary key columns which must have unique values.

12.5.6 UNIQUE

The UNIQUE constraint ensures that a column or a group of columns declared UNIQUE have distinct values. SQL:1999 permits NULL values in the UNIQUE column(s) since the language assumes UNIQUE to mean 'not equal' which implies NULL values are acceptable. Most practitioners recommend that NULL not be used in UNIQUE columns.

Figure 12.8 specifies a UNIQUE for a column of a given table. We are using the *Employee* table and have added an attribute *Telephone* and have assumed that the telephone number is unique.

```
CREATE TABLE Employee
    (EmpID NUMBER(6) PRIMARY KEY,
    Name CHAR(20),
    DeptID CHAR(10),
    Telephone INTEGER UNIQUE,
    Address CHAR (50),
    Position CHAR (20);
```

Figure 12.8 Specifying UNIQUE as a column constraint in SQL

Once again, Fig. 12.9 shows how the UNIQUE constraint may be specified as a table constraint. If more than one attribute together is to be declared unique then a table constraint needs to be specified. In Fig. 12.9 we are assuming that the combination of (*LName*, *FName*) attributes is unique.

```
CREATE TABLE Player
    (PlayerID INTEGER PRIMARY KEY,
    LName CHAR(15),
    FName CHAR(15),
    Country CHAR(20),
    YBorn INTEGER,
    BPlace CHAR(20)
    FTest INTEGER,
    UNIQUE (LName, FName));
```

Figure 12.9 Specifying UNIQUE as a table constraint

A UNIQUE constraint is enforced by the system by checking every time a new tuple is inserted to a relation or a tuple is modified to ensure that only unique values are permitted. If a violation is detected, the insertion or modification is rejected and the database is restored to the state that it was before the insertion or modification.

12.5.7 DOMAIN

A DOMAIN for a column may be specified when the table is defined or it may be specified in the domain definition. A DOMAIN specification defines the possible values of an attribute. The specification may include the following:

- The DOMAIN name
- The data type and the length
- Whether NULL values are acceptable
- The default values
- Constraints on the allowable values

The SQL clause used to define domains is CREATE DOMAIN as described in Chapter 4. An example of a domain definition is given in Fig. 12.10.

```
CREATE DOMAIN Name1 CHAR(15),
CREATE DOMAIN PlayerID1 INTEGER,
CREATE DOMAIN Name2 CHAR(15);
```

Figure 12.10 Specifying domains in SQL

The domain definition can be modified by using the ALTER DOMAIN clause. A domain definition may be dropped by using the DROP DOMAIN command.

12.6 SQL AND SEMANTIC INTEGRITY

The syntactic constraints comprise a number of important constraints including existential integrity and referential integrity constraints. However, they have little to do with the semantics of information in the database. The semantic constraints on the other hand limit the values that may appear in a relation. We will explain what that means.

SQL provides three constructs for specifying semantic integrity constraints. These are CHECK, ASSERTION and TRIGGER. We discuss each of them.

12.6.1 CHECK Constraints

The CHECK constraint is the most useful and perhaps the simplest semantic constraint in SQL:1999 since it allows specification for a wide range of constraints for tables in a database.

A CHECK constraint is a condition or business rule that must be satisfied when insertions, deletions or updates occur. It may be specified as a column constraint or as a table constraint, when it is to be specified for each tuple as a whole. The constraint may be specified over multiple tables similar to the way in which the WHERE clause of a query uses EXIST and NOT EXIST. The constraint may then involve subqueries.

Column-based CHECK Constraint

The CHECK constraint is often defined as an attribute declaration by specifying a parenthesized condition which may be a simple limit on an attribute value but could also be anything specified in the WHERE clause. Just as in the WHERE clause, the CHECK constraint also is often a condition like one of those listed in the table below.

	Possible conditions in the CHECK clause
1	attribute A > value v
2	attribute A between value v1 and value v2
3	attribute A IN (list of values)
4	Attribute A IN subquery
5	attribute A condition C1 OR condition C2
6	attribute A condition C1 AND condition C2

A column-based CHECK constraint is checked whenever a value of the column specified in the CHECK clause is inserted or updated. Once a CHECK constraint is defined, all the column values must satisfy the constraint.

Consider an example given in Fig. 12.11 where it is required that a player in the cricket database be born after 1950 (which obviously cannot be correct if we had information about some old ODIs in the database). We will use the CHECK constraint as a column constraint.

```
CREATE TABLE Player
    (PlayerID INTEGER PRIMARY KEY,
    LName CHAR(15),
    FName CHAR(15),
    Country CHAR(20),
    YBorn INTEGER CHECK (YBorn > 1950),
    BPlace CHAR(20)
    FTest INTEGER));
```

Figure 12.11 Using CHECK to specify a column constraint in SQL

The CHECK condition is specified as a search condition, like a condition that appears in a WHERE clause. It is also possible to specify two constraints or more in the same table for different columns or two or more constraints for the same column as shown in Fig. 12.12. Here it has been specified that a player must be born before 1999.

```
CREATE TABLE Player
    (PlayerID INTEGER PRIMARY KEY,
    LName CHAR(15),
    FName CHAR(15),
    Country CHAR(20),
    YBorn INTEGER CHECK (YBorn > 1950),
    CHECK (YBorn < 1999),
    BPlace CHAR(20)
    FTest INTEGER));
```

Figure 12.12 Using two CHECK column constraints in SQL

The two constraints in Fig. 12.12 can also be written as

CHECK (YBorn > 1950 AND YBorn < 1999)

It should be noted that when a CHECK constraint is specified as a column constraint, it cannot refer to any column other than the column with which it is associated. However, a table-based CHECK constraint may refer to a number of columns of the same table or even refer to other tables.

Table-based CHECK Constraint

Some conditions cannot be specified using a column-based CHECK constraint. Once again, the constraint could be anything that could be specified in the WHERE clause and may include any of the conditions defined earlier. The table-based CHECK constraint may include subqueries and may also include other relations or more than one row of the same table.

In the CREATE TABLE definition in Fig. 12.13, the CHECK constraint is defined at the table level. This CHECK constraint essentially applies to each tuple and uses more than one attribute and requires that a player must have played his first test match when he was older than 15[2].

```
CREATE TABLE Player
    (PlayerID INTEGER PRIMARY KEY,
    LName CHAR(15) NOT NULL,
    FName CHAR(1) NOT NULL,
    Country CHAR(20),
    YBorn INTEGER,
    BPlace CHAR(20)
    FTest INTEGER,
    CHECK (FTest > YBorn + 15));
```

Figure 12.13 A table constraint using CHECK in SQL

Although a column CHECK constraint cannot refer to any column other than the column with which it is associated, the table CHECK constraint may involve a number of columns and a number of conditions. For example,

CHECK (YBorn > 1950 AND YBorn < 1999 AND *FTest* > *YBorn* + 15);

CHECK constraint may also be specified in the CREATE DOMAIN clause as shown in Fig. 12.14. In these specifications, any insertion or update will be rejected if the condition following the CHECK is not true.

```
CREATE DOMAIN NRuns INTEGER
        CHECK (VALUE ≥ 0),
CREATE DOMAIN PlayerID1 INTEGER
        CHECK (VALUE > 12345)
```

Figure 12.14 CREATE DOMAIN with a CHECK constraint

2. Has any cricket player played his first test match before he was 15? Check it out!

Dynamic CHECK Constraint

Consider a more complex CHECK specification example given in Fig. 12.15 that uses a number of tables and would be checked after a change to any of the tables is specified. Such CHECK constraints are called dynamic CHECK constraints.

We need to use an employee database because the cricket database does not include sufficient information to specify a complex CHECK constraint. The database being used is given below.

DeptFinance(DeptID, Name, Head, Budget)
Employees(EmpID, Name, DeptID, Manager, Telephone, Address, Position, Salary)

In Fig. 12.15, two integrity constraints on the *DeptFinance* table are shown. The first constraint called *budget1* checks that the attribute *Budget* is NOT NULL and it has a positive value. The second constraint, called *salaries*, is a CHECK constraint that checks that the budget for a department is not less than the sum of the salaries of all employees in each department. These constraints are evaluated when a transaction that is updating the *Budget*, or inserting a new row in *DeptFinance*, attempts to commit.

```
CREATE TABLE DeptFinance
    (DeptID Number (6),
    Name CHAR(20),
    Head CHAR(20),
    Budget Number (15),
    CONSTRAINT PK PRIMARY KEY (DeptID),
    CONSTRAINT FK
     FOREIGN KEY (Head) REFERENCES Employees(EmpID),
    CONSTRAINT budget1
        CHECK ((Budget > = 0) AND (Budget IS NOT NULL)),
    CONSTRAINT salaries
        CHECK (NOT EXISTS
            (SELECT*
            FROM DeptFinance f
            WHERE Budget <
                (SELECT SUM (Salary)
                FROM Employees e
                WHERE e.DeptID = f.DeptID))));
```

Figure 12.15 Using a multirelation CHECK constraint in SQL

A CHECK constraint is enforced by the system by checking every time a new tuple is inserted to a relation or a tuple is modified to ensure that only values satisfying the constraint are permitted. If the constraint is violated by the new value, then the new tuple or modification is rejected and the database is restored to the state that it was before the insertion or modification.

We now discuss the ASSERTION constraint.

12.6.2 ASSERTION Constraints

ASSERTION constraints are database elements, like relations or views. They are stand alone constraints. They are not specified as part of a CREATE TABLE statement and therefore are not column constraints or table constraints. An ASSERTION is a constraint over an entire set of relations or database in contrast to CHECK constraints which apply only to an attribute or to a table. An ASSERTION constraint is defined by:

CREATE ASSERTION <name> CHECK <condition>

The ASSERTION constraint always requires a constraint name.

Similar to CHECK, an ASSERTION states what must be true and prohibits an action that would violate a specified constraint. However, unlike CHECK, it is evaluated every time a table involved in the constraint is modified. In this sense, CHECK can be thought of as a local constraint while an ASSERTION is a global constraint which may involve any number of tables. The condition in an ASSERTION can be anything allowed in the WHERE clause.

As noted above, an ASSERTION is defined independently of any table definition and is activated on any modification of any table mentioned in the ASSERTION. If a modification violates an ASSERTION, the modification is rejected. In some ways ASSERTION constraints are more effective but they can be less efficient than CHECK constraints.

A simple ASSERTION constraint is defined on a single table. As an example, consider the constraint given in Fig. 12.16 which ensures that there is no typing mistake in the table *Batting* such that the number of runs scored by a batsman is less than 4 times the number of fours plus 6 times the number of sixes the player had hit.

```
CREATE ASSERTION assert1
    CHECK (NOT EXISTS
        (SELECT *
        FROM Batting
        WHERE NRuns < 4*Fours + 6*Six));
```

Figure 12.16 Specifying an ASSERTION constraint on a table

A version of ASSERTION constraint presented in Fig. 12.15 is presented in Fig. 12.17.

```
CREATE ASSERTION Finance
 (CHECK (NOT EXISTS
    (SELECT *
    FROM DeptFinance
    WHERE (NOT EXISTS
        (SELECT *
        FROM Finance f
        WHERE Budget <
            (SELECT SUM (Salary)
            FROM Employees
            WHERE DeptID = f.DeptID)))));
```

Figure 12.17 An ASSERTION constraint for Fig. 12.15

The ASSERTION in Fig. 12.17 shows that constraints in Fig. 12.15 are specified in a more natural way, independent of the CREATE TABLE command, by using an ASSERTION. The CHECK constraints in both

Figs 12.15 and 12.17 are very similar but the constraint in Fig. 12.17 is independent. Just like in any SQL query, the table(s) must be specified in the FROM clause and then attributes of those tables must be used in the WHERE clause. To create an ASSERTION, the names of tables must be specified before the columns may be used in the WHERE condition.

When an ASSERTION is not needed any longer, it can be removed, using the DROP ASSERTION command as shown in Fig. 12.18.

```
DROP ASSERTION assert1;
```

Figure 12.18 Dropping an ASSERTION constraint

When an ASSERTION is specified, the DBMS tests for its validity. This testing may introduce a significant amount of computing overhead, thus assertions should be used carefully.

12.6.3 Constraints on Empty Tables

SQL has a rule about constraint checking; most constraints can be violated only if a table has one or more rows in it. If a table has been created and no data has been put in it, then it cannot violate any constraints defined on the table. This rule can sometimes lead to unpredictable results, for example, if a constraint required that there be at least five rows in a table. This constraint will not be violated if the table is empty. ASSERTION constraints on the other hand are always checked and an empty table will violate a constraint that the number of rows be at least five.

12.6.4 Trigger Constraint

The concept of triggers was introduced in SQL:1999. It is a named event-condition-action (ECA) rule that is activated by a database when any event (that is, insertion, deletion or update) takes place. In contrast to an ASSERTION constraint, which is also independent of CREATE TABLE statements, a trigger is always associated with a particular table. A trigger may not be associated with views according to SQL:1999.

We present an informal definition of a trigger.

> ***Definition—Trigger***
> *A trigger is a named event-condition-action rule associated with a particular database table that is activated by a database state transition and an optional condition which evaluates to true.*

In contrast to an assertion that requires that the constraint specified be true at all times, as noted earlier, a trigger is activated when certain events takes place. The action part of ECA is then carried out. A trigger therefore allows actions that may violate a constraint and hence it tests for the presence of a violation. An assertion does not permit a violation of specified constraints and hence it tests for the absence of the violation.

The difficulty with the ASSERTION constraint is that it usually results in checking almost every modification of the table that is involved in the ASSERTION. It can be expensive and therefore ASSERTION constraints are sometime not used. Trigger is an easier and more procedural version of ASSERTION that explicitly lists the events to be monitored and the action to be taken.

The general form of CREATE TRIGGER is presented in Fig. 12.19. For those who are not familiar with BNF, we note that INSERT | DELETE | UPDATE means either of the three INSERT or DELETE or UPDATE.

```
CREATE TRIGGER trigger-name
    {BEFORE | AFTER}
    [INSERT | DELETE | UPDATE] ON table-names
    FOR EACH [ ROW | STATEMENT ]
    [WHEN (<trigger condition>)]
    Trigger actions
```

Figure 12.19 General form of a trigger definition

We can see the event-condition-action structure of a trigger. The event is an insert, delete or an update. The condition may be specified in the WHEN clause and an action could be, for example, a ROLLBACK, a DELETE, a stored procedure, and so on.

We now look at the various components of the specification in Fig. 12.19.

1. *Name*—Refers to a unique trigger name which identifies the trigger in the CREATE TRIGGER command. A trigger name is needed so that it can be identified, for example, if it needs to be deleted later. Given a trigger's name, it may be redefined by using the "REPLACE TRIGGER trigger_name" command.
2. *Event*—Refers to a triggering event which could be one of the modification operations as we have noted earlier: INSERT, DELETE or UPDATE. Multiple events may be described by using OR. Since a trigger is defined for a table, the trigger will fire only if the INSERT, DELETE or UPDATE relates to that table. An event cannot take place in a SELECT SQL statement.
3. *Time*—Refers to an activation time which is BEFORE or AFTER executing the triggering event. Therefore, it may be BEFORE INSERT or AFTER DELETE or AFTER UPDATE.
4. *Granularity*—For example, FOR EACH ROW or FOR EACH STATEMENT. As described in more detail later, a trigger may fire after each row or after each statement.
5. *Condition*—A condition may be any valid SQL condition which is either true or false. The condition determines whether the action should be executed. If no condition is specified, the action will be executed once the event occurs. When a condition is specified, it is evaluated and the event is executed if the result is true.
6. *Action*—Refers to any valid single SQL statement or a sequence of SQL statements executed sequentially enclosed in BEGIN and END keywords. An external program may also be executed.
7. *Timestamp*—Refers to time when the trigger was created.

Triggers are simple but many triggers cause confusion. For example, a chain of triggers can be difficult to predict. There can be confusion about the difference between row level trigger and statement level trigger. A row level trigger is defined using the FOR EACH ROW clause and the trigger then executes once for each row AFTER (or BEFORE) the event. Thus, if the event updates 10 rows in a table, trigger is executed ten times, once for each row. If FOR EACH ROW is not specified, FOR EACH STATEMENT is assumed and the trigger executes only once.

Using a FOR EACH STATEMENT trigger, it is not possible to access old and new values of attributes but with a FOR EACH ROW trigger it is possible to do so using the REFERENCING clause of the trigger definition, since the trigger is executed once for each row. For example, for INSERT, the new value is; *NEW.columnname* while for a DELETE the deleted attribute value is; *OLD.columnname*. If however a row is being updated, the old attribute value is given by; *OLD.columnname* and the new value by; *NEW.columnname*. These old and new values may be used in comparisons. For example, it is possible to specify NEW.value >

1.5*OLD.value in the BEFORE trigger clause and specify an action to be taken if the condition is violated. The NEW and OLD must proceed with a colon in all references except using them in the WHEN clause. This just illustrates the complexity of triggers.

Triggers do not support for time actions. For example, one cannot specify an action to take place at midnight.

Triggers have a number of limitations. There is a limit to prioritization and optimization when multiple triggers are opened. Triggers are specified in a low-level language and are more difficult to deal with. Furthermore, each commercial DBMS has subtle differences in the language used for specifying triggers. Also, triggers only execute after data is finished modifying. External actions do not know if the trigger that executed it committed causing possible inconsistency. Increasing problems arise when there are many triggers specified for one relation. A further difficulty is related to interaction between triggers and other constraints. This can lead to some confusion regarding when the trigger and the other constraints will be enforced. Details of how triggers are executed when there are a number of triggers and other constraints defined on the same table are complex and are not discussed here.

Most trigger examples in the literature appear to be about salaries of employees (similar to the constraints in Fig. 12.15) since it is easy to specify salary constraints and harder to specify constraints for the cricket database. We therefore also present an example using an employee database in Fig. 12.20. The trigger ensures that if an employee's salary becomes greater than his manager's then the HR department is warned.

```
DEFINE TRIGGER trigger1
    after UPDATE of Salary
    ON Employees
    WHEN (EXISTS
        (SELECT *
        FROM Employees E, Managers M
        WHERE E.Salary > M.Salary
        AND E.Department=M.Department))
    informHR (EmpID);
```

Figure 12.20 A sample definition of a trigger

InformHR is a procedure stored in the database and can be called by the DBMS. When a trigger is not needed any longer, it can be removed using the DROP TRIGGER command as shown in Fig. 12.21.

```
DROP TRIGGER trigger1
```

Figure 12.21 Example of dropping a trigger

We should note the difference between ASSERTION and TRIGGER in the above condition. A trigger allows an action that may violate a constraint and hence it tests for the presence of the violation. An ASSERTION does not permit a violation and hence it typically tests for its absence.

It should be noted that some TRIGGER constraints may be enforced by using other integrity constraints which are easier to understand and then use of TRIGGER may not be necessary. TRIGGER constraints however are useful not just for integrity constraints since they are more flexible and powerful. They have many other applications including enforcement of a variety of business rules. For example, a trigger may be used to check a customer's credit limit or whether a customer is one of those who are on a preferred customer list.

12.7 ACTIVE DATABASE SYSTEMS

We have discussed the importance of semantic integrity constraints in this chapter so that a database is able to support database semantic constraints within the database itself. When introducing the concept of triggers in the last section, we noted the event-condition-action (ECA) rule that is activated by a database trigger whenever any relevant insertion, deletion or update takes place. The action is performed whenever one of the specified events arises. Active databases reflect this trend to support additional relevant semantics of the database within the DBMS itself rather than within the application programs.

The ECA may be described as follows. The *event* part of a rule describes a database happening to which the rule may be able to react. The *condition* part of the rule considers the context in which the event has taken place. The specified *action* is the task the DBMS is required to carry out if the relevant event has taken place and the relevant condition has been met.

We first present a definition of active database systems before discussing such systems further.

Definition—Active Database Systems
Active database systems are database systems that are able to monitor relevant events and react to them and take specified action if the given conditions are met.

Therefore, an active database system must provide facilities for the following:

- Event definition
- Condition detection
- Action to be taken

We briefly discuss these three components of an active database system.

Event Definition

All events of interest must be specified and registered with the database system. The events must be defined using a rule specification language which often is an extension of SQL. It is essentially the triggers discussed in Section 12.6.4 which must be defined and registered in the database catalog. Events of interest are often either primitive or composite. Primitive events are generally single low-level events, for example, inserting or deleting a row in a table or updating a column in a table. Primitive events may also include the time being some specified time. The composite events may be a combination of a number of primitive events, for example, updating one column of a table as well as updating another column of the same table. It may also be if an update happens at a particular time. Many other events are possible. We will not discuss them here.

Condition Detection

The ECA rules do not require a condition to be specified. It is optional. When the condition is specified, detecting primitive events like insertion, deletion and update is straightforward in relational database systems. Detection of composite events is somewhat more complex.

Action to be Taken

Action taken may include updating some part of the database, invoking a particular program, informing the user or the DBA that a particular event has happened or taking some other action from possible actions.

12.7.1 Examples of Active Database Systems

Active databases are likely to be useful in many applications. We list some possible examples.

- A user is trying to login to a database system unsuccessfully and has tried to login three times. The computer security personnel may need to be informed of such an incident. A user is logging in to a sensitive police database when it is known that the user is away on annual leave. Such events may be automatically checked if the list of users on annual leave is included in the database. This may trigger appropriate action including logging the event and informing appropriate authorities.
- A train is running late so that the connecting train in Chennai would leave before this train reaches Chennai. Action taken may include sending an email to all relevant Indian Railways officials.
- Due to heavy monsoon rains, a dam is receiving high volume of inflows. Checking of the volume of inflows event may result in action taken including releasing more water from the dam and informing the relevant authorities.

Active database systems is an active area of research. Many aspects are being investigated including powerful languages for event detection, algorithms for rules analysis and optimization, condition monitoring and tools for designing and debugging active applications.

SUMMARY

In this chapter we have discussed the importance of integrity in database systems. The following topics have been covered:

- The integrity of a database system is important.
- Definition of integrity is presented and why it is important is explained. Integrity ensures the transactions users are running are correct.
- Integrity can be syntactic integrity or semantic integrity. Differences between the two are explained. The syntactic integrity constraints are basic constraints which have nothing to do with the semantics of any table in the database while semantic integrity constraints deal with business rules of an enterprise.
- Integrity enforcement principles include what to enforce, where to enforce, when to enforce and how to enforce.
- Syntactical integrity constraints include existential integrity (PRIMARY KEY constraint), referential integrity (FOREIGN KEY constraint), NOT NULL constraints, and DEFAULT, UNIQUE and DOMAIN constraints and implementing each syntactic integrity constraint in SQL.
- Some constraints may be declared as column constraints while others may be declared as table constraints in CREATE TABLE commands.
- SQL commands for specifying semantic integrity constraints are described. These include GRANT and REVOKE commands.
- Differences between the semantic constraints CHECK, ASSERTION and TRIGGER are discussed. TRIGGER is a constraint on one table while CHECK and ASSERTION constraints may be on more than one table.
- ASSERTION constraint is declared separately from the CREATE TABLE statement.

- CHECK constraint checks the specified condition on one or more relations.
- TRIGGER is declared for only one table and is invoked when any of the events specified in the TRIGGER declaration happens.
- An active database is a database with associated triggers.

REVIEW QUESTIONS

1. What are the primary aims in specifying database integrity constraints? (Section 12.2)
2. What are the differences between syntactic integrity and semantic integrity? (Section 12.2)
3. What are the aims of existential and referential integrity constraints? Give examples to show how they can be specified for the tables in the ODI cricket database as column constraints and as table constraints. (Section 12.5)
4. In referential integrity, why should the referenced attributes be unique? Explain what would happen if this is not so. (Section 12.5.2)
5. What are semantic integrity constraints? Give two examples of semantic integrity constraints in a student database. (Section 12.6)
6. Show how CHECK constraint may be specified as a column-based constraint and as a table-based constraint. (Section 12.6.1)
7. Why is it not desirable to implement semantic integrity constraints through application programs? (Section 12.6)
8. List the four types of semantic integrity constraints. Give examples of constraints included in each class. (Section 12.6)
9. Give an example of ASSERTION constraint on the cricket database. (Section 12.6.2)
10. Give an example of a TRIGGER definition on the cricket database. (Section 12.6.4)
11. What are the main features of an active database system? (Section 12.7)
12. What is ECA? (Section 12.7)
13. How should an event be defined, detected and action taken once detected? (Section 12.7)
14. Give an example of an application where an active database system might be helpful. (Section 12.7)

SHORT ANSWER QUESTIONS

1. What is the most important aim of integrity constraints?
2. Why is existential integrity needed?
3. What could go wrong if referential integrity is not enforced? Give an example.
4. Give one example of syntactical integrity.
5. Give one example of semantic integrity.
6. Would you classify triggers as syntactical or semantic constraints? Why?
7. Give an example where UNIQUE might be useful.
8. Give an example of one or more CHECK constraints for the *batting* table in the cricket database.

9. What is the difference between assertions and triggers?
10. What is the purpose of domains? Give an example to explain its importance.
11. What could be the reasons for some data being NULL?
12. What is an ASSERTION constraint?
13. How is a TRIGGER different than an ASSERTION?
14. List the components of a trigger definition.
15. What are the three components of an active database?

MULTIPLE CHOICE QUESTIONS

1. Which one of the following is **not** a syntactic integrity constraint?
   (a) Primary key (b) Foreign key (c) Unique (d) Triggers
2. Which one of the following is **not** a semantic constraint?
   (a) No employee in the company is given a cut in salary.
   (b) No updates are allowed on the record of retired employees.
   (c) No department can have sum of salaries larger than the budget.
   (d) All employee numbers must be unique.
3. Which one of the following is true?
   (a) Integrity constraints may be specified in natural language to the DBMS.
   (b) SQL's default policy is to check constraints at the beginning of executing a SQL statement.
   (c) An integrity constraint may be enforced before the transaction execution, during the transaction execution or after the transaction execution.
   (d) SQL statements that violate a constraint are not rolled back.
4. Which of the following constraints are provided by SQL for semantic integrity?
   (a) CHECK (b) ASSERTION (c) Trigger (d) All of the above
5. Which one of the following is true?
   (a) Primary key may be a column based or a table based constraint.
   (b) Foreign key may be a column based or a table based constraint.
   (c) NOT NULL may be a column based or a table based constraint.
   (d) All of the above
6. Which one of the following is **not** true?
   (a) CHECK may be a column based or a table based constraint.
   (b) ASSERTION may be a column based or a table based constraint.
   (c) Trigger may not be associated with views.
   (d) UNIQUE may be a column based or a table based constraint.
7. When should semantic integrity constraints be enforced?
   (a) Before a transaction is executed. (b) During transaction execution.
   (c) After transaction execution. (d) All of the above are possible.

8. What is the primary aim in enforcing semantic integrity constraints?
   (a) Database efficiency
   (b) Database integrity
   (c) Database consistency
   (d) Reducing redundancy
   (e) None of the above
9. Which one of the following is correct?
   (a) Some integrity constraints deal with one or more database values being equal to given values.
   (b) Some integrity constraints deal with restricting the values of an attribute to some range of values.
   (c) Some integrity may constraints require that a relationship between some values hold.
   (d) All of the above
10. Which one of the following is true?
    (a) A CHECK integrity constraint is checked only when the attribute or the tuple in the constraint is modified or a new tuple is inserted.
    (b) The ASSERTION integrity constraint is checked only when the attribute or the tuple in the constraint is modified or a new tuple is inserted.
    (c) The TRIGGER integrity constraint is checked only when the attribute or the tuple in the constraint is modified or a new tuple is inserted.
    (d) All syntactic integrity constraints are checked only when the attribute or the tuple in the constraint is modified or a new tuple is inserted.
11. Which one of the following is **not** true in SQL?
    (a) A CHECK integrity constraint requires a CREATE CHECK command.
    (b) An ASSERTION integrity constraint requires a CREATE ASSERTION command.
    (c) A TRIGGER integrity constraint requires a CREATE TRIGGER command.
    (d) A TRIGGER integrity constraint may be viewed as an event-condition-action (ECA) construct.
12. Which one of the following is true?
    (a) CHECK integrity constraint may be specified in a CREATE DOMAIN command.
    (b) ASSERTION integrity constraint may be specified in a CREATE TABLE command.
    (c) TRIGGER integrity constraint may be specified in a CREATE TABLE command.
    (d) CHECK integrity constraint must be specified in a CREATE TABLE command.
    (e) None of the above
13. Which one of the following is **not** true?
    (a) A CHECK constraint may be dropped by the DROP CHECK command.
    (b) An ASSERTION constraint may be dropped by the DROP ASSERETION command.
    (c) A TRIGGER constraint may be dropped by the DROP TRIGGER command.
    (d) A DOMAIN constraint may be dropped by the DROP DOMAIN command.
    (e) All of the above are correct.
14. Which of the following may be specified as a single table constraint?
    (a) Trigger
    (b) NOT NULL
    (c) UNIQUE
    (d) CHECK
    (e) All of the above
15. Which one of the following may be specified as a multiple table constraint?
    (a) UNIQUE
    (b) CHECK
    (c) ASSERTION
    (d) Trigger
    (e) None of the above

EXERCISES

1. Construct a simple bank database. List a set of integrity constraints that apply to the database. How easy would it be to enforce these constraints?
2. What are the primary aims of integrity? How do the aims differ from the aims of recovery, concurrency, and security?
3. What are the aims of existential and referential integrity constraints? Give examples to show how they can be specified for the tables in the ODI cricket database. In referential integrity, why should the referenced attributes be unique? Explain what would happen if this is not so.
4. In referential integrity, a table *R* references a table *S*. What would happen if the table *S* also references the table *R*? Explain.
5. What are semantic integrity constraints? Provide examples to show how they differ from the two integrity constraints in the last question? Give two examples of semantic integrity constraints in a student database.
6. Why is it not desirable to implement semantic integrity constraints through application programs?
7. List the four types of semantic integrity constraints. Give examples of constraints included in each class.
8. Specify the following constraints in SQL using the CHECK command:
   - (a) All values of attribute *mark* in relation *enrolment* must be within 0 and 100.
   - (b) If the value of attribute *grade* is '*A*' then the *mark* must be more than or equal to 80. If the value of attribute *grade* is '*B*' then the *mark* must be less than 80 but greater than or equal to 70.
   - (c) If a student is enrolled in a subject offered by department 'ABC' then the age of the student cannot be less than 22. Assume *age* is an attribute in relation *student*, enrolment information is given in the relation *enrolment* and information about subjects and their departments is in *subjects*.
9. Show how the referential integrity constraint may be specified using a CHECK constraint. Give an example.
10. In semantic integrity constraints enforcement, which of the following is the best approach? Explain the advantages and disadvantages of each approach.
    - (a) The constraints to be enforced within the application programs.
    - (b) The constraints to be enforced by the DBA.
    - (c) The constraints to be enforced by the DBMS.
    - (d) The constraints to be enforced by the user.
11. Explain and describe the differences of the three semantic integrity constraints CHECK, ASSERT and TRIGGER allowed by SQL.
12. What does a TRIGGER constraint do? What are its three parts? Why are TRIGGERs difficult to understand and implement. Give an example using the cricket database or another database. Give an example of a TRIGGER using one of the examples given above.
13. A table in a database has a number of associated triggers and a number of declarative constraints. Describe what problems might arise in enforcing these constraints. How can these problems be solved?

PROJECT

1. Consider the following 13 tables that we obtained by mapping an E-R diagram to the relational model in Chapter 3. The E-R diagram is given in Chapter 3.
    - User (FName, LName, Login_Name, Address)
    - Program (PName, Code, Date, Version, Extension, Description, Language)
    - Programmer (Login, Code, FName, LName, Address)
    - DBMS (DB_name)
    - Relation (RName, PKey)
    - Attribute (RName, Attname)
    - Written_by (PName, Login)
    - Interact_with (PName, DB_name)
    - Administer (Login, DB_name)
    - Use (Login_name, PName)
    - Call (PName, PName)
    - Has (DB_name, Relation, RName, PKey)
    - Comprises_of (RName, Attname)
        (a) List 10 constraints that apply to this database.
        (b) Write SQL definitions for these constraints.
        (c) Implement three of the above integrity constraints as triggers.

LAB EXERCISES

1. Consider the simple airline database presented at the end of Chapter 9. List all the syntactic integrity constraints that need to be specified for this database.
2. List at least five semantic integrity constraints discussed in this chapter.
3. List all the semantic integrity constraints for the ODI cricket database.

BIBLIOGRAPHY

For Students

The paper by Tucker and Gertz provides a very good coverage of integrity constraint checking using SQL in a number of DBMS. For some of the new developments in integrity constraints in SQL:1999, students should either look at recent editions of database textbooks or look at a comprehensive introduction to SQL:1999.

For Instructors

The book by Doorn and Rivero is a good collection of papers on integrity constraints checking. The papers in the book edited by Paton, the papers by Paton et al., and Paton and Diaz provide good introduction to triggers and active databases. They also include description of a number of active database systems and the facilities provided by them. The book by Widom and Ceri also deals with active database systems.

Badal, D. Z., "Semantic integrity in centralized DBMS and distributed DBMS based on slow (geographically distributed) and fast (local area) networks", *Information Systems*, Vol. 9, pp 121-138, 1984.

Bernstein, P. A., B. T. Blaustein, and E. M. Clarke, "Fast maintenance of semantic integrity assertions using redundant aggregate data", *Proceedings of the 6th Very Large Data Bases Conference*, 1980, pp 126-136.

Ceri, S., R. J. Cochrane, and J. Widom, "Practical applications of triggers and constraints: successes and lingering issues", *Proceedings of the 26th Very Large Databases Conference,* Cairo, Egypt, 2000 pp 285-296.

Christiansen, H., and D. Martinenghi, "On Simplification of Database Integrity Constraints", *Journal Fundamenta Informaticae,* IOS Press, Issue 4, Vol. 71, 2006, pp. 371-417.

Dayal, U., E. Hanson, and J. Widom, "Active Database Systems", In *Modern Database Systems: The Object Model, Interoperability and Beyond*, Addison-Wesley, 1994.

Domínguez, E., J. Lloret, and M. A. Zapata, "Integrity Constraint Enforcement by Means of Trigger Templates", *Lecture Notes in Computer Science* 2547, pp 54-64, 2002.

Doorn, J. H., and L. C. Rivero (Eds), *Database Integrity: Challenges and Solutions*, Idea Group Inc, 2002.

Eswaran, K. P., and D. D. Chamberlin, "Functional Specifications of a Subsystem for Data Base Integrity", *Proceedings of the 1st Conference* on *Very Large Databases*, 1975, pp. 22-24.

Fernandez, E. B., and R. C. Summers and C. Wood, *Database Security and Integrity*, Addison-Wesley, 1981.

Gulutzan, P., and T. Pelzer, *SQL:99 Complete, Really*, R&D Books, Gilroy, California, 1104 pp.

Lee, D., W. Mao, H. Chiu, and W. W. Chu, "Designing Triggers with Trigger-By-Example", *Knowledge and Information Systems*, Vol. 7, Springer-Verlag, 2005, pp 110–134.

Nicolas, J. M., "Logic for Improving Integrity Checking in Relational Databases", *Acta Informatica*, July 1982, pp 227-253.

Paton, N. W., (Ed), *Active Rules in Database Systems*, Springer Verlag, 1999, 439 pp.

Paton, N.W., O. Diaz, M. Williams, J. Campin, J. Dinn and A. Jaime, "Dimensions of Active Behavior", *Proceedings of the Workshop on Rules in Database Systems*, Heidelberg, Germany, 1993, pp 40-57.

Paton, N.W., and O. Diaz, "Active Database Systems", *ACM Computing Surveys*, Vol. 31, No. 1, March 1999, pp 63-103.

Tucker, C., and M. Gertz, "Semantic Integrity Support in SQL:99 and Commercial (Object-) Relational Database Management Systems", *Journal of Very Large Database Systems*, Vol.10, No 4, pp 241-269, 2001. http://www.db.cs.ucdavis.edu/papers/TG00.pdf

Weber, W., W. Stuckey, and J. Karszt, "Integrity Checking in Data Base Systems", *Information Systems*, Vol. 8, pp 125-136, 1983.

Widom, J., and S. Ceri, *Active Database Systems*, Morgan-Kaufmann, 1996.

Jennifer Widom—Contributed to Active Database and Other Areas

Jennifer Widom has contributed to a number of areas in database management including active database systems, data warehousing, semi-structured data management, and stream database systems. Her 1990 ACM SIGMOD paper offered the first complete framework for incorporating production rules into a DBMS with well-defined semantics. In the area of semi-structured data, Widom's Lore system pioneered techniques for storing, querying, and managing semi-structured data, before the emergence of XML. Her CQL language is widely regarded as having brought structure and well-thought-out semantics to the problem of querying streams.

Professor Widom completed her PhD in Computer Science from Cornell University. She is currently the Fletcher Jones Professor of Computer Science at Stanford University. At the time of writing this book, she was the Chair of the Department of Computer Science.

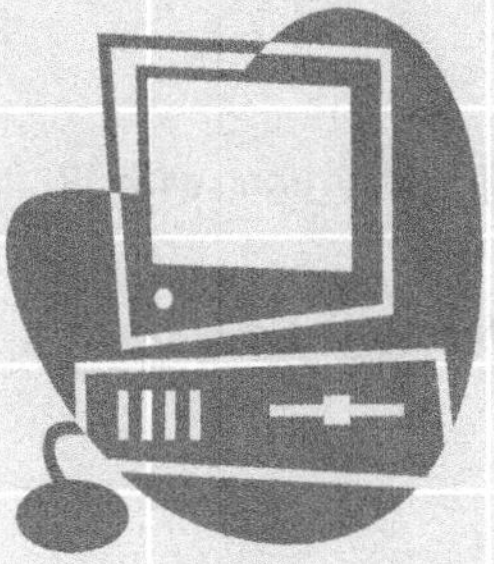

Distributed Databases

13

OBJECTIVES

- Discuss the motivation for distributed databases.
- Explain the basics of distributed database systems.
- Describe the features of a distributed database system.
- Present some examples of distributed database systems.
- Explain the advantages and disadvantages of distributed database systems.
- Discuss the objectives in designing a distributed database system.
- Explain how fragmentation of data may be implemented.
- Describe horizontal, vertical, derived and hybrid fragmentation.
- Explain the basics of replication.
- Explain how data can be distributed across sites.
- Explore how queries can be evaluated in a distributed database system.
- Discuss the issues in transaction management of distributed databases.

KEYWORDS

Distributed databases, 3-tier system, client-server system, features of distributed database system, examples of distributed database system, advantages, disadvantages, autonomy, expandability, design complexity, DDB design objectives, location independence, fragmentation independence, replication independence, network independence, data distribution, fragmentation, horizontal fragmentation, vertical fragmentation, hybrid fragmentation, derived fragmentation, replication, data distribution, distributed transaction management, distributed query processing.

The highest education is that which does not merely give us information but makes our life in harmony with all existence.

Rabindranath Tagore

13.1 INTRODUCTION

A distributed database system (DDS) is a union of two important technologies, viz., database management and computer networks.

Database technology basically involves centralization while computer network technology promotes decentralization. They can be combined in a distributed database systems to develop an integrated approach providing the benefits of both, which can match distributed organization of many enterprises.

We first provide a definition of distributed database system.

Definition—Distributed Database System

A distributed database system is a multiple, logically related database system physically distributed across several sites using a computer network that is normally under the control of a central site.

A distributed database system may include application servers, for example, web servers, and clients, that do not have a local database. The database sites, applications servers and the clients are usually connected by a high speed network. A typical distributed database system in shown in Fig. 13.2.

The reason distributed databases are desirable is that many enterprises have more than one branch and these branches often prefer to maintain their own database systems. Although it may be desirable to maintain local databases, an enterprise also needs an enterprise view of the database. A distributed database should be such that the impact of data distribution on the enterprise view of the database is minimal. This is why distributed databases are useful in large enterprises which have many locations.

Distributed databases are also desirable because they can be more reliable. If one of the sites in the distributed system containing some of the data goes down, the rest of the sites and their data continues to be available. Also accessing local data is often very efficient as compared to accessing data from a central database although with increased speed of networks it may not be such a problem.

13.1.1 Two-Tier Client-Server System

A client-server system may be considered a simple distributed database system in which all the data is stored in one or more interconnected servers and some of the application programs are stored and executed on a number of clients. Clients are often personal computers which provide a friendly presentation interface to the users and send the queries to the servers which might be running on powerful machines. The client-server architecture is popular in many environments since it allows much of data and processing to be carried out on powerful server machines. Client-server systems can be quite efficient if some data and basic functionality can reside with the client. Most common example of client-server architecture is a web server or a database server.

The way a client-server system works is that when a client is retrieving information from a database that is located on the server, the client makes a request perhaps in the form of a SQL query. The request is transmitted through the network and received by the database server that has appropriate DBMS to interpret the request, process the query and run it on the database. The result is then transmitted through the network to the client.

13.1.2 Three-Tier Server Architecture

As the name implies, a three-tier system has three levels. These levels are as follows:

- *First Level*—The client. This level is also called the presentation level and the client is usually a personal computer. The client may include some application programs as well as the presentation logic to display the results. It also has widely used software, for example, web browsers, email client, common application programs like Microsoft Office. The client handles input and output from the next level.
- *Second Level*—The application server or the middle tier. This level receives inputs from the client and returns results to it. This tier can carry out some processing which may include authentication and perhaps some parsing and checking of the query submitted by the client.
- *Third Level*—The database server. This tier handles all the requests that involve the database. It receives requests from the application server, carries out the processing required and returns the results or error messages to the application server.

Figure 13.1 illustrates these three levels.

Therefore, a three-tier system is different from the two-tier system as in the two-tier system the server is responsible for both the applications and the database, while in the three-tier system, the database and applications are divided into two different servers. The client therefore never directly deals with the database server.

As an example of the three-tier architecture, we may consider the client at the first level posing a SQL query which is then transmitted to the application server at the second level. This application server may carry out query optimization and transmits the resulting code to the database server which runs the query. The result of running the query is then transmitted to the next level down which in turn transmits it to the user's machine.

The two-tier and three-tier systems have a number of advantages. Since some of the functionality is separated, it is easy to replace any tier without affecting the others. Also, the separation of application and database functionality can assist in better load balancing. Furthermore, it is possible to enforce better security policies within the server tier which holds most of the important and sensitive information and software.

There are a large variety of distributed database systems and therefore we will make some simplifying assumptions. We assume that data is not moving dynamically between different sites although the nature and requirements of sites could well be changing with time. We also assume that all connections are of similar speed and will not worry about differences in the speeds of different network connections.

Presentation Tier This is the user interface. It translates tasks to send to the application tier and presents results to the user.	 User 1	 User 2	 Another user
Application Tier This tier processes commands from the user and carries out some applications and computation. It moves data between the tier 1 and tier 3.	Software to interact with surrounding layers and to carry out some computation. Allow user access to a variety of application software.		
DBMS and the Database The database is at tier 3. This tier also has the DBMS which carries out query processing and returns results to tier 2.	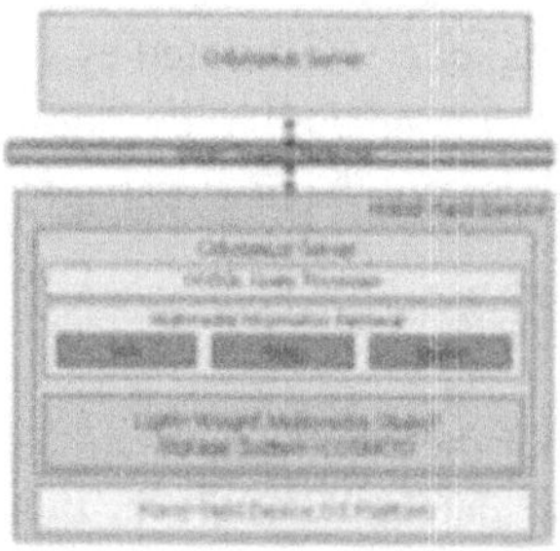 DBMS	 Database	

Figure 13.1 A three-tier database architecture

The chapter is organized as follows. First, the features of a distributed database are described in Section 13.2 followed by a brief introduction to different types of distributed database systems and some examples of large distributed databases in Section 13.3. Advantages and disadvantages of distributed databases are presented in Section 13.4. Section 13.5 deals with the objectives in designing distributed databases including a variety of transparencies. Database fragmentation is discussed in detail in Section 13.6 including benefits of fragmentation, horizontal fragmentation, vertical fragmentation, derived fragmentation and hybrid fragmentation. A number of examples illustrating horizontal fragmentation, vertical fragmentation and hybrid fragmentation are presented. In Section 13.7, data replication and data allocation techniques are discussed. Some issues in distributed query processing are discussed in Section 13.8. An example of query processing in presented in section 13.9. To conclude, transaction processing is discussed in Section 13.10.

13.2 FEATURES OF A DISTRIBUTED DATABASE SYSTEM

Distributed database systems have the following features:

- **Data is stored at a number of sites and each site is a logically independent single computer.**
  In a distributed system, data is distributed at a number of sites. Distributing the data enables individual groups to exercise local control over their own data making them less dependent on other sites in the database system.
- **Sites are interconnected by a high speed network rather than a multiprocessor configuration.**
  Given that high bandwidth connectivity is now common, the sites in a distributed database are connected by a high speed network.
- **Each site is a database system in its own right, running its own DBMS.**
  As discussed below, each site in a distributed database system has its own database system that is managed fairly autonomously. This database maintains local data on a local computer making it more efficient when local data is accessed locally.
- **The whole enterprise's distributed database system is logically a single database.**
  Although the distributed database system is distributed, one of the features of a distributed system is that the user views the whole distributed database system as a single system and is able to use it as such.
- **The distributed DBMS has full functionality of a DBMS.**

As noted above, although the distributed database system is distributed over many sites, the user views it as a single system and the system has full functionality of a DBMS.

Figure 13.2 presents a structure of a typical distributed database system.

More details of a distributed database are now presented. Consider a distributed database with four sites in the cities Delhi, Kolkata, Mumbai and Chennai. These four sites may have different types of facilities, for example, Delhi and Kolkata have local databases as well as their own local DBMS. In addition they are part of the distributed database system which allows their users to access the local database as well as the distributed database of the enterprise. The Mumbai site has no local database facilities and therefore the users in Mumbai directly access the distributed database system. Chennai users do not use the distributed database system. They use only their own local database but communicate with other sites using the national data network.

Figure 13.2 A distributed database system

The components of such a distributed database are shown in more detail in Fig. 13.3. Note that to communicate with the distributed database a site requires a copy of the distributed DBMS as well as a global data dictionary.

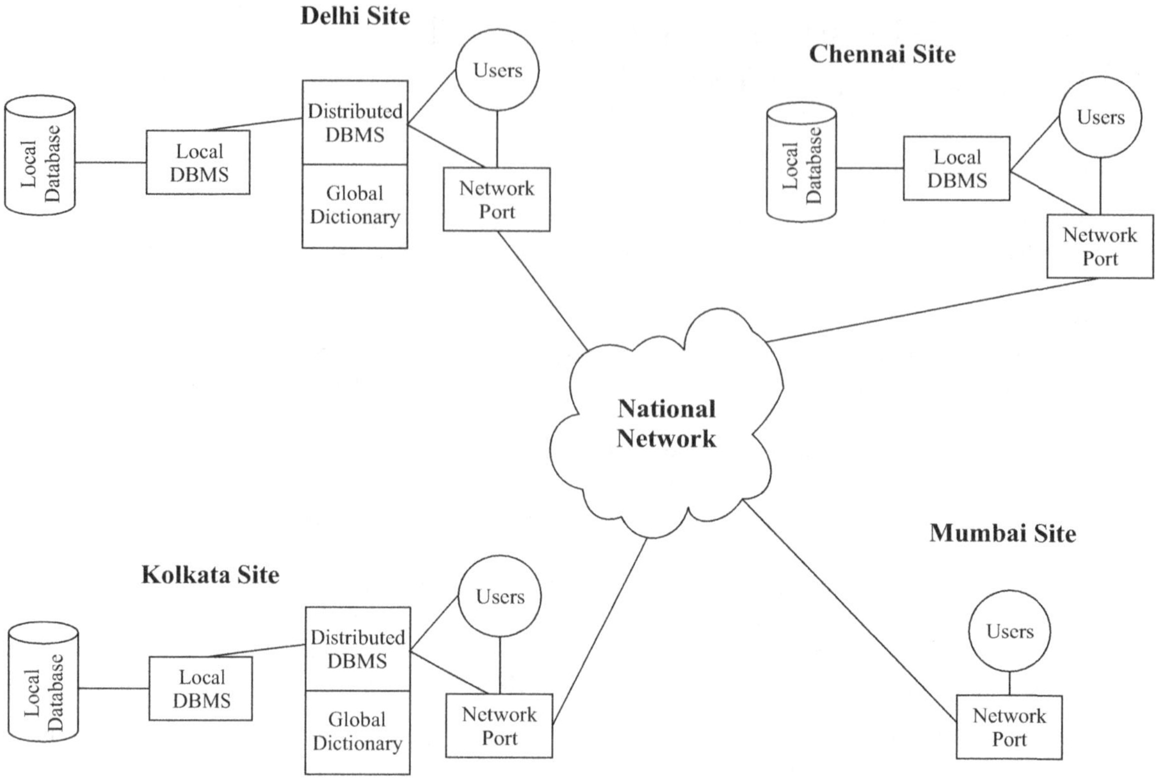

Figure13.3 Components of a distributed database system

13.3 TYPES AND EXAMPLES OF DISTRIBUTED DATABASE SYSTEMS

There are many different types of distributed databases as illustrated in examples ahead. One way to classify distributed databases is based on the network topology that connects the databases. Some possibilities are as follows:

1. *Fully connected distributed database system*—It is a network topology in which every database site is connected with every other site. Therefore, a distributed database with n sites will require $n(n-1)/2$ network connections. This is therefore quite costly but a very reliable topology.
2. *Partially connected distributed database system*—It is a network topology in which every database site is connected with a number of other sites. Therefore, such a distributed database requires fewer connections than the fully connected system and is therefore less costly and less reliable than the fully connected topology.
3. *Ring connected distributed database system*—It is a network in which every database site has exactly two other sites connected to it.

4. *Tree network connected distributed database system*—It is a network in which the database sites are connected in a hierarchical arrangement like a tree. The root of the tree may be nominated as the central site. This topology may lead to problems when a single site fails since that will result in partitioning two or more sites from the rest of the network.
5. *Star network connected distributed database system*—It is a network in which each database site is connected to a central site. The central site then rebroadcasts all transmissions received from any database sites to all other sites. All sites therefore only communicate with the central site which may become a bottleneck and the whole network may collapse if the central site goes down.
6. *Hybrid connected distributed database system*—It is a combination of any two or more topologies discussed above. Most networks are hybrid in nature.

Distributed database systems can also be classified as

1. *Homogeneous distributed database systems*—A homogeneous distributed database system is a system that is distributed over more than one database sites but uses the same DBMS, and all the clients use identical software. All the sites have the same degree of autonomy.
2. *Heterogeneous distributed database systems*—A heterogeneous distributed database system is a system that is distributed over more than one database sites but at least one of the sites is using a different DBMS and all the clients may not be using identical software. All the sites may not have the same degree of autonomy. In spite of these differences, the distributed database appears to the user as one database system. Some heterogeneous database systems are also called Federated Database Management systems.

We now present a number of examples of distributed database systems:

1. *Google*—Google has a large, petabyte[1] size, data across hundreds of thousands of commodity servers (estimated to be more than 500,000) that store the data. The data includes web indexing, Google Earth and Google Finance. This large number of machines is connected in some 200 clusters, each cluster containing up to 5000 machines. Google uses its own technology to store data on these machines. Two of the major software packages used by Google for data storage and retrieval are BigTable and MapReduce. Details of BigTable are given in the paper by Chang et al.
2. *Government services*—In India, government's e-governance services is trying to market principles such as economic efficiency, accountability and effectiveness of electronic services. Another proposed project is a web-based online library service connecting public libraries in India and integrating library services in a 'single window access'. More details about e-governance are available at http://unpan1.un.org/intradoc/groups/public/documents/apcity/unpan014672.pdf
3. *Airline booking systems*—An airline booking service may be using a number of sites, for example, four sites: Delhi, Mumbai, Chennai and Kolkata, with each site having its own computer with a database consisting of all the customers and flight details maintained at that site. Each branch has local reservations at the local site, which can be easily accessed from other places in India.
4. *Railways*—The Indian Railways reservation system could be designed to use a distributed database system. Reservation from one station to any other station can be given from a single window covering the round trip, which means passengers only have to stand in one queue. More information is available

---

1. A Petabyte is 1000 Terabytes, which is 10^{15} bytes of data. It is almost equal to storing all materials held in US academic libraries which has been estimated to be close to two Petabytes.

at www.indianrailways.gov.in/cert/CRIS.ppt and some other at http://www.wipro.in/newsroom/wiprointhenews/NC_tracking_solution_feb2k10.pdf

5. *Banks*—The Indian Overseas Bank has been reported to have implemented a cluster-based distributed database. The bank has 38 regional computer centres. The network connects more than 500 branches that are connected to 30 regional nodes that are in turn connected to each other through 1 Mbps or 64 Kbps leased lines.

   A case study about State Bank of India is available at http://www.tcs.com/sitecollectiondocuments/case%20studies/bancs_case_sbi.pdf

13.4 ADVANTAGES AND DISADVANTAGES OF DISTRIBUTED SYSTEMS

A distributed database system has a number of advantages as well as disadvantages over a centralized system.

13.4.1 Advantages of Distributed Database Systems

We list advantages of distributed database systems in Fig. 13.4.

- Matches distributed structure of enterprises
- Local autonomy
- Improved performance—most data available locally
- Improved reliability or availability
- Economics
- Expandability—modular growth
- Enhanced security

Figure 13.4 Advantages of distributed database systems

We now discuss each of these.

1. *Matches distributed structure of enterprises*—Distributed database systems match the distributed structure of many large enterprises, whether they are multinational corporations or the central government of a country, since both types of enterprises must provide services to local customers and staff. In such a situation, a database at the headquarters and perhaps smaller ones at regional offices may be required. Furthermore, different databases are sometimes needed to run particular business functions of an enterprise even at one location (for example, an inventory database and a human resources database, may be connected to form a distributed database system).
2. *Local autonomy*—When an enterprise is distributed all over a region, country or even internationally, it helps employees' morale if they are able to feel that they have some local autonomy of their own systems. Distributing a database system enables individual groups to exercise local control over their own data, making them less dependent on other sites in the database system. It is possible to make changes to the local site without risking functionality of the whole database system.
3. *Improved performance (most data available locally)*—A distributed database system can provide improved performance since local data is maintained locally. In addition, it is often easier to tune

the distributed system to match the workload. Workload problems can be more easily identified and resolved without affecting the whole system.

4. *Improved reliability/availability*—When a database is distributed over many sites, most sites will continue to operate even if one or two of them fail. Also, if some data from the failed sites has been replicated at other sites then the full functionality of the database system will continue to be available. Reliability of the database system is also improved if there is replication since the copies can carry out the role of backup copies when some sites are not able to recover from a failure. This improves the reliability of the database system in contrast to that of a single centralized system in which if the system fails, then all the functionality is lost. The same arguments apply to availability.
5. *Economics*—A distributed database system can be more economical to build and maintain since it can be build incrementally as opposed to a centralized system which must be built in one database development.
6. *Expandability (modular growth)*—Since the distributed database system is distributed over many sites, it is easier to expand it gracefully by upgrading some of the sites or adding more processors when required. If the enterprise is growing faster at one or two particular sites, it makes sense to expand the facilities at those sites or add another site rather than expand the whole system. This is easier to do than upgrading a large centralized system.
7. *Enhanced security*—In some ways a distributed system may enhance security of the database because the data is distributed over a number of autonomous sites and an intruder who is successful in penetrating one site may have difficulty accessing data from other sites. The data can be shared without sharing accounts and passwords. Each site can have its own administrator and its own set of accounts which can assist in keeping data secure.

13.4.2 Disadvantages of a Distributed Database System

Distributed databases also have a number of disadvantages as compared to centralized database systems. A list of these is presented in Fig. 13.5.

- Complexity of design and management
- Cost of development
- Distribution of control
- Security
- Integrity control is more complex
- Lack of experience

Figure 13.5 Disadvantages of distributed database systems

We discuss each of these disadvantages now.

1. *Complexity of design and management*—Designing a distributed database system involves extra work in design and maintenance of the multiple disparate systems, instead of a big one. Extra database design work must also be done to account for the distributed nature of the database. For example, joins become expensive when performed across multiple systems. Therefore, management of a distributed system is often more difficult than of a centralized database system.
2. *Cost of development*—As noted above, the increased complexity and more extensive infrastructure of distributed systems require additional manpower for the design effort and additional costs.
3. *Distribution of control*—Given that a distributed database involves many sites with local autonomy as well as a central site to manage the whole system, the control of the database is distributed.
4. *Security*—Although security was listed above under the advantages of distributed systems, security may also be considered as a disadvantage because it can be difficult to know and to control who is accessing

the database in a system which is distributed over many sites, which are operating autonomously. To control access, users to the system should be given no more access rights than absolutely necessary.

5. *Integrity control is more complex*—Given a number of sites and distribution of data, enforcing integrity over a network and the many sites becomes complex and often requires more resources. The design and realization of a distributed system involves management of many more integrity problems than does a centralized system.
6. *Lack of experience*—Distributed databases are complex and there is not much readily available experience in designing and maintaining them.

13.5 OBJECTIVES IN DESIGNING A DISTRIBUTED DATABASE SYSTEM

A distributed database system design would have many objectives. Some have already been noted. Twelve objectives (called commandments) were developed by C. J. Date. They include the distributed database system providing a number of transparencies:

- Location transparency
- Network transparency or Distribution transparency
- Replication transparency
- Fragmentation transparency

We now discuss the four transparencies followed by the other eight objectives. We will use the airline database used in earlier chapters as an example. The database has the following tables.

Consider a very basic airline booking system, let us call it Bharat Airlines, and let us assume we have implemented the following schema which is a rather primitive system:

Customer(CustomerID, Title, First name, Last name, Gender, Age, Address, TelephoneBH, TelephoneAH, Email)
Flight(FlightNUM, DepartureDate, DepartureTime, ArrivalDate, ArrivalTime)
Seat(FlightNUM, CustomerID, DepartureDate, SeatNUM, Class)
Ticket(SerialNUM, FlightNUM, DepartureDate, SeatNUM, CustomerID)

1. *Location transparency*—As noted earlier, the users do not need to know where the data is located. Location of data should be transparent to users and they do not need to know where the data is physically stored. To a user, a distributed database system should give the impression that all the data is stored at their own local site. In addition, data should be able to be transferred from one site to another without changes to users' queries.

   As an example of location transparency, consider a distributed database system of Bharat Airlines that flies domestically as well as internationally within three most popular airports, Mumbai, London and New York. It decides to establish a distributed database with sites in these three places with details of flights originating in USA stored in the New York database, of flights originating in UK stored in the London database and information about the remaining flights stored in the Mumbai database. In spite of this distribution of data, no travel agent or internet user should know which database is being used for their query. Furthermore, updates of the data should be possible without the user knowing where the data is. This is called location transparency.

Location transparency also requires a data-naming scheme that is not location dependent. The metadata should be able to deal with the issue of the location of data.

2. *Network transparency*—A distributed database system should appear like a centralized database even if different sites are running on different hardware and have different network types. The relations in the distributed system will be distributed over a number of different sites. However, a user is not required to know which relations are stored on which site. Also, the user queries should not be affected if the relations are moved from one site to another. The user requests should be stated in terms of relations and should take no account of the location or the network.

   It should be noted that in spite of fragmentation and replication each data item in a distributed database system must have a unique name. Given that one of the objectives of a distributed database system is to provide autonomy to all sites, naming of data objects becomes a serious issue. One approach is to use a central name server, but a better solution is to devise another system for generating names, e.g., site17.account.f 3.c2. Users obviously cannot be expected to remember names like site17.account.f 3.c2 and the distributed database system must translate user queries to queries on the data located at different sites.

3. *Replication transparency*—We discuss fragmentation in Section 13.6 and replication in Section 13.7. Fragmentation involves decomposition of a table in many parts while replication involves placing copies of each table or each of their fragments on more than one site in the system. In a distributed database system, in spite of data being replicated at several sites, a user is not required to know how fragments of a relation are replicated when using the system. Data replication is important since it provides increased reliability, increased availability and increased parallelism, but with an increased overhead on updates as discussed in Section 13.7. Replication also of course needs more storage. Nevertheless, the performance and reliability aspects of replication are too important and storage costs have now declined so much that one can ignore the increased storage factor.

   The user requests should be stated in terms of relations that take no account of replication. Using replicating copies effectively makes the retrieval, update and concurrency algorithms much more complex.

   As an example, we again consider the three-node distributed database of Bharat Airlines. The data in this system, for example, the table *Flight* as well as the other tables, must be replicated because the airline cannot afford to have one of the nodes going down or so overloaded that response time becomes unacceptable. It will probably be best to replicate data on all three nodes to ensure high level of availability and reliability of the system.

4. *Fragmentation transparency*—Fragmentation is discussed in the next section. It is dividing a relation in several fragments and storing the fragments on different sites. In a distributed database system, the user does not need to know about fragmentation or how many replicas of each fragment exist in the system. A relation in the system may be partitioned into a number of fragments and those fragments be replicated. User requests should be stated in terms of relations assuming they are not fragmented and replicated.

   As an example, continuing with the system of Bharat Airlines, as already noted, information about different flights is stored in different nodes but the information is replicated at all three nodes. For example, the table *Flight* is fragmented based on where each flight originates. There is no reason for a user to know how the tables have been fragmented and replicated.

5. *Hardware independence*—Sites may be running on different hardware so the sites probably have different operating systems and different network types. As noted earlier, Google has more than 500,000 machines all over the world and these machines must be using different hardware, since each year new and faster hardware becomes available and old hardware cannot be thrown away. It should not matter to the user what hardware is being used and the whole distributed database system should work like a central database.
6. *Operating system independence*—It is desirable not only to be able to run the same DBMS on different hardware platforms, but also to be able to run it on different OS platforms. Once again, let us consider the example of Google. Given that there are so many machines; one can only assume that these machines are using different operating systems like Linux, Windows, Mac operating system and other operating systems. It should not matter to the user what operating system is being used and the whole distributed system should work like a central database.
7. *DBMS independence*—It should be possible to use a variety of DBMS in a large international distributed database management environment as long as they support the same or similar interface. For example, it should be possible to run Oracle on some machines and IBM DB2 on others. A homogeneous distributed database system is based on using the same DBMS at all sites. In a heterogeneous distributed database system at least one of the sites is using a different DBMS than the other sites. This should however not impact smooth running of the system.
8. *Local autonomy*—As noted earlier, the sites in a distributed database system should be autonomous although total autonomy is not possible. Decisions about how the data will be stored, what hardware will be used and what security will be employed should generally be local issues. We list these issues in Fig. 13.6.

- All local data is owned and managed by the local site.
- All database operations at a site are controlled by the local site.
- Local data is managed at its site and the site is accountable for its data.
- The local site should determine security, integrity and storage issues.

Figure 13.6 Local autonomy issues in distributed database system

9. *No reliance on a central site*—A distributed database system should have no reliance on a central site for query processing and transaction management. Therefore, metadata management, query processing, concurrency control and recovery functions must be distributed. Also, it is important that if the central site fails, the whole distributed database system does not fail. Also, the central site may become a bottleneck if all sites depend on it.

   Continuing to use the example of Bharat Airlines, let us assume that the Mumbai node is the central site since we assumed, that the head office of the airline is located there. For the airline to work with a high level of reliability, the New York and London nodes must be independent of the Mumbai node because if the Mumbai node goes down even for one hour, it could create serious problems for airline bookings.
10. *Continuous operation*—A distributed system should provide greater reliability and greater availability than a centralized database system and therefore should keep working nonstop. As noted earlier, when the database is distributed over many sites, most sites will continue to operate even if one or two of them fail. Also, if some data from the failed sites has been replicated at other sites then the full functionality of the database system should continue to be available. It is clear that an airline or even

Google must be able to rely on their computer system to operate 24 × 7 without any down time. Adding and removing sites and installation and upgrade of software should be possible without too much disruption to the system.

11. *Distributed query processing*—In a distributed database system, the system should be able to find efficient ways of processing queries including processing a query from site *A* at sites *B* and *C* without the user knowing where the query was processed. A distributed system may need to transfer some data from one site to another to optimize query processing.

    Distributed query processing is particularly important for 24 × 7 operations of some international database systems. For Bharat Airlines, when it is day time in USA, it is night time in Mumbai and it is possible to distribute the query processing load between New York and Mumbai. Similar argument applies for Google. When a query is being posed in Delhi during the day time, who knows which machine located where is processing it; it might be in Edinburgh or Dallas or somewhere else.
12. *Distributed transaction management*—The system must be able to deal with issues like recovery and concurrency in a distributed environment. Since many large international databases like those for eBay or for United Airlines are busy all day and night, the systems must ensure that at no stage the integrity of their database is compromised. It is not acceptable to have more bookings made for a flight than there are seats on the plane allocated to the flight[2]. To provide high level of concurrency in a distributed database, the transaction managers at each site must cooperate to ensure appropriate concurrency control. We will discuss more about transaction management later in this chapter.

We list issues regarding distributed transaction management in Fig. 13.7.

- As noted in previous chapters, the major issues of transaction management are recovery and concurrency.
- Distributed transactions must conform to the "all or nothing rule".
- Distributed concurrency often based on the two-phase commit to protocol.

Figure 13.7 Distributed transaction management issues

A distributed system also needs to consider the following:

- *Level of Local Autonomy*—From low local autonomy to total autonomy although some central coordination is often required.
- *Level of Distribution*—We discuss fragmentation, replication and distribution later in this chapter. Distribution may include full replication and distribution to little distribution (e.g., client-server systems)
- *Level of Heterogeneity*—from all sites using the same hardware and same software to every site using different hardware and software.

2. Actually most airlines do book more seats than there are seats on the plane allocated for the flight assuming that some people having booked seats would not show up. This can obviously create huge problems on occasions. I myself have suffered from overbooking in India when many years ago Air-India told me at Palam airport (as it was then called) around midnight that I could not travel in spite of having a confirmed ticket. Overbooking is legal in most countries although I don't know if there is an overbooking law in India. These laws require that if there are too many passengers for a flight, reasonable compensation must be paid to those who are not allowed to board the flight.

13.6 DISTRIBUTED SYSTEM DESIGN–FRAGMENTATION

The design of a distributed database system involves making decisions on the placement of data and programs across the sites of a computer network. It is desirable that data is placed at sites where it is most likely to be accessed so that communication costs and delays can be minimized. Some highly sought after data may have to be replicated at all the sites but this then leads to problems of updating all the copies of the database when the data is to be updated.

Normally a relation is too coarse a unit of distributing data. A row or a column is too fine. Therefore, relations must be fragmented for distribution. In designing distribution of data in the system we will assume that there are no a prior constraints on how data is distributed. Furthermore, we assume that access patterns of data are relatively static and the design may be based on these access patterns. No replication of data is to be considered when designing data distribution.

The distribution of data involves two tasks:

- Fragmentation—to partition each relation of the database into fragments along its rows (that is, horizontally) and/or along its attributes (that is, vertically).
- Allocation—to decide the allocation of the fragments to various sites on the network.

13.6.1 Fragmentation Issues

We will discuss the following issues in distributed database design:

- Why fragment at all?
- How should we fragment?
- How much should we fragment?
- How to test correctness of decomposition?
- How should we allocate?

Why Fragment?

Even a centralized database may benefit from fragmentation, for example, attribute partitioning may improve performance of a centralized database. In a distributed system, fragmentation is not only advantageous but essential for efficient transaction processing. The unit of distribution may be a relation or a fragment although the fragment is often a more suitable unit since it allows parallel processing of a query. Decomposition of a relation into fragments facilitates concurrent and parallel query processing but fragmentation must provide completeness, reconstruction and disjointness.

Often application views are subsets of relations. Allocating a relation to one site may result in a high volume of remote data accesses which may be reduced by fragmentation.

Fragmentation can also have disadvantages. As noted earlier, replicating fragments at all sites causes update problems and is not desirable if storage is limited. Applications that involve more than one fragment may suffer performance degradation.

Fragmentation can lead to difficulty in semantic data control such as integrity checking.

How to Fragment?

Fragmentation may be carried out in a number of ways as listed below:

- Horizontal fragmentation
- Vertical fragmentation
- Hybrid fragmentation

In general, the applications that are run on the distributed database need to be characterized with respect to a number of parameters. The fragmentation is then determined according to the values of these parameters.

The parameters that are required in fragmenting relations include:

- A set of most often used queries in terms of the 20-80 rule.
- Types of queries, e.g., retrieval or update.
- Access frequency of each query or an estimate.

Generally speaking, the primary aim of fragmentation is to have user applications using only one fragment, which is smaller than the whole relation.

How much to Fragment?

Despite the advantages of fragmentation, fragmentation also has a number of disadvantages. These could include some performance penalty for some types of queries as well as lower efficiency in updating the database and difficulty in integrity checking. It is possible to have a level of fragmentation from no fragmentation at all, to the level where a table is fragmented in as many fragments as the number of rows in it. A balance must be found in the level of fragmentation and the cost of query processing.

Fragmentation Correctness

When relations are fragmented, it is important to ensure that the fragmentation has been carried out correctly. The following properties ensure that a fragmentation is correct:

- *Completeness*—If a relation R is decomposed into fragments r_1, r_2, ... r_n, each data item that can be found in R can also be found in one or more r_i's.
- *Reconstruction*—If a relation R is decomposed into fragments r_1, r_2,... r_n, it should be possible to define a relational operator so that $R = Op(r_i)$
- *Disjointness*—If a relation R is decomposed into fragments r_1, r_2,... r_n and data item d_j is in r_i then d_j should not appear in any other fragment.

How to Allocate?

This is discussed in Section 13.7 after a discussion on replication.

13.6.2 Horizontal Fragmentation

Horizontal fragmentation involves breaking up a relation into a number of subsets of rows. Each fragment therefore is essentially a selection on the base relation. We therefore need an algorithm to partition each relation. We first consider fragmenting a single relation horizontally.

Primary Horizontal Fragmentation

The primary horizontal fragmentation involves fragmentation based on predicates that define certain conditions on the attributes of the table of that relation. The question arises what predicates to use for fragmentation? Predicates could be based on frequency of access of different parts of a table assuming that the rows in each fragment are accessed with the same frequency. It is somewhat difficult to get an estimate of access patterns (the number of times a tuple is accessed per second or per minute) of different parts of a relation, so a designer often has to rely on his/her gut feeling. In some situations it is possible to obtain a rough estimate for access patterns of each application.

Derived Horizontal Fragmentation

In the relational database model, a relation often has many foreign key relationships with other relations. Given that these relationships carry a special meaning it is quite likely that a relation will be accessed with another relation that it is referring to, or is being referred to, when the two relations are involved in a join. It is therefore desirable that these relationships be taken into account when data is being distributed so that related tables stay together on the same site as much as possible.

Derived horizontal fragmentation therefore is based on one table propagating its fragmentation to other tables in an effort to keep related tables together. This is called derived horizontal fragmentation.

Primary Horizontal Fragmentation Based on Minterms[3]

As noted earlier, we need to know the predicates used in the application queries, at least the important ones. Based on these we can select predicates that can form the basis of horizontal fragmentation. Simple predicates might be of the form given below:

Salary > 30,000
City = 'Kolkata'
Title = 'Manager'

Let us assume we have a set of simple predicates like those listed above.

$$P_r = \{p_{i1}, p_{i2}, \ldots p_{im}\}$$

The predicates above are called *simple predicates*. From these we can compose complex predicates by using conjunction and negation. If we combine all simple predicates using conjunction and negation, we obtain a set of complex predicates called the *minterm predicates*.

$$M_i = \{m_{i1}, m_{i2}, \ldots m_{in}\}$$

These minterm predicates may be used to provide the basis of partitioning of the table under consideration. We will illustrate it using an example.

We consider a distributed database with a number of sites. Let us consider the *Player* relation in a distributed database. Two of the attributes in the table are *Country* and *YBorn*. Suppose we have some basis for choosing the following simple predicates for distributing the data. One condition is that players are from India; another is that players are from Australia and the third is that they were born before 1975. The predicates are given in SQL queries in Figs 13.8, 13.9 and 13.10.

---

3. A minterm is a logical expression of n variables consisting only of the logical and operator.

```
SELECT (*)
FROM Player
WHERE Country = 'India'
```

Figure 13.8 A selection query *Q1*

```
SELECT (*)
FROM Player
WHERE Country = 'Australia'
```

Figure 13.9 A selection query *Q2*

```
SELECT (*)
FROM Player
WHERE YBorn <= 1975
```

Figure 13.10 A selection query *Q3*

Using these simple predicates it is possible to derive eight minterms by combining them and using their negations as well. Some minterms will be meaningless as we will see. These then may be deleted and the remainder can be used as a basis of a fragmentation algorithm. Let the minterms be m_1, m_2, m_3, etc., given in Fig. 13.11.

Minterms	Predicates
m_1	Country = 'India' AND Country = 'Australia' AND YBorn <= 1975
m_2	Country = 'India' AND Country = 'Australia' AND YBorn > 1975
m_3	Country = 'India' AND Country ≠ 'Australia' AND YBorn <= 1975
m_4	Country = 'India' AND Country ≠ 'Australia' AND YBorn > 1975
m_5	Country ≠ 'India' AND Country ≠ 'Australia' AND YBorn <= 1975
m_6	Country ≠ 'India' AND Country ≠ 'Australia' AND YBorn > 1975
m_7	Country ≠ 'India' AND Country = 'Australia' AND YBorn <= 1975
m_8	Country ≠ 'India' AND Country = 'Australia' AND YBorn >1975

Figure 13.11 Deriving minterms based on three simple predicates

Note that the first two minterms are meaningless since no player can come from both India and Australia. The third and fourth minterms are about players from India and the seventh and eighth are about players from Australia. The fifth and sixth are about players who are neither Indian nor Australian and are meaningful only if we have players from other countries in the database. Our relation *Player* does have players from other countries.

A horizontal fragment R_i of a relation R consists of all the tuples that satisfy meaningful minterms m_i. These fragments are often called *minterm fragments*. We now present an algorithm in Fig. 13.12 based on the minterms.

Horizontal Fragmentation Algorithm

1. Find a set of simple predicates that are relevant in partitioning the input relation.
2. Derive minterms based on the simple predicates.
3. Eliminate meaningless minterms.
4. Use the remaining minterms to define the fragments.

Figure 13.12 Horizontal fragmentation algorithm using minterms

We now present the fragments of the relation *Player* based on the minterms derived in Fig. 13.10. We remind the reader that the first two minterms are meaningless.

The first fragment is Indian players born in 1975 or earlier based on the minterm m_3. It is presented in Fig. 13.13.

PlayerID	LName	FName	Country	YBorn	BPlace	FTest
89001	Tendulkar	Sachin	India	1973	Mumbai	1989
96001	Dravid	Rahul	India	1973	Indore	1996
90002	Kumble	Anil	India	1970	Bangalore	1990
96003	Ganguly	Saurav	India	1972	Calcutta	1996

Figure 13.13 A fragment using the minterm m_3

The second fragment is Indian players born after 1975 based on minterm m_4. It is presented in Fig. 13.14.

PlayerID	LName	FName	Country	YBorn	BPlace	FTest
25001	Dhoni	MS	India	1981	Ranchi	2005
23001	Singh	Yuvraj	India	1981	Chandigarh	2003
21001	Sehwag	Virender	India	1978	Delhi	2001
98002	Singh	Harbhajan	India	1980	Jalandhar	1998
27001	Kumar	Praveen	India	1986	Meerut	NA
27002	Sharma	Ishant	India	1988	Delhi	2007

Figure 13.14 A fragment using the minterm m_4

The third fragment is players from outside India and Australia born in 1975 or earlier based on minterm m_5. It is presented in Fig. 13.15.

PlayerID	LName	FName	Country	YBorn	BPlace	FTest
90001	Lara	Brian	W Indies	1969	Santa Cruz	1990
96002	Gibbs	Herschelle	South Africa	1974	Cape Town	1996
95002	Pollock	Shaun	South Africa	1973	Port Elizabeth	1995
99003	Vaughan	Michael	England	1974	Manchester	1999
92003	Ul-Huq	Inzamam	Pakistan	1970	Multan	1992
94004	Fleming	Stephen	New Zealand	1973	Christchurch	1994
93002	Streak	Heath	Zimbabwe	1974	Bulawayo	1993
93003	Kirsten	Gary	South Africa	1967	Cape Town	1993
95003	Kallis	Jacques	South Africa	1975	Cape Town	1995
94002	Vaas	Chaminda	Sri Lanka	1974	Mattumagala	1994
92002	Muralitharan	Muthiah	Sri Lanka	1972	Kandy	1992
91001	Jayasuriya	Sanath	Sri Lanka	1969	Matara	1991

Figure 13.15 A fragment using the minterm m_5

The fourth fragment is players from outside India and Australia born after 1975 based on minterm m_6. It is presented in Fig. 13.16.

PlayerID	LName	FName	Country	YBorn	BPlace	FTest
97004	Vettori	Daniel	New Zealand	1979	Auckland	1997
98001	Afridi	Shahid	Pakistan	1980	Khyber Agency	1998

Figure 13.16 A fragment using the minterm m_6

The fifth fragment is Australian players born in 1975 or earlier based on minterm m_7. It is presented in Fig. 13.17.

PlayerID	LName	FName	Country	YBorn	BPlace	FTest
95001	Ponting	Ricky	Australia	1974	Launceston	1995
92001	Warne	Shane	Australia	1969	Melbourne	1992
99002	Gilchrist	Adam	Australia	1971	Bellingen	1999
24001	Symonds	Andrew	Australia	1975	Birmingham	2004

Figure 13.17 A fragment using the minterm m_7

The sixth fragment is Australian players born after 1975 based on minterm m_8. It is presented in Fig. 13.18.

PlayerID	LName	FName	Country	YBorn	BPlace	FTest
99001	Lee	Brett	Australia	1976	Wollongong	1999

Figure 13.18 A fragment using the minterm m_8

The above fragments are not of similar sizes. Fragments in Fig. 13.15 and Fig. 13.17 are small but we are not concerned about them since all new players are likely to be younger and will go to these fragments.

It should be noted that the above fragmentation satisfies the three requirements of fragmentation, viz., **completeness, reconstruction and disjointness. Each tuple of** *Player* appears in one of the fragments, no tuples are duplicated and the union of all the fragments reconstructs the original relation *Player*.

13.6.3 Derived Fragments

We now present an example to illustrate derived fragments. Consider the three other relations in the cricket database, i.e., *Match*, *Batting* and *Bowling*. If we were to fragment *Match* then an obvious way might be to derive the fragments based on the fragments of *Player* obtained already. A simple approach might be to put tuples where *Team1* was *India* with Indian players, tuples with *Team1* as *Australia* with Australian players and the remaining with a fragment that has the remaining players. We have two fragments for India and two for Australia so we might just put three fragments of *Match* on three sites rather than six sites, since we cannot find a good way to fragment *Match* into six fragments.

We can use the same approach to fragment *Batting* and *Bowling*. The fragments for these two tables may be derived based on the fragments of *Player* obtained already. A simple approach might be to put tuples of *Batting* and *Bowling* on the same sites where their *Player* records have been put. We leave it as an exercise to determine the fragments of these two relations. We will only use *Match* to illustrate derived relations.

The first derived fragment of *Match* is when *Team1* is India. It is given in Fig. 13.19.

MatchId	Team1	Team2	Ground	Date	Winner
2440	India	Australia	Mohali	29/10/2006	Team2
2480	India	West Indies	Nagpur	21/1/2007	Team1
2493	India	West Indies	Vadodara	31/1/2007	Team1
2520	India	Sri Lanka	Rajkot	11/2/2007	Team2
2632	India	Australia	Mumbai	17/10/2007	Team1
2643	India	Pakistan	Guwahati	5/11/2007	Team1

Figure 13.19 A derived fragment of *Match*

The second fragment is when *Team1* is Australia. It is given in Fig. 13.20.

MatchId	Team1	Team2	Ground	Date	Winner
2675	Australia	India	Melbourne	10/2/2008	Team2
2688	Australia	India	Sydney	2/3/2008	Team2
2689	Australia	India	Brisbane	4/3/2008	Team2
2717	Pakistan	India	Karachi	26/6/2008	Team2

Figure 13.20 Another derived fragment of *Match*

The third fragment is when *Team1* is neither India nor Australia. It is given in Fig. 13.21.

MatchId	Team1	Team2	Ground	Date	Winner
2324	Pakistan	India	Peshawar	6/2/2006	Team1
2327	Pakistan	India	Rawalpindi	11/2/2006	Team2
2377	West Indies	India	Kingston	18/5/2006	Team2
2404a	Sri Lanka	India	Colombo	16/8/2006	Abandoned
2449	South Africa	India	Cape Town	26/11/2006	Team1
2611	England	India	Southampton	21/8/2007	Team1
2717	Pakistan	India	Karachi	26/6/2008	Team2
2750	Sri Lanka	India	Colombo	24/8/2008	Team2
2755	Sri Lanka	India	Colombo	27/8/2008	Team2

Figure 13.21 Another derived fragment of *Match*

This concludes the discussion on horizontal fragmentation. We now discuss vertical fragmentation.

13.6.4 Vertical Fragmentation

In vertical fragmentation a given relation R is broken up into fragments R_1, R_2, ... R_n, each of which contains a subset of R's attributes as well as the primary key. Just as in horizontal fragmentation, the aim of vertical fragmentation is to fragment so that each application needs to normally use only one fragment. Vertical fragmentation may be useful even in centralized databases.

To design vertical fragmentation one of the following heuristics may be used:

- Grouping (may produce overlapping)
- Splitting (produces non-overlapping)

Since it is a requirement that the original relation may be constructed from fragments, the primary key of the relation must be in each fragment. It causes problems but also has advantages (in integrity checking).

The aim of vertical fragmentation is to put together those attributes that are accessed together.

Togetherness is measured by affinity of attributes.

Let $Q = \{q_1, q_2, ... q_m\}$ be user queries and
$R = \{A_1, A_2, ... A_n\}$ be attributes.

Then we may define a matrix *use* as follows:

$use(q_i, A_j) = 1$ if references and 0 if not. *use* is then a matrix with 1s and 0s.

This matrix may now be used to compute affinity which could be the basis of partitioning.

As an example we use the following relation to illustrate vertical partitioning. The relations used in the cricket database are not suitable for vertical partitioning. The relation in Fig. 13.22 gives details of a number of Bollywood and Tollywood couples, some married and others not but reported as couples in the gossip columns of magazines[3]. We only give first names since the space does not allow full names to be included.

We should explain the meanings of the attributes of the table *IFC* in Fig. 13.22.

1. *ID* is just an artificial identification for each row.
2. *FName1* is the first name of the first partner (assumed female).
3. *FName2* is the first name of the second Partner (assumed male).
4. *NFilms1* is the number of films in which Partner 1 has acted.
5. *NFilms2* is the number of films in which Partner 2 has acted.
6. *YBirth1* is the year of birth of Partner 1.
7. *YBirth2* is the year of birth of Partner 2.
8. *City1* is the city of birth of Partner 1.
9. *City2* is the city of birth of Partner 2.
10. *LCity* is the city where the couple live.

The relation *IFC* can be easily divided into two vertical fragments since there are columns that relate to the males and others that relate to the females of the couples. The last column *LCity* is related to both since it is

3. We have tried to get accurate information for this table but it would surprise us if some of the information has not changed when the reader is reading it!

where they live. It may be put in either of the fragments, it does not matter which, but we cannot put it in both since that will violate one of the requirements of fragmentation.

ID	FName1	FName2	NFilms1	NFilms2	YBirth1	YBirth2	City1	City2	LCity
1002	Deepika	Ranbir	6	5	1986	1982	Copenhagen	Mumbai	Mumbai
1004	Katrina	Salman	19	75	1984	1965	Hong Kong	Indore	Mumbai
1011	Kareena	Saif	38	46	1980	1970	Mumbai	New Delhi	Mumbai
1050	Bipasha	John	40	26	1979	1972	New Delhi	Mumbai	Mumbai
1070	Freida	Dev	1	2	1984	1990	Mumbai	Harrow	Mumbai
1085	Gouthami	Kamal	50	17	NULL	1954	Andhra	Paramakudi	Chennai
1099	Latha	Rajnikanth	NULL	25	NULL	1950	NULL	Bangalore	Chennai
1235	Raadhika	Sarath	20	95	1963	1954	Chennai	New Delhi	Chennai
1137	Shalini	Ajith	21	48	1980	1971	Chennai	Chennai	Chennai

Figure 13.22 A relation called *IFC* (Indian film couples)

The first vertical fragment of *IFC* is called *IFCFemales*. It is given in Fig. 13.23.

ID	FName1	NFilms1	YBirth1	City1
1002	Deepika	6	1986	Copenhagen
1004	Katrina	19	1984	Hong Kong
1011	Kareena	38	1980	Mumbai
1050	Bipasha	40	1979	New Delhi
1070	Freida	1	1984	Mumbai
1085	Gouthami	50	NULL	Andhra
1099	Latha	NULL	NULL	NULL
1235	Raadhika	20	1963	Chennai
1137	Shalini	21	1980	Chennai

Figure 13.23 A vertical fragment called *IFCFemales*

The second vertical fragment is called *IFCMales*. It is given in Fig. 13.24.

ID	FName2	NFilms2	YBirth2	City2	LCity
1002	Ranbir	5	1982	Mumbai	Mumbai
1004	Salman	75	1965	Indore	Mumbai
1011	Saif	46	1970	New Delhi	Mumbai
1050	John	26	1972	Mumbai	Mumbai
1070	Dev	2	1990	Harrow	Mumbai
1085	Kamal	17	1954	Paramakudi	Chennai
1099	Rajnikanth	25	1950	Bangalore	Chennai
1235	Sarath	95	1954	New Delhi	Chennai
1137	Ajith	48	1971	Chennai	Chennai

Figure 13.24 Another vertical fragment called *IFCMales*

We are assuming that transactions would frequently access either *IFCFemales* or *IFCMales* although we really have no basis for making this assumption.

It should be noted that the above vertical fragmentation satisfies the three requirements of fragmentation, i.e., **completeness, reconstruction and disjointness. Each tuple of** *IFC* appears in both the vertical fragments, no tuples are duplicated and a join of the two fragments on the attribute *ID* reconstructs the original relation *IFC*. We now briefly consider hybrid fragmentation.

13.6.5 Hybrid Fragmentation

Hybrid fragmentation deals with using both horizontal and vertical fragmentation. We decomposed the relation IFC in Fig. 13.22 into 13.23 and 13.24. These can in fact be decomposed further horizontally as shown in Fig. 13.25, 13.26, 13.27 and 13.28. We will not go into the details of predicates for this partitioning and assume that a reasonable partition is based on the value of *LCity*. The predicates *LCity* = **"Mumbai' and** *LCity* ≠ Mumbai will be used as the basis of further portioning the tables in Figs 13.23 and 13.24.

The first hybrid fragment is presented in Fig. 13.25.

ID	FName1	NFilms1	YBirth1	City1
1002	Deepika	6	1986	Copenhagen
1004	Katrina	19	1984	Hong Kong
1011	Kareena	38	1980	Mumbai
1050	Bipasha	40	1979	New Delhi
1070	Freida	1	1984	Mumbai

Figure 13.25 *IFCF1*—A horizontal fragment of *IFCFemales*

The second hybrid fragment is presented in Fig. 13.26.

ID	FName1	NFilms1	YBirth1	City1
1085	Gouthami	50	NULL	Andhra
1099	Latha	NULL	NULL	NULL
1235	Raadhika	20	1963	Chennai
1137	Shalini	21	1980	Chennai

Figure 13.26 *IFCF2*—Another horizontal fragment of *IFCFemales*

The third hybrid fragment is presented in Fig. 13.27.

ID	FName2	NFilms2	YBirth2	City2	LCity
1002	Ranbir	5	1982	Mumbai	Mumbai
1004	Salman	75	1965	Indore	Mumbai
1011	Saif	46	1970	New Delhi	Mumbai
1050	John	26	1972	Mumbai	Mumbai
1070	Dev	2	1990	Harrow	Mumbai

Figure 13.27 *IFCM1*—A horizontal fragment of *IFCMales*

The fourth hybrid fragment is presented in Fig. 13.28.

ID	FName2	NFilms2	YBirth2	City2	LCity
1085	Kamal	17	1954	Paramakudi	Chennai
1099	Rajnikanth	25	1950	Bangalore	Chennai
1235	Sarath	95	1954	New Delhi	Chennai
1137	Ajith	48	1971	Chennai	Chennai

Figure 13.28 *IFCM2*—Another horizontal fragment of *IFCMales*

It should be noted that the above fragmentation also satisfies the three requirements of fragmentation, i.e., **completeness, reconstruction and disjointness. Each tuple of** *IFC* appears in two fragments, no tuples are duplicated and the union of the fragments in Figs 13.25 and 13.26 and those in Figs 13.27 and 13.28 followed by a join reconstructs the original relation *IFC*.

We now discuss data replication and allocation.

13.7 DISTRIBUTED DESIGN ISSUE—DATA REPLICATION AND DATA ALLOCATION

Once a database system has a number of sites, it needs to be decided what data will be stored at which site. The easiest approach is to let each local site store and manage its own data but this is not a particularly good approach because if one of sites goes down then the data stored at that site is not available to the users at other sites. Fragmentation and replication together are used to improve the reliability of a distributed database system.

13.7.1 Replication

Distributed database systems often involve replication of data, storing several copies of each relation or its fragments, to ensure that full database will be available to users in spite of one or more sites going down and therefore enhancing the reliability/availability of the database. Of course when a distributed database system has many sites, the chance of one of the sites going down becomes higher than a single site. Furthermore, replication allows more parallel processing and that may result in quicker response to user queries.

On the negative side, replication involves increased data storage costs, and more importantly, a much higher cost of updating relations.

We present an informal definition of replication.

Definition—Replication

Replication in a distributed database is a technique by which multiple copies of a table or its fragments are located at different sites to improve availability and performance of the database system.

The goal of replication is to improve availability in spite of failure of one or more sites in a distributed database system, since if a site fails, another site that has replica of information required by a query can be used. Replication also creates some challenges since when a table or its fragment needs to be updated, all replicas must be updated. One possibility to deal with this challenge is to implement one-copy serializability which involves updating all copies of a fragment when one copy is updated and not commit the transaction unless all copies have been updated. This approach can lead to other difficulties, in particular when one or more of the sites are down. One possibility is to propagate updates to all replicas in a particular order and ensure these updates are applied to a failed site when it recovers from the failure.

Replication can be classified into the following three types:

- *Fully Replicated*—As the name implies, fully replicated distributed database replicates every table (or its fragments) on every node of the system. That means that each node has a full copy of the database making it easier for query processing. Failure of a node has minimal effect on the operation of the database except for users that wish to use the failed node. The disadvantage of a fully replicated database is that updates become expensive and so does transaction management and concurrency. Furthermore, full replication requires much more storage than a system with no replication.
- *Partially Replicated*—A partially replicated distributed database replicates some or all the tables (or their fragments) on only a number of nodes of the system. That means that each node has a partial copy of the database making it more complex for query processing than in the case of full replication. Failure of a node in partial replication has minimal effect on the operation of the database if every table has at least two replicas except for users that wish to use the failed node. The disadvantage of a partially replicated database is that updates are expensive and so is transaction management and concurrency although it is better than fully replicated database. Furthermore, partial replication requires more storage than a system with no replication although the storage requirements are lower than a fully replicated database.
- *No Replication*—As the name implies, these database systems have no replication of data. That means that each node has the only copy of some tables or their fragments. This makes query processing quite expensive. The advantage of a such a database that has no replication is that updates become less expensive and so does transaction management and concurrency when compared with the other two replication methods. Finally, failure of a node in a system with no replication can have serious impact on the operation of the database if the node has tables that are used by many users at the other nodes. In summary, the benefits and disadvantages of replication are given in the figure below.

Task	Full Replication	Partial Replication	No Replication
Query Processing	Easy	Some difficulty	Some difficulty
Concurrency Control	Moderate difficulty	Difficult	Easy
Reliability	Very high	High	Low
Metadata Maintenance	Easy	Some difficulty	Some difficulty

Figure 13.29 Advantages and disadvantages of replication

13.7.2 Data Allocation

Data allocation involves making decisions regarding what fragments or tables will be allocated to which nodes and how much replication will be carried out. These decisions must be based on the requirements of the system including the query profiles, response time required and the level of reliability needed. If there are a lot of updates then the lower level of replication may be recommended. If however, the system is going to be fully replicated, then of course the data allocation has already been decided but decisions need to be made for partially replicated and nonreplicated systems. In partially replicated databases the decisions may be based on what data is being accessed by each node and try to ensure the data is where it is accessed more frequently. If there is no replication then various fragments will need to be allocated to different nodes. Some nodes may be allocated lot more data than others depending on the needs of the nodes. In fact, in a large network of nodes, some nodes may have no data at all.

13.8 DISTRIBUTED QUERY PROCESSING

We discussed query processing in Chapter 8. We described the process of query processing and listed the following five steps:

1. Parsing and Validating
2. Optimization
3. Code Generation
4. Query Execution

The same four steps must be followed in distributed query processing. We discuss these steps now.

13.8.1 Parsing and Validating

Parsing and validating in distributed query processing is essentially the same as discussed in Chapter 8 for centralized database systems.

13.8.2 Optimization

Optimization is also similar to optimization in a centralized database system but additional complexities are introduced due to fragmentation, replication, and distribution of the tables. The optimizer therefore must decide which site will be used to execute each operation and how each operation, for example, a join, will be carried out. Operations are different when the tables are fragmented horizontally and vertically. Many more options are available for computing a join when the relations are fragmented and replicated in the system. A number of plans must be generated including details of where each operation will be executed and their costs estimated including the cost of transmitting data and results from one site to another. The plans may be represented as query trees as discussed in Chapter 8 but these query trees must also include details of sites where the operations will be carried out and details of transmission of data and operations.

The plans may include fetching the data as the query requires or shipping the query to a site that has all or most of the data that the query requires. In other cases, it may make sense to ship some of the data from sites that have it and that is required by the query, to the query site even before the query needs it. Yet another approach may be shipping the query and then shipping some data so that the query and data are available at the same site.

In conjunction with possible shipping of query and/or data, a decision must be made regarding which site will carry out the query or an operation of the query. In summary, a selected query plan is likely to include the following information:

- Execution sequence—It is a sequence of operations to be executed.
- Processing sites—It determines what sites have been selected for processing each operation.
- Access path—For each operation access paths must be specified. For example, would index scan be required or a sequential scan?
- Processing algorithm—It determines what algorithm would be used to carry out the operation? For example, in computing a join, would nested-loop or sort-merge or hashing be used.
- Data transfer—For each operation, what data would be transferred and from where? Would a whole relation need to be transferred or only some fragments would be required?

13.8.3 Code Generation

Once the least cost plan has been selected, it must be transformed into an executable plan. This executable plan or code may be a sequence of algebra operations or may be a lower level language. If the query includes insertion, deletion or update of some tables then the code must also include algorithms for updating the different fragments and replicas of the table. The most common approach is to update the table or tables when the query is executed and propagate these updates to all replicas that are affected.

13.8.4 Query Execution

Query execution is usually based on algorithms similar to those used in centralized database systems but execution must deal with data shipment between nodes and modified algorithms for operations taking into account that data may not be available at a single site. The join algorithm is a particularly complex one when data is fragmented and replicated. Using the algorithms, the query plan may be executed by pipelining the results obtained from one operation to the next.

13.9 AN EXAMPLE OF DISTRIBUTED QUERY PROCESSING

Consider the cricket database which includes four relations, *Player, Match, Batting* and *Bowling.* Assume that each relation is fragmented into two or more fragments and each fragment is replicated once so two copies of each fragment are stored at two different sites.

Now consider a very simple query posed by Site 1, 'Find the names of all players from India who have made a century'. The query involves a selection, a join and a projection. How should the query be processed?

1. *Selection*—This will require identifying which copies of the fragments are to be used and then carrying out the selection.
2. *Join*—Let us assume the relations are fragmented into only two fragments. We therefore have two fragments each p_1, p_2 (of *Player*) and b_1, b_2 (of *Batting*) and each fragment has two copies stored on different sites. They are therefore located on eight different machines. We first need to decide which copies to use, carry out the selection and then decide which fragment will be moved to another machine for processing the join. It is not a trivial task.
3. *Projection*—Once we have the result of the join, a projection is then a straightforward operation.

The task of the global query optimizer in a distributed system is to

- **Translate a high-level query to a low-level plan.**
- **Develop an optimal plan including details of which operation will be carried out on which sites.**

Global query optimization is complex due to cost models, fragmentation and replication, and a large solution space to choose from.

It is necessary to be able to predict the cost of alternative candidate plans. Often the cost is a weighted combination of the input/output cost, CPU cost and communications cost. In early distributed systems when the networking was slow and expensive, the local processing cost was sometimes ignored since the communication costs were often dominant. Present networks are fast and cheap enough to make the local processing costs a significant component of the total cost. Often one of the two cost models is used, viz., total cost (time) or the response time.

Total cost is the sum of all the component costs while the response time is the elapsed time from the initiation to the completion of the query. Response time may be improved by increasing the degree of parallelism. Response time may reduce even if the total cost is increased. We note that the two major costs are given below:

- *Local Processing*—cost of CPU plus the cost of I/O.
- *Communication Cost*—fixed cost of initiating and receiving a message plus the cost of transmitting the message which is proportional to the number of bytes transmitted.

Often no account is taken of network traffic or the distance between the sites communicating.

Query optimization performed before query execution is called *static* optimization. If done during the execution, it is called *dynamic* optimization.

Static optimization is based on estimates of the size of intermediate relations and site loads. If these estimates are incorrect, the plan may be far from optimal. Dynamic query optimization can use the actual sizes of intermediate relations and site loads in designing plans. Of course, repeated query optimization is expensive.

13.9.1 Size of Intermediate Relations

One of the main factors affecting cost is the size of the intermediate relations produced during execution since the CPU time and communication cost of subsequent operations is determined by them. A number of statistics need to be maintained by a DBMS to enable reasonable estimates of the intermediate results.

These include the following:

- *For each attribute*—Length or the number of distinct values in each fragment.
- *For each attribute*—Minimum and maximum possible values (if order exists).
- *For each attribute*—Cardinality of the domain.
- *For each relation fragment*—The number of tuples.
- *For pairs of relations*—Join selectivity of frequent joins.

As noted earlier, even a simple query may become complex if the relation that it needs to access is fragmented and replicated. The system then must figure out which fragments are required and which copies of the fragments will be used. Furthermore, the system will need to make decisions about which site(s) will carry out the processing and which fragments, if any, will need to be transferred to those site(s).

13.9.2 Join Processing

The join could be computed by a number of plans, for example:

1. Send all relations to one site if the site is not Site 1, send the result to Site 1.
2. Send p_1 and p_2 to both sites *Site3* and *Site4* where b_1 and b_2 and stored and compute the joins there, and combine the results and send them to *Site1*.
3. Compute the four fragments of the join at the four sites (p_1 and b_1, p_1 and b_2, p_2 and b_1, p_2 and b_2) using as much parallelism as possible.

13.9.3 Semijoin

The above techniques involve quite a bit of transferring of data from one site to another. One approach that can reduce the network traffic when the result of a join is small is called *semijoin.*

When we want to compute a join of R and S which are on different sites, semijoin involves sending only the join attribute values of R to the site that has S. This information is used to select those tuples of S that will contribute to the join of R and S. These selected tuples are now sent to the machine where R is located and the join is now computed.

13.9.4 Updates

Given the fragmentation and replication, the system needs to decide which fragment(s) of a relation need to be updated and how all copies will be updated.

One approach that is often used is that one copy of a replicated fragment is designated as a *primary* copy and primary copies are distributed in the system. Once a primary copy is updated, the update is assumed complete.

13.10 DISTRIBUTED TRANSACTION PROCESSING–CONCURRENCY AND RECOVERY

We have discussed various aspects of transaction processing, for example, concurrency, recovery, security and integrity in Chapters 9, 10, 11 and 12. All these become more complex in distributed database systems.

Concurrency control in a distributed system is different since parts of a transaction could be executed on different sites of the system. For a transaction to commit, it must commit on all sites. Also, each table that is modified in the transaction must be propagated to all replicas of the table in order to maintain database consistency.

13.10.1 Concurrency Control

Each site has a *transaction manager* which participates in concurrency control as well as in recovery. As described for the centralized database systems in Chapter 9, distributed database systems also need to ensure that the schedules of transaction satisfy the requirements of serializability and often the distributed systems use a *two-phase* commit protocol.

Two-Phase Locking

A number of issues must be resolved when using two-phase locking in a distributed database system. We look at the major issue first. How would locking on relations or fragments be implemented when there are a number of replicas available on the system? This is followed by a brief discussion of deadlock detection and prevention. It is clear that when a data item is to be locked then that lock should be obtained on all copies of the item. We briefly consider the two approaches:

- *Centralized 2PL*—In a centralized 2PL implementation, a central site is responsible for managing all transaction schedules. Therefore, all locking and unlocking requests must go through the central site. This can create problems if the central site fails.
- *Primary Copy 2PL*—In a primary copy 2PL implementation, one copy of each table or its fragments is designated as the primary copy. All locking and unlocking requests must go through the node that has the primary copy. All updates then must be propagated to the other replicas.

There are other approaches that have been proposed in the literature. One of them requires that instead of locking all replicas, a majority of replicas be locked. This ensures that two transactions will not be able to lock the same data item unless it is a shared lock.

Deadlock Detection and Prevention

As discussed in Chapter 9, two-phase locking can lead to deadlocks which must be detected and then resolved. The concept of wait-for-graph was introduced in that chapter. A cycle in the graph meant there is a deadlock. Once a deadlock is detected it must be resolved by restarting one of the transactions.

To detect deadlocks in distributed database systems, each site maintains its own wait-for-graph. A local deadlock can then be easily detected but a deadlock involving two or more sites works differently when centralized 2PL is used or primary copy 2PL is used, since in centralized 2PL information about all locks is maintained by the lock manager on the central site. The lock manager then regularly checks for a deadlock and takes action when a deadlock is detected. The situation is more complex when the primary 2PL is used. One approach that has been proposed is hierarchical deadlock detection. It involves all the nodes organized as a hierarchy and deadlock detection is carried out at each node of the hierarchy.

As discussed in Chapter 9, it is possible to use deadlock prevention which involves restarting transactions whenever there is a possible danger of a deadlock.

13.10.2 Recovery

The issue of recovery in a distributed database is also more complex than in a centralized database system, since there are a number of other failures which may occur. For example, a site may fail, some messages may get lost or a link connecting two sites may go down.

In spite of these complexities of the distributed databases, if the recovery is log-based then the fundamental principle of DO, UNDO, REDO must be followed. There are a lot of complex details of log-based recovery in distributed databases that we are not able to cover here. These details include the following:

1. How the log of each node would be maintained and used when recovery is required?
2. How would the operations DO, UNDO and REDO work when each transaction may be running on a number of sites using different replicas of table fragments?
3. If one of the sites fails while others continue to work, what recovery is required? How is the recovery process affected by fragmentation and replication?

We will not discuss these issues any further in this textbook. Readers interested in detailed study may refer to the books listed in the bibliography.

SUMMARY

In this chapter we have discussed the meaning a distributed database system and its features. The following topics have been covered:

- A distributed database system (DDS) is a union of two important technologies: database management and computer networks.
- DDS and its features are described. The features include distribution of data at a number of sites that are interconnected by high speed network giving the user a feeling that it is logically a single database.
- There are a number of motivations for implementing distributed database systems. Perhaps the most important is that a distributed database matches the nature of many large enterprises that have a number of branches.
- Simple examples of DDS are two-tier and three-tier client server systems that are widely used today.
- A DDS can be of a number of types including a fully connected system, partially connected system or a ring connected system.
- A number of examples of distributes database systems are presented including the Google system with 500,000 commodity computers connected in 200 clusters.

- When a centralized database system is the best option and when a distributed database system may be better is explained. Perhaps a DDS is better when it matches the distributed structure of an enterprise although a DDS is complex to implement.
- Major objectives when designing a distributed database system include location transparency, network transparency, replication transparency and fragmentation transparency.
- Fragmentation is an important issue in the design of DDS. A number of issues need to be considered, for example, why fragment and how to make sure that the fragmentation is correct.
- Fragmentation may be horizontal fragmentation or vertical fragmentation and horizontal fragmentation may be primary fragmentation or derived fragmentation.
- Primary horizontal fragmentation is based on minterms; a minterm is a logical expression of a number of variables (or their complements) consisting of only the logical AND operator. An example of a variable is Country = 'India' or its complement. Examples of using such variables in minterms are presented.
- Derived horizontal fragmentation is also illustrated.
- Vertical fragmentation may be obtained based on an affinity matrix but all vertical fragments must have the primary key to ensure correctness. Hybrid fragmentation combines the two concepts.
- Use of fragmentation and replication in distribution of data across a number of sites is considered.
- Distributed query processing and distributed transaction processing including concurrency and recovery are briefly introduced.

REVIEW QUESTIONS

1. What are the motivations for using distributed database systems? (Section 13.1)
2. What is a distributed database system and what are its features? (Section 13.2)
3. What are the main advantages and disadvantages of a distributed database as compared to a centralized database system? (Section 13.3)
4. What is a two-tier client-server database system and a three-tier system? (Section 13.3)
5. Give two examples of a distributed database system. (Section 13.3)
6. What are three major objectives of distributed database design?(Section 13.4)
7. List three major advantages of distributed database systems. (Section 13.3)
8. List three major disadvantages of distributed database systems. (Section 13.3)
9. Give an example to illustrate the different types of fragmentation. (Section 13.5)
10. What is a minterm? (Section 13.5)
11. Describe primary horizontal fragmentation using minterms?(Section 13.5)
12. What is derived horizontal fragmentation? (Section 13.5.3)
13. What is vertical fragmentation and hybrid fragmentation?(Section 13.5.4)
14. Give an example when hybrid fragmentation might be useful? (Section 13.5.5)
15. Why is it useful to have fragmentation and replication of data in a distributed database system? (Sections 13.5 and 13.6)
16. Why is replication used in distributed databases? (Section 13.7)

17. Describe how data should be replicated and distributed in a distributed databases. (Section 13.7)
18. Describe the major differences between query processing, centralized query processing and distributed query processing. (Section 13.8 and 13.9)
19. List two major issues that need to be considered in distributed query processing. (Section 13.8 and 13.9)
20. List two issues that are important in distributed transaction management. (Section 13.10)

SHORT ANSWER QUESTIONS

1. Give an example of an Indian organization that will benefit from implementing distributed database system.
2. What do you think will be the benefits of implementing DDB for the organization you selected in Question 1?
3. List three features of DDB.
4. What is the major difference between a two-tier system and a three-tier system?
5. List three advantages of DDB.
6. List three disadvantage of DDB.
7. List five major objectives of distributed database design.
8. Give an example of a simple database where horizontal fragmentation might be useful.
9. Give an example of a simple database where vertical fragmentation might be useful.
10. Give an example of a simple database where hybrid fragmentation might be useful.
11. What is replication?
12. What are the different techniques of replication?
13. How should data be replicated if many updates are being performed on the database?
14. What is the biggest disadvantage of a system without any replication?
15. Name two rules of thumb used in centralized query processing that may still be used in distributed query processing.
16. What is query shipping?
17. What is data shipping?

MULTIPLE CHOICE QUESTIONS

1. Which one of the following is **not** part of the definition of distributed database systems?
   (a) It has multiple database systems.
   (b) There is no central controlling site.
   (c) The database systems are logically related.
   (d) The database is physically distributed.
2. Which one of the following is correct?
   (a) A client-server system may not be considered as a distributed database system.
   (b) A client server always has only one server.

(c) A client-server system always has only one client.

(d) A three-tier client-server system has a presentation tier, an application tier and a DBMS tier.

3. Which one of the following is correct?

(a) Each site relies on the central site for DBMS service and has no DBMS facilities of its own.

(b) Each site is a nothing-share commodity computer.

(c) The distributed DBMS has full functional capacity of a DBMS.

(d) Each site has a duplicate copy of the entire database.

4. There are a number of different types of distributed database systems. Which of the following may be classified as a distributed system?

(a) Fully connected (b) Partially connected

(c) Star connected (d) All of the above

5. Which one of the following enterprises probably does not require a distributed system?

(a) The University Grants Commission (UGC) (b) Indian Railways

(c) Indian Overseas Bank (d) Air India

6. Which one of the following is correct regarding fragmentation?

(a) Primary horizontal and primary vertical fragmentation are possible.

(b) Derived horizontal and derived vertical fragmentation are possible.

(c) Vertical fragments may be based on minterms.

(d) Fragmentation may be based on hybrid fragmentation.

7. Which one of the following is correct regarding vertical fragmentation?

(a) A relation *R* may be broken into a number of vertical fragments which only require that they together must include all attributes of *R*.

(b) One vertical fragment must include the primary key of *R*.

(c) Two vertical fragments must include the primary key of *R*.

(d) All fragments must include the primary key of *R*.

8. Which one of the following is **not** correct about vertical fragmentation?

(a) Vertical fragmentation may be based on a heuristic that groups the attributes even if it produces overlapping fragments.

(b) Vertical fragmentation may be based on splitting the attributes and producing non-overlapping fragments; each fragment including the primary key.

(c) Vertical fragmentation works well even for a table with only a few attributes.

(d) The procedure of vertical fragmentation may be based on using an affinity matrix before partitioning.

9. Which one of the following is unlikely to be an example of a distributed database?

(a) Google database of web pages (b) Indian electoral database

(c) A library catalogue database (d) Income tax department database

10. Which of the following are features of a distributed database?

(a) Data stored at a number of sites. (b) All sites connected by a high-speed network.

(c) Each site running its own database. (d) All of the above

11. Which of the following are advantages of distributed databases?
    (a) A distributed database matches distributed structure of enterprises.
    (b) A distributed database provides local autonomy.
    (c) A distributed database provides improved performance since most data is available locally.
    (d) All of the above
12. Which one of the following is **not a disadvantage of distributed databases?**
    (a) Complexity of design and management. (b) Cost of developing
    (c) Security concerns (d) All of the above
13. Which one of the following is **not an objective in designing a distributed database?**
    (a) Location transparency (b) Hardware independence
    (c) Replication transparency (d) Fragmentation transparency
14. Which one of the following is **not a correctness property of fragmentation?**
    (a) Completeness (b) Disjointness (c) Losslessness (d) All of the above
15. In fragmenting the table *Player* in the cricket database, assume that three simple predicates used are *Country* = 'India', *Country* = 'Australia' and finally *Country* = 'Sri Lanka'. Eight minterms may be derived from these simple predicates. How many of the eight are meaningless?
    (a) 2 (b) 4 (c) 3 (d) 6
16. For the table *IFC* in Fig. 13.22, a horizontal fragmentation is proposed based on simple predicates *NFilms2* > 30 and *LCity* = 'Mumbai'. How many fragments will be obtained based on meaningful minterms based on these simple predicates?
    (a) 1 (b) 2 (c) 3 (d) 4
17. A table with 10 rows is fragmented into four tables using hybrid fragmentation. How many rows in total will appear in the four tables?
    (a) 10 (b) 20 (c) 30 (d) 40
18. Consider the animal table given later for Project 3. Consider simple predicates "*Weight* > 100" and "Weight ≤ 50". How many minterms based on these predicates are meaningful?
    (a) 1 (b) 2 (c) 3 (d) 4
19. Assume that the relation *Player* has been fragmented in six fragments as shown in Section 13.6.2 and distributed to six sites. We now wish to derive fragments for relations *Batting* and *Bowling*. Using the minterms used in fragmenting *Player*, how many fragments of each relation *Batting* and *Bowling* may be derived?
    (a) 4 (b) 6 (c) 8 (d) None of the above
20. Consider the query, 'Find the names of all players from India who have made a century'. The query involves a selection, a join and a projection. The relations *Player* and *Batting* have both been fragmented into six fragments and have been replaced twice. Which of the operations require the most data communication?
    (a) Selection (b) Projection (c) Join (d) Each is about the same

EXERCISES

1. The issues of database security have not been discussed in this chapter. Explain how security issues in distributed database systems are different from those in centralized database systems.
2. Discuss the horizontal, vertical and hybrid fragmentation schemes. Explain the properties all fragmentation schemes must satisfy?
3. What is meant by transparency and autonomy? Why are these concepts desirable in distributed database systems?
4. What is meant by fragmentation transparency, replication transparency and location transparency? Describe why these are important in database systems.
5. Why is global query optimization difficult in distributed databases? Describe some of the issues in query processing in distributed systems.
6. How do the locks get managed in a distributed database given that relations are fragmented and replicated? What steps of the lock granting, deadlock prevention and deadlock detection are different in distributed database systems? Provide details.
7. Explain how concurrency control may be applied in distributed database systems. How do two-phase commit protocols and three-phase commit protocols work in distributed database systems?
8. Can the timestamping technique of concurrency control be used in a distributed database system? Describe how it might work in the distributed systems.
9. Explain how the recovery techniques used in centralized database systems need to be modified for a distributed database system.
10. What happens in a distributed system if the central database system node fails? How can the database continue to function and how would the recovery take place?
11. Find two simple predicates for the table *IFC* given in Fig. 13.21 and derive the minterms. Use the minterms to obtain horizontal fragmentation of the table.
12. Consider the query, 'Find the names of all players from India who have made a century'. The query involves a selection, a join and a projection. The relations *Player* and *Batting* have both been fragmented into six fragments and have been replaced twice. Describe how this query may be processed.
13. Discuss the major problems in concurrency control in a distributed database system.
14. How would views be managed in a distributed database systems? Describe in detail where the views may be defined and where the view definitions be stored and how queries including views will be processed.
15 Consider the problem of maintaining accurate metadata in a distributed database system. Explain how metadata should be maintained if the database is fragmented and fully replicated, fragmented and partially replicated and not fragmented and not replicated.
16. We posed the following questions regarding recovery in distributed database systems. Answer each of the questions.
    - How would the log of each node be maintained and used when recovery is required?
    - How would DO, UNDO and REDO work when each transaction may be running on a number of sites using different replicas of table fragments?
    - If one of the sites fails while others continue to work, what recovery is required? How is the recovery process affected by fragmentation and replication?

PROJECTS

1. We have not discussed integrity constraints for distributed database systems in this chapter. Consider each integrity constraint given in Chapter 12 and describe how implementation of the constraint will be different in distributed database systems.
2. Consider a distributed databases system which has a number of sites located all over the world. The sites are connected by a variety of networks which have different speeds. The sites also have computers that have different level of resources and their CPU speeds are quite different. From time to time data from one site must be transferred to another depending on the demand for that data. How would these factors affect distributed query processing and transaction management? Discuss in detail.
3. Consider the following table that gives information about a number of mammals, their weight, gestation period and composition of their milk. Find two simple predicates that may be used in horizontal fragmentation and derive the minterms. Use the minterms to obtain horizontal fragmentation of the table.

ID	*Animal Name*	*Size*	*Weight (kg)*	*Gestation Period (days)*	*Milk Protein*	*Milk Fat*	*Milk Lactose*	*Milk Ash*
1	Buffalo	L	500	280	5.9	7.9	4.7	0.78
2	Camel	L	400	405	3.5	3.4	4.8	0.71
3	Cat	S	10	60	10.1	6.3	4.4	0.75
4	Cow	L	400	270	3.9	4.9	5.1	0.8
5	Deer	M	75	200	10.4	19.7	2.6	1.4
6	Dog	S	25	60	9.3	9.5	3	1.2
7	Elephant	XL	4000	625	3.6	17.6	5.6	0.63
8	Fox	M	50	54	6.6	5.9	4.9	0.93
9	Goat	M	75	150	3.6	3.9	4.6	0.79
10	Guinea Pig	XS	2	21	7.4	7.2	2.7	0.85
11	Hippo	L	1500	237	0.6	4.5	4.44	0.1
12	Horse	L	400	330	2.6	1	6.1	0.35
13	Human	M	80	270	1.1	4.5	6.8	0.2
14	Monkey	M	40	165	2.2	2.7	6.4	0.18
15	Orangutan	M	50	180	1.4	3.5	6	0.24
16	Pig	M	60	110	7.1	5.1	3.7	1.1
17	Rabbit	XS	2	30	13.3	13.1	1.9	2.3
18	Rat	XS	2	20	9.2	13.6	3.3	1.4
19	Sheep	M	80	145	5.6	6.4	4.7	0.91
20	Whale	XL	20000	425	11.1	21.2	1.6	0.85
21	Zebra	L	120	365	3	4.8	5.3	0.7

4. After obtaining horizontal fragments in the last exercise, does it make sense to use those fragments and derive hybrid fragments? If not, why? Discuss.

LAB EXERCISES

1. For the table *Player* in the cricket database consider simple predicates "Country = 'India'" and "Country = 'Australia'". Which of the following are meaningful minterms?
   (a) Country = 'India' AND Country = 'Australia'
   (b) Country = 'India' AND Country ≠'Australia'
   (c) Country ≠'India'" AND Country ≠'Australia'
   (d) Country ≠'India'" AND Country = 'Australia'
   Discuss the remaining minterms and explain why they are meaningful or not.
2. Consider the cricket database that we have used in this book. Suppose the data is distributed amongst nodes in England, West Indies, Australia and India. Describe how you will fragment, replicate and distribute the data.
3. Assume that the database is fragmented and replicated. Select five different queries from Chapter 5 and discuss how they will be carried out.
4. When an ODI match is being played, the data is being updated as the game progresses. Describe how the updates of the data will be carried out in a fragmented and replicated database.

BIBLIOGRAPHY

For Students

There are not many new and good books on this topic. The book by Oszu and Valduriez is the standard book. The first book in the list below provides a good introduction.

For Instructors

A new book by Rahimi and Haug has recently been published and it is a comprehensive 700+ page book that deals with most aspects of distributed databases. The book by Oszu and Valduriez is quite good but is a bit dated. The book by Artre also provides a good introduction. The article by Chang *et al.* is an introduction to Google's BigTable. The manual on distributed Oracle database is also useful. The Kossman survey paper on distributed query processing; Bernstein and Goodman's paper on distributed concurrency; Mohan, Lindsay and Obermarck's paper on distributed transaction processing in R* and other papers on R* are all good papers on different aspects of distributed databases. The paper by Stonebraker et al., describes a wide-area distributed database system.

Apers, P., "Data Allocation in Distributed Database Systems", *ACM Transaction on Database Systems*, Vol. 13, 1988, pp 263-304.

Atre, S., *Distributed Databases, Cooperative Processing and Networking*, McGraw Hill, 1992, 256 pp.

Bell, D., and J. Grimson, *Distributed Database Systems*, Addison-Wesley, 1992, 424 pp.

Bernstein, P., N. Goodman, E. Wong, C. Reeve, and J. Rothnie, "Query Processing in a System for Distributed Databases (SDD-1)", *ACM Transactions on Database Systems*, Vol. 6, pp 602-625, 1981.

Bernstein, P., D. Shipman, and J. Rothnie, "Concurrency Control in a System for Distributed Databases (SDD-1)", *ACM Transactions on Database Systems*, Vol. 5, pp 18-51, 1980.

Bernstein, P., and N. Goodman, "Concurrency Control in Distributed Databases Systems", *ACM Computing Surveys,* Vol. 13, 1981, pp 185-221.

Bernstein, P., and E. Newcomer, Replication, Chapter 9, *Principles of Transaction Processing,* Second Edition, 2009, pp 245-279.

Bertino, E., L. Haas, and B. Lindsay, "View Management in Distributed Database Systems", *Proceedings of the 7th International Conference on Very Large Databases,* 1981, pp 166-178.

Burleson, D. K., *Managing Distributed Databases: Building Bridges between Database Islands*, John Wiley and Sons, 1995, 367pp.

Ceri, S., and G. Pelagatti, *Distributed Databases: Principles and Systems*, McGraw-Hill, 1984, 393pp.

Chang, F., J. Dean, S. Ghemawat, W. C. Hsieh, D. A. Wallach, M. Burrows, T. Chandra, A. Fikes, and R. E. Gruber, "Bigtable: A distributed Storage System for Structured Data", *Proceedings of the Operating Systems Design and Implementation*, OSDI'06 Conference, Seattle, November 2006, pp 205-218. http://static.googleusercontent.com/external_content/untrusted_dlcp/labs.google.com/en//papers/bigtable-osdi06.pdf

(PowerPoint of a talk about this paper is available at http://osnet.cs.nchu.edu.tw/powpoint/seminar/2009/Bigtable_A_Distributed_Storage_System_for_Structured_Data.pdf

Distributed Database Management, Oracle Database Administrator's Guide, Part VII, 10g Release. http://download.oracle.com/docs/cd/B19306_01/server.102/b14231/part7.htm

Date, C. J., "Distributed Database: A Closer Look", In C. J. Date and H. Darwen, *Relational Database Writings 1989-1991*, Addison-Wesley, 1992.

Fong, E., C. L. Sheppard, and K. A. Harvill, *Guide to Design, and Management of Distributed Databases*, US Department of Commerce, 1991, 53 pp.

Helal, A. A., A. A. Heddaya, and B. B. Bhargava, *Replication Techniques in Distributed Systems*, Springer, 1996.

Kossman, D., "State of the Art in Distributed Query Processing", *ACM Computing Surveys*, Vol. 32, December 2000, pp 422-469.

Lindsay, B. G., L. Haas, C. Mohan, P. F. Wilms, and R. A. Yost, "Computation and Communication in R*: A Distributed Database Manager", *ACM Transactions on Computer Systems,* Vol. 2, 1984, pp 24-38.

Lohman, G., C. Mohan, L. Haas, D. Daniels, B. Lindsay, P. Selinger, and P. Wilms, "Query Processing in R*", *In Query Processing in Database Systems*, W. Kim, D. Reiner, and D. Batory, (Editors), Springer Verlag, 1984.

Mohan, C., B. Lindsay, and R. Obermarck, "Transaction Management in R* distributed database management system", *ACM Transactions on Database Systems,* Vol. 7, 1982, pp 187-208.

Obermarck, R., "Distributed Deadlock Detection Algorithm", *ACM Transactions on Database Systems,* Vol. 11, 1986, pp 378-396.

Ozsu H. T., and Valduriez P., *Principles of Distributed Database Systems*, Third Edition, Springer, 850 pp. 2011.

Rahimi, S. K., and F. S. Haug, *Distributed Database Management Systems: A Practical Approach*, Wiley-Blackwell, June 2010, 896 pp.

Stonebraker, M., P. M. Aoki, W. Litwin, A. Pfeffer, A. Sah, J. Sidell, C. Staelin, and A. Yu, "Mariposa: A wide-area Distributed Database System", *The VLDB Journal*, 1996, pp 48-63.

Yu, C. T., and C. C. Chang, "Distributed Query Processing", *ACM Computing Surveys*, Vol. 16, 1984, pp 399-433.

Object-Oriented Databases 14

OBJECTIVES

- Explain the benefits of the object database model.
- Present an overview of the object database model.
- Explain the concepts of objects, literals, object identity, attributes and relationships.
- Discuss types, classes, inheritance and encapsulation.
- Describe the Object Definition Language (ODL).
- Explain the Object Query Language (OQL).
- Explore the differences between the relational model and the object model.
- Introduce the concept of object-relational databases and describe some object features of SQL:1999.

KEYWORDS

Object-oriented approach, objects, literals, OID, types, classes, object data model, inheritance, supertype, subtype, attributes, relationships, encapsulation, set, bag, array, list, dictionary, object definition language, ODL, object query language, OQL, transactions, constraints, object-relational, SQL:1999.

A customer is the most important visitor on our premises; he is not dependent on us. We are dependent on him. He is not an interruption in our work. He is the purpose of it. He is not an outsider in our business. He is part of it. We are not doing him a favour by serving him. He is doing us a favour by giving us an opportunity to do so.

Mahatma Gandhi

14.1 INTRODUCTION

Relational database systems have been very effective in dealing with most types of OLTP needs because of the simplicity of the relational model. The simplicity is relational model's strength and it is also its weakness for developing some complex applications as we will see in this chapter.

As we discussed in Chapter 3, the relational model consists of the following three components:

1. *Data Structure*—The data structure in the relational model is very simple since the data structure is a relation which represents either an entity or a relationship, and each tuple in a relation represents an instance of the entity or the relationship.
2. *Data Manipulation*—Three relational languages for data manipulation were presented. Two formal languages, relational algebra and relational calculus, were presented in Chapter 4. The third was a commercial relational language which has become the standard database language for current systems. It is SQL and it was discussed in detail in Chapter 5.
3. *Data Integrity*—Data integrity was briefly discussed in Chapter 3 and in more detail in Chapter 12. The basic integrity included existential integrity, referential integrity, domains and NULLS. More complex constraints like triggers have been introduced in SQL.

In modeling relational databases we used the entity-relational modeling technique which modeled an enterprise as a set of entities and relationships, both of them with attributes. To deal with some more complex situations we explored generalization and specialization.

After the relational theory was presented in the 1970s, many database vendors started calling their products relational. As a result, Codd proposed 13 rules that fully relational DBMS must satisfy. This standardization of the relational model and standardization of SQL helped the relational model achieve portability of database applications.

We will try to describe the object-oriented databases (ODMS) using a structure like that given above for the relational model. The relational model was defined by Codd. There is no such individual who has similarly defined the object model. A group of experts however, presented a manifesto (Atkinson et al., 1990) for object database systems in 1990. The manifesto, which we will discuss briefly later, was influential but another group of some 30 professionals, many representing companies that were producing object database systems, formed the Object Database Management Group (ODMG) in 1991 to formulate standards for the object-oriented database systems. The latest ODMG standard includes the *object model*, the *object definition language* (*ODL*) and the *object query language* (*OQL*). In addition, the standard defines bindings to three object-oriented programming languages. We will briefly discuss the standard and much of our discussion in this chapter is based on the work of ODMG which produced five revisions of its guidelines including versions ODMG 1.0, 2.0 and 3.0 before the group was disbanded in 2001. The work was then taken over in 2004 by the Object Management Group (OMG).

In 2006, the OMG formed the Object Database Technology Working Group (ODBT WG). This group is working on the 4th generation of an ODMS standard. References to ODMG and OMG publications are given in the bibliography at the end of the chapter.

We first define an object-oriented database system using a definition given by the ODMG.

> **Definition—Object Database Management System (ODMS)**
> *An ODMS is a DBMS that integrates database capabilities with object-oriented programming language capabilities.*

Therefore, an ODMS is a database which is a collection of objects. Objects are the essential structure of an ODMS. Objects are persistent, i.e., residing on a disk, while in object programming languages the objects are transient. ODMS is essentially built on top of object-oriented programming languages like Java and C++ which do not have persistence. We may therefore express it in the following manner:

ODMS (Persistent Objects) = Object Programming Language (Transient Objects) + Database Management (Persistence)

According to ODMG, there are three major components of the object-oriented model:

1. *The Object Model*—This essentially deals with the semantics of objects that may be stored in an ODMS.
2. *The Object Specification Language*—This deals with how objects are described to an ODMS using the Object Definition Language (ODL).
3. *The Object Query Language (OQL)*—This is the language that may be used to query a ODMS.

As noted earlier, in addition to these three major components, ODMG defines a number of language bindings, namely, for C++, Java and Smalltalk. We will not discuss the bindings in this chapter.

We first consider why the object approach is more appropriate in some applications.

14.1.1 Why the Object-Oriented Approach?

For some time the database community has started to recognize that 'one size does not fit all'. That is, the relational database systems are not the most effective database systems for all applications. For example, some web databases have abandoned traditional relational database systems for the so called "NoSQL" systems because such systems provide much higher scalability perhaps over thousands of nodes in a network. These systems provide little or no predefined schema and are very efficient for an environment where the system has to deal with many more readers than writers. Some vendors are modifying their relational systems to better deal with such newer applications.

Object-oriented database systems are another approach for some types of applications.

With increasing complexity of some applications, processing components of data processing are becoming more important. While storage and retrieval of data is still important, the focus is now on the actual operations performed on data. For example, in electronic banking the focus is on the operations that can be performed on accounts. This is because the operations are closer to what the user wants. Examples include opening an account, closing an account, transferring money to/from the account, making the account operable by others (e.g., joint accounts). These functions are more relevant than just the balance available in the account or the amount of money transferred. This is not to say that the values are not important, but from a user's perspective the values are only part of the overall behaviour.

In some other applications as well the relational model of a database in which the only data structure available is a relation is not always appropriate. Such applications include computer-aided design (CAD) and geographical information systems (GIS). In addition, the relational model also has problems dealing with entities that have multivalue attributes. If the multivalue attributes are represented using separate relations, some of the SQL queries become awkward.

One other point is worth noting here. Since SQL deals with sets and programming languages deal with one record at a time there is an *impedance mismatch* between SQL and procedural programming languages. It is because of this mismatch that complete application programs cannot be written in SQL and a host language, which does not understand relations and sets, must be used. The host language then uses a cursor that goes down the set returned by a SQL query. This mismatch does not occur in object databases since an object programming language may be used with a ODMS.

The differences between the relational model and the object-oriented model can be summarized as follows:

- Relational model is based on the concept of relations while object-oriented model is based on the concept of objects.
- Relational model requires that each element in a relation be atomic. The object-oriented model does not.
- Object model has a number of features that are not available in the relational model. These include
    - Immutable object identifiers
    - Inheritance
    - Encapsulation

As noted earlier, a richer data model is required for some types of applications. Object-oriented data model is an attempt to build such a richer database model.

We will discuss object database systems starting with the object model.

14.2 THE OBJECT MODEL

An object-oriented database is based primarily on the data structure called the *object*. The object concept originates from the concept of class which was proposed in the 1960s for the programming language *Simula*. The concept has more recently been used in a number of programming languages like *smalltalk, Java* and *C++*.

ODMG standard specifies the characteristics of objects, how objects can be related to each other, and how objects can be named and identified. It describes a number of constructs in the Object Model. The following list gives these constructs.

1. Basic primitives—the object and the literal

2. Type
3. State
4. Behaviour
5. Schema

We now discuss these constructs.

14.2.1 Basic Primitive—The Object

Objects and literals are the building blocks of the ODMG object model.

Humans interact with objects (living and otherwise) everyday. For example, students read books, use pens to write notes, and may play with a cricket ball. These objects have associated properties. A book has an author, a publisher and number of pages. A pen could be either an ink pen or a ball point pen. Both types of pen could have colour of ink as a property. It is possible to change this when using an ink pen by pouring in a different coloured ink or changing the ball point pen's refill. A cricket ball could be white or red, old or used.

Let us now define an object.

> ***Definition—Object***
> *An object is a combination of data which represents the state of the entity that the object represents and procedures which represent the object's behaviour.*

Therefore, an object is a combination of values and procedures or operations. In object terminology, the operations are called the object's *behaviour*. As we will discuss later, an object is identified by a unique identifier and possibly a name.

ODMG standard defines standard interface of each object as given in Fig. 14.1.

```
Interface Object{
Boolean same_as(in object other_object)
Object copy ();
Void delete();
}
```

Figure 14.1 ODMG standard for each object

ODMG standard describes a number of aspects of objects including their creation, their identifiers, names, lifetimes and structure. We discuss these aspects.

Object Identity

In the relational model, each tuple must have a unique identifier. Similarly in ODMS each object is uniquely identified by an unchangeable value given to it by the ODMS automatically when it is created. This value is called the *object identifier (OID)* and therefore an ODMS needs a reliable component within the system to generate OIDs and preserve them. In contrast to the primary key of a tuple in the relational model, the object identifier is not visible to the ODMS user. On the other hand, the primary key value of a tuple may be changed by using an update statement in a relational database thereby changing the instance of the entity that the tuple represents. The object model does not allow the object identifier to be changed during its life time. The OID is *immutable*.

Literals are not identified like the objects and have no identifier since literal values are essentially constant and their value cannot change.

Object Names

In addition to an OID, each object may also be given one or more names that can be used by the users. Essentially the system maps the name to the object identifier. Names are unique within a database but are not considered to be the same as keys.

Object Structure

Objects can be any of the three types, viz., atomic objects, collection objects, and structured objects. Each of these types supports a number of types.

- **Atomic Objects**—There are no built-in atomic objects. Therefore, all atomic objects are user-defined.
- **Collection Objects**—ODMG standard supports collection of objects, which may be collection of atomic types, or a collection of literals, or a collection in which each of them itself is a collection. A collection must have elements that are of the same type. The collections supported by the ODMG object model include the following:

    1. *Set*—It is a collection that is unordered and has no duplicates. The conventional set operations are allowed on the set.
    2. *Bag*—A collection that is unordered and may have duplicates. The union, intersection and difference operations are defined on this collection. It is also possible to find out how many times a particular element occurs in the bag.
    3. *List*—It is an ordered collection in which elements may be inserted. Operations on lists are positional, for example, it is possible to find the element given its position. Operations on lists are defined for selecting, updating, and deleting elements.
    4. *Array*—It is a dynamically sized, ordered collection in which elements may be replaced. Elements may be located by position and may be inserted, removed and the array may be resized.
    5. *Dictionary*—This is an unordered sequence of key-value pairs that maps keys to values. It has no duplicate keys. Operations to find, insert, delete and select entries have been defined on dictionary.

Standard interfaces are defined for each collection object. For example, an *array* has the following standard interface.

```
class       array : collection {
exception   Invalidindex{unsigned long index;};
exception   Invalidsize{unsigned long size;};
attribute   array<t> value;
void        remove_element_at(in unsigned long index)
              raises (InvalidIndex);
Object      retrieve_element_at(in unsigned long index)
              raises (InvalidIndex);
void        replace_element_at(in unsigned long index, in Object element)
              raises (InvalidIndex);
void        resize(in unsigned long new_size)
              Raises(InvalidSize);
};
```

Figure 14.2 ODMG standard interface for collection *array*

Dictionary has been defined to have the following interface.

```
class       dictionary : collection {
exception   KeyNotFound{Object key;};
exception   DuplicateName{string key;};
attribute   dictionary<t,v>value;
void        bind(in Object key, in Object value);
             raises(DuplicateName);
void        unbind(in Object key)
             raises(KeyNotFound);
Object      lookup(in Object key)
             raises(KeyNotFound);
boolean     contains_key(in Object key);
};
```

Figure 14.3 ODMG standard interface for collection *dictionary*

As shown above, all collections have a number of operations defined on them. For example, *set* and *bag* both allow operations for union, intersection and difference. List has a number of operations for removing an element, retrieving an element, replacing an element, inserting an element and concatenating two lists. As shown above, *array* allows removal of an element, retrieval of element and resizing of the array. Finally, as shown above, *dictionary* allows inserting, deleting and selecting entries in a dictionary object.

- **Structured Objects**—Lastly, ODMG data model defines the following structured objects, viz., date, interval, time, and timestamp.

  1. *Date*—Includes day, month and year and allows a number of operations including operations to check if a date is greater than a given date, less than a given date or equal to it. It is also possible to find the previous date, the next date, the date after a number of days. A number of other operations are also possible.
  2. *Interval*—Is a structured object that represents a duration of time in days, hours, minutes, seconds and milliseconds. Once again a number of operations are possible including checking if an interval is greater, less than or equal to another interval. Arithmetic operations are also possible on interval including plus, minus, product and quotient.
  3. *Time*—Is a structured object that defines time as a world time by specifying time in GMT and time zone. Operations like equal to, greater than and less than are defined on time.
  4. *Timestamp*—Is a structured object that defines the date and time. The usual operations have been defined on timestamp.

14.2.2 Basic Primitive–The Literal

Literals are different than objects, they have values and do not have identifiers. They may have a simple or a complex structure. ODMG standard describes a number of aspects of literals including types, copying, comparing, and equivalence. Literals can be any of the four types: atomic literal, collection literal, structured literal and null literal. Each of these types (except the null literal) supports a number of types of literals.

Atomic literals are basic data types that include numbers and characters and a number of other types, for example, short, long, float, char, and string. Enumeration types *Enum* is also included to declare values like (pass, fail) or (A, B, C, D, F). Collection literals are once again the same as defined for objects set, bag, list, array and dictionary. Structured literals include the same four that were discussed earlier for objects date, interval, time and timestamp.

Literals cannot be compared by identity since they have no identity. Comparison of literals is defined in detail in the ODMG standard.

14.2.3 Object Types and Classes

Each object is associated with an external specification including properties and operations which are visible to the user and one or more internal implementations which describe the internal aspects, for example, data structures and algorithms, which are not visible to the user. The external specification therefore is an abstract description of the operations and properties which the user may invoke. Thus the user may access the operations and the values of the state variables. As noted earlier, the internal implementation describes the data structures and algorithms. These are sometimes called *representation* and *methods*. For each operation, there is a representation and a method which are normally based on the language binding of the ODMS. The distinction between internal implementation and external specification is important and is the basis of information hiding and encapsulation that we shall discuss soon.

Objects are categorized by their types. A collection of objects of a given type share the same set of properties and common behaviour. An object associated with a type is called *instance* of that type. A class is a collection of objects of a type associated with an extent.

Classes play a role similar to the role that relations play in the relational model. A relation is a collection of entity (or relationship) instances. Similarly, a class is a means of organizing objects of the same type in a group. A class definition only defines the abstract behaviour and the state of the object type.

Extents

In the relational model, the database is defined by a schema which is then implemented as a set of relations. Similarly, in the object model, a distinction is made between a class and a set of objects in that class but the system designer must specify whether the system should maintain the extent of the class. The extent of a class, that is given a name other than the class name, is the set of all object instances of the class. To specify the distinction, the class name is followed by the keyword extent and the name chosen for the extent within parenthesis.

In some cases, a class with an extent may have identifying properties called *keys*. A key is called a *simple key* if it consists of a single property and called a *compound key* when it consists of a number of properties.

14.2.4 Attributes and Relationships

Attributes

Each object normally has a number of properties or attributes. Each defined attribute has a name and a value, and is a fact about the object, and is associated with a fixed type as described below. It is always either a literal or an object, and therefore object attributes can be quite different than the attributes in the relational model which requires attributes to be of atomic type. Some attributes may be designated as object identifier or object key which distinguishes an object from other objects. Some attributes may be implemented as procedures, for example, an attribute may be the batting average of a player which will be computed from all batting scores for the player.

Attribute types may include any of the following:

- *Atomic types*—These are the usual data types including integers, real numbers, character strings, Boolean, enumerators, etc. These are like PID, last name, first name, country name, place of birth and so on.
- *Collection types*—These include set, bag, list, array and dictionary collection types that we have discussed earlier.
- *Structure types*—These include record structures consisting of a number of components. It is similar to what is used in object programming languages. An example might be address.
- *Reference types*—These include references to another type. It is similar to pointers in some object programming languages.
- *Date*—It includes date, time and timestamp.

Use of attributes is demonstrated later when we define a number of objects.

Relationships

A relationship represents associations between different objects of different classes or the same class. In contrast to the relational model, the ODMG standard supports only binary relationships. Each relationship is given a name which identifies the relationship. The relationship also includes object identifiers of the related objects exactly like it does in the relational model. Each object in a relationship must have instances that may be referenced by its identifier.

Just like in the relational model, a relationship may be one-to-one, one-to-many or many-to-many.

An ODMS relationship is defined explicitly by declaration of traversal paths, each traversal path is declared as a pair, one for each direction of the relationship. Therefore, each relationship has a corresponding *inverse relationship*. Relational model of course allows inverse relationship in many-to-many relationship since such relationships are always represented by a separate table. For example, we are able to find the batting and bowling performance of a given player and for a given batting or bowling instance we can find the player.

As an example, the following relationship is included in the definition of the object *Player*. It defines a traversal path which allows the logical connection between the related objects. This relationship with the name 'bats' specifies that for each object of the type *Player* there is a relationship with one or more objects in *Batting*.

Relationship Set <*Batting*> *bats*;
    Inverse *Batting*::*batted*;

As noted earlier, traversal paths are always declared in pairs, one for each direction of the relationship. The inverse relationship is included in the definition of the object *Batting* as follows. The relationship with the name 'batted' specifies that in each object of the type *Batting* there is a relationship with only one object in *Player*.

Relationship *Player batted*;
Inverse *Player*::*bats*;

The above relationship between *Player* and *Batting* is therefore a one-to-many relationship. The cardinality is shown by using the keyword set and the angle brackets around the type *Batting* in the declaration for *Player* which indicates that each instance of *Player* is related with a set of objects in *Batting*. On the other hand, the declaration in *Batting* indicates that each instance of *Batting* is related to only one instance of *Player*.

In the above example of relationship we assumed that *Batting* is a class. In the entity-relationship model in Chapter 2, *Batting* and *Bowling* were many-to-many relationships, as tables, each with a number of attributes, between *Player* and *Match*.

In the object model, a relationship between the objects is specified in two complementary ways. Firstly, reference attributes are included in each of the involved objects. Secondly, a link connects the two objects, with an indication of the relationship cardinality. In a one-to-many relationship, the object on the 'one' side has a set reference attribute to the other object. In the case of a many-to-many relationship both objects have set reference attributes. Attributes of a relationship may be included by using a multiple value attribute.

Many-to-many relationships with many attributes may be more conveniently represented as a separate object. The object may then have one-to-many references to the the related objects. If a relationship is declared as an object then even ternary or higher relationship may often be represented in the object model. The object then has links to the other objects involved in the relationship. All the objects also include the reference attributes. It is somewhat similar to what we did in entity-relationship modeling. The use of reference attributes in an object that represents the relationship determines the degree of the relationship represented by that object.

There is no explicit integrity constraint declaration in ODMS like the foreign key constraint in the relational model. The ODMS is responsible for maintaining the bi-directional referential integrity. Integrity in ODMG model does not depend on key values. Therefore, if an object that is participating in a relationship is deleted then the traversal path to is also deleted.

14.2.5 Object Behaviour—Operations and Methods

As noted earlier, each object has associated with it certain operations that in the ODMG standard are called *operation signatures*. The operations are also called methods or behaviour. A signature is an executable code defined for a particular class. It has at least one object of the class as an argument. For example, the object *Player* may have associated with it a method that computes the age of the player or computes his age at the time of his first test. Each operation is defined on only a single type and the signature defines the name of the operation, a list of its arguments including their name and type. In addition, the types of values returned are defined and the names of any error conditions are listed. Some operations may have side-effects and return no value.

The behavior defines all the operations that may be done on an object and therefore defines how other objects may interface with it. These operations are the only ones that may be used to access and manipulate the object. This is somewhat different than what happens in the relational model in which each entity instance is a tuple and tuples may be manipulated by the same set of operations, for example, operations defined by relational algebra. Operations on objects can be executed by passing values like subroutine calls in programming languages. Operations therefore may be retrieval operations and update operations.

An object is therefore an entity that can have state and well defined behaviour. The facility by which data and its behaviour are integrated within an object is called *encapsulation* which we discuss in Section 14.2.7. Therefore, an object itself is a small little database in itself.

Interface

Interfaces define the ways the objects can interact with each other. An interface defines the abstract behaviour of an object since, ideally, the details of the implementation should be hidden. For example, the controls on a television allow us to change the channels, change the volume and mute the volume. But they do not define how these are actually implemented.

14.2.6 Class Hierarchies and Inheritance

We have dealt with the subtype-supertype (or type-subtype) relationship (also called ISA relationship) and inheritance in Chapter 2 when we discussed generalization and specialization.

Inheritance is a key concept in object database systems. Some experts consider inheritance to be the most important feature of object-oriented database systems. The concept is similar to the concept of inheritance that we discussed in Chapter 2 that allowed an entity to be a sub-entity of a super-entity. Inheritance allows objects to be instances of many types simultaneously. Usually the different entities in a complex system have some commonality. For example, in a drawing package, the user will be allowed to create different shapes. The drawing package will also provide a standard set of operations on these shapes including resize, copy, move and delete. One defines a *base* class which has all the common behaviours. The derived classes can define extra behaviour. If necessary, they are also allowed to change the common behaviour. So, the operations resize, copy, move, delete will be defined in the base class. If the drawing package supports drawing a circle, it could provide a derived class for circles. This derived class could define a special method to change the radius of the circle. The drawing package could also provide another derived class for rectangles. This derived class could define a special method to change the size of the sides.

Inheritance is therefore a relationship between classes that deals with sharing the implementation. This is called *class derivation*. In general, if class *C*1 is derived from class *C*2 then any public function belonging to *C*2 can be used by objects of class *C*1. However, *C*1 has the ability to override any function in *C*2.

As an example, we define an item that can be borrowed from a library. The data fields include the name of the item, the number of days it can be borrowed and if the item is actually available. This may be captured in the base class and is called 'borrow'.

Two derived classes may also be defined. The first class may be called Book which sets the borrowing limit to 21 days while the second class may be called Tape which sets the borrowing limit to 2 days. The constructors used in the derived class use the constructors in the base class.

To demonstrate inheritance, let us consider a generic bank account called Account. From the generic bank account we may derive specific bank accounts, for example, a joint bank account which looks similar to Account but has extra variable that shows the other owner of the account. The joint bank account inherits the properties of the object Account.

In the chapter on E-R modeling, we introduced the idea of specialization and generalization. These concepts included the idea of subclass/superclass forming class hierarchies in which a subclass inherited the properties of its superclass. An important concept in object data modeling is the concept of class hierarchies and inheritance.

14.2.7 State of an Object

The state of an object can be considered to consist of a set of values that the object contains. These values represent the object's properties. These properties, as noted earlier can be of two types, viz., *attributes* and *relationships*. An attribute is a fact about the object. It is has a name and a value, just like attributes in a tuple in the relational model. Some attributes may be designated as an object identifier or object key which distinguishes this object from other objects. A relationship represents associations between different objects. Each relationship is given a name which describes the relationship. The relationship also includes object identifiers of the related objects exactly like it does in the relational model.

The state may be constructed from other objects by using certain type of constructors.

Schema

Object model also has schemas, just like the relational model. The schema contains types of instances defined in the ODL and the ODMS is the based on the schema.

14.2.8 Abstraction and Encapsulation

The notion of an object provides the basics for *abstraction* and *encapsulation*. The concepts are related to abstract data types (ADT) and information hiding in object programming languages. The main advantage of these concepts is to localize the details. So to understand a certain aspect of the current system as well as make changes to them, one needs to study only a small part of the entire system. This is especially true if the system is very large.

Encapsulation is an important paradigm shift from relational model since encapsulation allows programming and persistent data to be integrated. Methods can execute in separate tier, caching data and offloading database server. Encapsulation and private attributes allow representation to be hidden. Full power of an object programming language can therefore be used.

Abstraction is the process of removing unnecessary or irrelevant details. There are two main types of abstractions, viz., procedural and data abstraction. Procedural abstraction removes the details of how procedures are actually implemented. They are usually specified in terms of high level behaviour. Similarly, data abstraction removes the details of how the data is actually represented. Aspects of the program that use the data use the procedures for manipulating the data and are not allowed to inspect the actual representation.

Encapsulation captures all the related behaviour in one entity. Thus the details are not available outside the object. So any behaviour that relies on the specific representation is prevented by encapsulation. This notion is similar to that of modularity where the source code for different objects is kept as separate modules. This allows for the code to be written and maintained independently.

Consider a record for a person. For the sake of this example, let us assume that we are interested only in their date of birth. An initial design could store the date of birth as an integer. Later the program is changed to store the date of birth as three integers (one each for the day, the month and the year). If information hiding was not implemented then all programs that used the age information must change to reflect the change in representation. However, if the internal representation were private, the class would have provided methods for the age. The only change would be to these methods but not the programs that were using these classes.

Example

Here is an example to illustrate abstraction and encapsulation. Initially a bank account may be represented by a positive number (say implemented as an unsigned integer). Later the bank decides to attach a character to the number to create a sting. The role of character is to signify the type of account (e.g., *S* for Savings, *C* for Chequeing). If the rest of the program relied on an account being a number, then one has to examine the entire program to be sure that one has changed all the relevant fragments.

This is error prone (how can one be sure one has changed all the fragments?). However, with abstraction and encapsulation only a small part that deals with the actual representation needs to be changed. The abstraction and encapsulation process would have hidden the details while providing functions to use the data.

Abstraction and encapsulation allows us to put together large and complex systems from simpler components which may be designed, implemented and tested independently of the other components. Within the large system, the simpler components interact with each other to exhibit the overall behaviour. For this to be effective, the simpler components need to have a well defined interface. Each aspect of the interface provides a well defined behaviour which can be invoked in a larger context.

14.2.9 Overriding, Overloading and Late Binding

Polymorphism is the ability for a class or procedure to handle a variety of types. That is, a given interface can be used in different situations. As an example, consider the function to sort data. The essence of the various sorting algorithms is not dependent on the data type. For example, in quicksort, one chooses a pivot and compares each value against the pivot to create two sub-lists. As long as a data type has a comparison function it is possible to use quicksort. This may be implemented using *overloaded* functions. An overloaded function is a collection of functions that have the same name but different specific semantics. So it is possible to write a quicksort function that operates on strings, as well as write another quicksort function that operates on integers. It is the system's task to select the right function using the type information. If the system cannot identify the correct function, an error occurs. In order to provide overloading functionality, the operation name must be resolved at run-time, this is called *late binding*.

14.2.10 Summary of Object Terminology

The table in Fig. 14.4 summarizes most of the object terminology.

Term	Definition
Object	An entity of interest that has properties and behaviour.
Object ID	A unique automatically generated object identifier that is immutable.
State	Attributes and relationships with other objects.
Type	Objects with the same state and behaviour.
Class	The implementation of a type is usually called the *class* to which the objects belong.
Extent	The extent of a class is the set of all object instances of the class.
Attribute	A property of an object that has a name and a value.
Signature	Each object has associated with it operations that are called operation signatures.
Inheritance	A relationship between classes that deals with sharing properties and implementation.
Encapsulation	All the behaviour of an object that is not available outside the object.

Figure 14.4 A Summary of Object Terminology

14.3 OBJECT SPECIFICATION LANGUAGES

The main aspect of object-oriented design is the identification of the types (or classes) required for the solution. Relevant relationships between these classes also need to be derived. The definition of classes should focus on the public interface as well as the data hiding that can be supported. While supporting data hiding, one should create the following: initial values inspector functions (functions that allow the state to be inspected) change functions (functions that allow the state to be altered). ODMG defines two object specification languages: Object Definition Language (ODL) and the Object Interface Format (OIF). We discuss the ODL.

14.3.1 Object Definition Language (ODL)

ODL is based on the ODMG object model that we have discussed. It is a definition language used to define the specifications of object types but is not a full programming language. ODL plays a role similar to the role of the data definition language (DDL) that we discussed for the relational model in Chapter 5 but is somewhat different than SQL DDL. The primary purpose of ODL is to create object specifications independent of any programming language.

14.3.2 Type Characteristics

A type may be defined by specifying its class. In such a definition, the characteristics of the class appear first. These may include supertype information, extent naming (no more than one is allowed) and specification of keys (more than one is allowed). The supertype of course requires its own definition.

A simple example for the class definition of a match is given below.

```
class Match
(extent Matches)
{
        attributes
```

```
                relationships
                operations
}
```

14.3.3 Instance Properties

A type's instance properties include the attributes and relationships of the instances.

Attributes

As described earlier, each type has a number of attributes that must be defined. Each attribute specification must start with the keyword as shown in the definition above.

Relationships

A relationship must define the traversal path. The specification will also include the cardinality of the relationship. For example, as described earlier, a relationship may look like the following:

Relationship Set <*Batting*> *bats*;
    Inverse *Batting*::*batted*;

This is a many-to-one relationship. The keyword relationship must be included in defining relationships.

14.3.4 Operations

ODL allows the operations to be specified when defining a class. Full details of standard operations are defined in ODMG standard.

14.3.5 Defining Classes

We will declare the classes corresponding to the tables we had created in Chapter 3 although we include some new information to illustrate inheritance. These classes are defined below in Figs. 14.5 to 14.10.

The additional information included is as follows:

- Information about officials involved in a test match will be included in the database. These people include umpires, TV umpire, match referee and reserve umpire.
- To illustrate inheritance we will create a class *Person*. All people participating in a test match will inherit properties from the object *Person*.

The basic form of specifying a class definition command is given below.

1. Each class definition includes a *class header* and a *class body*.
2. The class header defines the class properties including specification of supertypes, extent and keys.
3. The body of a class follows the header declarations. The body is contained in curly brackets {…}. The class body declares the state of each class instance including all the attributes and relationships. It also includes the instances behaviour. Therefore, the body may include.

    - Attributes
    - Relationships

- Operations
- Types
- Constants
- Exceptions

We now define a number of classes. Figure 14.5 defines the class *Person*. We have included attributes in this class that we expect to be common to all persons that are involved in a test match.

```
Class Person
(extent Persons)
{
    attribute ID;
    attribute string LName;
    attribute string Fname;
    attribute string Country;
    attribute integer Yborn;
}
```

Figure 14.5 Data definition for the class *Person* in ODL

Based on the class *Person* in Fig. 14.5 we now define a class *Official* in Fig. 14.6. The class *Official* now inherits all the properties of the class *Person*. Additional attributes have been included for officials including doneumpiring, doneTVumpiring and donematchrefereeing. These attributes record if the official has any previous experience of acting in a match. This class has a relationship with the class *Match* since each official is responsible for a match (and has been an official in many matches) and each match has a number of officials. Therefore, the relationship is many-to-many.

```
Class Official extends Person
(extent Officials)
{
    attribute boolean doneumpiring;
    attribute boolean doneTVumpiring;
    attribute boolean donematchrefereeing;
    Relationship Set Match officiates;
        Inverse Match::umpires;
}
```

Figure 14.6 Data definition for class *Official* in ODL

Figure 14.7 defines the class *Match*. Note that this class has the same attributes that the table *Match* did in Chapter 3. In addition, the definition has three relationships since each match has relationships with officials as well as with batting performance of each player that played in the match and with each player who has bowled in that match. Both relationships are many-to-one since a match has many batsmen and many bowlers but each batting record and bowling record relates to only one match. Also, each match has a numbers of officials.

```
Class Match
(extent Matches)
{
    attribute integer MatchID;
    attribute string Team1;
    attribute string Team2;
    attribute string Ground;
    attribute string Date;
    attribute string Result;
    Relationship Set <Batting> mbats;
        Inverse Batting::mbatted;
    Relationship Set <Bowling> mbowls;
        Inverse Bowling::mbowled;
    Relationship Set <Official> umpires;
        Inverse Official::officiates;
}
```

Figure 14.7 ODL Data definition for Class Match

Figure 14.8 defines the class *Player*. Note that this class has the same attributes that the table *Player* did in Chapter 3 since it inherits all the properties of the class *Person*. In addition, the *Player* definition in Fig. 14.8 has two relationships defined as part of the class. These relationships involve the player's batting performances and his bowling performances. The relationships are many-to-one since each player is allowed to have batted in more than one match and have bowled in more than one match.

```
Class Player extends Person
(extent Players)
{
    attribute string Bplace;
    attribute integer Ftest;
    Relationship Set <Batting> bats;
        Inverse Batting::batted;
    Relationship Set <Bowling> bowls;
        Inverse Bowling::bowled;
}
```

Figure 14.8 Data definition for class *Player* in ODL

Figure 14.9 defines the class *Batting*. Note that this class has the same attributes that the table *Batting* did in Chapter 3. In addition, the definition has two relationships defined as part of the class. One of the relationships (*batted*) is with the player whose batting it is, and the other relationship (*mbats*) is with the match in which the batting took place.

```
Class Batting
(extent Battings)
{
    attribute integer MatchID;
    attribute integer PID;
    attribute integer Order;
    attribute string Hout;
    attribute integer FOW;
    attribute integer Nruns;
    attributes integer Mts;
    attribute integer Nballs;
    attribute integer Fours;
    attribute integer Sixes;
    Relationship Player batted;
        Inverse Player::bats;
    Relationship Match mbatted;
        Inverse Match::mbats;
}
```

Figure 14.9 Data definition for class *Batting* in ODL

Figure 14.10 defines the class *Bowling*. Note that this class has the same attributes that the table *Bowling* did in Chapter 3. In addition, the definition has two relationships defined as part of the class. One of the relationships (*bowls*) is with the player whose bowling it is, and the other relationship (*mbowled*) is with the match in which the bowling took place.

```
Class Bowling
(extent Bowlings)
{
    attribute integer MatchID;
    attribute integer PID;
    attribute integer Novers;
    attribute integer Maidens;
    attribute integer Nruns;
    attribute integer Nwickets;
    Relationship <Bowling> bowled;
        Inverse Player::bowls;
    Relationship <Match> mbowled;
        Inverse Match::mbowls;
}
```

Figure 14.10 Data definition for class *Bowling* in ODL

To summarize, the class definitions illustrate the following:

1. Each class definition defines the external appearance of the class including attributes and relationships.

2. The definitions above include the extent, that is, collection of instances that have been given a name.
3. The definitions above are quite simple but in two cases they show inheritance and therefore, supertype/subtype relationships.
4. The attribute types are either boolean, integer or string.
5. Each class includes one or more relationships, many of which have been defined by relationship set indicating relationship with a number of objects and also an inverse relationship.

Now that the classes have been defined, we consider the object query language OQL.

14.4 OBJECT QUERY LANGUAGE (OQL)

The object model defined by ODMG does not include an object algebra although earlier research has defined an object algebra that includes, for example, the operation restriction to select objects that satisfy a given condition, the operation union to select objects from two collections, and other operations including intersection, difference, choose, join and so on. We do not discuss object algebra any further in this chapter.

We discuss Object Query Language (OQL) that is defined in the ODMG 3.0 standard.

The Object Query Language (OQL) is a declarative query language based on the ODMG's Object Model. ODMG followed an evolutionary approach in designing OQL and its syntax is in many ways similar to SQL although OQL has no update operator and no data definition commands, since they are included in ODL discussed earlier.

Many queries in SQL are also valid in OQL and have a similar meaning because OQL also uses the SELECT, FROM, WHERE structure. While every SQL query returns a relation as the result, OQL queries usually return a collection of objects which may be queried again. OQL may be invoked interactively or from within an object-oriented programming language for which an ODMG binding is defined. Many vendors do not support OQL interactive mode but have defined binding for Java.

Each query in OQL is called an *expression*. Every expression is built from typed operands and has a type which may be derived from the structure of the query.

We first deal with path expressions which allow us to navigate through an object database.

14.4.1 Dealing with Objects and Path Expressions

A collection of objects may be selected in OQL by specifying an attribute, a relationship or a method. This is done by using '.' which enables us to find the information we are after. For example, if *x* from *Players x* is an object in a class *Player*, then *x.a* may represent an attribute *a* of *x*, it may also represent a relationship of *x*. *x.a* may also represent a method *a* if the user wishes to apply the method to the object and retrieve the result.

This can be much more complex. For example *x.bats.mbatted.ground*, assuming *x* is a player, will find all his batting objects by traversing the relationship *bats* and then find all the matches by traversing another relationship *mbatted*, and finally find the grounds for each match.

Object Creation

Objects are created in OQL in a somewhat similar fashion as tables are created in SQL. To create an object a creation operation is invoked. The basic form of the object creation command that includes the keyword *class*, the name of the class and a list of properties is given below. Note that we have discussed the types of attributes and relationships earlier.

Person(ID: 21345, LName: "Ponting", FName: "Ricky", Country: "Australia", YBorn: 1974)

By specifying property names we are able to initialize them. Those that are not initialized are given default values.

Selecting Existing Objects

OQL allows a number of ways of selecting objects. For example:

1. A number of objects that are identified in a simple SELECT FROM, for example, SELECT x FROM Players x as shown in queries $Q1$ and $Q2$ below returns a collection of players.
2. A single object that is identified in a SELECT FROM WHERE query, for example, SELECT x FROM Players x WHERE x.LName = "Dhoni" returns details of the player Dhoni.
3. A collection of values or a single value often using a query like SELECT x.YBorn FROM Players x (returns a collection of values) or SELECT x.YBorn FROM Players x WHERE x.LName = "Dhoni" returns only one value. The first query may also be written as Players.YBorn without using the SELECT and the FROM clauses.

14.4.2 Simple Queries

The simplest type of OQL queries may be defined as follows:

<query> ::= <object name> | <literal value>

Given the above syntax of simple queries, the following queries are legal. These queries do not use the SELECT-FROM-WHERE clauses.

(a) Players
(b) Players.LName
(c) Players.YBorn
(d) "Ishant Sharma"
(e) 31
(f) 31*43
(g) 1.54
(h) True

The first three simple queries are object names or their properties. The first will return all the information from the collection *Players* while the second will return a collection of strings that are the last names and the third a collection of integers. The remaining queries return literals including a string, an integer, an arithmetic expression, a floating point number and a Boolean value respectively. Such queries may involve arithmetic calculations. These type of queries are obviously not useful when the query includes a condition like Country = "India".

The form of a simple OQL query using SELECT-FROM-WHERE clauses is given in Fig. 14.11. Similar to SQL queries, the meaning of this simple query is select objects from a collection <collection-object> where the condition specified by the <predicate> is true.

```
SELECT <variable>
FROM <collection-object> <variable>
WHERE <predicate>
```

Figure 14.11 Form of a Simple OQL query

The <collection-object> is usually an object name, for example, *Players*, but may also be another OQL query that returns a collection-object. The <variable> is just a variable that ranges over the collection objects. The variable name may be used in the SELECT clause, FROM clause and also the WHERE clause. This may be specified as presented above (*Players x*) or by formulating it as *x* IN *Players* or *y* in *x*.Country where *y* is a variable in the set *x*.Country which are the countries of players. Finally, the WHERE clause may include any predicate in order to select a number of objects that match the predicate. Join may be defined in the FROM clause by listing two collections, similar to what is allowed in SQL.

Using this OQL syntax, we may, for example, select all the objects from *Players* or some of the objects that have the value specified for a given attribute. UNDEFINED values are special literal values in OQL. This value may be tested by "is_undefined(*x*)" which returns true for undefined values. It is similar to NULL in SQL.

A method may be called within an OQL query. The notation for invoking a method is very similar to accessing an attribute or a relationship. The method may have parameters or it may be without any parameters. The result of executing the method is then returned.

We now illustrate OQL by presenting a number of queries.

- (*Q*1) Print all the objects *Player*.

Figure 14.12 shows how this query may be formulated in OQL.

```
SELECT p.ID, p.FName, p.LName
FROM Players p
```

Figure 14.12 OQL for query *Q*1

When the WHERE clause is omitted, all the objects in the collection are selected.

Note that the name in the FROM clause is a name of the extent of a class, which as we noted earlier, is a collection of objects from the class. The extent names in the four class definitions are *Players*, *Matches*, *Battings* and *Bowlings*.

- (*Q*2) Find all the information about objects *Players* from India.

Figure 14.13 shows how this query may be formulated in OQL. Since we are only interested in players from India, the WHERE clause is used to specify the condition.

```
SELECT x.FName, x.LName
FROM Players x
WHERE x.Country = "India"
```

Figure 14.13 OQL for query *Q*2

- (*Q*3) Find details of all matches played in Australia.

The WHERE clause specifies the condition that *Team1* is Australia as shown in Fig. 14.14.

```
SELECT m.Team1, m.Team2, m.Ground, m.Date
FROM Matches m
WHERE m.Team1 = 'Australia'
```

Figure 14.14 OQL for query *Q*3

14.4.3 Boolean Operators

In the last two queries we used a very simple predicate, for example, *x*.Country = "India". This type of conditions are sometime called atomic conditions but conditions can be much more complex using AND, OR and NOT. In OQL, AND and OR are specified by using *andthen* and *orelse*. We use these Boolean operators in the queries below.

- (*Q*4) Find all the information from the collection *Players* about players from India who were born after 1980.

Figure 14.15 shows how this query using arithmetic may be formulated in OQL.

In this query we are interested in players from India but only want players born after 1980. The conditions are specified using the WHERE clause.

It should be noted that the condition following *andthen* is evaluated only if the condition before the *andthen* is true. Furthermore, the arithmetic operations permitted are =, >, <, >=, <= and !=.

```
SELECT x
FROM Players x
WHERE x.Country = 'India'
ANDTHEN YBorn > 1980
```

Figure 14.15 OQL for query Q4

- (*Q*5) List matches played in which India or Australia was *Team1*.

The condition in this query is slightly more complex. Figure 14.16 shows how this condition may be formulated in OQL. The query could use aliases if the headings need to be changed. For example:

```
SELECT m.Team1 AS HTeam, m.Team2 AS Visitors, m.Ground, m.Date
FROM Matches m
WHERE Team1 = 'Australia'
ORELSE Team1 = 'India'
```

Figure 14.16 OQL for query Q5 using aliases for column names

Note that the condition following *orelse* is evaluated only if the condition before the *orelse* is false.

- (*Q*6) Find the *Player ID* of players who have made a century in each of the ODI matches 2755 and 2689.

The table *Batting* has a separate row for each innings. We can therefore either use a subquery or use a join. We use a join of table *Batting* with itself.

Figure 14.17 shows how this query may be formulated in OQL.

```
SELECT PID
FROM Batting b1, Batting b2
WHERE b1.PID = b2.PID
AND b1.MatchID = 2755
AND b2.MatchID = 2689
AND b1.NRuns > 99
AND b2.NRuns > 99
```

Figure 14.17 OQL for query Q6

14.4.4 Using DISTINCT and ORDER BY

- (*Q*7) Find IDs of all players that have bowled in an ODI match in the database and have claimed more than five wickets.

Figure 14.18 shows how this query may be formulated in OQL. A WHERE clause is not required since we want IDs of all players in the class *Bowling*.

```
SELECT DISTINCT b.PID
FROM Bowlings b
WHERE NWickets > 5;
```

Figure 14.18 OQL for query *Q7*

- (*Q*8) Display a sorted list of ground names where Australia has played as *Team1*.

This is a query that uses a WHERE clause to specify the condition that Australia is *Team1* and we use ORDER BY to sort the result.

Figure 14.19 shows how this query may be formulated in OQL.

```
SELECT m.Ground
FROM Matches m
WHERE Team1 = 'Australia'
ORDER BY Ground
```

Figure 14.19 OQL for query *Q8*

14.4.5 Checking for Undefined

- (*Q*9) Display the first and last name of an Indian player whose first test value is not defined.

The query is formulated as shown in Fig. 14.20 in which the *FTest* value is checked for being undefined.

```
SELECT x.FName, x.LName
FROM Players x
WHERE x.Country = 'India'
AND is_undefined (x.FTest)
```

Figure 14.20 OQL for query *Q9*

14.4.6 Using Joins

- (*Q*10) Joins may be used in a way similar to their use in the relational model. For example, consider the following query which retrieves the number of runs that Ponting has scored in the matches.

The query is formulated as shown in Fig. 14.21 in which the collections *Players* and *Battings* have been joined and a condition that the player is Ponting has been specified.

```
SELECT b.NRuns
FROM Players p, Battings b
WHERE p.id = b.id
AND p.LName = "Ponting"
```

Figure 14.21 OQL for query *Q10*

14.4.7 Using Subqueries

There are a number of formats for a query that uses a subquery. Three commonly used syntax formats are defined as follows:

<query> ::= <query> IN <query>
<query> ::= <query> <comparison_operator> [*SOME* | *ANY* | *ALL*] <query>
<query> ::= <query> [< | > | ≤ | ≥] <query>

The conditions involving SOME or ANY test for at least one in an object collection returned by the subquery and are therefore like existential quantifiers discussed in Chapter 4. A condition involving ALL tests for all objects in the collection returned by the subquery and is therefore more like universal quantification discussed in Chapter 4. We now illustrate these different types of subqueries.

• (*Q*11) Find *Match IDs* of all matches in the database in which Tendulkar batted.

As noted above, this query needs to use two classes as the player name is given only in the class *Player* and the batting performance is given only in the class *Batting*. We will use a subquery to obtain the *PID* of Tendulkar and use that information to obtain *Match IDs* of matches that he has played in.

This query is a simple use of a subquery. The subquery only returns a single constant which is compared with another value in the WHERE clause. If the comparison's result is true then the row in the outside query is selected otherwise it is not.

```
SELECT b.MatchID
FROM Batting b
WHERE b.PID IN
        (SELECT p.PlayerID
        FROM Player p
        WHERE p.Lname = 'Tendulkar')
```

Figure 14.22 OQL for query Q11

In a query like this in which the subquery returns only one value, *PID* IN could be replaced by *PID* = but if we are not certain that the result of the subquery will be a constant, then it is best to use the IN operator.

Figure 14.22 shows how this query may be formulated in OQL.

• (*Q*12) Find all the ground names where the umpire Buckner has officiated.

Figure 14.23 shows how the query *Q*12 may be formulated.

```
SELECT b.Ground
FROM Ground b
WHERE b.MID IN
        (SELECT p.MID
        FROM Officials p
        WHERE p.LName = 'Buckner')
```

Figure 14.23 OQL for query Q12

14.4.8 String Comparison

• (*Q*13) Find players whose name starts with 'Sin'

Figure 14.24 shows the OQL formulation for query *Q*13

```
SELECT p.FName, p.LName
FROM Players p
WHERE p.LName LIKE "Sin*")
```

Figure 14.24 OQL for query Q13

The query returns a collection of objects (or a bag) whose name starts with 'Sin'. The * denotes any string and therefore name Singh will match.

14.4.9 Using Aggregation

Just like in SQL, OQL allows aggregation using functions AVG, COUNT, SUM, MIN and MAX.

• (*Q*14) Find the maximum score of Tendulkar.

Figure 14.25 shows how this query may be formulated in OQL.

```
SELECT Max(b.NRuns)
FROM Batting b
WHERE b.PID IN
        (SELECT p.PlayerID
        FROM Player p
        WHERE p.Lname = 'Tendulkar' )
```

Figure 14.25 OQL for query Q14

14.4.10 Using GROUP BY and HAVING

Once again GROUP BY and HAVING clauses in OQL are similar to that in SQL. The OQL GROUP BY requires that it be followed by a field name, a colon and an expression. The HAVING clause is very similar to the HAVING clause in SQL.

- (*Q*15) Find the average runs scored by players that have an average score greater than 50.

```
SELECT b.PID, AVE(b.NRuns) AS Ave
FROM Batting b
GROUP BY PID: b.PID
HAVING (AVE(b.NRuns ) > 50)
```

Figure 14.26 SQL for query *Q*29

Very complex queries can be formulated in OQL since there may be queries included in the SELECT clause, in the FROM clause as well as in the WHERE, GROUP BY and HAVING clauses.

14.5 TWO 1990 MANIFESTOS

Two major manifestos were published in 1990. Both of them were considered the future of database systems beyond the relational systems. They have both been influential in the database community.

14.5.1 The ODMS Manifesto

The classical 1990 paper by Atkinson et al., presented a manifesto (a set of policies and aims) that according to a group of leading database experts each ODMS must support. The 13 mandatory features are the golden rules according to the manifesto and are listed below with brief explanations.

To meet the aims of the manifesto, an ODMS must support the following:

1. *Complex objects*—The ODMS must allow complex objects to be formed from simpler ones. It should be possible build complex objects from any object. Appropriate operators must be provided for objects that have been built.
2. *Object identity*—Each object in the ODMS must have a unique and immutable identifier (OID) that is independent of its value so that objects may be shared through references. Using object identifiers as in the relational model places the burden on the user to insure uniqueness of each object.
3. *Encapsulation of objects*—Each ODMS object has data and methods which consist of interface and implementation. There needs to be a clear distinction between the specification and the implementation of an operation. Furthermore, modularity is necessary for implementation by a number of programmers. Encapsulation provides a form of logical data independence.
4. *Types or classes*—The two concepts, type and class, are similar. The type summarizes common features of a collection of objects and has two parts; the interface and the implementation. A class is different than type. Specification of a class is the same as that of a type but it contains an object factory to create new objects and an object warehouse which is a set of objects that are instances of the class.
5. *Class or type hierarchies*—Classes will allow inheritance, i.e., each ODMS will allow class hierarchies so that specification and implementation may be reused. Possible inheritance may include substitution inheritance (inherit behaviour not values), inclusion inheritance (inherit structure not operations),

constraint inheritance (a type of inclusion heritance) and specialization inheritance (a subclass includes more specific information).

6. *Overriding, overloading and late binding*—This includes using the same name for different operations so that an ODMS method is redefined in subtype. Various versions of a method can exist in parallel and an appropriate method is selected at run time. This is called late binding.
7. *Computational completeness*—SQL is not complete but an OO database language should be computationally complete. Therefore, an ODMS must allow any computational function to be specified.
8. *Extensibility*—ODMS must allow users to define new types and there should be no difference between the system defined and user defined types.
9. *Persistent*—Data will be persistent. All data in an ODMS must survive after an application has finished execution.
10. *Secondary storage management*—An ODMS must provide all facilities needed for very large databases, as available in the relational databases. These include index management, data clustering, access path selection and query optimization.
11. *Concurrency*—An ODMS must provide concurrency as provided in RDBMS (ACID properties and serializability).
12. *Recovery*—An ODMS must provide recovery as provided in RDBMS (recovery procedures including logging of operations).
13. *Ad Hoc query facility*—It is a simple way of querying data. An ODMS must provide an ad hoc query language that is simple like SQL. The query language should therefore be high level, efficient and application independent.

In addition to the golden rules, the manifesto includes five optional rules. These are multiple inheritance, type checking and type inferencing, distribution, design transactions and versions.

It appears that the recommendations of the ODMG 3.0 meet many of the golden rules of this ODMS manifesto. Let us now look at another manifesto which was published about the same time. Yet another manifesto, this one for Object/Relational database systems was published as a book by Date and Darwen in 1998.

14.5.2 The Third Manifesto by the Committee for Advanced DBMS Function

The Committee for Advanced DBMS Function composed Michael Stonebraker, Lawrence A. Rowe, Bruce Lindsay, James Gray, Michael Carey, Michael Brodie, Philip Bernstein and David Beech. The Network and Hierarchical database systems were labeled the first generation database systems and the Relational Systems were labeled the second generation systems. The next generation database systems were called the third generation database systems. Although these two manifestos were announced more than 20 years ago, the third generation systems have been slow in coming to the market.

This manifesto presents three tenets[1] and 13 propositions that are listed below.

1. According to the Oxford dictionary, a tenet is a principle or belief, especially one of the main principles of a religion or philosophy. A proposition is a statement or assertion that expresses a judgement or opinion.

The Tenets of Third-Generation DBMS

- Tenet 1: Besides traditional data management services, third generation DBMSs' will provide support for richer object structures and rules.
- Tenet 2: Third generation DBMSs' must subsume second generation DBMSs. This is necessary given the huge investment in current OLTP systems.
- Tenet 3: Third generations DBMSs' must be open to other subsystems. There is a need to include 4GL, decision support tools, interfaces to spreadsheets and graphical interfaces.

Propositions Concerning Object and Rule Management

- Proposition 1.1: A third generation DBMS must have a rich type system. The rich types may include abstract data types, array type constructor, sequence type constructor, record type constructor, set type constructor, functions as a type, union type constructor, recursive composition of the constructors.
- Proposition 1.2: Inheritance is a good idea. As discussed in the previous ODMS manifesto, inheritance including multiple inheritance is considered essential.
- Proposition 1.3: Functions including database procedures and methods and encapsulation are a good idea. Once again this agrees with the rules discussed in the last section. Encapsulation is strongly supported.
- Proposition 1.4: Unique identifiers (UIDs) for records should be assigned by the DBMS only if a user-defined primary key is not available. A system defined UID is supported for situations where a user-defined never to change key does not exist.
- Proposition 1.5: Rules (triggers, constraints) will become a major feature in future systems. They should not be associated with a specific function or collection. Rules must be enforced by the DBMS but not bound to any function or collection.

Propositions Concerning Increasing DBMS Function

- Proposition 2.1: Essentially all programming access to a database should be through nonprocedural, high-level access language. The expressive power of a query language should be present in every database programming language.
- Proposition 2.2: There should be at least two ways to specify collections, one using enumeration of members and one using the query language to specify membership.
- Proposition 2.3: Updatable views are essential. It is often not possible to update relational views. Better approach for updating views is required. This may involve the user providing additional semantic information.
- Proposition 2.4: Performance indicators have almost nothing to do with data models and must not appear in them. Almost all performance issues are not data modeling issues.

Propositions that Result from the Necessity of an Open System

- Proposition 3.1: Third generation DBMSs' must be accessible from multiple high-level languages. These new DBMS need not be tightly connected to a particular programming language and it should be possible to write application programs in a variety of programming languages.
- Proposition 3.2: Persistent *X* for a variety of *Xs* is a good idea. They will all be supported on top of a single DBMS by compiler extensions and a (more or less) complex run time system. It is likely that a variety of persistent programming languages will be designed and each will require a compiler.

- **Proposition 3.3: For better or worse, SQL is intergalactic dataspeak. Since SQL is being used universally** for database queries, a new system must use it for commercial viability.
- **Proposition 3.4: Queries and their answers should be the lowest level of communication between a** client and a server.

14.6 ODMS VS RDBMS

We briefly discuss the strengths and weaknesses of the two database models; the object-oriented model and the relational model.

1. Relational database systems, sometime called the second generation database systems, mainly focus on business data processing applications and are inadequate for a broader class of applications.
2. Relational model is a corporate standard and a lot of data is already stored in relational databases. This data cannot easily be converted to object-oriented database systems.
3. Relational model is very simple, using only one simple data structure, the relation. It has very simple and powerful set operations.
4. Relational model is based on mathematical rigour.
5. Relational database systems provide very efficient implementations given that implementations have been refined and tuned over the last 20 years or more.
6. Relational model is poor in representing structural semantics since no semantics can be added to the simple data structure used. Simplicity forces all data to be accessed by using table names, key values and column names which results in the use of complex joins and subqueries.
7. Although views are useful in the relational model, the views are usually not updatable.
8. ODMS is more expressive using a richer data representation including behaviour of the information. This enables more complex relationships to be represented.
9. Objects can be organized in an inheritance hierarchy allowing some objects to inherit attributes and behaviours from other objects.
10. Relational model suffers from impedance mismatch which leads to application code complexity.

14.7 OBJECT-RELATIONAL MODEL AND OO FEATURES OF SQL

We now briefly discuss some object-oriented features that have been included in some of the relational database systems recently. In addition we briefly discuss the recent standards of SQL and the object-oriented features in the recent standards.

In the last section we discussed the strengths and weaknesses of the relational model. To overcome the weaknesses of the relational database systems, the relational systems have been extended. These extended systems are called *Object-Relational Database Systems*. The extended systems include features that are usually associated with the object-oriented model. These features include object identifiers, methods, inheritance and encapsulation. In addition, facilities have been included for complex entities.

New standards of SQL are large documents often difficult to comprehend fully. The standards consist of a number major parts which for draft SQL:2003 includes nine parts that in total are about 1000 pages long. Recent standards of SQL allow features that deal with objects and XML. There are two ways of modeling entities, either by a row in a table or by using abstract data types.

Other additions in SQL are as follows:

- *User-defined Abstract Data Types (ADTs)*—The idea of ADTs originated in the idea of information hiding in software engineering and later was adopted by object programming languages. The idea of ADTs in relational systems is to provide a facility similar to that of a class provided in the ODMS, since ADTs have attributes and behaviour:

```
CREATE TYPE (ADT_Name) (
Member_attributes_list
Methods Declaration);
```

- *Generalization and Specialization*—The supertype/subtype relationships are supported by SQL using ADTs. Inheritance not only appears in type hierarchies, it may also be used in table hierarchies. The construct used is CREATE OBJECT TYPE Player UNDER Person and is therefore very similar to what is used in ODMS. For example:

```
CREATE TABLE Player OF Person_type
CREATE TABLE Player UNDER Person
```

- *Assertions and Triggers*—These have been discussed in Chapter 12.

14.8 WHY ODMS ARE NOT USED MORE WIDELY?

During the 1990s, the object database technology seemed like a technology that will change databases in the same way the relational model changed databases during the late 1970s and the 1980s. It appears not to have happened. Why?

Some experts have noted that ODBMSs occupy a small niche market that has no broad appeal. While the relational DBMS market has sales revenue of more than ten billion dollars, the sales of ODBMS is even smaller than one-tenth of that amount.

ODBMS continue to be popular in areas like CAD/CAM and artificial intelligence and other applications that involve complex data structures.

SUMMARY

In this chapter we have discussed the following topics:

- Although relational model is widely used in database management, it is not suitable for complex applications like computer-aided design.

- The relational model is often maligned for impedance mismatch between SQL and procedural programming languages.
- Object-oriented databases were proposed in the 1980s. A group of experts proposed an object-oriented database manifesto in 1990 and another group (Object Database Management Group or ODMG) proposed recommendations in 1991. Our discussion is based on the recommendations of the ODMG.
- We define an object database management system (ODMS) as a database system that integrates the capabilities of a database system with that of an object-oriented programming language.
- The components of the ODMG include the object model, the object specification language (ODL) and the object query language (OQL).
- The details of the object model based on the work of the ODMG are described. These include the basic primitives (the object and the literal), type, state, behaviour and schema.
- Object data structures, attributes, relationships, collections, inheritance are described.
- An object may be atomic, a collection or structured. The collection objects may be a set, a bag, a list, an array or a dictionary.
- Class hierarchy is related to the concept of subtype-supertype. Inheritance deals with sharing of implementation between classes.
- The concepts abstraction and encapsulation are useful in localizing the details. Abstraction is the process of removing unnecessary details of an implementation. Encapsulation allows representation to be hidden.
- Overriding, overloading and late binding are additional characteristics of objects. These concepts relate to use of the same name for different operations. The term overriding is used when a function of a base class is redefined in a derived class. An overloaded function is a collection of functions that have the same name. In order to provide the functionality, the names of operations must be resolved at run time (not at compile time). This is called late binding.
- Features of the object specification language ODL defined by the ODMG are presented. These include defining classes.
- Features of the object query language OQL defined by the ODMG are presented. A number of examples of using the OQL including simple queries, Boolean operators, using DISTINCT and ORDER BY are presented.
- Description of two 1990 manifestos for object-oriented databases is presented. The first manifesto is published by Atkinson et al. and the second is by the Committee for Advanced DBMS Function.
- Differences between ODMS and RDMS are explained. These include simplicity of the relational model, using only one simple data structure, and their high efficiency. ODMS is more expressive and provides a variety of facilities (for example, inheritance, and encapsulation) that are not available in RDMS.
- To meet the demands of object-oriented community a number of object-oriented features have been included in SQL. These include user-defined data types and generalization and specialization.

REVIEW QUESTIONS

1. Explain the motivation for object-oriented database systems? Define ODMS. (Section 14.1)
2. Define an object and some of its properties. (Section 14.1)

3. What is ODMG and what are the three major components of the object model it has defined? (Section 14.1)
4. What are the components of the object model and how they differ from components of the relational model? (Section 14.2)
5. What is a literal? How is it different than an object? (Section 14.2.1)
6. What is object identity OID and object name? In what way is it different from a primary key of a relation in the relational model? (Section 14.2.1)
7. What are object type and a class? Explain the components attributes, relationships, hierarchies and inheritance. (Section 14.2.2)
8. Explain the attribute types allowed in the object model. (Section 14.2.3)
9. Explain how many-to-many relationship with a number of attributes will be represented in the object model. Give an example. (Section 14.2.3)
10. Explain what is meant by operations, methods and behaviour of an object? (Section 12.2.4)
11. Explain the motivation for introducing the concept of class hierarchy and inheritance. Why is it important? Give an example to illustrate. (Section 14.2.5)
12. What is an object state? (Section 14.2.6)
13. What is abstraction and encapsulation? (Section 14.2.7)
14. Give an example of overloading and late binding. (Section 14.2.8)
15. What is the aim of object specification languages and object definition language ODL? Compare SQL DDL with ODL? (Section 14.3)
16. List some of the commands of the object query language OQL including those that use a subquery, aggregation as well as GROUP BY and HAVING clauses. (Section 14.4)
17. Discuss the golden rules of the ODMS manifesto and compare them with the aims of the Third Manifesto of Stonebraker et al. (Section 14.5)
18. Compare the advantages and disadvantages of ODMS and RDBMS. (Section 14.6)
19. Describe some object features of SQL:1999. (Section 14.7)
20. Discuss the reason why object-oriented databases are not used more commonly? (Section 14.8)

SHORT ANSWER QUESTIONS

1. What is the origin of object-oriented approach?
2. What is the difference between an object and a relation?
3. What is a literal? How does it differ from an object?
4. What is an object identity? Can it be changed?
5. Describe the properties of an object identifier.
6. What is an object's state and what is a class?
7. Explain the two types of properties that an object state possesses.
8. What is an attribute?
9. How is a relationship specified in ODL? Give an example.
10. Do relationships have names? If not, how do we refer to them?
11. Give an example of specifying one-to-many relationship between *Match* and *Batting*.

12. What is an extent? When is it used?
13. What is object hierarchy and inheritance?
14. What is an object's behaviour?
15. What is meant by encapsulation?
16. What is an object interface?
17. What is object definition language? Is it just like a DDL?
18. Describe an object creation definition for *Player*.
19. What is an instance?
20. What is the difference between OQL and SQL?
21. Show an example of an OQL query using a subquery.
22. Show an example of an OQL query using GROUP BY, HAVING and an aggregation function.
23. How many different types of collection of objects OQL allows?
24. What is the difference between Set and Bag?
25. What is the difference between a List and an Array?
26. Define permissible operations on Dictionary.
27. List three most important golden rules of the ODMS manifesto.

MULTIPLE CHOICE QUESTIONS

1. Which one of the following is true?
   (a) ODMS is usually more efficient than RDBMS.
   (b) ODMS is more suitable for complex applications than RDBMS.
   (c) ODMS standard is based on the work of E.F. Codd.
   (d) ODMS is now being used widely.
2. Which one of the following is true?
   (a) Object is exactly like a tuple in the relational model.
   (b) Class is exactly like a relation in the relational model.
   (c) OQL is exactly like SQL in the relational model.
   (d) ODMS relationships are exactly like relationships in the relational model.
   (e) None of the above is correct.
3. Which of the following are major differences between the relational model and the object model?
   (a) Relational model is based on the concept of relations while object-oriented model is based on the concept of objects.
   (b) Relational model requires that each element in a relation be atomic while the object-oriented model does not.
   (c) Object-oriented model requires immutable object identifiers but the relational model does not.
   (d) Object-oriented model allows inheritance and encapsulation while the relational model does not.
   (e) All of the above

4. Which one of the following collection objects are supported in ODMG?
   (a) Set (b) Bag (c) List (d) Array
   (e) All of them
5. Which of the following structured types are supported in the ODMG standard?
   (a) Date (b) Interval (c) Time (d) Timestamp
   (e) All of them
6. Which of the following operations are possible on Date?
   (a) Is greater than (b) Is less than (c) Next (d) Is equal to
   (e) All of the above
7. Which one of the following **cannot** be represented as a structured data type?
   (a) Duration of time (b) Time specified in a time zone
   (c) Time specified in Greenwich Mean Time (d) Time specified as Indian Standard Time
8. Which one of the following is **not** correct?
   (a) Set and Bag both allow operations for union, intersection and difference.
   (b) List allows operations for removing an element, retrieving an element, replacing an element.
   (c) Array allows inserting an element and concatenating to arrays.
   (d) Dictionary allows inserting, deleting and selecting entries.
9. Which of the following are true?
   (a) Data structures and algorithms used in an object are not visible to the user.
   (b) Data structures and algorithms are called representation and methods.
   (c) A collection of objects of a given type share the same set of properties.
   (d) In an object model, there is a difference between a class and a set of objects in it.
   (e) All of the above
10. Which of the following are attribute types in ODMG?
    (a) Atomic (b) Collection (c) Structure (d) Reference
    (e) All of the above
11. Which one of the following is true about specifying relationships in ODMG?
    (a) Relationships in the object model are represented by relationship objects.
    (b) Relationships in the object model are defined explicitly by traversal paths.
    (c) Integrity must be maintained in ODMG by declaring foreign keys.
    (d) Relationships are defined as unary, binary or ternary.
12. Which one of the following is true?
    (a) OID can be modified by the user.
    (b) An object can have a name other than OID.
    (c) An OID can be specified by the user.
    (d) An OID is exactly like the primary key in the relational model.
13. Which one of the following is true?
    (a) Object type is same as data type in SQL.
    (b) Relationship specification in ODMS specify a one-to-one, one-to-many or many-to-many relationship.

(c) ODMS allows relationships to have attributes.
(d) ODMS relationships are always one way relationships.

14. Which one of the following is true?
    (a) The state of an object is true or false.
    (b) The state of an object includes attributes and relationships.
    (c) The state of an object is active or passive.
    (d) The state of an object shows if it is part of a class.
15. Which one of the following is **not** true?
    (a) The behaviour of an object is the set of operations defined on it.
    (b) ODMG defines an object's behaviour as a set of operation signatures.
    (c) Each operation may be defined for one or more types of objects.
    (d) Each operation must include a list of arguments including their names and types.
16. Which one of the following is true?
    (a) Abstraction and encapsulation are the same. (b) Schema and type is the same.
    (c) Behaviour and methods are the same. (d) OQL and SQL are the same.
17. Which one of the following are the same?
    (a) Polymorphisms and overloading (b) Dynamic binding and late binding
    (c) Overriding and overloading (d) Methods and messages
18. Which one is an advantage of ODMS over RDBMS?
    (a) Solid theoretical background (b) Well defined algebra and calculus
    (c) Simplicity (d) Ease of representing more expressive structures
19. Which one of the following is common to both the manifestos discussed in Section 14.5?
    (a) Updatable views (b) SQL or a similar language
    (c) Inheritance (d) Triggers
20. Which of the following object-oriented features are included in SQL?
    (a) User-defined abstract data types (b) Generalization and specialization
    (c) Assertions and triggers (d) Encapsulation

EXERCISES

1. Describe the problem of impedance mismatch in the relational model. Does it also occur in the object database model? Explain.
2. What are the three characteristics of an object? Discuss their importance.
3. What are attributes and relationships in OODBMS? Do both of them have names and values? How are these concepts different in the object data model as compared to the relational model?
4. What is the difference between a literal and an object? Do literals have identifiers? How many different types of literals are defined in the object data model? Explain.
5. Discuss the meaning of encapsulation and describe its benefits.
6. What is an interface? Why is this term used in the object data model?

7. What is inheritance? Is it similar to generalization and specialization that we discussed in Chapter 2? Discuss the benefits of inheritance using an example.
8. What is overloading? Give an example to illustrate the power of overloading.
9. How does the object data model represent more information semantics?
10. Explain the different components of an object and how these components represent structural and behavioural information?
11. Describe ODL and its components.
12. Identify the properties of an object. How is an object identified?
13. Discuss the relationship between data-hiding, encapsulation and abstraction.
14. Define a simplified interface for a web browser.
15. What is the difference between an object and a class? Give one example to explain the difference.
16. Explain how the cricket database may be represented in an OODB.
17. Describe the five optional rules of the ODMG 1990 manifesto. Discuss their importance and explain why they were not included in the set of golden rules.
18. Are there any major differences between the ODMG manifesto and the Third Manifesto of Stonebraker et al.? Discuss.
19. Which one of the golden rules of the ODMS manifesto can be included in a relational DBMS by modifying the DBMS? Explain how it can be done.

PROJECTS

1. In the 2007 White Paper, the Object Database Technology Working Group, discussed a new approach to ODMS. This approach is available at the website http://www.sbql.pl. Study this approach and compare it with the work of ODMG. Could this approach provide a better foundation for ODMS? Discuss.
2. This is a rather complex project which can be simplified to suit the needs of a class.

   The database is to be developed for buildings on a university campus and their maintenance. There are many buildings on the campus. Each building is identified with a unique name. Each building has a floor plan for each floor which needs to be stored. Every floor of the buildings has offices and laboratories. Each of them is uniquely numbered. Each office has one or more doors and one or more windows. For ease of reporting to maintenance, each of these must also be uniquely numbered for each building. Each office has furniture including one or more of the following, viz., desk, chair, bookshelf, white/black board on the wall, computer, filing cabinet, lights, power plugs, internet connection, cabinet to hang coat, etc., (this list may be adjusted to suit the local situation). Essentially, the database must include detail of everything in each building so the facilities manager can send a maintenance person to repair anything that is broken; even a power plug by giving the maintenance person the number of the power plug.

   Each building also has several doors that are uniquely numbered as well as one or more lifts (or no lift). It also has some facilities like the toilets that also have doors and toilets that are numbered.

   There might be some more equipment in each office. Some offices, like the Head of a Department's office, may have a fridge and/or a printer. The laboratories will have equipment; the computer labs will have several computers and printers.

   Design an object-oriented database for this problem and list all the object types that are needed.

LAB EXERCISES

1. Study the two manifestos in Section 14.5 and compare them with the recommendations of the ODMG. Discuss what is included in the ODMS report and what is not.
2. **Object Data Model**

   Explain the following terms and compare them with terms with similar meanings in the relational model.

   (a) Object
   (b) Literal
   (c) OID
   (d) Class
   (e) Attribute
   (f) Relationship
3. **OQL**

   Formulate in OQL some of the queries from Chapter 5 SQL. Assume that the relations *Player*, *Match*, *Batting* and *Bowling* have been defined using the same attribute names in ODL.
4. **A Cricket Database**

   In a cricket match, a company sells tickets, advertising materials and food during the match. These sales generate income. Staff must be paid wages. Cost of venue hired and of security is also the responsibility of the company. Current profit or loss needs to be calculated after each match. The stadium has a capacity and you cannot sell more tickets than the capacity.

   Explain how you will implement an object database to include all this information.
5. **Country/Rivers/Deserts/Mountains/Animals**

   A database of countries, their rivers, deserts, mountains and animals is to be developed. It is required to store a variety of information about the countries depending on availability of information. For rivers, we would want to store information like name, country or countries it passes through, source of the river, destination, river length, etc. For mountains, we would want to store information like name of the range, list of peaks, their names and heights, country or countries through which the mountain range passes, etc. For animals, we need to store information like name, type (mammal, bird, etc.), the names of countries where each is found, and some of their characteristics.

   Represent the data by using the object model. List the benefits of the object model compared with the relational model.

BIBLIOGRAPHY

For Students

The books by Eaglestone and Ridley and two chapters in the book by Garcia-Molina, Ullman and Widom are good references on object databases and they are relatively easy to read.

For Instructors

One of the first detailed document describing object databases is by Atkinson et al., (1989). The third Manifesto by Stonebraker et al., is also important and so are ODMG standards listed below. The ODMG version 3.0 is the most recent object database standard. An older version is also cited below. The books by Date and Darwen and by Stonebraker are worth consulting.

Agrawal, R., N. H. Gehani, "ODE (Object Database and Environment): The Language and The Data Model", *SIGMOD '89: Proceedings of the 1989 ACM SIGMOD International Conference on Management of Data, ACM*, 1989.

Atkinson, M., F. Bancilhon, D. DeWitt , K. Dittrich, D. Maier, and S. Zodnik, "The Object-Oriented Database System Manifesto", *Proceedings of the First International Conference on Deductive and Object-Oriented Databases*, pp 223-40, Kyoto, Japan, December 1989. Also appears in Bancilhon, F., C. Delobel, and P. Kanellakis, (Eds.), *Building an Object-Oriented Database System: The Story of O2*, Morgan Kaufmann, 1992.

http://www-2.cs.cmu.edu/People/clamen/OODBMS/Manifesto/htManifesto/Manifesto.html

Banerjee, J., W. Kim, H. Kim, and H. Korth, "Semantics and Implementation of Schema Evolution in Object-Oriented Databases", *ACM SIGMOD*, 1987.

Bertono, E., and L. Martino, *Object-Oriented Database Systems: Concepts and Architectures*, First Edition, Addison Wesley, 1993.

Carey, M. J., and D. J. DeWitt, "Of Objects and Databases: A Decade of Turmoil", *VLDB '96: Proceedings of the 22nd International Conference on Very Large Databases.*

Cattell, R. G. G., and D. K. Barry, (Eds.), *The Object Data Standard: ODMG 2.0*, Morgan Kaufmann, 1997, 270 pp.

Cattell, R. G. G., and D. K. Barry, (Eds.), *The Object Data Standard: ODMG 3.0*, Morgan Kaufmann, 2000, 280 pp.

Date, C. J., and H. Darwen, *Foundation for Object/Relational Databases: The Third Manifesto*, Addison Wesley, 1998, 495 pp.

Eaglestone, B., and M. Ridley, *Object Databases: An Introduction*, McGraw-Hill, 1998, 380pp.

Garcia-Molina, H., J. D. Ullman, and J. Widom, *Database Systems: The Complete Book,* Chapters 4 and 9, Prentice Hall, 2002, 1119 pp.

Kifer, M., W. Kim, and Y. Sagiv, "Querying Object-Oriented Databases", *SIGMOD '92: Proceedings of the 1992 ACM SIGMOD International Conference on Management of Data*

Kim, W., *Modern Database Systems: The Object Model, Interoperability, and Beyond*, ACM Press, 1995, 705 pp.

Kim, W., "A Model of Queries for Object-Oriented Databases", *VLDB '89: Proceedings of the 15th international Conference on Very Large Data Bases.*

"Object Database Technology Working Group, Next-Generation Object Database Standardization", *Object Database Technology Working Group White Paper*, September 2007.

Stonebraker, M., (with D. Moore), *Object-Relational DBMSs: The Next Great Wave,* Morgan Kaufmann, 1996.

Stonebraker, M., L. A. Rowe, B. G. Lindsay, J. Gray, M. J. Carey, M. L. Brodie, P. A. Bernstein, and D. Beech, "Third-Generation Database System Manifesto", *ACM SIGMOD Record*, Vol. 19, Issue 3, September 1990, pp 31 – 44.

Won Kim—Pioneer of Object-Oriented and Object-Relational Database Systems

Won Kim is one of the pioneers of object-oriented and object-relational database technologies. Professor Won Kim has published four books on database systems and object-oriented technology and has published over 150 research and technical papers in international conferences and journals. He received the VLDB 10-year Best Paper Award in 1995 and the ACM SIGMOD Test of Time Award in 2002.

Won Kim was Editor-in-Chief of ACM Transactions on Database Systems and founding Editor-in-Chief of ACM Transactions on Internet Technology. He was Chair of the ACM Special Interest Group on Management of Data. He received the 2001 ACM Distinguished Services Award and was elected an ACM Fellow in 1995.

Won Kim received a BS and MS from the Massachusetts Institute of Technology, and a PhD in Computer Science from the University of Illinois at Urbana Champaign. He is currently Professor and University Fellow at Sungkyunkwan University (SKKU) in Suwon, South Korea.

Data Warehouses and OLAP 15

OBJECTIVES

- Discuss why traditional database systems do not meet the needs of decision makers.
- Introduce the concept of separate databases for enterprise's operational work and decision making.
- Introduce the concept of an Operational Data Store (ODS).
- Introduce the concept of a data warehouse (DW), define and describe a DW.
- Describe the importance of data preparation and the process of data extraction, transformation and loading (ETL).
- Describe differences between an OLTP system and DW.
- Describe data warehouse modeling and implementation.
- Discuss the concept of Online Analytical Processing (OLAP).
- Describe the characteristics of an OLAP system.
- Discuss the concept of a data cube and how it relates to OLAP.
- Describe operations, roll-up, drill-down, slice and dice and pivot.
- Present guidelines for implementing OLAP.
- Describe a data warehouse case study.

KEYWORDS

OLTP systems, decision making, operational data store, ODS, data warehouse, DW, data warehouse modeling, dimensions, measures, facts, implementation, OLAP, data cube, multidimensional, drill-down, aggregation, roll-up, slice and dice, dimensions, pivoting, ROLAP, MOLAP, OLAP guidelines, case study.

Believe nothing, no matter where you read it, or who said it, no matter if I have said it, unless it agrees with your own reason and your own common sense.

Buddha

15.1 INTRODUCTION

So far we have described many features of conventional database systems, i.e., systems that help day-to-day running of an enterprise. Essentially these systems automate the work of office workers. Such systems are called Online Transaction Processing (OLTP) database systems. We first present an informal definition of OLTP systems.

Definition—Online Transaction Processing (OLTP) System

An Online Transaction Processing system is a database system which is used for time-sensitive, transaction-related information for immediate processing that is always kept current to assist the day-to-day operations of an enterprise.

The chapters so far have essentially dealt with OLTP systems. In this chapter we will discuss special types of database systems that are designed to help decision makers of an enterprise.

Major enterprises have vast amount of data in OLTP systems. For example, an enterprise with branches in many locations may have local OLTP systems as well as an enterprise system. Even a large enterprise with only one location may have a number of OLTP systems. For example, in a university with only one campus, the library may run its own catalogue and a borrowing database system while the student administration may have its own system running on another machine. There might also be a separate finance database system, a property and facilities management database system and yet another for human resources management.

This vast amount of information can be difficult to use for answering the type of queries that senior managers may want to ask the database systems, since the OLTP systems usually only store current data, and as noted above, the data may be distributed over a number of systems.

In the early database systems, and the file systems before that, whenever the managers required information for decision making purposes, a special application program had to be written to retrieve the information and print the reports required. The head office in most enterprises therefore had to have a computing section that could carry out such tasks. More recently, it has been found that this is not an effective way of providing decision making information to the managers, since the needs of decision maker's change frequently in the contemporary competitive environment. Reports requested by the management can be by region today, while the next day they can be by product.

The primary objectives of building a data warehouse are to provide a single version of the truth about information in the enterprise and to provide good performance for adhoc management queries required for enterprise analysis to manipulate, animate and synthesize enterprise information.

This chapter is organized as follows. In the next section, an example is presented to explain the type of queries that senior managers of an enterprise might wish to pose. Section 15.3 introduces the need for a separate enterprise database for decision makers. Section 15.4 introduces the concept of an operational data store and Section 15.5 deals with data warehouse and presents two definitions. Section 15.6 lists why an enterprise may want to implement a data warehouse and Section 15.7 explains why a data warehouse may not be appropriate for some enterprises. Section 15.8 discusses guidelines for implementing a data warehouse and explains the different steps. A typical architecture of a data warehouse is presented in Section 15.9. Section 15.10 describes the first major step in implementing a data warehouse, which is data preparation, and it includes extraction, transformation and loading, and is usually called ETL. The reasons for some data from source systems being dirty are discussed ahead. Designing a data warehouse requires modeling which is discussed in Section 15.11. This section includes discussion of star schema and snowflake schema.

Online Analytical Processing (OLAP) is discussed in Section 15.12. OLAP perhaps can be explained as using the database like a spreadsheet. In a spreadsheet, data is provided in a two-dimensional table, and all the summaries of columns and rows are easy to obtain and often very useful. Although a spreadsheet can only be two-dimensional or three-dimensional, OLAP can deal with many dimensions providing the management a variety of summaries and aggregations to assist in decision making. Section 15.13 lists a number of characteristics of OLAP systems. Section 15.14 introduces the multidimensional view and data cube. An example to illustrate these is presented in Section 15.14.1. Data cube implementations are discussed in Section 15.15 which includes description of ROLAP and MOLAP. Section 15.16 deals with data cube operations including roll-up, drill-down, slice and dice and pivot. Guidelines for implementing OLAP are presented in Section 15.17 and a case study describing a data warehouse implementation in Section 15.18 concludes the chapter.

15.2 EXAMPLE QUERIES MADE BY MANAGERS

Consider the following relatively simple student database in a university.

> student(S_id, SName, State, DOB, LAddress, PAddress, Mobile, HPhone,..etc)
> enrolment(S_id, D_id, Year, UnitsComp, GPA, ExpComp, ...etc)
> degree(D_id, Degree, Length, YIntroduced, Department, ...etc)

In each relation schema we have indicated that there might be many more attributes in a real life database. The student table could well have 25 or even 50 attributes.

Let us first consider a number of queries that might be posed by the university management to a similar database system of their university. We assume the major entities of interest are students, staff, degrees, and academic years.

1. What is the average number of students enrolled in the university from each Indian state over the last five years?
2. Show the trends in enrolments in each degree program in the last three years.
3. Show the trends in student drop-out rates in each degree program over the last five years.
4. Which degree programs have had less than 10 students enrolled in them during each of the last three years?

5. Which programs have been the three most popular degree programs over the last five years?
6. From which state did no students enroll over the last five years?
7. Show trends in enrolments for those states for which the enrolments are growing.

On how many different aggregations would the decision makers might want reports from such a system? How many different aggregations are possible? We can estimate the number of different aggregations possible as follows.

First we consider a university environment in which the managers only want aggregations on one variable (degrees). Only two types of aggregation queries are possible:

1. No variable value specified so there is only one possible aggregation. (e.g., how many students are there? Only 1 possible query.)
2. Only degree specified (e.g., how many students are doing BSc? 5 possible queries, if we assume 5 different degrees.)

We can easily formulate these six different types of queries using SQL and GROUP BY as shown below. The first query does not require a GROUP BY.

```
SELECT count(*)
FROM student
```

The remaining five aggregations can be obtained by running this GROUP BY query.

```
SELECT Degree, count(*)
FROM enrolment, degree
Where enrolment.D_id = degree.D_id
GROUP BY Degree
```

We assume these queries can be run on the OLTP system without much additional load.

What happens when the number of variables grows? Assume that the managers want aggregations on one variable (that is about degrees) as well as two variables (degree and state). The types of queries possible include the two types of queries listed above for one variable as well as the following two types.

1. Only state specified (e.g., how many students are from Tamil Nadu? 35 possible queries if there are 28 states and 7 union territories.)
2. Both degree and state specified (e.g., how many students from UP are enrolled in BCom? With 5 degrees and 35 different states and union territories we have 175 different queries of this type.)

Therefore, there are already 216 different possible aggregation queries with two variables. Once again we can formulate all these queries in SQL using GROUP BY.

With only one variable there are 2 types of queries and with two variables there are four types of queries. From this we expect eight different types of queries with three variables. Let us assume that there are three variables of interest (degree, state, year). We may then call it three-dimensional data. We list all the possible aggregates for these three dimensions. These include the four types of queries listed above for two variables.

1. No dimension value specified, so there is only one possible aggregation. (e.g., how many students are there? Only 1 possible query.)

2. Only degree specified (e.g., how many students are doing BSc? 5 possible queries if we assume 5 different degrees.)
3. Only year specified (e.g., how many students entered in 2009? 5 possible queries if we only have data about 5 years.)
4. Only state specified (e.g., how many students are from Tamil Nadu? 35 possible queries if there are 28 states and 7 union territories.)
5. Both degree and year specified (e.g., how many students entered in 2008 to enroll in BCom? With 5 degrees and 5 different years we have 25 different queries of this type.)
6. Both year and state specified (e.g., how many students from Kerala enrolled in 2010? With 5 years and 35 different states/union territories there are 175 different queries of this type.)
7. Both degree and state specified (e.g., how many students from UP are enrolled in BCom? With 5 degrees and 35 different states and union territories we have 175 different queries of this type.)
8. All three specified (e.g., how many students from MP joined in 2007 to enroll in BCom? With 5 degrees, 5 years and 35 states and union territories, there are 875 different queries of this type.)

In general, 2^n types of aggregations are possible for n dimensions.

These types of queries may also be formulated in SQL using GROUP BY. For example, the last query in the set above may be formulated using GROUP BY state, year and degree and the result will be the full results of all the 875 queries. In a large database such aggregation queries are likely to create a heavy load on the OLTP system.

As noted above, assuming that we have data for the last 5 years and the university offers only 5 different degrees and with 35 states and union territories there are $5 \times 5 \times 35$ or 875 possible different aggregations for type 8 aggregation queries as noted above. If all the first seven types of aggregation queries listed above are also included, the list is 1296 possible queries which is equal to $6 \times 6 \times 36$ since these include all the sums as well. Clearly for a typical university, the number of dimensions and number of values will be larger (for example, the number of degrees with Bachelors, Masters and the PhD degrees is likely to be larger than 5) so the total number of possible aggregations would be much larger, may be in millions for some enterprises. Obviously if a significant number of aggregation queries were being posed to the OLTP system, it could put substantial load on it.

Further complexity arises if the data is distributed over a number of systems. Suppose the student table is stored on the student record's computer, degree on the registrar's system and enrolment table on some other computer system, then the aggregations become difficult to process.

It is of course possible to meet the decision making needs of an enterprise's management by modifying its OLTP systems to support decision making and allowing managers to pose queries like those above to a mediator system. The mediator system then decomposes each query into appropriate subqueries for the OLTP systems that the query needs to access, obtains results from those systems and then combine and present the results to the managers. This is called *on-demand* query processing. Although this approach has some advantages since the query is able to access up to date information, it also has a number of disadvantages. The major disadvantage is that the management queries may generate such a heavy load on some OLTP systems that the performance of the systems becomes unacceptable for the managers as well as other users.

We now discuss another solution to meet this need of decision makers. It involves setting up a separate database designed for answering aggregation queries efficiently.

15.3 A SEPARATE ENTERPRISE DATABASE

A convenient way to develop an overall enterprise view of the data is to develop a separate enterprise database that only stores information that is of interest to the management. Such a separate database involves the needs of management staff to be analyzed and the enterprise systems that store some or all of the information identified. A suitable data model is then developed and the information extracted from various heterogeneous sources followed by cleaning, filtering and transforming the extracted information. The information is then loaded in the new database. Such a database is called a *data warehouse* (*DW*). Once a data warehouse has been built, the new database is used to answer management queries and the enterprise OLTP systems are not accessed for such queries.

A data warehouse therefore is a separate database derived from the vast amount of information stored in the enterprise's OLTP systems that are in many different formats possibly stored on different computers even perhaps using a number of different DBMS. A data warehouse must be able to manage and easily deliver complete, timely, accurate and understandable information to managers for decision making.

We also introduce the concept of another type of separate database that is sometimes useful as an enterprise database. It is called the *operational data store* (*ODS*). An ODS may be considered a special simple type of DW that only stores current data. Data warehouse on the other hand stores historical data as well, and therefore assists the decision managers in efficiently computing trends and aggregates. Implementing a data warehouse can be a complex task requiring substantial resources. It may also involve considerable research regarding requirements, tools available in the market and trial and error, but once implemented the benefits of a data warehouse can be significant.

We first introduce the concept of an operational data store.

15.4 OPERATIONAL DATA STORE (ODS)

As noted earlier, an ODS is an operational database that is separate from the OLTP systems. It consolidates data from multiple source systems and provides a near real-time, integrated view of volatile, current data for operational purposes. It can also be a staging area for a data warehouse, feeding data to the data warehouse. This can save the effort required for extracting information from the OLTP systems for the data warehouse. A data warehouse is a reporting database that contains relatively recent as well as historical data and may also contain aggregate data.

An ODS has been defined by Inmon and Imhoff as follows:

> ***Definition—Operational Data Store***
> *An operational data store is a subject-oriented, integrated, volatile, current valued data store, containing only corporate detailed data.*

We now define the terms used in this definition.

Term	*Meaning*
Subject-oriented	Information is organized around the major data subjects of an enterprise, for example, players, matches, grounds and so on.
Integrated	Information is a collection of subject-oriented data from a variety of systems to provide an enterprise-wide integrated view of the data.
Current-valued	Information is up-to-date and reflects the current status of the enterprise. Since the data in OLTP systems is changing all the time, information from underlying sources should refresh the ODS as regularly and as frequently as possible.
Volatile	The information in the ODS changes frequently as new information refreshes the ODS.
Detailed	The ODS is detailed enough to serve the needs of the operational management staff in the enterprise.

As noted earlier, an ODS may also be used as an interim database for a data warehouse. Since the contents of an ODS are updated frequently, it may also be used to quickly perform relatively simple queries (such as finding the status of a customer order), rather than complex queries on large amounts of data, typical of a data warehouse.

An ODS may be viewed as an enterprise's short term memory as it stores only very recent information; in comparison, the data warehouse is more like an enterprise's long term memory as it stores historical information relatively permanently.

An ODS can provide a number of benefits to an enterprise. For example, given that an ODS is a unified operational view of the enterprise, it can provide its users improved access to important operational data. An ODS can be much more effective in generating current reports without having to access the OLTP or legacy systems. As noted earlier, the ODS may also shorten the time required to implement and populate a data warehouse system. An ODS may also become a source of reliable information for some other applications.

We now consider the concept of a data warehouse.

15.5 DATA WAREHOUSE

A data warehouse can be a critical resource in a large modern enterprise and is designed to manage and easily deliver complete, timely, accurate and understandable information to managers for decision making.

We present a definition of a data warehouse[1]. The definition is similar to the definition of the ODS given earlier except that an ODS is a current-valued data store while a data warehouse is a time-variant repository of data. This is a widely accepted definition by Inmon.

1. Data warehouse has been defined in a number of ways in the literature; a number of other names are being used for similar technologies. A popular name is Business Intelligence (BI) which has been defined as "the computing processes, techniques and tools that support business decision making". Another term that is less frequently used is Information on Demand (IOD).

Definition—Data Warehouse
A data warehouse is an integrated subject-oriented and time-variant repository of information in support of management's decision making process.

We have defined earlier some of the terms that are used in the above definition except the term 'time-variant' which indicates that a data warehouse has much more than current information.

As noted earlier, modern decision making requires strategic use of information. For example, the student recruitment department in a university would want to study the profiles of students that have been recruited over the last few years. The department may also want to study the trends in student performance and student numbers from different states. A sales department of a music store would want to study the buying profiles of its customers. A government department on the other hand may want to study how the use of services provided has been changing over the last few years.

Therefore, in summary, a data warehouse is

- Corporate-wide in scope.
- Subject-oriented data organization.
- Nonvolatile database that is integrated, cleansed and derived from enterprise OLTP systems.
- Capable of storing historical data.

As noted earlier, a data warehouse is different from an OLTP system. The differences are summarized in Table 15.1.

Table 15.1 Comparing OLTP and Data Warehouse Systems (Based on Oracle, 2002)

Property	*OLTP*	*Data Warehouse*
Nature of the database	3NF	Multidimensional
Indexes	Few	Many
Joins	Many	Some
Duplicated Data	Normalized Data	Denormalized Data
Derived Data and Aggregates	Rare	Common
Queries	Mostly predefined	Mostly adhoc
Nature of queries	Mostly simple	Mostly complex
Updates	All the time	Not allowed, only refreshed
Historical data	Often not available	Essential

The table shows a number of differences, for example, an OLTP system is likely to be a relational database system which has been normalized to at least 3NF while the structure of a data warehouse is likely to be multidimensional. The data warehouse is likely to have more indexes and process more complex queries than an OLTP system. Furthermore, no updates are allowed to the data warehouse data although it is regularly refreshed.

The relationship between an OLTP system, an ODS and a data warehouse may also be shown as in Fig. 15.1. It shows that the data warehouse has much more information than OLTP systems, since it has a significant amount of historical data. The ODS does not have any information that is not current and therefore not available in the OLTP systems

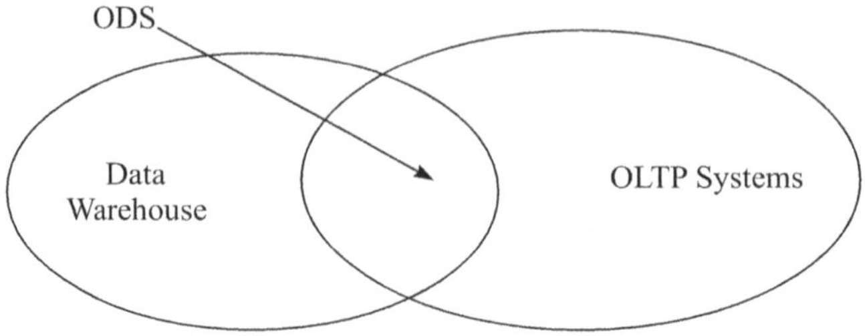

Figure 15.1 Relationship between OLTP, ODS and DW systems

The term data warehouse was not coined until the late 1980s. It was only in the early 1990s that tools for implementing data warehouses became available and enterprises started implementing these technologies. It appears that there are now hundreds of vendors that supply some aspects of data warehouse technology.

15.6 REASONS FOR IMPLEMENTING A DATA WAREHOUSE

We have already discussed some benefits of implementing a data warehouse. In this section we present a more comprehensive list of reasons why a large enterprise would benefit from implementing a data warehouse.

1. To perform decision makers' queries without using the OLTP systems of the enterprise since running decision makers' qtueries on OLTP systems may result in degrading performance
   Performance of OLTP systems is very important since they are being used for day-to-day running of the enterprise including dealing with customers' queries.
2. To carry out queries that would normally not only involve more than one OLTP system but that requires historical data.
   Many of the managers' queries deal with trends over the last few years. It is not possible to run such queries using OLTP systems because these systems do not normally have historical data. Given the importance of historical data, a data warehouse has important management applications.
3. To allow decision makers to query the database without much knowledge of the technical aspects of OLTP systems.
   The senior managers are unlikely to have much technical background and therefore cannot be expected to pose complex queries in SQL. They require special systems that are easier to use. The front end to a data warehouse can meet that need.
4. To provide a clean data depository that does not have errors. Therefore, a data warehouse can provide a 'single version of the truth'.

It is very important for an enterprise to have a single version of the truth about the enterprise's activities. I have come across more than one situation in a university where it was difficult to get accurate data about enrolments and finances.

5. To control access to OLTP systems by providing decision makers (who do not need such access) access to the data warehouse.

   A data warehouse can also assist in security of OLTP databases by controlling the number of people who can access the database. If there is no data warehouse, the decision makers must be given access to the OLTP systems. Once a data warehouse is implemented, such access to OLTP systems is not required.

15.7 WHEN IMPLEMENTING A DATA WAREHOUSE MAY NOT BE APPROPRIATE

Although we have listed a number of benefits of implementing a data warehouse in the last section, some enterprises are unlikely to benefit from using this technology. We list some reasons why data warehousing is not appropriate for all.

1. The importance of a data warehouse can vary. An enterprise should ensure that the data warehouse is going to assist the business before a lot of resources are invested in it.
2. It can be expensive to capture data and process it through the ETL process to provide clean data to the end user.
3. Given that data warehouse normally has historical data, a data warehouse can complicate decision making by including historical data that may not be currently relevant.
4. A data warehouse is expensive to build and maintain. It is difficult to find personnel who have experience in building them, and once built, it normally involves substantial training of personnel to make full use of it.

15.8 GUIDELINES FOR IMPLEMENTING AN ENTERPRISE DATA WAREHOUSE

We discussed an approach of building a database system in Chapter 1. A data warehouse is quite different than a relational database system and therefore we modify the guidelines given in Chapter 1 so that they are appropriate for building a data warehouse.

The modified guidelines are presented in Fig. 15.2.

All design processes are usually iterative processes. For example, the modeling phase may discover some inconsistencies in the requirements analysis phase which may need to be fixed before proceeding further.

We discuss the steps shown in Fig. 15.2 briefly.

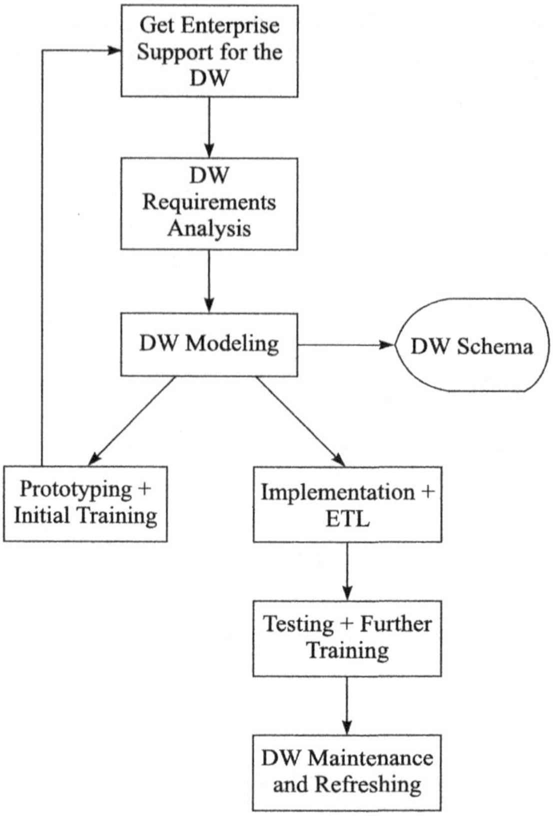

Figure 15.2 Data warehouse design cycle

15.8.1 Get Management Support

The benefits of building a data warehouse may not be obvious to some senior managers in an enterprise. Therefore it is particularly important that a data warehouse has such support from senior management and a senior person who is a DW champion. Implementing a data warehouse is an iterative process that involves working with the senior managers and other users.

15.8.2 Requirements Analysis

Each large software project involves requirements analysis to ensure that the software to be developed meets the requirements of the enterprise. For a data warehouse system, requirements analysis is somewhat different. It involves the implementers fully understanding what data is available in the OLTP systems and what data is required by the managers. These requirements must be explored in depth, ensuring that a clear and concise description of the requirements is prepared. Furthermore, the growth of the data in the future should also be considered. This can be a very challenging task.

A requirements specification document should be prepared based on all this information. This document must be accepted and signed by the senior managers of the enterprise. Once signed, the document is then used in implementation phases that follow.

15.8.3 DW Modeling

Once the first phase has been completed and the information content of the proposed data warehouse and the requirements specification document is available, the information must be modeled. The primary aim of modeling is to develop an enterprise view of the proposed data warehouse with the ultimate aim of achieving an efficient implementation that is suitable for the expected workload and meets the requirements.

15.8.4 Prototyping and Initial Training

Prototyping can be a very helpful phase of data warehouse design because it helps in improving communication between the designers and the clients. A prototype should be a quick and dirty implementation of a simplified data warehouse with some data loaded in it, in order to confirm the specifications developed in the requirements phase.

A prototype can also help in initial training for some users. These users should be able to learn the basic aspects of data warehousing so that they can pose some simple queries.

15.8.5 Implementation and ETL

Final decisions need to be made about what data will go into the data warehouse and plan ETL operations to load data once the data warehouse is implemented. Data may need to be requested from other parts of the enterprise. For reasons of politics, overwork, and just plain lack of knowledge of how data are physically stored in a system, the feeder system programmers may take a while to provide the data.

15.8.6 Testing and Training

Just like any software system, a database system must also be tested to ensure that the system is reliable, efficient, correct, and meets the needs specified in the requirements document. The testing phase should discover most of the errors that may have arisen during the modeling and implementation phases. Testing may also be used to show the client how the system is likely to appear and perform.

Users are likely to need more training about the system. Data is often not self-explanatory so metadata is required to answer users' questions. First time users need to be helped when they have a use for the data warehouse.

Although testing and training can go hand-in-hand, it is particularly important in the initial stages to encourage users to find mistakes in the data warehouse implementation. The errors may be due to lack of controls in feeder systems. Testing should also involve checking the correctness of aggregation logic and whether codes were assigned correctly.

15.8.7 Maintenance

In spite of thorough testing, any new system is likely to have errors and omissions and these need to be fixed during the maintenance phase. In addition, on using the system the clients may come up with new demands that require some modification to the system. Also, some users might find that some queries are not performing well and need performance improvement. The data warehouse administrator is of course in charge of resolving all such client requests. Maintenance of a system can become very expensive unless the system is well designed.

In addition to the above, a data warehouse requires regular refreshing of data. Refreshing may be considered part of data warehouse maintenance.

For the most part, use of data warehousing system in an enterprise is optional. Therefore the persons in charge of the data warehouse may have to identify potential users of the system and promote the benefits to the senior management.

15.9 ARCHITECTURE OF A DATA WAREHOUSE SYSTEM

We now present a typical architecture of a data warehouse system in Fig. 15.3. It shows that the system has a number of sources from which data is extracted through an ETL system and the data is then loaded into the data warehouse. Often some of the data from a data warehouse may be extracted for some data marts.

A data mart has been defined as follows by Gill and Rao.

> ***Definition—Data Mart***
> *A data mart is an implementation with a small and more tightly restricted scope of data warehouse functions, serving a single department or section of an enterprise.*

A data mart may be appropriate when all or some of the units of the enterprise primarily query data about their own units. For example, data marts may be appropriate for each faculty in a large university.

Since the data warehouse does not store real-time data, it does not require real-time updates. A data warehouse can be large but growing only slowly over time.

Figure 15.3 shows that an enterprise may have a number of source systems from which the data is extracted using ETL systems. After the ETL step, the data is deposited in the data warehouse. Decision support is based on extracting information from the data warehouse and supplying it to the managers. In some cases, the data may be deposited in data marts which may then be used by decision makers.

Although not shown in Fig. 15.3, a data warehouse must also include a subsystem to store warehouse metadata or the catalog. The catalog is particularly important for a data warehouse since it includes information about mapping of data from source to target as well as the usual catalog information about various data elements.

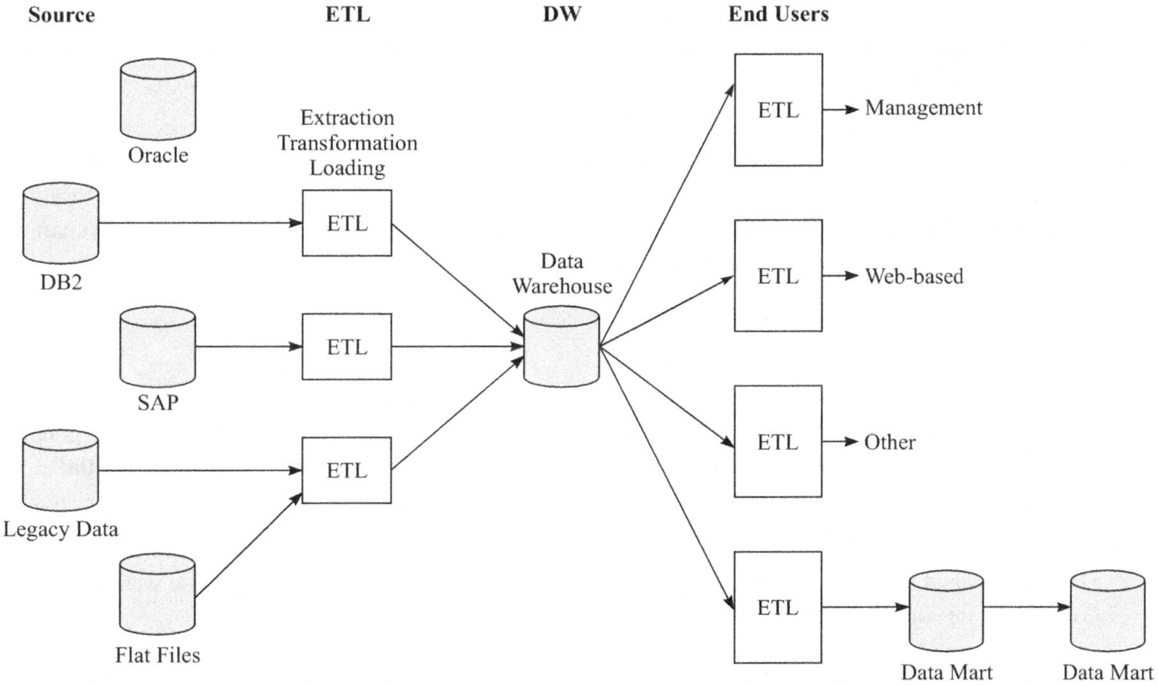

Figure 15.3 A typical architecture of a data warehouse system

A data warehouse not only takes the aggregate query load off the OLTP systems, it also provides the OLTP systems a facility to off-load data that the systems no longer require. If a data warehouse was not available, historical data may have to be downloaded to media that may not be available for online queries.

As shown in Fig. 15.3 data extraction, transformation and loading (ETL) is a critical part of the data warehouse architecture. We discuss it now.

15.10 DATA PREPARATION—EXTRACT TRANSFORM LOAD (ETL)

ETL involves identifying the data requirements, locating the computer systems that have the data, and extracting and transforming the data into the required format for the data warehouse. This is a nontrivial part of building a data warehouse and may take as much as 80% of the time spent in a data warehouse implementation. Spending resources to prepare data correctly is essential for the long term benefits of a data warehouse.

ETL is therefore a core technology needed for data integration. An enterprise may have several OLTP systems as well as some legacy systems. Extracting data from such a collection of systems could involve ad-hoc arrangements using custom-built software implementing business logic developed within the enterprise. The difficulty arises because changes may be made to some OLTP systems which results in costly and time-consuming modifications to the custom-built software. Furthermore, major problems may arise if the enterprise is involved in a merger or an acquisition. In order to solve these problems, a systematic strategy and a well established infrastructure for data integration is needed. Benefits of a unified approach are simplicity and reduction in time in developing an ETL system that works.

A recommended approach is to let all incoming data be intercepted by the ETL system. The data then undergoes necessary data transformation and is loaded in the data warehouse system. In addition to initial bulk upload and batch refreshing uploads at regular intervals, the ETL system can also listen to data changes occurring at the source systems and capture these changes.

15.10.1 Dirty Data

Since our aim is to implement a data warehouse that has clean data, we must deal with dirty data from the source systems. We list a number of reasons why dirty data may be found in the OLTP sources. It is not a complete list as a careful reader would understand by looking at the various websites dealing with the topic but we list the most common reasons for dirty data.

1. *Dummy Codes*—In older systems it was not possible to put NULL values and therefore dummy values like -99999 had to be used. These values were needed in older systems when the value was not known or to indicate some special status.
2. *Multipurpose Fields*—Since a number of source systems are needed to populate a data warehouse, it is necessary that same field names in different systems with different purposes be carefully identified. For example, the field 'status' may be used for different purposes in different source systems.
3. *Primary Keys Misuse*—A variety of problems can occur when sourcing data from OLTP systems. For example, we know the world of business is dynamic and products come and go. The primary key of a product that is not produced any more could be reassigned to a new product. On the other hand, a product or a customer may have been given more than one identifier. For example, some airline flights are double coded. A company may be identifying a customer in two or more different ways for some reason.
4. *Cryptic Data*—A friend of mine used to name his files as 'x' or 'xx' or 'xy'. This created some problems when I copied data from his hard disk to my memory stick because I had no way of knowing which file was which. Similar problems can arise in some source systems where it may become difficult for an ETL system and the person involved in the ETL to work out what a table in database was about.
5. *Inappropriate Use of Name and Address Lines*—This can be a real headache because there is a huge variety of names and addresses in India. Many South Indians have only one name and have initials that may relate to the person's village or person's father or something else. How should one deal with such problems. Furthermore, addresses come in many forms. Some addresses will have street number and street name while other might include phrases like 'Next to Jain College' or 'Behind the Fertilizer Warehouse' and, of course, there may be a number of addresses for the same person living at the same place.
6. *Violation of Business Rules*—Some data may violate business rules because of typos or other reasons. A salary figure may have been typed incorrectly and a person's date of birth may have been typed 2075 instead of 1975. Other more complex violations, for example, some systems may have salary as a month salary while others may have it as an annual salary of business rules may be discovered in the source data.

7. *Data Integration Problems*—As illustrated by problems listed above, data integration may become difficult if data that is related cannot be related and integrated due to, for example, two primary keys or two names not matching because of primary key misuse or inappropriate use of names and addresses. In the future, perhaps the use of UID would make data integration easier if every source system was using UID but that will take some time.

In spite of so many reasons for data being dirty, most of the data can be cleaned and loaded in the data warehouse. The level of effort required of course depends on the quality of data in the source systems.

We now describe some steps of the ETL process.

15.10.2 ETL Steps

We briefly describe the most common steps of the ETL process. There are many web pages that are full of advice on ETL. They are often promoting their own software to carry out ETL.

1. *Parsing*—
   - Parsing locates and identifies individual data elements in the source systems that are required by the data warehouse.
   - As noted earlier, major problems can arise in parsing the first, middle, and the last name; street number and street name; and dates, place and state. The change in state names in India does not help. For example, new states of Uttaranchal, Chattisgarh and, Jharkhand were created in the last few years. There has been some talk of a new state of Telangana. In fact, demands have been made to create 10 more states in India according to some reports.
2. *Correcting*—
   - Corrects parse individual data components using a variety of data intelligence, sophisticated data algorithms and secondary data sources.
   - Examples include changing the state name for Roorkee from Uttar Pradesh to Uttaranchal, changing University of Roorkee to Indian Institute of Technology, Roorkee, and changing postal codes where appropriate.
3. *Standardizing*—
   - This step involves applying conversion routines to transform data into the structure arrived at during data warehouse modeling.
   - Examples include changing the telephone numbers to standard representation, for example, +911129999888, adding street number and street name in an address when possible and standardizing people's names when possible.
4. *Matching and Consolidating*—
   - Careful searching and matching of records collected from different source systems is carried out, partially with the aim of eliminating duplicates. As noted earlier, this can be a challenging task since systems may have even reused the primary key, and as noted earlier, problems arise due to different versions of names and addresses.
   - Examples include identifying similar names and addresses using intelligent name searching and any secondary information, for example, the address.
   - Consolidation may involve collecting data about all individuals from the same family.

15.11 DATA MODELING FOR DATA WAREHOUSING

In Chapter 2 we considered Entity-Relationship modeling to model data. The data in data warehouses is somewhat different than data that can be modeled as entities and relationships that we considered in Chapter 2. Therefore, usually data warehousing modeling techniques are also different although some professionals suggest E-R modeling could still be used. As noted earlier, data in a data warehouse is normally subject-oriented.

We have already listed the steps that are required in implementing a data warehouse. We now consider how to model the data in a data warehouse. A list of typical management queries was given in Section15.2. By analyzing such queries it is possible to determine the dimensions that the managers need and therefore should be in the data warehouse.

15.11.1 Multidimensional Terminology

Since the data in a data warehouse is normally not entities and relationships, another approach of viewing the data is required. This view is called a multidimensional view. The terminology used in multidimensional view is explained in the table below.

Term	*Definition*
Dimension	A dimension is like an entity for which performance can be measured. It includes products, salespeople, market segments, enterprise's business units, geographical locations, country or state, or industry. In context of cricket it might be players, matches, grounds and countries.
Member	A dimension member is a name or identifier used to identify a data item within a dimension. For example, the dimension degree has BSc as a member.
Measure	A measure is a value that depends on the dimensions. It is data that helps measure the performance of the business. It includes quantities and amount. For example, money, sales volume, head count, inventory and profit. The measures are usually aggregated data (e.g., total sales). There may be more than one measure. For example, one may be interested in not only storing the number of items sold but also the total revenue.
Fact and Fact Table	A fact is a collection of related measures that are represented by the dimensions. The fact table is a collection of related data items, consisting of all values of dimensions of interest and the value(s) of measure(s).
Time	It is usually measured as daily, weekly, monthly, quarterly, or yearly.

We describe two methods for modeling multidimensional data. The first is called the *Star Schema* and the second is called the *Snowflake Schema*. We discuss them now. It should be noted that the data warehouse models will only include the data that has been identified by the managers. For example, a data warehouse would not include detailed information about the students or staff because management has no interest in such details.

15.11.2 Star Schema

The multidimensional view may be modeled as a star schema in which each vertex is a dimension that is usually implemented as a table. The middle of the star is the fact table which has a row for each dimension combination. The fact table therefore has values of each dimension and one or more measures. For example, there were 50 students (this is one measure) from UP that came in 2001 to do a BCom degree and on the Central Government scholarship (these are the four dimensions). Note that we have added another dimension, scholarship, so that we may show a model with four dimensions.

Fact tables can become large if the dimensions have many members and in a large fact table many values of the measures are zero.

A simple example of such a multidimensional view with the four dimensions is shown in Fig. 15.4 for a university where we assume that the number of students is the only measure, in fact the table that is determined by the four dimensions, degree, year, state and scholarship.

A characteristic of a star schema is that all the dimensions directly link to the fact table. A part of the fact table may look like as shown in Table 15.2. Examples of the four dimension tables are given in Tables 15.3 to 15.6. Note that if there were five different values of year, five values of degree, 35 states and union territories, and say 10 different scholarships, then the fact table will be very large but most rows will have no students and we may leave out these rows from the table.

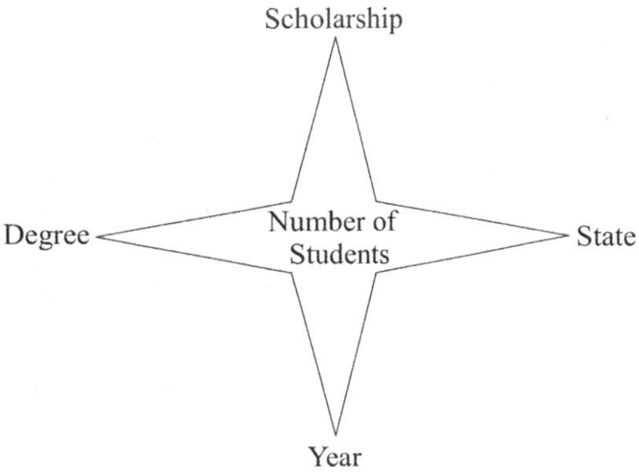

Figure 15.4 A simple example of a star schema

Table 15.2 An example of a fact table

Year	*Degree*	*State*	*Scholarship*	*Number of Students*
2003	BSc	UP	Central Government	35
1999	MBBS	MP	Krishna Foundation	10
2000	LLB	Maharashtra	Industry	22
2002	BCom	Tamil Nadu	Merit	7
2001	LLB	West Bengal	Bursary	2
Many more rows				

The first dimension is degree. An example of the dimension Table is table 15.3.

Table 15.3 An example of the degree dimension table

Name	*Faculty*	*Scholarship Eligibility*	*Program Length*
BSc	Science	Yes	6
MBBS	Medicine	No	10
LLB	Law	Yes	8
BCom	Business	No	6
BA	Arts	No	6
More rows if more degrees			

The second dimension is state. An example of the state dimension table is Table 15.4.

Table 15.4 An example of the state dimension table

Name	*Region*	*Literacy*	*Population (in millions)*
UP	North	60	150
MP	Central	65	60
Maharashtra	West	78	100
Tamil Nadu	South	74	60
West Bengal	East	70	80
30 more rows for the states and union territories			

The third dimension is scholarship. An example of this dimension table is Table 15.5.

Table 15.5 An example of the scholarship dimension table

Name	*Amount*	*Eligibility*	*Number*
Central Government	100%	All	6
Krishna Foundation	100%	Low Income	10
Industry	50%	Top 5%	8
Merit	75%	Top 5%	5
Bursary	25%	Low Income	12
More rows if more scholarships			

The fourth dimension is year. An example of the year dimension table is Table 15.6.

Table 15.6 An example of the year dimension table

Name	*New Program*
2005	Journalism
2006	Multimedia
2007	Biotechnology
More rows if more years	

We now present further examples of the star schema. Figure 15.5 shows a model where there are only two dimensions. Figure 15.6 shows a star schema for four dimensions.

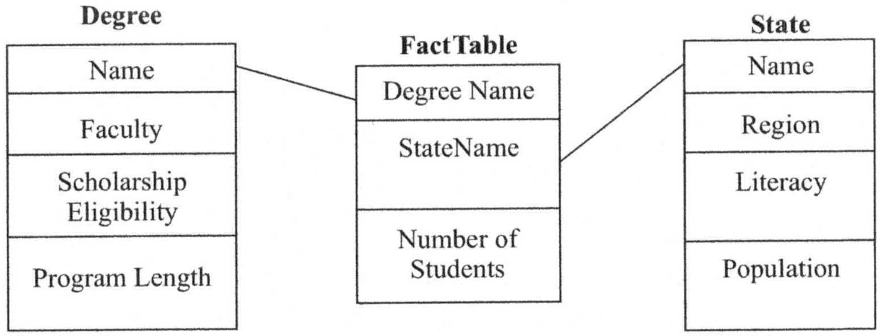

Figure 15.5 Star schema for a two-dimensional example

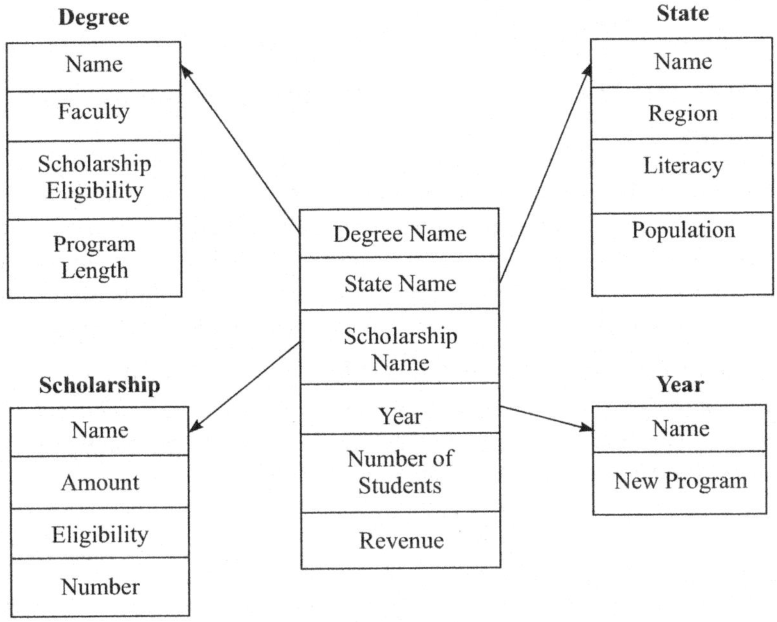

Figure 15.6 Star schema for four dimensions

15.11.3 Snowflake Schema

Star schemas can be refined into *snowflake schemas* if we wish to provide support for dimension hierarchies by allowing the dimension tables to have subtables to represent the hierarchies. For example, in Fig. 15.6 we may wish to include more information about regions or about faculties. This can be done by including subtables but the four-dimension model with subtables becomes a bit too large to display so we display a simple two-dimensional snowflake schema in Fig. 15.7. The model has two dimensions, degree and scholarship, and the model also includes more information about each faculty which is included in a separate table.

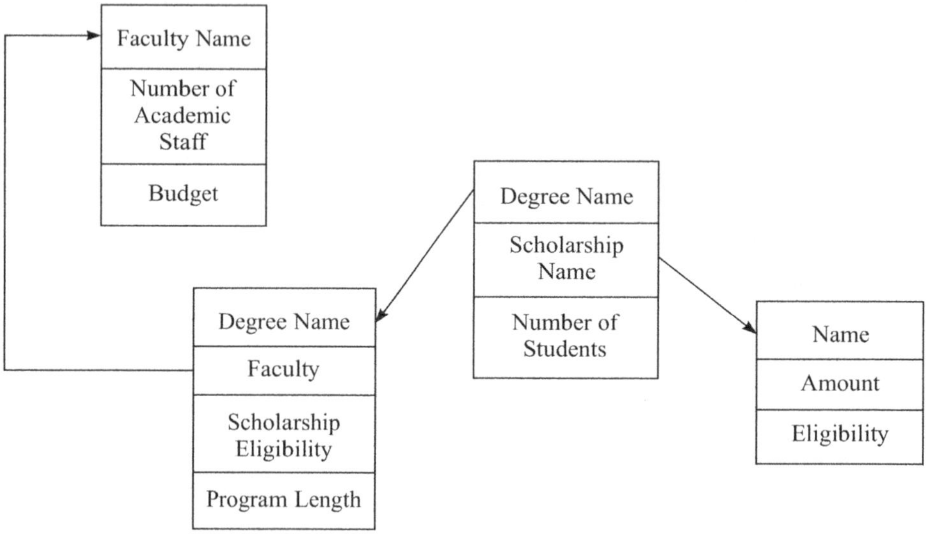

Figure 15.7 An example of a snowflake schema for two dimensions

The star and snowflake schemas are intuitive, easy to understand, can deal with aggregate data and are easily extendible by adding new attributes or new dimensions. They form the popular data warehouse modeling technique. Entity-relationship modeling is often not discussed in the context of data warehousing although it is quite straightforward to look at the star schema as an E-R model. Each dimension may be considered an entity and the fact may be considered either a relationship between the dimension entities or an entity in which the primary key is the combination of the foreign keys that refer to the dimensions.

The dimensional structure of the star schema or the snowflake schema is called a multidimensional model in online analytical processing (OLAP) which we discuss next. We will define the concept of a cube that can be implemented as a front end of a data warehouse and help in providing a very quick response to management OLAP queries regardless of the size of the data warehouse.

15.12 OLAP

OLAP systems are data warehouse front-end software tools to make aggregate data available efficiently to an enterprise's managers for advanced analysis.

In 1993, Codd presented this somewhat difficult to understand definition of OLAP:

Definition—Online Analytical Processing
OLAP is the dynamic enterprise analysis required to create, manipulate, animate and synthesise information from exegetical contemplative and formulaic data analysis models.

Essentially what this definition means is that the information is manipulated from the point of view of a manager (exegetical), from the point of view of someone who has thought about it (contemplative) and according to some formula (formulaic).

Here is another, much easier to understand, definition of OLAP.

Definition—Online Analytical Processing
OLAP is a software technology that enables decision makers to gain insight into data through fast, consistent, interactive access to a wide variety of possible views of information that reflects the real dimensionality of the enterprise as understood by the decision makers.

As discussed earlier, data warehouse and OLAP are based on a multidimensional conceptual view of the enterprise data. Data that is arranged by the dimensions is like a spreadsheet although a spreadsheet presents only two-dimensional data with each cell containing data or an aggregation. As an example, Table 15.7 shows one such two-dimensional spreadsheet with dimensions Degree and State, where the measure is the number of students joining a university in a particular year.

Table 15.7 A multidimensional view of data for two dimensions

	BSc	*LLB*	*MBBS*	*BCom*	*BIT*	*ALL*
UP	5	20	15	50	11	101
MP	10	0	15	25	17	67
Maharashtra	5	1	10	12	23	51
Tamil Nadu	2	2	10	10	31	55
West Bengal	5	0	5	25	7	42
Kerala	5	15	20	20	13	73
Bihar	0	2	20	15	19	56
ALL	32	40	95	157	121	445

Let Table 15.7 be information for the year 2005. We will use this table in an example later in the chapter. Similar spreadsheet views would be available for other years. Three-dimensional data can also be organized in a spreadsheet using a number of sheets or by using a number of two-dimensional tables in the same sheet. Spreadsheets are however not suitable for OLAP since they tie data storage too tightly to the presentation. It is therefore difficult to obtain other desirable views of the information. Furthermore, it is not possible to query spreadsheets and spreadsheets become unwieldy when more than three dimensions are to be represented, as often is the case with OLAP.

Data cube, which is discussed in Section 15.14, essentially generalizes spreadsheets to any number of dimensions.

In summary, a manager would want even the most complex query to be answered quickly. OLAP is usually a multi-user system that may be run on a separate server using specialized software. The major OLAP applications are trend analysis over a number of time periods, slicing, dicing, drill-down and roll-up to look at the data at different levels of detail and pivoting or rotating to obtain a new dimensional view. We will discuss these operations later in the chapter in Section 15.16.

15.13 CHARACTERISTICS OF OLAP SYSTEMS

Before we discuss characteristics of OLAP systems we compare OLTP and OLAP systems. The differences between the two types of systems can be summarized as in the following table.

Item	*OLTP*	*OLAP*
Users	Large number of office workers including call centre staff	Select group of managers
Function	Mission-critical day-to-day operations	Management-critical analytical investigations
Nature	Process customer records	Aggregate queries of data
Design	Application-oriented based on E-R Model	Subject-oriented based on multidimensional model
Time	Current	Historical
Operations	Read, write, insert and delete	No updates

Codd's 1993 paper listed 12 characteristics (or rules) of OLAP systems. Another six in 1995 followed these. He restructured the 18 rules into four groups. These rules provide a point of view of what constitutes an OLAP system. We do not discuss all the rules. Instead we consider 10 characteristics that we consider the most important.

1. *Multidimensional Conceptual View*—As noted above, this is the central characteristic of an OLAP system. It includes operations like slice and dice as a requirement.
2. *Accessibility: OLAP as a Mediator*—The OLAP software should be placed between data sources (e.g., a data warehouse) and an OLAP front-end.
3. *Batch Extraction vs Interpretive*—An OLAP system should provide multidimensional data staging plus partial pre-calculation of aggregates in large multidimensional databases.
4. *Multi-User Support*—The OLAP software should provide many normal database operations including retrieval, update, concurrency control, integrity and security.
5. *Storing OLAP Results*—Data generated as OLAP results should be kept separate from source data. Read-write OLAP applications should not be implemented directly on live transaction data if OLTP source systems are supplying information to the OLAP system directly.
6. *Extraction of Missing Values*—The OLAP system should distinguish missing values from zero values. If such distinction is not made, the aggregates are likely to be computed incorrectly.

7. *Treatment of Missing Values*—An OLAP system should ignore all missing values regardless of their source. Correct aggregate values will be computed once missing values are ignored.
8. *Uniform Reporting Performance*—Increasing the number of dimensions or database size should not significantly degrade the reporting performance of the OLAP system. This is a good objective although it may be difficult to achieve in practice.
9. *Generic Dimensionality*—An OLAP system should treat each dimension as equivalent in both its structure and operational capabilities. Additional operational capabilities may be granted to selected dimensions but such additional functions should be grantable to any dimension.
10. *Unlimited Dimensions and Aggregation Levels*—An OLAP system should allow unlimited dimensions and aggregation levels. In practice the number of dimensions is rarely more than 10 and the number of hierarchies rarely more than six.

15.14 THE MULTIDIMENSIONAL VIEW AND DATA CUBE

As noted earlier, the multidimensional view of data is in some ways a natural view of an enterprise for managers.

Earlier in the chapter, we noted that the SQL command GROUP BY is useful in formulating queries that involve aggregations. GROUP BY divides a table virtually into subtables based on the attributes' values in the GROUP BY clause and then aggregations over each subtable are carried out. SQL has a variety of aggregation functions but GROUP BY does not provide facilities for histograms, roll-up and drill-down facilities. Furthermore, no facilities are available for cross tabulation. Also, GROUP BY on several dimensions can become a performance bottleneck for OLTP systems.

Jim Gray introduced the concept of data cube which computes aggregates over all subsets of dimensions specified in the cube. A cube may therefore be looked at as the union of a (large) number of SQL GROUP BY operations. Generally all or some of the aggregates are precomputed to improve query response time. A decision has to be made as to what and how much should be precomputed since precomputed queries require storage and time for computation. We now present an informal definition of a data cube.

Definition—Data Cube
A data cube is a multidimensional structure that contains an aggregate value at each point.

A data cube is often implemented as a database in which there are dimension tables each of which provides details of a dimension. This database can be the data warehouse of the enterprise.

We illustrate the multidimensional view of data by using an example.

15.14.1 An Example

We go back to the student database that we presented in Section 15.2. It consists of the following three tables.

student(S_id, SName, State, DOB, LAddress, PAddress, Mobile, HPhone,..etc)
enrolment(S_id, D_id, Year, UnitsComp, GPA, ExpComp, ...etc)
degree(D_id, Degree, Length, YIntroduced, Department, ...etc)

We assume that there are a number of other tables in the OLTP systems of the university.

Sample tables for the above schema are given in Tables 15.8, 15.9 and 15.10.

Table 15.8 The relation student

Sid	*SName*	*State*	*DOB*	*LAddress*	*Other Columns...*
8656789	B. Natrajan	UP	1/1/1980	20 Govind Hall	....
8700020	Suresh Chandra	MP	2/2/1981	37 Govind Hall	.....
8900020	Arun Krishna	Maharashtra	3/3/1983	90 Nehru Hall	.....
8801234	Naresh Kumar	Tamil Nadu	4/4/1983	88 Gandhi Hall	.....
8654321	Reena Rani	West Bengal	5/5/1984	89 Gandhi Hall	.....
8712374	K. Muralikrishna	Kerala	6/6/1980	80 Azad Hall	.....
8612345	Samir Khan	Bihar	7/7/1981	11 Main Street	.....
8744223	Ramesh Ghosh	UP	8/8/1982	Null	.....
8977665	Sachin Singh	MP	9/9/1983	Null	.....
9234567	Rahul Kumar	Kerala	10/10/1984	Null	.....
9176543	Saurav Gupta	UP	11/11/1985	1, Tagore Drive	....
More rows					

In Table 15.9 below, the attribute *Year* is the year in which the student started the current degree.

Table 15.9 The relation enrolment

S_id	*D_id*	*Year*	*Other Columns*
8900020	1256	2002	...
8700074	3271	2002	....
8700074	3321	2002	....
8900020	4444	2000	....
8801234	1256	2001	....
8801234	3321	1999	....
8801234	3333	1999	....
8977665	3333	2000	....

In the Table 15.10 below, *Degree Length* is given in terms of the number of years it normally takes to finish it. *YIntroduced* is the year in which the degree was introduced.

Table 15.10 The relation degree

D_id	*Degree*	*Length*	*YIntroduced*	*Department*	*Other Columns*
1256	BIT	6	1995	Computer Science	....
3271	BSc	6	1920	Physics	....
3321	BCom	6	1986	Business	....
4444	MBBS	12	1960	Medicine	....
3333	LLB	8	1972	Law	....
More rows if more degrees					

Extracting Data for the Data Warehouse

It is clear that much of the information given above in the three tables, and similar information that is likely to be in other OLTP systems, although suitable for a student enrolment operational system, is not suitable for management decision making. The managers do not need detailed information about individual students or their enrolment. They are more interested in the trends in student numbers in different degree programs and from different states.

We first consider only two dimensions. Let us say we are primarily interested in finding out how many students from each state came to do a particular degree. We may therefore visualize the data as a two-dimensional State X Degree table. A table that summarizes this type of information for the year 2005 was presented in Table 15.7. Another table with 2006 enrolment details is presented in Table 15.11. We may call Table 15.11 that gives number of students admitted (in say 2006) a two-dimensional 'cube'.

Using this two-dimensional view we are able to find the number of students joining any degree from any state (only for year 2006). Other queries that we are quickly able to answer are as follows:

- How many students started BIT in 2006?
- How many students joined from MP in 2006?

We could tabulate similar data for other years:

Table 15.11 Two-dimensional table of aggregates for year 2001

	BSc	*LLB*	*MBBS*	*BCom*	*BIT*	*ALL*
UP	7	10	16	53	10	96
MP	9	0	17	22	13	61
Maharashtra	5	1	19	19	20	64
Tamil Nadu	2	2	10	12	23	49
West Bengal	8	0	5	16	7	36
Kerala	4	13	20	26	11	74
Bihar	4	2	10	10	12	38
ALL	39	28	97	158	96	418

Let us now imagine that Table 15.11 is put on top of Table 15.7. We now have a three-dimensional cube with *Year* as the dimension that is perpendicular to the state and degree dimensions. We may now put on top of these two tables another table that gives the vertical sums, as given in Table 15.12 below:

Table 15.12 Two-dimensional table of aggregates for both years

	BSc	*LLB*	*MBBS*	*BCom*	*BIT*	*ALL*
UP	12	30	31	103	21	197
MP	19	0	32	47	30	128
Maharashtra	10	2	29	31	43	115
Tamil Nadu	4	4	20	22	54	104
West Bengal	13	0	10	41	14	78
Kerala	9	28	40	46	24	147
Bihar	4	4	30	25	31	94
ALL	71	68	192	315	217	863

The three tables, Tables 15.7, 15.11 and 15.12, together now form a three-dimensional cube. The top table shown at the front in Fig. 15.8 provides totals for the two years and we are able to 'drill-down' to find numbers in individual years. Note that a cube does not need to have equal number of members in each dimension. Putting the three tables together gives a cube of 8 × 6 × 3 (=144) cells including the totals along every dimension. A cube such as we have described could be represented by *State* × *Degree* × *Year*.

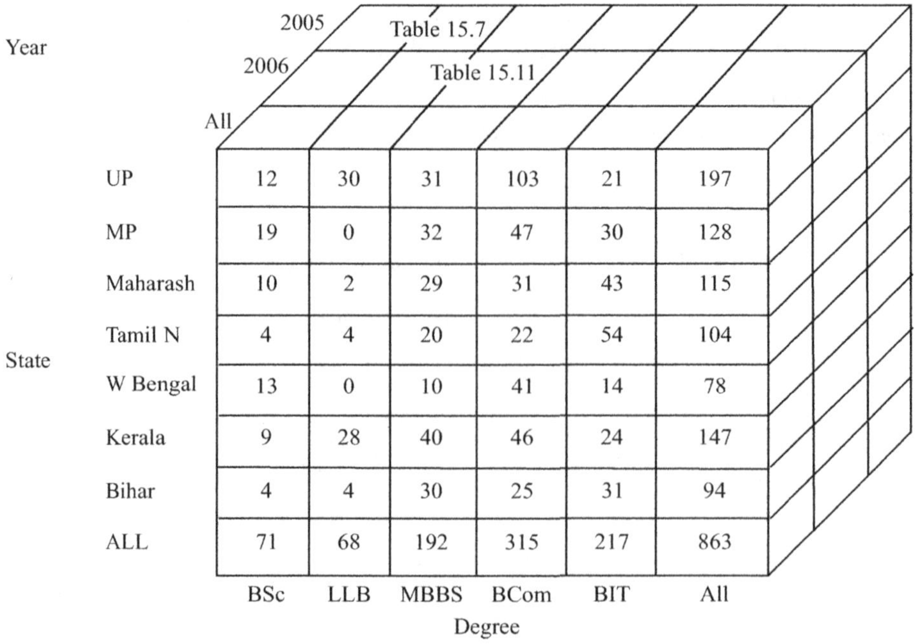

Figure 15.8 A three-dimensional cube formed by Tables 15.7, 15.11 and 15.12

Each of the three edges in the cube represents a dimension. Each dimension has a number of members. For example, the dimension *Degree* has members BSc, LLB, MBBS, BCom and BIT. Similarly, the dimensions *State* and *Year* have members. We have not defined any hierarchies on the dimensions but hierarchies are possible. Each of the dimensions may have attributes (for example, population of each state) that are not included in the cube. All the cells in the cube represent measures or aggregations. For example, a cell may provide the number of students from Tamil Nadu admitted to BCom in 2006.

We may have all the precomputed aggregates for a number of years, not only for years 2005 and 2006, if the university needs them. We are then able to quickly answer any of the following queries:

- How many students from MP started degree BCom in year 2005, 2006 and 2007?
- How many UP students joined the university in 2006?
- How many students started the BSc degree each year?

We have noted earlier that SQL may be used for all such queries although the OLTP system may not have all the historical data.

15.15 DATA CUBE IMPLEMENTATIONS

We identified many aggregates for the simple example and have noted that the number of aggregates can be much larger for a real enterprise. For example, if a university had 10 colleges, as many Indian universities do, we could have $35 \times 20 \times 10 \times 10$ or 70,000 aggregations. Millions of aggregates are likely in a large enterprise when there are more than three or four dimensions. Should all these aggregates be precomputed? Many of these aggregates are likely to be zero. How should they be stored? How should sparsity be managed? Some possible solutions are as follows:

1. *Precompute and store all*—Although it may appear like a reasonable approach, it involves perhaps millions of aggregates that need to be computed and stored. In some ways this is the best solution as far as query response time is concerned. The solution is also impractical since resources required in computing the aggregates and storing them will be prohibitively large. Indexing large amounts of data is also expensive.
2. *Precompute (and store) none*—It is the opposite of precompute all. This involves that the aggregates are computed on-the-fly using the data warehouse whenever a query is posed. This approach does not require additional storage for storing the cube but the query response time is likely to be poor for large data cubes.
3. *Precompute and store some*—This is the hybrid approach and involves the most frequently queried aggregates precomputed and stored and others computed as the need arises. We may also be able to derive some of the remaining aggregates using the aggregates that have already been computed. It may therefore be worthwhile to also precompute some aggregates that are not most frequently queried but help in deriving many other aggregates. It will of course not be possible to derive all the aggregates from precomputed aggregates and it will be necessary to access the source database (e.g., data warehouse) to compute the remaining aggregates. The more aggregates we are able to precompute the better is the query performance.

Each cell of a data cube may be identified by the values of its dimensions. For example, as noted at the beginning of this chapter, (BSc, Maharashtra, 2005) for dimensions (degree, state and year) describes a cell. It has been suggested that an additional value of dimension "ALL" be added to identify cells like (BSc, ALL, 2005). This gives us the number of all students who entered the university in 2005 to do a BSc. Such aggregates do not need to be materialized since one could obtain the aggregate on-the-fly by summing all cells like (BSc, ?, 2005) for all the states. If a cell's dimension values do not contain an 'ALL' value then the aggregate must be computed from raw data since there is no way to derive that aggregate but if it does contain ALL it can always be derived from other aggregates.

It can be shown that large numbers of cells do have an 'ALL' value and may therefore be derived from other aggregates. Let us reproduce the list of queries we had in Section 15.2 and define them as (*a*, *b*, *c*) where *a* stands for a value of the degree dimension, *b* for the state and *c* for the starting year:

1. (ALL, ALL, ALL) no value given (e.g., how many students are there? Only 1 query.)
2. (*a*, ALL, ALL) degrees (e.g., how many students are doing BSc? 5 queries.)
3. (ALL, ALL, *c*) year (e.g., how many students entered in year 2005? 2 queries given data only about 2005 and 2006.)
4. (ALL, *b*, ALL) state (e.g., how many students are from UP? 7 queries, given 7 states in our example.)
5. (*a*, ALL, *c*) degrees, year (e.g., how many students entered in 2005 to enroll in BCom? 10 queries.)
6. (ALL, *b*, *c*) year, state (e.g., how many students from MP entered in 2005? 5 queries.)
7. (*a*, *b*, ALL) degrees, state (e.g., how many students from MP are enrolled in BCom? 35 queries.)
8. (*a*, *b*, *c*) all (e.g., how many students from Kerala entered in 2005 to enroll in BCom? 70 queries given the information in the example.)

It is therefore possible to derive 74 of the 144 queries from the 70 queries of type (*a*, *b*, *c*). Of course in a very large data cube, it will not be practical to precompute all the (*a*, *b*, *c*) queries and decisions will need to be made which ones should be precomputed given that storage may be limited and we wish to minimize the cost of computing the aggregates.

Another related issue is deciding the residing location of data used by OLAP. We assume the data is stored in a data warehouse or in one or more data marts.

Data cube products use different techniques for precomputing and storing aggregates. They are generally based on one of two implementation models. The first model, supported by vendors of traditional relational model databases, is called the ROLAP model for Relational OLAP. The second model is called the MOLAP model for multidimensional OLAP. The MOLAP model provides a direct multidimensional view of the data whereas the ROLAP model provides a relational view of the multidimensional data.

15.15.1 ROLAP

ROLAP is relational OLAP and uses a relational DBMS to implement an OLAP environment. It is typically based on using a data warehouse that has been designed using a star schema. The data therefore is likely to be in a denormalized structure. A normalized database avoids redundancy but is usually not appropriate for high performance. The summary data will be held in aggregate tables. The data warehouse provides the multidimensional capabilities by representing data in fact table(s) and dimension tables. The fact table contains one column for each dimension and one column for each measure and every row of the table provides one fact. An OLAP tool is then provided to manipulate the data in these data warehouse tables. The advantage of using ROLAP is that it is more easily used with existing relational DBMS and the data can be stored more efficiently using tables. The major disadvantage of the ROLAP model is the poor query performance of ROLAP products.

15.15.2 MOLAP

MOLAP is multidimensional OLAP and is based on using a multidimensional DBMS rather than a data warehouse to store and access data. The multidimensional database systems do not have a standard approach to storing and maintaining their data. They often use special-purpose file systems or indexes that store all aggregations in the cube precomputed. Since MOLAP does not use a relational data warehouse as its basis, it is necessary to use proprietary software tools. These tools try to optimize storage usage and query execution times. The data for precomputed aggregates has to come from source systems and could also come from a data warehouse. The multidimensional DBMS is normally stored on disk but storing data in main memory can further boost the performance of the system. The precomputed aggregates are often stored in some form of array structure. MOLAP systems have to deal with sparsity since a very high percentage of the cells can be empty in some applications. The MOLAP implementation is usually exceptionally efficient. The disadvantage of using MOLAP is that it is likely to be more expensive than ROLAP, the data is not always current, and it may be more difficult to scale a MOLAP system for very large OLAP problems.

It has been suggested that MOLAP is easier to use and therefore may be more suitable for inexperienced users. Users who need a tool that they can use for frequently changing query requirements may be better advised to use ROLAP.

15.15.3 HOLAP

Hybrid OLAP or HOLAP attempts to combine the advantages of MOLAP and ROLAP. For summary-type information, HOLAP uses MOLAP type technology for faster performance of summary queries. When detail information is needed, ROLAP is used to drill down into the details.

15.16 DATA CUBE OPERATIONS

A number of operations may be applied to data cubes. The common ones are as follows:

- Roll-up
- Drill-down
- Slice and Dice
- Pivot

We describe these operations now.

15.16.1 Roll-up

Roll-up is like zooming out on the data cube. It is required when the user needs further abstraction or less detail. This operation performs further aggregations on the data. For example, from single degree programs to all programs offered by a school or department, from single state to a collection of states, and from individual years to a number of years. Often a hierarchy defined on a dimension is useful in the roll-up operation as suggested by the example of states and regions.

15.16.2 Drill-down

Drill-down is like zooming in on the data and is therefore the reverse of roll-up. It is an appropriate operation when the user needs further details or when the user wants to partition more finely or wants to focus on some particular values of certain dimensions. Drill-down adds more details to the data. Hierarchy defined on a dimension may be involved in drill-down. For example, a higher level view of student data gives student numbers for the two years for groups of states and groups of degrees. If one is interested in more detail then it is possible to drill-down for student numbers in each of the years, for each state and for each degree.

15.16.3 Slice and Dice

Slice and dice are operations for browsing the data in the cube. It refers to the ability to look at information from different viewpoints.

A slice is a subset of the cube corresponding to a single value for one or more members of the dimensions. For example, a slice operation is performed when the user wants a selection on one dimension of a three-dimensional cube resulting in a two-dimensional slice. Let the degree dimension be fixed as degree = BIT. The slice will not include any information about other degrees. The information retrieved therefore is more like a two-dimensional cube for degree = BIT.

The dice operation is similar to slice but dicing does not involve reducing the number of dimensions. A dice is obtained by performing a selection on two or more dimensions. For example, one may only be interested in degrees BIT and BCom and states West Bengal, Maharashtra and Kerala for years 2005 and 2006. The result is a three-dimensional cube.

Slice and dice often figure in interactive use of an OLAP system in which the user can navigate through the cube by specifying either one or two dimensions or values of all three dimensions that are of interest.

15.16.4 Pivot or Rotate

The pivot operation is used when the user wishes to re-orient the view of the data cube. It may involve swapping the rows and columns, or moving one of the row dimensions into the column dimension. For example, the cube consisting of Tables 15.7, 15.11 and 15.12 gives the dimension degree along the x-axis, state along the y-axis and starting year along the z-axis (or the vertical axis). One may want to swap the dimensions state and starting year. The cube will then consist of several tables like those given in Tables 15.13 and 15.14 on top of each other.

Table 15.13 One table on which other similar tables are piled up in a rotated cube (State Dimension Value = West Bengal)

	BSc	*LLB*	*MBBS*	*BCom*	*BIT*	*ALL*
2005	5	0	5	25	7	42
2006	8	0	5	16	7	36
ALL	13	0	10	41	14	78

Table 15.14 Another table that is part of a rotated cube (State Dimension Value = Maharashtra)

	BSc	*LLB*	*MBBS*	*BCom*	*BIT*	*ALL*
2005	5	1	10	12	23	67
2006	5	1	19	19	20	64
ALL	10	2	29	31	43	131

Clearly this rotated cube gives a different view of the same data. Such views can be particularly useful if the number of dimensions is greater than three.

15.17 GUIDELINES FOR OLAP IMPLEMENTATION

In this section we present a number of guidelines for successful implementation of OLAP. The guidelines are somewhat similar to those presented for data warehouse implementation in Section 15.8.

1. *Vision*—The OLAP team must, in consultation with the users, develop a clear vision for the OLAP system. This vision including the business objectives should be clearly defined, understood and shared by the stakeholders.
2. *Senior Management Support*—The OLAP project should be fully supported by the senior managers. Since a data warehouse may have been developed already, this should not be difficult.
3. *Selecting an OLAP tool*—The OLAP team should familiarize themselves with the ROLAP and MOLAP tools available in the market. Since the tools are quite different, careful planning may be required in selecting a tool that is appropriate for the enterprise.
4. *Corporate Strategy*—The OLAP strategy should fit with the enterprise strategy and business objectives. A good fit will result in the OLAP tools being used more widely.
5. *Focus on the Users*—The OLAP project should be focused on the users. The users should, in consultation with the technical professionals, decide what tasks will be done first and what will be done next. An attempt should be made to provide each user with a tool suitable for that person's skill level and information needs. The project can only be successful with the full support of the users.
6. *Joint Management*—The OLAP project must be managed by both the IT and business professionals. Many other people should be involved in supplying ideas. An appropriate committee structure may be necessary to channel these ideas.

7. *Adapt and Review*—As noted in the last chapter, organizations evolve and so must the OLAP system. Regular review of the project may be required to ensure that the project is meeting the needs of the enterprise.

15.18 DATA WAREHOUSING CASE STUDY

This case study by Watson, Fuller and Ariyachandra describes an interesting implementation of a data warehouse (DW) in a relatively large healthcare organization of 2.8 million members supporting 200 users in the areas of sales and marketing, financial services, corporate analysis and risk assessment, corporate audit and health quality improvement. The DW described draws data from 12 source systems, including 5 legacy systems, 6 external and third party systems and a new claims system. The system consists of 200 tables, 1500 data elements and 2.5 terabytes of storage running on a system with 17 nodes each with 4 processors.

The focus of the paper however is on governance, not technology. The quality of governance can make or break a high risk/high return data warehouse project. It has been shown that the primary reason for most DW project failures is organizational rather than technical. Although the idea of data warehousing is simple, implementing a DW is complex since it involves quite challenging technical undertakings and significant organizational issues.

The case study presents a discussion of issues that DW governance needs to deal with before the project starts. These include the usual tasks, viz., identifying the need, setting up project priorities, aligning them with company goals, and so on. The role of governance after the DW is operational and is also discussed. The implementation of the DW project is described. A team headed by a Vice-President manages the operations of the DW. The team consists of four groups (Decision Support Consulting, Business Information and Design and Architecture, Project Management and Development, and Operations and Quality Control). The governance structure consists of three strategic and operational committees each chaired by staff of the data warehouse group. These are the Vice-President Data Oversight Team (VPDOT), the Data Development Oversight Team (DDOT) and the Business Requirements Group (BRG). VPDOT provides the high-level direction to the entire project and is a cross-functional team that includes a business leader from each of the major divisions of the organization. DDOT deals with resource prioritization tasks while BRG deals with communicating project developments and issues with the users. Both the operational structure and the governance structure have evolved over time. In spite of changes at the senior management level of the organization, the role and support for DW has remained unchanged.

The project was started in 1997 and so the paper describes a number of years of experience in building, maintaining and refining the DW.

The paper concludes with the benefits of building a DW and the lessons learned. The most important benefit of course was that the organization had a 'single view' of truth. The lessons learned include that the senior management must be passionately involved in the project to be successful; committees are needed to deal with business and technical issues, and finally the importance of educating committee members about what the project is supposed to achieve.

SUMMARY

In this chapter we have discussed the need for an enterprise to have one or more separate databases to support the needs of management. The following topics have been covered:

- The types of database systems that we have discussed so far are called Online Transaction Processing Systems or OLTP systems. These systems support day-to-day operations of an enterprise.
- In addition to OLTP systems, most large enterprises need to have one or more separate database systems to support needs of the management. An example is presented to illustrate the type of queries that senior managers of an enterprise might wish to pose.
- Such management queries cannot be posed to OLTP systems because queries involving aggregates are likely to put substantial load on OLTP systems. Therefore a separate database is required. One such system is called a data warehouse (DW). Another system is called the operational data store (ODS).
- Two definitions of data warehouse are presented and the differences between a data warehouse and OLTP systems are explained.
- A data warehouse is designed to efficiently compute aggregates and trends for decision makers.
- Design of a data warehouse including requirements, design, testing and maintenance are described. Different steps in implementing a data warehouse are explained.
- Guidelines for implementation of data warehouse include full support of top management and appropriate consultation processes with all stakeholders.
- A typical architecture of a data warehouse system includes the source systems, the ETL system, the data warehouse itself, and the end users' interfaces.
- Use of extraction, transformation and loading (ETL) techniques is important for extracting and transforming data from source systems and loading it in the data warehouse.
- Designing a data warehouse requires modeling which may involve using the star schema or the snowflake schema
- Differences between OLAP and OLTP systems include large number of users for the OLTP systems and a select group of users for OLAP.
- OLAP involves using the database like using a spreadsheet. In a spreadsheet, data is provided in a two-dimensional table, and all the summaries of columns and rows are easy to obtain and often very useful. Although a spreadsheet can only be two-dimensional or three-dimensional, OLAP can deal with many dimensions providing the management a variety of summaries and aggregations to assist decision making.
- The concept of a data cube, multidimensional data model and cube implementation is explained. The implementation of OLAP may involve using ROLAP or MOLAP.
- Common OLAP operations such as roll-up, drill-down, slice and dice and pivoting may be carried out on the data cube. These operations allow a user to get less detail, more detail or only a part of the cube.

REVIEW QUESTIONS

1. Why do many enterprises need a data warehouse? (Section 15.1)

2. What are OLTP and OLAP database systems? (Section 15.1)
3. What types of queries do managers need to pose to the enterprise's database systems? (Section 15.2)
4. Discuss the need for a separate database for decision makers. (Section 15.3)
5. What is ODS and what is it used for? (Section 15.4)
6. What is a data warehouse and how is it defined? (Section 15.5)
7. What are the likely benefits of building an enterprise data warehouse? (Section 15.5)
8. List some aims of an OLTP system and a data warehouse system. (Section 15.5)
9. When is implementing a data warehouse is not recommended? List reasons for the same. (Section 15.6)
10. List guidelines for implementing a data warehouse. What is the most important step in implementing a data warehouse? (Section 15.7)
11. Describe the features of a data warehouse. (Section 15.8)
12. Explain why ETL must deal with dirty data when extracting information from the source systems. (Section 15.9.1)
13. Give examples to illustrate the major steps involved in the ETL process. (Section 15.9.2)
14. Explain the star schema technique of modeling a data warehouse. (Section 15.10.1)
15. What is the major difference in the star schema and the snowflake schema. (Section 15.10.3)
16. What are the differences between OLTP and OLAP systems and what are the characteristics of an OLAP system? (Section 15.13)
17. Explain multidimensional view of data. (Section 15.14)
18. What is a data cube? (Section 15.14)
19. How is a data cube implemented? Explain ROLAP and MOLAP. (Section 15.15)
20. Describe the operations, roll-up, drill-down, slicing and dicing, which are possible in a data cube. (Section 15.16)
21. List guidelines for implementing an OLAP system. (Section 15.17)

SHORT ANSWER QUESTIONS

1. List four types of queries that are possible with two variables.
2. What is an OLTP database system?
3. What is an ODS used for? How does it differ from a data warehouse?
4. Define a data warehouse?
5. Give three most important benefits of implementing a data warehouse for a large enterprise.
6. Give one important reason why data warehouse may not be recommended for a company.
7. What is the most important guideline in implementing a data warehouse?
8. Give two major components of any data warehouse system.
9. What is ETL?
10. Give two reasons for dirty data being extracted from source systems.
11. List four steps of the ETL process.
12. What is a dimension?

13. What is a measure?
14. What is a fact and fact table?
15. Show a four-dimension star schema.
16. Give a simple definition of OLAP.
17. List two major characteristics of OLAP.
18. Define data cube in your own words.
19. Illustrate a data cube of two dimensions.
20. Give a simple data cube implementation.
21. Are all data cube entries nonzero? If not, why?
22. What is the major difference between MOLAP and ROLAP?
23. What is the difference between drill-down and slicing?

MULTIPLE CHOICE QUESTIONS

1. Which one of the following is true about OLTP systems?
   (a) OLTP systems run day-to-day business of the enterprise.
   (b) OLTP systems are primarily for senior managers.
   (c) OLTP systems cannot be accessed by enterprise call centres.
   (d) OLTP systems never delete any historical data.
2. Which one of the following is true?
   (a) A separate enterprise database is needed to provide additional computing power.
   (b) An ODS is a special type of data warehouse.
   (c) A DW only has current values.
   (d) A data warehouse cannot be implemented without implementing an ODS first.
3. Which one of the following features must be present in a data warehouse?
   (a) Allow updates by the users.
   (b) Allow retrieval through the Web.
   (c) Data is organized around subject areas important to the management.
   (d) Is refreshed as soon as data in OLTP systems is updated.
4. Which one is **not** true?
   (a) ETL is essential to implement an ODS or a DW.
   (b) ETS involves extraction, transformation and loading.
   (c) ETL can be done after loading OLTP data in a DW.
   (d) ETL deals with dummy codes, multipurpose fields and cryptic data.
5. Which one is true?
   (a) OLAP is essentially the same as data warehousing.
   (b) ODS is essentially an OLTP.
   (c) ROLAP and MOLAP are same.
   (d) ETL is an essential part of implementing DW.

6. Which of the following is **not** a use of a data warehouse?
   (a) Manager's queries (b) Customer's enquiries
   (c) OLAP (d) Data mining
7. Which one of the following is **not** true?
   (a) OLTP systems are for office workers while OLAP is for managers.
   (b) OLTP systems are mission critical while OLAP are not.
   (c) OLTP systems process aggregation queries efficiently.
   (d) OLTP systems are used for updating information while OLAP systems are not.
8. Which one of the following is included in guidelines for OLAP?
   (a) OLAP implementation must have support of technical staff.
   (b) OLAP software should normally be built in-house.
   (c) OLAP system must focus on needs of operational staff.
   (d) OLAP must be managed both by technical and business professionals.
9. Given cardinality of tables *Players*, *match*, *batting* and *bowling* (each 100), which one is the true number of rows in the fact table?
   (a) 100 (b) 1000 (c) 10000 (d) 100000000
10. Which one of the following is **not** required in building a data warehouse?
    (a) Testing (b) Requirements analysis
    (c) Data Modeling (d) Data recovery
11. Which one of the following is **not** true?
    (a) OLTP systems are for office workers while OLAP is for decision makers.
    (b) OLTP is mission-critical while OLAP is management-critical.
    (c) OLTP systems allow insertion, retrievals and updates while no updates are allowed in OLAP systems.
    (d) OLTP systems may be accessed by managers and OLAP may be accessed by call centre workers.
12. Which one of the following is **not** true?
    (a) A cube is a multidimensional structure that contains an aggregate value at each point.
    (b) A cube allows a variety of cross-tabulations.
    (c) A cube does not allow a (ALL, ALL, ALL) aggregation.
    (d) A cube may be implemented in a number of ways.
    (e) All of the above are true.
13. Which one of the following is **not** a characteristic of OLAP systems?
    (a) OLAP systems do not allow multi-user support.
    (b) OLAP systems present a multidimensional view of data.
    (c) OLAP systems must ignore all missing values.
    (d) OLAP systems should not limit the number of dimensions.
14. Which one of the following is **not** true about data cube implementation?
    (a) ROLAP is a relational implementation.
    (b) MOLAP is a multidimensional implementation.
    (c) OOLAP is an object-oriented implementation.
    (d) HOLAP is a hybrid implementation.

15. Which one of the following pair is essentially the same?
    (a) Data warehouse and data cube
    (b) OLTP and ODS
    (c) Star schema and snowflake schema
    (d) Data warehouse and a data mart
16. Which one of the following is part of the extraction process in ETL?
    (a) Extracting all the data available in the enterprise.
    (b) Extracting all the data required in building a data warehouse.
    (c) Extracting data that has been loaded in the data warehouse.
    (d) Extracting data from the MOLAP system.
17. Which one of the following is **not** an ETL step?
    (a) Compiling
    (b) Combining
    (c) Matching
    (d) Standardizing
18. Which one of the following is a correct relationship between the dimension table and the fact table?
    (a) One-to-one
    (b) Many-to-many
    (c) One-to-many
    (d) Many-to-one
19. Which one of the following is **not** an option in data cube implementation?
    (a) Precompute and store all aggregations.
    (b) Precompute and store no aggregations.
    (c) Precompute and store some aggregations.
    (d) Find the zero aggregations and do not store them.
20. Which one of the following is true?
    (a) Roll-up is looking at more data than is available in the data cube.
    (b) Drill-down is looking at more detail than available in the data cube.
    (c) Slice is a subset of a data cube corresponding to a single value of a dimension.
    (d) Dicing involves reducing the number of dimensions in the data cube.

EXERCISES

1. Define the following terms:
    (a) ODS
    (b) DW
    (c) Star schema
    (d) Fact table
    (e) Dimension
    (f) Measure
2. What are the reasons for implementing a separate ODS and a separate data warehouse in an enterprise?
3. Use an example of a university data warehouse and model it using the star schema.
4. Discuss the following data cleaning issues:
    (a) Missing data
    (b) Duplication removal
    (c) Instance identity problems
    (d) Matching codes
    (e) Keyboard entry errors

5. What are the benefits and risks of implementing a data warehouse?
6. Present a list of guidelines that may assist in the success of a data warehouse project implementation?
7. What is the role of metadata for a data warehouse? Give some examples of data warehouse metadata and explain how it differs from metadata for OLTP systems.
8. Define OLAP and explain its relationship with data warehouse.
9. What is the difference between a dimension, member and a measure? Explain the difference between a fact and a fact table.
10. What is a data cube? What is it supposed to do and how does it achieve it?
11. What is the primary purpose of OLAP? Explain briefly.
12. What are ROLAP and MOLAP? Describe the two approaches and list their advantages and disadvantages.
13. Describe the operations roll-up, drill-down and slice and dice.
14. Does an OLAP system require an indexing system? What type of indexing would be appropriate? Discuss.
15. Describe how one should deal with a data cube when the system is refreshed.
16. Describe MOLAP, ROLAP and HOLAP. Discuss their differences and compare their efficiency. How would the operations roll-up and drill-down be computed differently in the three methods?

PROJECT

1. Consider an airline booking system and assume that the following database system has been implemented. Clearly the database schema is rather primitive.

    Customer(CustomerID, Title, First name, Last name, Gender, Age, Address1, Address2, Address3, Moble, TelephoneBH, TelephoneAH, Email, FrequentFlyerNumber)

    Flight(FlightNUM, DepartureDate, DepartureTime, ArrivalDate, ArrivalTime, PlaneType, Capacity)

    Seat(FlightNUM, CustomerID, DepartureDate, SeatNUM, Class)

    Ticket(SerialNUM, FlightNUM, DepartureDate, SeatNUM, CustomerID, CreditCardType, CreditCardNumber)

    (a) In your opinion, what are the dimensions of interest for the management?
    (b) What types of queries would the airline managers like to pose to this system? Make a list of at least 10 aggregation queries.
    (c) What information should be included in the airline data warehouse from these tables?
    (d) Select three most important dimensions and show them in a data cube using some artificial data.

LAB EXERCISES

1. List some aggregation queries that can be made to the cricket database.

2. Does it make sense to build a cricket data warehouse perhaps based on more information than that given in the database in this book? Consult the cricinfo website and look at the types of statistics that is available there.
3. How frequently would you need to refresh the airline data warehouse? Explain.

BIBLIOGRAPHY

The concept of a data warehouse was introduced by Inmon and the concept of ODS was introduced by Inmon and Imhoff. Codd et al., suggested the need for OLAP.

For Students

Watson et al. described an interesting case study which has been briefly described in Section 15.18. The Data Warehousing Information Center is also a good source of information about data warehousing.

For Instructors

The IBM Red Book, the Oracle Data Warehouse Guide and the SQL Resource Kit are easy to read but they are usually very long documents. They should be consulted for a much more thorough discussion on these topics. The classic references on data warehouses are by Inmon and Kimball. The paper by Widom has been highly cited. The papers by Gray et al., and Codd et al., are classic papers on the data cube and OLAP respectively. The paper by Harinarayan, Rajaraman and Ullman on implementing data cubes has been cited many times.

Agarwal, S., R. Agrawal, P. M. Deshpande, A. Gupta, J. F. Naughton, R. Ramakrishnan, and S. Sarawagi, "On the Computation of Multidimensional Aggregates", *Proceedings of the International Conference on Very Large Data Bases* (VLDB'96), Bombay, India, pp 506-521, September 1996.

Chaudhuri, S., and U. Dayal, 1997, "An Overview of Data Warehousing and OLAP Technology", *SIGMOD Record*, Vol. 26, No. 1, pp. 65-74.

Codd, E. F., S. B. Codd, and C. T. Salley, 1993, "Providing OLAP (on-line analytical processing) to User-analysts: An IT Mandate". http://dev.hyperion.com/download_files/resource_library/white_papers/providing_olap_to_user_analysts.pdf.

Gray, J., A. Bosworth, A. Layman and H. Pirahesh, "Data Cube: A relational aggregation operator generalizing group-by, cross-tab, and sub-totals", *Proceedings of the 12th International Conference on Data Engineering*, New Orleans, pp 152-159, March 1996.

Gray, J., S. Chaudhuri, A. Bosworth, A. Layman, D. Reichart, M. Venkatrao, F. Pellow, and H. Pirahesh, "Data Cube: A relational aggregation operator generalizing group-by, cross-tab and sub-totals", *Data Mining and Knowledge Discovery*, Vol. 1, No.1, pp 29-54, 1997.

Golfarelli M. and Pizzi S., *Data Warehouse Design: Modern Principles and Methodologies*, McGraw Hill, 2009.

Harinarayan, V., A. Rajaraman, and J. D. Ullman, "Implementing Data Cubes Efficiently", *Proceedings of ACM SIGMOD International Conference on Management of Data*, Montreal, Canada, pp 205-216, June 1996.

IBM, DB2 Cube Views: A Primer http://www.redbooks.ibm.com/abstracts/sg247002.html (very long, 760 pages)

Inmon, W. H., *Building the Data Warehouse*, John Wiley, Fourth Edition, 2002.

Inmon, W. H., and C. Imhoff, *Building the Operational Data Store*, John Wiley, 1996.

Kimball, R., *The Data Warehouse Toolkit*, John Wiley, Second Edition, 2002.

Kimball R., and Ross M., *The Data Wareshouse Lifecycle Toolkit*, John Wiley, Second Edition, 2008

Kimball R., and Ross M., The Kimball Group Reader: Relentlessly Practical Tools for Data Warehousing and Business Intelligence, Wiley, 2010.

Oracle9i Data Warehousing Guide, Release 2 (9.2), March 2002. http://www.lc.leidenuniv.nl/awcourse/oracle/server.920/a96520/toc.htm

"SQL Server 2000 Resource Kit", *Cubes in the Real World*, Chapter 22. http://www.microsoft.com/resources/documentation/sql/2000/all/reskit/en-us/default.mspx (long)

"SQL Server 2000 Resource Kit – Data Warehouse Design Considerations", Chapter 17. http://www.microsoft.com/resources/documentation/sql/2000/all/reskit/en-us/default.mspx

"SQL Server 2000 Resource Kit, Data Extraction, Transformation, and Loading", Chapter 19. http://www.microsoft.com/resources/documentation/sql/2000/all/reskit/en-us/default.mspx

Watson, H. J., Fuller, C. and Ariyachandra, T., "Data Warehouse Governance: Best Practices at Blue Cross and Blue Shield of North Carolina", *Decision Support Systems*, Vol. 38, pp 435-450. Copyright (2004), (with permission from Elsevier).

Weir, R., T. Peng and J. Kerridge, "Best Practice for Implementing a Data Warehouse: A review for strategic alignment", In *Data Warehousing and Data Mining Workshop*, Berlin, CEUR Workshop Proceedings, Vol. 77, 2003, pp 5.1-5.14.

Widom, J., "Research Problems in Data Warehousing", *Proceedings of the 4th International Conference on Information and Knowledge Management*, 1995, pp 25-30.

Bill Inmon—Inventor of Data Warehouse

William Inmon is sometimes called the Father of Data Warehousing. He is the creator of the Corporate Information Factory and more recently, creator of the Government Information Factory. He has many years of experience in database technology management and data warehouse design.

Inmon has written a large number of articles on a variety of topics about building, using, and maintaining data warehouse and the Corporate Information Factory. These articles have been published in major computing journals. He has also written many books. Bill Inmon has also established a number of companies.

Inmon received his Bachelor of Science degree in Mathematics from Yale University and his Master of Science degree in Computer Science from New Mexico State University.

Jim Gray (1944–2007)—Inventor of Data Cube

Jim Gray's profile is presented at the end of Chapter 9. His famous papers of 1996 and 1997 are listed in the bibliography for this chapter.

16 Data Mining

OBJECTIVES

- Explain what is data mining and when is it useful.
- List the steps involved in data mining process.
- Explain association rules mining and an algorithm for discovering rules.
- Introduce the concept of supervised classification.
- Explain decision tree building.
- Introduce the concept of clustering and a simple clustering algorithm.
- Introduce web mining and text mining.
- Briefly describe a number of data mining case studies.

KEYWORDS

Data mining, data mining process, association rules, case studies, support, confidence, itemsets, decision tree, clustering, supervised classification, training data, text mining, terms, concepts, web mining, web content mining, web structure mining, web usage mining, hub, authority, Apriori, K-means.

India is the cradle of the human race, the birthplace of human speech, the mother of history, the grandmother of legend, and the great grandmother of tradition.

Mark Twain

16.1 WHAT IS DATA MINING?

Almost all enterprises collect a variety of information electronically. In recent years there has been an explosive growth in the generation and storage of electronic information as operations of enterprises are increasingly being computerized due to technological advances in data acquisition (e.g., barcoding of products) and a continued decline in data storage costs. At the end of 2010, hard disk storage was estimated to cost Rs. 5 per GByte only.

It has been reported that a large chain of stores like Wal-Mart of the USA with more than 4500 stores worldwide in 2010 has to deal with a database of perhaps more than 500 Terabytes[1]. Wal-Mart deals with more than 20 million point-of-sale transactions every day. Some of the major telecommunications companies also collect a huge amount of data as do banks, some scientific research projects and some government agencies. With this growth in electronic information, most enterprises have started to realize that the information accumulated over the years constitutes an important strategic asset (some call it a gold mine of information) and there is potential business intelligence hidden in the large volumes of data. This intelligence can be the secret weapon on which the success of a business may depend. Given the volume of information and its growth (information is claimed to be doubling every 20 months), not even a small fraction of it could be looked at by a human eye. It is therefore no simple matter to discover business intelligence that might assist decision making. What is required are techniques that allow the enterprise to distil the most valuable information from mountains of accumulated data. The field of data mining provides such techniques.

Data mining or knowledge discovery in databases (KDD) is a collection of exploration techniques based on advanced analytical methods and tools for handling a large amount of information. The techniques can find novel patterns that may assist an enterprise in understanding the business better and in business forecasting as well. Many data mining techniques are closely related to some of the machine learning techniques that have been developed over the last 50 years. Others are related to techniques that have been developed in statistics, sometimes called exploratory data analysis. These techniques were developed some time ago and were designed to deal with a limited amount of data. The techniques have now been modified to deal with large amounts of data. Yet other techniques are relatively new. These include techniques used for web data mining.

Data mining may be defined as follows:

> ***Definition—Data Mining***
> ***Data mining is a collection of techniques for efficient automated discovery of previously unknown, valid, novel, useful and understandable patterns in large databases. The patterns must be actionable so they can be used in an enterprise's decision making.***

---

1. A terabyte is one trillion bytes or 10^{12} bytes. It is roughly equivalent to storing two million books. The 460 terabytes figure comes from a 2004 article "What Wal-Mart Knows About Customers' Habits" by Constance L. Hays in The New York Times, November 14, 2004.

As we have noted, we assume that we are dealing with a large or perhaps huge amount of data, certainly in gigabytes, perhaps in terabytes. Data mining techniques may be used for smaller amounts of data, but larger the data, the better the chance of finding something novel and interesting. Also, if something interesting is indeed discovered, the large amount of data provides confidence in the discovery. In other words, we want to ensure that what has been discovered is indeed something interesting about the process underlying the data that is being analysed and not simply a result of some random fluctuations. We want to ensure that the novel pattern that we have discovered is in fact consistent and replicable.

Conventional database systems provide users with query and reporting tools. To some extent, the query and reporting tools can assist in answering questions like "where did the largest number of students come from last year?" but these tools cannot provide any intelligence about why it happened. Data mining is an attempt at providing some intelligence that lets a manager understand his/her business better. In conventional analysis, a manager may have a question or hypothesis or perhaps just a hunch and he/she is interested in proving or disproving it. If the manager had a series of hypotheses, the process of proving or disproving them is likely to be time consuming and expensive. In data mining, the responsibility of the manager does not disappear entirely, but much of the work is shifted to the data mining software, thereby reducing the analysis effort required of the manager.

We now list a number of situations in which data mining may be helpful. We list some of the aims of an enterprise and the questions an enterprise poses. Possible data mining techniques that may be appropriate are suggested as answers.

The aim	*The questions*	*Possible methods*
To find more about customers of the enterprise	How many different types of customers are there? Can we identify groups of similar customers? Which customers are the most profitable?	Classification Clustering
Improving customer service	How do I retain customers for the long term? Which customers are likely to leave?	Classification Customer profiling
Anticipating health problems	Which patient has high risk of heart attack or breast cancer?	Classification
Reducing fraud	Which customers have an unusual pattern of activity?	Clustering customer profiling
How to improve the effectiveness of my website	Which pages are being visited most frequently and what is the location of these?	Web data mining
Designing a shopping mall	There will be 100 shops in the mall. How should they be arranged?	Association Rule Mining

Towards the end of this chapter we present brief descriptions of a number of case studies in which some of the questions listed above are asked and solutions have been suggested. Some of the areas of case studies include the following:

- Retail and Sales

- Banking and Finance
- Telecommunications
- Health Care
- Insurance
- Taxation
- Web and e-commerce

This chapter is organized as follows. We first discuss the data mining process in Section 16.2. A number of well known data mining techniques are described in sections 16.3 to 16.7. These include association rule mining in Sectin 16.3, supervised classification in Section 16.4, clustering in Section 16.5, text mining in Section 16.6 and web mining in Section 16.7. A set of guidelines for successful data mining are presented in Section 16.8. A number of case studies are then presented to illustrate these techniques in Section 16.9.

16.2 THE DATA MINING PROCESS

Data mining is a complex process that involves a number of steps before useful results may be obtained. Often data preprocessing including data cleaning is required. In the last chapter on data warehousing and OLAP, ETL techniques for extracting data for decision makers from the enterprise OLTP and legacy systems were described. For data mining to be effective a lot of careful work is needed in establishing a data warehouse.

A typical data mining process is likely to include the steps shown in Fig. 16.1 which are somewhat similar to the process described for implementing a data warehouse in the last chapter.

We now describe these steps briefly.

1. *Management Support*—Since the benefits of a data mining project will not be immediately obvious to the senior management, it is important to explain the benefits to them and get their full moral and financial support for the project. For data mining to be successful, a senior manager should be the enterprise data mining champion. This is perhaps the most important step in the data mining process.
2. *Requirements Analysis*—The enterprise decision makers need to formulate goals that the data mining process is expected to achieve. The business problem must be clearly defined. One cannot use data mining without a good idea of what kind of outcomes the enterprise is looking for. Furthermore, once the objectives have been clearly defined, it is easier to evaluate the results of the project. Once the goals have been agreed upon, the following steps are needed.

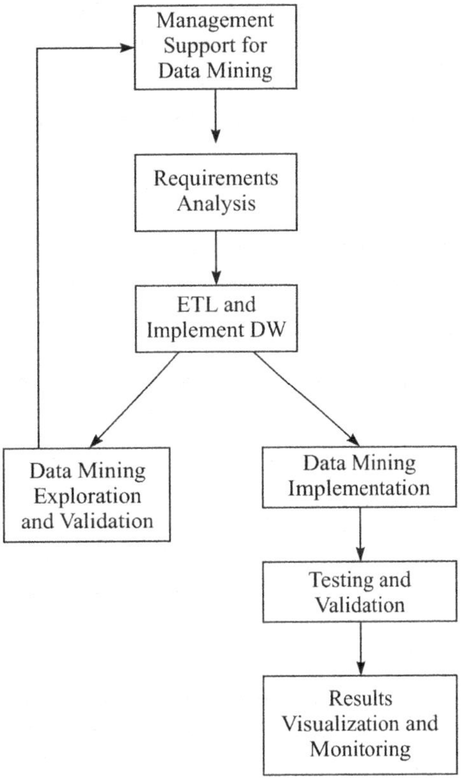

Figure 16.1 Steps of data mining process

3. *Data Selection, Collection and ETL*—This may not be an onerous task if a data warehouse containing the required data already exists. Otherwise, as explained in the last chapter, ETL can be very resource intensive. Details of ETL were presented in the last chapter.
4. *Data Mining Exploration and Validation*—Data mining exploration can now commence. Assuming that the user has access to one or more data mining tools, a data mining model may be constructed based on the enterprise's needs. For each technique the results should be evaluated and their significance interpreted. This is likely to be an iterative process which should lead to selection of one or more techniques that are suitable for implementation, testing and validation.
5. *Implementing, Evaluating and Monitoring*—The selected model can now be implemented. This may involve software development for generating reports or for results visualization and explanation to managers. It may be that more than one technique is available for the given data mining task. It is then important to evaluate the results and choose the best technique. Evaluation may involve checking the accuracy and effectiveness of the technique. Furthermore, there is a need for regular monitoring of the performance of the techniques that have been implemented. Every enterprise evolves with time and so must the data mining system. Therefore, periodical monitoring leads to the refinement of tools and techniques that have been implemented.
6. *Results Visualization*—Explaining the results of data mining to the decision makers is an important step of the process. Most commercial data mining tools include data visualization modules. These tools are often vital in communicating results to the managers although a problem dealing with a number of dimensions must be visualized using a two-dimensional computer screen or printout. Clever data visualization tools are being developed to display results that deal with more than two dimensions.

The approach given above is only one data mining approach. Other methodologies have been suggested. For example, SPSS uses the 5As approach which consists of five steps—assess, access, analyze, act and automate. SAS on the other hand uses another five-step approach that consists of steps—sample, explore, modify, model and assess. Another recommended approach consists of six steps—business understanding, data understanding, data preparation, modeling, evaluation and deployment. These approaches are similar but it needs to be understood that data mining is neither a simple nor an inexpensive process that anyone with a database can carry out.

16.3 ASSOCIATION RULES MINING

We now present a conceptually simple yet interesting example of analyzing supermarket data with the aim of discovering association rules. This is called *association rules mining* or *market basket analysis* and involves searching for interesting customer habits by looking at associations. The classical example is the one where a store in USA was reported to have discovered that people buying nappies tended also to buy beer. The association rules mining technique has many applications other than market basket analysis including applications in marketing, customer segmentation, medicine, electronic commerce, web mining, bioinformatics and finance.

Let us first describe the association rule mining task informally and define some terminology by using an example of a small food shop. To keep the example simple we assume that the shop sells only a small variety of foods as geven below:

- Pizza
- Chicken
- Sweets
- Juice
- Dosa
- Tea
- Biryani
- Bread
- Chat

We assume that the shop has a system that records what each customer purchases. Such records of ten customers are given in Fig. 16.2 below. Each row gives the set of items one customer bought.

Transaction ID	Items
10	Pizza, Chicken, Bread
20	Pizza, Chicken, Juice
30	Pizza, Dosa
40	Chicken, Juice. Dosa, Sweets
50	Chat, Tea, Sweets, Biryani, Bread
60	Chat, Tea, Sweets, Biryani, Dosa, Juice, Bread
70	Pizza, Chicken
80	Pizza, Chicken, Juice, Sweets
90	Pizza, Dosa
100	Chat, Tea, Sweets, Pizza, Dosa, Juice, Bread

Figure 16.2 Transactions for the 10 customers

The shopkeeper wants to find which products (call them items) are sold together frequently. If for example, chat and tea are two items that are sold together frequently then he/she might consider having a sale on one of them in the hope that it will not only increase the sale of that item but also increase the sale of the other. We will soon find a solution to this example.

16.3.1 Terminology

We first define some terminology. We assume that the number of items the shop stocks is n (for example, $n = 9$ for this shop) and these items are represented by $I\{i_1, i_2, ..., i_n\}$. We assume that there are N transactions ($N = 10$ for the shop data in Fig. 16.2). We denote them by $T\{t_1, t_2, .., t_N\}$ each with a unique identifier (TID) and each specifying a subset of items (possibly a small subset) from the item set I purchased by one customer. Let each transaction of m items be $\{i_1, i_2, ..., i_m\}$ with $m < n$. Typically transactions differ in the number of items. We now wish to find association relationships given a large number of transactions such that items that tend to occur together are identified. It should be noted that association rules mining does not take into account the quantities of items bought.

Association rules are often written as $X \rightarrow Y$ meaning that whenever X appears Y also tends to appear. X and Y may be single items or sets of items (in which the same item does not appear in both). X is often referred to as the rule's *antecedent* and Y as the *consequent*.

$X \rightarrow Y$ is a probabilistic relationship found empirically. It indicates only that X and Y have been found together frequently in the given data and does not show causal relationship implying that buying of X by a customer causes him/her to buy Y.

As noted above, we assume that we have a set of transactions, each transaction being a list of items. Suppose items (or itemsets) X and Y appear together in only 10% of the transactions but whenever X appears there is a 80% chance that Y also appears. The 10% presence of X and Y together is called the *support* (or *prevalence*) of the rule and the 80% chance is called the *confidence* (or *predictability*) of the rule. Essentially the support and confidence are attention-grabbing aspects of the rule. A high level of support indicates that the rule is frequent enough for the business to be interested in it and a high level of confidence shows that the rule is true often enough to justify a decision based on it.

Let us define support and confidence more formally. As noted earlier, the total number of transactions is N. Support of X is the number of times it appears in the database divided by N and support for X and Y together is the number of times they appear together divided by N. Therefore, using $P(X)$ to mean probability of X in the database, we have:

$$\text{Support}(X) = (\text{Number of times } X \text{ appears})/N = P(X)$$
$$\text{Support}(XY) = (\text{Number of times } X \text{ and } Y \text{ appear together})/N = P(X \cup Y)$$

Confidence for $X \rightarrow Y$ is defined as the ratio of the support for X and Y together to the support for X. Therefore, if X appears much more frequently than X and Y appear together, the confidence will be low. It does not depend on how frequently Y appears.

$$\text{Confidence of } (X \rightarrow Y) = \text{Support}(XY)/\text{Support}(X) = P(X \cup Y)/P(X) = P(Y/X)$$

$P(Y/X)$ is the probability of Y once X has taken place, also called the conditional probability of Y.

We summarize some of the definitions in the table below.

Term	*Definition*
Support (X)	Number of times X appears in the transactions divided by N, the total number of transactions.
Confidence ($X \rightarrow Y$)	The ratio of the support for X and Y together to the support for X.
Frequent	Items or itemsets that meet the minimum support requirement
Confident	Rules that have more than user-specified minimum confidence
Antecedent and Consequent of rule $X \rightarrow Y$	X is the rule's *antecedent* and Y as the *consequent*.

It should be noted that considerable care is needed in interpreting association rules. For example, if the consequent is very popular, like Coke, which is a very frequently bought item in most Australian supermarkets, then the confidence of the rule is likely to be high irrespective of whether the two items are associated.

16.3.2 The Task and a Naive Algorithm

We are now able to define our task more precisely. Given a large set of transactions, we seek a method to discover all association rules which have at least $p\%$ support with at least $q\%$ confidence such that all rules satisfying these constraints are found and the rules are found efficiently.

Example

Let us consider a naive brute force algorithm to do the task. Consider the following example which is even simpler than what we considered earlier in Fig. 16.2. We now have only four items for sale (Bread, Pizza, Juice and Sweets) and we have only the four transactions given in the Fig. 16.3; each transaction showing the purchases of one customer. We are interested in finding association rules with a minimum support of 50% and minimum confidence of 75%.

Transaction ID	Items
100	Bread, Pizza
200	Bread, Pizza, Juice
300	Bread, Sweets
400	Pizza, Juice. Sweets

Figure 16.3 Transactions for Example 2.1

The basis of our naive algorithm is as follows. If we can list all the combinations of the items that we have in stock and find which one of these combinations are frequent then we can find the association rules that have the confidence from these frequent combinations.

The four items and all combinations of the four items and their frequencies of occurrence in the transaction in Fig. 16.3 are given below in Fig. 16.4.

Itemsets	Frequency
Bread	3
Pizza	3
Juice	2
Sweets	2
(Bread, Pizza)	2
(Bread, Juice)	1
(Bread, Sweets)	1
(Pizza, Juice)	2
(Pizza, Sweets)	1
(Juice, Sweets)	1
(Bread, Pizza, Juice)	1
(Bread, Pizza, Sweets)	0
(Bread, Juice, Sweets)	0
(Pizza, Juice, Sweets)	1
(Bread, Pizza, Juice, Sweets)	0

Figure 16.4 List of all itemsets and their frequencies

Given the required minimum support of 50%, we find the itemsets that occur in at least two transactions. As noted earlier, these itemsets are *frequent*. The above list of frequencies shows that all four items (Bread, Pizza, Juice and Sweets) are frequent. The frequency goes down as we look at 2-itemsets (only two out of a possible six are frequent), 3-itemsets (none are frequent) and 4-itemsets (again, none are frequent). The frequent itemsets are given in Fig. 16.5.

Itemsets	Frequency
Bread	3
Pizza	3
Juice	2
Sweets	2
(Bread, Pizza)	2
(Pizza, Juice)	2

Figure 16.5 The set of all frequent itemsets

We can now proceed to determine if the two 2-itemsets (Bread, Pizza) and (Pizza, Juice) lead to association rules with required confidence of 75%. Every 2-itemset (A, B) can lead to two rules $A \rightarrow B$ and $B \rightarrow A$ if both satisfy the required confidence. As defined earlier, confidence of $A \rightarrow B$ is given by the support for A and B together divided by support for A.

We therefore have four possible rules and their confidence as follows:

Bread → Pizza with confidence of 2/3 = 67%
Pizza → Bread with confidence of 2/3 = 67%
Pizza → Juice with confidence of 2/3 = 67%
Juice → Pizza with confidence of 100%

Therefore, only the last rule Juice → Pizza has confidence above the minimum 75% required and qualifies. These rules have earlier been defined to be *confident*.

This is not an interesting example since there were only four items. We had to use a small number of items because Fig. 16.4 grows quickly with the number of items. There are 15 different combinations in Fig. 16.4 and if we include the null combination (a combination with no items) as well, we obtain 16 or 2^4 combinations. Therefore, if the example had six items it would have produced 64 combinations and if the number of items was 10 then we would have a table with 1024 combinations.

This simple algorithm works well with four items but if the number of items is say 100, the number of combinations is much larger, possibly in billions. The number of combinations becomes over a million with 20 items since the number of combinations is 2^n with n items.

16.3.3 The Apriori Algorithm

The basic algorithm for finding association rules, called the Apriori algorithm, was first proposed in 1993. This algorithm may be considered to consist of two parts. In the first part, the frequent itemsets (that exceed the minimum support requirement) are found. In the second part, association rules that meet the minimum confidence requirement are found from the frequent itemsets. The second part is relatively straightforward, so much of the focus of the research in this field has been to improve the first part.

First Part—Frequent Itemsets

The first part of the algorithm itself may be divided into two steps (Steps 2 and 3 below). The first step essentially finds itemsets that are likely to be frequent or candidates for frequent itemsets. The second step finds a subset of these candidate itemsets that are actually frequent.

The algorithm works as follows for a given set of transactions (it is assumed that we require minimum support of p%):

1. *Step* 1—Scan all transactions and find all frequent items. Let these frequent items be L_1.
2. *Step* 2—Build potential sets of k items from L_{k-1} by using pairs of item sets in L_{k-1} such that each pair has the first k–2 items common. Now the k–2 common items and the one remaining item from each of the two itemsets are combined to form a k itemset. The set of such potentially frequent k itemsets is the candidate set C_k. (For $k = 2$, build potential frequent pairs by using the frequent item set L_1 so that every item in L_1 appears with every other item in L_1. The set so generated is the candidate set C_2). This step is called Apriori-gen.
3. *Step* 3—Scan all transactions and find all k-itemsets in C_k that are frequent. The frequent set so obtained is L_k. (For $k = 2$, C_2 is the set of candidate pairs. The frequent pairs are L_2.)
4. Terminate when no further frequent itemsets are found otherwise continue with Step 2.

Second Part—Finding the rules

To find the association rules from the frequent itemsets, we take a large frequent itemset, say v, and find each non-empty subset a. The rule $a \rightarrow (v - a)$ is possible if it satisfies the confidence. Confidence of this rule is given by support(v)/support(a).

There are many other methods for solving the association rule mining problem but we will not discuss the problem further.

16.4 CLASSIFICATION AND PREDICTION

Supervised classification is a classical problem extensively studied by statisticians and machine learning researchers and is probably one of the most widely used data mining techniques. In classification it is assumed that the classes have been decided apriori and classification then consists of training the system so that when a new object is presented to the trained system the system is able to make a prediction by assigning the object to one of the existing classes. This approach is called *supervised classification*. Techniques are also available for unsupervised classification in which the classes are determined based on the given data. Those techniques are called clustering and will be discussed in the next section.

The training is based on a training sample, a set of sample data, where for each sample the class is already known. We assume each object to have a number of attributes, one of which tells us which class the object belongs to. The attributes may be of different types. Attributes whose domain is numerical are called *numerical attributes* while attributes whose domain is not numerical are called *categorical attributes*. Usually supervised classification assumes that the attributes are categorical. If some of the attributes are continuous-valued, they should be discretised by binning. For example, age values may be binned into the following categories (under 18), (18 – 40), (41 – 65) and (over 65) and transformed into A, B, C and D or more.

The class attribute is known for the training data but for data other than the training data (we call this other data the *test data*) we assume that the value of the attribute is unknown and is to be determined by the classification method. In supervised learning schemes, it is assumed that we have sufficient training data to build an accurate model during the training phase. The model that we build from the training data is never 100% accurate and classification based on the model will always lead to errors in some cases. In spite of such errors, classification can be useful for prediction and better understanding of the data.

There are a number of classification methods. We will only discuss the *decision tree technique*. A decision tree is a popular classification method that results in a flow-chart like tree structure where each node denotes a test on an attribute value and each branch represents an outcome of the test. The tree leaves represent the classes.

The decision tree algorithm is given below. It is a relatively simple top-down algorithm. The aim of the algorithm is to build a tree that has leaves that are as homogeneous as possible. The major step of the algorithm is to continue to divide leaves that are not homogeneous into leaves that are as homogeneous as possible until no further division is possible.

1. Let the set of training data be *S*. Put all of *S* in a single tree node.
2. If all instances in *S* are in the same class, then stop.
3. Split the next node by selecting an attribute *A* from amongst the attributes that best divides or splits the objects in the node into subsets and create a decision tree node.
4. Split the node according to the values of *A*.
5. Stop if either of the following conditions is met otherwise continue with Step 3:
   (a) If this partition divides the data into subsets that belong to a single class and no other node needs splitting.
   (b) If there are no remaining attributes on which the sample may be further divided.

In the decision tree algorithm, decisions are made locally and the algorithm at no stage tries to find a globally optimum tree.

The major step in the decision tree building algorithm is Step 3, where an attribute that best splits the data needs to be selected. We assume that only one attribute is to be used for the split, although methods that use a combination of attributes have been proposed in the literature. Therefore, the split rules in our algorithm are based on simple tests, for example, 'salary = high' while algorithms that use more than one split attribute may use split rules such as 'salary = high and age = A'.

To find a split attribute, all the attributes that have not yet been used need to be somehow given a *goodness* value that shows the discrimination power of the attribute. The attributes then may be ranked according to that value and the highest ranked attribute selected.

16.5 CLUSTERING

There are major differences between cluster analysis and supervised classification. In supervised classification, the user already knows the classes and training data that is already labeled by their class membership is available to train or build a model. In cluster analysis, the user does not know what classes or clusters exist in the data and the aim is to group the given data into meaningful groups. The idea in clustering is to find the groups or clusters so that intra-cluster differences are minimized (that is, all members of a cluster are as similar to each other as possible) and inter-cluster differences are maximised (that is, all members of different clusters are as different from each other as possible). Clustering has a number of applications, for example, clustering of patients with similar symptoms, or documents of similar nature, and as discussed in Section 16.9.6 in crime analysis, to find cluster of similar crimes.

There are a large number of cluster analysis methods available, which are often based on diverse underlying principles and they lead to qualitatively different results. In some ways cluster analysis is best used as an exploratory data analysis exercise when the user has no hypothesis to test. We will discuss only one cluster analysis method. In this widely used K-means method, it is required that the user specify the number of clusters and starting seeds for each cluster. In many applications it might be difficult to specify these without some insight into the data that the user may not have. Other methods can then be tried.

K-means is the simplest and most popular classical clustering method that is easy to implement. The classical method can only be used if the data about all the objects is located in the main memory. The method is called K-means since each of the K clusters is represented by the mean of the objects (called the centroid) within it. It is also called the centroid method since at each step the centroid point of each cluster is assumed to be known and each of the remaining points are allocated to the cluster whose centroid is closest to it. Once this allocation is completed, centroids of the clusters are recomputed using simple means and the process of allocating points to each cluster is repeated until there is no change in the clusters (or some other stopping criterion, e.g., no significant reduction in the squared error is met). The method may also be looked at as a search problem where the aim is essentially to find the optimum clusters given the number of clusters and seeds specified by the user. Obviously we cannot use a brute-force or exhaustive search method to find the optimum so we consider solutions that may not be optimal but may be computed efficiently.

The K-means method uses the Euclidean distance measure, which appears to work well with compact clusters. If instead of the Euclidean distance, the Manhattan distance is used, the method is called the K-median method. The K-median method can be less sensitive to outliers.

The K-means method may be described as follows:

1. Select the number of clusters. Let this number be k.
2. Pick k seeds as centroids of the k clusters. The seeds may be picked randomly unless the user has some insight into the data.
3. Compute the Euclidean distance of each object in the data set from each of the centroids.
4. Allocate each object to its nearest cluster based on the distances computed in the previous step.
5. Compute the centroids of the clusters by computing the means of the attribute values of the objects in each cluster.
6. Check if the stopping criterion has been met (e.g., the cluster membership of each cluster is unchanged). If yes, go to Step 7. If not, go to Step 3.
7. [Optional] One may decide to stop at this stage or to split a cluster or combine two clusters heuristically until a stopping criterion is met.

The method is scalable and efficient (the time complexity is of $O(n)$ and is guaranteed to find a local minimum.

16.6 TEXT DATA MINING

There is huge amount of useful information in piles of textual information published in newspapers, magazines, blogs, web pages and scientific papers. One of the objectives of text mining is similar to that of supervised classification. We wish to classify documents based on a number of documents that have been classified already. In the past, some of this work was carried out by librarians but given the amount of textual data being published today, we need an automatic knowledge-intensive classification technique.

Let us consider data mining any collection of documents. We assume that the documents have no particular structure but do have some patterns that are worth extracting. The volume of documents is now too large and therefore it is necessary to extract structure from them. One way of doing so is to extract terms which are often single words extracted directly from the documents using a term extraction algorithm. Concepts may also be extracted. Let us first define terms and concepts informally.

Definition—Term
A term is a single word or multiword phrases selected from a document.

Definition—Concept
A concept is a single word, multiword, whole clause, or even larger syntactical unit that is related to specific concept identifier.

Text mining essentially consists of discovering patterns in a document. A useful pattern to extract from a document collection is a frequent concept set. This is a set of concepts which occurs frequently enough (above a given threshold). Another useful concept may be associations. This is similar to what we discussed in the association rule mining (ARM). In text mining this essentially involves a pattern which is like $A \Rightarrow B$ meaning that when a concept A appears then the concept B also tends to appear.

Before any pattern discovery may be carried out, each document that is being studied must be preprocessed. Preprocessing usually involves representing each document as having a set of attributes or features. These features must be automatically extracted since the number of features is often large. Preprocessing in many cases also requires removing the most common words of the language (called stop words) and stemming (for example, replacing computer, computing, computation, etc., with a word like 'comput' even if that is not a word). A number of different types of features have been proposed including those based on terms and on concepts. A document then may be represented with a feature vector which may be used in data mining.

There are many techniques for text mining which include clustering, categorization, classification and association. These techniques have applications in searching large collection of legal documents, financial documents, patents, and life sciences. We discuss a somewhat different problem of comparing a number of documents and finding those that are identical or similar or have significant overlap based only on content. Some studies have considered the problem of analyzing a large collection of documents to find those that are similar. This is an *n*-to-*n* problem. Others have studied the problem in which one document is compared with documents from a given collection. This is a 1-to-*n* problem. Resemblance of two documents may be defined to be a number between 0 and 1; with 1 indicating that the two documents are identical.

A number of techniques for syntactic similarity analysis are based on fingerprinting. A system called COPS was developed at Stanford in the context of copyright protection based on dividing each document into chunks. A chunk is defined as a sequence of consecutive units (sections, paragraphs, sentences, or words) which could then be counted and compared.

Another technique uses fingerprinting based on a set of subsequences of characters from the document. A document of length N is divided into all possible substrings of length L. These $N - L + 1$ substrings are called *shingles*. Assuming $S(X)$ and $S(Y)$ to be the sets of shingles for documents X and Y respectively, resemblance $R(X, Y)$ and containment $C(X, Y)$ between the two documents may be defined as follows:

$$R(X, Y) = \{S(X) \cap S(Y)\}/\{S(X) \cup S(Y)\},$$

and $$C(X, Y) = \{S(X) \cap S(Y)\}/\{S(X)\}$$

where {.} represents the cardinality of the set. An algorithm like the following may now be used to find similar documents from a collection:

1. Choose a suitable shingle width and compute the shingles for each document.
2. Build a fingerprint for each document based on the shingles or their subset.
3. Compare the fingerprints for each pair of documents.
4. Identify those documents that are similar based on the number fingerprints that match.

In all fingerprinting techniques, the fingerprint must be small enough not to require too much additional storage and be efficient. In one study, fingerprints of 30 million documents were used to build clusters. 3.6 million clusters were found, most of which contained identical documents.

In another study, statistics of documents were collected. These included inverse document frequency[2] or *idf* for each term and then using the *idf* filtered the document, after removing the most common and most infrequent terms. A signature for each document was built and compared with other documents.

It should be noted that no syntactic similarity method that finds two documents to be similar can guarantee that the documents are indeed similar since most techniques, to save on storage and CPU time, use only a small fraction of the documents to analyze similarity.

16.7 WEB DATA MINING

Web mining is the application of data mining techniques to find interesting and potentially useful knowledge from web data including hyperlink structures of the Web and the web log data.

There is no agreed definition of web mining but we present one simple definition.

Definition—Web Mining
Web mining is the application of data mining techniques to find interesting and potentially useful knowledge from web data. It is normally expected that either the hyperlink structure of the Web or the web log data or both have been used in the mining process.

Web mining may be divided into three categories:

1. *Web Content Mining*—deals with discovering useful information or knowledge from web page contents. It goes well beyond using keywords in a search engine. In contrast to web usage mining and web structure mining, web content mining focuses on the web page content rather than the links. As noted earlier, web content is a very rich information resource consisting of many types of information.

2. Inverse document frequency is commonly used in text mining. It is useful to deal with the issue that some words may appear frequently in some documents like algorithm in a book on data structures and algorithm. IDF is defined as the logarithm of the ratio of number of documents in a collection to the number of documents containing the given word. For more information, look at the article "Why Inverse Document Frequency" by Kishore Papineni at www.aclweb.org/anthology/N/N01/N01-1004.pdf

For example, unstructured free text, image, audio, video and metadata as well as hyperlinks. The content of web pages includes no machine readable semantic information. Search engines, subject directories, intelligent agents, cluster analysis and portals are employed to find what a user might be looking for.

2. *Web Structure Mining*—deals with discovering and modeling the link structure of the Web. Work has been carried out to model the Web-based on the topology of the hyperlinks. This can help in discovering similarity between sites or in discovering important sites for a particular topic or discipline or in discovering web communities. Kleinberg at Cornell has developed a connectivity analysis algorithm called Hyperlink-Induced Topic Search (HITS) based on the assumption that links represent human judgement. His algorithm also assumes that for any query topic, there are a set of *authority* sites that are relevant and popular focusing on the topic and there are *hub* sites that contain useful links to relevant sites on the topic including links to many related authorities.
3. *Web Usage Mining*—deals with understanding user behaviour in interacting with the Web or with a website. One of the aims is to obtain information that may assist website reorganisation or assist site adaptation to better suit the user. The mined data often includes data logs of users' interactions with the Web. The logs include the web server logs, proxy server logs and browser logs. The logs include information about the referring pages, user identification, time a user spends at a site and the sequence of pages visited. While web structure mining shows that page *A* has a link to page *B*, Web usage mining shows who or how many people took that link, which site they came from and where they went when they left page *B*.

The three categories above are not independent since web structure mining is closely related to web content mining and both are related to web usage mining.

It should be noted that there are major differences between text mining and searching the Web:

1. *Hyperlink*—Text documents obviously do not have hyperlinks, while the links are very important components of web documents. In hard copy documents in a library, the documents are usually structured (e.g., books) and they have been catalogued by cataloguing experts. No linkage between these documents is identified except that two documents may have been catalogued to the same classification and therefore deal with similar topics. None of this is true for the web documents. The web hyperlinks provide important information. *A* link from page *A* to page *B* indicates that the author of page *A* considered page *B* of some value.
2. *Types of Information*—As noted above, web pages differ widely in structure, quality and their usefulness. Web pages can consist of text, frames, multimedia objects, animation and other types of information quite different than text documents which mainly consist of text but may have some other objects like tables, diagrams, figures and perhaps some images.
3. *Dynamics*—Text documents do not change unless a new edition of a book appears while web pages change frequently because the information on the Web including linkage information is updated all the time (although some web pages are out of date and never seem to change!) and new pages appear almost every second.
4. *Quality*—Text documents are usually of high quality since they go through some quality control process because they are very expensive to produce. In contrast, much of the information on the Web is of low quality. Compared to the size of the Web, it may be that less than 10% of web pages are really useful and of high quality.

5. *Huge Size*—Although some of the libraries are very large, the Web in comparison is much larger, perhaps its size is approaching 100 terabytes, that is, equivalent to about 200 million books. All the books in the US Library of Congress would fit in about 20 terabytes!

Another Web related topic is search engines. Search engines are huge databases of web pages as well as software packages for indexing and retrieving pages that enable users to find information of interest on the Web. Normally the search engine databases of web pages are built and updated automatically by web crawlers. When one searches the Web using one of the search engines, one is not searching the entire Web. Instead one is only searching the database that has been compiled by the search engine. Normally the huge search engine database is searched using an index that has been built.

16.8 GUIDELINES FOR SUCCESSFUL DATA MINING

Every data mining project is different but the projects do have some common features to. A very nice article describing these is by Lavrac, Motoda, Fawcett, Holte and Langley. First they discuss some basic requirements for a data mining project to be successful. These are as follows:

- The data must be available.
- The data must be relevant, adequate and clean.
- There must be a well-defined problem.
- The problem should not be solvable by means of ordinary query or OLAP tools.
- The results must be actionable.

Once the above basic prerequisites have been met, the following guidelines may be appropriate for a data mining project. A useful and much more detailed document is the CRISP-DM.

1. Data mining projects should be carried out by small teams with a strong internal integration and a loose management style.
2. Before starting a major data mining project, it is recommended that a small pilot project be carried. This may involve a steep learning curve for the project team. This is of vital importance.
3. A clear problem owner should be identified who is responsible for the project. Preferably this is not a technical analyst or a consultant but someone with direct business responsibility, e.g., someone with experience in a sales or marketing environment. This will benefit the external integration.
4. The positive return on investment should be realized within 6 to 12 months.
5. The whole project should have the support of the top management of the company.

Similar guidelines are presented in some other data mining literature regarding successful implementation of specific data mining techniques.

16.9 DATA MINING CASE STUDIES

We now present a number of case studies from a variety of data mining applications. The original papers describing some of these case studies as well as a number of other case studies are included in the book. These original case studies must be carefully studied to better understand the applications of data mining and the data mining process.

16.9.1 Aviation

Wipro has reported a simple case study of frequent flyer data from an Indian airline. Before carrying out data mining, the data was extracted and prepared. The study used only the three most common sectors flown by each customer and the three most common sectors for which points were redeemed by each customer. Much of the data supplied by the airline was incomplete or inaccurate and it was felt that the customer data captured by the company could have been more complete. The airline, for example, did not know customers' marital status or their income or reasons for taking a journey.

In spite of problems with the data, there were some interesting results including some simple facts that most customers fly between metropolitan cities of India. It was found that customers flying Mumbai–Delhi also flew to other cities, for example, Mumbai–Chennai, Mumbai–Kolkata and Mumbai–Banglore. Most customers flying Banglore–Hyderabad also travelled Delhi–Banglore. Those who flew Gauhati to Bagdogra did not fly back to Gauhati but instead flew to Delhi. These results provided the airline with a somewhat better understanding of its business and better quality data would have helped the airline to refine flight programming to better suit the customers.

16.9.2 Classification—Direct Marketing

In this case study, a direct mail company held a list of a large number of potential customers. The company's response rate had been only 1%, which the company wanted to improve. To carry out data mining, the company had to first prepare data, which included sampling the data to select a subset of customers including those that responded to direct mails and those that did not.

For each customer, there were more than 200 variables including basic personal information like the area where they lived, their gender, marital status, and their buying habits including when they last responded to a mailout, what money they spent the last time they responded, and the last product they bought.

Using the decision tree approach, the company was able to identify characteristics of customers who were more likely to respond and was thus able to reduce the number of customers it mailed while simultaneously improving the response rate.

16.9.3 Astronomy

An interesting area for application of data mining is astronomy. Astronomers produce huge amounts of data every night on the fluctuating intensity of around 20 million stars which are classified by their spectra and their surface temperature. Some 90% of stars are called *main sequence stars* including some stars that are very large, very hot and blue in colour. The main sequence stars are fuelled by nuclear fusion and are very stable, lasting billions of years. Smaller main sequence stars include the Sun (star type *G* in the table below). There are a number of classes including stars called yellow dwarf, red dwarf and white dwarf. We show the seven major classes below:

Star type	Colour	Approximate temperature	Average brightness (Sun = 1)	Average radius (Sun =1)
O	Blue	> 25,000K	> million	60
B	Blue	11,000 to 25,000K	20,000	18
A	Blue	7,500 to 11,000K	80	3.2
F	Blue to White	6,000 to 7,500K	6	1.7
G	White to Yellow	5,000 to 6,000K	1.2	1.1
K	Orange to Red	3,500 to 5,000K	0.4	0.8
M	Red	< 3,500K	0.04	0.3

Figure 16.6 Different types of stars

Using the enormous amount of data that is being collected, astronomers want to classify stars and galaxies and find any new classes of objects that might be present out there. Decision trees and cluster analysis techniques have been used for such data mining.

As an example, when a clustering program was used to group a large amount of astronomical data, four classes corresponding to stars, galaxies with bright central cores, galaxies without bright central cores and stars with visible 'fuzz' around them were found. The clustering program found unexpected but meaningful results without any understanding of astronomical data.

16.9.4 Classification—Banking

This case study by Hu in 2005 uses a number of classification techniques to analyze a large retailing bank's 750,000 customers of a loss-making loan product and identify those that have high probability to attrite.

938 attriters and an equal number of non-attriters were selected randomly and combined to make the training dataset. Monthly data for four months was combined into one record with 870 fields, which were reduced to 242 fields after filtering and sensitivity analysis.

Four algorithms, boosted naive bayesian, neural network, decision tree and selective naive Bayesian as well as a hybrid algorithm combining the four were used to rank customers from those most likely to attrition to those least likely. The decision tree algorithm was modified to do so. The effectiveness of each algorithm was evaluated by calculating 'lift' defined as the ratio of attritioners found in the top *p*% of the result to the number expected in a random sample.

Finally, the results were tested in a field trial in which top 4% of around 750,000 customers ranked by the hybrid method were chosen and divided into two groups of 15,000 customers each. Each customer in one of the groups was contacted by the bank and offered an incentive package while no contact was made with the other group. The attrition rate of the two groups at the end of two months was 0.12% and 5.6% respectively. Although the 0.12% result appears attractive, it may not be a good basis for action by the bank since over 94%

of the 15,000 customers who were contacted were not expected to attrition and the incentives were wasted on them.

16.9.5 Banking and Finance

Banking and finance is a rapidly changing competitive industry. The industry is using data mining for a variety of tasks including building customer profiles to better understand the customers, identify fraud, evaluate risks in personal and home loans, and better forecast stock prices, interest rates, exchange rates and commodity prices. In the field of credit evaluation, data mining can assist in establishing an automated decision support system which would allow credit card or loan providing companies to quickly and accurately assess risk and approve or reject an application.

The magazine Network Magazine India reports a case study about the Standard Chartered Bank (SCB). The bank established a group of 25 people in Bangalore to analyse the large amount of data from its 2.2 million customers and 1.3 million credit card holders. SCB discovered that a significant proportion of their business came from the upwardly mobile Indian women and this was likely to grow substantially. The bank successfully launched a specially designed women's international credit card with several features including discounts and zero interest rates on categories like jewellery, cosmetics, apparel, consumer durables, leather products, and mobile phones.

16.9.6 Clustering—Crime Prevention

A number of case studies have now been published about use of data mining techniques in analysing crime data. In one particular study, data mining techniques were used to link serious sexual crimes to other crimes that might have been committed by the same offenders. The data used related to more than 2000 offences (the number of offenders was much smaller since most offenders committed multiple crimes) involving a variety of sexual crimes.

As in most case studies, the data was not complete and there were errors and discrepancies in the data supplied by the police. Some of the values were also missing. Data was encoded and two sets of variables were selected for two different studies. In one of the studies, three clusters were identified. In the other study only one 'super cluster' was found. The results of the study were verified and it was found that the clusters did have strong similarities within them and they identified crime patterns that police officers, could agree with. SPSS data mining package Clementine was used for this study.

16.9.7 Healthcare

Data mining has been used in determining factors influencing the survival rate of heart transplant patients when survival rate data has been available for a significant number of patients over several years. It has been claimed that data mining may be able to identify factors that influence doctors' ability to recommend new drugs in the market. In Australia, the Health Insurance Commission has been able to identify doctors who tend to overservice their patients. In one data mining application, it was found that there were a small number of patients who tended to go doctor shopping, that is, they visited several different doctors during a month or a fortnight.

In a healthcare data mining study, data from a hospital was analysed. The aim of the study was to be able to predict the length of hospital stay for patients suffering from spinal cord injuries. The study was undertaken because spinal injury patients often had extended hospital stays and the hospital system wanted to know if the length of stay could be reduced and the efficiency of the hospital improved.

The study required data validation and data cleaning including manual checking to ensure accuracy and reliability. Many errors and in many cases missing values were found in the paper records. About 5000 data records were thus extracted. The data belonged to some 20 diagnostic categories of spinal cord injuries. The length of stay varied from one day to more than two years, with a mean of about two months. The data was visualised and after visualisation, it was decided to focus the study on patients who had stayed less than 40 days, since this duration included the vast majority of cases. Models were built which could correctly predict the length of stay in up to 80% of the cases.

16.9.8 Telecommunications

The telecommunications business is changing through consolidation in the market place and the convergence of new technologies, for example, video, voice, data and mobile phones. Furthermore, in some countries, on one hand there is an infrastructure capacity explosion and on the other hand the Internet and VOIP (voice on the Internet protocol) is impacting the telecommunications business significantly. In this environment, the carriers are offering a variety of products including packaged landline, broadband and mobile phone services.

A widely discussed data mining application in the telecommunications industry is churn analysis. Essentially, given the highly competitive nature of the industry, there is extreme competition to retain customers and to poach other companies' customers. Data mining can provide information about customers who are most likely to remain loyal and those who are most likely to switch. The industry places high importance on retaining customers since retaining a good customer is much cheaper than recruiting a new customer.

A telecommunications company has to deal with a large number of variables including cost of local calls, cost of international calls, mobile phone plans, installation and disconnection rates, customer satisfaction data or data about customers who do not pay their bills or do not pay them on time. Furthermore, companies would like to improve their profitability by identifying customers who might wish to buy new products and to profile customers' use of telephone cards in an attempt to reduce fraud. A number of data mining techniques are being used including data warehousing, OLAP, classification, clustering and association rules in the telecommunications sector.

SUMMARY

In this chapter we have explained what data mining is and have presented the following topics:

- Data mining is used for efficient automated discovery of previously unknown, valid, novel and actionable patterns.
- Because there is huge amount of data collected by OLTP systems, there is a reason to use data mining techniques to discover useful actionable information in the OLTP data.
- Just like in data warehousing and OLAP, there are a number of steps that are involved in the data mining process. Some of the steps are obtaining management support, requirements analysis and identification of source OLTP (or a data warehouse) systems.

- **Developing a data mining system requires a good understanding of the business as well as the data** mining techniques and available data mining software.
- **For data mining to be successful, it is important that a data mining model be built (e.g., for classification)** and it be tested and validated.
- **A number of data mining techniques are available including association rule mining (finding** associations in a market basket), supervised classification (building a model based on training data for prediction), clustering (exploring if the given data has clusters), text mining (finding structure in a large collection of documents) and web data mining.
- **Association rule mining (ARM) has been explained by using a simple shopping example and the** Apriori method has been described.
- **Guidelines for implementation of data mining include full support of the top management and** appropriate consultation processes with all the stakeholders.
- **A number of data mining applications in fields like aviation, marketing, banking, astronomy, crime** prevention, and health care are briefly described to illustrate the use of data mining.

REVIEW QUESTIONS

1. Explain data mining and define it. (Section 16.1)
2. Describe the features of OLTP systems, data warehouses and data mining. (Section 16.2)
3. What is the motivation behind association rules mining? List two situations where this technique can be useful? (Section 16.3)
4. Explain the terminology used in association rule mining. Why doesn't the brute force approach work? (Section 16.3)
5. What is the primary principle behind the Apriori algorithm? Describe the algorithm briefly. When does the algorithm becomes inefficient and which step of the algorithm becomes a bottleneck? (Section 16.3)
6. What is motivation behind supervised classification? What is a training set? In what situations can this technique be useful? How can a decision tree be constructed? (Section 16.4)
7. When is cluster analysis useful? Why can't we use supervised classification instead of cluster analysis? (Section 16.5)
8. Describe the K-means algorithm and discuss its strengths and weaknesses. How does the distance metric affect the result of clustering? (Section 16.5)
9. What is the motivation behind text mining? Describe the basis of text mining and its applications. (Section 16.6)
10. What is the difference between text mining and web content mining? Explain. (Section 16.6)
11. What is web data mining? In what situations can web data mining techniques be useful? What is a hub and an authority? (Section 16.7)
12. Is building a data mining system similar to building software? List some guidelines for building a data mining system? (Section 16.8)
13. List some of the major applications of data mining. (Section 16.9)

SHORT ANSWER QUESTIONS

1. What are the aims of data mining?
2. What is the major aim of market basket analysis?
3. What is support?
4. What is confidence?
5. What is a frequent itemset?
6. What step of Ariori is the most expensive for large databases?
7. What data is needed to build a decision tree?
8. Describe an application of supervised classification. Why can't cluster analysis be used for it?
9. What are the weaknesses of clustering?
10. What is the basis for K-means algorithm?
11. List one major difficulty with K-means algorithm.
12. Show how text mining can be useful.
13. What are the different types of web mining?
14. Give an example of text mining.
15. What is a term and a concept?

MULTIPLE CHOICE QUESTIONS

1. Which one of the following questions can be easily answered without using any data mining tools?
   (a) How many different types of customers are there?
   (b) What customers are the most profitable?
   (c) Which state did the most students come from?
   (d) Which patient has a high risk of breast cancer?
2. Which one of the following data mining must include?
   (a) Finding a pattern that the user already knew.
   (b) Finding structure that was derived from the data warehouse.
   (c) Aggregation complex queries
   (d) A novel pattern that is actionable.
3. Which of the following are features of data mining?
   (a) It is an automatic process.
   (b) It is about discovering novel patters.
   (c) It usually deals with large datasets.
   (d) The patterns must be actionable.
   (e) All of the above
4. Which one of the following is not a step in the data mining process?
   (a) Visualization
   (b) Report production
   (c) Requirements analysis
   (d) Testing and validation

5. Which one of the following areas has applications for data mining?
   (a) Telecommunications (b) Education
   (c) Health care (d) Astronomy
   (e) All of the above
6. Which one of the following is the most important step in the data mining process?
   (a) Getting management support (b) Data selection
   (c) Visualization (d) Monitoring
7. Which one of the following makes the brute force approach to finding association rules not viable?
   (a) Too many items (b) Too many transactions
   (c) Too many itemset combinations (d) Too many rules
8. Which one of the following is **not** true about association rule mining?
   (a) Support of X is equal to the number of times X occurs in the transactions.
   (b) An item is frequent if it meets the minimum support specified.
   (c) An association rule is confident if its confidence is above the user specified minimum confidence.
   (d) A candidate set of itemsets is potentially frequent set of itemsets.
9. Three frequent pairs (p, q), (r, s) and (t, u) have been found in association rule mining. What is the maximum number of rules that may be derived from these three pairs?
   (a) 3 (b) 4 (c) 6 (d) 8
10. Three frequent pairs (p, q), (r, s) and (t, u) have been found in association rule mining. What is the minimum number of rules that may be derived from these three pairs?
   (a) 0 (b) 1 (c) 3 (d) 6
11. Which one of the following makes the clustering problem difficult to solve?
   (a) Too much data (b) Too many attributes
   (c) Not all attributes are numeric. (d) The number of clusters is not given.
12. Which of the following belongs to web data mining?
   (a) Discovering authority sites (b) Clustering web pages
   (c) Understanding behaviour of web users (d) Web search
   (e) All of the above
13. Which one of the following is **not** a suitable text data mining application?
   (a) Clustering documents (b) Comparing documents
   (c) Categorization of documents (d) Text prediction
14. Which one of the following is **not** a data mining technique?
   (a) Association rule mining (b) Clustering
   (c) Multiple regression (d) Supervised classification
15. Which one of the following is true?
   (a) Association rule mining is same as market basket analysis.
   (b) Market basket analysis is same as computing correlation.
   (c) Clustering is same as classification.
   (d) Text classification is same as page rank analysis.

16. Which one of the following is true?
    (a) Support and confidence are the same.
    (b) Frequent item set and a candidate item set are the same.
    (c) Apriori algorithm may be used for supervised classification.
    (d) Association rule mining should not be used for medical applications.
17. Which of the following $X \rightarrow Y$ rules are the most interesting from a business point of view?
    (a) Support(X, Y) = 80% and Confidence ($X \rightarrow Y$) = 75%
    (b) Support(X, Y) = 10% and Confidence ($X \rightarrow Y$) = 80%
    (c) Support(X, Y) = 1% and Confidence ($X \rightarrow Y$) = 90%
    (d) Support(X, Y) = 50% and Confidence ($X \rightarrow Y$) = 50%
18. Let the support of three items X, Y and Z together be 20%. Which one of the following must be true about support for the two pairs X and Y and Y and Z?
    (a) Support(X, Y) = 20% (b) Support(Y, Z) = 20%
    (c) Support(X, Y) $\geq$ 20% (d) Support(Y, Z) $\geq$ 20%
    (e) Support(X, Y) < 20% (f) Support(Y, Z) < 20%
19. Let the support of the three itemsets (p, q, r), (p, r, t) and (p, q, s) be above the minimum support required. Now in attempting to find frequent 4-itemsets which of the following itemsets must be looked at?
    (a) (p, q, r, s) (b) (p, s, q, t) (c) (p, q, s, t) (d) (p, q, r, t)
20. Which one of the following is true if the classical algorithm was being used?
    (a) Association rules require numeric data.
    (b) Supervised classification requires categorical data.
    (c) Clustering requires categorical data.
    (d) All of the above are true.
21. Which one of the following is the main feature of supervised classification?
    (a) Training data must be available.
    (b) Data must be numeric.
    (c) Decision tree is the only technique.
    (d) Changing split technique can change the results.
22. Which one of the following is true about clustering?
    (a) K-means is the only method available.
    (b) Number of clusters must be specified.
    (c) Changing distance metric does not change the results.
    (d) Training data must be available.
23. Which one of the following is a part of web data mining?
    (a) Crawler (b) Indexer (c) Structure mining (d) Hyperlink mining
24. Which of the following is one of the guidelines for successful data mining?
    (a) The enterprise must have a data warehouse.
    (b) There must be a well defined problem.

(c) There must be good visualization tools available.
(d) The enterprise must have OLAP experience.

25. Which of the following are required in text mining?
(a) Terms must be extracted.
(b) Concepts must be extracted.
(c) Documents must be preprocessed.
(d) A feature vector must be built.
(e) All of the above

EXERCISES

1. Discuss the advantages of data mining over other approaches of analyzing data.
2. Consider an example with the following set of transactions that we wish to analyze using association rule mining.

TID	*Items bought*
001	B, M, T, Y
002	B, M
003	A, T, S, P
004	A, B, C, D
005	A, B
006	T, Y, E, M
007	A, B, M
008	B, C, D, T, P
009	D, T, S
010	A, B, M

Assume that we wish to find association rules with at least 30% support and 60% confidence. Find the frequent itemsets and then the association rules.
3. Suppose that a large store has a transaction database that is distributed among four locations. Transactions in each component database have the same format, namely $T_j: \{i_1, \ldots, i_m\}$, where T_j is a transaction identifier, and i_k ($1 \le k \le m$) is the identifier of an item purchased in the transaction. Propose an efficient algorithm to mine global association rules. Present your algorithm in the form of an outline. Your algorithm should not require shipping all the data to one site and should not cause excessive network communication overheads.
4. What kind of data is the decision tree method most suitable for? Briefly outline the major steps of the algorithm to construct a decision tree.
5. Use the K-means method to find three clusters in the data below. Let the three seeds be Indonesia, France and Thailand. Scale the data before clustering so that the magnitude of different attribute is similar.

Country	Exports of Goods and Services %	Distribution of Family Income (GINI index)	Olympic Medals per 10 Million Population since 1948
Australia	20	35	18.10
Bangladesh	14	34	0.0
Brazil	16	61	0.42
China	29	40	0.39
France	27	33	6.52
India	15	38	0.01
Indonesia	35	32	0.09
Malaysia	50	49	0.2
Philippines	49	46	0.06
Singapore	60	40	0.46
Thailand	65	41	0.17
UK	26	37	5.44
USA	10	41	5.68

6. Describe three major differences between the conventional textual documents and Web documents. What type of information do we wish to extract from a collection of web pages? Give an example.
7. Briefly describe data mining case studies in the following areas:
   (a) Astronomy (b) Marketing (c) Telecommunications
8. List some of the pitfalls in implementing a data mining application. What precautions are necessary to improve the chances of a successful data mining system implementation? State guidelines that have been recommended to ensure data mining is implemented successfully. Discuss their importance.

PROJECTS

1. **Designing a Shopping Mall**

   An interesting case study is to look at a shopping mall. So many shopping malls are opening in India that is why we consider how the enterprises that establish shopping malls decide what shops will go where. Looking at a number of shopping malls we find that some of the stores included in the malls are as given in the list below.

Formal apparel	Sports	Bedroom
Formal accessories	Restaurant	Kitchen
Men's casual wear	Food & Beverage	Dining
Luggage	Unisex Fashion	Living room
Women's casual wear	Ethnic formal	Electronics
Women's accessories	Gifts and celebration	Audio systems
Women apparel	Fashion accessories	Electricals and home appliances
Kids wear	Bathroom	Floorings
Furnishings	Music and movies	Mobile phones
Books and stationary	Toys	Tailor

(a) Explain how Association Rule Mining could be used in this shopping mall design. What data do you require?

(b) Assume that in an attempt to generate some data on which the company could base the design, the company issues shopping loyalty cards to shoppers that they must scan at every shop they go. To encourage scanning, the company announces that a few prizes will be offered to some of the shoppers who do the scanning.

(c) Now to generate some data for this project, hand out a list of these store names to all the students in your class and ask them what stores they are likely to visit when they go to the shopping mall. Also, ask them to mark the stores that their mother or sister is likely to visit. It may help if codes are assigned to all the 30 stores above. You will need at least 100 transaction records, more would help. Use association rule software from the Web or use weka from New Zealand to run this software using your data. Analyze the results and write a report.

2. Food in a shopping Mall

All shopping malls also have food malls which might include dishes like those given below. Use clustering to find structure in this data. You may use weka software.

Food Item	*Calories*	*Carbohydrates*	*Protein*	*Total Fat*
Aloo-Baigan	103	32	1	5
Aloo Curry	105	15	1	5
Bhindi (Okra)	161	12	4	11
Cabbage	131	7	2	5
Chole	74	3	4	4
Besan Khadi	100	15	3	5
Mutter Paneer	147	11	9	8
Pumpkin	67	7	2	4
Kofta Curry	147	13	3	9
Chana Dahl	99	13	5	3
Moong Dahl	211	31	13	4
Sambhar	5	3	15	2
Boiled Rice	111	25	2	0.2
Milk (Buffalo)	117	5	4	7
Milk (Cow)	67	4	3	4
Khoa	421	21	20	26
Cheese	348	6	24	25

3. Documents

Select some interesting key words, say "data mining, clustering, examples" or some other keywords, and find a number of documents using a search engine. Use a term extracting software (perhaps from the Web) and compare the frequencies of ten terms that are common in them all. Cluster the documents using these frequencies.

LAB EXERCISES

1. Consider the data in the table at the end of Chapter 13. Use clustering to find structure in that data.
2. Consider the data in the table below. Label each animal as bird or mammal or marsupial. Now build a decision tree using the data.

Name	*Eggs*	*Pouch*	*Flies*	*Feathers*	*Eats*	*Nocturnal*	*Habitat*
Bandicoot	No	Yes	No	No	C	Yes	Bushes
Cassowarry	Yes	No	No	Yes	O	No	Ground
Cockatoo	Yes	No	Yes	Yes	C	No	Trees
Crocodile	Yes	No	No	No	C	No?	Water?
Dingo	No	No	No	No	C	No	Forest?
Dugong	No	No	No	No	H	No	Water
Echidna	Yes	Yes	No	No	C	No	Ground
Emu	Yes	No	No	Yes	C	No	Ground
Kangaroo	No	Yes	No	No	H	Yes	Grass
Koala	No	Yes	No	No	H	Yes	Trees
Kookaburra	Yes	No	Yes	Yes	C	No	Trees
Penguin	Yes	No	No	Yes	C	No	Burrows
Platypus	Yes	No	No	No	C	No	Streams
Possum	No	Yes	No	No	H	Yes	Trees
Wombat	No	Yes	No	No	H	Yes	Burrows

3. Consider the following data about nutrients for a number of regional foods in Assam. This data is based on a paper "Nutrient Composition of Some Regional Recipes of Assam, India" published in Ethno-Med, Vol. 3, No. 2. 2009, pp. 111-117. Many more foods are listed in that paper if a bigger data set is required for analysis.

Food	*Water*	*Protein*	*Fat*	*Minerals*	*Fibre*	*Carbohydrate*	*Energy*
Mandhania Chutney	89.6	1.7	0.6	1.2	0.6	6.3	37.4
Kalmou Sak Bhaji	64.8	1.2	11.8	3.0	5.4	13.8	166.2
Aloo Bilahi Pitika	82.8	3.3	0.8	1.7	0.3	10.9	64.8
Bhat Kerala Bhaji	65.8	0.9	9.8	2.8	12.6	8.1	124.2
Rou Masar Tenga	81.9	2.0	2.7	1.7	0.2	11.5	78.3
Boriola Mas Bhoja	29.3	27.0	26.7	8.8	–	8.2	381.0
Bhoja Murgi	44.1	26.9	16.3	1.9	0.6	10.2	295.1
Pura Aloo Pitika	70.5	3.0	1.3	2.1	0.3	22.8	114.9

(a) Consider the data carefully and suggest what data mining technique could be used to find structure of this data.
(b) Would it help if we modified the above data by scaling and/or deleting some data?
(c) Use software from the Web to run an appropriate weka program and analyse the results.

BIBLIOGRAPHY

Different data mining books seem to have different focus. For example, the book by Han and Kamber is written from a database perspective while the books by Witten and Frank and Dhar and Stein deal with data mining issues from the perspective of machine learning. Both books by Berry and Linoff reflect a business perspective. The recent paper by Lavrac et al., is a very useful summary of what a person starting on a data mining project should know.

For Students

We list of a number of articles and tutorial slides that are easy to understand and may prove useful for students wishing to look at a different view of data mining. The book by Linoff describes a number of data mining topics using SQL and EXCEL. The book takes a very practical approach. The book by Bramer is written for undergraduate students.

For Instructors

The books by Berry and Linoff and the newer book by Linoff are easy to read and more practical. For more advanced treatment, refer to books by Han and Kamber and the one by Tan, Steinbach and Kumar.

Berry, M., and G. Linoff, *Data Mining Techniques for Marketing, Sales and Customer Relationship Management*, John Wiley & Sons, 2004.

Berry, M., and G. Linoff, *Mastering Data Mining*, John Wiley & Sons, 1999.

Bramer, M., *Principles of Data Mining,* Springer, 2007, 344 pp.

Chaudhuri, S., U. Dayal, and V. Ganti, "Database Technology for Decision Support Systems", *IEEE Computer*, Vol. 34, No. 12, 2001, pp 48-55.

"Two Crows Corporation", *Introduction to Data Mining and Knowledge Discovery*, Third Edition, 1999. http://www.twocrows.com/intro-dm.pdf

Dhar, V., and R. Stein, *Seven Methods for Transforming Corporate Data into Business Intelligence*, Prentice Hall, 1997.

DM Review, http://dmreview.com (A good source of current data mining information as well as data mining tutorials)

Fayyad, U. M.., G. Piatetsky-Shapiro, P. Smyth, and R. Uthurusamy, R., (Eds.), *Advances in Knowledge Discovery and Data Mining*, MIT Press, 625 pp, 1996.

Feldman, R., and J. Sanger, *The Text Mining Handbook: Advanced Approaches in Analyzing Unstructured Data*, Cambridge University Press, 2007.

Gupta, G. K., *Data Mining with Case Studies*, Prentice Hall India, 2006.

Grabmeier, R., "Techniques of Cluster Algorithms in Data Mining", *Data Mining and Knowledge Discovery*, Vol. 6, 2002.

Han, J., and M. Kamber, *Data Mining: Concepts and Techniques*, Morgan Kaufmann, Second Edition, 2005, 800 pp. The book's website is http://www.cs.sfu.ca/~han/DM_Book.

Hu, X., "A Data Mining Approach for Retailing Bank Customer Attrition Analysis", *Applied Intelligence* 22, pp 47-60, 2005.

Klösgen, W., and J. M. Zytkow, (Eds.), *Handbook of Data Mining and Knowledge Discovery*, Oxford University Press, 2002, 980 pp.

Lavrac, N., H. Motoda, T. Fawcett, R. Holte, P. Langley, and P. Adriaans, *Introduction: Lessons Learned from Data Mining Applications and Collaborative Problem Solving: Machine Learning*, Vol. 57, No. 1-2, pp 13-34.

Linoff, G. S., *Data Analysis using SQL and EXCEL*, Wiley, 2007, 645 pp.

Moore, A., *Statistical Data Mining Tutorials*, Tutorial Slides (Carnegie-Mellon University), http://www-2.cs.cmu.edu/~awm/tutorials/

"SQL Server 2000 Resource Kit, Effective strategies for data mining", Chapter 24. http://www.microsoft.com/resources/documentation/sql/2000/all/reskit/en-us/default.mspx, September 2004.

Tan, P. N., M. Steinbach, and V. Kumar, *Introduction to Data Mining,* Addison Wesley, 2005, 769 pp.

Thearling, K., *An Introduction to Data Mining*. http://www.thearling.com/dmintro/dmintro.htm

Wang, K., S. Zhou, Q. Yang, and J. M. Y. Yeung, "Mining Customer Value: Association Rules to Direct Marketing", *Data Mining and Knowledge Discovery*, Vol. 11, pp 57-79, 2005.

Williams, G. J., and Z. Huang, *KDD for Insurance Risk Assessment: A Case Study*, CSIRO Division of Information Technology, GPO Box 664, Canberra 2601, March 1996.

Williams, G., M. Hegland, and S. Roberts, *A Data Mining Tutorial*, 1998. http://wwwmaths.anu.edu.au/~steve/pdcn.pdf

Witten, H., Frank E. and Hall M.A. *Data Mining: Practical Machine Learning Tools and Techniques*, Morgan Kaufmann, Third Edition, 2011, 664 pp. The book's website is www.mkp.com/datamining. The *weka* software is available from www.cs.waikato.ac.nz/weka.

Rakesh Agrawal–Inventor of Association Rules Mining

Rakesh Agrawal has developed fundamental data mining concepts and technologies and has made contributions to key concepts in data privacy, including Privacy-Preserving Data Mining. Rakesh is the recipient of the ACM-SIGKDD First Innovation Award, ACM-SIGMOD Edgar F. Codd Innovations Award, ACM-SIGMOD Test of Time Award and the VLDB 10-Yr Most Influential Paper Award. He is a Member of the National Academy of Engineering, a Fellow of ACM, and a Fellow of IEEE.

Prior to joining Microsoft as a Microsoft Technical Fellow in March 2006, Rakesh was an IBM Fellow and led the Quest group at the IBM Almaden Research Center. Earlier, he was with the Bell Laboratories, Murray Hill from 1983 to 1989. He also worked for 3 years at the Bharat Heavy Electricals Ltd.

Agrawal received the MS and PhD degrees in Computer Science from the University of Wisconsin-Madison in 1983. He is a graduate of the University of Roorkee (now IIT-Roorkee).

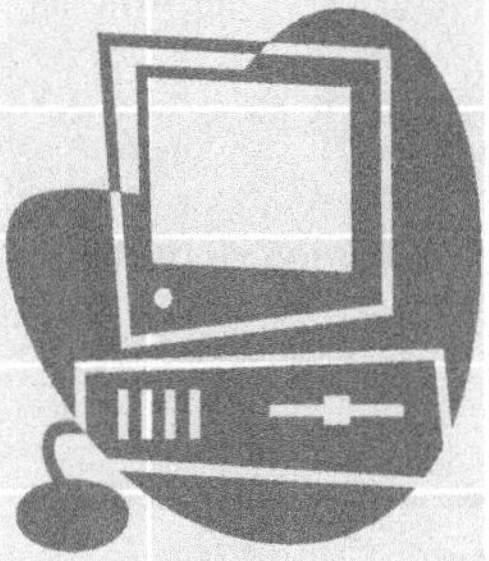

Web Databases and XML

17

OBJECTIVES

- Introduce the Web and its terminology.
- Consider the differences between searching the Web and the classical information retrieval problem.
- Introduce classical information retrieval and terminology.
- Explore building of the search engine database using the crawler.
- Consider indexing of documents on the Web, inverted index.
- Introduce techniques for querying the Web.
- Introduce markup languages and semistructured data.
- Describe features of XML.
- Explain a number of implementation details of XML databases using a relational approach and a native XML database approach.
- Introduce a query language for a XML database.

KEYWORDS

World Wide Web, documents on the Web vs text documents, classical information retrieval, search engine, search engine database, crawler, indexing, web query, inverted index, hubs and authorities, precision, relevance, recall, ranking, vector space model, term, XML element, attribute, document type definition, DTD, namespace, XML databases using RDMS, native XML database.

Our chief defect is that we are more given to talking about things than to doing them.

Jawaharlal Nehru

17.1 INTRODUCTION

The World Wide Web is the largest depository of documents and it is therefore natural that database technology is being used for storage and retrieval of the large collection of web documents. Web documents are not like the information we store in relational databases. In this chapter we consider the unique characteristics of web documents and how they may be stored and searched.

In a short time, say since 1995, the Web revolution has had a profound impact on the way we deposit, search and find information at home and at work. The exponential growth in the Web has been unbelievable. From the beginning in the early 1990s the Web has grown to more than 25 billion pages in 2010[1] with millions of people from all over the world (some estimates suggest almost two billion, including some 750 million in Asia, or about 30% of the world's population!) accessing it. In the USA, the use of the Web continues to grow and in 2010 about 75% of people went online and spent an average of more than ten hours per week online. The Web has become the number one source for information for Internet users although the credibility of web information appears to have declined somewhat recently according to a 2010 survey.

The Web is very dynamic. Millions of web-pages are added every day and millions of others are modified or deleted. Web pages are written in a variety of languages and they provide information in a variety of mediums including text, animation, images, photos, sound, music and video[2]. One of the most important features of the Web is the hyperlink by which one web-page provides links to other pages allowing a user to traverse the Web following links of interest to him or her.

The Web is an open medium. There is no one monitoring what is published and there is no mechanism to control the quality or appropriateness of the content. The Web has hate sites, love sites, pornography and anti-pornography sites, sites on hobbies, sports, politics, religion, medicine, cults, academic disciplines, music, movies, scams and everything else under the sun. The quality of these sites varies from awful to superb with most sites somewhere in between. The Web does not have a catalogue like libraries do but it has search engines, directories, portals and indexes to help users browse the information.

The openness has meant that the Web has grown exponentially which is its strength as well as its weakness. The strength is that one can find information on just about anything, however esoteric the topic. The weakness of an open Web is that there is the problem of abundance of information. For example, searching for the phrase "Web database" on Google in August 2010 found more than 800,000 pages. How does one plough

1. Our estimate is based on the number of pages indexed by Google in 2010. In practice it is only a lower bound since no search index is able to index the entire Web and a union of web-pages indexed by all major search engines is larger than what Google indexes. It is claimed that less than half the pages available on the Web are indexed by the search engines and this ratio has been declining. Also worth noting is that some 250 billion email messages are being sent every day. Most of these messages are also stored on the Web.
2. The Web has more than four billion photos on just one popular website. It is estimated that around 30 billion photos are uploaded to Facebook in a year. There are a large number of videos on sites like YouTube.

through such a large collection of documents to find those that are the most useful? How reliable is the ranking provided by the search engines that retrieve large numbers of documents by specifying a number of keywords?

In this chapter we first discuss the major differences between web documents and classical text documents. This is followed by a brief description of web terminology in Section 17.3 followed by a discussion of web structure in 17.4. Some information retrieval terminology is presented in Section 17.5 and classical information retrieval is briefly discussed in Section 17.6. This is followed by information storage and retrieval on the Web via the search engines. Section 17.8 deals with web crawler and indexing of web pages while Section 17.9 describes query processing and ranking of web pages. Section 17.10 briefly describes markup languages and Section 17.11 explains what we mean by semistructured data. This is followed by a description of XML in Section 17.12 including an example and introduction to XML elements, attributes, namespace, document type definition (DTD), document object model (DOM), XML schema and XQuery. Section 17.13 discusses XML databases, some details of the implementation of relational XML databases is presented in Section 17.14 and native XML are discussed in Section 17.15.

17.2 WEB DOCUMENTS VS CLASSICAL TEXT DOCUMENTS

In Section 16.7, we noted that there are major differences between searching using classical text retrieval and searching the Web. These include the use of hyperlinks in web documents, different types of information in web pages, dynamic nature of most web documents, the quality of many web pages and the huge size of the Web.

We present some basic web terminology followed by results of investigations about the structure of the Web.

17.3 WEB TERMINOLOGY

We define some web terminology based on the work of World Wide Web Consortium (W3C).

- The *World Wide Web (WWW)* is the set of all the nodes which are interconnected by hypertext links.
- A *link* expresses one or more (explicit or implicit) relationships between two or more resources. Links may also be established within a document using *anchors*.
- A *web page* is a collection of information, consisting of one or more web resources, intended to be rendered simultaneously, and identified by a single URL. A *website* is a collection of interlinked web pages, including a homepage, residing at the same network location.
- A client *browser* is the primary user interface to the Web. It is a program which allows a person to view the contents of web pages, and for navigating from one page to another.
- A *uniform resource locator (URL)* is an identifier for an abstract or physical resource, for example. a server and a file path or index. Each URL contains four distinct parts, namely, the protocol types (usually http), the name of the web server, the directory path and the file name.

- A *Web server* serves web pages using http to client machines so that a browser can display them.
- A *client* is the role adopted by an application when it is retrieving a web resource.

Obtaining information from the Web using a search engine is called information 'pull' while information sent to users is called information 'push'. For example, users may register with a site and then information is sent ('pushed') to them without them requesting it.

Now that we have the terminology we discuss the structure of the Web.

17.4 WEB STRUCTURE

An investigation of the structure of the Web was carried out based on an analysis of about 200 million pages and 1.5 billion links. The number of in-links (links pointing to a page) and the number of out-links (links pointing from a page) were analysed and it was found that most pages have only a few links pointing to them and only a few links being pointed by them.

The fraction of web pages with i in-links was found to be proportional to $1/i^{2.1}$ and the fraction of web pages with i out-links was found to be proportional to $1/i^{2.72}$. Thus there are only about 10% of pages that have three links pointing to them and there are only about 5% of pages with four links pointing to them. A similar law applies to out-links, with only a small percentage of pages pointing to say five other pages.

The structure of the Web has also been analysed and it was found that 90% of pages analysed form a single undirected graph. If we could follow both forward and backward links then the Web is a very well-connected graph, but considering the Web as a directed graph shows that most pairs of pages are not connected or are connected by a rather long chain of links.

It was found that the Web is not a ball of highly connected nodes. It displayed interesting structural properties (the structure appearing more like a 'bow-tie') and the Web could be conveniently divided into the following five components:

1. *The Strongly Connected Core (SCC)*—This part of the Web was found to consist of about 30% of the Web, which is still very large, given more than four billion pages were estimated to be on the Web in 2004. This core may be considered the heart of the Web and its main property is that pages in the core can reach each other following directed edges (i.e., hyperlinks).
2. *The IN Group*—This part of the Web was found to consist of about 20% of the Web. The main property of the IN group is that pages in the group can reach the SCC but cannot be reached from it.
3. *The OUT Group*—This part of the Web was found to consist of about 20% of the Web. The main property of the OUT group is that pages in this group can be reached from the SCC but cannot reach the SCC.
4. *Tendrils*—This part of the Web was found to consist of about 20% of the Web. The main property of pages in this group is that the pages cannot be reached by the SCC and cannot reach the SCC. It does not imply that these pages have no linkages to pages outside the group since they could well have linkages from the IN Group and to the OUT Group.

5. *The Disconnected Group*—This part of the Web was found to be less than 10% of the Web and is essentially disconnected from the rest of the Web world. These pages could include, for example, personal pages at many sites that link to no other page and have no links to them.

The deep Web includes information stored in searchable databases often inaccessible to search engines. This information can often only be accessed by using each website's interface. Some of this information may be available only to subscribers. The shallow Web (or indexable Web) is the information on the Web that the search engines can access without accessing the web databases. It has been estimated that the deep Web is about 500 times the size of the shallow Web.

We have noted above that the Web consisted of more than 25 billion pages in mid-2010. Assuming that each web page is on the average 15K in size, the Web in 2010 was more than 350 terabytes. If we include the size of the deep Web in estimating the size of the Web then the Web is much larger than one petabyte.

The links on web pages provide a useful source of information that may be harnessed in web searches. Kleinberg at Cornell has developed a connectivity analysis algorithm called Hyperlink-Induced Topic Search (HITS) based on the assumption that links represent human judgement. His algorithm found that for any query topic, there are a set of *authoritative* sites that are relevant and popular and focus on the topic, and there are *hub* sites that contain useful links to relevant sites on the topic including links to many related authorities.

17.5 INFORMATION RETRIEVAL TERMINOLOGY

In all types of information retrieval the user wishes to retrieve relevant items or been documents. Relevance has defined in a number of ways. We give an informal definition.

> ***Definition—Relevance***
> *Relevance refers to what extent the items retrieved matches the topic of the user's query or information need.*

Two other terms are frequently used in the information retrieval field. These are called precision and recall. We first define precision.

> ***Definition—Precision***
> *Precision is the proportion of items retrieved that are relevant. Therefore it is equal to the number of relevant items retrieved divided by the total number of documents retrieved.*

Recall is now defined.

> ***Definition—Recall***
> *Recall is the proportion of relevant items retrieved. Therefore it is equal to the number of relevant items retrieved divided by the total relevant items.*

Figure 17.1 below illustrates the relationship between precision and recall.

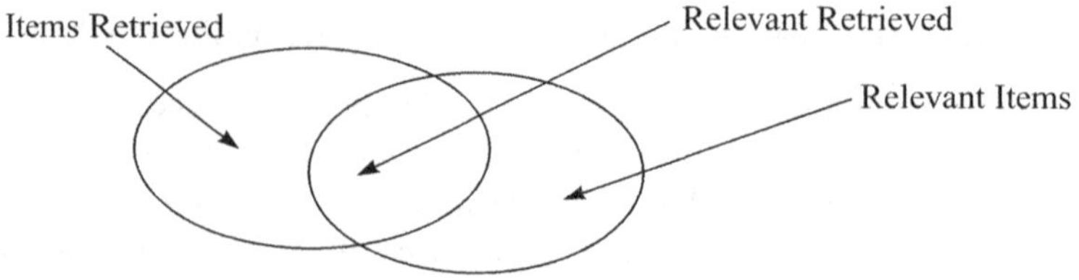

Figure 17.1 Recall and precision in information retrieval

Although recall and precision are appropriate concepts for evaluating an information retrieval system, the major problem with using these two metrics for web search is that recall is impossible to measure. We don't know and have no way of knowing how many relevant documents there are on the web given a query and thus cannot determine what proportion of relevant documents have been retrieved.

Furthermore, the recall and precision criteria require that each item be labeled either relevant or irrelevant. Often there are documents that cannot be put in either of these two categories.

Precision and recall usually have a trade-off relationship that is often shown by a precision-recall graph. It is well known that in this trade-off relationship:

1. Precision decreases faster than recall increases because to improve recall a lot more documents must be retrieved which reduces precision.
2. It is much more difficult to improve precision than improve recall because to improve precision the proportion of retrieved documents that are relevant must be improved which is difficult to do.

We now discuss classical information retrieval followed by information storage and retrieval on the Web.

17.6 CLASSICAL INFORMATION RETRIEVAL

Classical information retrieval (IR) deals with searching a collection of text documents but does not focus on how the documents are stored. The user inputs a query to a given collection of documents and the IR system retrieves the documents that are most relevant to the query. The main thrust of IR techniques is how to find the most relevant documents efficiently. A crude technique will return all documents that include at least one of the terms of the query but this obviously is not very satisfactory. The queries may be Boolean queries using AND, OR, NOT operators. Often the user wishes to retrieve documents that are ranked by their relevance. Ranking often depends on how terms in the query match the terms in the document and how frequently the query terms appear in the document.

We assume that the documents have no particular structure. One way of searching document collections is to first extract terms which are often single words extracted directly from the documents using a term extraction algorithm.

17.6.1 Vector Space Model

The vector space model is well known in IR. It involves representing each document as a high dimensional vector with each dimension per term in the document collection. The vector is often called a *term vector*. In the simplest form, the value of each term is either zero if that term does not appear in the document or a number, called *term frequency* (*TF*), which is the number of times the term appears in the document. These numbers are often called the *weight* of the term. The weight for a term is also determined by how frequently the term appears in the entire document collection. Thus the term vector may be normalized so that the most frequent terms in the entire collection are given lower weight in the document term vector, since the most frequent terms are not very useful in searches. Zipf distribution or the 80:20 rule is often found in many applications and it also is found in documents, which means that a small number of terms are very frequent even after removing the stop words. The normalization is often done by multiplying the term frequency in the term vector with inverse document frequency (IDF). IDF is the inverse of the term frequency of a term in the entire document collection and therefore results in lowering the importance of very frequent terms.

Further transformation may be carried out to perhaps scale the largest weight to 1. Similar term vector may be derived for a user's query. Given these term vectors for documents as well as for a query, the dot product of a query vector and a document vector gives a measure of similarity between the two. The documents that have the largest similarity are returned to the user who posed the query.

As an example, let us consider each section of this chapter as a separate document and the whole document as a collection of these documents. We found the term frequency of every term in this collection of documents[3] (that is, this chapter). There were 1,884 unique terms; many of them are stop words in this chapter that has 15,817 words. After removing the stop words, the top ten words in the collection and IDF for each of the words are given below:

Term	*Frequency*	*IDF*
Web	242	0.00413
XML	180	0.00555
Document	112	0.00892
Pages	105	0.00952
Information	102	0.00980
Documents	98	0.0102
Page	78	0.0128
Search	74	0.0135
Number	73	0.0137
database	70	0.0143

3. The word frequency count of a document may be obtained by pasting the document's text in the box at the site http://www.writewords.org.uk/word_count.asp and submitting it. The word frequencies are then returned.

Now if we find the term frequencies of each term in one document (that is, a section in this chapter) and build the term vector then the frequencies should multiplied by the IDF of the collection given above. Therefore, the number of times Web appears is multiplied by 0.00413 and the number of times database appears is multiplied by 0.0143.

We can see the problems created by not stemming the words since the words 'document' and 'documents' appear as two different words in the table above and so do 'page' and 'pages'.

17.7 STORAGE AND RETRIEVAL ON THE WEB–THE SEARCH ENGINE

A search engine is the primary vehicle for storage and retrieval of information on the Web. We therefore discuss the components in a typical search engine.

A search engine is a rather complex collection of software modules and carries out a number of tasks including the following:

1. *Collecting information*—A search engine would normally collect web pages or information about them by web crawling or by human submission of pages.
2. *Evaluating and categorising information*—In some cases, for example, when web pages are submitted to a directory, it may be necessary to evaluate and decide whether a submitted page should be selected. In addition it may be necessary to categorise information based on some ontology[4] used by the search engine.
3. *Creating a database and creating indexes*—The information collected needs to be stored either in a database or some kind of file system. Indexes must be created so that the information can be searched efficiently.
4. *Computing ranks of the web documents*—A variety of methods are being used to determine the rank of each page retrieved in response to a user query. The information used may include frequency of keywords, value of in-links and out-links from the page and frequency of use of the page.
5. *Checking queries and executing them*—Queries posed by users need to be checked, for example, for spelling errors and whether words in the query are recognisable. Once checked (and perhaps corrected), a query is executed by searching the search engine database.
6. *Presenting results*—How the search engine presents the results to the user is important. The search engine must determine what results to present (not all the information that the search engine has about the resulting items can be presented) and how to display them.
7. *Profiling the users*—To improve search performance the search engines carry out user profiling that deals with the way users use search engines.

Now we discuss building of a web database by employing a crawler to collect information about web pages and then building an index for the pages. Querying the web database via a search engine and ranking of pages that are retrieved will be discussed in Section 17.9.

4. Ontology is a philosophical concept that has a number of definitions. Ontology is about studying being or existence as well as the basic categories thereof trying to find out what entities and what types of entities exist. In computer science, ontologies help in representing knowledge. The aim of ontology is to create a shared understanding between humans and computers.

17.8 BUILDING THE SEARCH ENGINE DATABASE–THE CRAWLER

The search engine databases are built using different technologies by different search engine companies. For example, Google builds a database called Bigtable which distributes the web data over thousands of machines and is then able to process search engine queries in parallel.

The crawler (or spider or robot) is an application program that carries out a task similar to graph traversal. The traversal is given a set of starting URLs that it uses to automatically traverse the Web by retrieving web pages, initially from the starting set. Some search engines use a number of distributed crawlers. Crawlers tend to return to each site on a regular basis, perhaps once in two months, to look for changes. Often search engines have a list of sites that change frequently, for example, newspaper sites, and visit them much more frequently, even every few hours.

A web crawler must take into account the load (bandwidth, storage) on the search engine machines and sometimes also on the machines being traversed in guiding its traversal. For example, when a crawler is being run, the resources used by it should not be so high that it disrupts the use of the Web by other users. It is expected that a crawler would not swamp the network and would not swamp the individual Web servers. There are a number of ways to reduce network traffic, for example, avoiding large pages and avoiding sites with large multimedia material.

Each page found by the crawler is often not stored as a separate file otherwise four billion pages would require managing four billion files. Usually lots of pages are stuffed into one file.

Crawlers follow an algorithm like the following:

1. *Find base URLs*—A set of known and working hyperlinks are collected.
2. *Build a queue*—Put the base URLs in the queue and add new URLs to the queue as more are discovered.
3. *Retrieve the next page*—Retrieve the next page in the queue, process and store it in the search engine database.
4. *Add to the queue*—Check if the out-links of the current page have already been processed. Add the unprocessed out-links to the queue of URLs.
5. Continue the process until the stopping criteria are met.

The above algorithm shows that if a page is not linked to any page, the crawler can never find it and therefore the search engines will not show it in response to any query. Some search engines allow users to submit their web pages to them. If a page has been submitted in that way, it is more likely be indexed by the search engine.

The task of a crawler is rather large since as the crawler collects more pages it discovers more links and has even more work ahead of it. To understand the task, let us consider that a crawler was to collect one million pages a day (that is, 365 million pages a year). To do this task, a crawler needs to find 700 pages per minute! A search engine therefore cannot maintain up to date information even if it consists of more than one crawler. One expects a search engine crawler to at least manage to visit every site once a month.

A crawler would often have a traversal strategy. It may traverse the web breadth first, depth first or the traversal may be priority based. Breadth first traversal is claimed to perform better than depth first traversal since it better spreads load. Priority based traversal has been found to perform better since priority based traversal is often based on frequency of change of pages and PageRank of pages. The crawl order is important since it also impacts the quality of the index because a crawler is only going to crawl a part of the Web.

17.8.1 The Indexer

Given the size of the Web and the number of documents that current search engines have in their databases, an index is essential to improve query evaluation. An inverted file structure is often used in which each document is essentially indexed on every word other than the most common words. Google uses this approach. These indexes may be built while the crawler is collecting the web pages or could be done later. Indexing can be a very resource intensive process and is often CPU-bound since it involves a lot of analysis of each page. The search engines have refined indexing approaches ensuring that indexes can be updated quickly.

In automatic indexing of web documents, many parts of the documents are difficult to use for indexing. This, for example, applies to multimedia content. Keywords also need to be extracted from a wide variety of document formats including PDF, postscript and Microsoft Word. In the early days of search engines, most search engines only extracted terms from the title and some other parts of the documents (e.g., meta-tags) while some search engines used the full documents. The recent trend has been to use the full documents and store them in the search engine database. The information is not updated every day and may be somewhat stale given the dynamic nature of the Web.

An inverted index, rather than listing keywords for each page, lists pages for each keyword. The roles of keywords and pages have therefore been inverted although an inverted database normally still maintains a collection of pages including its content in some way.

An inverted index has the following components:

- Vocabulary of index terms in the collection.
- Some information about each term, for example, how many times the term appears in the collection and perhaps in each document.
- An inverted list of documents that have that term.

As an example of a simple inverted index consider the data structure in table 17.1. This index specifies a number of keywords and the documents (the documents are stored elsewhere) that contain the keywords. If we were searching for 'data Web' we look for documents for each keyword 'data' and 'Web' and then find the intersection of the two lists and obtain document numbers 26 and 41.

Table 17.1 A simple inverted index

Words	*Documents ID*
data	10, 18, 26, 41
Web	26, 30, 31, 41
search	72, 74, 75, 76
engine	72, 74, 79, 82
Google	72, 74, 90

The challenging part of such an exercise is when the two lists are large. For example, in Google 'data' appears in more than 1,570 million pages (on 1 June 2010) and 'Web' appears in more than 3,080 million pages. Finding an intersection of these very large lists takes time. The usual approach is to split the lists across many machines to find the intersection quickly. The task becomes easier if one of the lists is relatively smaller than the other. Also, the speed is improved if much of the inverted index is main memory based. Since a search engine might be using thousands of machines and each machine could have perhaps a few gigabytes of main memory allowing much of the index to be stored in the main memory.

Another problem is to search for phrases like 'Web database'. The above intersection will provide us a list of documents that have 'Web' and 'database' in them. Looking for the phrase 'Web database' requires that we find a subset of the list produced by the intersection of the two lists such that the subset has the phrase 'Web database'. One possible solution is to store the position of each word in the inverted index as well and then it is easier to determine if the two words are next to each other. Queries may also be disjunctive (using OR) and then the two inverted list may be combined to obtain a list that needs to be searched.

Given that the number of unique keywords (or terms) on the Web is several million (including proper names), the search engine inverted index is huge. It can occupy almost as much storage as the Web pages.

As the crawler updates the search engine database, the inverted index must also be updated. Depending on how the index is stored, updating may be relatively easy but at some stage after many updates it may become necessary to rebuild the whole index which normally takes substantial resources.

17.9 QUERYING THE WEB

There has been considerable research into the nature of search engine queries. A study carried out some years ago considered the information needs of users making a query. It was suggested that the information needs of the users can be divided into three classes:

1. *Navigational*—The primary information need in these queries is to reach a website that the user has in mind. The user may know that such a site exists (for example, a user knows that there is a website for Air India) or may have visited the site earlier but does not know the site URL.
2. *Informational*—The primary information need in such queries is to find a website that provides useful information about a topic of interest. The user does not have a particular website in mind. For example, a user may wish to find out the difference between an ordinary digital camera and a digital SLR camera.
3. *Transactional*—The primary information need in such queries is to go to a website to perform some kind of transaction. The user may or may not know the target website. An obvious example is to buy a book. The user may wish to go to amazon.com or to a local website if there is one. Another user may be interested in downloading some images or some other multimedia content from a website.

The study estimated the percentage of queries from each of these categories and found that the percentages were in the following ranges:

Navigational queries 20 – 25%
Informational queries 40 – 50%
Transactional queries 30 – 35%

Search engine query processing is quite different than query processing in relational database systems. In relational database systems, query processing requires that the attribute values specified in the query match exactly the values provided in the query. In search engine query processing, an exact match is desirable but not always required. A partial match or a fuzzy match may be sufficient. Often search engines assign a weight to each document that has been retrieved to indicate the 'goodness of fit'.

The web pages retrieved in response to a query are not always served by the host machine. The most common approach is to use web caches and proxies as intermediaries between the client browser processes and the machines serving the web pages. A web cache or proxy essentially mediates access to the Web for improved efficiency. Often, it is an intermediary that acts as a server on behalf of some other server by supplying Web resources without contacting the server.

Essentially a cache is supposed to catch a user's or client's request, get the page that the user has requested if one is not available in the cache and then save a copy of it in the cache. It is assumed that if a page is saved, there is a strong likelihood that it will be requested again by the same user or some other user. Also, the web has some very popular sites which are requested frequently. The proxy essentially satisfies such requests without going to the web server.

17.9.1 Ranking of Query Results and Results Presentation

Before presentation of results to the user, the results usually need to be ranked. Ranking is often based on page popularity in terms of number of other pages providing links to it.

How much of what has been found should be presented to the user and what is the best way to present it? Regarding how much, the number of items retrieved could be very large. Given the volume of a result, not all items retrieved can be presented to the user. It is therefore better to present only the 100 or 200 most relevant items given that users rarely look beyond a screen or two of the results. Most current search engines present the retrieved items as a list on the screen with some information for each item, for example, the type of document, its URL, perhaps the date of the document and a brief extract from the document description.

Different search engines follow different algorithms for ranking pages although they may still return the same pages at the top of their lists. Even if search engines return good documents at the top of the rankings, it is not uncommon for irrelevant documents to make it to the high rankings and appear in the top one or two pages. For example, searching for 'Computer Science Australia' in mid-2010 using Google, 'Christian Schools Australia' was returned as a highly ranked document.

When ranking pages, some search engines pay considerable importance to location and frequency of keywords and phrases in the page and some may consider the meta-tags as well. Some search engines may give more importance to pages that have the required keywords close to the top of the page, or in the title. This may be based on the assumption that if a page is important to the topic, it will mention the topic from the beginning.

Google has the most well-known ranking algorithm, called the PageRank algorithm that has been claimed to supply top ranking pages that are relevant. The PageRank algorithm is based on use of hyperlinks as indicators of a page's importance. It is almost like vote counting in an election. Every unique page is assigned a PageRank. If a lot of pages vote for a page by linking to it then the page that is being pointed to will be considered important. The voting is not fully democratic since votes cast by important pages are given more importance than votes cast by unimportant pages. Votes cast by a link farm (a page with many links) are given less importance than votes cast by an article that only links to a few pages. Internal site links also count in assessing PageRank. PageRank has no relationship with the content of the page.

PageRank was originally developed based on a probability model of a random surfer visiting a web page. The probability of a random surfer clicking on a link may be estimated based on the number of links on that page. The probability of the surfer clicking any link is assumed to be inversely proportional to the number of links on the page. The more links a page has, the less is the chance that a surfer will click on a particular link. For example, if we assume that the Web has a total of 100 pages and a page had a PageRank value of 2, it is supposed to indicate that the random surfer would reach that page on an average twice if he/she surfs the Web separately 100 times.

Therefore, the probability for the random surfer reaching one page is the sum of probabilities for the random surfer following links to that page. The probability model also introduces a damping factor to take into account that the random surfer sometimes does not click on any link and jumps to another page at random. If the damping factor is d (assumed to be between 0 and 1) then the probability of the surfer jumping off to some other page is assumed to be $1 - d$. The higher the value of d, the more likely the surfer will follow one of the links.

17.10 INTRODUCTION–MARKUP LANGUAGES

Every etext processing system, whether it is Microsoft Word or Latex, requires a markup language interspersed among the text to separate the logical elements of the document and to specify the functions (for example, formatting) to be performed on the elements. We present an informal definition of markup.

> ***Definition—Markup***
> *Markup is the text that is added to the data of a document in order to convey information about it. The markup text may specify how the logical elements of the document may be separated or specify the processing to be performed on those elements.*

Since electronic documents must be processed by computers, they must have markups that are explicitly or implicitly specified by the user. For example, markup is implicit in a Microsoft Word document which the user cannot see, since it is hidden from the user, while it is explicit in Latex, where the user explicitly specifies the markups using tags (for example,\title {My Document} or \end {My Document}).

There are a variety of markups that are used in markup languages. These include descriptive markup, reference markup, separator markup and processing markup. Using markup, a document may be represented as a tree structure in which each nonterminal node is the root of a subtree which may be called an element and each terminal node is data. Most markups include a way of specifying the document boundaries, a way of specifying paragraphs, lists, title and subtitle; a way of specifying indentations and nesting of elements, and a way of showing relationships between different components of the document.

Markups in a word processing document essentially involve three components. Firstly, the user must identify the structure of the document which may include titles, headings, paragraphs, lists, footnotes, references, tables, images and any other components. Markups must then be provided in the text to describe the processing instructions to the word processing system. The document is then processed using the word processing system that the user is using.

Most markup languages use control words which can be time consuming, error-prone and require a highly skilled person to properly instruct the system to produce a document that is being prepared. In the earlier systems, markups were different for different systems. To overcome the difficulties created by a number of different markup languages, generalized markup languages were proposed in the 1980s so that documents could be ported from one document preparation system, formatting style or processing system to another. This approach is somewhat different than that used say in Microsoft Word where a document prepared using a new version of the software may not even be displayed in an older version.

The generalized markup language approach is based on the following two postulates:

- Markup should be independent of the formatting style or the processing system and therefore must only describe the document's structure and other attributes rather than specifying processing to be performed on it.
- Markup should be rigorous so that a variety of processing techniques may be used.

A generalized markup language that follows these two postulates has a number of advantages since such a language reduces the cost of markup, reduces lead times in large document preparation and permits interchange between different document processing systems.

A number of markup systems have been developed over the years including the development of IBM's GML (Generalized Markup Language), SGML (Standard Generalized Markup Language) for documents, HTML (Hypertext Markup Language) for web documents and XML (Extendible Markup Language) for organizing and storing any type of information. One may in fact assert that XML is not really a markup language since it only provides a set of rules for building markup languages. XML does however include a number of features that were defined by the SGML ISO 8879 standard.

17.11 SEMISTRUCTURED DATA

Data comes in many forms. It may be structured like that in a relational database or it may be unstructured. It may be in the form of text, figures, diagrams, voice, music, photos or video. Structured data in relational databases or in object-oriented databases comes in chunks which can be entities or objects. They usually have attributes and a predefined structure. Unstructured data however has no structure. For example, it may just be a collection of words or numbers. Semistructured data on the other hand has some structure but some parts of data may lack structure, for example, a movie. Semistructured data may be available in chunks that have a meaning and similar chunks of data may be grouped together. However, one chunk may have more attributes than another chunk and the type of an attribute in one may be different than in the other. For example, web documents may be labeled unstructured since they are quite different than data in relational databases. They are also different than the usual text documents. In fact one could say that there is nothing common between a web page and a project report or information in a relational database.

When we store data in a relational or object-oriented database, we must define the structure of the data and then insert the data in the database. This is not necessary for describing semistructured data since data can directly describe and insert the data as shown below. For this reason semistructured data is sometime referred as self-describing. We give two simple examples below:

{playerid = 812345, name = "Tendulkar", Country = "India"}
{playerid = 812345, name {first = "Sachin", last = "Tendulkar"}, Country = "India"}

Note that pieces of data are of the same type except the name in the second has two components.

Semistructured data therefore is a collection of pairs that includes labels and values and not all data is of the same type and we are able to deal with variables.

Thus, semistructured data includes data that varies in structure and the data may include:

- Variable number of fields
- Repeated attributes
- Variable types of data for the same attribute

A formal machine-readable language is needed to express such semistructured data. We consider how XML may be used to define such data.

17.12 XML

Jim Gray once noted that XML is the solution to the clash between three cultures, i.e., everything is a relation culture, everything is an object culture and everything is a document culture. These three views have been irreconcilable for some time but XML may be the bridge that provides representation for all types of data on the Web since XML can store and organize all kind of information. It also has simple clear syntax that is easy to use.

XML (Extensible Markup Language) is a standard language adopted by the World Wide Web Consortium (W3C) in 1998. It is an emerging standard for data exchange on the Internet. We discuss XML, XML databases and one XML query language.

XML is a HTML-like markup language. HTML is used for defining web pages and is human-readable but it is not designed to be understood by computer programs since HTML was designed specifically to describe information presentation via the browser and not the content. HTML is a markup language in which the various pieces of text are marked with tags that determine how the web page would appear in a Web browser. HTML defines a fixed number of tags, like the bookends, for example, consider the following:

```
<head> ... </head>
<body> ...
<h1>
<b>
</body>
```

Each HTML tag like the ones above has a clearly defined meaning and the number of tags in HTML is fixed. For example, any text between <h1> and </h1> is assumed to be a header. Lower level headers may be included by using tags like <h2> and <h3> and so on.

XML on the other hand is designed to define the content, not its presentation. It is a language for transmitting data on the Web. It allows custom tags to be defined by the user. It also allows nested tag structure. XML does not focus on the presentation and allows arbitrary number of user-defined tags with no set semantics for such tags.

The problem of defining tags is overcome by defining a semantic layer on top of XML. Such layers are different for different applications and the tags are displayed by a browser using a stylesheet for each application. A stylesheet allows the browser to translate XML tags into HTML tags which can then be displayed.

A XML document has a tree structure in which a document consists of pieces called *elements* which may nest inside each other. The elements may be structurally related. The structure provides flexibility and therefore the number of nodes at each level is allowed to vary.

An Example

We now give an example of converting Cricinfo information about each test match into a XML tree. Note that the root node is a test match. There will be many such matches. For each match the following information is usually included (refer to cricinfo for the basis of this):

1. *Scorecard*—The scorecard has a lot of information in addition to the scores. Information about the dates of the test, a unique test number, ground where the test is played, who won the toss, who was the player of the match and other information like umpires, match referee, TV umpire, reserve umpire as well as information about each days play and so on is included in each cricinfo scorecard. We cannot show all this information in the tree below because we do not have sufficient space for it all.
2. *Bulletin*—A bulletin is usually posted after each day's play and the final bulletin is posted after the match is over. A bulletin would have a variable number of descendents assuming that all bulletins are to be saved. We have not shown any descendents of *Bulletin* because of lack of space. Each bulletin usually has text as well as one or two photos.
3. *Comments*—There are a variable number of comments after each day's play and after the match is over. Some comments are audio reports others are just text. Again some comments may include a photo or two.
4. *News*—Although we have included news about the test match in the scorecard, since that is where it is to be found in cricinfo, there are often a variable number of other news stories about injuries or the state of the pitch, etc.
5. *Plays of the day*—This often includes a variable number of plays which were crucial in the match.
6. *Gallery*—A collection of photos from the match

Other items can sometime appear for a test match. For example, during the July 2010 Sri Lanka – India test match there was a Tour Diary which included a report about the ground staff. In addition there were stories about Murali reaching the 800 wickets mark and his retiring from test cricket.

Note that each of the above items may have a separate web page and some pages have links to other pages. Thus, the information about a test match and the way it is displayed by cricinfo is complex and cannot be modeled easily for displaying in a textbook.

In Fig. 17.2, we have shown only two descendents for *Comments*, two for *News*, three for *Play of the Day* and three for *Gallery* but the number of descendents for all these is variable.

This data may be represented as follows in XML. Note that many of the elements in this definition are not defined. The tag <player> is called a start-tag and </player> an end-tag. Tags always come in pairs like parenthesis. There are no predefined tags like those in HTML.

Any properly nested piece of text between the two matching tags is called an *XML element*. Each element has a name given to it by the tags. The text between the tags is called the *content* of the element. The elements may have ancestor/descendent relationships between them. For example, *News* has decedents *Dates*, *Ground*, *Toss* and *Player of the Match* and its ancestor is *Scorecard*.

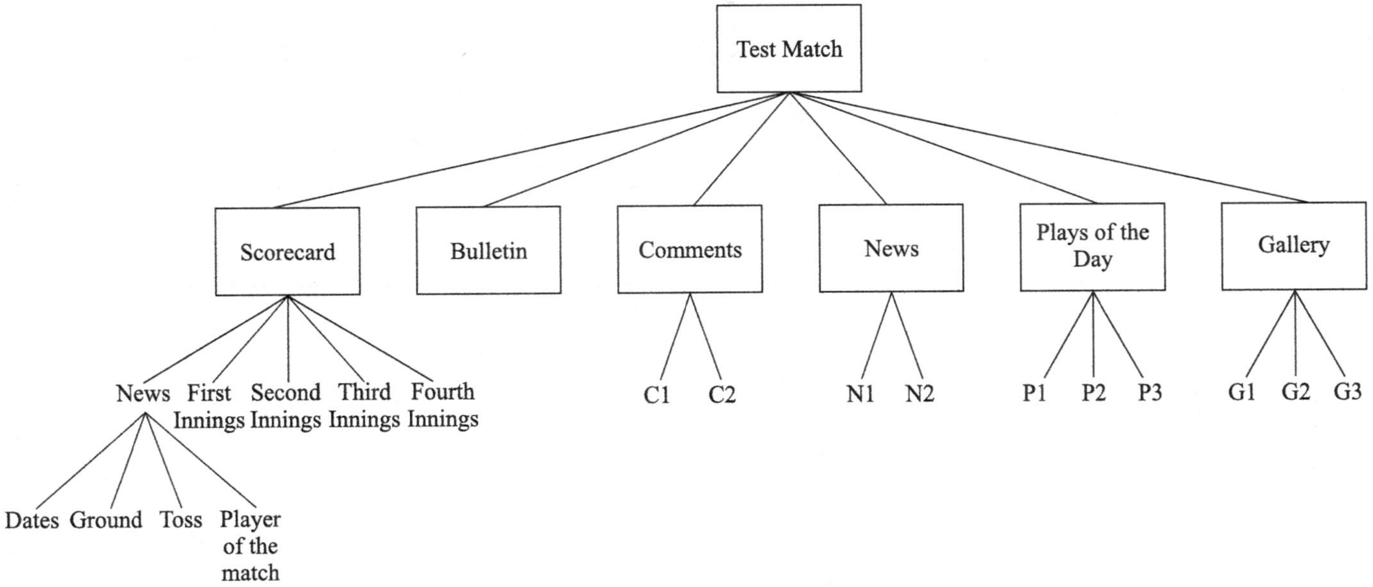

Figure 17.2 An example of modeling cricinfo test match data

With each line of XML in the Fig. 17.3 below we include a comment for each line. Unfortunately we have not included any data, except a few items, since including data will make the example very large. For example, the scorecard has information about the four innings (assuming there were four. Some matches only have three while others may have only one or two or even no play due to bad weather). Each inning has a lot of information including the eleven batsmen, how each got out, runs made, fall of wicket score, number of fours, and number of sixes and so on.

XML Code	Level	Comments
<?XML Version = “1.0” ?>	0	Mandatory Statement
<Title Value = “Test Match”>	1	Opening tag for title
<Scorecard>	2	Opening tag for Scorecard
<News>	3	Opening tag for News
<Date>22 July 2010</Date>	4	Content added
<Ground>Galle</Ground>	4	Content added
<Toss>Sri Lanka</Toss>	4	Content added
<POTMatch></POTMatch>	4	Content to be added
</News>	3	Closing tag for News
<FInnings></FInnings>	3	Content to be added
<SInnings></SInnings>	3	Content to be added
<TInnings></TInnings>	3	Content to be added
<LInnings></LInnings>	3	Content to be added
</Scorecard>	2	Closing tag for scorecard
<Bulletin></Bulletin>	2	Content to be added
<Comments>	2	Opening tag for Comments
<C1></C1>	3	Content to be added
<C2></C2>	3	Content to be added
</Comments>	2	Closing tag for Comments
<News>	2	Opening tag for News
<N1></N1>	3	Content to be added
<N2></N2>	3	Content to be added
</News>	2	Closing tag for News
<POTDay>	2	Opening tag for POTDay
<P1></P1>	3	Content to be added
<P2></P2>	3	Content to be added
<P3></P3>	3	Content to be added
</POTDay>	2	Closing tag for POTDay
<Gallery>	2	Opening tag for Gallery
<G1></G1>	3	Content to be added
<G2></G2>	3	Content to be added
<G3></G3>	3	Content to be added
</Gallery>		Closing tag for Gallery
</Title>		Closing tag for Title

Figure 17.3 XML code for crineinfo test match data

Although no comments are included in the code above, comments may be added.

17.12.1 XML Elements

As noted earlier, a XML document is composed of pieces called elements. An element is like a box of information that is surrounded by XML tags. Each element divides the document into its parts which may be images, text, or a diagram. The document with all the elements has a tree-shaped structure with the top element called the *root element*. An element may have elements nested within it. These are called the descendents or children and leads to ancestor/descendent relationships between elements.

As an example, let us look at more details of the scorecard that cricinfo has and represent it in XML in Fig. 17.4.

```
<India 1st Innings>
<Batsmen>
    <Player>
        <Name> G Gambhir </Name>
        <HowOut> lbw b Malinga </HowOut>
        <R> 2 </R>
        <M> 2 </M>
        <B> 2 </B>
        <F> 0 </F>
        <S> 0 </S>
        <SR> 100.0 </SR>
    </Player>
    <Player>
        <Name> V Sehwag </Name>
        <HowOut> c Paranavitana b Welegedara </HowOut>
        <R> 109 </R>
        <M> 175 </M>
        <B> 118 </B>
        <F> 19 </F>
        <S> 1 </S>
        <SR> 92.3 </SR>
    </Player>
    <Player>
        [.... Remaining batsmen ....]
    </Player>
</Batsmen>
</India 1st Innings>
```

Figure 17.4 Information about players in XML

It is clear that each innings has a lot of information since there could be 11 batsmen and then we need to include the bowling figures, fall of wickets and other information. Each innings could take several pages of XML to describe it. Note that <F> tag is used to indicate the number of 4s and <S> indicates number of sixes.

It should be noted that this type of XML markup does not specify how the content will be displayed as in case of HTML markup.

Each element begins with a tag that is surrounded by <tag name> ..</tag name>. The tag name must start with a letter or an underscore and may contain any number of letter, numbers, hyphens, underscores and periods. Therefore, all these tags as tgname, tg+name, tg.name, tg_name, tg_12name.44 and _tagn are fine but 4s and 6s are not legal. It should be noted that for each pair of tags the end tag must come after the start tag and the pair should have the same parent to maintain an unambiguous hierarchical structure.

17.12.2 Namespace

Since the users are allowed to develop their own tag names, it is natural to expect that the same tag names from different fields will have different meanings. This confusion can be avoided by using the concept of namespace and requiring that the name of every XML tag has two parts, viz., the namespace and the local name. One could for example, use namespaces match and player in a cricket setting by using tags like cricket:match and cricket:player (namespace:tag) while a document about properties may also talk about how a property matches needs of a family of four by using tags like property:match while most other tags for the two namespaces would be quite different. Another example could be documents relating to a matrimonial site which has details about requirement for a suitable match for a person. Many other tags are likely to be common in a number of applications, for example, name, age, gender, place of birth, citizenship and so on. The same tags may mean different things in different applications as we illustrated by using the two applications, cricket and matrimonial.

A namespace must be defined in the XML document before it can be used. The declaration usually appears in the root element and the declaration starts with the keyword xmlns: which informs the parser that this is a namespace declaration. This keyword is followed by a namespace prefix followed by an equal sign which a URL in quotes. For example, the following declaration is a namespace declaration. Note that the URL in the example does not exist. The namespace prefix can be any reasonable identifier.

xmlns:cricket="//www.cricketns.com"

The URL in the above declaration needs to be of an organization that maintains the namespace. The XML processor actually does not do anything with the URL and it is only a formality to provide the URL.

17.12.3 XML Attributes

XML elements may have attributes to describe details about the element that the element's name does not convey. These attributes are quite different than attributes in the relational model since XML attributes are properties of XML elements and are defined as (name, value) pairs. XML attributes are mostly used for annotating pieces of text that is enclosed between a pair of tags. These attribute values are not part of the text. Ordering of attributes in an element is not important.

Users may define any number of arbitrary attributes for an element but each attribute must have a unique name and be separated by spaces. The value of an attribute is always a string and therefore must be enclosed in quotation marks. A number of attribute names are reserved. These include xml:lang, xml:space, xml:link and xml:attribute. In fact it is best to avoid using an attribute name starting with the word xml.

We now present a short example to show how attributes are used in XML. There are two attributes shown for the element <player>. In one attribute the description is that the player is a top batsman. The other attribute notes that the player is still playing.

```
<player>
<description = "top batsman">
<fname status = "Still playing in 2010">
 Sachin </fname>
<lname> Tendulkar </lname>
<Yborn> 19973 </Yborn>
<Country> India </Country>
</player>
```

17.12.4 Document Type Definition (DTD)

The document type definition (DTD) is a way of modeling a document. A DTD defines the legal building blocks of an XML document; it defines the types of tags, elements, attributes and entities that may be used and the types of information the document may contain.

Using a DTD, each XML document may carry a description of its own format with it. A DTD is a set of declarations defining the names of the document components and can be declared inside an XML document or it may be an external reference.

For large documents the DTD declarations can include hundreds of element and attribute declarations. Keeping such a large collection of DTD declarations can be a challenge. In fact there are one or two complete books that describe how to declare DTDs, keep them organized, modularized, readable and bug-free. We list a number of rules of thumb to manage a large number of DTDs declarations. Some of these rules of thumb are similar to the naming conventions in Chapter 2.

- Each attribute and element name should come from their description, which has meaning to the user.
- Each name should normally be a noun, singular and current tense.
- A convention for names may be used (for example, the first letter is always uppercase).
- Where necessary, underscores should join the words.
- Names should not be abbreviated unnecessarily making them difficult to understand.
- All DTD declarations should be organized into sections by their functions.
- Comment all DTD declarations to improve readability of DTD declarations.

17.12.5 Document Object Model (DOM)

The XML DOM defines a W3C standard for accessing and manipulating XML documents. The DOM assumes that everything in a XML document is a node in a tree structure. The text of an element node is stored in a text node. As discussed earlier, the terms parent, child, and sibling are used to describe the relationships between nodes.

DOM is essentially a specification that defines the structure of the document. A DOM is an API that describes how programs interpret the structure and content of the document.

DOM includes a number of modules including the core module, the views module, and the stylesheet module. The core module defines the basic object types in XML documents including elements and attributes. The views module describes the interaction between the document and its views. The stylesheet module is an interface that helps derive stylesheet objects.

17.12.6 XML Schema

Some people have criticized DTDs as old and inflexible and therefore XML schema is an alternative to DTDs for document modeling. It is different from DTDs and may be defined in XML itself. The schema is also a way of modeling a document. It defines the legal building blocks of an XML document including types of tags, elements, attributes and entities that may be used and the types of information the document may contain. In contrast to DTDs, schemas have many additional capabilities that include datatype control and content restrictions.

Every element and attribute declaration in schema has type attribute. There are a number of predefined datatypes including string, decimal, float, long, Boolean, time and date as well as a number of others. Schema also includes patterns which are constraints on a datatype which may be a predefined pattern or which is created by using a <pattern> declaration. XML schema therefore allows finer detail of a document to be defined.

17.12.7 XQuery

A number of languages have been designed to query XML data. One of the languages is XQUERY which is the W3C standard query language for XML documents.

XQuery statements have some similarity with statements in SQL and those in OQL. FWR structure (meaning FOR, WHERE and RETURN clauses) is the basic structure of XQuery expressions. The FOR clause is similar to the FROM clause in SQL queries and is used to specify the documents that are to be used in the query. The WHERE clause has the same functionality in XQuery as the WHERE clause does in SQL. It is used for qualifying the results. The RETURN clause is similar to the SELECT clause in SQL since it defines the result.

17.13 XML DATABASES

There are a large number of XML DBMS on the market. A list may be found at http://www.rpbourret.com/xml/XMLDatabaseProds.htm.

Similar to relational databases, a XML database needs to carry out the basic DBMS functions efficiently. These functions include data storage for documents, query processing and presentation of query results. In a relational database, tables are stored, indexes are built, SQL queries processed and results are obtained. Similar steps are required for XML databases.

XML DBMS are usually one of the two types. The first approach, called the *relational approach*, involves XML data to be converted into a relational database. Some relational DBMS now support XML within the conventional DBMS. When XML data is managed by a relational DBMS, a database schema that defines a set of relations must be defined. The schema may be defined for each DTD or it may be defined independent of a DTD by describing the XML tree structure and the positions of elements in such a structure. A number of database vendors including IBM DB2, Microsoft SQL Server and ORACLE have developed tools to assist in mapping XML documents into relational representation. It should however be noted that mapping XML data into relations in some cases results in a large number of tables that may be unnormalized and it can be in some cases difficult to capture the rich structure of XML into a relational structure. Since a tree must be mapped into many tables, some of the queries can involve a number of joins.

The other approach is called the *Native XML database* approach. In this approach, the XML DBMS is developed from scratch using either an ODMS approach or one based on the document object model (DOM). In the ODMS approach, each XML element is mapped into a separate object leading to a large collection of objects for large documents. The XML DOM is a W3C standard and is a language-neutral interface, which allows programs and scripts to dynamically access and update the content, structure, and style of a XML document. DOM presents an XML document as a tree-structure and provides a standard set of objects for representing XML documents. According to DOM, everything in an XML document is a node and all nodes can be accessed through the tree. Their contents can be modified or deleted, and new elements can be created.

We now discuss the two approaches of building XML databases in some more detail.

17.14 RELATIONAL XML DATABASE

As noted earlier, there are many relational DBMS available for XML. The paper by Lu, Jiang et al., presents results of benchmarks of the following six relational DBMS and three native XML DBMS.

- Monet
- Edge
- XRel
- XParent
- Shared-inlining
- Shared-inlining with a path index

The different relational database systems use different ways of supporting XML. Therefore, if an application is developed with one RDBMS product then porting that application to another database system may require some effort.

The performance of a relational XML database depends on how the XML data is represented in the relational model. In order to represent XML as a relational database, there is a requirement to develop an efficient encoding scheme for the XML tree so that XML core operations on the document may be carried out efficiently. This is sometimes called *shredding* a XML document into rows of relational tables.

Many encoding schemes have been presented in the literature. We present three encoding schemes that are investigated in the paper by Tatarinov *et al.*

Global Order Encoding (GOE)

This encoding scheme involves assigning a number to each XML tree node such that the number represents the node's absolute position in the document tree. This encoding provides good support for XML queries that are order related, for example, *following* or *following-sibling* although node insertion requires changing, on average, half the codes of the nodes.

Local Order Encoding (LOE)

The LOE encoding scheme encodes a XML document tree by assigning a number that represents its relative position amongst its siblings. It therefore provides good performance for node insertion since an insertion only requires renumbering of the following siblings. The disadvantage is its poor performance of order related XML queries and therefore this encoding only has limited practical use.

Dewey Order Encoding (DOE)

This encoding is based on the Dewey system that is used in the libraries. Each node under this system is assigned a code that represents a path from the document's node to the leaf. In some ways this encoding may be looked at as a compromise between the global and local encodings, therefore, providing benefits of both those schemes. One of the schemes that uses this encoding is called ORDPATH.

Figure 17.5 illustrates the three encoding schemes for Fig. 17.2 that describes a test match.

Note that we did not include encodings for every node since the figure would then become crowded but the encodings given should be sufficient to illustrate how the three encodings work. Global encodings just go from 1 to the last node 26 (in Fig. 17.3). Local encodings restart at 1 for each level, going from 1 to 15 at level 3. The Dewey coding are different, for example, the first node at level 4 is 1.1.1.1 and the fifth node on level 3 is 1.1.5. It is clear that insertion is expensive in global encoding while easier in local encoding and Dewey encodings.

A relational table or shredding of Fig. 17.5 (page 727) is shown in Fig. 17.6 (page 728). Each node has now been transformed as a row in the table. Note that the ORDPATH numbers are given in the first column of the table. New nodes can be inserted by modifying the ORDPATH values of few other nodes if required. The parent of a given ORDPATH number may be obtained by removing the rightmost component of the given number. The smallest descendents of a given ORDPATH number may be obtained by adding *a* .1 to the number. The table may now be queried using SQL. One or more indexes may be built when the table is large.

Once shredding of an XML document is achieved and the document is stored in a RDBMS, the usual queries may be used to query the database.

We now briefly discuss features of native XML databases.

17.15 NATIVE XML DATABASE

Native XML databases aim to focus on efficient storage of documents, where a key issue is the document granularity. Granularity is important since some documents can be large and it may be necessary to access parts of the document without accessing the whole document. Therefore a document may be stored intact or not intact. A disadvantage of intact document storage is that for certain queries, it can take a long time to process a request although an advantage of intact document storage is its simplicity. The benefits of using a finer granularity include ability to reference an element within a document directly, ability to retrieve partial documents without parsing, efficient querying by materializing only those parts of a document necessary to evaluate the query and, finally, ability to modify a small piece of a large document.

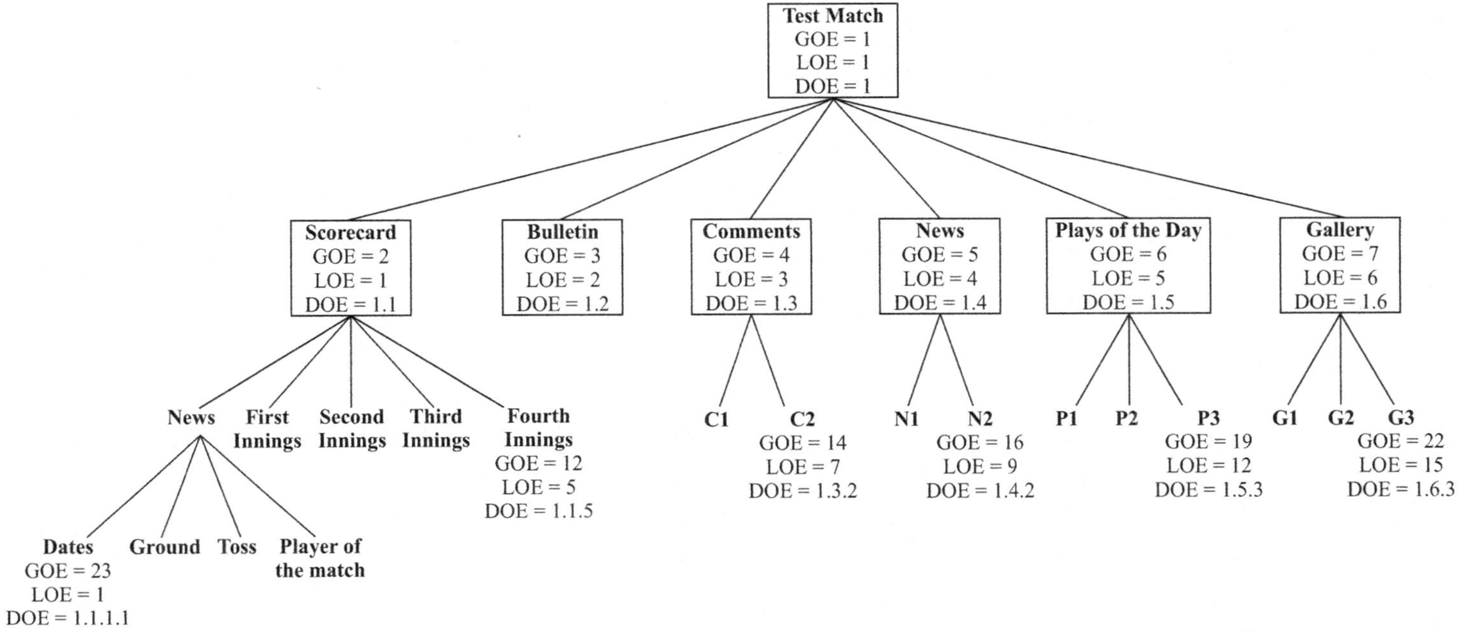

Figure 17.5 Example of Fig. 17.2 with node encodings

ORDPATH	Tag	Node Type	Value
1	Test Match	(Element)	To be defined
1.1	Scorecard	(Element)	To be defined
1.2	Bulletin	(Element)	To be defined
1.3	Comments	(Element)	To be defined
1.4	News	(Element)	To be defined
1.5	Plays of the Day	(Element)	To be defined
1.6	Gallery	(Element)	To be defined
1.1.1	News	(Element)	To be defined
1.1.2	First Innings	(Element)	To be defined
1.1.3	Second Innings	(Element)	To be defined
1.1.4	Third Innings	(Element)	To be defined
1.1.5	Fourth Innings	(Element)	To be defined
Ten more rows at Level 3			
1.1.1.1	Dates	(Element)	22 July 2010
1.1.1.2	Ground	(Element)	Galle
1.1.1.3	Toss	(Element)	Sri Lanka
1.1.1.4	Player_of_the_match	(Element)	Murali??
More rows depending on what is at Level 4			

Figure 17.6 Example ORDPATH shredding using Dewey encoding of Fig. 17.5

Native XML databases that store documents as fine-grained nodes must assign addressable node identifiers to each tree node. Node IDs are used to retrieve specific nodes during processing. Smaller nodes and node IDs mean better locality of reference and fewer disk accesses to read and write data. Some XML databases store document nodes in a B-tree. Node numbering is one of the more interesting issues in building a native XML DBMS. There are node numbering schemes that have the ability to allow insertion and removal of arbitrary nodes without renumbering and to allow query-relevant operations to be performed based solely on node numbers and indexes, eliminating node lookups. A XML database may use a numbering scheme that allows some direct relationship comparisons and attempts to minimize the need to materialize nodes for navigation. The scheme also avoids renumbering when a document is modified partially.

17.15.1 Indexing and Storage

In any database system, whether it is relational, object-oriented or XML, indexes are required for efficient processing of queries if the database is large. XML indexes can be of two types. One based on values and the others based on structures since XML documents can have complex tree-structure that includes ancestor-dependent or parent-child relationships.

Proper specification and use of indexes can increase query performance significantly. All indexes deal with elements, attributes and their respective text content. However, there is no standard or convention regarding how to specify indexes or even what is indexed and how. Different XML databases have made different choices regarding indexes.

Most native XML databases store documents in a collection. The scope of a given index is usually for a whole collection.

An XML document may be viewed as an ordered tree where the nodes correspond to document elements. To develop a structural indexing technique, each node of the document tree must be numbered in some sensible way so that relationships between different nodes may be determined relatively quickly. As noted earlier, a number of different schemes have been proposed. We discussed three techniques earlier. We note two others here. One of them uses a 3-tuple for each node that includes (document id, start position:end position, nesting level). The start and end positions are determined by the distance from the beginning of the document. The other possibility is to use a pre-order traversal number which can uniquely identify the elements of the XML tree. Although this is an attractive scheme, it does not provide a durable reference since insertions and deletions change the pre-order numbers of the document elements.

One of the databases, eXist, has four different indexes on the XML data stored in its database. All the four indexes are based on B^+-tree. The four indexes are as follows:

1. *Collection hierarchy*—Each collection is given a unique id and indexed.
2. *DOM*—All document nodes are stored according to the W3C DOM model and are indexed by the B^+-tree.
3. *Elements*—Top level elements are indexed by the B^+-tree.
4. *Words*—This is an inverted index associated with each word or phrase in the documents and where it occurs.

17.15.2 Query Processing using XQuery

There are a number of XML query languages including XPath, XSLT and XQuery. XQuery has been adopted as a standard by W3C. XQuery has a number of different types of expressions including comparisons and sequence manipulation, arithmetic, and logic. As noted earlier, XQuery and SQL are similar. XQuery has a FWR structure (FOR, WHERE and RETURN) and both XQuery and SQL have an ORDER BY clause which may be used for sorting. The FOR clause is similar to the FROM clause in SQL queries and is used to specify the documents that are to be used in the query. The WHERE clause has the same functionality in XQuery as the WHERE clause does in SQL. It is used for qualifying the results. The RETURN clause is similar to the SELECT clause in SQL since it defines the result.

Given the indexes that were briefly described above, different nodes of the XML tree can be accessed easily. As discussed in Chapter 8, a query must be parsed into an algebraic language which is optimized using the storage and indexing information which is in the metadata. The query plan now includes operators like selection, projection and join. Sorting is also included when results need to be sorted. The query evaluator then evaluates the query plan thus obtained from the query optimizer.

Information about XML databases is available in the references cited in the bibliography at the end of this chapter.

SUMMARY

In this chapter we have studied the following topics:

- The Web is the largest collection of documents. It has been claimed that there are more than 25 billion pages on the Web in 2010.
- The differences between classical information retrieval and searching the Web were described in Chapter 16.
- Web terminology, for example, a browser, a URL and a web server, has been explained.
- Web structure has been explored by some researchers and they found the structure to be like a bow-tie. The middle part of the Web is called the Strongly Connected Core (SCC) which is about 30% of the Web.
- Three most important concepts in information retrieval are relevance, precision and recall. Relevance deals with the relevance of documents retrieved, precision deals with the percentage of documents retrieved that are relevant, and recall deals with the percentage of relevant documents retrieved.
- Vector-space model has been used in classical information retrieval. It involves representing each document as a high dimensional vector with each dimension per term in the document collection.
- A search engine is a complex piece of software. The components of a search engine include a number of components, for example, crawler, indexer, and query processor.
- The role of a crawler in building a search engine database by traversing all the web pages and collecting information about them has been described.
- Another component of a search engine is the indexer. The index for web pages is built by indexer using an inverted index. This index is used in querying the Web.
- Before presentation of the results of a query, the pages must be ranked which may be based on page popularity.
- The role of markup languages is primarily in specifying a document's structure and the processing that is to be carried out on the document.
- Semistructured data including data with variable number of fields, repeated attributes and variable type of data for the same attribute is described.
- The language XML is introduced and an example of representing information about a test match as available at the cricinfo site in XML is presented. Components of a XML document including elements and attributes are explained.
- XML databases are implemented either as relational XML databases or as native XML databases. Details of their implementations have been provided.

REVIEW QUESTIONS

1. How are the web documents different than the documents in a library? (Section 17.2)
2. Explain some of the terminology used for the Web? (Section 17.3)
3. Describe the structure of the Web. (Section 17.4)

4. Describe some of the terms used commonly in information retrieval. (Section 17.5)
5. Review the basics of classical information retrieval and explain the vector space model. (Section 17.6)
6. What are search engine functionalities? (Section 17.7)
7. Describe the roles of web crawler and the indexer. (Sections 17.8)
8. Explain query processing by a search engine. (Section 17.9)
9. Describe how the ordering of the pages is determined by a search engine. (Section 17.9)
10. Discuss the role of a markup language in specifying the structure of a document. (Section 17.10)
11. Describe the features of semistructured data and how it differs from relational model data. (Section 17.11)
12. Review the language XML and its history. (Section 17.12)
13. Describe why attributes are used in XML documents and list some of their properties. (Section 17.12)
14. Write a simple XML code and represent it as a XML tree. (Section 17.12)
15. Discuss the relational technique of implementing an XML database. (Section 17.13)
16. Briefly discuss storage and indexing of XML database. (Section 17.13)
17. How does query processing work in XML databases? (Section 17.13)

SHORT ANSWER QUESTIONS

1. How large is the Web estimated to be?
2. Explain the meaning of a web page, a link and HTML.
3. What is the primary purpose of tags in HTML?
4. What is strongly connected core? How large is it?
5. What is deep Web?
6. What are a term, relevance, precision and recall?
7. What is semistructured data?
8. Why can't semistructured data be processed by a relational DBMS?
9. What did HITS algorithm discover?
10. What is the aim of a search engine?
11. What are the characteristics of a search engine?
12. How many pages does Google index?
13. How can documents be ranked?
14. What are a crawler and an indexer?
15. What is the vector space model?
16. Explain terms term vector, weight, term frequency and inverse document frequency.
17. Give an example of a markup language.
18. What is XML? What does XML stand for?
19. What are three major differences between HTML and XML?
20. What is an XML element?
21. What is a tag? Does XML predefine some tags?

22. What is a XML attribute? How does it differ from an attribute in the relational model?
23. What is the difference between a XML element and an attribute?
24. What is the difference between DTD and a XML schema/
25. Give a name of an XML database and the implementation approach used by it.
26. What are the advantages and disadvantages of implementing a XML database as a relational database?
27. What are the advantages and disadvantages of implementing a XML database as a native XML database.

MULTIPLE CHOICE QUESTIONS

1. Which one of the following is **not** a way to search for information on the Web?
   (a) Directories (b) Portals (c) Search engines (d) Catalogue
2. Which one of the following is **not** a major difference between classical information retrieval and information retrieval from the Web?
   (a) In classical information retrieval documents cannot be searched on keywords while Web can be searched on keywords.
   (b) Classical documents do not have hyperlinks while web documents do.
   (c) Classical documents are not dynamic but web pages are.
   (d) Documents are of high quality while web pages are of variable quality.
3. Which one of the following is **not** correct?
   (a) A URL is an identifier of a web resource.
   (b) A client browser is the primary user interface to the Web.
   (c) Searching the Web is called "information push".
   (d) All Web links represent human judgement about relationship between two web pages.
4. Which one of the following is true?
   (a) The Web in 2010 was about 5 billion pages.
   (b) The Web is a random collection of pages with no structure.
   (c) About 700,000 new pages are created on the Web each week.
   (d) Deep Web is much larger than the shallow Web.
5. Which one of the following is true about the structure of the Web?
   (a) About 25% of the web pages are not connected to any other web page.
   (b) About 50% of the Web is highly connected called the Core or SCC.
   (c) The Web has less than 10% of pages which cannot be reached from the core but do have links to other pages.
   (d) The Web has sites that are authorities on most topics.
6. Which one of the following is correct?
   (a) Relevance of a document indicates how much it matches the user's specification.
   (b) Precision is the total number of relevant documents retrieved.
   (c) Recall is the total number of irrelevant documents retrieved.
   (d) Precision increases faster than recall increase.

7. Which one of the following is correct?
   (a) Classical retrieval does not require preprocessing each document.
   (b) IDF is the same as term frequency.
   (c) Vector spaced model always involves building a vector of all the terms in the document.
   (d) The query vector is compared with each document's vector to determine the relevance of each document.
8. Which of the following are correct?
   (a) A search engine data is stored in a central database.
   (b) The search engine crawler collects information on the web pages.
   (c) Indexer builds an index using the B-tree.
   (d) Query server serves the results after ranking each page retrieved.
9. Which one of the following is **not** a component of an inverted index?
   (a) Vocabulary of index terms.
   (b) Information about the terms, for example, how many times each term appears.
   (c) For each term an inverted list of documents that do not have the term.
   (d) For each term an inverted list of documents that have the term.
10. Which one of the following is true about ranking search engine results?
    (a) There is only one technique for ranking pages.
    (b) The indexing of web pages is based on ranking of the pages.
    (c) PageRanks are usually based on hyperlinks to and from the page.
    (d) PageRank is an accurate reflection of a page's relevance.
11. Which one is **not** an example of a markup language?
    (a) SGML (b) Word (c) HTML (d) XML
12. Which one of the following is **not** a property of semistructured data?
    (a) It usually has a variable number of fields.
    (b) It may have repeated attributes.
    (c) It does now allow variable types of data for the same attribute.
    (d) It is self-describing.
13. Which one of the following is **not** a component of a XML document?
    (a) Elements (b) Attributes (c) Primary key (d) User defined tags
14. Which one of the following is **not** a component of a XML document?
    (a) Predefined tabs (b) Elements (c) Tags (d) DTD
15. Which one of the following is true about XML?
    (a) XML is not designed to define content.
    (b) XML is designed to define the document presentation.
    (c) XML documents must have a fixed number of nodes at each level.
    (d) The text between any pair of XML tags is called content.
16. Which one of the following is true about a relational implementation of a XML database?
    (a) DBMS like Oracle cannot be used.
    (b) The XML database must be converted to an E-R Model.

(c) Primary key and foreign keys must be defined.
(d) Although many tables may need to be created, the relational implementation can still work efficiently.

17. Which one of the following is a native XML database?
(a) Monet (b) Edge (c) XParent (d) eXist
18. Which one of the following is **not** a query language for XML databases?
(a) XPath (b) XSQL (c) XSLT (d) XQuery
19. Which one of the following is **not** an encoding scheme for XML trees?
(a) Global Order encoding (GCE) (b) Local Order encoding (LOE)
(c) Hybrid Order encoding (HOE) (d) Dewey Order encoding (DOE)
20. Which one of the following is **not** a component of a XML database?
(a) Query processor (b) Indexing
(c) Storage of elements (d) Domains

EXERCISES

1. Define the following terms:
(a) Browser (b) Uniform resource locator
(c) Domain name server (d) Cookie
2. Describe the 'bow-tie' structure of the Web. What percentage of pages forms the Strongly Connected Core? What is the main property of the Core?
3. What is the difference between the deep and shallow Web? Why do we need the deep Web?
4. (a) What is the distribution of in-links and out-links from web pages?
(b) Estimate the percentage of web pages that have only one in-link or no link?
(c) Estimate the percentage of web pages that have only one out-link or no link?
5. What are the major differences between classical information retrieval and web search?
6. What is precision and recall? How do they apply to web search?
7. What are the different components of a search engine? Describe them briefly and present a basic crawling algorithm.
8. What is the most important property of a web page in determining its PageRank?
9. Discuss the native XML approach of implementing an XML database.
10. Describe some of the features of a native XML database.
11. Describe how a XML document may be shredded into rows of a relational table.

PROJECTS

1. Find a recent issue of your local newspaper. Explain how the front page of the newspaper may be represented in XML. Draw the XML tree for the front page.

2. Convert the front page XML tree into a relational database and show the database schema. Explain any problems in this conversion. How many tables were created?
3. Now explain how the tree can be converted for storage in a native XML database. Is this better than the relational database? Why?
4. If time permits, the class can download and share an open source native XML database from the Web and use it to store your newspaper front page as XML. Describe what you have done.
5. List some queries that you may wish to pose to this document. Write the queries in XQuery.

LAB EXERCISES

1. Consider the following XML tree for information about a cricket team touring another country. The tree is about another set of cricket information. We have only included four tours that are taking place during the 2010 11 season, which is the Australian summer. Therefore, the root node has a child for each tour and each tour has a number of descendents depending on the number of matches being played on the tour. These may include first class matches, test matches, ODI and T20 matches. We have included very little information in the tree since the tree otherwise becomes quite big; too big to be included on a page.

   Each test match is labeled $T1$, $T2$, $T3$..etc., to indicate that it is a first test match of the tour or second test match of the tour and so on. As shown in Fig. 17.2 earlier, a test match has a large amount of information which we do not show in this figure. We only show information about the *Ground*, *Date*, *Teams* and *Result* but once again we note that we are not able to show a tree that has all the information. Show what the XML code would look like for this tree. Label each node with each of the three encoding schemes (global, local and Dewey). Represent it as a relational table using the Dewey scheme.

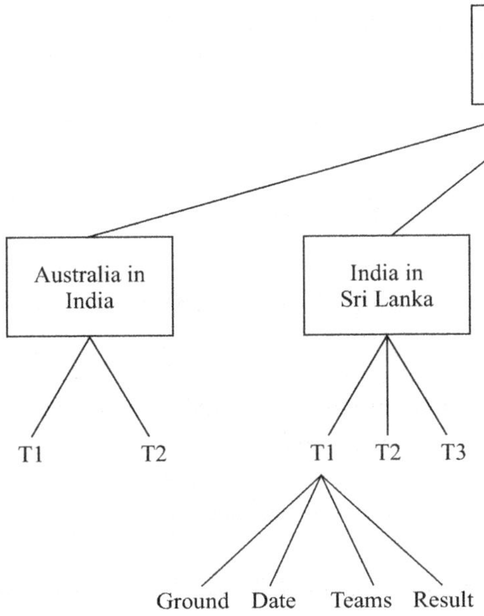

Figure 17.7

2. Consider the inverted index technique of storing web pages. Assume you wish to find documents that have the key words data and Web. In Google 'data' appears in more than 1.6 billion pages and 'Web' appears in more than 3.1 billion pages. How should the intersection of the two lists be found efficiently?
3. Assume that you have 10 computers (or 100 or even a 1000). Describe an efficient way of finding the intersection of the two very large lists using all the computers.
4. Find some XML trees from the Web. Study them and explain what documents they represent. Is this a good representation of the documents? Why?
5. Study the database techniques used in TIMBER. Write a 500 words summary of techniques used in this XML database.

BIBLIOGRAPHY

For Students

Huang's survey is good and Kleinberg's paper is interesting. Paper by Lu, Jiang et al., gives a lot of information about benchmarking XML databases.

For Instructors

We present two books that provide a lot of interesting information. XML database implementations are described by Jagdish et al., Tatarinov et al., and Meier. The book by Chaudhri, Rashid and Zicari is an excellent collection of papers on XML database management, including native XML and relational approaches, as well as applications of XML. The book by Brundage explains XQuery well.

Adamic, L., "The Small World Web", *Proc. 3rd European Conf. Research and Advanced Technology for Digital Libraries (ECDL)*, 1999, pp 443-452.

Arasu,A., J. Cho, H. Garcia-Molina, A. Paepcke, and S. Raghavan, "Searching the Web", *ACM Transactions on Internet Technology*, Vol. 1, No. 1, 2001, pp 2-43.

Huang, L., *A Survey on Web Information Retrieval Technologies*, Technical Report, Computer Science Department, State University of New York at Stony Brook, 2000.

Berry, M. W., and M. Browne, *Understanding Search Engines: Mathematical Modeling and Text Retrieval, SIAM*, Philadelphia, PA, 1999, 116 pp.

Borodin, A., G. Roberts, J. S. Rosenthal, and P. Tsaparas, "Finding authorities and hubs from link structures on the World Wide Web", *Proc. 10th Int. World Wide Web Conf. (WWW10)*, Hong Kong, 2001, pp 415-429.

Brin, S., "Extracting Patterns and Relations from the World Wide Web", *WebDB Workshop at 6th International Conference on Extending Database Technology (EDBT'98)*, Valencia, Spain, 1998.

Brin, S., and L. Page, "The Anatomy of a Large-scale Hypertextual Web Search Engine", *Proc. 7th Int. World Wide Web Conf. (WWW'98)*, Brisbane, Australia, 1998, pp 107-117. Also in *Computer Networks and ISDN Systems*, Vol. 30, Issue 1-7, April 1998, pp 107-117. http://www-db.stanford.edu/~backrub/google.html

Broder, A., "A Taxonomy of Web Search", *ACM SIGIR Forum*, Vol. 36, No. 2, 2002, pp 3-10. http://www.acm.org/sigir/forum/F2002/broder.pdf

Broder, A., R. Kumar, F. Maghoul, P. Raghvan, S. Rajagopalan, R. Stat, A. Tomkins, and J. Wiener, "Graph Structure in the Web: Experiments and Models", *Proc. 9th Int. World Wide Web Conf. (WWW9)*, Amsterdam, Netherlands, 2000, pp 309-320.

Chaudhri, A., A. Rashid, and R. Zicari, (Eds.), *XML Data Management: Native XML and XML-Enabled Database Systems*, Addison-Wesley, 2003.

Cooley, R., P. N. Tan, and J. Srivastava, "Discovery of Interesting Usage Patterns from Web data", *Advances in Web Usage Analysis and User Profiling, Lecture Notes in Computer Science*, Spiliopoulou, M. and Masand, B., (Eds.), Vol. 1836, Springer-Verlag, 2000, pp 163-182.

Dhyani, D., W. K. Ng, and S. V. Bhowmick, "A Survey of Web Metrics", *ACM Computing Surveys*, Vol. 34, No. 4, 2002, pp 469-503.

Florescu, D., A. Levy and A. Mendelzon, "Database Techniques for the World-Wide Web: A Survey", *ACM SIGMOD Record*, Vol. 27, September 1998, pp 59-74.

Gibson, D., J. Kleinberg, and P. Raghavan, "Inferring Web Communities from Link Topology", *Proc. 9th Conf. on Hypertext and Hypermedia (UK)*, Pittsburg, PA, 1998, pp 225-234.

Jagdish, H. V., S. Al-Khalifa, A. Chapman et al., "TIMBER: A Native XML Database", *The VLDB Journal*, Vol. 11, 2002, pp 274-291.

Kleinberg, J., "Authoritative Sources in a Hyperlinked Environment", *Journal of the ACM*, Vol. 46, No. 5, 1999, pp 604-632.

Kleinberg, J., R. Kumar, P. Raghvan, S. Rajagopalan, and A. S. Tomkins, "The Web as a Graph: Measurements, Models and Methods", *Proc. Int. Conf. on Combinatorics and Computing*, No. 1627 in Lecture Notes in Computer Science, Springer, Berlin, 1999, pp 1-18.

Kleinberg, J., "The Small-World Phenomenon: An Algorithmic perspective", *Proc. 32nd ACM Symposium on Theory of Computing*, 2000, pp 163-170.

Lu, H., H. Jiang, J. X. Yu, G. E. Yu, G. Wang, A. Zhou, and S. Zheng, "What Makes the Differences: Benchmarking XML Database Implementations", *ACM Transactions on Internet Technology*, Vol. 5, 2005, pp 154-198.

Pirolli, P., J. Pitkow, and R. Rao, "Silk from a sow's ear: Extracting usable structures from the Web", Proc. SIGCHI Conf. on Human Factors in Computing Systems, Vancouver, Canada, 1996, pp 118-125.

Pitkow, J. E., "Summary of WWW Characterizations", *Computer Networks and ISDN Systems*, Vol. 30, No. 1-7, 1998, pp 551-558. http://www.searchenginegenie.com/google-pagerankexplained.htm (long!)

Meier, W., "eXist: An Open Source Native XML Database", *Lecture Notes in Computer Science,* Vol. 2593/2009, 2009, pp 169-183.

Page, L., S. Brin, R. Motwani, and T. Winograd, "The PageRank Citation Ranking: Bringing Order to the Web", *Stanford Technical Report*, 1998. http://dbpubs.stanford.edu:8090/pub/1999-66

Brundage, M., *XQuery: The XML Query Language*, Addison-Wesley, 2004, pp 505.

Tatarinov, I., S. D. Viglas, K. Bayer et al., "Storing and Querying Ordered XML using a Relational Database System", *ACM SIMOD Conference*, 2002, pp 204-215.

Trevor, B., E. Weippl, and W. Winiwarter, *A Modern Approach to Searching the World Wide Web: Ranking Pages by Inference over Content*, INAP, Tokyo, Japan, 2001, pp 316-330.

Zobel, J., and A. Moffat, "Inverted Files for Text Search Engines", *ACM Computing Surveys*, Vol. 38, Issue 2, Article 6, July 2006.

Tim Berners-Lee—Inventor of the World Wide Web

Around 1990, Tim Berners–Lee at the European Laboratory for Particle Physics, which is better known as CERN, proposed a new protocol which was based on a system called hypertext, where embedded links in a text can be used to link to other texts. This developed into something which we now know as the World Wide Web.

Tim Berners–Lee directs the World Wide Web Consortium (W3C), an open forum of companies and organizations with the mission to lead the Web to its full potential through the development of Web technical standards, which he founded in October 1994. He is a Distinguished Fellow of the British Computer Society, and a Honorary Fellow of the Institution of Electrical Engineers, a Member of the American Academy of Arts and Sciences, and a Fellow of the Royal Society.

In 2004, Tim was made a Knight Commander of the Order of the British Empire (KBE). He is a graduate of Oxford University, England, and currently holds the 3Com Founders Chair at the Computer Science and Artificial Intelligence Laboratory (CSAIL) at the Massachusetts Institute of Technology (MIT).

Emerging Database Technologies

18

OBJECTIVES

- Discuss trends in emerging database technologies based on reports of two recent meetings of database experts.
- Explain cloud computing and cloud computing databases.
- Describe benefits and economics of cloud computing.
- Discuss security concerns of cloud computing.
- Introduce the importance of mobile databases.
- Describe characteristics of mobile devices.
- Consider mobile database challenges and location based services.
- Explain a new development called MapReduce. What is MapReduce? What is Hadoop?
- Explore the challenges of using a large collection of commodity computer for some large database problem.

KEYWORDS

Emerging database trends, Lovell meeting, Claremont meeting, cloud computing, CAPex, OPex, elasticity, variable demand, amazon.com, economics of cloud computing, data management, email, IaaS, Paas, SaaS, security concerns in cloud computing, security benefits, mobile databases, mobile device characteristics, mobile database challenges, location, query processing, intermittent connections, battery, MapReduce, Hadoop, map, reduce, clusters, massive data, large networks of commodity computers.

> *Any darn fool can make something complex; it takes a genius to make something simple.*
>
> **Peter Seeger**

18.1 INTRODUCTION

Identifying emerging technologies is not always easy. For example, in the database field, a group of about 25 senior database researchers have gathered every few years to survey the field and to identify technology trends. The forecasts from these panels are not always accurate because of new technological developments.

We briefly consider the deliberations of the last two such meetings. These are the 2003 meeting in Lowell, Massachusetts and the 2008 meeting in Claremont, California.

18.1.1 Lowell Meeting 2003

It is noted in the report of the Lowell meeting that the Internet and the Web were the main driving forces but science was emerging as another important area because it was generating large data sets. Another emerging major source of data was identified as cheap microsensor technology.

These change factors were summarised as follows:

Change Factors

- *Web, Science and e-commerce*—These were having an enormous impact on database technology.
- *Cheap microsensor technology*—This development was enabling most things of material value to report their location and/or state in real time. Sensor-information processing was expected to raise many interesting database issues, with a new set of opportunities.
- *Major DBMS challenges*—In areas like data models, access methods, query processing algorithms, concurrency control, recovery, query languages, and user interfaces.
- *Maturation of database technologies*—These included data mining, web search engines, combining some areas of artificial intelligence and database technology which could allow, for example, more effective handling of speech, natural language, reasoning with uncertainty, and machine learning.

Because of these change factors there were a number of areas of interesting database research.

Research Opportunities

Thirteen topics were listed. These topics and their brief descriptions are as follows:

1. *Integration of text, data, code and streams*—There is a need to rethink basic DBMS architectures that would support structured data, text, image and multimedia data, data types that include methods, triggers and data streams.
2. *Information fusion*—There is a need to investigate cross-enterprise information integration so that integration of perhaps millions of web information sources was possible.
3. *Sensor data and sensor networks*—As noted above, there is a need to study management of data generated by a very large number of low-cost sensor devices.

4. *Multimedia queries*—Since multimedia data is growing very rapidly, there is a need to develop much better facilities for management of multimedia data.
5. *Reasoning about uncertain data*—There is a need to investigate how a query processor may accumulate evidence to provide good answers to a user's queries when an exact answer is not available.
6. *Personalization*—There is a need to investigate if query answers should be influenced by a person's profile which might indicate that the user is an expert in the field or is a student or new to the field.
7. *Data mining*—There is a need to investigate if querying and data mining tools may be integrated to provide the user more useful information.
8. *Self-adaptation*—There is a need to investigate if DBMSs should recognize internal malfunction, data corruption, application failures and be able to resolve such difficulties without human intervention.
9. *Privacy*—There is a need to explore technical solutions to ensure that access decisions are based not only on who is requesting the data but also on what use it will be put.
10. *Trustworthy systems*—There is a need to explore issues related to unauthorized disclosure of data, protecting individual property rights and allowing private conversations.
11. *New user interfaces*—Given that database community has done little to improve user interfaces over the last 30 years and the current interface are not user friendly, there is a need to improve database interfaces and explore if visualization systems may be incorporated in them.
12. *One-hundred-year storage*—Since much of world's information is now stored digitally, there is need to investigate indefinite time electronic storage to ensure information is not damaged or lost.
13. *Query optimization*—There is a need to consider inter-query optimization involving large number of queries to improve the efficiency of some OLTP systems.

The report discusses how to proceed further. Looking back at the thirteen topics we can see that progress has been made in some areas while not much has happened regarding the others. The next meeting was held in 2008 and in a short period of only five years the concerns and interests of the database community have appeared to change significantly as we will discuss ahead.

18.1.2 Claremont Meeting 2008

This 2009 report can be dated to a May 2008 meeting, the seventh such meeting, of a group of database experts held in Claremont near Berkeley in California. This meeting also identified a number of change factors which are listed below:

Change Factors

It is noted in the report that there was a feeling in the meeting that the data management industry was at a turning point that provided rich opportunities for technical advances. The factors that were responsible for this feeling were identified and are listed below.

- *Excitement over big data*—As a result of many applications, for example, web applications, large volume of data has to be managed sometimes using a network of large number of machines. Some of the applications that involve large data in addition to the web search engines are astronomy, biology, earth sciences and social-networking analysis.
- *Data analysis as profit centre*—The use and value of data analysis in business has been growing and the market for data analysis software and tools has also been growing.

- *Ubiquity of structured and unstructured data*—The volume of structured and semistructured data is growing rapidly partly because of the information on the Web and the information that is being generated by mobile computing.
- *Expanded developer demands*—A growing user base of database systems is leading to developers' demands for more user friendly database systems.
- *Architectural shifts in computing*—Many changes are being witnessed in computer architecture including increasing use of cloud computing and large networks of commodity computers.

Given these factors, the members in the meeting felt that there was a need for a number of new data management technologies. There was an agreement that success of database research should be evaluated by helping new classes of users, powering new computing platforms and making conceptual breakthroughs. Consensus was reached on the following research opportunities.

Research Opportunities

1. *Revisiting database engines*—The current DBMSs still use the technologies developed in the 1970s and these technologies do not always meet the needs of current applications. Research in this area may include designing DBMSs that use clusters of a large number of commodity processors, exploiting remote RAM and flash memories, compressing and encrypting data, using nonrelational systems and trading off data consistency for performance.
2. *Declarative programming for emerging platforms*—Developing more powerful and efficient database languages to help developers deal with more complex problems.
3. *Interplay of structured and unstructured data*—The growth in the number of documents, emails and web documents requires that database systems be able to extract structure and meaning from unstructured and semistructured data.
4. *Cloud data services*—As discussed later, cloud services are growing in spite of some risks because the economics of cloud computing is driving the growth and dealing with the growth and the sheer scale of data management in cloud computing is challenging.
5. *Mobile applications and virtual worlds*—Not only cloud computing is growing; there is a huge growth in the use of mobile phones and other mobile devices. In India, about 20 million new phones are being added to the mobile networks each month and the total number of mobile phones at the end of 2010 is over 700 million (China has over 840 million and USA 300 million). The total number of mobile phones in the world will soon surpass 5 billion. Given such a huge user base, many database applications could be added for the users. Mobile databases require appropriate retrieval and storage systems and power-sensitive technologies.

In addition to the five topics listed above, a number of other topics were noted. These included a number of topics that were also included in the Lovell Report, for example, management of uncertain information, data privacy and security, personalization, and adaptive systems. Other topics included streaming and networked data, e-science, social networks, new hardware technologies and energy constraints.

We have selected three topics from the lists above to discuss in this chapter. These are cloud computing, mobile databases and MapReduce. MapReduce deals with huge amount of data using a cluster of commodity computers.

The chapter is organized as follows. We start by describing cloud computing in Section 18.2. This section includes discussion of characteristics of cloud computing, benefits of cloud computing, cloud computing architecture, some cloud computing applications, cloud computing economics, and security concerns in cloud computing. Section 18.3 is devoted to mobile databases. This section deals with characteristics of mobile devices, challenges of mobile databases and locality based services. Section 18.4 deals with MapReduce that is designed to handle huge amount of data that is usually distributed over 100s or 1000s of commodity computers.

18.2 CLOUD COMPUTING AND DATA MANAGEMENT

Cloud computing was identified as one of the emerging technologies in the Claremont Meeting.

What is cloud computing and why is there so much talk about it? In a recent interview, the new Infosys CEO Mr Gopalkrishnan identified cloud computing as one of the technologies on which Infosys is focusing.

Cloud computing is a concept we all are already familiar with since we all use emails from Hotmail, Gmail, Rediffmail, Yahoo! and so on. By using these email systems we access, store and send emails using someone else's computer and memory installed somewhere else. Gmail and Hotmail now claim to provide several gigabytes of memory to each email user for free. Therefore, we are using cloud computing! Somewhere out there someone is providing us computing and storage to use email. The comparing is in "The clouds" or we may say it is providing cloud computing for free.

Although email was first used in the 1970s as computer network became more widely used. Few people knew about email then but then networks became ubiquitous and the Web was invented. This led to the invention of Hotmail by Sabir Bhatia in California and that meant that we did not have to worry about our own computers managing the email traffic. Someone else's machine could do it all. We only had to connect to the Hotmail website and create a Hotmail account and use it from anywhere in the world. Currently we have Hotmail, Yahoo, Gmail and Rediffmail which altogether have almost one billion email accounts. From 2010, Monash University is moving all student emails to the clouds using Gmail and the university will stop worrying about some 50,000 student email accounts. The staff will also move to Gmail. It makes a lot of economic sense to do that.

In addition to email, the most popular cloud services include social networking sites (about 500 million people that use Facebook are being social in the cloud), microblogging and blogging services such as Twitter and WordPress, video-sharing sites like YouTube, photo-sharing sites such as Flickr, document and applications sharing sites like Google Docs, social-bookmarking sites like Delicious, business sites like eBay, and ranking, rating and commenting sites such as Yelp and TripAdvisor.

There are many definitions of cloud computing. We present an informal definition.

> ***Definition—Cloud Computing***
> *Cloud computing is computing services offered on the Internet that may provide computing resources such as processing, storage and software that are normally not physically present at the user's location and the user pays only for the computing resources and services used.*

The term *cloud* in cloud computing usually refers to a third party computing centre although it does not have to be a third party resource. Cloud computing can be done when the computing resources in the cloud are owned by the enterprise that is using it.

Many companies are now in the business of cloud computing, providing cloud computing for a fee. For example, it has been reported that amazon.com provides cloud computing services, for example, one could purchase 50 GB of storage for an annual fee. It then becomes an economic decision whether to purchase a hard disk or just purchase some storage from amazon.com or some other cloud computing company.

18.2.1 Characteristics of Cloud Computing

We list a number of characteristics of cloud computing:

- *On-demand computing resources*—This enables an enterprise not to worry about planning ahead for providing resources.
- *Ability to pay per use for computing resources*—Whether the need is short term or long term, the resources can be paid on the basis of what is used although the provider is likely to charge a premium for this facility.
- *Share nothing architecture*—The computing resource is usually a farm of networked commodity computers that share nothing.
- *Data and processing distributed over the network*—Given that the resource is a collection of hundreds or thousands of computers distributed possibly all over the world and networked, growing demand is more easily accommodated if the workload can be parallelized.
- *Data is replicated*—Given the above, the data may be replicated over large number of computers, possibly all over the world.

18.2.2 Benefits of Cloud Computing

The benefits of cloud computing are related to the characteristics listed earlier. We list the benefits as follows:

1. *Scalability*—Applications can grow and use more resources as required and use fewer resources if the demand goes down. One therefore does not have to deploy resources to handle peak demands. Also, one does not need to rely on forecasting to decide how much equipment to acquire because forecasts are not always correct. The user can feel that any amounts of computing resources are available on demand but it should also be understood that a cloud service provider charges a premium over the cost of owning or leasing equipment if it is fully utilized.
2. *Availability, reliability and security*—In today's world many applications are supposed to be running 24×7. Reliability involves an application never failing, for example, a telecommunications company's accounting system must not fail and a lottery system must not go off the air. Security ensures that unauthorized persons are not granted access. It also ensures that the system that the enterprise relies on does not fail and create serious problems. Cloud computing enables an enterprise to ensure that its resources are not dependent on one service centre since the provider is likely to have computing resources located at a number of sites.

3. *Economics of allocating funds to capital expenditure to operational expenditure*—Given the modern business environment and shortage of capital, it makes sense not to invest a lot of capital to start a project. Instead one can pay for the services as the resources are used. Therefore, there is no upfront capital expenditure (CapEx) and enterprise expenditure is spread over time since the enterprise pays for the service (OpEx) as it uses it. One may of course make an argument that CapEx does not have to be upfront since it may be possible to get a lease which may involve payments say over three years.
4. *Ability to quickly allocate and de-allocate resources*—Once again given the rate of change of business environment, it is desirable to allocate and de-allocate resources when required. Cloud computing provides much needed elasticity.
5. *Flexibility and agility*—Reduced initial costs in deployment of new business applications, as noted earlier, and ability to spread the computing workload to more than one vendor may be desirable.

We now describe three types of services that are usually offered by cloud computing providers.

18.2.3 Types of Cloud Computing Services

Cloud computing may be divided into three service models. Each of these service models addresses a specific business need.

- *Infrastructure as a Service (IaaS)*—This involves the customer purchasing computing processing power, storage and network support from a provider. IaaS is delivered as an operating system on a server with storage and network transfer. IaaS may be delivered as a single machine or as part of a collection of machines integrated into a network. The provider does not manage the services provided; just ensures that the facilities needed are available. IaaS is particularly attractive to meet on-demand infrastructure needs of a customer.
- *Platform as a Service (PaaS)*—PaaS involves the customer purchasing an application environment on top of IaaS. The advantage of PaaS is that the customer can buy a fully functional computing environment that can facilitate development and deployment of applications quickly without the cost of buying and managing the infrastructure. The services provided by PaaS may include programming languages, DBMS as well as development environment and tools. A variety of services may be available under PaaS.
- *Software as a Service (SaaS)*—SaaS involves the customer purchasing the complete use and support of an application software, for example, DBMS. SaaS provider hosts and manages the application required by the customer. The same service is provided to a number of customers but each customer feels as if he/she is the only customer using the service. Google Apps is one example of SaaS. Another example is salesforce.com that provides customer relationship management (CRM) software. Google is offering their Fusion Tables service for data management and collaboration including merging of multiple data sources, querying, visualization, and web publishing. This service is not a traditional database system focusing on SQL queries and transaction processing. The service also allows integration with a visualization API for a variety of ways to display data.

IaaS, PaaS and SaaS are the three major services provided by the cloud computing service providers. We now consider how data management may be done using cloud computing.

18.2.4 Data Management in the Cloud

Database management systems are being provided by some providers. They generally use open-source DBMS, for example, mySQL. Database applications in some cases are suitable for cloud computing since establishing a database system is quite expensive and using cloud computing provides an inexpensive alternative if a provider is able to provide suitable facilities. For example, most OLTP systems; for example, airline booking and banking, may be difficult to move to the clouds since cloud computing often uses a shared nothing collection of commodity computers which may not be suitable for OLTP.

Amazon Web Services recently announced the Amazon Relational Database Service (Amazon RDS), a new cloud computing service that Amazon claims makes it easy to set up a database and operate and scale the database in the cloud. Amazon RDS is based on the MySQL platform and is claimed to provide a cost-efficient resizable capacity while automating time-consuming database administration tasks.

It is necessary to look at how data management will be implemented in the cloud computing scenario. The issues that need to be explored are as follows:

- **How would query processing be carried out given a new architecture in which the user may be located** on another continent and data may be distributed and replicated amongst many computers? Obviously efficient query processing becomes more challenging.
- **How would transaction management be handled given that the database may be fragmented over many** computers that are geographically distributed? Since cloud computing normally uses a shared-nothing collection of computers, transaction management is challenging because most DBMS are not designed to run on such an architecture. Maintaining the ACID properties also becomes more difficult with such architecture.
- **How would concurrency and integrity be handled?—Once again, the data is distributed and replicated** making concurrency control and integrity maintenance more challenging.
- **How would the cloud computing provider ensure security of the database when many users may be** using the same DBMS? This requires a very reliable authentication and authorization regime.

Cloud computing therefore provides a number of advantages as well as a number of challenges when used for database management.

18.2.5 Cloud Computing Architecture

We know who supplies email but who supplies database management services and other cloud services, for example, storage for files and proper backup and security for them? We will discuss these issues in this section.

There can be several types of implementations of cloud computing. We discuss three.

1. *Public cloud computing*—It is offered by companies like amazon.com or google.com. In public clouds, an external third party organization is responsible for providing a variety of facilities and services. Using such cloud computing also means that the cloud computing provider is looking after the data which in some cases may be valuable. It should be noted that in public clouds, applications from a number of different customers may be running on the cloud provider machines but this should

have no impact on any of the customers. For customers that are particularly concerned about security, a public provider may provide exclusive resources to the customer for an additional fee.

2. *Private cloud computing*—It may involve an on-site facility or an off-site facility for exclusive use by the users in the enterprise. In private cloud computing the enterprise that owns it completely controls it and therefore the facility becomes somewhat like a computer centre that is managed by the owner enterprise. Private clouds do not provide some of the benefits of cloud computing since the capital expenditure must be incurred by the enterprise but a private cloud provides full control of the facilities and sensitive information may be better protected.
3. *Hybrid cloud computing*—It includes both private and public cloud computing. Hybrid cloud computing tries to combine the benefits of both public cloud computing and private cloud computing. Such an hybrid arrangement can be appropriate when sensitive information needs to be stored using a private cloud while other services that are not that sensitive may be carried out using public cloud computing. This arrangement provides some of the benefits of cloud computing as additional facilities may be purchased from the public cloud company when demand increases.

18.2.6 Economic Issues in Cloud Computing

We now consider how an enterprise buying its own hardware and software and running its own applications on them compares to running applications using a cloud computing provider such as Amazon (Amazon EC2 and Amazon S3), 3Tera (AppLogic Platform), Force.com (Apex), or Google (Google App Engine).

As we have noted, the key economic issues are listed below.

- Quick provisioning of computational resources.
- No installation or maintenance work required.
- Remote management of application resources.
- Paying for only what is used.

As noted earlier, cloud computing allows an enterprise to quickly allocate and de-allocate resources. Cloud computing therefore provides much needed elasticity.

Enterprise users may find it hard to resist the quick provisioning aspect and not having to deal with the installation and maintenance headaches, as well as only paying for what is used. Yet, what truly differentiates cloud computing apart from everything that preceded it is the remote management of the applications through the Internet.

Having briefly discussed the economic issues of cloud computing, we now discuss some of the security concerns when an enterprise's data and processing is carried out using a cloud computing provider.

18.2.7 Security Concerns in Cloud Computing

As noted earlier, cloud computing can provide significant benefits but it also poses significant security concerns, in particular, when sensitive personal information or critical applications are moved to the clouds, possibly overseas. Some of the concerns are listed below.

- *Security of data*—Given the multinational nature of many cloud computing companies, a cloud computing client would want to know where the enterprise data is stored and how it is protected. The client needs to be confident that unauthorized person will not be able to access the data and the cloud site is well protected from attacks like the denial of service attacks.
- *Security of authentication*—A cloud computing client would want to know how access to his/her data is controlled by the provider. Username and password authentication are weak and can be compromised by determined hackers. A more secure authentication is required.
- *Security to audit*—A cloud computing client needs to be able to periodically audit data access and data updates to ensure that no unauthorized access has taken place. There must be clear agreement how periodic data audit is to take place.
- *Security of support*—The customer needs to understand the HR practices of the cloud computing provider to ensure that the quality of employees that are employed by the provider is high. Only then the customer can have confidence in the support provided by the provider. It is also very important to ensure that every employee of the provider is properly screened before employment.
- *Security of cloud computing provider*—Given that the customer may be totally dependent on the cloud service provider, the customer needs to know how robust the provider is. For instance, in case of some global disaster, like the recent global financial crisis, would the provider be able to survive? The customer also needs to know how he will be able to access the services if by chance the provider fails.
- *Security of investigating violations*—Given the multinational nature of many cloud computing companies, the customer needs to know how any violations will be investigated and follow-up action be taken. Different countries have different legislations so this might be an important concern for the customer.
- *Security against disasters*—Given that many cloud computing providers have their computing resources distributed, the customer needs to know how the provider is ensuring that the resources are protected against disasters like earthquakes, hurricanes, floods and tsunamis.

The issues listed above show that security concerns must be considered by an enterprise when it is considering using cloud computing services. On the other hand, cloud computing can also improve security. We discuss the security benefits next.

18.2.8 Security Benefits of Cloud Computing

We have listed a number of security concerns of cloud computing. There are also a number of arguments in favour of better security in the cloud computing environment. We list these arguments.

- *Better authentication*—A cloud computing service provider is likely to have better authentication and authorization practices than an enterprise.
- *Auditing*—A cloud computing service provider is likely to have appropriate auditing tools that ensure that each access is logged and therefore full audit trail is available.
- *Cost of security*—Since a cloud computing provider will be providing similar security controls to a number of customers, the cost of providing and testing security is shared and therefore reduced.
- *New developments*—A cloud service provider is more likely to quickly implement any new developments in the field of security given the pressure from customers and therefore customers will be able to benefit from such developments.

- *Reduced chances of losing data*—Since cloud computing provides access to data to authorized users from almost anywhere, the need for carrying data on memory sticks or laptops or other portable devices is reduced. This means that if one of these devices is lost, the chances of losing data are reduced.
- *Monitoring security and investigating breaches is better*—A cloud service provider is likely to have much better monitoring of the security systems. Furthermore, any breaches of security are likely to be investigated quickly.

Given the security concerns and security benefits of using cloud computing, security issues for each situation must be considered carefully.

18.2.9 Summary of Cloud Computing

We have briefly discussed the benefits and concerns of using cloud computing. In spite of the fact that some people believe cloud computing is only brilliant marketing, cloud computing is likely to continue to grow in the next few years. In fact, Gartner in its annual forecast for 2010 and beyond[1] highlights cloud computing and claims that by 2012 India-centric IT services will represent 20% of the leading aggregators in the world markets.

18.3 MOBILE DATABASES

Given the widespread use of portable devices[2], including small devices like a mobile phone, a smart phone like the iPhone and tablets like iPad as well as devices like laptops, it is becoming important for mobile users to be able to connect to the enterprise central database through these devices to access information from the database. Mobile databases offer many benefits to mobile users, for example, offline access to data without a network connection. They also pose a number of technical challenges.

We illustrate the growth in mobile computing by presenting some recent figures about mobile computing.

The Gartner study noted earlier, forecasts that the mobile phones will overtake PCs as the most common web access device worldwide. It has been noted that in 2010 more than 150 million users were accessing Facebook through their mobile devices. One study forecasts that the number of mobile web users in the world will be close to one billion by the end of 2010 and may reach 1.7 billion by 2013. India and China are likely to have more than 400 million mobile web users by 2013 although some studies forecast that the number of users will be much larger.

We provide an informal definition of mobile databases.

---

1. The annual report of Gartner is available at http://www.gartner.com/it/page.jsp?id=1278413. Another forecast by Gartner is that by 2014, over 3 billion people in the world will be able to transact electronically via mobile or Internet technology. Gartner is an international IT company that carries out analysis about a wide variety of IT issues.
2. It has been estimated that there will be more than two billion mobile computing devices in the world by 2011 and about half of them will be in India and China.

Definition—Mobile Databases
Mobile databases refer to database applications and services that users can use while on the move, using a mobile device.

A mobile database system includes a number of components. The first is that the database system being used is a full DBMS. It must be accessible using mobile equipment from anywhere and anytime.

We assume that we are dealing with a mobile client and a fixed host. This is the most common environment in which a travelling employee is using a portable device to access the company's database. Such mobile databases are becoming important in a variety of applications. For example, a policeman who is moving around may require access to the database. At the current time, when a policeman stops a suspect, he/she must phone the police station and ask an operator to provide the details about the particular person. If the policeman had access to a mobile database, it would not be necessary to contact an operator for information. Also, in some cases the operator of such a telephone service could become a bottleneck if many calls are coming during the peak time. Other mobile applications include database use by salesmen and mobile offices.

18.3.1 Characteristics of Mobile Devices

There are a number of characteristics of most mobile devices that need to be considered in designing mobile databases. Some of these are as follows:

1. *Intermittent connections*—There are many reasons why a mobile connection may disconnect without the user disconnecting it. Coverage can be a problem, for example, a train going through a tunnel may cut off the connection. Some part of the country may not have the coverage, for example, while the user is driving outside urban areas. There may be interference from other services. A number of techniques may be used when the user is disconnected.
2. *Expensive communications*—In many countries mobile communication is relatively expensive. This, for example, is true for Australia. A recent OECD study shows that Australia is the most expensive country for communication services. High prices of wireless data communication is at least partly responsible for slow rate of developments in the field in some countries.
3. *Short battery life*—Most mobile devices have short battery life although a mobile device in a car can usually be connected to a recharger. Generally though one has to be sensitive to a mobile device's power consumption. It is not expected that an innovation is likely to overcome this serious limitation in the short term.
4. *Limited device capabilities*—Most mobile devices are resource-poor compared to desktop machines. The mobile devices, for example, have limited processing power, bandwidth, memory, disk storage and display size. Mobile communication is often slow except perhaps devices like a laptop or an iPad. Most mobile devices have limited memory although memory sizes have been growing. The display sizes are usually quite small although the displays are also becoming larger in some devices, for example, laptops and iPad.

The characteristics of mobile devices listed above make effective use of mobile databases challenging that requires balancing between the competing characteristics of unreliable and low-performance networks while being aware of mobile device's power consumption. We now list mobile database design challenges.

18.3.2 Mobile Database Challenges

We now look at how data management is implemented in mobile databases. The issues that need to be explored are as follows:

- How would query processing be carried out given a new architecture in which the user may be located on another continent?
- How would transaction management be handled given that the database may be fragmented over many computers that are geographically distributed?
- How would concurrency and integrity be handled?
- How would the mobile database provider ensure security of the database when many users may be using the same DBMS?

We consider the above issues keeping in mind, the characteristics listed in last section as well as some others mentioned below.

1. *Low reliability of wireless connections and slow or expensive networks*—Slow speed and intermittent connectivity of a wireless connection can make it difficult to transmit large results to a mobile device. As noted earlier, intermittent connectivity is a common problem in wireless environment since mobile clients may get disconnected at any time due to poor network coverage at the user's location or due to problems with the mobile device's battery. Assuming that the client's tower has a cache for storing information, a disconnection makes it impossible to refresh the information in the client's device. A disconnection should be detected immediately although the server may keep sending fresh information to the client. When the connection is re-established, there is a need to synchronize the client's information with the server's information. Intermittent connectivity therefore requires that the server detects disconnection and then the re-connection, so that it is able to take appropriate actions to synchronize.
2. *Security and privacy issues of mobile access*—Mobile applications includes commerce, banking, e-commerce and emergency services. These applications involve transmitting personal information. Therefore, security in mobile databases is important. To ensure security, a mobile database system requires reliable user authentication, server-enforced access controls, authorization and encryption. Encryption and decryptions should take place at the client side to prevent any disclosure of data in transmission or at the server.
3. *Data management and synchronization*—This is a major database issue between a remote client and the database server because a disconnected mobile client, for example, a laptop, may continue to work on the information residing in the mobile device and therefore create two different copies of the same data. Once the connection is re-established, conflict resolution between the two copies must take place. This may involve the mobile client sending its copy to the database server as soon as possible. Much research has been carried out on data synchronization. One approach is based on enforcing the properties of causability preservation, intention preservation and convergence.
4. *Performance*—Mobile databases are expected to provide access to the mobile clients quickly and at anytime and anywhere in spite of limited storage capacities of the clients. Improving performance of mobile databases requires a number of techniques including improving the cache memory performance. Due to the low bandwidth and low reliability of wireless channels, it is important for a mobile client to cache its frequently accessed database items into its local storage. This improves performance of database queries and improves availability of database items for query processing during disconnection.

5. *Query processing*—(location based queries)—Query processing can be challenging in mobile databases since the amount of data returned to the device may need to be minimized. As discussed in the following section, there are a number of types of location based queries and processing them may require considerable computations.
6. *Mobile transaction management*—It is important that consistency of a mobile database be maintained and transactions are managed effectively in spite of intermittent connections from some devices. A mobile database therefore must have robust techniques for handling unplanned disconnections. Problems may arise when concurrent operations on both the mobile device and the database are being carried out perhaps due to disconnection. Another scenario is that a mobile client issues a transaction and is then disconnected. How should the transaction then be committed when the user is not online?
7. *User interface*—Given that the screen size of most mobile devices is small, user interface and the size of data returned to the device become important issues. One possibility is for the database to serve 4-5 rows of results at a time. User interface should also provide a convenient way to interact with the database including querying the database. Information that is designed to display on larger screens can be displayed by using vertical and horizontal scroll bars to view the complete information. Another possibility is to break the information into several parts and display the part that the user wishes to view next. Both approaches clearly have limitations. Yet another approach is to design the information so it will display well on small screens. Furthermore, there are some web browsers who present information so that the information just fills the screen although such displays can be almost impossible to read when the information on the page is complex.
8. *Data caching and replication*—Performance of a mobile device is seriously affected by caching and replication. We would like to ensure that any requests for data that is available in the mobile device does not require any I/O. Data caching on a mobile device may require different metrics of cache performance than are normally used in computer systems. The primary aims of caching in mobile computing are to improve availability of information even when a disconnection has taken place, reduce the communication overheads and reduce power consumption.
9. *Mobility issues (dynamic data, placing data, moving computations)*—Mobility involves a number of issues in mobile databases including the impact of mobility on the database server, the network, and the mobile client. The client may be moving either on foot or in a vehicle, perhaps a car or a bus or a train. This movement may mean that the server will have to deal with another tower that is nearby. The server and the client therefore have to decide when to hand-off to another tower and how to do it. This may require the old base-tower to pass on information about its interactions with the client to the new tower. This will at some stage involve initiating a hand-off, transferring the client's interaction information and then committing the hand-off.
10. *Failure recovery*—As noted earlier, a mobile connection may be intermittent that can lead to loss of communication and possibly data. Recovery techniques in mobile databases may use a no-logging approach or a logging approach. In the no-logging approach the state of the mobile client is saved at the base-tower on every write event by the client. In the logging approach, the mobile client carries out periodic checkpointing and logs all write events between checkpoints. These are then transferred to the server. Techniques have been proposed that take into account mobility as well as failure rate and the mobility rate of the mobile user. Therefore, checkpointing rate may be different for different users. Recovery on reconnection starts with the server sending the latest checkpoint and the log to the mobile client which is then replayed to arrive at a consistent state.

18.3.3 Location Based Services

It is not difficult to imagine many useful location based services. One may want to find out a good restaurant close to one's current location. One may need to find a taxi. An amusing application suggested by Japanese company was to find if any friends were in the shopping centre. Location therefore plays a key role in determining the types of query a mobile client might pose to the server database. Most location based services are considered continuous as the user may be walking or be on a bus or in a car and therefore query results will change as the user moves.

- *"Where am I?" Type Queries*—Some queries relate to the mobile client's location and navigation. Such capabilities allow users to find where they are and find their way to a destination.
- *Proximity Query*—The aim here is to find all objects within a certain range. It may be easier to compute an answer to a rectangular range query; computing answers to radial range query is somewhat more difficult although the range query may first be transformed into a rectangular range query using a minimum bounding rectangle.
- *K-nearest Neighbour Query*—It is a complex query with the aim of finding the K-nearest objects. To find the result, the query with the support of indexes may scan a number of objects only once and from them select the K-nearest neighbours. Another approach involves scanning the candidate objects several times and counting the number of objects returned and then counting the nearest K of the objects.

Many other location based services are possible and some new ones are being developed. New applications of location-based services will need to deliver relevant, targeted and timely information to the mobile users at the time and place of their choice. Given the forecast growth in mobile devices and mobile computing, a lot of new developments are expected to become available in the future.

18.3.4 Summary of Mobile Databases

We have noted the dramatic growth in the number of mobile devices in recent years and the growth is likely to continue with the introduction of smart phones like iPhone and devices like iPad. Gartner forecasts that by 2013, mobile phones will overtake PCs as the most common web access device worldwide since the number of smartphones and browser-equipped enhanced phones will exceed the 1.82 billion installed base for PCs. This growth will fuel the growth in mobile databases which in turn will lead to new developments in mobile database technologies.

18.4 DEALING WITH MASSIVE DATASETS–MAPREDUCE AND HADOOP

We now discuss MapReduce which was designed by Google to deal with massive amounts (multi-terabytes) of data using thousands of share-nothing commodity computers in reliable fault-tolerant networks. In India, with the advent of the UID, it will be necessary to store data for about more than 500 million people, each of them including a variety of information and the images of ten fingerprints. A single fingerprint may be as large as 10 MByte of data although it can be compressed. In spite of compression, the UID database is likely to have massive amount of data.

Big data is becoming a fact of the real world and therefore we need to develop techniques for dealing with large datasets. Furthermore, in a number of applications large amounts of data leads to better testing of hypotheses. Applications like high energy physics, astronomy and DNA sequencing are some examples of very large datasets. More recently because of the advent of the Web, most enterprises have to deal with a variety of data including text, structured data, images, videos and so on. All this data need to stored and processed efficiently. We may call this type of technology data-driven technology.

18.4.1 Features of MapReduce

Lin and Dyer list the following features of processing large data using a large number of computers using a system like MapReduce.

- *Assume machine failures are common*—Large farms of computers will experience a number of failures a day. Software that uses a large number of machines must therefore cope with failures gracefully.
- *Move processing to the data*—Since many massive datasets are not computation demanding, it makes sense to move processing around.
- *Process data sequentially and avoid random access*—Since very large datasets must be disk resident, it makes sense not to spend too much time reading and writing from the disk. Therefore, random access of data should be avoided. MapReduce may be considered and designed for batch processing over large datasets.
- *Hide system-level details from the application developer*—MapReduce provides an abstraction that isolates the application developer from system-level details.
- *Seamless scalability*—To cope with growing amount data it should be possible to increase the size of the cluster of machines and still process data quickly.

Our discussion of MapReduce is based on the original 2004 paper by Dean and Ghemawat and the papers that have followed.

MapReduce is designed to deal with large amounts of data, for example, crawled web documents, set of frequent search engine queries, graph representations of the Web and large datasets in linguistics research. In all these problems simple computations are required but the datasets can be very large.

MapReduce derives its name from functional programming. A MapReduce query is usually divided into independent chunks which are processed by a number of machines in parallel. The MapReduce system takes care of scheduling tasks, monitoring them, re-executing the ones that failed and collecting the results as described in the two steps below.

- *The Map Step*—This step involves the master node taking the user input and dividing the query into a number of smaller subqueries, perhaps by splitting the files. These subqueries are then distributed over the nodes that are available to process the query. The master node does not need to be a separate node. The map function receives an input that often is the name of the document and its content, and carries out operations specified by the user. The intermediate result from map is another set of document names and their contents.

- *The Reduce Step*—This step involves the master node collecting the intermediate results from the map nodes and combining them and distributing them to the reduce machines to carry out the reduce task specified by the user to generate a set of documents as the output to the user.

The pieces distributed to the map and reduce machines are typically much larger than the number of machines used since one does not want the work to be spread too thinly across the machines.

We now present an informal definition of MapReduce.

> **Definition—MapReduce**
> *MapReduce is a programming framework for expressing distributed computations on massive data sets so that the computations may be carried out on a large cluster of commodity machines. It involves a map function that processes a key/value pair to generate a set of key/value results which for the same intermediate key are merged using a reduce function.*

It is interesting to now discuss how an application is implemented using the MapReduce software running on a large farm of share-nothing computers. We discuss it briefly.

18.4.2 Overview of MapReduce Applications

The steps involved in MapReduce are listed below and shown in Fig. 18.1. They are based on details provided in the paper by Dean and Ghemwat.

1. *Step 1*—Split input files—The input files are split typically into pieces of 16–64MB. This is controlled by the user. Copies of the program are started on a cluster of machines.
2. *Step 2*—Master program—One of the copies of the program is special and is called the Master. The rest are assigned work by the master. The master picks idle machines and assigns each one a map task or a reduce task.
3. *Step 3*—Map task—A machine that has been assigned a map task reads the contents of the corresponding input file fragment. It then parses key/value pairs out of the input data. Each pair is passed through the user-defined map function. The resulting key/value pairs are stored in the machine's memory. The locations of these pairs are passed back to the master who forwards them to reduce machines.
4. *Step 4*—Reduce task—When a reduce machine is notified by the master about the locations of the intermediate results, it reads the results from the map machines and sorts them by the key value so that all occurrences of the same key values are grouped together. The corresponding set of intermediate values are now passed to the user's reduce function. The output of the reduce function for this map machine is appended to a final output file.
5. *Step 5*—Output—Once all map machines and reduce machines have completed their tasks, the master communicates with the user program and returns the results.

The output files may be passed to another MapReduce call.

Many information retrieval tasks require a similar approach that essentially deal with a large number of records which may be searched on many machines and the results then aggregated. Key/value pairs are the basic data structure in such problems.

MapReduce is a patented programming framework developed by Google to deal with data management of massive data sets which are becoming more common now[3].

The top part of Fig. 18.1 shows the files that have been split into pieces for distribution over many machines. Map phase carries out the computations specified by the user and the results are then processed and passed on to the map phases. After the map phase, the results are collected and passed on to the user.

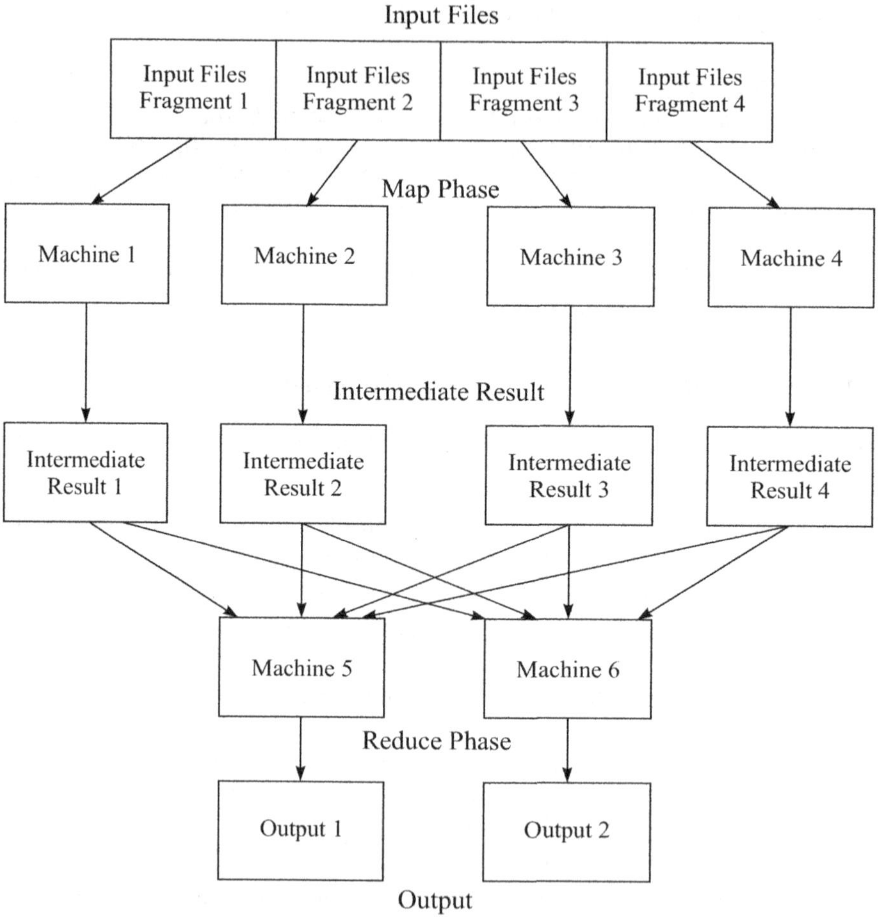

Figure 18.1 Overview of a MapReduce Application

MapReduce has a number of implementations. The most well known implementation has been developed by Apache and is called Hadoop. Another implementation is called SQL-MapReduce developed by Aster Data. SQL-MapReduce functions are integrated within the SQL language and therefore SQL may be used to manipulate the data and provide the user with results.

3. The book by Lin and Dyer claims the following. Google was processing 20 petabytes of data a day in 2008. eBay was processing 150 billion new records per day. Facebook in 2009 had 2.5 petabytes of user data, growing by 15 terabytes each day (that is, almost 6 petabytes a year).

The papers of Dean and Ghemavat present results of performance evaluation of MapReduce and discuss a number of different applications at Google and other places for which MapReduce has been used. One of these applications produces the indexes used for the Google search engine using the 20 TB or more web pages data that is retrieved by the crawler.

18.4.3 Hadoop

Hadoop is an open-source implementation of MapReduce.

Although the Hadoop framework is implemented in Java, MapReduce applications need not be written in Java. Hadoop essentially consists of two layers. The first layer is a block-structured file system for data storage called the Hadoop Distributed File System (HDFS). The second layer provides the MapReduce functionality.

The MapReduce functionality is provided in a way that is similar to what is described in Fig. 18.1. The Hadoop job is submitted to the master (called JobTracker) which is broken down into map tasks based on the size of the files and the number of available machines. The master manages a collection of TaskTrackers. The master assumes the responsibility of distributing the software configuration to the TaskTrackers, scheduling tasks and monitoring them, providing status and diagnostic information to the job client.

18.4.4 Summary of MapReduce

Although the MapReduce systems are being labeled by some as database systems others are calling them similar to the ETL (Extract, Transform and Load) systems discussed earlier in Chapter 15. It is of course clear that MapReduce and Hadoop systems for dealing with massive datasets are very different than a relational database system. Given that very large datasets are now being generated in a number of application areas, the use of MapReduce systems is only going to grow.

SUMMARY

- **Forecasting emerging database technologies is not always easy as illustrated by the recommendations** of the last two meetings of database experts held in Lowell, Massachusetts, in 2003 and in Claremont, California, in 2008.
- **The forecasts of the both meetings included recommendations like personalization, privacy and** adaptive systems. There were also differences in the two set of recommendations, for example, cloud computing was included in the 2008 report but not in the 2003 report.
- **The forecasted importance of cloud computing in the future and economic factors are driving the** growth in cloud computing. Cloud computing provides an enterprise a number of benefits including scalability, availability, flexibility and agility. It provides a flexible approach for meeting the computing resources needs of an enterprise. Cloud computing also provides a 'pay as you use' basis for computing hardware and software.
- **Cloud computing may be private, public or hybrid. Each of these arrangements has their own benefits.** For example, an enterprise that is highly concerned about security should perhaps choose a private cloud computing solution.

- Cloud computing services include services like IaaS (infrastructure), PaaS (platform) and SaaS (software).
- It is important to consider the economic as well as the security aspects of cloud computing before deciding whether cloud computing offers the best solution for an enterprise.
- Given the widespread use of mobile devices in India and other countries, mobile databases are likely to become very important in the future.
- Mobile devices have a number of characteristics including intermittent connections and short device battery life.
- For mobile databases to become widely used, a number of challenges in the field that must be met include security and privacy of mobile access, performance of mobile databases, failure recovery, and low reliability of wireless connections.
- Important applications of mobile databases include location based services.
- MapReduce is a new technology to deal with the problem of searching very large datasets. It has been designed to solve some other problems as well. The main components of Google's MapReduce include the map step and reduce step.

REVIEW QUESTIONS

1. Review two recent forecasts for the future of database systems (the Lowell meeting and the Claremont meeting). (Section 18.1)
2. What kinds of services are provided by cloud computing providers? What are the benefits and risks in using cloud services? (Section 18.2)
3. How data management can be implemented in cloud computing? (Section 18.2)
4. Describe public, private and hybrid cloud computing. (Section 18.2.5)
5. Give examples of security concerns and security benefits of using cloud computing if the services IaaS, PaaS and SaaS are used. (Section 18.2.7 and 18.2.8)
6. Importance of mobile databases and reasons for the growing importance of mobile computing. (Section 18.3)
7. Characteristics of mobile devices and how they impact mobile computing. (Section 18.3.1)
8. Location based services and queries. (Section 18.3.3)
9. The issues of intermittent connection, mobility of the client and limited display size. (Section 18.3.2)
10. What types of applications is MapReduce most appropriate for? (Section 18.4)
11. List the differences between relational databases and MapReduce. Is MapReduce a database technology? List its features. (Section 18.4)
12. What is MapReduce and what is Hadoop? List some of the features of Hadoop. (Section 18.4.1)
13. What is map and reduce? What do these steps involve and who specifies them? (Section 18.4.2)
14. List the steps involved in implementing a MapReduce application. (Section 18.4.2)
15. Discuss the role of each step in the MapReduce application. (Section 18.4.2)

SHORT ANSWER QUESTIONS

1. Define cloud computing and explain the motivation that is driving this technology.
2. What is shared-nothing computing?
3. Name two advantages of cloud computing?
4. What might be the disadvantages of using cloud computing?
5. What is IaaS?
6. What is PaaS?
7. What is SaaS?
8. Name two companies that provide cloud computing services.
9. Name three security concerns if a university starts using cloud computing for its examinations.
10. Name the three different types of cloud computing.
11. What is a mobile database?
12. Why are mobile databases becoming important?
13. How many mobile phones are estimated to be in use in India?
14. List three characteristics of mobile devices?
15. List three challenges in the field of mobile databases.
16. List three types of location based queries.
17. How do databases deal with the mobile client's intermittent connection?
18. What problems are caused by the size of the mobile client's display?
19. What needs to be done when a mobile client is moving?
20. Give an example of a suitable application of MapReduce.
21. List three major steps of a MapReduce application.
22. Who developed MapReduce? What application was it designed for?
23. Name two companies that are using MapReduce technology.
24. List the five steps of a MapReduce program.

MULTIPLE CHOICE QUESTIONS

1. Which one of the following services is **not** provided by Cloud Computing?
   (a) Infrastructure (b) Consulting (c) Platform (d) Software
2. Which one of the following is **not** a benefit of cloud computing?
   (a) Scalability (b) Cheap compute power
   (c) Flexibility and agility (d) Availability when needed
3. Which one of the following is **not** included in IaaS?
   (a) Operating system (b) DBMS (c) Communications (d) Storage

4. Which one of the following is **not** included in PaaS?
   (a) Compilers (b) Development environment
   (c) Communications (d) Programming languages
5. Which one of the following is included in SaaS?
   (a) Operating system (b) DBMS (c) Communications (d) Software support
6. Which one of the following is **not** a step in MapReduce?
   (a) Split the files (b) Distribute them to map machines
   (c) Distribute also to reduce machines (d) Combine results
7. Which one of the following is **not** true about MapReduce?
   (a) It uses share-nothing commodity processors.
   (b) It uses a farm of geographically distributed computers.
   (c) It includes a powerful central master processor.
   (d) It is more like batch processing.
8. Which one of the following is true?
   (a) Hadoop is a mobile database system.
   (b) Hadoop is primarily a RDBMS.
   (c) Hadoop has a master-slave architecture.
   (d) Hadoop only deals with shared-everything architecture.
9. Which of the following are **not** true about a mobile database?
   (a) It always has a mobile database server. (b) It always includes mobile clients.
   (c) It cannot carry out transactions. (d) It cannot carry out location based queries.
10. Mobile database systems face a number of challenges. Which one of the following is **not** one of them?
    (a) They must deal with intermittent connections.
    (b) They must deal with short battery life of mobile clients.
    (c) They must deal with limited capabilities of the mobile clients.
    (d) They must deal with a variety of DBMS.
11. Which one of the following is not a security concern in cloud computing?
    (a) Security of data (b) Security of authentication
    (c) Security of support (d) Security against disasters
12. Which one of the following is **not** a feature of MapReduce computing?
    (a) It hides system-level details from the developer.
    (b) It represents data in a relational form.
    (c) It assumes that machine failures are common.
    (d) It moves processing to data.
13. Which one of the following is **not** true in MapReduce computations?
    (a) The user specifies the map function. (b) The user provides the reduce function.
    (c) The user provides the files. (d) The user selects the master processor.
14. Which one of the following is true about MapReduce?
    (a) It only works with massive amounts of data. (b) It only works with thousands of computers.
    (c) It only works with textual information. (d) It only works with Web data.
    (e) None of the above

15. Which one of the following is true about mobile computing?
    (a) There is a fixed host.
    (b) The clients are mobile.
    (c) There is a reliable connection.
    (d) There is inexpensive communication.
16. Which one of the following is **not** a mobile database challenge?
    (a) Low reliability of wireless communication
    (b) Failure recovery
    (c) Transaction management
    (d) Physical data structures
17. Which one of the following is **not** a location based query?
    (a) Proximity query
    (b) K-nearest neighbour query
    (c) Sorted distance query
    (d) Sorted time to reach destination query
18. Which one of the following is **not** true about Hadoop?
    (a) Hadoop is a open source software.
    (b) Hadoop includes a master machine called JobTracker.
    (c) Hadoop includes a number of machines called TaskTrackers.
    (d) Hadoop includes one machine called the ResultTracker.
19. Which one of the following is true about MapReduce?
    (a) The idea of Map and Reduce came from Google founders.
    (b) MapReduce is open source software.
    (c) Map and Reduce tasks are specified by the user.
    (d) MapReduce relies on random access of data to improve efficiency.
20. Which one of the following is true about mobile databases?
    (a) It only works with a mobile client.
    (b) It only works with cheap communications.
    (c) It only works with limited client display.
    (d) It only works with location-based queries.
    (e) None of the above.

EXERCISES

1. Discuss the major issues listed in the two database research meeting reports. Which topics were common in both reports and which were different? Discuss the thought behind the two reports and why some topics were included and others excluded.
2. Discuss briefly the key challenges in adopting cloud computing.
3. How should one determine whether an enterprise should buy some cloud services or purchase the hardware and software locally to carry out the computing in-house? Explain.
4. List the major security concerns when a database storing personal information is stored on machines owned by a cloud computing company. How can you ensure that the security of information is maintained?
5. Describe different types of services that cloud computing providers are providing. What cloud computing services could Infosys provide to international companies and how would the company meet the concerns of its international customers?
6. Describe the major differences between mobile databases and centralized databases.

7. Discuss the characteristics of mobile devices and list a number of location based services that could be provided using mobile databases.
8. Discuss briefly the key challenges in building a mobile database.
9. Discuss how the major database issues of performance, query processing, transaction management and integrity may be dealt with in mobile computing.
10. Why is there a need for MapReduce? What does the MapReduce approach do that a large relational database system cannot?
11. Present an overview of use of MapReduce to run an application like building an index for a large number of web pages. Explain every phase of the process in detail.
12. Describe some of the features of Hadoop. How is it different than a distributed relational database system? Discuss.
13. Discuss why an enterprise should use services of a cloud computing provider. Note that the provider may not be able to support the platforms and configurations the enterprise has been using. Also, consider the issue of licensing, for example, database licensing. Also consider security risks and the risks of exposing data sources to the provider.
14. Discuss briefly the key challenges in implementing a MapReduce application.
15. It has been claimed that MapReduce is not a database but instead it is more like an ETL system. Discuss it.

PROJECTS

1. Make a list of all the computing facilities and services in the university that you are studying at. Now identify all those facilities and services that may be outsourced to a cloud computing company. Prepare a list of advantages and disadvantages for using cloud computing for each of the services that you have selected.
2. What data do you think will be stored in the UID database? How much data is expected to be stored for each person? Assume that the data will include images of the ten fingerprints and perhaps one or more photos. Collect as much information as possible for the UID database. Now assume that the UID database has information about 500 million people. What is the size of the whole database? How would this data be managed efficiently? Describe what you will do if you had to manage the system.

LAB EXERCISES

1. Make a comprehensive list of advantages and disadvantages of cloud computing.
2. Why would an Indian company like Infosys be so interested in cloud computing? What kind of business opportunities are there in cloud computing for an Indian IT company?
3. How many mobile phones are there in India? How can these phones be used as clients for mobile databases? Describe some likely applications of mobile databases in India. How would mobile database technology change as the next generation of smart phones become available?
4. Study the objectives of MapReduce and think of an application for which it might be appropriate to use MapReduce. Who in India may benefit from this technology?

BIBLIOGRAPHY

For Students

The reports of Lowell and Claremont meeting are easy to read. For cloud computing, the article by Sun Microsystems provides a good introduction and so does the paper by Won Kim. The book by Lin and Dyer provides a good introduction to MapReduce.

For Instructors

The reports of Lowell and Claremont meeting are worth reading. For cloud computing, the article by Abadi deals with data management in the cloud and the Berkeley Group provides a good introduction. The paper by Nori and the one by Ilarri, Mena and Illarramendi are good.The papers by Dean and Ghemawat are the primary references and have been highly cited. The book by Lin and Dyer provides a good introduction to MapReduce. Venner's book deals with Hadoop.

Abadi, D. J., "Data Management in the Cloud: Limitations and Opportunities", *Bulletin of the IEEE Computer Society Technical Committee on Data Engineering*, March 2009, pp 3-10.

Abiteboul, S. et al., "The Lowell Database Research Self-Assessment", *Communications of the ACM*, Vol. 48, No. 5, May 2005, pp 111-118.

Agrawal, R. et al., "The Claremont Report on Database Research", *Communications of the ACM*, Vol. 51, No. 6, June 2009.

Abouzeid, A., K. Bajda-Pawlikowski, D. Abadi, A. Silberschatz, and A. Rasin, *HadoopDB: An Architectural Hybrid of MapReduce and DBMS Technologies for Analytical Workloads*, VLDB'09, August 2009, Lyon, France, pp 922-933.

Armbrust, M., A. Fox, R. Griffith, A. D. Joseph, R. Katz, A. Konwinski, G. Lee, D. Patterson, A. Rabkin, I. Stoica, and M. Zaharia, "Above the Clouds: A Berkeley View of Cloud Computing", *Technical Report Number UCB-EECS-2009-28*

Bernard, G., J. Ben-othman, L. Bouganim, G. Canals, S. Chabridon, B. Defude, J. Ferrié, S. Gançarski, R. Guerraoui, P. Molli, P. Pucheral, C. Roncancio, P Serrano-Alvarado, and P. Valduriez, "Mobile Databases: A Selection of Open Issues and Research Directions", *ACM SIGMOD Record* , Vol. 33, Issue 2, June 2004.

Dean, J., and S. Ghemawat, "MapReduce: Simplified Data Processing on Large Clusters", *USENIX Symposium on Operating Systems Design and Implementation (OSDI)*, 2004.

Dean, J., and S. Ghemawat, "MapReduce: A Flexible Data Processing Tool", *Communication of the ACM*, Vol. 53, No. 1, January 2010.

Ilarri, S., E. Mena, and A. Illarramendi, "Location-Dependent Query Processing: Where We Are and Where We Are Heading", *ACM Computing Surveys*, Vol. 42, No. 3, Article 12, March 2010.

Kim, W., "Cloud Computing: Today and Tomorrow", *Journal of Object Technology*, January-February 2009, pp 65-72.

Lin, J., and C. Dyer, *Data-Intensive Text Processing with MapReduce,* Morgan & Claypool Publishers, California, 2010, 165 pp.

Nori, A. K., "Mobile and Embedded Databases", *Bulletin of the IEEE Computer Society Technical Committee on Data Engineering,* 10 pp. http://www.sites.computer.org/debull/A07sept/nori.pdf

Pradhan, D. K., P. Krishna, and N. H. Vaidya, "Recoverable Mobile Environment: Design and Trade-off Analysis", *IEEE Proceedings of the 26th Annual International Symposium on Fault-Tolerant Computing (FTCS '96)*, 1996

Sun Microsystems, *Introduction to Cloud Computing: White Paper*, June 2009. http://www.scribd.com/doc/17028937/Cloud-Computing

Stonebraker,M., D. Abadi, D. J. Dewitt, S. Madden, E. Paulson, A. Pavlo, and A. Rasin, "MapReduce and Parallel DBMSs: Friends or Foes?", *Communications of the ACM*, Vol. 53, No. 1, January 2010, pp 64-71.

Stonebreaker, M., "The End of a DBMS Era (Might be Upon Us)", *ACM Communications of the ACM Blog*, June 30, 2009.

Venner, J., *Pro Hadoop*, Apress, Berkeley, 2009, 407 pp.

Weinman, J., *The 10 Laws of Cloudonomics*, Gigaom.com, September 7, 2008. http://www.gigaom.com/2008/09/07/the-10-laws-of-cloudonomics/

White T., *Hadoop: The Definitive Guide*, Second Edition, Yahoo Press, 624 pages, 2010.

Appendix A

Answers to the Multiple Choice Questions

Chapter 1

1. (b) 2. (d) 3. (b) 4. (d) 5. (d) 6. (e) 7. (e)
8. (c) 9. (c) 10. (e) 11. (b) 12. (d) 13. (c) 14. (b)
15. (e) 16. (e)

Chapter 2

1. (e) 2. (e) 3. (d) 4. (a) 5. (d) 6. (d) 7. (e)
8. (b) 9. (c) 10. (b) 11. (e) 12. (d) 13. (d) 14. (d)
15. (d) 16. (d) 17. m:n, 1:n, 1:1, m:1, 1:n 18. (e) 19. (a) and (b)
20. (c) 21. (d) 22. (d) 23. (a)

Chapter 3

1. (a), (b) and (d) 2. (b) 3. (d) 4. (b) and (d) 5. (d)
6. (d) 7. (a) and (d) 8. (c) 9. (b) 10. (a) 11. (d) 12. (d)
13. (a) and (b) 14. (d) 15. (a) and (c) 16. (d) 17. (b)

Chapter 4

1. (c) 2. (b) 3. (a) 4. (a) 5. (e) 6. (b) 7. (a) and (d)
8. (a) 9. (d) 10. (e) 11. (e) 12. (a) and (d) 13. (b)
14. (d) 15. (e) 16. (d) 17. (d)

Chapter 5

1. (b) 2. (e) 3. (a) and (c) 4. (c) 5. (a) 6. (d)
7. (c) 8. (d) 9. (d) 10. (e) 11. (e) 12. (b) 13. (c)
14. (b) 15. (d) 16. (d) 17. (d) 18. (c) 19. (a) 20. (a)
21. (a) 22. (c) 23. (a) 24. (a) 25. (d) 26. (a) 27. (a)

28. (a) 29. (b) 30. (e) 31. (b) 32. (c) 33. (b) 34. (d)
35. (c)

Chapter 6

1. (a) and (b) 2. (b) 3. (a) 4. (a) 5. (a) and (b) 6. (a)
7. (a) 8. (d) 9. (b) 10. (d) 11. (d) 12. (d) 13. (d)
14. (b) 15. (b) and (d) 16. (b) 17. (d) 18. (c) 19. (b)
20. (d) 21. (c) 22. (b) 23. (b) 24. (e) 25. (b) and (c)
26. (b) 27. (d) 28. (d) 29. (a) and (b) 30. (b) 31. (b)
32. (d)

Chapter 7

1. (d) 2. (a) and (b) 3. (d) 4. (e) 5. (a) and (b)
6. (e) 7. (a) 8. (d) 9. (d) 10. (a) 11. (a) 12. (c)
13. (d) 14. (c) 15. (a) 16. (b) 17. (b) 18. (a) 19. (c)
20. (a) 21. (a) and (b) 22. (d) 23. (e) 24. (b) 25. (d)
26. (a) 27. (c) 28. (c) and (d)

Chapter 8

1. (e) 2. (b) 3. (a) and (d) 4. (e) 5. (c) 6. (b)
7. (c) 8. (a) 9. (d) 10. (a) 11. (c) 12. (d) 13. (a)
14. (a) and (c) 15. (b) 16. (b) 17. (b) 18. (c) 19. (b) 20. (a) and (b)
21. (a) 22. (c) 23. (d)

Chapter 9

1. (d) 2. (d) 3. (b), (c) and (d) 4. (a) 5. (a) 6. (d)
7. (d) 8. (a) 9. (b) 10. (d) 11. (a) 12. (b) 13. (b)
14. (d) 15. (b) 16. (d) 17. (c) 18. (e)

Chapter 10

1. (d) 2. (d) 3. (a) 4. (d) 5. (b) 6. (d) 7. (b)
8. (d) 9. (d) 10. (a) 11. (a) 12. (a) 13. (c) 14. (b)
15. (a) 16. (a) 17. (a) 18. (d) 19. (c) 20. (d)

Chapter 11

1. (b) 2. (a) 3. (c) 4. (d) 5. (c) 6. (e) 7. (b)
8. (b) 9. (a) and (b) 10. (d) 11. (a) and (b) 12. (b)
13. (a) and (b) 14. (d) 15. (c) and (d) 16. (c) 17. (d) 18. (d)
19. (a) and (d) 20. (d)

Chapter 12

1. (d)	2. (d)	3. (c)	4. (d)	5. (d)	6. (b)	7. (d)
8. (c)	9. (d)	10. (a)	11. (a)	12. (a)	13. (a)	14. (e)
15. (c)						

Chapter 13

1. (b)	2. (d)	3. (c)	4. (d)	5. (a)	6. (d)	7. (d)
8. (c)	9. (c)	10. (d)	11. (d)	12. (d)	13. (b)	14. (c)
15. (c)	16. (d)	17. (b)	18. (c)	19. (d)	20. (c)	

Chapter 14

1. (b)	2. (e)	3. (e)	4. (e)	5. (e)	6. (e)	7. (d)
8. (c)	9. (e)	10. (e)	11. (b)	12. (b)	13. (b)	14. (b)
15. (c)	16. (a)	17. (b)	18. (d)	19. (c)	20. (a) and (b)	

Chapter 15

1. (a)	2. (b)	3. (c)	4. (c)	5. (d)	6. (b)	7. (c)
8. (d)	9. (d)	10. (d)	11. (d)	12. (c)	13. (c)	14. (c)
15. (d)	16. (b)	17. (a)	18. (c)	19. (d)	20. (c)	

Chapter 16

1. (c)	2. (d)	3. (e)	4. (b)	5. (e)	6. (a)	7. (c)
8. (a)	9. (c)	10. (a)	11. (d)	12. (e)	13. (d)	14. (c)
15. (a)	16. (c)	17. (b) and (c)		18. (c) and (d)		19. (a) and (d)
20. (b)	21. (a)	22. (b)	23. (c)	24. (b)	25. (e)	

Chapter 17

1. (a)	2. (a)	3. (c)	4. (d)	5. (d)	6. (a)	7. (c) and (d)
8. (b) and (d)	9. (c)	10. (c)	11. (b)	12. (c)	13. (c)	14. (a)
15. (d)	16. (d)	17. (d)	18. (b)	19. (c)	20. (d)	

Chapter 18

1. (b)	2. (b)	3. (b)	4. (c)	5. (c)	6. (c)	7. (c)
8. (c) and (d)	9. (d)	10. (c)	11. (d)	12. (b)	13. (d)	14. (e)
15. (b)	16. (d)	17. (d)	18. (d)	19. (c)	20. (e)	

Index

E

T

Made in the USA
Monee, IL
08 November 2026

68144950R10439